Contemporary
Literary Criticism

Guide to Gale Literary Criticism Series

When you need to review criticism of literary works, these are the Gale series to use:

If the author's death date is: **You should turn to:**

After Dec. 31, 1959
(or author is still living)

CONTEMPORARY LITERARY CRITICISM

for example: Jorge Luis Borges, Anthony Burgess,
William Faulkner, Mary Gordon,
Ernest Hemingway, Iris Murdoch

1900 through 1959

TWENTIETH-CENTURY LITERARY CRITICISM

for example: Willa Cather, F. Scott Fitzgerald,
Henry James, Mark Twain, Virginia Woolf

1800 through 1899

NINETEENTH-CENTURY LITERATURE CRITICISM

for example: Fedor Dostoevski, Nathaniel Hawthorne,
George Sand, William Wordsworth

1400 through 1799

*LITERATURE CRITICISM FROM 1400 TO 1800
(excluding Shakespeare)*

for example: Anne Bradstreet, Daniel Defoe,
Alexander Pope, François Rabelais,
Jonathan Swift, Phillis Wheatley

SHAKESPEAREAN CRITICISM

Shakespeare's plays and poetry

Antiquity through 1399

CLASSICAL AND MEDIEVAL LITERATURE CRITICISM

for example: Dante, Homer, Plato, Sophocles, Vergil,
the Beowulf Poet

Gale also publishes related criticism series:

CHILDREN'S LITERATURE REVIEW

This ongoing series covers authors of all eras. Presents criticism on authors and author/illustrators who write for the preschool through high school audience.

SHORT STORY CRITICISM

This series covers the major short fiction writers of all nationalities and periods of literary history.

ISSN 0091-3421

Volume 46

Contemporary Literary Criticism

Excerpts from Criticism of the
Works of Today's Novelists, Poets,
Playwrights, Short Story Writers, Scriptwriters,
and Other Creative Writers

Daniel G. Marowski
Roger Matuz
EDITORS

Sean R. Pollock
Robyn V. Young
ASSOCIATE EDITORS

Gale Research Company
Book Tower
Detroit, Michigan 48226

STAFF

Daniel G. Marowski, Roger Matuz, *Editors*

Sean R. Pollock, Robyn V. Young, *Associate Editors*

Jane C. Thacker, Thomas J. Votteler, Bruce Walker, *Senior Assistant Editors*

Kent Graham, Michele R. O'Connell, David Segal, *Assistant Editors*

Jean C. Stine, *Contributing Editor*

Derek T. Bell, Melissa Reiff Hug, Anne Sharp,
Debra A. Wells, *Contributing Assistant Editors*

Jeanne A. Gough, *Production & Permissions Manager*
Lizbeth A. Purdy, *Production Supervisor*
Kathleen M. Cook, *Assistant Production Coordinator*
Suzanne Powers, Jani Prescott, Lee Ann Welsh, *Editorial Assistants*
Linda M. Pugliese, *Manuscript Coordinator*
Donna Craft, *Assistant Manuscript Coordinator*
Jennifer E. Gale, Maureen A. Puhl, Rosetta Irene Simms, *Manuscript Assistants*

Victoria B. Cariappa, *Research Supervisor*
Maureen R. Richards, *Research Coordinator*
Mary D. Wise, *Senior Research Assistant*
Joyce E. Doyle, Kevin B. Hillstrom, Karen D. Kaus, Eric Priehs,
Filomena Sgambati, Laura B. Standley, *Research Assistants*

Janice M. Mach, *Text Permissions Supervisor*
Kathy Grell, *Text Permissions Coordinator*
Susan D. Battista, *Assistant Permissions Coordinator*
Mabel E. Gurney, Josephine M. Keene, *Senior Permissions Assistants*
H. Diane Cooper, Anita L. Ransom, *Permissions Assistants*
Eileen H. Baehr, Melissa A. Kamuyu, Martha A. Mulder,
Kimberly F. Smilay, Lisa M. Wimmer, *Permissions Clerks*

Patricia A. Seefelt, *Picture Permissions Supervisor*
Margaret A. Chamberlain, *Picture Permissions Coordinator*
Pamela A. Hayes, Lillian Tyus, *Permissions Clerks*

Copyright © 1988 by Gale Research Company

Library of Congress Catalog Card Number 76-38938
ISBN 0-8103-4420-3
ISSN 0091-3421

Computerized photocomposition by
Typographics, Incorporated
Kansas City, Missouri

Printed in the United States

Contents

Preface   7

Authors Forthcoming in *CLC*   11

Appendix   451

Literary Criticism Series Cumulative Author Index   467

Preface

Literary criticism is, by definition, "the art of evaluating or analyzing with knowledge and propriety works of literature." The complexity and variety of the themes and forms of contemporary literature make the function of the critic especially important to today's reader. It is the critic who assists the reader in identifying significant new writers, recognizing trends in critical methods, mastering new terminology, and monitoring scholarly and popular sources of critical opinion.

Until the publication of the first volume of *Contemporary Literary Criticism (CLC)* in 1973, there existed no ongoing digest of current literary opinion. *CLC,* therefore, has fulfilled an essential need.

Scope of the Work

CLC presents significant passages from published criticism of works by today's creative writers. Each volume of *CLC* includes excerpted criticism on about 45 authors who are now living or who died after December 31, 1959. Nearly 1,900 authors have been included since the series began publication. The majority of authors covered by *CLC* are living writers who continue to publish; therefore, an author frequently appears in more than one volume. There is, of course, no duplication of reprinted criticism.

Authors are selected for inclusion for a variety of reasons, among them the publication of a critically acclaimed new work, the reception of a major literary award, or the dramatization of a literary work as a film or television screenplay. For example, the present volume includes Vladimir Nabokov, whose recently translated work *The Enchanter* is considered a preliminary sketch for his controversial novel *Lolita;* Alice Walker, whose novel *The Color Purple* was adapted into an acclaimed film; and Ken Kesey, whose retrospective collection of stories and essays, *Demon Box,* received significant critical attention. Perhaps most importantly, authors who appear frequently on the syllabuses of high school and college literature classes are heavily represented in *CLC;* Louise Bogan and Jean Genet are examples of writers of this stature in the present volume. Attention is also given to several other groups of writers—authors of considerable public interest—about whose work criticism is often difficult to locate. These are the contributors to the well-loved but nonscholarly genres of mystery and science fiction, as well as literary and social critics whose insights are considered valuable and informative. Foreign writers and authors who represent particular ethnic groups in the United States are also featured in each volume.

Format of the Book

Altogether there are about 650 individual excerpts in each volume—with an average of about 14 excerpts per author—taken from hundreds of literary reviews, general magazines, scholarly journals, and monographs. Contemporary criticism is loosely defined as that which is relevant to the evaluation of the author under discussion; this includes criticism written at the beginning of an author's career as well as current commentary. Emphasis has been placed on expanding the sources for criticism by including an increasing number of scholarly and specialized periodicals. Students, teachers, librarians, and researchers frequently find that the generous excerpts and supplementary material provided by the editors supply them with vital information needed to write a term paper, analyze a poem, or lead a book discussion group. However, complete bibliographical citations facilitate the location of the original source and provide all of the information necessary for a term paper footnote or bibliography.

A *CLC* author entry consists of the following elements:

- The **author heading** cites the author's full name, followed by birth date, and death date when applicable. The portion of the name outside parentheses denotes the form under which the author has most commonly published. If an author has written consistently under a pseudonym, the pseudonym will be listed in the author heading and the real name given on the first line of the biographical and critical introduction. Also located at the beginning of the introduction to the author entry are any important name variations under which an author has written. Uncertainty as to a birth or death date is indicated by question marks.

- A **portrait** of the author is included when available.

- A brief **biographical and critical introduction** to the author and his or her work precedes the excerpted criticism. However, *CLC* is not intended to be a definitive biographical source. Therefore, *cross-references* have been included to direct the reader to these useful sources published by the Gale Research Company: *Contemporary Authors,* which includes detailed biographical and bibliographical sketches on more than 89,000 authors; *Children's Literature Review,* which presents excerpted criticism on the works of authors of children's books; *Something about the Author,* which contains heavily illustrated biographical sketches of writers and illustrators who create books for children and young adults; *Dictionary of Literary Biography,* which provides original evaluations and detailed biographies of authors important to literary history; *Contemporary Authors Autobiography Series,* which offers autobiographical essays by prominent writers; and *Something about the Author Autobiography Series,* which presents autobiographical essays by authors of interest to young readers. Previous volumes of *CLC* in which the author has been featured are also listed in the introduction.

- The **excerpted criticism** represents various kinds of critical writing—a particular essay may be normative, descriptive, interpretive, textual, appreciative, comparative, or generic. It may range in form from the brief review to the scholarly monograph. Essays are selected by the editors to reflect the spectrum of opinion about a specific work or about an author's literary career in general. The excerpts are presented chronologically, adding a useful perspective to the entry. All titles by the author featured in the entry are printed in boldface type, which enables the reader to easily identify the works being discussed.

- A complete **bibliographical citation** designed to help the user find the original essay or book follows each excerpt.

Other Features

- A list of **Authors Forthcoming in *CLC*** previews the authors to be researched for future volumes.

- An **Appendix** lists the sources from which material in the volume has been reprinted. It does not, however, list every book or periodical consulted during the preparation of the volume.

- A **Cumulative Author Index** lists all the authors who have appeared in *CLC, Twentieth-Century Literary Criticism, Nineteenth-Century Literature Criticism,* and *Literature Criticism from 1400 to 1800,* along with cross-references to these Gale series: *Children's Literature Review, Authors in the News, Contemporary Authors, Contemporary Authors Autobiography Series, Contemporary Authors Bibliographical Series, Dictionary of Literary Biography, Something about the Author, Something about the Author Autobiography Series,* and *Yesterday's Authors of Books for Children.* Users will welcome this cumulated author index as a useful tool for locating an author within the various series. The index, which lists birth and death dates when available, will be particularly valuable for those authors who are identified with a certain period but whose death date causes them to be placed in another, or for those authors whose careers span two periods. For example, Ernest Hemingway is found in *CLC,* yet a writer often associated with him, F. Scott Fitzgerald, is found in *Twentieth-Century Literary Criticism.*

- A **Cumulative Nationality Index** listing the authors featured in *CLC* alphabetically by nationality, followed by the volume numbers in which they appear, is included in alternate volumes of *CLC.*

- A **Cumulative Title Index** listing titles reviewed in *CLC* in alphabetical order from Volume 1 through the current volume is included in alternate volumes of *CLC.* Titles are followed by the corresponding volume and page numbers where they may be located. In cases where the same title is used by different authors, the author's surname is given in parentheses after the title, e.g., *Collected Poems* (Berryman), *Collected Poems* (Eliot). For foreign titles, a cross-reference is given to the translated English title. Titles of novels, novellas, dramas, films, record albums, and poetry, short story, and essay collections are printed in italics, while all individual poems, short stories, essays, and songs are printed in roman type within quotation marks; when published separately (e.g., T.S. Eliot's poem *The Waste Land*), the title will also be printed in italics. A separate offprint of the Author, Nationality, and Title Indexes is also available.

Acknowledgments

No work of this scope can be accomplished without the cooperation of many people. The editors especially wish to thank the copyright holders of the excerpted essays included in this volume, the permissions managers of many book and magazine publishing companies for assisting us in securing reprint rights, and the photographers and other individuals who provided portraits of the authors. We are grateful to the staffs of the Detroit Public Library, the Library of Congress, the University of Detroit Library, the University of Michigan Library, and the Wayne State University Library for making their resources available to us. We also wish to thank Anthony Bogucki for his assistance with copyright research.

Suggestions Are Welcome

The editors welcome the comments and suggestions of readers to expand the coverage and enhance the usefulness of the series.

Authors Forthcoming in *CLC*

To Be Included in Volume 47

Louis-Ferdinand Céline (French novelist, essayist, and dramatist)—Best known for his novels *Journey to the End of the Night* and *Death on the Installment Plan,* Céline combines fractured syntax, Parisian argot, and obscenities to portray the chaos of Europe during World War I. The posthumous publication of *Conversations with Professor Y* has renewed critical interest in this controversial author.

James Dickey (American poet, novelist, critic, and essayist)—Widely acclaimed for his novel *Deliverance* and his National Book Award-winning poetry collection *Buckdancer's Choice,* Dickey has garnered critical attention for his recent novel, *Alnilam,* which details a blind man's search to learn the truth about his enigmatic son, who died in an airplane crash.

Michael Frayn (English dramatist, novelist, journalist, and scriptwriter)—A satirist of human foibles and contemporary society, Frayn is best known for his farcical play *Noises Off,* in which he examines the dichotomy between art and reality. Recent dramas to be covered in his entry include *Wild Honey,* adapted from Anton Chekhov's *Platonov,* and *Benefactors.*

John Masefield (English poet, novelist, short story writer, autobiographer, and dramatist)—The Poet Laureate of England from 1930 until his death in 1967, Masefield gained notoriety with his long narrative poems containing epithetic, colloquial language and vivid descriptions of the sea.

Marianne Moore (American poet, critic, essayist, and dramatist)—A prominent figure in twentieth-century American literature, Moore wrote poetry characterized by her technical and linguistic precision, acute observations, and detailed descriptions. Recent collections of her works to be covered in this entry include *The Complete Poems of Marianne Moore* and *The Complete Prose of Marianne Moore.*

Elsa Morante (Italian novelist, short story writer, essayist, and poet)—Best known for her novels *Arturo's Island* and *History,* Morante often focuses upon Marxist and Christian themes in her works. Criticism of *Aracoeli,* a novel published shortly before her death in 1985, will be featured in this entry.

R. K. Narayan (Indian novelist, short story writer, and essayist)—One of India's most celebrated contemporary authors, Narayan is noted for his creation of Malgudi, a mythical town in southern India, which provides the setting for much of his fiction. Criticism of his recent novel, *Talkative Man,* will be included in Narayan's entry.

Walker Percy (American novelist, essayist, and critic)—Percy's philosophical novels often depict Southern characters who attempt to rise above the deadening routine of modern existence and attain spiritual happiness. In his recent best-selling work, *The Thanatos Syndrome,* Percy uses elements of the thriller to explore the moral implications of social engineering.

Georges Simenon (Belgian-born French novelist, short story writer, autobiographer, essayist, and nonfiction writer)—With more than five hundred titles to his credit, Simenon is quite possibly the world's most prolific living writer. Simenon's entry will focus upon his novels and short stories featuring detective Jules Maigret.

Tristan Tzara (Rumanian-born French poet, dramatist, and essayist)—Tzara was the founder of Dadaism, an intellectual movement of the World War I era that espoused intentional irrationality and repudiated traditional values of art, history, and religion. Tzara's nihilistic precepts continue to influence contemporary artists of all genres.

Jorge Luis Borges (Argentinian short story writer, poet, essayist, critic, and scriptwriter)—Among the most eminent and distinctive contemporary Latin American authors, Borges is particularly noted for his innovative short stories, in which he blends imaginative fiction with historical detail and philosophical speculation. Criticism of *Seven Nights,* a collection of essays on literary topics, will be featured in Borges's entry.

Loren D. Estleman (American novelist and short story writer)—Writing in the "hard-boiled" detective tradition established by Dashiell Hammett and Raymond Chandler, Estleman employs a terse yet vividly descriptive prose style to examine the sordid world of urban crime. Among the novels to be covered in his entry are *Sugartown, Kill Zone,* and *Roses Are Dead.*

Sheila Fugard (English-born South African novelist and poet)—A respected author who examines life under apartheid in South Africa, Fugard combines feminism and the Gandhian concept of nonviolent resistance to address her country's social problems in her recent novel, *A Revolutionary Woman.*

Ellen Gilchrist (American short story writer, novelist, and poet)—Gilchrist is best known as the author of the short story collection *Victory over Japan,* for which she received the American Book Award in fiction. Her recent volume of stories, *Drunk with Love,* has elicited significant critical attention.

Julien Gracq (French novelist, critic, short story writer, dramatist, and poet)—Influenced by Surrealism and the work of André Breton, Gracq creates phantasmagoric novels characterized by elegant prose and evocative imagery. Gracq's third novel, *The Opposing Shore,* won the Prix Goncourt in 1951.

Tina Howe (American dramatist)—Best known for her humorous plays about human interaction, Howe often sets her dramas in such unlikely locations as art museums, restaurants, and fitting rooms. Among her recent works are *Appearances, Painting Churches,* and *Coastal Disturbances.*

Tommaso Landolfi (Italian novelist, short story writer, critic, poet, dramatist, essayist, and translator)—Among the most innovative stylists in modern Italian fiction, Landolfi demonstrated a surreal vision and a preoccupation with language similar to Franz Kafka and Italo Calvino. His most respected books include *The Moon Stone* and *The Two Spinsters.*

Medbh McGuckian (Irish poet)—McGuckian is praised for her innovative and descriptive verse imbued with a feminist sensibility. In such volumes as *The Flower Master* and *Venus and the Rain,* she experiments with language and conveys personal themes.

Vernon Scannell (English poet, novelist, critic, autobiographer, scriptwriter, and editor)—A respected figure in post-World War II English literature, Scannell is best known for his unaffected traditional verse through which he passionately examines themes related to war, violence, and the dangers inherent in the modern world.

Yevgeny Yevtushenko (Russian poet and novelist)—Among the most outspoken and controversial poets to emerge in the Soviet Union since the death of Stalin, Yevtushenko has written two recent novels, *Wild Berries* and *Ardabiola,* in which he expands on the personal themes of his poetry.

Alice (Boyd) Adams

1926-

American novelist and short story writer.

In her fiction, Adams focuses upon well-educated, upper middle-class female professionals whose lives undergo numerous transformations during their ongoing search for happiness and independence. Anne Tyler characterized these heroines as "perceptive . . . intelligent and a bit world-weary." Adams employs polished, graceful prose replete with subtle nuances through which characters and conficts become progressively intertwined. After drawing attention for short stories published in various magazines, particularly the *New Yorker,* Adams secured her reputation with the novels *Families and Survivors* (1975) and *Listening to Billie* (1978). These early works are noted for such playful narrative intrusions as foreshadowing of events and asides directed toward the reader. Adams's later novels are more wistful and exhibit briskly efficient use of detail.

Adams frequently employs incidents from her own life in relating the adventures of her protagonists. These women often become involved in passionate but destructive love affairs, endure separation or divorce, and struggle to rebuild their lives by entering more stable relationships and dedicating themselves to their vocations. Adams, who was married at an early age, was divorced in 1958 and moved to San Francisco, where much of her fiction is set. She published her first novel, *Careless Love* (1966), at the age of forty. This work, which follows Daisy Duke from divorce to eventual romantic bliss, was generally regarded as a sentimental romance. *Families and Survivors,* her next novel, traces thirty years of love and disappointment in the lives of two sisters. Through the parenthetical remarks of an omniscient narrator, a common feature in her early work, Adams foreshadows events and introduces subtle twists of plot. The title of *Listening to Billie* refers to blues singer Billie Holiday, whose mournful songs reflect the feelings of Eliza, the novel's protagonist. Eliza wallows in grief following the suicides of her husband and her father but eventually finds meaning and happiness through writing. Adams's next novel, *Rich Rewards* (1980), concerns a divorcée who attempts to reorder her life following several disappointing love affairs. Reviewers praised the novel's central character, Daphne, who generously cares for her acquaintances while trying to make sense of her own problems. *Superior Women* (1984) elicited comparisons to Mary McCarthy's novel *The Group,* as both novels concern several female college students from diverse backgrounds.

Adams's short stories are collected in *Beautiful Girl* (1979), *To See You Again* (1982), and *Return Trips* (1985) and frequently appear in annual anthologies representing the best in short fiction. Critics compared the stories in *Beautiful Girl* to works by John Cheever and F. Scott Fitzgerald, citing their poignant focus on private emotions. In several stories, Adams gently mocks the preoccupations of her characters while expressing compassion for their concerns. The pieces in *To See You Again* deal predominantly with well-educated, financially secure protagonists who nevertheless are dissatisfied with their lives. Adams was praised for her deft social observations and exploration of her characters' fragile personal relationships.

© Thomas Victor 1987

The stories in *Return Trips,* according to Susan Schindehette, are examples of "sublime subtlety, of nuance and quiet perception—stories from a writer who is quite clearly an accomplished, absolute master of her craft." Schindehette continued: "[It] is Adams' gift to reveal the tremendous inner workings beneath the apparent tranquility and make characters come to life in her spare, elegant style."

(See also *CLC,* Vols. 6, 13; *Contemporary Authors,* Vols. 81-84; and *Dictionary of Literary Biography Yearbook: 1986.*)

SHEILA WELLER

I fell in love with Alice Adams two years ago, by way of ***Listening to Billie,*** her exquisite chronicle of the life of a young female poet over several decades. In a prose style that was somehow both grave (even ominous) and unlabored almost to the point of being dashed off, she showed how time burnishes character, how we come to accrue what we refer to as the "lessons" of life. It was this powerful wistfuless that sent me back to ***Billie*** three—or has it been four?—times, and to Adams's previous novel, ***Families and Survivors.*** In both, she created the fullness of a saga without any of a saga's lugubrious weight.

She was, I realized, a wonderfully old-fashioned writer. The Dickensian coincidence, the solemn omniscience, the sense of lives destined to intertwine: in lesser hands one would hear the organ music of a TV soap opera through these techniques; not in Adams's. And, in an era of the cloyingly accessible ''I,'' her formal third person allowed us the pleasure of *stealing* glimpses into the minds of characters who were provocatively complex. (pp. 18, 20)

I was still in rapture (a dangerous state) when I picked up her newest—fourth—novel, *Rich Rewards.* Yes, happily, we were back in San Francisco with another world-weary heroine. (Daphne, a 40-year-old interior designer, had gone through a French socialist, an American junkie, and a British lawyer in Paris, New York, and Boston before coming West to decorate the home of her similarly patrician/bohemian friend, Agatha.) Yes, all the people in these two women's circle would fatefully interlock. Yes, yes, yes . . . but as I began reading, something seemed distastefully awry. Adams was writing in the first person now—through Daphne's point of view. And Daphne's point of view was awfully chatty and glib, even—could it be?—trite. ''Orgasms.'' ''Sexist.'' ''Sixties.'' *Newsweek*-cover-story words kept cropping up. . . .

The action that Daphne dips into and out of centers around a Marin County family—philandering, self-made husband; neurotic wife; ''bad guy'' carpenter son; ''good guy'' sculptor daughter—whose various charms and brutalities are far more described than revealed. I was not distressed that I knew these people would end up destroying one another—eerie foreshadowing is a wonderful Adams tease—but I was distressed that I didn't *care* that they did. Eventually Daphne herself did become genuine to me; more than genuine, someone I might share a bottle of wine with. And so did Agatha. But then only they, of all the characters, had a *history*. Their cool, weathered intimacy—the footnotes in their talk, even in their silences—gives Adams her only chance in the book to do what she does best. The novel has a wildly, perfunctorily happy ending. I felt cheated out of enjoying a sumptuous meal because I wasn't hungry.

Would this novel have sprung off the page if Adams had made it her usual scrapbook, instead of a snapshot? Given the story years, not months, to brew? Or if she had freed herself from the coy, cramping ''I'' and let the other characters (on whom, after all, she placed the burden of interestingness) expand under our own gaze? Probably, but that's not the point. The point is: I miss her gravity, her irony, her old-fashionedness, her *wistfulness*. All of which are luminous. And all of which I, like any sad-but-hopeful lover, demand to see again. (p. 20)

Sheila Weller, ''Timely Goes Trendy,'' in Ms., *Vol. IX, No. 3, September, 1980, pp. 18, 20.*

ANNE TYLER

This is the kind of thing that makes Alice Adams (or, rather, her central character [in *Rich Rewards*]) nervous: You go to a friend's house for lunch, she asks if you'd like some wine, you accept and she instantly fetches two glasses that have been waiting, already filled, in the refrigerator. Trivial, on the face of it, but then again, what depths of anxiety, edgy control, unsettling efficiency are implied by those two glasses!

The central character's name in *Rich Rewards* is Daphne, and she is not only perceptive but intelligent and a bit world-weary. She's a true Alice Adams heroine, in other words: close kin to two old friends in *Families and Survivors,* or to the independent Eliza Quarles in *Listening to Billie.* Unattached, she has made her way through any number of lovers, some of them extremely ill-chosen, but her genuine friendships tend to be with other women.

It's because of one of these women, an old schoolmate named Agatha, that Daphne seizes the opportunity to break off her latest affair and move to San Francisco, in order to act as decorator for Agatha's new house. There, she becomes involved with a family who might (except for the fine writing that delineates them) have stepped from a television soap opera: the handsome, philandering Royce Houston, his half-crazed wife, eyelash-batting girlfriend, malevolent son and a daughter beaten senseless by a man she refuses to name. Moving among these people, accidentally interrupting the tryst of one and paying a condolence call on another, Daphne is a sort of thread that links their lives. She wonders occasionally, what significance these people are meant to have for her:

> For a long time, it now appeared, I had been making a career out of personal relationships, and on the whole that had not worked out too well. It had led me, seemingly, to this network of violence and craziness in California. And since in a supersitious way I do not quite believe in accidents, I could not believe that my presence, there and then, among these particular people was entirely accidental. I was there for some purpose, which sometimes seemed to be a negative instruction: Do not go on as you are, it will lead to nothing good; you have to change.

But change is the last thing we'd wish for her. She is such a tactful and observant friend, so sensitive to the slightest shift in emotional climates, that you can't help hoping she'll continue as she is forever. (p. 13)

This is a marvelously readable book. It's mysterious in the best sense—not a setup, artificial mystery but a real one, in which we wonder along with the heroine just what all the chaotic events are leading up to. Another element of suspense is provided by Daphne's old love affair with [a] French Socialist—does she have a chance of resurrecting it some 20 years later? Is there any significance to the fact that his name keeps popping up the minute she begins her new life in San Fancisco?

But for me, at least, the real interest lies in Daphne herself—in her independence, her sensitivity, her openheartedness. If the conclusion seems a bit sudden and easy, lacking the texture of the rest of the story, it is also the ''rich reward'' that Daphne deserves. Draw a moral, if you like: Daphne is one of the most admirable female characters in recent fiction. She behaves honorably throughout, and it's only right that she be granted a happy ending. (p. 20)

Anne Tyler, ''An Honorable Heroine,'' in The New York Times Book Review, *September 14, 1980, pp. 13, 20.*

VICTORIA GLENDINNING

For a newcomer—like myself—to Alice Adams' fiction, which has been highly praised, *Rich Rewards* is a puzzle. How can a novel combine so much to admire with so much to object to, so much skill with so much that is undistinguished?

Daphne, a divorcée escaping from a destructive English lover, comes alone from Boston to San Francisco, where the only person she knows is her old school friend Agatha. Her flight is a retreat into the quiet life, comforted by what she sees as the "extreme localness" of the city. But she cannot escape the past. She sees in a newspaper a disturbing reference to her lost lover of 20 years back in Paris—Jean-Paul, now a famous left-wing economist; later she finds that he is coming to lecture at Berkeley. "Everywhere is dangerous."

Particularly dangerous is the Houston family, friends of Agatha's, who become "for me, *the* Californians".... Our heroine becomes observer and confidante as all four Houstons, and Agatha, fall apart in violence and alienation. At first she is over-involved, but as her own horizons widen, and the Houstons each go their own weird ways, she becomes free of them and free to seek out the only man she has ever loved, Jean-Paul.

Daphne is an interior decorator by trade, and the domestic settings of her new friends are obsessively described. Her thoughts about details of form and decor, often symbolic, are balanced by a preoccupation with her own inner, mental coloration: "Like many people of my generation and my sort of education . . . my friends and I did a lot of emotional temperature-taking, so to speak. We were always very interested in how we were."

Daphne's generation is that of people in their early forties, and her age is very important. The decades through which she has lived are repeatedly evoked and characterized. She notices the "mid-Seventies opulence" of the silk and velvet clothes worn at the Houston's party, and thinks that she herself is a "Seventies person"—"temporarily asexual, earning too much money.". . . It is time for radical change, for opening out and for optimism. Making love, she and Jean-Paul find, is better "after forty," and another advantage of age is that "when you're really happy you know you are."

So far so good. Daphne says her favorite book is *Howards End,* and one can see the relevance of this information. A strong family atmosphere in both books influences and alters outsiders. And the pattern of *Rich Rewards*—the way in which the closed worlds of Daphne and Agatha, on one hand, and the Houstons on the other, meet and mesh and go on, changed, is pleasing. What is disappointingly bad is the actual writing. No one in his right mind would complain of a novel being written lightly, but this one seems often written carelessly. Sentences beginning with "Well . . ." or "Actually . . ." give the book a conversational feel. And as one does in conversation, the author repeats herself. Daphne shares her creator's easy garrulousness.... Daphne has a literary bent, and her "intuitive flashes" too are made much of. But the banality of most of her insights about life and behavior do not merit the importance they seem to be given.

The other main problem springs from the "outsider" position of Daphne in relation to the action. In order for her— and us— to follow the desperate dramas of the Houstons, the author has to manufacture a series of often artificial-seeming visits, telephone calls, summonses and surprise encounters, which suggest the episodic construction of a soap opera. There is also a lot of useless linking material about driving and parking cars and going up in elevators, etc., of a kind that provides wordless continuity on film, but blunts written narrative. (pp. 9, 14)

Victoria Glendinning, "Nice Life, Old Flame," in Book World—The Washington Post, *October 12, 1980, pp. 9, 14.*

LAURIE STONE

[*Rich Rewards*] is a grownup novel full of randy riffs delivered without winks. How nice. Adams's women are every bit as curious and reverent as men are about anatomical wonders, just as delighted sometimes to place the whole person behind his parts. In *Rich Rewards,* women think this way not because they've been besmirched by heterosexist pornoganda but because they're animals, because, like men, they think about sex—remember it, want it, resist it—most of their waking and sleeping hours.

Adams writes a graceful, simple prose that seldom calls attention to itself. Daphne, with her too-large breasts and "far from beautiful" face, is a clear-eyed floater, and like so many of Adams's women, has moved through Boston, the South, and finally San Francisco. As the novel opens, she's doing interior design for people with too much money and blondness. . . .

Daphne is a very appealing character as she camouflages the grotesque proportions of California houses, befriends a scrumptious carpenter, forgets Derek, her latest mean-hearted lover, and pines for Jean-Paul, long-lost Socialist. . . . Friendship and the sexual imperative matter more to her than anything else, and, with no worldly ambition for balance, her psyche is suitably striped. Daphne knows she has never adequately separated from male-need—never felt entirely alive or whole unmanned and alone—and she knows this isn't good and hopes that younger women live less vulnerably. She rides out the novel observing other people's lives, and clearly something has to happen to her, too. But Adams makes a terrible choice: Jean-Paul comes to San Francisco to lecture. The two meet. Daphne goes back to Paris with him to live happily ever after, and the novel dies.

Jean-Paul is always a shadowy figure, a Beatrice smiling from the mists. It's impossible to believe that their coupling will work out—not because Daphne hasn't quite gotten it together before her rescue, and not because sex is her primary raison d'etre—but because Adams never shows them together. Romantic women don't have to end like Emma Bovary, but Adams's fairytale finish is even more depressing than a lonely Daphne would have been. Jean-Paul is a fantasy whom we are asked to accept as real. That Adams can't give a fully created woman a flesh-and-blood man suggests that such a union is, in reality, impossible—unimaginable.

But the problem may not be Adams's imagination so much as the myth it's hooked into. Maybe there are no Jean-Pauls. Maybe they're as false as the angel/whore myth of women, and maybe it's time the Mr. Rochesters and the Mr. Knightleys were buried—or were at least shown to be no less self-serving and petulant in marriage than the average boor.

Laurie Stone, "Shlong Song," in The Village Voice, *Vol. XXV, No. 48, November 26-December 2, 1980, p. 43.*

BENJAMIN DeMOTT

Author of four novels, including the highly praised *Listening to Billie* (1978), Alice Adams is also an accomplished short story writer whose work has been represented in each of the last 10 O. Henry collections. *To See You Again* is her second volume of stories; about half the tales it gathers appeared first in *The New Yorker*. Their setting, usually, is San Francisco and the Bay area. The characters are, for the most part, bright, well-educated, reasonably well-off architects, painters, magazine writers, academicians, youngish widows and the like. And the feelings and impulses explored lie close to the core of contemporary emotional life.

Chief among these feelings is hunger for change. Alice Adams's heroes and heroines are ever on the lookout for means of trading current attachments, selves, environments, repressions for something fresher. When they review a canceled marriage or revisit a childhood scene, they're moved less often by nostalgia than by longing to confirm the absolute pastness of the past—to prove to themselves that yesterday can't lay a glove on them. And on the rare occasion when one or another figure in *To See You Again* is gripped by an objectionably adhesive memory Miss Adams arranges matters so that the action of the story frees the person straightway from bondage. . . .

Everywhere in the book "relationships" hardly begun are abruptly ended. Back-to-back stories—**"The Break-In"** and **"True Colors"**— tell of women who, off on journeys with men they think they're in love with, decide the chaps in question won't do after all, and resourcefully light out on their own, alone. And repeatedly in Miss Adams's pages people discover the pleasures of shedding old friends. In **"The Party-Givers"** Hope and Josiah, newly married, decide to end their friendship with another couple, Gregory and Clover; at the time they're making this decision, Gregory and Clover are arriving at a similar decision about their friendship with Hope and Josiah. (p. 7)

Lots of moving on, in short. Miss Adams's manner is good-humoredly ironic and understated, and she's a deft social observer. (Her Las Vegas, sketched in one tale in this collection, is closer to the "reality" than Hunter Thompson's.) Readers in north central middle age will doubtless be heartened, moreover, by the lively desire and splendid resiliency of this author's senior citizen-changelings. (The best story in the book—**"Greyhound People,"** about a widow who, aided by a California bus pass, is in process of transforming herself into a new-style picaresque heroine—is admirably alert to the possibilities of social, as distinguished from sexual, adventure.) And it's at least arguable that the short story is, finally, a happier form for Miss Adams's gifts than the novel. Moral vacancy, nervous shuttling in and out of relationships, weightless life commitments and plans—these items are better suited to brisk, won't-take-a-minute short stories than to the huff and puff of novelese. I'm saying that both Miss Adams's story collections seem stronger books to me than either *Listening to Billie* or *Rich Rewards* — the novels of hers that I've read.

Yet I'm afraid it doesn't follow that *To See You Again* is a wholly satisfying experience. Life in this book is indeed lived, as I said, in easygoing obedience to the key emotional imperative of the age (Change Your Life). None of Miss Adams's people ever tears a passion to tatters; she herself is blessedly disinclined to harangue us about meaninglessness, narcissism, ego enclosure and the rest; only here and there, in a proper name such as Yvonne Soulas (soul-less?), does a critical reservation about a character break the smooth surface. But these stories do suffer from lack of tonal variety. By the middle of the book I found myself in need of change, desirous of esthetic (not moral) relief—wanting to hear, say, the sound of a voice of full-hearted social hope, or to look at somebody at least

capable of imagining grief, or to be surprised by behavior signifying belief (however benighted) that loyalty is a good thing or that duty can still call.

Miss Adams frets a little about this problem, interrupting herself once with a story about Mexican peasant life that's removed in tone from the other 18 pieces in the collection. (The story comes late and it's too marginal to have impact.) Once or twice, as in **"Related Histories,"** she allows a glimpse of a settled life that's marked by "fairness . . . honesty and kindness." But the glimpse comes only in a closing paragraph, and is unaccompanied by any sense of the inner texture of the life. About the author's power to penetrate a calm mind there can't be serious doubt; though more than once in the past she's brought her jittery folk to the edge of a stillness, forced them to stop fidgeting for a while. (I think in particular of **"A Pale and Perfectly Oval Moon,"** a resonantly truthful, impressively grounded, narrative about sex, marriage, cancer and death, in *Beautiful Girl,* her first collection of stories.)

But in this outing practically everybody in sight is wild to start over. The change-obsessed members of Miss Adams's audience, thus invited to see themselves again and again, will surely be amused for a time, but there's a chance that even they may find the performance a shade too monotonic before the end. (pp. 7, 17)

Benjamin DeMott, "Stories of Change," in The New York Times Book Review, *April 11, 1982, pp. 7, 17.*

STEPHEN GOODWIN

To See You Again is [Adams's] second collection of short stories. . . . Her readers will recognize their formidable worldliness. This worldliness is more than an attitude, a matter of style or sophistication; it amounts to a metaphysics, the wisdom of the world. Adams casts a cold eye on romance, nostalgia, anything that smacks of sentiment. She is staunchly on the side of those who believe that happiness, if it lies anywhere, lies in reality. She is alert to the smallest self-deceptions, all those little illusions that are anything but innocent, the fine cracks in the teacup which ought to warn us that sooner or later that teacup is simply going to fall apart.

Nothing lasts, least of all the relationships between men and women. Adams' fiction, including this new collection, is populated with women who are divorced, widowed, or between affairs. Willingly or not, they are on their own, and the tricky lesson they all must learn is how to live without men.

These women have not completely sworn off men. They can't; they enjoy them too much. The erotic currents are murky and powerful. Sex, not love, is the great mystery in Adams' fiction. The men swim by like so many fish, brilliant and colorful in the moment before they disappear, as they inevitably do. The women respond to their grace and beauty with a sensual gusto that is the traditional response of men to women. Though not in the least romantic, Adams is a marvelously sexy writer.

The conflict—not the outward conflict between men and women, but the private and inward conflict of individual women—runs through all of Adams' work. Her women value men but they prize their own independence. She treats the conflict as a given, a tension so familiar and commonplace that it requires no explanation. She is not particularly interested in the observation of emotional and psychological niceties. She would rather show us how people act than how they feel.

The result, of course, is that her stories have a decidedly moral cast. They can be read much as Hemingway's stories were and sometimes still are read, as advice. In fact, her fiction does for women something very similar to what Hemingway's fiction did for men: it embodies a code.

Several of the key rules of this code are stated forthrightly in the description of the young woman in **"An Unscheduled Stop."** Flying over the town where she grew up, she has burst into tears.

"The young woman . . . who is not on drugs, or drunk, has been deeply mortified by those tears, which came on her like a fit, a seizure. Generally she is a disciplined person; she behaves well, even under emotional stress. She does not make scenes, does not cry in public, rarely cries alone.". . . (p. 4)

A "disciplined person"—this woman has created herself through an effort of the will. She tells herself that she has made "precisely the sort of 'unconscious' mistake that people who pride themselves on rationality, on control, are most prone to make . . . it is how they do themselves in, finally." The code is not easy to apply.

It requires more than resolution and intelligence of the women who adopt it; it requires fortitude. The woman in **"Berkeley House"** learns that her stepmother, from whom she is estranged, is going to sell the house in which she grew up. "If I can't have it no one will, she wildly thought, at that most vulnerable predawn hour." In the very next sentence comes the reassertion of control: "She had no right to any of these emotions." Yet she cannot censor her dreams, which are frequently of the house. She regards the dreams as "unbearably sentimental, not to mention infantile." Here, again, the "unconscious" has impinged, bringing with it its residue of grief and rage. The code requires her to bear her loss and her dreams in silence. She doesn't allow herself to tell her lover about her dreams until the dreams have ended.

There are many other similarities between these two stories, including a professional resemblance—one woman is a painter, the other a magazine writer. In both stories the encroachment of the "unconscious" is assimilated into their work. The painter finishes a landscape—"its tidiness possibly being a counter to the confusion in her mind"—and without showing it to anyone takes it to her gallery, where it is immediately sold for enough money to live on for several months. The code emphasizes the importance of work as a source of self-expression and self-esteem. And the code has a bottom line: money, usually in short supply for Adams' women, is always the condition of their independence.

Provide, provide—this is, after all, the wisdom of the world, its most ancient wisdom. Alice Adams has updated and adapted it: her women are sane and civilized and frequently gallant; her stories are true and contemporary, a part of the history of our own times. Her books are eagerly awaited, and her readers, I am sure, find their own lives reflected in them.

I am equally sure that I will only sound like a dog in the manger when I say that the wisdom of the world is not enough. It aims low; it is a strategy for cutting your losses. No wonder Alice Adams' characters move so fast—something might be gaining on them. (p. 6)

Stephen Goodwin, "Alice Adams's San Francisco Chronicles," in Book World—The Washington Post, *May 9, 1982, pp. 4, 6.*

ROBERT PHILLIPS

[Alice Adams's] first collection, *Beautiful Girl* (1978), was intelligent and well-crafted, mostly stories about love. *To See You Again* shows a widening of range and subjects, and an admirable ability to shift point-of-view from character to character.

While the majority of her stories are set in California, where she now lives, others collected here are set in Mexico, Europe, the South, and Washington D.C. The Mexican stories show Ms. Adams at her best and worst. When she writes of tourists or expatriates, she is marvelous, as in **"At the Beach,"** a story of the uncertainties of older age. . . . It is when Ms. Adams attempts to write of the unworldly that she gets into trouble. In **"Teresa"** she tries to get under the skin of a Mexican native girl who suffers two tragedies. It is a more primitive tale than Ms. Adams's usual story of quiet epiphanies—more Isak Dinesen than Elizabeth Bowen. Teresa is the least convincing protagonist in the book. It is as if the author needs the trappings and familiar actions of "civilization" to fully comprehend her characters' motivations.

The other unsatisfactory story in the volume, curiously enough, is the title piece ["**To See You Again**"], which seems a sketch for a much longer story. We really do not know enough about the heroine's husband and marriage to understand his hold on her. But in a big collection of nineteen stories, Ms. Adams is forgiven two misses.

The usual Adams character does not give in to his or her fate, but attempts to shape it, however misguidedly. In both **"The Girl Across the Room"** and **"By the Sea,"** women become aware not only of missed opportunities, but also of life's endless possibilities. Alice Adams is not overly pessimistic. In both **"Lost Luggage"** and **"Berkeley House,"** serenity is achieved through great loss. She is a highly knowledgeable writer of psychological states. **"The Break-In"** is fashioned upon Oedipal rivalry, and **"Related Histories"** explores coincidence and similarity in the lives of separated lovers—Jung's synchronicity. "Reality" is no concrete thing in her imagination; after reconstructing the life of one Carstairs Jones, in **"Truth or Consequences,"** she admits, "But of course I could be quite wrong about Car Jones. He could be another sort of person altogether; he could be as haunted as I am by everything that ever happened in his life."

One of my favorites in the book is **"At First Sight,"** in which a poor little rich boy spends his youth in his long room in a cold, modern odd-shaped house, telling himself stories in which he is the son of some very plain but substantial midwestern people who live in a big plain square house that was warm. By the end of the story, now an adult, he has found his surrogate family in the place he least expected to find them. He also has found the love of his life. Ms. Adams accomplishes all this with great economy. William Blake said, You never know what is enough unless you know what is more than enough. Alice Adams knows the latter. She suppresses and condenses, allowing the reader to make vital connections between situation and character. (p. 190)

Robert Phillips, "Missed Opportunities, Endless Possibilities," in Commonweal, *Vol. CX, No. 6, March 25, 1983, pp. 188-90.*

BARBARA KOENIG QUART

In [*Superior Women*], Alice Adams focuses on five women who become friends at Radcliffe in 1943 and then watches them evolve over the next 40 years.

Not at all systematically, to be sure, and with fairly thin references to the extraordinary events of those turbulent decades, still, Adams holds us firmly with a lively narrative pace. She creates an almost gossipy interest in what happens to her characters; and she can't write a bad sentence, though hers is the kind of fine unobtrusive style that you notice only if you're looking for it.

Then is the book's very ambition the problem? Is it because Adams takes on so much more than she generally aims for, that it works less well? Or maybe a distinction has to be made here between being engaged with a book and being deeply engaged.

Certainly Adams tries hard enough to engage us. The group she sets up is carefully diverse—varied personality types, varied locales of interest. The heroine, Megan Greene, carries suggestions of older American classic themes: raw Westerner comes east to where the culture is. Also, ashamed young woman flees tacky Mom and Dad in California, for the richest, most sophisticated-looking "in " group at Radcliffe, presided over by the thinnest and blondest of elite dream girls, Lavinia. Part of what the book is about is the diminution of Lavinia and all that she represents—a redefinition over time of what, socially and morally, constitutes a "superior woman." All to the good, though Lavinia communicates little to the reader of the seductive power she is said to wield over everyone, a serious weakness since she is one of the book's two central characters.

Still, the novel does very well in evoking what it felt like to be a nubile young woman in the 1940s: all the waiting for and obsessing over men, the urgent centrality of which one to choose, the sexual fierceness (women's as well as men's here) presented euphemistically as "kissing" and "necking"—and the ways the women friends are brought together or are cut off from one another by all this. Adams catches the painful and bewildering sortings out of "suitable" couples for marriage— marriages that later miserably fall apart, or more miserably stay together. The book also evokes how what once looked luminous, looks to the same woman 20 years later—with pity and affection for that younger innocent self.

Adams has a wonderful way of capturing the multilayered reality of what passes between people in a moment in time. For example: a foursome that doesn't work right and their own sense of pointlessness under the animated talk or the sexual undercurrents in the flat talk between Megan and George Wharton, her knight from Harvard Yard. (One of the nicest things in Adams is the way that her women convey the deliciousness they find in sex, their observation and appreciation of men's bodies, their delight in the unconventional beauty of a man's face.). . .

The temptation for Adams of the fabulistic almost runs the whole novel up on the shoals in its final pages, with an idyllically happy ending for the 1980s that reads like a parody of feminism. . . .

But the book has keen things to say about women past and present, and is pleasurable, intelligent reading, even if it's not all it could have been.

Barbara Koenig Quart, "A Woman's 'Naked and the Dead'," in Ms., Vol. XIII, No. 3, September, 1984, p. 28.

JONATHAN YARDLEY

This inert lump of a book is the latest entrant in the Group-stakes, that ongoing competition among American writers to copy the formula that Mary McCarthy patented in *The Group*. That novel, published two decades ago, told the stories of eight young women who graduated from Vassar College in 1933 and attempted to make their way through a difficult and puzzling world: it contained ample doses of social satire and, by the standards of the day, sex; it aroused a certain degree of heated chatter in those circles where books have the power to cause controversy, and it enjoyed a commercial success sufficiently terrific to arouse the envy of just about every other writer then and since. It spawned countless imitations, by writers of both sexes, some of which managed to duplicate the formula but none of which came close to the best-seller lists.

Now comes **Superior Women,** which contains all the ingredients of the formula except interesting characters, interesting plot and interesting prose. Its author, Alice Adams, has received favorable comment for her earier books, but on the evidence of **Superior Women** it is difficult to see why. What is not difficult to see, by contrast, is the cranking of the machinery as she hauls out the McCarthy formula and runs it through her own typewriter; there's formula aplenty in **Superior Women,** but there's precious little else.

The time is the summer of 1943, 10 years after McCarthy's octet made its way out of Vassar. Now, under an accelerated schedule designed to accommodate the needs of wartime, five girls are matriculating at Radcliffe College. They have been cast, appropriately enough, according to the foxhole theory made so popular in Hollywood war movies of the period:

Megan, the heroine if that is the word for her, is a Californian of little means. . . . She is attractive but somewhat overweight, and possessed of appetites that lead her to believe "that in a sexual way she is indeed different, not quite like other girls."

Lavinia is a rich, beautiful—well, "scrupulously analyzed, Lavinia's features are not actually beautiful; she simply gives a strong impression of beauty"—Southern belle to whom life has been handed unsullied on a silver platter but who manages, of course, to tarnish it quite satisfactorily with her unhappy marriage and not much happier love affairs.

Peg is your basic "jolly noisy old good-hearted" rich girl. . . .

Cathy is a "withdrawn, and enclosed" Catholic from Philadelphia, who "is generally hostile to new impressions, new ideas, and heaven knows hostile to new people, generally." . . .

Janet is from Brooklyn and is Jewish, and that's about all there is to be said about her. . . .

There they are: The Group. At Radcliffe they learn all manner of things, many of them having to do with the pleasures and frustrations of love, not to mention the mysteries of the opposite sex. "Men are different," Lavinia discovers, for some reason failing to add the obligatory "Eureka!". . . [None] of these women understands men, and none of their men understands women, and what we have here is a failure in communications.

What we also have is a shopping list of public events, causes and fads. As the women leave Radcliffe and enter the world, Adams dutifully trots them through everything from civil rights to Watergate; some of the men they meet turn out to be homosexuals, and one of the five ladies turns out to be a lesbian, which makes her very happy in the end; dear Lavinia, spreading her favors as she may, manages to become passionately involved—successively, and almost simultaneously—with an aristocratic communist and a high official of (!) the Committee to Re-Elect the President. All of this romancing is heady stuff,

18

precious little of it ends up satisfactorily, and it leaves Megan wondering: "Are some men put off by extremes of intelligence or even attractiveness in women—put off by superior women? This is a new thought, highly puzzling, unwelcome, and difficult to digest. And it is true; she is quite sure of that."

This, alas, is how Alice Adams writes: nearly 400 pages of breathy little sentences, almost all of them in the present tense. As she writes at one point, "Lavinia and Peg often address each other in this sort of semi-baby talk, but today Megan finds it especially embarrassing." Well, what Adams writes comes embarrassingly close to baby talk too, and reading it at such length is approximately as pleasurable as spending several hours scraping one's fingernails on a blackboard. Given the choice, I'd take the latter.

> Jonathan Yardley, "That Old Gang of Hers," in
> Book World—The Washington Post, *September 2,
> 1984, p. 3.*

LOIS GOULD

Some writers have such lovely voices they always make you want to hum along. Alice Adams is like that; she is fond of the word "perfect," and it suits her. What does a poor college girl see while poking about a rich classmate's messy dormitory room? "A pair or earrings that, if real, are diamonds and rubies, lie across an open book, and the book turns out to be Hobbes, instead of some romantic poetry, as it should be, for those earrings."

But the tune being called in *Superior Women* is tricky. It lulls you, and surely the author means it to, with its harmonious form—five brave girls and how they grow. Since Louisa May Alcott, and perhaps earlier, American woman writers have been drawn to this form. By now, thanks to Mary McCarthy's masterly *The Group* and other novels, it deserves to be called a classic genre, parallel to the male novelist's coming-of-age model, the *Bildungsroman,* wherein a single young protagonist sets out on life's first perilous journey, the quest for manhood (through college, war or love). For the woman writer, "the group" is a kind of interior quest, a portrait of the artist as several different young selves—contrasting, perhaps warring, images that are ghosts of her adult destiny. She exorcises them by giving each self her own life. The group portrait thus releases the "other" women within the mature writer—all those women she chose not to be when she grew up.

For Miss Adams, applying her elegant, rhythmic style to the form, the challenge lies in making it new, fitting it to her own literary place and our time.... We know from Miss Adams's earlier novels and beautifully crafted stories that there will be tenderness and bite, awkward sex that turns graceful with a stroke of wit and a surprise inside every smile....

We can tell [the women] are superior, even in their teens, by the simple fact of Radcliffe. In the 1940's and 50's, getting into Radcliffe, choosing to go there, was so vivid a mark of excellence and ambition that it could, like serious acne, scar a young woman for life.

But the author does not burden us—or them—with their brilliance. They rarely talk of anything but men, sex (necking, not doing "it") and each other. The book of Hobbes is never cracked, and when rich, beautiful Lavinia (she almost never appears without her string of adjectives) says, "Proust has always been my absolutely favorite writer. I feel so at home in Proust," we are meant to laugh a little meanly along with

her envious friends. Two of them will graduate with highest honors, Proustian Lavinia will scrape through with a mere *cum laude,* and the others will drop out for marriage. Fat, odd Peg, in fact, will get pregnant and have to marry her first, only and dreadful blind date. Abortion, for a superior woman, is out.

By now we have begun to discern the complexity of Miss Adams's tune. Each of the women must come, we understand, to a series of bad ends, and the author, with a fine, wry logic, will make us see that disappointment, bitterness, waste, all come with this territory. Is it the terrible cost of being superior—or wanting to be? But she is at pains to tell us these women don't feel strong, don't want to scare away their men, their happiness; it just works out that way.

Perfect Lavinia marries beautifully and is bored, even with her glamorous adulteries and dining room furniture....

Intense, Jewish Janet marries brilliant, nasty, non-Jewish Adam, a playwright, who whisks her off to Paris for a while but then dumps her in White Plains with their child, who bites people, while he runs off with a beautiful black model. Janet goes back to school, becomes a doctor; her son turns out to be a homosexual. Big, miserable, marriage-trapped Peg has so many children she doesn't know what to do; a nervous breakdown, shock treatments and the civil rights movement of the 1960's finally help her escape to her old, odd self. There is an occasional, distressing confusion when the outside world intrudes on these private lives; a fashionable 1956 party has hard rock music, marijuana and "blockbuster writers"; hippies appear on the streets of New York in the early 60's.

Meanwhile, wry, Catholic Cathy manages to finish graduate school and become an economist but then commits a shocking sin of the flesh in California with a priest and condemns herself to unwed motherhood, loneliness, cancer and death. She will not help the economy. Miss Adams has told us Cathy's story before, movingly, in the short story **"What Should I Have Done?"** In both tellings, it is the waste of Cathy's life that haunts us and the author, far more than the figure of Cathy herself or the priest or the fatal love affair.

As for ambitious Megan, who comes as close to a heroine as the author will give us, it is she who has the "success" story. She has a career as a literary agent, makes a lot of money and love and derives little lasting pleasure from any of it. Megan ("overweight, bosomy, overshy") came to Radcliffe from the provinces (Palo Alto, Calif.) pursuing the larger life—rich, Eastern, perfect—as in a Henry James novel, as personified by Lavinia. First she finds a rich young man who likes to kiss her violently but won't take her home to meet his family, teach her to sail on Cape Cod or go clamming with her.... Years later Megan has a brief reunion with the young man who didn't take her clamming. By now she too is thin and rich, with her powerful job, expensive clothes, glamorous New York life. The young man, now tall, thin and gray, says, "By God! I wouldn't have recognized you, you've got so, so—" " 'Thin?' Megan helps him out. But perhaps he has not meant simply thin? Had he, conceivably, meant beautiful, or rich? Very likely not—just thin."

In college, nursing her early wounds, Megan planned to write a thesis about the significance of private incomes in Henry James. It makes us smile—the author is joking? But she rarely does. The final trick of Miss Adams's melancholy chorale is that her subject is not, after all, superiority or growing up or even friendship—they were friends, the dying Cathy says, "who possibly never really liked each other." The novel is rather about the severity of America's class system and the futility of outsiders' dreams. Rich, poor, fat, thin—even, perhaps especially, superior—women are outsiders. Still, if Miss Adams had had the good fortune to meet Henry James, I think they would have had fun, clamming.

Lois Gould, "Life after Radcliffe," in The New York Times Book Review, *September 23, 1984, p. 9.*

JOHN UPDIKE

Alice Adams, the distinguished short-story writer, has come up with *Superior Women,* which takes five Radcliffe students—Megan Greene, Lavinia Harcourt, Peg Harding, Cathy Barnes, and Janet Cohen—from their first meeting, in June of 1943, in Cambridge, to a June exactly forty years later, in northern Georgia. Readers of Ms. Adams' short story **"Roses, Rhododendron"** will be reminded of it—it, too, tells of female friendship dating from the forties and sustained by letters, though the girls are ten instead of seventeen. As in the pairing of Lavinia and Megan, the one girl is cool and Southern and the other is needy and "hot," with an eccentric mother and the antique business in her background; superficially antithetical, both girls are intelligent and bookish and become, somehow, one. Such female alliances repeat throughout *Superior Women,* in a number of forms, across an American landscape of great breadth and sharp detail. . . . As happened in *The Group* twenty years ago, a natural short-story writer's avidity for the telling detail becomes, extended over a wide-ranging plurality of characters and events, rather actuarial, and a certain bleakly notational texture overtakes the survey, and the reader feels that he is not so much enjoying vicarious experience as overhearing gossip.

The first hundred pages of *Superior Women* move slowest and least skimmingly; they take place at Radcliffe between 1943 and 1946. . . . The intricacies of remaining "technical virgins," the degradations of dating drunken and inept college boys, the rise and fall of romantic passions, the subtle but intensely felt shifts of closeness among the young women are lovingly and expertly laid bare. . . . [The] book in its latter stretches has so much plot, so summarily relayed, that it reads like the class notes crowded at the back of an alumnae magazine. Children and traumas and political movements are reduced to rumors that pop up in letters or conversations among the rapidly aging old friends; it all bounces along so briskly that the author seems to assign no importance to these events save a demographic one: this is what tends to happen to you if you graduated from Radcliffe in 1946. Typically, you marry, are miserable, have some miserable children, and take comfort in pills and romantic affairs (Lavinia) or communal living and liberal activism (Peg).

Though there is a good deal of ethnic cross-reference in the text of *Superior Women,* its many characters fall almost entirely into four groups: blacks, Jews, Irish-Americans, and upper-class Wasps. The Wasps are the heavies, with their ghastly clubbiness and haughty prejudices; just their melodious names—Lavinia Harcourt, George Wharton, Potter Cobb, Connie Winsor, Cameron Sinclair, Price Christopher—would make even a middle-of-the-road reader see red, and when the toniest name of them all, Henry Stuyvesant, turns out to have no money and to have once joined the Communist Party we still find it hard to love him. Whereas the blacks are beautiful people. . . . The Jews, too, are beyond reproach. Whatever the job set before them, they do it. . . . Blacks and Jews, in this book,

are invariably figures of comfort. Wasps represent privilege and power. . . . Only the Irish have in them the potential to be good or bad—to be human, in short. . . . Megan Greene, the heart and heroine of the novel, oscillates between her "strong, eager needs" and her habit of getting top marks, her sexual and intellectual prowess, her passion for the circumspect Henry James and her headlong falls into love.

Lavinia and Megan are, like the two little girls of **"Roses, Rhododendron,"** matched opposites: "tall thin blond, impeccably expensively dressed Lavinia—and plump dark Megan, in her slightly wrong California clothes." The compounded attraction and repulsion between them should be the axis of the novel, around which its many lesser worlds turn. If this doesn't quite work, it is not for any failing of vitality and believability on Megan's part but because Lavinia doesn't get, as a character, a fair shake: her purported intelligence ("Actually, perhaps surprisingly, Lavinia herself has a remarkably high IQ; in those numerical terms the two girls are identical") is buried under the reflexive snobbery, the feral schemingness, the ossified narcissism that the author loads upon her, for political reasons; she symbolizes the sterility of the haves. Too rarely is Lavinia allowed to shed the accoutrements of her class. . . . Megan, self-described as "poor and innocent and slightly simple," is intended to command our sympathy, and does; but are we supposed to feel something lamely collegiate about her life's culmination, in 1983, at a feminine dormitory in the Georgia hills, meddling in good works among the Atlanta underclass and snuggling into her weekend visitations from a Chapel Hill professor? Are we supposed to suspect that her tried-and-true beau, his physical charms detailed down to (or up to) his giraffelike eyelashes, is just a senior wimp? They once intended to marry, but put it off for one of the strangest reasons in romantic fiction: they were depressed by the election of Richard Nixon as President. . . . *Superior Women,* indeed, makes much of Nixon, who may end by finding his way into more works of the literary imagination than any executive since King Arthur. The Second World War whisks by in a hazy flecking of uniforms, and of Korea and Kennedy's assassination there is not a mention, but Nixon and Watergate get right into bed with Ms. Adams' characters, causing impotence in one instance and celibacy in another.

Internal references indicate that the author had in mind, as models for this narrative, the schoolgirl novels of Jessie Graham Flower and Jane Austen's novels of female education and (as a graduation prize) marriage. The superior women, at college, entertain no expectation higher than the materialization of "the knight (ah! Mr. Knightley!), the perfect figure of romance." As Nina Auerbach, in her fine "Communities of Women: An Idea in Fiction," has pointed out, the women in Austen are waiting for the door to open, and the gentlemen to enter. . . . Over a century later, the girls of Barnard and Bertram Halls are still pinning their chance of pleasure on the male visitors, though the dates as described are horror shows of compulsory drunkenness and frantic fumbling. The girls stagger back to the dorm like shell-shocked soldiers from the front, and even good-natured Megan is hard-pressed to find the beauty of being pawed on the cold dirt underneath a Charles River bridge. And yet, though four of the five become career women of a sort, their careers are chronicled in terms of amorous discovery and conquest, of multiple orgasms and helpless heartbreak. . . . As the novel progresses, the reader's heart comes to sink whenever a white heterosexual male enters the scene, for to a man they are crude, exploitive, and ultimately feckless. The black Jackson Clay doesn't disappoint, of course, nor do

Megan's Paris pal Danny and her New York pal Biff; both are homosexuals. Naturally, Megan asks herself, "Are gay men really nicer than so-called straight men?" Adam Marr, for whom she has always felt an unaccountable sneaking fondness, turns out to have been a closet homosexual, which explains the fondness. The plight of the superior woman, as he once explained it to Megan, is that "just any old guy won't do. You wouldn't like him, and even if you did your strength would scare him. . . Inferior men are afraid of you." Since, on the evidence marshalled here, all men are inferior, the plight is universal. Stop watching the door, ladies, and ask yourselves to dance.

The novel, written in a swifter and less parenthetical style than Alice Adams sometimes employs, reads easily, even breathlessly; one looks forward, in the chain of coincidences, to the next encounter, knowing that this author always comes to the point from an unexpected angle, without fuss. Momentous scenes are dispatched in a page or two; Cathy's life, especially, seems more rumor than reality. Though not short, the book feels edited, by a racing blue pencil that leaps the years. One would have liked to spend more time with these people, who seem even visually underdeveloped. . . . And this reader would have gladly absorbed even more bits of specifically feminine wisdom than are granted. We learn, for example, that sex is good for your skin and that "it is extremely important, always, to pretend to believe whatever a man is saying . . . Never accuse them of lying." These insights are courtesy of Lavinia; Megan perceives that men who dislike women express it by marrying a lot of them, and that, sadder still, there is "a connection . . . between crippledness and romantic extremity." Only the deformed and self-loathing can really love—that is, idealize—another. To such stark but not unbearable conclusions Megan's pilgrimage brings her, and to a relationship in which, we are assured, the man and she "exchange a small smile, of the most intense affection." The traditional joys of motherhood find no place in *Superior Women;* the children are sad and deplorable where they are not mercifully absent. Megan's main discovery, as she approaches sixty, is herself as a daughter; her path has led backward, to the primal superior woman, her mother. (pp. 160-70)

John Updike, "No More Mr. Knightleys," in The New Yorker, *Vol. LX, No. 38, November 5, 1984, pp. 160-70.*

MICHIKO KAKUTANI

It's a fitting title, *Return Trips,* for the characters in Alice Adams's novels and short stories are almost constantly traveling, on the road, on the move—changing jobs, moving from home to home, relationship to relationship, with the improvisatory skill of veterans of the 60's. For the most part, they're intelligent, well-heeled women, now in late middle age, who have long since traded the domestic loyalties of the 50's they were raised on for the more selfish imperatives of society today. Many are on their second or third or fifth marriages; others have settled into a period of unattachment, but all of them feel, in some very basic way, separate and alone.

In such previous books as *Listening to Billie. Rich Rewards* and *To See You Again,* Miss Adams seemed to want to validate, even celebrate, the independence of her women. She seemed to regard them as brave banner-carriers of the women's movement who had managed to put ill-considered marriages and dependencies behind them, who in "finding themselves" had

succeeded in leaving behind a muddled past. In this latest collection of brisk, gracious short stories, however, the past—often in the shape of a former lover, an ex-husband—returns to haunt Miss Adams's characters. They are not exactly nostalgic for what they've left behind, but they have at least become aware of the after-effects of continually moving on, and the persistence of personal history.

In "Sintra" and the title story "Return Trips," a woman finds that a previous—and very passionate—affair casts troubling shadows over her current involvement with a man, and in both cases is forced to re-evaluate the claims of each liaison. In "Return Trips," as in "My First and Only House" and "Molly's Dog," a particular place also has the effect of triggering memory: whether it's a childhood home or the site of a former love affair, this place exerts a ghostlike hold on the characters' lives, serving as a stubborn reminder of the innocence they've lost.

In this volume, in fact, the emotional consequences of dislocation are everywhere, leaving Miss Adams's characters with an unshakable sense of the precariousness, the random hazards, of life. Having drifted about for the better part of their lives, many of these women now find themselves with only the most tentative or incomplete connections to other people, trying on—and discarding—best friends and lovers with the same haphazard nervousness with which they might try on a new suit or dress. . . .

For these characters, there is too much risk, too much responsibility, attached to more full-time commitments. The lonely narrator of "A Public Pool," for instance, turns down the offer of companionship made by a young man she's glimpsed at the local gym, she would rather keep him at a distance, one of the many strangers whose lives are merely tangent with her own. . . .

Although her heroines often seem to lead strangely unexamined lives—they are constantly wondering how it is they ever ended up marrying the men they did—Miss Adams herself writes about their emotions and the shape of their lives with clear, omniscient skill, summarizing patterns of behavior and ironies of timing with candor and dispassion. At its worst, this approach results—as in *Superior Women,* Miss Adams's last, and peculiarly schlocky novel—in schematic, overly manipulative story lines that simply turn the characters into pawns in the author's master game plan. Yet if a few of the lesser stories in this collection (namely, "You Are What You Own: A Notebook," "Separate Planes" and "Elizabeth") give evidence of this same weakness, most are saved—if not thoroughly redeemed—by the translucent clarity of Miss Adams's prose and her evident compassion for her creations.

Michiko Kakutani, in a review of "Return Trips," in The New York Times, *Section 3, August 21, 1985, p. C17.*

BEVERLY LOWRY

Nobody writes better about falling in love than Alice Adams. The protagonists of her stories, almost always women, often professional women—lawyers, art historians, illustrators, journalists—with a number of years and a good deal of experience behind them, know exactly what is about to happen: no nitwits, never victims or too gaga, they have been there before. They fall with eyes open, knowing full well that the man in question might be inappropriate—married or too self-involved ever to commit totally. Such women think they should know better.

They do know better. That is the glory of an Adams heroine, she is that smart and still goes on. "Ah," she says to herself, sighing, "this again: *love*." And plunges in.

Return Trips is the third collection of short stories Alice Adams has published. It is slimmer than *Beautiful Girl* and *To See You Again* and more wistful by far. Her characters are older. Desperate not to suffer more loss than has already come their way, they keep tripping over a past they have heedlessly let slip through fingers, thinking there would always be time for other opportunities, new adventures. Often, friends, husbands are dying or have died. The survivors make do, but there is an essential sadness to them now, and even their most hopeful statements are often filled with nostalgia. A sentence from **"Waiting for Stella"** echoes a recurrent feeling in this collection: "The condition of youth now seems to Baxter a club from which he has abruptly and most unfairly been excluded." In another, the narrator says, "I am now going back to a very early time . . . before anyone had died." These are not morbid people, only smart and anxious, pensive and extremely touching.

Return Trips has a wonderful opening:

> Some years ago I spent a hot and mostly miserable summer in an ugly yellow hotel on the steep and thickly wooded, rocky coast of northern Yugoslavia, not far from the island of Rab. I was with a man whom I entirely, wildly loved, and he, Paul, loved me, too, but together we suffered the most excruciating romantic agonies, along with the more ordinary daily discomforts of bad food, an uncomfortable, poorly ventilated room with a hard, unyielding bed, and not enough money to get away. Or enough strength: Paul's health was bad.

The story is entirely equal to the tightly packed beginning. Paul knows he is dying and so he sends Emma, the narrator, away, back to graduate school and a moderately successful career. When Paul then dies, the summer in Yugoslavia takes a permanent position in Emma's mind and memory as the great, the irretrievably wonderful time. . . . The present never quite seems to match up to Emma's memories of the past. How could it? She is probably too old and common-sensical now to expect it to. Yet she yearns. And that yearning is the essence of an Alice Adams story. The trick the author pulls off is that readers yearn with Emma. Even clever readers, who think they should know better. . . .

Return Trips contains 15 stories in less than 200 pages. Obviously, they do not dwell in one spot overlong. Like a watercolorist whose every brush stroke must be perfect, this author's hand is lightning fast and brilliant. Of necessity, she must work with confidence and from a large and very certain store of information, as well as a brisk and full imagination. Which she does. Rereading all her stories yields much amazement. How can one person know so much?

Like Colette's, Alice Adams's world is—praise be, these times—an altogether adult one. Long may she explore that world and make her swift reports.

Beverly Lowry, "Women Who Do Know Better," in The New York Times Book Review, September 1, 1985, p. 5.

ELIZABETH WARD

Alice Adams' reputation is as a connoisseur of contemporary American relationships, a specialist in the affairs of white, middle- or upper middle-class, well-educated, well-traveled women, growing up liberal but coming truly into their own in the self-regarding, rather humorless '70s. Her big novel, *Superior Women* (1984), might have been expected to stand as her definitive effort in this minor genre.

But the aptly titled *Return Trips,* a collection of 16 gentle, pedestrian stories, gives us more of the same, though none of the stories has the pace, the sheer gossipy pizazz, which made *Superior Women* a best seller. Only one, **"New Best Friends,"** seems to me really successful. Two, or perhaps three, are moving. The rest are so studiedly insubstantial that they barely manage to lodge in the memory. It is not just that the characters are often dilettantish ("Very cautiously we began to be in love") or that the predominantly minimalist style is choked up with parentheses, qualifiers and strings of synonyms. The problem is, more profoundly, that Alice Adams's idea of meaning in human life is so depressingly tenuous. One quickly tires of so much intensity being brought to bear on so much triviality.

Yet *Return Trips* is not a random collection, thrown together without thought. The stories are all in one way or another about "trips," whether inward journeys of memory, imagination or desire, or real journeys to exotic places, sometimes both, as people at least try to make a little sense of their lives. . . .

Alice Adams' heroines are not in the least contemptible. They are sincere, likeable, sometimes even thoughtful people. In **"New Best Friends,"** the best of the stories, Adams succeeds in conveying with real feeling the pain and mortification of a young New York couple in a mid-Southern town snubbed by local people whom they had believed to be their friends. The material is typically attenuated, but Adams captures convincingly the fine nuances of several overlapping relationships.

Perhaps the biggest practical difficulty with writing unironically, as Alice Adams does, about ordinary, self-absorbed people like these is keeping their ordinariness and self-absorption, their cliché-molded dullness, out of the actual prose. Even Adams' better-educated characters can be appallingly banal, and there is very little saving sense of distance between the characters and their creator. . . .

There is much solipsism in these stories, very little wit or joy. In the end, style and vision coalesce, creating a world of stringently limited possibilities. V. S. Pritchett has said that the short story is "the glancing form of fiction that seems to be right for the nervousness and the restlessness of contemporary life." The stories in *Return Trips,* however, serve to remind us that nervousness and restlessness are not themselves literary virtues.

Elizabeth Ward, "Alice Adams' Chronicles," in Book World—The Washington Post, *September 15, 1985, p. 5.*

SUSAN SCHINDEHETTE

[The stories collected in *Return Trips* are examples] of sublime subtlety, of nuance and quiet perception—stories from a writer who is quite clearly an accomplished, absolute master of her craft.

The characters in Adams' stories tend not to be enmeshed in life's more dramatically external cataclysms. There is no physical violence, no outward brutality, little in the way of sensational vulgarity. Their lives appear to be relatively placid.

Yet it is Adams' gift to reveal the tremendous inner workings beneath the apparent tranquility and make characters come to life in her spare, elegant style. She writes, with marvelously-crafted specificity, of unresolved love, life's harsher deals, of the vague and sometimes unnameable yearnings that grow from lives spent in aloneness and disconnection.

She is equally adept at conjuring, in a few brush strokes, both the external sense of place . . . and its larger significance. . . .

Return Trips is not a collection of unstructured mood pieces or cerebral ruminations. Characters learn things about themselves and the people they have loved—sometimes with stunning emotional impact. Throughout, there is the deep resonance of truths, large and small, told with glistening accuracy.

There are many slivers of light in these stories of Alice Adams, which altogether form a shimmering brilliance. (p. 74)

Susan Schindehette, in a review of "Return Trips,"
in Saturday Review, *Vol. 11, No. 6, November-December, 1985, pp. 73-4.*

John Banville

1945-

Irish novelist, short story writer, critic, and editor.

Among the foremost contemporary authors to experiment with the format of the traditional Irish novel, Banville makes extensive use of metaphors, literary allusions, and elements from various genres to create complex aesthetic effects. His narratives are usually enigmatic and ambiguous, reflecting his belief that reality cannot be accurately mirrored by the conventional realistic novel. Banville's plots often contain such classical components as murder, evil, and love, and he explores such themes as personal freedom, truth and order, the importance of the commonplace, and the tensions between art and reality. Although critics occasionally fault Banville for obfuscated plots and a tendency to indulge in fashionable literary trends, he is consistently praised for sophisticated and masterful prose and for demonstrating the ability to synthesize a highly original style from diverse influences.

Banville's first work, *Long Lankin* (1970), is a collection of short fiction loosely united by common conflicts arising from personal relationships. In these works, he addresses such topics as guilt, loss, destructive love, and the pain inherent in attaining freedom. *Nightspawn* (1971) is a parody of several genres in which Banville endeavors to expose the limitations of the traditional novel through an intentionally chaotic narrative. Set on a Greek island, the story involves a potential military coup, a highly sought-after document, a plenitude of sex, and a murder. *Birchwood* (1973), a modern-day Gothic novel about a decaying Irish estate and a disturbed family, centers on Gabriel Godkin, the son and heir, who gains independence and maturity through his involvement in a circus and a revolutionary coup.

In the mid-1970s, Banville began a series of novels influenced by *The Sleepwalkers: A History of Man's Changing Vision of the Universe,* Arthur Koestler's study of notable astronomers. *Doctor Copernicus* (1976), a historical novel for which Banville received the James Tait Black Memorial Prize, is a fictional reconstruction of the life of Polish astronomer Nicolaus Copernicus, who formulated the heliocentric theory of the solar system. The novel is noted for evoking the squalor and superstition of fifteenth-century Europe as well as Copernicus's struggle to reconcile his theory of the cosmos with those of prevailing religious authorities. In *Kepler* (1981), Banville examines the life and ideas of German astronomer Johannes Kepler, who developed scientific laws concerning the motions of planets in their orbits. In this work, Banville contrasts the Renaissance mathematician's doubts and triumphs with the political and religious strife of his era. In *The Newton Letter* (1982), Banville departs from historical reconstructions. This novel centers on a contemporary scholar who rents an Irish cottage in order to complete his study of Isaac Newton but who becomes more interested in a neighboring family. He makes crucial mistakes in his judgment of the family, however, underscoring Banville's theme that reality cannot be determined by indiscriminate assumptions.

Banville's recent novel, *Mefisto* (1986), reveals the influence of Samuel Beckett in its examination of evil and its relationship to language and memory. In the book's first section, "Mari-

Courtesy of John Banville

onettes," Gabriel Swan recounts his lonely childhood, during which he sought order and form through the pursuit of mathematics. The book's second section, "Angels," depicts Gabriel's quest for harmony despite the influence of Felix, a satanic mentor who Gabriel believes may be his deceased twin brother.

(See also *Contemporary Authors,* Vol. 117 and *Dictionary of Literary Biography,* Vol. 14.)

STANLEY REYNOLDS

Not surprisingly from Ireland comes a ray of hope for the future of fiction. . . . [In *Long Lankin*], Mr Banville displays an amazing sophistication. This is an Irish novel, but it is not Pat and Mike as Trinity students discussing life over a stout in Mooney's but a faintly allegorical tale full of extremely intelligent and articulate characters. They talk with a poetic precision while they move about in a magic sort of world. The plot is classical—incest, murder, and the exorcism of devils—in which the loss of love and happiness is the price of freedom. There are not many writers around, and certainly few of Mr Banville's age, who are capable of having a character say, in answer to being asked what he wants: 'O the word is too big for me to say it without laughing.' Mr Banville not only has his people talk like this, he gets away with it. The theme is ambitious and the form of the novel is far from usual, but Mr Banville is masterly enough to carry both off. He is obviously a man to watch. . . .

Stanley Reynolds, "Artful Anarchy," in New States-man, Vol. 79, No. 2029, January 30, 1970, p. 157.

THE TIMES LITERARY SUPPLEMENT

Long Lankin is divided into two sections: the first consists of nine separate episodes, the second of a continuous novella-length narrative which brings together many of the characters encountered in the earlier section. The themes which lend co-herence to this structure are complex ones, but can be defined simply enough: loss, guilt, mutually destructive loves, the pain of becoming free. Taken individually, the stories vary little as far as quality goes—they are, most of them, excellent. Without having to resort to histrionics, without pushing his characters into dramatic extravagances, John Banville strings the stories together on a single line of tension. Nobody overacts, no one's part is overwritten, yet the feeling of emotional tautness is seldom lost.

This is not to say, though, that the writing is drab, or the stories uneventful; and the knowledge that the novella is there to lend cohesion provides the reader with a sense of anticipation and the stories with a necessary congruity. Possibly the episode titled "Nightwind"—a sombre, subtle story of a party going sour—provides some of the best examples of Mr. Banville's ability to produce a looked-for sense of unease and emotional strain. Characters become known to us without reliance on a run-down on their appearance and antecedents and the sensi-tivity which makes this possible is brought to bear on descrip-tions of the world the characters inhabit. In "Persona", the story which closes the first section, a man is wandering through his empty house and the deadness and strangeness he feels, and upon which the story depends, are swiftly and subtly con-veyed. . . .

The overriding seriousness of [*Long Lankin*] does lead, at times, to an uncharacteristic self-indulgence. Because each of the characters must be provided for in the second section, the party at which they finally meet becomes a little too savage, too obviously climactic; and here Mr. Banville is sometimes tempted to overload a prose which depends for its effect on balance. But the book is more often truthful and perceptive; and for a writer in his early twenties, is an impressive first appearance.

"Rightly Reticent," in The Times Literary Supple-ment, No. 3545, February 5, 1970, p. 127.

AUBERON WAUGH

Mr Banville's last book [*Long Lankin*], which I have not read, was greeted [by Stanley Reynolds (see excerpt above)] as 'A ray of hope for the future of fiction'. Kay Dick, in *Queen*, hailed 'A quite brilliant new talent . . . poetically literate, dra-matically exciting, structurally original and genuinely crea-tive.'

Perhaps Mr Banville's first novel was all these things, but if it was anything like his second then Stanley Reynolds of the *New Statesman* and Kay Dick of the *Queen* need their heads

examined. And one sees similarly rapturous reviews appearing for *Nightspawn*. The only purpose, so far as one can judge, of this utterly pointless book is to impress gullible reviewers with its own cleverness. It is a mystery without a solution and without any very clear problem. It comprises unconnected and inexplicable episodes linked by clumsy lumps of descriptive 'prose poetry'—'the gutters ripe with discarded prophylactics' (of course) and 'Darkness drifted slowly down like soft black glass, from out of a pale sky.' What on earth would black glass look like if it were slowly to drift down from out of a pale sky; how can glass be soft?

Nightspawn might be about a revolution in Greece, or it might be about five people going mad. There are too few clues for the reader to work up much of an interest either way. The tragedy is that Mr Banville—by a vivid passage of description here, an original character there, several powerful passages of narrative—shows that he could write an extremely good book if he felt inclined or were forced to do so, or perhaps (and this is the gloomiest possibility of all) if someone were to teach him where he goes wrong.

But for as long as publishers allow it and moonstruck reviewers encourage it, we must all prepare to put up with this self-indulgence. It may be fun to write (although I doubt it) but it is a blinding bore to read. (p. 287)

Auberon Waugh, "The Rest of the Iceberg," in The Spectator, Vol. 226, No. 7444, February 27, 1971, pp. 287-88.

THOMAS LASK

Nightspawn has a grand opening. The setting is splendid too: a dead, arid, forsaken Greek island surrounded by a stupefying sea. Life on it is fitful, torpid, dying. Awaiting special visitors on the dock is Ben White, a writer manqué, a pusillanimous busybody and the narrator of the story. The visitors arrive: a German journalist and political commentator who knows ev-erything, a man of singular and graceless appearance. His male companion is a crippled sinister Greek. There are also other visitors not expected by White: a trio consisting of a clubfooted Englishman, his young (very much young) wife, and her brother, ideally handsome, languorous and a dope. These three arrive in their own white, trim yacht, persons of undeniable wealth and hidden power.

An appointment has been set up by White for the German to meet a mysterious courier at a witching hour of the night. But before anyone can say Lord Byron, the courier is assassinated in a public square by an agent of the local authorities, and the German's room and belongings are ransacked with a thor-oughness that makes the place look like the haunt of war. White, having accepted an invitation for a drink extended by the Englishman, finds himself rubbing knees with his hostess. A number of Greek officials in various states of confusion and fear make up some of the other dramatis personae. *Nightspawn* certainly has the makings.

But something happens after this promising beginning; the story goes every which way and never makes up its mind what it is. In a superficial way, it is a thriller involving a potential army coup, which can be prevented by a threat of making public a document dangerous to the plotters. Everyone wants to get hold of the document, including a bunch of sleazy henchmen. But there is not enough suspense, clever tracking or strict story line to maintain that side of the novel.

It could have been a black comedy. One of the larger incidents is a party in which the pièce de resistance is a gadget full of wires, wheels and gears designed to let a bomb explode at the appropriate hour. And the love affair between White, vulgar, bawdy, athletic, and the young bride, surface prim, ladylike and proper, also has the ingredients of ludicrous comedy. Characters can, after all, move like puppets and still be perfect in their roles in a comedy of manners. But in *Nightspawn* the wires and armatures are so visible that they take the play away from the dangling men.

Nightspawn might also have been a study in decadence. There is a whiff of incest, homosexuality, of unnatural alliances. But in the end it is none of these things and it isn't a successful amalgam of any of them. The fictional tone breaks too often for consistent effect. Ben White himself is made up of odd shaped chunks that don't go together. He can get off a long, delicate and quite lyrical ode to the island of Delos and her past and woo his lady love as if he were Kowalski in *A Streetcar Named Desire*. It's possible, of course, but the combination doesn't ring true here. . . .

People come and go according to the author's whim, not according to any demand in the story. When he needs them, they pop up like figures in the Punch and Judy show. Clack? they get a knock on the head and disappear the same way. . . .

The dialogue is full of rhetorical, repetitive questions, elliptical statements, half uttered thoughts. All of it is supposed to be fraught or pregnant with meaning. Too often it is just boring. . . .

Mr. Banville, an Irish journalist and novelist, seems to be divided between writing of Greece in what might be termed the classical manner, lyrical, serious, evocative, or in a way that mocks, undercuts and kids the popular reaction to the "Isles of Greece." It's a confusion that spoils what might have been a modestly successful entertainment.

Thomas Lask, "How Not to Make It in Greece," in *The New York Times*, September 25, 1971, p. 29.

ELSA PENDLETON

John Banville's *Nightspawn* [is] a surrealistic tale of love, murder, and political intrigue of various obscure kinds. The narrator, a young author living in Greece, becomes enmeshed in plot-and-counter-plot schemes involving the overthrow of the government. Other prominent characters include a family plucked from Greek mythology, a political journalist and his hunchbacked associate, a Greek Army colonel, and a large supporting cast partly composed of doppelgangers and imaginary shapes dimly seen hiding under things.

Chaotic and ambiguous though the story may be, the final impression is that Banville has achieved the result he wanted—an extended metaphor of trouble and despair as experienced by a sensitive man confronting a malignant universe. The real richness of *Nightspawn* is in the language. Banville, a dryly humorous man, enjoys words, and this is the rare book containing passages which can be enjoyed for the language, quite apart from the story. Additionally, the book abounds with puns, anagrams, and literary allusions, most of them difficult. The impression which remains after reading *Nightspawn* is that it represents the darker underside of the Looking Glass chess game. (pp. 49-50)

Elsa Pendleton, "Fantasy in Fiction," in The Progressive, *Vol. 36, No. 2, February, 1972, pp. 49-50.*

AUBERON WAUGH

John Banville's first novel, *Long Lankin,* was hailed in the *New Statesman* by a reviewer called Stanley Reynolds as "a ray of hope for the future of fiction." Obviously what he meant was that he had found *Long Lankin* jolly good and wished to recommend it. Quite apart from the ineptitude of his wording and the fatuous prejudice which it reveals in Mr Reynolds's approach to the task of reviewing a novel, one shuddered for the effect which this type of praise might have on an impressionable young man like John Banville. If novelists are taught to despise the English novel in order to seek this sort of approval, then the future of fiction might indeed be bleak. In fact, having lived all my life in houses which were plentifully stocked with novels from every period of English novel writing, I honestly believe that more English and American novelists are producing first-class novels now than at any time in the world's history. The only flies in the novelist's ointment are the free library system, which has taken away his livelihood, and the obstinate mediocrity of a handful of literary editors who have effectively destroyed all intelligent interest in the novel by their cretinous anxiety to be thought 'highbrow.'

I mention these dismal truths in the context of John Banville's new novel [*Birchwood*] because I am worried about the lad. He is quite plainly a writer of startling originality, with a most vivid and unusual imagination and rare ability for sustaining interest in a narrative which obeys none of the rules of logical progression. Time and again I found myself gasping with pleasure at some unexpected development. Why then, does Mr Banville wear an angry scowl in his photograph, like some provincial university lecturer who has been passed over for a fellowship? And why does he make the first twenty-one pages totally unreadable, a compendium of deliberate mystification and every silly literary trick which inane fashion or pretentious whimsy has contrived?

The story concerns a boy who lives on an Irish estate in the last stages of decay. He is taught by an aunt, who brings her bastard to live in a menial capacity with the household, which consists of a senile, timorous grandfather, a tyrannical grandmother, a cynical and self-indulgent father, a timid, devoted mother, who soon goes mad, the boy himself and attendant old servants. One day, the grandfather dies, found in the wood with his false teeth embedded in the bark of a tree. Next the grandmother inexplicably explodes. Aunt Martha is burnt to death. The boy (Gabriel) runs away from home in search of phantom sister, joins a travelling circus and witnesses the great Irish potato famine. Many more people die in gruesome circumstances: a coffin inexplicably explodes; Gabriel's cousin is revealed as his twin brother, the offspring of Aunt Martha's incestuous relationship with his father; a revolution takes place in which Gabriel is inexplicably on the winning side, his brother, a member of a transvestite revolutionary group called the Molly Maguires, obscurely the loser. He comes into his inheritance and sits down to write his memoirs.

The reader has to stay on his toes to unravel that much of the plot. Incidents have a way of being slipped into treacly, nature descriptions about plashy fens and luscious blackberries, of a sort to make the aged, cancer-ridden town rats who nibble at these things exclaim about the beauty of Mr Banville's prose. But he is an extraordinarily tough writer, this Banville. Admitting in conclusion that half the loose ends have been left untied, he explains that all these things happened for the same reason—"the reason that does not have a name." And of course he will get away with it, as he deserves to do. In a totally inconsequential death scene which lasts for less than a page—one of the circus company is murdered by soldiers—he is able to summon as much anguish, as would take Dickens twenty pages. He has a quite exceptional talent, as I have said.

Which takes us back to the opening. The first sentence is "I am, therefore I think." Is that clever, Mr Lambert? Is that to your liking, Mr Ratcliffe? What about that, then Dr Steiner? Next, he has us back to the womb:

> And since all thinking is remembering, what
> for instance did I do in the womb, swimming
> there in those dim red waters with my past time
> all before me? Intimations survive. Often a sound
> heard throbbing at dusk from the far side of a
> hill seems an echo of the wallop of their bellies
> as they coupled.

Sounds pretty highbrow to me. What do you think, Michael? Perhaps we should telephone George to make sure it's as significant as it sounds.

Next we have a retrospective preview of Gabriel's first sexual experiences. . . . Then we go on to something really important, a discussion of reality, memory and human perception as they affect the writing process:

> Such scenes as this I see, or imagine I see, no
> difference, through a glass sharply. The light
> is lucid, steady, and does not glance in spikes
> or stars from bright things, but shines in cool
> cubes, planes and violet lines and lines with
> planes, as light trapped in polished crystal will
> shine. Indeed, now that I think of it, I feel it
> is not a glass through which I see, but rather a
> gathering of perfect prisms.

Not bad, that about "through a glass sharply," eh, George. Geddit, Jack? You with us, Stanley Reynolds? Ever so poetic, I must say. It's years since I've seen a really nice gathering of perfect prisms. One may wish to God that young Banville would shut up and let someone buy him a Guinness at such moments as these, but a more serious suggestion is that he should stop reading his reviews. (pp. 171-72)

Auberon Waugh, "Potato Crop," in The Spectator,
Vol. 230, No. 7546, February 10, 1973, pp. 171-72.

THE TIMES LITERARY SUPPLEMENT

"What does it mean? That is a question I am forever asking, what can it mean?" Well might young Gabriel Godkin ask himself that. Granny Godkin has just exploded from spontaneous combustion in the summer house ("those smuts on the wall"). . . . Gabriel goes off (no wonder) to join a travelling circus, or rather a very symbolic Magic Circus; famine and warfare rage; and in the last chapter [of *Birchwood*] much is revealed—incest, inheritances, twins, treachery, illegitimacy, murder.

But what *does* it mean? A jump, evidently, on to a fashionable fantasy bandwagon (or rather circus wagon); an inordinate number of adjectives such as "mysterious", "sombre", "nameless", and "strange"; a scattering of loaded surnames in the manner of Patrick White—Lawless, Godkin, Prospero, Rainbird,

Strongbow; and a profundity or two about Time, the passing of. If it were not that John Banville, according to the book jacket, has won considerable praise for two earlier novels, one might sometimes suspect him to be a *pasticheur* from the *New Statesman* competition pages spreading himself at greater length. Clearly this kind of fantasy demands more, not less, authenticity than realistic fiction.

Still—if this is a recommendation—*Birchwood* does achieve some moments of real gruesomeness.

"Truly Gruesome," in The Times Literary Supplement, *No. 3702, February 16, 1973, p. 169.*

J. A. CUDDON

In recent years Mr Banville, who is still well on the right side of thirty, has published two other novels: **Long Lankin** and **Nightspawn,** both of which were considerably praised (and rightly so, in my view) for their wit, exuberance and originality. Now—*Birchwood,* no less witty and exuberant; and its originality springs for the most part from Mr Banville's lyrical gifts as a dexterous stringer together of words.

'I am, therefore I think.' (he begins) 'That seems inescapable. In this lawless house I spend the nights poring over my memories, fingering them, like an impotent casanova his old love letters, sniffing the dusty scent of violets. Some of these memories are in a language which I do not understand, the ones that could be headed, the beginning of the old life.' This sets the tone and tune for the novel which describes a very 'Irish' family (I feel the events could only happen in Ireland though they would be possible in Russia or parts of the South Slav lands), the Godkins, who live in the eponymous white elephant house of Birchwood.

Gabriel Godkin, our 'hero', grows up in this crumbling mansion, whose decay (even, at times, actual disintegration) symbolises the decadence of its inhabitants and the immediate environment. He grows up in company with his drunken, feckless and negligent father, a Machiavellian and plotting aunt, a somewhat loopy mother, his ruthless and autocratic grandmother . . . and her husband who is also halfway off his coconut. This, you might think, is really too much, but the characters are wholly convincing and fully dimensional as human beings: dotty, eccentric, egoistic, impossible—but very endearing. The main narrative is a haunting and rather melancholy (at times very funny) kind of *recherche du temps perdu.* . . .

[The story] at times, in the author's own phrase, is informed by a kind of 'mordant gaiety'. Ireland is being ruined by famine and revolution. Birchwood is rotting into the ground. The hero sets forth on a journey to find a sister who *may* exist. In the course of this journey he sees the effects of famine and revolution. Eventually he goes back to Birchwood—to start again. It's a moral tale (in which some episodes, like those in the circus, may be taken as symbolic) which is continuously alive with Mr Banville's sardonic humour, invention and verbal ingenuity. 'Violets and cowshit,' Gabriel Godkin says to himself, 'my life has been ever thus.' Here, it seems to me, he summarises that state of 'chassis' and chaos which Ireland has so often been in—and is in once again more disastrously than ever.

J. A. Cuddon, in a review of "Birchwood," in Books and Bookmen, *Vol. 18, No. 12, September, 1973, p. 83.*

JULIAN BARNES

John Banville's novel [*Doctor Copernicus*] has the qualities—earnestness, ambition, and stern historicity—which appeal to the judges of glittery literary prizes, and the defects—clotted prose and humourlessness—which deter readers. It reminds one of Johnson's comment on Congreve's *Incognita,* that he would rather praise it than read it. Nor has Mr Banville exactly picked one of the more gripping greats: Koestler describes Copernicus as 'perhaps the most colourless figure among those who, by merit or circumstance, shaped mankind's destiny'. Mr Banville naturally plays up the man-for-our-time side: the astronomer is sceptical, detached, secretive out of disgust at the world's pretences, and half certain that the whole set-up is absurd. He inhabits a world in political and religious chaos, full of arbitrary suffering, vain scholarship and joyless whoring.

Mr Banville presents this background with some informed vigour, especially the sense of cosmic claustrophobia which agonised Copernicus into the idea of the heliocentric universe. But as for his prose, the best that can be said is that it is, in all its awkward sincerity, at least his own. He favours those inelegant nominal marriages (nerveknot, cloudshadow, dogmerd) which claim vainly to add up to more than their partssum. The attempt to describe mental processes drives him to empty, hulking metaphors. Copernicus has a head 'packed with granite blocks of knowledge'; on the next page he 'ventures out in the frail bark of his thoughts' (a wonder he doesn't capsize); and when he makes his famous breakthrough, the solution arrives 'like a magnificent great slow golden bird alighting in his head with a thrumming of vast wings'. At such vital moments it would be profitable to switch to Koestler, both for the astronomy (*The Sleepwalkers*) and for the intellectual processes (*The Act of Creation*).

Julian Barnes, "Getting On," in New Statesman, *Vol. 92, No. 2384, November 26, 1976, p. 766.*

STEPHEN CLARK

John Banville misses few chances in his retelling of Koppernigk's life [*Doctor Copernicus*]: the sundial he constructed in his schooldays under Canon Wodka, nicknamed Abstemius; the confrontation with Brudzewski of Cracow, the great Ptolemaist whose lectures the youthful Koppernigk did not attend; a clumsy attempt by the Neoplatonist Novarra to enlist him against the Borgias; a syphilitic brother; and the manic-depressive Rheticus to persuade him to publish. Koppernigk's talents, as statesman in the long struggle with the Teutonic Order and as physician, are given ample scope.

His great failure as an astronomer (more impressive than most men's success) is fully displayed: the Copernican system had eight more epicycles than the Ptolemaic, and mistakenly reduced planetary distances; it was not even, technically, heliocentric—the sun stood arbitrarily to one side of the centre. To be sure the navigational tables produced eight years after Koppernigk's death were more accurate than the Ptolemaic, but it was neither accuracy nor simplicity that made the revolution. Koppernigk, in effect, saw the world as Nicholas of Cusa's infinite sphere: and as modern cosmology returns us to a finite universe, we can look back and consider the post-Copernican infinities of empty space. More important still, Koppernigk attempted a realistic description of the world beyond sight, rejecting Ibn Rushd's defence that "Ptolemaic astronomy is nothing so far as existence is concerned, but it is convenient for computation of the non-existent". Andreas Ossiander's editorial preface, attempting to make Copernican astronomy a similarly non-realistic model, could not diminish its radical effect.

Mr Banville's Koppernigk is a scientific mystic, whose vision is traduced and distorted in the working out, and who devotes himself ever more distrustfully to the intellect and its intelligibles. Human companionship and the world of flesh are repulsive to him; his brother Andreas, a sinister Italianate figure, "the bent bow from which he propelled himself beyond the filthy world". Only on his deathbed can he repent. That engaging homosexual, Rheticus of Wittenburg, is allowed to tell his story, though from a standpoint less friendly to Koppernigk than his constant efforts to publicize the master's work would suggest. Certainly he had cause for hostility. Koppernigk gave him no mention in *De revolutionibus,* doubtless from senile forgetfulness and, as Tiedemann Giese put it in a conciliatory letter to Rheticus, his constant inattention to matters non-philosophical.

Psychological speculations on the roots of science do not make a novel. The strength of Mr Banville's work lies in his pictures of Koppernigk and Rheticus. He perhaps underplays Koppernigk's real practical ability—he was also an early economist, urging a unified national currency—and perhaps exaggerates his coldness. Rheticus makes more amusing reading, as he bounds and plunges about the room, tearing his hair over the hideous complexity of the orbit of Mars. And as a spokesman for the common world of sense which Koppernigk wished to transcend he is more convincing than Andreas Koppernigk. *Doctor Copernicus* is good enough as a historical primer; as a novel it is better than most.

Stephen Clark, "Eclipse of the Earth," in The Times Literary Supplement, *No. 3900, December 10, 1976, p. 1533.*

THE ECONOMIST

Nicolas Koppernigk lived in times that even our age might not envy—born into a world of fading medieval certainties, he left it an utterly changed thing, changed by his own ideas from the central essential point of the entire universe (and hence a place, no matter how imperfect and vile, in which men could believe themselves chosen to be masters of all) to a wandering and comfortless vehicle of doubt swimming in a limitless sea of chaos. It is almost impossible for us, at this distance, to understand the terror and despair into which Copernicus' heliocentric theory could plunge his contemporaries; and the treatment of this effect—and how the theory itself became so quickly and widely known, in spite of Copernicus's refusal to publish—is not the most satisfactory aspect of Mr Banville's otherwise outstanding novel. But on Copernicus's own struggles to fend off the vileness of his world, to reconcile the horrors among which he lived with the purity of his vision of the cosmos, Mr Banville is superb, as he is in dealing with the price that men of awesome vision pay in insulation from the comforts and splendours of being human. There are not many historical novels of which it can be said that they illuminate both the time that forms their subject-matter and the time in which they are read: *Doctor Copernicus* is among the very best of them.

"Brief Lives," in The Economist, *Vol. 261, No. 6955, December 18, 1976, p. 131.*

PAUL TAYLOR

As a historical novelist Banville is amazingly adept at evoking the flavour and the feel of the period he is writing about, while as an expositor of the scientific and philosophical ideas of his hero he is admirably fluent and lucid. Not the least of the pleasures to be derived from *Kepler* is the way Banville's tactile, sensuous prose coils itself confidently around everything—from Tycho Brahe's disconcertingly metal nose to Kepler's most abstract theories on the *harmonia mundi,* from the "throb" of oranges in a pewter dish (Kepler sees oranges for the first time when he visits Prague) through to the revolutionary ellipse laws of the *Astronomia Nova.* All is presented (to borrow a phrase from the novel) with a "tense inexorable thereness".

Kepler contrives to be both a novel of ideas and a novel of character, and one moreover which shrewdly adumbrates the influence of character *on* ideas. Out of the emotional and financial mess of Kepler's life (shunted as he was, thanks to anti-Lutheran laws, a parsimonious wife and the caprice of patrons, from refuge to refuge), there emerged a psychological compulsion to find an all-embracing universal order, a desire which gave rise ultimately to Kepler's law of world harmony which states that "the squares of the periods of evolution of any two planets are to each other as the cubes of their mean distances from the sun". In its bare prose formulation, this does not seem much to get worked up about. It is Banville's achievement to charge each of Kepler's discoveries with the sublimity and the poetry that they held for the astronomer himself.

But the book is not so unsubtle as to suggest that Kepler's was a steady march of mind onward and upward to the light of truth. Europe was still riddled with superstition and the astronomer himself was not entirely untainted by it. Employed as Imperial Mathematician to Emperor Rudolph (in succession to Tycho Brahe), Kepler is dismayed to find that the main service required of him is to plot astrological charts, but he is quick to defend astrology from the root-and-branch attack made on it by Feselius. For Kepler, God was to be found in the geometrical relationships set up in nature and in the heavens.

There were, however, more harrowing clashes between Kepler's science and his superstition. As Europe slid into the Thirty Years' War, the astronomer began to wonder if it was a demon risen from the closing pages of the *Harmonia Mundi* which was inciting the turmoil. He found it increasingly difficult to separate his own inner confusions from those of the outside world and feared for his sanity. When Kepler's mother is tried for dabbling in witchcraft, Banville is very acute in bringing out the perverse sense of anticlimax which is felt by her family. Kepler realizes "with amazement, and a sick heave, that he was, yes, it was the only word, disappointed. Like the rest of them, including even, perhaps, his mother, he had wanted something to happen; not torture necessarily, but *something,* and he was disappointed." Banville is especially good at showing how his characters are caught in the unsettling cross-currents between essentially medieval and modern outlooks.

If the novel has a fault it is in its rather moist and uncritical attitude to Kepler. It cunningly exploits the age-old narrative rhythm of progress-setback-progress, but often the setbacks . . . are milked for more pathos than seems warranted: there are echoes of that cloying sentimentality which sometimes threatens to vitiate Chaplin's art, similarly preoccupied as it is with the depiction of little put-upon idealists. Banville's novel is at its worst when it is most starry-eyed about its heroic star-gazer. *Kepler* survives these blemishes, however, and emerges as a first-rate historical novel which manages to cram in more detail, verve and insight than many a novel three times its length.

Paul Taylor, *"Head in the Stars,"* in The Times Literary Supplement, *No. 4061, January 30, 1981, p. 107.*

ALAN BROWNJOHN

"I have abandoned my book", writes John Banville's unnamed narrator at the very beginning of *The Newton Letter,* "real people keep getting in the way". The real reader could be forgiven for hoping that the brief span of the novel will indeed allow flesh and blood to elbow their way through the introspective musings of the historian who is telling this tale instead of finishing his life of the great astronomer. As it is, people receive too rare a chance to emerge from the all-too-delicate prose and unobtrusive symbolism. This is a slim book inside which a fatter one is struggling to get out.

The historian has rented a holiday cottage somewhere within reach of Dublin to get on with his work. The place is the former lodge at the approach to Fern House, which stands a couple of hundred yards away, visible and fascinating to a lonely scholar. The inhabitants of this broken-down mansion are equally interesting: the middle-aged Lawlesses, Edward and Charlotte, he drunken and tamely boorish, she graceful and distant; Ottilie, their niece, twenty-four, blonde, purposeless and vaguely handsome; and a child who might belong either to the older couple or to Ottilie. The narrator assumes they are protestants and patricians; the trappings of aristocracy have disappeared and "only style remains". The life of Newton recedes into the distance.

In the midst of what might seem an inevitable affair with Ottilie, the narrator senses a secret sharer attending on his enthusiastic yet uneasy love-making, and he becomes aware that he has fallen in love with Charlotte (who has hardly spoken to him), instead. In an elusive way, these passages are sensitively contrived: Ottilie is the more real; Charlotte is a passion of the mind, and their relationship always "would teeter on the brink of being something". Thus it is with the novel itself. Its apparent message is that reality is not to be deciphered by casual assumptions. The mysterious child belongs to neither woman, and has been adopted by the childless older couple: he revealed eventually as dying of cancer, she cocooned in tranquillizers. But all this is less convincing than some almost incidental episodes in this short tale: *The Newton Letter* is on the brink of being something when the author occasionally lifts his gaze from the tiny, enigmatic scenes which he finds so absorbing.

Two compelling moments when the outside world walks into Fern House suggest the vigour which has been inexplicably rejected in favour of a minimalism which ends up as merely decorative and slight. . . . In both scenes the atmosphere is perfect; and Mr Banville sets his characters in motion at last with a speed and sureness of touch which give more than a hint of the life that could have been injected into these frail, melancholy existences.

Alan Brownjohn, *"A Matter of History,"* in The Times Literary Supplement, *No. 4132, June 11, 1982, p. 643.*

MIRANDA SEYMOUR

Mr Banville's most recent and highly-praised books were imaginative reconstructions of Copernicus and Kepler. Newton seemed the logical successor. Instead, [in *The Newton Letter*], we have the letters of a middle-aged modern academic whose study of Newton has given way to the study of his neighbours, the Lawless family. As he puzzles over the reasons behind Newton's nervous collapse in his fifties, he fails to recognise the parallel situation in his own life. The Lawless family are glibly assessed by him and—as it turns out—tragically misconceived. The narrator's obtuseness here is as artfully conveyed as that of Dowell in Maddox Ford's *The Good Soldier*. His fantasies of cerebral adultery with Charlotte Lawless while bedding her niece Ottilie owe more than names to Goethe's *Elective Affinities*.

Well, it is all grist to the reviewer's mill—how satisfactory to spot the derivations!—but I couldn't help feeling that Mr Banville was playing too many literary games for the good of his book and that this was a pity. It is beautifully constructed and written. He can conjure up with suddenness a hot afternoon, a squalid bedroom, a decaying house. He is both acute and evocative when he writes of the moment when 'the worst and deepest fear of the heart will drift out with the dreamy innocence of a paper skiff on a pond.' Only occasionally does love of language get the better of sense. Try as I will, I cannot suppose that making love to a woman is really like entering Venice in the 'blue shade of her pavements. Here was a dreamy stillness, a swaying, the splash of an oar . . . the great square, the sunlight . . . a flock of birds scattering with soft cries in my arms.' Shall I look at Venice with different eyes in the future? I think not. (p. 27)

Miranda Seymour, *"Burning Sappho," in* The Spectator, *Vol. 248, No. 8032, June 19, 1982, pp. 26-7.*

MARTIN SWALES

The unnamed narrator of John Banville's novel [*The Newton Letter*] is an academic who spends the summer on a run-down country estate in Ireland where he hopes to put the finishing touches to a book on Isaac Newton. Gradually, his research takes a back seat as he becomes fascinated with the family on whose property he is living. Edward Lawless is a wreck of a man, clumsy, inarticulate, frequently drunk; his wife Charlotte is noble, suffering, strangely withdrawn; Ottilie, Charlotte's niece, is blonde, somewhat graceless, but physically available. Even in the physical abandon of his love-making with Ottilie, the narrator's heart—and mind—are not in it. Inwardly, he is obsessed with Charlotte, and it is her image which informs—and, to a certain extent, deforms—the relationship with Ottilie. By the end of the story the narrator learns a number of lessons: he realises that many of the images and patterns he has established for himself and for those around him are false. The Lawless family are not genteel Protestant aristocracy in decline; Edward is not the brute of the narrator's account, he is dying of cancer; Charlotte's mysteriousness has more to do with the tranquillisers she has been taking in order to cope with the horror of her husband's decline than with any mysterious Iris Murdoch-like spiritual drama. The 'illustration from a Victorian novelette', the 'old novels', the 'echo of some old brown painting'—such exercises in cultural image-making founder before the authority of simple fact. The narrator comments: 'I dreamed up a horrid drama, and failed to see the commonplace tragedy that was playing itself out in real life.' The sophisti-

cation of the knowing mind proves brittle and irrelevant. As Ottilie puts it: 'You think you're so clever, but you don't know a thing.' The ordinary has the last word.

This breakthrough of the commonplace is linked with the breakdown of the book on which the narrator is working. He is fascinated by Newton's nervous collapse in 1693, a crisis which is no mere psychological disturbance: Newton's (fictitious) letter to Locke reports a profound change whereby the 'lofty verities of science', the austere splendour of laws and patterns, have crumbled before the abundant truth of commonplace, unremarkable being. Newton's crisis, then, is of a piece with his biographer's.

'Shall I say, I've lost my faith in the primacy of the text?' the narrator asks at the beginning of his account. Well, yes and no. Given that the theme of Banville's novel is the destruction of certain kinds of textuality, one would assume that its actual mode would necessarily be overtly unpatterned, devoted to unmediated rawness of the 'let-it-all-hang-out' school—or to a kind of *chosiste* prose of constatation. But this is far from being the case. *The Newton Letter* is no loose baggy monster. Rather, it manipulates a particular kind of intertextuality in order to supplant one kind of text by another. The discovery of humble being, of the radiance inhering in the particular, of the truth of objects in their 'innocence', 'their non-complicity in our affairs', is part of a particular intertextual continuity. . . .

Compounding this density of textual reverberation, we have the all-pervasive, formative presence of Goethe's novel *The Elective Affinities*. The names of the characters (Charlotte, Edward, Ottilie, Mittler), the 'spiritual adultery' of the narrator's relationship with 'Charlottilie'—all this makes it clear that Banville is inviting us to perceive his novel as a debate conducted with—and through—Goethe's unforgettable study of the place of image, picture and pattern within the flux of human eros ('knowing' in both senses of the word). Goethe, with his dislike of Newtonian science, would have approved. He would also have approved of Banville's refusal to be reductive. Commonplace facts—Edward's cancer—may have the last word. But inseparable from *that* matter-of-factness is the celebration of humble things and circumstances that are outside (but not excluded from) the human acts of perception, comprehension and symbolisation. The narrator writes of Edward: 'I can't recall what he said, what words he used. The subject was the countryside, farming, something banal. But what he was talking about, I suppose, was his sense of oneness now with all poor dumb things, a horse, a tree, a house, that suffer their lives in silence and resigned bafflement, and die unremarked.' At one level, the process the narrator undergoes is one of moral growth. His stylistic love affair with drainpipes, wellington boots, with concrete particulars, serves to redeem the physical (but not *merely* physical) truth of his feelings for Ottilie.

John Banville has written a compassionate and vibrantly intelligent novel—and also a timely one. Readers . . . will find here a book whose indebtedness to other literary works has nothing to do with derivativeness—nor with a self-regarding pan-literariness. Rather, Banville reminds us of the ways in which, and of the extent to which, literature can legitimately be made out of the issue of its own mode and being—and can thereby address profound issues of human cognition and behaviour.

Martin Swales, *"Creative Affinities," in* London Review of Books, *July 15, 1982, p. 22.*

RUSSELL McCORMMACH

Instead of writing a conventional fictional biography [in *Kepler*, Banville] presents episodes, varying in length from one day to several years, from Kepler's life. We meet Kepler at the moment of his auspicious meeting with the Danish astronomer Tycho Brahe, upon whose observations of Mars he would base the new astronomy; we leave him during his last illness as we met him, waking from a dream of cosmic mystery. Of the 30 years in between, Mr. Banville chooses three periods that illuminate three aspects of Kepler's life. He shows us Kepler the frustrated scientist during his transition from Tycho's collaborator to his successor as court mathematician in Prague, all the while seeking a theory to fit Tycho's observations of Mars. Next he shows us Kepler's emotional roots by describing his visit home to Swabia after completing the "New Astronomy" in 1608. Finally the author portrays Kepler the public figure through fictional letters from 1605 to 1612, a period of personal, professional and political turmoil.

Within these episodes, Mr. Banville vividly evokes details of 17th-century society. He also fills in much of the rest of Kepler's life, but he does not do so systematically, as the reader soon learns when he confronts seeming contradictions and large gaps and reversals in time. This scrambling of events serves a literary purpose; it allows Mr. Banville to depart from the techniques of the biographer and the writer of popular fictional biography. Drawing an analogy with Kepler's cosmos, he organizes the book as a series of orbital motions by Kepler through repeated way stations—Graz, Prague, Linz and a few other places. Kepler's motions, forward and retrograde, are bound to centers of influence, much as the motions of the planets are bound to the sun. While Kepler is spiritually independent . . . , the political and religious forces of his day drive him to attach himself to whatever center of power will sustain him.

Mr. Banville's attempt to express the novel's content through its structure is intriguing but does not succeed. The reader who is not already familiar with the historical Kepler and his achievements is likely to become lost, and he will remain confused about the development of Kepler's scientific work. A related and more serious shortcoming is the portrayal of Kepler as a scientific thinker. A novel about an actual scientist promises to re-create not only the daily life he had in common with his contemporaries but also a mental life of great interest. This is particularly true when the scientist is Kepler, who left behind a rare and intimate autobiographical record of his route to scientific discovery. Aside from a few glimpses into his scientific preoccupations—twice in the novel the "sleepwalking" Kepler stumbles onto a scientific insight—Mr. Banville does not show us Kepler at work. He includes little about the content of Kepler's works (there is an unfortunate typographical error in the statement of his third law, making "revolution" appear as "evolution") and leaves the reader with a feeling of incompleteness.

As one who is interested in the possibilities of the fictional depiction of scientists and their work, I hope that Mr. Banville will write more on this subject. Despite its shortcomings, *Kepler* is an informed and lively account of an important time and personality by an author of seriousness and talent. (pp. 10, 12)

> Russell McCormmach, "He Remodeled the Cosmos," in The New York Times Book Review, May 29, 1983, pp. 10, 12.

BARBARA HARDY

The first page of John Banville's dazzlingly individual new novel [*Mefisto*] resounds with ancestral voices. His hero, Ga-

briel Swan, makes his first appearance in male metonymic guise as a tiny swimming sperm heading for 'the burning town, the white room and Castor dead', images which transmute Yeats' "Leda and the Swan" to anticipate what's to come, and begin the mythical permutations. Lower down on the page the narrator borrows and straightens out Beckettian contradictions to assert, as mythical hero, narrator, and novelist, 'I could go on. I shall go on'. When swimmer has been successfully matched with the minimised female part, conception is followed by a birth in which he survives while his monovular twin drowns in air. We eventually follow him into a Joycean education, punishment, and precocious imaginative exercises. He will later extend his swan and dove aspects to claim relation with Icarus. So the novel uses, perhaps to exorcise, three modern masters—four, if we include Flann O'Brien, a pervasive influence. In an interview . . . , Banville complained of the lack of an Irish tradition, instancing Joyce and Beckett as extrovertedly looking to Europe. But for one who sees the ancestors as 'other', not regionally insular, he certainly uses their forms, voices and symbols in some very Irish ways. The chief guide in this quest/novel, is Felix, culpable and diabolical, with a nice line in rude address and blasphemy which unmistakably echoes the priestly fun-and-games of Buck Mulligan ('Your absurd name, an ancient Greek' and 'A little trouble about those white corpuscles'). Felix teases Gabriel about his name, 'Swansir', 'birdboy', and 'whooper', but is a more sinister and powerful figure than Mulligan, an elusive authorial force. Traditions and influences are mostly comic gracenotes, not anxieties. But Beckett's presence seems integral.

The narrator reflects, Beckett-like, on imagination, the chase of reality by art, and language. Banville presses on words, slowing them up as they speed past. . . . [The novel's] refreshing scrutiny of dulled words is very like Beckett. So too is the expressive two-part structure, in which the binary formula, imprinted on the lone twin, is used to break, not construct, sequence. A whole new set of characters and events arrives, more or less out of the blue. Banville uses Beckett in ways which normalise the older artist's disruptions of linear moves, providing some continuity as Gabriel grows from the passivity of the first section, "Marionettes", to a more demanding metaphysic and ethic in the second half, "Angels". It's more like *Godot* than *Molloy* or *Watt*.

If I labour this debt—and I could go on—it's certainly not because it is not fully repaid. Banville may be the only writer to use Beckett and keep his head, like Beckett with Joyce. Banville's weird world is all his own. He shares with Beckett and Flann O'Brien the ability to make a world familiarly, even provincially, Irish, yet beyond nature. The happenings are ordinary and plausible—embraces, dyings, crimes, researches, state sponsorship of sciences—but presented discretely, stripped of motive, bare of background, denuded of history, to act as surreal images and structures. The language also separates as well as joins, producing laconic statements, isolated verisimilitudes, odd witty figures. . . . But not everything is bizarrely innovative. Banville is strong on sensation, and gives a virtuoso account of a nightmare recovery from a bad burning, awakening from pain to pain. He's good on thought, in many inventive accounts of imaginative calculation, essential in a portrait of the artist as mathematician, struggling for formula against flux. He's not interested in character, but animates his mythy doves, swans, devils, angels and puppets by shame, disgust, horror, fear, lust, aspirant desire.

The blurb says the book is about the Yeatsian man caught between life and work. Yeats himself made that grand affirmation about having to choose between perfection of life and of work, but was himself no 'Yeatsian man'—he applied himself creatively to life and art, falling short like everybody, doing better than most. Banville's hero and novel can't be so reduced. Gabriel's emergence from the obsession with harmony coincides with his exit from the author's grip, and the attempts to break, make and remake forms, to pit art against life and life against art, seem more like Beckett than Yeats. 'Is it my imagination? Was it ever anything else? He'll be back, in one form or another, there's no escaping him.' Let's hope he will.

Barbara Hardy, "Birdboy," in Books and Bookmen, *No. 371, September, 1986, p. 26.*

PATRICIA CRAIG

The hero of John Banville's novel *Birchwood* is called Gabriel Godkin, and he's looking for his missing twin. This twin motif keeps recurring in Banville's work. In *Mefisto,* another quest novel, another Gabriel—Gabriel Swan—misses the ghostly twin, his embryonic *Doppelgänger,* who didn't survive his exposure to a new element: "He drowned in air." The dualistic character of the new novel, with its positive and negative elements, is established straight away. "Even yet I cannot see a one and a zero juxtaposed without feeling deep within me the vibration of a dark, answering note." Gabriel, prodigiously numerate, finds in pure mathematics an answer to the rage for order which possesses him, even in the face of inescapable randomness. . . . The search for symmetry leads to disintegration.

Gabriel's surname is significant. Zeus, Leda, Castor and Pollux, Icarus, Daedalus: take "Swan" as a starting-point, and all these emblematic associations, and more, will follow. "Birdboy" is an early nickname applied to Gabriel by his evil genius Felix-Mephistopheles, or—as it may be—Felix Virgil, the guide who steers Gabriel through a particular kind of underworld, at a time when he feels himself to be enduring his own season in hell. He has survived an accident, but only just, coming round in hospital after being appallingly burnt. Weeks, months of pain and disorientation follow—and there's a sojourn among tramps and drunks, dustbin pickers, drug addicts. The unnamed city in which these people are observed and occasionally encountered is presumably Dublin; this is section two of the two-part novel, called "Angels".

In the first part ("Marionettes"), set in an Irish town resembling Wexford where John Banville grew up, we have Gabriel's sedate and fateful childhood, his rigorous schooling, the local Big House, Ashburn by name, with its lofty family on the verge of extinction. . . .

In *The Newton Letter,* John Banville seems to suggest, among other things, that fiction itself is only one way of imposing a pattern on events and perceptions, and a hit-or-miss way at that. *Mefisto* departs from a standard narrative pattern by going in for deliberate dislocations, by withholding a good deal of everyday information, and by having a profusion of contexts for its symbolic overlay. Part Two of the novel seems not so much a continuation of Part One as a more complex version of it: the peripheral figures, odd and astray; the lures for Gabriel—first a mathematical notebook, then a computer. None of this is irritating; the author's strength of purpose and ingenuity keep us engrossed. Whatever he has gained from other authors—Beckett and Joyce in particular—Banville, in the end, shapes his material in unprecedented ways, and enshrines his extended metaphors, his unsettling evocations and moments of ordinariness in resonant and lucid prose.

Patricia Craig, "A Rage for Order," in The Times Literary Supplement, *No. 4358, October 10, 1986, p. 1131.*

WILLIAM KELLY

Readers familiar with Banville's previous work will not be surprised by his latest novel [*Mefisto*]. It is, like all the others, a writer's rather than a reader's book. That is to say, we cannot expect to understand or even like it at first reading. Nor can we expect the novelist to be troubled by this. His books are written not to be enjoyed but to be endured. Idlers be warned. *Mefisto* is therefore a "writerly" novel which, in the conventional modern idiom, continually questions its own fictionality. The title, attaching to no character in the text, floats freely over it as if challenging the reader to interpret the story by its uncertain light. Yet it identifies by default the Faustian narrator and protagonist, Gabriel Swan, whose obscure preoccupation with "the banality of gemination" suggests that his mysterious mentor, guardian angel, or evil genius, code-named Felix, might also be his phantom twin.

The narrative takes the form of Gabriel's life history, told, after the manner of *Tristram Shandy,* from the moment of his conception. . . . What follows is like the opening of a leaf from a tightly-folded bud. Gabriel reviews the events of his life in the order of growth. If what he records is beyond the plausible limits of memory, this is no reason to doubt his story. His imagination is free to invent what he cannot be expected to remember. . . .

However, when the question of plausibility is raised, Gabriel is ready with his answer: "Can that be possible? It's what I remember, what does it matter whether it's possible or not?" What is the reader to make of a narrator who says that his memory of events, not the events themselves, constitutes their fictional reality? It's as if the novelist was saying to his readers: abandon your naive preference for experience over imagination, a preference much pandered to in "realistic" fiction; everything in my book is a product of my character's imagination, even though I employ the tactic of giving him a memory as well.

And yet in some curious way well understood by, say, 18th-century novelists, the illusion declared is not the illusion dispelled. Gabriel's willingness to confess his inability to recall a lost detail somehow gives *him* a reality which his fiction lacks: "I had come to tell her, let me see, to tell her—oh, what does it matter. I can't think of anything." On the other hand, his habit of surrendering invention to fact has the effect of cancelling the distinction he tries to make between them. Thus, on his way out of the hospital, where he has just identified his mother's body, he looks for a nun in an elaborate, winged head-dress that he saw on his way in: "The nun with the head-dress was gone, had winged away, leaving the ledger open on the desk. No, there was no nun. I invented her." But of course it is too late for this now, because in fiction, as Gabriel's narrative frequently reminds us, nothing can ever be struck off the record.

This is a meticulously crafted, utterly self-conscious novel. It specializes in telling rather than in showing, apparently subordinating the latter mode to the overriding potency of the poetic voice. Every character, with the significant exception of the Mephistophelean Felix, is frozen in the intricate lattice-work (metaphor supplied) of Gabriel's narrative. . . .

For all this, *Mefisto* succeeds in hauling the reader through moral horrors that seem anything but fictional. . . . If a book, as Kafka put it, should serve as an ice axe for the frozen sea within us, then this one is hard enough for the job.

William Kelly, "John Banville's Great Expectations," in Irish Literary Supplement, *Vol. 6, No. 1, Spring, 1987, p. 15.*

Donald Barthelme

1931-

(Has also written under pseudonym of Lily McNeil) American short story writer, novelist, essayist, and author of children's books.

A preeminent writer of experimental fiction, Barthelme creates humorous and often unsettling stories by juxtaposing incongruous elements of contemporary language and culture. His prose has been described as a verbal collage in which words are intended to function as objects and are intentionally stripped of meaning by their unlikely combinations. Barthelme's writing is characterized by the absence of traditional plot and character development, disjointed syntax and dialogue, parodies of jargon and cliché, and a humor, according to Thomas M. Leitch, that arises "from a contrast between outrageous premises and deadpan presentation." His work contains allusions to literature, philosophy, art, film, and popular culture, and he considers such themes as the ability of language to express thought and emotion, the function of art and the role of the artist in society, the complications of sexuality, the frailty and transience of human relationships, and the fragmentary nature of reality. Although some critics perceive a destructive impulse to subvert language and culture in much of his fiction, Barthelme has enjoyed widespread critical acclaim and is particularly praised as a stylist who offers vital and regenerative qualities to literature.

Barthelme's first stories appeared in literary periodicals during the early 1960s. In these works, many of which were first published in the *New Yorker* and subsequently collected in the books *Come Back, Dr. Caligari* (1964), *Unspeakable Practices, Unnatural Acts* (1968), *City Life* (1971), and *Sadness* (1972), Barthelme incorporates advertising slogans, comic-book captions, catalogue descriptions, and jacket blurbs from records and books into a style that features verbal puns, non sequiturs, and fractured dialogue and narrative. These volumes contain some of his best-known and most highly praised stories. Although some critics expressed concern over the monotonous tone and the apparent meaninglessness of many of the pieces, most praised Barthelme's inventiveness and technical skill.

Guilty Pleasures (1974) and *Amateurs* (1976) are retrospective compilations of Barthelme's uncollected writings. Promoted as nonfiction, *Guilty Pleasures* contains miscellaneous parodies and satirical pieces that were originally written for the *New Yorker,* while *Amateurs* includes short stories from the 1970s. In *Great Days* (1978) and *Overnight to Many Distant Cities* (1983), Barthelme invests his various characteristic methods with new elements. Almost half of the stories in *Great Days* consist of what Robert Towers described as "a staccato dialogue form in which two speakers bounce phrases off one another at high speed; sometimes the phrases answer each other, often they do not." *Overnight to Many Distant Cities* is composed of typical Barthelme stories and very brief, dreamlike monologues. While some critics faulted the collection for Barthelme's idiosyncratic use of literary devices, others noted the presence of hope in many of the pieces as well as an uncharacteristic willingness by Barthelme to confront and reflect emotions.

Barthelme's first novel, *Snow White* (1967), is a darkly comic and erotic parody of the popular fairy tale. Set in contempoary Greenwich Village, the title character is an attractive yet unsatisfied young woman who shares an apartment with seven men. Composed largely of fragmented episodes in which undistinguishable characters attempt to express themselves in jargonistic and often nonsensical speech, *Snow White* has commonly been interpreted as an examination of the failure of language and the inability of literature to transcend or transform contemporary reality. *The Dead Father* (1975) is often considered one of Barthelme's most sustained and cohesive narrative works. The central character, the Dead Father, is described by Thomas R. Edwards as "a Gulliverian figure, God, machine technology, civil and economic law, an idea of the world as ordered, equitable, and perhaps benign, an embodiment of collective selfhood and its history." In this novel, a surrealistic, mock-epic account of the Dead Father's journey to his grave and his burial by his son and a cast of disreputable characters, Barthelme weaves mythological, biblical, and literary allusions to create a story, according to Hilton Kramer, that lends "a sense of mystery and complexity and a certain decorative appeal to what . . . is actually a rather simple fantasy of filial revenge." In his third novel, *Paradise* (1986), Barthelme uses spare, formalistic prose marked by both a sense of playfulness and sorrow to relate the story of Simon, a fifty-three-year-old architect recently separated from his wife and teenage daughter who is sharing his New York City flat with three women. The accounts of Simon's exotic and often erotic experiences with his housemates are interspersed with sections of revealing dialogue involving Simon and what appears to be either his psychologist or his alter ego. One of Barthelme's more traditionally structured works, *Paradise* has been called a male fantasy that is simultaneously funny, disturbing, and deeply moving.

In addition to the critical acclaim accorded his adult works, Barthelme's children's book, *The Slightly Irregular Fire Engine: or, The Hithering Thithering Djinn* (1971), received the National Book Award for children's literature. *Sixty Stories* (1981) contains a selection of his short fiction as well as miscellaneous prose pieces and an excerpt from *The Dead Father.* Barthelme has also adapted his novel *Snow White* and seven stories from *Great Days* for the stage.

(See also *CLC*, Vols. 1, 2, 3, 5, 6, 8, 13, 23; *Contemporary Authors,* Vols. 21-24, rev. ed.; *Contemporary Authors New Revision Series,* Vol. 20; *Something about the Author,* Vol. 7; *Dictionary of Literary Biography,* Vol. 2; and *Dictionary of Literary Biography Yearbook: 1980.*)

THOMAS M. LEITCH

Perhaps the most striking feature of Donald Barthelme's fiction is the number of things it gets along without. In Barthelme's fictive world, there appear to be no governing or shaping beliefs, no transcendent ideals or intimations, no very significant physical experience, no sense of place or community, no awareness on the part of his characters of any personal history or context of profession or family or, for the most part, personal relationships, no psychology of character, indeed no characters at all in the usual sense of the term, no guarantee, at the level of incident, of verisimilitude or of rational causality or of plot itself, no thickness of circumstantial detail which might make his world seem more densely realistic, and no considerable exploration of such themes as love, idealism, initiation, or death.

Of course, there are exceptions, or apparent exceptions, to each of these rules. **"110 West Sixty-First Street"** (in *Amateurs*) concerns a precisely defined location. **"Robert Kennedy Saved from Drowning,"** (*Unspeakable Practices, Unnatural Acts*) is a collection of episodes ostensibly intended to provide insight into the character of a politician named Robert Kennedy. **"Florence Green Is 81"** (*Come Back, Dr. Caligari*), like most of Barthelme's work, is full of sharply realistic, indeed photographic, detail. And *The Dead Father* is all about families, physical experience, and death. Each of these exceptions, however—and there are many others—is peculiarly suspect. We know from his title that Barthelme is writing about Robert Kennedy or 110 West Sixty-First Street, and to a certain degree these stories depend on these identifications: "Abraham Lincoln Saved from Drowning" would be a profoundly different story, and the title "61 West 110th Street," changing only the neighborhood of New York, would make that story nonsense. But these identifications, however central, are curiously disengaged. . . . In Barthelme, love, death, fatherhood, and Robert Kennedy are always ideas or objects, never experiences which engage emotional commitment.

For this reason it might be more accurate to say, not that Barthelme's stories are never about passion, idealism, and death, but that the word *about* has a special, narrowly focused meaning in Barthelme that makes his fiction unusually difficult to summarize. A summary of a story, say in a review article, normally describes the subject of the story. To describe Barthelme's stories by reference to their professed subjects, the things they are about, is possible but thoroughly misleading. **"The Glass Mountain"** (*City Life*) is about a man trying to climb the side of a glass mountain. **"Cortés and Montezuma"** (*Great Days*) is about the subjugation of the Mexican ruler by the Spanish conquistador. **"The Temptation of St. Anthony"** (*Sadness*) has a subject accurately defined by its title. In each case, however, an accurate summary is inadequate or misleading or simply irrelevant because it fails to describe the important ways in which Barthelme's stories elude the genres his subjects imply. **"The Glass Mountain"** is not, despite its subject, a fairy tale: it diverges at too many points from the rules for fairy tales. **"Cortés and Montezuma"** is not a historical anecdote, **"The Temptation of St. Antony"** an exercise in hagiography, **"Robert Kennedy Saved from Drowning"** a political or personal profile. These stories could more aptly be described as parodies of the genres their subjects imply; the point is simply that the subjects themselves would give anyone who did not already know Barthelme's stories a false impression of them.

It might be objected here that summary gives a false impression of any story whatsoever, and to a certain extent this is no doubt true. But the summary of most fiction is likely to be a plot summary: in saying what a given story is about, we tend to recapitulate, or at least to suggest, the plot. "Young Goodman Brown" is about a man who has an intense experience of evil at a real or imagined witches' sabbath. "The Beast in the Jungle" is about a man who spends his entire life waiting for an experience to which he feels doomed. "A Good Man Is Hard to Find" is about the confrontation between a Georgia family, especially the grandmother of the family, and an escaped convict. Each of these situations implies a plot that is itself expressive of the author's view of the world. Even on a higher plane of generalization, the respective situations—the equivocal role of the imagination in the perception of evil, the perils of well-bred but implacable egoism, the offering of grace in a moment of supreme physical and spiritual danger—each implies a plot, and, as Aristotle says of tragedy, "the incidents and the plot are the end [*telos*]" of the whole work. Aristotle contends that "the end is the chief thing of all," and this dictum holds for many dramatists and novelists, but not for Barthelme, whose fictive situations characteristically fail to imply any *telos* in the sense of coherent plot development. Barthelme's stories are organized around situations (or suppositions or hypotheses) that commit him to no particular line of narrative development, or indeed to the very conception of development. (pp. 129-31)

All of Barthelme's stories might well have begun with *Suppose.* Suppose a thirty-five-year-old man were inadvertently placed in a sixth-grade class (**"Me and Miss Mandible,"** *Come Back, Dr. Caligari*). Suppose a giant balloon appeared one night over Manhattan (**"The Balloon,"** *Unspeakable Practices, Unnatural Acts*). Suppose a dog fell from a third- (or fourth-) floor window and landed on an artist passing below (**"The Falling Dog,"** *City Life*). Suppose Edward Lear, foreseeing his death, turned it into a public event (**"The Death of Edward Lear,"** *Great Days*). In nearly every case, the hypothetical situation, instead of being subjected to a single chosen line of development, is revolved or considered under different aspects, so that Barthelme's stories often seem to assume the form of meditations. Writers such as Hawthorne, James, and O'Connor tend to choose characteristic subjects: their stories are generally variations on a typical situation or theme. But thematic analysis is largely irrelevant to Barthelme's work because his situations are themselves arbitrary and haphazard: what is characteristic, instead of thematic development, is the tone of Barthelme's handling. However illogical, disruptive, or outrageous the situations are, they are always treated circumstantially, in the same deadpan tone. Stories such as **"I Bought a Little City"** and **"The Captured Woman"** (both in *Amateurs*) might have been titled "Some of the Unexpected Problems I Faced After Buying Galveston, Texas" or "Situations and Adventures That Arose Between Me and the Woman I Had Captured." In each case the premise is gratuitous: the town is already purchased, the woman captured, when the story begins, and no explanation is ever given why anyone would want (or how he would be able) to buy towns or capture women, or why towns or women would stand for such treatment. (p. 132)

The discordance between the fantastic situation and the determination to cope with it logistically, more than any summary or catalogue of situations, gives the flavor of Barthelme's world. In this respect, at least, his work seems less kindred to that of other short story writers than to that of other figures associated with *The New Yorker,* in which most of Barthelme's stories first appared—figures such as S. J. Perelman, James Thurber, Saul Steinberg, and Woody Allen, whose humorous effects arise from a contrast between outrageous premises and deadpan presentation. "I can't get in touch with your uncle," a Thurber medium tells her dismayed client, "but there's a horse here that wants to say hello." The trick is to intimate and deflate metaphysical or teleological pretenses as economically as possible, as in Woody Allen's aphorism: "Not only is there no God, but try getting a plumber on weekends." The fictional form most dependent on this rhythm of presentation is of course the cartoon, itself an essential avatar of *The New Yorker*'s sensibility, and Barthelme's stories might themselves be considered cartoons that resemble those not only of *New Yorker* artists like Thurber and Steinberg but also of such recent figures as B. Kliban and Monty Python. Kliban's straightforward acceptance of outrageous premises—his cartoons include "Gondolier Attacked by Rabbis" and "Never Give a Gun to Ducks"—rivals Barthelme's own; the graphic work of the British comic troupe Monty Python, which freely adapts, juxtaposes, and animates stolid Victorian graphic designs, undercuts its targets very much as Barthelme's work does, and looks a good deal like Barthelme's own graphic work in **"At the Tolstoy Museum,"** and **"Brain Damage"** (*City Life*), **"The Flight of Pigeons from the Palace"** (*Sadness*), **"The Expedition"** and **"A Nation of Wheels"** (*Guilty Pleasures*).

Barthelme's fiction, like the graphic work of Kliban and Monty Python, produces its effects by combining materials calling for different responses which are undercut by the process of juxtaposition. A print of a wheel and another of a hastily barricaded city are perfectly serious; but when they are put in the same frame in different scales, they imply a situation whose patent absurdity (America becomes a nation of wheels in the sense that wheels take over the country) suggests in turn the perfect deadpan caption: "All defenses were found to be penetrable" (*Guilty Pleasures*). Barthelme has called this structural procedure "the principle of collage . . . the central principle of all art in the twentieth century in all media," and explained:

> New York City is or can be regarded as a collage, as opposed to, say, a tribal village in

which all the huts . . . are the same hut, duplicated. The point of collage is that unlike things are stuck together to make, in the best case, a new reality. This new reality, in the best case, may be or imply a comment on the other reality from which it came, and may be also much else. It's an *itself,* if it's successful: [an] . . . "anxious object," which does not know whether it's a work of art or a pile of junk.

Barthelme's observation that any collage, including his own fiction, is "an *itself*" suggests a dimension, not only of his work, but of all fiction, which critics are often unable to appreciate or discuss systematically. Short stories and novels, like ritual tragedy, normally have a teleological dimension, an end toward which the events of the plot are moving. Aristotle uses *telos* in the double sense of unity of plot (as the plot of *Oedipus* or *Macbeth,* for example, rushes forward to an end) and unity of thought, conception, or purpose. . . . The end or *telos* implies both a line of development for the plot and a rationale which allows a literary or dramatic work to be apprehended as a unitary whole and for which, in an ultimate sense, the work was written.

This comprehensively end-oriented or teleological quality, however, is neither exhaustive nor always primary. . . . A narrative situation normally implies not only a plot and rationale—or numerous rationales, of which a given writer can be expected to choose one—but myriad possibilities for spectacles, situations, or effects to be enjoyed for their own sake, on their own terms, purely as display. (pp. 133-34)

By displaying narrative situations as objects with no necessary direction or meaning, Barthelme emphasizes the objective dimension of his fiction, a dimension implicit in all fiction. His method is itself displayed most simply and economically in **"Nothing: A Preliminary Account,"** which sets out to define nothing by making an exhaustive catalogue of things nothing is not: "It's not the yellow curtains. Nor curtain rings. Nor is it bran in a bucket, not bran, nor is it the large, reddish farm animal eating the bran from the bucket, the man who placed the bran in the bucket, his wife, or the raisin-faced farmer who's about to foreclose on the farm . . ." (*Guilty Pleasures*). Despite the undoubted accuracy of such observations and the pleasure they may arouse, what they assert about their subject is precisely nothing.

"Nothing," like the other pieces collected in *Guilty Pleasures,* feels even less like a short story than the work in Barthelme's other collections. The miscellaneous quality of the pieces in *Guilty Pleasures* reveals how Barthelme's stories are based on, and tend to elide into, forms outside prose fiction: New Journalism, book reviews, interviews, political satire. Despite the satires in the second part of *Guilty Pleasures,* Barthelme is not primarily a satirist arguing from a well-defined corrective viewpoint like Horace or Moliére nor a romantic ironist like Schlegel but rather a parodist, again like S. J. Perelman or Woody Allen. (p. 138)

In general, however, there is an important structural difference between Allen's work and Barthelme's. In Allen's parodies and films, the basic compositional unit is the joke, implying a rising and falling rhythm from exposition to deflation of a given situation, repeated indefinitely. In Barthelme's best stories—for example, **"Daumier"** (*Sadness*), **"The Indian Uprising"** (*Unspeakable Practices, Unnatural Acts*), and **"Views of My Father Weeping"** (*City Life*)—the reductive or parodistic impulse has become so inveterate that there are no punch lines and so no stable and discrete compositional units whatever. Allen's parodistic stance commits him, if not to a moral belief, at least to a given series of effects: anyone who failed to find the jokes in *Love and Death* funny could justly claim to have been cheated. Barthelme, who escapes this commitment, incurs another one far more difficult to fulfill: his situations must be worth displaying on their own terms, despite their lack of purpose or implied *telos*. His stories succeed as anxious objects or not at all, because there is nothing else for them to be.

It is excessively difficult to establish a critical vocabulary for a fiction that so resolutely resists structural closure. Some problems of analysis might be resolved by classifying Barthelme's stories as anatomies, to use the word by which Northrop Frye designates certain works by such writers as Petronius, Apuleius, Rabelais, Erasmus, Swift, Voltaire, and Peacock. The anatomy, according to Frye, "deals less with people as such than with mental attitudes" and "presents people as mouthpieces of the ideas they represent." In such works, Frye observes, "the intellectual structure built up from the story makes for violent dislocations in the customary logic of narrative." Although "a magpie instinct to collect facts" is a hallmark of the anatomist, short anatomies have been written in the form of "a dialogue or colloquy, in which dramatic interest is in a conflict of ideas rather than of character." In Frye's terms, Barthelme would be an anatomist, not of manners or ideas, but of objects, artifacts of human culture, junk. (pp. 139-40)

[Barthelme's catalogues of cultural debris achieve their] eerie and dazzing effect by removing each object from the context that would give it meaning: as William H. Gass has shrewdly remarked of Barthelme, "Anything dropped in the dreck *is* dreck, at once, as an uneaten porkchop mislaid in the garbage." The fear of objects losing their meanings, as when they are sold at an auction that deprives them of the context they had for their owners, underlies a good deal of recent American fiction, including Gass's *Omensetter's Luck*, which begins with an auction, and Thomas Pynchon's *Crying of Lot 49,* which ends with one. Such anxiety accords well with what Frye calls the "highly intellectualized" temper of the anatomy. Unlike Gass and Pynchon (and, for example, John Barth), however, Barthelme does not present lists of objects in order to assimilate them into a coherent intellectual stucture. The form of the anatomy implies, if not a teleology of plot, certainly an intellectual *telos* or rationale. But Barthelme's work makes neither of these teleological commitments because it projects neither an order for the situations, facts, and objects it presents nor an intelligible attitude toward them. Barthelme is more truly a magpie than the writers Frye considers because he has a magpie's interest in his material, displaying it not because it implies a *telos* but because it is bright and eye-catching. (pp. 140-41)

Barthelme's narrative situations are less often teleological than tellable, to use the term Mary Louise Pratt has borrowed from the linguist William Labov and applied to literary texts. Tellable assertions, explains Pratt, "must represent states of affairs that are held to be unusual, contrary to expectations, or otherwise problematic." (p. 141)

Pratt points out that because "what literary works chiefly do is elaborate on the states of affairs they posit," fictive narration can be "exceedingly redundant"; an author, like an oral storyteller, "can pile detail upon detail, and can even be blatantly repetitive, because he is understood to be enabling his audience to imagine and comprehend the state of affairs more fully and

to savor it for a longer time." Tellable narratives are to a great extent both retellable and capable of practically endless elaboration; indeed, the better an audience already knows a narrative, the less concerned it is that the narrator get to the point.

An important implication of Pratt's discussion, though one she does not make explicit, is that often the process of elaboration itself can make a narrative tellable: that is, insofar as the point of a narrative is display rather than *telos,* elaboration, repetition, and discursiveness are precisely what make the narrative tellable. . . . To the extent that any fiction elaborates a given situation without implying a *telos,* or without altering the *telos* the situation itself implies, it seeks to make that situation more tellable. Sometimes, as often in Barthelme, the main point of the elaboration is its pointlessness—a point by which audiences are understandably bewildered. (p. 142)

Although writers like Barthelme . . . are unusually discursive, narrative fiction in general is shaped by both a structural imperative, an impulse in the broadest sense teleological, and a discursive or elaborative impulse. Narrative tellability can be based on either teleology or elaboration—circumstantial detail, for example, establishes a sense of verisimilitude and an elaborative range that can both make a narrative more tellable—and no narrative, not even Barthelme's, works absolutely in isolation from either impulse, though their relative importance may vary widely from one narrative to the next. Barthelme's resolute emphasis on narrative elaboration, which reduces the importance of *telos* to a minimum, is significant principally as a challenge to the limitations of thematic and structural analysis and as a reminder that the first requisite of a narrative, the merit on which all other merits depend, is that it be worth telling. (p. 143)

Thomas M. Leitch, "Donald Barthelme and the End of the End," in Modern Fiction Studies, *Vol. 28, No. 1, Spring, 1982, pp. 129-43.*

EDITH OLIVER

Herewith some brief impressions of *Great Days,* . . . [theatrical] adaptations by Donald Barthelme of seven of his short stories, six of which first appeared in these pages. The good adaptations are very good—funny and arresting, managing in dramatic form to preserve intact Mr. Barthelme's eccentric vision and style; the others are only fair. . . . Good or fair, though, all seven stories play surprisingly well—surprisingly, that is, because Mr. Barthelme's stories, much as I've enjoyed them, have never struck me as particularly theatrical. That they are so is at least partly attributable to the work of the splendid troupe: there is no reciting here, only true acting. The evening springs to life at the start with **"Momma,"** in which . . . [two brothers] discuss to a jazz beat all the things that "Momma didn't 'low." My other favorites are **"The Apology,"** with . . . [two women] looking out an invisible window at some poor, desperate fellow below, and **"Morning,"** with . . . [two men], travellers on a train, admitting to some mighty peculiar things that frighten them.

Edith Oliver, in a review of "Great Days," in The New Yorker, *Vol. LIX, No. 19, June 27, 1983, p. 75.*

RICHARD GILMAN

Donald Barthelme is one of the American writers I most admire, and I found admirable things in his play *Great Days.* . . . In the end, however, the play bears out Jarry's dictum; its characters don't really feel at home on the stage, don't unquestioningly belong there. I speak of characters, but that's for convenience. The actors speak lines taken from a collection of Barthelme's stories, also called *Great Days,* in which there are no recognizable characters but only voices, figures in a series of shifting, plotless dialogues. Such handicaps make it all the more remarkable that Barthelme has succeeded as well as he has in converting his fiction to the theater.

The play is in seven sections, or scenes, six of them taken from the book—I haven't been able to find the source of the seventh—and they vary greatly in interest. . . . There are hardly any props and little physical activity—two men carry drinks in one sequence—so that the actors, three men and three women, have almost nothing to do except talk.

The talk is often delicious, with Barthelme's characteristic blend of slang, argot, classical allusions and literary speech. In a segment called **"Morning"** a man says he's not afraid of life because he has a "smoke detector, tickets to everywhere and a guardian angel." In **"Apology"** someone says, "There are many ways a grown woman can spend her time. Lacemaking. Feeding the Golden Carp. Higher mathematics." And in **"The Leap,"** my favorite, there's a wonderful discussion of faith, which one can "leap away from" as well as toward, and of love, which "allows us to live together, men and women, in small grubby apartments," as well as a number of those lovely casual observations with which Barthelme's highly sophisticated, deeply ironic prose is tempered, like "a day when you accidentally notice the sublime."

It isn't enough. If it's a commonplace to say that talk isn't necessarily drama, one still has to say it about *Great Days.* Beckett's stage works are also mostly composed of talk, but they have a dramatic quality, which comes from several sources. One is the sense Beckett conveys of speech struggling with silence, meaning with non-meaning. Another is the older theatrical tradition behind the text; used up, banal, it nevertheless remains as a ghostly presence or a model that's been pared down to essences. (pp. 124-25)

The trouble with Barthelme's play, as with his earlier dramatization of his novel *Snow White,* is that for all its rich wit and fine verbal precision, there's little sense of silence pressing against speech and no dimension of tradition denied, refused or played with. Everything comes forward immediately as speech in isolation—clever, wise or affecting as it often is, but without depth—lacking connection to other realities, especially the reality of theater. . . .

The result is not an entity, an organism, but a series of epigrams, a splintering of bright language, a shower of stars. (p. 125)

Richard Gilman, in a review of "Great Days," in The Nation, *New York, Vol. 237, No. 4, August 6-13, 1983, pp. 124-25.*

JONATHAN PENNER

[*Overnight to Many Distant Cities*] consists of 24 pieces, which we may as well call "stories" and "not-stories." They alternate: not-story, story, not-story, story, and so on to the end of the book, giving us 12 each. Each category is diverse. But many of the not-stories are characterized by extreme brevity (typically two or three pages); by the use of a "we" narrator; and a vaguely futuristic, dystopian quality—a sense of waiting menace.

Further emphasizing the discreteness of the two groups, the not-stories are printed in italics, with ragged right-hand margins; the stories have justified margins and are set in Roman. Each story has its own title page, but the not-stories have no titles at all. (The table of contents lists them by their opening words, followed by ellipses).

These distinctions seem so purposeful that the reader tests hypotheses—for instance, that the not-stories will prove to be a single story if read consecutively. But there is no code here to crack. And thus comes a valuable first lesson in reading this book: not to apply the brain to what is meant solely for the senses, notably the sense of design and the sense of disorder.

One story, **"The Palace at Four A.M.,"** is beautiful, moving, and memorable. King Duncan of Ho is writing his autobiography, the opening pages of which recall his love for one Hannahbella, a "bogle." (Bogles are "semispirits," smaller than humans but otherwise similar.)

The king has caused these pages to be sent to Hannahbella, now living in exile, and the story comprises excerpts from them, together with comments by a servant entrusted with their transmission. (The servant is merely a voice, and the comments may actually be those of the king himself—a mirrors-and-shadows device typical of Barthelme.) This fairy-tale king and his nymphal lover, though creatures of whimsy, are human to unexpected depths, and the king's final plea for Hannahbella's return is eloquent with pain.

That Barthelme can write such a story—one that startles without stupefying; one that stylizes the world but doesn't destroy it; a story amused by, rather than hostile to, conventions of literary genre—will only deepen many readers' disappointment with most of this collection. (pp. 3, 10)

"The little girl dead behind the rosebushes came back to life, and the passionate construction continued." That is the last sentence of **"They called for more structure . . . ,"** one of the dozen snippets I have called not-stories. An unusual statement in any case, but especially strange as a final sentence here, because this is the first we have heard of either the girl (alive or dead) or the rosebushes.

Until we reach this startling conclusion, we have been reading about the construction of some city-of-the-imagination, told by a "we" that represents the construction workers collectively. Is the building of the city a metaphor for artistic creation? For civilization? For the principle of order itself? The reader wonders. Then, as though to rebuke his wondering—as though to show the irrelevance of all speculation—comes that final sentence, inventing and resurrecting its dead child.

The principle operating here and through much of this book is that the further you read the less you understand. That is the author's intention; that is what he wants your experience to be. Many of these pieces are designed to be not "difficult" but impossible. However you put it together, it's wrong, and the more materials you are given the harder it is to make anything from them. . . .

Evident throughout the book is an agnosticism, a reductive solipsism, that denies not only the integrity of art but also the possibility of knowledge itself. If this view was ever truly fresh, by now it has surely been propagated unto surfeit, and handled practically to pulp. Fiction never grows stale, but messages quickly do, and it is tiresome to be told (as in **"The Sea of Hesitation"**) that "There is no particular point to any of this behavior. Or: This behavior is the only behavior which has point. Or: There is some point to this behavior but this behavior is not the only behavior which has point. Which is true? Truth is greatly overrated. . . .''

Too often, Barthelme's is a destructive art, an art of vandalism: the drawing of mustaches on billboards. Frequently his methods are ingenious, and sometimes the results are funny.

But to readers who honor fiction partly as it honors us, most of these stories and snippets present a face of ice. What this book says is that nothing can be said. Its message is ''Disregard previous message.'' Life means nothing, art is false, understanding is impossible.

What is wrong with such fiction? That it's destructive, moralists would say. Esthetically, what is so disturbing is that it seems so easy. To create a world, as Barthelme does in **''The Palace at Four A.M.,''** is difficult and noble, the work of a champion. It doesn't require a writer as good as he—it doesn't take more than a bystander's malice or boredom—to stick out a foot and watch the champions fall. (p. 10)

Jonathan Penner, ''Donald Barthelme's Just-Not Stories,'' in Book World—The Washington Post, *November 27, 1983, pp. 3, 10.*

ANATOLE BROYARD

''Overnight to Many Distant Cities'' is composed of stories separated by italicized spoken interludes, which serve as a sort of mood or atmosphere for the more formal pieces. It seems to me that Donald Barthelme also intends these interludes to function as footnotes to the stories, like T. S. Eliot's notes for *The Wasteland.*

The first interlude opens with ''They called for more structure,'' and my hopes rose in anticipation of those antic structures for which the author is already famous. The speaker in this passage proposed to build a new city—''Oh radiant city!''—which would ''make architects stutter.'' For architects, perhaps we should read literary critics. Mr. Barthelme appears to be hinting at his esthetic.

The new city will have its own witch doctors, which I read as short story writers for *The New Yorker.* ''By the light of the moon,'' the anonymous speaker says, ''we counted our chisels and told stories of other building feats.'' Areas of the city have been designed ''to rot, fall into desuetude,'' and this is as we might have expected, for we know the author as a connoisseur of rotted culture and language that has fallen into desuetude.

The speaker calls our attention to ''the ferocious integrity of the detailing'' in his new city, and nobody writing today has more ferocious integrity in his details or his diction than Mr. Barthelme at his best.

So far, so good. This is a brilliant beginning to *Overnight to Many Distant Cities.* Unfortunately, the book doesn't live up to these brave promises. In fact, this has become almost a pattern in the late Barthelme work: the promise is grand, but then the author, rather than the architects, stutters. It's not our culture that rots and falls into desuetude to be wittily chronicled by Mr. Barthelme: it's the stories themselves.

In a typical piece, he will seize a metaphor, as a man seizes a woman or as a policeman seizes a thief. The air will be full of suspense. But then Mr. Barthelme will abuse the metaphor, kick it around and mock it until it loses its meaning for us. . . .

In a story called **''Lightning,''** a reporter is sent out to interview nine people who have been struck by lightning. The Donald Barthelme of *Unspeakable Practices, Unnatural Acts,* of *Come Back, Dr. Caligari,* or *Snow White* could certainly have conjured with that—but somehow the piece dribbles off into a love affair with a beautiful black model. The non sequitur, Mr. Barthelme's special province, is not a gorgeous discontinuity, a comment, but a last gasp, a grab at any old thing.

One of the interludes begins very well with garbage cans disappearing from the speaker's neighborhood, and again the reader is aware of the possibilities in the image, while the author seems uninterested in them. The absence of garbage cans, we read, leads to rats, and the neighborhood dry cleaner, who owns an airplane, offers to drop lethal cleaning fluid on them. The image is lame, the garbage cans don't even clatter.

In **''Conversations With Goethe,''** all the supposed fun comes from clichés uttered by Goethe, which is hardly a new device. There are in *Overnight to Many Distant Cities* quite a few other stock devices: the sudden switch from a mock-formal style to the vernacular, the introduction of arcane irrelevancies, the deadpan presentation of the lowest denominator of small talk, the catalogue of improbabilities and so on. . . .

It's easy to quote Mr. Barthelme against himself, and perhaps he intends us to. ''He has learned nothing,'' he writes of a character, ''from the gray in his hair; the additional lenses in the lenses of his spectacles have not educated him.'' In **''The Sea of Hesitation,''** the narrator says, ''that there was 'behavior' at all seemed to me a small miracle.'' There used to be something recognizable as behavior in Barthelme stories, and I think they were better for it. For such a talented man to surrender, without resistance, to the absurd is absurd.

Anatole Broyard, in a review of ''Overnight to Many Distant Cities,'' in The New York Times, *December 9, 1983, p. C33.*

JOEL CONARROE

Many of these 24 pieces [in *Overnight to Many Distant Cities*] appeared originally in *The New Yorker,* long receptive to Mr. Barthelme's mildly daring variations on the *roman nouveau.* His heart also seems increasingly to belong to *New York* magazine, that boisterous guide to what, where and who is currently in. A dropper of brand names, he has perfect pitch about a certain type of urban sensibility, circa 1983. Like nearly everyone else in Manhattan, he is, for one thing, preoccupied with food; we discover not only the right places to eat but what to order (vitello tonnato) and even what to drink. Nonculinary icons show up too, if only in passing—*The Village Voice,* thigh-reducer courses (''fat, fat, fat, fat''), Pinchas Zukerman, the Art Theater, Mary McFadden and Bells, ''a club frequented by disconsolate women in the early afternoons.'' Here is New York in all its irresistible dazzle and drive—and resistible foolishness.

Besides being a resident scholar of city life (with an honorary degree in Domestic Angst), Mr. Barthelme has long been a recorder of strange objects, a poet of the palpable. There are memorable images in these stories—a T-shirt that reads ''Buffalo, City of No Illusions,'' a psychiatrist who spends a Mexican vacation ''in perfect dread, speaking to spiders,'' a woman who illuminates manuscripts having to do with ''the waxing / waning fortunes of International Snow.'' I also admire, don't ask why, the "leper armadillo, white as snow, with a little bell around its neck."

Much of the poetry of this book, though, lacks resonance, and the overall effect of the stories, with a couple of exceptions, is curiously vacuous. The exceptions are **"Visitors"** and **"Lightning,"** the first of which describes a night in the life of Bishop, a character familiar to readers of Mr. Barthelme's earlier work. "It's three o'clock in the morning," the story begins, reminding us of F. Scott Fitzgerald's statement that in the dark night of the soul it is always 3 A.M. This portrait of a man waiting out the dawn is poignant: he is Updike's Rabbit translated to Greenwich Avenue, a man pushing 50 who weighs too much, drinks too much and is obsessed by women and their mysterious ways. At the tale's end he watches two old women in an apartment across the way having breakfast by candlelight, the image highlighting his absurd solitary life.

"Lightning" is also appealing. On assignment for Folks magazine to interview several individuals who have been struck by lightning, Edward Conners is himself struck, as it were, falling instantly in love with a black fashion model. Among the story's several eccentric characters, the most winning is a loquacious bald monk whose joy in life is listening to rock music on his Sony Walkman. (p. 8)

A swatch of surrealistic prose follows each story, this interpolated material, depending on one's tolerance for other people's dreams, either enhancing or sabotaging the book's overall rhythm. The 12 unconventional passages differ from anything in Mr. Barthelme's earlier work and are dramatically at odds with this book's more domesticated fiction. The publisher's blurb in fact refers to these passages as "visionary texts" that provide "a dynamic counterpoint," but less partisan readers may find them private intrusions that communicate little beyond self-satisfaction. . . .

It is difficult to picture the adult whose ribs would be tickled by some of Mr. Barthelme's humor. Perhaps his ideal reader is a very young person blessed with a low risibility threshold. What we find in this book, with a few wonderful exceptions, is not the sort of comic virtuosity we associate with Stanley Elkin, say, or Philip Roth, but rather an excess of cuteness. . . .

Not only is the fun generally precious, but the jokes tend to be stretched beyond the breaking point. . . .

I don't mean to suggest that the Emperor of Bleecker Street has no clothes. I do, though, increasingly get the impression that his suit is, as one of his characters might put it, threadbare, threadbare, threadbare. (p. 22)

Joel Conarroe, "Some Tame, Some Wild," in The New York Times Book Review, *December 18, 1983, pp. 8, 22.*

JAMES C. ROBISON

From the prominence of *The New Yorker*, Donald Barthelme . . . exerted a formidable influence on the short story. . . . Of recent writers of short experimental works (such as John Barth, Robert Coover, and Ronald Sukenick), Barthelme has had the most visible and enduring impact on American fiction.

A virtue he shares with most successful experimental writers is a piercing eye for the absurdities of conventional behavior, an awareness that seems to have been the starting point for most experimentalists. He has a fine ear for language and can make trenchant social criticism by his use of idiom and vernacular.

Barthelme's stories can be classified according to clarity: the obscure stories (**"The Piano Player," "Views of My Father Weeping,"** and **"City Life"**), which are amusing, coherent, subtle, and clear; and the didactic stories (**"A Shower of Gold," "The Glass Mountain,"** and **"Kierkegaard Unfair to Schlegel"**), which proclaim theme at the expense of subtlety. These classifications that straddle either side of the so-called balanced story contain difficulties that often trip writers of new fiction. Experimentalists tend to reduce coherent action and depth of character in favor of manipulating form and word-play. When they fail, they can either land in the hole of meaningless obscurity or in the safety net of flat didactic statements.

Come Back, Dr. Caligari (1964) contains stories that contributed substantially to Barthelme's reputation, and are representative of tales found throughout the body of his work. **"The Piano Player"** presents much of what Barthelme's critics have attacked: deteriorating absurd conversation, repeated incantation of a key term ("ugliness" in this case), incongruous and incoherent action, and a chaotic conclusion (the daughter's piano strikes the father dead). The story is fragmented and strained by clashs of images and ideas.

Quite different from the obscure stories is **"A Shower of Gold,"** in which the sculptor Peterson conducts a TV talk show that the producers have determined should be a platform for expressing twentieth-century alienation. After playing along for a while, he rebels and announces his credo to the audience: "In this kind of world . . . absurd if you will . . . there are opportunities for beginning again . . . How can you be alienated without first having been connected?"

Balanced stories, such as **"Me and Miss Mandible"** and **"Marie, Marie, Hold on Tight,"** find the middle ground and effectively combine incongruity and commitment to theme. The first appears as the diary entries of a thirty-five-year-old who has been unaccountably put back into the sixth grade. The story points out the arbitrariness of social convention and the necessity of conformity as the narrator learns that he must "pick up the clues" to prosper in a baffling society. The second story tells the agony of three men who "demonstrate against the human condition" by picketing a church, asking, "Why does it have to be this way?" After they are beaten by thugs, one returns and delivers a speech the next night. The narrator explains, "He was very eloquent. And Eloquence, Henry Mackie says, is really all any of us can hope for." In this allegory of the modern writer performing his role, human warmth conveys humor and makes a resonant statement.

City Life (1970) is generally a weaker collection than *Caligari*. **"The Tolstoy Museum"** and **"Brain Damage"** are presented through words and illustrations, and they achieve an occasional sharp stroke of satire. **"The Glass Mountain,"** a didactic first-person-absurd story of a man scaling a skyscraper, appears in the form of one hundred brief entries (mostly single sentences) that are the allegory of a romantic hero's quest for excellence in a corrupt society. **"City Life"** is the story of two young women suffering various hardships of involvement in society, deciding that they dislike city life, but surrendering to it at last. The final despair is clear. **"Views of My Father Weeping"** is told by a bewildered first-person narrator, and the story is obscured by a montage of incongruous elements: a mixture of nineteenth-century and twentieth-century images and motifs from cowboy movies and Freudian psychology. By contrast, the meaning of **"Kierkegaard Unfair to Schlegel"** is clear because it is a philosophical discourse rather than a conventional story. The reader is finally led to believe that irony is not satisfying, but it is acceptable, rather like the eloquence mentioned in **"Marie, Marie, Hold on Tight."** Here there is less of the dramatic texture of the earlier story.

As such stories illustrate, Barthelme tends to use either the coldly objective third-person narrator or the bewildered first person. Both techniques keep the reader at a distance from the characters and, to use Wayne C. Booth's term from *The Rhetoric of Fiction*, at a distance from the "implied author." When the author strikes an indifferent pose toward his characters, it is hard for the reader to care about them.

"Daumier," from *Sadness* (1972), is one of Barthelme's finest stories, complex but ultimately rewarding. Daumier complains of his "hankering" and "rapacious" feelings. He proposes to compensate for his imbalance by creating a world in which everyone's flaws are balanced out by his surrogate form. This world is made of Western-movie characters and plot devices. The counterpart of Daumier's real-life Amelia is Celeste (a parody of a Corinne Calvet character from a Western about mail-order brides), who is voluptuous and speaks in broken English and French. (pp. 78-80)

The story is written in brief titled sections through which the "real" and created narratives run parallel and finally mix. By an act of will, Daumier rescues Celeste from the substitute world and ends up with both her and Amelia, the moral to the story being, "The Self cannot be escaped, but it can be, with ingenuity and hard work, distracted." As in earlier stories, Barthelme offers eloquence and irony as stays against futility.

In *Great Days* (1979), the title story and many others are unnarrated dialogues, a form seen earlier in **"Kierkegaard Unfair to Schlegel."** In a sense, Barthelme is writing one-act plays, and the influence of Samuel Beckett, whom he admires, is not far beneath the surface. A major difference between the two, however, is that at his best Barthelme is more concerned with the nobility of his characters than with their absurdity. At their weakest, these stories are bitterly glib, such as **"The Crisis."** At their strongest, they become a mixture of lampoon and paean. **"The Leap"** subjects Kierkegaard's "leap of faith" to the kind of argument Beckett might raise. . . . As the argument deepens, Barthelme is at his seriocomic best: "He who hath not love is a sad cookie." The nameless characters finally resolve not to act today, but soon. **"Great Days"** continues the focus on struggling with dignity and the importance of doing "our damnedest." The subject of this conversation-story is the agony of doing the right things while facing daily discouragement. Amid the undertow of despair and lines that bring the tension of police distress calls, come words that are both self-mocking and sincere: "I find you utterly delightful. Abide with me. We'll have little cakes with smarm, yellow smarm on them." Borrowings from a hymn title and the slang of the society set bring the speaker's aspirations down to reality and suggest that dreams for the future are not based on naivete but on sobering experience. At the conclusion, the man and woman remain, as do most of Barthelme's characters, dissatisfied. They have the only hope that Barthelme offers throughout his fiction: the solace of eloquence, the relief of irony, and the comfort of each other.

Donald Barthelme has influenced contemporary fiction, but unfortunately, he has also too often been praised for the wrong reasons. The obscurity of his work is readily visible and therefore has drawn critical praise under the label of inventiveness. His surface innovations work best when they are supported by a narrative energy and ironic humor that would strengthen any type of fiction, from the most radical to the most conservative. (p. 81)

James C. Robison, "1969-1980: Experiment and Tradition," in The American Short Story, 1945-1980: A Critical History, *edited by Gordon Weaver, Twayne Publishers, 1983, pp. 77-110.*

GEOFFREY STOKES

"The principle of collage is the central principle of all art in the twentieth century in all media," an extremely sure-of-himself Donald Barthelme told *The New York Times* 14 years ago. This was, at best, a problematic statement about all the century's arts, and it is by now only superficially useful in discussing Barthelme's own fictions. But since the surfaces of his work are so kaleidoscopically mesmerizing, they are not a bad place to begin. . . .

In a more recent interview with Jerome Klinkowitz, Barthelme expanded this notion: "The point of collage is that unlike things are stuck together to make, in the best case, a new reality. This new reality, in the best case, may be or imply a comment on the other reality from which it came, and may also be much else. It's an *itself*, if it's successful." In other words, the collection of facts or opinion once contained in that scrap of newspaper glued to a canvas is less important than its shape, its shape less important than its placement. Collages eat meanings the way we eat cornflakes—and in that elusive best case, the digested matter becomes bone and sinew, the structure beneath the skin. Fiction, wrote Barthelme 20 years ago, isn't "an authoritative account of the world delivered by an expert," but "*there,* like a rock or a refrigerator."

The theory is easy enough to embrace in the case of purely visual art, but words—unlike bits of torn tissue—inescapably *mean,* and for an artist working in the medium of words to make their contractually agreed meanings disappear into a new "itself" is a tricky piece of business. The most straightforward way is to treat words fundamentally as objects, the method employed by concrete poets and (at least sometimes) by William Burroughs, and then to shuffle them around like furniture. In [*Overnight to Many Distant Cities*], Barthelme initially hints that he will adopt this strategy as his own. In the opening piece—one of the short italicized fugues that alternate with the book's dozen stories—the narrator is building a city: *"They called for more structure, then, so we brought in some big hairy four-by-fours from the back shed and nailed them into place with railroad spikes. This new city, they said, was going to be just jim-dandy, would make architects stutter, would make Chambers of Commerce burst into flame."* . . . Finally, high in the air, on a skyscraper setback, they looked down and *"saw the new city spread out beneath us, in the shape of the word FASTIGIUM. Not the name of the city, they told us, simply a set of letters selected for the elegance of the script."* But the word is magic nonetheless: *"The little girl dead behind the rosebushes came back to life, and the passionate constructions continued."*

At least one reviewer has groused that the rest of the book fails to live up to the promise implied in this introductory passage [see excerpt above by Anatole Broyard], but the more pertinent point, I think, is that the promise is inappropriate. In architecture (a longtime preoccupation of Barthelme's), in painting, sculpture, collage, even in performance art, (mere) elegance of structure can awaken a sleeping soul, but Barthelme's medium is awash in connotation and denotation. Freighted words are the tools with which a literary performer must amaze the dead into quickness, and in *Overnight*, Barthelme approaches his chosen task not by denying the meaning of word-objects, but by loading them with new and unsettling meanings, as when a character says "that if I did not abstain from further impertinence she would commit sewerpipe." *Sewerpipe??* This would, I think, slow down even Evelyn Wood.

To be stopped so, brought up short in the midst of this otherwise conventional structure, is to shift from consumer to collaborator. . . .

Precisely because Barthelme is here assembling something more complex than "pure" colors or bits of burlap, . . . [his writing] forces the reader into participation. . . . (p. 38)

This is, of course, Barthelme's aim. "The reader reconstitutes the work by his active participation," Barthelme wrote two decades ago, "by approaching the object, tapping it, shaking it, holding it to his ear to hear the roaring within. It is characteristic of the object that it does not declare itself all at once, in a rush of pleasant naivete." Though he was writing of *Finnegans Wake*, Barthelme could as well have been discussing his own work. Perhaps for this reason, he did not go on to mention that the reader could also flip the object skyward and continue strolling along the beach. We may be psychologically impelled to ask the questions Barthelme thrusts upon us, but we are hardly obliged to invest ourselves in answering them. To make the reader a part of his collage—to make the other pieces he's assembled a part of us—Barthelme has to convince us that the game is worth the candle. In this sense, *Overnight* is a mixed success.

When the magic works, when we are convinced that neither the questions nor the answers are trivial, it is usually because the challenge thrown at us is ethical as well as aesthetic. Barthelme isn't exactly a moralist, but neither do his more interesting characters wish merely to be happy; they wish to be good as well. (pp. 38-9)

Like [his characters], Barthelme regrets giving up superficial beauty when the demands of sub-surface reality intervene, but this doesn't at all mean he is willing to sacrifice the principle that his stories take place not so much on the page as on an imaginary scrim located between his readers and his words. One can see this principle working in many of the revisions to the older stories included in this selection. About a third of them date from the earliest years of the '70s, and the revisions to **"Henrietta and Alexandra"** (which appeared as **"Alexandria and Henrietta"** in *New American Review 12*, 1971) are typical: in the new lead, the characters are specifically reader and writer, and an extraneous character has been completely excised from the story, gentling the principals somewhat. Most dramatically, that which was demi-pornographic—and by definition cast the reader as voyeur—has become evocative, an invitation to more than masturbation:

> 1971: "Alexandria looked at herself in the mirror. She admired her breasts, her belly, and her legs, which were long and white.
>
> "'Now I will go into the other room and ball Henrietta, who is also beautiful.'
>
> "Alexandria and Henrietta were sweating, in their very large bed. Alexandria's head was

between Henrietta's legs and Henrietta's head was between Alexandria's legs. All of the legs were long and white and extremely well-formed."

> 1983: "Alexandra looked at herself in the mirror. She admired her breasts, her belly, and her legs, which were, she felt, her best feature.
>
> "'Now I will go into the other room and astonish Henrietta, who is also beautiful.'"

This revision, though it serves Barthelme's theoretical purposes, is more than technical. Like the transformations of "girls" into "women" in **"The Sea of Hesitation"** (and the satisfying shift of Thomas from womanizer to an altogether more complex and interesting figure), the revisions connect the reworked object with the world that has changed around it. By their very existence, the changes imply the non-trivial nature of what Barthelme is attempting. Indeed, with the exception of **"Conversations with Goethe,"** a sort of one-trick pony, all the newer stories seem willing to confront and reflect the world—including the world of emotion, which the younger Barthelme disdained—directly. (p. 39)

Geoffrey Stokes, "Over Decades to Many Distant Cities," in The Village Voice, *Vol. XXIX, No. 3, January 17, 1984, pp. 38-9.*

ROBERT MURRAY DAVIS

For those who study the shape of a career rather than individual stories or collections, *Overnight to Many Distant Cities* will make a statement about the directions in which Barthelme is moving or, more accurately, is failing to move after *Sixty Stories* (1981), which summarized and defined his early career. Whether one terms the process momentum or inertia, the stories in *Overnight* embody much the same themes in many of the same methods as Barthelme's earlier work. (p. 277)

[The] stories have familiar characters and situations: Barthelme's recurrent, often unnamed protagonist—urban without being urbane, intelligent without being wise, able to analyze but not to change—is a bit further along in years; a husband and wife fail to make contact but live on, more or less together, not too unhappily—this a new turn; a reluctant subject is cross-examined about the ownership of various objects in Beckettian dialogue; a film character, here Captain Blood rather than the Phantom of the Opera or King Kong, appears in a problematic modern context; a major reputation—here Goethe rather than Tolstoy—is undercut; realpolitik and censorship are introduced into a fairy tale. New—at least as separate entities—are what the dust jacket calls "brief visionary texts," printed in italics between the longer stories, like the interchapters of Hemingway's *In Our Time*. Some of them read like transcriptions of dreams (**"I put a name in an envelope"**), some like monologues undercutting current fashions or fads (**"Well we all had our Willie & Wade records"**). Three of them—**"They called for more structure," "Financially the paper,"** and **"The first thing the baby did wrong"**—compress into a page and a half a coherent world of fantasy or obsession as brilliantly as anything Barthelme has done.

The problem with judging Barthelme's work in a given story or as a whole is that he is witty and inventive, and the humorous and surprising turns, found in anything he publishes, can disarm casual criticism. On my first reading of this volume, I was so delighted by individual sentences and paragraphs that I failed to ask questions about the quality of the stories as stories. . . . I came back to *Overnight* and discovered that about a third of the stories are better than competent and that a fourth of the "visionary texts" are brilliant and the rest dross.

Perhaps it is more useful—certainly it is easier—to explain why "Visitors," "The Sea of Hesitation," "Lightning," and ["Overnight to Many Distant Cities"] succeed than why "Captain Blood," "Affection," "Wrack," and "The Palace at Four A.M." do not. The first four have, for one thing, a single speaker or focal character who by the very act of speaking or observing or reflecting on the disparate and inconclusive fragments of his life imposes the form of the quest for Barthelme's grail-substitute, "What is wonderful?" The dilemmas and failures and momentary joys are not sociologically different from those in "Affection," but the lack of narrative focus in this story leaves it a series of fragments rather than an imaginative whole. One of his earlier characters says, "Fragments are the only forms I trust," and Barthelme selects and presents them wittily and sharply, but they cannot be trusted to themselves.

Even when a successful piece is more conventionally coherent than, say, "The Sea of Hesitation," the coherence is imposed by the characters rather than by the form. . . . In contrast, the fantasy of "The Palace at Four A.M." is externally imposed, built into the premises: an imaginary kingdom; a broken liaison between an ass-headed king and a diminutive, beautiful, and sexually adventurous semi-spirit of the race of bogles; anachronistic mixtures of armor and breathalyzer tests; fairy-tale situations undercut by the language of image-conscious official autobiography. The story is too busy for its own good, so mannered that there is no room left for matter. And the frame—a letter to the bogle from the king's secretary—remains only a frame.

On a smaller scale, Barthelme is funniest, most moving, and most effective when he begins with the individual voice, with characters attempting to explain themselves eloquently, ruefully, and with a guarded hope. He is least effective when he depends upon pure dialogue or lists, when he relies upon fanciful fantasy—the bright idea—or when he borrows a structure from Beckett or Borges or a continental philosopher, and forgets native models like Ambrose Bierce, Don Marquis, Mark Twain, and perhaps James Thurber. He transcends these models, in part because he knows a good deal about Modernist and postModernist writing, but he does best when he does not abandon them. (pp. 278-79)

> *Robert Murray Davis, in a review of "Overnight to Many Distant Cities," in* Studies in Short Fiction, *Vol. 21, No. 3, Summer, 1984, pp. 277-79.*

MICHIKO KAKUTANI

Simon, the hero of Donald Barthelme's third novel [*Paradise*], is a 53-year-old architect, prominent enough to be featured in *Progressive Architecture* and vain enough to think that his work could drive Louis Kahn's ghost mad with jealousy. . . . Although he's always wanted "to be a hearty, optimistic American, like the President," he's long since settled "for being a competent, sometimes inventive architect with a tragic sense of brick."

For readers of Mr. Barthelme's previous novels and short stories, Simon's practice of architecture may sound an awful lot like a tongue-in-cheek version of the author's own approach to fiction. Like Simon's buildings, his prose is stylized and formalistic, and it's marked by a similar sense of playfulness and sadness. What's more, the accusations leveled at Simon in his private life echo criticisms Mr. Barthelme's own work has received: as various characters put it, Simon is unserious, he doesn't care about people as individuals and his "cheapo irony" reduces people's emotions to the status of glib jokes. "You worry about the way I say things," a woman tells him, "but you don't worry about what I mean."

Certainly such charges are irrelevant when it comes to such works as *Snow White*, **"Robert Kennedy Saved From Drowning," "Views of My Father Weeping"** and **"The Indian Uprising."** . . .

The author's weaker efforts, however, could very well be found guilty of the charges leveled at Simon—here, wit and intellectual one-upmanship dwindle into fun and games; detachment into mechanism; narrative fragmentation into mere absurdity for absurdity's sake. Unfortunately, this is the case with *Paradise*.

All of Mr. Barthelme's well-known devices are on display here: characters indulge in pointed refrains ("Catch my drift?" "Catch my drift?" "Catch my drift?"), sport funny T-shirts ("Arm the Unemployed," 'Ally Sheedy Lives!") and speak in long series of ridiculous non sequiturs. Name brands, meant to give us a sense of contemporary life in New York, are generously dropped (Conran's, the Palladium, Dannon yogurt), and odd, dreamlike images proliferate throughout the text: extra beds lie stacked in a room "like a means test for a princess," a "dead bear in a blue dress" lies face down on the kitchen floor and three naked young men named Harry hatch from an eight-foot-high plaster egg.

As for the novel's structure, it's predictably idiosyncratic—fairly conventional chapters of exposition alternate with chapters of Q and A in which Simon talks to his psychiatrist (or perhaps a version of himself) about adultery, guilt and the future. Together these chapters tell a pretty straightforward story: Simon, who's recently separated from his wife, has come to live in New York in a large, empty apartment. He meets three would-be models from Denver in a Lexington Avenue bar and offers to let them stay at his house. They move in and soon make themselves at home in Simon's bed. Sometimes one of them goes off to have another affair; sometimes Simon goes off to have another affair. Time passes and the three women eventually leave.

In the course of this story, we learn certain things about Simon—that he thinks of himself as a giraffe or a palm tree, that he likes to listen to the radio, that he has a long history of adultery. And we learn certain things about the women—that they used to work for a place called Frederick's of Hollywood of Denver (that had "nothing to do with the real Frederick's of Hollywood"), that they're having a hard time finding jobs, that two of them are blondes and one is a brunette. Other than this, all of them are ciphers—vaguely unpleasant, cartoony people whose inner life is so tenuous that everything they do and say feels like a series of random events.

Simon is a classic male chauvinist: he believes the women have only two choices—"they could join the under-employed half-crazed demi-poor, or they could be wives." And as portrayed by Mr. Barthelme, the women come close to fulfilling Simon's worst suspicions—they're dumb, incompetent and incessantly whiny. Further, they're virtually indistinguishable from one another—half the time we don't even know which one of them is talking.

Mr. Barthelme occasionally notes that Simon is "existing in a male fantasy, in hog heaven"; and given the book's title (and a reference to a book called "On Adam's House in Paradise"), it seems as though he's trying to make some sort of point about the disparity between reality and dream life, and the difficulties of understanding the opposite sex. In the end, though, we're never really made to care about such issues, so half-hearted and perfunctory are the author's efforts. Except for the occasional funny one-liner, *Paradise* has little of the vitality or inventiveness of Mr. Barthelme's earlier work and none of its provocative intelligence. In this case, his narrative pyrotechnics do not enhance his subject; rather, they trivialize the now very tired theme of the male midlife crisis.

> *Michiko Kakutani, in a review of ''Paradise,'' in*
> The New York Times, *October 22, 1986, p. C24.*

ELIZABETH JOLLEY

Although Donald Barthelme has written 12 previous books of fiction—containing some of the most innovative, influential stories of our day—reading *Paradise* is a shock and a revelation. It is a revelation of a known and existing world that is fresh because the approach is unique. The writer offers an energetic prose controlled at all times by a powerful restraint. It is a very funny novel; I laughed aloud, a rare thing while reading contemporary fiction. It is also a sad book. Its form is dramatic; the drama is built up in fragments of conversation. Sometimes it is not easy to be certain who is saying what, but it is important that the things are said. The impact of these conversations is enhanced by their sparseness. . . . The actors in the drama are 53-year-old Simon and three tall, good-looking, temporarily homeless women who have moved in with him. The situation is vividly introduced and continued at intervals by an internal dialogue consisting of an exchange of questions and answers. A tantalizing first chapter is followed directly with the arrival and reactions ("Boy is this place empty") of the three women. His spacious New York apartment is practically unfurnished. "I said I didn't know what we were going to do for beds." The women are models who have just finished a lingerie show in a bar. That sort of thing is often sordid and tedious in real life but not in this book: "Bikini pants burning at eye level" and "The white lacy *Büstenhalter* encompassing the golden breasts nudging your arm." Details in the novel that could be described as "sexy" are never dull and never salacious; rather, they are natural and necessary, ridiculously funny and tender as in real life.

Simon, an architect with "a tragic sense of brick," after discovering a pipe bomb wired under his Volvo, has left his job and his wife, giving himself a sabbatical, his first for 14 years. In reality he has left not because of the bomb, but because of "the prospect of listening to his wife's voice for another hour, another minute." The pipe bomb and its implication are not mentioned again.

Other characters are Simon's mother, occupied with her own life, outspoken but only by telephone ("What fool bought brisket?"), and Simon's wife. "In bed, he was almost asleep. She came in and threw four quarts of icewater at him." Their relationship is now conducted by telephone (she calls him) and correspondence from a lawyer (hers). . . .

The three women, who have given all their money to fight hunger in Africa, emerge in compact scatterings of conversation. They have no prospects for the time being of further employment. They all have their individual ways of walking; sometimes they bump into one another. They talk a great deal, to one another and to Simon and about Simon, even within his hearing. They have their own standard of honesty and morality and seem to live in the immediate present. Simon seems expected to respond to extraordinary sexual advances. Are some of these fantasies? Can you wake up with six breasts hanging over you? And can two women kiss one spot at the same time? The women enjoy food and drink, they cook and wash together making a lot of noise. They make love with Simon, sometimes singly, sometimes in pairs, turning from him to each other.

Their unfurnished and easygoing existence is punctuated by truths from the outside world. There are some splendid passages of satire. . . .

It is the rhythm of speech, the laconic tone, that transforms the content. There are some very specific erotic passages, but owing to their tone they do not bore, as such descriptions often do. One of the women states quite simply that Simon is not exactly perfection but she's had more orgasms with him than with anyone else. Some readers might be offended; but, in that case, the book is not for them.

Simon's marriage comes to an end. We cannot know what is wrong between Simon and his wife. Throwing ice water over a husband in bed is the action of a frustrated woman who is too angry to think of the consequences—that she will either have to set to and change the bedclothes or sleep in a wet bed. But Simon is the husband who has left the wife. . . .

The three women become restless and argumentative and Simon is told, "Thirty-five percent of all American women aren't allowed to talk at dinner parties. Think about that."

"How do you know?"

"It's in a book." Many authors, strident in the feminist cause, will never achieve the immensity Mr. Barthelme achieves quietly in that small exchange.

The women will be leaving and Simon accepts this. His nightmares are universal. The wisdom offered in the conversations can reach many. Anger is universal. "Each person could be angry at any given point with one, two, or three others, or angry at the self. . . . He reached forty-nine possibilities before his math expired."

Donald Barthelme is a writer to be read and admired and read again. *Paradise,* made up of the collision of brilliant moments, cannot be summed up. It is a picture of human needs and wishes and fantasies. Is Simon in hog heaven? It is a criticism without judgment on contemporary American life. Is it just America? In addition to being funny and deeply moving, *Paradise* is a disturbing book because it is a fantasy of freedom in a world where there is no freedom. Is this just America?

> *Elizabeth Jolley, ''Is Simon in Hog Heaven?'' in* The
> New York Times Book Review, *October 26, 1986,*
> *p. 7.*

PAUL STUEWE

Barthelme's short, cryptic tales of contemporary anomie established a new literary fashion when they began appearing 25 years ago, but his attempts at expanding them into novel-size narratives have been uniformly unsuccessful. *Paradise* is no exception: its thin story-line and slightly sketched characters remain undeveloped in ways that are emphasized by the book's inordinate length. The absence of meaningful intellectual or emotional content, which seemed daring and even profound when Barthelme's work was first published, has by now become the kind of cliché that calls for parody rather than imitation. Die-hard Barthelme fans who remember when he was one of the brightest lights of post-modern fiction are in for a hell of a disappointment.

Paul Stuewe, "A Lively Deal . . . Tubeside Companion . . . Stellar Stella," in Quill and Quire, *Vol. 53, No. 1, January, 1987, p. 33.*

MICHAEL FEINGOLD

Simon, an aging architect [and the protagonist of *Paradise*], has just gotten divorced and moved into an unfurnished apartment. Instead of objects, he finds himself furnishing it with a middle-aged man's fantasy come true—three beautiful young models, encountered in a bar under circumstances of such extreme unlikelihood they invite you to take the story as a fairy tale which just happens to have a 1980s Manhattan setting and a throng of naturalistic details. The mixture of wish-fulfillment high and reality bringdown isn't new: Both of Barthelme's previous novels, *Snow White* and *The Dead Father*, trafficked in it, as do some of his best short stories, like **"The Glass Mountain,"** which ends with the flat assertion that its subject matter doesn't exist. What makes *Paradise* fresh is a sense that the author is trying to realize the fantasy for his readers, instead of just toying with it conceptually. If the three young women aren't strikingly characterized, there's at least an effort to give them differing pasts and personalities; the events take place in an idyllic world, but one that's believably everyday, not turned upside down by Barthelme's usual giant balloons, heat-seeking pencil sharpeners, and dwarves who manufacture Chinese baby food.

Apart from its central situation, the fantasy-tripping in *Paradise* is confined mostly to Simon's unspoken thoughts, and to a series of Q-and-A dialogues between him and an unidentified voice that starts out sounding like a shrink but soon develops into one of those eerie, discontinuous voices that sing the signature tune of the typical Barthelme short story. This interrogative voice goes from amiable low-key queries ("Ever been subject to epilepsy?") to lengthy, surreal expositions of its own fantasies, which Simon ends by partly sharing—apparently along with some mood-changing drugs. ("Do you want some of these little green ones? They're supposed to be good.") One wonders if Barthelme isn't suggesting that the end of Simon's three-model idyll may drive him onward to some final binge or mental collapse—an unhappy ending delicately adumbrated, as if including too much of it would spoil the fairy tale.

While the idyll lasts, though, it's shot through with rue and comic discomfiture: The women treat Simon as a sexual object, discussing his shortcomings among themselves while they're in bed with him. They go on buying sprees, or date younger men, exercising just enough reserve to make him feel he isn't being used or betrayed. Magic moments keep getting interrupted by phone conversations with his ex-wife, his college-age daughter, his all-knowing mother. . . . And the daily round of New York craziness keeps breaking in—jury duty, skin surgery, attempted muggings, and storekeepers who have epileptic fits. Simon's harem fantasy collapses as readily and as often as a leaky beach ball. It may be a sort of paradise, Barthelme seems to be saying, but it isn't Eden; contemporary life is a series of footloose coincidences which, in Simon's case, just happen to have lined up in a particularly enticing pattern.

The bemused, affectionate way Barthelme's style looks at Simon (who often seems to be looking at himself the same way, wheels within wheels) keeps *Paradise* from being an erotic indulgence, crystallizes its wishful thinking in a work of art which is both a picture of life and, as art tends to be, an implicit criticism of the life it pictures: a paradise for its readers rather than its hero. Simon seems to know this, too. In the last of *Paradise*'s brief chapters, a Q-and-A, he responds to his interrogator's put-down of the sculptor Giacometti by saying, "He's got a razor in his shoe," something said earlier about a street tough. Art, like the city, has hidden dangers, the ominous capacity to cut at unexpected moments, and *Paradise* is a slice of life which also, teasingly, slices off a little taste of heaven.

Michael Feingold, "Beautiful Schemer," in The Village Voice, *Vol. XXXII, No. 5, February 3, 1987, p. 51.*

H(erbert) E(rnest) Bates

1905-1974

(Also wrote under pseudonyms of Flying Officer X and John Gawsworth) English short story writer, novelist, nonfiction writer, critic, author of children's books, biographer, autobiographer, essayist, dramatist, and scriptwriter.

Bates was a prolific author who enjoyed several phases of popularity during his lifetime. He initially established himself as a promising author with novels and short stories set in the rural English midlands. In these works, Bates employs pastoral imagery and a lush prose style to vividly evoke mood and atmosphere while focusing on seemingly ordinary events that significantly affect his characters. During World War II, Bates was commissioned by the Royal Air Force to write about the exploits of fighter pilots, leading to a series of fiction and nonfiction works that examine the effects of war on soldiers and civilians. Later in his career, Bates returned to rural settings and themes, frequently depicting poignant incidents in the lives of children or elderly characters. Among Bates's most popular later works are a series of novels about the Larkins, a spirited rural family who vigorously pursue the sensual pleasures of life and nature. Bates garnered consistent praise from reviewers throughout his career, and several of his books were bestsellers.

Bates is perhaps best known for his short stories, particularly those he wrote during the late 1920s and 1930s. In these early works, noted V. S. Pritchett, "[Bates's] setting was usually the traditional life of the small farms, cottages and holdings, his people the hedgers, ditchers, thatchers and local carriers—a horse-and-cart England in the main, the England of rural hagglings and feelings which had changed very little for centuries and often sounds Chaucerian and ripe in speech." Critics frequently compare his early stories to those of Anton Chekhov, citing Bates's ordinary characters engaged in everyday activities, his minimal use of plot, and his lucid evocation of atmosphere and feelings. In his first two collections, *Day's End and Other Stories* (1928) and *Seven Tales and Alexander* (1929), Bates established his ability to engage the reader with lyrical descriptions of nature and human emotion. For example, in the story "Alexander," from the second collection, Bates describes a day in the life of a boy who accompanies his uncle to gather apples and visit acquaintances. Bates focuses on the boy's sensual impressions of the lush natural environment and his mysterious feelings when encountering a farmgirl. "This is all the story," commented one critic. "But Mr. Bates manages to capture in it, as successfully as any one has ever done, the difficult emotion of pre-adolescence, the sharp and yet diffuse impressions of youth." Several critics, including Graham Greene, claimed that Bates's talent as a short story writer matured in *The Woman Who Had Imagination and Other Stories* (1934). The title story of this volume concerns members of a young chorale whose boisterous and flirtatious interaction is contrasted with the strained relations between a couple with whom they lodge.

Several of Bates's early collections contain stories that center on Uncle Silas, a wily, pleasure-seeking elderly man who relates his humorous, fabulistic adventures to his nephew. These stories are represented in the volumes *My Uncle Silas* (1939)

and *Sugar for the Horse* (1957) and are collected in *My Uncle Silas* (1984). Bates's most accomplished later volumes of short stories include *Colonel Julian and Other Stories* (1955), *The Daffodil Sky* (1957), and *The Watercress Girl and Other Stories* (1959). Set in rural locales, the pieces in these collections often focus on youthful or elderly characters and examine local concerns as well as the effects on rural England of World War II and encroaching industrialization. "Colonel Julian," for example, depicts a retired veteran of the English wars with India who attempts to share his heroic adventures with World War II soldiers but becomes disillusioned upon learning of the horrors of modern warfare. *The Watercress Girl* has been called Bates's "paean to youth." In the often-anthologized story "Great Uncle Crow," for instance, Bates writes from the perspective of a young boy who vividly pictures the anecdotes his nostalgic uncle relates to him.

In his novels, Bates lushly describes natural images to mirror the moods of his characters while relating poignant incidents in their lives. He secured recognition with his first book, *The Two Sisters* (1926), which concerns two siblings, one of whom is demure, the other lively, who take care of their troubled father and brothers. The sisters are torn apart when they become involved in a love triangle and reconcile only after having suffered several tragedies. Bates's next two novels, *Catherine Foster* (1929) and *Charlotte's Row* (1931), were not as well received. The former work involves a woman who attempts to escape her dull marriage through an affair with her husband's seamy brother, while the latter centers on life among the inhabitants of an impoverished district in a small city. Bates's next three novels, *The Fallow Land* (1932), *The Poacher* (1935), and *Spella Ho* (1938), were more roundly praised and helped secure his reputation as one of the most accomplished English writers of the 1930s. *The Fallow Land* depicts the painstaking efforts of a vagabond's wife to provide for her family by farming her poor tract of land. *The Poacher* chronicles the life of Luke Bishop from his happy youth spent with his father as an unlawful hunter and trapper to his disillusioned adult life as a respectable townsman. Margaret Wallace commented: "Beautifully and without affectation Mr. Bates has expressed through the story of Luke Bishop's life his deep feeling for the life of the English countryside, for the changes which have come over it in the last half-century and his own nostalgic regret for the order which has passed." *Spella Ho* follows Bruno Shadbolt from his impoverished youth through his adult relationships with several women, who instill in him the qualities necessary to attain material prosperity. The title of this work refers to a manor that Bruno eventually acquires and from which, as a youth, he stole coal to heat his mother's lodgings.

During World War II, Bates was commissioned by the British Royal Air Force to produce works detailing the exploits of fighter pilots. His nonfiction book *There's Something in the Air* (1943), published under the pseudonym Flying Officer X, offers straightforward, unglorified anecdotes of various sacrifices made by pilots in order to further the Allied war effort. *Fair Stood the Wind for France* (1944) is a novel about a pilot who is forced to crash-land his airplane in Occupied France. Bates relates the injured pilot's struggle to escape from enemy territory and the heroic efforts of the French civilians who aid him. Bates also wrote a best-selling trilogy of novels set in the Far East which examines themes related to war: *The Purple Plain* (1947) concerns an acerbic English flight commander in Burma who gradually finds happiness through love; *The Jacaranda Tree* (1949) relates the evacuation from Burma to India of English citizens threatened by advancing Japanese forces; and *The Scarlet Sword* (1950) is set in Kashmir during a time of social turmoil.

Bates's later novels include five books detailing the adventures of the fun-loving Larkin family, whose members enjoy bucolic pleasures and a carefree lifestyle. *The Darling Buds of May* (1958), generally considered the best of the Larkin books, introduces the family and portrays a stolid tax collector who investigates the Larkins's failure to pay income taxes but who eventually grows to appreciate their way of life. Several critics suggested that Bates wrote this book in response to the dark social satire of the Angry Young Men, a group of English writers, including Kingsley Amis, John Wain, and John Osborne, who became prominent during the 1950s. According to Max Cosman, "[*The Darling Buds of May*] is Mr. Bates's riposte to younger contemporaries, angry or otherwise disturbed. It takes up their challenge that life is something of a pain in the neck and retorts there is more to say than that." While this work is appreciated as a rollicking farce, subsequent books in the series were unfavorably reviewed, as critics questioned the merits of the Larkins's hedonistic existence. One reviewer stated: "[To] anyone who respected Mr. Bates's talent as a serious novelist or his spontaneous Uncle Silas humour, the Larkin interlude is disturbing and sad—a crude travesty of the whole pastoral tradition." The five Larkin novels are collected in *Perfick, Perfick!: The Story of the Larkin Family* (1985)

In addition to his novels and stories, Bates is respected for his work in several other literary forms. Two of his novellas, *The Cruise of "The Breadwinner"* (1946) and *The Triple Echo* (1970), are considered among his finest works. The former is set on a small sea vessel that is used to rescue downed fighter pilots and details a boy's initiation into the glories and horrors of war. *The Triple Echo* concerns the nature of love and the effects of war in its study of the emotional involvement between a wife of a prisoner of war and a troubled soldier. Bates also wrote children's books, nonfiction works about life in the country, and a respected literary study, *The Modern Short Story: A Critical Survey* (1941). *The Best of H. E. Bates* (1981) offers a sampling of his work in a variety of genres. In a review of this volume, Valentine Cunningham stated: "What H. E. Bates does best, and what this superb selection aptly shows him best at, is satisfying his characters' and his readers' deep cravings for pastorals. Repeatedly he proves the delights that attend life in the pastoral enclave, the garden enclosed, shut off from discontents and disturbances."

(See also *Contemporary Authors*, Vols. 93-96, Vols. 45-48 [obituary].)

EDWARD GARNETT

In calling attention to **The Two Sisters** I think critics of insight will agree that the novel is a signal example of a rare species, and one, moreover, easy to be overlooked in the yearly cataract of fiction. A friend, a story-teller of reputation, was at first surprised that a novel of so poetical a character should emerge to-day, but after consideration he agreed: 'Yes, what we need now is the novel of essentials, for the realistic chronicle novel threatens to suffocate us by mere weight.' Perhaps. But if this is so it is because most novelists will insist on telling us too much. . . . Just as the ordinary room holds unnecessary furniture so the ordinary novel is crowded with an excess of detail, with a plethora of information and a congestion of comments. One sighs for the sparse line, for grace of outline, for the rare gift that extracts the essential word from the shallow rapids of conversations. One longs to get back to essentials, especially to the essential of beauty. And the element of beauty that our utilitarian civilization pushes out more and more with its 'tubes' and 'wireless,' with its newspapers and telephones and other disseminating, speeding-up mechanics of life, is an element that pervades **The Two Sisters**.

The author, of course, has the advantage over most of us of being quite young. His novel is about Youth at the period when youth absorbed in its own ardours and frustrated longings can make grief itself into a luxury of passion. And his achievement is that, while identified with his creations, Jenny, Tessie and Michael, the author has known how to detach himself from these figures of eternal youth and show them, with all their tumultuous, passionate emotions, in a beautiful mirror. That is remarkable in an author of twenty years. (pp. 7-8)

[In] little scenes the author guided by his sure instinct, instead of over-loading his descriptions with details, has pierced to the spirit of things by swift intuition and intensity of perception. . . . Great is artistic economy. I may be excused for dwelling on this aspect for we moderns have forgotten that it is the begetter of grace and beauty. Truth to essentials, implying both precision of insight and precision of touch in the writer, is exemplified by [Bates's] treatment of the tensity of feeling, growing and growing between Tessie and Jenny and Michael. . . . This is the bloom of youth's ecstacy of feeling, like the bloom on youth's cheek.

The author's artistic handling of dramatic suspense is evident throughout the story, but nowhere more so than in the remarkable River chapter . . . where the unforeseen happens. The claim that **The Two Sisters,** wherever it may fall short, is of a rare poetical order, is attested by the opening scene of Jenny's homeward journey and clenched by the atmospheric truth and beauty of the angry River ending.

This said, it is best to hazard no conjecture about the author's future work. There is the path of art endlessly difficult and the path of facile achievement and it depends on the youthful writer's star which he shall follow. (pp. 9-10)

> *Edward Garnett, in a foreword to* The Two Sisters *by H. E. Bates, Jonathan Cape Limited, 1926, pp. 7-10.*

LOUIS KRONENBERGER

The Two Sisters is in sharp contrast, structurally, to one of the most popular forms of contemporary fiction—the novel of detail. It is almost impossible nowadays to encounter a biographical or chronicle novel which does not pursue the experiences of its chief characters from the day of their birth to the day of their death, amassing a multitude of facts about them, and describing minutely their adventures, their thoughts, their emotions, their manifold interrelationships. Mr. Bates has a story to tell of the lives of two sisters, yet he does not tell it as the day-by-day record of many years. His method is different. **The Two Sisters** is not a spare outline of scenes cut to a minimum; it is, if anything, slightly longer than the usual full-length novel. But it seeks quintessences instead of a heap of details. It is conceived in the poetic spirit and presented, as in a mirror, almost indirectly, that its poetic truth and reality may be the more direct. Its beauty, its drama, its tragedy reach us without that superficial and immediate quality of realism which is achieved by a marshaling of facts; but we get them in essence, in a universal sense rather than a specific, with that lingering quality of realism which is achieved through the imagination. When we get this in the highest degree we have, of course, a work of genius. Mr. Bates has not quite given us that, often has not nearly given us that. But, all question of his age left out, he has written an unusual and lovely book.

The Two Sisters is the story of Jenny and Tessie Lee and of Michael Winter, all three of them living near a small English town called Bromsweald. Jenny, the older of the sisters, is the more serious and the more sensitive to responsibility, and because their mother is dead, maternally watchful over Tessie. Tessie is far more emotional and lively. The real drama of the story begins with Michael's coming and Tessie's falling in love with him. He does not respond and Tessie becomes upset. When Jenny upbraids him, she learns it is she with whom he is in love, and suddenly discovers how much she reciprocates his emotion. The truth drives Tessie away from home. Later, her father, an absorbingly queer but not wholly successful creation, dies. . . .

Mr. Bates concludes his story with a scene years after, a mellow and beautiful scene showing the two sisters linked together by common memories of a common love. It is in keeping with Mr. Bates's already discernible excellences as a novelist that

the scene is kept free of all sentimentality. It is a scene, too, so thoroughly poetic in temper that it lacks a sense of personalities—it is like a picture, an almost universal embodiment of two people healed by sharing a joint sorrow. In a sense it overcomes the feelings one had earlier of a weakness on Mr. Bates's part in so little characterizing the sisters. Jenny, perhaps, is adequately characterized, but Tessie not at all. But in the portrayal of Michael we have a weakness the sense of which persists to the end. One feels that the nature of his attraction and charm for the two girls should have been communicated to the reader, and one is given instead a man of whom one knows nothing, a mere symbol. It is the one glaring shortcoming of the book, however much it seeks for essentials, since the amount of space expanded with subordinate effect on the girls' father could much better have gone toward the creation of a living Michael. . . .

The book moves slowly. The first forty pages describe Jenny's return home from the village. But into them Mr. Bates gets not only an excellent sense of what she is like as a child, but the whole mood and tone of the book as well. Thereafter the simple story unfolds without haste, increasing its tempo only at times of stress, such as Jenny's scene with her father and the fine river passages. There is a remarkable quality to the account of Michael's last night on the river, of Jenny's frenzied passage from house to wharf and back again, of Tessie's superhumanly controlled waiting in the "morbidly quiet" room. In its writing, too, the book, though often lacking in sure mastery, shows a very definite talent. It lacks, no doubt, a certain guiding power as it lacks insight into character, strict narrative unity, and a continuously compelling interest. But these are compensated for by less usual merits, and even many of its shortcomings are justified by the aims of the book.

> *Louis Kronenberger, "A Return to 'The Novel of Essentials'," in* The New York Times Book Review, *September 26, 1926, p. 11.*

NEW YORK HERALD TRIBUNE BOOKS

Instead of the slender volume of verse which is the characteristic output of a young writer at nineteen, Mr. Bates wrote a novel [**The Two Sisters**] and poured into it the lyricism and the adolescent agony more commonly reserved for poetry. The result is a story which is intense, unrelievedly serious and often beautiful. When the book opens, Jenny is trying to right herself in a child's world sent reeling by the death of her lovely and understanding mother. Still a little girl, she is thrown into the captaincy of a household of clouded and troubled spirits: her father, violent and finally insane; her younger sister, Tessie, antagonistic and pleasure loving; the two brothers, brutal Jim and epileptic Luke. The two girls grow older, hating and fearing, yet loving each other. Then Michael, a simple river man, comes their way. He seems to be attracted by Tessie, and she grows thin and anxious waiting for him to speak his mind. But it is Jenny he loves, and Jenny also loves him. In this common love, which spells pain for one and ecstasy for the other, the two sisters are reconciled. . . .

This bare outline of the story gives more of a feeling of plot than one is conscious of in reading the book. **The Two Sisters** is a record not of event, but of moods—of golden moods, like the early morning sunlight through a blossoming orchard; of dark moods which spread like a thunder cloud to darken a day's living. It is distinctive as a novel in that it shows us the interior life not with the analytical eye of introspection, but with the directness of emotion remembered and reproduced. Its process is apprehension, not comprehension.

The essentials of *The Two Sisters* are not the essentials distilled out of life lived to the full or the wise and humorous folktale of a grown people; but the essentials of defeated youth, turned in on itself and content to die if death is the price of feeling. The beauty and the sureness of Mr. Bates's telling is the proof of the clearness with which he recalls that bitter-sweet torment.

> *"The Bitter-Sweet Torment of Defeated Youth," in* New York Herald Tribune Books, *Vol. 3, No. 13, December 12, 1926, p. 10.*

CYRIL CONNOLLY

[The stories collected in *Day's End and Other Stories*] are very good indeed. All are written in the same vein, which would, in lesser writers, be described as poignant. Actually they are studies in diffidence or tenderness described with great reticence of style and feeling. . . . Mr. Bates is interested in the obscurer forms of emotional breakdown—sudden panics, hastily checked; silent, unnoticed crises of fear, despair misinterpreted, or the eternal contrast of our daydreams and our limitations. These he describes by delicate understatement. All his stories have just enough point to make a story, and soon he will be able to make one out of nothing at all. They mostly leave an aftertaste of regret. It is characteristic that when there is a story of a channel crossing, it should be of the Styxlike transit from Gravesend to Rotterdam; when a river is described, it is as it appears to a homesick boy spending his first night on a barge. The mother is shown adoring the child of whose vulgarity so far only the reader is aware, and the father is seen weeping in public houses for the death of a daughter he beat till she ran away. The most beautiful effects are the quiet descriptions of English scenery or the half-tones which reveal the distress and *malaise* of avenging youth. The author sometimes trembles on the verge of sentimentality, but usually his delicacy avoids it.

> *Cyril Connolly, in a review of "Day's End," in* New Statesman, *Vol. XXXI, No. 795, June 21, 1928, p. 484.*

THE NEW YORK TIMES BOOK REVIEW

When *The Two Sisters* appeared, critics hailed its young author, H. E. Bates, as a star of first magnitude in the English literary firmament. . . . Thus Mr. Bates's second book, *Day's End and Other Stories,* comes to a public prepared for and expectant of something important in these twenty-five short stories.

The long first story, [**"Day's End"**], is of Israel Rentshaw, whose seventy years are drawing to an end. Due to ill fortune, he has been a failure as a farmer. His daughter, Henrietta, has long wanted him to move into the village. His rented farm is about to be sold. Indecision as to what to do—whether to try to buy the farm or give it up—heart attacks and passing days bear down on him heavily. At last he comes to his day's end. The story is beautifully felt, but heavy at times with a useless tautology—Henrietta was "homely and plain-looking." . . .

Most of these stories are of individuals beaten by themselves, or what they think about themselves. Unlike Chekhov's stories they lack that relentless combining of circumstances which make for power against a nature not strong enough to fight. And unlike Katherine Mansfield's stories there is no play of light and shade to delight the reader, no happy choice of subject matter. And no tightening of his throat muscles as he reads. These are moods, done quietly in one color. As stories, they will add nothing to the reputation of the author, and many of them, such as **"Nina,"** would better have been left as character sketches in the author's notebook to await the time when they would fit like bits of mosaic into a large pattern.

> *"Stories by H. E. Bates," in* The New York Times Book Review, *October 14, 1928, p. 28.*

NEW STATESMAN

[Mr. Bates] has what is essentially the poet's seriousness, the poet's reverence for emotion even in its slightest manifestations. With Mr. Bates, "the winged joy" quickly becomes an ecstasy whose tragedy is its own transience, and whose flight, in an unfeeling world, is its own reward.

He is a writer whose sensibility deepens and intensifies more surely than his imagination widens. In tragic atmosphere and skilfulness of treatment there is probably nothing in this volume that excels the title story of *Day's End,* his earlier book; but this is not to say that *Seven Tales and Alexander* shows no development in his talent. He is more sparing with his wilder metaphors; he has discovered a sense of humour; above all, he is ripening without vitiating an exquisite childlike sensitiveness. There has always been something of the mood of Gray's *Elegy* about his work, but in this book his faintly elegiac gravity is moving out of the shadow of the churchyard into the light of memories of a rustic childhood.

Four of the eight stories of this book are about children, a fifth—the least successful—is *for* children; and the remaining three are concerned with inarticulate people who are scarcely more than children in the secrecy and muteness of their hopes and disappointments. . . . Mr. Bates takes the emotions of even his most comic or pathetic creatures seriously, without dropping into the "awfu' solemn" on the one hand or blurring the subtlety of their outline by a lyrical fog.

"Alexander," a long story, is perhaps the most characteristic piece in the book. It describes merely how a little boy goes out for the day with his uncle to gather apples in the orchard of an eccentric old lady, how on the way they call at a cottage to see a sick man, and finally the return. All the curiosities, fears, calculations, the elusive joys, inarticulate regrets and wonderings of childhood are in this beautiful piece of work. The observation of people and scenes, the renderings of changing mood, are delicate and alive, so that one can almost hear the beating of the child's heart, and smell the still, warm air of the cottage gardens. Mr. Bates's descriptions are less inclined to be imposed and static; they emanate naturally from events. . . .

Mr. Bates is still tending to encumber the situation with his own feeling, that he endows children with a sensibility that is almost morbidly self-conscious and excessive; but he has, by seeing with a child's eyes, found a world of marvellous and strange beauty, and has given the smallest shades of change and emotion the magnitude and drama they have in the minds of children and poets.

> *"Mr. Bates's Short Stories," in* New Statesman, *Vol. XXXIV, No. 870, December 28, 1929, p. 398.*

THE NEW YORK TIMES BOOK REVIEW

Mr. H. E. Bates is a young English novelist already well known for the delicacy and flexibility of his prose, and for the elusive charm of his characterizations. [*Seven Tales and Alexander*] brings to maturity some of the talents displayed in his earlier books. Mr. Bates has a leaning toward fantasy which seems to rise naturally from the necessities of his style, which is sometimes delicate and tenuous to the point of obscurity. While it is not fair to say that he is more successful in fantasy than in any other medium, at least one can say that his success in it is more consistent. In dealing with the world of reality, he still has little to do with portraying strong and clear, logical or passionate emotions. He is most at home with elusive sentiments and sensations, with impressions only half understood and half remembered, the emotions of childhood and early adolescence, or of simple-hearted and uninquiring old age.

"Alexander," the longest tale in the present volume, and by all odds the finest, excellently illustrates Mr. Bates's peculiar talent. Its plot is so simple as to be nearly non-existent. A young boy, 11 or 12 at the most, sets out with his uncle in a horse-drawn cart. They are going to pick fruit at a farm some distance away, and will return the same day. They stop on the road at a house where his uncle is acquainted, and are asked in for refreshment. While his uncle gossips with old friends, Alexander, cake in hand, wanders off toward the orchard. He encounters the daughter of the household, a girl about 15, and they talk together, sometimes with the unconstrained chatter of children, sometimes with the shy inarticulateness of approaching maturity. Alexander is stirred by a new and strange emotion, half-painful and half shadowily romantic. Although he knows nothing about the girl, not even her name, the rest of the day, spent with his uncle, is mysteriously filled with her presence. . . .

This is all the story. But Mr. Bates manages to capture in it, as successfully as any one has ever done, the difficult emotion of pre-adolescence, the sharp and yet diffuse impressions of youth. . . .

None of the other stories in the volume quite equals this one— not even the exquisite sketch of a child who gazed through a tinted window pane until, irresistibly allured by a lemon-yellow beach filled with bathers, she threw off her clothes and ran down to the sea, outraging the sensibilities of fat women in bathing suits. In the fantasy of "**The Peach Tree,**" and in the fairy story of "**The King Who Lived on Air,**" his effect is overambitious. Either—and one cannot be sure which is the case—his allegories are too obvious to warrant a setting so elaborate, or they are too obscure to fulfill his intention.

"Stories of Childhood," in The New York Times Book Review, *October 12, 1930, p. 7.*

THE TIMES LITERARY SUPPLEMENT

Mr. H. E. Bates is at once a new and a traditional writer. Traditional in kind, new in degree. No one writes quite as he does, yet he approaches familiar subjects in a familiar way. There is no sense in reading him of a new tip of consciousness budding and reaching out, as for example in much of the work of D. H. Lawrence; yet in his pages experience is continually born anew, seen pristine and beautiful. *The Fallow Land* is by far the most sustained novel he has yet written. It is a poem of the English countryside which never loses its lyric intensity, its delicacy and yet its strength, from first to last. . . .

[His] precision of detail, always subdued to the total theme, is the book's most notable quality. It extends equally to the characterization. Mr. Bates's men and women, his children, too, have a consistency not logical, but intuitive; they are real creations. The story is of an English farm, and one woman's life on it, over nearly fifty years. Deborah is a mere girl, servant to an eccentric lady in the village, when she weds old Mortimer's son Jess and goes to live on the farm with them. She bears two sons. Jess leaves her. She, the old man, and the boys carry on. The War comes to bring unhappiness, the later years more sorrow still. . . . [The story] may seem simply sad, or simply lovely. It may miss the full epic quality, which indeed it does not seem to have aimed at; it is too typically English, of the softer southern counties, for that. It may even be held to have idealized some aspects of the life it portrays, though certainly it does not shirk distress, pain, sorrow. But to the limits of its chosen vision it is as true as it is beautiful.

A review of "The Fallow Land," in The Times Literary Supplement, *No. 1601, October 6, 1932, p. 708.*

THE NEW YORK TIMES BOOK REVIEW

The character of Deborah [in *The Fallow Land*], though cramped in by narrow horizons and surrounded for the most part by dreary and inferior natures, stands out only the more vigorously and nobly in her struggle to make something of the land she has almost accidentally acquired, and her unselfish and almost impersonal determination is skillfully made to gain by contrast with the feeble slackness of her husband and son. . . .

She was a servant girl—in fact, the only servant—in the house of an invalid and half-crazed old lady when she first met Jeff Mortimer at a country fair and was horrified by his extravagance at the cocoanut-shies and merry-go-rounds. Their courtship followed a laconic, unemotional course, until one Winter's day when Jeff's mother suddenly collapsed and died, and it seemed necessary to both of them that Jeff should marry at once so that there might be a woman at the farm. Mrs. Mortimer had been no miser, but her whole life had been centred in Jeff and she had pinched and scraped every penny for his sake; some months after the birth of her first child, David, Deborah discovered that her husband's mother had hidden away the incredible sum of 150 golden sovereigns. When Jeff got hold of the money he became lazier than ever and began to drink, and when Benjamin, the second son, was about six years old, he left the farm in a towering rage and did not reappear. Her father-in-law died at about the same time and Deborah was left alone to cope with the fast-decaying little farm. It was then that her shrewd character, full of determination and sound common sense, asserted itself; and after a few years of her good management the farm was prospering again. . . . As Deborah grew older she saw her accomplishment grow with her up to a certain point, then wither away again as Benjamin came back from the war with no taste for farming, nor indeed for anything except mechanism, drink and vulgarity. The return of Jeff proved the final emotional stroke which was too much for Deborah to bear.

The fallow land was a field near the house, barren enough, which was in a way symbolical of Deborah's life and of all the personages in it. The Mortimers, father and son, continually laid plans for cultivating it but failed to get started; Deborah, who hated sloppiness and indecision, by infinite toil wrung good crops from it; it was the first thing which drew her attention when she began to take an active interest in the farm, and the last thing she thought of as she realized, dying, that Jeff was letting it slide again.

Nor is the book altogether such a tragic affair as it may seem from this description. Mr. Bates's characters, especially his women, are extraordinarily lively and accurate, even down to the subtle distinction between Mrs. Mortimer, who respected Deborah because she was "in service," and her sister, who kept a public house and despised her for the same reason. Deborah herself, kind, clever, patient and strong-willed, with "no nonsense about her," is a memorable person. But perhaps the best thing about the book is the lovely prose in which it is written, matter-of-fact and yet half poetic, in which each word and phrase is so unobtrusively right as to be almost unnoticeable.

> *"An Indomitable Woman,"* in The New York Times Book Review, *January 15, 1933, p. 7.*

HORACE GREGORY

The title story [of **The Black Boxer**] serves as a key to the entire collection.... ["**The Black Boxer**" depicts] an American Negro at an English fair, not about to die, but to endure an experience of greater dissolution than death itself, which is the realization of his waning powers. This exhibition of his skill is not his last fight, nor will it be his last effort to win a purse for his shrewd cockney manager. Sullivan, whose traveling boxing show has its counterpart in the carnivals that settle for a week or two in summer on the outskirts of American small towns.

Zeke Pinto, the boxer, was past forty, and Sullivan had half guessed the fact, for Zeke had developed a growing lassitude while in action—the youthful animal lust for fighting had left him some time ago, only superior skill remained, a skill that might be readily overcome by the crazy onslaught of a younger man, some local favorite in a provincial town. The Negro could be driven to victory only through the fear of losing his job, and Sullivan had the shrewdness to keep alive that fear within the Negro's blood, the fear of old age and final defeat.

Despite its danger of running head on into cheap emotional values and then down full length into sentimentality, H. E. Bates tells the story with great effectiveness; the action in the ring, the Negro's encounter with a local hero, is beautifully timed, and Pinto's hollow victory (on a foul) is given genuine dramatic value. Mr. Bates's prose is crisp and clear, but this quality is not to be confused with Hemingway's so-called hard-boiled manner, for it is used to contrast the beauty of the English countryside with the embittered lives of his characters.

The best of the stories in the book ["**Charlotte Esmond**"] is of the "long short story" length, and its effect is that which is usually obtained in a novelette. It is the story of Charlotte Esmond, the cooked-meat shop woman, a widow, whose daughter, Effie, becomes her successful rival for the love of a genial draper. The older woman's defeat is carried over into the actualities of tragic experience, and it is given full significance by her responsibility for the death of Effie's baby, her single grandchild. This death, which was purely accidental, breaks off Charlotte's last contact with life, nor has she the strength of will to lock the doors of her meat shop and follow the pilgrimage of her sons to America. She is imprisoned within herself, surrounded by the horror of the child's death, and is at last doomed to complete resignation....

With the exception of Katherine Ann Porter there is no one of the younger generation of short story writers in America who can equal Mr. Bates's command over form and yet give the definite conviction of having something to say. He belongs to a small company of younger English writers, poets as well as novelists, who are participating in a genuine literary revival.

> *Horace Gregory, "Master of the Short Story," in* New York Herald Tribune Books, *Vol. 10, No. 1, September 10, 1933, p. 11.*

THE NEW YORK TIMES BOOK REVIEW

Like H. A. Manhood and Malachi Whitaker, H. E. Bates is deservedly reckoned to be one of the best of the younger English short-story writers. Like theirs, too, his work is cool, restrained, a little fragile. The power of a William Faulkner and the intensity of a Sherwood Anderson are quite foreign to him, but for compensation he has an exquisite clarity and chastity of style, a kind of muted tenderness which lends distinction to even his slightest sketches.

For the most part Mr. Bates chooses to write of simple, fairly inarticulate people—catching them at a time when the whole quality and drift of their lives are crystallized in a moment of emotion....

The stories [in **The Black Boxer**] vary a good deal in merit. "**A Flower Piece**" and "**Sheep**" are somewhat too tenuous. "**A Love Story**" misses fire. "**The Russian Dancer**" verges on the banal. One could ask for nothing better, however, than "**The Hessian Prisoner**," a singularly touching tale of two old country people who hire, quaking and fearful, a man from a prison camp to do their work, and who becomes so attached to their big gay German that his death leaves them utterly desolate. Excellent, too, are "**Charlotte Esmond**"—a more ambitious story than the rest—and the lovely "**Death in Spring**."

H. E. Bates's work may be too quiet-toned, too simple, too austere, for our brisk, full-blooded taste. If so, it is America's loss. He is a very genuine artist, even if a minor one, and his stories are as good as any that are being written in England today. If he should seem alien, a difference in national temperament and tempo is to blame.

> *"Tales by H. E. Bates," in* The New York Times Book Review, *September 17, 1933, p. 6.*

THE TIMES LITERARY SUPPLEMENT

Mr. H. E. Bates is, to the critically minded reader, a continuously exciting writer, for with all his accomplishment he has not yet ceased to grow. His development, indeed, has never seemed swifter or more certain than within the past year or so, and there are half a dozen tales in **The Woman Who Had Imagination and Other Stories** which, taken together with **The Fallow Land**, or even alone in their own right, suffice to set him in the front rank of living English writers under thirty. Had he staying power? it used to be asked, had he penetration? The former can be no longer in doubt, while the latter increases steadily. He remains primarily an objective writer, implying rather than presenting psychological processes; the result leaves us sometimes wondering whether we have quite grasped all that was meant to be implied, but much more seldom prepared to assert that any other method could have been more successful; and where on occasion method and matter meet in a perfect marriage the triumph is absolute. There is one such story here, perhaps the briefest and yet the most memorable. It is **"The Gleaner,"** a study in seven pages of an old woman working in a field alone, all through the late summer day. Not once do we enter her consciousness; simply, we watch her at her work, described in her minute particularity, without a word too few, a word too many. And as we watch, by some unobstrusive magic in the words she becomes not one but universal, not *a* gleaner but all gleaners and a veritable symbol of humanity itself winning its bread by patient toil from the earth.

There are other stories, only less lovely, which display more plainly Mr. Bates's richly varied talents and, in addition, his technical virtuosity. The change and succession of the moods in [**"The Woman Who Had Imagination"**] is notably dexterous, the scene shifting from crowded brake in noon sunlight to deserted house shaded against afternoon heat, and then from evening twilight beside the lake to the return under the midnight stars, variety attractive and refreshing in itself but always subtly subordinated to the emotional rise and fall the theme demands.

A review of "The Woman Who Had Imagination," in The Times Literary Supplement, *No. 1674, March 1, 1934, p. 142.*

GRAHAM GREENE

The influence of a great writer is as dangerous as it is valuable: it is valuable in so far as it is a purely technical influence, dangerous if it is a spiritual influence, especially the spiritual influence of a writer of different race. No writer without losing his independence can adopt another's outlook, as Miss Mansfield adopted Tchechov's. There seemed some danger that Mr. Bates might follow the same road. He had mastered Tchechov's technique, in particular that accumulation of objective detail, of which the real importance is that it precedes a sudden abandonment of objectivity. For this was Tchechov's legacy from the conventional *conte;* the point of his story was often contained in the last paragraph, but the point, instead of being the conventional surprise, was a change of tone from the objective to the subjective, a spiritual summing up of the mood which had dictated the story. Here Mr. Bates very closely followed him. . . .

The Woman Who Had Imagination is, to my mind, the first volume of Mr. Bates's complete maturity. In his previous books he has worked out all the superficial aspects of literary influence, and in his new volume he shows himself an artist of magnificent originality with a vitality quite unsuspected hitherto. I cannot enough admire [**"The Woman Who Had Imagination"**], of which the framework is an excursion to a country house of the Orpheus Male Voice Singers with their wives and sweethearts to take part in a competition. The dresses and slang (which perfectly convey the period of the story), the heat of the afternoon striking up into the crowded brake from the country road, the return at night, the sleepy gossip and the dying away of drowsy flirtations: these frame, in the setting of the country house, an odd romantic episode. But the sureness of Mr. Bates's tact is seen in this: the unusual (of which the treatment is not quite on a level with the rest) is kept in its place and is not allowed to do more than to throw into relief the lovely realism of the choir's outing. This story and at least one other, **"The Wedding,"** containing an excellent character, the bawdy old reprobate Uncle Silas, who figures in three of these tales, seem to me to deserve a place among the finest English short stories.

Occasionally, as in **"The Gleaner,"** Mr. Bates is too purely pictorial; very rarely, in **"A German Idyll"** for example, his sentiment becomes a little lush; and, although the strength of his stories partly lies in his firm sense of a country locality (his pictures of slum life seem by contrast rather literary), his treatment of nature is sometimes over-romantic. . . . Sometimes, too, he indulges in a sketch which was hardly worth the while. And yet it is in his trivialities that one can see most clearly Mr. Bates's integrity as an artist. For these trivialities have been studied from the first word: such a sketch as **"Innocence"** has been as carefully designed as a novel; the reader has the satisfying knowledge that he is not being fobbed off with something careless, with something easy, that has occupied only half the author's attention.

Graham Greene, in a review of "The Woman Who Had Imagination," in The Spectator, *No. 5516, March 16, 1934, p. 424.*

THE NEW YORK TIMES BOOK REVIEW

Most readers who are interested in the modern short story are already familiar with the work of H. E. Bates. This young Englishman has experimented widely with the short-story form and has attempted, by abandoning the familiar and confining formulas, to expand it into a freer and more sensitive medium of expression. To this endeavor he has brought an evident artistic sincerity, a finely drawn imagination, and a supple and polished prose—all attributes which serve to offset a certain thinness in the material he habitually selects. . . .

[*The Woman Who Had Imagination and Other Stories*] maintains the artistic standards of Mr. Bates's previous work; but only one or two of the stories presented here have sufficient substance in themselves to justify the carefully wrought setting Mr. Bates has been at pains to give them. The title story, **"The Woman Who Had Imagination,"** is brilliantly suggestive, but it leaves one in the end with a feeling of vague dissatisfaction. The history of a tragic marriage is given to us, indirectly and in fragments, as it is seen through the uncomprehending eyes of a young shop assistant on a holiday. Mr. Bates achieves his particularly ironic effect by contrasting the girl's unhappy story with the background from which the young man emerges, with a day's outing of an English country chorus and the ribald merriment of the junketing choristers.

The longest, and perhaps the most complete and ponderable story in the collection, is **"A German Idyll."** Its narrative outlines are excessively simple, but its emotional effect is inescapable. . . .

The other pieces in the collection are much shorter. Some of them, indeed, are scarcely stories at all, but are rather character sketches or episodes, depending for their effect upon a kind of reticent irony. There is **"Millennium Also Ran,"** the story of a sentimental young reporter who laid a wager on a horse race, meaning to assist with his winnings a destitute young widow whose plight had caused him to reflect, for a brief hour, that civilization is out of joint. The more amusing and robust character sketches are **"The Lily," "The Wedding,"** and **"The Death of Uncle Silas"**—all of them dealing with the adventures of Uncle Silas, that stout, virile and incredibly ancient gentleman who is one of Mr. Bates's most delightful creations.

"Stories by H. E. Bates," in The New York Times Book Review, *August 12, 1934, p. 7.*

THE TIMES LITERARY SUPPLEMENT

The author of *The Poacher,* it was affirmed in these columns less than a year ago (March 1, 1934) [see excerpt above] must be deemed to stand in the front rank of living English writers under thirty. It might have been at once more generous and no less precise to have declared him frankly and without further qualification the occupant of a place of his own among our contemporary novelists and short-story writers of whatever age, though neither in justice to him nor in deference to plain fact must the matter of his relative youth be entirely overlooked. If Mr. Bates should write no more, still something of his, if only a handful of short stories, would stand as a contribution to current literature unique in its own kind.

To suggest this assurance in his short stories above his novels is not to diminish the latter in the least, at any rate so far as his later work is concerned. He is, from whatever cause, a primarily lyrical writer, and his impulse has so far found its purest though not necessarily its fullest expression in his briefer fictions. His total qualities may nevertheless be as well or better studied in his maturer novels, and perhaps nowhere so aptly as in his newest and maturest story *The Poacher.* It is in almost all respects a highly typical piece of its author's work, as fresh and in parts as moving as anything he has written, but with no surprises. It is the history of a poacher from his youth in the early 'eighties until after the War, the span practically of *The Fallow Land.* The setting is the same as in all Mr. Bates's novels and most of his other work, the Nen valley country of Eastern Northamptonshire. But, again as in all his work, neither period nor topography is intrusive. The reader is made to realize the past from the most incidental remarks or passing details of costume; similarly, while some of the descriptions (especially of the countryside) are beautiful in their precision, principally the book is a study of a man. Luke Bishop may draw his early fecklessness from a feckless environment, but his country longings are bred in the bone. Buck Bishop, piecework shoemaker and the most skilful of poachers, is his father and hero, and their night expeditions together are the bright adventures of his youth. These adventures and Buck in his role as trainer of young running or boxing hopefuls are described at some length with a fine vigour and freshness. So, too, is Luke's flight from a dead keeper, pursued by police but taking refuge on a remote farm, where he finds a wife with whom he returns home to set up as a smallholder on the edge of the town. Thenceforward comes an increasing foreshortening of events. Two or three years have occupied nearly two hundred pages; the next forty will fill barely a hundred more. Their story is one of Luke's growing loneliness—his strong-willed wife developing her own career and moving apart from him, his daughters learning to despise him. Only with his son-in-law Walter and presently his grandson Edward has he any community of spirit; and even this is frowned upon by the womenfolk who see him but as bringing disgrace upon the family by a recrudescence of his old habits leading him to prison and thereby to dispossession of all that still makes his life worth living.

It is all, as a whole, admirably told, with vivacity, spontaneity of incident, sensitiveness in understanding, clear character-portrayal and consistent power of evocation. Everything, in the telling, appears adequate and natural. A living relation is established between the characters in the very tones as well as the terms of their dialogue. They are all, even Luke, objectively viewed, and, what is not beside the point, they are also all simple characters, instinctive rather than intellectual creatures, and none ever more than momentarily self-conscious. They

live in moods and scenes, which is, save for brief linking passages, the story's mode of progression.

These are the common qualities of the bulk of Mr. Bates's stories and novels. From what is said of *The Poacher* both the merits and limitations of the rest of his work should be deducible. It is not to be blinked that he is, in his published work, a limited writer. The simplicity of his characters has been noted, as has been too their detachment from period and place. Countrymen close to the soil, artless girls or domestic women, children—these are his favourite and most convincing types, beings of small horizons for whom the death of a mare or the fall of a tree at the bottom of the garden is more than they will ever read in the newspapers. Even his town-dwellers in the slum of *Charlotte's Row* are instinctive countryfolk at heart, cheated of their heritage by forces they do not and in the main make no effort to understand. Mr. Bates has never drawn a fully conscious man, or even, persuasively, a markedly educated one. In the result the modern world, as such, can scarcely be said to exist in his pages. His world is in the main hardly more than a narrow strip of lovely South Midland countryside, set with some pleasant villages and an ugly town or two. To this one can add, from the short stories, but the briefest glimpse or two of a detestable London and again of an idyllic Rhineland. Politics, even the War, are matters heard afar off. All these things are limitations—they are not necessarily defects. Whether they are or are not the latter, must depend upon their origin in strength or weakness. It would be quite plausible to urge their birth directly from an unwavering poetic instinct for essentials, to argue that Mr. Bates writes of common men, because he is concerned with the most universal emotions, and deliberately avoids the quality of contemporaneity because he would not obscure the unchanging issues of birth and love and death, the ceaseless pattern of mortality, by interweaving with them the irrelevant because passing preoccupations of this year or that. Men and women are born, and live their lives, and grow old and die; their true analogue is not the counting of the office calendar but rather the eternal recurrence of the seasons from winter to winter, each cycle beginning anew as if those before had never been.

> The field lay rough and fallow, without a furrow turned. It looked to him just as it had looked in his father's time, as though it had never been touched, the same old field difficult to plough and worse to reap, never worth the trouble of seed or harvest.

Some such vision does undoubtedly lie at the root of all Mr. Bates's writing. It is the frame of his picture of life, obvious in the very schemes of *The Poacher* and *The Fallow Land* and some of the short stories from *Day's End* forward, and implicit in many more. . . .

It is a tragic vision of existence, but also a humanizing one. We meet a thousand men upon the road to Death and they all are our brothers. Mr. Bates recognizes the tragedy, but acquiesces, finding beauty at once in its universality and inevitability. Sometimes, it may be felt, especially in relation to his earlier work, the acquiescence is too easy; the suspicion arises that he has not himself faced imaginatively the situation into which he thrusts his characters. The beauty, too, is not always devoid of the taint of facility, having on occasion an air of being draped about rather than derived from the essential conception. . . . There is, in the later writing, short stories and novels alike, a notable increase in imaginative austerity; there is in that superb little study, **"The Gleaner,"** scarcely a superfluous word or image. Even more striking has been the development of character, the ultimate test of imaginative reality in any form of fiction. It is a long step from the shadowy figures shifting at their author's whim across the blurred word-tapestry of *The Two Sisters* to the clear-cut autonomous individuals of *The Poacher,* and it is a most hopeful sign that each book between has marked an evident pace forward. . . .

Mr. Bates's basic intuition, we have intimated, is tragic, but also human. By very reason of his knowledge, his sense of the brightness and activity and even humour of life is heightened. His tales may sometimes be sad—they are seldom gloomy. They can be—and it is a vein he seems to work increasingly—really funny without losing, as farce does, human reality. There is in *The Poacher* no lack of lively scenes—the opening eviction, Buck Bishop and the woman at the inn, Buck as trainer, Luke and his aunt, Luke and the farmer Thompson, and presently Luke and his grandson. None of these is specifically comedic, but the salt of a living humour born of clash of character is in each one. In some of his best short stories—**"The Lily," "The Woman Who Had Imagination,"** that oddly pleasing trifle **"Innocence"**—the comedy is one of the conditions of their moving beauty. . . .

He remains, in the sense we have sought to define, a limited writer, but whether that be a matter of conscious or instinctive choice his roots are in sound soil, his inspiration is authentic. He may in the course of time and growth discover the necessity to transcend those limitations, to turn from lyric to what may be called by contrast epic expression, and to more complicated, if not more final, fields of interest. . . . If he can grow thus, in his own good time his future development should prove even more remarkable than his past has been.

> *"Mr. H. E. Bates," in* The Times Literary Supplement, *No. 1721, January 24, 1935, p. 45.*

MARGARET WALLACE

[In *The Poacher*] H. E. Bates gives evidence of a splendidly developing talent. Best known, at least in [the United States], for his volumes of short stories, he cannot help but become better known with the publication of *The Poacher*. His atmospheric and delicate short stories were uniformly fine in workmanship but rather tenuous in substance. Little of them remained to the reader after the book was laid aside except an impression of the writer's conscious skill in expressing something which seemed, in retrospect, hardly worth the expenditure of so much industry and talent.

In this novel, however, Mr. Bates has found a subject better suited to his powers and has created a character—commonplace enough, it is true—who happens to be impressively real. Luke Bishop's father was a poacher—a big, cunning, soft-footed man with no taste at all for honest work. Luke admired him extravagantly. The most thrilling nights of his boyhood were spent scouting the countryside with his father, eluding the gamekeepers, setting snares for rabbits, or putting up nets, and hunting with ferrets. The secrecy, the skill, the spice of danger, the silent beauty of the woods at night, were all a part of the spell of this outlawry.

The tempo of the book changes in its latter half, although the effect is not at all inharmonious. The story merely gathers speed, covers more ground in a briefer space—as a man's own life seems to in its latter half. . . .

Living more and more in the past as the years rolled by, Luke was revived to the present by the birth of his grandson and began to plan for the boy's future. What money he had inherited after his aunt's death he made over to young Edward's father to be expended on his education. And in his own way he began to contribute to that education, teaching the boy the ways of the fields and woods, how to make and set a snare, how to break a rabbit's neck with a single light blow from the side of the hand. His parents not unreasonably protested, especially when the child got himself arrested with a snare in his possession.

The final episode of the tale, one last ill-fated poaching expedition which lands the aging Luke in jail and from which he returns to find himself homeless and a pauper, is a fitting conclusion to this chronicle of a deep and simple nature. Beautifully and without affectation Mr. Bates has expressed through the story of Luke Bishop's life his deep feeling for the life of the English countryside, for the changes which have come over it in the last half century and his own nostalgic regret for the order which has passed.

> *Margaret Wallace, "A Moving Novel of English Country Folk," in* The New York Times Book Review, *March 17, 1935, p. 7.*

THE TIMES LITERARY SUPPLEMENT

Are there half a dozen novelists to-day who offer as much pleasure as Mr. Bates in his best work? There are certainly not more. One comes to him in the knowledge that he has no taste for a show of sophistication, none of the pretensions of the novelist with a purpose, no affectations of prose style, nothing of the latest touch that is so soon out of date. These things apart, one does not easily tire of the varying poetic moods of his stories, the freshness and grace of his descriptions of the countryside, the intuitive delicacy of his studies of old people and children. Like every good storyteller, he creates freely within boundaries of his own choosing. A small canvas with two or three characters only in the foreground serves him best. In his novels, as in his short stories, it is the illumination of a small familiar scene, of a moment of unambitious experience, that enables him to take beauty, as beauty must be taken, by surprise.

Spella Ho, his latest novel, is a longer and more elaborately designed book than any he has attempted hitherto. Mr. Bates sets out to follow the fortunes of Bruno Shadbolt from the seventies of the past century, when he was a wretchedly poor, illiterate, almost brutish village youth, to lonely and memory-ridden old age in the great house in which he had served, which he had coveted and eventually made his own. As soon as he had learned to reason Bruno, like the hero of a Balzac novel, came to see that only two things mattered in life, women and money. It is his pursuit of these ends that principally engages Mr. Bates. And, with the best will in the world, it is impossible to say that he has made a success of his story. There are scenes and incidents that are recognizably his and his alone, winter and summer landscapes of an enchanting exactness. But the vision of distant horizons that he seeks to fashion in the experience of his hero is shifting and cloudy, as though the experience itself were imperfectly realized. If one may venture the suggestion, the theme he has chosen here does not match his distinctive talent.

The potential greatness that Mr. Bates tries to uncover in Bruno Shadbolt is never apparent to the reader. Passion flickers for a moment in him, and here and there one can glimpse a thwarted groping towards beauty; but for the most part he is merely powerful and dumb, a lustful and intensely masculine creature of instinct that is only dimly apprehended. . . .

Paradoxically enough, a novelist has often most to fear from his greatest gifts. Mr. Bates in this novel too frequently resorts to an apt and charming descriptive passage when what the story would seem to require is a deepening of emotion or an increase of tension. His mastery of the short-story technique has led him, we think, to over-simplify the treatment of his subject here and so fall short of his effects. Criticism over, there remains much for which one is grateful. As in **The Poacher** and other novels of his, there are pictures of snow falling on the fields that stay in the mind. There is too, a quite unsentimental and unforgettable picture of poverty in the early part of the book, when the half-starved Shadbolt children march round the icy-cold room to keep themselves warm, singing hymns at the bidding of their mother, herself dying and dead that same night. Here is the true and vivid perception, with the added touch of authentic strangeness, that makes Mr. Bates's best work a poetic and moving interpretation of life.

"The Village Satyr," in The Times Literary Supplement, *No. 1909, September 3, 1938, p. 567.*

JANE SPENCE SOUTHERON

Mr. Bates, though only thirty-three years of age, has a pageful of titles to his credit—and to his credit in every sense. *Spella Ho* would seem, decidedly, to top the lot. It has a protagonist who has no prototype in literature; though, so far as actual life is concerned, most people will feel he is a kind of man vouched for by experience; a sort of Beethoven of business; rugged, moody, dreamy, incalculable, instinctive and deriving impetus from his relations with women but motivated, fundamentally, by a primitive urge that compels him to fulfill himself. . . .

He has a fatal fascination for women and, besides casual encounters that satisfy only one side of his nature and leave him virtually unaltered, there are four, all as different from each other as it is possible for women to be, who exercise extraordinary influence, beneficent and apparently though perhaps not really baneful, over his life. . . .

It is a queer book, full of queer folk, queer emotions and mental states and reactions and queer situations; but there is nothing that is bizarre. It is the queerness of life itself that is caught and fixed, in instantaneous literary photography, by a writer attracted less to the commonplace than to the exceptionally unusual; and the queerness is given an everyday aspect by the ordinariness of the background—an English township changing, as was many an American one during the same years, from mid-nineteenth century material backwardness to what we, today, style modernism.

The queerest thing in the book is, as in life, the queerness of contrast! Bruno Shadbolt, at 20, ingrainedly dirty because he has never realized the need for washing; half-starved, fiercely determined to save his fanatically honest old mother from perishing of cold, creeping up to the great house, "Spella Ho," that stood above Caster, and stealing coal. At the other end of his long life we watch him, a fine old man who has made Caster and bought the beautiful mansion in its magnificent acreage, patiently and with characteristic modesty replying to the pert criticism of a young woman who, with modern sureness, relegates his lifework to a nothing summed up in hide-

ousness. There is, he feels, "no record" of anything beautiful he has produced; but the record is there in himself—a grand old man wrought, through the divine spark of hidden genius, from a boorish, lumpish human creature lower than peasant and almost as inarticulate as the earth he trod on.

And there is the contrast between his women. The fairly young widow, "easy and just a little flash," to whom he sold stolen coal and who taught him to wash and roused in him the first wholly unexpected rush of physical passion; and Lady Virginia, an idealist, who, much later, appealed to every side of the man and whom he was to have married but for the strange waywardness of fate. Before that there had been gentle, devoted Louise who, more than any of them, set him free by helping him along the first painful stages of the road to education; Gerda, the warmly passionate German wife of a stupid English doctor, who was torn from him by an impelling personal longing; and Italian Jenny, the lovely but meretricious dancer who egged him on to carry out materialistic schemes that made him rich, but were entirely against the grain.

Hardly less important are the men who meant so much to him in his career and the miserly old woman who gave him, at "Spella Ho," which changes hands four times during the story, his first monetary start. But, all said, it is his delineation of physical passion in its countless variations and permutations that is Mr. Bates's most outstanding contribution to fiction in his latest novel.

Jane Spence Southeron, "A Striking Novel by H. E. Bates," in The New York Times Book Review, *October 30, 1938, p. 6.*

THE TIMES, LONDON

The imagination that has inspired the stories of *The Flying Goat* is not remote or cold. The humour, indignation, or sympathy with which some of them were written is only enhanced by the austerity of the expression; and the level of accomplishment still allows an extraordinary variety of mood. At the one extreme is **"I Am Not Myself,"** and at the other the farcical and fantastic **"A Funny Thing,"** another of the Uncle Silas episodes. The first is a story of insanity in a young girl, and in this piece there is no sort of barrier between the reader and the characters. He hears the silences in this grave, unnatural circle, feels the visitor's spontaneous love for the girl who seems only to be living on two planes, notices with him the change in the eyes, the change from presence to absence, and experiences the same unreasoning necessity for flight. **"Perhaps We Shall Meet Again,"** which records a chance conversation between a starving girl and a woman who wants to get thin, and **"The Late Public Figure,"** which discovers the truth about him, are more obvious, but both of them are forceful and both contain many instances of the extraordinarily quick eye for personal idiosyncrasies for which the author is famous. **"The Ox"** is a shorter, compressed version of Miss Fanny Hurst's "Lummox," **"The Flying Goat"** itself has the cheerful absurdity of a true nonsense story, and **"Shot Actress—Full Story"** gives an excellent example of the obstinacy and ruthlessness of gossip. None of the rest is poor, but one remembers with particular pleasure **"The Ship,"** in which a sailor comes home with a coloured bride.

A review of "The Flying Goat," in The Times, *London, September 15, 1939, p. 11.*

FRED URQUHART

Only two of these sixteen stories [collected in *The Flying Goat*], the title story and "The Wreath," are slight and relatively unimportant. Admirers of Bates will not be disappointed with the others, although they will probably find in them echoes of themes which have interested him in the past. In "**Every Bullet has its Billet**," we find a favourite Bates theme: the awakening of love for a married man in the heart of a young girl. Readers of his first novel, *The Two Sisters,* will recognize the nostalgia for strange countries and the preoccupation with madness in "**The Ship**" and "**I am not Myself.**" And in "**The White Pony,**" a delicate and sensitive tale of a boy's love for a pony, we are introduced again to the boy, Alexander, who figured in the early story of that name, a story which the late Edward Garnett at one time regarded as Bates's highwater mark. But this story is streets ahead of the earlier one. It is tighter and far more economical. And in general this applies to the whole collection. There are none of these thumb-nail sketches of which Bates was so prolific in the early stages of his career, sketches which although lyrical were so slight that they really made little impression. Every one of the present group is brilliantly executed, and joined together they are in my opinion the most satisfying collection that he has given us. Especially satisfying are three stories which have great social significance. In these days when art and propaganda are so entwined, it is heartening to find a writer of Bates's calibre writing stories like these. He has always been ready to pick holes in the shoddy fabric of our civilization, but nowhere, I think, to such good purpose as in "**The Late Public Figure,**" where he unstrips with calm deliberation, the newspaper proprietor who was such a sham and a hypocrite. In "**Perhaps We Shall Meet Again,**" an upper-class woman who, gorged on public dinners, has grown so fat that she thinks seriously of dieting, sits down on a bench in a public park and talks about her difficulties to a girl who is starving. And in "**The Ox,**" a study of an incredibly stupid woman, Bates is much more effective than dozens of highbrow textbooks deploring the lack of education among the lower classes. For these stories alone this volume is memorable.

Unfortunately there is only one story here about Uncle Silas. In it we find that lovable old rascal, more bloodshot of eye than ever, getting the better of Uncle Cosmo, a character who looks as though he might outrival Uncle Silas in popularity. This story, "**A Funny Thing,**" has no difficulty in living up to its title. (pp. 289-90)

H. E. Bates writes mainly of the country, of the English farming and labouring classes; occasionally of the industrial workers in small manufacturing towns. In an article of this length I have not space to examine the social significance of his work, but it strikes me as curious that many left-wing theorists who laud the work of his upper-class intellectual contemporaries have not paid greater attention to it. If his books were given to people whom the Marxists wanted to convert, they would have much more effect than plays in blank verse about mother-complexes and pseudo-homosexuality. An ordinary working man or woman would understand and appreciate the difficulties of Bates's young farm-girls and stolid labourers much better than they would understand the spiritual hunger of the inhabitants of Bloomsbury. Two of his best novels, *The Fallow Land* and *The Poacher,* depict phases of English country life, knowledge of which is vital in the present class-struggle: the decay of the countryside and the industrialization of the land.

Probably the trouble is that Bates does not beat the big drum. He writes dispassionately, never calling upon his reader to see the injustices that his characters are undergoing. Or it may be due to the fact that his characters and situations are so commonplace. By this I do not mean to be disparaging. I mean that the characters are the sort of everyday characters that one is always meeting. Writing of him in 1934, David Garnett said: "Bates's work is liable to be undervalued . . . because he is not a very original writer; his great merit is not originality, but sensibility. His sensitiveness to beauty and to character is astonishing; it is, I think, greater than the sensibility of any other living writer." Nowhere is this sensibility better demonstrated than in Bates's portraits of old people and children. His stories about children are among the best in the language. And everybody knows his Uncle Silas. (pp. 291-92)

Fred Urquhart, "The Work of H. E. Bates," in Life and Letters To-Day, London, Vol. 23, No. 28, November, 1939, pp. 289-93.

MEYER BERGER

Here is sheer beauty in writing. This little volume of short pieces [*There's Something in the Air*] will give the reader a clearer conception of the combat's thinking, fighting, living, than anything that has come before. The little tales are gems cut from purest carbon, handed down so that they spit cold fire.

It is done with quiet little words. Emotion is superbly checked in every passage, yet the full impact flows through the reader. Night scenes that come within the bomber pilot's vision over England, over the Channel, over Brest and Germany are painted so crisply that they crackle. . . .

No other book on the British flier—or any other flier for that matter—has the sharp, authentic note Flying Officer Bates has written into this work. Commissioned by the English Government as Flying Officer X, he got all his material first hand, and he has made it come alive. If there were decorations for this sort of thing, H. E. Bates would have the highest.

"**The Young Man From Kalgoorne,**" the tale of an Australian pilot, is perhaps a little better than some of the rest of these gems. It tells the story of a youth whose farmer parents managed to keep from him, on their remote acres, the news that war had come to Britain and that London and the English countryside were crumbling under Nazi bombs. It tells how he finally learned of it, anyhow, and how he went to England to learn how to pilot a Stirling and how he went out again and again to repay the German pilots for their deadly gifts. It tells how he came to have a "popsy"—a girl—who would wait for him each night when his Stirling was on operations, and of her bitterness one night when he did not come back. . . .

These are tales told in impressive quiet, tales that are innocent of even the suggestion of flagrant heroism that colors so many stories about combat pilots. The tone is so even and the flow so temperate that the reader is apt to wonder, when he has done with the book, how this effect was achieved. An ordinary writer would have used angry words, words closer to hand. Flying Officer X seems to shun them, yet all the feeling of a magnificent anger and of heroic achievement seems to burn into the reader's soul.

The finest example of this magical literary technique, I think, is "**The Sun Rises Twice.**" It is the story of a Stirling pilot who won no medals though he flew faster and farther on most operations than any of his decorated flying mates. It is a model of simplicity—nothing more than a literary hors d'oeuvre—but the taste lingers. . . .

There's something in the air and pretty soon every one must be aware of it. It is something miraculously clean and clear. It is the writing of Flying Officer X.

Meyer Berger, "British Combat Pilots," in The New York Times Book Review, *May 16, 1943, p. 3.*

VIRGILIA SAPIEHA

Mr. Bates, widely known as an English short-story writer, has used his talent and experience to celebrate, in [*There's Something in the Air*], the magnificent few to whom so many owe so much. Here, in these sketches of R.A.F. fliers at a bomber station in England, the author does not so much describe his series of brave young men as introduce them to us with a few rapid clues to their background and then let us fly off with them and judge them for ourselves.

Our whole history is illumined with tales of extraordinary individual courage in the unequal struggles, of men against nature and the terrible struggles of men against men. But there has never before been such material for heroic stories as is provided today in the embattled skies.

The story called **"The Greatest People in the World,"** the title under which part of this book was published in England, is about young Lawson, who had never wanted to do anything else but fly. His father had cut hedges and dug ditches in Somerset, while his mother worked at the local rectory and helped in the fields at harvest time, and together they had never earned much more than two pounds a week, yet with endless skimping they had managed to secure for their only child the education he most wanted. Although when he became a flyer Lawson's new life lay far apart from that of his parents, he never forgot what they had done for him. At the flying field Lawson met a stretch of bad luck, beginning with the night when his plane would not take off. Careful and steady as he was, this anticlimax gave him nightmares, and he lost confidence. Another time, when he had flown only a short way, icing began, the plane reeled and Lawson had to jettison his bombs and turn home. The brakes did not work in landing, the under-carriage was smashed. He was afraid he would be grounded. Then Lawson got a telegram. He went home on "compassionate leave" to see the charred ruins where his parents had been killed. After that he never ran into any more bad luck. When he roared over the English fields on his way back from bombing and saw the tiny figures of a man and a woman working, he remembered his parents, the greatest people in the world, and his whole life was clear. . . .

There is the story of the girl whose parents do not want her to go out so often with her pilot friend, since there is no future in it; the story of the man from an Australian sheep farm whose parents hid from him for a whole year that England was at war with Germany, and who, when he discovered it, was the angriest young man in the world; and too, the story of Canadian Sergeant Carmichael, who keeps alive his three companions in a storm-tossed dinghy through the night and gets them safely to the shore. Into this little book are crowded the stories of some twenty nerve-taut, daring, infinitely shy young men. At the end of the series there is a short glossary to explain the new words with which these young men cover up their dangers and their deeds.

The root of all these stories of R.A.F. flyers is sacrifice. But Mr. Bates, being a true Anglo-Saxon and a true writer, keeps this root well underground. Sacrifice, implicit in every action, is never mentioned. No high-blown praise mars the account of daily heroism which is beyond words or praise. On the contrary, Mr. Bates writes so reticently, with so much understatement, and his young flyers exchange such brief and almost shame-faced talk about their feats, that only the streamlined modern Anglo-Saxon mind could appreciate the tribute which he pays them.

Virgilia Sapieha, "The Few to Whom So Many Owe So Much," in New York Herald Tribune Weekly Book Review, *Vol. 19, No. 40, May 30, 1943, p. 3.*

BEN RAY REDMAN

Readable and absorbing as it all is, part of [*Fair Stood the Wind for France*] is readable as writing that aspires to be literature, and succeeds, while the remainder of it is readable as fiction of the now popular escape-from-German-occupied-territory school. One can have no quarrel with the author's choice of subject, or with his handling of it through the better part of his narrative; it is only when he slips from sincerely thoughtful writing into an overworked and somewhat slovenly pattern that one suffers disappointment and is moved to protest. After which one reads on, still pulled by the tow of the yarn, but on a different level. Fortunately, however—and let it be emphasized—the change occurs late.

Fair Stood the Wind for France is the story of John Franklin, R.A.F. bomber pilot and captain of a Wellington crew. We meet him in the third summer of the war when he is flying back across the Alps after completing a mission to northern Italy. Behind him is almost a year of active operations, beginning with Bremen and Cologne; and of his crew of four sergeants, three have been with him all this time. Behind him is fear, that he has learned to screen even from himself. Behind him is the learned "habit of foreshortening the focus of his mind: so that he never looks forward beyond the next moment of darkness.". . . Behind him, between operations, is a lot of drinking and a lot of dancing and love-making, all calculated to hold back "tides of apprehension and pain"; behind him, "screaming nights in the local towns, crashing traffic lights, with girls screaming in the back of the car, everyone having a wizard time. Wizard: the word has grown crusts on it. What fun!" John Franklin, at the age of twenty-two, thinks that he has a sizable chunk of life behind him. He does not know that a broken airscrew, a crash landing in Occupied France, a severed artery in his left arm, and the beginning of a new and more meaningful life lie just a few minutes ahead.

In the new life an arm is lost and a girl is found, and long steps are taken toward John Franklin's maturity. . . .

Mr. Bates tells the story simply, but with little or none of the pretentious "simplicity" paraded by writers who follow Hemingway at too great a distance. He is particularly skilful in the communication of physical sensations—indeed, he is body-conscious to a remarkable degree—and the sensitive reader will often feel a probe go home. He is skilful, too, in the creation of suspense, and in the precise, measured, slow-motion writing that can increase almost to the breaking-point the tension of a dramatic scene. John Franklin, in the story's telling, grows from a mere name into a character of considerable substance; while the other airmen matter not at all, with the exception of O'Connor who, to my mind, serves the novel ill rather than well. Françoise, the girl, does not grow, because she is complete to begin with—strong, true, loving, tender, capable, courageous. If any captious critic objects that such a character is a mere dream-girl, let him take a look at some of literature's most successful heroines.

As to the pattern of the story, it is enough to have suggested its nature without reducing it to a synopsis that might rob some readers of the pleasures of discovery and surprise. It is often a deeply moving story, always an exciting one.

> *Ben Ray Redman, "Endurable Fragments in France,"*
> *in* The Saturday Review of Literature, *Vol. XXVII,*
> *No. 21, May 20, 1944, p. 18.*

HERBERT KUPFERBERG

[*Fair Stood the Wind for France*] seems likely to go down as one of the most exciting and moving stories of [World War II]. Filled with suspense, written in a taut prose that fairly crackles, it is at once the tale of a wounded British flyer's effort to escape capture by the Germans in France, and of a fallen nation's effort to regain its soul.

The story goes back to the summer of 1942, when France still was divided into occupied and unoccupied zones. British flyers who "conked out" over occupied France had to make their way southward to the Vichy zone, eventually to Marseilles, where passage might be gotten to Spain and thence to Britain. Only by a miracle did they ever escape capture: travel was down back roads, over fields, along streams—always by night, of course, when it was easier to elude German sentries at bridges and crossroads.

Dealing with the French was a tricky business—to reveal yourself was to put yourself in some one else's power. Sometimes you hit it right and stumbled into a sort of underground railway system where friendly hands provided you with forged identification papers and peasant clothes and directed you to the next stop along the line. Other times you stumbled into the Nazis' grasp.

Having a badly injured arm complicated matters no end. That was John Franklin's trouble. He had been the only one hurt when the Wellington crash-landed in a French marsh; the other four were unscratched. So when a friendly French family gave them refuge and managed to get four sets of forged papers, Franklin stayed behind while his crewmates struck out in an attempt to reach Marseilles.

It's hard to think of a more deeply stirring picture than the one Mr. Bates gives of the French peasants who hide the young flyer. Realization of what they were doing for him came slowly even to Franklin. After all, he would merely become a war prisoner if caught, but they would be executed.

But helping Franklin and others like him was their way of fighting. . . .

These magnificent people, magnificently portrayed, are what gives *Fair Stood the Wind for France* its stature. The old woman was surviving her third war with the Germans. (It was her belief that the 1914 war—the only one France won—had ruined the nation for good.) For Francoise, the girl, it was her first war, and she had enough faith and love (after Franklin came) to live through it. Her father resisted because he was a Frenchman. . . .

In his perilous travels through France, Franklin ran across knaves and heroes; met people who would help him because of love, because of honor, because of money—and some who would not help him at all. Far more than his own flying missions, it made him realize what war really was.

This is story telling of a high order—the kind that deals with people one can believe in, with whose fortunes and misfortunes one can be deeply concerned. You'll go a long way in war novels to find an episode to keep you on edge as does Franklin's river journey in a rowboat toward unoccupied France. Nor will you soon forget what happened in the tiny, desolate town where he got a glimpse of the other France—the part that had lost its courage and become brutalized.

> *Herbert Kupferberg, "One of the Most Exciting Sto-*
> *ries of the War," in* New York Herald Tribune Weekly
> Book Review, *Vol. 20, No. 39, May 21, 1944, p.*
> *3.*

THE TIMES LITERARY SUPPLEMENT

Mr. Bates's new novel [*Fair Stood the Wind for France*] follows a frankly popular, almost too frankly popular, design. It is about the pilot of a R.A.F. bomber which crashed in occupied France in the summer of 1942 and his love affair with a French girl. There are nice things in the novel, as was only to be expected, but they are fewer and altogether less individual in stamp than might have been hoped for. Mr. Bates has always been happier with the short-story form than with the full-length novel, but the extended short story which he has given us on this occasion is disappointingly close to the magazine variety. . . .

The whole thing is readable enough, sometimes more than readable. There are neat sketches of some of the minor figures in the tale, and the small landscape pictures that he manages as a rule with charming intimacy are not absent. But Mr. Bates, if one may say so, appears to have taken less trouble than usual with them. He is very fond here of descriptive similes that are merely literary or extravagant—an open eye like a black cherry, pear branches that swing like ropes of solid yellow bells, and so on. In short, although his popular touch is probably well calculated, this is not a novel that adds to Mr. Bates's reputation.

> *"The Pilot's Wooing," in* The Times Literary Sup-
> plement, *No. 2231, November 4, 1944, p. 533.*

JAMES STERN

In this racy, sexy, rollicking tale [*The Darling Buds of May*], tossed off, one feels, during a month of glorious spring weather among the hop fields and blossoming orchards of what surely must be Kent, Mr. Bates assures his readers that if people like the newly rich Larkins don't live literally like royalty it's only because they are vociferously happy living the way they do.

For "Pop" Larkin on his farm everything was "perfick." What's more, and more important, Pop was determined that all visitors, including the horsey and impoverished local gentry, should share with his family the "perfick" things of life; above all the colossal meals cooked by Ma (whose "great continent" of a body was about to produce a seventh child), and Pop's drinks which he produced from a monster cocktail cabinet known as the "Spanish galleon." ("A Guide to Better Drinking" was the only book Pop had ever read.) (p. 4)

The young visiting tax-collector, Mr. Charlton, is as staggered by the Larkins' appetite and lavish way of living as Pop is to learn that he should have filled up a form to pay the taxes on his past year's income. Fill up a form? "I got no time for forms," roars Pop. "Gawd Awmighty, I got pigs to feed. Turkeys to feed. Hens to feed. Kids to feed." Mr. Charlton is about to express his very serious view of the situation when he sees, floating across the immediate Larkin hen-and-pig-scape, a very different kind of form in the Larkins' 18-year-old daughter, Mariette.

With Mariette's silken legs brushing against his under the tea-table, all the Larkin children stuffing themselves . . . , Ma cooking three geese for supper and Pop pouring whiskey into his tea ("relieves the wind, frees the kidneys and opens the bowels"), the stunned, underfed Mr. Charlton is soon, and in all senses of the word, undone.

Only occasionally in the crowded, dreamlike days to come, during the strawberry and hop picking season, does the be-mused tax-collector remember his mission. These Cockney hop-pickers, for instance, they ought to be paying taxes on what they earn! Taxes, cries Pop, "dammit, if they was taxed, they wouldn't come. Then you wouldn't have no beer!"

The logic of this argument Mr. Charlton finds as crushing to his last shreds of reasoning as the reader should find this prolific writer's latest creation—or should we say a perfick piece of entertainment? (pp. 4, 24)

James Stern, "The Larkins' Cup of Tea," in The New York Times Book Review, May 25, 1958, pp. 4, 24.

MAX COSMAN

[*The Darling Buds of May* is] Mr. Bates' ripost to younger contemporaries, angry or otherwise disturbed. It takes up their challenge that life is something of a pain in the neck and retorts there is more to say than that. It rests its case on the Larkin ménage.

Not for a long time has there been so earthy a group. First, of course, is Pop Larkin, a veritable anaconda at roast goose and turkey, buns and jams, ketchup and Guinness. (p. 356)

Pop's abetter in physicality is none other than Ma Larkin. Her dimensions are on the scale Lachaise has accustomed us to. Certainly they are an earnest of the endless eating in which she no less than the others of the household engage. Perhaps as indulgent in another way, she has already given six pledges of love to Pop and has no intention of crying quits. Indeed, shortly before *The Darling Buds of May* comes to its robustious end, she informs him of "a funny feeling it might be twins." Since she has not been wrong before, he promptly accepts the news as "perfick" and begins to study what to call those who are due.

For the Larkins have always been believers in "jolly good names." Since Ma's favorite flowers are Zinnia and Petunia, the twins she already has naturally could not be called other-wise. As for Primrose, showing up in the spring, what else was there for her but Primrose? And so too Victoria, for ar-riving in plum time, and Montgomery for reminding one of the general. Only Mariette is different. She owes her name to a Larkin malapropism for Marie Antoinette.

It is she who first spots Cedric Charlton hovering about the family farm *cum* junkyard. Naive fellow, he has come down

from the office of the Inspector of Taxes to right a little matter of income return for the last year. Has he a chance with his buff-yellow form? No. Pop baffles him with the cunning of an up-and-coming entrepreneur. Ma sates him with huge meals. The twins select his lap for sitting on in the landaulette. And Mariette overwhelms him with the charms of a Lilith and an Eve's assurance that he is her Adam.

Willy-nilly, Cedric becomes the honored guest. In this begin-ning is his end. He relaxes, he eats heavily, he drinks daringly, he earns money at strawberry time, he takes a long vacation from the office, he proclaims his love for Mariette and is accepted—in brief, he turns into true Larkin.

Underneath this jollity, Bates is serious too. Like his master in the pastoral-comical, he is funnily mad but north-north-west. When the wind is southerly he also knows his hawks from handsaws. He can put the finger on T.V. uplift or Welfare State sick-leaves with the sharpest of younger cynics about. And he is as deft as any older contemporary at more traditional ribbing. His handling of gymkhana gentry, for example, is out of the same manual Waugh used for exemplars of rank in *Vile Bodies*. As a matter of fact, Angela Snow, good sport at Pop's party, is a dead ringer for Cynthia Runcible.

The Darling Buds of May, then, is a switch on Bates' usually tense bucolics. It offers gusto instead of agony; Rabelais (adapted to English propriety) rather than Webster. The result is a de-lightful conte which, if it has no great future, at least has an entertaining present. (pp. 356-57)

Max Cosman, "Rabelais Adapted to English Pro-priety," in Commonweal, Vol. LXVIII, No. 14, July 4, 1958, pp. 356-57.

VALENTINE CUNNINGHAM

The best of H. E. Bates? With so much to choose out of the cornucopia of a lifetime's fictional stuff—twenty-five novels, a score and more volumes of short stories—some devotees are bound to want to argue about that. No one, though, is very likely to dispute that what's here [in *The Best of H. E. Bates*] does include revealingly good examples of Bates's most char-acteristic work: there is, for instance, one of the Uncle Silas stories; there are stories such as **"The Simple Life"**, about a snootily urban woman's conversion to the country and to sex in the country, and **"The Little Farm"**, about an illiterate farmer's short-lived affair with a woman who answers his ad-vertisment for help; and there is *The Darling Buds of May*, first of the ribald Larkin novels. And only the most argumentative of Bates-fanciers would want to question the inclusion of the novella *The Triple Echo* (1971), one of the finest of Bates's later returnings to wartime themes; *The Purple Plain,* first of the great trilogy of novels that he wrote in the 1940s about Far Eastern theatres of conflict in the Second World War; and, of course, *Fair Stood the Wind for France* (1944), with reason thought by many to be the best British novel of the war.

What H. E. Bates does best, and what this superb selection aptly shows him best at, is satisfying his characters' and his readers' deep cravings for pastorals. Repeatedly he proves the delights that attend life in the pastoral enclave, the garden enclosed, shut off from discontents and disturbances. Take, for example, the eternal summer of memory, where time is forever suspended in a Huck Finn boyhood. The blessed in Bates's fiction cannot only recall when the "medder were yeller", "yeller as a guinea", but—like Uncle Crow in **"Great Uncle**

Crow''—they can actually recreate those times. A model of avuncular beneficence on Dickensian lines, nicely lubricated by doses from his ''neck-oil'' bottle, Crow conjures up for Lukey Boy the entrancing edible components of his own blissful past: watercress (''He found the watercresses in the bucket, cool in the shadow of the little house''), moor-hens' eggs (''Now you put the cresses on that there plate there and then put your nose inside that there basin and see what's inside''), spring-water to boil the eggs, salt to ''frost'' the cress, and slices of ''thick brown bread'', ''pasted'' with ''summery golden butter'': all nature's goodness, in fact, handed to the lad on a golden plate. ''But not on a golden plate?'', he inquires. But yes, for ''the sun was a gold plate in the sky''.

This generous artfulness with the powerful components of idyll has become, of course, so much the desired effect of bad novelists and devisers of television advertisements for brown bread and such that better writers tend now to shy away from it. Happily, H. E. Bates had got into the swing of Uncle Crow's business before the copywriters (and, for that matter, the television adapters of his own stories, whose work does rather blur into the golden margarine purveyors' material) could deter his relish for it. He likes nothing better than creating the isolated space, the place islanded from trouble and war, within whose calm precincts love can live, feelings of time-off can reign, and recollections of childish innocence are inevitable. Escaping through France by bicycle in *Fair Stood the Wind*, the flyer Franklin ''rode sometimes with his feet on the handlebars, as he had done when a boy, and was very happy''.

The grace of such moments can be afforded under varying circumstances, just as some circumstances can mock the absence of that grace even as they evoke it: Franklin ''persuaded himself for one moment'' that the fraught train journey towards the Spanish frontier ''was a holiday''; condemned to trudge through nightmarishly hot wastes in *The Purple Plain*, the airman Forrester thought ''the picture was of some holiday scene, with slightly distorted differences, taken at the seaside''. Happiness comes to Franklin when he is shut up in a mill and hiding under a tarpaulin in a rowing boat. . . .

June, July and August are Bates's particular months. He likes his fictions to be out and about when there's some chance of the day being the hottest one of the year. His pages gorge themselves on the sights and smells of peaches and apples, plums and strawberries, gooseberries and damsons. Wherever the fiction is set Bates's prose is zestfully busy, touching and tasting and sniffing at things that grow—the yuccas in France, frangipani and lime and jasmine in Burma, the apples and pears that will remain forever English. . . .

Naturally, this abundance can on occasions seem overdone. . . . But the lushness is always savingly rooted in country lore—life-savingly sometimes, as when Franklin warns his men not to cross a sugar beet field (''Going through will make a hell of a noise'') or Forrester ekes out his water-supply by sucking pebbles (''He remembered how, as a boy, he had gone to stay with an uncle, on a Suffolk farm, in harvest-time; and how in the August heat, in the dry eastern fields, the labourers had taught him to suck a pebble, to quench his thirst''). And the sprawling adjectives always sound convincingly precise.

Bates's eye always alights acutely on the object. The unseeing eyes of the impercipient have, in fact, to be educated into the author's, the countryman's way of acute noticing, ''Oh! no'', Roger of **''The Simple Life''**, a boy with ''exceptionally bright'' eyes, keeps correcting townee Mrs Bartholomew's misimpres-

sions of marshland wildlife. And in their distinctly quiet way, Bates's adjectives prove continually as telling as Auden's best. . . . Bates is always working manifestly hard for the exact description. He will modify adjective by adjective. *Golden-pink, grey-green, green-pink, tawny-purple, rosy-purple, green-white:* how these double-barrelled exactitudes pile up. But his prose does not only accumulate its impressions, it keeps on confidently selecting, seeking out the sharpest of comparisons from the widest fields of metaphorical possibility. Water lilies in **''Great Uncle Crow''** are ''as big as china breakfast cups''. ''There was so much ham in the rolls'', in **''The Major of Hussars''**, ''that it hung over the side like pink spaniels' ears''. In the heat of *The Purple Plain* a towel dries ''to the unkindly roughness of a loofah husk''. Some poets have rested their main claim to distinction on being able to manoeuvre metaphor like that: but it is only one among many shots in Bates's crowded locker. Not that the power of metaphor is not, however, at the heart of Bates's pastoral. It is, for by it he keeps underscoring the force of his women as part of the natural world.

Bates is one of the most tenderly affectionate describers of desirable women in English literature (*tender, tenderly, tenderness* are, not surprisingly, among his most used vocables). His narratives love women of all sorts, and love to dress, as well as undress, women in all kinds of clothes. Bates is obsessed by cloth of every sort, especially cloth with a woman's body beneath it. But, noticeably, he does prefer his women dressed in green—the green skirt of Françoise in *Fair Stood;* the pale green blouse of Forrester's girl in *The Purple Plain*, the lime-green silk dress of Mariette in *The Darling Buds of May,* the vivid emerald taffeta of Mrs Boorman in **''The Wild Cherry Tree''**. And these green-clad creatures become more evidently still the aptest of pastoral beloveds in the transformations wrought on them by Bates's metaphors. Like the fruits of the earth, they become good things to eat, their skin *milky* and *creamy,* their hair *coffee-brown,* their mouths *plum-like* or like the strawberries they chew (''Mr Charlton looked up to see the lips of Mariette parted half in laughter, half in the act of biting into some glistening arc of lovely dark ripe flesh''). The eye of Françoise, open as she prays, is ''like a black cherry held against her partly opened fingers''. Boorman's boorishness is evinced by his angry ripping up his wife's green dress; conversely, Mrs Boorman's ideal love affair with a passing stranger is enacted when she's discerned to be, as it were, an apricot: ''Then suddenly he caught sight of the apricot dress.''

Mrs Boorman seemed to her lover ''actually to be walking as if in fact she were a myth''. The stuff of Bates's pastoral is, like that of all pastorals, a mythically prelapsarian business; and that can never be sustained entire because our arts are all more or less fallen ones. In the case of Bates, a 1930s author who kept on writing into the 1970s, the Fall repeated itself many times. The *entre deux guerres* his writing grew up in turned out to be no consolatory pastoral enclosure away from distress and violence, but a cage into which writing and writers were willy-nilly locked, a prison infiltrated by wars and rumours of wars, whose boundaries were not defensive pales but threatening borders across which, in 1939, the world was violently shoved into yet more slaughter. And after the war, there descended a wintry greyness (as Bates perceives it) of socialism and taxation and the accelerated ruination of the land by petrol-driven machines, transistorized vulgarity, and barbarians in their weekend cottages. All of which, however, Bates also bravely acknowledges, sternly facing his gentle mythologies with the harder realities of our times.

So his fine pastoral enclaves keep being smashed apart. Sophie swims among the water-lilies on a hot summer's day in **"The Four Beauties"**, but drowns shortly after. All too soon the Military Police winkle *The Triple Echo*'s deserting soldier out of his farm hideaway and, with mixed feelings, his beloved shoots him and his captor dead. . . .

[One] of Bates's astutest stratagems for coping with the end of pastorals as he has known them is to reconstitute the Garden of Eden ironically, making its grotesque modern inheritors, the Larkins, blackly but also endearingly funny.

The Larkins, with their tax fiddles, their exploiting of the "National Elf lark", with Pop's swish old Rolls, their ignorance and illiteracy and their host of tellies, their gruesome booziness and grimly excessive gourmandizing, with lumberingly fat Ma's dismayingly transparent nightie and the family's refinements of sexual "technique", the Larkins are everything that Leavis and the old Organic Communards feared most. As they prosper, the older denizens of the countryside, the Brigadier, the Anglo-Indian ladies, Sir George Bluff-Gore, go down the hill, fraying and patched, diluting their whisky sadly, wondering whether Bluff Court might as well be sold to Pop for scrap. Yet, rough Cockney pastoralists though the Larkins be, they've tapped the genuine Keatsian intensities. After all, Keats himself was a noisy Cockney sensationalist, not unlike them. And though the burping and the frank chat about bowels, not to mention the menu chez Larkin—ice-cream with jam and chips, iced-buns with tomato sauce and lurid cocktails—might turn the better-bred stomach, Pop's "Perfick", as he surveys his Paradise Garden and anticipates the fruit-picking, the June strawberries, the July cherries, the August apples and plums and pears, the September hops, seems just the right verdict.

Much against the prevailing odds, whether there are perturbing modern violences or loud Larkin uncouthnesses, the quiet strains of Bates's preferred rural world are continued. Bates is always paying tribute to survivors who cling fiercely to life—that crowd of women who trekked north to escape the Japs in *The Purple Plain*, or Forrester in the same novel who toughly carries the burned Carrington back to civilization ("aware of a fierce kind of affection for the very livingness of the boy"). And despite everything working to the contrary, Bates makes trust and comradeliness, love and tenderness—for which no one has a more delicate touch than he; the repeated silent scenes where male lovers softly touch or kiss the naked breasts of their female beloveds never fail to compel—makes these virtues seem feasible as well as worthwhile survivors. It amounts, of course, to a faith in the continued virtues of ordinary people, "the little people" that *Fair Stood the Wind* so sticks up for, the inhabitants of the "little" farms that lofty Franklin has to come acceptingly down among. It's a belief, too, in the importance of keeping up the humane tasks of the traditional novel. It is no accident that the lovers' long row to safety in *Fair Stood the Wind* should remind one so piercingly of Pip and Magwitch trying to escape by boat in *Great Expectations*—that journey where their love emerges triumphantly as they hold hands at last—nor that when O'Connor performs his final act of self-sacrifice at the end of the same Bates novel he should be turning himself so movingly into a convincing latter-day Sidney Carton.

Valentine Cunningham, "Pastoral Perfick," in The Times Literary Supplement, *No. 4058, January 9, 1981, p. 27.*

WALTER ALLEN

It was probably due to the dominance of Coppard that during the Twenties the short story in England often appeared as a specifically bucolic form registering a scene and ways of life that had scarcely changed since those depicted in Hardy. Parallels with Georgian poetry abound. At his best, Coppard himself rose above these criticisms and, at his best, his true successor was H. E. Bates. He never, as Coppard does from time to time, surprises with a fine excess but he was an exceedingly careful craftsman who kept up a consistent excellence. . . . [This] careful craftsmanship was infused with a sensitivity to beauty and character that led David Garnett to write that 'his best stories have the extreme delicacy and tenderness of Renoir's paint'. Having been read once, some of his stories exist in the mind as pictures, often as still life, as does **"The Gleaner"**, probably the most famous of his early stories. Movement in it seems arrested almost to the point of having been frozen. (p. 262)

The impression he creates of stillness, of stasis, seems at times akin to the rendering of a state of trance, as in the late long short story **"Death of a Huntsman"**, published in 1957, almost a quarter of a century after **"The Gleaner"**. **"Death of a Huntsman"** shows admirably, by the way, Bates's range of social types and scenes, which is considerably wider than one at first thinks. (p. 263)

Generally, prose-poetry is a pejorative phrase: that Bates's prose has a genuine relation to poetry is shown by the frequency with which his rendering of nature in its minute particulars especially, as in the description of the quince-trees on the tiny island, reminds us of poets, of Tennyson for example. At the same time, he wrote some splendid heroic stories. This was a development in his talent brought to fruition during the war, when as 'Flying Officer X' he was commissioned in the Royal Air Force to write stories of the war in the air. The finest of these is perhaps *The Cruise of "The Breadwinner"*, which appeared over his own name in 1946. [*The Cruise of "The Breadwinner"*] is a characteristic British wartime improvisation. A small lugsail fishing boat, she patrols the Channel looking for the pilots and crews of shot-down aeroplanes. Her skipper is Gregson who appears to Snowy, the cabin-boy as a 'man of unappeasable frenzy', and Jimmy is the engine-man.

When the story opens, Snowy is still a boy, pining for a pair of binoculars (for he is also the plane-spotter), but when he returns from the day's cruise he is a boy no longer. (p. 265)

The Cruise of "The Breadwinner" is an austere work in which there are no heroics and no sentimentality. Among other things, it is a story of initiation into manhood. The characters are drawn boldly and simply, and this gives them a representative quality. The British officer partakes of the stereotype of the RAF pilot of the day, and Bates allows for this. He sees the pathos and the paradox of the stereotype: '. . . his words transcending for the first time the comedy of the moustache'. Gregson is beautifully rendered and Snowy is the epitome of boy at that moment in national history: he is defined completely in terms of one or two simple symbols, his prowess as a plane-spotter, his lust after the binoculars, his awe of Gregson. *The Cruise of "The Breadwinner"* is among the masterpieces of the years it celebrates. (p. 267)

Walter Allen, "Bates," in his The Short Story in English, *Clarendon Press, Oxford, 1981, pp. 262-67.*

DEAN R. BALDWIN

One reason for Bates's present obscurity may be that he is very much outside mainstream modern British fiction. For one thing, Bates took no part in the experiments which marked much of the significant writing early in the century. He uses straight-forward, naturalistic narrative, devoid of symbolist or stream-of-consciousness techniques. For another, he did not participate in any of the century's literary coteries nor in any of its intel-lectual movements. His fiction espouses no political, social, or religious point of view; thus no movement or ideology used his work for its own purposes. Moreover, while most modern writers have turned to urban characters, settings, and themes for their fiction, Bates has remained a largely rural interpreter, writing most often and most powerfully about people and events far removed from modern urban concerns. And finally, while much of modern literature represents a conscious departure from romantic themes and ideology, Bates exhibits a strong, persistent streak of romanticism—Wordsworthian romanticism at that. Bates is, in other words, an anomaly, a naturalist in technique at a time when the realist-naturalist traditions in fiction were declining in significance, and a romantic at a time when most authors were striving for a new classicism. (p. 132)

One of his most successful creations was Uncle Silas, a char-acter about whom he published two volumes of stories [*My Uncle Silas* (1939) and *Sugar for the Horse* (1957)]. . . . These stories are not characteristic of Bates's other novels, stories, and novellas, but they are the best indication of his romantic temperament and a highly entertaining body of fiction. They deserve to be better known. In what follows, therefore, I would like to examine the Uncle Silas stories as examples of Bates's romanticism and to analyze their appeal.

Much of Bates's best writing deals with the countryside and people he knew as a boy growing up in Northamptonshire, but most of his characters are imaginary creations. Not so with Uncle Silas, whom Bates transferred to the written page directly from his model, a great uncle named Joseph Betts. . . . Part of Uncle Silas' appeal, therefore, may lie in his authenticity. Knowing that such a character lived and did many of the out-rageous things Bates narrates imparts an added dimension to the tales. It may also be partly responsible for the liveliness and color of the tales themselves. Bates always wrote with great vividness about the country, but there is a special sharp-ness in the Uncle Silas tales, a hearty robustness animated by the comic spirit.

An author careless in managing such materials might easily allow an Uncle Silas to become a merely sentimental character, a male version of the clichéd prostitute with the heart of gold, or perhaps a countryfied tough-guy who is all gentleness and love of mother inside. Occasionally, Bates borders on just such sentiment, but Uncle Silas is spared this fate because Bates refuses to blink away Silas' very real faults. (pp. 132-33)

Silas is something of an outcast, certainly a strong individualist. He lives on the fringes of civilization, in a picturesque cottage surrounded by a well-kept garden that makes him almost as self-sufficient as a medieval lord of the manor. He grows his own vegetables, raises pigs, brews wine from cowslips, elder-berries, and parsnips, and supplements his diet with game poached or legally taken. The romantic appeal of such a life is obvious. . . . The problem . . . is to preserve this charm with-out allowing it to dissolve into escapist fantasy or nostalgia. That Bates himself preferred this brightly colored pastoral to modern industrial grayness cannot be doubted, but his artistic problem was to keep the appeal of this romantic scene without reducing it to sentimental mush.

The chief device by which Bates tempers the inherent romanti-cism of his materials is comedy. Not all of the tales are

humorous, but all but one or two contain many light moments. Essentially then, Silas inhabits a comic world against which his own strengths can stand out to good advantage and in which his own weaknesses seem harmless. Good examples can be seen in stories like **"A Funny Thing," "Silas and Goliath," "The Race," "The Foxes,"** and **"The Eating Match,"** in which Silas gets the better of someone (usually a local braggart or bully) by combining shrewd psychology and downright guile. **"Silas and Goliath"** *(My Uncle Silas)* is typical. The villain is a brag-gart and bully named Porky Sanders, who offends one of Silas' lady-friends. Silas challenges him to a fight and then enlists the lady to work on Porky, convincing him to train on nothing but cucumbers and beer—liberally laced with salts. By the time of the fight, "what with the bellyache from the beer and the bellyache from the cucumbers, Porky turned up for the fight looking as green as a boiled frog." Silas easily disposes of the bigger man by butting him into a creek. In these tales, Silas is portrayed as something of a hero, even though his means of victory are less than honest. His adversaries, being braggarts and bores, deserve their defeat, and Silas' trickery thus serves to make the tales more humorous. If Silas' repu-tation is unduly enhanced and if his romantic role threatens to make him seem larger than life, all is saved by exuberance and comedy. Silas' devilishness is excusable for its being devoted to a good cause, while the romantic elements of the tales can be enjoyed because they do not become mawkish. In these respects, some of the Silas stories have the appeal of folktales, where moral judgment is momentarily suspended and the tale stands on its own as entertainment, irrespective of the fabulous elements that could stretch credulity too far.

Even comedy cannot by itself neutralize the ill effects of a romantic hero who continually triumphs over opponents de-serving defeat. Other ways are needed to keep Silas from be-coming a sort of rustic superman. Important in this respect is Bates's skillful manipulation of point of view as a way of keeping Silas in perspective. Three points of view are used in the stories. Most of the tales are related by Silas himself, often to the narrator (presumably Bates himself) as a young boy. Others are told to the narrator as an adult, and a few are given entirely in the third person—told by the narrator about Silas. Each point of view carries its own ironies, calculated to un-dercut the romanticism of character and setting.

When Silas is himself the narrator and his audience "the boy," his tendency, naturally enough, is to exaggerate. Silas partic-ularly enjoys playing on the innocence of the lad in tales of ribald double entendre. **"Finger Wet, Finger Dry," "The Bed-fordshire Clanger," "The Double Thumb,"** and **"The Wid-der"** all fit this category. The boy is not merely a passive listener, however, for like all children he has a healthy skep-ticism about adults and their tendencies to fib. In such tales, there are thus two plots, one in the story Silas is telling, the other in the interaction between Silas and the boy. **"Finger Wet, Finger Dry"** illustrates the type. Early in the story, Silas claims that the venison on the dinner table comes from a deer he shot with a bow and arrow. The boy pesters Silas about making him a bow until Silas relents, makes a crude bow and some arrows, and "proves" that he killed the deer by shooting a hapless cow in the rump. . . . [The] marvellous interaction between Silas and the boy makes the stories particularly rich in humor and comic ironies. Silas' devilment is indeed a source of pure comedy. Simultaneously he develops as a romantic individualist, caring as little for social taboos as he does for the strict truth of a tale. How much is fact and how much fabrication we—like the boy—cannot tell. And so the joke is as much on us as on him; we share his innocent delight in the exploits and perhaps even more so in the "proof" Silas offers to authenticate them.

In the stories told by Silas to the mature narrator, this innocence-experience theme necessarily almost disappears, and the focus accordingly shifts to the exploits themselves. "The Lily" and "The Revelation" (from *My Uncle Silas*) and "Queenie White," "The Blue Feather," and "The Fire Eaters" (from *Sugar for the Horse*) are of this type. On the whole, their tone is less rambunctious, the humor less pointed; in some a melancholy or even a sour note slips in, helping to offset the sunny, romantic world which threatens to overwhelm the tales. (pp. 134-36)

Finally, there are the stories told about Silas by the mature narrator. In these, Silas retains his salty ways and individualistic assaults on respectability, but he is also occasionally seen as something of a buffoon. Included in this category are such stories as "The Wedding," "The Sow and Silas," "The Shooting Party" (all from *My Uncle Silas*), "Sugar for the Horse," "The Foxes," and "Little Fishes" (in *Sugar for the Horse*). . . .

As a boy growing up in Northamptonshire, H. E. Bates absorbed the last remaining drops of ancient English rural life. As long as he lived his fiction drew strength from the people and their ways. His is a tough, uncompromising, sharp-eyed view of these people, their strengths and weaknesses, their hard work, dignity, suffering, and triumphs. Beneath the tough manner of his fiction, however, lies a great respect for rural ways and traditions and an understandable nostalgia for ways of life already dead or rapidly dying. Small wonder, then, that in the character of Silas, Bates's romanticism would find full scope for expression. If I have dwelled at length on the devices the author uses to control the inherent romanticism of his materials and his own romantic tendencies, it is because casual readers may too easily dismiss these stories as escapist entertainment. Entertaining they are, but these tales are "light" in the best sense of that word: simple, direct, entertaining, but also finely crafted, well told. (p. 137)

> *Dean R. Baldwin, "Uncle Silas: H. E. Bates's Romantic Individualist," in* West Virginia University Philological Papers, *Vol. 28, 1982, pp. 132-39.*

DENNIS VANNATTA

By 1946 Bates was already a veteran of writing about men at war. Even though *The Cruise of the Breadwinner* is another story about World War II, however, it marks something of a departure, and perhaps something of a risk, for Bates. Bates had gleaned a wealth of observations and experiences as Flying Officer 'X,' and he had an established, enthusiastic audience for works drawing upon those experiences. But *The Cruise of the Breadwinner* does not heavily draw upon those experiences, although it does involve a downed R.A.F. flyer; it is a work almost entirely of imagination. Another element of risk was the timing of the book. The Flying Officer 'X' stories were published at a time when all Englishmen's thoughts were filled with the war; England needed and appreciated stories showing the dauntless courage of her young warriors. But by 1946 England was adamantly and defiantly tired of the war. Could another war novel find a receptive audience? *The Cruise of the Breadwinner* proved that it could; and Bates—and many other novelists such as Nicholas Monsarrat (*The Cruel Sea*, 1951) and Charles Morgan (*The River Line*, 1949)—continued

throughout the 1940s and early 1950s to write commercially successful novels set during World War II, although none of the English literature of the Second World War approached the tragic brilliance of the World War I poets and novelists.

The Cruise of the Breadwinner is more than simply an analysis of the horrors of war. In his introduction to *Six Stories*, Bates compares his novella to its thematic predecessor, *The Red Badge of Courage*, in that both involve a naive youth who confronts war in its bloody, palpable horror and returns "strangely grown in stature and refined by fire." Thus, *The Cruise of the Breadwinner* is more than an account of a harrowing incident of war; it is a fictional *rite de passage*, a dramatization of a boy's psychic journey from youth to maturity.

The boy, Snowy, works aboard *The Breadwinner*—a small fishing vessel converted to a patrol craft—with the captain, Gregson, and the cynical engineer, Jimmy. All patrols to date had been uneventful affairs, and Snowy yearns to witness some exciting event from the war. . . . (pp. 62-3)

Snowy gets his wish when they hear an aerial battle out to sea and sail off in search of possible downed pilots. Soon they rescue an English pilot swimming in the sea, and then his adversary, a German. Both are wounded, both colorful, and Snowy ached "to be part of the world of men." Below deck making tea for the pilots and crew, Snowy hears running on deck. "He had at that moment reached the fine and rapid conclusion that war was wonderful." But war turns from wonderful to hideous when he hears machine-gun fire bursting out above him, ascends to the deck and sees the results of a strafing attack: Jimmy blown to bits beside the Lewis gun and Gregson and the two pilots in a bloody heap. Gregson, miraculously, is unharmed, but the pilots' fresh wounds will soon prove fatal.

The remainder of the story concerns Gregson and Snowy's efforts to comfort the dying pilots and get the disabled *Breadwinner* back to shore. (p. 63)

In contrast to the majority of Bates's previous work, *The Cruise of the Breadwinner* plot and characterization are more important than atmosphere. Equally interesting and important to the theme is a "sight pattern" of sorts—a motif incorporating images, items, references, and actions suggesting sight, vision, blindness, similar to the one found in *King Lear*—which parallels Snowy's maturation process.

For instance, the one thing for which Snowy yearns above all else is a pair of binoculars—the better to see the glamorous events of the war, of course. Gregson had promised him a pair long ago but not delivered, and Snowy covets those worn by the German pilot. What Snowy in fact needs is vision, maturity of vision. Ironically, he is noted for his ability to identify aircraft at great distances, even by their sound; but significantly, the one time that his talent is put to the test, he fails. "Spit pilot?" he asks the English pilot. "Typhoon," he is corrected. Thus, the binoculars underscore his need not only for sight, but insight into the true nature of war, suffering, death.

But the "sight pattern" involves much more than simply the symbolic binoculars. Almost all suggestions of maturity or immaturity, ignorance or experience, are couched in terms of vision or blindness. Thus, when Snowy hears the machine-gun fire and rushes up to the deck—just after reaching the "fine and rapid conclusion that war was wonderful"—"he became for some seconds quite sightless, as if he had stared at the sun." He is numbed by what he sees. The air feels suddenly cold, "then still colder on his eyes, shocked stiff by what he had seen of the engineer." He runs off "like a blind man. . . . He had seen the dead." (p. 64)

Snowy's immature vision has been dispelled, only to be replaced by blindness and confusion, certainly not maturity. He begins, however, to take tentative steps toward a more balanced, mature vision. . . .

The end underscores his maturing vision in a sight image: "He had been out with men to war and had *seen* [italics mine] the dead. He was alive and *The Breadwinner* had come home."

The Cruise of the Breadwinner was a popular success because it was an exciting story, trim and direct, with sympathetic characters; it was a critical success for the same reasons, in addition to having an important theme and characters not only sympathetic but human enough to engage us in their psychological as well as physical conflict. Bates followed this success with three novels in four years set in the Far East [*The Purple Plain, The Jacaranda Tree,* and *The Scarlet Sword*], all based, at least in part, on Bates's observations while serving with the Air Ministry in India and Burma. The three far exceeded *The Cruise of the Breadwinner*'s popular success but fell short of its critical acclaim. (p. 65)

Of the three, *The Purple Plain* (1947) most nearly rises above the "best-seller" tag. The protagonist's conflict is engaging, the setting hypnotically painted, and the plot is frequently exciting. Equally important, Bates weaves a rich tapestry of imagery that underscores plot, theme, and characterization.

The protagonist is Forrester, an R.A.F. flight commander at an isolated airstrip bordering the scalding plain (the purple plain) of Burma. The germ for Forrester's inner conflict came to Bates on the very day of his demobilization. A fellow officer remarked upon a pilot who had gotten to be a much-decorated hero by the dubious method of trying to get himself killed. It happened that his wife had been blown out of his arms and killed by a German bomb while they were dancing on their honeymoon. Thereafter, he went into the air hoping to be killed, only to down plane after German plane instead. . . . Bates appropriated this dilemma for his suicidal hero, Forrester, in whom subordinates and fellow officers see clearly "the signs of fiber disintegration, the moral breakup, the end."

Almost unbeknown to Forrester, however, some genuine feeling for life still stirs him occasionally. He craves solitude yet still feels stabs of pity for his detestable tent-mate, Blore. He is contemptuous of his own life yet is stunned by the fiery death of a fellow pilot. He longs for death with each flight yet subconsciously scans the terrain below for avenues of escape in the event of a crash. The commingling of Forrester's death wish and life urge is reflected in the war, of course, but also in the dual nature of Burma itself: overabundant with life yet permeated with cruelty and death. . . . Finally, Burma's three-year drought reflects Forrester's spiritual drought, yet Burma has a saving grace: its people, represented by Anna, who helps rescue Forrester from his spiritual wasteland.

Anna is an educated young Burmese woman who, along with a very few others, survived a long trek from Rangoon to escape the advancing Japanese. She survived terrible hardships while watching most of her companions die, so like Forrester she is an intimate of life's horrors. Yet she has achieved a serenity and implicit balanced view of life that allows her to enjoy the beauty that life offers while recognizing and fighting against its depredations. Her alliance with the more fertile side of

nature is signified by the pale green dress that she wears and the frangipani flower (its blossoms last forever, seemingly) caught in her hair.

Almost immediately upon their first meeting Forrester is captivated by Anna's beauty and even more by her wise, earned serenity. He leaves that first meeting terrified by his previous desire for death, and when he sees a fellow pilot die in a plane crash the next day, he realizes how very much he wants to live. (pp. 66-7)

Structurally, *The Purple Plain* breaks into two distinct halves: the first half at the airstrip and nearby village where Anna lives and the second half on the plain. To say that the two halves do not fit together is not entirely accurate; we have already shown that the struggle on the plain, carrying Carrington "piggyback," tests Forrester's desire to live and his commitment to his fellow man. Yet nagging problems remain for the reader. Forrester's spiritual demon is his desire for death, yet for all practical purposes that demon is exorcised in his first visit to Anna in the second chapter. His aching hollowness at the loss of his wife is assuaged in the sixth chapter, only a third of the way through the novel, when he holds Anna in his arms during a bombing attack. This scene mirrors the one in which Forrester lost his wife, so we know that he has found a replacement.

Thus the novel ends, thematically, before it is half over. At no time in his struggles on the plain do we doubt Forrester's will to live or his desire to get back to Anna. We gain no new insight about him as a man or about man's condition in a world rich in life and death. Bates's account of the trek across the plain is a masterful *tour de force* of action and description—the equal of any in Bates's long career—and it is worth reading for that alone; yet it would be just as satisfying had it been published alone as a novella, apart from the story of Anna. (pp. 67-8)

If we wonder whether at this point in his career Bates was teetering on the edge between serious fiction and more purely popular fiction, a look at his next two novels of the Far East will not be very encouraging.

The Jacaranda Tree (1949) was even more popular than *The Purple Plain* and presents even more problems for the discriminating reader. A brief summary of the plot seems to indicate a novel that could not help but be diverting, even exciting. Peterson is the English manager of a mill in a small Burmese town when news comes that a Japanese advance is imminent. Peterson organizes the British inhabitants of the village, together with his Burmese mistress and her brother, for what he hopes will be an orderly evacuation to India. (pp. 68-9)

To be fair, the novel is exciting in places, and Bates's well-established descriptive powers occasionally enthrall us, although never with the force seen in the last half of *The Purple Plain*. The problems with *The Jacaranda Tree* are twofold: tone and characterization. The novel is peopled for the most part with characters who are dangerously oblivious to the enormous changes taking place in their world. Vestiges of the Britsh Empire, they can hardly comprehend the imminent danger of the Japanese invasion, much less the more sweeping currents that are rapidly washing away the remains of the empire. . . .

[The] first third of *The Jacaranda Tree* has more nearly the flavor of an English comedy of manners moved to Burma than a serious study of civilians caught up in the horrors of war, and it is here that the novel is most original and interesting. It is when the tone changes to what we expected all along that we begin to lose interest. Knowing Bates's considerable skills, we would expect the novel to have great power and suspense once the action shifts to the long flight up the road to India, but too often it does not. (p. 69)

The novel might still have been saved from its inconsistency of tone and flaws in the dramatic action if we were presented with one strong character to build an engaging theme and conflict around, but unfortunately we are not. Peterson, the protagonist, is largely a mystery, and a confusing, not an engaging, mystery. Bates presents Peterson in the first chapter as an irritable man, frequently drunk. His servant-boy, Tuesday, gauges his moods by the number of aspirin he demands each morning; and while Tuesday worships his master, he also stands poised to dodge in case Peterson slings a glass or bottle at him: evidently a common practice. What is the cause of Peterson's unhappiness, irritation, dipsomania, or whatever it is? We never know. (p. 70)

About the only question that the reader has is how soon will the bad fellows (Portman, Betteson, Mrs. McNairn) get their due, and how much trouble will they cause the good fellows before that happens. In other words, in *The Jacaranda Tree* Bates comes closer than ever before to the facile conflicts and resolutions of the best-seller.

In some ways, the last novel of Bates's Far East trilogy, *The Scarlet Sword* (1950), is the most satisfying of the three, in some ways the least. The story of an English mission in Kashmir pillaged during the bloody days of the Indian partition, *The Scarlet Sword* avoids both the flawed thematic structure of *The Purple Plain* and the inconsistency of tone and characterization of *The Jacaranda Tree;* and it very nearly avoids the sentimentalism that caused Bates to kill off the unpleasant characters and save the likable ones in both. Indeed, the violence and horror in and about the mission strike the innocent and guilty, the holy and unholy alike (although early on we do sense quite correctly that the violence will spare the protagonist, his new love, a likable priest, and a courageous nurse).

The virtue of *The Scarlet Sword* is its single-mindedness. It evokes the violent world of rape, murder, and torture that marked the India partition with a relentlessness that forces the reader to keep turning the pages. But if this single-mindedness allows Bates to avoid the pitfalls of structure and tone that flawed the previous two novels of the Far East, it also prevents him from engaging us on any other level. (pp. 70-1)

The Scarlet Sword opens with a host of characters—tired, cynical, and frightened—and closes with a much-reduced host, laughing. We can only guess why they are tired and cynical in the beginning or why they are laughing at the end: unless it is that it is very nice to be alive when one might have been dead, and that is hardly revelation enough to build a novel around.

Bates had spent two decades building a reputation as a writer who could skillfully and engagingly weave stories and novels that told us a good deal about individuals, specific segments of society, specific epochs of history, and the human condition. With the three novels of the Far East, he seems to be attempting the same thing in an altered setting; but for all their sweeping action, varied characters, colorful and exotic settings, we do not learn much about men or man, place or time in the three novels. We are left primarily with violent action and love affairs, the stuff of best-sellers. We can easily see why Bates was reaching an ever-expanding audience, while at the same

time leaving behind old friends who longed for him to return to the settings and characters of the Midlands. (pp. 71-2)

Bates had written fictions which might qualify as novellas before the later years of his career, most notably *The Cruise of the Breadwinner* (1946). Yet the sheer number of novellas which he produced between 1953 and 1970—twenty-two, five collections and one published separately—indicates that the novella acquired a fascination for Bates rivaling the novel and the short story. By all accounts the novella is a difficult form in which to work but one whose rewards are great. (p. 108)

Bates's [second] collection of novellas—*Summer in Salander* (1957)—was published only four years after *The Nature of Love,* and in many ways it is a thematic extension of its predecessor. All the novellas deal with love relationships, and all end unhappily. In *The Nature of Love,* however, love most often translates into degrading lust; in the present collection we occasionally encounter relationships that—had conditions been happier—might have developed into something resembling a healthy love. Another major difference in the collections is in their respective tones. The novellas in *The Nature of Love* envelop the reader in a suffocating fog of gloom, whereas in two of the *Summer in Salander* selections we are refreshed with an occasional ray of humor. (p. 112)

The Grapes of Paradise: Four Short Novels (published in England as *An Aspidistra in Babylon,* 1960) continues Bates's analysis of not the nature of love but the nature of bad love: frustrated love, painful love, joyless love, love that ends in violence. Each novella offers a variation on the traditional love triangle, with one or more of the participants blinded by passion to the reality of the situation. Only one offers even a hint of hope in the end. (pp. 116-17)

The Triple Echo is Bates's last novella, and it shares with *The Cruise of the Breadwinner* (1946) the distinction of being his most fully realized. . . . In this novella of love and death, war and embattled peace, Bates skillfully blends plot, characterization, atmosphere, and image into an organic whole. Moreover, whereas in many of his works in the later period Bates exhibits an inclination to make emphatically a thematic point (not always to the detriment of the story, certainly), *The Triple Echo* is strikingly evocative, as reverberating in its implications as its title suggests. Indeed, several of Bates's thematic concerns come to a head in his last novella; the devastating effects of war, the forbidding prospect of a life of loneliness, the destructiveness of suffocating passions.

War's impact on all concerned is established in the novella's opening passage. "My husband's a prisoner with the Japs," states Mrs. Charlesworth. "I'll probably never see him again. That's all I know." Mrs. Charlesworth lives on a secluded farm in rural England, apparently as far removed from the war as one could be, but war intrudes in her thoughts of her husband, and its effects are seen in the sorry condition of the farm itself—in a progressive state of decay since her husband's absence.

Worse, with her husband gone and her farm "cut off from the main road,"... Mrs. Charlesworth is almost totally isolated from humanity. Ironically, instead of being peacefully locked away from the war, she reacts to her isolation like an embattled soldier.... We might judge the young woman to be hardy and self-reliant, yet Bates makes it clear that her situation is desperate. Her eyes "had something of the lost glassiness seen in the eyes of birds imprisoned in cases, with only dead grass and ferns for company."

The image of Mrs. Charlesworth being an imprisoned bird initiates a pattern of bird imagery throughout the first section of the story. Birds, particularly nightingales and skylarks, frequently appear in Bates's fiction as symbols for the liberated spirit . . . ; significantly, when young soldier Barton intrudes upon Mrs. Charlesworth's isolation, he is enthralled by a nightingale's song, but she is oblivious. As the first section progresses, she begins to be attracted to the shy young man and realizes how much she has missed human contact. By the end of the section both listen attentively to the nightingale's song.

Barton is on leave from the nearby army camp, and he despises the military with bitter intensity. . . . (pp. 125-26)

Barton returns again and again to do odd jobs for Mrs. Charlesworth, but as his leave nears its end it is obvious that their relationship will take a romantic turn. The scene of what was to be Barton's last visit to the farm represents Bates at his best. A storm approaches on the hot, sultry afternoon, and nature abounds in images of tension, impending conflict. . . .

Mrs. Charlesworth invites Barton to spend the night, and they begin to feel themselves "sort of in a vacuum. You're just two people and you're here and nothing outside matters. There isn't anybody else. There isn't any war." Of course, there is a war, and Mrs. Charlesworth feels that she is skirting too near it when Barton announces that he is never going back to the army, that he is going to live on with her. That Barton has made a decision in accordance with nature as opposed to civilization and its wars is emphasized by the reappearance of the nightingale. (p. 126)

Mrs. Charlesworth finally agrees to let Barton stay, but to prevent discovery she makes him wear a dress, a padded bra, and lipstick. He becomes "Jill." Changes in wearing apparel are significant throughout *The Triple Echo*. It is when Barton changes from his uniform to civilian clothes that Mrs. Charlesworth becomes sexually attracted to him. In the same way, when she dons a skirt and blouse after wearing work clothes, Barton shows an interest in her. But the morning after he first spends the night, he puts on his uniform again, and their relationship becomes strained.

Thus, when Barton wears woman's clothes for weeks on end and allows his hair to grow long, Mrs. Charlesworth begins to think of him as a woman. Her love for Barton has a suffocating intensity, while at the same time she resents having the responsibility of head of the household placed on her shoulders. As a result, she alternately fawns over him and explodes in vituperation. (pp. 126-27)

The Triple Echo is a story of echoes and reverberations: the lost husband—perhaps the most pitiful victim of all—who intrudes only at the beginning and end of the novella; the passions which arise out of the vacuum of Mrs. Charlesworth's isolation only to reverberate with expanding consequences throughout the story; the hints of homosexuality and lesbianism—subtle but disturbing echoes behind the interplay of mannish woman and womanish man; and most important, the war which crashes and roars in the world at large and echoes throughout Mrs. Charlesworth's isolated life. And in the end the war enlists her in its ancient routine of violence, blood, and death.

The Triple Echo is the richest of Bates's novellas—one that the reader can return to with great rewards—and it represents a fitting climax to his fiction career. (pp. 127-28)

Dennis Vannatta, in his H. E. Bates, *Twayne Publishers, 1983, 147 p.*

V. S. PRITCHETT

H. E. Bates was one of the gifted English artists in the [short story] genre, especially in what he wrote in the Twenties and Thirties. He was a poet by nature. His setting was usually the traditional life of the small farms, cottages and holdings, his people the hedgers, ditchers, thatchers and local carriers—a horse-and-cart England in the main, the England of rural hagglings and feelings which had changed very little for centuries and often sounds Chaucerian and ripe in speech. We know how his people talk, eat, work, drink, love and die. Their habits had not yet been touched by the industrialization which changed village life after the last war. The people are not the generalized 'Loamshire' folk of radio and television, and for that reason are real in their past. . . . Bates is interested in people for their own curious sakes. In one of his finest stories, **"The Mill,"** a tragedy is left to tell itself. It is a tragedy set in motion by the meanness of a country trader in scrap. Bates was often lyrical but here he exposed the sourness and silences of rural poverty and the unprotected sight of innocence abused. The story has remained in my mind for forty years. But Bates was a writer of many kinds of stories. He could be lyrical, dour, even luscious and comic too. In the remarkable **"The Woman who had Imagination"** we . . . see a vulgar group of cheery villagers boozing, itching and singing on a charabanc trip to give a rural concert in the grounds of a country house; and in the series of stories called *My Uncle Silas* hear a genial rapscallion in his nineties telling extravagant lies about his sinful life to a boy.

Do not mistake the Uncle Silas stories for old-style bucolic farce. Every detail of Silas's unwashed ugliness and of his domestic habits as the village liar and boozer is truthfully put before us, as if we were sitting in his house with him or had been sent down to the cellar to bring up another dreadful bottle of his home-made wine. And Bates has had the art to make us see the villain through the memory of a small boy who is fascinated by the old man, if also, every now and then, skeptical. Silas has the arts of the rural story-teller who drops into long evasive silences and then takes up the tale to add to its enormities, deedily watching his audience. Cats come out of the bag one at a time: that is art and artfulness. He can suggest even more by an unfinished phrase, by a mastery of innocent metaphor or *double entendre*. (pp. 3-5)

Is Uncle Silas a preposterous exaggeration? Not entirely, for two reasons. Bates knows how to make silences pregnant and then the boy is his passive, wondering audience. The listening of the boy makes the stories almost genuine. The second justification is that Uncle Silas is an expert in the techniques of rural story-telling, that is to say he is the villager talking, when an hour will pass while one person and then the next will join in and add some fantasy out of village memory to the tale. He is rumour itself. It will succeed if told in a flat, casually dry passage; until it reaches an open-ended silence for the next speaker to go one better, out of village memory. Uncle Silas is in fact the scandalizing village memory at work. One is listening to something in the genre of **"The Miller's Tale;"** and, in any case, every villager has samples of every kind of man and woman in the world at hand. Well, not every kind, but some very insinuating examples. Like most good short stories from Chekhov onwards, Bates had the art that enabled him to write many kinds of story. The poet could be the comedian, saved from slapstick by his resources of style and observation. And he was always at his best in the country landscape of his childhood where the hours seemed fuller and longer. (p. 6)

V. S. Pritchett, in an introduction to My Uncle Silas *by H. E. Bates, Oxford University Press, Oxford, 1984, pp. 3-6.*

DEAN R. BALDWIN

From the early 1930's until his death in 1974, H. E. Bates was considered one of the finest short story writers in England. A prolific author, he published well over two hundred stories in seventeen volumes, in addition to novels, novellas, country essays, and an influential study of the short story [*The Modern Short Story*]. An output this large necessarily means that his works are of uneven quality, but as a short story writer he maintains an astonishingly high level of achievement in a wide variety of moods and subjects. On the one extreme are stories of harsh naturalism like **"The Mill"** and **"The Ox,"** while at the other are tales of unabashed romanticism like **"The Cowslip Field"** and **"The Watercress Girl."** Most of his stories are in a tragic or sombre mood, but in two collections of Uncle Silas stories and in occasional flights of high spirits like **"A Couple of Fools"** and **"A Party for the Girls"** he shows a rare and genuine comic gift. Considering both the quantity and quality of Bates's output, it is surprising that he is not better known or more highly regarded among academic critics or historians of the genre. Very little has been written about him, though there are signs that his achievement is finally gaining recognition. This trend deserves to continue, as Bates is unquestionably a master story-teller whose excellences have thus far been largely overlooked.

On the surface, stories by H. E. Bates seem extremely conventional and straightforward. Readers will instantly recognize the influence of Chekhov in his technique of building stories out of trifling events and suggestion rather than through dramatic plot; in the rural stories of the 1930's particularly, the influence of A. E. Coppard is equally obvious. But to categorize Bates as a purveyor of rural idylls or Hardyesque studies in pain and endurance is to deny the wealth and variety of his achievement and to miss the individual stamp of his talent. Perhaps it is the surface simplicity which is deceptive. Bates seldom deals in complex characters or subtle psychology; his people are drawn from the lower social and economic strata where feeling and impulse dominate, thought has little subtlety, and ideas are few. The young, the inarticulate, and the innocent are the usual subjects of his stories. His plots are similarly straightforward and direct: a fall from innocence or the eternal love triangle are at the center of a great number of his stories which are spun out with few complications and a minimum of elaboration. Complexities of emotion rather than of plot or character are his trademark, and he almost never ventures into political commentary, social criticism, or abstract ideas. The interactions of people with one another and their immediate, natural environment are the focus of his interest. Yet for all their apparent simplicity, Bates's stories have an intricate structure and a subtle texture that makes them curiously powerful and resonant. By and large their substance derives from his handling of atmosphere; the intricate interplay of mood and scene in relation to character and event is the basis of Bates's considerable art as a short story writer.

One aspect of Bates's romanticism manifests itself in stories of luminous natural beauty, often set on warm spring or summer days. **"The Mower"** is typical of these, depicting a hot June day on which a family of three is cutting a field of hay by hand. The physical atmosphere of the story is permeated by images of heat and light. . . . Throughout the story the colors yellow, white, and green appear and reappear, as do reminders of the sun's relentless heat. Reflecting these motifs are the woman and a hired hand named Ponto, a mower of prodigious skill and strength emanating danger and sexuality. Their illicit passion is joined to the natural scene by the woman's white blouse and green skirt, green being an ancient symbol of fertility.

In addition to this link between the heat of the day and the passion of Ponto and Anna, there is an air of expectancy and tension that permeates the story. At the beginning, this is created by uncertainty over whether Ponto will actually come to help with the mowing. Once he arrives, the question shifts to whether they will be able to complete the mowing that day. These two feelings, expectancy and passion, are joined in the relations between Anna and Ponto, for in spite of the physical attraction that draws them together, they are prevented from consummating their love by the prying eyes of her husband, her boy, and even the sun. At one point they snatch a few moments alone, but that is all. Moreover, Ponto's swaggering confidence in his own sex appeal contrasts sharply with the woman's submissive devotion, adding another layer of tension to the atmosphere. All three are maintained throughout the story, but gradually a fourth emerges, the suggestion of death. The act of cutting hay itself recalls the Biblical proverb, "As for man, his days are as grass; as a flower of the field, so he flourisheth," while the swaggering, carefree Ponto in his skill and power suggests the grim reaper. In the end, none of these tensions is resolved so that the story culminates in a remarkable effect—that on the one hand nothing significant has happened on this hot, lazy summer day, yet everything is quivering with suggestion and possibilities. Thus the story's effect lies not in its characters or incidents so much as in the aura created by the interaction and tension of its various elements. (pp. 215-17)

Among Bates's best stories are a number which recreate scenes of his boyhood, a time just after the turn of the century when the ancient world of horsepower and manual labor was being replaced by automobile and machinery. In tales like **"The White Pony," "Alexander," "Great Uncle Crow,"** and **"The Cowslip Field,"** the atmosphere is usually as golden and sunny as that of **"The Mower."** In evoking this Eden, Bates calls upon his considerable powers of description and his intimate knowledge of the countryside. **"The Watercress Girl"** joins this sense of innocent beauty to an air of mystery in a tale uniquely evocative of childhood and overlain with a melancholy nostalgia of rare piquancy. (p. 218)

In the sharpest possible contrast to the sunny romanticism of these stories is **"The Mill,"** one of Bates's undisputed masterpieces of naturalism. From first to last it maintains a relentlessly grim atmosphere which Bates himself once described as "emotionless negativity." At the center of the story is Alice Hartop, an adolescent girl so browbeaten by her father that she has literally no personality or will of her own. To supplement the family income, she is sent to care for Mrs. Holland, suffering from dropsy and living in a disused mill. Bates's description of Alice's arrival typifies the story's mood of static nullity. . . . (p. 219)

Equally severe is the atmosphere of plodding futility that surrounds every human activity in **"The Ox."** The mood is set at the beginning in the description of the Thurlow's house. . . . Here the loneliness and exposed situation of the house suggest the condition of the Thurlows themselves, particularly Mrs. Thurlow who exists in an endless round of cleaning and washing for other people, daily pushing her bicycle laden with laundry and other burdens from house to house. "Her relationship to it was that of a beast to a cart." Her husband is equally alienated, having suffered a head wound on the Marne which left him with a silver plate in his head and periodically excruciating headaches. The Thurlows are not even a family but a collection of isolated individuals with no affection for one another. The only bond is Mrs. Thurlow's mindless dedication to the future welfare of her sons as she slaves at her cleaning and laundry, hoarding her money under a mattress. This is the environment in which the rest of the story takes place: Thurlow's murder of a man who doubts the existence of the silver plate, his theft of his wife's money, his capture, trial, and conviction. In the process, Mrs. Thurlow loses even her sons, for they prefer living with their prosperous uncle. In the end, she is left with her bicycle, her work, and the dull Midlands mud, which "seemed to suck at her great boots and hold her down."

Between these extremes of romanticism and naturalism are a great number of stories, usually involving love triangles, which combine elements from both approaches. Atmosphere in these stories is less obvious but no less important in determining the overall effect. (p. 221)

It would be wrong to suggest that Bates's talent as a short story writer lay solely in his ability to create and manipulate atmosphere, for he possessed complete technical mastery, including a flexible and lucid style, a rare gift for natural description, and the ability to draw convincing characters with great economy. However, his use of atmosphere distinguishes many of his stories and marks them as among the best produced by any British writer in this century. (p. 222)

Dean R. Baldwin, "Atmosphere in the Stories of H. E. Bates," in Studies in Short Fiction, *Vol. 21, No. 3, Summer, 1984, pp. 215-22.*

Wendell (Erdman) Berry

1934-

American poet, novelist, short story writer, essayist, and translator.

In his poetry and prose, Berry documents the rural lifestyle of his native Kentucky. He often draws upon his experiences as a farmer to evidence the dangers of disrupting the natural life cycle and to lament the passing of provincial American traditions. The thematic unity evident throughout Berry's writings has prompted many critics to praise his control of several diverse genres. Like Henry David Thoreau, with whom he has been compared, Berry is also admired for his pragmatic and even-tempered approach to environmental and ecological issues.

Berry has resided in Kentucky for most of his life. After briefly holding teaching positions at New York University and the University of Kentucky, he followed the five previous generations of his family and began farming. Berry rejects modern methods and farm machinery in favor of more traditional and conservational means. In his verse, he uses conventional techniques to demonstrate how the ordering and healing qualities of nature should be allowed to function in human life. In such volumes as *The Broken Ground* (1964), *Openings* (1968), *Farming: A Handbook* (1970), and *Collected Poems, 1957-1982* (1985), Berry often adopts an elegiac tone to convey his agrarian values. The affinities to nature that Berry displays in his poetry induced John Lang to comment: "Berry envisions the marriage of man and nature, God and world, the human and the divine. His poems often begin as acts of attention to the physical world and end as invocations to the spirit at work in that world."

Berry is equally distinguished as a writer of prose. His first novel, *Nathan Coulter* (1960), traces the title character's transition from youth to maturity as he begins to accept responsibility for the care of his family's farm. Berry's subsequent fiction is set in the fictional Kentucky town of Port William, which serves as a microcosm of conflicting opinions on the ethics of land usage. *A Place on Earth* (1967; revised, 1983) portrays agricultural life in Port William during one year at the end of World War II. *The Memory of Old Jack* (1974) depicts nearly a century of the protagonist's experiences to illustrate humanity's growing alienation from nature. *The Wild Birds: Six Stories of the Port William Membership* (1986) evidences Berry's thematically integrated shorter fiction. Berry's nonfiction essays, collected in *The Long-Legged House* (1969), *A Continuous Harmony: Essays Cultural and Agricultural* (1972), *The Unsettling of America: Culture and Agriculture* (1977), and *Standing by Words* (1983), reiterate the prevailing themes of his fiction and poetry.

(See also *CLC*, Vols. 4, 6, 8, 27; *Contemporary Authors*, Vols. 73-76; and *Dictionary of Literary Biography*, Vols. 5, 6.)

© *Thomas Victor 1987*

JOHN LANG

From his earliest volumes of poetry (***The Broken Ground*** and ***Findings***) through his most recent collection (***A Part***), Berry has consistently sought to convey his double vision of nature's physical presence and the divinity manifest in nature. The early poem entitled **"Observance,"** for example, depicts a religious rite directed toward what the poet calls "the god of the river," a god whose human worshippers, we are told, "sing renewal beyond irreparable / divisions." In his two earliest volumes, Berry emphatically dissociates himself from institutional Christianity and all other-worldly religious traditions. "Christ is stillborn once a year / in the cavities of churches," he remarks in ***Findings***. And he parodies the concept of Eternal Life by reducing it to "the interest / compounded on an investment / . . . payable / to the insured upon his demise." With the church's musty "heirloom rituals," Berry contrasts the green of summer trees and the love of mother and child. "I've worn out all allegiances but these," he declares. "I choose and sing these shapes and breathings of the ground."

Neither of these first two volumes uses the term "mystery"; yet both clearly establish the poet's commitment to the physical world. In many of these poems, however, this commitment is called into question by the fact of death. As the example of Whitman suggests, any poet who seeks to identify with nature must confront the problem of change and the body's dissolution. If, as Berry writes in a poem entitled **"Canticle,"** "What death means is not this— / the spirit, triumphant in the body's fall, / praising its absence," how *does* one define the individual's—and nature's—relationship to death? The question is one to which Berry returns almost obsessively in volume after volume. One of his most extended responses to it occurs in **"The Handing Down,"** a sequence of fourteen poems that constitute nearly a third of *Findings*. In this poem, Berry describes an old man's growing awareness of his approaching death. Section 7 of the poem, entitled **"The heaviness of his wisdom,"** reveals the old man's awareness that "the worst possibilities are real." "The terrible justifies / his dread of it," Berry admits. Yet the old man "trusts the changes of the sun and air: / dung and carrion made dirt, / richness that forgets what it was." Loving the earth he will become and nourish, the old man descends peacefully into his death. His attitude reflects that of his author, for whom resurrection is a fundamental principle of nature, not simply a religious doctrine. *Findings* concludes with yet another elegiac poem, one in which an old man's death is described in the following terms: "He's hidden among all that is, / and cannot be lost."

As these lines suggest, the vision of life that informs Berry's poetry is cyclic rather than linear. The individual and nature are joined in a process involving birth, growth, decay, and rebirth. Loving the earth, the individual can be reconciled with death. (pp. 260-61)

Starting with his third collection of poems (*Openings*), Berry begins to invoke the concept of mystery explicitly and regularly. The first poem in that volume, a poem entitled **"The Thought of Something Else,"** again illustrates his concern for a literature attuned to other life than men have made. . . . Elsewhere in this volume Berry anticipates "a resurrection of the wild," "the second coming / of the trees." To apply such theological terms to natural objects and processes is one of Berry's characteristic strategies. Through this device he calls attention to nature's sacramental qualities and at the same time associates divine providence with nature's beneficence. Grace, like mystery, is a key term in Berry's poetry. But he rarely thinks of grace as an abstraction. Instead he observes its operations within and through nature. We thus read not of God's grace but of "the river's grace" and "the grace of the world." Many of Berry's poems, in fact, seem to move toward a pantheistic identification of God and the world. . . . Rather than thinking of the divine as disembodied spirit, Berry conceives of it in one poem as "the unseeable animal." But this mysterious divinity assumes flesh in Berry's poems; it becomes substantial. At the same time, however, nature grows transparent to the poet's eye. In and beneath physical forms the spirit reveals itself. Of the sycamore, for example . . . :

I love it as I have seldom loved anything.
I recognize in it a principle, an indwelling
the same as itself, and greater, that I would be ruled by.

It is the phrase, "and greater," that saves Berry's poetry from pantheism. Yet Berry undoubtedly places far more emphasis on God's immanence than the Judaeo-Christian tradition typically has. Envisioning his poetry as a necessary corrective to the excerpting of the Creator from the creation, Berry has focused most explicitly on nature, on what he calls "close mystery." As the title of his most recent collection of poems suggests, however, Berry realizes that he has chosen to celebrate *A Part*. Yet the part implies the whole. There is a double movement in Berry's work, a dialectical development. The

sacred re-enters the world and is incarnate there, but the world also reveals a spirit that transcends it—which is "the same as itself, and greater." Berry's poetry reflects this double movement. . . . "The blessed and blessing trees" of another poem in *A Part* also express this double vision. Nature both blesses and is blessed. It receives God's grace and in turn mediates that grace to mankind. Honoring "the grace that keeps this world," Berry discovers a power that he addresses in traditional Christian terms as "the Holy Spirit," a spirit that dwells "far off and here, whole and broken."

Thus, although Berry's primary aim is to celebrate "close mystery," a mystery immanent in nature, the terms in which he does so continually introduce what Flannery O'Connor would have called "the added dimension," the realm of transcendent mystery. Berry's nature poetry springs from a profound religious impulse. But the object of that impulse extends beyond nature itself, as Berry's repeated use of the term "creation" indicates. Far more than a synonym for "nature," "creation" implies the existence of a creator. That nature surpasses human making is one of the poet's central themes. But that nature surpasses *nature's* making is also implicit in his writing. Berry's work seems to illustrate what theologians would call the doctrine of continuous creation—a doctrine intended to avert the very disjunction of God and world against which Berry protests. Moreover, in his recent writing, Berry has given increasing emphasis to the term "creation" by capitalizing it whenever it refers to nature. This practice suggests not only his vision of nature's holiness but also his experience of the indwelling presence of the Creator. Such capitalization stresses the connection between God and the world. It seeks to secure respect for nature by underscoring nature's divine origin and by reminding us of our responsibilities as stewards of the creation.

To signal both the presence of mystery and the appropriate human response to its presence, Berry employs the related metaphors of song and silence. The two terms appear throughout his poetry, defining and structuring his vision. Music and song become significant symbols for Berry because they denote an underlying harmony within the creation. . . . Berry envisions the marriage of man and nature, God and world, the human and the divine. His poems often begin as acts of attention to the physical world and end as invocations to the spirit at work in that world. . . . He joyfully attends to the song in the world, and to that song he adds his own psalm of praise. Moreover, in and beyond his own and nature's songs, he detects the music of the spheres: Job's morning stars singing together, today as at creation's dawn.

Linked, somewhat paradoxically, to this metaphor of song is that of silence. For Berry, this silence attests not to the failure of communication—as silence often does for Kafka or Beckett—but rather to the presence of a reality that transcends language. The silence witnesses to the ineffable. It awakens a sense of what Rudolf Otto in *The Idea of the Holy* calls the numinous. In this classic study Otto notes, moreover, that Western art has traditionally relied on two means to express the consciousness of religious mystery: silence and darkness. Berry uses both. Yet although that mystery escapes man's comprehension, it permits communion. What Berry calls "the sweet of speech" must periodically be abandoned if we are to hear both the song and the silence to which nature gives voice. (pp. 261-64)

Darkness, like silence, often represents the numinous in Berry's work. The darkness preserves mystery. It places limits on human reason. To the spirit of being at work in the world, the poet proclaims:

> That we do not know you
> is your perfection
> and our hope. The darkness
> keeps us near you.

To accept this darkness, to submit to mystery, is to acknowledge our creaturehood. . . .

For Berry, as should be evident, to venture into the realms of silence and darkness and mystery is not to find oneself wandering aimlessly in a meaningless universe. It is to go by singing and to be attended by song. Mystery, though represented by darkness, paradoxically illuminates the human condition by clarifying its boundaries. (p. 265)

[Berry] writes poems that articulate what he calls "a reverence for the order and grace that I see, and that I trust beyond my power to see." . . . Berry's work reaches not toward a supreme fiction but toward a supreme being. Though Berry, as a farmer, recognizes that mankind invents *some* species of order, he presupposes that such human order remains faithful to reality only when it "accommodates itself both to other order and to mystery."

Berry's poetry invites us into a natural wilderness that, though dark, is "graceful." . . . Berry withholds final assent to Christianity—as if he suspects it of harboring an ineradicable antipathy toward the earth. Nonetheless, in its affirmation of "the sense of eternal mystery surrounding life on earth," his poetry remains deeply religious. It testifies to the ongoing incarnation of a spirit by whose "divisions and returns," as Berry proclaims, "the world lives." (pp. 267-68)

> *John Lang, " 'Close Mystery': Wendell Berry's Poetry of Incarnation," in* Renascence, *Vol. XXXV, No. 4, Summer, 1983, pp. 258-68.*

NOEL PERRIN

The Wheel is Mr. Berry's eighth volume of poetry. I find it no worse and perhaps a little better than the earlier seven. There is no line that passes the old test of making one's skin prickle as one reads it, and there are many that seem indistinguishable from prose. (p. 8)

[But there] is also one poem, the longest in the book, that has real distinction. Mr. Berry is at his best when he resurrects the past and makes it live into the present. This he does in **"Elegy."** In a dream, the dead of his own past gather to meet him on what was once their land and now is his. "They knew me, / but looked in wonder at the lines on my face, / the white hairs sprinkled on my head," he writes.

The reader then encounters these dead, and each encounter is moving. Not sentimental, not even sad. Moving, as Dante is moving, though in a different (and, of course, greater) way, in the *Inferno.* There is no outstanding line or passage, nothing that will pluck out as a quote; and yet the whole poem does make one's skin prickle. It is a true addition to our literature. This cannot be said of many of Mr. Berry's poems. I think him a minor poet in an age of minor and even minimal poets. (It is both funny and repellent to read the reviews poets write of each others' books and to note the special heightened language they have evolved to dignify one another's modest achievements.)

Standing by Words is Mr. Berry's third collection of literary essays. I find it as good, as learned, as full of deep common sense, as unpretentious as the other two. There is no special, heightened Appreciatese here.

Most of the essays concern poetry. Mr. Berry takes poetry even more seriously, perhaps, than most poets do; he also sees its function quite differently. (pp. 8, 16)

In all six essays, Mr. Berry is eloquent and clear—and very much out of harmony with the prevailing thought of our time. He is also, I think, not quite adequate to the task he has set himself. The minority that shares his views will like *Standing by Words* very much, but most in the fashionable majority will remain unpersuaded. They will, in fact, sneer at his insistence on such concepts as decorum and hierarchy. It is hard to give a positive sense to these words in 1983. The book reminds me of a frigate standing bravely into an enemy fleet, the gun crews trained to perfection but the metal too light. A ship of the line is needed, but, unfortunately, that was beyond the shipwright's capacity.

Happily, warships are not the only kind of craft. The third of Mr. Berry's new books is the novel *A Place on Earth,* and here (spared by the novelistic form from the need to argue) I think he has succeeded very well indeed.

The book has a curious history. It was originally published in 1967, and at that time it was 550 pages long. It was (and still is) the interwoven stories of about a dozen people in the small Kentucky town of Port William during the last year of World War II. Mat Feltner is a farmer living on the edge of town; Wheeler Catlett is his lawyer son-in-law; Jayber Crow is the town's barber; and so on. All are fully realized characters. The Muse of Inspiration and the Muse of Realization were working in perfect tandem from the first.

But in the 1967 version, Mr. Berry indulged his love of finely observed detail rather too freely, and he allowed himself too much comment on the action. It was a poet's novel, and it tended to drag. Now he has cut it by about a third, rewritten just a very little—and the result is magical. After what is still a slightly slow start (the reader needs about 50 pages to live his way into Port William), one reads entranced to the end. The book has the remorselessness of fate. . . .

The book also has the tenderness one would like to imagine God has as He watches a human community act and interact, be brave and cowardly, convert experience into life into meaning. It has two or three of the great comic scenes in our recent literature. It has an overwhelming sense of place. It never uses words like "decorum," though one sees the concept in action in such things as Old Jack Beechum's relation with his daughter, who married a banker and lives in Louisville. It has so much, in fact, that the despairing reviewer is inclined to fall back on the heaped adjectives of praise, only to realize that they have been worn so smooth by other reviewers (and, alas, himself) as to be useless.

So I shall resort to a noun. Reviewing the original version for this paper in 1967, Henry Mitchell called it a good if over-ornamented novel—no masterpiece but perhaps the "harbinger of a masterpiece to come." He was right in a way he could not have foreseen. It was the harbinger of itself. The revised version of *A Place on Earth* is a masterpiece—the best thing Wendell Berry has done, a book not to be missed. (p. 16)

> *Noel Perrin, "More Than One Muse," in* The New York Times Book Review, *December 18, 1983, pp. 8, 16.*

WYATT PRUNTY

On one level, Wendell Berry's *The Wheel* is a series of elegies. On another level, however, it is a series of reclamations. Overgrown fields are cleared, and new springs bring new plantings. But there are always the harvests too. In **"Elegy,"** with "crops . . . in the barn," Berry greets a dead friend of whom he says, "The best teachers teach more / than they know." What his friend has taught him is the order created by the rhythms of the family farm, the seasonal work one performs year after year. In **"The River Bridged and Forgot,"** Berry says that work "teaches the mind / resemblance to the earth / in seasonal fashioning." The rhythms of the land are an analogue by which we understand ourselves. The external world is a model by which we organize the mind's internal world. For Wendell Berry this is cause for celebration, "departures and returns / of song." Activity and understanding are joined. (p. 958)

Wendell Berry's particular displacement, the loss over time of those he loves, leads him to a myth built out of the activity of farming, something central to the American imagination. His garden has its serpent, the machine. And its fall, described in **"Elegy,"** which requires living "by the sweat of [one's] face," eating one's bread "assured that cost was paid." (p. 959)

The Wheel is a collection of poems which opt for song rather than individual assertion, the conversational voice. Berry would prefer to speak with the collective voice of a chorus. At the same time he is a subtle, skilled writer who takes advantage of all the noises our language provides him. He has a fondness for the iambic tetrameter line, but only after he has hit that line with a hammer. The order Berry makes of nature through the practice of farming he also makes of human experience through the practice of poetry. For him a farm is a form. So is a poem. In Wendell Berry's understanding, history curves into myth. The forms he finds for that myth elevate utterance. (p. 960)

> *Wyatt Prunty, "Myth, History, and Myth Again,"*
> *in* The Southern Review *(Louisiana State University), Vol. 20, No. 4, Autumn, 1984, pp. 958-68.*

DAVE SMITH

Wendell Berry is a maverick poet whose work reflects ties to the Black Mountain aesthetic circle as well as to Southern Fugitives. The common denominator is a hunger for ultimate answers to the problems of a world believed in collapse. In **"Below,"** Berry says, "What I stand for / is what I stand on." He means he has faith in the sustaining earth, a farmer's faith, but the laconic and bulldog ring of his conviction is typical of his *Collected Poems.* American poetry has been and is essentially pastoral, with the visionaries often extolling soil, tillers of soil, and virtues of the plain life. E. A. Robinson, Masters, Frost, Tate, Ransom, Davidson, and Gary Snyder—these are the ghosts in Berry's poetry. They would agree with Berry's idea the modern world is wrong:

> I dream an inescapable dream
> in which I take away from the country
> the bridges and roads, the fences, the strung wires,
> ourselves, all we have built and dug and hollowed out,
> our flocks and herds, our droves of machines.

Behind this view stand the tenets of Romanticism, and Berry echoes Thoreau when he speaks of "thing-ridden men" as victims of a self-blinded, materialistic world. Yet in Berry we do not often see or feel the problems; we hear about them as causes of answers which through his twenty-five years of poetry remain the same, an optimism somewhere between Jefferson and Emerson. Berry is a nature worshipper who believes the ruined world will be returned. . . . (p. 40)

Asserting rather than dramatizing his vision of ultimate Unity is an evangelical characteristic, and it turns out there is an emergent Christianity in his later books which causes Berry to say of "the community of knowing" that "There is not only no better possibility, there is no / other, except for chaos and darkness." If we may regard Berry's seamless answer of yeomen husbandry as a metaphor of the right world, his spiritual counsel has depth, vigor, and sometimes poetry. But when he moves upon us in a faith that is Mormon-optimistic, we might watch for the evidence of what he calls "the enrichment of pain"—which is only Puritan elbow grease in service of conversion. The weakest of Berry's poems possess a slippery Emersonianism that sounds like Zen koans or the graffiti of the '60s. It isn't simply that his answers are too simplistic or that he seems curiously ignorant of much beyond himself—his neighbors, boredom, failures, daily intrusions, the urban world— but that he refuses to plant his high sayings in dramatic soil. One wishes he would remember himself saying, "Better than any argument is to rise at dawn / and pick dew-wet red berries in a cup."

Nevertheless, Wendell Berry's *Collected Poems* is a welcome testament, rich with the feel and shape of a life that has character. Berry is gifted with descriptive powers and his farm is real in his mind and his words. His meditations remind me of George Herbert, his love poems of Roethke, his moral relentlessness of Adrienne Rich. But his talent is surely the elegy, the portrait of love celebrated, a man-speech that can howl and hum as Berry likes. (p. 41)

> *Dave Smith, in a review of "Collected Poems: 1957-1982," in* Poetry, *Vol. CXLVII, No. 1, October, 1985, pp. 40-2.*

DAVID RAY

Wendell Berry's [*Collected Poems: 1957-1982*] is a validation of his decision nearly 20 years ago to give up the literary life in New York and seek a deeper bond with his ancestral home, a hillside farm in Henry County, Kentucky, on the Kentucky River. His straightforward search for a life connected to the soil, for marriage as sacrament and family life, affirms a style that is resonant with the authentic. The lyricism is not forced, but clearly grows out of a deep bond with the earth and its generosity, with all of nature. He mocks little except man's arrogance and destructiveness, and he can be said to have returned American poetry to a Wordsworthian clarity of purpose. Nor is Wordsworth's piety out of place in Mr. Berry's world; the rustic and the rural are honored and celebrated with seldom if ever a touch of doubt for the course undertaken, a deeply committed life.

Mr. Berry's poetry is, then, a manifestation of character, and the articulation of that character's honest vision. A man is somehow blocked, Schopenhauer wrote, until he "has in some degree acquired real self-knowledge." There can be no doubt Mr. Berry has labored for that knowledge, which he shares through his poems. One can feel the effort to say rightly what must be said. . . . The pursuit of virtue, Schopenhauer wrote, "can only be followed with seriousness and success when all claims that are foreign to it are given up, when everything else is renounced . . . a man must know what he wills, and know what he can do; only then will he show character, and only then can he accomplish something right.'' Mr. Berry's poems speak of this search, and of the joys of doing something right by farming and loving well.

But his celebration of the farm, and doing things right, is hardly a retreat from the world. As strongly as any contemporary, he has spoken up against war and madness. . . .

Just as eloquently, Mr. Berry has fought for ecology and sound conservation of resources, and he has a way of voicing his indignation without being preachy; yet the voice is strong and unambiguous. The ethical life is a necessity for peace and happiness in his view. At times, a wizened humor breaks through, particularly when he is speaking with his ''Mad Farmer'' persona: ''Don't own so much clutter that you will be relieved to see your / house catch fire.''

Mr. Berry is doctrinal in recommending organic farming, the use of horses instead of tractors, and even in being quite happy with the audience his poems find when they are published in Organic Gardening magazine. There are times when we might think he is returning us to the simplicities of John Clare or the crustiness of Robert Frost. . . . But, as with every major poet, passages in which style threatens to become a voice of its own suddenly give way, like the sound of chopping in a murmurous forest, to lines of power and memorable resonance. Many of Mr. Berry's short poems are as fine as any written in our time.

His *Collected Poems: 1957-1982* is important because it will inspire; there is nothing naïve about the straightforward course recommended by a poet who is willing to be ''an unacknowledged legislator.'' Treasured for its nature and love poems, reread for its insights and passionate advocacies, the book will probably be valued most of all for its **''Elegy''** on the farmer Owen Flood. (p. 28)

David Ray, ''Heroic, Mock-Heroic,'' in The New York Times Book Review, *November 24, 1985, pp. 28-9.*

ROBERT McDOWELL

Over the last twenty-five years, Wendell Berry has developed a career that is a blueprint for anyone who would understand what it means to be a modern Man of Letters. Formerly a teacher, currently a farmer and occasional lecturer, he has written novels in the tradition of Sherwood Anderson, essays on language, land use, and conservation, and eight volumes of poetry. [*Collected Poems: 1957-1982*] gathers together nearly two hundred poems and brings into focus the full weight and conviction of Berry's poetic achievement. His strength as a poet is elegy, and an elegiac tone is remarkably consistent throughout his career. . . . In the authoritative third person of **''The Man Born to Farming,''** the poet clearly defines the gift that is the farmer's way of life: ''. . . to him the soil is a divine drug. / He enters into death / yearly, and comes back rejoicing.''

Ultimately, behind this solitary celebration lies loneliness, and this best defines Berry's sense of community. Neighbors, observed from an emotional distance, are admired for steady labor, for fitting into the natural cycle, which governs farming as it governs nothing else. In this world, community is that which drives one deeper into what one does every day. This is fundamentally different from the sense of community usually created in an urban setting. There the impulse is to blunt ex-

ternal forces and cultivate those relationships that divert attention from the daily grind.

But most of us live in cities. What, then, does this poet have to say *to us?* For one thing, he implicitly confronts our wish to be evasive. His poems make us examine anew the thousand poses we slip in and out of each day, dodging to remain untouched, unscathed. And if we are lucky, we feel self-conscious. Then we begin to explore the possibility of conduct based on those actions—working in harmony with the environment, loving without greed or malice, accepting what comes—that bring us together rather than keep us apart. For another, Berry reminds us that Community begins with the awareness that individuality is meaningful only when it fits harmoniously into the life-death cycle that is the rural *and* urban experience. The key to this knowledge is useful pursuit, labor done well that contributes to the lives of neighbors and gives back to the environment what it uses.

This philosophy is *not* new, it is as old as the oldest story. And it is just as timely—and necessary—as it was when first uttered around a fire. (pp. 681-82)

Robert McDowell, ''Poetry: Changes & Channels,'' in The Hudson Review, *Vol. XXXVIII, No. 4, Winter, 1986, pp. 681-94.*

GREGORY L. MORRIS

Wendell Berry is most generally known as a writer of poems and essays, as a celebrant—and sometime eulogist—of a specifically rural way of life. Berry, however, has also translated that particular agrarian vision and voice into fiction, busy over the last thirty years at chronicling the ways and works and workings of the town of Port William, Kentucky, a town drawn largely upon Berry's own hometown of Port Royal, where he continues to live and write and farm. The Port William cycle began with the novel *Nathan Coulter;* expanded itself in the novel *A Place on Earth;* and evolved into a trilogy with the publication in 1974 of *The Memory of Old Jack* (the only novel yet to appear in an unrevised edition—perhaps an indication of Berry's growing self-assurance as a writer of fiction). Berry also supplemented his prose portraits of his Kentucky River farmtown with a play (though nearly a long dramatic poem, in its rhythms and intonations) entitled *The Bridge of Water,* published as part of his book of poems, *Farming: A Hand Book.*

Most recently, though, Berry has taken up the short story in pursuing his biography of town and people. The six stories in *The Wild Birds,* which span the years from 1930 to 1967, takes up the life of the Port William Membership—that collection of men and women (though Berry focuses upon the men) who work and farm and sustain the memory and spirit of their intimate community. This sense of community, of shared moral and social value, of shared sense of place and heritage, is central to Berry's work. When a citizen of that community (a community which assumes the world as ''ruled by instinctive decency'') abandons or renounces that community, he or she forfeits an almost secret emotional connection with the profounder life of the town. . . . Berry places his emphasis upon the *rightness* of relationships—relationships that are elemental, inherent, inviolable. Work—right work, good labor—becomes a ''dance,'' an intuitively choreographed movement of physical and spiritual harmonies.

Death, too, is part of that synchronous movement of man and time, and one of the things we witness in *The Wild Birds* is the natural and right decline *and* replenishment of the Membership, new and younger men moving in to replace, to assume the ritual-dance of labor of those lost to time and death. (pp. 102-03)

Even in those stories that deal less centrally with Berry's ethic of work and land and love of place—stories like **"Thicker Than Liquor,"** where familial love reclaims the most destitute of relations, and **"Where Did They Go?"** which describes an initiatory revelation of age and sex and elemental need—even in stories such as these, Berry's concerns remain consistent. People work to "come through," to endure, to make a passage onto some kind of personal *and* communal peace. Berry's stories are constructed of humor, of elegy, of prose that carries within it the cadences of the hymn. The narrative voice most successful in Berry's novels speaks—or more appropriately, *sings*—here in these stories; it is the voice of the elegist, praising and mourning a way of life and the people who have traced that way in their private and very significant histories. (p. 104)

Gregory L. Morris, in a review of "The Wild Birds: Six Stories of the Port William Membership," in Prairie Schooner, *Vol. 60, No. 4, Winter, 1986, pp. 102-04.*

CAROL POLSGROVE

The places and people of *The Wild Birds* are familiar from [Berry's] earlier fiction. Here, in six stories scattered across a thirty-seven-year period, we meet them in either younger or older incarnations or in relations that change our perceptions of them.

For those who have read *A Place on Earth,* the most satisfying story in the new collection may be **"The Boundary,"** in which Mat Feltner, a man still in his prime in the novel, has grown old. Taking his last walk upon his land, he gives Berry the opportunity to do what he does best: trace the movement of a mind across place and time. (p. 626)

To those who know country life, there may be too much tender elegy in Berry's rendering. Mat Feltner's life has been touched by sadness, sorrow, but not by meanness, in the sense of cruelty or of days devoid of meaning. Berry does not intend to carve out a slice of rural life. He is dreaming life as it can be, not necessarily as it is. His dreams take shape out of the rural life he's known, but they are still dreams. His fiction is almost utopian.

"I'm not just interested in people as they are," he says. "I'm interested in the possibilities that are suggested by people as they are. There are some stories in *The Wild Birds* that reach toward that kind of realization—not just what community has in fact meant in my experience but what is suggested by my experience of community."

One of those stories, **"It Wasn't Me,"** the most overtly philosophical in the collection, is, indeed, a virtual essay by the end. When Old Jack Beechum dies, he leaves his farm to his city-dwelling daughter. But, in an unconventional move, he leaves half the purchase price to the tenants of the farm, a young couple who have cared for the land. To his lawyer and friend Wheeler Catlett he leaves the task of making the transaction work.

Here the chill shadow of a city ethic falls over the story. To Jack's daughter and her banker husband, the farm is property, and they mean to sell it, not to the tenants at the price Jack set, but at auction to the highest bidder. In answer to Wheeler's plea that Old Jack not only wanted "to put the good people and the good farm together" but that he also loved his tenants, the daughter replies, "My father's loves are not mine."

And so the story connects the obligations of blood, friendship and love to the obligations people have to the land. In Berry's mind, a world that treats land as property is also a world in which a daughter would refuse to carry out her dying father's wish. Set against that broken world is the "Port William Membership"—a community joined not just by friendship, blood and sharing of a common place, but by knowledge. "The land expects something from us," Wheeler says. "The line of succession, the true line, is the membership of people who know it does."

In **"The Wild Birds,"** another story on the theme of unconventional inheritance, Wheeler's friend Burley Coulter—a careless, kind and sometimes comic character in earlier fiction—comes to him with an irregular request: Burley wants to leave his land to the illegitimate son he has loved but never acknowledged. The surprise of seeing that even in a small and close community a man may live a secret life, have a secret self, is sharper in this story than in any others. But one of the pleasures of reading Berry's fiction lies in watching characters go in and out of focus—appearing and reappearing, now on center stage, now on the periphery.

We also get a sense of the past still spreading throughout the present in these stories. That sense has been heightened for Berry because he lives in the place he knew as a child and writes about as an adult. "I've always had to think about the past not as recalled but as a cause and influence in the present in which I'm living. You need to see what things have led to before you understand them."

Thus he explains why **"The Wild Birds,"** the last of the stories, takes place almost twenty years ago, at about the time he moved back to Kentucky. Even then, the decay of rural life had started to become visible in the empty stores and empty streets of a once busy country town. Finishing the story and the volume I felt the incompleteness of the larger story Berry has been telling throughout his fiction. In *The Wild Birds* he has only just begun to write about the change he's seen in rural life and chronicled so well in his nonfiction—not just economic change, but change in spirit, as farmers are pushed to the very margins of our culture. Unless he moves forward in time and confronts the difficult rural present, Berry's fiction may too easily be read as nostalgic fantasy—not the moral challenge he means it to be. (pp. 626-27)

Carol Polsgrove, "Unsettling the Land," in The Nation, *New York, Vol. 242, No. 17, May 3, 1986, pp. 626-27.*

BRIAN SWANN

Berry is well-known in environmental circles as an untiring and eloquent advocate of "sustainable" farming methods. But he is not as well-known as he should be to the rest of us for what he is: one of our most versatile and prolific writers. Why isn't he better known? Perhaps in a country that admires excess and consumption, rapidly changing excitement, and the quick fix, Berry's virtues of discipline, balance, and responsible restraint might seem old-fashioned and "irrelevant." As might his use of certain uncurrent words. In his essays on poetry in *Standing by Words,* as in his essays on the land in *Recollected Essays,* Berry has loaded words such as "sin," "pride," "ignorance," "love," "obedience" with a new/old meaning, and uses these words naturally and unself-consciously.

He takes words as seriously as he takes farming, and for him poets are the bearers of our culture. The true poet has "larger responsibilities." He works from and embodies a concept of order (by which he means "the possibility of responsible action"), and an "ecological intelligence" of temperance and obligation superior to himself. In closely argued, original, and passionate essays in *Standing by Words,* Berry castigates the egotism of the Romantics, particularly Wordsworth and Shelley, while asserting that our richest and most responsible tradition is to be found in such writers as Milton, Dante, Pope. He has little time for the modern "specialization of poetry," and the "religion of art."

It is no accident that Berry admires Milton and Dante, since he too is possessed of an eschatological imagination. The great truths of Christianity are reworked into an environmental ethic in the largest sense, an ordering of the world that can best be described as hierarchic, a "just hierarchy," not the inflexible or totalitarian kind: a kind of updated Great Chain of Being. There is no need to make up such laws, Berry says. We just need to rediscover them. Because there is an absolute truth: the truth of the nature of our existence on earth. An ecological truth. Berry's aim in everything he writes, from story to essay to poem, is to "restore the broken connections" through love, right work, and community. (pp. 345-46)

Berry's themes do not vary from book to book, or from genre to genre. There is an interweaving and a kind of spiritual manuring. Nothing is wasted. Everything gets recycled and renewed. If there is one main theme Berry starts from it is that "we have been for some time in a state of general cultural disorder and that this disorder has now become critical." This disintegration is seen in all aspects of society, from language (the theme of *Standing by Words*) to the basic biological or cultural unit, marriage or domestic order (two of Berry's most impressive essays are **"Poetry and Marriage"** in *Standing by Words,* and **"The Body and the Earth,"** with its moving interpretation of the *Odyssey,* in *Recollected Essays*).

Whether he is writing about canoeing on the Kentucky River or hiking the Red River Gorge; buying or repairing a home; writing stories about Wheeler Catlett; telling stories of his childhood; writing about **"Discipline and Honor"**; writing about form in poetry and culture; making poems distinguished for their scope and detail—or on any other subjects, in whatever form, Wendell Berry is extraordinary. In one of his essays he says that "to live in the place that is one's subject is to pass through the surface." Berry passes through the surface of everything he cares about. Which is just about everything. And he is accessible. The style of his writing is always elegant and balanced, always passionate. It doesn't call attention to itself, and the subject shines through. Always we sense "an eagerness that is felt only by those who are doing what they want passionately to do," the eagerness of a man whose aim is "a decent, open, generous relation between a man's life and the world." His poem **"The Silence"** asks the question: "What must a man do to be at home in the world?" Everything Berry has written attempts to answer that question. (p. 346)

Brian Swann, "The Restoration of Vision," in Commonweal, *Vol. CXIII, No. 11, June 6, 1986, pp. 345-46.*

Louise Bogan

1897-1970

American poet, critic, editor, and short story writer.

A major American lyric poet whose darkly romantic verse is characterized by her use of traditional structures, concise language, and vivid description, Bogan is known particularly for her honest and austere rendering of emotion. Douglas L. Peterson noted that she wrote "mainly of highly personal and painful experience—of personal losses suffered through death and the betrayal of intimate and deeply valued personal relationships, of time passing and of her acute awareness of the fragility of all things caught in time." Bogan's work is often compared with the short lyrics of such seventeenth-century poets as Thomas Campion, John Dryden, and Ben Jonson, and she shares with these writers an emphasis on musicality and craftsmanship as well as a subdued sense of grief and despair. Also a distinguished critic who served as a poetry editor for the *New Yorker* from 1931 to 1970, Bogan is known for her exacting standards and her penetrating analyses of many of the major poets of the twentieth century.

Bogan's personal life was marked by turbulence and instability. Her mother was prone to unpredictable and often violent behavior and would periodically abandon her family. Bogan entered her first marriage in part to escape her unstable home life, but the relationship ended shortly after the birth of a daughter in 1917; a 1925 marriage also failed. During these traumatic years, Bogan experienced severe depressions, for which she underwent psychoanalysis and was briefly and voluntarily institutionalized. Although these experiences are considered central to the development of her personal and artistic vision, some critics contend that Bogan's best poems are objectively distanced from the events and instead focus upon the resulting psychological and emotional states. Extolling the significance of Bogan's verse at a memorial tribute in 1970, W. H. Auden stated: "What, aside from their technical excellence, is most impressive about her poems is the unflinching courage with which she faced her problems, her determination never to surrender to self-pity, but to wrest beauty and joy out of dark places."

Bogan's initial poems were published in *Poetry* magazine in 1922 and were subsequently included in her first collection, *Body of This Death* (1923). Concerned with such themes as betrayal, the limitations of time and beauty, and the relationship between knowledge and passion, these poems have been viewed as a young woman's examination of the trials of heart and mind. Bogan was praised for her technical mastery and for the intensity of her verse. *Dark Summer* (1929) gathers the most significant poems from Bogan's first book as well as several new poems. Progressing toward a more purely lyrical mode, the new pieces expand upon Bogan's concerns with love, betrayal, passion, and wisdom. The poems in *The Sleeping Fury* (1937) are generally considered to display greater depth and power than much of Bogan's earlier work. This book contains some of Bogan's most highly regarded and frequently anthologized poems, including "Italian Morning," "Roman Fountain," and "Kept."

Poems and New Poems (1941) comprises works gathered from Bogan's three previous books and a selection of sixteen new

pieces in which she occasionally experiments with meter and rhyme. Although the new poems are generally considered less successful than the poems in *The Sleeping Fury*, Babette Deutsch described *Poems and New Poems* as a volume "distinguished by the testimony it bears to the integrity of so accomplished a poet." Bogan's most successful writings from her previous volumes appear with several new works in *Collected Poems, 1923-1953* (1954). In her later poems, critics noted Bogan's attempts to confront difficult personal themes relating to inner conflict. The last volume of poetry Bogan published during her lifetime, *The Blue Estuaries: Poems, 1923-1968* (1968), adds twelve pieces to *Collected Poems*.

Bogan's accomplishments as a poet are enhanced by the respect she received and the influence she possessed as an editor and critic. *Achievement in American Poetry, 1900-1950* (1951) contains Bogan's brief but incisive sketches of many seminal figures in twentieth-century American verse. Bogan's other publications include two volumes of critical pieces, *Selected Criticism: Prose, Poetry* (1955) and *A Poet's Alphabet: Reflections on the Literary Art and Vocation* (1971), and a survey collection of poetry for young people, *The Golden Journey: Poems for Young People* (1965), which she edited with William Jay Smith. Details of Bogan's personal and professional relationships are revealed in *What the Woman Lived: Selected Letters of Louise Bogan* (1973), which collects her correspondence. *Journey around My Room: The Autobiography of Louise Bogan, A Mosaic* (1980) is a pastiche of journal passages, letters, poems, stories, criticism, and conversation.

(See also *CLC*, Vols. 4, 39; *Contemporary Authors*, Vols. 73-76, Vols. 25-28, rev. ed. [obituary]; and *Dictionary of Literary Biography*, Vol. 45.)

MARK VAN DOREN

It is impossible to say what these twenty-seven poems [included in *Body of This Death*] are, and it would be difficult to say what they are like. The temptation is to speak of them only in images, for they are not susceptible to paraphrase; they take effect directly upon the imagination. One thing about them, however, seems plainly, prosaically sure. The thirty pages which they cover are packed as tightly with pure poetry as any thirty pages have been for a generation. The poet would be rare at any time who could achieve so much concentration and so unquestionably sustain it. Practically every one of these bare, stricken lines is suggestive of riches; the words dig deep, bringing up odors of earth and life that will live a long time in the memory. There is no rhetoric—hardly a phrase could be reduced by a word—but there is the sheer eloquence of passion; there is no tunefulness, but there is music "from music's root," "a fine noise of riven things."

Under a diversity of forms Miss Bogan has expressed herself with an almost awful singleness. Again, however, it is impossible to say what it is she has said; again one must resort to an image—or to her images. One can be certain that experience of some ultimate sort is behind this writing, that something has been gone through with entirely and intensely, leaving the desolation of a field swept once for all by fire. But the desolation is not vacancy or lassitude. The charred grass is brilliantly black, and the scarred ground is fascinating in its deformity. There still is life, hidden and bitterly urgent. . . .

Miss Bogan has spoken always with intensity and intelligent skill; she has not always spoken clearly. Now and then her poetry comes too immediately from a personal source to mean very much to others. Nevertheless, this first volume places her near the lead of those poets today—Anna Wickham, Charlotte Mew, Genevieve Taggard, and others—who are passionately exploring the endless, narrow paths of woman's (and man's) experience. It is absolutely individual, yet it reaches toward the race. It may be a classic.

> *Mark Van Doren, "Louise Bogan," in* The Nation, *New York, Vol. CXVII, No. 3043, October 31, 1923, p. 494.*

ROBERT L. WOLF

Louise Bogan's *Body of This Death* has more than anything else the quality of direct, simple, almost cruel statement. In a kind of contained twilight frenzy, without excuse or hesitation, the poet lays her hand deliberately upon the central key of a mood, and follows her own instruction. . . .

The material of the book is, in symbol or simple fact, the love experience of a modern woman, in Miss Bogan's case tinged with a tragedy that is not less impressive for being nameless. (p. 335)

Except for the early "**Macaw**" with its beautiful eleventh line, and its less authentic other thirteen, there is hardly any waste motion in the book, and hardly any ornamentation. Miss Bogan's fault lies in the other direction. Her words too often lockstep upon themselves, like prisoners of some terrible intensity. She needs, if anything, to deliver herself more loosely and luxuriously to her art. Even "**Chanson un peu Naive,**" perhaps the most beautiful poem in the book, has an occasional gasp of constriction that mars its hauntingly clear music; and "**The Frightened Man**" runs down-hill into an inconclusive ending. . . . (p. 336)

In its extraordinary economy, the texture of Miss Bogan's verse is perhaps nearer to Mrs. Wylie than to any of her other contemporaries. But Miss Bogan is never obscure, like Mrs. Wylie, from fantasy or reticence. Where Miss Bogan is difficult—and she often is—it is because she has too much to say; it is because each word is pregnant with such extreme intensity that she has not woven language that will bear the burden.

Of those of her fellow-poets to whom she has been so far chiefly compared, she is by no means so breath-taking as Edna Millay, but perhaps even more austere and ruthless; she lacks the warm richness of Genevieve Taggard, but makes up with an individual and lean athletic quality; and if she can not pack words as deftly as Mrs. Wylie, her speech is much more vital. Or to change the metaphor, in the orchestra of the younger women poets, as some one else has said, Louise Bogan plays the 'cello, while Edna Millay is probably first violin, Genevieve Taggard improvises on the organ, and Elinor Wylie is active at the xylophone and triangles. Miss Bogan is the newest and least flawless. She is molding a technique for herself where each word has the importance of a deliberate and separately thrown grenade; but she is not yet quite at full ease with her method—she is not able to play with it in the spacious carelessness that denotes real freedom. (p. 337)

> *Robert L. Wolf, "Impassioned Austerity," in* Poetry, *Vol. XXIII, No. 6, March, 1924, pp. 335-38.*

YVOR WINTERS

[*Dark Summer*], Miss Bogan's second volume, includes the best poems from her first, so that a reading of it offers a complete view of her talent to the present time. The chief stylistic influence discernible is that of E. A. Robinson, and that only here and there. Two of the early poems reprinted in this book—"**Portrait**" and "**The Romantic**"—close on a typically Robinsonian epigram; and there are a good many similar passages in her first book, *Body of This Death*. She has either escaped or absorbed this influence in her later work, progressing toward a more purely lyrical mode that culminates in "**The Mark,**" "**Come break with time,**" and "**Simple Autumnal**"; poems that demand—and will bear—comparison with the best songs of the sixteenth and seventeenth centuries, whether one selects examples from Campion, Jonson, or Dryden. . . .

She has certain technical limitations. She apparently has little or no understanding of free verse, and her more regular unrhymed verse (one hesitates to call it blank verse), though extremely interesting from a purely metrical standpoint, divulges an inability to treat the long line and the long poem as such—she treats them rather as series of stylistic and perceptive incidents that would probably have gone into short rhymed lines had they been able to gather about themselves a little more symbolic value. They almost drop from the limb that bears them into separate identity, but never quite; neither, most of the time, are they quite organically necessary to that limb. And the movement of the long unit is hopelessly impeded by—one is tempted to say, made up of—minor, decorative digressions. This, from any standpoint, is an incorrect technique for a long poem, whether narrative or philosophical. . . .

The intricacy of some of the best of Miss Bogan's poems is, I imagine, an intricacy of feeling, and hence of style, rather than of idea. The basic ideas of her work do not appear to be particularly complex. The writer of our period finds himself tempted, on one side, by the roads to rhythmic salvation offered by the various sects of tree-climbing mystics, and on another by the faint moribund murmurs of transatlantic, Middle-Western, and middle-aged Whitmanism: these, and related manifestations of our democratic era and of its Pragmatic Providence, our educational system, have to be avoided. Miss Bogan, one suspects, has avoided them as a cat avoids water rather than as a philosopher avoids nonsense—and the result is a kind of instinctive distrust of certain ranges of experience that either might or might not involve some kind of spiritual looseness. She plays safe and allows no implications to enter a poem that are not defined in its subject-matter: she thus achieves the irreproachable mastery of her best poems, but she also causes each poem to be a sort of insulated unit, even pushing the quality occasionally, as in **"Old Countryside,"** to a certain dryness. Thomas Hardy, writing a twelve-line lyric on the passage of time, often seems to involve the tragedy and the wisdom of the whole of human experience; there is a kind of emotional current passing into the form from the formless recollections of the man; the gesture, the cadence, the pauses, indicate a richness of wisdom and experience not defined in the meaning of the words. In Miss Bogan's poems, as in those of Jonson or Landor, this is the case, if at all, to a very limited degree. The poem is a sharply defined segment of experience, raised to something very near to major power by the sheer brilliance of the craftsmanship. But if the poem deals with the message of time, it deals with that and nothing more, in its effect on an isolated entity as such. (p. 247)

But Miss Bogan's subject-matter, or rather attitude, if it seems limited in the way I have indicated, is as central, as fundamental, as any attitude so limited could be. It would take only a turn, a flicker, to transform her into a major poet; it is conceivable that the flicker may be taking place as I write, that it may even have occurred in her book, *à mon insu*. The least that the most defamatory of critics can say in her praise is that she suffers no diminution by comparison with the best of the English lyricists, that she is certainly as good in every respect as a great many of the best, and that she is beyond any doubt one of the principal ornaments of contemporary American poetry. (pp. 247-48)

Yvor Winters, "The Poetry of Louise Bogan," in The New Republic, *Vol. LX, No. 776, October 16, 1929, pp. 247-48.*

POETRY

Richness of intellectual and emotional experience is present in every detail of Miss Bogan's poetry. *Dark Summer*, like *Body of This Death*, is the product of strict selection and rigid discipline in the practice of her art. Where each page yields its memorable phrase and where every stanza is slowly turned to the final perfection of statement and suggestion, any suspicion of meagre inspiration may be dismissed immediately. With a creative patience rivaled by that of few other living poets, she

has brought her verse to a state of ripe completeness; it does not seek its reward through stylistic variety or the diversity of its ideas and pictures, but rather in the fine unity of purpose and craftsmanship it achieves. (pp. 158-59)

Since her artistry insists always upon a fine intensity of statement and upon as complete a reduction of poetic content as possible, the two longer poems in this book—the analytical narrative called **"The Flume"** and the dialogue **"Summer Wish"**—do not present her best work. To draw out to the length of full analysis an experience or problem requires a greater control of externals, of the real events which surround and condition the activities of the mind. Miss Bogan lacks Lola Ridge's lively understanding of the reality of action. Drama—except of the allegorical or suggestive kind she employed in her earlier poems, **"A Tale"** and **"Fifteenth Farewell"**—is outside her range. Insight produced by a quick sympathy and interest is present, but not in sufficient quantity to stir into life the people with whom she is concerned. Her finest poems grow as ideas which seek their embodiment in nearby symbols. The discriminating reader would not for a moment think of doing without **"The Flume"** and **"Summer Wish"**; their exquisite imagery and the skill whereby they snare elusive meanings make them far too valuable for that. But their presence in this book, surrounded by the sharp austerity of the lyrics and sonnets, is enough to reveal limitations of which Miss Bogan herself is aware. She usually restricts herself to a kind of lyric poetry in which her mastery remains sure and undisputed.

Signs of this mastery are abundant in *Dark Summer*. The delicate use of imagery is probably first among them. Instead of employing irrelevant pictorial devices or garnishing a poem with elaborate ornaments and decorations, she carves the image out of the concept with scrupulous care. The poem finds its substance in the mind and its shape grows around the symbol which the mind selects from experience. (pp. 159-60)

In **"The Romantic,"** one of several fine poems she has reprinted from her first book, she outlines with memorable skill the tragedy of a life frustrated by discipline and authority, and the exquisite **"Chanson un peu naïve"** gives expression to the same problem in terms of a haunting melancholy. In **"The Crossed Apple"** a rich humorous balladry is suggested, while **"Old Countryside"** and **"Simple Autumnal"** reveal a subtle interest in homely realism. (pp. 160-61)

"Fiend's Weather" and **"I Saw Eternity,"** by their clear eloquent phrases, and **"Tears in Sleep"** and **"Sonnet,"** by their poignancy, go further in showing that this collection, which at first glance seems marked by severe austerity and formality, has a real range of feeling and expression. Miss Bogan may be trusted to explore that range further, but never to produce a weak or careless line. By her fine craftsmanship and sure judgment, she has made herself a master of her art, and given us, in her second book as in her first, a rare and beautiful group of poems. (pp. 161-62)

M. D. Z., "The Flower of the Mind," in Poetry, *Vol. XXXV, No. 3, December, 1929, pp. 158-62.*

EDA LOU WALTON

We have had no book from Louise Bogan since her small and exquisite first volume *Body of This Death*. Those poems were as delicate as bone, but they reflected like a crystal an intense and bitter mind intent upon the analysis of its betraying heart, punishing itself in a kind of proud confessional. A spiritual pride and a heart wiser than its desires were there written down in flawless perfection of language. No other poet in America has a more inevitable sense of the exact word to be employed than has Miss Bogan. In *Dark Summer* the same immaculate spirit and restless heart continue their discourse in language which shows no flagging of the poet's critical employment of her tool. The tool is the same and the creator the same; only the season has changed. For in *Body of This Death* a young woman examined the warfare of mind and heart and found brief respite in passionate interludes, whereas in *Dark Summer* a mature woman examining the same warfare finds it deathless.

Here is an immortality unique with Miss Bogan: no harvest fills the bins while the cycle of years spins by so rapidly that images of spring and summer must be forever in the mind's eye. Memory will not give us pause even in autumn. The heart must bleed and the mind be unaccepting even while the flesh chills. Therefore these unquiet lives. In the long narrative poem **"The Flume"** a woman protected by love cannot be convinced of love in any way save by betrayal. In the dialogue **"Summer Wish"** the first voice must protest against the violence of memory which makes Spring a repetition, while the second voice argues for an acceptance of promised beauty. Inescapable beauty must destroy the shell-like spirit and yet the voice be proud to speak:

> Within the mind the live blood shouts aloud;
> Under the breast the willing blood is burned,
> Shut with the fire passed and the fire returned.
> But speak, you proud!

The intensity of *Dark Summer* is the intensity of fear always alive in the mind though the heart be at home in love:

> The willing mouth, kissed never to its own beauty
> Because it strained for terror through a kiss,
> Never quite shaped over the lover's name
> Because the name might go.
>
>   (pp. 682, 684)

At the time when so much of poetry is merely energetic echoing or forced attempt at individuality, we have among us those few, and among them Louise Bogan, who are not only excellent technicians but true poets in that they have an extremely sensitive approach to their physical world and a definite poetic outlook concerning it. (p. 684)

> *Eda Lou Walton, "Verse Delicate and Mature," in* The Nation, *New York, Vol. CXXIX, No. 3361, December 4, 1929, pp. 682, 684.*

EDA LOU WALTON

[Bogan's *The Sleeping Fury*] is unmistakably the poet's most mature and distinguished volume. Miss Bogan's admirable precision of language and expert craftsmanship remain unchanged, but the conflict between emotional intensity and an intellectual analysis almost equally violent—so characteristic of all her work—is in these poems resolved.

Betrayal has long been Miss Bogan's theme. At first it was the betrayal inevitable in love. Now this poet sees betrayal as common to all, as a betrayal by life itself. It is life itself which so changes body and spirit that they become their opposite. This is the ultimate, bitter truth. And whatever of personal bitterness there was in Miss Bogan's earlier lyrics becomes in these later poems either a deep impersonal hatred of human fate or an austere acceptance of that fate. . . .

Distinguished is the word one always thinks of in connection with Louise Bogan's poetry. Whatever form she tries, her art is sure, economical, and self-definitive. There is never in her poems a wasted adjective or phrase but always perfect clarity and a consistent mood precisely set down. She can write the completely artless lyric or the very subtle poem worked out through complex imagery. Sensuousness is here but it is always reined in by the strict mind. Poems like **"Italian Morning"** express perfectly the atmosphere of the old carved rooms and the sense of timelessness in contrast with personal time and loss. The sheer passion to create in words is behind much of this poetry and is the theme of one of the loveliest lyrics in the book **"Roman Fountain."** This passion, the poet believes, persists despite defeat in life. . . . And so, in the end, one is impressed by a kind of wisdom in these poems, the wisdom of profound intuition and of a rapier analysis turned inward rather than outward.

> *Eda Lou Walton, "Henceforth from the Mind," in* The Nation, *New York, Vol. 144, No. 17, April 24, 1937, p. 488.*

FORD MADOX FORD

There is one word singularly useful that will one day no doubt be worn out. But that day I hope is not yet. It is the word "authentic." It expresses the feeling that one has at seeing something intimately sympathetic and satisfactory. (p. 158)

I had precisely the same sense and wanted to use that same word when I opened Miss Bogan's book [*The Sleeping Fury*] and read the three or four first words. They ran:

> Henceforth, from the mind,
> For your whole joy . . .

Nothing more.

I am not any kind of a critic of verse poetry. I don't understand the claims that verse poets make to be (compared with us prosateurs) beings set apart and mystically revered. Indeed if one could explain that, one could define what has never been defined by either poet or pedestrian: one could define what poetry is.

But one can't. No one ever has. No one ever will be able to. You might almost think that the real poet, whether he write in prose or verse, taking up his pen, causes with the scratching on the paper such a vibration that that same vibration continues through the stages of being typed, set up in print, printed in magazine, and then in a book—that that same vibration continues right through the series of processes till it communicates itself at last to the reader and makes him say as I said when I read those words of Miss Bogan's: "This is authentic." I have read Miss Bogan for a number of years now, and always with a feeling that I can't exactly define. More than anything, it was, as it were, a sort of polite something more than interest. Perhaps it was really expectation. But the moment I read those words I felt perfectly sure that what would follow would be something stable, restrained, never harrowing, never what the French call *chargé*—those being attributes of what one most avoids reading. And that was what followed—a series of words, of cadences, thought and disciplined expression that brought to the mental eye and ear, in a kind of television, the image of Miss Bogan writing at the other end of all those processes all the words that go to make up this book.

There are bitter words. But they are not harassingly bitter. . . . There are parallel series of antithetical thoughts, but the antithesis is never exaggerated. . . . There are passages that are just beautiful words rendering objects of beauty. . . . And there are passages of thought as static and as tranquil as a solitary candle-shaped-flame of the black yew tree that you see against Italian heavens. . . . There is, in fact, everything that goes to the making of one of those more pensive seventeenth century, usually ecclesiastical English poets who are the real glory of our twofold lyre. Miss Bogan may—and probably will—stand somewhere in a quiet landscape that contains George Herbert, and Donne and Vaughan, and why not even Herrick? This is not to be taken as appraisement. It is neither the time nor the place to say that Miss Bogan ranks with Marvell. But it is a statement of gratification—and a statement that from now on, when we think of poetry, we must think of Miss Bogan as occupying a definite niche in the great stony façade of the temple to our Muse. She may well shine in her place and be content. (pp. 159-61)

Ford Madox Ford, "The Flame in Stone," in Poetry, *Vol. L, No. 2, May, 1937, pp. 158-61.*

MORTON DAUWEN ZABEL

Louise Bogan's earlier books, *Body of This Death* in 1923 and *Dark Summer* in 1929, won their fame for sufficient reasons. Their rigor of form and emotion was an immediate reproach to the lyric slovenliness around them. They showed a poetry that said nothing that did not come from the deepest sources of personal and poetic sincerity, and that allowed no word or phrase to remain untested by an extreme pressure of creative necessity. Her new book [*The Sleeping Fury*] is as spare and severely compiled as its predecessors, and in a new decade it points a similar distinction and moral. Whether it will be greeted by the same high respect is beside the point. Fashions in poetry may change but not the accent and austerity of poetic truth, a phrase that has its meaning refreshed by the finest entries in this volume—[**"The Sleeping Fury"**], **"Italian Morning," "To My Brother," "'Roman Fountain," "Kept," "Man Alone,"** the first and final songs. Here there is nothing to disguise, prop or confuse the thing said: no front of "beliefs," no leaning on borrowed arguments or literary and political allusion, and none of that fretting preciosity which has become a recent lyric fashion. The word, phrase and stanza have their simplest construction (Miss Bogan is still at her best away from free verse or experimental forms); the imagery is simple and final; the symbol stamps the mind with an indelible impression and shows the poignance of meanings extracted from a depth of mind and consciousness that alone ensures a compelling form of truth. It is because they show so firmly what this depth can yield that these poems bring the finest vitality of the lyric tradition to bear on the confusions that threaten the poets who, by satire or prophecy, indignation or reform, have reacted against that tradition and cast it into contempt. Poets like Yeats and Rilke met this crisis of sincerity in their careers, and comparison loses its odium when Miss Bogan's finest lyrics are set in the company of theirs. She has kept to the hardest line of integrity a poet can follow and has sacrificed the easier victories of many of her contemporaries. Her work, instinctive with self-criticism and emotional severity, speaks with one voice only; her rewards and those of her readers have a common source in the discipline to which the clarity of her music and her unsophistic craftsmanship are a testimony. It should be a model for poets in any decade or of any ambition. (pp. 391-92)

Morton Dauwen Zabel, "Lyric Authority," in The New Republic, *Vol. LXXXX, No. 1170, May 5, 1937, pp. 391-92.*

MALCOLM COWLEY

Critics writing about Louise Bogan have usually discussed her technique, and there is good reason for this emphasis. What seemed to be the subject matter of her first two volumes was not at all striking—love that is all-powerful but fleeting, chastity that is a lie, tears shed alone at night; in general the themes that were being treated by dozens of women poets during the 1920's. But her real subject, implicit in her manner of writing, was always poetry itself. She was saying by her example that the duty of the poet is to crowd all possible meaning into a few short lines; to find the exact word, the one right image, the rhythm just awkward enough to vary the pattern without breaking it entirely. She was saying that such poetry is terrifyingly difficult to write, but worth all the years and pains one devotes to it. And she was saying that art is fearful as well as beautiful; it is the Gorgon's head that can forever fix an evanescent landscape:

> The water will always fall, and will not fall,
> And the tipped bell make no sound.
> The grass will always be growing for hay
> Deep on the ground.

With such a theory of art, it is difficult or impossible to write a great deal. *Poems and New Poems* is not a big volume, but it contains everything that Miss Bogan thinks is worth saving from her work of the last twenty years. There are seventy-two poems, mostly short lyrics, taken from her three earlier books; and sixteen others written in various manners since *The Sleeping Fury* appeared in 1937. Other poets publish more in a single season. Even quantitatively, however, Miss Bogan has done something that has been achieved by very few of her contemporaries: she has added a dozen or more to our small stock of memorable lyrics. She has added nothing whatever to our inexhaustible store of trash.

Nevertheless, I hope she now decides to make some change in her theory and practice of the poet's art. Together they have been confining her to a somewhat narrow range of expression. Her new poems—meditative, witty and sometimes really wise—suggest that she has more to say than can be crowded into any group of lyrics; and that perhaps she should give herself more space and less time. Most American poets write too much and too easily; Miss Bogan ought to write more, and more quickly, and even more carelessly. (p. 625)

Malcolm Cowley, "Three Poets," in The New Republic, *Vol. 105, No. 19, November 10, 1941, pp. 625-26.*

BABETTE DEUTSCH

In the four years that have elapsed since her last volume was published, Miss Bogan, working with her accustomed scrupulousness, has produced comparatively little. As the title of the present collection [*Poems and New Poems*] suggests, most of the lyrics it contains will prove familiar to her public. . . . But so profound and intimate is the emotion that beats in most of these lines, so deliberate the art controlling it, that one ends by greeting the old lyrics and welcoming the new with almost unqualified delight.

There are two strains in Miss Bogan's poetry that contend with and support one another as in counterpoint. One is the influence of the Metaphysicals—indeed, **"I Saw Eternity"** is the work of a twentieth-century Traherne; the other is the expression of a modern woman, self-probing, passionate and ironic. One has heard these voices before, notably in the performance of Elinor Wylie, of which not a few of Miss Bogan's lyrics are reminiscent. One has heard them, more thinly and more purely, in the exquisite verse of Léonie Adams. One hears them sound again from these pages, with renewed resonance. If Miss Bogan, like the English poets of the seventeenth century, compresses subtle speculations in a little space, it is not surprising that, like them, she should sometimes be obscure. And if, with a feminine pathos which the male poet not seldom exhibits, she confides matters of purely private import to her verse, it is natural that she should not always find the objective correlative that will give the poem a more general validity. For the most part, however, Miss Bogan sustains her performance at a level to which the fewest of her contemporaries can rise, matching an uncommonly responsive and penetrating sensibility with an equally rare technical felicity. . . .

It is indicative of Miss Bogan's sensitiveness to the weight and color of her syllables that so many of her poems should be about music or written to be sung. Thus, one finds **"Juan's Song,"** **"Chanson un Peu Naïve,"** **"Girl's Song,"** **"Song for a Slight Voice,"** **"Spirit's Song,"** **"Song for a Lyre,"** **"To Be Sung on the Water,"** not to mention simply **"Song"** and **"Second Song."** It is noteworthy that in no case does Miss Bogan offer the verse equivalent of songs without words: however clear and fluent her melody, there is always a given base of thought or feeling, distinguishable from the song yet related to it.

So careful a craftsman would, of course, be scornful of poetic fashions, and the character of Miss Bogan's work has not altered noticeably in nearly twenty years. It is therefore odd to find her including a piece originally published with the subtitle "Imitated From Auden" and honoring neither the model nor the copyist. She is wittier when she imitates nobody but herself. The more memorable poems from her previous book, *The Sleeping Fury,* the title-poem, **"Single Sonnet,"** **"Baroque Comment,"** among others, differ from her earlier work only in showing greater depth and power. They are not exceeded, nor, indeed, equaled by any of her more recent poems. The present collection is as a whole distinguished by the testimony it bears to the integrity of so accomplished a poet.

Babette Deutsch, "Collected Lyrics New and Older," in New York Herald Tribune Books, *December 28, 1941, p. 8.*

STANLEY J. KUNITZ

On the jacket of [*Poems and New Poems*, an] omnibus volume of Louise Bogan's work containing in all some ninety poems, Allen Tate is quoted in praise of Miss Bogan as "the most accomplished woman poet of our time." The praise, to my mind, is justified; but I suspect that to be perennially classified and reviewed as a "woman poet" must prove discomfiting, at the least, to a poet of Miss Bogan's superlative gifts and power. It is true that she is a woman and a poet and that her motivations and themes, like those of her sister poets, relate essentially to her special experiences in a man-world—and why not?—but the virtue of her work is not a quality of gender. (p. 40)

Miss Bogan's work is occasionally pretty, with a deliberately wrought elegance of lyric style; it is never, or almost never, girlishly arch or matronly sticky. She is exempted from sentimentality by her respect for her art; by her discipline in self-seeing; by that implacable capacity for self-disdain without which the romantic poet, in an age of non-romantic values, no longer can endure.

Miss Bogan understands form: she writes a poem from beginning to end, disdaining the use of filler. Her ear is good: she is sensitive to verbal quantity and quality. When she succeeds—and she succeeds remarkably often—the surface of her poem is only the other side of its substance, without holes to fall through. . . . The distillation of her talent is in a deceptively simple quatrain, so just in style, so mature and witty in sensibility, that a long life can safely be predicted for it:

> Slipping in blood, by his own hand, through pride,
> Hamlet, Othello, Coriolanus fall.
> Upon his bed, however, Shakespeare died,
> Having endured them all.

Aside from this quatrain and two other pieces, **"The Dream"** and **"The Daemon,"** her new poems seem to me less consummately organized than before. (I am not discussing the silly section of *New Yorker*ish verses, which might well have been omitted.) In the new poems there are indications that Miss Bogan is experimenting in an effort to release her poetic energies more fully and to extend her range. Her long-held ideal of geometric perfection, her creative illusion of "cool nights, when laurel builds up, without haste, / its precise flower, like a pentagon," has undoubtedly, in some respects, fettered her talent, so that one feels at times that she has reworked her materials to excess, at the expense of associative spontaneity. I should like to see further manifestations of the mood of savage irony that produced **"Hypocrite Swift"**; and I find in **"Kept,"** with its cold abnegating pity—"the playthings of the young / get broken in the play, / get broken, as they should"—a kind of writing that no one else can do half as well.

But I am persuaded that the true world of Miss Bogan's imagination, of which she has up to now given us only fragmentary impressions, is "the sunk land of dust and flame," where an unknown terror is king, presiding over the fable of a life, in the deep night swarming with images of reproach and desire. Out of that underworld she has emerged with her three greatest poems, spaced years between, of which the latest is **"The Dream."** . . . In the body of Miss Bogan's work **"The Dream"** stands with **"Medusa"** and **"The Sleeping Fury"** in violence of statement, in depth of evocation. They give off the taste of pomegranates: Persephone might have written them. (pp. 41-3)

Stanley J. Kunitz, "Pentagons and Pomegranates," in Poetry, *Vol. LX, No. 1, April, 1942, pp. 40-3.*

LOUIS UNTERMEYER

Miss Bogan's title [*Achievement in American Poetry, 1900-1950*] gets her keen and remarkably compact book off to a bad or, at least, an off-balance start, for it soon becomes apparent that Miss Bogan measures "achievement" chiefly in terms of "the breakthrough of a modern esthetic" and hence regards "social content" with little more than bare tolerance. Stressing tone, texture, and techniques, faintly deriding "moralistic values" as leftovers from the Victorian sideboard, she is half-reluctantly but inevitably drawn to what was once praised as "art for art's sake" with its consequent accent on preciosity. Yet, in spite of her debatable approach, there can be no question about the rightness of her direction. Constant experiments may lead to strange twists and thorny turns, but it is a better guide to progress than a broad path flanked by immovable traditions. And it is no discredit to Miss Bogan that she is more at ease helping her readers through difficult terrain than she is on smooth and well-marked highways.

Miss Bogan is particularly persuasive when she charts the uncertain and often circuitous route traversed by American poetry during the last half-century. Widely traveled in the arts, she collates the influence of various mediums and significant forms: symbolist prose and verse, post-impressionist painting, functional architecture, atonal music, intransigent essays, and the exotically "primitive" ballet. Maintaining for the most part a severe impartiality, she recognizes the important part played by the vigorous "renaissance" (1912-1917), the forgotten "little magazines," and the voices of the tortured Twenties which "broke up more social and moral pressures than any comparable period of ten years in the past." Hers is the first measured tribute to the contribution of the once-overpraised and now belittled Imagists—an appraisal which is balanced, just, and historically correct. . . . (p. 21)

Eminently precise . . . are her appreciations of Yeats, Pound, and (particularly) Eliot. The intricate relations between Eliot and Pound and the contrary course of their careers are traced with unusual understanding; the accomplishments of such experimental talents as those of Hart Crane, William Carlos Williams, Wallace Stevens, and Marianne Moore are assessed with sympathy and analyzed with critical perception. Her brief but pithy judgments of the three Midwestern poets, Masters, Lindsay, and Sandburg, are neatly discriminating, although they make her estimate of Frost seem unnecessarily niggling. Even her praise of Frost sounds grudging when it concludes:

> He began to play with the role of self-conscious homespun philosopher. He began to give reasons for his innate, countryman's conservatism, and not only reasons, but arguments which were half-apologies. . . . He has come to hold so tightly to his "views" that they at last have nearly wiped out his vision.

Such a lopsided summary is accentuated by the appended thirty-one page anthology or sampler which is obviously intended to illustrate America's poetic achievement during the last fifty years. It is a queer collection. It includes most of the imperative "names," but the proportions are surprising and the very choices of poems seem arbitrary and capricious. There is, to begin with, a commonplace sonnet by Louise Imogen Guiney, composed of the very conventions which Miss Bogan elsewhere derides; but there is nothing by such far more representative women poets as Amy Lowell, Genevieve Taggard, Elizabeth Madox Roberts, and Muriel Rukeyser. There is not a single poem by Conrad Aiken, mentioned in the body of the book only in connection with his introduction to the *Selected Poems* of Emily Dickinson published in England, nothing by Archibald MacLeish, John Gould Fletcher, E. E. Cummings, the Benéts, Horace Gregory, Mark Van Doren, Robert Penn Warren, James Agee, John Berryman, Merrill Moore, and Randall Jarrell, and other less well-known but valuable contributors to the poetry of the period. There are two poems by T. S. Eliot, one of which is in French and is scarcely a measure of achievement in American poetry; and there are two pieces by Gertrude Stein which presumably reveal how, according to Miss Bogan, "her

sense of style, her feeling for words, and her peculiar wit combined to make them unforgettable."

My objection is a limited one. It is not to Miss Bogan's style, which is taut and never trivial; nor to her taste, which is sensitive, if eclectic. My objection centers about the implications of her title, which is a promise and which the book only partially fulfils. (pp. 21, 38)

Louis Untermeyer, "About Trends in Poetry," in The Saturday Review, *New York, Vol. XXXV, No. 5, February 2, 1952, pp. 21, 38.*

JOHN CIARDI

Louise Bogan's poetry has much in common with Miss [Léonie] Adams's. Here are the opening lines of three of Miss Bogan's early poems:

> In fear of the rich mouth
> I kissed the thin,—

and

> I make the old sign.
> I invoke you,
> Chastity.

and

> Now that I know
> How passion warms little.

At that point at least—and down to the Puritan marrow of Miss [Elinor] Wylie's bones—Miss Adams and Miss Bogan were surely sisters in the same aesthetic convent; and while I must confess that I have often wondered why that sisterhood insisted on wearing its chastity belts on the outside, poetry nevertheless remains wherever the spirit finds it. If that starting illusion was necessary to the poem, what matters is that the poems came—clean, hard, rigorously disciplined, and reaching to the nerve. Miss Bogan's capture in such an early piece as **"Medusa"** is enough to justify a whole burial ground of Puritan marrows.

But—speaking as one reader—if I admire objectively the poems of the first three (the earlier) sections of [*Collected Poems, 1923-53*], with the poems of section four, I find myself forgetting the thee and me of it. I am no longer being objective about the excellences of a poet who leaves me shrugging down to the Neapolitan marrow of my bones. I am immediately engaged. Miss Bogan began in beauty, but she has aged to magnificence. . . . One has only to compare **"The Dream"** . . . with the poems whose openings I have already cited to see how much more truly Miss Bogan sees into herself in the late poems—and not only into herself, but deeply enough into herself to find within her that jungle—call it the Jungian unconscious if you must—that everyone has in himself. **"The Dream"** is not only Miss Bogan's; it is everyone's.

Beginning with the poems of section four, that is, Miss Bogan leaves the convent. She comes out of timelessness into time. Nor is this a matter of topical reference. No such thing. It is, rather, that the kind of inward perception that marks the later poems speaks not only an enduring motion of the human spirit but an enduring motion that is *toward* the timeless *from* the times. (pp. 445-46)

John Ciardi, "Two Nuns and a Strolling Player," in The Nation, *New York, Vol. 178, No. 21, May 22, 1954, pp. 445-46.*

RICHARD EBERHART

Louise Bogan's poems adhere to the center of English with a dark lyrical force. What she has to say is important. How she says it is pleasing. She is a compulsive poet first, a stylist second. When compulsion and style meet we have a strong, inimitable Bogan poem.

There is relatively little technical innovation in her poems. She writes mainly in traditional verse forms, handled with adroitness and economy. The originality is in the forceful emotion and how this becomes caught in elegant tensions of perfected forms. She has delved in antique mysteries and brought up universal charms from deep sources, from a knowledge of suffering and from full understanding of the lot of man.

Some of her short lyrics [included in *Collected Poems, 1923-53*] have been known for a long time. To these she adds an arsenal of profound and beautiful poems. Her struggle is to throw off the nonessential, to confront naked realities at their source. Her poems are rich in passionate realizations, expressing in turn irony, bitterness, love and joy.

Her attitudes come down to a deep sincerity, the result of her strongly searching quality. A profundity of psychological knowledge works in the poems. One feels the truths of life, death and love have been confronted and uncompromising answers given.

Miss Bogan writes portrait poems like **"The Romantic"** and satirical poems like **"At a Party."** There is a small body of sententia, as **"To an Artist, to Take Heart."** She has a group of story or parable poems, such as **"The Crossed Apple," "Medusa," "Cartography"** and **"Evening in the Sanitarium."** I made a list of what I call her universal poems. This was quite long, including **"My Voice Not Being Proud," "The Alchemist," "Men Loved Wholly Beyond Wisdom," "Memory"** and **"Cassandra."**

This is a rich vein. I also made a list I called pure lyrics, a long list including **"Song for a Slight Voice," "I Saw Eternity," "Old Countryside," "Exhortation," "Man Alone," "To My Brother," "Spirit's Song," "Heard by a Girl"** and **"The Dream."** Her finest work is also in this vein.

Miss Bogan, who reviews poetry for *The New Yorker*, has year to year devoted careful thought to other poets, presenting their work in review with precise commentaries. She has developed these to a fine point of critical interest and sagacity. One had the notion that she wrote sparingly herself. This book is most welcome in giving the reader for the first time the full dimension of her poetic talent. The feeling is of somber strength, of a strong nature controlling powerful emotions by highly conscious art. There is marked skill in her restraint. Her best poems read as if time would not be likely to break them down.

> *Richard Eberhart, "Common Charms from Deep Sources," in* The New York Times Book Review, *May 30, 1954, p. 6.*

KENNETH REXROTH

Louise Bogan has always seemed to me a considerable problem. It is most illuminating to give her work to classes in the analysis of poetry. At first you can see only the special hyperesthesis, the trance state so common in the poetesses of the first quarter of the century. It is very easy to be misled, because some of her earliest poetry is certainly in this idiom. As you read on, you discover a fundamental, all important difference.

Louise Bogan really means what she says. Read any of her more mature poems. It is obvious that you have an honest, yet piercing awareness of life as fundamentally tragic. The hyperesthesis is there, but it is embroiled in life, it handles and judges life in real terms. This is simply the difference between responsibility and irresponsibility, which is the difference between art and sentimentality, tragedy and melodrama.

Besides this, or because of it maybe, there is another thing in Louise Bogan—that inescapable accent of the real poet, words that really seize the mind, something poetry either has or hasn't. It can be analyzed, but it can't be defined. I would make bold to say that [*Collected Poems, 1923-53*] is the carefully considered life work of one of America's very best poets.

> *Kenneth Rexroth, "Among the Best Women Poets Writing Now in America," in* New York Herald Tribune Book Review, *July 4, 1954, p. 5.*

LÉONIE ADAMS

The immediate significance of [*Collected Poems, 1923-53*] is twofold. It provides, in an admirable arrangement and with some fine additions, work whose excellence had been recognized, but which had been for some years out of print, and it provides occasion for calling it to the attention of the wider audience it deserves.

Self-possessed, from the beginning intact, Miss Bogan's talent has never been in dispute, nor had the unhappy, often questionable merit of "eluding" definition. Since the brilliant and early beginning of *Body of This Death*, she has not stood still, nor advanced by fits and starts. After the poems in *The Sleeping Fury*, though still to bring forth those true fruits which always surprise, she could hardly exceed herself in her characteristic mode. With the publication of *Poems and New Poems*, the distinguished quality of her work had been asserted and as far as possible perhaps discriminated by some of those most competent to do this. The present reviewer feels no need for revision of their essential estimate. Indeed an old jacket reminds one that things were said of her poems in 1923 which are still, in effect, being said with perfect soundness in 1954.

What there is need of, and opportunity for, is to repeat and labor a little the estimate alluded to. The virtues of her writing which have been most often spoken of are, I should suppose, firmness of outline, prosodic accomplishment, chiefly in traditional metrics, purity of diction and tone, concision of phrase, and, what results in craft from all these, and at bottom from a way of seizing experience, concentrated singleness of effect.

The description might well delimit the classic form of the short lyric, any time, any place, abstractly, and so hold for any example, and none. Actually its elements have seldom, and never for long periods, been held in English verse in any serenity of balance, and this poet's particular management of them remains to be discussed.

Louise Bogan has not written a large body of work, nor addressed herself—though this will seem less true by concentrating on the later sections of the book—to peculiarly modern preoccupations. Just as a certain inner rhythm can be found—and some other effects of sound patterning cannot—only within freely absorbed metrical forms, a certain lyric reduction can perhaps be reached only for recurrent norms of experience, a little beneath and apart from immediate phenomena. The evidence of the poems is that this poet has rarely written except when impelled by the strong experience of the private person.

Though adhering more closely to traditional forms than many poets find will meet their case, the language of the poems is as well of now as not, their temper of mind and presuppositions perfectly so.

A large part of their moral force derives from the refusal to be deluded, or to be overborne. The learning of the unwanted lesson, the admission of the harsh fact, a kind of exhilaration of rejection, whether of the scorned or the merely implausible, the theme appears in the earliest work, and reaches maximum power in Section III. To mention some of the well known pieces there, **"The Sleeping Fury,"** like **"The Dream,"** finds an image for such admission within the self; **"At a Party"** situates its scene; the finely sustained **"Putting to Sea"** encompasses both these, the elegiac tone of innocence, and the deeper one of some inclusive mystery of survival. **"Henceforth from the Mind"** is the theme's more abstracted song.

Yet despite this theme's prevalence, though there are pieces which might be classified as small ironic portraits (**"The Romantic," "The Alchemist," "Man Alone"**) and even an epigram or so, the true vein of her work is not ironic in the usual sense, nor satiric, but something at once simpler and more desperately human. In the best of these poems what makes possible their strong charging of the formal balance is this: the explicit matter is unimpeded delineation; its cost, seldom adumbrated, resounds. (pp. 165-67)

Miss [Marianne] Moore has written of Louise Bogan's "compactness compacted." It is not the concentration of density, dazzling or murky, to be found in some modern work, but of rapid elucidation, and its secret is again that of the poise of elements in the poem. A few examples of the early period, in the symbolist-imagist manner, do more to develop the reserves of the image, and the last poem in the book does so magnificently; any number of phrases throughout are witness to "sensibility" for objects. "Listen but once" she oftenest tells that faculty and refuses to freight the poem with more than can be brought incisively to its light. She has always seen the use of the dramatic figure or mask, not for elaboration, but statement of the essence of a situation. (Longer pieces, like **"The Sleeping Fury," "Summer Wish,"** are a progressive unfolding, in the same style.) Her musicianship works for what Hopkins distinguished as "candour, style" (harmony of tone) rather than "margaretting" (pearling with musical effects?). Many of her best poems should be related—for the lyric has other ancestors than the spontaneous cry—to the sort of choric lyric which speaks its comment nearest to the scene.

It is an art of limits, the limit of the inner occasion and of the recognized mode. This is part of its relevance, when writing often reminds us that there is no end to the remarks to be made, the matters to be noted; or, on the other hand, that the literary vegetation abounds less with forms, as in Mr. Stevens' phrase, than with techniques for exploitation.

Ranging only as far as may be from a personal center, this is a civilized poetry. (pp. 168-69)

> *Léonie Adams, " 'All Has Been Translated into Treasure'," in* Poetry, *Vol. LXXXV, No. 3, December, 1954, pp. 165-69.*

MARIANNE MOORE

[The essay from which this excerpt is taken was originally published in Poetry, *March-April, 1956.]*

This writing [in *Selected Criticism: Prose, Poetry*] has fiber. The subject matter, reprinted from various sources, is arranged chronologically except as it has been regrouped for clarity. Miss Bogan's first book of poems was published in 1923; and in 1924 her first book review, in the *New Republic*. Her contributing of verse criticism to the *New Yorker* began in 1931, "at first as 'omnibus reviews' which covered the year's books at six-month intervals. From 1937 her *New Yorker* reviews have appeared as a regular subdepartment of 'Books' under the heading 'Verse.'"

An extensive survey, this; which includes besides Emerson, Emily Dickinson—and her father "who stepped like Cromwell when he went to gather kindling"—Thoreau, "wholesome Thoreau-like Robert Frost," Henry James, Hardy, G. M. Hopkins, W. B. Yeats; also, as coloring their respective periods, Wyndham Lewis, Ezra Pound, T. S. Eliot, Wallace Stevens, E. E. Cummings, W. C. Williams and others; Edmund Wilson and R. P. Blackmur (as critics), Gide's Journals, Collette, Virginia Woolf, Robert Graves, and poets 1944-1955.

As precursors of modernism in literature, mingled sensibilities, tendencies, and inter-related experiments are accounted for by Miss Bogan and brought into sequence. "The population after the Cuban war," she says, "was infatuated with power . . . an era of gilt wicker furniture, hand-painted china, lace curtains, and 'sofa cushions,'" of "the pulp magazine" and "a taste for 'sordid elegance,'" "attacked by Thorstein Veblen and others from the left." "American realism finally broke through": we had Dreiser's novels, "'disguised autobiographies,'" and free verse. Wagner and Villiers de L'Isle-Adam, Debussy and Mallarmé, post-impressionist "anatomizing of nature" and the Armory show in 1913, are correlated. We have Gertrude Stein in Paris, Imagist poetry in England and America, and "the novel as a Luciferian universe in the hands of Joyce."

"With an eye to virtues rather than defects," Miss Bogan does not overbear. She has no literary nephews; her pronouncements are terse, rendered with laboratory detachment. Unmistakable emphasis is placed on two capacities as indispensable to achievement—instinctiveness and "coming to terms with one's self"—instinctiveness as contrasted with Henry James' Mona Brigstock, who was "all will." Goethe's central power is seen as "interpretive imagination," an interior compulsion linked with integrity. In *The Family Reunion*, "an integration," Miss Bogan sees T. S. Eliot "in complete control of himself." Was Joyce in *Finnegans Wake*, she asks, "the farceur" or have we here "immaturity transcending suffering"?—a query one connects with Henry James' observation in discussing Turgenev's fiction: "The great question as to a poet or novelist is, how does he feel about life? What in the last analysis is his philosophy? This is the most interesting thing their works offer us. Details are interesting in proportion as they contribute to make it clear."

These compact, unequivocal studies are set off by a kind of dry humor-incognito which is idiosyncratically eloquent. Henry James "really was a great poet and profound psychologist," Miss Bogan says. "He has been thought genteel when he had become the sharpest critic of gentility, a dull expatriate when his books flashed with incisive American wit." "He must be approached as one approaches music," she says. "He continuously shifts between development and theme, never stops, never errs." She affirms Rilke's conviction that "we must adhere to difficulty if we would make any claim to having a part in life" and feels that we have in Rilke "one of the strongest antidotes to the powers of darkness"; "often exhausted, often afraid, often in flight but capable of growth and solitude—he stands as an example of integrity held through and beyond change.''

The combination of open writing, unstereotyped insights, and daring, is most attractive, as when Miss Bogan says, ''Yeats and Pound achieved modernity. Eliot was modern from the start.'' We have Ezra Pound, ''whom,'' Miss Bogan says, ''time will in the end surely honor,'' delineated in his statement, ''I am trying to use not an inch rule but a balance''; and perhaps with his tendency to diatribe in mind, she says, ''Pound's ideal reader is a person who has experienced real discomfort in being shut up in a railway train, lecture hall, or concert room, with well-modulated voices expressing careful, well-bred opinions on the subject of the arts.'' (pp. 229-31)

W. H. Auden is especially well observed. ''He gives humanity a hard unprejudiced stare,'' Miss Bogan says—but is capable of gaiety which can even be ''hilarity.'' ''He points up and freshens the language,'' ''describes with great originality the power drives of succeeding eras,'' and in *Poets of the English Language,* has participated, with Norman Pearson, in ''a peculiarly modern achievement.'' His ''lack of hatred, his fight against intellectual stupidity as well as outer horror'' are noted. . . . We have in Mr. Auden, Miss Bogan feels, ''a poet, one of whose urges always will be to transcend himself.'' . . . ''The Letters of Rainer Maria Rilke and the study of Gide's Journals reveal the bristling amateur who fears to be soft''— show what philosophy that is equity can be; and typical of the whole temper of the book—Miss Bogan says of Yvor Winters, a writer ''very nearly without listeners, let alone friends and admirers, his interest appears limited only because he has made choices, proof of probity and distilled power in unlikely times. These facts should delight us.''

A fascinating book, abounding in important insights such as, ''Loose form must have beneath, a groundswell of energy''; ''If one hates anything too long . . . one forgets what it is one could love''; the advice of W. B. Yeats that we ''write our thoughts as nearly as possible in the language we thought them in.'' And we are warned against ''stubborn avant-gardism when no real need for a restless forward movement any longer exists; the moment comes,'' Miss Bogan says, ''for a consolidation of resources, for interpretation rather than exploration.''

One has here mastery of material and associative creative insight—a conspectus of the transition from fettered to new writing—''from minor to major art''; to precision and ''a transcending of the self through difficulty.'' The book rises above literariness, moreover, and fortifies courage, in practicing a principle which is surely Confucian; implying that one need not demand fair treatment, but rather, see that one's treatment of others is fair. (pp. 231-32)

> *Marianne Moore, ''Selected Criticism,'' in her* A Marianne Moore Reader, *The Viking Press, 1961, pp. 229-32.*

THEODORE ROETHKE

Two of the charges most frequently leveled against poetry by women are lack of range—in subject matter, in emotional tone— and lack of a sense of humor. And one could, in individual instances among writers of real talent, add other esthetic and moral shortcomings: the spinning-out; the embroidering of trivial themes; a concern with the mere surfaces of life—that special province of the feminine talent in prose—hiding from the

real agonies of the spirit; refusing to face up to what existence is; lyric or religious posturing; running between the boudoir and the altar, stamping a tiny foot against God; or lapsing into a sententiousness that implies the author has re-invented integrity; carrying on excessively about Fate, about time; lamenting the lot of the woman; caterwauling; writing the same poem about fifty times, and so on.

But Louise Bogan is something else. True, a very few of her earliest poems bear the mark of fashion, but for the most part she writes out of the severest lyrical tradition in English. Her real spiritual ancestors are Campion, Jonson, the anonymous Elizabethan song writers. The word order is usually direct, the plunge straight into the subject, the music rich and subtle (she has one of the best ears of our time), and the subject invariably given its due and no more. As a result, her poems, even the less consequential, have a finality, a comprehensiveness, the sense of being all of a piece, that we demand from the short poem at its best.

The body of her complete poetic work is not great, but the ''range,'' both emotional and geographical, is much wider than might be expected from a lyric poet. There is the brilliant (and exact) imagery of her New England childhood; there is also the highly formal world of Swift's Ireland; the rich and baroque background of Italy called up in the evocative **''Italian Morning.''** And, of course, her beloved Austria. Her best lyrics, unlike so much American work, have the sense of a civilization behind them—and this without the deliberate piling up of exotic details, or the taking over of a special, say Grecian, vocabulary.

Invariably these effects are produced with great economy, with the exact sense of diction that is one of the special marks of her style. Even out of context, their power, I believe, is evident. (p. 13)

[From] the poem **''Italian Morning,''** the lines:

> The big magnolia, like a hand,
> Repeats our flesh. (O bred to love,
> Gathered to silence!) In a land
> Thus garnished, there is time enough
>
> To pace the rooms where painted swags
> Of fruit and flower in pride depend,
> Stayed as we are not.

The ''garnished'' and the ''painted swags'' are triumphs of exactitude in language—suggest the elaborate background without recourse to merely baroque diction.

This is only one, and by no means the best, of Miss Bogan's poems on time, on change, on the cessation of time. Even in her earliest work, she seems to be seeking a moment when things are caught, fixed, frozen, seen, for an instant, under the eye of eternity.

A very early piece, **''Decoration,''** printed in her first book, *Body of This Death,* but not in the *Collected,* is, I believe, a beginning, a groping toward this central theme. . . . (p. 14)

[**''Decoration''**] is a vulnerable poem, in spite of certain felicities (the fine ''and all the simple evening passes by,'' for instance). But the uncharitable might say hardly beyond magazine verse. And even though Miss Bogan disarms us with her title, the poem remains *too* static, not very interesting syntactically, and the final line plays upon one of the clichés of the twenties: ''A crystal tree lets fall a crystal leaf.'' Still, the scene is looked at steadily and closely; the poem is what it is.

Another early piece, **"Statue and the Birds,"** is already a much better poem on essentially the same theme. However, the **"Medusa,"** printed on the page opposite **"Decoration"** in the first book, is a breakthrough to great poetry, the whole piece welling up from the unconscious, dictated as it were. . . . (p. 15)

One definition of a serious lyric—it may come from Stanley Kunitz—would call it a revelation of a tragic personality. Behind the Bogan poems is a woman intense, proud, strong-willed, never hysterical or silly; who scorns the open unabashed caterwaul so usual with the love poet, male or female; who never writes a serious poem until there is a genuine "up-welling" from the unconscious; who shapes emotion into an inevitable-seeming, an endurable, form.

For love, passion, its complexities, its tensions, its betrayals, is one of Louise Bogan's chief themes. And this love, along with marriage itself, is a virtual battleground. But the enemy is respected, the other is *there,* given his due; the experience, whatever its difficulties, shared. (pp. 16-17)

Many of the best Bogan poems in this vein are of such complexity and depth that the excerpt is virtually impossible, particularly since Miss Bogan often employs the single developed image with usually at least two levels of meaning. And often, within a very short space, she effects an almost intolerable tension, a crescendo in rhythm, as in **"Men Loved Wholly Beyond Wisdom"**; or builds up the theme powerfully, as in the remarkable **"Feuer-Nacht,"** and then takes a chance with a generalization without losing the momentum of the poem. . . . (p. 17)

Some of her best pieces begin with the object perceived, as it were, for an instant, and the image remembered, fixed in the mind unforgettably.

However, she is not, as I have said, a poet of the immediate moment, as say, Lawrence, but of the time *after,* when things come into their true focus, into the resolution, the final perspective. Listen to **"Roman Fountain"**:

> Up from the bronze, I saw
> Water without a flaw
> Rush to its rest in air,
> Reach to its rest, and fall.
>
> Bronze of the blackest shade,
> An element man-made,
> Shaping upright the bare
> Clear gouts of water in air.
>
> O, as with arm and hammer,
> Still it is good to strive
> To beat out the image whole,
> To echo the shout and stammer
> When full-gushed waters, alive,
> Strike on the fountain's bowl
> After the air of summer.

For me, the opening lines are one of the great felicities of our time: the thing put down with an ultimate exactness, absolutely as it is. Perhaps the two appositives "Bronze of the blackest shade / An element man-made" in the next stanza are a bit "written"; but "gouts of water" saves everything. Nor do I care much for the evocative outcry—and the arm and hammer image. Yet the poem resolves itself with characteristic candor. We have come a long way in a short space.

I believe this poem will stay in the language: its opening alone demands immortality. Yet it exists, too, as a superb piece of

observation; as a phallic poem; as a poem about the nature of the creative art in the no-longer young artist.

In the last lines of this piece, we hear the accent of the later work: a tone of resignation, an acceptance of middle age, a comment, often, on the ironies of circumstance. Of these, I believe **"Henceforth, From the Mind"** to be a masterpiece, a poem that could be set beside the best work of the Elizabethans. . . . And certainly **"Song," "Hommunculus,"** and **"Kept,"** at the very least, are among our best short lyrics. (pp. 17-18)

I find my rather simple method of "pointing out"—at which Miss Marianne Moore is such a master—has omitted or underemphasized certain qualities in Louise Bogan's work, and of necessity passed by remarkable poems.

For example, the great variety and surety of her rhythms—that clue to the energy of the psyche. Usually the movement of the poem is established in the very first lines, as it should be. . . . And she is a master of texture, yet always the line is kept firm: she does not lapse into "sound" for the sake of sound, lest the poem thin out into loose "incantatory" effects. (pp. 18-19)

Louise Bogan rarely, if ever, repeats a cadence, and this in an age when some poets achieve a considerable reputation with two or three or even *one* rhythm. The reason for this is, I believe, her absolute loyalty to the particular emotion, which can range from the wry tenderness and humor of **"A Crossed Apple"** to the vehemence of **"Several Voices Out of a Cloud."** . . .

I have said that Miss Bogan has a sharp sense of objects, the eye that can pluck out from the welter of experience the inevitable image. And she loves the words, the nouns particularly, rich in human association. **"Baroque Comment"** ends:

> Crown and vesture; palm and laurel chosen as noble and
>   enduring;
> Speech proud in sound; death considered sacrifice;
> Mask, weapon, urn; the ordered strings;
> Fountains; foreheads under weather-bleached hair;
> The wreath, the oar, the tool,
> The prow;
> The turned eyes and the opened mouth of love.
>
> (p. 19)

The imagery in some of the last poems is less specific, yet still strongly elemental; we have, I think, what Johnson called the grandeur of generality. They are timeless, impersonal in a curious way and objective—not highly idiosyncratic as so much of the best American work is. Her poems can be read and reread: they keep yielding new meanings, as all good poetry should. The ground beat of the great tradition can be heard, with the necessary subtle variations. Bogan is one of the true inheritors. Her poems create their own reality, and demand not just attention, but the emotional and spiritual response of the whole man. Such a poet will never be popular, but can and should be a true model for the young. And the best work will stay in the language as long as the language survives. (p. 20)

*Theodore Roethke, "The Poetry of Louise Bogan,"
in* Michigan Alumnus Quarterly Review, *Vol. LXVII,
No. 10, Autumn, 1960, pp. 13-20.*

WILLIAM MEREDITH

Now that we can see the sweep of 45 years' work in this collection of over a hundred poems [*The Blue Estuaries: Poems,*

1923-1968], we can judge what a feat of character it has been. The verse character of John Crowe Ransom is a similar accomplishment. The diction, rhythms and forms of the two poets body forth assertions of strong, but never merely eccentric, individuality.

Miss Bogan's diction, as Theodore Roethke pointed out [see excerpt above], stems from the severest lyrical tradition in English, She uses this Elizabethan language without the irony Ransom uses to mock his own brocaded speech. With Miss Bogan it is simply a passion for grammatical and etymological accuracy. Here is a language as supple as it is accurate, dealing with things in their own tones. . . .

Reading this book with delight, I was struck (as Roethke must have been in 1961) by how Louise Bogan's reputation has lagged behind a career of stubborn, individual excellence. I hope *The Blue Estuaries* may set things straight.

> William Meredith, *"Poems of a Human Being," in The New York Times Book Review, October 13, 1968, p. 4.*

HAYDEN CARRUTH

Miss Bogan is one of our finest poets. She has written twenty or twenty-five poems that are unforgettable; they may be the best of their kind in American literature. And what we get from them, I think, aside from our delight, is the recognition of her basic poetic wisdom. She has not resisted her temptations, for she has seen that resistance can produce only poems which are crafty and correct but rarely interesting. Instead she has yielded; she has taken her temptations as they came, and has outsmarted them. Let the poem be conventional, public, and occasional, since that is the mask one must wear—so she might have spoken—but let each poem reveal just enough of a private inner violence to make the surface move without breaking. A passionate austerity, a subtle balance; and only perfect poetic attention, far beyond technique, could attain it.

Not that the technique isn't marvelous. Readers who take joy in prosodic effects for their own sake can find passages in every poem [in *The Blue Estuaries*] to study; the first stanza of **"Roman Fountain,"** for instance, which is famous, and which will remain famous as long as any ear is tuned to standard English metric. It is a miraculous example of the power to bend the reader's actual bodily attitude, through phrasing, meter, and rhyme, to the movement of the poet's own vision. (p. 330)

But other readers will seek for something more, the intact poetic experience, and they will go more often to simpler poems, **"Women," "Henceforth, From the Mind," "Short Summary," "To My Brother," "Man Alone," "Song for the Last Act,"** and others. These are the poems in which the balance is exactly struck.

The Blue Estuaries adds twelve poems to Miss Bogan's *Collected Poems* of 1954, which has been out of print for some years, but it is still a small book to represent forty-five years of work; only 136 pages altogether. Perhaps it could have been smaller yet. But that isn't important, for in another sense—the sense of a quality that we cannot do without—this book's best pages make it fundamentally irreducible. (p. 331)

> Hayden Carruth, *"A Balance Exactly Struck," in Poetry, Vol. CXIV, No. 5, August, 1969, pp. 330-31.*

CHOICE

[*A Poet's Alphabet: Reflections on the Literary Art and Vocation* is a virtually] complete collection of the criticism of the late Louise Bogan arranged in a convenient alphabetical order and ranging from American literature through Yeats. Bogan writes a criticism that is discovery and that invites discovery. In her own phrase, her ideas are "large and centered." She has the penetrating intelligence of the best academic minds but is without the narrowness often associated with academic writing. Her ability to talk about what is interesting is unerring. She persistently shows the courage of judgments. She has wisdom and grace, wit and humor, and a felicity of language that often becomes classic utterance. This is a book that belongs . . . on the shelf of every literate person with an interest in modern letters.

> A review of *"A Poet's Alphabet: Reflections on the Literary Art and Vocation," in Choice, Vol. 8, No. 1, March, 1971, p. 62.*

NANCY MILFORD

Letters at their best, and [*What the Woman Lived: Selected Letters of Louise Bogan, 1920-1970*] is a fine selection, provide a sort of informal biography. They permit us to move through the private voice of their author into her life. And that's the excitement, the sheer fun. For although letters are a more casual form of writing than poetry is, and something quite different is at stake in their writing, in reading them one is linked to the past. Reading becomes an act of connecting in which the past is made personal.

Louise Bogan was 32 when she wrote John Hall Wheelock, the poet who was her editor at Scribner's: "I refused to fall apart, so I have been taken apart, like a watch. . . ." (p. 1)

These breakdowns were apparently recurring, but they are never clearly spelled out in this edition of her letters. I mention this because I do not understand why a simple chronology of her life was not given at the beginning of the book. I could arrive at her date of birth only by being nimble at subtraction. When she writes Rolfe Humphries in 1924, "I'll be 27, Rolfe. O God, I thought I'd be a great poet by 27 with fat works ranged on shelves," you figure that she was born in 1897.

Many of the notes are excellent and helpful, but an early and important one does not make clear the simplest facts of her life. To "child" in the sentence, "I had a suitcase, half doz. apples, a child, and a copy of The American Mercury," the following note is keyed: "the child, Maidie Alexander, had been born to LB and her first husband, Curt Alexander, in the Panama Canal Zone, a few years earlier. Alexander, an army officer, died in 1920." One cannot know from this note either the age of the child or the date of the first marriage, or even whether or not it ended in death or divorce. I am also bothered that her editor, Ruth Limmer, has nowhere made clear why there are no letters to her first husband, to her second, to her mother, her father, or her daughter.

Ruth Limmer has, however, served her well in the selections themselves, for when she writes in her Introduction, "It is no small thing to know, as precisely as Louise Bogan did, what it is to be a woman," we believe her. Theodore Roethke is unknown and in trouble when she writes to him "—I, too, have been imprisoned by a family, who held out the bait of a nice hot cup of tea and a nice clean bed. . . . the only way to get away is to get away: pack up and go. Anywhere. I had a child, from the age of 20, remember that, to hold me back, but I got up and went just the same, and I was, God help us, a woman.''

It is to Edmund Wilson (''Edmund dear'' she almost never calls him Bunny, and only once in a fury addresses him as ''Dear Ed'') that she first confides that Roethke is her lover.

> I, myself, have been made to bloom like a Persian rose-bush, by the enormous love-making of a cross between a Brandenburger and a Pomeranian.... He is very, very large (6 ft. 2 and weighing 218 lbs.) and he writes very, very small lyrics. 26 years old and a frightful tank. We have poured rivers of liquor down our throats ... and in between, have indulged in such bearish and St. Bernardish antics as I have never before experienced. * * * Well! Such goings on! A woman of my age!

She is not quite 38 (and I for one would love to know what those three asterisks replaced). From then on Ted, as she calls him, is her ''lamb pie,'' her ''duck,''—''my fine boy-o,'' ''my pickled pear,'' ''my coney.''

Being a woman alone with a child to support was not easy; she was poor, she was evicted once, and she fretted when she missed deadlines.... Yet for all this there was remarkably little complaining or begrudging anyone of anything.

When she was young, she told Rolfe Humphries not to get mad because Frost got the Pulitzer. ''By the time we're 48 we'll get it.'' In 1969, when she knew she had lost it for the last time and her final volume of poetry, *The Blue Estuaries,* was passed over, she wrote her friend Ruth Limmer: ''My poems seem to have fallen down that deep, dark well. Not a review! This doesn't bother me much.'' But it did hurt to be dismissed, and to Robert Phelps who was working on an edition of her criticism she said, ''Let's not give it another thought.... The Pulitzer comes from a school of *journalism,* we must remember.'' At the close of her life she saw her daughter once a week and a young psychiatrist twice a month; she was lonely and irritated with herself for feeling it. She called it ''A slight failure of nerve.... But I hate it, and wish it would go away.'' She was pleased to be elected to the American Academy of Arts and Letters; and when she left *The New Yorker* after 38 years on the staff she seemed relieved. ''I've had it. No more pronouncements on lousy verse. No more *hidden* competition. No more struggling *not* to be a square.'' Four months later, alone in her apartment, she died. (pp. 1-2)

> Nancy Milford, ''Through a Poet's Private Voice into Her Life,'' in The New York Times Book Review, *December 16, 1973, pp. 1-2.*

BRAD LEITHAUSER

Publication of Louise Bogan's autobiography promises the arrival of a fascinating and thoughtful book. Hers was a full and ultimately triumphant life. Author of six fine books of verse, poetry critic of *The New Yorker* for 38 years, friend to Auden and Edmund Wilson, mentor and brief lover of the young Theodore Roethke, she exerted—as poet, critic, literary friend— a three-sided influence on American poetry from the '20s, when she first began to publish, to her death in 1970. As critic, she could be taxingly severe, but was always, as the pared slimness of her collected poems suggests, most demanding on herself.

Journey Around My Room: The Autobiography of Louise Bogan is indeed a fascinating, thoughtful book, although not for the reasons one might expect. The title is somewhat misleading, for this is not a true autobiography, and little of Bogan's activities—her friendships, her two disastrous marriages, her nervous breakdowns, her relationship with her daughter—is presented here. The book is, in the words of its compiler Ruth Limmer, a ''mosaic,'' a mix of ''journals, notebook entries, poems ... sentences and paragraphs from her criticism, portions of letters, a lecture, answers to questions ... short stories, recorded conversations, scraps of paper.'' Bit by bit, this mosaic becomes the portrait of a temperament, the mental lineaments of a woman of candor, tenacity, and catholic intellect. That this mosaic does not, despite its variety of sources, have a makeshift, tessellated feel attests to Ruth Limmer's craftsmanship.

Bogan's short story **''Journey Around My Room''** has been cut into sections and used as a ''frame,'' opening and closing the volume. The choice was an apt one. The story's subject (the baffling casual links between one's past and present) and imagery (the mind equated to a room) are the subject and imagery of much of the book. The story's narrator asks herself, ''How did I reach the window, the walls, the fireplace, the room itself; how do I happen to be beneath this ceiling and above this floor? ... Some step started me toward this point, as opposed to all other points on the habitable globe.'' In search of these buried influences, Bogan turns repeatedly throughout the book to the turmoil and privation of her childhood, and to childhood's complementary store of comforts, particularly those of vanished light. She resurrects mornings when the kitchen ''was floating in sunlight,'' towns where the sun ''falls incredibly down through a timeless universe to light up clapboard walls.'' Bogan writes convincingly of childhood, conveying without self-pity or any distancing solemnity its terrors and solaces and anguished appetites. (p. 4)

Much of this book derives from Bogan's journals. When excerpted in 1978 in *The New Yorker,* the entries were presented chronologically. In this volume, Ruth Limmer has grouped them thematically, and here and there has unobtrusively added or altered a phrase for clarity. Of course any alteration of a writer's journal must carry attendant losses. In this case, Limmer has paid for greater coherence and cumulative power by sacrificing some of the journal's quietness and haphazard grace. The exchange nonetheless proves a profitable one. Bogan has been respectfully and sympathetically served.

Enjoyable as this volume is (and I would recommend as companion piece *What the Woman Lived,* her collected letters), it is through her poems that Bogan's achievement must be tested. In poetry, the boundary that separates the old-fashioned from the timeless is often unclear, and it is in this hazy region that many of Bogan's poems lie. (p. 10)

> Brad Leithauser, ''Portrait of a Temperament,'' in Book World—The Washington Post, *January 18, 1981, pp. 4, 10.*

DOUGLAS L. PETERSON

In the years following the publication of *Blue Estuaries: Poems, 1923-68* Louise Bogan has been all but forgotten. The reasons are obvious enough. She was a formalist during a time when the main lines of development in American poetry were radically experimental. There is little evidence in her verse to indicate that she was much interested in Imagism or the experimental techniques of Pound, Eliot, and Williams, or that she found much that was useful to her in the works of the Symbolists. She was a poet who relied mainly on the old modes of logic and the metrical forms which since the sixteenth century have been used to accommodate discursive statement. The neglect of her verse, then, is hardly surprising: it does not conveniently fall into the categories of Modernism that have been codified by academic authorities, and it has offered little in the way of precedents to follow for aspiring young writers whose tastes have been fashioned by the trendy quarterlies of the sixties and seventies.

But my concern here is not only to call attention to the distinguished and neglected poet; it is also with style and with the kinds of questions which, given the current state of American poetry and the notions about style which seem to have shaped it, strike me as being especially cogent at this time. (p. 73)

Bogan's reasons for adopting a specific style are ethical and rhetorical. The style she fashioned out of the precedents with which she began represented for her a set of ideal attitudes toward her own experience and the world in general, which she endeavored to realize in the way she lived as well as in the way she wrote.

From her earliest poems on she writes mainly of highly personal and painful experience—of personal losses suffered through death and the betrayal of intimate and deeply valued personal relationships, of time passing and of her acute awareness of the fragility of all things caught in time. Her way of securing and maintaining some kind of control of self in the face of such experience was to cultivate a discipline of withdrawal, denial, and indifference. Even though she soon came to realize that attempts to deny the claims of feeling and to seek serenity by withdrawing from the world into the self were not only life-denying but an impossibility, it is clear from *The Blue Estuaries* that she continued in those attempts throughout her life and, further, that the writing of verse in the severest of forms came to be a means of exercising herself in a stoic discipline.

It is not surprising, then, that she discovered when she first seriously began to write, useful precedents in the firmly controlled verse of her New England predecessor E. A. Robinson and in the tradition of the Elizabethan plain-stylists. Robinson's method of reflective summary narrative in poems like ''For a Dead Lady,'' ''Lost Anchors,'' and ''Eros Turannos,'' along with his characteristic manner of stoic forbearance, are evident throughout *Body of This Death,* her first collection of poems.... Robinson's detached, objective manner of treating personal experience by way of a fictional character and situation; his controlled discursive statement, often in the form of reflection on what is presented as irrevocably a part of the past; and, above all else, his consistent attitude of dignified forbearance are qualities which Bogan found especially attractive.

Similar qualities distinguish the best work of the plain stylists of the English Renaissance, and such poems in *Body of This Death* as ''Song,'' ''Knowledge,'' and ''The Alchemist'' indicate that Bogan began early in her career to read carefully in the work of Nashe, Jonson, and the anonymous writers of Elizabethan song. The results are not always successful. On some occasions, as in ''Knowledge,'' the austere forms employed exclude so much that all that remains are summary statements whose authority resides only in a rhetoric of flat statement and the resonances of firmly controlled and sensitive rhythms.... [Yet] Bogan has made the style her own. The final lines, in which the discovery of the futility of the stoic

effort is stated without any trace of rhetoric, have the authoritative ring of a truth which, however obvious, has finally been personally won.

Other poems in the collection disclose a talent for using natural description that is the equal of the best of her contemporaries. When she employs that talent to convey a state of mind, the results are often original and unforgettable. **''Last Hill in a Vista,''** a modern-day pastoral in the octosyllabic line perfected by the Renaissance plain-stylists, provides a good example.... Whatever reservations one may have about the attitude toward self expressed in the opening lines of each stanza, the writing elsewhere is typical of Bogan at her best. The use of feminine rhyme and syntactical parallelism to create cadenced rhythms and the variation through the use of runovers from the norm established by those repeated rhythms are Elizabethan techniques, but they have been completely assimilated and employed to a use that is Bogan's own. The use of descriptive detail to convey a state of mind is of course also traditional and, in fact, common among her contemporaries. Bogan's originality in her use of the technique is in her discipline and restraint. (pp. 75-8)

Neither *Dark Summer* (1929) nor *The Sleeping Fury* (1937), Bogan's second and third collections, shows anything in the way of an attempt to experiment with styles or of a desire to move on either to new subjects or to new ways of dealing with old ones. Renunciation and practiced indifference remain her only means of dealing with loss and betrayal. What does emerge in these volumes is a growing awareness and preoccupation with time and mortality. Technically, the major precedents continue to be those offered by the Elizabethans. **''Henceforth, from the Mind,''** a poem remarking with a gentle but firm irony that what the will is unable to achieve in the way of tranquility by rejecting desires and passion, the passing of time guarantees, employs a refrain technique frequently used by the Elizabethans. **''Kept,''** too, is a poem containing traces of the techniques of the plain-stylists of the late sixteenth century. Whereas in ''Henceforth, from the Mind,'' Bogan employs summary statement almost exclusively, here she develops a metaphor. Both the trope and the attitude established in the opening lines are reminiscent of Campion's ''Now Winter Nights Enlarge.'' The refrain from Shakespeare's song from *Cymbeline* . . . also comes to mind. Again, the ''repetitive harmony'' of the old tradition comes to life in this poem and in ways that remind us of its richness as a resource.... The description of how we come to identify our possessions with self and of the consequences is simple and disturbingly true.

The influences of Elizabethan song are even more pronounced in **''Come, Break with Time.''** The effects here, however, are strikingly different from those of **''Henceforth, from the Mind''** and **''Kept.''** The austere diction, the two-beat line, the heavy, repetitive cadences, and the sequence of terse, summary statements suggest Nashe's ''In Time of Pestilence''; but the imitative effects of rhythm that are so much a part of the poem are Bogan's own creation.... The value of imitative rhythms has been exaggerated in critical commentary and handbooks of poetry in recent years; and demonstrations of imitative rhythm more often than not turn out to be mere impressionistic excursions. The principal value of rhythms achieved by means of traditional meters has always been and will continue to be in establishing and sustaining tone. Occasionally, however, the achievements of imitative rhythm are real and indisputable. The measured regularity of the opening line of Bogan's **''Simple Autumnal''**—''The measured blood beats out the year's delay''—is one such instance. The suggestion in "Come, break with time" by rhythmic means of the swing of a clock's pendulum surrendering to the gravitational pull of the "earth's heavy measure" in the final line of **"Come, Break with Time"** is another.

"Division" and **"The Mark,"** in which Bogan also addresses the subject of time, suggest more recent models. The convention Bogan employs in each is a favorite among the Romantics and one which in our own century Hardy, Robinson, Frost, Stevens, and Roethke have found useful. The poet-observer is alone in a natural setting; something attracts his attention—an animal, a bird's song, a tree, or a scene—which stirs him to serious reflection. The originality of Bogan's poems is in her choice of objects and in the brilliant and precise description. The illusion created in **"Division"** is again, as in **"Medusa,"** of having successfully recorded a moment. . . . (pp. 80-2)

"The Mark" is similar to **"Division"** not only in theme and method, but in the symbolic use of shadow, as well. Here, the tree and the shadow it cast upon the door of the house in **"Division"** are replaced by the upright figure of a man and the shadow it casts upon the ground. The latter is "the mark," "the spear of dark in the strong day / Beyond the upright body thrown," an inescapable reminder of "time's long treason." The final stanzas are among the most impressive in all of Bogan:

> Stand pinned to sight, while now, unbidden,
> The apple loosens, not at call,
> Falls to the field, and lies there hidden,—
> Another and another fall
> And lie there hidden, in spite of all
>
> The diagram of whirling shade,
> The visible, that thinks to spin
> Forever webs that time has made
> Though momently time wears them thin
> And all at length are gathered in.

The brilliant exploitation in these stanzas of the relationship between verse and syntactical units, first to sharpen the contrast between two aspects of process—the slow, methodical ripening of the apples and the whirling shade of the visible world—and then to support rhetorically the final summary statement, is another example of how effectively the techniques of the pre-modernist verse tradition can still be employed by the poet who takes the trouble to master them. There is no retreat in these lines to orthodoxy. The ancient trope of falling apples to represent the cyclical process of the seasons (it was commonplace long before Touchstone's melancholy reflection in *As You Like It,* "And so, from hour to hour we ripe and ripe / And then, from hour to hour, we rot and rot") and the "diagram of whirling shade," the view offered by modern physics of the circular movement of cosmic and subatomic bodies, are juxtaposed to articulate a new and deepened awareness of each end of the process which is fundamental to being, itself.

There are other impressive poems in *Dark Summer* and *The Sleeping Fury,* among them **"At a Party," "Italian Morning,"** and **"Winter Swan"** but there is also something disturbing about these collections. The more familiar one becomes with them, the more aware one becomes of a limiting sameness. It is as much a matter of tone and technique as it is of subject and concern. Bogan herself is aware of the problem. In **"Summer Wish"** she wants to turn to new areas of experience. . . . The search for serenity by retiring into the self has failed. To continue to look inward is to continue to rely upon the mind

and the mind has proved to be an unreliable guide. . . . Nature seems to offer in its bright assurances of renewal a promising alternative—new subjects and new hopes and ways of feeling:

> In the bright twilight children call out in the fields.
> The evening takes their cry. How late it is.
> Around old weeds worn thin and bleached to their pith
> The field has leaped to stalk and strawberry blossom.
> The orchard by the road
> Has the pear-tree full at once of flowers and leaves,
> The cherry with flowers only.

These lines in themselves are lovely and hold the promise of further growth. But the later collections do not fulfill that promise. **"Evening in the Sanitarium," "Train Time," "After the Persian," "Several Voices out of a Cloud," "Poem in Prose,"** and **"Animal, Vegetable, and Mineral,"** poems which first appeared in *Poems and New Poems* (1941), are modest attempts at experimentation. But of these, only **"Animal, Vegetable, and Mineral,"** a dryly ironic attack on the reductiveness of the scientific account of pollination that is represented by glass models in the Ware collection in Harvard's Botanical Museum, is really distinguished, and it is experimental only as an essay into satire. Its effectiveness, in fact, is due to Bogan's mastery of the pentameter line and of rhyming patterns. . . . In the poems which appear for the first time in *Blue Estuaries* further signs of experimentation are evident. The line is freer and more varied and stanzas are irregular. Rhyming, too, is often irregular and sometimes abandoned. But the method remains discursive and descriptive. The best of these late poems is **"The Dragonfly,"** a sad but beautiful representation of what life finally amounts to in Bogan's view. . . . (pp. 83-6)

It may be tempting to some to speculate about what Bogan might have accomplished if she had begun earlier to experiment with freer forms, and even to suggest that she might have been a more significant figure in the history of American poetry if she had adopted Modernist techniques. Such speculation is both pointless and misleading. The style she initially adopted represented for her a way of managing experience. Although one may point to other and perhaps potentially more successful ways that she might have chosen and, thus, to other styles that she might have found less confining, each of us makes our way as best we can when dealing with the cold business of life. That Bogan chose to adopt a form of stoicism is her own business. Ours is to consider the results of that choice in her poems.

The discipline and control she develops in the use of traditional forms enabled her to write cleanly and with great connotative effect about the visible world and to exploit the rhythmical potentialities of traditional prosody in ways that few of her contemporaries were able to approach. At the same time, her mastery of traditional forms led her sometimes to substitute formal control for spiritual control. On those occasions the disciplined surfaces of what she writes are belied by feelings that hint at self-pity and even hysteria. That Bogan was herself aware of what she was vulnerable to is evident in **"Single Sonnet,"** an apostrophe to the sonnet form itself as a "heroic mold" which offers to her the possibility of relief by assuming a burden which she has carried so long alone:

> Too long as ocean bed bears up the ocean,
> As earth's core bears the earth, have I borne this;
> Too long have lovers, bending for their kiss,
> Felt bitter force cohering without motion.

Staunch meter, great song, it is yours, at length,
To prove how stronger you are than my strength.

Finally, what is true of the style she adopted is true of the stoicism she practiced. The effort to win serenity through withdrawal and indifference is for the poet, as she eventually realized, I think, really suicidal. It leads to the systematic narrowing of the range of one's concerns, and when the end is attained, one is left with neither the desire to write nor subjects about which to write. Nevertheless, along the way to that end subjects familiar and important to us all continue to demand attention. Death and time, for Louise Bogan as for Marcus Aurelius so many centuries earlier, continued to matter to her, as the beautiful and powerful **"Dragonfly"** indicates, to the very end. (pp. 86-7)

Douglas L. Peterson, "The Poetry of Louise Bogan," in The Southern Review (*Louisiana State University*), *Vol. 19, No. 1, Winter, 1983, pp. 73-87.*

Antonio Buero Vallejo

1916-

Spanish dramatist.

One of Spain's leading dramatists, Buero Vallejo has contributed significantly to the revitalization of postwar Spanish theater. Eschewing the frivolous plots and comforting sentimentality of much early twentieth-century Spanish drama, Buero Vallejo writes deeply serious, moralistic plays that frequently depict characters consumed by despair and frustration. Commonly regarded as a tragedian, Buero Vallejo advances a conception of drama characterized by the redeeming presence of hope. He suggests that by inviting people to confront reality without self-deception, the writer of tragedies raises issues fundamental to human existence which have as their ultimate end the improvement of society.

Buero Vallejo rose to prominence as a dramatist following his six-year imprisonment by the conservative Nationalist government of Generalissimo Francisco Franco for his activities as a Loyalist medical assistant during the Spanish Civil War. While many of Spain's best-known artists chose to flee the oppressive social and political conditions that existed under Franco's regime, Buero Vallejo remained in Spain after his release from prison and began concealing his criticisms of governmental policy in dramas that make extensive use of symbolism and metaphor. His first play, *Historia de una escalera* (1949), depicts tenement life in Madrid through two generations of a poor family who attempt to reconcile their miserable economic condition and their seemingly futile aspirations.

Buero Vallejo's significance derives particularly from his use of what have been termed "immersion effects." Described by Martha Halsey as devices that "enable the audience to share certain sensory perceptions of [Buero Vallejo's] protagonists that are not perceived by the other characters," these techniques represent, according to William Giuliano, "a striving for psycho-physical [audience] participation emphasizing the spiritual, with elements of Brecht on one hand and Beckett on the other." *En la ardiente oscuridad* (1950), Buero Vallejo's first play to contain these innovations, evidences his initial use of mental and physical impairment to symbolize the condition of Spanish society. This play concerns the psychological conflict between two students at a school for the blind. Ignacio, a new student whose reluctance to accept his blindness disrupts the school's tranquil atmosphere, is confronted by Carlos, who becomes jealous of his girlfriend's reaction to Ignacio. Carlos eventually kills Ignacio, but not before being affected by Ignacio's spirit and adopting some of his rebellious traits. Commonly interpreted as a thinly-veiled metaphor of the Spanish populace's passive acceptance of totalitarianism, this play features a moment in which the theater lights are extinguished to simulate Carlos's and, by extension, Spanish society's blindness.

Other plays in which Buero Vallejo employs similar techniques include *El sueño de la razón* (1970), *Llegada de los dioses* (1971), and *La fundación* (1974). *El sueño de la razón* is based upon Spanish artist Francisco de Goya's resistance to the tyranny of King Ferdinand VII. To dramatize Goya's deafness, Buero Vallejo's characters engage in incoherent dialogue and

use sign language or notes to communicate with the protagonist. Buero Vallejo projects Goya's famous Black Paintings at the rear of the stage to reflect the cruelty and terror Goya experienced at this time. One of Buero Vallejo's most pessimistic plays, *El sueño de la razón* is also among his most acclaimed works. In *Llegada de los dioses,* Buero Vallejo again darkens the theater so that spectators may experience the protagonist's sightlessness. A condemnation of Spain's bourgeois society, this play concerns the sudden psychological blindness of a young radical caused by his inability to reconcile his ideals with reality. In *La fundación,* Tomás, a political prisoner awaiting sentence, perceives his squalid cell to be furnished with such items as a comfortable bed, a complete bar, a telephone, and a breathtaking view of the countryside. While the audience shares Tomás's vision, the other characters attempt to convince him that he is hallucinating. As the play progresses, the luxurious elements gradually disappear, and Tomás and the audience return to reality. Throughout this work, prisoners engage in discussions on the nature of political power and oppression, concluding that even though power corrupts all who possess it, they must continue to oppose those who abuse the freedoms of others.

In all of his works, Buero Vallejo emphasizes the need to temper idealism with reality in order to solve the problems of Spanish society. His many other plays include *El concierto de*

San Ovidio (1962; *The Concert at Saint Ovide*), the story of a blind musician who rebels against exploitation by a manipulative entrepreneur; *La doble historia del Doctor Valmy* (1968), considered Buero Vallejo's most virulent attack on totalitarianism, in which a member of the Special Police is forced to assist in making a prisoner impotent and consequently becomes impotent himself; and *Caimán* (1981), in which a woman's refusal to accept her young daughter's death results in her own demise. Buero Vallejo has received numerous awards and honors for his role in the renaissance of Spanish theatre. These include the Premio Lope de Vega for *Historia de una escalera* and his inauguration into the Real Academia Española in 1972.

(See also *CLC*, Vol. 15 and *Contemporary Authors*, Vol. 106.)

WILLIAM GIULIANO

Today's heroes are sometimes tomorrow's villains, and unfortunately, to a limited extent, that is the unhappy lot of Antonio Buero Vallejo, whose play *Historia de una escalera (Story of a Staircase)* in 1949 injected new life into the stagnant Spanish theater and inspired many young dramatists to write serious plays, directly or indirectly criticizing the political, social, and economic policies of Spain. A prisoner for six and a half years, under sentence of death for eight months, Buero was released in 1946 and soon after won the Lope de Vega prize for *Historia de una escalera,* which became an instant hit. Within several years, he and another outstanding young dramatist, Alfonso Sastre, became symbols of liberal opposition to the Franco regime.

Unfortunately, the two playwrights became involved in a polemic which severed their friendship and paved the way for a gradual undermining of the reputation of Buero as a sincere exponent of Spanish liberalism. (p. 223)

The youth of Spain in Buero's early years as a dramatist rallied behind him and Sastre as bulwarks of courageous resistance against a repressive political environment. The youth of twenty years later, however, began to lose faith in Buero, thinking, as Sastre had earlier, that he had capitulated to government censorship. He encountered disfavor not only ideologically but also esthetically. He was severely criticized for persisting to use a technique which gave him, as author, full control of the text, instead of permitting greater audience participation in the manner of the Living Theater.

Although he had deliberately sought to involve the audience in his plays (as early as 1950 in *En la ardiente oscuridad (In the Burning Darkness)*), the theater lights were completely extinguished for a moment to make the audience feel the darkness of the blind protagonist), Buero refused to involve the audience actively. On seeing *Orlando Furioso*, directed by Luca Ronconi, Buero expressed his ideas on the performance. Ronconi inspired much action, he observed, but this was purely physical. Unless the spectator is spiritually as well as physically involved, such participation is purely illusive. . . . His own technique represented a striving for psycho-physical participation emphasizing the spiritual, with elements of Brecht on one hand and Beckett on the other (Brechtian *Verfremdungseffekt* and Beckett's Theater of the Absurd).

In 1970, after not having produced a play for three years, Buero presented the theater public with a drama that embodied the

principles of audience participation as he had evolved them. The play, entitled *El sueño de la razón (The Sleep of Reason)*, which was not approved by the censors for five and a half months, is based on the life of Francisco de Goya at the age of seventy-six, when, refusing to accept the tyranny of Ferdinand VII, he retired to his country home and created the famous Black Paintings. Goya was deaf at this time, and Buero skilfully makes the audience see and feel everything through his eyes. When Goya is on the stage, the other characters communicate with him by writing, gesturing or using sign language. They move their lips, but the audience does not hear them. Goya, of course, does speak. There are voices which the painter and the audience hear, but the other characters do not. Among other sounds Goya hears laughter, the howling of cats, the screeching of owls, the braying of donkeys, and the cackling of hens. Dozing off, he sees grotesque figures which attack him. Through these dramatic means, the audience feels intimately the solitude of deafness and the terrible fear which slowly grips Goya, who refuses to submit to Ferdinand by begging forgiveness for derogatory remarks made about him. Later, however, threatened by the king and his soldiers, the aged Goya finally breaks down in terror and asks father Duaso, his friend, to beg the king's forgiveness and permission to leave the country.

Buero, who had previously become more Brechtian in his estrangement technique, now identifies the spectator completely with his main character, a procedure which he declared did not necessarily prevent *Verfremdungseffekt*. Obviously Ferdinand represents the twentieth-century dictator and Goya, the liberal resister. There are references to censorship, the Holy Inquisition, and religious and political oppression. In this play, however, Buero is more pessimistic than he has ever been. The Black Paintings, which are flashed on the back of the stage, and the action of the play reflect the malice, hypocrisy, greed, cruelty, and terror which overwhelm man with only a faint ray of hope to offset their devastating effects. Goya is defeated, and the play consequently would seem to reveal the triumph of tyranny, but there is one saving grace. Father Duaso, Ferdinand's official censor, and doctor Arrieta, an avowed liberal, are hostile to each other in the beginning, but later both men forget their differences to help Goya avoid the wrath of the king, both realizing that they must mitigate the undue violence that is an integral part of both factions. These two characters may symbolize the opposing sides of the Spanish Civil War, both of which must suppress extreme elements to effect a peaceful synthesis.

This play has been one of Buero's most widely acclaimed. It was performed in Italy, Russia, East and West Germany, Czechoslovakia, Hungary, Rumania, and other countries, and although it was a triumph at home as well as abroad, the youth who had criticized Buero before continued to do so.

Undoubtedly a desire to answer his youthful critics motivated the writing of the next play, *Llegada de los dioses (Arrival of the gods)*, produced in 1971. In it Julio, a young painter, suddenly becomes blind for one of two reasons which the author deliberately leaves open to question: the first, Julio learns that his father, [Felipe], years before, had been a member of the military and tortured prisoners; the second, several days later, immediately after Julio's exhibition has met heartbreaking failure, his father, who is an amateur painter, informs him of the great success of his own exhibition. (pp. 224-25)

As in *El sueño de la razón*, the action is seen through the eyes of the protagonist, Julio. When Julio enters the stage for the first time, the stage becomes totally dark. A spotlight is focused on him, then on Artemio, his father's best friend. Artemio has horns protruding from his head: the sign of the cuckold, since his wife, Matilde, who appears with the head of a fox, has been deceiving him with Felipe, who appears with smoked glasses. These and many other stage effects are used to make the audience see everything from Julio's point of view.

Julio represents the young well-to-do Spanish radical who likes to talk about revolution but does nothing concrete while he still enjoys the benefits of what he considers his father's ill-gotten wealth. . . . When his father dies, Julio recognizes his own shortcomings. He had considered himself a "god" come to right wrongs, but now he realizes that he is merely a sick person in a sick world, and other gods (other young people) more sincerely dedicated must come to purify society.

Angel Fernández Santos, in his review of the play, finds the stage effects unnaturally superimposed on the action in contrast to the brilliant integration of effects and action in *El sueño de la razón,* and he declares that *Llegada de los dioses* "has justified his [Buero's] many detractors." He also criticizes the structure of the play, declaring that Buero merely poses questions without coherent development. In an interview with the same Angel Fernández Santos, Buero clarifies the significance of the role of Julio. . . . Buero explains that Julio represents only a segment of Spanish youth. . . . [He is] still tainted by the bourgeois world in which . . . [he lives], and Julio's rebellion may be caused more by his failure as a painter than by his horror at his father's black deeds. Finally, Buero affirms that his play is a condemnation of the bourgeois society of Spain and concludes: "I do not attempt, therefore, to bring out the deficiencies of an apparently rebellious young man in order to justify the actions of his parents but I do try to study his deficiencies in confrontation with his parents who are not all in the right and who, in part, are the cause of these deficiencies."

Obviously *Llegada de los dioses* did not endear Buero to the hearts of the younger generation, nor did his inauguration into the Real Academia Española (Royal Spanish Academy) in May 1972 (he had been elected early in 1971). This acceptance of an honor closely related to the Establishment put Buero on the defensive from another quarter. Some labeled it a surrender to the forces of conservatism, but Buero's friends of long standing did not desert him. Francisco García Pavón, the noted critic and novelist, defended him in an article approving Buero's decision to accept the honor. He excoriates those who remain in Spain but maintain silence and those who fled the country. Buero, he says, has had the courage to stay in Spain and speak his mind, using symbols imposed by circumstance (obviously censorship), but nevertheless speaking out. Emilio Gascó Contell also supported Buero, declaring that this unexpected honor was totally unforeseen but clearly earned. (pp. 226-27)

As usual, Buero delayed a long time in preparing his next play, *La fundación (The Foundation),* for performance in Madrid in 1974. The action of this play takes place in the jail where Tomás and other political prisoners await sentence. Again we have audience participation in the Buerian sense. The spectators see the cell as Tomás sees it, with nice beds, fine glassware, a good bar with drinks, a telephone, et cetera. The other prisoners do not see these things. They are all a dream world created by Tomás to escape reality—the reality of having betrayed his fellow revolutionaries. Asel, the eldest of the prisoners, slowly brings Tomás back to reality. The luxuries imagined by Tomás disappear one by one until he finally realizes

his true situation. Asel has been trying to get them transferred to a punishment cell by behaving improperly, but they are not removed. When Max is called out, Asel tells Tomás and Lino of a plan to escape from the punishment cell to the outside. They suspect that Max has told the authorities of their wish to be transferred. Their suspicions are confirmed. Asel is called for execution, and while the door is open, Lino, in retaliation, hurls Max over a railing to his death. Tomás and Lino are ordered to pack their belongings. They know that they are going to be executed or taken to the punishment cell. Tomás, who had opposed Asel's plan to escape, is now inspired by Asel's words and actions to declare that he will try to escape if taken to the cell.

Asel summarizes the main theme of the play when he tells the others that they live in a violent world in which men are killed for fighting injustice, for belonging to a particular race or religious creed, a world in which even children are killed and maimed by napalm bombs (reference to Vietnam?). Even they, the oppressed, may become the oppressor. He tells Tomás: "This time we are the victims, my poor Tomás, but I tell you something . . . I prefer it so. If I should save my life perhaps someday I would be the hangman." In spite of this, Asel continues, they must keep fighting in order to stop all atrocities and oppression. They should, however, try to distinguish between justifiable cruelty and unjustified violence, a difficult procedure because the enemy makes no distinction (Part I).

In his review of the play, Miguel Bilbatúa criticizes Buero for being unspecific about the political society he is portraying and for being ambiguous: "Some will say it [the play] is a marvel in being able to avoid the obstacles of censorship, others will say it is a fine example of how to swim and keep your clothes dry." According to Bilbatúa, Buero is evidently telling us that violence will always exist and the oppressed will be the oppressors when they come to power. This interpretation, however, would seem to be based on the speech of Asel quoted above without reference to the limitations he added immediately after. Angel Fernández Santos also finds that the play is subject to varying, even diametrically opposed, interpretations, but calls it one of Buero's most daring works in which the author is playing with fire.

The apparent paradox—the resort to oppression by the oppressed come to power—is the inevitable result of a world steeped in hatred, evil, and cruelty, and even though a revolutionary must also have recourse to cruelty, he must seek to control his natural inclination to violence, continue the fight for freedom, and strive to establish the rights of man. This is the lesson taught Tomás by Asel. (pp. 228-29)

It is clear that Buero has lost favor with many of those with whom he wished to be associated, and in particular with the younger generation. We ask ourselves why this has come about; and this writer finds a number of reasons for it. The young who have not known the horrors of the Civil War resent the lack of political freedom and feel the urge to act—hence the constant student demonstrations that have closed the universities so many times for so long. They do not understand that an author cannot do individually what they do collectively. To write exactly what he thinks is impossible—a rigid censorship determines every single work to be published, every line an actor can speak. The censors sometimes license plays that are very critical of the regime, but performances are limited to one night stands and university functions, or they are otherwise restricted. Thus, this type of play is usually seen only by those who are already in sympathy with the author's views. In order to receive a license for the commercial theater which will give him the widest audience, an author must resort to subterfuge if he wishes to be critical of conditions in Spain. Buero usually does this by choosing a well-known story or a well-known figure from the past as the basis for a play in which the discerning spectator easily perceives an analogy to conditions in the present. He does this so effectively that even the members of the society he is attacking find his plays so different, so artistically superior to run-of-the-mill commercial drama, that they welcome and praise each new one. (pp. 230-31)

La doble historia del doctor Valmy should silence many of Buero's detractors. The granting of a license by the censors astonishes this writer, for this play is unquestionably Buero's most virulent, direct attack on the police state. In it Daniel Barnes, a member of the Special Police, is engaged in torturing prisoners. One day he is forced to assist in making a prisoner permanently impotent. From then on he cannot fulfill his sexual obligations with his wife. He consults Doctor Valmy, who narrates the story to the audience. The doctor informs Barnes that he feels guilty for having deprived the prisoner of his virility and consequently has annihilated his own desires in punishment. Daniel's wife, Mary, who had not known of his torture activities, is horrified. Daniel tries to resign, but he is not permitted to do so. Mary believes he does not wish to resign, and one day she seizes his pistol and tells him not to come near her. He does approach her, and she kills him. The other case history is that of The Gentleman and The Lady, neighbors of the Barneses, who occasionally interrupt the action to tell the audience that the Barnes story is false. They represent the guilty who refuse to see repression and consequently do nothing about it.

This brief outline is enough to reveal the play as a powerful indictment of dictatorship. Intensely dramatic, it moves rapidly and smoothly from one scene to another without the interruption of a curtain. It is Brechtian in technique and one of Buero's best plays. Certainly if Buero has compromised his principles, he would not permit the performance of this play. It will be interesting to assess the reaction to it. If nothing else, *La doble historia del doctor Valmy* should inspire respect for a man who has suffered much to play his part in restoring the dignity of man and who has steadfastly and courageously been true to himself. (pp. 231-32)

William Giuliano, "The Defense of Buero Vallejo," in Modern Drama, *Vol. 20, No. 3, September, 1977, pp. 223-33.*

JAMES R. STAMM

The theater of Antonio Buero Vallejo . . . is the most innovating and varied dramatic product of the 1950s and 60s. In terms of theme, scenic effect, and originality of presentation, Buero stands out among his contemporaries as a writer of subtle and imaginative sensibility. . . . His first work, *Historia de una escalera (History of a Staircase)*, was produced in Madrid in 1949 with enormous success. Here, the lives of lower-middle class families are interwoven, with their frustrations, rivalries, and very limited hopes of bettering their economic conditions. Buero says nothing directly about the war or politics, but the implications of social injustice which reduce a generation to poverty and very limited personal horizons are clear. Two major plays deal with the blind: *En la ardiente oscuridad (In the Burning Darkness)* and *El concierto de San Ovidio (The Concert of Saint Ovid)*. In the first, the dramatic tension is generated from within the group of sightless inmates of an asylum for the blind; in the second, a small band of blind musicians is victimized by an unscrupulous promoter who exhibits them as a curiosity, as if they were trained seals. The metaphor of sightlessness is clear and perhaps oversimple. A group of people handicapped by lack of vision and the inability to organize their own lives are in one way or another victimized and frustrated by their limitations; an obvious and ironic parallel to the situation of a majority of the population of post-Civil War Spain.

Buero develops another system of metaphor in a series of biographical historical plays. In *Las Meninas*—the title is that of a major work of the painter Diego Velázquez—he dramatizes a critical episode in the life of the great baroque artist. Velázquez has painted a nude Venus, against the prohibitions of the Inquisition, and also, according to envious courtiers, portrayed members of the royal family as simple human beings rather than as glorified and majestic figures. Finally, after striking blows for human and artistic freedom and dignity, the play ends with the exoneration of the artist and his restoration to the king's favor. *El sueño de la razon* deals with the later years of the painter Francisco Goya, and takes its title from one of the master's etchings. The action takes place in the most degraded period in the reign of Fernando VII, a period of terror, torture, dynastic absolutism and foreign support of a tyrant. Goya, aged, deaf, and fatally ill, becomes a target for the vindictiveness of a reign which, having no popular support, vents its rage on all non-conformists: painters and writers and liberal politicians alike. Buero calls upon his extraordinary gifts as a scenarist to give great visual presence, with lights, projections of the most horrific paintings of Goya's "black period," and rapid shifts between the royal palace and the painter's studio in the outskirts of Madrid, to the rapid and violent movement of the action. Goya's deafness is an integral part of the play. When the elderly painter is on stage, the other actors speak in growls, squawks, and the cackling of hens; a totally incomprehensible cacophony, as the deaf Goya might have heard their speech. When the painter is absent, the actors speak clearly and in normal tones. Buero's political metaphor goes farther here, to tell us that a period of desperate tyranny and senseless, terrified repression can only result in injustice, pointless social paralysis, and total incommunication with the most civilizing and creative forces of the epoch. Buero's critics point out that, in these historical plays, he often exaggerates events, distorts history, and makes up characters and situations which have no historical foundation. The author replies with a shrug; he is writing plays, not textbooks, and is more concerned with generalities of human experience than with historical detail.

El tragaluz departs from historical biography to present a confusing futuristic survey of contemporary problems. Two "beings" from the twenty-second century appear on stage and announce that the audience will see a recreation of a problem from the twentieth century. The problem is one of contemporary middle-class melodrama. An unscrupulous parvenu is making a great deal of money in questionable and chancy business transactions, and having an affair with his secretary. His younger brother has an idealistic repulsion for the shadier aspects of his brother's wheeling and dealing, and supports himself minimally through some translation and proof-reading for his brother's publishing house. The key character—and he is a marvelous realization—is the senile, half-insane father of the two men. The old man spends his days cutting out figures from magazines and postcards, wondering who these strange people are, convinced that he has seen or known them somewhere, sometime. The play comes to a thundering conclusion when the father stabs the entrepreneur son with his ever-ready scissors, aware at last that the son has caused the death of a younger sister during the war years. The inevitable melodramatic touch is added when the idealistic proof-reader son decides to marry the pregnant mistress of his adventurous brother to save her from the street.

In all of Buero's work there is an irreducible element of soap-opera, of melodrama and the gimmick. *El tragaluz*—the title refers to the street-level windows which illuminate one of the interior sets—infuriates the sophisticated spectator because its flaws could be so easily remedied with a bit more taste and maturity of concept. Yet his dialogue is excellent, if a bit slow moving, his creation of dramatic character is very solid, and his sense of what will play scenically is outstanding. His painter's vision never fails him in the use of space and light, but his timing is poor. Speeches are often too long and carry too much message, too little feeling. Usually the message is obvious from the outset: he is talking about repression and social injustice, and the conditions of post-war Spain make it necessary for him to speak his piece from a temporal distance and in a historical or masked context. Buero's choice of heroes, the blind, the deaf, and in *La doble historia del Dr. Valmy,* the sexually impotent, make it clear that he sees around him a deformed and incapacitated society, capable now and then of joy, but ordained to battle against crushing social pressures. (pp. 226-30)

> *James R. Stamm, "Spain in the Twentieth Century," in his* A Short History of Spanish Literature, *revised edition, New York University Press, 1979, pp. 201-62.*

HANNA GELDRICH-LEFFMAN

Blindness is one of the recurring themes in the work of the contemporary Spanish playwright Antonio Buero Vallejo. He sees the mission of the writer as that of the conscience of his society, and the unifying purpose of his own writings as that of opening eyes ("el de abrir los ojos"). His theater has been characterized as one of basically tragic orientation. His heroes are agonizing characters, who show man's pain and suffering in this world and who end in apparent defeat, while their ideas often live on and offer hope to future generations. . . . As Buero Vallejo says, tragedies are expressions of a faith which doubts; the ultimate and major moral effect of a tragedy is that of an act of faith. For him tragedies are animated by a subtle religious spirit and the deaths of their heroes have the characteristics of sacred sacrifices. Thus his heroes very often show characteristics of sacrificial victims, whose search for truth and understanding lead them into conflict with society and very often into death, a death that nevertheless offers possibilities of redemption for others in the future. (pp. 678-79)

The search for truth is the central preoccupation of Buero Vallejo's theater. Very often this search is expressed in symbols of light and darkness, vision and blindness. Therefore, blind characters play a central role in his theater as symbols of human blindness confronting life and its problems and their own nature and destiny and the concomitant search for light and illumination. Some critics have called Oedipus the "prototype of the tragic protagonist of Buero's theater." (pp. 679-80)

For the blind critic Jean-Paul Borel, blindness is the symbol of man's tragic solitude, his loneliness. On the other hand for some of Buero Vallejo's characters blindness is not a negative quality, but provides a deeper insight and a deeper sensitivity and is therefore likened to the figure of Tiresias. Thus, we can see the two sides of the image: on the one side blindness as evil, as the absence of knowledge, truth and life; but also on the other side as the truest and deepest knowledge attained by only a few, the victim figures and the seers. (p. 680)

In *En la ardiente oscuridad* (1950) and *El concierto de San Ovidio* (1962) the blind are the central characters of the play; in *La llegada de los dioses* (1971) it is the blindness of the protagonist Julio, which is the central theme; even in some of his other plays, blind characters appear. In *La tejedora de sueños* (1952) it is the old nursemaid, Euriclea, who will be the only one to perceive the coming of the furies, the mysteries lurking behind the apparent realities to which the other characters are blind. Buero Vallejo himself noted the parallelism to Tiresias. In *Las Meninas* (1960) it is the half-blind Pedro Briones, the only friend of Velázquez, who "sees" and understands not only his paintings but also the true reality of the crisis of Spanish society. At the end he dies at the hands of the authorities, one of Buero Vallejo's victim figures. In *Un Soñador para un pueblo* (1958) it is the figure of the old blind man who sells papers and Piscator's forecasts for the year who has the double function of the choir in Greek tragedy, to announce a date and to foretell the future. Blindness in these minor figures is associated with an oracle; it is the tool to see deeper and further, to go beyond appearances. A similar role is also assigned to principal characters in some of his other plays.

In *En la ardiente oscuridad* all the main characters are blind, and the action itself takes place in a special school for the blind. Into this tranquil world of blind students who have accepted their blindness comes the rebel Ignacio, who cannot and does not want to conform and to accept his situation of a life without sight. He tries to show the other students the lie of their existence and to make them aspire to something better, to something beyond. Ignacio tries to bring them hope, the hope of light, but Carlos, the representative of the students from the school, rejects this hope. A situation of conflict arises between the idealist and dreamer, Ignacio, and the practical conformist, Carlos. It is a conflict over a woman, Juana, loved by both, but also over an idea. Ignacio, talking to Juana, accuses them of living a lie and contrasts their cold conformity with his ardent crusading spirit. He sees himself as a saviour figure; Carlos, on the other hand, calls him "un mesiánico desequilibrado" who yearns for death. Carlos presents himself as the defender of life, but it is a life based on falsehood and thus necessarily sterile and leading to death. The conflict between the two ends tragically with the death of Ignacio at the hands of Carlos. Yet it is a death that brings hope, for Ignacio had been able to transmit his ideas to the reluctant Carlos, whose speech at the end of the play uses almost the same words Ignacio used earlier. So truth has finally been "seen" and accepted by Carlos, and the medium of language used throughout the play by him and by the school to obscure this truth can now finally shine forth in its true purpose as the revealer of truth in the same way as Ignacio intended.

Buero Vallejo was not admittedly concerned so much with the social message of the situation of the physically blind; he wanted the play interpreted symbolically to call attention to the spiritual blindness in all of us. The blind students can be seen as ". . . man in general, who has created a world in his own image and likeness, [and] Ignacio [as] the mystic who brings to them the message of a transcendent world to which most men are spiritually blind." Theirs is a world of falsehood, based on a lie, constructed according to an order that gives refuge and permits

its inhabitants to live in peace, but the peace is based on the fiction of apparent normalcy. The students are also a symbol of what, in today's political systems, we call "the silent majority," which is the basis of many of these systems: a majority of satisfied, untroubled, and not to be troubled citizens. Ignacio, on the other hand, is a man of despair and of immense hope. He is a rebel bringing war, the sword, who hopes for the impossible and whose words open the eyes of the others to their limitations; they now know that they are blind and long for the light.

The main themes are the search for self-realization, for the truth about oneself and about the world, and man's constant Faustian striving. The individual may fail in his quest, but he is saved because he was able to establish a relationship with the other who can take up the fight and convert it into a reality; in this way, Buero Vallejo gives us an example of his version of tragic hope. (pp. 680-82)

A similar theme is presented in Buero Vallejo's other drama in which the blind play the central roles, *El concierto de San Ovidio*. The action takes place in 1771 in Paris during the time of Louis XV and is based partially on an historical occurrence. A group of blind men, grotesquely dressed to attract the public, are made to give concerts by a man called Luis María Valindín, who shamelessly exploits them. One of the blind, David, rebels against this attack on their human dignity, but the rest of the group does not follow him. He can accomplish his purpose only by killing Valindín, and eventually he is hanged for his deed. The historical figure of Valentín Haüy, founder of an institute for the education of the blind and inventor of raised type writing, later perfected by Braille, is shown as being inspired to his humanitarian work by the sorry spectacle of this orchestra in this play.

Although the emphasis here seems to rest on the social implications, the blind representing an example of the oppression exercised by the strong on the weak, there is a parallel between this play and *En la ardiente oscuridad*. We are shown a picture of a corrupt society, where for Valindín the other is a being that can be manipulated, that can serve simply as an object. His attitude toward the blind is expressed in his scornful "¿Qué sabe un ciego? ¡Nada!", and later when David rebels against the role of fools that Valindín assigns them, he says: "Ciegos, lisiados, que no merecéis vivir!" It is in the role of David that the parallel to the previous drama becomes more pronounced. He has been compared to Ignacio, as a dreamer yet a man of action, a man of unshakable faith, whose struggle represents the conflict between free will and necessity. Not only does David rebel against the role society assigns the blind, but also, he, like Ignacio, is a man in search of light, truth, knowledge, as the only means to set man free. (pp. 682-83)

The play *La llegada de los dioses* has been seen as a reelaboration of the myth of Oedipus, with the figures of both Oedipus and Tiresias contributing important aspects to it. Julio, the young painter, has become blind after learning from the son of one of the victims who had died after becoming blind, that his own father, also a painter, was in the secret police during the war and tortured prisoners. Julio's blindness has been diagnosed as psychological by several specialists. It represents perhaps Julio's way of expiating the sins of his father. But, since his blindness, he has become more perceptive, he "sees" more than the others: "Veo mejor desde que he cegado," he says to Verónica, his mistress, who has come to help him and show her true love. Blindness has given him the insight to see behind the façades of the lies of middle class insincerities, the lies that cover up the dark past of his father and the dark side of society, a society bent to destroy itself through wars, bombs, and pollution of its resources. But blindness has also given Julio a faculty, like that of Tiresias, to see into the future, a faculty that frightens and disturbs him. However, Julio is also Oedipus seeking the truth without knowing *what* truth he is seeking. The relationship with his father is one of conflicting antagonism and love. One critic has pointed out that his blindness in this relationship has several meanings: he wants to expiate his father's sins, but at the same time he also imposes a punishment on his father and rejects the world of his father, a world of wars, violence, materialism, and insincerities. But he is also unable to accept his father as he really is, and he is unable to accept his own love and hatred for his father. He is not yet ready to see what Verónica tries to show him, that perhaps it is also his own failure as a painter, this complex of artistic castration, which made him go blind. He is not yet ready to see inside himself and to accept his own limitations and insecurities. Only at the end will he understand and have the courage to face ambiguities and contradictions, that is to face life and go towards it courageously with the help of Verónica. (pp. 684-85)

Although she clearly stands for truth or the search for truth, [Verónica's] own validity and truthfulness are doubted by Julio, who questions her loyalty, and, again in the Freudian Oedipal sense, imagines her abandoning him for his father, Felipe. It is during the scene of jealousy that his eye-sight returns. (p. 686)

But sight also brings temptations, especially for the artist; the temptation of beauty and with it the temptation of giving up insight for sight. And again it is Verónica who understands: "Se puede ver sin olvidar".

The catalyst of the drama is Nuria, a girl of fifteen, the goddaughter of Felipe, who turns out to be his daughter, fruit of an illicit love-affair between him and Matilde. She will be the innocent victim, destroyed by the collision of the opposing forces whose death will bring the resolution of the tragic conflict. The threat of incest noticed by Verónica is not accepted by Felipe even though the innocent love of Nuria for Julio might in time turn into an incestuous love. Julio's proclamation of the truth about Nuria's relationship to Felipe brings only a denial from him. But later when Nuria dies in an accident (an explosion when the jumper given her as a present by Felipe strikes a buried grenade left over from the war), Felipe's anguish explodes into the truth, a truth that cannot be hidden anymore: "Es mi hija!" But it is too late, and this truth also kills the father, who collapses after a heart-attack.

Just as hearing the truth about his father's violent past apparently caused his first blindness, now the admission of Felipe's sexual guilt blinds Julio again, and darkness surrounds him. The second and final blinding has been seen as a punishment for Julio's almost succumbing to the temptation of his father's world. But it coincides also with Julio's attainment of understanding about himself: "Yo te amaba . . . Y vine a matarte". So knowledge does not bring certitude but only points to the ambiguity of truth, life and blindness. Julio, who is very much in need of help now, will finally seek it from the one who had offered it all along, from Verónica. . . . (pp. 686-87)

Just as *El concierto de San Ovidio,* this play also presents a social critique, an accusation against capitalistic society, against war and torture; it urges the transformation of man as the only possible solution. But again, as do all of Buero Vallejo's plays, it really centers around the problems of man himself. (p. 687)

In all the plays of Buero Vallejo discussed above, the figures of Oedipus and Tiresias embody the central preoccupation of the author and point to the basic meaning of blindness. In the three major plays death is the necessary reality that effects the resolution of the conflicts. Only after the death of the victim is insight attained by the "other" or by society. In *En la ardiente oscuridad* Carlos accepts his reality only after killing Ignacio; in *El concierto de San Ovidio* Valindín's death frees the blind from the oppression of society and sets the stage for Haüy's reforms; and in *La llegada de los dioses* Nuria's death leads to Felipe's admission and thus to the attainment of insight by Julio. In each case neither victim nor "killer" is wholly innocent, nor wholly guilty, not even the almost-child Nuria, tainted already by her world through her love for her brother. All this serves to show the existence in tragedy of what Girard calls the "concept of alternation," the presence of both good and evil in each character, so that neither extreme has a hold but represents one part of the "double" and its expression of mimetic rivalry.

In this connection, a progression in the plays of Buero Vallejo can be noted in that the conflict, the mimetic rivalry, is embodied visually in two antagonists opposing each other over the figure of a woman: Juana and Adriana respectively in the two first plays, while in the last play, although the mimetic rivalry is exteriorized between father and son possibly also partially over a woman, Verónica, and the possibility of incest looms as a threat, the antagonistic forces are basically both housed in Julio. And even though the "evil" of blindness, much more prominent in *En la ardiente oscuridad* and *El concierto de San Ovidio* is not denied here, physical sight is equated with blindness to the realities of this world, whereas only physical blindness offers possibilities for real insight and thus salvation. (pp. 688-89)

Hanna Geldrich-Leffman, "Vision and Blindness in Dürrenmatt, Buero Vallejo and Lenz," in MLN, *Vol. 97, No. 3, April, 1982, pp. 671-93.*

MARTHA HALSEY

The tragic theater of Buero Vallejo presents us with images of hope for the future. Through the revolutionary force of his art, the playwright helps us to understand and assess, not only a reality that already exists, but a reality that may someday be. Prophet and seer, he anticipates and helps render this new world possible through his craft. Conscious of the fact that it is not enough to denounce the ills of the present—because peace, for example, is not the same as the absence of war—Buero creates positive images or symbols of the reality he envisions. These images often take the form of idealized landscapes, imagined, or perhaps glimpsed, by his dreamer-protagonists. These landscapes, suggested verbally in the earlier plays but depicted visually in more recent works such as *La Fundación* (1974) and *Caimán* (1981), are a means of leading us to identify with the point of view of his characters, of immersing us in the future heralded by his romantic visionaries.

Buero's first use of a landscape to suggest an ideal is seen in *Aventura en lo gris* (1963), one of the very earliest plays he wrote. Silvano, a history professor in an imaginary country defeated in war, describes his recurrent dream of peace to his companions in a refugee shelter. . . . However, the end of the drama sees the arrival of enemy soldiers with machine guns rather than Silvano's smiling angels. (p. 252)

In *La Fundación* and *Caimán,* as in *Aventura,* an idealized landscape functions clearly as an image of hope. In these two more recent works, however, the role of this landscape assumes a much greater importance, becoming the key to the meaning of the dramas and to Buero's dialectical vision of reality. At the beginning of *La Fundación,* we find ourselves in what we are led to believe is an elegant research center for writers and scientists. . . . Rainbow-hued morning light, which seems somewhat unreal, floods the room. The "Pastoral" from Rossini's romantic "Overture to William Tell," is heard as the protagonist, Tomás, contemplates the vista beyond the window. This music becomes associated with the idyllic landscape. Tomás compares the purity of its melody to the fresh cool of dawn, when the sun first appears, and expresses his pleasure at listening to it on such a radiant morning, when the countryside with its green forests and silver lake sparkle like jewels. The serene "Pastoral," with its English horn melody echoed by the flute, seems, in fact, to suggest such a delightful scene. (p. 253)

There comes a moment, however, when Tomás—and the audience—guided by skillful questions of the former's companion, Asel, begin to become increasingly conscious of the strangeness of his landscape, with its dazzling light that falls constantly from the same direction, morning, afternoon, and even night. Finally, Tomás and the audience see the landscape darken and even disappear, along with the music. Indeed, its disappearance is the last in an extensive series of changes undergone by the set. Fine crystal, silver, linens, television, stereo, as well as other comfortable, even luxurious furnishings of the "Foundation," and finally, the picture window and vista vanish one by one until, at the end, we find ourselves, not in the pleasant room of a research center, but in a squalid prison cell whose inhabitants are political dissidents condemned to death.

Incapable of facing this situation, Tomás has rejected reality. He suffers, it becomes obvious, a type of schizophrenic delusion. Since we see reality through his eyes and thus identify with him, we too become victims of a delusion; however, when we share, also, in his return to lucidity, our experience results in a clearer understanding of our own situation. When the set has been dismantled, when Tomás' fictitious world has crumbled and reality has emerged, we see our own world for what it is and always has been. Asel's words, after Tomás has returned to lucidity, represent a counterimage to the illusion of the "Foundation," whose scholars Tomás believed he saw strolling among its pavilions, laughing beneath the morning sun. The former's words . . . [describe] a "civilized" world where the favorite sport is the ancient practice of human slaughter, where people are beheaded, starved, shot, and condemned by secret tribunals for reasons of race, religion, or politics, and where even children are burned and mutilated. The result, Asel states, has been rivers of blood throughout the ages. "El mundo no es tu paisaje," he tells Tomás, "está en manos de la rapiña, de la mentira, de la opresión."

Nevertheless, Asel's conviction is that this world can be made as beautiful as Tomás saw it in his delusion. . . . Through Asel—an author surrogate—Buero expresses his hope for a better future which, even though glimpsed only through the eyes of delusion, may become reality. Hope is thus much more explicit here than in the preceding dramas, although the conclusion of none is closed.

In the dialectical process depicted metaphorically by the drama, the reality of the prison vanquishes the imaginary "Foundation.'' Nevertheless, the ideal symbolized by the luminous . . . landscape remains. Our strength is that we can maintain our vision in the face of the worst type of adversity. . . . Buero enables the spectators to share this ideal through the most extended effect of interiorization or ''immersion'' in the plays presently under consideration.

The ''immersion'' effects in these dramas enable the audience to share certain sensory perceptions of his protagonists that are not perceived by the other characters. . . . [We] hear the Rossini ''Pastoral'' and see the ''Foundation'' with the marvelous view that Tomás imagines during most of the drama. The ''immersion'' technique lends itself to an increasingly subjective theater in which Buero utilizes more extensively the view point of his protagonists, enabling us to better share their vision.

At the end of the drama, the music and the fictitious landscape appear once again as new occupants—who obviously include the spectators—are invited to enter the comfortable room. If we believe that the ''Foundation'' and the landscape already exist, we are as deluded as Tomás, who thought the future already his. If, however, we accept the landscape as the idealized image of a liberated world we ourselves must create, this final vision can sustain us. (pp. 253-54)

The water garden envisioned by Rosa of *Caimán* is no less real, Buero suggests, than the . . . landscape seen by Tomás. Rosa's fantastic garden is the hallucination of a poor woman driven to insanity by the loss of her daughter, just as Tomás' lake and mountains are the product of his delusion. This garden becomes associated with the reproduction of one of Monet's large *Water Lilies* that occupies a prominent place on the wall of Rosa's apartment. We shall see that, despite her mental unbalance, Rosa, like Tomás, is the bearer of Buero's message and that the playwright's purpose is to bring us to share her vision.

Like Tomás, Rosa refuses to accept reality, in this case, the death of her eight year old daughter, Carmela, who fell into an opening to the sewer left in a construction site that had been abandoned as the result of a real estate swindle. For Carmela and her friends who played there, the site, in the poor neighborhood where they live on outskirts of Madrid, was a storybook palace or garden. Unlike Tomás, Rosa, at least initially, knows what the real facts are, even though she rejects them. Nevertheless, since the body of her daughter was never found, she desperately hopes, each time knocks are heard at the door, that it is Carmela. (p. 255)

The significance of the Monet water landscape becomes clear when Rosa explains the legend of the cayman, the subject of a play she is writing. This piece is to be performed by the children of the neighborhood center where Rosa directs dramas as part of her and her husband's efforts to bring culture to the neighborhood. In the Indian legend, an ancient chief, swallowed by a cayman, calls out to his son to save him and is rescued unharmed. Rosa believes that, in the same way, her daughter will rescue her from the jaws that entrap her and her poor neighbors—the jaws of poverty, exploitation, and preparation for nuclear war. For such is the sad reality Buero's drama depicts. . . . The Monet garden, painted as the world darkened with war and as the artist's eyesight dimmed, celebrates and renders eternal the beauty of earth, presenting an innocent, fresh vision that approaches music and poetry. The ''fusion of realism and lyricism'' that characterizes the *Water Lilies* sequence makes the painting quite appropriate for Buero's purpose, given the poetic nature of *Caimán*. The painting,

with its beauty that is both plastic and ideal, is used to suggest the better world Rosa envisions. Like Tomás' Turner landscape, it is an image of utopia. Whereas Dionisio pretends, for his own selfish reasons, to believe that Rosa's fantasies are possible, Néstor insists that she can escape only through her own efforts, for example her work with the neighborhood center. Her mission is to live for those other children who need her. Utopia, he suggests, can be realized not through impossible dreams but through action.

As in *La Fundación,* it is the counterimage that vanquishes the imaginary garden, although the ideal remains. *Caimán* is a denunciation of various problems of Spain in the early 1980's: the economic crisis that brought increasing unemployment, political instability, social injustice, and exploitation by the powerful, as well as delinquency, street violence and terrorism. All of these problems affect the lives of Rosa and her neighbors, as the consequences of the real estate scandal demonstrate. Buero depicts a society that, in one critic's words, ''grita desde la entraña del caimán por la salvación.'' This counterimage is seen most clearly when Rosa hears a young girl's voice calling for help from the abandoned building site. It turns out that the voice belongs, not to Carmela, as Rosa hoped, but to a young girl from her theater who is being raped. It is this experience, together with Rosa's trip to the morgue to view a badly decomposed body found in the sewers that Néstor insists is their daughter's, that marks the beginning of the disillusionment that destroys her, ''la invasora sustitución del jardín fantástico por un cielo negro''.

Rosa's refusal or inability to accept reality leads, finally, to her death. As Néstor insists that the corroded buckle on the shoe of the unidentifiable child in the morgue was Carmela's, it becomes obvious to Rosa that she can expect no help from either Néstor nor Dionisio in searching the supposed underground antinuclear shelters where she now imagines her daughter to be. The dialectical struggle between Rosa's fantasies and the remaining bit of sanity she preserves is suggested by an ''immersion'' effect. As she imagines her daughter alive, the blue lights appear, Carmela's voice speaks to her suggesting that she is coming through the blue garden to meet her mother, and first the girl's photograph and later the Monet painting radiate a strange brilliance. Then, as Néstor suggests that Rosa must live with the truth of Carmela's death, a reproduction, on the wall, of Max Ernst's *The Obscure Gods* begins to gleam. Despite its bright blue and other colors which radiate in the darkness, the painting, with its strange bird figures is disturbing, suggesting the sense of horrible foreboding produced, in Rosa's mind, by Néstor's words. However, it is Rosa's hopes and fantasies that finally prevail as mysterious flashes of light turn the apartment into a sparkling diamond. Shortly thereafter, when Néstor and Dionisio realize that Rosa has escaped to the construction site to look for Carmela, to find the marvelous garden where she believes her daughter awaits her, it is too late.

Rosa's refusal to accept reality, like Tomás', is shown to be a grave error. Néstor, the union activist and political militant who, like Asel of *La Fundación,* has spent years in prison and who now leads his neighbors in their demonstrations on behalf of social justice, explains that the legend of the cayman is poetry, not reality, that it exalts the impossible. (pp. 255-56)

Néstor, who works actively to build a better world, thus represents hope for the future. The narrator states that he was only an insignificant individual but that it is to persons like him that we owe our strength. Without them, the cayman would have devoured us long ago. . . . (p. 256)

[With *Caimán,* the playwright restates a conviction present in each of the plays under consideration:] the need for dreams. We must dream of a better world, but without deluding ourselves into believing that it already exists or thinking it can be achieved without a concerted, sustained effort in solidarity with others. Such are the errors of Tomás and Rosa.

To realize our dreams, it is necessary to create positive images that can sustain us. This is what Buero does in his tragic theater. In opposition to a twentieth-century landscape of war, prison, torture, violence, and exploitation, he creates aesthetic landscapes of the imagination in order to both provoke in us a consciousness of the imperfections of our own society and to inspire hope for its future transformation. The importance of such a creative act is seen in the last play, when the narrator states that the only justification for her life is having authored a work called *Caimán.* These words undoubtedly reflect a conviction held by Buero himself.

In Buero's dialectical theater the conclusion is always left open; hope remains, for the audience if not for the characters. The beautiful landscapes of the future seen in *La Fundación* and *Caimán* are real even if they exist so far only in dreams or on the painter's canvas. Buero has spoken recently of his own convictions in this regard, his own "esperanza irrevocable en la sociedad liberada que simboliza el ficticio paisaje que cree ver Tomás." The politics of theater is a politics of imagination. Buero imagines or envisions this better society; however, he does not provide any particular solutions or answers as to how it may be achieved. His plays thus transcend the limitations of any particular ideology. He postulates the possibility—if not always the probability—of the ultimate realization of our dreams. However, this realization rarely occurs on stage. Rather it depends upon the spectators whom the playwright, both visionary and realist, seeks to move through the images he creates. Of course hope is present implicitly in all Buero's plays that denounce the ills of our world, even those that present no such images. If it were not for a world that might be, it would be futile to condemn the world that is. (p. 257)

Martha Halsey, "'Landscapes of the Imagination: Images of Hope in the Theater of Buero Vallejo'," in Hispania, *Vol. 68, No. 2, May, 1985, pp. 252-59.*

Andrei Codrescu

1946-

(Has also written under pseudonyms of Betty Laredo, Tristan Tzara, and Urmuz) Rumanian-born American poet, memoirist, editor, and journalist.

Codrescu writes spare, forthright poetry noted for its exacting language and imagery and playful, irreverent wit. His subject matter is largely autobiographical, often consisting of recollections of his youth in communist Rumania and his experiences as an expatriate living in Rome, Paris, and the United States. Codrescu eschews polemic in favor of a self-denigrating, mock-revolutionary pose and a disillusioned yet resistant attitude. He is frequently commended for perceptive insights into American culture as viewed from a foreigner's perspective. His poetry, which reveals the influences of the Dadaist and Surrealist movements, has been likened to the works of Walt Whitman and William Carlos Williams for its replication of American vernacular. According to M. G. Stephens, "Codrescu has a mastery of English that comes from using a language essentially foreign to his experience. . . . The beauty of his work lies in his usage of American idioms in metaphors and similes with an outsider's ear tuned to natural speech rhythms and patterns."

Codrescu began writing poetry at the age of sixteen. He became involved with his country's literary intelligentsia prior to publishing several poems critical of Rumania's communist government, which contributed to his exile. After receiving his master's degree from the University of Rome, Codrescu emigrated to the United States, where he was hailed as a promising young poet with the appearance of his first collection, *License to Carry a Gun* (1970). In this volume, Codrescu explores his psychological inclinations through three distinct personas: Julio Hernandez, a Latin American poet and political prisoner who represents the exiled revolutionary; Peter Boone, a Vietnam War veteran and American expatriate who displays fascist tendencies; and Aurelia, a woman who symbolizes feminine, creative qualities. In his next collection, *The History of the Growth of Heaven* (1971), Codrescu rejects tradition, history, and order to create introspective, surrealistic poems on urban themes. Representative verse from Codrescu's career appears in *Selected Poems, 1970-1980* (1983).

The Life and Times of an Involuntary Genius (1975) is a colorful, poetic memoir in which Codrescu expands upon and embellishes his life in Rumania and recounts his surprise and delight in discovering the 1960s American counterculture. According to one reviewer, the book imparts "a haunting sense of the meaning of exile that carries it well beyond mere autobiography." *In America's Shoes* (1983), a companion volume to *The Life and Times of an Involuntary Genius*, details Codrescu's emergence into the American way of life. Written in a warm, humorous tone while evidencing Codrescu's critical views on bureaucracy, the book features personal vignettes and irreverent portraits of such figures as Kenneth Rexroth, Robert Bly, and Bob Dylan.

Comrade Past and Mister Present (1986) is a collection of Codrescu's recent work. This volume contains several long poems as well as prose and journal pieces consisting of rem-

Photograph by Gloria Frym

iniscences and wry philosophical insights into moral, sexual, and political topics. A regular speaker on the National Public Radio program "All Things Considered," Codrescu demonstrates the broad range of his monologues in the collection *A Craving for Swan* (1986). Codrescu has contributed poetry to various magazines under the pseudonyms of Tristan Tzara and Urmuz and is also the editor of *Exquisite Corpse,* a monthly magazine of "books and ideas" which he founded in 1982.

(See also *Contemporary Authors,* Vols. 33-36, rev. ed. and *Contemporary Authors New Revision Series,* Vol. 13.)

JEROME CUSHMAN

[In *License to Carry a Gun*], Codrescu assumes the roles of a political prisoner, an American beatnik in Europe, and a woman involved with her own eroticism. This bold and exciting technique does not come off because there is not enough tonal distinction in the voices. Yet it permits the poet to explore many of the concerns of today. The poet often indulges in annoying obfuscation; yet when he is precise with his nomenclature of feelings, the poems project a fierce intensity. (p. 2489)

Jerome Cushman, in a review of "License to Carry
a Gun," in Library Journal, *Vol. 95, No. 13, July,
1970, pp. 2488-89.*

M. G. STEPHENS

[Andrei Codrescu is a] Rumanian poet (exiled from his country
in the early '60s) who emigrated to America four years ago.
He arrived in New York not knowing a word of English, and
once told me how the taxi driver who drove him from the
airport into Manhattan charged him $17 for the trip, leaving
him $3, a bundle of Rumanian poems, and a good knowledge
of Italian his first time in the Village.

From there he wandered to Detroit (because he read about that
city in Celine's *Journey to the End of the Night*), hooked up
with John Sinclair's Artist Workshop, and learned, as on a
tabula rasa, the American language via the street, hippies,
radical poets, rock records, and later from runaway girls he
picked up on 8th Street, the countermen at Blimpie's on Sixth
Avenue, and other unaccountable American sources. Codrescu
has a mastery of English that comes from using a language
essentially foreign to his experience. The beauty of his work
[in *License to Carry a Gun*] lies in his usage of American idioms
in metaphors and similes with an outsider's ear tuned to natural
speech rhythms and patterns, as in the poem **"for sarah"**:

> I can't empty myself of you,
> goddamn beatnik
> I don't think you ever got to
> rome.
> someone raped you and carved
> your fine bones
> with fertility masks.
> it's what i should have done.
>
> (p. 6)

[Codrescu divides *License to Carry a Gun*] into three parts,
each part written by a fictitious poet who inhabited Andrei's
flesh at certain points in his life. They are: Julio Hernandez,
a Cuban poet in jail for an unknown crime; Peter Boone, a
mystical fascist returned from Vietnam; and Alice Henderson-
Còdrescu, his wife in real life and the woman inside him in
these poems. Each section is preceded by a picture of a fictional
poet and accompanied by explanatory notes by Codrescu.

For those who don't know Andrei, the set-up is confusing,
since the reader is never given any signs whether Andrei is the
editor of this book or whether he really wrote these poems
himself. (The current *Books in Print* lists him as the editor,
giving the names of his creations as the poets.) But what the
book does is to present three sides of an extremely complex
writer: revolutionary in exile, machismo fascist, and the feminine in man. The resources available to the poet are endless,
and he uses them, he never slights his poems. They read simple
at first, even a bit raw to those not familiar with his work, but
the words grow out of their simple structures, they grow fantastical with a few readings.

In the Julio Hernandez section, a poem called **"for marguerite,
real love"** combines most of the passions driving the poet, and
yet retains a simplistic meter. . . . (pp. 6, 40)

But the Julio section does not stand up as well as the other
two sections. The poems often don't go beyond surfaces, they
remain flat and one-dimensional when compared with the Peter
Boone and Alice Henderson-Codrescu sections. This doesn't
mean that particular part of the book is slight; the book as a

whole has faults, but the raw potential of the poet attests to
his poetic sensibility; Andrei is probably the only poet I know
under 30 who has the potential to become a major voice. His
voice has a maturity that few writers achieve and he has the
energy to sustain that voice.

> as usual
> the tangerines are rotten
> twisted inside like a bundle
> of eyes.
> fred is out in the woods
> chasing nymphs.
> paul is under water
> hunting greek boys.
> i alone
> with a bundle of indian eyes

The preceding poem is from the Peter Boone section, **"All
Wars Are Holy."** The poet has committed himself to darker
sciences in this section, where violence, hate, the flag, all
become glorious American symbols. They are poems that would
make George Patton salute him, they are fierce mystical poems
written with the blood of the poet. Andrei emerges from Peter
Boone as the counterpart of Charles Manson on the Yeatsian
gyres. Where the latter never achieves a transcendence of evil,
Andrei emerges from the morass a black saint, a holy devil.

The Aurelia section of the book has the most appeal, though,
because of its male/female timeliness. In the introduction the
poet says, "The woman in man is maybe the most unknown
woman ever; this fascinated and obsessed me for a few years."
What the poet does is to be impertinent enough to assume the
feelings of a woman and write these feelings down.

A poem called **"dream dogs"** in the Aurelia section shows
this beautiful man from Transylvania at the peak of his craft:

> years ago it was easy to dream of wolves
> and wake up your lover
> to show him the blood on your hip
> the wolves had ties
> and followed after every sentence
> rather polite.
> now there are police dogs
> using tear gas and the lover next to you
> doesn't wake up.

A friend once told me that a man who doesn't know himself
is carrying a concealed weapon. Possession of this book in
some countries could get you a sentence that would make you
wish you had a machine gun found in your hotel room instead.
While the feds still don't know about these poems, you should
buy at least one copy before the apocalypse. It is still legal.
(p. 40)

M. G. Stephens, "These Poems Are Loaded," in
The Village Voice, *Vol. XV, No. 53, December 31,
1970, pp. 6, 40.*

KIRKUS REVIEWS

I, I, I is the essence of both the success and the failure of this
collection of poems [*The History of the Growth of Heaven*] by
the much-touted young poet [Codrescu], who considers "staying loose" the gist of his art. This he can do, sometimes
wonderfully . . . but too often the spontaneity goes and we are
left with the poet straining, burning out slush: "my mind is
filled with the snowflakes of soft things." Hyperbolic posturing

("I lie! I lie a lot!''), repetition, and whimsical imagery ("A languishing pregnancy / pushes its lazy way through the tenth / year!'') have a tendency to substitute for energy. Enjoyable as those poems can be, the best come when the poet abandons his "up" persona and settles for himself.... The book is disappointing because it could have been so much better; the poet seems content with his short quick punches (never more than a page long), with feelings and ideas he is already competent to express; the rather melancholy case of the grasp exceeding the reach.

> *A review of "The History of the Growth of Heaven,"*
> *in* Kirkus Reviews, *Vol. XLI, No. 13, July 1, 1973,*
> *p. 723.*

PUBLISHERS WEEKLY

[Codrescu] has shown in [*The History of the Growth of Heaven*] and two earlier books that he is among the most gifted of the newly emerging Americans who write poetry. Fresh and unforced in his use of language, form and image, he demonstrates an artful spontaneity while remaining very much a poet steeped in the enjoyment of a kind of game he is playing with the reader. This keen self-awareness may be imbued with self-mockery—one thinks of the painter Dali (who also has written some prose wearing many faces). At times Codrescu identifies himself as a monk; but the grin discernible between the clear caustic lines is sensuous, satanic. A poet to watch and enjoy through the stages of a maturity that holds great promise.

> *A review of "The History of the Growth of Heaven,"*
> *in* Publishers Weekly, *Vol. 204, No. 8, August 20,*
> *1973, p. 76.*

CHOICE

The poems in [*The History of the Growth of Heaven*] ... are urban poems, surrealistic poems, poems in the American tradition of Whitman and William Carlos Williams. But Codrescu is not obsessed with place and the American scene as these earlier poets were; his landscape is introspective, internal.... Still, like Whitman and Williams, Codrescu, although more hysterically, writes poems as if no one had written one before. Here are the opening lines from "Good morning": "sometimes when they shut off the faucets / i think of chinese mailmen / how they must feel holding / birds full of letters." Codrescu wants his poems to read like miraculous jottings; they begin and end as the original impulse or perception began and ended, flashes of ecstasy or despair. As he says, the real danger in the development of a monk "is the magic he can perform / after he gets his head together / in regard to the world." These poems are startling, fresh fragments.

> *A review of "The History of the Growth of Heaven,"*
> *in* Choice, *Vol. 10, No. 12, February, 1974, p. 1863.*

JOHN R. CARPENTER

At first glance Andrei Codrescu seems to be an anti-traditional poet. Nothing happened until I was here, he says [in *The History of the Growth of Heaven*]:

> allowing for the thousand distortions
> that make us laugh, tell me,
> has anyone ever said anything?

Like the Dadaists he denies the existence of tradition, although this itself has become a well-known tradition. He treats the world as a newly created *tabula rasa* for his imagination. This is brash, but it has advantages. Perceptions are fresh, and there is genuine psychological realism; when experiences occur in life they often seem totally unique and the comparing process occurs only after the event. It is hard to be true to the experience and to the intellect at the same time.

Many actions in the poems are stated rather than evoked. Often the language is rather flat, without nuances, and there are some mistakes in English. After an interesting description of sex in New York and thousands of intertwined limbs, tongues, and genitals, the poet concludes: "A ball of flame floats permanently around the city.'' This is a disappointing stock image. Or: "things look real / they freak me out". Or: "All resurrection must begin right away.'' Miraculous things occur and the poet presents many metaphors which are quite original but usually directly stated, with only a dime-store finish, and not evoked. There is freshness and magic in these poems; there is little intense feeling, but I think this is the intention of the author. He assumes that the world makes no sense, and because he believes each of his experiences is totally new he refuses to put himself in anyone else's shoes. He cannot speak for others, nor for what has happened in the past; he cannot compare. He gains in spontaneity, but loses in participation; the freshness is specialized. There are many good poems in this book: "**To the Virgin as She Now Stands**" and "**Late Night, San Francisco**" are strong poems with powerful endings. (pp. 166-67)

> *John R. Carpenter, "The Big Machine," in* Poetry,
> *Vol. CXXV, No. 3, December, 1974, pp. 166-73.*

PUBLISHERS WEEKLY

Codrescu's memoir [*The Life and Times of an Involuntary Genius*], pungent and intense, offers eloquent testimony to the craving for individual expression that has driven many creative talents to leave their homelands behind the Iron Curtain and seek fulfillment in America. It is an absorbing work.... Codrescu experienced in his boyhood the shock of the Nazi occupation; through the postwar years right up to the Hungarian uprising he was enmeshed in a feverish search for identity that came to a head when the rift widened between himself and his young Party-oriented friends. The culture shock he suffered when he fled to Italy and later when he arrived in the United States still echoes in his writing, giving his memoir a haunting sense of the meaning of exile that carries it well beyond mere autobiography.

> *A review of "The Life and Times of an Involuntary*
> *Genius," in* Publishers Weekly, *Vol. 207, No. 9,*
> *March 3, 1975, p. 68.*

THOMAS A. WASSMER

[Andrei Codrescu is] considered by many writers to be one of this country's most imaginative poets, with talents similar to those of Walt Whitman and William Carlos Williams.... Collections of [Codrescu's] poetry have appeared in numerous small press chapbooks and in two full-length books: *License To Carry a Gun* and *The History of the Growth of Heaven*. His poetry has been characterized as a "magnificent clash of words," touched by an imagination that is magical, a clearer penetration into the soul of America by a foreigner than any by a native American poet.

All of these tributes are made to his poetry and it would be overly generous to extend these same characterizations to all of his prose writing. This autobiographical account [*The Life and Times of an Involuntary Genius*] is a procession of short jerky sentences that tell the story of the poet's childhood spent in a haunted castle in the dark hills of Transylvania. His grand-mother lived in just two rooms on the lower floor which were the former servants' kitchen next to the big old kitchen. The other inhabitants of this dreary place were spiders, bats, ghosts, and various astral species. Andrei would see his mother on occasions whenever "her men left her" and then "she would go into unending fits of despair and would threaten to wash the world away with her tears." Bursts of his poetic powers appear in almost every description of his parents, his grand-mother, his young associates. (pp. 69-70)

The autobiography races rapidly through early adulthood and the worthless struggles with communist power which the poet experienced as an unbearable burden because of his scorn for authority. His early attempts at writing were belittled by the critics and he was expelled from the university and served notice for military conscription. He decided to escape from his country without money, friends, or any knowledge of other languages and he wandered through the ghettos of Paris, Rome, Detroit, and New York's Lower East Side, and finally reached California. These accounts are full of adventure and colorful experiences with many bizarre characters and they move with spirit and brio. America becomes a place for him where the people "smile dazzlingly and bang their Cadillacs into one another." Two Frenchmen whom he meets there at the corner of Bleecker and MacDougal in the Village had the ingenious way of making money by working with a Sperm Bank. Andrei worked at the famous 8th Street Bookstore before he finally migrated to San Francisco "that wicked town filled with the most marvelous Mediterranean air and suicidal fog."

The imagery and the freshness of the descriptions never cease to come, one after the other. It may be the greatest tribute to Codrescu that his prose drives a reader to the magical language of his poetry. (p. 70)

Thomas A. Wassmer, in a review of "The Life and Times of an Involuntary Genius," in Best Sellers, *Vol. 35, No. 3, June, 1975, pp. 69-70.*

CHOICE

[Codrescu's] poetry has elicited praise from people who know something about the medium. . . . But [*The Life and Times of an Involuntary Genius*], a survey of his adolescent and adult difficulties with contemporary political events, is a pretentious and foolish affair that will do nothing to enhance his reputation. Codrescu, who became a U.S. citizen in 1971, is a "revolu-tionary" who believes in monarchical government. Page 149 contains the insight that "democracy is, essentially, an ac-knowledgment of the banality of collective needs," which, while true, happens to be an extremely banal truth. The dust jacket informs us that "this then is the story of Andrei Codrescu who journeyed across two different worlds in search of nothing special." Which is what is offered to the reader.

A review of "The Life and Times of an Involuntary Genius," in Choice, *Vol. 12, Nos. 5-6, July-August, 1975, p. 680.*

STEPHEN KESSLER

The typical Codrescu text throughout *Selected Poems* is short, quickly paced rather than discursive or meditative, surreal, erotic, intermittently violent, full of surprising turns of phrase and image—images and phrases enigmatic enough to invite more than one reading—and pervaded by a playful sense of humor. For Codrescu, even the most serious poetic utterance is a kind of joke, often a joke on the poet, told with the glee of a naughty little boy, which he clearly enjoys being. He revels in the shifting identities of the creator's role, explaining an aspect of his strategy in this piece from *Secret Training:*

> I sell myths not poems. With each poem, goes a little myth. This myth is not in the poem. It's in my mind. And when the editors of magazines ask me for poems I make them pay for my work by passing along these little myths which I make up. These myths appear at the end of the mag-azine under the heading ABOUT CONTRIB-UTORS or above my poems in italics. Very soon there are as many myths as there are poems and ultimately this is good because each poem does, this way, bring another poet into the world. With this secret method of defying birth con-trols I populate the world with poets.

The writer is having a good time, engaging in mischievous and ironic activity even when writing from the depths of sadness and depression, but not in a manner to set him brooding on the artist's tragic fate. No, the poet's art is magical, miraculous, and therefore comic for Codrescu: it can turn grief into fun simply by a twist of the sinewy mind, a turn of the tongue, his tongue, which is all the more amazing because it speaks in a second language, American English, which he wields with remarkable facility, felicity and fire.

Selected Poems is a sprightly book, light and smart like the banter of streetwise city boys after a horror movie, charged with a nervous youthful energy, sexy, a little menacing at times and clever in the best and worst of ways. At worst Codrescu's work comes off as evasive, cute or frivolous—"Creative Jive"— but at least these pieces make no pretense of their own im-portance. Most of the poems have a refreshing gleam in their eyes, a good-natured slash at the sensitive ego so often wounded by delusions of significance. At best they resonate very mys-teriously, offering lively proof of the power of imaginative play. . . . (p. 5)

In America's Shoes is a parallel tale in prose which documents the period during which the poems were written, a warmly humorous narrative account of the poet's emergence as an American. It is a sequel to Codrescu's earlier "autobiogra-phy," *The Life and Times of an Involuntary Genius.* While continuing with what purports to be his own life story—a some-times fanciful mixture of legend and confession—he focuses on several of his friends of the 1960s and '70s, portraying them not only as interesting characters but also as cultural arche-types, poets and hippies and borderline bohemians with whom he shared various adventures, tragedies and revelations in the course of coming of age, marrying, and fathering two children.

The book opens with a very funny account of the author's induction into American citizenship. His perspective as an im-migrant with a wickedly sardonic sense of the oppressive stu-pidity of all governments makes his testimony deliciously dis-illusioned yet cheerful. There is much shrewd, cynical insight into the workings of bureaucracy, and at the same time a tender appreciation of the sweetness and solidarity of friendship in the land of the free, where he now writes within earshot of a baseball stadium.

Because of his East European Jewish background, Codrescu becomes a kind of grandfather figure to many of his American contemporaries. He has an almost protective understanding of the fragility of yankee innocence and rootlessness while relishing the freshness of that innocence and mobility, enthusiastically cultivating those qualities in himself. Like any wandering rascal poet he experiments with experience, making assorted urban and rural scenes from coast to coast, meeting eccentric people, taking drugs, making love, and writing it all down.

What makes Codrescu's story more than just another personal tale of the life and loves of a roving rogue is his keen apprehension of American culture as only an outsider can see it. He claims, paradoxically, "I've always been an American," and he is, in some ways even more profoundly than his native friends. The restlessness of his energy, his optimism, his refusal to be a sober adult—these are a few of his typically American traits. The book is an essay on US cultural history in the '70s, informally chronicling the massive turn toward guru-worship and the marketing of the psyche as suffered by some of his dearest comrades from the counter-culture.

In America's Shoes is also an interesting glimpse, or kaleidoscope of glimpses, into various poetry "scenes"—especially of the San Francisco Bay area—of the '60s and '70s whose participants continue to make waves, or stagnant pools, in the swamps of American writing.

Codrescu is gossipy, alive to what's happening, young but seasoned enough to discount cultural icons or joyfully skewer their presumed authority. Kenneth Rexroth, Robert Bly, Jack Hirschman, and Bob Dylan are among the figures he sketches with delightful insight and irreverence. He seems an unusually happy person and his happiness radiates from the pages of his prose even more generously than from the poetry. The writing is a celebration, a festive song of gratitude for his good luck in the New World, and is pleasantly free of literary pretense even though he moves in literary realms.

In Baltimore, where he now lives, Codrescu writes a column for the Sunday *Sun* and co-edits the new journal *Exquisite Corpse,* "a monthly of books and ideas," whose first few issues have been a dynamic mixture of opinion, polemic, satire and otherwise stinging commentary on current events in contemporary culture. If the *Corpse* survives, it promises to be a notable contribution to the country's maelstrom of little magazines. The wit and energy of his efforts give me the impression that Codrescu's presence as a poet and all-around cultural agitator will matter more and more. *Selected Poems* and *In America's Shoes* are suggestive evidence of a versatile writer whose gifts are swiftly evolving. (pp. 5-6)

> Stephen Kessler, "Good Luck in the New World!" in San Francisco Review of Books, Vol. VIII, No. 4, Winter, 1983-84, pp. 5-6.

RAY OLSON

The Romanian-American poet who has been broadcasting weekly essays on National Public Radio's "All Things Considered" since 1983 finally collects some two years worth of them [in *A Craving for Swan*]. It is astonishing that he has produced so regularly, even more that his range is so wide and his imagination so fertile. Week after week, he has taken a concept, a bit of history, something he saw on the street, a trivial newspaper report, an incident from his own life, etc., and made a few minutes' entrancing spiel of it. Sometimes he's a bit off base, e.g., the *Titanic* went down in 1912, so it doesn't represent the "gilded age between the wars." More often, he's right on, as when he demurs from Eugene McCarthy's statement that U.S. poets suffer a fate worse than imprisonment, to wit, "They are ignored." . . . Witty, profound, or both at once, his commentaries read as well as they sound.

> Ray Olson, in a review of "A Craving for Swan," in Booklist, Vol. 83, No. 6, November 15, 1986, p. 467.

CHARLES BISHOP

In this delightful book [*A Craving for Swan*] Rumanian émigré poet Codrescu has gathered about 150 of his radio commentaries for National Public Radio. . . . [The articles are] about a page and a half each, and the topics include leg warmers, time, Madonna and her cult, aging, telephones, the Statue of Liberty, and New Orleans. Codrescu is a witty and insightful commentator whose unique background, gift for language, and radical common sense make this a recommended book.

> Charles Bishop, in a review of "A Craving for Swan," in Library Journal, Vol. 112, No. 1, January, 1987, p. 89.

BRUCE SHLAIN

When one reads the young Codrescu, one imagines an artist who wants to burn the museums. But he has written 15 volumes of poetry and two autobiographical prose works. Today he teaches at Louisiana State University after a stint at Johns Hopkins and is a regular commentator on National Public Radio's "All Things Considered." In the contemporary world of accelerated pace and dislocation, his expatriate sensibilities of wonder and detachment seem ever more timely.

In *Comrade Past & Mister Present,* his splendid new collection of poetry, prose and journal entries, this perpetual outsider offers ample evidence that even as his life grows more settled, he continues to push at his own outer limits, all the while treating the derangement of his senses with uncommon spontaneity and wit. Perhaps Flaubert was right when he suggested in his letters that one should live as a bourgeois, so that one can be wild and free in one's art. In ["**Comrade Past & Mister Present**"], he has successfully found a meeting place for his prose and poetry. He has left the characteristic movement of his earlier work, which was posing questions, taking them out of context and then allowing his diabolically dialectical mind to eat up the question itself. "**Comrade Past**" is an elliptical, extended poem with longer lines, designed like a series of opening doors or peeled-off layers. . . .

For Mr. Codrescu, images are embedded in language "like anchovies in a pizza," as he puts it. He may play games, but if his intent is to take the reader's head off, he gently unscrews it and places it in one's lap. He shifts effortlessly from comic surrealist to naturalist, philosopher to saint to madman, but he is always the seeker after transcendence, in thrall to the unknown:

> And so the mystery burns
> giving off only enough light for the enormous job
> of making oneself.

In Mr. Codrescu's native Transylvania, poets are social spokesmen, and that perhaps explains his fearlessness of treading on the languages of philosophy, religion, politics, science or popular culture. His focus on a pet theme, oppression, is as much concerned with the private as with the public. He ominously begins the poem **"Momentary Bafflement With Return Home at Dawn"**: "Extremely logical circumstances are in effect / we are in danger of behaving as expected." Mr. Codrescu has a knack for bringing out dichotomies in matters moral, sexual and political, as when asking the perplexing question in the poem **"Dear Masoch"**: "What do you do if you're a masochist but have been placed / in a position of power?"

His journal entries, entitled **"The Juniata Diary: With Timely Repartees,"** range from remembrances of losing his virginity at the Museum of the Communist Party to explorations of "sleep linguistics" for a university of the future and reflections on those who have influenced his work (he eulogizes the late poet Ted Berrigan, much venerated as the "Gulf Stream of Consciousness," as a mentor and a father). In this diary Mr. Codrescu also includes some of the rigorous intellectual gymnastics that find lyrical expression in the poems. Even when his sharp observations yield little more than dime store philosophy, it is a most interesting and frequently dazzling dime store presided over by one of our most prodigiously talented and magical writers.

> *Bruce Shlain, "Memory, Recovered or Redeemed,"
> in* The New York Times Book Review, *January 25,
> 1987, p. 15.*

Don Coles

1928-

Canadian poet and critic.

In his verse, Coles examines such traditional lyric themes as romantic love, beauty, and mortality, and emphasizes the nature and effects of time. Coles was in his mid-forties when he published his first book of poetry, *Sometimes All Over* (1975); this maturity, manifested in his confident and controlled style, is one of the qualities critics admire in his work. According to several reviewers, Coles's compassionate vision of the human condition occasionally borders on sentimentality yet remains one of the strengths of his verse. Coles has won praise for his clear, precise use of imagery and his skill in expressing transcendent ideas through ordinary objects and events.

In *Sometimes All Over* and his second collection, *Anniversaries* (1979), Coles explores themes relating to time and the significance of everyday things in his characteristically lyrical, personal style. In *The Prinzhorn Collection* (1982), his preoccupation with time becomes a meditation on loss and aging, as in "Landslides," considered one of Coles's finest achievements. In many of the poems in *The Prinzhorn Collection*, Coles draws upon his extensive travels in Europe and his interest in European culture and history. The title poem, for instance, concerns a collection of writings and artworks produced by inmates of a German insane asylum in the late nineteenth century. *Landslides: Selected Poems, 1975-1985* (1986) contains pieces from his previous volumes as well as twelve new poems in which he further elaborates on time and mortality.

(See also *Contemporary Authors*, Vol. 115.)

Photograph by Luke Coles. Courtesy of Don Coles.

SAM SOLECKI

Sometimes All Over is Coles's first book but it reveals a technically confident writer who is able to project a consistent tone, voice and personality; like A. R. Ammons or Tom Wayman he is a poet whose self, both social and private, is at the very centre of his poetry. Like Wayman he is a superb evoker of everyday life in terms of everyday language. He is particularly good at registering the importance of those moments or events whose significance—because of their very evanescence—is often overlooked and lost. Poems such as **"Moving Day," "The House"** and **"Photograph,"** among many others, repeatedly focus on those moments in Coles's life when "time hollowed a space around me." The poems record or re-enact personal situations in which some kind of domestic and secular revelation occurred. (p. 647)

> Resting once after play you looked at me and said,
> "Daddy,"
> and "Daddy" until I had time
> and you said, "Someday I will fly away—like
> Peter," and
> again, "like Peter," you said
> meaning Peter Pan, the story we had read

> And I don't suppose you noticed what happened next
> but
> time hollowed a space around me then, the words
> moved in that space
> I could have wept, probably did not but then I don't
> weep enough generally

The music of the verse is unobtrusive, the rhythm, diction and situation are all casual but the tone is already tending towards the reflectiveness of the poem's ending. Like so many of the poems in the collection this one ["**For My Daughter, Now Seven Years Old**"] is concerned with memory and consequently it functions on at least two levels of time: Coles begins by recalling an event that occurred when his daughter was five years old and he concludes by asking whether he is "doing what I said thirty years ago to whoever was listening." The commonplace situation—a father thinking about his daughter's age and comparing her youth to his own—is typical of a Don Coles poem. I assume that this very sense of the commonplace or everyday accounts for at least part of the poem's convincingness and charm.

I'm usually suspicious of poetry that tends toward the sentimental and *Sometimes All Over* repeatedly almost dares the reader to dismiss it as just that. I assume that most readers agree with my assumption that sentimental poetry is usually

107

bad poetry. Coles himself seems to be aware of the perils of an indulgently emotional poetry and several poems contain lines similar to the following: "To be moved by these people must seem / sentimental." The line, by itself, indicates an awareness which is a register of that mature and unsentimental sensibility which pervades the volume.

Sometimes All Over is an impressive first book; I look forward to reading more of Don Coles's work. (pp. 647-48)

Sam Solecki, in a review of "Sometimes All Over," in Queen's Quarterly, *Vol. 82, No. 4, Winter, 1975, pp. 647-48.*

DOUGLAS BARBOUR

Sometimes All Over is a strong first book from a poet whose careful intelligence manifests itself in every poem. Don Coles has waited longer than usual to publish his work; the result is a book of substance and occasional profound power. Coles is obsessed with time and time's influence on us all. His best poems are personal meditations on time's touching his loves, his relations or himself. They look to a past now lost and unchangeable or to a present all too swiftly becoming irrevocable past. In these poems people and events emerge with clarity and precision to beguile and intrigue us. Coles's language is concrete and cuttingly personal; it co-opts our emotional assent to the pain or joy he explores. In other poems, more clearly a result of Coles's reading or research, the thought is still interesting but the language is slacker, more abstract, and the edge of tension which can be felt in such poems as **"Separating"** or **"Six Meditations after the Event"** is missing. I can enjoy the intellectual games of **"Death of Women"** but it doesn't call me back as does the truly moving meditation on family history in **"Photograph"**, a piece about Coles's grandparents. *Sometimes All Over* is a welcome book, heralding as it does a new poet of genuine power in our midst. With all its misses, it contains a number of palpable hits, poems which in their smoky passion, the tension of their wayward rhythms, and the process of discovery they map, insinuate themselves into our lives.

Douglas Barbour, in a review of "Sometimes All Over," in The Dalhousie Review, *Vol. 55, Winter, 1975-76, p. 749.*

A. F. MORITZ

[Coles's second volume, *Anniversaries,* is an] impressive book full of music and variety, wit and meditation. Coles's voice is supple and urbane as it ranges with no lack of passion over the traditional lyric themes of beauty, age, loss, decision, how to live, what to live for, the struggle to make terms with death.

But this is not disembodied reflective poetry. Coles does not—and cannot—engage these subjects except in and through the realities of our time and his own experience. His poems fill with closely observed people and things, from television wrestlers to a girl in a terminal ward, from a lake to a 1918 newspaper clipping, from a photo album to a group of war veterans. And his music modulates to suit them all.

Perhaps most impressive is the precise, intelligent, yet deeply involved style of such major poems as **"Always the Effort to Gather It All"** and **"Old,"** a sequence of brief internal speeches to a dying girl that includes these lines:

> As you grow so comprehensively down to it
> Is the world terrible?
> Are our voices insect wings?
> Do memory's glints humiliate?
> When I go do unsilhouetted tides resume?

Also effective is the style that combines agile thought with verbal ingenuity and dense imagery à la middle Auden and MacNiece. It is the vehicle of such fine poems as **"Guide Book," "Codger,"** and **"On a Bust of an Army Corporal Killed . . . in the Boer War,"** which hauntingly leaves the statue looking across the town green at night,

> Finding it odd, still, those distant, paused horsemen,
> That roaring hurt, reins gone slack,
> In Africa.

As a whole, *Anniversaries* shows a poet who is earnestly weighing human accomplishment against the sorrows of nature and the human condition. (p. 11)

A. F. Moritz, "Bone Hurt and Battle-Weary," in Books in Canada, *Vol. 8, No. 4, April, 1979, pp. 10-11.*

RICK JOHNSON

According to the blurb on the back cover of Don Coles's second volume of poetry, *Anniversaries,* his poetry purports to deal with that interface of reality between "the private, observing self and the outer world of experience." I'd always assumed that any poetry worth its salt grew out of that polarity; and, that any contemporary poet (read Canadian) who would speak to me as my favourite poets have, would have to make me see and feel that familiarity anew. My request is simple: astound me with your language.

Don Coles's poetry does and does not. Some of the poems merely tell about or describe the self-conscious self coming upon itself. Other poems invite you into a mind and heart admirably fitted to the external world. Some of the imagery, alas, is inert and trite, speaking only to our superficial, sentimental selves; some astounds with its concrete and concise aptness. . . . Sometimes you get the feeling that Coles tries too hard; you want to tell him that it's enough to suggest: let us use our imaginations. When he tries to direct our attention his energy and sensitivity become diffused.

It is unfortunate that the volume begins with **"Old"**, "eleven unvoiced conversations with a female patient in a chronic (=helpless & dying) ward." (Again, we should not be given the parenthetical sleeve-tugging.) Anyway, in this poem the language is generally descriptive, inappropriate for the obviously overwhelming feeling in the sensitive observer. I say unfortunate because this protracted poem gives a false impression of most of the rest of the volume. Many of the ensuing poems indicate Coles's ability to make poems that grow out of the minute particularities of life, what Henry James called creative "germs" that stimulated his imagination. This serendipitous felicity for fashioning universal, human value out of tiny facts of life is Coles's strength. Poems that grow out of the activity of the self-conscious imagination ruminating over keepsakes, photographs, names on gravestones, old newspapers lining trunks, the bust of a soldier killed in the Boer

War give voice to the individual at the centre of the vast eddy of time and circumstance groping to make sense of the world.

Generally, then, Coles's poetry does please with its "clear-crafted images." His poetry reaches into the dim places where our humanity crouches, from which comes the strength to oppose the forces that would make us merely mechanical. He also reveals the necessary humility of the poet who knows that what he says is always so much less than what he wants to say.

Rick Johnson, "Interfaces," in The Canadian Forum, Vol. LIX, No. 691, August, 1979, p. 30.

PETER STEVENS

The striking thing about [*Anniversaries*] is the sense throughout of a consistent voice, which establishes a personality around which the poetic statements cohere.... This is not a poetry that is private in the confessional sense, nor is it writing that obscures its impulse by too much private reference. Running through the book is a notion of the difficulty of getting things right in words, the temptation to remain silent because of that, and yet the persistent attempt to gather experiences in order to place them. One of [Coles's] poems is called **"Always The Effort To Gather It All,"** and yet he confesses in another poem that his old temptations are "stillness and silence."

Silence remains a quality in the book, not only as a calmness which might contain a knowledge of both disturbing and joyful experience but also as a response to overwhelming, perhaps incomprehensible events. In **"Veterans"** he ponders the discrepancy between the gathering of ex-soldiers "every November in business suits / Clumping the main street" and the tremendous dangers they endured, dangers they, like the poet's father, are now vague about. The poem continues as a meditation, ironically expressed in almost that off-hand way the veterans use to describe the risks and escapes from death, about the inability to express such shattering experiences and so the inability to connect through language with following generations with their "own / bad news." Perhaps some writer occasionally gets it "almost straight" but the poem closes by stating that probably all that we have "to remember them by, or to go on" is "that famous understated / 2-minute / Silence of theirs."

That tone, somewhat bemused and diffident, yet worrying at the anxieties and wonders, the shocks and the pleasures of life, is reminiscent of the tone in the poetry of Philip Larkin, and, as such, is perhaps un-North-American, the persona, like Larkin's cyclist in "Church-Going," shabby-genteel, his trousers still clipped, letting slip through his awkwardness and unease with words a curse at the rottenness of the world or a reverent acknowledgment in awe of some vision larger than himself.

Coles sometimes places simple objects as emblems of his awe so that they take on the semblance of epiphanies. The very existence of certain things and people are sufficient in themselves and so a simple presentation is all that is required in the poem. A memory of his aunt, now old and three provinces distant, swimming after supper as it grows dark and his uncle taking towels down to the shore for her, results in the epiphany of the closing line: "Those white towels on the bank!" In the same way he writes of a vicar taking an early walk every morning to pray. It is a "Simple repetitive act / which asks no complex comment" for it "deserves / To escape the diminishing visitation / Of words." Such an act carries its own

meaning, so the poem closes with the short line, "He is there." This belongs in the category of what he calls in another poem "enormous commonplaces."

Yet often, Coles suggests, words are not enough or can obscure the experience, as in the lighter-toned poems like **"Guide Book"** in which the inflated language of that kind of publication has not obliterated the ecstatic communion of love.

Language is only an approximation, but even more obfuscating and destructive is time. He calls it a "catastrophe" for it unsettles relationships and brings on old age and death. Coles's poems contain a steady view of old age and dying and, in spite of his dissatisfactions with language, some poems memorialize those older dead and dying persons, ironically preserving them in poems. The opening poem, **"Old,"** a sequence of five-line poems on a dying patient in hospital, is a case in point, for the sequence contains within its short takes acute observations of both the other patients and the hospital staff. Within this setting, though, is the poet himself, not this time the shambling, Larkin-esque figure, but here the intellectual, whose worrying at dying and death comes through other writers' words—Wittgenstein, Taylor, Musil. At first, these references seem strained in such a poem, but finally, I think, they are integrated in the sequence because the poet's tone presents them ambivalently: as genuine comment but also as mere intellectual postures in the face of life and death. The final poem in the sequence offers his real "thought-shelter": "Sunlight, Father, Book, Leaf / My breathing."

At times the tentative qualifications, the whittling down as if for clarity become prosaic. In contrast to Larkin, there is no sudden break into the coarsely colloquial. The calmness remains in place, even as the poet discusses unhappiness (there is a peculiar non-distinction between the comic and the serious, and this discrepancy sometimes undermines the language in certain poems). At other times the name-dropping becomes obtrusive and one or two poems remain simply anecdotal. Sometimes the ironic bathos used manages to reduce poems to the commonplace level Coles so often celebrates in other terms.

Coles certainly finds sermons in stones and other common objects, not in a preachy fashion, for he nearly always allows the objects themselves, the context and the tone of presentation to make the point. (pp. 505-07)

Peter Stevens, in a review of "Anniversaries," in Queen's Quarterly, Vol. 88, No. 3, Autumn, 1981, pp. 505-07.

ANN GUNNARSSON

The pleasures of reading Don Coles are various, but I'd like to start with a story that gets to the nub of my own enjoyment. I first read *Sometimes All Over* at a friend's flat in Montreal. I found it gracious, intelligent, endearing, tremendously accomplished for a first book of poems, somewhat attitudinizing and post-adolescent in sensibility, and thoroughly gentle (I think I mean 'gentil'). I liked the book but I didn't know if it mattered all that much.

Then I got stood on my head. Not by the poems, though; by falling in love. And it was a doozer. Things came alive, the familiar glow and tingle started up—not just in my body and feelings, but in the world at large. I'd forgotten how powerful the transformation is, when you open out and begin to know streets, skies, another person, yourself, in that expanded luminescence.

One day in this condition I pulled *Sometimes All Over* off the shelf again. (By this time I was residing with the friend, so it was handy.) And saw what the book had been about all along.

It wasn't just that Coles writes good love poetry . . . though he does; he's something like a Leonard Cohen for grownups. Which is not to deprecate Cohen, merely to situate Coles. But more than that—the whole of *Sometimes All Over* turns on a singular impulse: the craving to know the world as marvellous—to live ecstatically. By falling in love; by cherishing past lives till they become luminous; by just sitting still, caught up in the moment's dimensions. However. To taste the world as miracle is, in Coles's first book, the one thing that makes life worth living. It's a spirited, risky obsession. And the poems have paid their dues; they *know* what it's like to let that obsession run your life.

It wasn't till I found myself in my own state of incandescence that I was able to appreciate how first-hand the poems were. And with what a sure artistic touch Coles was charting the way we move towards that occasional grace of the marvellous, go incandescent, lapse out the other side . . . Whew! I didn't know anyone's work had caught it so well. My estimate of the book went up a long way; in fact, for a while I found it indispensable reading.

I don't mean you have to be in love to read it. But I mean something not far from that. *Sometimes All Over* will come most alive for a reader who is already familiar with the condition, 'living in a luminous world'. The book treats that condition, almost unreflectingly, as its centre of gravity. Miss that (as I did at first), and you'll miss three quarters of the excitement. . . .

Coles is a poet to re-read; for a denizen of the marvellous, he is remarkably austere. The poems don't gush or editorialize, and they come into focus only gradually. (p. 32)

Sometimes All Over [is] distinctive in two respects. First, some 90% of the poems deal in one way or another with the experience of secular transcendence (including with its lack). And secondly, the book takes it for granted that day-to-day life is to be tested, understood, and in fact lived with 'experience of transcendence' as the central point of reference. Somehow or other, I hadn't perceived either of those things—though they hit you smack in the eye. But then my own brief sojourn in the marvellous put the experience front and centre. And I was able to recognize that poem after poem in *Sometimes All Over* assumes, quite matter-of-factly, that the meaning of life comes down to the ecstatic experience available to a person in the secular world. (p. 33)

So far, we have identified Coles's subject matter. But writing about ecstasy and writing well have no necessary connection. What I find particularly compelling are the places where Coles doesn't simply speak *about* the experience of the marvellous, but where the dislocated murmur of the lines itself recreates the experience, and where in reading we start to enter the bewitched timeless condition he hankers after. (p. 34)

There aren't all that many writers whose subject is the firsthand experience of the marvellous. They don't have an easy time of it, either, because the experience is, precisely, ineffable—beyond, beneath, or outside words. Writing an article like this one, I can get away with saying that Coles's subject is ecstasy, transcendence, the world as miracle; it's one more pigeonhole, it's like saying his subject is bumblebees or separatism. But if Coles began a poem by telling us, "I had this really good

ecstasy last week," we'd yawn, or put up active resistance. "I don't believe you," would be our immediate response. The real experience of ecstasy prevents people from brandishing labels that way. They know what they have known, and they're usually impressed with how hollow words feel when they speak of it. Especially, large abstractions like "ecstasy." If a Don Coles tries to name directly the thing he's speaking of—to announce or describe it in the language of rational categories—he is guaranteed to fail even before he begins.

I find only one example of this in the book. His five-year-old daughter tells him, "Daddy . . . someday I will fly away—like Peter." And the words trigger an epiphany, which is described as follows:

I don't suppose you noticed what happened next but time hollowed a space around me then, the words moved in that space

". . . Time hollowed a space around me": this is about as close as Coles gets to bald labelling. The phrase is OK; but it just sits there, it doesn't recreate the experience. Coles seldom falls into that trap.

How does he deal with the challenge?

As far as I can figure out, it's by starting with a maximum of concrete, physical, sometimes dramatic content—some specific, credible locus of the marvellous, which he already knows in rich detail—and then handling it with a maximum of intellectual discrimination, verbal fastidiousness, and rhythmic/syntactic fidelity to the jerky yet hushed locomotion which (for him) seems intrinsic to the experience of ecstasy. It is this fusion of immediate human experience with a highly sophisticated sensibility—rather as in some of the metaphysical poets—that keeps Coles from mere sappy emoting, on the one hand, and mere arid word-spinning on the other. It's a mark of his integrity, I think, given the highly loaded and 'romantic' nature of his material, that a casual reader is more likely to find him arid than sappy. But as I discovered, there is a proper way of reading Coles; and from within it you recognize that extreme poignancy and extreme discrimination co-inhere in his work—fused in its austere, ecstatic poetic speech. (pp. 34-5)

For the freedom of his eccentric, elliptical syntax—and perhaps for his masterly way with line-breaks—Coles is presumably indebted to John Berryman. But whatever he has stolen, he has made his own. Berryman's idiosyncratic syntax has its own point; it embodies a sensibility constantly at the breaking point, achieving its fine unexpected leaps only as a last-minute exit from disintegration. . . .

Coles's murmuring yet rigorous voice invites us into a gently fractured sense of the quotidian. We aren't being coaxed beyond daylight speaking because it is bourgeois or square, philistinely repellent; merely because there's still more to the world than our 9-to-5 has dreamed of.

Coles likes to prolong an individual sentence, so we feel the fingertip probing of an intelligence, indeed a whole person, which knows the exquisite particularity of what it has experienced, and will be satisfied only by complete fidelity in recreating it. In the process, he often introduces a series of qualifications to what he's trying to say, sometimes in the form of double negatives; moves ahead by unexpected collocations of adjectives and nouns, which turn out to be exactly right once we discern what on earth he's talking about; and leaves us suspended in mid-syntax for line-break after line-break, till the end of the sentence's exploration and a full-stop in the line-endings finally coincide, with a distinct little click of resolution. (p. 35)

There are dangers in the way Coles writes.

The first is simply that a reader misconstrue the deliberate flatness or awkwardness he introduces (''it's those character analyses you left me with / that I find myself living alongside of''), or misconstrue the more elevated and impersonal tone he moves into (''Darker now, the edges of your admired white body / soften towards me''). These things can make the poems seem merely talky, heady, a bunch of words—perhaps not worth the effort of acclimatization they demand; if you unravel the syntax, will there be anything inside? And that's a pity, because once you do acclimatize you realize that the poems are this formidably articulate—and then this quirkily offhand—precisely because the experience they mediate is specific and passionate and delicate in the extreme, and mustn't be violated by any facile blat of emotive language. The distancing effect of the style releases an even greater power in the subject, the experience of the marvellous in daily life.

Another danger is that Coles's signature techniques could become mannerisms, exercised by reflex. (p. 36)

Finally, there is a larger question: how long can anyone live a life devoted to seeking perfect gestures of epiphany? Rigorous though this poetry may be, doesn't it finally deal with a self absorbed and self-indulgent way of living? It never degenerates into the sappy outpour that such a stance usually leads to, of course. . . . But what about children? mortgage payments? Biafra? Those issues are not created by the existence of Don Coles's poetry. But they are real issues, with which the project of his poetry inevitably intersects. It is no more credible that the poetry should be able to postpone them indefinitely—or treat them as mere background to its runs at private beatitude—than it would be for an elderly person who wrote extremely resonant, humane poems to never come to grips with an aging body, the loss of friends, approaching death. To be hideously gauche: shouldn't this poetry Grow Up?

Sometimes All Over is hardly the work of a blissed-out idiot. And yet . . . and yet . . . How *does* one live a good life, when so much of it is necessarily light-years away from incandescence? And don't his poems have to wrestle directly with that dilemma?—whether or not they have anything by way of a solution?

Saying this is not a matter of criticizing Don Coles, about whose personal life I know nothing. But we have a right to ask whether the poetry recognizes the limitations of its own stance; and if it does, how it responds to them as poetry.

The answer, in *Sometimes All Over,* is that the poetry does at times recognize the limitations; the title poem [**"Sometimes All Over"**], and the one about being unable to extend the 'hard grace' to all of life, are examples. But it can do no more than occasionally register their existence—at times with a teasing irony which is at once honest, fun, and self-indulgent in a fresh way. (pp. 36-7)

The danger of this poetry is that it drift into mere masturbation, when it is seeking to be invocation of the marvellous. But perhaps good masturbation and good invocation aren't always opposed. Maybe the god isn't always outside us. And besides, no one poet can be expected to cope with all the tensions of being alive. If Coles can do artistic justice to the part of us that aspires to be simpler and more whole than we are, if he

can recreate the direct experience of the marvellous, isn't that enough? . . . (p. 37)

Ann Gunnarsson, *"Touching the Marvellous," in*
Brick: A Journal of Reviews, *No. 14, Winter, 1982,
pp. 32-7.*

MARK ABLEY

Canadian poetry began as an outpost of imperial culture, but in recent decades the strongest influences on its language and ideas have come from south of the border. One notable exception to the pattern is Toronto poet Don Coles, whose work stands squarely in the tradition of European civilization. His third book, *The Prinzhorn Collection,* begins with madness and ends near death—an all too common approach in modern poetry, some might say. But these poems never submerge themselves in the bleak events they describe. They feast on memory, irony and paradox in a style that somehow manages to be rich and elliptical at once. Much of Coles's writing could be described as an exploration of his heritage, for he knows that our past is implicit in every word we speak, every action we take. The settings of many of these poems (Bavaria, Russia, Scandinavia), together with their attitudes and style, reflect a temperament fascinated by history as it affects the poet's own life.

Many contemporary poets seek merely to present experience in a sharp, clear light unadorned by explanation; Coles begins where they leave off. His writing is an effort to comprehend, to make sense of an ancient, dishevelled world. When one of his characters gives up the struggle, ''chaos drinks him.'' When he visits an elderly woman in a Gericare Centre, Coles thinks of ''all that / Chaos is repossessing behind the / Widening night-glittering moat.'' His tense battles for order and his exact command of words make this a powerful text—the sort that may still be finding readers in 20 years' time, when many of today's better-known authors will have been deservedly forgotten. (p. 50)

Mark Abley, *"Searchers for a State of Grace," in*
Maclean's Magazine, *Vol. 95, No. 21, May 24, 1982,
pp. 50, 52.*

JON PEIRCE

[*The Prinzhorn Collection*] takes us through both contemporary Europe and Europe of the late nineteenth and early twentieth centuries. Along the way, we're introduced to some of the history, literature, and architecture of that earlier period, as well as to some of its more notable personalities, such as Ibsen, Tolstoi, and Rilke.

In many ways *The Prinzhorn Collection* is both innovative and ambitious. Coles' range of learning is impressive, and his craftsmanship is unquestioned. The title piece is of particular interest, since it's one of the best sustained dramatic monologues ever written by a Canadian poet. All the same, the collection isn't totally satisfying. Even as we admire the technique, we can't help regretting that Coles didn't do more with the wealth of material at his disposal.

Let's consider, for example, [**"The Prinzhorn Collection"**]. As Coles explains in a note, the poem was inspired by a collection of letters, journals and drawings made by the inmates of a mental institution near Munich during the late nineteenth century and preserved by Dr. Hans Prinzhorn, the institution's director during the period just before Hitler came to power.

As the narrator of the poem (presumably the curator of the gallery in which the collection is being exhibited) admits, this is ''strong stuff.'' And well it might be; we are, after all, talking about Bismarck's era, the era which gave rise to Thomas Mann's *Buddenbrooks* and Hermann Hesse's *Beneath the Wheel*.

To understand what Coles has missed here is to imagine what a poet like Robert Browning would have discovered—a comparison that doesn't seem unfair, in view of the Browningesque note which Coles strikes both at the beginning and the end of the poem. In the hands of a poet like Browning, the Prinzhorn collection would have been the occasion for an impassioned comment on the repressiveness of German society, on the treatment of mental patients and presumably on Prinzhorn himself about whom Coles has disappointingly little to say. From *that* kind of poem we would have come away as from ''My Last Duchess,'' the Browning monologue it most closely resembles, knowing and caring more both about nineteenth-century Germany and about twentieth-century Canada. From Coles' poem we emerge as from a dusty museum, our curiosity more sated than piqued. Seldom, if ever, do we get the feeling that Coles really cares very deeply about all the ''strong stuff'' he has seen.

One problem is that Coles spends a lot of time and energy on the mechanics of his documentary (making translations from German into English, for instance). At times this involvement with such mechanical details is so obsessive that it gets in the way of more important matters. A more serious problem is that, for reasons that still aren't entirely clear, he simply doesn't show us very much of the collection. All that we're given in any detail are the letters of one of the patients, Joseph Grebing, to his father. These letters do help us to feel some sympathy for poor Joseph, who seems to have been institutionalized merely because he was a bit difficult for his co-workers (in his father's firm) to get along with. But they aren't enough to make up for what Coles leaves out: the men's drawings, the women's letters, conditions in the institution generally, and Prinzhorn himself. In no area does Coles' inferiority to Browning stand out so clearly as in his lack of attention to such important details.

The narrator poses a different kind of problem—one of tone. It's hard to know what to make of a man who, having shown someone things as grisly as the Prinzhorn works, can address his visitor in such words as these:

> . . . I return, stooping
> A little, towards my competency,
> The visible. The Prinzhorn
> Collection moves to Düsseldorf in
> March, there are no plans for it
> After that, it will be dismantled.
> A sculpture exhibition is due here
> From Berlin at that time . . .
> Perhaps you will come, your students
> Will be nice, they will allow you,
> We will talk. Yes? Try. This long
> Letter, sorry. More *sangfroid*
> Next time. I am sorry for this.

Moreover, if Coles was after the callousness and cynicism that this kind of talk seems to suggest, he could have conveyed that callousness and cynicism more effectively if the curator had first shown the collection ''warts and all!'' Such difficulties with the narrator's voice point toward a larger difficulty with the poem as a whole. What, finally, has been Coles' purpose in showing us the Prinzhorn collection? After several readings

of the poem, I confess to being no nearer answering that question than I was after one reading. But one possibility intrigues me, namely, that the present poem is merely one point of view on the Prinzhorn collection, a kind of dress rehearsal for a longer and more sustained tour. With all its faults, the present poem is well worth returning to. If Coles were to do the collection full justice, the result would be poetry truly of world class.

Most of the other short poems in the collection with the exception of the delightful ''**Major Hoople**,'' a portrait of a grotesque who might have done Daumier or Browning credit, suffer from the same problems as [''**The Prinzhorn Collection**'']. As in the case of the longer poem, we come away from most of these shorter pieces feeling as if our travel has been merely escape. And again we're so caught up in the mechanics of time and space translations that we aren't able to enter into the hearts and minds of the people Coles is describing.

''**Landslides**,'' the other long poem in the collection, is quite a different proposition. This poem, based on visits to a ''Gericare Centre,'' uses time travel as a means of discovery—in this case, discoveries about the old women resident in the institution. There's real compassion in Coles' voice as he imagines an old woman as a little girl skating out ''along the Chateauguay'' or with her uncle driving a cart into an abandoned barn during a rainstorm. My only objection to the piece is its lack of unity and the rather didactic note (most uncharacteristic of Coles) on which it ends. On the whole, ''**Landslides**'' seems much the most fully realized poem in the book. (pp. 27-8)

Jon Peirce, ''The Poet as Traveller,'' in The Canadian Forum, *Vol. LXII, No. 722, October, 1982, pp. 27-9.*

PAUL STUEWE

Don Coles's *The Prinzhorn Collection* includes one poem (''**Major Hoople**'') based upon a mass-cultural source, although Rilke, Tolstoy and Ibsen are more apt to figure as spurs to its author's sensibilities. Given the high level of excellence achieved by this volume, it is tempting to hypothesize that the intrinsic quality of the source may be directly related to the resultant quality of the literary product; and if this sort of thinking isn't logically compelling, it does indicate how impressed this reader was with the exhibits on display in *The Prinzhorn Collection*.

The exhibits viewed in [''**The Prinzhorn Collection**''], which describes an art gallery's reconstruction of life in a nineteenth-century German ''madhouse,'' are characteristic of Coles's methods and materials. These graphically-described drawings, letters and journals are presented as emblems of madness rather than its direct physical analogues, and their significances are gradually unveiled in a discursive and ultimately very effective way. The form of the poem, itself epistolary, contributes another layer of meaning through our dawning realization that its writer is also under a great deal of strain, and the final revelation of one inmate's hopeless despair is echoed by the exhausted tone of the narrator's farewell. This technically stunning performance also displays sustained powers of imaginative invention, and one can't help but wonder if such standards will be maintained in the remainder of the volume.

They largely are, although an occasional infelicity or miscalculation establishes that the author can err with the rest of us humans. ''**I Long for People Through Whom the Past**'' and

"**Collecting Pictures**" impress as accumulations of miscellaneous memories that haven't been shaped into coherent wholes, and Coles sometimes chooses to end poems on Hemingway-like downbeats that have no discernible relation to what has preceded them. More typically, however, the reader is treated to a feast of deftly-handled assonance and near-rhyme, evocative cultural references and vividly-described interior and exterior landscapes. (p. 1038)

Coles's venture into Browning's *Men and Women* territory, "**Natalya Nikolayevna Goncharov,**" is a fine act of homage in its own right as well as yet another indication of the exceptional range of his talent. Its perhaps self-reflexive observation that "To pour images is fine, drowning however / Is no joke" sounds the note of sincere, craftsmanlike concern so characteristic of Browning's best work, and its concluding outburst of words and phrases expelled under increasing psychological pressure seems as authentic as it does aptly chosen. On a rather different literary turf, Coles's figurative language can be almost as sharp as Raymond Chandler's. . . . And where only an overwhelming effusion of emotion will do, as in "**Abrupt Daylight Sadness,**" it is memorably provided. . . . *The Prinzhorn Collection* is a marvelous book, as great a pleasure to re-read as it is to experience in the first rush of enthusiasm, and I cannot recommend it too highly. (pp. 1039-40)

Paul Stuewe, "Attending the Masses: The Media and Some Canadian Poets," in Queen's Quarterly, *Vol. 90, No. 4, Winter, 1983, pp. 1034-41.*

EVA TIHANYI

As his new work [in *Landslides: Selected Poems, 1975-1985*] in particular shows, Coles is a poet who has hit his stride: the right word in the right place, poems that feel finished. "**Somewhere Far From This Comfort**", with its mesmerizing use of repetition and its elegiac tone, is especially deserving of attention, as is "**In the Dream of My Grandmother's Tree**" where the poet looks up at "the transparent heart of things" and remembers "how / Strange I used to feel looking up / Knowing I would be old sometime." Childhood, aging, the merciless passing of time are almost obsessions with Coles. There is a nostalgic mood in many of the pieces that deal with these subjects, but Coles does not resort to mere sentimentality nor does he indulge in pathos for its own sake. There is the odd poem such as "**Running Child**" which is strikingly trite in comparison to the two poems mentioned above, but such a lapse is rare.

It is perhaps also worth noting that although Coles is by no means a funny writer, he is not completely devoid of humour—the dry, ironic kind reminiscent of Margaret Atwood—as in "**Nostalgie de Bonheur**" where he decides that "Nothing is so much to be avoided / As unhappiness" and ends by saying that:

> The moon is more beautiful
> Through the strayed curtains
> Of a man who knows this much
> Than it is over all the Americas.
> I'll see how this turns out.

Despite much that is praiseworthy in *Landslides,* there is the occasional false note: the poet's lover's "white rib-cage and its bobbling / Breasts" in "**Imprudent Lover**", for instance, or the irritating overuse of the word "and" in "**Moving Day**". The piling up of conjunctions is a noticeable stylistic habit of Coles'. His poems often have a run-on, stream-of-consciousness quality, which although effective in some cases does seem forced in others. In contrast, there is a different kind of "running on" in the lengthy narrative poem "**The Prinzhorn Collection**" based, as the author explains in a note, on a "collection of letters, journals, and drawings made by inmates of a mental institution near Munich during the late nineteenth-century." The poem is the conclusion of a "letter" being written about the exhibition of this collection, which might account for its prosy long-windedness, but I must admit I missed the usual mellifluous Colesian word-flow (even when it gathers conjunctions as it goes) more and more with each stanza.

Usually in Coles, the voice suits perfectly what is being said, and what is being said tends to be about relationships, connections between past and present, self and family, individual and individual. A sampling of titles from the book's second section provides a good introduction, I think, to his close-to-home concerns: "**Divorced Child**", "**Photograph**", (the photograph is one of Coles' favorite images), "**Sandcastle**", "**For My Daughter**". It is much to Coles' credit that he leaves the reader feeling not that something obvious has been restated yet again, but that something *not* so obvious has been discovered near at hand and brought to light. (p. 42)

Eva Tihanyi, "Different Voices, Equal Quality," in Cross-Canada Writers' Quarterly, *Vol. 8, Nos. 3 & 4, 1986, pp. 42-3.*

LOUISE McKINNEY

Coles has never confused making poems with making a name, and his new anthology, *Landslides: Selected Poems 1975-1985* is a display, an unfolding, of his talent that confirms the old adage about quantity and quality.

Landslides is breath-taking in its scope, variety, and omniscience. The collection presents the best of his earlier work (with minor tinkering) and adds a new parcel called Dark Fields. Throughout, Coles undertakes traditional lyric themes—time, ageing, growth, love, and death—with compassion and wisdom. Yet his sights are fixed on the particular, those homely experiences that, as he says, "can sensitize us . . . can illuminate areas of life for us". Here, as Thomas Hardy would say, is a poet with "the seeing eye".

Louise McKinney, in a review of "Landslides: Selected Poems, 1975-1985," in Quill and Quire, *Vol. 52, No. 6, June, 1986, p. 39.*

Robert (Lowell) Coover

1932-

American novelist, short story writer, dramatist, poet, and critic.

A leading contemporary experimental writer, Coover uses his fiction to startle and fascinate the reader, believing, with John Barth, that literature has reached a state of exhaustion. In his search for new approaches to literature, Coover produces works in which the distinction between fantasy and reality becomes blurred. By placing standard elements from fairy tales, biblical stories, or historical events in a distorted context, Coover strives to deconstruct the myths and traditions which people create to give meaning to life. Robert Scholes cited Coover's work, along with that of Barth, Donald Barthelme, and William Gass, as examples of "metafiction," a term he defines as writing that "attempts, among other things, to assault or transcend the laws of fiction."

In his first novel, *The Origin of the Brunists* (1966), Coover describes the formation of a religious cult, the Brunists, after Giovanni Bruno claims that he was saved from death in a coal mine disaster by divine intervention. In this work, Coover investigates the human need to create myths, to impose order and purpose on chaos and inexplicable tragedy. Coover develops this theme further in his second novel, *The Universal Baseball Association, Inc., J. Henry Waugh, Prop.* (1968). An expansion of Coover's short story "The Second Son" (1962), this novel portrays a lonely, middle-aged accountant who devises a world for himself through a table baseball game played with dice. In obvious parallels to God, particularly the Hebrew God Yahweh, J. Henry Waugh creates the players, their histories, and their futures. The plot climaxes when the dice dictate that a favorite player must die; at this point, Waugh has become so involved with the game that the reality of his life merges with the reality of the game. Coover blurs the lines between the two realities and leads the reader to question which of the worlds is invented.

Coover's next work, *Pricksongs and Descants* (1969), is a collection of short stories, some of which were written early in his career. By making readers aware that they are reading fiction and by subverting myths, Coover attempts to induce his audience to recognize significant new literary patterns. Coover based these stories on such sources as the Bible, fairy tales, and familiar, everyday events, arranging them into original, unexpected forms. In the story "The Brother," for example, Coover relates a tale about Noah's brother, who helps build the ark and then is left by Noah to drown. Along with other pieces, *Pricksongs and Descants* contains "Seven Exemplary Fictions," with a prologue in which Coover explains his literary intentions. He contends that "great narratives remain meaningful through time as a language-medium between generations, as a weapon against the fringe-areas of our consciousness, and as a mythic reinforcement of our tenuous grip on reality. The novelist uses familiar mythic or historical forms to combat the content of those forms and to conduct the reader . . . to the real, away from mystification to clarification, away from magic to maturity, away from mystery to revelation. And it is above all to the need for new modes of perception and fictional forms able to encompass them that I . . . address these stories."

Photograph by Stathis Orphanos. Courtesy of Georges Biorchardi, Inc.

Coover's next novel, *The Public Burning* (1977), brought him widespread critical notoriety. In this work, he uses facts from the 1953 conviction and execution of Julius and Ethel Rosenberg and features then-Vice President Richard Nixon as narrator. Creating bizarre scenes of perversity and violence, Coover emphasizes the destructiveness of some of America's self-conceptions. He said of this book: "I originally felt back in 1966 that the execution of the Rosenbergs had been a watershed event in American history which we had somehow managed to forget or repress. . . . I was convinced, one, that they were not guilty as charged, and, two, even had they been, the punishment was hysterical and excessive. . . . [It] was important that we remember it, that we not be so callous as to just shrug it off, or else it can happen again and again." Due to the controversial subject matter of *The Public Burning,* Coover had great difficulty securing a publisher for the book.

A Political Fable (1980) is an expanded version of Coover's short story "The Cat in the Hat for President" (1968). In this novel, Coover presents the zany character from Dr. Seuss's children's books as a presidential candidate. Despite its broad farce, the book ends with the cat's murder, symbolizing the death of artistic, creative energies. *Charlie in the House of Rue* (1980) is a novella which proceeds in the manner of a silent film. After beginning in a slapstick mode, the story soon becomes horrifically surreal, as the Chaplinesque protagonist unwittingly helps the heroine commit suicide and then frantically tries to save her. Coover manipulates such techniques as pratfalls and sight gags to show their inherent violence. *Spanking the Maid* (1981), written in the mode of the *nouveau roman*, or antinovel, is built around repetitions of a single scene. Richard Gilman stated: "*Spanking the Maid,* whose eroticism is a lure toward metaphysical awarenesses, delighted me with its daring and supple handling of the theme of time as ritual and obsession." The short story collection *In Bed One Night and Other Brief Encounters* (1983) demonstrates Coover's talent for transforming standard occurrences into extraordinary events. In these pieces, Coover focuses on the act of writing in order to explore the relationship between art and reality.

In the novel *Gerald's Party* (1985), Coover subverts the conventions of the English parlor mystery, as an enigmatic homicide at a party seems less important than the bizarre behavior of the sophisticated guests. Amid murders, copulations, and destruction of property, Gerald and his friends urbanely ruminate on art, time, love, and memory. Coover creates a disorienting, kaleidoscopic effect through continual disruptions of dialogue and action and extensive use of non sequiturs. Although the book is intended to be outrageous, *Gerald's Party* raises serious issues, including "the intransigence of death, the persistence of regret, the inadequacy of memory, [and] the unfathomability of causation," according to Robert Christgau. *A Night at the Movies* (1987) consists of short works which overturn the traditions of such classic Hollywood films as *Casablanca* and *High Noon*. "Feature-length" pieces are interspersed with brief vignettes similar to such early movie-house staples as previews, cartoons, short films, and an intermission. Michiko Kakutani noted that by reversing such stock cinematic motifs as good triumphing over evil and by refuting the essential human faith in cause-and-effect, "Mr. Coover is able to make us question our most fundamental social and cultural preconceptions."

(See also *CLC*, Vols. 3, 7, 15, 32; *Contemporary Authors*, Vols. 45-48; *Contemporary Authors New Revision Series,* Vol. 3; *Dictionary of Literary Biography,* Vol. 2; and *Dictionary of Literary Biography Yearbook: 1981.*)

ROBERT A. MORACE

That Robert Coover's novels, plays, and short fictions are strangely unsettling, both for the reader and the critic, is certain. His inconclusive plots and open-ended endings extend well beyond Hawthorne's "device of multiple choice," Melville's "ambiguities," and Whitman's "open road" to the characteristically modern confrontation between the reader and the indeterminate text. It would be a mistake, however, for the more tradition-minded reader to dismiss Coover's Borgesian "forking narratives" as the narcissistic play of the metafictionist who distrusts and therefore disrupts the political and philosophical implications of the "totalizing novel" (as Mas'ud Zavarzadeh has aptly termed it). Although his work is narratively and philosophically disruptive, it is (except for a few of his short fictions) accessible and compelling rather than hermetic and merely clever. Moreover, the stories he tells concern the typically American theme of the autonomous self, or more specifically, the individual's quest to create a meaningful fictional universe. . . . Against what Henry Adams called "the

bourgeois dream of order and inertia," Coover posits the creative and liberating possibilities of the human imagination. His characters lose their freedom when they passively accept roles in mythic systems that are, as Larry McCaffery has persuasively argued, "ideological" rather than "ontological" in nature. And what further complicates their situation, making their autonomy the more precarious, is the fact that they must mediate between various opposing extremes—self and society, fiction and experience, order and indeterminacy—as successfully as Coover mediates between the analogous poles of metafiction, with its characteristic stress on individual consciousness, and traditional narrative, with its more broadly social emphasis.

"To be obsessed by mystery, by the impossible Self and the tyrant Other, by paradox and flux . . . is a malady, to be sure, but a malady of some ('human' is the word) dimension." This quintessentially human obsession that Coover [in his essay **"The Last Quixote"**] finds in the work of Samuel Beckett is equally characteristic of his own distinctively American writings. His art, too, is "an exemplary settling down into the Self through all its pseudoselves and posturings, disguises, imaginative displacements, with no illusions, doubting even the wherewithal." In Coover, as in Beckett, there is a desperate, if at times clownish, concern for establishing the realm of the existentialist's authentic self. The individual's search for self-awareness and authenticity informs all of Coover's writings. But the "need to be cut off" that his characters feel is invariably qualified: "cut off for awhile." Against the desire for authenticity, they feel the counter desire to be "in there, with them." And therein lies the problem Coover's characters must face, for as Coover learned from his reading of Emile Durkheim, the dynamics of communal gatherings require the repression of individual freedom so that intensification of group power can result. Despite the flagrant and often grisly excesses of what Durkheim called the "collective effervescence" (the public burning of Julius and Ethel Rosenberg, for one), Coover's writings evidence a sympathetic understanding of the human need for community and ritual even in its most outrageous or ludicrous manifestations. Yet at the same time Coover clearly shows—as did Hawthorne, Whitman, Twain, and other typically American authors before him—how opposed this need is to the individual's desire for self-definition and imaginative freedom.

In its most elemental form, the conflict between self and other, which constitutes the basic plot of Coover's plays, stories, and novels, pits one archetypal character against another: the pattern-keeper, who accepts the determinacy of a teleological universe, versus the pattern-breaker, who embraces indeterminacy and imaginative freedom. Because it is usually the pattern-keeper (or the pattern-keeping half of the self) that emerges victorious, the individual's need for a receptive, flexible community is more often frustrated than fulfilled in Coover's work. Moreover, Coover's least imaginative characters are the ones most susceptible to becoming trapped in the plots of "the tyrant Other" or—what amounts to the same thing—trapped in that rigidity of character which Bergson has identified as the essence of comedy. Confusing the factitious with the real, the epistemological with the ontological, they restrict their lives to a narrow and unsatisfying plot in which there exists neither time nor space for the reflectiveness, spontaneity, imaginativeness, and play that would humanize them. In effect, they passively renounce the rich and bewildering variety of life that Coover asks his readers to acknowledge and accept, either directly, as in his "pricksong," **"Romance of the Thin Man and the Fat** lady,'' or more obliquely, in *The Kid*, a play about a communal plot gone awry. (pp. 192-94)

In *The Kid,* as in other Coover works, language is power. . . . [The] fact that figuratively or even literally mute characters appear quite frequently in Coover's work—for example, *The Kid,* **"The Wayfarer,"** **"A Pedestrian Accident,"** *Charlie in the House of Rue*—suggests that Coover is not especially optimistic about the individual's ability to control his linguistic environment. Rarely does he express the hopeful determination that characterizes the similarly postmodern fiction of, for example, Italo Calvino: "above us stretches another roof, the hull of words we secrete constantly. . . . There is no time to lose, I must understand the mechanism, find the place where we can get to work and stop this uncontrolled process." Calvino's reader believes man will prevail; Coover's reader is considerably less assured.

The problem of linguistic freedom—of the individual's ability to control his language and metaphors rather than be controlled by them—is, of course, central to those Coover works that deal specifically with the relationship between the artist and his audience. In his most explicit treatment of the artist-audience relation—presented, significantly, in the form of a pantomime—a magician uses hats, doves, rabbits, sex, and violence in a seemingly frantic and apparently unsuccessful attempt to win the approval of his easily jaded audience. If the magician does fail, then the story presents, as Neil Schmitz says, nothing more than the record "of his incapacity, his desperate striving." But to read **"The Hat Act"** in this way, it is necessary to regard the ending as unambiguous, which it clearly is not. The magician's failure to pull his assistant out of the hat can be read as evidence of his "incapacity" or as the magician's final and intentional illusion. If the assistant's death is an illusion, then the trick serves to free the magician momentarily from the demands of his voracious audience, and it also suggests that his already "desperate striving" will perforce become even more desperate in subsequent performances. The magician is free, but his freedom cannot last.

The magician's hat acts, the writer's fictions, the individual's imaginings, and the society's myths are alike in that they are simultaneously "empty" and "useful," meaningless and meaningful. We "pass our lives, or something like them," Coover has written, "fearfully encircling the voided core, minds averted." His work shows a dual emphasis: the existential self must recognize the absurdity of his existence, and at the same time he must find relief from that knowledge by devising fictions that create meaning and, by reason of their self-evident fictiveness, their play aspect, bring the "voided core" into even clearer focus. The struggle against a culture's mythic content that would overwhelm the self must be wedded to the struggle against the void that would deny the self any significance whatsoever. To create myths and fictions and to "test them against the experience of life" are both necessary human activities, Coover maintains. Though the appropriate relation between the two may best be described as one of perfect balance, it is precisely this equilibrium that his characters usually fail to achieve. Instead, they seem to move erratically along an arc that has system and closure at one end and indeterminacy at the other. (pp. 195-97)

Robert A. Morace, "Robert Coover, the Imaginative Self, and the 'Tyrant Other'," in Papers on Language & Literature, *Vol. 21, No. 2, Spring, 1985, pp. 192-209.*

CHARLES NEWMAN

Robert Coover has given us some of the most distinguished fiction of his generation. *The Origin of the Brunists* (1966), *The Universal Baseball Association* (1968) and long sections of *The Public Burning* (1977) are enduring works, demonstrating a total command of idiomatic American speech with a philosophical acuity rare in American literature. These are political and sexual parables at once deadly serious and deadly funny. In his most recent novel, however, Mr. Coover has both compressed and exploded his signature techniques well beyond comprehension. *Gerald's Party* is one we have all reluctantly been to, in both contemporary life and fiction, and the point is there will be no relief until it is over. A cranky courage is nevertheless operating here; as the narrator tells us, straight-faced: "The mirror, as parodist, did not lie—on the contrary—but neither did it merely reflect: rather, like a camera, it *created* the truth we saw in it, thereby murdering potentiality." And of all the murders in this book, the novel's own self-slaying is the only one with clear motivation and ruthless intent.

What we are given as propitiatory offering is the English parlor mystery—a gathering of eccentric characters, the sudden discovery of a body known to them all and the inevitable appearance of the detective. In the conventional entertainment genre, while the characters reveal themselves (and their social relations) through laconic, dispassionate conversation, the sleuth presumably maintains narrative momentum through deductive reasoning, eliminating suspects until we have a plausible accusation. The superior man of reason solves the crime, and we can turn out the light on yet another night mercifully foreshortened by the knowledge that if we could only gain a little distance and diffidence, the pattern of human behavior would reveal itself and justice be done. What Mr. Coover has done is to take all the elements of such conventional escapist literature, stand them on their head and create a literature of absolute affront. The mystery is not "who done it," but the inexplicable behavior of *all* the characters, including the author, an inexplicability not by default but by design.

"I disbelieved in fate, hated plays and novels whose plots were governed by it," the narrator tells us, and so the plot is one of random accretion, not momentum, impossible to summarize, but creating a kind of weird camaraderie between the readers and characters, as they both struggle against the author's willfulness. (p. 1)

As the avalanche of guests arrive, each to participate in what the news-media call "gratuitous sex and violence"—the point here seems to be that sex and violence are no more gratuitous than anything else—the characters become *less* clear the more they talk, until it is literally impossible to tell them apart. Worse than their criminal appetites is their predilection to philosophize on Art and Life. This is a reference not to their own debased condition but an instance of the author's use of fraudulence as a deliberate technique to subvert the conventional novel. After murdering his best friend, the narrator is asked, "How do you feel about nihilism as a viable art form?" It is very difficult for a reader who is pulling for an author while struggling with him, particularly one whose career is deserving of the greatest respect, to be told repeatedly that there are interesting theoretical reasons for his letting you down. So it is not the actual content of the book which is shocking, as much as the manner of the author in relating it, rubbing your nose in *his* conduct, perversely encouraging you to quit on him and cheering you on at the moment you are ready to chuck the whole thing.

Inspector Pardew is a wonderful character in spite of this, caught in a maze of police chalk lines which attempt to give a shape to the action, but end up only creating their own abstract design, an act of post facto criticism totally without reference.

Pardew is victim of the whole post-Miranda criminal-rights jargon, a specialist in high-minded relativism as irrelevance. But Mr. Coover is not being cheaply nihilistic here, for the distinct moral message of the book is clearly that in America, anybody—including the author—can get away with anything. The population can no more be outraged than the literary audience can be engaged.

By the time Pardew finally fingers the murderer, the initial crime seems the least of the horrors that have been perpetrated. It is a measure of Mr. Coover's relentlessness that we have been inured, like his characters, to *any* criminal behavior, and the culprit is not only "unlikely," but you have to reread the book to find out where he came in. The point being of course that the solution to the crime is the most inconsequential and arbitrary part of the mystery, that guilt, accountability and justice are mere literary conventions projected by the stupefied reader.

Among other things, the book is a fiendishly calculated study in interruption. No one gets to finish a sentence or sex act, much less a thought or coherent narrative, before he is interrupted by another's speech. Even the narrator's first person is invaded by parenthetical second guesses, memories and idle speculation, and while the texture is airless in the extreme, it remains technically fascinating and conveys perfectly the hallucinatory disconnectedness of a drunken party. But once the effect is achieved, it is flogged mercilessly and redundantly, typical of an esthetic which sneers at its own results while insistently trying to sell you on its method.

The real question the novel raises is—and it is a question supremely relevant to contemporary literature—can a work of art be truthful to the milieu it describes, truthful in its own procedures, truthful in its evisceration of literary conventions, and still be so willfully artless that you don't care about the truth—or the question in the first place?

It should be clear that Mr. Coover's book goes far beyond black humor and self-parody. It is a work of the purest, unremitting malevolence. (pp. 1, 21)

> Charles Newman, "Death as a Parlor Game," in The New York Times Book Review, *December 29, 1985, pp. 1, 21.*

MALCOLM BRADBURY

Gerald's Party has been described as a mock murder mystery, but the drawing room detective story is only one of many art forms played with and parodied in this novel of strong, sustained invention and impersonation. The party becomes a theater, a film, a fairy tale, and an ever-accelerating trade over the space between the real and the fantastic. It is a field of desire always dissolving and reforming, a sequence of pratfalls and interrupted fornications, of extraordinary rituals: "Butcherblock Blues," "The Host's Hang-Up" and "Candid Coppers" are only some of the dramas staged for our delight.

Stories are seen as cunning deceptions; here they turn into every kind of tease, transfigured by the erotic laws of estrangement, deception and reversal. The mystery is solved, in perfunctory fashion; it really doesn't matter. The sexual pursuit by Gerald of Alison, the girl he dreams of, turns through pratfalls into disaster. What holds the reader is the manipulation of an amazing cast of ever-moving figures, the constant multiplying of styles and situations, and above all the unremitting babble of voices.

Gerald's Party is a very erotic and also very esthetic novel, a flamboyant display of the writer's repertory. The book has many Postmodern habits—the characters are virtually characterless, they are voices, clothes and bodies constantly changing into other clothes and other bodies. There is clear philosophical dimension, to do with the relation of form to reality, as well as the relation between the storyteller's and the lover's habits of foreplay and combination. There are many deaths and various Gothic brutalities, all held within the frame of comedy.

The guests, those who survive, confess—after 312 pages in the same house, on the same evening—that they have had a very good time. You were probably out of town that night and missed it, which may have been wise. But you certainly should not miss what Gerald says about that infinitely memorable evening in the brilliant display that is *Gerald's Party*.

> Malcolm Bradbury, "Scenes from an Evening's Revelry," *in* Book World—The Washington Post, *January 19, 1986, p. 5.*

RICHARD GILMAN

I've always admired Robert Coover's fiction a little more than I've enjoyed it. The pleasures of his work aren't obscure. *The Universal Baseball Association* especially recommended itself; years ahead of Coover's protagonist, I had as a boy invented a baseball game using cards and dice, organized a league with imaginary players, and so, like J. Henry Waugh, lived for a while in a surrogate, compensatory reality. *Spanking the Maid,* whose eroticism is a lure toward metaphysical awarenesses, delighted me with its daring and supple handling of the theme of time as ritual and obsession. Even *The Public Burning,* Coover's erratic, distended grotesquerie about the Rosenbergs and Watergate, has set pieces of great cleverness and charm.

Still, Coover's ideas often outrun his means. It's easy to get fatigued or irritated by his fiction, and yet honor its intentions—which is the way I feel about much of Barth, Hawkes, Gass, Barthelme, Pynchon, and Gaddis, the best writers we have. This has everything to do with the writers' seriousness, with the ambition of Coover and the others to make fiction do more or other than its conventional job of reflecting, exposing, comforting, diverting, or tacking meaning onto our actualities. . . .

For all the different forms it takes, the project of these writers is to force language to reveal itself, and narrative modes to reveal, by analogy, ontological or metaphysical conditions. Unlike the classic 19th-century novel, such fiction (like theater that has stopped trying to "represent") offers very little assured hold on our experience beyond the page. The writing is the experience, functioning in one or more of these ways: as trap, fertile lie, jest, weapon, game, dirge.

It's a noble, nearly impossible attempt to bring us out of chaos and deceit, and sometimes an exhausting one. (p. 28)

Coover's new novel [*Gerald's Party*] is ambitious, original, bizarre, harrowing, and often tedious, a book unlike any other long piece of fiction I know, although there are some technical resemblances to Nathalie Sarraute's work, *The Planetarium* in particular, and to Gaddis's *JR*. *Gerald's Party* takes place over a single evening and night. On the surface it seems to be at once a parody of detective fiction, a satire on our hedonism, a tale of life as theater, and interspersed with everything else, a set of reflections on time. It is indeed all of these, but only, as rapidly becomes clear, as strategies and instigations toward something deeper and more complex.

Gerald and his (unnamed) wife are giving one of their famous parties. The guests are all "creative" or pseudo-creative types, in their 30s and 40s mostly. At the center of the night's events is a woman they all know, a celebrated sexy actress named Ros, who is found murdered on the living room floor as the book begins. The police come and set up a zany "laboratory.". . . More guests arrive, mayhem breaks out, more killings take place, toilets are stuffed up, the house is wrecked, sexual activity sprouts in every corner, chaos ensues, and the mystery is finally "solved."

Quickly the reader becomes aware that something is very wrong with the depiction of these events, that something "unlifelike" is going on at the heart of so seemingly naturalistic a tale. On the one hand Coover is exquisitely precise in his dense physical descriptions. . . . On the other hand, everyone behaves with extraordinary inappropriateness. The police aren't called for several hours. The bodies are allowed to lie around throughout the night. A film is undertaken with the dead Ros as its "star." In general, all the horror that would normally be felt at such carnage is transposed to an emotional and moral key of astonishing remoteness from the facts, a business- (or fun-) as-usual mood that has the effect of framing the action in disjunction, under a harsh philosophical light. (p. 29)

Behind the weirdly irrelevant or dreamily incongruous responses to the horrific or revolting events . . . is an impressive aesthetic and philosophical intention that, as nearly as I can make out, resembles in good part the one Coover ascribed to Cervantes: to fight against out-worn and inherited modes, to create "new complexities," and finally, to encompass the unsynthesizable.

At the risk of oversimplifying, one can say that the discrepancy between act and reaction leaves a space for moral sensibility to work by undermining, in the interest of new consciousness, our expectations of narrative. What we anticipate—overt or implicit dismay, disgust, indictment—is untrustworthy, Coover suggests, because such reactions tell us nothing new at the same time that they invariably mask a residue of barbarism, the fascination we secretly have with disaster and excess.

More than that, the events immediately lend themselves—openly to the characters, covertly to us as voyeurs—to a theatrical impulse. Life is seen as a series of dramas, a set of impersonations: victim, lover, murderer, artist, host, policeman, wife. "What is life, after all," a character in a Coover story asks, "but a caravan of lifelike forgeries?" Things happen so we can enact or witness them. Inauthentic role-players, we await our cues. Conventional fiction, through "identification," reinforces this. In a crucial comment on the novel Gerald thinks: "Memories always come before the experiences we attach to them. . . ."

Memories are sundered from experience, actions from values; and one task of commonplace fiction is to jam them together again. In the same way, formal, traditional theater provides us with activities to which we can instantly assign value—value that otherwise floats above us in a realm of abstraction. But, as *Gerald's Party* is trying to demonstrate, our whole lives have become fictional, theatrical. All is matter for our histrionic cravings.

Theater, Gerald says, is "an atavistic folk rite," a "hallucination at the service of reality." Hence the obscene use of Ros's body for a film, the frequent monologues, the continual arrival of new "cast" members, the conversations that sound scripted. All is performance. (pp. 29-30)

And yet there are difficulties. Coover's project of synthesizing disparate experience leads him to a novel whose structure of utterance and idea is thoroughly discontinuous, though moving along in a rough chronology. It is fragmented, jagged, elliptical, and centrifugal; the book proliferates rather than proceeds. Conversations are interrupted by thoughts and vice versa. Speeches are broken up by physical descriptions and then resumed. Much of the time the characters don't really talk to each other but as if to an invisible audience; the phenomenon is what the Germans call *aneinandervorbeisprechen*—to speak "past" another, to fail to connect verbally.

The purpose of all this disjunction and solipsism, as both the novel's subject and its style, is to sweep up in one net, as it were, the discontinuity and jumble of our behavior, to exhibit our values evading our actions and the other way round, to show how we act from primitive, unacknowledged motives. The aim is to make cognizable the disorder, illogic, and atomization of our social and psychic beings. Presiding over this valorous, quixotic endeavor is a dream other writers have had: to create an effect of synchronicity, of simultaneity, as a blow against the illusion of progression—to write a play, a poem, or a story in which everything exists, as nearly as possible, all at once.

But what problems for the mind, or to begin with, for the eye! I don't know another novel in which there are so many quotation marks, dashes, dots, parentheses. A dizzying profusion of punctuation separates the parts yet holds them together. One is hard put to keep track of who's speaking to whom, what exactly is happening. More than that, the constant breaks force you to keep casting your mind backward to the beginnings of interrupted sequences to pick up the threads, to separate speech from thought, to *follow*. The style also has the effect of diminishing the distinctiveness of the characters, who tend to merge or overlap with one another, to blur or to decompose. It's exhausting to have to keep identifying them, connecting them with what they did or said before. At times I longed for one of those lists of characters in Russian novels, which you consult to keep the names straight.

I battled with the book throughout. Yet at times I also yielded to it. Apart from the ambitiousness and the inventiveness, there's an accretion of incidental insight and wisdom. (p. 30)

Richard Gilman, "Invitation to Mayhem," in The New Republic, Vol. 194, No. 12, March 24, 1986, pp. 28-30.

ROBERT CHRISTGAU

In theory, Coover stretches us every time out, nowhere more thoroughly than in *Gerald's Party,* the fourth novel of a prolific and varied two-decade career. Coover says his latest book "contains almost all the elements of my previous novels," which is the kind of thing you might expect him to claim for his first full-length work since 1977 and is true nevertheless. Ostensibly an Americanized English murder mystery complete with shrewd sleuth and houseful of suspects, *Gerald's Party* reveals its recondite purposes almost as quickly as one of Coover's short ''fictions,'' the controlled environments where he conducts his frankest experiments. Thus it's like all his novels, only more so. All of them tell a synopsizable story that parodies/subverts/exploits the folk/popular with explicit mythic/metaphoric intent; all descend from relatively calm and solid narrative into a whirlpool of violently orgiastic incident. But over the years each of these usages has shown the taste for its own tail that is to be expected from any artist with Coover's highly conscious interest in form as form. Plot—not to mention character—atrophies; folk/popular content transmutes into form; myth and metaphor parade around with their clothes off; calm seems less prelude than illusion, sex-and-violence not metaphor but the ground of all being. . . .

[In] *Gerald's Party,* the whodunit quickly disappears beneath a bacchanal of snatched conversation, theatrical ritual, and of course sex-and-violence. When it's finally ''solved''—almost by the bye mostly to prick our underlying assumptions—it's impossible and probably inappropriate to care who murdered the first of the novel's numerous decedents, a nymph whose loss the male reader, at least, is inclined to mourn.

It isn't very metafictional of Coover to make Ros so lovable. . . . In fact, identifying with characters as if they were human beings is so frowned upon in this artistic microcosm that not just Ros but the novel's other sympathetic figures—host-cocksman-narrator Gerald, the nearest Coover's come to an autobiographical protagonist since Miller the newspaperman in *The Origin of the Brunists;* Gerald's flame, Alison, a paradigm of intelligent lust; painter Tania and author Vic, who philosophize with some cogency before the novel kills them—may well represent a misstep on Coover's aestheticist path. Of course, by choosing the metaphor of an arty party he's inviting identification from his arty readers, and as his partisans will no doubt huff, he's probably just testing us. Ros is a porn fantasy, Alison and Tania and Vic get theirs, and in due time the book undermines not only Gerald's credibility but the self-probing self-satisfaction that makes him sympathetic. We like Tania's or Vic's ideas, an affection artificially enhanced by the skill of Coover's dramatization, and then make the mistake of extending this affection into some illusory ''personal'' realm, where it's doomed to drown in the bathtub or get shot through the heart. Gerald's parties deliquesce inevitably into disaster, and his love for the ladies isn't so supreme that he can muster the wherewithal to protect Alison, who winds up getting gangraped in the basement, or his loyal, hard-working, nameless wife, who a few hours after the cops have searched her rectum joins Gerald for a great lay and then pads off to sleep, leaving our protagonist in utter existential solitude as Ros yanks ferociously at his balls (don't worry—it's only a dream, or a rehearsal, or an image, or a mistake, or The End).

For all the telegraphic description and dependent clauses of this synopsis, it doesn't begin to suggest the novel's hectic mood. It's impossible to keep the thing straight, which is what Coover wants. There are too many characters, some of whom go the way of all flesh by hearsay only, not even bothering to show their corpses. Ros's entire acting troupe commandeer house and guests in improvised obsequies. Though the novel is mostly dialogue, no conversation proceeds uninterrupted for even a page, and Coover enjoys sticking random remarks from passing onlookers into the middle of crucial (and not so crucial) utterances and ruminations. Yet at the same time, *Gerald's Party* (like all of his novels) *moves,* something no one can claim for Hawkes's *Second Skin* or, God knows, Gass's *Omen-*

setter's Luck. And while Coover's transcriptions of speech aren't totally free of annoying condescension, his fascination with American idiom adds a richness of texture you won't find in Barth or Barthelme or Hawkes, who for their various reasons are all more British in diction and/or rhythm than has been common in our literature. There really is something Rabelaisian in Coover's sense of humor, and his raunch is juicy enough to alarm reviewers. So we're hit with a potent combination—a formal scheme that makes a proper metafictional mockery of teleological narratives yet doesn't disdain all the amenities we associate with them.

In theory, this is swell, but in fact, *Gerald's Party* is the least of Coover's novels. I suppose I prefer it personally to his most popular book, *The Universal Baseball Association.* . . . But the formal intensifications of Coover's latest effort sell him short. The master of rhetoric who brings forth the dazzling fictions of *Pricksongs & Descants* and fleshes out *The Public Burning* hardly pokes through the tangle of dialogue here, and the crafter of flawless descriptive prose is choked altogether. Though Coover's political ideas are marred by an elitist's japes and an exile's exaggerations, I miss the political impulses that inform much of what he's published in the last decade. And though it's unreasonable to expect stone genius of any writer, I admit that I was hoping for something on the order of *The Public Burning*'s Nixon, a mind-boggling creation not least because his namesake's status as a historical personage confounds the kind of character-identification metafiction warns us to mistrust.

In theory, *Gerald's Party* is the poppest of all Coover's novels; in fact—and probably as a direct consequence, given the distaste of pretentious white American men for full-fledged pop—it's the most rarefied. Though you have to hand it to Coover for continuing to produce novels in the face of the metafictional void, something only Hawkes has managed readily, *Gerald's Party* would seem to betray a certain groping around for material. Despite his fondness for the American idiom, Coover has spent large parts of his adult life in England and Spain, returning for the teaching jobs that now seem to have made him a permanent resident again, and his novels have manifested an accumulating distance—first a good philosophical yarn rooted in personal observation [*The Origin of the Brunists*], then a more fantastic book reflecting his baseball-fan boyhood [*The Universal Baseball Association, Inc., J. Henry Waugh, Prop.*], then a researched historical novel [*The Public Burning*], and finally an arty party, one thing fringe academics generally know plenty about. Considering what he's given himself to work with, it's small surprise that the non-ostensible subject of *Gerald's Party* turns out to be about as innovative as the wild party itself. If I'm not mistaken, it's Coover's hope to unravel or discover or understand our basic underlying assumptions about—oh dear—Time.

Maybe I'm too young to fully appreciate such things, but I've always felt that novels about Time succeed (Proust) or fail (*Ada*) irrespective of their metaphysical revelations. No matter what's contraindicated by subatomic physics or mystico-philosophical introspection, the events of which almost all these novels still (ostensibly) consist take place in something like a sequential, diachronic dimension, a dimension that's *physically* human (mammalian, say) in scale, and the novelist is hard-pressed to dislodge them without resorting to the kind of sci-fi devices that are beneath pretentious white American men. This isn't to dismiss such excellent Time-related themes as the intransigence of death, the persistence of regret, the inadequacy of memory, the unfathomability of causation, all of which *Gerald's Party* does its erudite yet idiomatic bit with (while keeping its distance from their corn quotient, of course). I'll go along with Vic, for instance, when he argues that "rigidified memory, attachment to the past" is the only crime (only I wouldn't say only), and I know why Tania insists that "art's great task is to reconcile us to the true *human* time of *the eternal present,* which the child in us *knows* to be the real one!" But I'm afraid Tania is getting a little too close to Inspector Pardew, who posits a world in which space is fluid and time fixed and eventually concludes that Ros was done in by a satyrical dwarf who makes his entrance well after the guests notice her body on the floor. Even worse, I'm afraid Coover is setting Pardew up to do the hard part for him—to jar events into a properly metafictional dimension, to deprive us of the teleological comfort that no reader interested enough to get to the end of this book is likely to feel much need for. Maybe Pardew is just venting his anti-satyr prejudice, or maybe he knows something about the dwarf's movements that omnipotent Gerald doesn't bother to mention. Maybe he's fitting facts to theory, or maybe he's creating truth with it. It's hard to know what Coover thinks. And impossible, or inappropriate, to care.

One reason it's inappropriate is the games Coover plays with authorial authority, but nowhere is it harder to take him at his word—there's just too much self-congratulation built into metafictional practice. Consider Gerald's genius in bed. As in Hawkes's *The Blood Oranges,* a clearer and more disturbing book in which the narrator-protagonist is cooler about but no less possessed by his sexual prowess, it's a peachy metaphor for authorial omnipotence and—in Coover's case, not Hawkes's—its discontents. But either way it has the convenient side effect of making the *author* (as opposed to the narrator) look like an ass man. After all, mandarins generally think quite a lot of themselves. Just as in Beckett (a key influence on Coover, who went on to Joyce through him) the act of writing stands as a not-so-mute corrective to the nearly absolute pessimism of its (ostensible) message, so in Coover the act of showing off counteracts any pretensions to self-critical humility—which may be yet another conscious contradiction for us to chew over, and so what? (pp. 7-8)

Coover is one of those select contemporary writers who is genuinely awestruck by the pervasive power of the tools of his trade, an honorary citizen of structuralism's vast domain. As a pretentious white American man, he has no built-in beef with American society that Richard Hofstadter didn't long ago win a Pulitzer for complaining about, and thus he's free to peer at it from outside and above, like an astronaut photographing the whole earth; he's a formalist at least partly because he was given the chance to be. Though like most formalists he's strongest when he struggles willy-nilly against formalism's confines, if you strip his ideas down you'll find a good many middlebrow commonplaces—his carefully ironized male chauvinism, his political despair, his black humor itself. So it's his focus on form, and on words themselves, that we read him for—less the way he breaks apart the comforting rigidities of conventional storytelling than the way he builds up the sharp, diverting pleasures of the other kind. Still, there's an attractive intellectual strand there, a skeptic's fascination with simple faith that's heartier and more democratic than anything comparable you can pick out in his colleagues, sort of a cosmic counterpart to his abiding passion for the words he instructs us not to believe in. If you happen not to be a convinced formalist yourself, you could even say his work has content.

And maybe one way of explaining what went wrong with *Gerald's Party* is that his skepticism overcame his fascination and made the book brittle.

Or put it another way. I wouldn't say the best of Coover's work achieves any eternal present—that dream of synchrony is an old one among art-for-art's-sakers, obsessed as they understandably are with focusing their frustrated religious yearnings, and as Coover makes clear, it's impossible—but maybe it offers a dirty glimpse of it. And maybe in *Gerald's Party* Coover wants to make sure we concentrate on the window. (p. 8)

Robert Christgau, "What Pretentious White Men Are Good For," in VLS, No. 44, April, 1986, pp. 7-8.

ROBERT TOWERS

Robert Coover's *The Public Burning* (1977) is a good example of a novel in the bullwhip-and-manacles mode. Prolix, dazzling in its reproduction of American speech patterns, wildly and often farcically inventive, it is also remorseless in its determination to hold the reader captive in a situation that includes not only the prolonged agony of Ethel Rosenberg but the sodomization of Richard Nixon by that raunchy, goat-bearded old wind-bag, Uncle Sam. Though Coover's new novel lacks the political savagery of its predecessor, *Gerald's Party* is equally relentless in its pursuit of outrage and its attempt to reduce the reader to a condition of helpless and exhausted voyeurism. It is also a work of considerable comic vitality, full of inspired mimicry and parody, gleeful in its unabashed sadism.

"None of us noticed the body at first"—so the novel begins. The party at Gerald's house has been under way for hours, though only one guest has so far passed out. Gerald is busy refilling drinks and his wife (who is never given a name) is busy supplying food—activities which they will both conscientiously pursue throughout the ensuing chaos. The victim, Ros, has been lying on the living-room floor while the guests mill around her obliviously. . . .

Coover's technique of constant distraction and interruption—ranging from broken-off conversations to *fellatio interrupta*—creates a jerky, strobe-lit effect that is augmented by the ceaseless coming and going of the huge cast of guests—Chuck, Naomi, Sally Ann, Soapie, Tania, Dickie, etc. The reader is bombarded with fragments of scenes, with snatches of disembodied talk, with dizzying non sequiturs. . . .

Through the nightmarish din and flickering lights of the novel certain characters emerge with a kind of Dickensian clarity of outline. One is Gerald's wife, who moves imperturbably, if sometimes a bit wearily, through the novel, not only dishing out food but cleaning up the awful recurrent messes, introducing newcomers, and helping with the various crises as they occur. "I do wish people wouldn't use guns in the house," she complains mildly after a guest has been shot.

Then there is Inspector Pardew, who mouths such pronouncements as

> Murder, like laughter, is a muscular solution
> of conflict, biologically substantial and inevitable, a psychologically imperative and, in the
> case of murder, death-dealing act that *must* be
> related to the *total ontological reality!*

Just before the revelation (if it is that) of Ros's murderer, the inspector ruminates, pipe in hand, on crime as a "form of life depreciation." . . .

A kind of maniacal laughter rings through *Gerald's Party*. Middle American rituals of conviviality, the pretensions of home-grown theatrical groups, the mangled ethos of the sexual revolution, the conventions of pornographic writing and of the detective novel—all are fed into Coover's satanic mill. Coover, with his attuned ear for blather and eye for the unconscious buffoonery of our times, can be wonderfully funny. Yet *Gerald's Party* is a punishing book. It never lets up. Like *The Public Burning* before it, the novel goes on too long, burdening the reader with a sensory overload from which there is no respite. If *Gerald's Party* were half its length, it would be, I think, a small masterpiece of comic outrageousness. But as things stand, nothing depicted in the book is quite so perverse as Coover's insistence on benumbing us—his reader-victim—with a plethora of repeated effects. I enjoyed much of *Gerald's Party,* but well before the end I was ready to reach for the nearest Trollope.

Robert Towers, "Screams and Whispers," in The New York Review of Books, *Vol. XXXIII, No. 7, April 24, 1986, p. 38.*

MICHIKO KAKUTANI

Of all the post-modernist writers, Robert Coover is probably the funniest and most malicious, mixing up broad social and political satire with vaudeville turns, lewd pratfalls and clever word plays that make us rethink both the mechanics of the world and our relationship to it. The targets of his manic imagination are large—including religion (*The Origin of the Brunists*), baseball (*The Universal Baseball Association, J. Henry Waugh, Prop.*), the Presidency and anti-Communist fervor (*The Public Burning*)—and the methods he employs are often equally subversive of literary and philosophical conventions. In *Pricksongs and Descants,* he rewrote the stories of Joseph and Mary, Little Red Riding Hood, and Hansel and Gretel. In *Gerald's Party,* he refashioned the old-fashioned mystery story, turning its orderly narrative process into a mirror of mayhem and fear.

Now, in *A Night at the Movies,* Mr. Coover does a similar number on old-time Hollywood films—a perfect subject, when you think about it, for his malevolent magic. Not only do such movies rely upon conventional (and easily parodied) forms, but in doing so, they also tend to reinforce traditional values—a faith that good will triumph over evil, order over chaos, as well as a more basic belief in cause and effect, sense and sensibility. Thus, by inverting such conventions, Mr. Coover is able to make us question our most fundamental social and cultural preconceptions. . . .

Certainly the three full-length "features" in this volume (billed ironically enough as "Adventure!" "Comedy!" and "Romance!") do a thorough job of destroying all our fondest expectations, while serving, at the same time, as wittily observant exercises in mimicry. In **"Shootout at Gentry's Junction,"** the Sheriff—"'a tough honest man with clear speech and powerful hands, fast hands, fair hands and sure'"—sets out to rid his town of the notorious Mexican bandit Don Pedo. Though the Sheriff's a tidy—and often very funny—compilation of every good guy-western cliché ("there was no sun in his eyes, here in his office, but still he squinted as he stared toward the old screen door"), he fails miserably in his showdown with

Don Pedo, who winds up killing all the good guys and making off with their women.

In *Charlie in the House of Rue,* the rules of comedy are similarly subverted. In this case, Chaplin's Little Tramp—meticulously described in terms of gestures and idiosyncratic mannerisms—is placed in a booby-trapped house of horrors. Things begin normally enough—Charlie looks about, does a lot of business with his hat and cane—but they quickly escalate into chaos: not only do objects defy him (as they do in the original movies), but people also begin to act very strangely. By the end of Mr. Coover's little drama, a woman has hanged herself, another woman has sexually assaulted Charlie and Charlie himself is left stranded in this surreal world, in which the reassuring conventions of slapstick humor no longer apply. . . .

Although each of [the] segments of *A Night at the Movies* is unnecessarily repetitious, although each is somewhat predictable in its willful perversity, they all manage to engage the reader's attention, thanks largely to Mr. Coover's wonderful ear for language and his eye for cinematic detail. His impersonations of famous screen personalities are initially so convincing that we're lulled into believing the characters we're reading about are the same ones we've come to know and love on the screen. Consequently, we're shocked and dismayed when they fail, in Mr. Coover's hands, to continue to fulfill their designated roles.

The technique of setting up a familiar scenario and then destroying it is also used in other portions of this volume. **"After Lazarus"** mixes up motifs from artsy European films with ones from old horror pictures, while **"Intermission," "The Phantom of the Movie Palace"** and **"Cartoon"** all play on the blurring of lines between life and fiction, reality and art. The idea will no doubt remind one of Woody Allen's *Purple Rose of Cairo,* but the arch tone and darkly subversive viewpoint are distinctly Mr. Coover's own. If his aim in these stories is to discomfit his readers, while amusing them, he has defiantly succeeded.

Michiko Kakutani, in a review of "A Night at the Movies; or, You Must Remember This," in The New York Times, *January 7, 1987, p. C24.*

JOHN BLADES

Even though he calls the chapter, **"You Must Remember This,"** you'll scarcely recognize the scene from *Casablanca* that Robert Coover describes in *A Night at the Movies.* Coover does, however, use a familiar episode as the framework for his wickedly inventive and sacrilegious sendup of the film. It comes midway through the picture: With Victor Laszlo off at the underground meeting, Ilsa pays a surreptitious visit to Rick in his apartment above the *Cafe Americain,* the first time they've been alone since Paris. She draws a gun, demands the letters of transit. He refuses, saying: "Go ahead and shoot. You'll be doing me a favor." She swoons, drops the gun, and collapses in his arms. Fade to black.

What happened during that fadeout was discreetly left to the imagination of movie audiences, one of those romantic ellipses for which the old Hollywood is so affectionately remembered. In his shamelessly unaffected amplification on that scene, Coover leaves nothing to the imagination. And while few moviegoers presumed that Ilsa and Rick's relationship was platonic, they probably never dreamed it was quite so uninhibited—or so hilarious. "This is love in all its clammy mystery," Coover observes, in one of the few reprintable passages, "the ultimate connection, the squishy rub of truth, flesh as self-consuming message. This is necessity, as in woman needs man, and man must have his mate."

As the last sentence indicates, Coover is not only determined to sabotage the romantic pretensions of *Casablanca,* and other Hollywood monuments, but to transform the classic dialogue, even the lyrics from "As Time Goes By," into ribald punch lines and double entendres. . . .

The *Casablanca* sequence is the last chapter in Coover's book of short "fictions," all of which demonically spin off from the conventions and cliches of old Hollywood films, with allusions to *High Noon, Top Hat, Gilda,* Charlie Chaplin comedies, cartoons, previews of coming attractions, selected short subjects, and Saturday afternoon serials. There's even a scene in a projection booth, a "phantom" tour of an old movie palace, and an intermission, which also turn into a series of B-movie escapades.

If anything else in Coover's post-modernist montage were half as clever or funny as his night in *Casablanca,* the book would be a howling success. But the only other mildly amusing episode is his Western parody, **"Shootout at Gentry's Junction,"** in which Sheriff Henry Harmon . . . has to shoot it out with Don Pedo, who is both a comic caricature of a gold-toothed Frito bandido and a notorious sodomist.

Never a gentle or ironic humorist, in such sociopolitical fables as **The Public Burning,** Coover is not so much out to mock and lampoon Hollywood cliches as to destroy them, and, with one exception, there's almost no pleasure in his performance. Coover seems to have almost nothing but contempt and disrespect for audiences as well as movies. "Maybe the real world is too much for most people," he notes in an aside. "Maybe making up stories is a way to keep them all from going insane." But until we arrive in Coover's hardcore Casablanca, *A Night at the Movies* is itself an often maddening experience, like being forced to read interminable descriptive passages from a stack of unproduced, and unproducible, movie scripts.

> *John Blades, "A Night to Remember in Coover's 'Casablanca'," in* Chicago Tribune, *January 18, 1987, p. 3.*

EDMUND WHITE

Erwin Panofsky, the great art historian, recognized that to know a painting requires recreating it within the mind as an "object of inward experience." Robert Coover has extended this doctrine to the movies. His new collection of short fictions [*A Night at the Movies*] doesn't refer to the bewitching influence of films on receptive minds, as did Walker Percy's novel *The Moviegoer* and Woody Allen's film *The Purple Rose of Cairo.* Nor, at some other literary extreme, does Mr. Coover simply write a whole novel that turns out to be an epic movie, as Thomas Pynchon did in *Gravity's Rainbow.* Robert Coover has made literary art out of a total immersion in the movies. He isn't merely recycling old movie plots or drawing on the glamorous atmosphere of Hollywood. Rather, what he's doing is enlarging his literary technique by forcing it to assimilate cinematic conventions and to approximate filmic style. To say so perhaps makes the book sound stiff, but *A Night at the Movies* is as vivacious and entertaining as it is one hundred percent American.

The book gives us a long, exhilarating evening at an old-fashioned movie palace. In fact it begins with **"The Phantom of the Movie Palace,"** a sort of celluloid delirium that in 24 pages comes off as the most sustained display of verbal pyrotechnics I've encountered in years. . . .

The first short of the evening is **"After Lazarus,"** an arty horror picture from Eastern Europe or Scandinavia, perhaps. It's a chilling, stylized film, which Mr. Coover narrates in the language of a scenario ("Slow even tilt down to a village . . ."). As the title indicates, the tale is about rising from the dead, but the results are ghoulish and not at all miraculous. Mr. Coover confines his overflowing imagination by restricting himself to describing the soundtrack and the camera work, nothing more. Just as painting was enriched by its supposed enemy, photography, so literature is profiting from contact with the movies.

At the same time, Mr. Coover defiantly demonstrates the greater precision and flexibility of the written word. In **"Lap Dissolves,"** for instance, one scene blends into another but through puns and metaphors, never through the superimposition of visual images. When a woman about to be slaughtered by a pirate's cutlass bites his nose off and chews it "like a cow chewing its cud," a second later she is milking a cow on a peaceful farm, dreaming of adventures ("the milk squirting into the bucket between her legs echoes her excitement or perhaps in some weird way *is* her excitement"). Transitions (the "dissolves") through metaphor and metonymy are all purely verbal.

In **"Shootout at Gentry's Junction,"** the funniest piece in the book, sex, violence and racism mingle and savagery triumphs over law and order. Don Pedo, the Mexican bandit with the luminous gold teeth, imposes his reign of terror and lust on the lily-livered cowboys and their ladies. Indeed, the whole book slowly reveals that it is a pandemonium of anarchic passions, aberrant scripts, unleashed imagery.

Mr. Coover has understood the potential of the movies to persuade and to subvert but also to go out of control and through collage to hybridize unexpected nightmares. Thus in **Charlie in the House of Rue** the Little Tramp meets Poe, and Chaplin's pranks turn into sinister acts of violence. Or in **"Cartoon"** the ical collides queasily with the animated. In a different vein, **"Milford Junction, 1939: A Brief Encounter"** scrupulously sets the scene for a bittersweet Noël Coward love story—but then hilariously releases into this hushed milieu an eruption of animal and terribly un-British sexual desire.

Chaplin, Bogart, Fred Astaire, Valentino as the Sheik—these are a few of the myths re-imagined in this breviary of cinematic legends. Mr. Coover, to be sure, has always been attracted to mythology, as have the other postmodernist masters of his generation, each in his own way. . . .

But Robert Coover needs precisely the fixed boundaries of pop mythology to corral the toros of his anarchic imagination, somewhat as Joyce required the Ulysses myth to limit the proliferating possibilities of his technique. In an earlier collection of stories, **Pricksongs & Descants,** Mr. Coover drew on Hansel and Gretel as well as Noah, Falstaff (in a television panel game), Chronos (devouring his children in a train station) and Joseph and Mary. . . .

In his most recent novel, **Gerald's Party,** Mr. Coover doesn't evoke either pop or classical mythology, but he does begin to mix the reality of an all-night, orgiastic suburban party with the fantasy of the media (television programs and pornographic films that start to slide off the screen)—a vertiginous collage technique that anticipates the disturbing comedy of *A Night at the Movies*.

Early on in his career Mr. Coover invoked the spirit of Cervantes and complained that "the optimism, the innocence, the aura of possibility you experienced have been largely drained away, and the universe is closing in on us again." But in fact, as his dazzling career continues to demonstrate, Mr. Coover, though never innocent or optimistic, is a one-man Big Bang of exploding creative force.

> *Edmund White, "Splice Memory," in* The New York Times Book Review, *February 1, 1987, p. 15.*

Len Deighton

1929-

(Born Leonard Cyril Deighton) English novelist, nonfiction writer, short story writer, scriptwriter, and editor.

Deighton is a popular author of spy fiction whose first novel, *The Ipcress File* (1962), became a best-seller and set the standards by which critics appraise his later works. Deighton has been commended for creating a protagonist who, unlike most heroes of the genre, is working-class, cynical, wary of authority, and, most importantly, susceptible to human frailties. Along with John le Carré, Deighton is regarded as an innovator in the spy genre due to his realistic depictions of cold war espionage. His complex plots are narrated in an elliptical style which reflects the chaos of intelligence work.

Deighton's early spy thrillers are perhaps his most highly regarded novels. In *The Ipcress File,* which focuses upon the abduction of British scientists by criminals who intend to sell their services to a foreign power, Deighton introduces an anonymous narrator who reappears in several of his subsequent works. *Horse under Water* (1963) concerns drug trafficking and is written in the same style as *The Ipcress File. Funeral in Berlin* (1964), considered by some critics to be Deighton's best spy novel, depicts his hero's struggle to rescue a Russian scientist from East Berlin. This book was frequently compared to le Carré's masterpiece, *The Spy Who Came in from the Cold. The Billion Dollar Brain* (1966) portrays the agent's attempt to dismantle a computerized spy organization run by a conservative Texas millionaire. In *An Expensive Place to Die* (1967), Deighton examines the treachery inherent in intelligence work. Deighton's later suspense novels, *Spy Story* (1974), *Yesterday's Spy* (1975), and *Twinkle, Twinkle, Little Spy* (1976), although perceived by some critics as formulaic, were fairly well received.

Deighton has composed several works of fiction outside the spy thriller genre. *Only When I Larf* (1968), a humorous novel that focuses on a trio of con artists, is told in separate sections by each character. *Bomber: Events Relating to the Last Flight of an R.A.F. Bomber over Germany on the Night of June 31, 1943* (1970) is a fictionalized account of a World War II aerial battle. This extensively researched story is narrated alternately from the point of view of Allied flyers and their enemies. *Close-Up* (1972), which was well received by critics, concerns an author who agrees to ghostwrite an autobiography for a famous actor but decides instead to write the true story in novel form after researching the star's seamy past. *Declarations of War* (1971) collects Deighton's short stories about modern warfare and includes tales of the American Civil War, World Wars I and II, and guerilla warfare in South America. *SS-GB: Nazi-Occupied Britain, 1941* (1975) and *XPD* (1981) are speculative accounts of World War II. *SS-GB,* which details life in London and Europe based on the premise that Germany won the war, displays Deighton's ability to create convincing backgrounds. *XPD,* which John Sutherland termed an example of "the 'secret history of the war' genre," depicts the discovery of "the Hitler minutes," a transcript of a fictitious meeting between Adolf Hitler and English prime minister Winston Churchill in which Churchill offered to surrender on almost traitorous terms. *Goodbye, Mickey Mouse* (1982) is set in wartime Britain and

Photograph by Mark Gerson

tells of a pair of American fighter pilots who fall in love with two English women.

Deighton has also achieved recognition as a competent military historian. *Fighter: The True Story of the Battle of Britain* (1977) recounts the strategy, weaponry, and daily events leading to the first important combat fought exclusively in the air and Germany's first major defeat of World War II. Deighton conveys the significance of this battle and deflates various myths and legends about the Royal Air Force. *Airshipwreck* (1978) traces the relatively brief history of zeppelins and their numerous crashes. *Blitzkrieg: From the Rise of Hitler to the Fall of Dunkirk* (1979) is an account of Hitler's "lightning war" of sudden, overpowering offensives. While offering little new information, Deighton concentrates on the combination of technology, personalities, and luck which produced this military force.

With *Berlin Game* (1983), Deighton returned to the spy novel. This book, along with *Mexico Set* (1984) and *London Match* (1985), form a trilogy in which British agent Bernard Samson undergoes several career and personal crises. *Berlin Game* revolves around Samson's attempts to force a traitor in a British intelligence organization to reveal himself. At the end of the novel, Samson discovers that his wife, who is also employed by British intelligence, is a high-ranking Soviet agent; she is exposed and escapes to East Germany. In *Mexico Set,* Samson is suspected of being a double agent and attempts to vindicate himself by convincing a KGB officer to defect. However, the agent's defection is suspected to be part of a larger scheme to further discredit Samson. In *London Match,* Soviet misinformation hinders Samson's attempt to expose yet another British double agent. While concluding his trilogy, Deighton describes the deceit and betrayal among the personnel of intelligence agencies. *The Ipcress File, Funeral in Berlin, The Billion Dollar Brain,* and *Only When I Larf* have been adapted for film.

(See also *CLC,* Vols. 4, 7, 22; *Contemporary Authors,* Vols. 9-12, rev. ed.; and *Contemporary Authors New Revision Series,* Vol. 19.)

ROBERT OSTERMANN

Len Deighton has nobody but himself to blame if his new novel *The Billion Dollar Brain* is judged in relation both to *Funeral in Berlin,* his previous novel, and to John Le Carre's earlier and widely acclaimed *The Spy Who Came in From the Cold.* Mr. Deighton shares with Mr. Le Carre the achievement of having rejuvenated the field of espionage fiction; he helped establish the standards by which both writers must be judged. And by these standards *The Billion Dollar Brain* is a disappointment. . . .

[*Funeral in Berlin*'s] determined refusal to glamorize spying or promote heroics out of its material encouraged one to think Mr. Deighton might extend his range in his next novel.

He hasn't. In *Brain* the anonymous British agent of *Funeral* and Mr. Deighton's earlier *The Ipcress File* tangles with a private American espionage organization (Facts for Freedom: FFF) run by one General Midwinter, a Texas multi-multi-millionaire with a set hatred of Russia and a certainty that the United States is rushing to its doom under weak and irresponsible leaders. Midwinter programs his group's operations on a gigantic computer complex (the "billion dollar brain") buried deep in a Texas hillside. An FFF maneuver in the Baltic area endangers a British intelligence network there, and British and Russian forces quickly collaborate to put the general out of business.

Very little of this comes through as really credible, despite Mr. Deighton's documentary-like appendices, his serious attempt to accurately portray the contemporary moment, and some closely observed and felt local scenes as the British agent hops between Helsinki, New York, Leningrad, Riga in Latvia, Texas, and London. Credibility was one of *Funeral*'s strongest points; the book read as if the events could have happened only the way they were set forth. *Brain* fails to deliver this kind of conviction, although the conspiracy in which the British agent finds himself is relatively simple compared with that of *Funeral,* where the plots were laid on in layers of interlocking deception.

A conspicuous clue to *The Billion Dollar Brain*'s failure is available on page 214. The agent has successfully infiltrated FFF, and is in the New York headquarters talking with Midwinter. He thinks: "I was weary of war and sick of hate. I was tired, and frightened of Midwinter because he wasn't tired. He was brave and powerful and determined."

And that's how much of the novel goes. Talk, talk, talk. Words that tell, not words that show. Statements about feelings and analyses of feelings—but underneath, no real feelings. Scenes without validity and actions without motivation, because Mr. Deighton has devised no adequate dramatic equivalents to the novel's ideas about national conduct and international policy.

All sorts of inconsistencies crop up in the novel as a consequence, the worst occurring in FFF's defeat. Following his conversation with Midwinter, that same "tired" man proceeds to dismantle the Midwinter organization and render it ineffective as if he weren't half trying. It's too easy; what was all the fuss about? The ominous Texas hillside had labored and, like the mountain in the fable, had brought forth a mouse. You had to believe that *Funeral* happened. You can't believe that *Brain* happened.

> Robert Ostermann, "Spy-Story Writer Is on a Downhill Track in 'Brain'," in The National Observer, Vol. 5, No. 4, January 24, 1966, p. 21.

JOHN DICKSON CARR

I am no unconditional admirer of Len Deighton, whose British Intelligence narrator-hero is a kind of determinedly proletarian James Bond. But it must be conceded that *The Billion Dollar Brain* has its points. With all his usual dexterity the author suggests a world in which, if we are not careful, machines may be ruling men. Triggered by the murder of a Finnish political commentator, action shuttles between London and Helsinki, over to Leningrad and Riga, across the ocean to New York and San Antonio, Texas, then back to Europe for the payoff. The anti-heroine here is Signe Laine, a Finnish blonde with some curious traits; the bad guys are represented by Harvey Newbegin, neurotic American agent, and General Midwinter, that wicked conservative.

The day is long past when Americans in English novels (John S. Blenkiron of the Richard Hannay saga, for instance) talked a jargon no American in history has ever talked. The late Ian Fleming could draw admirable American scenes and characters. Alistair MacLean can do it. So can John Gardner. . . . Mr. Deighton's unnamed narrator manages tolerably well except when—his overmastering passion—he tries to be too in. Of him one American character is made to say, "He doesn't know a squeeze play from a loud foul." Do they hit many loud fouls in *your* league? The narrator understands baseball as little as he understands conservatives; in fact, with regard to so many things American, he doesn't know his you-name-it from third base.

> John Dickson Carr, "Murder Fancier Recommends . . . ," in Harper's, Vol. 233, No. 1394, July, 1966, pp. 84, 86, 88.

ANTHONY BOUCHER

Len Deighton is always a pleasure to read. He offers crisp prose, fast action, vivid scenes and an anonymous agent-narrator whose attitude is cynical, professional and completely of the 1960's. This, I suppose, is quite enough to account for his success; but serious Deighton-fanciers must, by now, have noticed a marked difference in the quality of the stories which, with these resources, he chooses to tell. His second novel (*Funeral in Berlin*) had a beautifully constructed and cogent plot; his first and third (*The Ipcress File* and *The Billion Dollar Brain*) were helter-skelter—absorbing at any given moment but never quite adding up. His fourth, *An Expensive Place to Die,* falls somewhere in between—that is, it has a good unified workable plot, if something short of the brilliance of *Funeral.*

This time the nameless narrator is stationed in Paris, and the case is not really his, but forced upon him by the Americans—a delicate matter of conveying secret data on atomic fallout to the Chinese, as a rational deterrent. This involves him with the pleasure house of a peculiar amateur scientist of emotions, and with the ambivalent ex-wife of a Sûreté inspector, who may be at least a double agent. [*An Expensive Place to Die*] is easily Deighton's second-best novel; and second place after *Funeral* is, like losing a mile to Jim Ryun, no real disgrace.

> *Anthony Boucher, in a review of "An Expensive Place to Die," in* The New York Times Book Review, *May 21, 1967, pp. 42-3.*

THE TIMES LITERARY SUPPLEMENT

[Mr. Deighton's] apparatus [in *An Expensive Place to Die*] is one of ambiguous loyalties, and his successes have been achieved by circumstantial documentation on the one hand and oblique narration on the other. In *An Expensive Place to Die* the first device is carried to the length of a miniaturized file laid in to the volume, containing such things as a letter from the White House endorsed in holograph: "George: See to this. H. W." For many readers this will seem to have gone beyond plausibility into parody, just as the central feature of the plot, a Paris "clinic" catering for sexual perversions which enables its proprietor to gain both secret information and a hold on its exalted clientele, belongs to the fundamentally silly world of Ian Fleming rather than the quite serious viewpoint of much of Mr. Deighton's previous work. (Even the culinary side of life, on which he is usually so strong, lacks conviction here: a meal that starts with smoked salmon and goes on to sole is altogether too fishy.)

The narrative technique has a severe disunity, too. The story is mainly seen through the eyes of a middle-aged British agent and is related in Mr. Deighton's familiar and effective cinema style—the presentation of the mere image, explication largely depending on the gradual accumulation of images. But sections of a third-person narration are inset, and these are more conventional, less plausible, and sometimes quite boring.

> *"Grand Gimmickry," in* The Times Literary Supplement, *No. 3405, June 1, 1967, p. 491.*

JOHN HEMMINGS

Only When I Larf is assured of a huge sale, and partly deserves it, for Mr Deighton is not just a writer of popular thrillers, he has bigger talents that one could imagine put to nobler uses. His gang—one leader and two stooges, two men and one woman—forms a trio of individuals, nothing stock about them. Each takes it in turn to tell part of the story, but there are short overlaps, and minor variants in the double record which tell us more about the characters than they ever could by themselves. To say that Mr Deighton is a fine novelist who has ceded to a best-selling one would be unkind. But perhaps not untrue. (p. 478)

> *John Hemmings, "Hogamus, Higamus," in* The Listener, *Vol. LXXIX, No. 2037, April 11, 1968, pp. 477-78.*

MAURICE RICHARDSON

Boldly, because they are such difficult subjects, Len Deighton gives us confidence tricksters for a change [in *Only When I Larf*]. His three, who take it in turns to tell the story, are Silas, the middle-aged brain, Liz, his mistress of all work, Bob, his tough apprentice. They pull off an elaborate swindle in New York, move to London and just fail to sell a load of non-existent arms to an African diplomat, then try a huge too-easy fraud on a Lebanese bank. I would have liked some more carefully documented criminal expertise; or perhaps you need to be a con man yourself to put across the confidence trick with its cunning play on human cupidity. But it's just zestful enough, with lively patches of sleazy luxury living on the run in between coups.

> *Maurice Richardson, in a review of "Only When I Larf," in* The Observer, *April 21, 1968, p. 28.*

THE TIMES LITERARY SUPPLEMENT

In *The Distant Laughter* Bryan Forbes made the mistake of saddling his main character, a film director, with integrity, both artistic and moral. (This is not to say that there's no place for integrity in the film world, only that there's no place for it in film-world novels.) Len Deighton, in [*Close Up*], is far more enjoyably tendentious: he shows that beneath the movie-man's glitter, beneath all his hypocrisy, narcissism and greed, beneath the gaudy and hysterical exterior, beats a heart of ice.

Marshall Stone (né Eddie Brummage), a middle-aged pretty-boy with twenty years of stardom behind him, commissions his ex-wife's husband—Peter Anson, author-surrogate and transmedial hack—to write his biography, or rather to ghost his autobiography. . . . Anson investigates, and uncovers a past full of predictable seaminess: lies about his war-record, professional and sexual unscrupulousness, bribes, and general nastiness. Finally, Stone's producer tries to talk Anson into writing the "official" life, but Anson says he is going to write the true story in novel form, calling it *Close Up*. But the significance of this symmetrical touch eluded the reviewer. . . .

Mr Deighton's achievement is to make Stone likable. Because Stone is hardly a person at all, more a sum-total of how he is seen by others. The lust for reassurance (after a slight he knows he will be unable to hold his food for days), the pathetic yearning for compliments, and the total inability to relate to anything outside himself: Stone's life becomes the sort of pleasureless game that one would be ashamed to laugh at—or laugh at too long.

The film industry is in many ways the ideal subject for Mr Deighton's talents. In a business so obsessed with surface he can exploit his eye for what one might (reluctantly) call the "furniture" of the world. And only occasionally does the writing become as slack as the world it describes; for example, "hands" which "carve dreams from tobacco smoke" is the kind of metaphor that Harold Robbins probably mutters in his sleep. On the whole, though, Mr Deighton seems to have got over his tiring revolts against style—as evidenced in those studiedly incomprehensible spy stories—and to have settled down to what he does best: reporting, lucidly and readably, on what his imagination sees.

> *"Be My Ghost," in* The Times Literary Supplement, *No. 3668, June 16, 1972, p. 677.*

JOHN COLEMAN

Himself no stranger to the movie business (four of his novels have been made into films so far, the last of which he co-produced, and his was the uncredited script for *Oh! What a Lovely War*), Len Deighton has now turned from thrillers and computerized epics (*Bomber*) to the kaleidoscopic portrait of a star, his henchmen, and manipulators. The internationally famous Marshall Stone, born Eddie Brummage in Leeds and dreading the approach of his 50th year, has suggested an old acquaintance of his should write his biography. This Peter Anson, at one time married to Stone's ex-wife Mary, decides at the end that all he can do with the warty material he has unearthed is to convert it into a novel. Hence *Close Up*. . . .

No one would deny Deighton his customary measure of expertise. There is enough of the intricate wheelings and dealings that lie behind the smiley front of showbiz to satisfy those who like to feel themselves in the presence of an inside job. Front money, deferment clauses, collateral, and the growing threat of the cassette market—the jargon is all there. The book seems equally at home on the studio floor, with its professional chatter of "brutes," pancakes (the sort of thing tiny Alan Ladd used to stand on), and the lighting Haskell Wexler used in *Medium Cool*. There are one or two shrewd cracks about the current stress on youth and the vexed question of whether stars really matter any more: *Close Up* claims they do. But these are ingredients of a recipe, as Deighton—no slouch in the kitchen himself—must know; not the achieved dish. . . .

What is so badly wrong with this departure from the world of Harry Palmer is that it is so casually written, a compound of cliches. It has no flavor. Unwisely, there are those extracts from the prose of presumably very different characters: They have a horrifying sameness. . . .

Away from the smoke-filled rooms of filmdom, our author is oddly out of touch. Pete Anson's steady job, we are informed, is that of entertainment editor on a posh English Sunday newspaper: but his copy . . . is hardly up to tabloid standards. . . .

And then there is the egregious Marshall Stone, pivot of the revels. Actors are notoriously hollow men. One argument runs they wouldn't be actors otherwise. But, for all the plotting that embroils him, he still occupies quite a slice of the novel *in propria persona*. There is only so much mileage to be extracted from his daytime use of mascara, his terror of wrinkles, his utterly self-centered musings and meditations on his craft. It is very hard to believe in this creature—no Burton or Olivier, he—as one of the great Hamlets of 20 years back. And even (as is just conceivable) could such a shell give such a performance, then it is the performance that is truly interesting, not the shell.

John Coleman, "A Fading Star and His Satellites," in Book World—The Washington Post, *June 25, 1972, p. 7.*

GENE LYONS

[It] is surprising, but still understandable, that when Deighton turns to the short story, as he does in *Eleven Declarations of War* [published in England as *Declarations of War*], he should prove so relatively heavy-handed and anxious to make a point that the moral ironist in him quite overthrows the maker of fictions. In "**Winter's Morning,**" for example, the first story in the book, a lovingly detailed reconstruction of a dawn patrol by a World War I flying ace is rendered pompous by the author's withholding until the final words that the man is a German and not an English pilot as the reader had been deliberately allowed to assume. In "**Bonus for a Salesman**" a traveling English munitions peddler complains bitterly and humorously about his having been forced into helping a South American guerrilla band. It is only at the very end, once again, that the reader is let in on the secret that the man has now become "General Alberto Sampson" and is running the squalid place. The habit of withholding vital plot information of that kind is not a good one for a short story writer to get into. Too often, regardless of the seriousness of the point being made, the form is simplistic and predictable, and if the punch line is: "like any professional assassin he took pride in seeing a victim die. Only such men could become aces," it will not be very long before the reader loses interest altogether.

Not all of the stories in the collection are so bald as that, but most of them depend, in one way or another, on making explicit ideas and judgments that should remain implicit in a work of fiction, or which should more properly provide the conflict of which the story is made, rather than its conclusion. It is one thing to affix epigraphs from the "Tacwargame" manual or the rules of chess to chapters in a spy novel and have the characters ponder their status as pawns, another to come thundering in near the end of an otherwise beautifully rendered episode in the American Civil War with the realization that "the infantry were litmus paper to see if it was safe to put the artillery there." What one wishes is to see then what happens inside men when they realize that that is what their mission amounts to. Rather, we see them die.

I don't want to be too hard on Deighton, for some of these stories are fascinating, if not as fictions, then as what strikes one as extremely accurate, well-researched and carefully chosen fragments of what one might call the social history of modern warfare. Deighton seems to be blessed with a historical imagination that is if anything too vividly acute for him to bother himself overmuch with the subtle nuances of character when he has larger things in mind. Almost every one of these stories might easily have become the subject of a novel or a screenplay. My favorite among them is "**Brent's Deus ex Machina**" in which a World War II bomber pilot of murky London origins rejects as "upper class gibberish" the patriotic speech of an R.A.F. doctor who will not disqualify him from flying simply because he sees double out of fear. Up until the last sentences, that is, when the narrative takes a cinematic step backward to reveal that the flier has become a hero out of sheer social resentment. One can understand and sympathize with Deighton's admirable intentions while maintaining one's suspicion that of all the subjects for epigrammatic ironies, war is one that has been done to death that way. (pp. 10, 12)

Gene Lyons, "Blood on His Hands, Not Custard on His Face," in The New York Times Book Review, *April 13, 1975, pp. 5, 10, 12.*

JULIAN BARNES

Len Deighton gets so much mileage out of the tension between ill-assorted operatives working on the same job that it's almost a substitute for narrative. In the early novels it was smooth Old Harrovian roughing up bright self-made Harry Palmer. Lately, he's concentrated more on a Brit-Yank pairing: [in *Twinkle, Twinkle, Little Spy*], fearsomely efficient, arm-punching Major Mann is teamed with an uneasily admiring English narrator (still Palmer, one presumes). In fact, there's little enough excuse given for the latter's presence in this American-based yarn about a defecting Russian egghead who's mastered everything from pulsars to masers (posh lasers); but clearly Deighton feels happiest leading with a grizzling, wrangling duo, even one whose language is oddly undifferentiated. Mann's sarky, tough Yankee jibes are from much the same mould as Palmer's sarky, tough Cockney jibes. This style of chat is infectious—a German-born spy's moll suddenly hits out with feisty wisecracks—making dialogue at times as uni-toned as Racine.

Pace, though, is what Deighton is the master of, and *Twinkle, Twinkle, Little Spy* shows all the familiar control. The lead-in is a routine pick-up of the defector in mid-Sahara, which goes smoothly except for an unlucky Arab getting snuffed; then a long, deceptive protection-and-debriefing section, packed with CIA info and burgeoning loyalties. Just when Deighton seems to be coasting, and you don't feel such a bubblebrain after all, in he jumps with a piece of smartly faked violence, the chase begins, and you zip around the world realising that the placid intro was not only full of hints but of hints which still have you foxed. Thereafter, the trail of murder, suicide, and hijacking is fast, probable, and very cleverly worked: the best spy story since . . . well, the last Deighton.

> Julian Barnes, "Nice and Nasty," in New States-man, *Vol. 91, No. 2361, June 18, 1976, p. 822.*

JOSEPH McLELLAN

Atmosphere is Deighton's strong suit—the feeling of a place, usually exotic and with a high potential for tension, where spies gather to prey on one another. In [*Catch a Falling Spy,* published in England as *Twinkle, Twinkle, Little Spy*], the place is the mid-Sahara for the novel's beginning and end (the middle is spent along the East Coast of the United States, with one episode at a marvelous inn that specializes in an environment of total nostalgia). The scene is presented with the same immediacy that Deighton has given to cold-war Berlin and to a submarine under the Arctic ice in other novels. Some characters are familiar, as types if not as individuals—a ruthlessly efficient American intelligence officer, assorted KGB baddies, and Deighton's usual rather neutral and faceless hero. But the plot revolves around a quite original creation, a Russian scientist who is intent on communicating with other planets and thinks he can do it better in the United States than at home. The story of his escape and manipulation by the American and Russian intelligence bureaucracies has a full quota of horror and Deighton's usual wheels-within-wheels intricacy; as happens more and more in suspense fiction, the subject is not so much espionage as meta-espionage: the search for information on the espionage apparatus itself rather than for the kind of data on war plans and materials that used to preoccupy spies. This novel may be a shade below the level of Deighton's best work (*The Ipcress File* and *Funeral in Berlin*), but it remains well above the average for this genre.

> Joseph McLellan, in a review of "Catch a Falling Spy," in Book World—The Washington Post, *September 12, 1976, p. H3.*

ERNEST K. GANN

Airshipwreck, by the very talented novelist Len Deighton and book designer Arnold Schwartzman, is another fine addition to aeronautical history, albeit without much nostalgia or per-sonal material. Zeppelins will always hold a certain mystique for groundlings as well as the air-minded, and their relatively brief heyday is here displayed in a text that is up to Mr. Deighton's high standards. His words are supplemented by a rare collection of photographs depicting the unhappy fate of almost all the rigid lighter-than-air craft. Mr. Deighton's extensive research makes *Airshipwreck* an essential book for any comprehensive aviation library. Though he provides the usual stories of heroism as the great gas bags encountered various hazards both natural and manmade, readers may well be more impressed by man's perseverance in trying to fly in the face of repeated calamity. (p. 13)

Airshipwreck is a valuable log of every rigid-airship crash. Mr. Deighton takes the reader from the earliest flights in contraptions that were nearly as much fantasy as fact, through the relatively ineffective zeppelin bombings of England during World War I and on through to the final night of the Hindenburg. Its explosion at Lakehurst, N.J., in 1937 stunned the world and brought an end to any real hopes for rigid airships. (p. 45)

> Ernest K. Gann, "Early Birds," in The New York Times Book Review, *May 20, 1979, pp. 13, 45.*

HARPER'S MAGAZINE

[*Goodbye, Mickey Mouse*] seems to promise the same serviceable formula [Deighton's] tinkered with in his other World War II books, most notably *Bomber* and *SS-GB*. Set in wartime Britain, it is the story of a motley group of American fighter pilots based in the muddy fenland of East Anglia. When not hurling their battered Mustangs through aerial combat over Germany, they find themselves embroiled in more mundane hostilities with the locals outside the pub at Steeple Thaxted on a Saturday night. As their numbers slowly dwindle, the men quarrel and bitch about creeping damp, botched leadership, and war.

Aficionados of Deighton's work might reasonably expect to be offered here: the lives and loves of men at war, revelations of cowardice or treachery, quaint British stuff, brave boys proving their mettle, the West Point martinet hated-by-his-men, death in battle, dense clumps of useful information—and, above all, a sturdy plot guided with such a swift and skillful hand that readers will gratefully overlook clunky characterization or wooden dialogue en route to the denouement.

Many of these delights are delivered. But the sad truth is that Deighton has unwisely opted for character this time, leaving the plot to lumber along without any coherent narrative thread. The denouement is too late and perfunctory to be convincing. In the meantime, the dawdling reader has had the opportunity to notice, for example, the stilted dialogue . . . ; the two-dimensional characters; the awkwardness of the sex scenes . . . ; and Deighton's grotesque idea of women. . . . Devoid of emotional authenticity, the book is oddly anemic—except on the subject of fighter planes. Deighton's obsession with planes makes the combat sequences lurid and exciting. If only the rest of the book were too.

> H. R., in a review of "Goodbye, Mickey Mouse," in Harper's Magazine, *Vol. 265, No. 1590, November, 1982, p. 76.*

PETER ANDREWS

When Len Deighton is in his usual good form, he makes it difficult for a reviewer to do his job properly. The narrative moves along so smoothly I forget to take notes, and once the action begins I don't want to stop to take any. After finishing *Goodbye, Mickey Mouse,* I felt as if I were back in school trying to fake a book report for Mr. Suitor's English class—"I liked this book a lot. I learned many things I didn't know before, and it was very exciting."

Not a particularly penetrating analysis, I am afraid. But Mr. Deighton's latest World War II adventure novel is such a plain, old-fashioned, good book about combat pilots who make war and fall in love that it defies a complicated examination. Capt. James Farebrother and Lieut. Z. M. Morse, known as Mickey Mouse, are a pair of skilled Mustang jockeys fighting in the air war over Europe who fall in love with two Englishwomen. Both affairs are brutally affected by the war in a final plot turn that stretches plausibility a bit but remains well within the acceptability range for a popular novel; in fact, the bittersweet ending is quite satisfactory. There are some additional plot complications, but that's just about it. What could have been little more than a routine Saturday Evening Post novella, however, in Mr. Deighton's hands becomes a tight, satisfying novel.

Few authors have written about flying as tellingly as Len Deighton in fact or fiction. Here he draws on some excellent research to give his fiction just the right tone.... *Goodbye, Mickey Mouse* is high adventure of the best sort but always solidly true to life.

Nor is it the kind of novel that "soars aloft but gets stuck on the ground," as critics are fond of saying. Mr. Deighton has a good cynical eye for the ways of the professional military. The squadron commander, Col. Dan Badger, has to juggle decisions about who will live and who will die and not forget the requirements of furthering his own career. He is after all a professional soldier, and no war lasts forever.

In air-war novels love scenes are usually something I simply try to bear while the planes are being gassed up and re-armed. But Mr. Deighton has brought as much skill to these elements as he has to combat material. Victoria Cooper, who loves Farebrother, and Vera Hardcastle, who loves Mickey (although she has a husband fighting in Burma), are both arresting, fully drawn characters.

There is a plenitude of spirited action in *Goodbye, Mickey Mouse,* including a murder that is made all the more appalling by its quiet inevitability. But Mr. Deighton's most compelling moments are the small, deft touches that dapple his narrative. Victoria and James fall in love in two brief paragraphs that are as sweet as anything you are likely to read. Even as he watches a B-17 plunge into a fatal spin in combat, Colonel Badger has the time to wonder what it is that a pilot, pinned to the controls by centrifugal force, thinks about in the final seconds of a too short life.

It is a delight to read a straightforward commercial novel that has been put together by a craftsman as conscientious as Len Deighton. You can read 100 or so pages of Mr. Deighton's seamless prose at a clip and never once get a sense of a novelist busy at work with his little collection of devices that are supposed to add to the plot but serve mainly to draw attention to the author. Len Deighton serves his story and his readers well by keeping it swift and simple.

I liked this book a lot.

> *Peter Andrews, "Pilots and Lovers," in* The New York Times Book Review, *November 14, 1982, p. 15.*

T. J. BINYON

After a long involvement in history and fiction dressed up as history Len Deighton has now returned to the subject—intelligence agencies—and the style—first-person narration—of his early novels, from *The Ipcress File* (1962) to *Twinkle, Twinkle, Little Spy* (1976). But his hero-narrator [of *Berlin Game*], described once as "an upstart from Burnley, a supercilious, anti-public school technician", and resolutely anonymous—except in the films, where he took the name Harry Palmer... has mellowed over the years. He now calls himself Bernard Samson (the surname is a distressingly obvious key to the plot), has married the beautiful and rich Fiona Kimber-Hutchinson, whose money he refuses to touch, and has two small children, a nanny and a Portuguese housekeeper.

The long lay-off has had its effects. The language creaks over the first few pages, and it takes Deighton some time to get away from the bland, featureless, international thriller style of his last book, *XPD,* and back to the quirky originality of the first novels. Accuracy of detail has suffered too; most noticeably when some of the top brass in British Intelligence, finishing off a large Sunday lunch in the country with a game of billiards, are discovered to be solemnly anointing the ends of their cues with resin, rather than chalk.... However, by the time Samson flies into Berlin to find out why Brahms Four, the East German who has been sending back economic intelligence to London, wants to quit, Deighton is back to the old mid-season form. Berlin, as before, brings out the best in him.

In a sense, *Berlin Game* is Deighton's *Tinker, Tailor, Soldier, Spy,* being concerned, like that novel, with the winkling out of a traitor in the upper echelons of British intelligence. Although the manner is almost as elliptic as le Carré's, the matter is much less richly textured—which is perhaps no bad thing. Once over the initial hump, the narrative runs downhill all the way, gathering momentum and suspense as it goes: the last few episodes, set on the other side of the Berlin Wall, are as good as or better than anything Deighton has done before.

Yet, in the end, the book is something of a disappointment. Earlier Deighton had shown his hero's superiors and colleagues, though hard and efficient in their work, to be nearly without exception men obsessed with social status or official position: the power struggle within the organization often appears almost as important as the conflict without. Now this has been taken to the extreme. Snobbery, *arrivisme,* and the desire for power within the system are the only forces which motivate the characters. Samson and the traitor alone are allowed to have integrity, ideals and a sense of duty. And the effect, sadly, is to make some parts of *Berlin Game* read like a parody of the earlier Deighton.

> *T. J. Binyon, "Brahms Four Fugue," in* The Times Literary Supplement, *No. 4203, October 21, 1983, p. 1170.*

DAVID QUAMMEN

Has success spoiled Len Deighton? Have his recent novels been composed into a tape recorder on a patio somewhere beside a swimming pool? If not, why are they no longer so dense, so wry, so freshly imagined, so quirky and convincing as his earlier wonders, like *The Ipcress File* and *Funeral in Berlin.* If not, why is such a talented, droll and original spy novelist now producing thrillers that seem slapdash and conventional? This isn't a matter of a brilliant artist whose flame has flared out prematurely; it's a matter of missing craftsmanship and care. Why should a writer of demonstrated excellence write a book—like the new *Berlin Game*—that is merely good?

Berlin Game is a decent entertainment that rattles swiftly along to its payoff. Two things especially recommend it—a devious contrivance of plot that has probably never been used before in an espionage novel; and the city of Berlin, mecca to spies and spy novelists. The second is the greater asset. Although the book is elaborately plotted, its best moments derive from the setting and from the force of this particular setting upon behavior and psychology.

Mr. Deighton knows Berlin well. He vividly depicts its nuances of language, its grand old houses, its streets and tunnels on both sides of the Wall, the East-West checkpoints. His main character, a British intelligence officer named Bernie Samson, is an apt guide for a spy tour of the divided city because he is divided himself—a second-generation spook who grew up in Berlin while his father was posted there and who speaks German well enough to pass. He provides, among other exotic trivia, the arbitrary logic explaining the jagged line along which the city was partitioned. We see the footbridge over the River Spree used by the last fugitives from the Führerbunker, and the Charité Hospital, in whose mortuary the Red Army found the bodies of the men who had conspired to kill Hitler in July 1944, their corpses kept on ice by the Führer's personal order. There are instructions on how to sneak underground into the East sector, what to wear for the mission, how to be smuggled back out by truck. . . .

As in most good spy novels, friendship and love and personal betrayal are the themes of *Berlin Game.* While Bernie Samson travels back and forth between London and Berlin, crosses back and forth between the Western sector and the East, he also gropes his way through some difficult moral terrain of conflicting loyalties. His marriage, his career, his oldest friendships are all on the line, as well as his commitment to a long-term British agent working in East Germany who goes by the code name Brahms Four. Samson is an admirable fellow who, despite frustrations and a weakness for gin, endangers himself repeatedly while trying to keep his hold on each of those loyalties. His crisis arrives when Brahms Four and a Soviet agent, who is operating within British headquarters in London, become mutually aware of, and therefore threatened by, each other. To say much more would hint away that plot contrivance upon which the story turns.

Although the crucial plot twist seems clever in the abstract, it turns out, as executed, to be predictable. Possibly it is just too clever, too cute, to be kept well hidden, and as one nears the end of the novel it becomes evident. So the conclusion, though plausible, is rather a fizzle.

Berlin Game is easily competent enough to make the best-seller lists but just not good enough to delight Deighton fans who ask for wit, graceful exposition, freshness of vision and deft prose. For all that, better to go back to *Funeral in Berlin.*

> David Quammen, "Second-Generation Spook," in
> The New York Times Book Review, *January 8, 1984,*
> *p. 24.*

T. J. BINYON

Mexico Set is the second volume of a projected trilogy; at the end of the first, *Berlin Game,* published last year, the hero Bernard Samson discovers that his wife Fiona is his Delilah:

while working with him in a Whitehall intelligence department, she has been a high-ranking mole, a KGB colonel no less. Exposed, she leaves in a hurry for East Germany, failing in a last-minute attempt to take her (or his) two children with her.

The second volume opens—unsurprisingly—in Mexico City, whither Samson and his boss Dicky Cruyer have come to investigate the sighting of a KGB major, last seen interrogating Samson in Berlin. As before, Deighton projects the view of an intelligence service whose members (with the exception of Samson) are more involved in the power struggle within the system than the one outside. Cruyer has "taken a PhD in office politics"; he might be "a little slow on languages and field-work, but in the game of office politics he was seeded number one." The slipshod, meaningless nature of the second image (players are seeded at Wimbledon, not in tennis) reflects the generally tired and flaccid narrative tone of the opening episodes, with local colour as thick as guacamole.

Gradually things improve. When Samson's sister-in-law tells him not to "start all that working-class-boy-makes-good stuff", she's mocking an obsession of Deighton's earlier books; and once the intrigue reaches Berlin, the story is up and running with all the old verve and energy. Using treachery to split the Samson family was a stroke of genius, for it enables Deighton to see the conflict between two intelligence services as one between separated man and wife, heightened by their intimate knowledge of one another, and sharpened by their struggle for the children. At the same time there's something inescapably comic and implausible about the transformation of the rich and beautiful, Sloane Rangerish Fiona (née Kimber-Hutchinson) into a Rosa Klebb lookalike. It will be interesting to see whether Deighton's got anything up his sleeve to counter this in the third part of the trilogy, presumably to be entitled *London Match.*

> T. J. Binyon, "The Intelligence Game," in The Times
> Literary Supplement, *No. 4263, December 14, 1984,*
> *p. 1457.*

ROSS THOMAS

The first novel in Len Deighton's new espionage trilogy was *Berlin Game.* Now comes *Mexico Set* and keener intellects than mine already will have anticipated a third novel to be called *Someplace-or-other-Match*—thus completing what I suspect will be referred to as the tennis trilogy.

I confess that I didn't tumble to the game, set and match conceit until after finishing Deighton's entertaining second novel in this trilogy that again features fortyish Bernard Samson, the British spy who is afflicted with far more than the usual amount of both career and domestic difficulties.

But as in all trilogies, the problem is the back story. The author has to fill it in for those who haven't read the first novel without irritating those who have. Having previously read *Berlin Game,* I wasn't at all bothered when Deighton again tells of Samson and his rich, beautiful, upper-middle-class wife, Fiona, who both work for the British secret intelligence service until . . . Well, I won't spoil the first book for those who want to start the series at the beginning.

Mexico itself doesn't provide much more than a routinely exotic locale and Deighton gives us a mere sidelong glance at it—certainly not the long, cool, sometimes almost loving stare that he has turned time and again on Berlin and London and even Paris. Mexico is only a backdrop, a place where a passed-over KGB major might be approached by a British agent to see if he is interested in defecting to the West. (p. 1)

But while Samson is traipsing around Mexico, his rivals back in London are jockeying for position in the spy bureaucracy. Suppose, it is murmured, that the traitor uncovered in *Berlin Game* fled East only to deflect suspicion from the real KGB mole who is still burrowing into the department? And who else could the real mole be but Bernard Samson?

Deighton manages to bring it all off nicely, as he usually does, writing with perhaps less sprightliness than in his previous novels, but with complete authority and control. When it comes to pitting working-class sharpies against Oxbridge twits, Deighton has few equals. He even gives us an American who has wormed his way up into the British spy hierarchy and is now lusting for a knighthood to show off back in the States. The American somehow is utterly believable. (pp. 1, 5)

However, it's Bernard Samson himself who deserves and gets both our attention and sympathy—Samson with his problems of civil service pay, motherless children, a vengeance-bent wife, unsympathetic and even jealous superiors, and a job—the only job he knows—that could very well either kill him or land him in jail.

We go from Mexico to London to Berlin and on to Paris in this novel about greed and deceit and treachery, which are the essential ingredients of all good thrillers. And once again Deighton has woven an intricate and wholly satisfying plot, peopled it with convincing characters, and even managed to give a new twist or two to the spy story. But then he is a master of the form, and *Mexico Set* is one of his better efforts.

Game. Set. And match. I now can't help but wonder where match will be set. (p. 5)

Ross Thomas, "Len Deighton: Dark and Devious," in Book World—The Washington Post, *January 27, 1985, pp. 1, 5.*

JULIUS LESTER

The "game" of *Berlin Game* went to Fiona, Bernard Samson's wife, who defected to Russia when Bernard exposed her as a K.G.B. agent. The "set" was won by Bernard, persuading Fiona's chief assistant, the K.G.B. Major Erich Stinnes, to defect [in *Mexico Set*]. Or is his defection a K.G.B. ruse to penetrate British intelligence and disseminate misinformation?

That is one of the puzzles Bernard Samson faces in *London Match,* as he moves back and forth between the city of the title and Berlin. Because Fiona had been a double agent, Samson also remains under suspicion. When he uncovers information indicating that another mole may be hidden in the higher echelons of British intelligence, he keeps it secret and undertakes his own investigation. All evidence points to Bret Rensselaer, the wealthy, American-born naturalized British citizen and one of Samson's superiors, whom Samson suspects of having had an affair with Fiona. When Stinnes fingers Rensselaer, his guilt seems certain. But Rensselaer comes to Samson as the only person he can ask to help exonerate him.

Though *London Match* is the most complex novel of the trilogy, the feeling it conveys of being trapped in a maze of distorting mirrors is almost a cliché in spy novels now. Despite Mr. Deighton's slickness in constructing the maze, the devotee of the genre will not be misled.

The strength of *London Match* is not in its plot but its characterization. . . .

Mr. Deighton portrays each character of his large cast fully and sympathetically. However, the best character is the city of Berlin. It is a living presence, and in some of the descriptions one can almost hear the stones breathing. Through the minor German characters, Mr. Deighton etches moving portraits of the country during and immediately following World War II, creating sympathy for the people but not for Nazism.

The novel's primary weakness is the attention lavished on the office politics of British intelligence. . . . The petty concerns of most of the characters for the advancement of their careers slow down the pace of the novel to the point where the reader begins not to care who wins the game. Some suspense is created by emotional questions: will Samson overcome his silly feeling of guilt for having an affair with a file clerk just past her 19th birthday and allow himself to fall in love? What will happen when he meets his traitorous wife, a scene the reader knows will be the novel's climax?

The subject of Len Deighton's novel—the mole in a position of authority within the intelligence establishment—is as current as recent news stories. And like those news stories, it lacks a sobering ethic, something that would provide a moral underpinning for a secret world that appears to have no morality. While Mr. Deighton creates characters with whom it is a pleasure to spend time, the reader comes to the end of *London Match* feeling that he has observed an elaborate and meaningless game. One misses the catharsis that would come if at least a single character knew it was meaningless, too.

Julius Lester, "Samson and Mole," in The New York Times Book Review, *December 1, 1985, p. 22.*

J. I. M. STEWART

Len Deighton published *Berlin Game* in 1983, followed it up with *Mexico Set* and now comes forward with *London Match*. The analogy with tennis is sketchy, since a good many games have to be played to win a set and several sets to win a match. But we are, I suppose, meant to conclude that by the end of the present volume there has been a decisive climax to a long and complex action, and that one player or side has gained a victory. The characters, however, turn out to have little sense of this. "It's not game, set, and match to anyone," the protagonist says on the final page. "It never is."

Is this perhaps a neat way of hinting that there may be more to come about Bernard Samson of London Central, his wife Fiona—whose sheer inconceivability establishes once and for all the robust character of Mr. Deighton's imagination—and a prodigal array of men and women nearly all of whom have some connection with espionage? If this be so, the writer is well entitled to his reluctance to have done with them and their environments in London, Mexico City, West and East Berlin. The characters, although liable to bore a little during their frequently over-extended verbal fencings, are tenaciously true to themselves even if not quite to human nature. Ben Jonson himself would have approved of them. The places, whether urban or rural, can be described only as triumphs alike of painstaking observation and striking descriptive power. (p. 1)

Sometimes, indeed, Mr. Deighton's linguistic resourcefulness is at odds with *vraisemblance*, but this happens less frequently than in the earlier books. In *Mexico Set,* for example, we come on somebody with "a hard unyielding face, smooth like a carefully carved *netsuke* handled by generations of collectors, and darkening as elephant tusk darkens when locked away and deprived of light." It seems not probable that this elegant fancy should come to Samson when it does....

With what he thinks of as an English upper crust Mr. Deighton is linguistically less assured. Thus a woman called Daphne has, we are told, the loud voice and upperclass accent that go with weekends in large unheated country houses, where everyone talks about horses and reads Dick Francis paperbacks. This is fair enough, down even to Dick Francis. But then Daphne suddenly says, "I'm sorry we can't go into the lounge." In England (as Mr. Deighton, who is London born, ought to know) only quite shockingly vulgar and plebeian people call a drawing-room or living-room a lounge. Lounges are located in hotels or at airports. Daphne has let Mr. Deighton down.

London Match is full of this class stuff, which is conceived of largely in terms of expensive dressing and eating and drinking, with plenty of authentic brand names thrown in.... This general expensiveness, although irritating and often seemingly no more than inconsequent padding, is by no means without its function in the total picture. It all comes to us from Bernard Samson on a note of ready compliance masking alienation, and we thus feel him to be what a secret agent should essentially be: a loner in disguise.

But what is this book—what are these books—*about?* The answer, if it has to be given in a word, is treachery.... Is such-and-such a man or woman a double agent, or susceptible of being "turned"? If apparently successfully "turned," is the success illusory and the agent's true allegiance still where it began? In *Berlin Game,* indeed, there is somebody in East Berlin who has been transmitting to England specific information in the field of economics and finance. But in general the rival secret services are concerned only with their rivalry.... And at London Central, there is another and wholly interiorized network of suspicions and treacheries. Everybody—to express the thing loosely—is after everybody else's job. Almost everybody, moreover, is after—or suspected of being after—everybody else's husband or wife. The spectacle is not without a certain power to entertain. But, like Restoration comedy, it is a purely speculative scene of things. (p. 14)

J. I. M. Stewart, "Len Deighton's Tournament of Spies," in Book World—The Washington Post, *December 15, 1985, pp. 1, 14.*

Peter De Vries

1910-

American novelist, short story writer, poet, and editor.

Widely considered one of America's best comic writers, De Vries satirizes various aspects of modern American society, including marriage, love, sexuality, religion, and conformity. Using a combination of puns, parodies, aphorisms, and burlesque, De Vries depicts characters who recognize their absurdity yet who courageously search for meaning in a purposeless, disordered world. Leonore Fleischer summarized his singular skill: "Peter De Vries gives black humor an extra half-twist. He invents a comic situation, as comfy as a TV family comedy, fills it with gags and, when you're laughing your head off, he pulls away the grinning clown's mask and shows you the grinning skull beneath it."

De Vries shuns complex characterizations and orderly plots, relying instead on character types and incident to animate his works. His protagonists are usually middle- or upper middle-class males who embark on a quest for the "true" self amidst the pressures of familial and career responsibilities. De Vries's own strict Dutch Calvinist upbringing informs much of his work, as many of his heroes wrestle with guilt caused by abandoning faith and indulging in promiscuous sex. Ultimately, these characters discover that marriage offers effective solace in an essentially absurd world, and they become, if not formally religious, then humanistically agnostic. Conformity and domesticity, in De Vries's view, are essential to surviving the chaos of modern life.

While lacking the depth and sophistication of his later works, De Vries's initial novels, *But Who Wakes the Bugler?* (1940), *The Handsome Heart* (1943), and *Angels Can't Do Better* (1944), introduce the themes and character types that recur throughout his work. In *The Tunnel of Love* (1954), *Comfort Me with Apples* (1956), and *The Mackerel Plaza* (1958), which are among his best-known early books, De Vries's stylistic virtuosity, his keen sense of life's ironies, and his shrewd social observations are entertainingly and cogently integrated.

The death from leukemia of De Vries's daughter in 1960 brought a deeper cynicism and black humor to many of his works that appeared in the following decade. This somberness is most apparent in *The Blood of the Lamb* (1962), which many critics consider De Vries's most important novel. In this book, Don Wanderhope's belief in the existence of God is challenged by the death of his daughter from leukemia. In a mournful rage, he throws a pie at the face of a statue of Jesus Christ and tosses his crucifix into the woods where he and his daughter had walked. Wanderhope concludes that chaos is an inherent element of modern existence. In *Through the Fields of Clover* (1961), *Reuben, Reuben* (1964), *Let Me Count the Ways* (1965), and *The Vale of Laughter* (1967), De Vries assimilates the points of view of youthful and elderly narrators, traditionalists and ultraliberals, and extremely literate and less educated characters. *The Cat's Pajamas and Witch's Milk* (1968) consists of two novellas that further express De Vries's gloomy opinion of the human condition. *The Cat's Pajamas* tracks the descent of Hank Tattersall as he renounces mainstream society by leaving his wife and resigning his positions as college professor

© Nancy Crampton

and advertising writer. Opting for bizarre occupations and a marginal existence, Hank's grip on reality becomes increasingly weaker until he eventually freezes to death. In *Witch's Milk,* a young boy's death affects his parents in different ways. While the mother becomes bitter and nihilistic, the father discovers order and meaning in the world. The characters of both novellas come to understand that they must reconcile themselves to a godless world and seek a supportive ethos by which to live.

De Vries's novels of the 1970s lack much of the existential turmoil of his 1960s work and focus on such sociological phenomena as the sexual revolution, the feminist movement, and gender role-reversal. *Mrs. Wallop* (1970) disputes the concept proposed by such books as Philip Roth's *Portnoy's Complaint* that mothers engender psychological problems in their children. Although critics have accused De Vries of creating female characters of little depth, most agree that Mrs. Wallop is his most fully realized feminine protagonist. In *I Hear America Swinging* (1976) and *Madder Music* (1977), De Vries satirically exposes the shortcomings of excessive sexual freedom. He emphasizes in these novels that marriage is a most beneficial institution, an attitude rarely found in contemporary American fiction.

De Vries's novels of the 1980s display more optimism than most of his earlier work. He frequently burlesques contemporary America's faddish lifestyles through the use of ludicrous plot twists and unreliable narrators. In *Slouching Towards Kalamazoo* (1983), De Vries irreverently updates Nathaniel Hawthorne's novel *The Scarlet Letter* by setting the story in the suburban Midwest and by making a 15-year-old student and his teacher the principal characters. In *The Prick of Noon* (1985), De Vries lampoons the inordinately tolerant values of wealthy suburbanites when a fashionable clique accepts a pornographic filmmaker into its ranks. *Peckham's Marbles* (1986) lightheartedly satirizes the publishing industry, literary agents, and the differences between escapist and serious literature.

(See also *CLC*, Vols. 1, 2, 3, 7, 10, 28; *Contemporary Authors*, Vols. 17-20, rev. ed.; *Dictionary of Literary Biography*, Vol. 6; and *Dictionary of Literary Biography Yearbook: 1982*.)

JOHN GROSS

Eddie Teeters (and in the course of Peter De Vries's new novel [*The Prick of Noon*] he frequently does, right on the brink) is a poor boy from Backbone, Ark., who has temporarily come to rest amid the broad suburban acres of Merrymount, Conn. One summer afternoon at the local country club, he is fatally smitten by a poolside princess called Cynthia; a single appraising stare, and he imagines himself conjugating his way into a major romance—"Favor, fervor, fever." But how can he hope to get to know her and win her, hemmed in as she is by her smart friends? As he overhears their sophisticated prattle, he is more painfully aware than ever of his own lack of polish, of all the books he hasn't read and all the words he keeps meaning to look up in the dictionary. . . .

Eddie's character is an interesting one. If it is hard to take him very seriously as the last anti-Puritan, defiantly raising his maypole in Merrymount, Conn., as his 17th-century forbears once did in Merrymount, Mass., he makes a memorable study in social mobility. There is a note of genuine—and refreshing—sourness in his private reflections about Cynthia's country-club friends, and a black realism in the conclusions he eventually draws about the persistence of class—"The jockey can't ever hope to marry into the horsey set"—and the power of money.

He is also a walking cultural paradox, a brilliant thieving magpie. He laments the gaps in his education, which certainly exist (when he takes umbrage he spells it "umbridge"), but which don't prevent him from quoting Proust in the right way at the right moment. He envies [the publisher] Chirouble's suave vocabulary, but his own words bubble along with as much sparkle as—well, as Peter De Vries's. Does the man who is afraid that he may have made "a delible impression" really need to increase his wordpower? Or the man who can describe an art show as consisting of "second-wave Abstract Expressionism, or maybe Express Abstractionism"?

As always with Mr. De Vries, virtually every page of *The Prick of Noon* is enlivened by a happy invention. Images linger—the hamburger that looks like "a hockey puck on a bun" or the new pair of shoes that meow. Snatches of dialogue reverberate—"Money is one of the fondest things I'm of"; "I like that blouse. Red, green, orange and blue are my favorite colors." And along with the quickfire jokes, there are some fine set pieces, notably the account of Eddie's delirious ravings when he is ill, a sustained surreal tour de force.

The obvious danger with such writing is that it can easily become too frenetic, too determined to raise a laugh at any cost. It is not a danger that Mr. De Vries has always escaped in the past, but here he has things well under control. *The Prick of Noon* ranks among his better books, and it is a measure of its success, and of his comic gift, that the potential sleaziness of his theme is kept wholly at bay.

John Gross, in a review of "The Prick of Noon," in
The New York Times, *April 5, 1985, p. C25.*

R. Z. SHEPPARD

Crack a Peter De Vries novel at random and you are likely to find a Mid-westerner trying just a little too hard to keep from making a fool of himself among the sophisticates of the Northeast. The journey from Pocock, Ill., to Decency, Conn., has been played forward, backward and sideways, sometimes strictly for laughs and often, as in *The Blood of the Lamb,* to illustrate that comedy is not the opposite of tragedy but its Siamese twin.

The serious side of De Vries has been subject to considerable analysis, most of it attempts to align the author's dour Dutch Calvinist upbringing with his development as a comic writer. To borrow a De Vriesian analogy, such treatment is like putting the reader into a diving bell and taking him down 3 ft. His latest novel [*The Prick of Noon*] counters that effect by granting his fans a chance to wet their feet once again in the forbidding shallows of sex, money and social class.

There is, of course, the usual danger of getting nibbled to death by puns. . . . The book's conspicuous title can have a number of meanings, all socially redeemed because the line is Shakespeare's ("The bawdy hand of the dial is now upon the prick of noon," *Romeo and Juliet,* Act II. Scene 4). But there are no star-crossed lovers, only heavenly bodies tumbling from orbit to bounce in the bed of Eddie Teeters, a producer and sometime actor in pornographic videocassettes piously merchandised as sex-education films. . . .

De Vries relies on literary parody, verbal burlesque and a baleful eye for "life-styles". The result is a deftly improvised confusion in which the suburbs become the stage for fragments of Elizabethan comedy, bits of Wodehouse farce and a generalized send-up of *The Great Gatsby*. There is even a climactic courtroom scene in which Teeters must defend himself against charges of smut peddling. Unfortunately, he has arrived in Merrymount one beat behind the conservative backlash and cannot convince a jury that his cassettes are the visual equivalent of *The Joy of Sex*.

The trial is oddly didactic. It is as if De Vries suddenly said, "To be serious for a moment," and then contented himself with a dramatization of research into sexual censorship cases. Neither the subject nor the ways of the law seem to arouse his inventiveness. Why else sour this section with such statements as "Cutter rumbled on in much the same vein, repeating himself to an extent that seemed to wilt the judge's briefly revived interest" and "Nothing was said for or against censorship that you haven't heard a thousand times"?

But then, the bludgeoning formalities of the bar were bound to numb a writer of De Vries' talents. His language has never been a weapon but an instrument of delight and celebration. Even his weakest puns and gibes are forms of appreciation for the unaccountable variety that is the raw material for his humor. *The Prick of Noon,* his 22nd novel, may not be his strongest performance. But at 75, De Vries still projects a vision that is fresh and sensuous. His is a comedy that does not reduce character with sociology and psychology but sees instincts and folly through the eyes of a naturalist.

R. Z. Sheppard, "Uncle Gatsby in Connecticut," in
Time, *New York, Vol. 125, No. 16, April 22, 1985,*
p. 69.

CLANCY SIGAL

It's getting harder to be funny these days, especially in the comedy of manners of which Peter De Vries is such a master. De Vries's splendid precocity has always consisted, in the past, of a deeply serious, even puritanical attack on the morals and living styles of the gracious set, or the mob that in [*The Prick of Noon*] he calls the "bohemian bourgeoisie." His famous puns ("It's the tale that dogs the wag") and tricks of language habitually are at the service of a genuinely old-fashioned sensibility. . . .

[In *The Prick of Noon,* De Vries's] arrow follows a rather disappointingly meandering path and thuds off-target though, as he would probably love to mix the metaphor, somewhere in the ballpark of malice and delight.

Eddie Teeters, a.k.a. Monty Carlo, is a porn king, an "abominable showman" who leads a double life. He produces and acts—only from the neck down—in skin flicks thinly disguised as training documentaries for Sexucational Films. But, as a Backbone, Arkansas-bred boy, he is also anxious to socially climb up the hill to Merrymount, Conn. . . .

Eddie is a high-school dropout who "flunked almost everything but nonchalance." His main tactic as a social striver is to lift from books phrases or even entire passages that, of course, often become transformed into "gross usages and corny cracks intended out of sheer vindictiveness to grate on the very people I strive to measure up to." In other words, he resents the smart set he aspires to. He's a Jay Gatsby as played by W. C. Fields.

Predictably in a De Vries caper, the hero sprays puns and smart-aleck ripostes like a machine gun gone out of control. Alas, it runs in the family. Eddie's father, caretaker of the local cemetery, insisted his was "a grave responsibility." A chip off the old blockhead, Eddie is also a compulsive teller of awful gags, such as "When it comes to chauffeuring, I don't take a back seat to anybody." Or, when he's in the hospital and the nurse tells him he's due for an esophagoscopy, he replies: "That's easy for you to say." At an ultramodern art show Eddie opines—a word he's fond of—"I too believe in every kind of experimentation. . . . But somewhere he's got to draw a line."

That's a fair sample of Mr. De Vries's whimsy. Even if you have a taste for this sort of thing—and I do—the plot and characters are more formless than usual. Eddie is obsessed with Cynthia Pickles, an "aloof poolside patrician," a good-natured, strictly raised WASP career woman. But his attentions are also drawn to a buxom country club waitress, Toby Snapper, irksomely given to twee cockney speech. Eddie desperately tries to conceal his double identity from both women and from their friends. Ironically, he is most easily accepted by the Merrymount sophisticates when his pornographic activities are exposed and he is hauled before a Moral Majority judge. I think Mr. De Vries is trying to make a point here about permissiveness, the anything-goes syndrome that makes a celebrity more rather than less socially acceptable after his or her run-in with the law has been publicized. . . .

[*The Prick of Noon*] is Peter De Vries at his most mechanical and amiable, not the best recipe for sharp parody. I have always admired him in his darker mode, as when he lambastes liberal religion in *The Blood of the Lamb,* or attacks the sinlessness of modern sin in *The Mackerel Plaza.* A bit more structure and a more vengeful bite in *The Prick of Noon* might have made it easier to swallow such puns as the author's definition of a semi-conductor—"Leonard Bernstein sawing himself in two with his own baton."

Clancy Sigal, "Paronomasiamania," in The New
York Times Book Review, *May 9, 1985, p. 16.*

JAMES BOWDEN

It is an odd thing for someone who has written an approving book on Peter De Vries [see excerpt in *CLC,* Vol. 28] and who also has testified in court against pornography to find a book by that agreeable author, more or less, on that disagreeable subject. In *The Prick of Noon* there is a familiar De Vries type, a social climber, in this case one Eddie Teeters from Backbone, Arkansas, a fellow who has made it to the upper economic echelons by producing what he calls sexucational films.

That is, he claims they are educational. That some of them depict "group sex" is all right for Eddie, since those films show how *not* to do it. Are we to believe this? Are we even to believe that Eddie believes it? It's difficult to determine: although there are certain similarities to *The Great Gatsby,* also about a parvenu who has taken a low but fast road to wealth, there are certain differences. For one thing, the book about Gatsby is told by Nick Carraway, who gives us a more detached perspective on the heroic figure than we get here, where Eddie himself tells his own tale. There is a sophisticate available to do the telling, one Jerry Chirouble—inherited-rich and set up as a publisher just to have something to do, though he never publishes any of the manuscripts he solicits. But he's only in the narrative as the desideratum. In that regard, then, the book is similar to what *Gatsby* might have been had Jay Gatsby told it himself.

In that case, we probably wouldn't have learned that the narrator's real name was James Gatz; in this one, the withheld name is Monty Carlo, Teeter's professional tag, which of course goes in the opposite direction socially, as if Gatz had an underworld name (Kid Guts? Jimmy-the-Gat?) he hid from his neighbors. Another difference is that while Gatsby already has his fake Norman castle in place, Teeters goes shopping for his. And he's never known a Daisy.

One thing Gatz and Teeters do have in common is a general approval of The American Dream, at least as it might be conceived of by a mafioso. (p. 14)

Often, as Roderick Jellema (one of his early critics) has said, De Vries' work has suggested that "sin isn't all it's cracked up to be." De Vries' people certainly are often disappointed in the trip after arriving at their destination. The human situation is still whatever it was to begin with, even in Merrymount, Connecticut (the setting for *Noon*), except it's more sophisticated, more aware, more *New Yorker*ish. For someone as witty as De Vries, and for his fans, that may be as much as there is. In *Noon,* though, the hero is not quite the same as in the 20-plus other De Vries novels where the fellow who has made it in advertising comes to this disillusion. The typical De Vries protagonist may have produced heavily suggestive commercials exploitative of women and pandering to men, but that's still not porn. Or, when the narrator was a writer, he may have written erotically, but that's not porn. (Eros is the sophisticate's porn?) And always he groans at women who say *ices* (I sez), at men whose *hopefully* modifies nothing.

Here it's good ol' boy Eddie Teeters, though, who is the gauche one. At the novel's opening, he is only six months past mispronouncing *epitome* (how does he do on *epigone*?) and now wants to get so well set in exurbia that eventually he can have children who will reject him and all he's striven for as "plastic." A different perspective, then. Very soon he meets *his* Daisy, his first "nice" girl. She is Cynthia Pickles, a toothsome sophisticate who wants backers for an avant-garde journal she is editing. (pp. 14-15)

There is, as is usual in De Vries books, an alternative female for the narrator to choose, a woman who is usually a bit too tacky or prurient or too tackily prurient to be ultimately satisfactory as a mate. In this instance Toby Snapper, a waitress in the converted club, is available: she is available indeed, but since Teeters hopes to raise himself "by his own . . . petard," she doesn't seem quite right. As usual, there are other female asides—De Vries *loves* women in their variousness—but these are dropped threads: a Wellesley lit major who has a summer job as a swillperson (drives a garbage truck) probably is there for the fun of seeing such a one in such a job, and Roxy, an assistant to Chirouble, is in too indeterminate a position to be developed—she's about halfway (ascending) between Toby and Cynthia. One gets used to this sort of smorgasbord of sexual opportunities that De Vries presents in his works, though one wishes he would pare it down a bit (art is supposed to). (p. 15)

Toby is the one who pairs with Teeters, finally, showing that *Noon*'s opening line is right, that "the trouble with treating people as equals is that the first thing you know they may be doing the same thing to you." Cynthia, who had manipulated Teeters to climax while they watched him (she ignorantly) act or perform in one of his own films, marries Chirouble. It seems Teeters does the close-ups himself, from the neck down, at least, leading up to, as he calls it, *la mort douche.* Toby recognizes him by a mole he has, and Cynthia finds out; neither cares.

Ought they? Ought anyone? A California court recently convicted a porn-film producer on the basis of that state's anti-pimp law: the court ruled that anyone who hired women to perform sexually was a pimp—and his employees prostitutes. At Teeters' trial, De Vries has the defense refer obliquely to *Ulysses* and *Lady Chatterley's Lover,* then goes on to contradictory experts who cancel each other out on the artistic merit of sexucational films. The real question for De Vries seems to be whether it would seduce susceptible personalities, but the asinine pregnant teenager (who says *kwee* for *could we*) who testifies cannot be taken seriously.

The part about the expert witnesses I believe: in the case where I testified, a social worker and a sociologist/sex therapist said the films in question were innocuous films (they were the sort usually advertised as XXX Rated), in which the people involved were merely being "friendly." My counter was that literature ordinarily has two- and three-dimensional characters, flat ones and round ones (cf. E. M. Forster's *Aspects of the Novel*), those who are not integral to the story and those whose personalities are developed fully. In pornography, the characters are not even flat, not even two-dimensional: they are one-dimensional. Pornography treats people, especially women,

as Things. This seemed to convince the jury, though the $15,000 fine was of no consequence. These films are produced by organizations that, as Meyer Wolfsheim says in *Gatsby*, have "gonnegtions."

Not so in *The Prick of Noon:* Eddie Teeters apparently has no underworld gonnegtions and is broken financially by his suspended sentence. Teeters has to drive his Land Yacht for hire, but he's happy being married to Toby, who is pregnant—see, pornographers are normal after all, yearn for a regular life—and he's trying to place a script of his own. At the close, he's having a hard time raising money, though he has faith he can do it.

Which, of course, is the heart of the whole thing: in a Marketplace Economy, that which can be sold will be sold, and that which can't be won't be. Probably that's better than a Planned (Censoring) Society, but De Vries doesn't address this issue directly, no more than he explores the infrastructure of pornography. Nor does he ask what its actors are like: his star is named Mea Culpa, a woman who thinks it's like Mia Farrow's name. We never get to know Mea, for she remains a flat character. On screen, I'll bet she was one-dimensional. (pp. 15-16)

James Bowden, "Gatsby without Clothes," in Chronicles of Culture, Vol. 9, No. 12, December, 1985, pp. 14-16.

JULIAN BARNES

Peter De Vries is a democrat among jokesters. Not just the strong and the rich are admitted to his republic of laughter. Look, here come the halt and the lame and the short of wind: all clapped on the tush and propelled into his fiction. An unco-operative driver [in *The Prick of Noon*] retorts, 'When it comes to chauffeuring I don't take a back seat to anybody'; a parvenu advises himself, 'You have faultless taste, Teeters, so let's try to hide your tasteless faults'; and is *noli me tangerine* much of a pun?

The Mr De Vries whose eye has vetted a million cartoon captions at the *New Yorker* wouldn't have let any of these through; but then, who vets the vetter? Fans of Mr De Vries will be glad of at least equal evidence of what made them fans in the first place: the wry characterisations ('I had flunked almost everything but nonchalance'); the poker face broken by a wink ('We have a rather substantial heterosexual community in Merrymount, Conn., where it's said they can always spot one of us'); the purloining or invention of jargon (a 'pre-existing infidelity' is a fine phrase for a sexual partner who, because he or she antedates the present lover, doesn't really 'count'); and the familiar, shimmying comic slide from high style into the vernacular.

The new novel is set among the not-very-smart country-club brigade, and the plot runs along traditional de Vries lines: partly a matter of sexual pursuit, partly one of puritan backlash to all sexual pursuits. Nominally set in the present, the novel often feels older than that, with its band of Hell's Angels (whose regular appearances never add up to a plot-function) and its rather *Playboy* descriptions of women. . . .

Indeed, the world of late (or, presuming less, latest) de Vries is an increasingly stylised place, increasingly dogged by the wisecrack. Character is subservient to joke. . . .

It's no doubt churlish to complain that a writer isn't doing now what he was doing 15 books ago, and to mention again with admiration *The Blood of the Lamb.* Samuel Butler advised us to eat a bunch of grapes downwards, so that each grape gets bigger and sweeter. Perhaps you should read Mr De Vries backwards, so that each book will seem funnier and truer. New readers, in that case, start here.

Julian Barnes, "Pundamental Sex," in The Observer, *January 26, 1986, p. 51.*

ANN HULBERT

In *Peckham's Marbles,* Peter De Vries turns on its head the conventional tale of literary corruption. His hopelessly highbrow protagonist, Earl Peckham—whose recent novel, *The Sorry Scheme of Things Entire,* has sold a total of three copies—does not undergo the familiar rude education in the ways of the publishing world. Instead, he gets to hold forth on the subject of how not to sell too well. Peckham's protégée is Poppy McCloud, author of the blockbuster *Break Slowly, Dawn* and a fellow writer on the Dogwinkle and Dearie list. (p. 42)

Peckham's role as mentor grows out of his romance with Poppy, begun while the two of them are traversing the country. (She's signing books by the thousands, he's making a pilgrimage to the only three bookstores in the country that have ordered copies of *Sorry Scheme.*) Poppy responds willingly, and De Vries develops the conceit deftly. Peckham distills spare, sophisticated *New Yorker* stories from Poppy's purple prose and engineers her emergence as one star in a new and fashionable literary school. He gives the school a name: "He had decided against 'The Dirty Romantics' . . . in favor of 'The Vagabonds,' which would emphasize the fact that their characters were all sexual itinerants wandering from one ephemeral relationship to another," and he successfully primes the media.

But in the denouement De Vries lets his comedy of standards get muddled. Poppy dumps Peckham, offended when she discovers that he once called her book "trash" (even though she's never pretended to write anything but potboilers), and she disappears from the story. Peckham is adrift, in a literary as well as a romantic way. He lapses into the stock impossibly-out-of-it-novelist role he played at the outset, even though he's just shown a wittier, savvy side to his character. Thus De Vries abandons his most subversive and interesting theme: in the reprocessing of Poppy for more sophisticated tastes, he has shown that high culture is hardly exempt from calculating compromises. (At the same time he has implied that lowbrow authors can at least claim a certain pragmatic honesty.) The erosion of standards, he suggests, isn't a simple matter of decline. The disorientation is more radical than that, as editors, publishers, advertisers, and writers look anxiously upward as well as greedily downward in search of values, however vacuous, to steer by. (pp. 42, 44)

Ann Hulbert, "New Glitter Street," in The New Republic, *Vol. 195, No. 3739, September 15, 1986, pp. 38-42, 44.*

WILLIAM RICE

Peter De Vries is among the heartiest of America's comic perennials, an author who has been tickling funny bones for three decades through books such as *Slouching Towards Kalamazoo, Reuben, Reuben,* and *The Tunnel of Love,* to cite a title from each decade. His latest, *Peckham's Marbles,* a tale

of how an acerbic English professor fails to save America from pop romance fiction and ends up as the most happy fellow in a loony bin called Dappled Shade (he marries the owner), is sure to bring indulgent chuckles from faithful readers. Even when he's off form, as he is here, there are still more laughs in a 250-page De Vries novel than in a season of TV sit-coms.

The book is essentially an Earl Peckham monologue, with straight lines delivered by a number of cartoon-like characters. As the curtain opens, Peckham is at Dappled Shade recovering from hepatitis and twin tragedies: "Two years before," we're told, enrollment in his creative writing course "had dwindled to one. And last year it had fallen off a little." More recently sales of his novel *The Sorry Scheme of Things Entire* had leveled off at three.

That doesn't stop Peckham from firing off zingers at anyone within ear-shot. "Nothing like a bout of hepatitis to make a chap look on the world with a jaundiced eye," he says while trying unsuccessfully to captivate Nelly DelBelly, Dappled Shade's owner.

Presumably Peckham is Groucho Marx wrapped in academic robes. At least that premise suggests itself when Dame Nelly is compared to Margaret Dumont, Groucho's foil in films. But Peckham isn't in the same league as such memorable De Vries characters as Gowan McGland of *Reuben, Reuben,* much less Groucho.

William Rice, in a review of "Peckham's Marbles," in Chicago Tribune, *October 19, 1986, p. 6.*

JOANNE KAUFMAN

Pity the poor souls assigned the task of reviewing a Peter De Vries novel. For no matter how desperately creative the critics, they'll never be able to come up with a fresh, new way to describe [him]. . . .

After all, Mr. De Vries has already been called the master of antic angst, has already been compared to Robert Benchley, Corey Ford, Frank Sullivan, P.G. Wodehouse, Pagliacci, Laurence Sterne, Cervantes, James Thurber, Max Beerbohm, Evelyn Waugh and S. J. Perelman, to name a few.

Mr. De Vries uses his antic angst to create slightly off-center characters who lead lives not of quiet desperation but of noisy confusion. A case in point is Earl Peckham, the title character in *Peckham's Marbles.* . . . He's a failed teacher (exactly one student signed up for his last creative-writing class; when enrollment dropped off, the university quite reasonably refused to grant Prof. Peckham tenure), a failed novelist (his last book, *The Sorry Scheme of Things Entire* sold exactly three copies) and a failed lover (in spite of his best efforts, Earl has been unable to score with either Nelly DelBelly, the Junoesque proprietor of the rest home where he's recuperating from a bad case of hepatitis, or with Mrs. DelBelly's luscious niece Binnie Aspenwall).

One thing Earl can do alarmingly well, as all his would-be conquests observe, is "work his mouth pretty good." Sometimes too good. "The chief obstacle to Peckham's progress with Mrs. DelBelly lay undoubtedly in his inability to chew the rag or chew the fat. . . ."

It's not that Earl doesn't try to "masticate the old suet" or "chomp the proverbial tallow"; he and Mrs. DelBelly, a woman of mean understanding, little information and piles of money, would be chatting cozily, say, about the passing of the flyswatter from the American scene, when he would dilate "on a nostalgic artifact once a staple of every household." Hoo boy, as Earl's grandfather might say. So much for singing the body electric with Nelly.

Well-aimed threats from luscious Binnie's loathsome fiance send Earl out into America's heartland to locate the three readers of his novel. But Earl finds more than a copy of *Sorry Scheme* in Omaha, Neb.; he also finds love in the form of Poppy McCloud, whose five-pound best-selling novel *Break Slowly, Dawn,* Earl denounced as trash to a newspaper reporter during an earlier stop in Cedar Rapids. Hoo boy.

In no time at all the ill-matched pair is living together in Poppy's upstate New York home; in no time at all, Poppy is at work on her second novel. . . .

But Poppy, an avid fan of *Sorry Scheme,* wants to learn from the master. She also wants to stop smoking. She gets both her wishes when Peckham, visions of Svengali dancing in his head, uses hypnosis on his lady love: "After I clap my hands three times you will have a passion for excellence. Pick my brains; they are yours for the plucking."

But since this is Peter De Vries country and since there are still 100 pages left, and since pride goeth before a fall, there are—hoo boy—several obstacles to Peckham's progress, and several complications before he finds peace of mind and peace from plucking.

Peckham's Marbles, which owes a debt to *Rebecca, Trilby* and, in its last paragraph, to *The Great Gatsby,* is sometimes rather slow going. Still, there is the sense that if you don't like the page you're on, you're bound to like the next one.

Certainly, the wordplay that is the mark of De Vries's oeuvre is as reliable as ever. "One of the greatest navigators of all time," Peckham notes of Christopher Columbus. "But put him on dry land and he was completely at sea." Later, using blandishments to calm the rough waters with Poppy, Peckham observes that "some marriages founder on deception, others are founded on it." Still later, when a freelance evangelist beseeches the beleaguered Peckham "to make a decision for Christ," Earl comes up with the only possible DeVriesian response: "Why can't he make his own decisions?"

If *Peckham's Marbles* doesn't quite deserve a bag of puries, it certainly rates a handful of keepers.

Joanne Kaufman, "The Misadventures of a Sorry Ex-Professor," in The Wall Street Journal, October 28, 1986, p. 32.

RALPH C. WOOD

[*Peckham's Marbles*] is the usual De Vriesian fare—outrageously punning, inside-out, upside-down. Many of De Vries's books can be as forgettable as they are amusing since their plots and characters serve as mere gossamer excuses for his wild humor. *Peckham's Marbles* is truly memorable. Peckham himself sticks in the mind because his plight is real: how does a man of wit and sensibility comport himself in a trite and banal world?

Peckham's curse is that he is unwilling to chew the rag, to indulge the American penchant for bromides and chestnuts. "Masticating the old suet," he calls it, "chomping the proverbial tallow." Peckham hates platitudes because they cheat life of its moral complexity and spiritual comedy. Without an ironic distance on oneself and the world, everything is flattened into a shallow sincerity and seriousness. "If God has no humor," says Peckham, "then we're not made in his image. On the other hand," he adds ruefully, "it gives you the willies to think of being governed by a Divine Being who'd split a gut" over what usually passes as humor.

Peckham's quest for a life without cliché is complicated by his dealings with women. He is twice divorced because, as he says, "to love women is to know them." Yet Peckham can do without women even less than he can live with them. Thus is this waggish man in his late 50s put in ardent and arduous pursuit of two younger women, Binnie Aspenwall and Poppy McCloud. They both prove themselves incapable, alas, of living the life of paradox. . . .

As a true humorist, Peckham turns his irony chiefly upon himself. He knows that his books do not sell—*The Sorry Scheme of Things Entire* has had just three buyers—because they spin too many "silken subtleties." Ms. McCloud accuses him of writing "loopy arcane stuff" full of "hemisemidemiquavers." "Angel's hair," she calls it. Peckham's colossal unsuccess reduces him, therefore, to self-mocking rage. . . .

Nelly DelBelly tells Peckham that he ought to have his marbles examined. This wonderful splintering of a phrase helps reconcile Peckham to the inevitable. Not within a paradise of punsters will he be able to live and move and have his being, but within the trite world of the truism. Human existence, he discovers, is more like a soap opera than an epic tragedy or comedy. To live amid threadbare predictabilities is the real human task.

Such a life requires what De Vries's novel so splendidly provides: a special mercy, a heroic ordinariness, an ironic acceptance of unrecognized irony. Finally, therefore, Peckham marries Ms. DelBelly, the woman he didn't want and doesn't deserve but graciously gets. They are joined as one flesh and one mind because they are able both to fight and to forgive: "Thus did hostility again move in its mysterious ways its wonders to perform. A marriage in name only lay in fragments at their feet, never to be pieced together again." Peckham has all his marbles and keeps them too.

Ralph C. Wood, in a review of "Peckham's Marbles," in The Christian Century, Vol. 103, No. 40, December 24-31, 1986, p. 1182.

Stephen R. Donaldson

1947-

(Has also written under pseudonym of Reed Stephens) American novelist and short story writer.

An author of fantasy fiction, Donaldson has enjoyed popular success with a series of novels collectively known as *The Chronicles of Thomas Covenant, the Unbeliever*. The trilogy, as well as its sequel, *The Second Chronicles of Thomas Covenant, the Unbeliever*, has drawn comparisons to J. R. R. Tolkien's *The Lord of the Rings* and C. S. Lewis's *Narnia* series for their inclusion of legend, mythology, folklore, and labyrinthine plots. In a genre in which most heroes are unrealistically good, the protagonist of these books, Thomas Covenant, is an anomaly. A leper, a misanthrope, and a skeptic, Covenant endears himself to readers by his vulnerability and fallibility, traits not usually associated with fantasy heroes. Although several critics have faulted Donaldson's verbosity and his reliance on obscure words and strained metaphors, others have praised his colorful characterizations and thematic range. One reviewer remarked: "What distinguishes Donaldson's work from the common run of fantasies is not just his more elaborate prose (which at times is too pedantic), but his approach to power. . . . Donaldson sees it as a corrupting temptation."

The Chronicles of Thomas Covenant, the Unbeliever is composed of the novels *Lord Foul's Bane* (1977), *The Illearth War* (1977), and *The Power That Preserves* (1977). Covenant, a successful author who is shunned by his wife and society because of his leprosy, is transported to an alternative world known as "the Land" and finds himself appointed savior because of his resemblance to a legendary hero whose return had been prophesied. The leaders of the Land desire Covenant's wedding ring, for its white gold possesses supernatural power in their world. Confronted by the Creator with a choice of remaining a leper on earth or attaining immortality in the Land, Covenant reluctantly agrees to fight the evil Lord Foul even though he believes the Land to be a hallucination. Covenant triumphs but disappoints the Land's inhabitants by sparing Lord Foul. John Calvin Bachelor stated that "although Donaldson writes dense and strangled prose, *Chronicles* has, at its heart, an unqualifiedly sublime idea—that the last shall be first."

The Second Chronicles of Thomas Covenant, the Unbeliever encompasses the novels *The Wounded Land* (1980), *The One Tree* (1982), and *White Gold Wielder* (1983). Set ten years after Covenant's victory, these books introduce Linden Avery, a female physician who joins Covenant in the Land to try to thwart a resurgent Lord Foul, who has tainted the Land's magic—known as Earthpower—with the blood of innocent people. In this trilogy, Covenant believes that the Land is real, but he lacks the power to detect evil, an ability he possessed in the first series and which Avery now holds. Both Covenant and Avery must overcome their guilt and depression in order to conquer Lord Foul. Critics generally rated the second trilogy inferior to the first. Contending that the initial novels are more successful "because of colorful, cinematic imagery, exciting action scenes, and epic and arcane language," Sam Frank complained that the later works include "more lurid dialogue

and debate than before, more gratuitous exposition, less epic vision and more redundant violence."

In *The Mirror of Her Dreams* (1986), the first volume of a projected two-book series entitled *Mordant's Need*, Terisa Morgen, like Covenant an outcast, becomes involved in a predicament which helps her discover her identity. Morgen, a self-deprecating young woman who adorns her apartment with mirrors to confirm her existence, is chosen by an ineffectual sorcerer to rescue the fantasy kingdom of Mordant, where mirrors have magical capabilities. Morgen's naiveté leads to catastrophe, but Donaldson leaves the ending inconclusive. Although some reviewers maintained that *The Mirror of Her Dreams* suffered from excessive description, others detected a sparer style and more humor than exhibited in the trilogies. In *Daughter of Regals and Other Tales* (1984), a collection of six stories and two novellas, Donaldson incorporates several styles, including medieval fantasy, science fiction, the spy thriller, and the modern horror story. Donaldson also has written two detective novels, *The Man Who Killed His Brother* (1980) and *The Man Who Risked His Partner* (1984), under the pseudonym Reed Stephens.

(See also *Contemporary Authors*, Vols. 89-92 and *Contemporary Authors New Revision Series*, Vol. 13.)

JOHN CALVIN BATCHELOR

Stephen R. Donaldson calls his Satan-figure Lord Foul, though, as with Satan in medieval romance, Lord Foul has a myriad of names, such as Corruption, the Despiser, and Gray Slayer. Donaldson's painfully long trilogy—*Lord Foul's Bane; The Illearth War; The Power That Preserves:* all under the collective title, *The Chronicles of Thomas Covenant, The Unbeliever*—concerns itself exclusively with the contest between the destructive urges of Lord Foul, who aims to rule if not rent asunder an alternate world called the Land, and the benign though uninformed urges of the heroic Thomas Covenant, a young writer from our Earth whom the Creator drops into the Land in order to save it from Despite, the power of evil.

Thomas Covenant, however, is no ordinary superstar. Sometime before his involuntary adventure, he contracted leprosy, which transformed what had been a successful (even smug) writer, husband, and father, into a self-pitying outcast who hates himself just a little more than he hates everything else. Covenant is Donaldson's genius, and I would be delinquent if I didn't say that although Donaldson writes dense and strangled prose, *Chronicles* has, at its heart, an unqualifiedly sublime idea—that the last shall be first.

Lord Foul has his day first, however. Foul is the first to confront Covenant as he awakens in the Land (an ecological paradise—indeed, another name for Foul could have been Industrial Waste). Foul makes a heady prediction, the gist of which is that the only thing that can prevent Foul's supremacy in "seven times seven years" is Covenant's white-gold wedding ring, which, in a world where there is no gold, gives Covenant a wild magic that is theoretically more powerful than Foul's Despite. . . .

Three times Covenant is called to the Land (thus three books), and each time he gets a little closer to besting, however inadvertently, Lord Foul—for whom I rooted throughout. Meanwhile, Foul tortures and desecrates the Land, where dwell a closetful of zippy folk like Giants, Viles, Wraiths, Lords, and Bloodguards. The real surprise of the tale comes not when Foul is expectedly undone, but rather when Covenant is returned by the Creator to Earth to die of an allergic reaction. The Creator offers the unconscious Covenant a reward for his service, however—either life as a leper on the real Earth, where Covenant is a believer in himself; or life as an immortal hero in the seemingly unreal Land, where Covenant was always an unbeliever in everything. I confess I don't entirely fathom Donaldson's choice of fates for his protagonist, and can only suppose the resolution, as well as the leprosy motif, speaks to some very personal melancholy of the author's. (p. 79)

John Calvin Batchelor, "Tolkien Again: Lord Foul and Friends Infest a Morbid but Moneyed Land," in The Village Voice, *Vol. XXII, No. 41, October 10, 1977, pp. 79-80.*

JUDITH T. YAMAMOTO

A head injury catapults Thomas Covenant, best-selling author and leper outcast, into a fantasy world where he sheds his physical affliction but retains a leprosy of the soul stemming from his belief that the experience is a dream or hallucination. In the war against the spirit of evil, Lord Foul, he progresses, to become the savior of the Land and its people, achieving at the same time his own internal salvation. While occasionally the language becomes uncomfortably precious . . . , and the ending is a bit of a cop-out, [*The Chronicles of Thomas Covenant, the Unbeliever*] shows promise and makes absorbing reading. Plenty of adventure is well-coordinated with a revealing study of the leper's psyche. (pp. 2184-85)

Judith T. Yamamoto, in a review of "The Chronicles of Thomas Covenant, the Unbeliever," in Library Journal, *Vol. 102, No. 18, October 15, 1977, pp. 2184-85.*

PUBLISHERS WEEKLY

[In *The Wounded Land,* the first volume of Donaldson's *The Second Chronicles of Thomas Covenant: the Unbeliever*], Covenant, a leper and the reincarnation of a legendary hero, returns to the magical world of the Land after 10 of our years and finds that thousands of years have passed since his defeat of the evil Lord Foul. That malign spirit has regathered his strength over the centuries and has now corrupted nature to blight the Land with the Sunbane, a neverending series of plagues. Once again Foul threatens to destroy the world and escape the prison made for him by the Creator. Covenant will fight to prevent this, of course, but his situation is complicated by the presence of another person from Earth, Dr. Linden Avery. . . . The many who enjoyed Donaldson's first trilogy will be eager to read this beginning of a new one, but familiarity with the earlier work isn't necessary to be caught up in the sweep of Donaldson's grim fantasy. (pp. 78, 80)

A review of "The Wounded Land: Book One of the Second Chronicles of Thomas Covenant," in Publishers Weekly, *Vol. 217, No. 15, April 18, 1980, pp. 78, 80.*

ROSEMARY HERBERT

With *The Wounded Land,* Donaldson begins a second trilogy set in the Land, a fantasy world once rescued from an evil power by the efforts of Thomas Covenant, a leper. Covenant again finds himself thrust from contemporary America into the affairs of the Land, this time in the company of a young doctor who, like Covenant, must fight her own guilt and despair in order to battle the larger forces of evil pervading this strange world. . . . [Dr. Linden Avery] is a believable character for new readers to follow into the Land, and fans of the first trilogy will appreciate her different way of responding to Covenant's world. (pp. 1411-12)

Rosemary Herbert, in a review of "The Wounded Land," in Library Journal, *Vol. 105, No. 12, June 15, 1980, pp. 1411-12.*

PUBLISHERS WEEKLY

When Brew accidentally shot his brother, a police officer who was chasing a thief, his life changed drastically: the private investigator lost his license and became an alcoholic. At the start of this tightly written mystery [*The Man Who Killed His Brother*], Brew is on a drinking binge, when his ex-partner, Ginny, seeks him out and tells him that his niece, Alathea, has disappeared. The 13-year-old's mother has hired Ginny, a smart, strong-willed investigator, to find the girl. Ginny helps Brew sober up, and the two begin to look for clues to Alathea's mysterious disappearance. . . . [They] learn that there have been six previous cases in which attractive girls of Alathea's age have vanished. The pattern is ominous: each has been found dead after several months. Their bodies showed evidence of heroin use and "intensive sexual activity.". . . There is nothing astonishing about the puzzle's solution, but Stephens fits the pieces together neatly.

A review of "The Man Who Killed His Brother," in Publishers Weekly, *Vol. 218, No. 18, October 31, 1980, p. 83.*

PUBLISHERS WEEKLY

This slim book [*Gilden-Fire*] is a specialty item for the many fans of Donaldson's Thomas Covenant stories. It's a brief episode that had to be cut from *The Illearth War* for reasons of logic and length, and which really cannot stand on its own as a novel, as Donaldson admits in his introduction. He explains that he is allowing it into print now because the logic problem is moot for readers who have completed the trilogy . . . and because of his fondness for the characters who are given more attention here. The story concerns the mission of Lords Hyrim and Shetra to the giants of Seareach as experienced by the sleepless Blood-guard Korik. It's a well-told fragment, however. . . .

A review of "Gilden-Fire," in Publishers Weekly, *Vol. 220, No. 24, December 11, 1981, p. 53.*

PUBLISHERS WEEKLY

In [*The One Tree*] Covenant finds that his role as savior of the Land must be shared with another from our world, Dr. Linden Avery. Like him, she has some deepseated problems of relevance to the plot, and their continuing exposition makes this more her story than his. To stop Lord Foul's terrible concatenation of plagues, the Sunbane, they sail with giants on a granite ship in search of the One Tree. Covenant hopes to fashion from it a new Staff of the Law to restore the natural order Foul has overturned. . . . What distinguishes Donaldson's work from the common run of fantasies is not just his more elaborate prose (which at times is too pedantic), but his approach to power. In pulpier sword-and-sorcery works power is relished and used with abandon. Donaldson sees it as a corrupting temptation, and this theme well complements the angst of his two protagonists. This is an impressive nonescapist fantasy. . . .

A review of "The One Tree: Book Two of the Second Chronicles of Thomas Covenant," in Publishers Weekly, *Vol. 221, No. 8, February 19, 1982, p. 62.*

NEIL K. CITRIN

When [Stephen Donaldson] began the second cycle of the *Chronicles of Thomas Covenant* two years ago with *The Wounded Land* I doubted his wisdom. How long could any reader stay interested in the constant, agonizing self-doubt of leper Thomas Covenant as he struggled to save the Land from the evil Lord Foul? After [*The One Tree*], the second in the new trilogy, I doubt no longer.

The first book began ten years (Covenant's time) after the events of the first trilogy. Two thousand years have passed in the Land, with traumatic changes wrought by Lord Foul. The Sunbane, fed by the blood of human sacrifices, has replaced the beneficial energy of Earthpower. Only Linden Avery, a doctor from Covenant's world, retains the ability to sense good or bad health once common in the Land. She must guide Covenant riddled by venom feeding on the power of his white gold ring, in his quest to cure the Land. As this book begins Cov-

enant and Avery ride with the tireless and loyal Haruchai and a party of Giants in search of the magical One Tree. From it Covenant hopes to replace the Staff of Law, destroyed at the end of the first cycle. He believes it will help him control the wild power of his ring as well as heal the Land.

Donaldson tells most of his tale through Avery. She finds Covenant's power and his ability to accept guilt while continuing singlemindedly toward his goal very attractive; she also feels that her indecision, her past, and her own dark hunger for power renders her unworthy of him. These forces battle inside Avery disrupting her relationships with her companions as they struggle to overcome one obstacle after another. . . . Tolkien fans may cry "blasphemy!" but the *Covenant* books equal the scope and power and beauty of the master's *Lord of the Rings* trilogy. Adding a generous helping of realism, the writer creates a story the equal of anything currently available in fiction today.

Neil K. Citrin, in a review of "The One Tree," in West Coast Review of Books, *Vol. 8, No. 4, July, 1982, p. 36.*

TIMOTHY ROBERT SULLIVAN

The best that can be said of *White Gold Wielder* by Stephen R. Donaldson is that it ends the Second Chronicles of Thomas Covenant, a fustian maxiseries that has been galumphing along since the publication of *Lord Foul's Bane* in 1977. All six of the Convenant books have proved immensely popular, usually lingering on the bestseller list with Asimov and the *Astounding* boys. After reading one of them, one can only wonder what so many people see in this stuff.

It's ironic that the first word in the text of *White Gold Wielder* is "awkward," for that word summarizes the considerable flaws of Donaldson's new book with cruel precision. As one burrows deeper into the inflated text it soon becomes apparent that the rules, not to mention the standards, of good fiction are violated repeatedly on every page. For example, people seldom say things. Instead, they spit, snarl, breathe, sigh, articulate, swallow, murmur, intone, rasp, grunt and otherwise make noises usually reserved for the lower orders on the Great Chain of Being.

Attempts to evoke a Tolkienesque world through a pseudo-medieval nomenclature are common in contemporary fantasy fiction, but few writers do it as ineptly as Donaldson. One glance at a term such as *ak-Haru Kenaustin Ardenol*, which sounds like a headache remedy for samurai, is enough to provoke gales of laughter from the little boy in one and snickers in the adult. . . .

Everything in this verbal quagmire takes three times as long to describe as it should, largely due to Donaldson's attempts at what he doubtless believes to be colorful language. As for the characters, well, the notion of an anti-hero in an epic fantasy work is all right, but it was pioneered by Michael Moorcock in the albino Elric of Melniboné. Donaldson tries to do Moorcock one better, featuring a misanthropic leper as his protagonist. The dubious charm of this casting-against-type has long since dried up after nearly a million words of Chronicles, however.

At least Donaldson is making lots of money. One imagines him sitting earnestly at the word processor, thesaurus at his elbow so that he can look up ever more outlandish synonymns for perfectly ordinary things until his prose takes on a hallucinatory tinge. Perhaps this is what appeals to his legion of fans, who must all be adults, for no child would be taken in by such decrepit linguistic mummery as Donaldson has to offer.

Timothy Robert Sullivan, in a review of "White Gold Wielder," in Book World—The Washington Post, *June 26, 1983, p. 10.*

SAM FRANK

The Thomas Covenant fantasy trilogies are a must for soap opera fans. All six books—especially *White Gold Wielder*—are loaded with misery and misplaced, overblown guilt. The first trilogy [*The Chronicles of Thomas Covenant: the Unbeliever*] had enough momentum and verbal sorcery to mitigate some of the angst, but the second trilogy is tiresome. It almost becomes a contest in which Covenant and his female companion, Linden Avery, who thinks she is responsible for the deaths of her parents, vie to determine who is more deserving of contempt. . . .

Though it's marred by a lot of breast-beating about leprosy and its seemingly unsympathetic hero's lack of humor, the first trilogy worked because of colorful, cinematic imagery, exciting action scenes, epic and arcane language and characters such as Saltheart Foamfollower (my favorite), a giant with a loving devotion to Covenant. The saga was addictive, carrying one through hundreds of pages of dire calamities and probing, introspective observations.

In this last installment, Linden Avery shares Covenant's dream, and when they emerge in the Land, they discover that since he left it 4,000 years ago by fantasy time, all that he accomplished has been undone by a resurrected Lord Foul. The Land is literally being laid waste by a corruption of nature engendered by Foul.

By the time Covenant and Avery reach the final plot machinations of *White Gold Wielder* the story has become repetitiously overextended. The author assumes an unfamiliarity with the first trilogy, and Covenant forgets lessons learned earlier. There is more lurid dialogue and debate than before, more gratuitous exposition, less epic vision and more redundant violence. One feels relieved rather than exalted when the whole, arduous journey is finally over.

Sam Frank, in a review of "White Gold Wielder," in The New York Times Book Review, *August 14, 1983, p. 13.*

PATRICIA HERNLUND

[Stephen Donaldson] has to be taken seriously. His first volume [*Lord Foul's Bane*] quite naturally, had the most force but the least technical perfection. His problem over six volumes was to keep the intensity while adding polish, clarity and control. He succeeded in keeping intensity, maintained and deepened his characterizations, and wrote better prose in the last three, but he does not yet have the clarity and control of a major writer. His sincerity and intense involvement with his characters are the greatest successes of the books, compelling the reader's involvement even when the prose is unclear, the vocabulary too lush, and the metaphors stretched. However, the language is improving: *White Gold Wielder* is by far the most controlled and direct of the Covenant novels, and the plot moves at a good pace. . . . Linden Avery, the heroine, is overshadowed by Covenant, but in any other book would be called

an excellent characterization. The supporting characters throughout the books are rich and satisfying. The giants, from Saltheart Foamfollower in [*Lord Foul's Bane*] through Pitchwife, The First, and the others [in the latest book] are easily the equal of any previous aliens or exotics in fantasy.

The theme of [*White Gold Wielder*] and the entire six volumes, is a Gandhi-like appeal for passive resistance as the ultimate weapon: more powerful than universal evil and available to any hero, even a leper, if it is profoundly believed. This theme is not just a reviewer's regurgitation of Donaldson's biography; it is the heart of *White Gold Wielder.* Covenant refuses to kill to prevent killing; that is, he refuses to wield the white gold. Lord Foul, the embodiment of evil, cannot foresee such a refusal and therefore cannot forestall or fight it. Linden Avery, Covenant's love and a doctor, cannot rationally understand the healing inherent in Covenant's non-action, but at the last instant loves and trusts him enough to provide her essential help. Her doubts, and those of other characters, help readers who do not hold Donaldson's beliefs about pacifism to believe the actuality and worth of Covenant's decision: he loses his life but gains his soul and saves the Arch of Time, our world, and The Land. As in classic tragedy, his death is a surprise even though it is completely consistent with all six books. It satisfies and completes the reader and the story through developing pity, terror, and purgation of these emotions with a return to order. Covenant's flaw is that he cannot act, cannot commit himself, but he turns his inaction into victory. The values advanced are saint-like, and the theme is important. Donaldson's victory is that he makes us feel Covenant's tragic decision as a real event. Donaldson's failure is in the skill to communicate the idea intellectually as well as emotionally. A writer of lasting value must make his books clear and convincing to those who are not tuned to his precise wave length. That is asking a lot, but Donaldson is headed in the direction of lasting value, because of the scope of his themes, and great success of his characterizations, and his ability to make readers emotionally committed, over thousands of pages, to a hero who is a leper and a disbeliever. (pp. 24-5)

Particia Hernlund, in a review of "White Gold Wielder," in Science Fiction & Fantasy Book Review, *No. 19, November, 1983, pp. 24-5.*

KIRKUS REVIEWS

[*Daughter of Regals* consists of eight] tales, including six reprints—. . . a reasonably varied if sometimes poorly thought-out bunch. For *Thomas Covenant* fans, there's an out-take from *The Illearth War* enlarging on the adventures of Korik of the Bloodguard. Thankfully, however, Donaldson elsewhere abandons the gnarled, pretentious prose of the *Covenant* sagas for writing that is merely labored and wooden. "Animal Lover" is fairly orthodox sf, in which a vengeful molecular biologist creates an army of genetically enhanced, firearm-wielding animals. There are some middling fantasies: a man in a placid, machine-like future turns into a unicorn; a powerful husband-hunting sorceress sets prospective suitors a series of tough puzzles; an angel without memory, incarnated as a street bum, saves a sculptor's soul from the devil; and a monstrous centipede causes trouble between an already quarreling couple. But elsewhere the plotting is often painfully obvious. . . . [This collection is hardworking], mannered, and fairly ordinary overall. . . .

A review of "Daughter of Regals and Other Tales," in Kirkus Reviews, Vol. 52, No. 4, February 15, 1984, p. 173.

PUBLISHERS WEEKLY

Of the eight stories [in *Daughter of Regals and Other Tales*]—including two novellas written for this collection—only one, *Gilden Fire*, an "outtake" from *The Illearth War*, involves "the Land" of Thomas Covenant, setting for Donaldson's two bestselling trilogies. The others demonstrate that his intense style and offbeat approach can be quite effective in other realms. For example, "**The Conqueror Worm**" is a modern horror story focused on a crumbling marriage, and "**Animal Lover**" is SF, complete with a cyborg secret agent and a Moreau-like scientist. [*Daughter of Regals*] is a fantasy set in a Platonic reality where very few things are truly real, and the heroine must prove she is or lose her throne. The gritty "**Unworthy of the Angel**" offers a refreshingly untraditional view of the nature of angels.

A review of "Daughter of Regals and Other Tales," in Publishers Weekly, Vol. 225, No. 9, March 2, 1984, p. 86.

PUBLISHERS WEEKLY

More half-baked than hard-boiled [*The Man Who Risked His Partner*], set somewhere in the Southwest, tells what happens when Mick ("nobody calls me Mick") Axbrewder and his depressed girlfriend/boss, Ginny Fistoulari, take a case that they know they shouldn't. Their client, Reg Haskell, a smooth-talking accountant at the Puerta del Sol National Bank, wants protection from the local mob chief. . . . Axbrewder, a tenuously sober alcoholic, takes the job, hoping that it will snap Ginny out of her depression. (She previously lost her hand in a bomb blast.) Written in a sort of bludgeon-the-reader, first-person style, this book offers lines like, "Why in the name of all the hamburgers in the world that ever tasted like lard held together by sawdust hadn't [Captain] Cason hauled Haskell if not me in to find out what the hell we thought we were doing?" And with little more than a haphazard plot to its credit, *The Man Who Risked His Partner* risks losing its readers on every page. (pp. 76-7)

A review of "The Man Who Risked His Partner," in Publishers Weekly, Vol. 226, No. 8, August 24, 1984, pp. 76-7.

ROBERT J. EWALD

Stephen Donaldson, successful chronicler of the adventures of Thomas Covenant, decided after six Covenant books to collect eight of his shorter efforts [in *Daughter of Regals and Other Tales*]. Two novellas, *Daughter of Regals*, and *Ser Visal's Tale*, were written especially for this collection and show the improvement in depth of characterization and in story-telling ability one would expect from the experience of writing a double trilogy.

Both tales belong to that genre of medieval fantasy on which Donaldson has built his reputation. *Ser Visal's Tale*, although stretched out much too long, is a tale of a nobleman's encounter with a witch in a land terrorized by a priestly caste and has a surprise ending worthy of O. Henry. . . . *Daughter of Regals* recounts the ascendancy of a young girl, supposedly without

magic, to the seat of power of three kingdoms kept at peace by the magic of her ancestors, the Regals, dragons and basilisks in human form. . . .

"**The Conqueror Worm**" is a delightfully piquant modern horror story about a loveless marriage. "**Unworthy of the Angel**" is a religious fantasy; an angel sent to Earth in the form of a derelict contends with a demon disguised as an art dealer for the souls of a sculptor and his suffering sister (who is afflicted with very curious stigmata). "**Animal Lover**" and "**Mythological Beast**" are both SF. The former, a spy thriller complete with a mad scientist, could well have been published in *Thrilling Wonder Stories*, and the latter is an engaging allegory of a man mutating into an unicorn in defiance of a medically-controlled future society. . . .

[I] easily agree with Donaldson's self-assessment that he is basically a storyteller, and as Patricia Hernlund perceives in her review of *White Gold Wielder* [see excerpt above], his forte is excellent, believable characters. Nevertheless, excluding some unclear passages, stretched metaphors, and long passages badly in need of cutting, each one of these stories has a touch of originality and a sweep that keeps the pages turning.

Robert J. Ewald, "Donaldson Succeeds in Shorter Form," in Fantasy Review, Vol. 7, No. 9, October, 1984, p. 28.

C. W. SULLIVAN III

[In *The Mirror of Her Dreams*], Terisa Morgan, a wealthy but rather ineffectual young woman from this world, is transported through a mirror by powers she does not understand to an essentially medieval kingdom called Mordant which is in desperate need of a champion. Geraden, the young apprentice responsible for her journey, is so inept that he seems destined never to be a Master. In this case, he was supposed to bring back a fighting man; instead, he has brought this woman. Is she the sought-for champion? She doesn't think so, and neither does anyone else—except maybe Geraden. In fact, most of the people in Mordant don't think she's real.

Most of this (first of two) book develops the main characters (especially Terisa and Geraden), discusses the theories concerning the mirrors, describes the land and its people, and sets the stage for whatever the main action is to be.. All of this happens with typical Donaldson thoroughness and, at times, a bit of overwriting. Once or twice, a description is repeated almost word for word. There are too many references to Terisa's unpleasant relationship with her parents. At a few points, the reader may be annoyed with how slowly the characters catch on to what's happening. In the last third of the book, however, the action picks up and Donaldson's writing becomes crisper, so that by the end of the novel—a good cliffhanger ending—the reader is anxious for the next one.

If *Mirror of Her Dreams* has some typical Donaldson weaknesses, it also has abundant strengths. Mordant is an interesting place and is quite different from The Land of the *Covenant* books; there are a number of interesting characters. . . .

In *The Mirror of Her Dreams*, Donaldson reinvigorates the mirror/gateway (which dates to Lewis Carroll and George MacDonald at least) as a fantasy device. Mirrors in Mordant do not reflect but show scenes from other times and places. The Masters and their apprentices not only make and focus these mirrors, but are also able to translate the images out of the mirrors and into Mordant. (Donaldson seems to be inviting the reader to compare the mirrors to such ultimate sources of power as atomic energy which can be used constructively or destructively.) A mirror focused on a watery world might, for example, provide water to irrigate an arid part of Mordant. But someone, perhaps the arch-Imager Vagel (whom everyone thought dead) is translating monsters out of the mirrors and loosing them in Mordant. Hence the need for a champion.

Final judgment on some matters, especially thematic ones, will have to wait until the concluding volume, *A Man Steps Through,* for Donaldson does not reveal much in this first book. *The Mirror of Her Dreams* is a very good start, though.

> *C. W. Sullivan III, "A Mirror of Donaldson," in* Fantasy Review, *Vol. 9, No. 10, November, 1986, p. 28.*

JOHN CLUTE

Instead of a truculent and willful male leper [who is the hero of *The Chronicles of Thomas Covenant*], the protagonist of [*The Mirror of Her Dreams*] is a wispy self-effacing, virginal young woman who is also afflicted with a form of obsessive Unbelief; in this case, however, she finds it almost impossible to give any credence to the fact that she herself actually exists, while at the same time supinely accepting the reality of the implausible high fantasy land of Mordant. And instead of limning for his readers a colorful outdoor phantasmagoria of high mountains and tiny elves, of swordplay and magic and derring-do under a sky bluer than ours, Donaldson keeps this self-doubting lady indoors for almost the entire volume. Outdoors it seems to be snowing or raining most of the time. The snow is dirty.

The plot itself also violates the high fantasy model, not only because it features a desperately insecure woman, and not only because it takes place almost entirely inside. High fantasy is a form of Romance, with its roots in Malory and Spenser, where clear-cut conflicts between good and evil are acted out by clear-cut heroes waging the good fight against clear-cut villains. Out of the Machiavellian maneuvers which dominate *The Mirror of Her Dreams*, no villain emerges, no action whose consequences are not ambiguous, no self-assertion which does not prove to be pyrrhic, and no hero or heroine not thoroughly confused by the jumble of events. If someone is indeed pulling the strings, then poor Terisa Morgen has only the vaguest inkling who, though the reader may be ahead of her here, and she hasn't a clue why he's muddying the waters.

That reader may also guess that it all has something to do with chess—or in this case, a form of checkers called hop-board. Long before the tale begins, the land of Mordant had been created (like Germany last century) out of a batch of quarrelling though consanguineous principalities by young King Joyse, who also organized the Imagers of the land into a kind of Round Table union called the Congery, with strict ethical rules about Imaging. In Mordant, a flat mirror will entrap the soul of anyone unlucky enough to look into it; the task of the Imager is to construct subtly curved mirrors through which weapons and produce and humans may be translated from one reality to another.

After decades of security, with Mordant once again threatened by external enemies and King Joyse occupying his apparent senility with hop-board, the Congery sends well-born, hapless, hamfisted young Geraden through a mirror to extract a Champion. The Champion they have viewed (as the reader knows, though they do not) is a figure from science fiction, a space-armored, laser-bearing human defending his spaceship from aliens. Unfortunately, Geraden seems to make a mistake, lands in the mirror-coated room in Manhattan that Terisa uses to convince herself she exists and persuades her to come with him back to Mordant. Once in King Joyse's ramshackle labyrinth of a castle, strongly reminiscent of Mervyn Peake's Gormenghast, Terisa soon finds herself bewilderedly embroiled in disputes over the aptness of her translation, over her loyalty to King Joyse, over the right course to follow in the defense of the realm; nor can she decide between Geraden and a Realpolitiking Imager, who vie for her affections. Only slowly does she even begin to half-suspect that the King is not senile at all, that the game of hop-board may model not only the plot but the world of Mordant itself, and that her passive intrusions into these fantastical imbroglios may be pivotal to their outcome.

The Mirror of Her Dreams is very long and sometimes seems interminable as pawns betray pawns, Terisa broods and King Joyse seems to maunder. It is also intricate, madcap, involving and not at all foolish.

> *John Clute, "Through the Looking-Glass," in* Book World—The Washington Post, *November 23, 1986, p. 9.*

SUSAN SHWARTZ

The Mirror of Her Dreams, [Donaldson's] first novel since *White Gold Wielder* (1983) and first in the projected two volume series *Mordant's Need,* demonstrates steady growth. Though he has replaced the tortuous, almost impenetrable, language that proved such heavy going in the *Chronicles* with the leaner, suppler prose of his novellas, Mr. Donaldson still focuses on outcasts.

This time his protagonist is Terisa Morgan, a modern-day Rapunzel so numbed psychologically that she surrounds herself with mirrors to prove she exists. Her unlikely rescuer is Geraden, the clumsiest apt, or apprentice, in the Congery of Imagers, a magicians' guild in the appropriately named land of Mordant. The Congery does its magic with mirrors, and Mr. Donaldson develops a whole metaphysics of optics. In Mordant, for instance, flat glass is thought to drive people crazy, since one image cannot exist in two places. And only Imagers have mirrors—huge, curved and carefully guarded against outsiders.

Mordant's need is desperate. It faces war, its king has retreated into a kind of moral atrophy, and Havelock, its chief Imager, is a madman. So the remaining Imagers spy out a champion through a specially designed mirror and send the expendable Geraden through the looking glass to fetch him. Bumbling as ever, Geraden crashes instead through the mirrored wall of Terisa's room, promptly decides that she is the promised champion and persuades her to return with him.

For a woman unsure that she exists, Terisa has a violent effect on the politics of Mordant. King Joyse confides in her, his daughter befriends her, and Geraden trips over his feet—and hers—to protect her. This is no small task: in rapid succession, Terisa faces assassination, seduction, treachery and a siege.

Her naïve involvement with the kingdom's politics results in disaster, both for Terisa and for readers, who reach the end of the book only to be told to look for the sequel, *A Man Rides Through,* if they want to know how the remarkably complex plot resolves itself.

Despite this cliffhanger ending (a ploy too much in use these days among fantasy writers), *The Mirror of Her Dreams* is an impressive, if occasionally frustrating, performance. Mr. Donaldson has created a galaxy of idiosyncratic, neatly described characters.

Mr. Donaldson's characterizations falter only when he deals with sex. Terisa's passivity, which renders her perhaps the weakest character in the book, makes it almost impossible to understand why even a lecherous magician would bother with her, let alone lapse into such steamy pillow talk as "I will take possession of your fine beauty utterly," or why, in her presence, the mad magician Havelock jumps around, yelping about fornication. Though Havelock's behavior echoes the imagery of the mad scenes in *King Lear,* his craziness seems more ludicrous than tragic.

The greatest success of *The Mirror of Her Dreams* lies in the complexity of its language, a fit vehicle for the intricate plot. Mr. Donaldson's style—shimmering and full of ambiguities and puns—resembles the curved mirrors of Mordant. If he strikes occasional false notes, however, they are the inevitable consequence of a talent like his: large, turbulent and hastening toward maturity too quickly to avoid a mistake here and there.

Susan Shwartz, "Surrounded by Glass," in The New York Times, *Section 7, November 30, 1986, p. 16.*

Gavin (Buchanan) Ewart

1916-

English poet, critic, editor, author of children's books, and librettist.

One of England's preeminent writers of light verse, Ewart combines an inventive use of poetic form and technique with an irreverent, often scatological sense of humor. Initially influenced by the work of W. H. Auden and later by such poets as John Betjeman and Peter Porter, Ewart tempers his satiric and ironic observations of contemporary life with a delight in sensuality and a genuine concern for the plight of modern humanity. He is respected for combining playful use of language with technical mastery of such poetic forms as the limerick, the clerihew, and the sestina. Although critics have expressed disapproval with the trivial nature of some of his work, most laud his enriching contributions to the light verse tradition.

Ewart began his career as a professional poet in 1933, when his poem "Phallus in Wonderland" appeared in Geoffrey Grigson's literary magazine, *New Verse.* Exceptionally fluent in his command of rhyme, meter, and syntax, he also demonstrates in his early poems a flair for imitating the styles of other poets, whether in outright parody, as in "Phallus in Wonderland," or in sincere tribute, as in "Audenesque for an Initiation." His most famous composition of this period is "Miss Twye," an early experiment in playful eroticism. Ewart would explore this style more fully in the liberal atmosphere of the 1960s and 1970s.

Following the publication of his first collection, *Poems and Songs* (1939), Ewart virtually abandoned poetry. After serving in the Royal Artillery in Italy during World War II, he began a career as an advertising copywriter. "The war was somehow a knockout blow," he explained in a 1983 interview. "I probably wrote only about a dozen poems during it, and when I got back to England I felt that my gift had more or less gone." In 1959, however, with the encouragement of Alan Ross, editor of *London Magazine,* he began to write and publish new poems. His second collection, *Londoners* (1964), which Ewart calls "a book of topographical pieces," describes the architecture and inhabitants of London in a humorous style that reflects the influence of Betjeman's light verse. Ewart's reputation was solidified with *The Pleasures of the Flesh* (1966). In this volume, he experiments freely with new verse forms and offers satirical, humorous, and tender lyrics on the human condition.

During the 1970s and early 1980s, Ewart was a prolific poet of consistent achievement. Philip Larkin commented: "What are we to say of this astonishing unstoppable talent? . . . The more he writes, the less likely [a typical Ewart poem] becomes. And this is what underlies his claim on our attention, this ability from time to time to pull out of the bag a new Ewart." In such volumes as *The Gavin Ewart Show* (1971), *Be My Guest!* (1975), *No Fool like an Old Fool* (1976), *Or Where a Young Penguin Lies Screaming* (1977), and *The New Ewart: Poems, 1980-1982* (1982), he has further developed his penchant for wordplay, inventing new forms of light verse and indulging in clever variations of traditional verse forms. He also parodies the works of such poets as Philip Larkin, Gerard Manley Hop-

Photograph by Mark Gerson

kins, and Christopher Smart. In these poems, Ewart adopts the persona of an aging but still lusty man yearning for the pleasures of youth. Bawdy sexuality remains the hallmark of his verse, although critics note that his work accommodates a wide range of themes and moods. This versatility is evident in *The Collected Ewart, 1933-1980* (1980). Reviewers admired his compassion, his ability to express the significance of ordinary objects and people, his tolerant commentary on human frailty, and his warm, caring attitude toward other people. Ewart's humanistic social and political attitudes, reflected by allusions to Communist ideals in his early verse, emerge in such later pieces as "The Gentle Sex," an unsettling poem that describes a brutal political murder in Northern Ireland. Since the 1986 publication in the United States of *The Gavin Ewart Show: Selected Poems, 1939-1985* and *The Young Pobble's Guide to His Toes,* Ewart's poetry has begun to receive more widespread recognition.

(See also *CLC,* Vol. 13; *Contemporary Authors,* Vols. 89-92; *Contemporary Authors New Revision Series,* Vol. 17; and *Dictionary of Literary Biography,* Vol. 40.)

PHILIP TOYNBEE

When I first met him, in 1934, Gavin Ewart belonged to a very bright group of Wellington schoolboys, strongly recessive to the dominant strain of that near-military academy. He was the poet of the gang even then; just as Esmond Romilly was the runaway rebel and Giles Romilly the melancholy homosexual intellectual.

Much of Ewart's early verse was strongly influenced by Auden, and much of it, in the manner of the time, was concerned with his public school; later with Cambridge. This preoccupation has been heavily frowned on by later generations of non-public school poets and critics; but it is really very hard to see what other material was available to us under that weird regime. Packed off to boarding prep-schools at 8 or 9, to public schools at 13, to Oxbridge at 18 or 19, we can hardly be blamed for being somewhat obsessed by the hot-house institutions in which we had been inescapably cultivated.

The point, surely—and it is a point made again and again throughout [*The Collected Ewart, 1933-1980*]—is that the poet's subject is wherever he happens to be; whatever he happens to see, or think, or feel. . . .

I met Gavin Ewart once or twice during the war, wearing officer's uniform, and I formed the melancholy impression that his military experiences had made a man of him. The kind of man, I mean, who would certainly have written no more poetry; and it is a strange fact that only 18 poems appear in this collection between his 1939 volume *Poems and Songs* and *Londoners,* published in 1964. Ewart, it seemed, had done a sort of mini-Rimbaud: and those of us who remembered his early verse with affectionate admiration often wondered what had happened to his muse. In fact he made a passionate appeal to all nine of them in a poem which must have been written towards the end of his 'Ethiopian' period. At least two of them seem to have promptly responded; namely, Thalia, the muse of comedy and idyllic poetry; and Erato, the muse of erotic poetry and mime.

The 1964 volume was most reassuring, for it showed that whatever Ewart had been up to during the long interval the poet had not been killed by a military or a commercial gent but had been quietly maturing under whatever outfit was now being officially worn. In the sparse poems of 1939 to 1964 one can see him fall under the influence of Betjeman, add this to his other influences, rather like a Red Indian adding scalps to his belt, and begin to assimilate all his influences and develop a genuine voice of his own. Several of the London poems are very good, effectively combining historical knowledge with that almost aching contemporary sensibility which has become Ewart's most notable quality in so many of his later poems.

These are not poems of the flashing and quotable phrase: each of them, about a page long, builds up the total impression with an easy manner but much careful precision. From this volume to the latest one of 1977 there is no remarkable heightening of his powers, but there is a considerable broadening of his sympathies and interests.

Ewart has often been thought of as the quintessential 'light' poet of his generation: and it is plain from some of his waspish answers to critics that this has caused him much exasperation. But I think the word is all right so long as it is properly understood, namely as the opposite not to 'serious' but to 'heavy.' There is a full range of light verse, from the great to the abysmal, just as there is an equally full range of heavy verse: and one might add that bad light verse is not quite so horrible as bad heavy verse. The worst of Herrick is less insufferable than the worst of *Paradise Regained.*

One of Ewart's superb qualities is that he is democratic in the best sense of the word. He has continued to write satire, and his targets seem perfectly appropriate to me; but the satirical is not his most individual tone. What he continually shows is true sympathy; a real fellow-feeling for many kinds of people who are normally despised or, at best, overlooked. There are even times when the dread word 'compassion' is the most fitting: dread because it is so over-used as a cover-all O.K. word, often covering a multitude of sins. Ewart's verses to a vivisected rabbit are violent in feeling, though beautifully controlled in technique. But a principal theme is the sadness of erotic longing, and erotic failure; a subject close to the heart of most ageing and many young men: no doubt, though I know less about this, of many women too. . . .

But this light poet is usually a serious one, even when he is being very funny, which is often. One of his poems attacks a reviewer who was guilty of the poisonous putdown: 'It's hard to dislike Ewart.' Shall I 'scape whipping if I write that it is hard, when he is in his best fighting form, not to like and admire Ewart very much?

Philip Toynbee, "A Poet First and Last," in The Observer, *June 1, 1980, p. 28.*

RUSSELL DAVIES

[Gavin Ewart] has a well-controlled but still developing fondness for himself as a third-person topic.

Perhaps he was driven to this by reviewers. Certainly he's been called "quirky" so many times that you can't blame him for holding "Ewart" at arm's length from time to time, to see if it's true. He has done a lot of answering back, too, in his time, and repeated references to jaws and teeth suggest that he nourishes a small horror of having his work "consumed". His frustration is understandable. My impression is that even his most faithful fans have found it difficult to say what it is they really like about Gavin Ewart's work. A negative approach is easier: hence one of the angrier poems in this comprehensive collection [*The Collected Ewart, 1933-1980*], "**It's Hard to Dislike Ewart**"—a title phrase attributed to a *"New Review critic"* (who turns out to have been Colin Falck). The poet's response to this judgment is distinctly shirty, or as his Scottish ancestors might have had it, sarky. . . .

The early pages of *The Collected Ewart* bring us lengthy reminders that he was once the Public School Prodigy, the freak of Wellington. . . .

First in this book comes "**Phallus in Wonderland**", a poem in many voices which more than fulfils the promise of its title (the least it could do). It "was excluded by me from my first book of verse", Ewart writes, "because of its immaturity". He now includes it, I presume, for the same reason. Every man respects his origins, even when he hates them; and Ewart, in any case, had immersed himself in a richer marinade of influences than he is commonly given credit for. There was poetry in his head before Auden arrived there. "**Phallus**", says his footnote "shows very clearly the influences of T. S. Eliot, the Pound of *Hugh Selwyn Mauberley,* and Ronald Bottrall. Auden, in 1933, was not yet making his presence felt." There was scarcely room for him as yet in these little verbaceous borders of the pupil Ewart, where rhyme is thought and the bulk of the thing is reputation. . . . By the time Ewart's first collection of *Poems and Songs* appeared in 1939, a new voice had broken through, the voice of a responsible, faintly pre-fectorial radicalism. . . . Auden has clearly arrived; and Ewart, catching from him the jingling, list-making bug, at times seems likely to depart in the same direction as MacNeice.

> For the island that's not on the chart,
>   For the whistle that isn't a bird,
> The sly beckoning-on of the heart
>   To admit that all action's absurd,
> For the rationalisation of fear,
>   For the man who's turned in and not out,
> For the sudden refusal to cheer,
>   All patrols look out! . . .

Among the other phenomena to which all patrols are alerted are two Audenesque favourites, "the virgin malicious and ill" and "the man who has seen his mistakes"; and Ewart's own prototypes of these characters make their appearance in two short early poems which show him operating at opposite ex-tremes of his taste. **"Miss Twye"**, a famous fragment much reprinted, is scarcely more than a momentary snigger, but a memorable one:

> Miss Twye was soaping her breasts in her bath
> When she heard behind her a meaning laugh
> And to her amazement she discovered
> A wicked man in the bathroom cupboard.

A nursery rhyme for adults, and a demonstration of the odd sense of inevitability the half-rhyme can sometimes induce. As for the man who has seen his mistakes, Ewart is growing up to be him. . . . In **"Home"** (reprinted under the heading "Other Pre-War Poems"), Ewart throws youth a filthy farewell glance. **"Written in 1938"**, remarks the excusing footnote, "unem-ployed and living at home, full of adolescent rebelliousness and bad temper." The very qualities the decade had so often prized, you might think, though Ewart's envoi does perhaps suggest a young man reversing almost self-destructively into a backwater: "O could one imagine an atmosphere fitter / To make one depressed, antisocial and bitter?"

Ewart produced no more books until the 1960s. He passed the war busily as an anti-aircraft officer in North Africa and the Mediterranean, and has said that he felt overwhelmed by the scale of events. It must have been disconcerting, too, to be part of a campaign whose purposes overall were so much more laudable than the day-to-day patterns of life. Ewart may well have felt as though he were back in the Old School, but deprived now of all good reason to rebel. His creative record during the war, at all events, seems to me wholly understandable—I'm surprised there weren't more like him. He wrote little, just a handful of war-poems, but several of them are among his best. **"Officers' Mess"** is a conversational set-piece, a barroom monologue built of Forces banter and embodying much the same comic virtues (against a grimmer background) as today's supposed letters of Denis Thatcher in the magazine *Private Eye*. . . .

The masque-like construction of Ewart's first verses had sug-gested that he might take pleasure one day in reconstituting tones of voice, and here for the first time he lets one rip for a page or so; and the result (preferred by Larkin for his *Oxford Book of Twentieth Century Verse*) is a triumphant marriage of speech-rhythm and poetic rhythm: there is no single phrase in it that the average braided barfly couldn't or wouldn't have spoken. Nor is there a single knot of moral complication, just

a hook at the end to connect the experience to the next one of its kind. . . .

By the 1960s, Ewart was established in advertising, in London, which had suddenly become a fashionable centre for most ac-tivities, even poetry. To look at *Londoners* now is to gain the momentary impression that Ewart is swinging a leg high on to the passing bandwagon—the book begins, after all, with **"Chelsea in Winter"**, and **"Chelsea in Winter"** begins "It's a long pull down the King's Road"; but Ewart's King's Road runs "down to the Pier Hotel" and thence, via a couple of rhymes, to "the streets of hell". They are "trodden by Mr Eliot's feet", some of these streets, and one gets the impres-sion, here and there, that Ewart would be comforted if some of the old faces (including his own) were to round the corner and make him feel at home again. The poems are long and discursive and have the air, especially in the Madame Tussaud's sequence, of keeping themselves amused while waiting for something to turn up. . . .

Pleasures of the Flesh followed in 1966. It's at this point that it becomes clear how perfectly Ewart's creative life has con-formed to the butterfly system. An active and noticeable cat-erpillar in youth, and twenty years a chrysalis, he struggles out stickily in *Londoners* and bursts forth, at last, into a gaudy maturity with *Pleasures*. The title, and the opening lines of the scene-setting **"Anti-Poem"**, identify the release as a sexual one: admitting to lust will be one of Ewart's richest themes from now on, and the exercise of his hormones will remain an index to the health of his talent (it works both ways). . . . Plain use, and exhibitionism, are cheerfully flung together: there is no roped-off section of his work marked "Fun". In *Pleasures of the Flesh,* there is certainly no need for one, since the whole collection carries a tone of manic resistance to the ageing pro-cess. It helps to remember that London in those days was slightly potty with its own success; it was a New Elizabethan Age in PVC boots, non-stop raciness under the Red, White and Blue. Plagued by the thighs of teenagers, Ewart is begin-ning to feel what it must be like to be old. . . .

But fantasy is never at an end, and it goes battering on through these pages, flirting merrily with Surrealism, sneaking Ewart into the calmer head of Sigmund Freud (the "S.F." in the title is, for once, the nearest we get to Science Fiction), and even predicting the end of Ewart's long servitude in offices: "It is better to be a scribe / than hacking in the salt-mines . . . / Ev-erybody wants to be a scribe."

Ewart has been a scribe almost throughout the 1970s, display-ing an unmanageable copiousness which he's possibly right in believing that critics resent, somewhere behind those ferocious jaws of theirs. (With his seven or eight books in the decade, Ewart has, for one thing, taken a hefty slice of their reviewing space.) Of this magnificent overproduction Anthony Thwaite has written that "there is something both attractively and dis-dainfully offhand about Ewart's poems", and this remains true. Since the offhand poem is something his heavy-verse contem-poraries are keen to avoid, Ewart actually stands to gain by this. Verses that seem to care little whether they succeed, fail, or suddenly let themselves down, begin to have their extra curiosity value.

Since 1971 or so, Ewart has been, for good or ill, the star of his own production. The very title of *The Gavin Ewart Show* proclaims it. In a curious way, he has become the sort of poet whom one "follows", as one might an actor or a sportsman or a singer. Ewart never produces a tight, interlocking performance at book length, but nor do singers with their "albums"; yet there are always one or two songs you play over and over. To have established this kind of career at all is a very considerable achievement. It involves Ewart in producing a great many jokes, whose charm is great at first but not slow to wear away ("Noel Coward has been handed down to us. Noel Coward is a flower that's free"); and Ewart's recent habit of adopting the metrical patterns of famous verses (filling out forms, you might call it) often strikes me as more of a help to Ewart, as a stratagem for getting poems written, than of emotional use to the reader. (A notable exception is **"The Gentle Sex"**, his Hopkins-inspired factual horror-story from Northern Ireland, where the nastiness of the events themselves entirely kill off the playful side of the emulative process.)

As for Ewart's "world" (and his satirical taste for duff marketing devices will surely lead him one of these days to entitle a volume *The World of Gavin Ewart*), he has described it thus:

> For us the world is one huge object found,
> random with art and wars and income tax,
> the very lack of pattern is a pattern.

And so it is with the work that pours out of Ewart. His constants are a dread of poetic plod (was it from Wellington that the public school world at large derived "boring" as its favourite expression of disgust?) and a flaming eroticism that would sound furtive and sex-in-the-head if you overheard it, but which Ewart sets down boldly as sex-on-the-page. I feel there is an element of perfectly conscious campaigning in this—Holbrook and Whitehouse are the pilots of the enemy tandem—and there is no doubt that Ewart will have blanched many a bluenose in his time. . . .

Two epitaphs, in all but name, close the collection, one in the body of the book, one banished to its dust-jacket. Their judgments are not easily gainsaid. The first: "There's more of him that we expected . . ." (yes, but not yet too much) "He wrote some silly poems, and some of them were funny" (yes, certainly, as far as that goes). The second: "He's typical of his age." Well, here I'm not so sure. It is an age characterized by (in Ted Walker's phrase) a "cautious husbandry of grief". There is parsimony even in suffering. With Ewart, instead, we have the generosity of desperation, and a roistering remorse. It is the oddest mixture, and I don't pretend to be fully used to it yet. But having taken the long way round himself, Ewart presumably won't mind waiting for the rest of us to catch up.

Russell Davies, "Roistering Remorsefully," in The Times Literary Supplement, No. 4033, July 11, 1980, p. 774.

ANDREW MOTION

Converts can usually be relied on for zeal. If Gavin Ewart is anything to go by, so can those who return to a fold they once inhabited and later abandoned. His first collection, *Poems and Songs*, appeared in 1939 and over the next 25 years he wrote only 18 poems. But in 1964 he completed a topographical sequence, *Londoners*, and has subsequently produced an extraordinarily fast-growing body of work: a poem written most days and a fattish collection published every two years or so. Simply in quantitative terms it's a remarkable achievement, and in qualitative ones it has established him as one of the foremost minor poets of his gifted generation. Apart from a few obvious examples—like **"The Larkin Automatic Car Wash"** or **"The Gentle Sex"**—his poems are less impressive individ-

ually than they are in bulk. And since *The Collected Ewart* is what it says it is—a collection rather than a selection—he has never appeared to better advantage. It's not just that he's unflaggingly entertaining and inventive, but that he's a remarkably compassionate writer. His facility, which might have led merely to loquaciousness or lack of discrimination, has in fact been used to express unhesitating concern.

Ewart dried up during the war for the same reason that he has written so well since: because of his indebtedness to the senior Thirties poets. He has said that experience of the army 'squashed' him, and what this seems to have meant is that having begun by adopting an identikit Auden manner, he was confronted in the early Forties with a range of subjects which made it feel inadequate. But after copying his master's voice so absolutely, he had trouble finding his own. The process didn't involve discarding his original allegiances altogether, but injecting into Auden's more discursive style a worldliness reminiscent of MacNeice. (p. 20)

Ewart's candour about his borrowings from other writers is an aspect of his generosity, and it shouldn't be allowed to obscure the extent to which he's an original. With his last three or four collections he has done for sex and death in poetry what Woody Allen has done for them in the cinema. The accent is different, of course, but the concentrated focus and the combination of hilarity and desperation is similar. Book by book his 'uneasy writing' gets uneasier: the more he longs for the simple life and the pleasures of being 'bedroomised', the less satisfying and available his aims become. . . . Many poets' conscious and single-minded devotion to a particular theme inhibits their development. But since for Ewart sex has an everyday importance, it's a short step from considering its frustrations and rewards to involving himself with the ordinary in all its aspects. This is partly a matter of his deliberately inclusive approach to the world, but it's also manifested by the marvellous, prized inconsequentiality of thoughts which are thrown up by the requirements of form. . . .

It's not surprising to find Ewart professing modesty about his abilities. Not to do so might be to make himself vulnerable to the same charge of hubris that he occasionally levels against others. But his own judgment—'They'll say (if I'm lucky): / he wrote some silly poems and some of them were funny'—is more than a method of defence. It's also a way of encountering the world. Because he keeps a low profile no one sees him watching and as a result he's able to write tenderly, as well as satirically, with a pronounced lack of self-consciousness. (p. 21)

Andrew Motion, "Bedroomised," in New Statesman, Vol. 100, No. 2575, July 25, 1980, pp. 20-1.

ALAN BROWNJOHN

Both Vernon Scannell and Gavin Ewart are heirs to that gentler sort of English modernism which paid its respects to Eliot (though not to Pound, or any insistently American or European modernism), took root in the early Auden and most of MacNeice, and branched out in individual ways in the work of poets like Roy Fuller and the late A.S.J. Tessimond. It is a poetry which embraces the immediate, wears and describes the scars of ordinary living, is plain (including plain frightened and plain indignant) about life and death and moral problems, rarely intricate, rarely delicate, always absorbing in its firm yet friendly insistence that the here-and-now of modern urban existence is what almost all of us have to fit into for most of the time. (pp. 64-5)

Unlike Scannell's, Gavin Ewart's has not been a steady, uninterrupted progress: in *The Collected Ewart,* the gap in the middle—where the war broke in on the exuberant precocity of his 1930s writing and slowed him down to nine poems in six years—is really very long indeed. He is only back into his stride again when he reaches *Londoners,* the 1964 book—and nothing of what happened later could have been predicted from that. *Londoners* was a very tentative re-start, in a Betjeman-esque vein, but in leisurely free verse: an informative topographical ramble through London scenes, from **"Chelsea in Winter"** to **"Strawberry Hill."** . . . (p. 66)

Not calculated to make an impression on admirers of either Ted Hughes' *Lupercal* (1960) or Philip Larkin's *The Whitsun Weddings* (1964), let alone Ginsberg's *Howl* or Lowell's *Life Studies, Londoners* seems now, with some wisdom of hindsight and in the context of *The Collected Ewart,* to be rather less artless and casual than it looked. It reads like an assembling of backdrops for all those later (but not much later) poems which people such scenes with grotesquely authentic inhabitants of our own time: ad agency monsters, house party cads, "the whole satirical setup." It was as if Ewart had not felt sure enough to pick up the threads where he had dropped them (though among the war poems, highly characteristic pieces like **"Officers' Mess"** and **"Oxford Leave"** were pointing the way, and could almost have been written 30 years later), but needed to recreate his world before he could recover his voice.

Just two years later, *Pleasures of the Flesh* is really very different. The later Ewart begins here, in a substantial collection which takes up and develops the themes and styles of his very early work, the brilliant and artfully-fashioned squibs of **"Phallus in Wonderland."** The key poem is no doubt **"The Muse":**

> A boy was kissing me left right and centre
> But something nasty crept into his quatrains.
> I left for thirty years. I haven't changed
> Though he's grey at the edges. Now I'm back
> We live together in uneasy joy.
>
> My lovely mouth; his bitter tainted kiss. . . .

Ewart is now the shyly outrageous poet daring to voice the hidden thoughts of urban man (scandalous ruminations, he says in *All My Little Ones,* which are actually in the mind of everybody except Mrs Whitehouse), and defining an area of decency in the midst of a cityscape of meretriciousness and violence. The disgust can be almost Swiftian, as in **"Variation on a Theme of A. Huxley":**

> See them revel in their beer and their beastliness,
> Egged on by sherry, the bit between their teeth,
> Ginned up for chambering and wantonness,
> As round a hot frilled leg they garter a parsley wreath.

Or hilarious, in **"The Spirokeet":**

> The Spirokeet is a terrifying brightly-coloured bird with
>   a flesh-tearing beak,
> It spends a lot of time in the palm trees squawking and
>   spouting Greek.
> It can curdle the blood-stream and shut teenagers up in
>   clinics,
> It reads Ibsen in the original and its friends are all old
>   cynics.

A point often forgotten about Ewart is that under the often exuberantly Rabelaisian surfaces, or between the elaborate jokes, there is a committed seriousness. There is joy in the nailing

down of the **"Office Primitive"** ("Me likum girlum. Hatum work. / Smokum. Drinkum. Strokum pussy.") and the caveat against **"Literary Unions",** but there is also uneasiness, and more behind **"The Argument for the Benevolent God"** or sonnets like **"At the Villa Madeira,"** about a famous murder. . . . (pp. 66-7)

Ewart is among the most prolifically ingenious poets we have: his sense of the right form is infallible, his jokes are invariably excellent, his feet planted firmly in recognisable experience. But in all his later books he has also used the comic as a means of stating views—simple, no-nonsense, compassionate opinions—and it would be insensitive not to notice the lacings of humane wisdom, even of moral severity, which go down with the draughts of scabrous humour. (p. 67)

Alan Brownjohn, "Going Concerns," in Encounter, Vol. LV, No. 5, November, 1980, pp. 64-70.

TERRY EAGLETON

Gavin Ewart may not quite measure up to Ben Jonson, but he is surely our comic balladeer *par excellence,* in whom the wan lusts and small suburban hopes of contemporary society find themselves transmuted into a more than "occasional" art. *The Collected Ewart* presents us with four hundred pages of unremitting randiness, including an interesting glimpse of where it all started in Ewart the Thirties poet: the flip, jocular, seedy yet politically committed iconoclasm of some of these earlier Macspaunday-like pieces, the "period" blendings of the ironic, tender and hard-boiled, reveal a Ewart who is in one sense in surprising continuity with his past, in another sense eternally contemporary. Like all fine comedians, he combines an eye for the contingent outlawed by tragic ideologies with a democratic impulse equally alien to them, a shrewd sense of what rhyme, inversion or antithesis will release the most pleasurably disturbing tensions in as many readers as possible, in the collective unconscious which unites his audience beneath their social or cultural differences:

> Hands that wiped arses
> are holding glasses,
> lips that fellated
> are intoxicated,
> parts that were randy
> have counterparts handy—
>
> but the fact of a quorum
> preserves decorum,
> and the social function
> inhibits the function
> of the natural passions
> concealed by the fashions.
>
> Tongues that liked scrota
> don't move one iota
> from the usual phrases
> that the century praises,
> the undisturbed labia
> are deserted Arabia. . .
>
>   (**"The Select Party"**)

'The *natural* passions' is important: comedy can mystify by cynically deflating history to an unbudgeable Nature, but it also helps to restore the positive sense of 'natural', the shared biological and material life which is the basis of all politics. It is in this sense that all the great comedians, from Rabelais to Joyce, have been materialists, in a way that most tragic ideologists have not been.

'The usual phrases that the century praises': for Ewart, in a sense, everything has been said before and his poems consist in recycling or reshuffling proverbs, clichés, mottoes, single-liners that are chunks of congealed social attitude, portable pieces of tattered meaning, packaged, instant or ready-made responses. Everything can come to sound like a parody of something else: phrases are threadbare emotional notations clotted with automatic connotations. . . . And indeed where else has language been so reified for instant recycling than in monopoly capitalism, within which Gavin Ewart was for some years an ad-man? Discourse in such conditions is, you might say, as rigorously codified, as subject to *genres* and conventions, as instantly emblematical as it ever was in the great periods of classical culture it consigns to the dust-heap. It's this historical coincidence which is the secret mechanism of Ewart's work: for if on the one hand he flirts with the computerised feelings and stock verbal cues of consumer society, he's also an un-flaggingly *literary* poet, something of a scholar on the side, given to esoteric Latin word-games and lexicographical sports which mime in their self-enclosedness and ingenuity something of the *genres* of the advertising agency. At the very historical point where advanced capitalism ousts the great classical codes, it reinstates a grisly parody of them as its own sub-*genres*. Ewart manages to satirise these sub-*genres* without implying a patrician nostalgia, so that in resurrecting a cliché ('rising to the occasion', or evening-dressed women 'making a clean breast of it') he at once exposes its paucity and turns it to productive use, unites the critical eye of the poet with the generous tolerance of the populist. (pp. 75-6)

Terry Eagleton, in a review of "The Collected Ewart, 1933-1980," in Stand Magazine, *Vol. 22, No. 4, 1981, pp. 75-6.*

CATHERINE PETERS

The New Ewart is more of the same, rather than any unexpected move forward or away from *The Collected Ewart* of 1980, which will be recommendation enough for those who are already hooked on Gavin Ewart's poetry. For those who haven't had the good fortune to come across him before the new collection is a good place to start.

The first thing one notices about Ewart is his stunning technical virtuosity; he seems to be at home in every verse form from ballad to sestina to elegiac ode (he is the best writer of English hexameters since Clough). He is a wicked parodist, who can catch the exact tone and form of another poet, either affectionately, as he does in **"Old Larkinian"**, or **"Jubilate Matteo"**, a cat hymn that updates Kit Smart; or less kindly in burlesques of Auden and MacNeice. He is the most reliably entertaining poet we've got.

English readers are traditionally suspicious of entertaining poets: Byron's fault in 19th-century eyes was not just that he wrote about sex, but that he was funny about it. Recognition of Ewart's talent was slow in coming, and even now he is sometimes categorised as a writer of light verse, rather than a true poet. The variety of his forms lends an air of parody even to poems which might otherwise be taken as straightforward statements. He can seem untrustworthy, a bar-room teller of tall tales, a satirist of genuine human feeling. Yet in spite of his infinite variety there is a recognisable Ewart tone, and a consistent personality and a view on life do emerge when the poems

are read as a collection. To begin with, there is, as in Byron, a hatred of cant allied to a truthfulness about sex. Ewart can celebrate lust without romanticising it: in two poems about Circe he manages the difficult feat of making copulation sound simultaneously disgusting and irresistible. But he can be tender too. A poem that begins 'In an exciting world of love-bites' ends with the acknowledgement that

> no one can sleep in the arms of an
> enemy, however charming.

"Conversation Piece," about his mother and aunt: "their total age is 181" echoes Larkin's "An Arundel Tomb" in its conclusion:

> There should be writing, writing on the wall:
> *All sex shall fail, but love shall never fail.*

'We'd be called tender, if we had our rights' he says of himself and Dickens, both entertainers, both knocked sideways by the charms of young girls.

Ewart *is* an Old Larkinian in many ways (though he was writing Larkinesque poems before Larkin was himself free of Yeats). Both have rejected the 'myth-kitty' and have a poetic integrity which comes from a self-made attitude to life rather than a system of belief or a carefully guarded tradition. But Ewart seems to me to have a wider, more flexible range of sympathies than Larkin, which shows no signs of narrowing with age. He can be scaldingly bitchy about the bitchiness of literary ladies on writing courses: a typically unsentimental poem compares the death of his mother with the death of his cat. Like Larkin, he can both feel for, and dislike, the young and the old. But where "An Arundel Tomb" draws its qualified affirmation from the inanimate, **"Conversation Piece"** gains its strength from personal human connections. In one of his **"So-called Sonnets"** (in sonnet form, but unrhymed) Ewart says that:

> Happiness is the one emotion a poem can't capture

yet the vigour of even his most attacking poems does convey just that.

Catherine Peters, "Byronic," in The Spectator, *Vol. 248, No. 8019, March 20, 1982, p. 23.*

PETER PORTER

The new Ewart has not shaken himself free of the old Adam, thank goodness. Indeed this generously filled book [*The New Ewart*] attains happy scatological depths not quite reached in Gavin Ewart's extensive previous career. As always, his dirty pieces are among his most inventive and humane: here, especially **"A Ballad of the Good Lord Baden-Powell"** and **"The Ballad of Erse O. Reilly,"** both showing that parody is a living way of writing well and not just something done at the weekend to win literary competitions.

By now most buyers will know that a new book from Ewart is indispensable, but for waverers I list several innovations and stylistic tropes present in this collection. **"The Literary Gathering"** is a surprising and sensible use of that dry form the sestina, where the recurring end-words are the names of the poem's dramatis personae. Cute arbitrariness is thus replaced by dramatic pointing. **"Sonnet: The Greedy Man Considers Nuclear War"** expands a brilliant metaphor of warring nations seen as men fearing to lose good things to eat—'I suppose you all realise we shall lose the sizzling sausages / and the mild mountains of mashed potatoes! Boiled silverside with dumplings, raspberries and cream! / We shall vanish from the peck-ing order of the tikka chicken.' **"The Meeting"** repeats its end-word in each pair of lines, bringing out the blankness and monotony of the occasion which is its subject. **"My Children's Book"** is new as an idea, fantasising Grimmly but Pre-Freud-ianly on the cruelty of fairy stories ('In the Great Jungle are child-eating orchids / (Rhodesia-Boysonia)'). **"They Flee from Me"** is a lovesong made wholly of unrecycled clichés:—

> I was not hallucinating.
> But with regard to that one
> my permissiveness
> has landed me in a foresaking situation.
> The affair is no longer on-going.

"The Germanic Day," puffed out with portmanteau words, reads like Tony Harrison among the Greeks. Best of all is **"A Glastonbury Cricket Match,"** a lovely spoof of the style of J. C. Powys. . . .

Amid all the high spirits, there is a constant note of elegy. Many of the poems lament deaths—of pet animals, old friends, parents and colleagues. Nor is Ewart a disciple of strength through joy: he may believe that a little reciprocated sex will untangle our mournful natures, but his mind soon returns to older fates and options. Dying animals, lost loves, alcoholic lives move through his pages. And he can find new images for the superior creatures who control our existence, as in a poem of unexplained disquiet, entitled **"The Owls Are Leav-ing"**:—

> The owls are leaving town, with no hint of passion.
> They shuffle forwards, they are calm and good.
> Their feet expect the texture of the roadway.
> They never loved us. They are birds that go.

> Peter Porter, *"Low Thoughts and High Spirits," in*
> The Observer, *March 21, 1982, p. 31.*

ALAN JENKINS

Gavin Ewart's poems . . . have never been afraid to approach the condition of undistinguished prose—from which they are held back, just, by sheer technical verve, a tightrope-walking act sustained with such metrical panache that one begins to ignore the acrobat's predicament and admire the skill that goes into the performance (and performance, this time, has nothing problematic about it: it proceeds unashamed). Ewart is so good at flirting with the dangers of triviality or bathos as he goes through his turn that we cease to notice whether he actually manages to pull back in time; instead we watch, delighted and amazed, as his gestures grow more daring. It would be easy, for example, to acknowledge how—with only a slight dimi-nution of his powers, only the merest slackening of tension or relinquishing of poise—all the truisms turn out to be true, how effortlessly *The New Ewart: Poems 1980-1982* lives up to the encomiums heaped on *The Collected Ewart:* well-shaped . . . imagination hand in hand with virtuosity . . . compulsively readable, devastatingly funny . . . cleverer and funnier as the years go by . . . heroically unpretentious . . . unflaggingly en-tertaining . . . weighty. . . . It would be easy, too, not to see how mordant and touching and determinedly *un*funny many of these recent poems are.

For example, from **"The Semi-Sapphics"**:

> Looking at mirrors never makes them feel much better.
> The best you can wish them is someone to like them,
> the frank confidence, the reciprocated cuddle.
>   That might improve them.

There are plenty of dead or dying animals here, also **"The Animals at the Adelaide Zoo"** (which Ewart described at a recent reading as a poem about the comfortably-off Western democracies and the Third World: well, maybe. . .). Many more poems are about ageing and approaching death, illness, receding hair and sexual opportunity, and about how terrible it is that "As you settle into peace, or dourness, / That bitter-sweet, that sweet-and-sourness, / is a vanished taste"; a few look back to the War, including the incomparable **"Gritty"**, and this, from **"Pian dei Giullari"**, as the poet revisits the scene of a Wartime love affair ("Never go back, they say. Never go back. / I went back." . . . The poem, ceasing to be plangent, becomes piercing.

To offset all this, of course, there is the metrical variety and virtuosity in abundance; there are the glorious rhymes ("tes-ticulate or clitorate/literate"); the parodies and pastiches (Joyce, Emily Dickinson, Smart, Longfellow, an utterly surreal J. C. Powys, and every imaginable register of fatuity, every vintage of English "Veuve Cliché"). There is a rough-and-ready, no-nonsense, knock-down-and-drag-out philosophy behind much of it ("It's so true we all want something—and that something might be someone— / that the only problem left is: do we do it sad, or gaily?") and a moralist's distrust of the "Puritans", the enemy, against whom Ewart's poems wage all-out war.

Do Ewart's poems have to be called "serious" or "light"? He can sound like Larkin ("It's when the slow darknesses loom?") or like Ogden Nash, he is happiest to be compared to Burns; yet his true master is Auden. Particularly, perhaps, the late Auden, who out of the accents of High Table and studied conversation among old friends brewed his own "so-cial" manner, whereas Ewart, while recognising the value of the relaxed, intimate tone—at its worst, merely chatty—lets his infatuation with doggerel and the demotic carry him nat-urally towards the idiom of popular song, the overtones of Noel Coward ("Strange how potent cheap music is!"). Perhaps he is simply our greatest living lyricist. (pp. 59-60)

> Alan Jenkins, *"A Barbarous Eloquence," in* En-
> counter, *Vol. LIX, No. 2, August, 1982, pp. 55-61.*

MICHAEL O'NEILL

The New Ewart: Poems 1980-1982 impresses most when Ewart's exuberant delight in craft whets the satiric edge of his verse. **"Sestina: The Literary Gathering"**, one of the funniest poems in the collection, shows Ewart's unerring ear for inflections of speech:

> There was a hint of dark Satanic mills about Carl,
> a contained intelligence; no fly-by-night Jeremy, he
> hadn't the open character of Ursula,
> in this respect he was more like Jane
> or the sheep and the cattle. And only Sheila
> seemed to understand him—except for Ursula.

The penultimate line's poker-faced descent into slapstick is beautifully managed. As is the case with many good comic poets, he commands an enviable social tone, one which allows him to bring poetry into the domain of the familiar, to stir in us what Johnson, discussing *The Rape of the Lock,* described as 'all the appetite of curiosity for that from which we have a thousand times turned fastidiously away'. There aren't, though, many poems where the observation of others is as pleasingly shrewd as **"Sestina: The Literary Gathering"**: perhaps **"The Meeting"**, **"The Semi-Sapphics"** and **"Hear the Voice of the Bard"** are candidates.

There are two kinds of poems Ewart writes which aren't so satisfactory. The first is the glorified *New Statesman* competition entry, the poem whose comedy is solely a matter of verbal high-jinks. The best of this group is **"The Germanic Day"** which excels by virtue of its disinterested absorption in its linguistic subject: 'Reports from salesmen take up working-time / My brainpan rings with what the farsound says'. More usually, though, this kind of poem involves ingenuities one smiles at once and feels no desire to read again: 'The sex-lives of the poets! And Miss God flounces in! / Who cohabits and who coits / And with what sense of Sin—'(**"Miss God"**). The coinage of 'coits' is droll. But the absurdities of sexual hypocrisy don't, for all his obsession with them, detain Gavin Ewart's imaginative gifts. (pp. 59-60)

The second group of poems which awaken doubt about their success are the serious ones. Seriousness is a ground Ewart finds difficult to occupy without sounding uneasily literary. Take the Larkinesque conclusion to **"25A Norfolk Crescent"**:

> that house is now a ghost
> within a house, where others now
> live and suffer.
> Tall in the anxious air.

When, abandoning such preciosities, he decides to bulldoze his way into deep emotion, the effect is of bluster: 'I say they were the patient venturing lions / and I the mean dog that stayed alive' (**"A Contemporary Film of Lancasters in Action"**). Doubtlessly the self-laceration is strongly felt, but the poem is too declamatory to possess imaginative sincerity. It's only fair to say, though, that such failures and near-misses are more than compensated for by a clutch of poems in *The New Ewart: Poems 1980-1982* that show the poet at his humane and amusing best. (p. 60)

> *Michael O'Neill, "Once More with Feeling," in* Poetry Review, *Vol. 72, No. 3, September, 1982, pp. 56-60.*

BRUCE BENNETT

Mr. Ewart was one of the small number of poets mentioned seriously for the poet laureateship a few years ago. Yet, lacking an American publisher, his work has remained almost unknown here. Now, happily, with the publication of *The Gavin Ewart Show: Selected Poems 1939-1985* and the availability of *The Young Pobble's Guide to His Toes,* we can discover what we have been missing.

Most obviously, we are in the presence of a clever, lively, often extremely funny writer with wide literary and cultural reference and extraordinary technical facility. Like Auden, whom Mr. Ewart credits as one of his masters (*The Gavin Ewart Show* begins with a poem called **"Audenesque for an Initiation"**), he is a virtuoso of forms; his work is a display case of inventiveness and adaptation, which includes numerous "homages" in the Poundian sense—Byron, Wordsworth, Tennyson, Browning, Hardy, Kipling, Philip Larkin and Ogden Nash are merely some of those whose manners he slyly or affectionately

slips into. Also like Auden, Mr. Ewart is a master of the conversational mixed tone, an urbane blend of knowingness, satirical edge, wisdom and tolerance, which is an aspect of what he refers to as "Auden's wonderful hybrid rose that crossed the comic with the tragic.". . . .

Mr. Ewart's dexterity of form and tone enables him to encompass the shocking and violent (**"The Gentle Sex"** chronicles a brutal Northern Ireland murder in the stanzas of Gerard Manley Hopkins's "Wreck of the Deutschland") as effortlessly as the farcical and frothy (**"The Importance of Being Earnest"** retells Wilde's plot in limericks). His ear for dialect of all sorts, sharpened by a distaste for jargon, is exquisitely tuned. . . . One entire poem, **"Love in a Valley,"** consists of Valley Girl slang, while another, **"The Inventor of Franglais?"** expands devastatingly on affectations found in an entry of Pepys's *Diary.* Ever playful, the poet engages in "semantic poetry," substituting Oxford English Dictionary definitions for the words of a bawdy limerick to create a delightful puzzle-piece. As if to bear out his own observation that "all writers (Shakespeare included) are, in the last analysis, in the entertainment business," Mr. Ewart is consistently—one might say compulsively—entertaining.

He is certainly entertaining about sex, one of his most frequent topics. . . . **"To a Plum-Coloured Bra Displayed in Marks & Spencer"** is a paean to a mass-produced look-alike that evokes ecstatic reminiscence: "You're a bra made in millions, promiscuously sold— / but your sister contained something dearer than gold." Yet, into sex as into other subjects he cuts deeper, revealing the dark side with unexpected depth of feeling. Venus and the Muse materialize, or dematerialize, to chastise and provoke errant devotees. Mr. Ewart portrays frustration, deviation, desolation and lack of fulfillment, less from disillusion with himself than with human nature.

He also writes movingly about his childhood, his relationship with his father and the suffering of children and animals. There are very affecting poems that confront head-on the indignity of age. . . .

"In the Old People's Home (1914)" allegorizes about such vessels as H.M.S. Incontinent, H.M.S. Repetitive, H.M.S. Wanderer and H.M.S. Vainglorious in their "last anchorage," attended by "the officious tugs *Snapper* and *Orderly*." Mr. Ewart seems haunted by the realization that "a good many lasts have taken place already" and outraged by what awaits everyone in indifferent and sterile modern institutions.

Part One of *The Young Pobble's Guide to His Toes* (a selection from it is also included in *The Gavin Ewart Show*) opens with the title poem announcing a central theme—the stoic coming to terms with loss and failing faculties—in a light-hearted way:

> Everything comes, everything goes.
> Some day you must say goodbye to your toes—
> all bitten off by the beasts of the sea
> or fading away by a gradual degree.

Part Two, "The So-Called Sonnets," features nine ruminative, loosely-rhymed or unrhymed sonnets. Part Three contains mainly light and unabashedly raucous pieces—formal exercises, take-offs on epigraphs, parodies, songs, tributes to friends and reactions to news stories, television, advertising and reading.

"You were good, and very British. / Serious, considered 'funny,' / in your best poems," he writes of Sir John Betjeman, "strong but sad, we found / a most terrific pleasure." Those lines could apply to Mr. Ewart. In an earlier poem, **"The Black Box,"** he claimed:

> As well as these poor poems
> I am writing some wonderful ones.
> They are all being filed separately,
> nobody sees them.
>
> When I die they will be buried
> in a big black tin box.
> In fifty years' time
> they must be dug up,
>
> for so my will provides.
> This is to confound the critics
> and teach everybody
> a valuable lesson.

While no one has access to that "black box," we are now the richer for possessing nearly five decades of Gavin Ewart's sane, shrewd, large-spirited and delightful verse.

> Bruce Bennett, *"From Rueful to Raucous," in* The New York Times Book Review, *August 17, 1986, p. 26.*

C. B. McCULLY

Gavin Ewart knows a thing or two about turning a line, but on the whole I found *The Young Pobble's Guide to His Toes* rather lamely entertaining. This is probably because Ewart has an unfortunate tendency to shoot himself in the foot: all the technical guile in the world cannot redeem puerile oversimplification or preoccupation with one's own limp humour. He comes to this volume with a big reputation . . . but I often felt the comic means to be jejune, and the gaiety consequently forced. For example, it is one thing to acknowledge Auden's continuing influence; it is another to write around it (in a metrical borrowing) as follows:

> He certainly gulped sex like food,
> quite the reverse of any prude,
> and, wholly greedy,
> he wolfed huge helpings that he carved—
> his cock was never stinted, starved,
> or poor and needy. . . .

> ("A Pilgrimage")

It is rather too easy, of course, for even the most splendid sub-academic hack to get sniffy about rankly indecorous verse. My objection, though, to pastiche like this is essentially that it is conceptually flawed: when comic means are a nudge and a wink, the ends are as tasteless as one of those cartoon seaside postcards. But Ewart seems to revel in that dreary 'fun'. . . . (p. 73)

Nevertheless, despite my reservations as to tacky rudery, despite the misprints ('Bramwell' for 'Branwell' four times in a sequence on the Brontës), and despite a hearty sickness brought on by exclamation marks (in **"Came Away with Betjeman . . ."** there are nine in twelve lines), I did enjoy some of the collection, notably **"A Wordsworthian Sonnet for Arnold Feinstein, Who Mended My Spectacles in Yugoslavia"**, **"Don't Make Me Hate You!"**, **"Can A Woman Be A Shit?"**, and **"De Quincey's Three Opium Dream Sonnets on the Wordsworth Family"**. These last read well, and they are comic, largely because Ewart's ear is so accurate—the first requirement of a parodist or pasticheur. . . .

The latest collection is, then, a work for Ewart enthusiasts. For the faint-hearted among us, I should add that many of the poems are far better read aloud; they do become attractive that way—but should lively recitation mask what is really sloppy, ill-considered, or crude? This is a central question when we consider the idea of Audience: an Audience is entertained by verbal ingenuity, but it may also be entertained by having its own preconceptions gratified in mediocre verse, and this is a danger. Some people like verse because it is audible confectionary, some want their souls shampooed: Ewart plays up to both. (p. 74)

> C. B. McCully, *"Voices Off," in* PN Review, *Vol. 13, No. 1, 1986, pp. 73-6.*

LINCOLN KIRSTEIN

The very notion of poet laureate summons up a figure of fun. This in no way denigrates our present national incumbent [Ted Hughes], certainly a most appropriate choice. But if one admits the faint risibility of certain verses by past laurel-crowned Britons, the chief of current comedians in the observance of public occasions is Gavin Ewart, now finally well introduced to the American audience [with the publication of *The Gavin Ewart Show: Selected Poems, 1939-1985* and *The Young Pobble's Guide to his Toes*]. Recently, he was runner-up for the butt of Canary wine traditionally awarded by the Sovereign to his or her most loyal bard. This time Ted Hughes won, but it was the victory of a poet of lyric sensibility over a virtuoso ironist, not of nature raw in tooth and claw, but of soldiering, board rooms, urban discontent, family joy and horror, and sex, sex, sex. Gavin Ewart, by virtue of profligate prolificity, as well as response to every noteworthy incident of immediate history except its official reaction, is England's most legitimate successor to John Betjeman. . . .

Ever since the Hitler war, Gavin Ewart has been volunteer laureate. Although almost annual publication now claims for him a national readership, there are difficulties in making his work available to an American following. It is by no means that his idiom is parochial, although his language, like Kipling's and Betjeman's, takes advantage of every shifting rage and fad of common taste and parlance. His imagery derives from the music hall, the corner pub, literary luncheons, board-room military slang, the argot of cities Anglican and Mediterranean. And the subject is life as it's lived in and out of newspapers, plus sex, sex, sex.

In both the exposure of a very broad personal sensitivity and the exploitation of language by rhetoric, imagery, meter, and rhyme, Ewart pushes all the old familiar (and very unfamiliar) possibilities. He is unafraid of the positive declarations of sentiment (or affection) for wife, son, daughter; cats, experimental animals, inequities of Northern Ireland and the City of London; and sex. Philip Larkin, another volunteer and much lamented laureate, was prompted to write that "the most remarkable phenomenon of the English poetic scene during the last ten years has been the advent, or perhaps I should say the irruption of Gavin Ewart." One of the more important functions of art, as Cocteau knew, was "a rehabilitation of the commonplace." . . .

Ewart has written in depth about large subjects of which he has had considerable firsthand data; for example on **"The Bofors A A Gun"**. . . . He's written delightful, extended summations of London by evoking its monuments; Madame Tussaud's Chamber of Horrors becomes a chart of historical myth via the daily sensationalist press. The museums of South Kensington, the Natural Science Museum, (What Man Is); the Victoria and Albert, (What Man Creates); the Brompton Oratory, (What Man Believes); the Science Museum, (What Man Knows); ending with "Excavation Road," (Man Is a Political Animal). . . . (p. 35)

Many of Ewart's most thoughtful, depressing, yet impressive verses concern sex. He could be hailed as the most persuasive celebrator of heterosexual love-hate since D. H. Lawrence. Praising the female in her every form—infant, girlfriend; mother, mistress, wife; bitch, goddess, witch, muse, friend—this preoccupation is a hopeless yet happy obsession. He denies it and adores it in something akin to the itch and agony of Rochester, Herrick, and Swift. It's the flesh that arouses and repels, tantalizes and mesmerizes, in all of its odors, wetness, fur, balefulness, and bliss. . . .

It is not possible to demonstrate the acrobatics of his versifying spectrum with every advantage and complexity of form from Horace through the troubadours to Lallan Scots and today's Liverpudlian. He does not disdain doggerel where it wags well, and he has rifled every anthology from hymnbook to the *Spectator*'s weekly competitions. Here is a very astute critic and appreciator who praises and complains in the identical measure of his heroes and victims. . . .

There are few poets today who regard their craft as sport rather than confessional. Verse streams out of him like a tidy fountain, the pressure almost at an energetic constant. Mandarin sensibility, the iteration of a self-projected persona owns the success of easier marketing. Give us the fingerprints and we've got the goods. An individual voice comes to be recognized as a staple; what is often available is a self-reflective invention, a response to its mirror imagery. When a poet declines to posit his self against the awesome specifics of time's passage as history, payment is in the charge of pretentiousness. The attraction of Ewart is in a depersonalized persona, a ruddy Englishman, aging slowly, with the light weight of his full and active years, and their correspondence to a lively tradition of verse as urbane action. . . .

Ewart's map is a secular mosaic, its tiny tesserae deftly cut, brightly colored, precisely placed. When we are curious about the administration of the British raj in India, ambiguities in the Boer War, craft in civil engineering and the spark in military matters in the first third of this century, we go to Kipling for true tales. For a funny, vivid, and centered conspectus of the years and their raw action since World War II, Gavin Ewart offers something not unlike, in style, wit, and warmth uniquely wondrous. (p. 36)

Lincoln Kirstein, "Provocateur," in The New York Review of Books, *Vol. XXXIV, No. 1, January 29, 1987, pp. 35-6.*

Richard Ford

1944-

American novelist, short story writer, essayist, and critic.

In his fiction, Ford contemplates existentialist themes and conflicts. His novels feature restless and alienated male protagonists who are haunted by painful experiences that render them incapable of emotional commitment. Although some critics have contended that Ford's use of techniques derived from the Southern literary tradition is imperfect, he is frequently commended for his keen sense of place, vivid descriptive powers, cynical humor, and evocation of American vernacular.

A native Mississippian, Ford set his first novel, *A Piece of My Heart* (1976), in his home state. He focuses upon Robard Hewes, an Arkansas drifter who leaves his wife to pursue an affair with his married cousin. Robard is warned by Sam Newel, a Chicago law student returning to the South, that his intentions are self-destructive. However, he ignores Sam and, ironically, is shot and killed by a youth for trespassing. While some critics faulted Ford for heavy-handed symbolism and for unsuccessfully attempting to assimilate William Faulkner's techniques into his prose, several reviewers acknowledged his ability to skillfully evoke the setting of the South and the temperament of its people. *The Ultimate Good Luck* (1981) revolves around a disaffected Vietnam War veteran who becomes involved in his ex-lover's attempt to free her brother, a convicted drug dealer, from a Mexican prison. Most critics considered Ford's blend of existential novel and hard-boiled thriller to be humorless and limited in comparison to his first book.

Ford's next novel, *The Sportswriter* (1986), chronicles the life of Frank Bascombe, an affable, introspective sportswriter who seeks solace after his young son dies and his marriage collapses. To cope with his grief, Frank drifts into dreamy states through which he disengages himself from reality. Although some critics considered Frank a bland and uninteresting protagonist, others maintained that his meditations on marriage, sports, suburbia, and the craft of writing are the novel's strongest aspects. Robert Towers deemed *The Sportswriter* "a reflective work that invites reflection, a novel that charms us with the freshness of its vision and touches us with the perplexities of a 'lost' narrator who for once is neither a drunkard nor a nihilist but a wistful, hopeful man adrift in his own humanity."

(See also *Contemporary Authors*, Vols. 69-72 and *Contemporary Authors New Revision Series*, Vol. 11.)

LARRY MCMURTRY

The South—dadgummit—has struck again, marring what might have been an excellent first novel. *A Piece of My Heart* shows obvious promise, but it also exhibits all the characteristic vices of Southern fiction. Those vices, in my view, are so numerous that there would not be space to list them all, but it won't hurt to tick off a few, starting with portentousness.

What we have here is a fairly mundane story of working-class adultery, in which the adulterer gets shot, not by the husband he has cuckolded, but by an indifferent youth who happens to be guarding a boat he makes off in. It would have made a creditable spare short novel. It does not, however, lend itself well to constant overtones on the fall of man.

If the vices this novel shares with its many little Southern cousins could be squeezed into one word, the word would be neo-Faulknerism. It reads like the worst, rather than the best, of Faulkner. It reminds us of the Faulkner whose passion for rhetoric so often swamped his instinct for syntax.

Richard Ford's frequently interesting narrative shows a distressing tendency to keep sliding backward, toward a past that is not half so interesting as its present. Even if it were interesting it would be hard to figure out who it is happening to, thanks to the author's preference for pronouns, rather than proper names. This too is a Faulknerian preference. (p. 16)

Portentousness, overwriting, pronouns drifting toward a shore only dimly seen, a constant backward tilt toward a past that hasn't the remotest causal influence on what is actually happening, plus a more or less constant tendency to equate eloquence with significance: these are the familiar qualities in which Mr. Ford's narrative abounds. From the tone, one might think that something of great moment is happening, but one would be wrong. A construction worker is having a guilt-ridden, largely unsatisfactory affair with the wife of a minor league pitcher. Fortunately for us the construction worker had to drive all the way from Nevada to Mississippi to consummate this affair, allowing for some interesting movement in the earlier parts of the book. Without that we would have had nothing but the $8.95 tour of the delta, accompanied by a chronically puzzled Chicago law student.

Indeed, women and old men seem to be the only characters in Southern fiction who aren't chronically puzzled. The Woman and the Old Man in this book are wonderfully done: articulate, profane and totally confident. It is the men who are forced to carry the narrative who invariably discover that they are also carrying the burden of Southern history. In this case, as in so many others, it squashes them into a mulch of pronouns and pulpy adjectives, of which "imponderable" is the one I personally have come to dislike most. . . .

One would hope that, in Mr. Ford's case, their vices won't prove incurable. His minor characters are vividly drawn, and his ear is first-rate. If he can weed his garden of some of the weeds and cockleburrs of his tradition, it might prove very fertile. (p. 18)

> Larry McMurtry, "With the Vices of the Genre," in The New York Times Book Review, *October 24, 1976, pp. 16, 18.*

VICTOR GOLD

Southerners, said Faulkner, are different from Northerners. Yes, answered Malcolm Cowley, they have more legend. In his first novel [*A Piece of My Heart*], Richard Ford, a 32-year-old Mississippian, enhances the legend of the mystic Mother Region that Wolfe could not go home to and Faulkner could not escape. Ford, similarly torn, solves his problem, at least in a literary sense, by the unique device of splitting his protagonist in halves. He tells the story, in tandem, of Robard Hewes, the Arkansas drifter drawn home from the Golden West by the most primal of attractions, and Sam Newel, the Mississippi drifter about to get his law degree in Chicago, who returns South, in the classic theme of the legend, to find a missing part of himself somewhere in the land and its people. . . .

The two men are mirror images: their fates intertwined, to be resolved during a brief and surreal stay on a river island between Arkansas and Mississippi. The publisher's cover blurb calls this "An extraordinary first novel," which, given the hyperbolic standards of today's literary marketplace, is mere understatement. I have read this book once, to learn which of the returnees has come to stay—*permanently* to stay—and which escapes. I am reading it again, as one brought up in the South, for the pure enjoyment of the author's authentic feel for the Mother Region, the beauty, ugliness, humor, and violence of its people. I will probably read it a third time, to pick up nuances I missed in the first two readings. On the other hand, if you are a reader who belongs back up in Lake Michigan, once may suffice.

The Hewes-Newel story opens, literally, with a bang. One of the two returnees has been shot, killed for no reason other than the mindless enforcement of a no-trespassing ordinance. His killer is a young boy—one of several monster children inhabiting Ford's literary landscape. When asked about the identity of his victim, the boy shrugs, "Damned if I know. Whoever

it was, though, he didn't have no business being here. I'll tell you that . . ."

The line and the boy are symbolic. The river island, there but somehow missing from the U.S. Geological Survey map, is symbolic. On and near the island there are a man with a mechanical larynx, a man hard of hearing, and a man with a war-wound-disfigured mouth. In addition, the characters in this novel all seem to have some tic involving the rubbing, reaming, and massaging of eyes. These, too, are symbolic. Mr. Lamb, the host and the lessee of the island (the lease being held by a Chicago corporation), is one of the most colorful, cantankerous, Southern fictional characters since Faulkner's Big Daddy. But he, too, is symbolic . . . H*ewes*-N*ewel*, the lamb with his *ewe.* (p. 1240)

[Ford's] poet's vision of a Mother Region littered with decay and deformity, where violence and death are shrugged off as integral to the life-force itself, is clear and unsentimental. This book may indeed be a classic of the genre, first novel or tenth. Ford is a superb storyteller who can relate a vignette of pure horror or a comedy of rustic manners with equal brilliance.

But that symbolism! Let Ford be cautioned that once a minstrel of the legend invites (as he has, with a vengeance) the attention of the symbol-hunters, there is no escaping their critical warp. . . .

Richard Ford is too good a storyteller to suffer such a fate. I don't much care whether the U.S. Geological Survey locates that island; but a little symbolism can go a long way. In future novels he should do something about all those eyes, ears, and throats. Send them to Lake Michigan for the cold, wet treatment. (p. 1241)

> Victor Gold, "The Far Side of Yoknapatawpha County," in National Review, *New York, Vol. XXVII, No. 43, November 12, 1976, pp. 1240-41.*

NOLAN MILLER

The great wonder of this quite affecting and gripping novel [*A Piece of My Heart*] is that ultimately it works. For some two hundred pages the focal characters, the sex-driven Robard Hewes, the self-pitying, memory-obsessed law student from Chicago, Sam Newel, seem dim, undefined, and so unsympathetic as to be often repugnant. . . .

The thematic substance of this murky but stylistically beguiling narrative at last lifts like morning fog. Hewes and Newel are both hollow men lost in the heart of darkness; Hewes is psychical, without past or future; Newel is a man who cannot face a future except with a past consciously realized. But little does it matter. Sensual or mental, the life of the moment is the only life we can know. Death holds the stop-watch.

Faulknerian in setting and atmosphere, the novel reveals a writer with his own cadence and tone. His descriptive passages are of transcendent beauty. His handling of minor characters, always in focus, always at one and the same time grotesque, even ridiculous, yet touchingly funny, are unforgettable. . . . With the exception of tricky, italicized flashbacks now and then, here is a novel without a page of tedium. With Richard Ford a fresh talent has arrived.

> Nolan Miller, in a review of "A Piece of My Heart," in The Antioch Review, *Vol. 35, No. 1, Winter, 1977, p. 124.*

SUSAN WOOD

[*A Piece of My Heart*] suffers from its own excesses, excesses seen far too often in Southern fiction of the last 30 years: an atmosphere of gloom and doom interlaced with black and bitter comedy; bizarre characters, sometimes called "Southern grotesques"; a situation *in extremis,* full of purposelessness and random violence; a certain circularity of style, sometimes known as the "Southern floodwater" school of writing, in which the prose goes on and on, turning in on itself, slowly building up to overwhelm the reader in a great torrent. The problem is that it is impossible, and senseless, to do what Faulkner did first—and best.

Despite these criticisms, Richard Ford is a writer of considerable talent and there are moments when the novel rises above its limitations: in odds and ends of wonderfully realized detail, in the character of Mr. Lamb, in his wife's story of how she acquired her glass eye, in a memorable mishap on a fishing trip. It is not that Ford cannot tell a story but that he has not found his own story to tell. Given his gifts, he will no doubt find that story and, with it, his own voice.

> Susan Wood, in a review of "A Piece of My Heart," in Book World—The Washington Post, February 20, 1977, p. N3.

KIRKUS REVIEWS

As Ford [in *The Ultimate Good Luck*] goes about setting up his initial scene—a rootless, alienated American in Oaxaca, Mexico, picks up an equally rootless girl and takes her to a boxing match where one of the fighters promptly has one of his eyeballs punched out—you begin to get a sinking feeling. When you learn that the American, Harry Quinn, is in Oaxaca in order to arrange for his lover's brother (a drug-dealer) to be sprung from a local prison, you sink a little lower—then lower still when you're introduced to Rae herself, Quinn's disaffected, zombie-oid lover. And things hit just about rock-bottom when these flat, clichéd characters begin to be surrounded by Ford's dreadful macho/psychological prose, a syrup boiled down from the worst tendencies of everyone from Hemingway to Robert Stone. . . . [Ford's combination of] pretentious/empty verbiage with the existential-thriller formula becomes a numbing one, and the plot itself, involving drug-traffickers, offers no surprises: thanks to a double-cross, Quinn and Rae never do get Rae's brother out of jail, and some shoot-ups ensue. True, *A Piece of My Heart* (though somewhat weighed down with similarly broody, hollow prose) did show a talent for Southern milieu, violent atmosphere, and loner characters. But this second novel fulfills none of that promise, settling instead for dismal posturing and imitative melodrama. (pp. 230-31)

> A review of "The Ultimate Good Luck," in Kirkus Reviews, Vol. XLIX, No. 4, February 15, 1981, pp. 230-31.

WALTER CLEMONS

Four years ago Richard Ford made an odd, original debut with a novel that has stuck in my head since. *A Piece of My Heart,* which recounted the convergence of two self-destructive men in a Godforsaken Mississippi backwater, was at once meandering and ominous, laconically funny and menacing. Even at its most laid-back comic moments, the reader was alerted to danger.

The Ultimate Good Luck is a tighter, more efficient book, and a good one, though Ford has jimmied himself into the confines of the existentialist thriller with a conspicuous sacrifice of his robust gift for comedy. His Vietnam veteran hero, Harry Quinn, arrives in Oaxaca to rescue his girl's brother, jailed for drug dealing by the Mexican authorities. Quinn is a loner without plans, who tries to live moment by moment. . . . His girl, Rae, left him because, she said, "I couldn't ever tell what your life was in behalf of," and he hopes his present errand, and Rae's arrival with the money to spring her brother, will enable him to win her back. (pp. 89-90)

Ford's sense of place is extraordinary. His Oaxaca, perpetually strung with Christmas lights and wire-mesh bells ("Mexicans thought Americans wanted it to be Christmas every day"), is a tourist town under military law. . . . Quinn the by-stander, who just wanted to get in and get out, is drawn into a labyrinth of betrayals, double deals and murder.

Sentence by sentence, *The Ultimate Good Luck* is the work of a formidably talented novelist. My dissatisfaction with it is that Quinn and Rae seem laboratory animals in a demonstration that Quinn's belief in living without attachments is an insufficient code: "The best thing you could do," Quinn thinks, "is take events one at a time, in order, and hope one wouldn't cut you up too much." Rae resents his guarding against feeling, and when she finally asks, "Do you think you're old enough to live your life unprotected, Harry?" we feel that Ford has known Quinn's answer from the book's start—has, in fact, locked himself in with a macho hero less humane and intelligent than he is. Ford's virtuosity is exciting here, but he has larger capabilities. (p. 90)

> Walter Clemons, "Uneasy Rider," in Newsweek, Vol. XCVII, No. 19, May 11, 1981, pp. 89-90.

C.D.B. BRYAN

"In the war," Quinn tells us [in *The Ultimate Good Luck*], "you maintained your crucial distance from things and that kept you alive, and kept everything out in front of you and locatable." Richard Ford keeps the crucial distance in his writing, too. His prose has a taut cinematic quality that permits him to record the color, the architecture, the movement, the violence occurring in front of him with the Cyclopean detachment of a wide-angle lens affixed to a camera on an exploratory spacecraft landing on an alien planet. It is a style that bathes his story with the same hot, flat, mercilessly white light that scorches Mexico, and it captures exactly that disquieting sense of menace one often feels lurking there just off the road.

Richard Ford's cool portrait of Quinn, the Vietnam vet whose alienation from the past and dislocation from the future render him incapable of emotional commitment beyond the here and now, seems exactly right, too. There is something comfortingly familiar about Quinn, a hint of the disillusioned, hard-boiled big city cop/newspaperman/private-eye hero of film and fiction we've come across before. (p. 13)

If Richard Ford's novel were to achieve the wide audience it richly deserves and a thoughtful, careful film version did result, then *The Ultimate Good Luck* could do for Mexico what the Paul Newman film *Fort Apache* has done for the South Bronx. (p. 51)

> C.D.B. Bryan, "Mexican Coke Rap," in The New York Times Book Review, May 31, 1981, pp. 13, 51.

GILBERTO PEREZ

[*The Ultimate Good Luck* explores] nasty and brutish territory.... I won't attempt to summarize a plot that seems intended to obstruct comprehension: something to do with cocaine smugglers in Mexico and an American who travels there to try to get his girlfriend's brother out of a messy situation. This American, a Vietnam veteran who might have been sent in by Central Casting for the role of an inarticulate tough guy, doesn't succeed in getting the brother out of anything, only in killing a lot of people. Through the gratuitous violence that fills this novel, Ford is attempting, one gathers, to make some kind of statement on the senseless violence around us all; but his book merely indulges the tough-guy mystique.... *The Ultimate Good Luck* calls to mind a cheap action picture in which hastily collaborating hacks didn't quite manage to put a story together—except that in Ford's book there's a leaden affectation in his adopted blood-and-guts mode and in his mannered slangy prose. (p. 620)

Gilberto Perez, "The First and Other Persons," in The Hudson Review, Vol. XXXIV, No. 4, Winter, 1981-82, pp. 606-20.

MICHIKO KAKUTANI

Frank Bascombe, the protagonist of Richard Ford's powerful new novel [*The Sportswriter*], is a sportswriter the way Walker Percy's famous hero, Binx Bolling, was a moviegoer. Frank admires athletes, regards them as "people who are happy to let their actions speak for them," and he envies their capacity to live "within" themselves.... As a young man, Frank himself possessed "the lanky, long-loose-arm grace of a natural ball player," but he was never much good at the game, afflicted as he was by a crippling self-consciousness, "an inbred irony" that cramped his instincts and his timing. So today, Frank works as a writer for a glossy sports magazine—watching, observing and annotating the actions of others. It is a job, he tells us, that he rather enjoys, a job that teaches you "there are no transcendent themes in life," that "things are here and they're over, and that has to be enough."

Like Harry, the hero of the author's last novel (*The Ultimate Good Luck*), Frank is an observer, a loner who's wary of getting too involved in the lives of others; and in telling his story—or rather, in allowing Frank to tell it himself in his own rambling, philosophical voice—Mr. Ford has succeeded in writing his finest book to date, a book that can stand alongside such works as Mr. Percy's *The Moviegoer* and Richard Yates's *Revolutionary Road* as a devastating chronicle of contemporary alienation.

As Frank tell us, his life has been a fairly unextraordinary one.... He'd given up work on his novel to take the sports-writing job, but he says he "was happy as a swallow"—it was a relief to trade the solitary rigors of fiction for the more immediate gratifications of journalism; and besides, Frank liked the ordinariness of his life in suburban New Jersey....

Things, however, have not turned out exactly as Frank might have expected. His 9-year-old son, Ralph, dies suddenly of Reye's Syndrome, and as Frank tries to cope with his death, he finds a kind of "dreaminess" seeping into his life, softening the edges of his hurt but also insulating him from everything and everyone around him. He finds himself drifting away from his wife, spends more and more time paging through mail-order catalogues, fantasizing about things he can't afford, and

he begins to carry on desultory affairs with women he's met while traveling out of town. He likes the sense of mystery and possibility afforded by these anonymous liaisons, but when his wife discovers his infidelity and subsequently leaves him, he starts to miss "the sweet specificity of marriage, its firm ballast and sail."

Though Frank says he believes that people put too much emphasis on the past, these fragments of a former life—recalled to us, in minutely detailed flashbacks—clearly dictate his current state of emotions. Convinced that he is too damaged to risk further pain, Frank has elevated his natural inclination toward detachment into a guiding principle of life, and this emotional reticence has left him stranded in a sort of twilight zone: he has acquaintances but no good friends, lovers but no one with whom to share his secrets and his dreams....

There are times when Frank's discursive monologue on his life, past and present, becomes long-winded and overly meditative—the novel would probably have benefited by being edited by some 50 pages—but his voice, as rendered by Mr. Ford, is so pliant and persuasive that we are insistently drawn into his story. It is a journalist's voice—observant of people and places, astringent in its attempt to eschew the sentimental—and quite clearly the voice of someone attuned to the random surprises of daily life, its discontinuity and its capacity to startle and wound.

As for Mr. Ford, he writes with a great deal of compassion for his hero, but his affection is tempered by a certain tough-mindedness; and so we come to see Frank not only as he sees himself (hurt, alienated, resigned to a future of diminishing returns) but also as he must appear to others—essentially kind and decent, but also wary, passive and unwilling to embrace the real possibilities for happiness that exist around him. In fact, as the events of the one weekend framing this novel—an abortive interview with a former football player, a visit to his girlfriend's parents, the suicide of a friend—accelerate, Frank is forced to reassess his own image of himself and the readers of *The Sportswriter,* too, are made both to see and experience the gathering sense of loss and disorder in his life.

Michiko Kakutani, in a review of "The Sportswriter," in The New York Times, February 26, 1986, p. C21.

ALICE HOFFMAN

Richard Ford, the author of the highly praised first novel *A Piece of My Heart,* focuses on one member of a shattered family in *The Sportswriter,* his third novel. Less about sports than about alienation, this moody chronicle is narrated by a father and former husband, Frank Bascombe. As he tells the story of his detachment—what he calls his "dreaminess" ... —the novel's cool, flat tone reflects his interior state. Bascombe's estrangement is charted with unsettling irony: the wife who has divorced him (after finding what she mistakenly believes to be a cache of love letters) is referred to only as X, and one of his surviving children, a daughter named Clary, appears only briefly nearly 300 pages into the narrative. Compulsively cerebral and self-absorbed, he searches for release in the ordinary and the unexamined. It is this yearning for a regulated world, rather than a love of sports, that has led him to turn from fiction to sportswriting. His vision of the athlete is one of immutable and childish simplicity, an egoism that is purer than his own:

Athletes, by and large, are people who are happy to let their actions speak for them, happy to be what they do. . . . [An athlete is] never likely to feel the least bit divided. Or alienated, or one ounce of existential dread. . . .

To quiet his own existential dread, Bascombe looks to his surroundings—the pleasant, highly unremarkable New Jersey suburb of Haddam. It is Bascombe, not his wife and children, who has remained in the family house. . . .

Because he is a perpetual escapee (from Manhattan, from fiction, from the rigors of family life), it makes sense that in telling his story Bascombe chooses to ignore tangled, emotionally charged family relationships, fixating instead on non-relationships and non-events. Of his parents and his youth, he tells us little:

> My own history I think of as a postcard with changing scenes on one side but no particular or memorable messages on the back. You can get detached from your beginnings. . . . And so we might as well think about something more promising.

What seems more promising, or so Bascombe insists, is his affair with a nurse, a relocated Texan, Vicki Arcenault, who ministered to his wound—a thumb cut by a lawn mower blade. As he is drawn to the suburb of Haddam, so he is drawn to Vicki, choosing both for their ordinariness and limited intellectual and emotional claims. Though he hopes to marry her, Vicki is not as easily satisfied as Bascombe would have her. After Easter dinner with her family. . . . Vicki tells him: "We don't have none of the same interests, doesn't look like. . . . I just figured that out sitting at the table. . . . I just don't love you enough to marry you. . . . I don't love you in the right way."

Bascombe's attempt at arranging an unexamined life for himself is thwarted not only by Vicki. The Divorced Men's Club he belongs to—a group that favors mute commiseration and good-humored fishing trips rather than soul-searching—has a disruptive presence in its newest member, Walter Luckett. Haunted by his wife's betrayal and a brief homosexual encounter, Walter seeks Bascombe out and insists on presenting his confession and tormented self-analysis. Bascombe will not react; he remains tolerant and aloof. In a world where human contact is dangerous business, Walter's suicide is not unanticipated. Though his death has negligible emotional effects on Bascombe, the act is meant to be pivotal: the note Walter leaves behind dispatches Bascombe on a search for Walter's nonexistent child—a posthumous push toward action and accountability.

The death of a son and a history of marital stress pushed to the limit by a husband's gloomy indifference are central not only to *The Sportswriter* but also to Anne Tyler's most recent novel, *The Accidental Tourist*. These novels display an uncanny series of similarities. In each we find a major character who is a workmanlike, rather than a creative, writer, a father and former husband who insists on continuing a suburban life after his family has left him, an intellectual nit-picker drawn to an unsuitable woman whose vitality and pragmatism attract him. But in spite of their corresponding characters and themes, the novels could not be more different in tone or consequence. Though *The Sportswriter* aims for a tougher, more realistic stance than *The Accidental Tourist,* it suffers from a lack of compelling action and an emphasis on Bascombe's dry med-

itations that obscures and minimizes the complex domestic structure the author initially presents.

Mr. Ford is a daring and intelligent novelist, but in choosing Bascombe as his narrator he has taken a risk that ultimately does not pay off. The authorial voice is so weakened that we are left only with the observations of an emotionally untrustworthy narrator. This is not to say that the author doesn't allow us some access to Bascombe's psyche. Certainly, his observations about a former athlete hold true for himself, for what he needs "is to strap on a set of pads and beat the daylights out of somebody and quit worrying about theories of art." He never trades theorizing for action. His inability to write fiction, which should illuminate his inability to connect emotionally, instead seems trivial. Even mourning is replaced by self-analysis, so that Bascombe's lost son seems less a ghostly presence than a tiny piece of glass set in the kaleidoscope of self-scrutiny.

That characters undergo great transformation is surely not a prerequisite of a satisfying novel. It is quite believable that at the close of the novel Bascombe seems as much in spiritual exile as when we first meet him. And yet he tells us: "It is possible to be married, to divorce, then to come back together with a whole new set of understandings that you'd never have liked or even understood before in your earlier life, but that to your surprise now seems absolutely perfect."

This is a jarring and contradictory evaluation of the emotional landscape we have just experienced. If there are layers of irony and perception, they are too subtle and diffuse. Mr. Ford's admirable talents, which include an extraordinary ear for dialogue and the ability to create the particulars of everyday life with stunning accuracy (on Bascombe's trip to Detroit with Vicki, for instance), are not well served in a novel given to abstract analysis. Perhaps the author is telling us that family connections are too impenetrable not only to understand but to record. Certainly, what is at the heart of Frank Bascombe's sorrow remains, for the reader, a mystery.

> *Alice Hoffman, "A Wife Named X, a Poodle Named Elvis," in* The New York Times Book Review, *March 23, 1986, p. 14.*

JONATHAN YARDLEY

Frank Bascombe, the narrator of Richard Ford's third novel [*The Sportswriter*], is a 38-year-old writer for "a glossy New York sports magazine you have all heard of," a career he pursues as a relatively easy alternative to the more demanding one of writer of fiction, for which he had originally seemed intended. A couple of years ago his eldest child, Ralph, died of Reye's syndrome; since then he has separated from and divorced his wife. He continues to live in their large old house in a New Jersey suburb; his ex-wife and their two surviving children live in another house not far away. His current romantic interest is Vicki Arcenault, a pneumatic nurse lately moved north from Texas; she is sweet and sexy and accommodating, but self-preoccupied and unsophisticated as well. . . .

Emotionally and professionally, Bascombe is a loner and an outsider. He genuinely wants intimacy and affection, yet he is neither strong nor mature enough to seize love when it is offered. He is a decent man who wants the best as much for others as for himself, and whose sympathies are easily negated, yet his instinct invariably is for escape and flight. Sportswriting, which permits him to a be a spectator and to report on the triumphs of others, is an apt occupation for one who is divorced from the action in his own life. This distancing, which he describes as "feeling dreamy," he traces back to his son's painful, protracted death; he thinks of his dreaminess as "a response to too much useless and complicated factuality."...

Bascombe can't make lasting connections with family and friends, so he turns instead to a fortune-teller, Mrs. Miller, whom he visits frequently. She is both impersonal and welcoming, and thus in his imaginings becomes *"the stranger who takes your life seriously,* the personage we all go into each day in hopes of meeting, the friend to the great mass of us not at odds with much," and he believes that "her philosophy is: *A good day's a good day. We get few enough of them in a lifetime. Go and enjoy it."* This may not seem unduly weighty as philosophies go, but it is ample for Bascombe, whose own philosophy is: "Things happen." Roll with the punches, is his motto: "If there's [one] thing that sportswriting teaches you, it is that there are no transcendent themes in life. In all cases things are here and they're over, and that has to be enough."

It may be enough for a private philosophy, but it's hardly enough to keep this novel moving. *The Sportswriter* is intelligent and compassionate, but it's terribly difficult to sustain the reader's interest in a narrator/protagonist who is not himself interesting. Though there are lively passages here and there—Ford is especially good when writing about suburbia in general and New Jersey in particular—most of the novel simply drones along just as Bascombe does, maintaining an amiable curiosity about things but never getting fully engaged with anything. The result is a book oddly deficient in energy, one that lazes around in circles without managing to go anywhere. Readers who are attracted to Frank Bascombe may want to make this trip, but their numbers are not likely to be legion.

Jonathan Yardley, "The Agony of Defeat," in Book World—The Washington Post, March 30, 1986, p. 3.

WALTER CLEMONS

Frank Bascombe, the sportswriter hero of Richard Ford's excellent third novel [*The Sportswriter*], is deceptively amiable, easygoing and sweet natured. As he tells his story in a chipper, uncomplaining tone, we gradually learn that he's a damaged man who's retreated into cushioned, dreamy detachment to evade grief and disappointment. Bascombe's eldest son has died, and his wife, whom he calls only X, has divorced him. Their life together in the green New Jersey suburb where they continue to live apart was "a generic one," he says mildly: "I looked out my window, stood in my yard sunsets with a sense of solace and achievement, cleaned my rain gutters, eyed my shingles, put up storms, fertilized regularly, computed my equity, spoke to my neighbors in an interested voice—the normal applauseless life of us all."...

The more Bascombe tells us he's sensible and unremarkable, the more Ford makes us feel the pain and alienation that underlie Bascombe's surface equanimity. The book's casual, flexible narrative voice is a superlative achievement. Though Ford can't always avoid the monotony inherent in working inside such a damped-down outlook, Bascombe is a big improvement over the macho protagonist of his previous novel, *The Ultimate Good Luck* (1981). Bascombe is tenderly observant, with welcome flashes of humor and malice. He has a funny airport encounter with his internist, Fincher Barksdale, "the kind of southerner who will only address you through a web of deep and antic southernness and who assumes everybody in ear-shot

knows all about his parents and history and wants to hear an update on them at every opportunity."...

Bascombe is likable even when his behavior is less than admirable. Most readers, males particularly, will sheepishly admit to sharing his inertia, his reticence, his desire for a life without complications. Only a scrupulously honest novelist could make us sympathetic to such an unheroic nature. Ford makes us feel we're more like Bascombe than we often care to admit.

At 42, Ford is one of the best writers of his generation.... [His] extraordinary stories, such as **"Winterkill," "Communist"** and **"Rock Springs,"** deserve collection in book form. Each of his works, *The Sportswriter* most of all, shows an original fictional intelligence. He's crafty, subtle and surprising.

Walter Clemons, "The Divorced Men's Club," in
Newsweek, Vol. CVII, No. 14, April 7, 1986, p. 82.

ROBERT TOWERS

The Sportswriter, which is Richard Ford's third novel, is a remarkably gentle and meditative book which belies the suggestion of hearty extroversion contained in its title. Rather the book steeps us, almost moment by moment, in the consciousness of its central character during three crowded days that mark a somewhat inconclusive shift in the direction of his life. What happens during that time is amplified by a series of extended flashbacks that have a direct bearing on Frank Bascombe's present condition, which might be described as that of a man more badly wounded than he cares to admit....

"My life over these twelve years has not been and isn't now a bad one at all," he tells us at the start. "In most ways it's been great." Just how great it's been—and is—forms a question that we are implicitly asked to consider as we track Frank over the course of the Easter weekend.

The action begins at dawn on Good Friday when Frank meets his ex-wife (referred to throughout merely as X) for a little ceremony of remembrance at the grave of their son, Ralph, who had died four years earlier of Reye's syndrome. (p. 38)

What follows is not in any sense a plotted novel with a rising action and a buildup of suspense. Instead we are given a series of detailed, vividly written episodes that succeed one another casually, almost haphazardly. One of these takes place outside of Detroit, where Frank (accompanied by his current girlfriend, Vicki) goes in order to interview a famous pro football player now crippled and confined to a wheelchair. Another occurs on Saturday night, when Frank, returning late to Haddam, finds an acquaintance named Walter waiting for him at his house. Walter, whom Frank has met through the Divorced Men's Club, is distraught over an unexpected homosexual incident with a married man and seeks Frank's acceptance and reassurance. (pp. 38-9)

These and other episodes are expertly rendered, but our chief interest throughout is in Frank's response to them. Ford has achieved, I think, a triumph in his characterization of Frank Bascombe, a decent man, kindly and always eager to see the hopeful side of things. As he moves from encounter to encounter, he wants to proclaim the goodness of life but is often bewildered or hurt by what he actually experiences. He is immensely accepting of people and the myriad ways in which they live. Walter's confession doesn't faze Frank, though in

161

general he dreads confessions; when Walter, misconstruing Frank's tolerance, suddenly kisses him on the cheek, Frank is upset ("I would kiss a camel rather than have Walter kiss me on the cheek again") but has no wish to react in a two-fisted way—he merely tells Walter to go home.

Frank is subject to prolonged states of dreaminess—a condition that became acute before his marriage ended and prevented him from taking steps to forestall a divorce that neither he nor X really wanted.

> "My son had died," he says, "but I am un-willing to say that was the cause, or that any-thing is ever the sole cause of anything else. I know that you can dream your way through an otherwise fine life, and never wake up, which is what I almost did. I believe I have . . . nearly put dreaminess behind me, though there is a resolute sadness between X and me that our marriage is over, a sadness that does not feel sad."

That last phrase sums up what we come to perceive as Frank's estrangement from his true feelings, of which the dreaminess is a symptom. He pretends to himself that he has "faced down" his grief over Ralph and his regret over his divorce. But of course these are the two very things that cause him to bleed—quietly and internally—throughout the book.

There are plenty of sad lives all around Frank. Walter is an example. So is the crippled football player, Herb Wallagher, about whom Frank hoped to write an "inspirational" article but who turns out to be not only embittered but more than a little crazy. Yet the emotional tone of *The Sportswriter* is any-thing but depressive. One of the chief pleasures of reading the novel comes from its sense of lively absorption in the varied details of contemporary American life that it conveys. Frank's embrace of these details—including the most banal—reaches beyond acceptance to something approaching active celebra-tion. Drive-ins, bars, airports, a glitzy hotel room in Detroit,

New Jersey housing developments, even the hodgepodge land-scape of New Jersey itself—all of these receive Frank's en-raptured attention. He relishes the lives of lower-middle-class people without even a hint of condescension; not only Vicki Arcenault, the feisty, literal-minded hospital nurse who is his girl-friend, but her father Wade, who collects tolls on the New Jersey Turnpike, and her stepmother Lynette, and her brother Cade are all recipients of his sympathetic and enlivening in-terest. . . .

Ford has fashioned a relaxed, colloquial style for Frank's rev-elation of himself and the world around him, a style with much of the breeziness but few of the clichés that we associate with sports writing. It moves easily from description to commentary and merges seamlessly with passages of dialogue that char-acterize the speakers in all their variety of social and regional background.

One wonders however about the thematic significance of the Easter weekend. Despite the recurrent ringing of church bells, the possible allusion to Judas in Walter's kiss, and the presence of a near-life-sized figure of the crucified Jesus on the Arcen-aults' lawn, I doubt that Ford intends us to seek anything allegorical in the Christian symbols. Frank, though a man of sorrows in certain respects, is hardly a Christ figure himself. Rather, he is distinctly a post-Christian man of a good will trying to find his way in a world bereft of the certainties of its religious past. He hears, but cannot respond to, the summoning of distant bells.

The Sportswriter is not a "big" novel. It is slow-paced and, like its protagonist, lacks a clear sense of direction; it arrives nowhere, so to speak. The book is, instead, a reflective work that invites reflection, a novel that charms us with the freshness of its vision and touches us with the perplexities of a "lost" narrator who for once is neither a drunkard nor a nihilist but a wistful, hopeful man adrift in his own humanity. (p. 39)

> *Robert Towers, "Screams and Whispers," in* The New York Review of Books, *Vol. XXXIII, No. 7, April 24, 1986, pp. 38-9.*

Ian Frazier

1951-

American essayist and journalist.

Frazier is well known for his humorous essays which display his imaginative, offbeat observations and droll wit. His first book, *Dating Your Mom* (1985), consists of pieces that were originally published in the *New Yorker*. Incorporating puns and gags into many of his essays, Frazier parodies such elements of contemporary culture as liner notes to record albums, popular literature, and autobiographies written by celebrities. The title piece is an outrageous satire of self-help manuals in which Frazier offers advice to single men on how to successfully date one's mother. Mordecai Richler observed: "Mr. Frazier owns just about every piece of equipment essential to a humorist's arsenal.... [He] is an elegant miniaturist, a much-needed mockingbird with a fine eye for the absurd."

Nobody Better, Better than Nobody (1987), Frazier's second book, contains essays which further demonstrate his descriptive powers and comedic talents. With the exception of the title sketch, a madcap account of Frazier's attempt to locate the author of the syndicated newspaper column "Hints from Heloise," the essays in this volume detail Frazier's travels to various locations in the United States and the people he encountered. Robert R. Harris noted that Frazier's "wit is restrained, but his remarkable powers of observation are set at full throttle."

© *Thomas Victor 1987*

CHRISTOPHER LEHMANN-HAUPT

There are flowers and pink ribbons on the cover of Ian Frazier's first book, *Dating Your Mom.* The ambiance is redolent of sentimental Mother's Day cards and barbershop quartets singing "I want a girl just like the girl that married dear old Dad."

But when we get to ["**Dating Your Mom**"], we are taken aback. "Dating your mother seriously might seem difficult at first," Mr. Frazier writes after modestly proposing that true love begins at home, "but once you try it I'll bet you'll be surprised at how easy it is. Facing up to your intention is the main thing, you have to want it bad enough." . . .

This is satire, obviously—a carrying to absurd extremes everything from Momism through the single-parent movement to those therapeutic best sellers that advise you to self-indulge. But there's more to the piece than that: there's a sinister anarchism here, as well as several surprising dramatic developments.

That's how all the best pieces work in this wickedly funny collection, most of which first appeared in *The New Yorker*. Like his precursor there, S. J. Perelman, or his wildly inventive colleague Veronica Geng, Mr. Frazier often takes off from an item he's come across in print or from a coupling he's dreamed up that is as provocative as courting one's mother. . . .

But even wittier than the ideas he comes up with are the odd directions in which his sketches sometimes twist. In "**The Bloomsbury Group Live at the Apollo**," what starts out as "Liner Notes From the New Best Selling Album" first turns into a reminiscence of "little Ginny Stephen" ("But man, that chick could *whale*") and John Maynard Keynes ("That cat took classical economic theory and bent it in directions nobody ever thought it could go"). Finally, it becomes an interview with Virginia Woolf herself: "The hardest thing about being a member of the Bloomsbury Group is learning how to be a person at the same time you're being a star. You've got to rise above your myth. We've reached the point where we're completely supportive of each other, and that's good." . . .

Dating Your Mom is . . . about language and writing, and everyone from pretentious book reviewers to novelists who use Nazi Germany as a plot device are targets for his wicked wit. He even takes aim at himself. In "a note on the author" that follows one short piece, he writes, "Ian Frazier is a writer who soaks up experience like a sponge. He experiences life as vividly and adjectivally as he writes about it. His appetite for life is as large as the man himself, or even somewhat larger, since Ian Frazier is of average size and his appetite for life is way above average."

But as this parody proceeds he inadvertently pays himself a considerable and deserved compliment. "He has that type of courage which one finds so rarely in an adult in our society, and that is the courage to play." . . .

A reviewer of his book must reaffirm his self-compliment. The only problem is, when you're as talented at play as Mr. Frazier is, it really doesn't take that much courage.

> *Christopher Lehmann-Haupt, in a review of "Dating Your Mom," in* The New York Times, *December 23, 1985, p. 15.*

MORDECAI RICHLER

Possibly because so many military secrets are now being bought and sold in parking garages and you can't even trust your neighborhood defector any more, conspiracy theories seem to be the order of the day. Is Kim Philby actually a British agent in place? Was Svetlana Alliluyeva sent back to Russia by the C.I.A.? The truth is, given the temper of the times, everybody is now suspect, even writers. Though I am only a very occasional reviewer in these pages, I have, in the last six months, heard from two probing reporters. They weren't horsing around. They wanted to know if the last book I pronounced on in *The Book Review* had been written by my brother-in-law or the loan officer at my bank, or maybe a cherished friend, or if I had praised it only because I was angling for a free lunch from the author's publisher.

So, for the record, let me say that Ian Frazier has never bought me a drink. I don't owe him any money. We weren't at school together. In fact, at this point in time, to the best of my knowledge, I have yet to meet him. But, yes, there is a connection. A few years back when I edited *The Best of Modern Humor* I was delighted to include a piece by him. It was called **"Dating Your Mom,"** and it is the title essay in his first collection. I included it because I hoped it would make me look good. I thought it was a deft, original and funny piece, and now I can see, happily, that it is only one of many—well, one of 25 to be precise—for *Dating Your Mom* is a deft, original and funny collection. Very welcome indeed. . . .

Mr. Frazier owns just about every piece of equipment essential to a humorist's arsenal. Obviously he cannot abide pretension or pomposity. He not only abhors clichés but has an engaging way of mangling them so that they are never quite the same again. Here he is, in **"Morris Smith: The Man and the Myth,"** on that trendy blight, the sexologist, whom we have seen interviewed again and again in the living or home sections of our local newspapers:

"'So, you see, it's awfully hard to generalize about the profession as a whole,' Dr. Smith continues. 'The best you can say is that all sexologists are human beings, and I think it's important not only for the public but also for the sexologists themselves to try and keep that in mind. We're people, too. We put our pants on one leg at a time—and, of course, I should add that some of the greatest sexologists in history have been women.'"

The insufferable children of Dr. Smith are grateful to him because "he always brings us neat stuff from his office. Anatomically correct dolls and stuff." His perfect wife says, "When your husband is in a demanding, high-risk job, you learn to love him when you can. . . . And you learn how to let go. If he didn't live for that big, shiny clinic of his, he wouldn't be Morris, and if he weren't Morris I guess I wouldn't love him." . . .

In **"Into the American Maw"** Mr. Frazier demolishes that overworked form of the deep-thinking writer's journal of a car-canoe-train trip across America, taking the nation's pulse, as it were. Meeting the literary obligations of the prescient traveler, he mourns lost American innocence and finds emptiness everywhere. "New York City, of course, is a woman. In fact, the entire tri-state area, including New York, Connecticut, and New Jersey, is a woman. But L.A.—L.A. is the City of the One-Night Stands. Or at least that's what I had heard. Just to be sure, I decided to call L.A. long-distance, my voice crying through wires across the vast, buffalo-scarred dreamscape of a haunted republic. I told L.A. that I was coming out for four days, and could I possibly get a three-night stand. They said no, sir. They said I had to get three one-night stands. Q.E.D."

Mr. Frazier is an elegant miniaturist, a much-needed mockingbird with a fine eye for the absurd, and his collection is a pleasure to read. That much said, at this point in time, to the best of my knowledge, he owes me a drink, if that's the way things really work now.

> *Mordecai Richler, "Samuel Beckett Is His Co-Pilot," in* The New York Times Book Review, *January 5, 1986, p. 5.*

RHODA KOENIG

Ian Frazier is the latest in a long line of *New Yorker* humorists, a breed whose traits are unmistakable the minute it puts its nose into the room—literary allusiveness; mania for funny names; innocent perplexity about politics, business, how to open a pickle jar; air of whimsical desperation. In addition, Frazier is representative of the new *New Yorker,* the one that says yes as often as Molly Bloom. There's a wonky, disconnected sensibility here and a casual knowingness about sex. . . .

[*Dating Your Mom*] starts out like a parody of how-to-have-a-relationship books. . . . But at the end, Frazier lets this entertaining sliminess dribble away—it turns out that what the narrator wants of Mom is to be fed while he sits in an adult-size high chair. Only kidding, folks! . . .

In other pieces, Frazier tries to wring laughs out of the more-than-obvious (a hospital's public-address system pages Dr. No, Doc Severinsen, and Dr. J) or to stretch a single, small joke past the point of extinction. A sample entry in **"Kimberley Solzhenitsyn's Calendar"** ("May 12—Remind Al—bring patio trays up from basement. Nobel Prize winners' Spaghetti Dinner. Get Al's marimba fixed") is enough for you to imagine the rest. **"The Bloomsbury Group Live at the Apollo"** jocularly answers the question "What if the Bloomsbury writers had been jazz musicians?"—a question I can answer much more briefly with "Well, they weren't." Then there's one titled **"Igor Stravinski: The Selected Phone Calls,"** a lengthy elaboration of an idea that could have provided one paragraph in a piece called "Forthcoming Books," that old standby of hungry humorists. (p. 52)

I quite liked Frazier's fantasy of Samuel Beckett as an airline pilot ("Gray bleak final afternoon ladies and gentlemen this is your captain your cap welcoming you aboard . . ."), and I really liked his satire on the Nazification of best-sellers (Goebbels, head of the Führer's Plot Restructurement Corps, reports, "We have already removed the structurally impure elements from all the major literary works of the English and have inserted fear-of-Nazi-menace as the main instrument of plot." Then he reads the new opening of Shakespeare's "The Elsinore Agenda"). Both of these pieces let Frazier play with funny voices, which have a lot more scope than funny names, and the latter goes on long enough to be a story instead of a *spritz.*

Both pieces, as well, are grounded in fact. Samuel Beckett, we learn from an epigraph, did once express a desire to become a commercial pilot, and a swastika on a book cover does guarantee a respectable sale. I can't say exactly why, but, at least for me, a basis in fact means the difference between truly funny and merely irritating. Most of the sketches here, though, are too detached, too fey, and, just like novels with superficial characters and a shortage of plot, they left me unmoved. (pp. 52, 54)

In fact, some of Frazier's pieces are so goofy I had trouble even figuring out what the joke *was*. I've noticed this a lot in *New Yorker* humor of the past few years. Ideas, adjectives, allusions with nothing in common except their incongruity are thrown together in a kind of silly soup; as it bubbles away, you hear the voice of the humorist, tittering at himself. This kind of writing reminds me of the grown-ups who try to make children laugh by making comical faces or pretending to be big woof-woofs. There are many children who like this sort of humor, and millions of adults (look at all the fans of Danny Kaye, or John Belushi), but I don't let them in my play group. (p. 54)

> *Rhoda Koenig, "Is Postmodernism Funnier than Sex?" in* New York *Magazine, Vol. 19, No. 2, January 13, 1986, pp. 52, 54.*

DAVID BERREBY

Everywhere I went with this book, people took me for the kind of guy they hope their daughters never meet. Whan a Bloomingdale's type in a restaurant knocked it off my table with a swoosh of her mink, she sniffed, "that *belongs* on the floor." Reading along on the subway, *I* knew I was engrossed in a collection of cool and literate sketches from *The New Yorker*, but the other passengers saw a pervert smirking and wheezing helplessly over something titled (in rather large letters, unfortunately) *Dating Your Mom*.

Ian Frazier's perversities, however, are purely intellectual, and most, like ["**Dating Your Mom**"], are very, very funny. He does satire as well as anyone around (I won't be able to read a lame Sunday-section Serious Person Profile without thinking of "**Morris Smith: The Man and the Myth**"), but he also writes something much rarer—simple, graceful, funny pieces with no obvious target. They amble along until they suddenly trip over a double meaning and go flying into the air. . . . *Dating* begins with a set of liner notes for the Bloomsbury group's latest album. . . . It continues with "**Kimberley Solzhenitsyn's Calendar**" ("May 24—. . . Al's slide-show at Church Guild— 'Russia: Land of Contrasts'").

By the time you get to "**Igor Stravinsky: The Selected Phone Calls**," you may think you've figured out Frazier's Perelman-esque way of constructing a story. This will make you feel smart, but it won't make you stop laughing. Even after you're on to him, Frazier provides the deep anarchic pleasure of seeing the rules upended. . . .

Frazier's writing is so graceful and controlled that all these pieces have the feel of an effortless romp. I just hope he calls his next book *War and Peace* or *The New Testament*.

> *David Berreby, in a review of "Dating Your Mom," in* VLS, *No. 42, February, 1986, p. 5.*

PUBLISHERS WEEKLY

[The essays in *Nobody Better, Better Than Nobody* are] a masterly blend of detailed observation and subtle humor. . . . The opening piece describes an unusual festival, the small Kansas town of Oberlin celebrating an anniversary with the descendants of Cheyenne Indians who raided the town in 1878. Frazier's love of fishing and the state of Montana are reflected in "**An Angler at Heart**," a profile of an unusual purveyor of fishing tackle near New York's Grand Central Station, and "**Bear News**," which tells almost as much about Frazier as about Montana's bears. The work of a true listener and observer, these reportings are Americana at its idiosyncratic best.

> *A review of "Nobody Better, Better than Nobody," in* Publishers Weekly, *Vol. 231, No. 11, March 20, 1987, p. 58.*

ROBERT R. HARRIS

In *Nobody Better, Better Than Nobody,* [Ian Frazier's] wit is restrained, but his remarkable powers of observation are set at full throttle. When Mr. Frazier walks through Grand Central on his way to Jim Deren's shop, he notices how the garish Kodak display, with its overblown photographs, overwhelms the terminal's concourse and affects the space's lighting. Driving from Chicago to Texas, he feels that something important is missing when he notes that as "Interstates 55 and 70 cross into Missouri at St. Louis, there is no sign on the bridge identifying the river underneath as the Mississippi." . . .

It is his keen powers of observation and eye for detail that connect Mr. Frazier with John McPhee, the best practitioner, it seems to me, of the kind of journalistic essay that *The New Yorker* is justly famous for. Like Mr. McPhee, Mr. Frazier writes longish articles on seemingly obscure topics, but from them we learn things we most likely won't learn elsewhere and, best, we enjoy ourselves immensely.

Stylistically, Mr. Frazier also has mastered certain devices familiar to readers of the nonfiction that appears in *The New Yorker*. Two examples are the long run-on sentence that both captures a voice and conveys a great deal of information (sometimes it seems *New Yorker* writers compete with one another to see who can write the longest of these sentences and still manage to maintain a semblance of meaning) and the long series that not only makes a fascinating list, but also, taken as a whole, is funny. . . .

Mr. Frazier is a patient observer. . . . He is also restless, always on the move—across town, across the country, off to Paris at the spur of the moment. And that combination of patience and wanderlust results in some wonderfully dry and droll reporting. If you missed any of his fine essays the first time round, give yourself a treat and catch up with them in *Nobody Better, Better Than Nobody*.

> *Robert R. Harris, "Observation at Full Throttle," in* The New York Times Book Review, *May 3, 1987, p. 9.*

PAUL GRAY

On the surface, it would appear that Frazier does not exactly knock himself out with work. In fact, he confirms this impression, openly admitting to lallygagging on the job. In the first sentence of "**An Angler at Heart**" [included in *Nobody Better, Better Than Nobody*], he confesses that he has often "taken a walk from the offices of *The New Yorker* along Forty-third Street—across Fifth Avenue, across Madison Avenue, across Vanderbilt Avenue—then through Grand Central Terminal, across Lexington Avenue, up to Forty-fourth Street, into the elevator at 141 East Forty-fourth Street, up to the third floor, and through the belled door of a small fishing-tackle shop called the Angler's Roost, whose sole proprietor is a man named Jim Deren.''

Having found a bucolic niche in the heart of midtown Manhattan, Frazier eases himself into a story that is partly a profile of Deren, a guru to flycasters the world over and the ''greatest man I know of who will talk to just anybody off the street.'' The author also digresses into a three-page list of the inventory in Deren's store and reminisces about his own fishing experiences and misadventures: ''The woman told me to hold still and the dog wouldn't bite me. I held still, and the dog bit me in the right shoulder. I told the woman that the dog was biting me.''

Frazier approaches his subjects like a man who does not want to move too fast and frighten them away. In [''**Nobody Better, Better Than Nobody**''], he decides to find out a little something about Poncé Cruse Evans, the woman who writes the syndicated column ''Hints from Heloise.'' This involves, for some reason, driving from Chicago to San Antonio, where Evans lives. ''In Muskogee, Oklahoma,'' Frazier confides, ''I saw a Taco Hut, a Taco Bell, and a Taco Tico.'' Then he has to find a suitable motel (''I wanted a locally owned one'') and assess his impressions so far: ''I had not been in Texas long before I started having millions of insights about the difference between Texas and the rest of America. I was going to write these insights down, but then I thought—Nahhh.''

The astonishing thing is that Frazier does come up with a detailed profile of Evans and her mother, who founded the column and whose name really was Heloise. . . .

This episode ends happily, and so do all of Frazier's stories. The reader winds up laughing and knowing a great deal about subjects—bears in northwestern Montana, a pair of madcap Soviet émigré artists—that most people can live without. The author's loopy laziness is a pose; he works carefully and hard to make everything look like fun.

Paul Gray, ''Lallygagging,'' in Time, *New York, Vol. 129, No. 21, May 25, 1987, p. 67.*

Jean Genet

1910-1986

French dramatist, novelist, and poet.

Among the most controversial and innovative of the generation of French authors that included Jean-Paul Sartre, Albert Camus, and Jean Cocteau, Genet is best known for his surreal poetic dramas in which he utilizes the stage as a communal arena for enacting bizarre fantasies involving dominance and submission, sex, and death. Genet, whom Cocteau dubbed France's "Black Prince of letters," is linked to such amoral, antitraditional writers as the Marquis de Sade and Charles Baudelaire by his use of rich, baroque imagery, his deliberate inversion of traditional Western moral values, and his belief that spiritual glory may be attained through the pursuit of evil. Although Genet first won international recognition for his lyrical novels about prison life, most critics contend that his dramas represent the most refined synthesis of his characteristic style and themes.

Abandoned as a child by his mother, a prostitute, to a state orphanage run by the French Assistance Publique, Genet was sent to a reformatory for boys at an early age for stealing. There he embraced the role of convict and devoted himself to crime, subsequently spending much of his youth and young adult life in European prisons for such offenses as theft, smuggling, and male prostitution. While in prison, Genet turned to writing. In 1948, he was deemed unreformable and threatened with life imprisonment by the French judicial system. Sartre and Cocteau, who discovered Genet's novels in the early 1940s, interceded, however, and with the aid of other prominent literary spokesmen obtained for Genet a pardon from French President Vincent Auriol. Genet never again returned to prison.

Genet's novels, which are fraught with exotic imagery and metaphors, French argot, and scatological language, all take the form of nonchronological, semi-autobiographical narratives which alternate between the first and third person. According to Richard Howard, Genet's novels "are the great affair in his career primarily because they are the first and perhaps the only texts to set forth for the Western imagination an explicit realization of homosexual eros." By rejecting the morality of what he perceives to be a repressive, hypocritical society which punishes its least powerful social castes for crimes universal to all classes of humanity, Genet seeks to create in his literature what Sartre termed in his influential study, *Saint Genet: Actor and Martyr,* "a black ethic, with precepts and rules, pitiless constraints, a Jansenism of evil." In his first novel, *Notre dame des fleurs* (1942; *Our Lady of the Flowers*), Genet inverts traditional Western values to replace ideals of goodness with ideals of evil, courage with cowardice, love with betrayal. Thus, evil is transformed into good, suffering into joy, and shame into glory. The book, described by Sartre as "the epic of masturbation," was written beneath a blanket in Genet's cell at the prison of La Fresne. Through his fantasies, Genet describes the loving revenge of a submissive homosexual prisoner, Divine, on his dominant pimps and cellmates, Darling and Our Lady, whom he resents supporting through male prostitution. Genet ultimately deems Divine's betrayal of Our Lady, a murderer Divine delivers to prison officials for execution, to be a tribute to supreme evil. By betraying his lover, Divine is

© *Jerry Bauer*

able to identify with both victim and executioner and to assume the universal burden of criminal responsibility.

In Genet's universe, to sin against the bourgeois moral order through theft, rape, or murder is to bring moral censure upon oneself; through a socially imposed sentence of death or imprisonment, the criminal is martyred by society and may thus attain the rank of sainthood. This proposition is explored in Genet's second novel, *Miracle de la rose* (1946; *Miracle of the Rose*). Written in La Sante and La Tourrelle prisons in 1943, the book describes in lyrical terms Genet's conversion from a submissive feminine "chicken" at the boy's reformatory of the Colonie de Mettray to a dominant, masculine homosexual at the prison at Fontrevault, where he is later imprisoned for theft. The novel's symbolism assumes religious dimensions as Genet professes his love for both the prison's vicious medieval atmosphere and for Harcamone, a young man driven to random acts of violence and murder whom Genet envisions emerging as a saint on the day of his execution. Keith Botsford called *Miracle of the Rose* "a deliberately lyrical and literary novel, the rose of the title being at once the anus, love and death, a perversion of our normal ethic and esthetic of the true, good, and beautiful."

Genet's later novels do not utilize prison settings or themes. *Querelle de Brest* (1947; *Querelle of Brest*) is a light *nouveau roman,* or antinovel, in which a ship's steward commits a series of devious crimes before escaping from his author and becoming his "own, singular being." *Journal du voleur* (1948; *The Thief's Journal*) describes Genet's experiences in the criminal underworld of Spain, Belgium, and other European countries in the 1930s. In his last novel, *Pompes funèbres* (1953; *Funeral Rites*), Genet addresses the moral question of how he may mourn for his dead lover, a French Resistance fighter killed in 1944 by a Nazi collaborator, without rescinding his opposition to traditional ethics. By creating his own ceremony as an antisocial act and by offering himself sexually first to his lover, then to his lover's murderer, and finally to members of the Nazi militia, Genet effectively defies the existing moral order while identifying with the suffering of his dead lover.

For Genet, the theater offered the most effective literary form for the incantatory expression of dream and ritual. His early plays, while true to the inverted universe detailed in his novels, reflect the influence of Sartre's drama *No Exit* and his dictum, "Hell is other people," in their stylized and abstract portrayals of inescapable personal rivalries. Genet's first produced play, *Les bonnes* (1947; *The Maids*), was based on the actual murder of an upper-class mistress by her female servants. In this ritualistic drama of uncertain identities, two sisters assume the roles of sadistic employer and submissive maid in enacting their fantasies of power and revenge. When their attempts to kill their real mistress fail, the sisters must satisfy themselves with killing her image, and the play ends with the dominant sister committing suicide as her submissive counterpart reads a eulogy. This conclusion echoes Genet's contention, expressed in *The Thief's Journal,* that "acts must be carried through to their completion. Whatever the point of departure, the end will be beautiful." Genet blends naturalism and fantasy in *Haute surveillance* (1949; *Deathwatch*), about the ritualistic efforts of a petty criminal, trapped in a cell with two killers, to achieve the saintly designation of murderer. Because, unlike his cellmates, he has not killed without reason or motive, he is ridiculed for his immoral inferiority.

Genet's later plays center increasingly on the illusory nature of social roles as well as on the rituals of the theater and their relationship to reality. These works, which are generally regarded as Genet's masterpieces, reveal the influence of Antonin Artaud's Theater of Cruelty in their emphasis on violence and sadism and make use of such theatrical devices as mirrors, masks, exaggerated costumes, and choreographed gestures to reveal symbolic meaning. The protagonist of *Le balcon* (1956; *The Balcony*), is Madame Irma, the opportunistic proprietess of a brothel known as the Grand Balcony, where clients act out their fantasies of authority, sex, and power. As a revolution occurs offstage, Irma's clients assume the roles of bishop, judge, general, and police chief; they are subsequently persuaded by government officials to assume their fantasy roles in public to restore order among the populace. As the old regime retains its power through these new leaders, Madame Irma's establishment comes to represent a microcosm of society in which her client's fantasies emerge as reality. According to Robert Brustein, *The Balcony* is based on Genet's "understanding that since revolution is dedicated to the destruction of artifice, its greatest enemy is playacting."

Uncertain and changing identities are again central to *Les nègres: Clownerie* (1959; *The Blacks: A Clown Show*). In this drama, fantasies of racial revenge are enacted by black actors, half of whom, painted in whiteface and occupying the stage's highest point, represent white society as blacks view them—pompous, hypocritical, and repressive. The remaining blacks are positioned at the stage's lowest point to reflect how they regard themselves and how white society views them. As a revolution rages offstage, the blacks enact the ritualized rape and murder of a white woman and escape to a cannibalistic existence in the jungle. Although the blacks overthrow their white oppressors, they finally reinstate the major authority figures of the previous government, illustrating that repressiveness and hypocrisy are not racially defined qualities. Genet's last play, *Les paravents* (1961; *The Screens*), his longest and most ambitious work for the theater, utilizes colonialism in North Africa as a metaphor for humanity's worst traits. Although Genet indirectly condemns France's involvement in the Algerian War, the drama is nonrevolutionary in intent. The major contribution of *The Screens* to contemporary drama lies in its innovative staging technique. As the scenes progress, settings are suggested by camera projections onto a series of folding screens or are sketched on canvases by actors.

Genet also wrote poetry in prison in the 1940s prior to creating his novels and dramas. "Condamné à mort," an elegy written after Genet's friend, Maurice Pilorge, was executed in 1939, is collected with the early love poem "Un chant d'amour" in *Poèmes* (1948).

(See also *CLC*, Vols. 1, 2, 5, 10, 14, 44; *Contemporary Authors,* Vols. 13-16, rev. ed.; *Contemporary Authors New Revision Series,* Vol. 18; and *Dictionary of Literary Biography Yearbook: 1986.*)

In this volume commentary on Jean Genet is focused on his novels.

JEAN-PAUL SARTRE

[*The essay from which this excerpt is taken was originally published in Sartre's study* Saint Genet: Comédien et martyr *in 1952.*]

Our Lady of the Flowers, which is often considered to be Genet's masterpiece, was written entirely in prison . . . in the solitude of the cell. The exceptional value of the work lies in its ambiguity. It appears at first to have only one subject, Fatality; the characters are puppets of destiny. But we quickly discover that this pitiless Providence is really the counterpart of a sovereign, indeed divine freedom, that of the author. **Our Lady of the Flowers** is the most pessimistic of books. With fiendish application it leads human creatures to downfall and death. And yet, in its strange language it presents this downfall as a triumph. The rogues and wretches of whom it speaks all seem to be heroes, to be of the elect. But what is far more astonishing is that the book itself is an act of the rashest optimism. (p. 447)

One is bored in a cell; boredom makes for amorousness. Genet masturbates: this is an act of defiance, a willful perversion of the sexual act; it is also, quite simply, an idiosyncrasy. The operation condenses the drifting reveries, which now congeal and disintegrate in the release of pleasure. No wonder **Our Lady** horrifies people: it is the epic of masturbation. The words which compose this book are those that a prisoner said to himself while panting with excitement, those with which he loaded himself, as with stones, in order to sink to the bottom of his reveries, those which were born of the dream itself and which are dream words, dreams of words. The reader will open

Our Lady of the Flowers, as one might open the cabinet of a fetishist, and find there, laid out on the shelves, like shoes that have been sniffed at and kissed and bitten hundreds of times, the damp and evil words that gleam with the excitement they arouse in another person and which we cannot feel. . . . There is only one subject: the pollutions of a prisoner in the darkness of his cell; only one hero: the masturbator; only one place: his "evil-smelling hole, beneath the coarse wool covers." (pp. 448-49)

This work of the mind is an organic product. It smells of bowels and sperm and milk. If it emits at times an odor of violets, it does so in the manner of decaying meat that turns into a preserve; when we poke it, the blood runs and we find ourselves in a belly, amidst gas bubbles and lumps of entrails. No other book, not even *Ulysses,* brings us into such close contact with an author. . . . This self-intimacy is traversed by an ideal separating surface, the page on which Genet writes *Our Lady of the Flowers.*

But, at the same time, this work is, without the author's suspecting it, the journal of a detoxication, of a conversion. In it Genet detoxicates himself of himself and turns to the outside world. In fact, this book *is* the detoxication itself. It is not content with bearing witness to the cure, but concretizes it. Born of a nightmare, it effects—line by line, page by page, from death to life, from the state of dream to that of waking, from madness to sanity—a passageway that is marked with relapses. *Before Our Lady,* Genet was an aesthete; *after* it, an artist. But at no moment was a decision *made* to achieve this conversion. The decision *is Our Lady.* Throughout *Our Lady* it both makes and rejects itself, observes and knows itself, is unaware of itself, plays tricks on itself and encumbers itself everywhere, even in the relapses. . . . At times the art of the tale aims only at bringing the narrator's excitement to its climax, and at times the artist makes the excitement he feels the pretext of his art. In any case, it is the artist who will win. Seeking excitement and pleasure, Genet starts by enveloping himself in his images, as the polecat envelops itself in its odor. These images call forth by themselves words that reinforce them; often they even remain incomplete; words are needed to finish the job; these words require that they be uttered and, finally, written down; writing calls forth and creates its audience; the onanistic narcissism ends by being stanched in words. (pp. 449-50)

Under his lice-ridden coverings, this recumbent figure ejects, like a starfish, a visceral and glandular world, then draws it back and dissolves it within itself. In this world, creatures wriggle about for a moment, are resorbed, reappear and disappear again: Darling, Our Lady, Gorgui, Gabriel, Divine. Genet relates their story, describes their features, shows their gestures. He is guided by only one factor, his state of excitement. These figures of fantasy must provoke erection and orgasm; if they do not, he rejects them. Their truth, their density, are measured solely by the effect they produce upon him.

Here is Divine. Divine is Genet himself, is "a thousand shapes, charming in their grace, [that] emerge from my eyes, mouth, elbows, knees, from all parts of me. They say to me: 'Jean, how glad I am to be living as Divine and to be living with Darling.'" Genet objectifies himself, as we all do in our dreams. As a sovereign creator, he cannot *believe* in the real existence of Darling; he believes in him through Divine. As Divine, he has the disturbing and voluptuous experience of aging; he "realizes" his dreadful fear of growing old. She is the only one of his creatures whom he does not desire; he makes her be

desired by the others. She excites him through Darling or Gorgui. Divine is an ambiguous character who serves both to bring his entire life into focus in the lucidity of his gaze and to let him plunge more deeply into sleep, to sink to the depths of a cozy horror, to drown in his opera.

The others—all the others, except the girl queens—are the creatures and objects of his feminine desires. The whole graceful procession of Pimps, those lovely vacant-eyed does, are the means he chooses for being petted, pawed, tumbled and entered. (p. 450)

To us who are not sexually excited, these creatures should be insipid. And yet they are not. Genet's desire gives them heat and light. If they were conceived in accordance with verisimilitude, they would perhaps have a more general truth, but they would lose that absurd and singular "presence" that comes from their being born of a desire. Precisely because *we* do not desire them, because they do not cease, in our eyes, to belong to another person's dream, they take on a strange and fleeting charm, like homely girls who we know are passionately loved and whom we look at hesitantly, vaguely tempted, while wondering: "But what does he see in her?" Darling and Divine will always baffle the "normal" reader, and the more they elude us, the more true we think them. In short, we are fascinated by someone else's loves.

As soon as the character is modeled, baked and trimmed, Genet launches him in situations which he evaluates according to the same rules. He is telling *himself* stories in order to please *himself.* Do the situation and the character harmonize? Yes and no. The author is the only one to decide whether or not they do. Or rather, it is not he who decides, but the capricious and blasé little fellow he carries between his thighs. Depending on Genet's mood of the moment, Darling will be victim or tyrant. The same male who cleaves the queens like a knife will stand naked and dirty before the guards who manhandle him. Does he lack coherence? Not at all. Amidst his metamorphoses he retains, without effort, a vital, ingrained identity that is more convincing than the studied unity of many fictional characters because it simply reflects the permanence of the desire it arouses. At times Genet submits to the Pimps, at times he betrays them in secret, dreaming that they are being whipped. But in order for his pleasure to have style and taste, those whom he adores and those who are whipped must be the *same.* The truth about Darling is that he is both the glamorous pimp and the humiliated little faggot. That is his coherence. (p. 452)

Genet shows everything. Since his only aim is to please himself, he sets down everything. He informs us of his erections that come to nothing just as he does of those that come off successfully. Thus, his characters have, like *real* men, a life *in action,* a life involving a range of possibilities. Life in action may be defined as the succession of images that have led Genet to orgasm. . . . The possibilities, on the other hand, are all the images that he has caressed without attaining orgasm. Thus, unlike *our* possibilities, which are the acts that we can and, quite often, do perform, these fictional possibilities represent simply the missed opportunities, the permission that Genet pitilessly refuses his creatures. He once said to me: "My books are not novels, because none of my characters make decisions on their own." This is particularly true of *Our Lady* and accounts for the book's desolate, desertlike aspect. Hope can cling only to free and active characters. Genet, however, is concerned only with satisfying his cruelty. All his characters are inert, are knocked about by fate. The author is a barbaric god who revels in human sacrifice. This is what Genet himself calls the ''Cruelty of the Creator.'' He kicks Divine toward saintliness. The unhappy girl queen undergoes her ascesis in an agony. . . . Moreover, the author himself, that owl who says ''I'' in the heart of his darkness, hardly comes off any better. We shall see him strike and dominate Bulkaen, or slowly get over the death of Jean Decarnin. Later, Jean Genet will become ''the wiliest hoodlum,'' Ulysses. For the time being, he is lying on his back, paralyzed. He is passively waiting for a judge to decide his fate. He . . . is in danger of being sent to a penal colony for life. Yes, *Our Lady of the Flowers* is a dream. Only in dreams do we find this dreadful passivity. (pp. 454-55)

Yet, by the same movement that chains him, in his work, to these drifting, rudderless creatures, [Genet] frees himself, shakes off his reverie and transforms himself into a creator. *Our Lady* is a dream that contains its own awakening.

The reason is that the imagination depends on words. Words complete our fantasies, fill in their gaps, support their inconsistency, prolong them, enrich them with what cannot be seen or touched. (p. 455)

Here and there we come upon sentences which seem to have been written without a pause and which give the impression that Genet, completely taken up with lulling his dream, has not reread what he has set down. Certain sentences limp because they have not been looked after; they are children that have been made to walk too soon: ''I might, just as she herself did to me, confide that if I take contempt with a smile or a burst of laughter, it is not yet—and will it be some day?—out of scorn for contempt, but rather it is in order not to be ridiculous, not to be reviled by anything or anyone, that I have abased myself lower than dirt.''. . . [At] this level the words are inductors with relation to each other; they attract and engender one another, in accordance with grammatical habits, within an unheeding consciousness that wants only to weep tears over itself. The sentence takes shape all by itself; it is the dream. But immediately afterward, Genet writes, parenthetically: ''I left out the *d* in blindly, I wrote 'blinly.''' This time he reflects *on the sentence,* hence on his activity as a writer. It is no longer the love of Divine and Darling that is the object of his reflection, but the slip of his sentence and of his hand. This error in spelling draws his attention to the meaning of the sentence. He contemplates it, discovers it and decides: ''Divine will take up this phrase to apply it to Our Lady of the Flowers.'' This time we feel we are reading a passage from *The Journal of Crime and Punishment* or *The Journal of The Counterfeiters.* A perfectly lucid writer is informing us of his projects, goes into detail about his creative activities. Genet awakens; Darling in turn becomes a pure and imaginary object. . . . In the end [Genet] seems to merge with himself as the pure will that keeps the fantasies well in hand, for he writes, with sudden tranquillity:

> It is Darling whom I cherish the most, for you realize that, in the last analysis, it is my own destiny, whether true or false, that I am laying (at times a rag, at times a court robe) on Divine's shoulders. Slowly but surely I want to strip her of every kind of happiness so as to make a saint of her. . . . A morality is being born, which is certainly not the usual morality. . . . And I, gentler than a wicked angel, lead her by the hand.

But this very detachment seems suspect. Why plume oneself on it, why bring it to our attention? Is it that he wants to shock us? Where does the truth lie? Nowhere. This lucid dreamer, this ''wicked angel,'' retains within himself, in a kind of undifferentiated state, the masturbator, the creator, the masochist who tortures himself by proxy, the serene and pitiless god who plots the fate of his creatures and the sadist who has turned writer in order to be able to torture them more and whose detachment is merely a sham. *Our Lady* is what certain psychiatrists call a ''controlled waking dream,'' one which is in constant danger of breaking up or diverging under the pressure of emotional needs and which an artist's reflective intelligence constantly pulls back into line, governing and directing it in accordance with principles of logic and standards of beauty. By itself, the story becomes plodding, tends toward stereotypes, breaks up as soon as it ceases to excite its author, contradicts itself time and again, is enriched with odd details, meanders off, drifts, bogs down, suddenly reappears, lingers over trivial scenes, skips essential ones, drops back to the past, rushes years ahead, spreads an hour over a hundred pages, condenses a month into ten lines, and then suddenly there is a burst of activity that pulls things together, brings them into line and explains the symbols. Just when we think we are under the covers, pressed against the warm body of the masturbator, we find ourselves outside again, participating in the stony power of the demiurge. This development of onanistic themes gradually becomes an introspective exploration. The emotional pattern begets the image, and in the image Genet, like an analyst, discovers the emotional pattern. His thought crystallizes before his eyes; he reads it, then completes and clarifies it. Whereupon reflection is achieved, in its translucent purity, as *knowledge* and as *activity.* (pp. 461-63)

Genet, like all great writers, is a storyteller, and we shall find in *Our Lady* several accounts of specific and dated events, for example the murder of old Ragon or the trial of Our Lady of the Flowers. . . . Genet, who is both a realist and an idealist, shows himself in his accounts to be both an empiricist and a Platonist. These accounts offer at first the resistance and irrational opacity of the event only to be metamorphosed all at once into classifications and descriptions of essence. In Plato, the hierarchy of ideas represents the immutable truth; the myth introduces time, space and movement into this calm sphere. In Genet, the relations are reversed, but in any case it is art, art alone which, in both writers, links truth to the myth. Art alone enables *Our Lady of the Flowers* to be both the ''golden legend'' and the botany of the ''underworld.'' It is art that gives this tear- and sperm-soaked manuscript the air of being a ''Mirror of the World.'' G. K. Chesterton said that the modern world is full of Christian ideas run wild. *Our Lady of the Flowers* would surely have confirmed him in his view. It is an ''Itinerary of the soul toward God,'' the author of which, run wild, takes himself for the Creator of the universe. Every object in it speaks to us of Genet as every being in the cosmos of St. Bonaventura speaks to us of God. Sabunde, following Lully, declares that the Creation ''is a book,'' that God ''has given us two books,'' that of Holy Scriptures and that of Nature. Genet reverses the terms. For him, the Book is the Creation of the World; Nature and the Holy Scriptures are one and the same. This is not surprising since, in his view, words contain within themselves the substantial reality of things. The being of the thief is contained in the name ''thief.'' Hence, the being of trees and flowers, of animals and men, is contained in the words that designate them. For the medieval philosophers, ''life is only a pilgrimage to God: the physical world is the road that leads us to Him. The beings along the way are signs, signs that may at first seem puzzling to us, but if we examine them carefully, faith, with the aid of reason, will decipher, behind characters that are always different, a single word, a call that is always the same: God.'' Replace God by Genet and you have the universe of *Our Lady of the Flowers,* whose only reason for being is to express Genet—who has written only in order to be read by Genet—and to recall him constantly to love of Genet. (pp. 474-75)

Since the pariah and God are alike external to nature, it will suffice for the pariah, in his cell, to dare invent being: he will be God. Genet creates in order to enjoy his infinite power. However, his too-human finiteness makes it impossible for him to conjure up the celestial sphere and the globe in the detailed distinctness of their parts; he sees the world as a big, dark mass, as a dim jumble of stars, *as a background.* Genet fakes; unable to follow the royal progression of Creation, he creates his heroes *first* so as to introduce *afterward* into each of them a primordial and constituent relation to the universe. (p. 479)

To us, this overweening pride and reckless unhappiness often seem exquisitely naïve. The just man, immersed in his community, determines each individual's importance, including his own, by means of an infinite system of reference in which each man serves as a measure for all and each. . . . But Genet, who is shut in, has no point of comparison. If he serves a two-year sentence, he is equidistant from Brazil and the Place Pigalle, that is, two years away. He does not touch the earth; he soars above it. Since he is equally absent from everything, his imagination is omnipresent; he is not in space. Every object therefore takes on for him the dimensions his fancy confers upon it, and these dimensions are *absolute,* that is, they are not given as a relationship of the object with other objects but as the immediate relationship of the thing to its creator. They can increase or diminish without those of the other varying, and since Genet wishes to ignore the severe and disagreeable laws of perspective—which are all right for the free citizens of French society—a hoodlum in Montmartre and a star in the sky seem to him equally close. . . . This ghastly book has at times the naïve poetry of the early astrolabes and maps of the world. Against a background of oceans, mountains or fields of stars appear animals and persons,—the Scorpion, the Ram, Gemini—all of the same size, all equally alone. But this strange freshness is only an appearance. We sense behind it the maniacal will—which has become exacerbated in prison—to regard the Nay as the symbol of the Yea and the Nought as the symbol of the All. Precisely because he feels lost ''when confronted with the universe,'' he wants to delude himself into thinking that he is creating the universe. . . . The God of the Middle Ages wrote ''the book of creatures'' to reveal his existence to man, his only reader. Similarly with Genet: his ''book of creatures'' is *Our Lady of the Flowers,* and he intends it for only one reader, only one man, himself. By their suffering and purity, Our Lady and Darling, saints and martyrs, bear witness before this wonderstruck man to his Divine existence.

So Genet has become God in reverie. He creates the world and man in his image; he manipulates the elements, space, light-years; he has gone quite mad. But the awakening is contained in the dream, for in the depths of his delirium this imaginary creator of Reality connects with himself as a real creator of an imaginary world. His feeling of omnipotence leaves him with a taste of bitterness and ashes. His characters are too docile; the objects he describes are both blinding and too pallid. Everything collapses, everything ends; only the words remain. . . . It is not through their self-sufficiency that the creatures escape their creator, but through their nullity. Genet and Jouhandeau, ambushed in Nothingness, hoped to avoid the gaze of God,

who sees only Being. Their fictions play the same trick on them. Owing to the modicum of reality that Genet communicates to her, Divine *is Genet.* She merges with him; she dissolves into a kind of turbidity, into moistness and swoons. She can *be Divine* only insofar as she is not Genet, that is, insofar as she is *absolutely nothing.*

Thus, the characters in *Our Lady of the Flowers,* born, for the most part, of Genet's fancy, change into quiet exigencies; they will live only if he believes in them. Genet the creator therefore calls Genet the reader to the rescue, wants him to read and be taken in by the phantasmagoria. But Genet cannot read his work; he is too aware that he has put into it what he wanted to find in it, and he can find nothing in it precisely because he cannot forget what he has put into it. So long as he fondled them in reverie, the figures seemed domesticated and familiar; when they are set down on paper, they are reproaches, shadows that can neither take on flesh and blood nor vanish, and that beg *to be.* . . . And since Genet is powerless to animate them, to confer *objectivity* upon them, they beg to exist for all, through all. If the ''book of creatures'' was composed in order to tell men about God, there had to be a God to write it and men to read it, and Genet cannot be God and man at the same time. Now that his dreams are written down, he is no longer either God or man, and he has no other way of regaining his lost divinity than to manifest himself to men. These fictions will assume a new objectivity for him if he obliges others to believe in them. And at the core of all his characters is the same categorical imperative: ''Since you don't have faith enough to believe in us, you must at least make others adopt us and must convince them that we exist.'' In writing out, for his pleasure, the incommunicable dreams of his particularity, Genet has transformed them into exigencies of communication. (pp. 479-81)

Jean-Paul Sartre, in his Saint Genet: Actor and Martyr, *translated by Bernard Frechtman, George Braziller, 1963, 625 p.*

LIONEL ABEL

Our Lady of the Flowers, Genet's first novel, written in the prison of La Fresne, and certainly a masterpiece—the greatest novel, I should say, since Faulkner was great—is also, to my mind, the book of Genet which best reveals his style of thinking. It is a style of thinking which derives its order and assumptions from the ''I''—the style first taught by Descartes.

I have chosen, though, to connect Genet with Descartes through still another writer—one not too well known in this country, but perhaps the greatest and most original of all Cartesians, and who has the advantage, for me, at least, of being, like Genet, a modern: the philosopher Edmund Husserl. Now it may seem strange to compare a purely theoretical work like Husserl's *Cartesian Meditations,* composed mainly of lectures he gave at the Sorbonne, with any novel, let alone a novel apparently at such a remove from questions of theory as the one written by Jean Genet in the prison of La Fresne. However, the efforts of Husserl and Genet are not at all dissimilar. About the *Meditations:* In this work the German thinker attempted the perhaps impossible task of scaffolding our common world on the structures of the solitary ego; he tried to set up, within the confines of the self, a world shared, or sharable, with other selves—on which public world, in turn, all scientific communication could rest. Now Husserl's effort has been called a failure. Was not his common world rather like the brothel designed by Leonardo, which each client could enter and quit without the risk of meeting any other client? For there seems little "danger" of the ego's meeting another ego in the maze of Husserl's *Meditations*. Just the same it remains one of the seminal works of this century. (p. 7)

Our Lady of the Flowers is not a failure. But what I must explain is how this novel about homosexuals and criminals suggests comparison with Husserl's *Meditations*. The German thinker began with solipsism. Genet, isolated on his prison bed, begins, as radically, with narcissism: Genet is masturbating. And in order to make masturbation effective he calls up images of the pimps, whores, and criminals he has known or imagined himself to be. . . . Sartre [see excerpt above] calls the novel "the epic of masturbation." I cannot agree. The novel is purely lyrical, and the word "epic" gives, I think, a wrong impression of it: an erection is brief, an epic long-lasting. Moreover, the book is not *about* masturbation; it is about all those figures Genet could make real to himself while masturbating. Masturbation was his aim and end: but it was also his method and means; by it he elaborated his personal world into one he could share sexually with others, and finally into the actual social world of criminals and homosexuals, male whores and pimps, which he had known. This world, to my knowledge, has never before been described by any writer: Genet in his novel constitutes it for us almost out of his own substance; in any case, out of the very substantial sexual pleasure he took in remembering and contemplating it. Thus it is that the social world of homosexuals and criminals in *Our Lady of the Flowers* has a freshness, a spontaneity—a sweetness, even—scarcely approached by those novelists who describe the world "objectively."

But did not Proust begin as radically, with his own impressions, and constitute, out of his sensations and memories, the French society of his time? Proust did indeed begin with his impressions, but out of these he wrought only those characters who could move him deeply; the French society of his time he described objectively. Often Proust reads like Balzac. Now Genet—at least in *Our Lady of the Flowers*—never reads like Balzac, but always like Genet: even when describing "objectively" the criminal and homosexual hierarchy he knew, Genet always seems most intent on remembering his own homosexuality, his own crimes.

It may be asked: If Husserl could not make of the private self the architect of a world with others in it, then how was Genet on his narcissist's couch able to construct such a world? Can it be said that Genet, the novelist, succeeded where Husserl, the philosopher failed? Let me make myself clear on this point: *Our Lady of the Flowers,* though a beautiful book, does not merit comparison with such works as *The Human Comedy, War and Peace,* and *The Red and the Black.* And Genet's novel would have to be as inclusive and universal as these to seriously challenge "objective" thinking—even in literature. I do claim for Genet that in *Our Lady of the Flowers* he created out of his narcissism a world with others in it. But this world is subject to a severe limitation: the others whom Genet is able to reach out to narcissistically are essentially narcissists themselves, as strictly separated from one another as Genet is from them. But Genet has this very great strength: the only world he wants to describe is the only world he can describe subjectively, the world of criminals and pederasts. To deal with any wider forms of social life he would have to attenuate, by objectifying, his method of description.

I have said that Genet's *Our Lady* is lyrical: it is necessarily that given its method of composition. The fable or plot of the book is suggested at the outset by an image:

> . . . I wanted to swallow myself by opening my mouth very wide and turning it over my head so that it would take in my whole body, and then the universe, until all that would remain of me would be a ball of eaten thing which little by little would be annihilated: This is how I see the end of the world.

Let me designate Genet's lyricism more precisely. It is that of the *passive* homosexual, as will be seen if one compares the image cited above with an image from Lautréaumont which expresses the feeling of the homosexual who is *active*.

> Oh that the universe were an immense celestial anus! I would plunge my penis past its bloody sphincter, rending apart, with my impetuous motion, the very bones of the pelvis.

The action of the novel is one of revenge: the revenge of Divine, a passive homosexual, on Darling and Our Lady, active pimps Divine loves—and supports by whoring. Darling is a thief as well as a pimp and Our Lady has the special glamor of being wanted for murder. The motive for revenge is "normal" jealousy made drastic by Divine's feeling of inferiority at being unable to play a male role. Darling finds another whore; Divine manages to get him arrested. And when Our Lady unexpectedly submits to the Negro Gorgui in front of Divine, the latter, despairing of sex, attracts the police. Our Lady is sentenced to the guillotine. But my point is that the lyrical passage about swallowing the world, which expresses Divine's passivity, is written into the very plot of the narrative, and is also indistinguishable from Divine's motives. The image can no more be separated from the rhythm of the story than the images of a poem from what it says.

Does Genet succeed in creating real characters? Divine, the balding male whore, who, when provoked by the assembled queens to prove that he is truly regal, takes out his denture and places it on his head (Genet remarks that it took much more grandeur of soul to replace the denture) is certainly a true, and even a great, character. Of course, Divine, as Sartre has pointed out, is a projection of Genet. But did the novelist create even one character in this book who is not a projection of himself? Without at least one such character, *Our Lady of the Flowers* would be a failure, even taking into account its limited scope. But Our Lady, the murderer, is no projection of Genet. He is less interesting than Divine, and has less psychological depth, but what Our Lady says and does has the surprisingness of a person we find real, in fiction or in life. When at Our Lady's trial the judge asks him: "Why did you kill?" the murderer replies: "I was fabulously broke." This is an answer which was surely not dictated by the author to his character. Narcissism does have creative resources, though Genet is probably the first author since Sade to have tapped them fully.

No doubt most of Genet's characters are roles the author has played or wanted to play. And here we see the limits of his theater, which relies not on character as we normally understand it, but on the different roles played by persons who apart from their roles would be quite interchangeable. What distinguishes Claire from Solange in Genet's play *The Maids*? Only the special roles they have decided to play. They even exchange names. And are not the Judge, the Bishop, and the General in *The Balcony* virtually the same? They differ only when they have put on their particular costumes and gotten up on stilts. Sometimes Genet writes as if other persons were real only when invested by him with some special authority. In fact, I think it must be very hard for him to think of anyone but himself as real. In *Our Lady of the Flowers,* though, I think Genet has made his greatest effort to give independent life to others and to treat them as more than actors in his own drama. This is his most realistic work.

Genet has written three other novels: *The Miracle of the Rose, Funeral Rites,* and *Querelle of Brest.* All are extraordinary and should be translated. But I think only one of them, *Funeral Rites,* is comparable in quality to *Our Lady of the Flowers,* and this is the only other novel by Genet in which he relies as radically on what I have called his "Cartesian" thought. *The Miracle of the Rose* and *Querelle of Brest* are at times subjective, and at times objective in the manner of other novelists. Only in *Our Lady of the Flowers* and in *Funeral Rites* does Genet's subjectivity, pushed to the point of paroxysm, donate whatever objectivity they have to others, things, and the environing world. I am not going to claim that the characters in *Funeral Rites* are very real. They are essentially roles, more so even than the lesser figures in *Our Lady of the Flowers,* and in *Funeral Rites* there is no social world, not even one like the world of pimps and queens Genet described in his first book. But the problem with which *Funeral Rites* begins is a genuine, even a "social" and "objective," problem: How mourn for the dead? Jean D., Genet's lover to whom the novel is dedicated, was a member of the French Resistance and had been killed by a French militiaman. With what ceremony should the living Jean grieve for the dead Jean D.? The whole novel, in fact, is nothing but the elaborate study of what such a ceremony might be.

A ceremony is a social act. Genet in *Funeral Rites* creates his own ceremony out of his own subjective needs, just as in *Our Lady of the Flowers* he created a whole social world in order to pleasure himself sexually. The ceremony Genet invents for mourning his lover is very peculiar, most perverse. Jean, Jean's lover, has been killed, as I said, by a French militiaman. The funeral has not yet taken place. And the living Jean, wondering how to mourn for the dead, goes to the cinema and there sees a newsreel fight between members of the French Resistance and French supporters of Pétain. Jean sees a young French patriot killed by a young French pro-Nazi; he imagines that the man killed is his lover, Jean, and has an immediate impulse to give himself to the killer. This fantasy is pursued throughout the novel, in which there is much about German pricks. In an imaginative flight, Jean thinks of the prick of Eric Seiler, a particularly brutal Nazi, who had begun his career as the lover of the headsman of Berlin, as the V-I protecting Hitler himself. In fantasy throughout the novel Genet is buggered in his own person—or in the person of French thugs or pro-Nazis with whom he identifies himself—by brutal Germans; at the end of the novel by Eric Seiler. Is this a way of mourning for a hero of the Resistance, a man valued for patriotic virtue? Or did Genet hate his lover for having this virtue which he himself did not possess? Genet identified himself, as he makes perfectly clear, with those French supporters of Hitler who took Nazi orders simply to get revolvers in their hands. So Genet could hardly mourn sincerely as a Frenchman for his lover. Moreover, Genet is a narcissist; his grief to be sincere had to be avowedly a narcissist's. And how does a narcissist grieve for the death of another? Would he not have to have died himself in order to understand the meaning of a funeral rite? But at the end of his book Genet makes clear what his ceremony really is and must be. The living Jean will eat the dead Jean, at least in fantasy; and the fantastic giving of himself to the dead Jean's killers is a mere preliminary to the real fantasy: the ceremonial

eating of the dead Jean. This is the great moment of the novel and Genet's description is magnificent. Personal, sexual, and religious feeling, half hidden from one another in most of us are called up imperiously by the author's words and united by them into a mighty spell. . . . (pp. 7-8)

Certainly this imaginary rite will disgust many readers. But I would ask them to consider what ways are at their disposal for giving ceremony to their grief for the dead. No doubt the funeral ceremonies of the established religions were at one time the result of some genuine subjective thought or feeling. But our sensibilities are quite different now from the sensibilities of those who invented the rites which we still entrust our feelings to. Who has not wanted to invent his own ceremony, be it of grief or of joy? I do not like Genet's way of mourning, but it does seem to me a real one, created out of his own substance. All the same this creation of a rite, though something more than a subjective act, is not equal in my view to the creation of a world shared with others, a world with the warmth and spontaneity of a real society. So remarkable rhetorically and spiritually as is *Funeral Rites,* I cannot place it on the same level with *Our Lady of the Flowers.*

I must add, too, that Genet's plays—*Deathwatch, The Maids, The Screens*—even *The Balcony* and *The Blacks*—seem inferior to me as intellectual efforts to *Our Lady of the Flowers* and *Funeral Rites.* Possibly the theater and its needs have imposed on Genet too many objective problems; his thought proceeds most surely when he begins with his intimate feelings and out of these tries to construct the world. But who knows? Perhaps some day this writer will give us a thoroughly Cartesian play. In any case, is it not remarkable that centuries after the death of Descartes, a male whore and hoodlum, speaking Descartes's language and using his method, should have given life to the novel, once the chief glory of French letters—and which without Genet's efforts would be moribund in France today. (p. 8)

Lionel Abel, "The Genius of Jean Genet," in The New York Review of Books, *Vol. 1, No. 4, October 17, 1963, pp. 7-8.*

BRIGID BROPHY

[*The essay from which this excerpt is taken was originally published in* London Magazine, *June, 1964.*]

The first thing to realise (and Sartre, it seems, *doesn't* realise the first thing—or most of those that come after) is that Genet virtually *is* Baudelaire. Not that he's—except in the deliberate re-reverberations—an imitator. *Being* Baudelaire means being as original as Baudelaire. Genet is, however, a Baudelaire of the twentieth century, with the result that he writes finer poetry in prose than in verse. **"Le Condamné"** is tinged with Reading Gaolery. It is the prose of *Notre-Dame des Fleurs* which defines and realises the most cogent mythology of poetic images since Baudelaire's. (p. 296)

The fashion for scarcely noticing Genet's imagery is set by Sartre, who stands sentinel over this edition in a long introduction [see excerpt of original essay above]. . . . True, Sartre has a section headed "The Images"; but he turns out to mean things like Genet's 'will-to-unify', his desire to '*verify* his *conceptualism*' and his Platonism—which 'one would think . . . at times' is 'a kind of Aristotelianism'. He is noble and grotesque, this impresario who, apparently blind and deaf to the talents of his prodigy, nonetheless intuitively—and generously—feels there is *something* in him, and goes stumbling round and round while he tries to think what on earth it can be. (Brilliance of metaphor, melody of language—you can shout the answers; but he only turns in another muddled circle, trying with good will to catch what you're saying.) There he stands, the gangling and admirable professor, goggling through his global spectacles, making lunges with his butterfly net—and above him swoops, sombre and solid, dazzling in smoothed black-and-white marble, a vast, wing-spread, baroque angel of death.

Genet's images are all of death: to be more precise, all of funerals. His is the imagery of the *chapelle ardente*. It is in seductively beautiful bad taste. The book starts with a shrine of faces torn from the illustrated papers, photographs Genet has stuck to the wall of his prison cell and whom he takes as his imaginary lovers when he masturbates. . . . All these handsome young men are murderers who have been executed. The heads, cut off in the photographs, have in fact been cut off by the guillotine. For 'the most purely criminal' of them Genet has made frames—'using the same beads with which the prisoners next door make funeral wreaths'. The form of the book is the stringing together of images into a funeral wreath. It is part meditation, part memory, part masturbation. The whole book is, according to Sartre, 'the epic of masturbation', but epic it is not: it is *not* a story, though it includes episodes of masterly narrative; and it is about sainthood, not heroism. (pp. 297-98)

Calling the book an epic, Sartre has ignored the information Genet gives: 'I raised egoistic masturbation to the dignity of a cult.' The whole nature of the book is stated in the *cult*. Genet does everything, strings his entire wreath, with—in the Catholic sense—an intention. . . . The book begins and ends with the death of Divine: in between, she has betrayed herself to the police for a minor crime, and a murderer has betrayed himself and been executed. Genet is having a masturbation fantasy, but he is also dedicating an altar. As he tells us at the start, meditating before his shrine of assassins, 'c'est en l'honneur de leurs crimes que j'écris mon livre.'

Noticing the insistence on hosts and masses, and the tributary garland of the title itself (in fact Notre-Dame des Fleurs is the name of the handsomest young murderer), Sartre mistakes the psychology of religious observance for religious faith, leaps at the notion of the ages of faith and hammers in his introduction at the idea of a medieval Genet. It is a ghastly howler, of the sort liable to be made by the tone-deaf. Anyone with an ear for a style—any antique dealer or auctioneer—could have told Sartre Genet is baroque. His essence is that he's post-Counter-Reformation. . . . Like the 'litanies' and the 'ex-voto dans le goût espagnol' of Baudelaire's vocabulary, Genet's is the over-blown, peony-sized language of devotional flowers that did not come into existence until faith had been challenged from outside. It is necessary, precisely, to *counter* the Reformation: you must screw your eyes tight shut and *exclude* the outside world—that is, you must *induce* the images.

As it happens, faith has been emptied out from this tight-shut imaginary world. The idiom of rites and cults is employed to induce a state not of grace but of mind. Genet says nothing about religion, either way. It is his literature, not his faith, that is Catholic. Linguistically and psychologically, the idiom of the erotic and the idiom of the religious are the same; therefore the two are wholly the same for Genet, who is utterly a psychological linguist. When Notre-Dame des Fleurs is . . . penetrated by Mignon . . . , he is Bernini's St Teresa pierced to the heart of ecstasy by an angelic spear. . . . The *cambrioleur*

is interchangeable with the saint. The confessional is interchangeable with the outdoor lavatory in the country (in both places 'the most secret part of human beings came to reveal itself'). . . . For Genet, the essential item throughout is that rites are performed with an intention, gestures are, like masses, offered—whom or what for is not the point. First, induce the images. When they exist to be dedicated, you can offer them to whom you will, just as the 'thou' of a sonnet can be equated with whatever initials you care to write at the top.

Sartre is for once construing Genet right when he traces to masturbation fantasies the peculiar technique of Genet's story-telling, whereby he admits to making up his characters as he goes along, dithers visibly about what form to make them up in, signals in advance that such a one will presently enter the book and sometimes leaves the reader free to imagine the dialogue two of them have on meeting. He is a resurrectionist, treating his characters like zombies. Even Divine, who is Genet, has to be led by the hand by Genet—to sainthood. . . . (pp. 299-301)

The technique of ushering his characters into the book permits Genet to create effects of baroque theatrically, as if he were seeing them onto the stage down a *trompe l'œil* avenue. Thus 'Our Lady of the Flowers here makes his solemn entrance through the door of crime, a secret door, that opens on to a dark but elegant stairway.' This is *trompe l'œil* indeed, for having effected Notre-Dame's entrance into the book Genet continues 'Our Lady mounts the stairway . . . He is sixteen when he reaches the landing'—and at this point the narrative merges into actuality; the character is on a real landing, about to knock and go into a room and murder an old man.

The rhythm, whether of masturbation or of Genet's prose, is designed to induce the images to take on enough solidity and durability to be dwelt on. And it is interesting that Divine's sex life is lived almost wholly in the imagination. It is not only that most of the narrative is the product of Genet's masturbatory fantasy: even when the narrative steps wholly inside the play-within-a-play, the sexual acts with partners do not replace masturbation, on which Divine still depends to 'finish off'. The acts with others do not advance Divine towards direct sexual satisfaction; they serve to consolidate and sharpen the contrast on the images—so that in the end the images almost take off into a detached sex life, coupling and enjoying the process on their own.

Indeed, it is the images rather than the characters that Genet animates, which is why he is more poet than novelist. The independent life he charges them with is so erotic that it is no surprise to find them combining; they themselves are the population of a gallant and promiscuous society. Since the images combine, Genet's mythology is metamorphotic. (p. 301)

[The] entire language of *Notre Dame des Fleurs* is built up from the grammatical metamorphosis of 'il' into 'elle'. From this flowers the queer *argot*—which is used only by 'male' queers; for Divine to use it would be as unseemly as 'whistling with her tongue and teeth . . . or putting her hands in her trousers pockets and keeping them there'. Even so, the metamorphosis is never fixed. It is a film Genet can run backwards at will—and which he does, when, with the meticulous and dispassionate love of an early watercolourist recording exotic fauna, he describes that bizarre change of life that comes to queers at thirty, the moment when a beloved crosses over and becomes a lover. Suddenly Divine does whistle, does put her hands in her pockets—until she discovers that after all she 'had not become virile; she had aged. An adolescent now excited her . . .'

I feel tolerably sure that this particular metamorphosis has a reflection in Genet's own name. . . . Take him straight and he is *un genet,* a jennet, a Spanish horse—an image, to his mind, as another of his transformation scenes demonstrates, of virility: but put, as surely his own imagination often does put, a circumflex on the second *e,* and he becomes some kind of flowering gorse or furze—a companion to all those secondary characters named Mimosa who weave a decorative and feminine garland through the book. (pp. 302-03)

The most astounding metamorphosis of all is the one which transforms the images that activate Genet's personal erotic tastes (which few do and some cannot even expect to share) into poetry, poetry being, precisely, a universal imagery of eroticism, which provokes the imagination to an intangible but all the same completely sensual erection—a universal love-language which is, however, in fact understood by fewer readers than French and practised by fewer devotees than the most esoteric sexual perversion. (p. 303)

Brigid Brophy, "Genet," in her Don't Never Forget: Collected Views and Reviews, *1966. Reprint by Holt, Rinehart and Winston, 1967, pp. 296-306.*

ROBERT HATCH

[*The Thief's Journal*] is a work of almost unparalleled intensity. It is a quest for personal consistency, carried out with an all-absorbing persistence that few of us could imagine, let alone document with such tormented nicety. Genet's book is a portrait of the artist as a work of art. In this context, it becomes irrelevant to ask whether it is a true biography; Genet lived his life and then he created it.

Ostensibly, the *Journal* covers the years of his young manhood, years spent in criminal vagabondage, principally in Spain and Antwerp, but crossing, usually at the demand of the police, almost every frontier of Europe. As the title says, Genet was a thief; he was also a prostitute, a forger, blackmailer, and dope peddler. He lived habitually in the filthiest surroundings and consorted exclusively with the most depraved individuals. (In that period, Genet recoiled, as though instinctively, from what he occasionally refers to as "your world"; it is his only acknowledgment that there is a reality other than the surreal one he shapes for himself.)

How, then, make a work of art from such material? "Acts," says Genet, "must be carried through to their completion. Whatever their point of departure, the end will be beautiful. It is because an action has not been completed that it is vile." And his concern, almost superhumanly vigilant—at least in retrospect—is to act so that every deed becomes the ultimate expression of that deed. That, of course, is how mystics and saints behave. Genet is a mystic, intoxicated by self-absorption; and he has been called a saint—by Sartre for one, and by himself for another.

Abandoned in childhood, Genet set out to get even with the world by being as wicked as possible. Most readers will recall similar schemes to surpass the worst expectations of their elders. But Genet differed from the rest of us both because he had a capacity for really extreme wickedness and because he was endowed with one of those hyperdiscriminating nervous systems that can detect infinite gradations of tone in a situation customarily seen as black-and-white.

That is his greatness and his curse. It permits him to depict his own feelings, his relationship with others, their appearance and manner, the content of an emotion, the quality of a sky, the dampness of a night, the taste and smell and feel of every contact available to the senses, with a refinement of observation that produces a microcosm of dazzling intricacy and precision. And it is his curse because the prismatic subtleties of his discrimination make only more elusive the perfection that haunts him.

The Thief's Journal is a major celebration of the human spirit—moving, astonishing, frequently acridly exciting, sometimes witty, occasionally boring. The last it becomes in part because, with the best will, few readers can care as passionately as does Genet for the ultimate nuance of his smallest scruple, and in part because even the most elegant self-taught mind will from time to time cry "Eureka" long after the event. The fact that in Genet's case the truths emerge with the expected values reversed does not always conceal their currency. (pp. 90-1)

Robert Hatch, "Peering In with the Outsiders," in Harper's Magazine, *Vol. 230, No. 1376, January, 1965, pp. 90-1.*

THE TIMES LITERARY SUPPLEMENT

If bibliographies are reliable, and if Genet himself is to be believed, *The Thief's Journal* was his fifth prose work to be published. . . . "You who regard me with contempt", he tells the readers of the account which he gives of his mean and poverty-stricken adventures between 1932 and 1940,

> are made up of nothing else but a succession of similar woes, but you will never be aware of this and thus will never possess pride, in other words, the knowledge of a force that enables you to stand up to misery—not your own misery, but that of which mankind is composed.

This moral self-assurance, this conviction that we are all tarred by the same brush and that the only difference between Genet and ourselves is that he is bad and knows it whereas we are worse and do not, also probably stems from the fact that by 1946 Genet had met Sartre. He could not have failed to draw from his ideas and personality some kind of philosophical justification for his own art and attitude, and Sartre's influence is indeed visible in several places. "This book, *The Thief's Journal,* pursuit of the Impossible Nothingness" reads like a title chapter from *Saint Genet, Actor and Martyr,* and there is also a self-conscious and pseudo-philosophical attitudinizing in the book which is, like the quotations from Sartre that Genet's publishers will insist on printing on the dust jacket, intensely irritating. Genet is no doubt "sincere" in the liking for theft, treason and homosexuality which he proclaims in this book—though a little more detail about the practical problems of theft would not have come amiss—but he has become far too aware of his audience. The presentation of the joys and miseries of the criminal in *Our Lady of the Flowers* was spontaneous, tormented and convincing. The world of the thief is used in this book as the excuse for too many theological disquisitions for it to provide the compulsive reading which a "scrofulous French novel" promises.

This is not to say that Genet, who admits at one point in the text to writing "pornographic books", has entirely lost his touch. The details of the bad taste which the pimp Silitano achieves in his search for elegance—a pair of green and tan crocodile shoes, a brown suit, a white silk shirt, a pink tie, a multicoloured scarf and a green hat—are but examples of the originality that Genet can put into his depiction of his world. This is what the non-theologically minded reader buys Genet for, and even the person whose interest in the "impossible quest for saintliness" is relatively limited cannot remain wholly unmoved by Genet's description of how he would take Communion in order to learn, through the nausea which the host provoked, "the magnificent structure of the laws in which I am caught". Similarly, the ecstasy which the Gestapo evokes in Genet is not without considerable social overtones for any country whose policemen are not all entirely wonderful. . . .

If *The Thief's Journal* is a less satisfactory book than *Our Lady of the Flowers* or *Miracle de la rose,* this is not wholly a result of the Sartrian philosophizing which constantly intrudes on the narrative and strikes so artificial a note. It is also because Genet is wholly indifferent to such literary considerations as plot, characterization and the logical development of ideas. There are, of course, a number of reasons for this. Genet's own life in the 1930s was a formless and itinerant one, so that it is fairly natural that any description of it should be rather meandering. Genet is also, though we can scarcely criticize him for this, essentially an autodidact, and all his prose works have a contempt for form which is understandable in someone who managed to acquire an education without ever being subjected to any scholastic discipline. Yet it would be unfair to Genet himself, as it would be misleading for his admirers, to claim that his books could not be improved. A more rigorous construction, a readiness to revise, an ability to resist the temptation to indulge in philosophical digressions, even some attention to the old-fashioned concept of plot, could save him from becoming an existentialist freak with occasional flashes of brilliance and turn him into a really great artist. It by no means necessarily follows that a man who has the courage to reject society's moral laws also has the right to demand that the reader always take him on his own very particular aesthetic valuation. A strong dose of Boileau would do Genet—and Sartre for that matter—a world of good.

> *"It's a Thief's World,"* in The Times Literary Supplement, *No. 3298, May 13, 1965, p. 376.*

F. W. J. HEMMINGS

[*The Thief's Journal*] provides enough Genet to give one either a taste for him or else an invincible distaste.

The distaste is less likely to be aroused by the freezing accounts of homosexual lovemaking than by the unexampled solipsism of the author. At the time, no doubt, Genet stole and prostituted himself out of a dislike of getting his bread in more conventional and less exhausting ways. But his *Journal* is, as he insists, not a record of his life, 'not a quest of time gone by, but a work of art whose pretext-subject is my former life.' He is trying to reinterpret it in terms of an ethic constructed *ex post facto,* to see it all as 'a highly delicate ascesis'. In episode after episode, he returns to the same vomit, a delighted contemplation of his own abjectness. . . . He retells the story of the French ex-mistress of a Nazi officer who got married at Charleville after the war. The townspeople presented her with a floral swastika when she left the church. Genet would have 'given the world', so he says, to have experienced her moment of exquisite shame.

The flamboyance, the sham-bold perversity of *The Thief's Journal* put Genet squarely at the bottom of the long line of romantic outlaws that starts with Schiller's Karl Moor. But the flaw in the myth of the Great Rebel can't be altogether concealed by its transformation into the myth of the petty rebel: for the rebel remains inexorably dependent on his encapsulation inside a law-abiding society. Robinson Crusoe couldn't have broken the eighth commandment if he'd wanted to. Genet is forced to value a policed society because nothing else can provide him with a morality to defy—and to feel ashamed of defying. In his wanderings through Europe, he was uncomfortable in only one country—Hitler's Germany.

> If I steal here, I perform no singular deed that might fulfil me. I obey the customary order. I do not destroy it. I am not committing evil. I am not upsetting anything. The outrageous is impossible. I'm stealing in the void.

In this last sentence I suspect an untranslatable pun (*je vole dans le vide*). Genet can't fly in the void: he needs an atmosphere, legality to earn himself the right to go to prison, decency without which he couldn't contrive a 'shocking' book. The solipsism is both distasteful and self-contradictory.

> *F. W. J. Hemmings, "For Shame," in* New Statesman, *Vol. LXX, No. 1792, July 16, 1965, p. 89.*

ROBERT TAUBMAN

Querelle of Brest is nearly a novel, much as Genet is nearly a poet—if there's anything at all in the claims made for him ('the poet of evil of our times'). It's less autobiographical than usual, but not more inventive: only more artificial. There's a lot of pure pantomime: two identical brothers, a chorus of sailors and a hero as strapping and equivocal as a Principal Boy. If there's also sex and violence, Genet emphasises that this, too, is a game of let's pretend. He comes and goes himself, arranging things; he hints that Lieutenant Seblon, who meditates on the sailors in his Gidean journal, isn't *in* the story at all. It's odd, the fussy and defensive manner, when, as always, he's also inviting you to share his dream. And when all that really counts is the hold the dream has on you.

The dream depends largely on sensation—the feeling for coaldust or the various body fluids is oddly aesthetic, a sort of inverted Pateresque, but at least it's conveyed. But why is it all so undisturbing? Partly, no doubt, because it also depends on ideas, and with less success. Genet's amoralism seems to me a feeble pretence. Morality isn't overthrown, it turns up in one of its dreariest guises: 'an undisputed moral authority, a perfect social organisation, a revolver and the right to use it.' For the rest, the mock-intellectual content merely cancels out. A criminal, Genet is saying, must accept responsibility; he murders 'of his own free will'. But he's also saying this is impossible, for what he evokes most lovingly is a dream-like fatalism—which is also his contribution to psychology: the rich live in hopes of being robbed, people due to be murdered *want* to be murdered, 'the victim becomes his own executioner.'

Sea, murder, uniforms ('uniform envelops the criminal like a cloud')—he gets a certain resonance out of them, just as Housman did out of uniforms, hangmen and football. Perhaps the effect seems less mainly because Genet is trying to convey more. He tries to convey evil, and fails. Like the cat Macavity, Querelle has broken every human law; but this isn't so amazing as some of his ways of proving it to himself. At night he 'peoples the shadows with the most dangerous of the monsters dwelling within him' in order to subject them to his will 'by breathing hard through his nose'. He displays the same baffling zeal—an excess of zeal over effect—when it comes to murder, and it's far from helping to establish that murder has actually taken place. However you regard the homosexual scenes—as frank or sickening or merely unlikely—nothing accounts for the peculiar quality of evil that's willed onto them. If Genet doesn't disturb, it's because he can't for a moment make one believe in evil. Hard breathing won't do it (and Macavity's not there). His characters seem to know this: the time comes when even Querelle relaxes and only feels 'sad and rather wicked'—a big let-down, and the moment when he nearly becomes plausible. (pp. 878-79)

> *Robert Taubman, "Straw Jesus," in* New States-man, *Vol. 72, No. 1865, December 9, 1966, pp. 878-79.*

THE TIMES LITERARY SUPPLEMENT

Genet seems to insist that we should hold reactionary views about crime and homosexuality, not for our own benefit but for his. He lays great store in *Querelle of Brest* by the fact that society condemns love between two men as unnatural and horrifying, because this makes such love a noble thing. The notion of "consenting adults" could only be an impoverishment. The book's hero, Querelle, is a muscular and god-like "hors-la-loi", a sort of Vautrin with hair, set free from the restraints of society because he is a sailor, a sodomite and a murderer. The morality that plays around his head is therefore all his own, even if it too at times comes to seem like a simple inversion of the norm. When Querelle murders, for example, he also steals, but he does not murder in order to steal, he steals in order to murder. . . .

The proposition that what is most degrading is thereby most noble becomes a tiring one, as all such closed systems must. Genet leans too heavily on what he sees as our innate respectability, until we resent it. For so long as he limits himself to describing the various moves in the power-game, as played between two homosexual lovers, he is very economical and very funny—there is a fine description of a meeting in Beirut between Querelle and an eager yet timid Armenian. Generally though, Genet, Romantic that he is, assumes that our world and his are mutually independent, and it is his pimps, prostitutes and policemen who alone offer an opportunity of mediation, together of course with himself, the "poet".

But if Genet is a poet it is to his language that we must look and not simply his viewpoint. His translators are faced with a difficult task, and *Querelle of Brest* shows many signs of strain. . . . Writers like Genet or Céline, with their reliance on argot, pose impossible problems and point to the lack in England of a truly classless equivalent. Some of what gets said in this version brings to mind the school playground rather than the Brest waterfront.

> *"Pastoral Cares," in* The Times Literary Supple-ment, *No. 3381, December 15, 1966, p. 1165.*

BERNARD GREBANIER

The miracle in *The Miracle of the Rose* is connected with the figure of Harcamone at the prison of Fontevrault, where [Genet], in his thirties, is sent for stealing a ring. Since its jailbirds "are much more vicious than those elsewhere," Fontevrault was, for the boys at the reformatory where Genet previously lived, "the sanctuary to which our childhood dreams aspired." Until the final pages Harcamone remains a shadowy figure, but he is the criminals' exemplar. "I," says Genet, "aspired to heavenly glory, and Harcamone had attained it before me, quietly, as the result of murdering a little girl, and fifteen years later, a Fontevrault guard." At 16 Harcamone had raped the frightened child ("the shuddering little bitch"), who, when she tried to scream, was strangled by him—an act which grants Genet "the vision of an ascension to the paradise which is offered me."

Sentenced to jail until he is 21, Harcamone thinks death "the only way of shortening his captivity." That escape he found by "a rather trivial act," cutting the throat of the guard who had been kindest to him, "a man almost insolent with mildness." Luckily, this murder differed from his first; "all too often people overlook the sufferings of the murderer who always kills the same way." Genet haunts the vicinity of the condemned man's cell and sees "The burden of saintliness" on Harcamone's chain cause it to be transformed "into a garland of white flowers." As Harcamone approaches death, Genet is vouchsafed a succession of three visions, the most imposing of which reveals the heart of Harcamone's heart as "a red rose of monstrous size and beauty."

This anti-novel does not proceed in ordered narrative but by free association. It moves back and forth from the reformatory to Fontevrault, the time element being deliberately vague. The method is justified because the ideals and protocol of the reformatory set those for the prison; the method is largely an effective one. But it has two difficulties: occasionally the reader is unsure where he is, and, more seriously, because of the emphasis on the reformatory, one keeps thinking of the Genet at Fontevrault as still a child, when he is actually a man in his thirties. (The author might here remind us that he has said that all prisoners are children.) It is important that we should be remembering that it is an adult who is behaving like an adolescent.

On the purely literary side there is enough to admire in this work—most of all, I feel, a quality which is peculiarly French, the discerning eye for significant detail. It is a trait that lifts French medieval sculpture above the general undiscriminating sculpture of the rest of western Europe at the time; it is what lifts the tragedies of Racine to the plane of exquisite refinement; it persists down to our own century, for instance in Proust and Cocteau. (p. 5)

Genet, whom Sartre, by an inversion of the word's definition, has dubbed a saint, has throughout his career made a religion of evil. . . . Because of this worship of evil he has been compared to Baudelaire—without reason, I believe, for there is little of the latter's Satanism (Catholicism in reverse) in Genet. The quintessence here is closer to that of Hitler, whom he cannot help admiring. ("I have murdered, ravaged, robbed, betrayed. A sum of glory!")

Because of his long history as a thief, Genet has also been compared to Villon, but he has none of Villon's breezy vagabondage. His holy arts of thieving and murder are inextricably linked with homosexuality to the extent that "thief" or "pimp" equals "homosexual." In the reformatory, to which he was sent as a boy, from the toughs' "open files . . . there escaped . . . the scent of tea roses and wisteria"; he himself suspects that the incentive to become a thief was his discovery that thieves kissed each other. . . . (pp. 5, 49)

Speaking from prison, which Genet knows to be his natural habitat, he says: "Each object in your world has a meaning different for me from the one it has for you." True enough. And since he is currently so much venerated I would like to make clear just what we are venerating: a man who has openly declared his efforts at self-dehumanization and has succeeded in this ambition very well. . . .

[When Genet's play *The Blacks* appeared in New York, the] production's long run was ascribable to a general feeling that somehow the play was contributing to better interracial relations, but the fact is that the piece, intended by the dramatist only for white audiences, heaped abuse and scorn upon them and offered for Negroes the amiable solution of a return to the cannibalism of the jungle, a solution no Negro is likely to accept, but consistent with Genet's hatred of society.

Genet is beyond question a stylist, a minor magician in the weaving of words—thereby undermining the easy platitude of his fellow-countryman that "the style is the man." He says, "I . . . love only beauty," and to an impressive degree he knows how to re-create it on occasion. He is, for instance, almost obsessed with the loveliness of flowers, as many passages and the titles of his first two novels witness. Nevertheless, beauty is for him more basically rooted in crime ("Theft is beautiful"), cruelty, bloodshed ("I want to sing murder, for I love murderers")—even filth and ordure.

Since *Miracle of the Rose* deals chiefly with his various love affairs at the reformatory and the prison, Genet conscientiously pursues, though to a lesser degree than in his first novel, his determination to be pornographic. The four-letter words describing anatomical matters, sexual congress and various excrements, like Genet's worship of evil, I find as dull and boring as (and much like) mid-Victorian euphemisms and worship of respectability. Both are merely a species of sentimentality. Victorian sentimental hymning of virtue was smothered in floridity, and Genet's sentimental hymning of vice is smothered in flowers. (p. 49)

> *Bernard Grebanier, "Author, Saint, Beggarman, Thief," in* The New York Times Book Review, *February 19, 1967, pp. 5, 49.*

TOM F. DRIVER

In addition to his five plays, two volumes of poems, and minor works, Jean Genet has written five books, of which I think, disagreeing with Sartre, that the most beautiful is *Miracle of the Rose*. . . . [The book] is a major achievement of modern literature, yet so unlike most other modern writing that comparisons are difficult. The novel must be judged on its own terms and according to the power that it generates by its own peculiar method.

Like *The Thief's Journal,* which was written later, *Miracle of the Rose* is autobiographical. We learn of Genet's experiences and loves during the time he was a prisoner, first at the reformatory known as the Colonie de Mettray, when he was sixteen, and then at the prison of Fontevrault some fifteen years later. . . . The intention of *Miracle of the Rose* is not to recount "what happened" but to reveal the spiritual content of Genet's mind. From a moral point of view the book's overwhelming characteristic is its honesty, even though Genet's dishonesty and indeed the inherent perfidy of his character are repeatedly made apparent.

The world we enter here is that of delinquents, homosexuals, pimps, burglars, and murderers. Aside from virtually anonymous turnkeys and wardens, these are the only characters. The reader may regard them as "unfortunates" or riff-raff; in Genet's eyes, and in each others', they are heroes and the attendants of heroes. They have the mark of fatality upon them, especially the murderer in Fontevrault's death cell, Harcamone, whose presence dominates the entire prison although he is seldom seen. It is Harcamone with whom Genet identifies himself in order that his own weakness and humiliation may be vicariously transformed into glory.

Genet's imagination is rooted in homosexual passion. He spares no anatomical detail his fancy dwells upon, and the homosexual act, in its several postures, is frequently described. He tells of sexual assaults made upon him by older boys when he arrived as a "chicken" at Mettray. He tells of his concubinage to Villeroy, whom he adored, and to Van Roy, whom he did not. He tells of his "marriage" in a clandestine ceremony to Divers, from whom he was separated the next day and whom he did not see again until fifteen years later, when he sighted him in the disciplinary hall at Fontevrault in the act of defecation. . . .

Sordid as all this is, *Miracle of the Rose* is not a dirty book. Rather, it is a book of moral transvaluations. The novel traces a biographical change in Genet from passive and feminine behavior to "masculine" homosexual love. This growth, if we can call it that, and I think we can, reflects Genet's affirmation of his destiny and his identity as a member of a "condemned" society. Therefore it is accompanied by a series of transvaluations: good into evil, evil into good, shame into glory, suffering into joy, humiliation into honor, and death into apotheosis. It becomes Genet's intention, as if he were a kind of messiah, to take the suffering of all upon himself. He becomes the spokesman and the atoner for all who are condemned, by sharing their guilt and by carrying it to its logical extreme. To take suffering upon himself is to fulfill what he calls his vocation of "saintliness."

It was then a fine poetic justice that made Genet an inmate at Fontevrault, for this prison had once been an important abbey, and its past lived on in the present. Genet and other prisoners walked like monks in its corridors. They were subject to the discipline of their superiors. They wore homespun and paced barefoot in the yard, frequently lost in meditation. Cloistered from the diurnal, dispossessed of worldly goods and responsibilities, these "monks" were the bearers of a secret glory, no less religious for the fact that sexuality was its principal sign and mystery. They lived in a communion of desire, awesome in its dedication to evil, its glorification of murder, and the ease with which it justified betrayal.

Since what is banal and what is outré are both in fashion nowadays, Genet's backside view of the world runs the risk of being praised and dismissed for the wrong reasons. To call white black, the superficial profound, or the ugly beautiful is not much of a verbal trick, and if Genet's art consisted only in this he would be no more than a passing curiosity. His genuine power, however, resides in other qualities, of which I shall mention three.

First, Genet has a very rare capacity for psychological self-revelation. He can make the reader believe in his integrity even though it is clear that much of what he says is a put-on. Psychological truth in Genet is always layered truth, and this is what is finally convincing and revealing. (p. 36)

Second, Genet is able to picture with utter vividness the actual scenes of his memory. This quality is the more remarkable because his narrative is seldom straightforward. Scenes dissolve into each other by principles of mnemonic association. The portrayal of a place and an incident may be broken off as soon as begun, not to be resumed for twenty pages, while the interval is filled with a dozen remembered fragments from Fontevrault, Mettray, and the burglary jobs done ''outside.'' Yet although we are led through a maze, detail is never lost. The bend of the stairs at Fontevrault, the dim lighting there, the walls and the windows . . .—all these and more are so specifically evoked that one feels he has lived in their presence. Genet's descriptions are not those of an objective reporter, though he sometimes displays a surprising detachment; they are the descriptions of one who has become aware of himself by increasing his awareness of the things around him. It is Genet's Fontevrault, Genet's Mettray we are shown, but they are all the more vivid for that. The same is to be said of the characters, whose vividness is surprising since Genet actually intends that all of them shall merge into a single figure.

Finally, by sheer force of imagination Genet transforms experiences of degradation into spiritual exercises and hoodlums into bearers of the majesty of love. Imagination is to Genet what prayer is to the man of God.

We are used to hearing that the imaginative writer creates a world. Genet seems not so much to create a world as to realize one. The world he presents to us is the real world of experience raised to a higher level of potency and thus, paradoxically, a higher level of actuality too. This strange work of the imagination is both a betrayal and a fulfillment of the real. To see a god in a psychopathic murderer is of course perverse, and Genet knows that. Yet it is also to recognize what power inheres in the human being—namely, the power to transcend, even by flaunting, the limits of humanity and thus to place oneself in the sphere of the demonic and the divine. It is this transcendence of given fact and given order that fascinates Genet and is identical with his imaginative fecundity. The given fact may be lust, animal pleasure, or merely sexual play of children: the transcendence is the mind's gradual transformation of these desires into love. The angelic is a potentiality of the bestial, and only when the latter is clearly in focus can the beauty of the former arise. (pp. 37, 113)

Evil though the desires of Jean Genet surely have been, there is something holy in his bearing. Sartre was not wrong to refer to him as a saint. Genet had already said it, and not entirely with irony. The imagination may devote itself to evil, but it cannot *be* evil. When pushed to the extremes of moral reality, it shows itself as the carrier in man of what is holy as well as evil. It becomes diaphanous, and one feels that he should indeed walk barefoot in its presence. It has been given to a pervert, thief, and coward named Jean Genet to come closer than the man of rectitude to the holy. Genet's head is full of violence, but his heart contains the rose of peace. (p. 113)

　　　　Tom F. Driver, ''An Exaltation of Evil,'' in Saturday
　　　　Review, *Vol. 50, No. 10, March 11, 1967, pp. 36-7,*
　　　　113.

STEPHEN KOCH

Twice during Jean Genet's *Miracle of the Rose* (near the beginning and near the end) the writing gets off the ground and really sails. The flights are spectacular enough, but not in the fashion of the blasting skyrockets to which book reviewers customarily compare such feats. The trajectory is more like the path of a great blue heron moving downstream, its vast wings scarcely moving in the still air as the bird scans the landscape, turning its head from left to right. Everything seems to fall silent as the unearthly vision floats by.

Both of these moments are among the more beautiful and absorbing in modern French literature. . . . But the book offers much more: I mention them only because they are the two moments of sublimity in a complex, self-undermining narrative the ultimate object of which is precisely that—sublimity. As such, they sound a little silly out of context. The first occurs (in a characteristically degraded situation) as Genet and his fellow convicts stand in a corridor of Fontevrault, the French penitentiary which is the novel's setting, and see a murderer named Harcamone being led by guards to the death cell, there to await the guillotine. . . . Suddenly the manacles on the martyr's wrists begin to be transformed into links of white roses. The guards see nothing, and Harcamone keeps walking. The iron door of the cell slams shut.

Following this vision, Harcamone (who is the book's patron saint, invisibly leading it to its conclusion) disappears from the scene, only to reappear in the final pages, though not in the flesh. He invades Genet's dreams in the form of a huge colossus on which crawl judges, jurors and executioners (emissaries from the middle class, against which Genet measures the strength of his private world of demons and martyrs) as termites might creep across the Colossus of Rhodes. These homunculi slowly descend into Harcamone's body (through the mouth) and discover it transformed into a dolorous wonderland—''more decked with black than a capital whose king has just been assassinated.''

I am not sure a simple critical description can make either of these passages sound very promising; Genet's motifs often sound merely grandiose without the concentration of imaginative energy that buoys them up and gives them their substance. But the final passage in particular is tremendously powerful, even for Genet: the judge's descent into Harcamone's flesh is a descent into a spiritual mystery, and every phase of the surreal fantasy is given both a tough, concrete presence and a peculiarly mute, admonitory ''significance,'' like the indecipherable totems of some lost civilization, staring out of ruins at the startled explorer. (pp. 761-62)

Mettray—a former convent, with encircling walls of stone—was Genet's mother. Fontevrault penitentiary was the arena of his perverse movement into manhood. Mettray was Genet's idyll, his pastoral; at Fontevrault that idyll was ripped to shreds. Genet's whole effort in this book is to reassemble a shattered and fragmented paradise. This is the immemorial motive that lies at the center of his art, making him the romantic he is—the only first-rate romantic genius of postwar world literature.

Romantic nostalgia can take the standard form of a flight from the present, in which fantasy wafts the mind back to some real or imagined moment of perfection. But it can also wear its struggle with the world on its sleeve and supply the energy for a creative act bound to the present, in which the artist attempts to achieve some kind of spiritual state that overcomes a wounding reality. The individual does not evade the moment, but struggles with it openly—and the struggle is an angry one, directed not only against an unacceptable world but also against time itself. Such a person sees himself as alone. . . . Genet's nostalgia erects a demonic ego, fighting a present he never stops facing, and overcoming it on his own.

The nature of this demonic, romantic egoism, its infinitely complex dialectic, and its ethical and aesthetic ramifications have been encyclopedically explored by Sartre in *Saint Genet* (it is an encyclopedia without an index), and I refer anyone interested in the philosophic dimension of Genet's romanticism to that maniacally analytic work. I don't see how anything more can possibly be said on the subject. Some feel that Sartre's dialectics fail to grasp the real genius of Genet: the sensuous glory of the spectacle. I don't agree with this argument—Genet is a philosophic novelist, and his work is inseparable from the serpentine subtlety of his intellect. But it is true that *Saint Genet* is more important to an understanding of Sartre's intellectual position than it is to a reading of Genet, and there is no need to resort to it to grasp what is, I would argue, a philosophic spectacle rendered in strictly poetic terms.

Still, this spectacle creates a strange kind of poetry in 1967. Genet seems to be an increasingly isolated figure in current literature . . . ; isolated particularly in France where the classical austerity of the new novel has moved in the opposite direction from his hyperbole, and even in America, where such would-be poets of the ego as Norman Mailer have run into a dead end—failing to get in touch with the poetic resources that keep Genet's prose aloft—and thus have been forced to use every journalistic ploy . . . to keep the glorious ego out in front and running.

I think the explanation of his artistic isolation lies in the facts of Genet's life. Like Mailer, Genet is inordinately aware of his audience, but as a *real* (rather than self-appointed) outcast he sees his audience as a mass of aliens, as those who have cast him out, as *them*. His first three books (including this one) were written in a prison cell, under a blanket at night, and hidden in the toilet (where else?) during the day. Genet's whole life has been determined by a real—and very clearly defined—sense of transgression. And for Genet's variety of romanticism, transgression is really a formal property which gives the art its substance and seriousness. (p. 762)

The central portion of *Miracle of the Rose* moves in a single, uninterrupted block, although one richly strewn with the wherewithal for Sartrean dialectics. This part of the book is much more talky than is either *Our Lady of the Flowers* or *Funeral Rites* (a novel whose structural technique is considerably more inventive than either). Genet's prose is always rather episodic. Typically, he is excited by some real event (meeting a handsome convict on the stairs, seeing a fist fight in the prison yard) and proceeds to expound on it, using his unique mixture of fantasy and intellectual reflection. The other two novels find devices to make this stop-and-start narration more clear-cut and lucid than it is in *Miracle of the Rose,* which sometimes allows its energy to be wasted in talk rather than in keeping things moving at the relentless clip they require.

Some readers (not myself, however) may find this talkiness sufficient compensation for the aesthetic lapse. This is the book in which Genet most extensively discusses his ideas as ideas; here the sociology of his prison life is most fully presented. (Both ideas and information, by the way, are of considerable interest and are expounded with great intelligence.) Needless to add that these expositions are not for "our" benefit—Genet neither amuses nor instructs his audience (at least not consciously). He seems more concerned with clarifying his life and intellectual position for his own benefit, and getting it down on paper. But to my mind, these maneuvers (evidently a necessary step toward his own maturity) make parts of the central portion of the book somewhat clumsy, in contrast to *Funeral Rites.*

These are minor failings in view of the book's whole achievement. The transgression succeeds on a profound level that has nothing to do with sexual mores or one's opinion as to whether Jean Genet is or is not a nasty man. In a period in which most art is moving in other directions, *Miracle of the Rose* is a monument to a peculiarly virile kind of energy: an act of transgression and completeness that puts before "us" the determination to create itself autonomously, to stand on its own terms. It begins in rebellion and ends as a work of self-contained beauty which no longer needs "us" to give it meaning. (pp. 762-63)

Stephen Koch, "A Romantic of the Wretched Life," in The Nation, *New York, Vol. 204, No. 24, June 12, 1967, pp. 761-63.*

JOHN UPDIKE

[*The essay from which this excerpt is taken was originally published in* The New Yorker, *November 4, 1967.*]

[*Miracle of the Rose*] is as subjective and compulsive as one could wish. . . . [Genet's first novel, *Our Lady of the Flowers*], proclaims itself, and is acclaimed by Sartre in his introduction, as a jailbird's masturbatory fantasies. *Miracle of the Rose* springs, as it were, from the same aesthetic:

> I carried Bulkaen off in the depths of my heart. I went back to my cell, and the abandoned habit of my abandoned childhood took hold of me: the rest of the day and all night long I built an imaginary life of which Bulkaen was the center, and I always gave that life, which was begun over and over and was transformed a dozen times, a violent end: murder, hanging, or beheading.

Reality and fantasy are inextricable. *Miracle of the Rose* seems slightly more earthbound than *Our Lady of the Flowers*—a touch less brilliant and soaring, a shade more plausible and didactic. Genet's own person emerges somewhat more solidly; while the earlier novel made the reader marvel that a criminal had become a writer, now it seems stranger that such a writer became a criminal. We are permitted glimpses—in categorical phrases like "a region to which irony has no access," in a critical disquisition on the vulgarity of placing slang words in quotation marks—of a depraved man whose vocation, nevertheless, from boyhood on has been literary. As a thief, he stole books! (pp. 358-59)

As in *Our Lady,* the story line of *Miracle of the Rose,* obeying no known gravitational laws, flies back and forth among the men Genet loves: Harcamone, the condemned man invisible in the death cell; Bulkaen, the young weakling covered even to his eyelids with tattoos; Villeroy, the big shot whose chicken Genet becomes at the boys' reformatory of Mettray; Divers, Villeroy's successor, who marries Genet in a mock ceremony and reappears fifteen years later, at the state prison of Fontevrault, and again possesses his bride. . . . The prison Fontevrault was once a monastery; when Genet arrives, manacled, the doorways are lit up as if for Christmas. Christianity permeates his confinement there. He suffers a series of mystic visions centered upon Harcamone, and indeed the prison world, "the eternal gray season in which I am trapped," does approximate the religious view of the world. Abasement gives rise to transcendent consolations: "And as our life is without external hope, it turns its desires inward. I cannot believe that the Prison is not a mystic community," "Your pride must be able to undergo shame in order to attain glory." . . . These testimonies, obtained under pressures of deprivation comparable to the oppression in which primitive Christianity thrived, cannot be dismissed as blasphemous any more than the pervasive erotic content can be dismissed as "homosexual." Genet is one of the few writers to make homosexual love credible, both in concrete detail—"Our shaved heads rolled around each other, with our rough cheeks scraping"—and in inner essence, in the tenderness and hysteria it shares with all sex.

Some months ago, the Reverend Tom Driver . . . [see excerpt above] admired *Miracle of the Rose* for showing Genet's transformation from a passive, "female" homosexual, the concubine of Villeroy, into an aggressive "male" one, the assaulter of Bulkaen. The improvement, to Driver, seemed self-evident, but three angry letters responded, one refusing to renew a subscription, another deploring "the literary morass of this decade," and a third likening Genet to the Nazis. Indeed, Genet, whose wartime efforts consisted of weaving, while in prison, camouflage nets for the Germans, does write kindly of the occupation forces. . . . It must be admitted, especially by those of us admiring of his rhetoric, that Genet, in his submission to rigidity and his quest for the resplendence of emotional extremes, is led into a moral realm where no conventional liberal, or even civilized person, can follow. . . . He worships Harcamone, who gratuitously murders a guard at Fontevrault; at Mettray, he admires Van Roy, who betrays an escape plot and thereby has "dared make a terrible gesture" demonstrating that "the strongest big shots were squealers." He is nostalgic for the superior—compared to mature criminals—ferocity of adolescents and remembers his own cruelty: "My cruelty, when I was sixteen, made me stab the left eye of a child who, frightened by my pitiless stare and realizing that his eye attracted me, tried to save it by putting his fist to it." Consistent with this savagery toward others is a fervent death wish: "My love of beauty (which desired so ardently that my life be crowned with a violent, in fact bloody, death) . . . made me secretly choose decapitation." Genet's outlawry is more thorough than de Sade's, who at least blamed God for the existence of pain; Genet says, "God is good. . . . He strews so many traps along our path." Only the desert saints of early Christianity, perhaps, would so blithely have burned the world to produce visions.

Is *Miracle of the Rose* an avant-garde novel? Genet does not claim it to be. . . . Certainly it lacks description in the sense of giving persons and objects an appearance of autonomy. The characters, apart from their names, are no more distinguishable than the mosaic figures aligned within a Byzantine dome. The dome is Genet's skull: he is absolute Creator within this universe, not only of persons but of the laws that control their motions. The humanization of nature, which Robbe-Grillet would eliminate from fiction, here operates with a vengeance; everything is transmuted into metaphor, nothing is more than what it means to Genet. The very prison melts so that, at the book's climax, Genet can mystically join Harcamone on his walk to the guillotine. The novel is a loose form, but *Miracle of the Rose* seems to me to fall outside it and to belong rather to that older stream of French literature, contributory to the novel, of essay and *pensée*, memoir and letter, confession and self-revelation. "We belonged to the Middle Ages," Genet says of his fellow-convicts, and when he writes of entering through Harcamone's gullet a country landscape detailed down to "the remains of a country fair: a spangled jersey, the ashes of a

campfire, a circus whip," his untrammelled hyperbole belongs—in defiance of intervening centuries of bourgeois empiricism and objectivity—to Rabelais. (pp. 359-62)

John Updike, "The Avant Garde: Grove Is My Press, and Avant My Garde," in his *Picked-Up Pieces*, Alfred A. Knopf, 1975, pp. 352-65.

JOHN LEONARD

Perhaps the only thing more irritating than a novel [such as *Funeral Rites*] by Jean Genet is a critical text on his fiction. Indeed, it sometimes seems as though he were a figment of the diabolical imaginations of Jean-Paul Sartre and Susan Sontag. "His intention," says Sartre, "is to harm, and his work aims at being an evil action." It is, Miss Sontag adds, "an extended treatise on abjection—conceived as a spiritual method." They agree that some sort of "transubstantiation" is involved, whereby the "onanistic meditator" annihilates the world we know. Whoopee. If then you graft to this palette of apocalyptic posturings a little Black Mass and an overmuch of resurrection myth . . . , and apply a urethane spray of prose that is gorgeously smutty, what esthete wouldn't swoon? We have apparently reached the terminal stage of a cancer of the culture, where the surgeons unzip flesh-flaps and gasp in admiration at the rioting cells. . . .

Funeral Rites is exemplary in its noxiousness. It purports to mourn the death of Genet's young lover, Jean Decarnin, a Resistance hero slain by a Nazi collaborator in 1944. It is actually (1) an exercise in cannibalism and necrophilia; (2) the proclamation of an esthetic of fascism; (3) a masturbatory fantasy that should shame Portnoy all the way to Sweden for an organ transplant; and (4) an outrageous bore.

It is outrageous on a moral level. We have been fed a lot of nonsense recently about the conceptual autonomy and moral "neutrality" of art. The loftier criticism today by special dispensation exempts literature from moral categories; it is considered sufficient to identify the artist's intention and to report on how much damage he has done to your sensibilities. All the rest is agitprop.

Yet Western art since the Greek tragedians has presupposed a moral dimension to creative utterance, and the utterer is no more "neutral" than Jack-the-Ripper or St. Augustine. We must live together and we must die alone, and that tension is one of the things that art will always be about; either it relates to morality or it doesn't relate to life. And the novel especially is a prose transaction which assumes the existence of readers who will absorb or reject or modify or misinterpret the organizing vision of the novelist.

Genet has an organizing vision; and, if we are to take him at all seriously, we must cope with it. *Funeral Rites* is a calculated series of degradations—first, of society; then of love (or the memory of it); and finally of consciousness itself. . . .

[Genet's] imaginings are themselves a theft. Knowing the heroic Jean D. to have been a secret homosexual, Genet "steals" him from society. The safely dead and therefore cherished love must then be betrayed by his submitting himself to Jean D.'s murderers. At the last, his mockery of himself obliterates even the fantasy. An ultimate solipsism, an ultimate permissiveness, is proposed: a consciousness capable of experiencing others only through manipulation and total control, employing and enjoying brutality, at once death-camp commandant and eager victim.

Unless we refuse this vision, we deserve it. To be neutral about it is to flirt with our own personal fascism; it is either a failure of nerve or . . . immoral. I find it odd that the very critics who postulate an autonomous esthetic despair of politics and are professional indignitaries, as though there were no connection between individual and society, between psyche and social condition.

Funeral Rites is also a bore, simply because it says the same things Genet has said in *Our Lady of the Flowers* and *Thief's Journal*. Once more we are offered a self-portrait of the artist on his back, metamorphosing himself from brutalized child to wicked angel. Once more we are asked to endure a self-swallowing infantile narcissism, a lust for the integral sloth of nullity: I am the Universe; the Universe is Nothing; I am Nothing, and therefore I'm free. To make a career of narcissism is to become a bore, no matter how sumptuously expressive that bore may be.

John Leonard, *"Portrait of the Artist as Narcissistic Hitler,"* in The New York Times, *June 19, 1969, p. 43.*

TOM BISHOP

The third of Genet's four novels, *Funeral Rites* testifies clearly to the strength and severe limitations of his fiction, and allows us to understand—and to applaud—Genet's decision to abandon the novel for the theater.

Like his other novels, *Funeral Rites* is a homosexual's masturbatory fantasy, wildly excessive and self-indulgent and yet astonishingly poetic in its evocation of a private inferno. It is the first of Genet's works that was not written in jail, and it lacks that particular prison universe of *Our Lady of the Flowers* and *Miracle of the Rose;* but it shares with these earlier books the preoccupation with the glorification of evil and the metaphysics of betrayal. (p. 36)

Funeral Rites is a perverted elegy to the memory of Genet's lover, Jean Decarnin, a Resistance fighter killed during the street battles that helped liberate Paris in August 1944. Genet, writing in the first person singular and in his own name, tells of meeting Decarnin's brother, Paulo, apparently a collaborator; their mother, and the lover she is hiding, a tall, blond, handsome German tank commander named Erik Seiler. He then postulates that Decarnin was shot by a member of the Militia— that most disreputable group of Frenchmen who fought alongside the Germans—and invents for the role a beautiful sixteen-year-old boy, whom he names Riton. The rest of the book takes place mainly in Genet's imagination.

At first, he is totally preoccupied with memories of his dead lover and he even envisions eating his body in order to absorb him completely, to assimilate him, to be totally possessed by his manliness. Initially, too, he despises the supposed killer, Riton; but gradually, through a delicate exploration of the paradoxical link between love and hate, Genet idealizes Riton and *wants* him to shoot Decarnin. Thus, by loving rather than hating the killer of his friend, Genet asserts himself and contradicts the normal order of the universe. His fantasy wills that Riton meet Erik in their last hours as they are being hunted down during the Liberation. Riton falls in love with the German officer, and after a *Götterdämmerung* of lovemaking on the roofs of Paris, Riton shoots his partner in an apotheosis of passion, despair, and betrayal.

In another of Genet's flights of fancy, Erik receives his homosexual initiation in Germany before the war, in the arms of an executioner. Here, as elsewhere, the author takes delight in parading his characters' pederasty; but his showing-off seems so deliberate and so repetitive that *Funeral Rites* succeeds in being neither pornographic nor erotic. In the most scandalous sequence Genet pictures Hitler making love to Paulo, Decarnin's brother, especially imported to Berchtesgaden for the occasion. It is scandalous not because it is obscene, but because of Genet's intense identification with his distorted image of the Nazi leader. . . . Hitler is Genet's ultimate hero—which means, of course, that he is the most abject and contemptible figure.

To portray his characters' thoughts and acts, Genet uses sometimes the third and sometimes the first person. That is, he writes, say of Hitler both from the outside and the inside, switching for no apparent reason and achieving no structural ensemble. It is this flawed narrative technique that makes *Funeral Rites* Genet's weakest novel. Curiously, the most marked defects may be attributable to Sartre's influence. The technique of constantly changing focus, as well as some of the incidents themselves (the killing of a cat, Riton's awaiting death on the rooftop) echo—but all too faintly—Sartre's *The Paths to Freedom*. Genet even indulges in some pseudo-philosophic speculation. . . . This kind of thing is not Genet's true métier.

Despite this over-all diffuseness, there are passages of great beauty and undeniable power. Erik's wanton shooting of a child in order to feel himself virile is a brief, horrifying gem; a longer, even more harrowing section recounts the betrayal and execution of a score of young insurgents in prison. Genet endows these incidents with an overwhelming feeling for evil that is quite extraordinary. Much more surprising is the sensitivity and sympathy with which he portrays a lowly maid who had briefly been Decarnin's mistress and who is humiliated by his selfishly pharisaic mother. She prefigures the subjugated heroines of *The Maids,* and Genet treats her with gentle compassion. In these, the best moments of the novel, the language sparkles with evocative imagery. . . . (pp. 36-7)

In *Funeral Rites* more than in his other novels, Genet delves into the paradox of love-hate and the multiple masks behind which men live. It is in his theater, however, that he will find the suitable structure and discipline to bring these themes fully to life. (p. 37)

Tom Bishop, in a review of "Funeral Rites," in Saturday Review, *Vol. 52, No. 28, July 12, 1969, pp. 36-7.*

THE TIMES LITERARY SUPPLEMENT

The first thing to be said about *Funeral Rites* is that it is an overwhelmingly *private* novel. The question, "why was it written in this way?", is largely answered by Genet within the novel; it is in trying to answer the more insistent question, "why then did he write it at all?", that we may catch a glimpse of the elusive Genet. . . .

[The] fact that Jean D's death has made him a national hero prescribes in detail the patterns of mourning; Genet's surge of spontaneous grief simply aligns him with these. How can Genet the social leper accept this coincidence without appearing to act out a sacrilegious masquerade, and so betray his love? On all sides he is being welcomed into the camp of the virtuous, for the wrong reasons. Genet's answer is to invent his own masquerade: to embrace gladly everything that Jean D stood against. To counterweight Jean D's communist militancy he will, catching at a face seen in a newsreel, create and idealize Riton, of the loathed Militia, and put him beside Erik, the bull-necked German tank-driver; to forestall the pious clichés which greet a love stopped by death he will linger searingly on sodomic practice; and all this so shaped as to isolate him from us. There is not even the possibility that this is all an aberrant attempt to disguise ''orthodox'' grief behind repellent trappings. Then why?

Part of the answer lies in the patterns of behaviour offered. For all the fascination of the overlap with ''real'' history and its reflection in narrative episodes, there are no characters and no episodes in this book. What we have is what Genet himself calls a ''prismatic decomposition''—of himself; a projection into alien flesh of tendencies, experiences and imaginings that are his own. In a world which, he believes, has denied him the use of moral and psychological criteria, he cannot evaluate his experience; and so he ''tries himself out'' in Riton, in Erik, in the bedraggled little maid (also bereaved), even in that ''supreme actor''—and universal villain—Hitler. Since there is no one to reflect, to ''place'' his feelings, he must rely on consciousness. And if, within the novel, the ''prismatic decomposition'' is a first step towards seeing his grief, the novel as a whole allows him a view of how far his words have enabled him to experience, and at the same time comprehend, intensity of feeling. It had to be written.

Tentative, irregular in rhythm, in many ways childlike, *Funeral Rites* is also horrifying; but if its search for honesty leaves Genet totally estranged, it is an estrangement on his terms, not on ours, nor even on those of Sartre, for all his—because of his—*intellectual* sympathy. It is to art, not to psychological analysis, that this appalling book belongs. This indeed is verbal victory.

''Verbal Victory,'' in The Times Literary Supplement, *No. 3528, October 9, 1969, p. 1146.*

RICHARD HOWARD

On April 16 the *New York Times* headline . . . read: ''Jean Genet, The Playwright, Dies at 75.'' There is a kind of revisionary thrust in those words, and though I admire Genet's plays, identification of him as a dramatist seems to me to be a tendentious error. . . . Genet's plays are an important development of his art and were valuable for him, since they enabled him to escape Sartre's imprisoning comprehension. But Jean Genet was not ''the playwright.''

He was, first of all, the author of five novels, if texts so lyrical, so drastic, so autobiographical can be called novels. . . . After Genet had written his last play, *The Screens,* in 1961, a silence in his literature ensued, though his publisher . . . announced at least five works as ''forthcoming.'' We know now that Genet destroyed all of these. He has left only *Un Captif Amoureux,* a prose text of over 200 pages concerning the Palestinian issue. . . .

Genet's great texts—his novels, his fictions, his romances—are the great affair in his career primarily because they are the first and perhaps the only texts to set forth for the Western imagination an explicit realization of homosexual eros. They do this by the most elaborate rhetorical armory to be marshaled by a French writer since Chateaubriand: although the tradition of the *mauvais garçon* from Villon to Rimbaud is often adduced, Genet's real achievement is not such brief, inveterate miracles of poetry, but rather a narrative comprehensiveness that makes his ''style,'' like his moral stance, capable of every enormity and of every delicacy, in order to fulfill his passion. He will transform himself by language until he is on the other side of that invisible barrier where all values are reversed, where abjection becomes sanctity and self-hatred a kind of divinity. This is not a transformation likely to be celebrated . . . but it seems to me the crucial point of Genet's achievement. As it happens, this achievement was silenced by Sartre's great study of 1952, *Saint Genet, Actor and Martyr,* which Genet said ''laid me bare, stripped me naked, quite unceremoniously.'' (p. 41)

Thinking about Genet's activism on behalf of Algerian independence, Vietnamese and Japanese dissidents, all demonstrations against racism, and of his defense of the Baader terrorists, I am only too convinced of where that Palestinian codicil will lead us all, prisoners as we are of his theatrical celebrity: it will lead us further into the debacle of a writer who must, by a kind of moral bravado, determine his salvation by a murderous theory. After all, Genet once said that he had probably never committed a murder because he had written his books. And he had stopped writing books. . . . I think of what Annette Michelson (married to Genet's translator . . .) told me when we spoke about Genet's death: ''You know what Jean always said: 'I couldn't care less about celebrity, it's glory that matters to me!' '' It is celebrity, of the theatrical, *New York Times* kind, that we have had from Genet for the last 25 years: celebrity and silence. It is glory that we will have in all the years to come, the glory of those five books—literature as personal salvation, social reintegration, literature as betrayal, sexuality, and love. (p. 42)

Richard Howard, ''Genet's Glory,'' in The New Republic, *Vol. 194, No. 20, May 19, 1986, pp. 41-2.*

Maureen Howard

1930-

American novelist, short story writer, critic, and editor.

Howard has garnered widespread critical acclaim for her novels about women searching for identity amid their career aspirations and within their socially prescribed roles. She celebrates the assertion of the human will to affect change, yet such action does not insure a happy or conclusive ending to her works. Critics have commended Howard's precise use of language, her double-edged humor, and the loose structure of many of her novels, which allows readers to draw their own conclusions about characters and incidents. Howard has also demonstrated a tendency toward digression, reflecting, stated Anne Tyler, ''a conviction that life is not so much a single straight line as a kind of mosaic, unreadable to ordinary humans but endlessly fascinating nonetheless.''

Howard's first novel, *Not a Word about Nightingales* (1962), focuses on the disruptions within a family when the father decides to pursue a life of ''feeling'' during a vacation in Perugia. Eighteen months later, his wife sends their daughter to bring him back; by this time, he has lost his enthusiasm for a hedonistic, unfettered existence and returns without much resistance. Howard wrote in her autobiography, *Facts of Life* (1978), that she wanted *Not a Word about Nightingales* to reflect a sense of order ''as I knew it in the late fifties and early sixties . . .—that our passion must be contained if we were not to be fools.'' This theme runs through most of Howard's fiction, including her second novel, *Bridgeport Bus* (1965). This work is structured around the experiences and impressions of Mary Agnes Keely, a middle-aged spinster who leaves her home in Connecticut for a different lifestyle in New York. As Ag records in her notebook, reality is not as enchanting as she had imagined, and the book ends with her unmarried and pregnant. The novel's conclusion marks the beginning of a new self-awareness for the protagonist, however, for she writes: ''I will say to my child, your mother burst forth upon the whole dry world and knew . . . she had triumphed, that it was no great sin to be, at last, alone.''

Before My Time (1974), Howard's third novel, has been viewed as a series of interrelated stories about numerous minor characters. At the center of this work is the relationship between Laura Quinn, a forty-year-old journalist and homemaker who has become bored with the restrictions of her life, and Jim Cogan, her cousin's teenage son, who is charged with drug possession and conspiring to destroy a public library. While advising Jim to avoid prosecution by running away, Laura rediscovers her own life-affirming motivation, which provides her the means to overcome her ennui and to foresee a brighter future. Howard investigates similar themes in *Facts of Life* in an attempt to come to terms with her own painful past. She portrays her parents' conflicting personalities and their ''diseased attitude toward money'' and examines the consequences of her strict Catholic upbringing. Howard also discusses the academic and publishing institutions which have shaped her adult life. *Facts of Life* received the National Book Critics Circle Award for general nonfiction.

In her later novels, Howard again creates characters who rediscover the possibilities of a fulfilling existence. The protag-

onist of *Grace Abounding* (1982) grows to understand and accept human mortality and cultivates a renewed appreciation of life following the death of her husband. *Expensive Habits* (1986) is the story of a writer who tries to correct her past mistakes after learning that she has a potentially fatal heart disease. Although reviewers faulted the novel as a personal narrative, *Expensive Habits,* in Michiko Kakutani's estimation, ''is most effective when it's addressing the question of fiction and its consequences.'' Howard's short stories and essays have appeared in such publications as the *Hudson Review*, the *Yale Review*, the *New Yorker,* and the *New York Times Book Review*.

(See also *CLC*, Vols. 5, 14; *Contemporary Authors*, Vols. 53-56; and *Dictionary of Literary Biography Yearbook: 1983*.)

NOEL PERRIN

In the four novels—all good—she has published over the past 20 years, Mrs. Howard has been a women's writer in several quite different ways. First and most traditional, she has been consistently concerned with how women deal with their families, and especially their mothers. The women and the mothers are nearly always Irish, as Mrs. Howard is herself. Clearly Irish mothers take a lot of dealing with, if only because they have Mother Church right behind them, an advantage Jewish mothers lack.... Maureen Howard writes brilliantly about mother-daughter relations—and father-daughter too, in those cases where the father is still alive.

The second way that Mrs. Howard is a women's writer is hard to describe without being ponderous (something she herself never is). I think I can approach it best by telling a little true story about the New England village I live in.

Some 15 years ago, a retired general and his wife bought the biggest house in our village and spent a year and a great deal of money remodeling it into what they themselves called Williamsburg North. Then they invited the entire village to a housewarming: the grand kind, with silver and china, tea being poured at one end of a long table, coffee at the other.

To that splendid soiree came almost every woman in the village, the handful of middle-class men and such other men as were firmly under their wives' thumbs. It awed me to see how every woman knew just how to hold her paper-thin teacup and praise the marvelous new curtains, while the men huddled in clumsy groups and tried to talk about deer hunting. How could the wives be sophisticated and the husbands such clods? I eventually concluded it was because in our culture as it then was, boys had a fixed identity from the start, while girls had a fluid one. They didn't even know what their names would be when they grew up and married. The boy was merely himself, while the girl was possibly Mrs. General and possibly Mrs. Farmhand. I saw it all as giving women an imaginative edge.

Mrs. Howard sees it quite differently. She sees it as giving women a problem in becoming authentic. With so many possibilities, at least in the mind, how can a woman ever know who she really is? What seems to be her real life may be just another acted role. There's a section in Mrs. Howard's autobiography, *Facts of Life* (written when she was about 30 years younger than the people who write such books usually are), in which she describes some curious girlhood lessons she had. They came from a lady elocutionist who taught her the Attitudes: "Rejection, Fear, Love (both open and guarded variety), Laughter (head tossed, eyes dancing) and my favorite, Sorrow." In all her novels, Mrs. Howard shows women trying to get past the Attitudes into true feeling—sometimes succeeding and sometimes not. I don't know a writer who has done it better.

In her new novel, *Grace Abounding,* she becomes a women's writer in a third way. There is some sex and quite a lot of sexual fantasy in the book, all of it experienced, fantasized or remembered by women. To someone raised as I was on books where men (if anyone) did all that, it's like seeing the world under some hitherto unsuspected spectrum of light. Fascinating, if slightly uncomfortable.

Grace Abounding is more nearly the story of one person than any of Mrs. Howard's other novels. That person is Maude Dowd, who, as the book opens, is a good-looking Irish Catholic widow with a 14-year-old daughter and a senile mother. She is 43, two years a widow, living in a big house in Connecticut.

In the first section, called "Sin," Maude seems to have the double sins of acedia and lust. Her life as action barely exists. About all she *does* is take a long drive three days a week to visit her mother, and share some of the housekeeping with her

daughter. The rest of her time is devoted to spinning sexual fantasies (one of which presently blooms into a real affair) and to watching the very odd neighbors through field glasses. These neighbors, especially two aged spinsters, Miss Jane and Miss Mattie Le Doux, are two enormously significant characters, both in the book and in Mrs. Howard's work. Miss Jane (so people think) is a reclusive poet; Miss Mattie, huge and garish, is still in her old age an active slut. The house is a mess.

In the second section, called "Sorrow," 10 years have passed. Maude is remarried, living in New York with her foundation-executive husband, Gilbert Lasser. She herself has acquired a Ph.D. in psychology and is a children's therapist. The sorrow in this section does not come from her marriage—it's a good one—but from two other causes. One is the death of a 3-year-old patient . . . ; the other is simply the aging process. Maude is now 53. . . .

Sin, sorrow, and death is the usual series, but the third section is called "Minor Chalazion." At first I wondered if this was some obscure monastic order. Actually, it's a small growth on the eyelid, in this case Maude's. It requires surgery. This serves both as a premonition of death and as part of the process of final eye opening. One of the things then seen is the truth about Miss Mattie Le Doux—who and what, underneath 70 years of playacting, she has authentically been. It would be unfair to the novel to detail that truth in a review—but one can say that in her size and physical strength (Mrs. Howard has always been partial to big women), her wild mixture of vulgarity and brilliance, her confident eccentricity, Mattie expresses something pretty close to the life force as Mrs. Howard sees it. One of its avatars, anyway.

Grace Abounding is not the most successful of Mrs. Howard's novels. It is a little too short for its plot, and there are places where she shamelessly tells the reader what to think or feel.

Furthermore, the book does not quite come together at the end. It was never meant to do so in the tie-up-all-the-threads sense; Mrs. Howard has always avoided tidy endings. But a novel can avoid closure and still give a sense of completion. *Grace Abounding* does not, or not sufficiently.

It does give a sense of lives as they are really lived such as only a small minority of novelists in each generation can or even want to manage. Mrs. Howard, even at second best, is a writer to read. Here the sensibility. There the intelligence. (p. 24)

Noel Perrin, "Mothers and Daughters," in The New York Times Book Review, *September 26, 1982, pp. 7, 24.*

ANATOLE BROYARD

Grace Abounding is a baffling book. It's not that Maureen Howard can't write—her talent is unmistakable—but it's as if she won't. This book seems to be filled with a brilliant impatience, as Miss Howard picks up characters and drops them in the middle of an incompleted motion. There's a lot of rhetoric that reminds one of the famous definition: "The attempt of the will to do the work of the imagination." There are too many characters for 175 pages. The very length of the book suggests the author's unwillingness to put up for long with the people she herself has created.

Maude Dowd is a 43-year-old widow with a 14-year-old daughter and a head full of rather coarse sexual fantasies. It's not clear what drives her to obsess in this way. She is attractive, intelligent and ostensibly normal. If she wants or needs sexual satisfaction, there are conventional social forms for providing it.

Instead she indulges in a rather seamy affair with a man who is married to a disabled woman and then spends her unoccupied hours spying with binoculars on two old spinsters who live next door. One of these spinsters is a poet, and the reader waits for the connection. I found myself waiting for connections all through the book.

Now, there are writers who don't believe in connections and I've learned how to read them, but Miss Howard is not one of these. Rather, her book sounds as if some of the pages had fallen out, as if she had led up to connections that were subsequently lost or blighted. . . .

Maude's senile mother has a nurse who talks like a writer. Both the nurse and Maude's mother die "in tandem," almost at the same time, and one can almost hear Miss Howard saying. "That's enough of them. Let's do something else." One of the spinsters dies. When Maude becomes a child therapist, a 3-year-old patient of hers dies by falling out of a window. But he falls, in the words of a poet, "as apples fall, without astronomy." You might say that they all fall without gravity.

Mattie, the surviving spinster, is a big, fat, nymphomaniac poet who tells us that "dying, my father had to watch me read the poems of William Butler Yeats, in his last agony watch me slowly turn the pages of 'Responsibilities.'" By now, I no longer asked why I surmised that the significance of each of these baffling episodes lay in some sort of Cubistic superimposition.

I began to try to make it out. When Gilbert Lasser, Maude's new husband, visits his Jewish son in Florida and finds him working as an assistant pastor in an Episcopal church, he becomes disgusted. But when I searched for meaning in his disgust, I found it too abrupt, for his son does have some redeeming qualities. When Maude has a minor eye operation that gives its name to a whole section of *Grace Abounding,* I thought that here, certainly, was a signpost, an alteration in her way of seeing, but this reading too did not seem to advance us. . . .

Though I've read some symbolic novels and some that deliberately avoided symbols, I don't understand how I'm expected to approach this one. I can't call it a failure, because Miss Howard writes too well to fail in that simple sense. I would say rather that *Grace Abounding* is a refusal. I think it's a useful description, perhaps even a category to describe those books in which a talented writer has not been willing, for whatever reason, to effect a transaction with the reader.

Anatole Broyard, "One Widow's Story," in The New York Times, *October 2, 1982, p. 17.*

ANNE TYLER

In one of her earlier novels (**Bridgeport Bus,** 1965), Maureen Howard described a butcher enrolled in an adult English class. This man's composition on Peru started out prosaically enough ("Truly, Peru is a land of contrasts"), but then took a sudden wild swerve: . . .

> His wife, Gloria, had come into the refrigerator down at Western Beef one day and said how disgusting, and made like she was going to be sick, but Al thought it was natural to want to

see what you were eating before you got it on a plate with a mess of potatoes. 'The tin industry alone,' Al's paper went on, 'constitutes over eighty per cent of the gross national income and employs nearly three-fourths of all unskilled Peruvian workers.'

The English teacher, predictably, was not impressed, and counseled the class against falling into "the pit of disorganization." But to readers, that vision of Gloria gagging in the refrigerator was a pure delight—and to longtime Maureen Howard fans it was a familiar, much-hoped-for delight; for one of the qualities that make her writing so absorbing and so intensely personal is precisely the kind of lunge into "disorganization" that Al the butcher enjoyed. (p. 35)

It's not really disorganization at all, we begin to realize. Instead, it's a distinctive view of the world, almost a philosophical statement: a conviction that life is not so much a single straight line as a kind of mosaic, unreadable to ordinary humans but endlessly fascinating nonetheless.

Grace Abounding, her fifth novel, tells the story of an attractive widow named Maude and her daughter Elizabeth. As the book opens, Maude is locked into an existence that seems lonely and confined. She has thrown away all her late husband's belongings, redecorated the house in a pretty, rather fussy style, and resigned herself to coping with her aged mother's gradual disintegration. Meanwhile it's up to Elizabeth, aged fourteen, to fix Maude's meals and conscientiously set aside certain periods each day to keep her company.

Bleak, you'd say, and probably doomed to remain that way; but not in Maureen Howard's hands. For starters, there's Maude's rich, subterranean fantasy life, which mostly centers on sex. There's the hauntingly described atmosphere she moves through—her own high white house contrasted with the "mad filth and shambles" of the shack next door. The repeated evocation of this atmosphere—certain landmarks called up several times over, in a circular way, demonstrating Maude's dogged ritualism—is very like poetry.

There is, in addition, the endearing character of the daughter, Elizabeth. Stodgy, almost matronly, far too bright for her small-town school but forced to remain there by Maude's need to have her close by, Elizabeth fends off an oddball reputation among her peers by solemnly memorizing popular songs. . . . Elizabeth has, in addition, a secret. In the back of her closet, in a box that pictures "a boy and girl in ecstasy over an optics set with test tubes and microscopes glittering behind them," she keeps the personal effects sent home from the hospital after her father's death: clothing, a ring, a watch she keeps wound, a comb, a wallet, and a love note from another woman.

A lesser writer would make more of that love note—dissect the mystery, for instance; or use it as an excuse for some emotionally charged scene. Maureen Howard does neither. This is not to say that she ignores the note. It's brought up again, years later; we discover Maude knew of the woman all along, with what effect we can only imagine. That's the really important fact: her knowing. It reinforces the sense we're given, in all of Maureen Howard's books, of the delicate balance and tensions in any configuration of people.

A swoop, then: a leap more startling than any glimpse of Gloria in the butcher shop. We're all at once moved ahead in time. Maude has remarried and is living in New York City. Elizabeth is married and pregnant. Maude has a new profession as a child psychologist and Elizabeth *did* have a profession, of the most unexpected sort (classical singing), before she gave it all up for domestic life. There are several new characters—the two husbands, naturally, but also some surprising extras: among others, a seriously disturbed little patient with a Snow Queen mother; and Maude's husband's grown son, who's a priest in Florida.

Well, it's baffling, of course. For instance, none of the book's established characters ever actually meets with that priest, but here he suddenly is, displayed in the center of his routine. In fact, he provides the book's conclusion.

Does it work? For the most part, yes, if you're willing to relax and enjoy the ride. That's not always easy. There were moments when I felt a little testy; I was just getting settled into a scene when the rug was pulled out from under me. In general, though, the effect is refreshing, even exhilarating. We're reminded of the wealth of enigmas surrounding every human being. Interlocking lives, plots that travel out into space on daring tangents—isn't that going on in our own world, too, if only we stopped to consider? (pp. 35-6)

> Anne Tyler, "The Mosaic of Life," in The New Republic, Vol. 187, No. 14, October 4, 1982, pp. 35-6.

DORIS GRUMBACH

It is hard to understand how a writer of Maureen Howard's elegance, sharpness, sensibility and tenderness has escaped widespread public notice for so long. . . . For all I know, **Grace Abounding** will not noticeably advance her fame, yet it is another of her meticulously observed and beautifully written short studies of women caught in the world of men, lost to themselves, and finding little meaning in what they do.

It may seem that, if this book has a flaw, it is that both the events and the characters are somewhat underdeveloped. They are spare, sparsely suggested, in the way that Willa Cather admired when she complained in her essay, "The Novel Démeublé," that "the novel, for a long while, has been overfurnished." Maureen Howard writes fiction with Edward Hopper's eye and an ear that might have been tutored by John Cage. A great deal happens in a short space. To my taste this is a virtue because it leaves the reader space to expand, to conjecture, and to create parallel structures from his own experience.

The heroine and point of consciousness, for most of **Grace Abounding** is Maude Dowd. . . . We see from the outside and from her unsettled and often confused interior her relation to her senile mother, to her gawky adolescent daughter Elizabeth, to her husband who is dead, to her frightened lover who runs a religious gift shop in their town in Connecticut, to the two odd ladies who live across the street—one of whom is regarded by the town as "our Emily Dickinson"—and to, eventually, her child-patients in psychotherapy and to her second husband. Time passes, Maude sees her daughter grow up to develop a beautiful voice professionally only to abandon it for a shallow suburban marriage. A small cyst appears on [Maude's] eyelid which goes by the romantic-sounding name of "chalazion," and suddenly her mortality and pity for her limbo-selves flood in upon her. At the same time her daughter discovers the truth about the two old ladies in the decayed farmhouse in Connecticut, Maude's Jewish husband spies upon his Episcopal-priest son and "finds him out" in a strange way, and Elizabeth begins to sing again. The final "grace note" to the story of

Maude and her connections is left for the priest who performs his function for a young couple and then stumbles home drunk to his solitary life.

The paragraph above is purposefully long and unbroken to suggest the crowd of event and character that make the tapestry of Maude Dowd's consciousness. There is the sense of a much larger tapestry than 175 pages can contain; there is the feeling of intimacy with the people, drawn in with swift and telling strokes, which the length of the descriptions cannot explain. Maureen Howard distills what she knows; what is left in the alembic is all the serious reader needs to enter into her world.

The long frieze of women in this novel—mother and her doomed housekeeper, heroine and her daughter, decaying old sisters— does not constitute the whole of the story. Howard is a writer in the feminist tradition only because the dominant sensibility is most often that of a woman. But she suffers no myopia when it comes to men: husbands, lover, priest-son are all very real and very central to the whole splendidly arranged and securely conceived structure. Women without men, to turn Hemingway's phrase about, is never her subject but rather women searching for their lost selves in a male world in which most of the men are also adrift.

> Doris Grumbach, "Maureen Howard's Understated Elegance," in Book World—The Washington Post, October 10, 1982, p. 3.

ADA LONG

Much in **Grace Abounding** is familiar from Maureen Howard's earlier books, both fictional and autobiographical. There is the family of ex-Catholics in Connecticut, where certainties of any kind—whether false or true—are harder to come by than in New York, the contrasting culture, where attitudes are a survival tactic. The family members themselves have parallels in past books: the mother, who is sensitive, self-dramatizing, and—although successfully or potentially professional—resistant to acknowledging her own competence, attracted more to the mysteries of memory and imagination than to the clearer demands of simple ambition; the father figure, usually a lawyer, orderly and out of reach; the grandmother, who is that "doomed" creature, a "lady"; a brother, vital and irresistible, but lost, in this case to grotesque mid-life change; and the child, beloved, elusive, and disappointing.

Familiar also is Maureen Howard's method: the many fragments, "stories within stories," which combine more than connect to tell the whole tale. The point of view, usually third-person but occasionally first, shifts from character to character, allowing each one at least a moment at the center, so that none is "minor."

Despite the familiar elements, however, **Grace Abounding** is full of surprises. It is a more concentrated work than any of Howard's previous books, and in its rendering of the characters a gentler and more convincing one.

Especially in her most recent books—**Before My Time** and **Facts of Life,** an autobiography—Howard seemed so intent on avoiding sentimentality and predictability that her narrative often became tense, and her characters sometimes fell victim; there was something disagreeable about them. While there is no sentimentality or predictability in the new novel, neither does one feel the strain of their exclusion. The characters, with their tragic and comic weaknesses, are shamelessly likable but nonetheless mysterious, unsettling, and original.

The novel also has a stronger plot: not the "exposition, character development, psychological motivation," and "rickety" suspense that Howard listed as the "bald techniques of cheap fiction" in *Facts of Life,* but an accumulation of startling events, changes, and discoveries that arouse curiosity. While the novel entices us to wonder what really happened, and what will happen, and why, it does not invite us to predict or even to want any answers. The events in the novel are not controlled by cause and effect or the comfort of understanding, but create the pattern of a life through mistakes and misunderstandings.

Maude Dowd is mistaken about almost everything. In the first and best section of the book, she is a forty-three-year-old widow living with her daughter in Shrewsbury, Connecticut (the year is 1971). . . . She has settled almost comfortably into a routine of lassitude and self-delusion. Three times a week she drives to visit her aged and dotty mother, a fulfillment of duty which only she—certainly not her mother—appreciates. At home, she administers token maternal gestures to her daughter, who in fact is mothering her, while she nurtures an obsession with two old spinsters who live next door, about whom she knows little, understands less, and invents much, all of it wrong. She always keeps a "good" book within arm's reach but reaches for trash, which she forgets even before she puts it down.

And she fantasizes. Her energy, which is considerable, and her anger go into fantasies which are pornographic in their lust for humiliation, victimization. . . . Her final fantasy is the seduction of Paul Deems, an antique-store owner married to a wheelchair-ridden espouser of liberal Catholic causes. Maude, wrong as usual, believes Paul to be saintly in his role of dutiful husband, and—in a fantasy of mutual victimization—has him taking her money while she takes his virtue. When the fantasy is acted out, it becomes only a drab suburban love affair.

Yet Maude is neither pitiable nor contemptible. There is a comic edge to both her fantasies and her affair that saves her. Rather than the products of neurosis or stupidity, they seem an odd counterpoint to the evening news, where brutality is rendered insipid by an "ambitious parrot" (as Maude's daughter describes the anchorwoman) in a "beautiful dress and beads," or where diplomacy centers on a ping-pong table. Nothing in Maude's world seems quite real, so, without impediment, she stubbornly keeps on making mistakes. Her stubbornness is almost admirable.

When we encounter Maude in the second section of the novel, she is a changed woman. She is over fifty now and has a new husband, a new name (Maude Lasser), a new home (in New York), a new profession as a child psychologist, and a new obsession with efficiency and purpose. Torpor and aimlessness have been supplanted by schedule and punctuality—by a professionalism that is, again, almost admirable.

At first the change strains one's credibility, and Maude Lasser hardly seems the same woman as Maude Dowd. We eventually learn the events that preceded the change: the death of Maude's mother, the disappearance of Paul Deems, and the discovery of the talent of Maude's daughter as a singer—which prompts a move to New York for voice lessons and provides an occasion for Maude, with naïve earnestness, to attend graduate school and become a would-be culture maven. But these events are not causes, and, even if the "psychological motivation" had been more explicitly mapped out for us, it would still be less significant in making the change credible than the fact that Maude's new life is really a refracted image of her old life. It is a matter of redirected energy. A big improvement, certainly,

but not a miraculous success story or exemplum of women's liberation.

The miracle is not that Maude has changed but that, in a basic and mysterious way, she has not changed; her circumstances have. She still keeps on making mistakes—about her patients, her family, herself. . . . In neither the private nor the public world can one ever understand motives, know causes, predict effects, or control events; to keep discovering this, as Maude does, and then to keep going is a worthy accomplishment.

Near the end of the book, Maude indulges in self-pity and anger after she has a minor eye operation, and exerts the same hysterical energy she had previously lavished on her fantasies. Among her grievances is her daughter:

> With no further provocation, I started on Elizabeth as I tottered to the bedroom with the mail and my magazine. Ungrateful girl. I had made a world for her. The costly years of training: her scales and noisy exercises—maddening while I worked over my courses for Columbia, preparing myself for life. . . . While the great waste went on around me—her Steinway, Italian lessons, diction, fencing, dance. I remembered the outrageous price of her georgette recital gown. In this version I had sold my house for her. Left a warmhearted circle of friends. On Seventy-sixth Street I had waited up for my daughter at night, long after the heat went off, . . . until her key turned in the latch. Supper for her on the stove at midnight. Oh, I was glad to be of any use.

One cliché after another. But the comic self-awareness of "in this version" is her salvation, her abounding grace—not the grace that was available to John Bunyan in *Grace Abounding to the Chief of Sinners,* but still, for now, grace enough.

I have made Maude seem much simpler than she is, for she does indeed exist in many versions. The other characters in the novel have wildly disparate impressions of her, and I suspect that readers will too. And besides, her story is but one among many. She is part of a large cast of characters who range from the mundane to the grotesque. . . . (pp. 46-7)

All the characters have a mysterious and complex integrity. By writing about them on their own terms—as they stumble and collide with one another and live through the accidents, illusions, deceits, and misunderstandings of their lives—Maureen Howard is able to make them surprising and more interesting than we would ever expect: a mark of first-rate fiction. (p. 47)

Ada Long, "Surprises," in The New York Review of Books, *Vol. XXIX, No. 19, December 2, 1982, pp. 46-7.*

JONATHAN YARDLEY

By contrast with Maureen Howard's four previous novels, *Expensive Habits* is long and, in the conventional sense, ambitious: the other books are delicate miniatures, elegantly crafted and somewhat elliptical in narrative method, but *Expensive Habits* attempts to paint a relatively large canvas and does so in a rather straightforward manner. The novel appears . . . to be Howard's attempt to reach for a larger readership than she has thus far enjoyed; it is an honorable effort, and in no way does Howard compromise her exceptionally high standards in the process, but *Expensive Habits* is an odd book that is more likely to provoke curiosity and respect than affection and admiration.

Readers familiar with Howard's earlier fiction and her fine autobiography, *Facts of Life,* will find much here that is agreeably familiar. She writes equally well about two strikingly different milieus, both of which are present in *Expensive Habits:* the domestic life of genteel but threadbare Roman Catholic families, and the bitchy, narcissistic world of the New York illuminati. Her prose has a distinct and refreshing individuality; she moves with ease between high and low styles, changing gears so smoothly that the reader rarely feels she is calling attention to herself. The sense of irony that permeates all of her work is uncommonly acute, yet it becomes merely judgmental; she recognizes all the weaknesses and self-indulgences of the people she describes and the fashionable ideas they embrace, but her satire is tempered by sympathy, even when silliness is endemic.

There is a good deal of silliness in *Expensive Habits,* much of it committed by the central character, Margaret Flood. She is a 46-year-old writer who has just been told that she suffers from a heart condition that will kill her in a matter of months. . . .

[She] drags herself from New York down to Baltimore, undergoes bypass surgery, and emerges from it with an opportunity to live a new life.

But the brush with "death's bright angel" has had a traumatic effect on this difficult, demanding, temperamental, arrogant woman: it has forced her to examine her past and its many errors, to attempt a rewriting of that past. Before leaving for the hospital "she had worked with a frenzy to set the record straight, as though she were ripping out the seams of her life." After the surgery she does not abandon this effort but continues it with new determination, possessed as she is by the conviction that her books, which are the story of her life, have told that story wrong—that they are riddled with self-serving falsehoods that have damaged others.

Chief among these, she believes, is her first husband, Jack Flood, whom she married while he was in medical training; they divorced following her discovery that he was having an affair with a nurse. This became the subject of her first novel, in which she portrayed him as altering the results of his medical research in order to obtain an NIH grant; all of these years she has known that "I contracted with myself to write a revenge tragedy, to make an unsupportable thesis of my marriage to Jack Flood." Now it is to him, a distinguished surgeon, that she turns not merely for medical help, but also for forgiveness for "bitter words and fancies, my only consolation, having lost the game."

It is one of many she has lost, thinking she has won: thinking that by reordering life, by faking it in fiction, she can recoup her losses and heal her wounds. But then she is made victim of an irreplaceable loss, one that shakes her house of fiction down to its foundation, and she confronts life's inescapable truth. . . .

[The] discovery of her mere humanity is arrived at by more routes than those provided by Jack Flood and a terrible personal calamity. Others with whom she must contend include her present husband, Pinkham Strong, a spineless patrician from whom she is separated; their son, Bayard, a 16-year-old of exceptional character and maturity; her first editor, Philo Pierce,

a cynical fellow traveler in literary and political circles; . . . a Hispanic maid, named (with an excess of irony) Lourdes, whose idle chatter has dreadful consequences; and a small band of ancient radicals—"grand men and women—flawed, perhaps fallen, but gods in their day"—about whom she is attempting to write a book.

It is, on the whole, a larger cast of characters (and the themes they bring along as baggage) than the novel can comfortably contain. Although it is clear what Howard means to do with each particular person, these schemes don't always seem necessary to the central concerns of the book; even when their connection to the major themes—fate, history, nostalgia, illusion—is clear, their presence can seem gratuitous. . . . Howard can't let sleeping themes lie, but pokes away at them with a didacticism that is most uncharacteristic. Neither does it help matters that Margaret Flood is never really brought to life, never really takes control of her own story; we are meant to feel a sympathy for her that she never manages to earn.

But if *Expensive Habits* is a disappointment, it is principally so by comparison with Howard's earlier work: those terse, elusive books that are so much larger than the sum of their parts. By comparison with most contemporary American fiction, on the other hand, it is a serious and accomplished piece of work. Here as in her other work Howard writes about the fads and fashions of the day, about a society eager to cash in on any passing joy or sorrow, but she is having none of that herself; she stands apart, observing "the dumb glory of it all" with an eye that is sharp but kind. If *Expensive Habits* is not [a] major work . . . , it is certainly a book rich in integrity and elegance, by a writer who matters.

Jonathan Yardley, "Maureen Howard: Satire and Sympathy," in Book World—The Washington Post, May 11, 1986, p. 3.

MICHIKO KAKUTANI

The heroine of Maureen Howard's fifth and latest novel [*Expensive Habits*] is a writer, the author of "wonderful books" and "thrilling scripts," a "tested marvel," who is wined and dined by both old guard leftist intellectuals and slick new Hollywood impresarios. At 45, though, Margaret Flood is also a "sick woman in her middle years, betrayed by one man, abandoned by another," a lonely casualty of two spoiled marriages, who is now lying in a hospital room, dying of heart disease.

Like many of Miss Howard's heroines, Margaret suffers from something of an identity problem—called upon to fulfill multiple roles (daughter, wife, mistress, mother, career woman), she finds it difficult to settle upon a self that feels real. And in Margaret's case, matters are complicated further by the fact that she's a writer—someone engaged full time in remaking, revising and reordering the stuff of her own life.

As a result, we are treated to a succession of scenes presenting various versions of Margaret—mainly Margaret as she defines herself in terms of assorted men. We see the young Margaret, as the resourceful wife of Jack Flood, an up-and-coming doctor . . . ; Margaret as the eager would-be novelist, decked out in a lavender tweed suit to meet Philo Pierce, the man who will become her mentor and literary conscience; Margaret as the rich and famous author, serving as a consort to Sol Negaly, a movie producer . . . ; and Margaret as the golden partner of the irrepressible Pinky Strong, a handsome preppie turned radical celeb.

With her swift eye for detail, Miss Howard is able to make these men materialize instantly before our eyes, and she proves equally adept at sketching in the worlds they inhabit. . . . She can conjure up a New York City bourgeois childhood with a handful of details . . . and she can give the reader a precise sense, too, of what it's like to be a kid, shuttling back and forth between estranged parents.

The trouble is that Miss Howard's pointillist descriptions frequently fail to run much deeper. All too often, she seems in a rush to get on to the next scene, the next character, the next incident; and consequently, the narrative of *Expensive Habits* can sound like a breathless account of a shopping expedition, spilled out in a staccato tumble of images and exclamations. We end up getting an impression of what the minor characters look and sound like, what sort of jokes and stories they like to tell; but we never get to know what they're like inside, what differentiates them, really, from other members of their class and profession.

As for Margaret Flood, we're given a number of views to choose from: besides getting to hear from her maid, her son and Margaret herself, we get to read Margaret's fictional representations of her own life. . . .

Just how all these versions of Margaret's life are supposed to add up is never made clear. Perhaps that is just Miss Howard's point—that character is something intangible, a collection of costumes and roles and reflections picked up in other people's mirrors. Still, Margaret's willful elusiveness tends to give the book a somewhat hollow center; and it's even more perplexing, in light of Miss Howard's determination elsewhere to manipulate the reader's emotions, to almost physically maneuver the story line into obedience. Not only does she use tired, obvious metaphors—much is made of Margaret's heart condition, and its relation to her spiritual afflictions—but she also resorts to soap-opera contrivances (including the violent murder of Margaret's son) to make her story of soul-searching and redemption hit the requisite emotional marks.

For this reader at least, *Expensive Habits* is most effective when it's addressing the question of fiction and its consequences. Though she's essentially remapping territory previously staked out by Philip Roth in such works as *My Life as a Man* and *Zuckerman Unbound*, Miss Howard succeeds here in making the dilemma of a writer like Margaret Flood both palpable and moving.

Michiko Kakutani, "Life and Fiction," *in* The New York Times, *May 24, 1986, p. 11.*

GEOFFREY WOLFF

In *Facts of Life* (1978), Maureen Howard told the story of her childhood and self-education in Bridgeport, Conn., among Irish-American Catholics. Now, her fifth novel [*Expensive Habits*] opens with an echo of the blunt priestly send-off from a confessional: "Go and sin no more." The second word of this novel's title resonates with the word for a nun's outfit, but "habits" spreads a wider net than costume can define.

The habit for which Maureen Howard's protagonist, Margaret Flood, has paid dearly is less a show of style than a principle of feeling. Her scarab-hard carapace of manner reveals hardheartedness, and Margaret Flood's combat against her meaner reflexes of thought and feeling provokes the friction that provokes the heat of a smart, sharp novel that might have—given a smaller purpose than Miss Howard's—been cold.

Margaret Flood enters *Expensive Habits* at 45, a celebrated novelist dying in New York of a heart disease. Her deeper disease is bitterness, an unlocated anger that her two husbands have let her down, that she has somehow failed her teen-age son, that her editors have been frauds and bullies, that her celebrity has failed to make her happy, or healthy. . . .

Margaret Flood, like her maker, is a writer of wit and precision, shrewd at seeing the dust beneath the rug, sardonic, an accurate mimic, wised up to pretense, suspicious of enthusiasm and sentiment, quick to anger. The self-revelations of *Facts of Life* invite my otherwise presumptuous connection between character and creator. As hard on herself as on others in that book of memories—and plenty hard on others—she wrote that "my parents took my anger as a joke. Disgust swelled from me: I was not ready for compassion."

Margaret Flood, dying and rescued from a failure of heart, dealt the worst cards a mother (or father) can be dealt, sick of her habits, is ready for compassion. She does not invite it from others, but longs to give it. . . .

In the crisis of her diseased heart [Margaret Flood] cannot say precisely what she wants to be (she is too honest for that), but she begins to see, with flickering acuity, what she wishes no more to be. To want is not to have, of course; this is a story about pain, alcoholism, crime, betrayal, the violent death of kin and of dreams. But "from back, far back, from grammar school, [Margaret Lynch Flood] remembers a pretty nun who did not like Margaret Lynch . . . does not like that smart little girl, calls her in front of the class, says cruelly, 'A little learning is a dangerous thing.'"

This passage abounds in Maureen Howard's stylistic signatures. *Expensive Habits* runs dangerous (and sometimes costly) risks with shifts of tense and voice, answering the imperative not of logical consistency but of her narrative instinct. The stakes seem always high, so the novel seldom relaxes. The prose is terse, epigrammatic, truncated, exact, dense with multiple suggestions. It inclines toward monologue, a partiality of point of view surrendered sometimes to secondary characters but recentering itself relentlessly in Margaret Flood's idiom and self-knowledge.

She knows herself so well, she thinks she knows everyone else—the most expensive vice of the habit of solipsism. Watching herself, she is also watching her first husband, second husband, maid, editors, old friends. Equipped with a superb intelligence, she is always on, and her instinct for center stage, so unappealing in a precocious schoolgirl, is intolerable in a grown-up and can wear on a reader as well. She is too smart to whine, but not yet wise enough to shut up and listen. On the final page of *Expensive Habits,* Margaret Flood is still "too smart for her own good." . . .

Margaret Flood, heart diseased, bypassed and broken, has embarked on a mission of self-repair, seeking to recover simple, sane kindness. She labors mightily, that is, for what seems an attainable end, a bit of human generosity.

Her son Bayard, every bit as smart as his mother, tragic at 16, spends himself first on the heavens (staring through a telescope) and then on a girl, good sweaty sex. (To reveal more about Bayard here is to compromise the exquisitely timed progress of Margaret Flood's destiny.) As attentively as he studies stars, focusing precisely, his mother looks at herself. It is another's observation, but her idiom, that hears her "disorderly heart, off beat, jazzy as a drummer's riff." She celebrates "the pure world of the sick.'' To see her after her bypass is to regard ''a beautiful incision.'' This is the heart of Miss Howard's art, too, a surgical procedure gorgeously executed; the cutting warrants attention; life-saving is by the way. . . .

Maureen Howard is a brilliant comic writer. To have played against her epigrammatic power is to have tried something serious, and difficult. When she surrenders most casually to that power she may hit notes with fell accuracy, pitch perfect, as with such minor characters as Tina, the young wife of a movie director (''The seasons are not Tina's thing. What's the big deal? Spring—it's so New York. Sunshine—whee!''), or with Margaret Flood's maid, Lourdes, whose own domestic troubles run a tragic counterpoint to Margaret's. But in the grip of her zeal for caricature, Miss Howard may also reach casually for easy parody, as with Jack Flood's idiotically smug wife, or the movie director, or a nasty editor, rodentlike Fred Peach: here she indulges a bully's tactics, setting up contemptible characters merely to punish them with contempt.

That Maureen Howard, in her ambition to set Margaret Flood against her worst instincts, has sometimes failed in generosity and complexity of sentiment does not undo the intelligence and honor of her ambition. This is a rich novel, deeply felt, smart, by God *written*.

Geoffrey Wolff, ''Hardhearted Margaret,'' in The New York Times Book Review, *June 8, 1986, p. 9.*

ANITA BROOKNER

[*Expensive Habits*] is a good, substantial, improving novel for those who think that nothing ever happens. It opens flamboyantly and goes on to better things; by the end the heroine, who began with a heart bypass operation, is left with literally not a leg to stand on. In between these two near fatalities several illusions have been demolished, reputations destroyed, marriages blown up, crimes committed, and lives abruptly ended. The interesting thing is that although the novel seems to promise one of those valiant though vulnerable, over-achieving yet victimised heroines so popular today in a certain kind of American fiction, the crazy and irritating Margaret Flood in *Expensive Habits* does in fact possess truly heroic qualities of courage and impassivity in the face of blind fate of a strain less frequently encountered now than was the case two generations ago. The amazing spectacle of a woman displaying the sort of pride that has become so unfashionable lifts the novel out of the ordinary and spreads a remarkable glow of optimism over the whole enterprise. One feels that something commendable has been attempted. (p. 31)

There are moments of genuine exaltation in this novel which make it hard to categorise. Maureen Howard has given the stereotyped woman's story—one woman against the world, her struggles, triumphs, loves, fears, etc.—and grounded it in something more persuasive. Low on sex and high on purpose, it reflects a stoicism conspicuous by its absence in contemporary feminist writing. It also reflects a sense of context. Maureen Howard's Margaret experiences more than mere consciousness of her own struggle and yet remains a heroine of

the old-fashioned type, designed for women to emulate. This is an intelligent novel which manages to please on several levels without quite destroying one's expectations of a traditional good read. (p. 32)

Anita Brookner, ''Unfashionable Pride Defeats Our Prejudice,'' in The Spectator, *Vol. 257, No. 8261, November 8, 1986, pp. 31-2.*

PEARL K. BELL

[It is] difficult to figure out what Maureen Howard had in mind in her fifth novel, *Expensive Habits*. Though she has declared (in that slick temple of trendiness, *Vanity Fair*) that her theme is ''celebrity as an American disease''—a promising idea—this is not borne out in the novel. True, Howard's heroine is, or once was, a best-selling novelist, but this doesn't automatically make her a celebrity. (pp. 107-08)

Howard does not endow her heroine with the rapacious craving for the limelight of a genuine celebrity. Nor does the fact that Margaret tarted up her shanty-Irish family in one book and defamed her first husband in another mean she's sold out to the bitch goddess. Novelists always distort and exaggerate, and they want to write successful books. This doesn't mean they're corrupt, but that's what Howard want us to believe about Margaret Flood. When she is felled by heart disease, the refining fire of mortality makes Margaret reach for redemption in the form of a notebook that will tell her clever young son (a precocious sixteen-year-old who says ''I live by my wits'') the truth she left out of her novels, not only about family and husband but ''the material of a decade,'' the radicals she hung around with in the fifties, McCarthyism, the peace movement.

This is an admirably ambitious scheme, but Howard does not bring it off because she has trussed her large-minded intentions in a style that defeats them at almost every turn. Theoretically there's nothing wrong with trying to capture the nervous staccato rhythms of a woman's mind as she is waiting for open-heart surgery: the fits and starts, the leaps and stumbling of her anxious monologue as she clutches at elusive patches of memory for reassurance. But Maureen Howard's fidgety, chopped-up prose disintegrates into a pseudo-Joycean muddle. . . . (p. 108)

[Maureen Howard's] design is intellectually spacious, and she shuttles energetically between past and present, between middle class and underclass (the world of Margaret's Puerto Rican housekeeper), between politics and illness. She is an old-fashioned modernist who doggedly believes that a story told through the disorientations, the lurch and stumble of a fitful consciousness, can dramatize complexities that straightforward narrative neglects. But this approach can succeed only when the writer clearly knows what she is trying to say. Maureen Howard has not defined her psychological or intellectual destination, and gets nowhere. ''It's a dark book,'' she told *Vanity Fair*. Darker than she knows. (p. 109)

Pearl K. Bell, in a review of ''Expensive Habits,'' in Partisan Review, *Vol. LIV, No. 1, 1987, pp. 107-09.*

Witi (Tame) Ihimaera

1944-

New Zealander novelist, short story writer, editor, and non-fiction writer.

In his fiction, Ihimaera, a member of the native Maori tribe of New Zealand, explores the traditional familial values of his people and the cultural changes which have resulted from European colonization. Recurring themes in Ihimaera's works include social conflicts between Maoris and the *pakehas,* or white Europeans; the loss of Maori reverence for their own tradition; and the disintegration of cultural identity brought about by attempts of younger Maoris to assimilate into the more affluent and urbanized *pakeha* society. Despite his fear that the Maori way of life may be disappearing, Ihimaera usually tempers his doubts with a cautious optimism and belief in the indestructible Maori spirit. According to one reviewer, Ihimaera's sensibility "contains, and controls warmth, a humorous affection, [and] makes the drabbest of detail, the commonplaces of rural and urban poverty, come alive, human, and acceptable."

Ihimaera intended his first collection of short fiction, *Pounamu, Pounamu* (1972), to be read by both Maori and *pakeha* children in New Zealand secondary schools. In these stories, Ihimaera illuminates Maori cultural values by examining the clash of loyalties and generational conflicts resulting from the transition of a primitive, communal society to an individualistic, industrial civilization. This dilemma is related through stories concerning *pakeha* attitudes toward Maoris as well as others celebrating Maori custom and ritual. The title of one story, "Tangi," is the Maori word for the mourning ceremony following a death in the community. Ihimaera expanded the story to create *Tangi* (1973), the first full-length work of fiction written in English by a Maori author. This novel concerns the death of a father and its effect on his son, Tama Mahana, a Maori educated by *pakeha* society who is a recurring character in Ihimaera's fiction. The narrative, which alternates between past and present, explores Tama's thoughts and memories as he shuttles between industrial *pakeha* society and his rural birthplace. Through recollections of his father's belief in Maori tradition, Tama learns to affirm life in the presence of death and to understand his spiritual inheritance of Maori customs and ideologies. H. Winston Rhodes deemed *Tangi* "a dramatic poem in prose, an elegiac evocation of the past, a triumphant acceptance of the future, an amalgamation of myth and legend with the reality of the present."

In his next novel, *Whanau* (1974), Ihimaera expands upon the theme of the spiritual bonds of Maori society first presented in *Tangi.* The word *whanau* refers to the Maori concept of family, which includes the village community as a whole. Ihimaera emphasizes the importance of the group over the individual by not designating a central character, and the *whanau* thus emerges as a collective protagonist. The novel depicts Maori village life by focusing on events of a single day in Waituhi. Celebrating the brief revival of family cohesion resulting from the search for the village's oldest member, who has disappeared, Ihimaera posits the possibility of a renaissance of Maori culture and values. Ihimaera's next book, the short story collection *The New Net Goes Fishing* (1977), is his most

direct examination of racial tension and *pakeha*-inspired aspirations. Harsher in tone than his previous works, this volume is framed by an opening story about the movement of young Maoris to the city and a concluding piece involving the return of a Maori to his village following years of urban living.

Ihimaera's recent novel, *The Matriarch* (1986), relates the attempts of Tama Mahana to understand the tribal inheritance assigned to him by his grandmother, the matriarch of his *whanau.* In a narrative that alternates between past and present and blends expository prose, polemic, and historical record, the woman delineates her prominent ancestors and manages to reconcile family and tribal rivalries through a mysterious charismatic power. Ihimaera has also written *Maori* (1975), a nonfiction work on Maori life, and has coedited an anthology of Maori fiction, *Into the World of Light* (1980). He presently serves as New Zealand's consul to the United States.

(See also *Contemporary Authors,* Vols. 77-80.)

THE TIMES LITERARY SUPPLEMENT

This collection of short stories [*Pounamu, Pounamu*] is not just a collection. The stories constitute a whole: they are all firmly and deeply grounded in the life of Maoris of today, a life seen through a Maori eye and a Maori memory which fuse truthfulness, faith to the facts, with love. . . . Witi Ihimaera's realism is like sunlight which conceals nothing but which, because it contains, and controls warmth, a humorous affection, makes the drabbest of detail, the commonplaces of rural and urban poverty, come alive, human, and acceptable.

The talent revealed is all the more welcome because this is not only Mr Ihimaera's first book but the first work of fiction . . . in which the Maoris of our time have emerged through the imagination of a Maori writer of such skill and power.

The repeated word of the title, *pounamu,* however translucent to New Zealanders, will be opaque to the English reader. It means "greenstone", a New Zealand form of jade, evocative of a past when it was the prized material of axe and ornament; and evoking also an early novel by William Satchell, *The Greenstone Door,* in which Satchell, a pakeha, tried to do from the outside for the epic times of the Maori wars and in the romantic idiom of a former day what Mr Ihimaera has now done from within for a time of transition, when the heroic has faded.

The problems of the Maori, making their transition from a communal primitive society to an atomized industrial society, lie behind many of these stories, and the inevitable clash of generations, conflict of loyalties, the pull of the past and the push of the present. Mr Ihimaera handles all this with subtlety and restraint, rightly making the creation of people his priority and leaving their problems to present themselves implicitly through the way his characters behave.

There are few writers who can write from love without stumbling into bathos or sentimentality. Mr Ihimaera can. This is the most interesting new writing to come out of New Zealand for a long time and implies a promise of more.

> *"Modern Maoris," in* The Times Literary Supplement, *No. 3701, February 9, 1973, p. 141.*

H. WINSTON RHODES

The influence of tradition on critical judgement is frequently unrecognised and rarely explored. Yet *Tangi,* the first novel published by a Maori writer, is such an honest and unusual book that differences in cultural background and artistic conventions should be frankly acknowledged. It is far from easy to discriminate and evaluate without a firm basis for comparison, and dishonest to praise or blame without turning a critical eye on one's own emotional and literary heritage.

Tangi describes 'the Maori values placed on life; and on aroha, love and sympathy for each other'. It gives expression to 'the village family unity of rural Maori life,' and 'is written in the hope that such a life, and the values of that life, will never be lost.' These fragments taken from lines that serve as an unorthodox introduction to *Tangi* are not necessarily an aid to understanding, but are rather a statement of intent. The fulfilment of the implied promise depends both on the author's skill as well as on the reader's ability to appreciate the values of the world he is invited to enter, and the ways in which that world is presented. The opening paragraph of the introductory declaration suggests that Witi Ihimaera is working within a tradition perhaps accessible to but nonetheless remote from the consciousness of the pakeha:

> My mother was the Earth.
> My father was the Sky.
> They were Rangitane and Papatuanuku,
> the first parents, who clasped each other so
> tightly that there was no day. Their children
> were born into darkness . . .

'Judge if you must, but first understand' is a daunting reminder of responsibilities, and of the difficulties encountered when trying to adjust to the unaccustomed ramifications of a different tradition. An even harder saying for the critic is 'Judge not, that ye be not judged.' For almost any comment on 'otherness' is likely to provoke a legitimate retort, and a reviewer is as prone to self-revelation as the author himself. 'Otherness' in tradition creates obstacles to complete understanding that are by no means confined to language and mythology. As *Tangi* illustrates, values, emotional tone and structure are all involved, and only the rash and insensitive reader can afford to ignore them.

At the centre of *Tangi* is the familiar, but in this instance unfamiliar, relationship between father and son, a relationship here so close, so intense and sometimes so suffocating that to this unregenerate but (I hope) normally dutiful pakeha it seems to belong to an alien world. Those of us who, it could be said, have for too long been brought up on a diet of novels in which the central and youthful character must escape from the ghosts of the past before he can become himself, who have been seduced by the catch-phrases of psychology, and have remained unaffected by the mystique surrounding the patriarchal family, may find it difficult to enter confidently into this world of oppressive sentiment, or to identify with the twenty-two-year-old Maori narrator, Tama. 'Judge if you must, but first understand.'

Our entry is made even more difficult because the mode of expression to which we have become accustomed inclines towards the laconic, prefers under-statement to over-statement, and what from the pakeha point of view may be deep and sincere emotion is often concealed by the language of restraint. As its title indicates *Tangi* is concerned with death, the death of Tama's father, and with its effect on the son and all the members of the extensive Maori family. The death of Rongo Mahana is always before us, accentuated by uninhibited lamentations and the phraseology of grief. One needs to remember that in the words of the author this 'is a poetic drama in prose, about a young man and his father . . . an account of death, but also an affirmation of life.' Nevertheless the repetitive and continual emphasis given to the distress of the mourners, and particularly of Tama himself, reveals once again the 'otherness' that is so intimately bound up with social tradition. Sensitive though even a pakeha may be, he could experience difficulty in accepting without a quiver continual variations on such passages as the following:

> It is sweet sadness to press noses in the hongi.
> It is sweet sadness to mingle my tears with the
> tears of my people, my family. I am more than
> my father's son. For these people I am son,
> friend, father too. They are to me in turn, my
> sons, daughters, fathers and mothers. That is
> the Maori way: not to talk of one family for
> we belong to each other, not only family living
> but family dead. . . . The tears fall, among us

mingling. The deep sighs of sadness are the winds gathering from Waituhi our home. The winds gather, the winds join; from the desolate emptiness of Rongopai they come.

Those of us who belong for better or worse to another tradition are suspicious of anything that smacks of sentimentalism. Yet *Tangi* cannot justly be accused of sentimentality. The Maori way is not the pakeha way, and should not be approached through pakeha traditions. (pp. 348-50)

The design of [*Tangi*] is not one that immediately becomes apparent to the inattentive reader, and its time-scheme at first seems curiously disconcerting. It is only when the reader is finally involved, for despite what has been said he does become involved and this is a measure of Witi Ihimaera's achievement that he succeeds in drawing even an unregenerate pakeha into his world, that he realises that Tama in successive chapters is returning home to the tangi, and travelling back to Wellington after it is over. On his flight to Gisborne his thoughts are with his father and everything reminds him of the past. On his long train journey to Wellington to arrange his affairs for a final return, his mind is likewise filled with memories. . . . The two journeys, together with the whole vivid description of the tangi, serve the double purpose of enabling Witi Ihimaera to tell the story of Tama's life in the midst of his family and of focussing attention on the underlying theme—'This is *Tangi*, an account of death, but also an affirmation of life.' It is indeed a dramatic poem in prose, an elegiac evocation of the past, a triumphant acceptance of the future, an amalgamation of myth and legend with the reality of the present. The structure of the novel is such that the present is involved with the past, and the past with the future. (p. 350)

Tangi becomes accessible to the pakeha reader provided that the latter is patient with his own misunderstandings, aware that literary conventions are closely related to social traditions, and willing to acknowledge the value of different traditions, to recognise that 'otherness' is other as well as significant. This first novel by a Maori writer is an impressive attempt to communicate between two cultures which, however much they may mingle, are likely to remain different until that remote and unforeseeable time when the traditions on which they are based become indistinguishable. (p. 351)

H. Winston Rhodes, in a review of "Tangi," in Land-fall, Vol. 27, No. 4, December, 1973, pp. 348-51.

THE TIMES LITERARY SUPPLEMENT

Tangi is the kind of novel that claims notice for reasons that are only peripherally connected with the business of fiction. It is in the end an unfair kind of worthiness that its author, Witi Ihimaera, finds himself rather laudably loaded with. . . . *Tangi*, his second book, is the first novel written by a Maori ever to get into print. All that is distinction of a real enough sort, but it rather sneakily tends to predispose the reader in Mr Ihimaera's favour without actually guaranteeing anything in the way of fictional merit. Anthropology keeps jogging criticism's elbow. And that's not the end of it: *Tangi* . . . levers the liberal critic into grudging acceptance by trading on his subterranean post-colonial guiltiness. Such fictions (let alone, one supposes, their publishers) are eagerly prone to remind us that it's our fault, after all, that creative Nigerians and Indians and Maoris have ended up writing in English and not in some more native and natural tongue, and that it is tough luck if they cannot find a slot on the Old Country's bookshelves.

So *Tangi* is hard to refuse, and if it's much less hard to put down, it makes you feel rotten for admitting so. It concerns itself, with a degree of open feeling that would embarrass *The Old Curiosity Shop*, with the dilemma of a young Maori caught between two cultures—the threatened traditions of his people and the modernity of present-day white New Zealand. Tama Mahana's father dies, and the young man returns piously from his job in the city of Wellington to, as he repeatedly insists, "where his heart is", that is, the home place, the painted Meeting-House of his tribe and the old ceremonies of mourning. But he is not altogether reclaimed by the past: there's a girl back in Wellington, and his clothes and livelihood are there. So the novel has him frequently in transit, shuttling back and forth by train and plane: over-clamantly, perhaps a symbol of the educated, new Maori, torn between two worlds.

But the many journeys at least give Tama a lot of time for recalling his dad, his lore and his love, and the family's long struggles to break out of poverty and quit other people's tatty shacks for their own farm. Some of this recollecting is just gush, but some of it manages to be very moving. And there are occasions when the novel compels attention on grounds other than the ethnic-colonial-anthropological. Like Tama's frequent and increasingly urgent questioning of his father, "What's a Maori, dad?"; or the taut account of the time when he was told a white school-friend's birthday-party was cancelled because of illness, and his mother insisted he take along the birthday present they had bought—only to discover the party in full swing. Moments like that would command respect in anybody's novel, anywhere. But most of the time there is too heavy a reliance on the reciting of strings of exotic names . . . , the rehearsing of strange beliefs, and the charting of, to us, uncustomary religious customs. . . . Even a Maori novel needs to be bulked out with something other than dollops of native lingo, endlessly reiterated. The blurb itself gets into the act, anxious to endorse this way of stunning readers. *Haere mai, haere mai, haere mai,* it chants, without letting on about the meaning of these evidently important words. It's a reticence the novel chooses never to make good. And mere exotica, even in large quantities, aren't enough. Sometimes Mr Ihimaera is prepared and able to give us more; too frequently he is not.

"Maori-Go-Round," in The Times Literary Supplement, *No. 3775, July 12, 1974, p. 741.*

MARTHA MILLER

[Ihimaera's second novel, *Whanau*], is a wistful celebration of what remains of Maori village life and *whanau* (family). In the village of Waituhi, family cohesion has declined and is mourned—so is the death of the great hockey tournaments of the 1940s; new zoning laws threaten further break up; in the painted meeting-house, old shadows and voices mass, and dust collects. Waituhi's villagers, identified in brief, domestic scenes, are characterized chiefly by their attitude to the community. There are stalwarts, sloggers and gossips—and sprightly children (August, Crete, Anzac) who steal chocolate, make kites and run away from the washing-up. There are renegades who, made bad or sad by failure in Wellington, have limped back to Waituhi to swill beer and sing "The Last Waltz" in a tin shack; and ambitious or disgruntled teenagers who dream of getting out of Waituhi and into diamonds, furs and universities. Everyone peppers his speech with "crikey dicks" and "blinking hells". But when Nanny Paora, oldest inhabitant of the village, wanders off, they all band together under the cry "our *kaumatua* is missing"—and find him. The air of anxious instruction with which Mr Ihimaera warns of such village phenomena as "an old *korua* with his *mokopuna*", together with chirpiness of dialogue, steers **Whanau** into the area of the geography textbook. Having a real subject and arranging it adroitly makes it likable.

> Martha Miller, *"Now Is the Hour," in* The Times Literary Supplement, *No. 3809, March 7, 1975, p. 260.*

CHARLES R. LARSON

[It] is encouraging to realize that the most recent writing from [the South Pacific] retains the exceptional level of quality set by works of the past few years. Consider, for example, Witi Ihimaera's ***The New Net Goes Fishing,*** the second volume of short stories by this gifted Maori writer. The tales themselves offer a kind of symbolic unity, balancing two aspects of contemporary Maori life: the traditional rural patterns of the greenstone country and the more recent adjustment to city dwelling. As in his earlier works, Ihimaera's poetic voice is tempered with bawdy humor as well as the more serious aspects of New Zealand racialism. The panorama of characters caught in the net of urban living is always colorful, particularly the depiction of their frustrations and the moments of beauty in their secret lives. (p. 247)

> Charles R. Larson, *"Anglophone Writing from Africa and Asia," in* World Literature Today, *Vol. 52, No. 2, Spring, 1978, pp. 245-47.*

NORMAN SIMMS

In our age of sociologists and all their minute analyses of Maori village life and the problems of the urban migration, what is needed is not a Maori Zola to transcribe with unyielding determination the reality of the Maori situation; rather the poet with his imagination firmly in harmony with the archetypal rhythms of Maori myth and ritual who can thus transform the clutter of sociological detail into sharp and moving images of truth, of the truth of the Maori experience in the modern world.

Witi Ihimaera makes this attempt and yet so far fails. I want to look at the three books he has so far published, show their strengths, but also try to point out why they fall short of success—of providing that satisfactory sense of truth one feels in Faulkner or Gorky or Stancu.

It has been said that there is a raw nerve at the heart of a culture which only the most sensitive of artists can touch without offending. For a people only now recovering from "the fatal impact" of European invasion, it may still be too soon to touch that nerve with English words. Nevertheless, a great artist—and this may be what ultimately makes him great—can create the imaginative structure in which that nerve, the centre of the Maori world, is shown without touching it, and so not causing pain to run through the community.

In ***Pounamu, Pounamu*** Ihimaera moves through apologetics and sentimentality towards that vital centre. In ***Tangi*** he comes rather close, but holds back, playing with extraneous technical games and once again putting up the veil of sentimentality. And then in **Whanau** he tries to depict the outsides of Maori life and use that to hint at the raw nerve, but this book greatly disappoints as a Maori novel because it tries too hard to succeed as a Pakeha narrative. Its real centre, which might have broken the structures of a European sensibility, should have been the

rebuilding of Rangopai, the physical embodiment of the village-family, the Whanau. As it stands, the novel has no centre and nothing real happens in it. That, alas, is the affectation of the modern European novel which a Maori literature must avoid if it is to be true to itself.

From his first collection of short stories, ***Pounamu, Pounamu,*** it is clear that Witi Ihimaera has as clear a grasp of the short story as any writer now working in New Zealand, and that his value as an author comes before his novelty of being the first Maori to respond to Bill Pearson's complaint about the absence of Maori writers of fiction in English.

It is also clear that Ihimaera does not begin with experiments in language, such as preoccupy [fellow New Zealand writer] Patricia Grace. Rather he shows a sure ease in writing Maori words and phrases to develop character and set the tone of a scene, allowing context or an unobtrusive repetition in English to serve instead of a glossary. Indeed, by the end of a first reading of ***Pounamu, Pounamu*** one is familiar enough with the language to accept it as a normal part of the fictional reality.

Having put the language custom into perspective, as it were, Ihimaera turns to the deeper questions of characterization and interpretation of events. But here is where problems arise that are only partly solved in this first collection of short stories and in the two subsequent novels, ***Tangi*** and **Whanau**. Depicting Maori situations involves coming to grips, first with the external reality of Maori life in relation to European culture—a reality in which, for good and for bad reasons, the Maori people have not fully succeeded in coming to grips with urban and technological bourgeois life—and, second, with deeper reality of Maori myth and ritual and the spiritual values, such as *aroha* (love),—a reality difficult to describe as a living matrix of feelings, images and ideas, and certainly not in the cold terms of anthropology or social psychology. In these problems Ihimaera tends towards a sentimentality and a patronizing superficiality, though there certainly are moments of deep pathos and balanced weight. But as we have remarked, touching the raw nerve of Maoriness is as difficult and as dangerous as it is necessary to the writer if he wants to be more than a Maori writing English literature about Maori themes.

By sentimentality I mean, not the focus on sentiments in the characters, but the rousing of sentiments in the reader at the expense of a nuanced and diverse appreciation of characters and events. Hence even a story like, **"Fire on Greenstone"** which contains the image of the greenstone in the title of the book, Ihimaera only uses the loss of the treasured family relic to raise tears, first in the narrator and the sympathetic characters of the story, and then in the readers. The rich cultural significance of the object is hinted to in highly emotive, but ultimately vague terms—

> It was a big piece of greenstone, not the valuable dark green kind, but a smoky green like opal. But I used to like to hold it to the sun and look into it, and feel the soft luminous glow flooding around me. And I used to whisper to myself, 'Pounamu . . . pounamu . . . pounamu . . . , and almost hear the emerald water rushing over the clay from where the greenstone had come.

The pounamu is, of course, linked ultimately with Nanny Tama, the old man, and his rich treasure house of memories. As well as his homestead rich in the treasures of the *Whanau*—the trophies and photographs, the whakapapa or genealogy sheets, and the ceremonial garments and objects of Maori culture.

The evocative power of *pounamu* to encapsulate the overflowing profusion, lost when the house burns down, instead of being developed into a sustained imaginative exploration of myth and custom is devalued by two sentimental ploys, one positive and one negative. In a positive way, when the homestead is ablaze, the whole village rushes to try to put out the fire, and in that communal effort some of the old *aroha* in the family group, the *Whanau*, is articulated; but there is barely one long sentence on this action. The negative way also dissipates the value of the symbol, in that it sets up a ridiculous straw man, an unfeeling European.

> Afterwards a Pakeha had tried to comfort Nanny Tama by saying, Never mind. He hadn't understood when Nanny Tama had said to him: All my family, all this Whanau, were in that house. All . . .

The question of the Pakeha's attitude towards the Maori is looked at in particular in **"The Other Side of the Fence"**, in which an immigrant English family, the Simmons, try to make sense of their Maori neighbours, the Heremaias. If the Simmons family come off in a stilted way as good-natured but bumbling moralists who come to a bemused tolerance of the Heremaia children's escapades and the touchy pride of the Heremaias senior, the Maori family is equally caricatured and the effect of their skittish and irrational behaviour viewed without the benefit of any insight into causes or the dynamic of their own alienation.

Two stories in **Pounamu, Pounamu** turn specifically away from effect towards cause, and attempt to portray the inside of the Maori condition from the perspective of myth and rituals, **"The Whale"** and **"Tangi"**. As the latter is in small the basis for the novel of the same name, I would like to look closely at **"The Whale"** and discuss its implications as a model for a specifically Maori literature in English.

It is the story of a *Kaumatua*, the elder of the *Whanau*, in his final vision of the world. "The world has changed too much and it is sad to see his world decaying". Most poignantly, as he declines into death, he has no one to pass on his knowledge to, no one except the young Hera; "she'd been one of the few of his mokopuna who'd been interested in the Maori of the past . . . Only in Hera had he seen the spark, the hope that she might retain her Maoritanga. And he had taught her all he knew." We are told something of what he has passed on, but then even Hera felt the pull of the Pakeha world. . . . Other memories of the decline of hope and aroha in the Whanau haunt the old man as he sits waiting for death, waiting to return through death to the people and the events that give meaning to his life. The final image of the poem, when the old man goes down to the beach, is of

> a whale, stranded in the breakwater, threshing
> in the sand, already stripped of flesh by the
> falling gulls.

and asking, "No wai te he . . . Where lies the blame:" the kaumatua watches the great beast die:

> And the whale lifts a fluke of its giant tail to
> beat the air with its dying agony.

The whale is partly a symbol of the old man himself, a dying species stranded out of his element and attached by petty crea-

tures of the new world, and also an emblem of Maoritanga itself, the extended Whanau operating by love, now useless and abandoned.

If this were all, however, we would again have a merely sentimental story of a pathetic old man divorced from his former culture seeking in illusions, memory and death—the rest a busy modern and confused world cannot afford to living fossils. What raises the story is partly the revelations of the significance of the physical objects of Maoritanga, especially the meeting-house as an image of the family past and present, and partly the recalled episode of the kaumatua breaking the lock on the door of the storeroom, so that late guests to a *hui*, a wedding to that moment apparently filled with aroha, can be fed, despite the shocking refusal of the hosts to perform this essential act of Maori etiquette. For in this story the raw nerve is not merely hinted at; it is touched. We have the beginning of a sustained description and explanation of the meaning and spiritual value of the meeting house, of the Whanau, of aroha, and we see in action and memory images the extreme power they have through deprivation on the old man. . . . He is the house, the house is the embodiment of the ancestors; the ancestors are bound together by love; the love sustains the village—but the young are departing, and so the old man, like the great whale, thrashes out, and then dies.

Tangi is certainly the book that made Ihimaera's reputation. But it is an overwritten work and fails because of an unsteady and unclear focus. The themes, images, and even the characters and events first tried out in the stories of *Pounamu, Pounamu* are looked at again in *Tangi,* to a great extent the novel being a major expansion of the story called **"Tangi"**. They even use many of the same flash-back techniques and the attempt to co-ordinate several simultaneous events—the recollection of the whole experience as the hero returns home from the funeral (*tangi*) of his father, the preparations and the journey home for that sad occasion, and the ceremonial of the tangi itself. Interspersed are revelations of characters and events associated with Tama, his family (in its extended form and in association with tribal lands and history, *whanau*), and, to a lesser extent, the larger context of New Zealand society.

Where the short story ["**Tangi**"] begins, "One step further now", the novel [*Tangi*] opens with "This is where it ends and begins". The scope is ostensibly more ambitious, but the result is I feel, not a sustained novel, not a coherent and incisive deepening of experience, but still a fragmented set of sketches. The main effect is to break a sentimentality in the repetitious grief—appeals of the young man achieving manhood—"The tangi marks the end of one life, the beginning of another"—which works counter to the dignity of the Maori ceremonial itself.

That ritual, when described, has a special dignity in its open emotions, its formal wailings and speeches, its assertion of communal identity with the whole history of Maoris since even before the landing of the canoes in Aotearoa. The meaningfulness of rite and myth to Tama is brought home both through his response to his mother's role in the tangi and in his recollection of his father's instructions. Indeed, the movement of the novel's spirit is twofold, matching the two kinds of movement in the structure: the journeys by plane and train to and from the little Maori village near Gisborne, and the movement of the tangi ceremony from the welcoming of relatives and friends on to the marae to the deposition of the deceased in the burial grounds. This double spiritual movement is Tama's journey from his pakeha (European) life in Wellington to a new understanding of Maoritanga (the customs and ideology of Maori culture) and an associated movement from virtual rejection of his family and rural existence to an intense commitment to return as head of the family and to carry on the ambition of his father to establish a viable farm in the community.

What does come out clearly enough is Ihimaera's insistence that success in the Maori sense is quite different from that of the Pakeha New Zealander's sense: it is not financial independence or personal fulfilment. Rather what Tama's father, Rango, was seeking, and what Tama himself comes to desire above all, is to live well in the Maori community, the whanau; to be independent of external pressures, but integrated into the emotional and ceremonial life of the village; to grow and earn enough so as to share with the village and take on the responsibilities of the whanau's whole emotional, ceremonial, and economic life. It is a vision of life that, at the same time as it is painfully aware of the transience of individual existence, as well as the precariousness of the communal identity in an overwhelmingly alien environment, is nevertheless courageous in its loyalty to the historical continuity of Maori life.

In one early conversation, Tama asked his father, "E pa, what is a Maori?" Rongo, answering in "fierce pride", recounted the list of the first canoes to bring the tribal ancestors from the mythic lands of origin. But the essence of the catalogue lies not in the ancient prerogatives of the Maoris to the land but in the all important spiritual corollary:

> To manawa, a ratou manawa
> Your heart is also their heart.

This proverb becomes a pulsating refrain in the novel; it is this that sustains what is best in the book from its most pathetic sentimental ploys. There is a real unity of hearts between every Maori now alive, and every Maori who lived before. In the threatened world of the Maori, this faith in the quintessential continuity of all his people, and all his ancestors is bulwark against loss of identity, loss of dignity, loss of significance. "And if even I was confused again," writes Tama, "all I needed to do was to recite the legendary names to calm my heart."

Tama's difficulty, though, is that he gave his faith corporeality in the person of his father. "He was the axis of my universe; my world took motion from him." So when Rongo dies, Tama feels the world coming apart, meaning falling away, identity running out.... In the city, under the pressures of Pakeha time, Pakeha regularity, Pakeha ambitions, when Tama forgot what being a Maori meant—he could not forget that he was a Maori—"I discovered that all I needed to do was remember Dad and my whanau, my big Maori family, and my world would right itself". With his father dead, Tama has to learn where the calm point is and how to calm the whirlwinds.

What seems to be at fault in the novel is precisely this: that learning comes sentimentally. Not that sentiments are wrong or even that it is untrue to see that the waves of varying feeling awash over Tama in the course of the story as the very source and process of his realization: but that the novelist seeks to evoke sentiments in the reader to make him accept the reality of the change, and in doing so does not disclose the process of that change so that it can be seen as valid. For what Tama must learn is that the calm point in his father is also in him and that the ability to calm whirlwinds is his—not merely as a given, a social and biological trait he inherits from his father and which is expected of him by his relatives; but an ability

he must establish by an act of the will, partly as acceptance and partly by assertion.

"Now he is dead and this place is a place of storms." This is what Tama tells himself. But in what sense is he talking to himself in such passages? For Tama is both addressing his father, in an act of expiation, and himself, in an act of self-assertion and self-discovery, and as he expresses his fears—"In an aimless life where people walked in and out of that life, you were my only strength"—that very voice becomes more than his own. It becomes the voice of the Maori spirit: "Kia kaha, Tama. Be strong". Because of the identity of hearts, Tama can find in himself the strength of his father and his whanau, yet not easily and only with the support of the family and the ceremonial. This is asserted in the novel, and we hear in the overlapping time scheme the clarifying of alternatives, but we are not convincingly shown the process of that struggle itself. (pp. 338-45)

The third book [*Whanau*] in what Ihimaera calls a trilogy on the people of Waituhi, the village of the Whanau A Kai, focuses mostly on Tama's father, Rongo, and his struggles to keep the family group viable. But the novel is also an attempt to give a realistic account of the rather grubby existence of a poor, isolated farming community. (p. 345)

While there is a greater attempt at social realism in *Whanau* than in *Tangi*, there is still a lack of coherence, and again the novel exists as fragments—interwoven sketches and tales. Ihimaera tries too hard to interlink various characters and events in the village, and overlooks, or at least does not exploit, the obvious centre of events, the meeting house.

In just a few pages, the description and history of the meeting house, Rongopai, are given, virtually in the same words used to refer to it in *Tangi*. The brief glimpse is tantalizing, frustrating to the reader seeking to follow through its implications for the present precariousness of life in the village and its significance in the enduring qualities of the spiritual bond holding the Maori people to their land and their history. (p. 346)

We know, from *Tangi*, that the old meeting house will be the setting for the great *hui*, the ceremonial gathering of the family from all parts of the country, and that in their grief over the death of Rongo, and especially in the new commitment of Tama to Maoritanga, there is hope. "Perhaps, Perhaps".

But the sentimental exaltation of *Tangi* is tempered by the cutting vignettes of *Whanau*—the drab, boring setting of the village; the escape into drink and squabbling; and the gradual departure of more and more young people to the cities, to Pakeha life. As one European company official puts it: "You Maoris will just have to learn to live with the times".

What tends to spoil the novel is not only the fragmented focus in the sense of incompletely controlled narrative strands and in the failure to exploit the symbolic value of the meeting house—even the decision to clean up and repaint Rongopai after an Auckland art critic suggests purchasing it and transporting it to the city for exhibition. What spoils the novel is the contrived sentimental conclusion. A young boy, Pene, with all the innocence of the ingenue whose naive acts cut through the layers of laziness and frustrated compromise, runs off with the village's Kaumatua, their most respected elder, Nanny Pana, an old sick man, whom the daughter married to a Pakeha wishes to send to hospital. By taking the old man into the rain, Pene causes a crisis for the Whanau; petty squabbles, drunken bouts, and superficial distinctions of culture disappear in the mixture of sentimental concern for an old sick man and tribal duty to the elder. The family is brought together, it works together, and its Maori identity reaffirmed: and, of course, fittingly, boy and Kaumatua are found huddled up cold in the meeting house.

Yet the rhythms of the narrative and its shirking of real issues—the way in which feelings and thoughts operate, the difficult process of decision and redefinition—focus on the aroused sentiments in the reader, rather than the exploration of sentiments in the characters. . . . That the village should be brought together by a child and a sick old man is patently a ploy, a trick—an avoidance of seeing through the problems seen among young and mature adults, of confronting the problem of Maoris growing up in a world dominated by Pakeha and European ways of seeing, doing, and valuing.

Because of this, the mythic vision at the very end does not ring true. It is too facile to conclude like this—

> The village sleeps.
> Rongopai, the painted meeting house, still holds up the sky.

A Maori literature cannot hold up a sentimentally contrived version of its own myths and legends, its oral literature, as a counterweight to the psychological and social complexities of a European novelistic reality. The depth and complexity of the traditional modes must be mastered and given new form in writing for the balance to hold true, or even to tip in favour of the Maori version. Witi Ihimaera has not yet given full weight to his own heritage. (pp. 347-48)

Norman Simms, *"Maori Literature in English Prose Writers: Part Two, Witi Ihimaera,"* in Pacific Quarterly Moana, Vol. III, No. 3, July, 1978, pp. 336-48.

NORMAN SIMMS

[In *The New Net Goes Fishing,* the] first book in Ihimaera's second trilogy of tales about the New Zealand Maori in pakeha (European) society, the new generation casts its net into the midst of the other society, Wellington, with casual and reflective glances back to the old way of rural life on the East Coast, around Gisborne. The stories in this collection are less well-made short stories per se, however, than sketches, characters, parables, cautionary tales, anecdotes—in short, an impressionistic set of glimpses into Maori character and life as it confronts the modern urban world of European New Zealand.

The collection is not casually arranged. Framed by two tales which show first the coming of Maoris into the city, ambitious, frightened and awed by what they see before them, and then the departure of the father after his children have grown up, his wife has died and his aspirations have been transformed into something more spiritual and profound, the impressionistic sketches and characters fall into three main types, each suggesting a step toward resignation, reconciliation and rejection of the confrontation between Maori and pakeha. We are shown either Maoris who drop out meeting with those who assimilate to white society, sometimes the drop-out being the reflection of the assimilator himself in memory, or those Maoris who think they have "passed" facing up to overt or covert acts of racial discrimination. Woven through these two kinds of tales is a third: episodes and anecdotes concerning the hero and family of Ihimaera's rural trilogy, Tama and the *whanau* (extended family clan). These tales reveal the essence of that Maori quality which is always hinted at in the other stories—hinted at but never clearly defined, analyzed with a sustained insight

or shown in action as a coherent whole. The self-doubts of the Maoris and the partial visions of the sympathetic or hostile pakehas always seem to miss this quality.

The *aroha* (love) of the family and *whanau*, the concern to reproduce the *whakapapa* (genealogy) burnt in a house fire, the search for the missing *pounamu patu* (greenstone ceremonial weapon) which bursts into light and vibrates with its own dynamic life—all these are part of that central Maori quality. . . . With such a mythopoeic vision underlying his writing, it would be only crass to demand of the author a European-style analysis of character and event; but we look forward to the time when he will attempt a major, sustained examination of the people and events he here examines only in impressionistic sketches and anecdotes.

Norman Simms, in a review of "The New Net Goes Fishing," in World Literature Today, Vol. 52, No. 4, Autumn, 1978, p. 696.

BILL PEARSON

It is not surprising that the two outstanding Maori writers of fiction [Patricia Grace and Witi Ihimaera] have continued the preoccupations of the pioneer, less prolific Maori writers in English whose stories appeared in [the magazine] *Te Ao Hou* in the fifties and sixties. . . . The recurrent concern was a cultural identity crisis, provoked by the rapid shift of Maoris to the cities and the passing of the old spiritually relaxed, emotionally assured way of life that had prevailed in villages for half a century or more, involving the personal sustenance and obligations provided by the extended family, mutual aid, and a sense of fulness of living. What is new in these two writers, Patricia Grace and Witi Ihimaera, is their greater literary skill, their familiarity with a range of English literature, and a less didactic spirit than that of the earlier writers . . . , a recognition of the special, and limited, role of the short story as an imaginative opener of the mind to unsuspected understanding. (p. 166)

Ihimaera's skill as a writer has, I suspect, been obscured by the initial acclaim from reviewers and by the publisher's promotion of him as 'the first Maori novelist'. Since my name was cited on the jacket of *Pounamu, Pounamu* as the author of an essay that prompted him to write, I have an interest, and must say that though it is a pleasure to know that one's criticism has been, to use Eric McCormick's term, a fertiliser rather than a weed-killer, I have no doubt that Witi Ihimaera would have started writing sooner or later. The acclaim and promotion have produced an undercurrent of muttering, from some pakeha writers and critics, that he owes his success to the commercial exploitability of his Maoriness, or to the adulatory and unintentionally patronising Pakeha public which is thirsty, just now, for a deep draft of ethnicity, as R. D. Oppenheim has put it in an informed but unkind review. But it is a mistake to think that, because the literary personality Ihimaera presents in some of his protagonists in his first collection is naive, he is a primitivist in literary skill. In fact he draws on an unusual range of English literature, on Maori myth, and frequently has in mind analogies with European music and pre-European Maori chant. He has a passion for Italian opera, both verismo and bel canto; and he told an interviewer he hopes one day to write a song based on Maori texts like Joseph Canteloubpe's *Songs of the Auvergne*.

Pounamu, Pounamu, he said, he looked on as his moteatea, each story a song. Witi Ihimaera has that lyrical gift of composing in thanksgiving for the gift of life, each story a gift itself. It behoves one to receive his stories in the spirit in which they are offered. I do not see this as precluding criticism. If one is pleased with, or disappointed with a gift, one needs to understand why. What it does preclude is superciliousness.

On the other hand his stories have disappointed some Maori political activists who think writing by Maoris should advance the cause of Maori rights: 'uncle Tom', 'middle-class Maori', 'pakeha pet' are some of the names he has been called. Yet a Maori MA student, a native speaker of the language and a man of high mana among the Ngati-Porou people, told me he could immediately sense the Maoriness of Ihimaera's writing, and an urban Maori secondary school teacher of English has told me that the only literature he can get some of his Maori students to read is written by Ihimaera.

Clearly Ihimaera invites one to, demands that one, question the critical assumptions one brings to him, as H. Winston Rhodes acknowledged [see excerpt above], finding himself embarrassed by the suffocating intensity of the bereft son's feeling for his father in *Tangi.* The dominant modes in Ihimaera are comedy, elegy and lyricism and his characteristic mode is a blend of all three. If there are occasional embarrassments in the apologetics and sentimentality, it is because Mr. Ihimaera's boldness in emotionality leads a sophisticated reader to expect the spurious, which in fact does not come. Tenderness is followed by the bouncy optimism or cheerful self-mockery that is the recurrent author's tone in *Pounamu, Pounamu,* and the sentimentality and the implicit moralising are as acceptable, even as welcome, as they are in an early Charlie Chaplin film. For readers trained in the current fashions of irony, paradox, complexity and a disenchanted view of human nature, it requires an effort of humility to respond to simplicity, innocence and cheerfulness, an effort as great as responding, say, to William Blake's *Songs of Innocence* if one did not have *Songs of Experience* to offset them.

It is probably the cocky cheerfulness that has made these stories so popular with adolescent students, and that led Ihimaera's publishers to see in the first batch of stories he offered them a collection aimed at secondary schools. Ihimaera has seen a virtue in this and it would be easy to explain the simplicity as chosen for this audience. Perhaps it was, but re-reading some letters Witi wrote to me before the book was published I see that he had originally written the stories with the aim of a wider audience and was a little disappointed that the range of the stories selected for his first volume was so limited. It is characteristic of him that he blamed himself for not having extended himself to a wider range in the first place. The fact that two of the stories not selected for *Pounamu, Pounamu,* **"The Liar"** and **"My First Ball"** (which have since been selected by other anthologists for secondary schools), play up the shy, gauche, bouncy persona, rather than tend to social moralising, suggests that a slightly false impression was created by the tone of the ten stories selected for *Pounamu, Pounamu.* Also omitted was the very human, not necessarily Maori story of two sisters, **"Queen Bee"**, (in which the whole situation was suggested by the image with which the story closes, of a queen bee flying off in splendour, after killing another bee).

Mr. Ihimaera would be the first to disclaim any monopoly of spokesmanship for Maori values. However, he welcomed the opportunity to reach the minds of schoolchildren: 'I want them— those kids back at Te Karaka and all the little places—to read that book, to know just what they might lose, just what might disappear.'

In fact the first story with a Maori subject that Ihimaera wrote (he had written several 'pakeha' stories before, none of them published) was on this very theme: **"Halcyon"** is a nostalgic idyll . . . , a memory of a long holiday of a town-dwelling boy and his sister with an aunt and uncle and cousins at a remote East Coast beach, the strange experience of living with a big family, fishing for paua and crayfish, catching and riding horses, a day and a night in Ruatoria. The idyll ends sharply and poignantly with the comment that he never saw his Nanny again or went to her tangi, and that when he saw his cousins again they had little to say to each other. Poignancy and pathos are effects that Ihimaera can deftly extract from situations much simpler than those which sophisticated readers demand before they will yield such responses: for example, the situation of the old woman who had cheated and squabbled her way through countless games of cards and died in the middle of one, still squabbling, while her friend, replying to her insult, kisses her; or of the child who looks after his Nanny whose mind has wandered since her husband died.

But the story in [*Pounamu, Pounamu*] in which Mr. Ihimaera extends himself most fully is **"One Summer Morning"**, an unsentimental close-up, (close to reported monologue), of a thirteen-year-old impatient to be a man, conscious of already being one since his first emission, resentful of all the regular chores he has to do, aware that they will increase when his parents recognise his manhood. He bickers with his sister, talks about sex with his cousin Tom, has a fantasy of himself as a gunman in a western film, gathers with other boys around a secret-agent story with its superman hero, sees himself as a conqueror of women and recalls the actuality of his shy encounter with a girl at the school dance. A sense of adolescent wonder, of unknown possibilities, is evoked as he watches a flock of wild geese pass over him. The boy's thoughts are presented dramatically, with frequent recursion to speech or exclamations, and continual self-mockery. In style the story ranges from the reported monologue which is the staple of the story during the basic action of Hema's milking the cows on the morning of his birthday; to first-person monologue in his recurring reminiscences of earlier events; to parody of a James Bond novel, comic debate or stichomythia between himself and the mirror; and to a sudden shift of point of view where the boy is seen (in comic deadpan third person reportage) by the alarm clock, as he prepares himself for the chill of the dawn by getting dressed under the bedclothes. The boy's hopes are imbued with a cocky confidence that is equal to every setback.

I find myself embarrassed by **"The Other Side of the Fence"**, because the parabolic intention is too obvious. It is not a cliché contrast between stereotypes, like the dull conventional pakeha obsessed with work and possessions and the ebullient Maori who knows how to live, but the juxtaposition of well-meaning kindly pakeha liberals and Maori neighbours who have their attractive qualities but are endlessly infuriating to the kind of proprieties the Simmonses live by. It is a cultural conflict; and I can imagine myself being as irritated as Jack Simmons by the Heremaias. The story offers no solution, since the conflict will continue, other than mutual cheerfulness and goodwill. I expect the reason for my dissatisfaction with Jack Simmons is that his thoughts and personality are too simple.

One of the stories of which Ihimaera is proudest and which 'cost . . . much pain and agony to write' is **"The Whale"**, the lament of an old man watching the disappearance from the minds of the young of the values he has lived by. It is one of those stories, like **"Queen Bee"** and **"Cicada"**, where the closing image symbolises the events that have preceded it—in this case a stranded whale uselessly beating its tail against the gulls that are stripping its flesh. In the central incident of the story, the old man recalls an occasion when he took an axe to the storeroom to feed the visitors who had come late. He was ashamed of the young who received them churlishly. In theme, mood and even in phrase, this story draws on Old English elegy, in particular the 9th century West Saxon poem *The Wanderer,* a poem studied by Mr. Ihimaera at university both at Auckland and Wellington. . . .

It is not surprising that a Maori should respond, once he had penetrated the barrier of language, to the literature of a people of a tribal society with strong ties of kinship, pursuing agriculture and war, to a literature in which age connotes dignity, wisdom and a long memory. But there is between these two passages an obvious difference in spirit. The Old English exile is without kinsmen or princely protector. The kaumatua is a leader whose descendants have turned away from the old values. It is not Fate but modern corruption of old traditions that is to blame.

The image of the whale and the gulls is a less optimistic version of the metaphor of the fire that destroys Nanny Miro's homestead, 'the manawa, the heart of the whanau, the heart of the family, and my Nanny Tama's heart too'. The fire represents the ravages of time and change, but if the house is flammable, there is a big piece of smoky greenstone, with a soft luminous glow, which is a symbol of an indestructible Maori spirit. (pp. 167-170)

If *Pounamu, Pounamu* was Ihimaera's songs of innocence, *The New Net Goes Fishing* is his songs of experience. The poignancy takes a harsher note; pakeha contempt is recognised and impatience not explained away: the aggressive, impersonal city threatens to overwhelm the traditional virtues. The reader is left to draw his own conclusions. Repeatedly Ihimaera tests, and is tentatively reassured by, Maori solidarity; repeatedly he takes comfort when, in reaction to pakeha slight, a Maori character reacts angrily and finds courage to assert himself. But there are defeats, and any optimism is tentative. (p. 172)

The poignancy, exquisite in some of the *Pounamu* stories, has become sour in **"Big Brother, Little Sister"** where the two children who run away from an unhappy home, venture into the menace of the city at night, reach a deserted railway station and return sadly to their neglectful mother and her cruel lover. The poignancy becomes sardonic in **"Cousins"** where a student attends the funeral of a cousin he never knew, among elderly relatives he does not know, and laments 'those happy village years when the hills and sea had formed the accustomed circumference of my life . . . when I had been like a kingfisher skimming across the green landscape of Maori country'; and again in **"I, Ozymandias"** where the narrator is persuaded by a pakeha friend to drive through a prison farm. He sees, at a moment when he is carelessly laughing, the close friend of his boyhood, a prisoner, who is hurt and made angry by the apparent exultation of his old friend sitting in comfort in a car with an arrogant pakeha whose system of justice has put him where he is. The teller keeps trying to unwish it, but the harm is ineradicable. So too, **"The Seahorse and the Reef"**, the reef where for years his parents had gone for sea-food is permanently polluted by sewage.

In some stories the kind of Maori who currently draws the attention of the police and the headlines is presented in such a way as to engage our sympathy—innocent and trusting beneath the unattractive behaviour. The three boys and a girl in **"Passing Time"** who gather daily on the railway station to insult and harass passers-by, waiting for the inevitable arrival of the police, are observed with understanding by a pakeha who keeps the magazine stall; and they come to trust her enough to tell her it is a game to pass the time. They are unemployed and their life is a cycle of boredom, parties, bikie gang raids and police harassment. So **"The Kids Downstairs"** are befriended by the professional-class Maori and his pakeha wife who have the upstairs flat, and respond to their kindnesses. There are five of them, living on the earnings of one girl who has a job and on what they can get on tick from the grocer. When they leave the flat without telling the landlord, Rangi and Susan upstairs take their side and remind the landlord that Rangi is Maori.

> —Oh, but you're different, he smiled. You're married to Mrs. Johnson.
>
> Rangi felt the rage rising inside him as he began to laugh.
>
> (pp. 172-73)

A greater number of these stories are told in the third person, sometimes from the point of view of a main character, sometimes from that of an observer like the magazine-stall keeper. Mr. Ihimaera told me at the time of writing these stories that he saw himself as 'trying to develop a new style, a new net, which will handle ably enough stories set in that difficult area of Maori-pakeha relations'. He aimed at providing as many viewpoints as he could, so that the reader would be forced to make his own judgements. There are two stories involving Api the radical and George the moderate who has a number of pakeha drinking mates. In **"Clenched Fist"**, after an argument with Api, George sees a Maori woman almost knocked down at a pedestrian crossing by a pakeha driver who calls her a black bitch. George recalls Api's words: 'In the end, brother, even you will join us' and asks 'Was he wrong after all?' It is interesting to see the changes made to this story from its first version in *Islands*. That version was told by George in the first person; it was told in a tone of greater immediacy as if it had just occurred and George was still simmering, and it ended on a more committed decision: 'Without even thinking, I raised a clenched fist against the sun.' In the revised version, the reader is distanced further by the third-person narration, the ending is less certain, leaving the reader himself to answer the question. In **"Tent on the Home Ground"**, again told by George in the third person, George and Api are drinking in a pub with George's pakeha mates, one of whom rises uncompromisingly to the challenge of Api's militance and after Api has left calls him a black bastard. George goes to the Maori protest tent in Parliament House grounds to join Api. He has found his answer to the question asked in **"Clenched Fist"**.

One story in which the reader is obliged to look for his own judgement is **"The Truth of the Matter"**, in which four different people give their version of an incident, each version distorted by self-interest, shame and the impression the teller wishes to make on the hearer. The facts are plain: a taxi-driver has been jabbed in the face with a broken bottle and his takings stolen, and his two Maori passengers have been found guilty and sentenced to two years' gaol. The sequence of events, the motives and the subtleties of circumstance on which one bases moral judgement, however, are not at all clear. The taxi-driver cannot be wholly believed, complaining to a friend after the trial about the lightness of the punishment; nor can the big guy, boasting to a cellmate in prison; nor can the other guy who is excusing himself to his father, though there are several points of corroboration between his version and that of the driver. Then we are given a version by the woman whose appearance catalysed the hitherto implicit racial tensions into explosion: a girl walking home late at night from a party wearing nothing but a raincoat that blows open as she waits for the lights to change. Since she is not involved, one might expect at last to get a reliable version. In her account (to her boyfriend five months later) it is the taxi-driver, not the big guy, who smashes the bottle and threatens the two passengers with it; so that if this is true, the driver was injured by a weapon he had threatened to use himself. But the girl's story is not reliable either, since she was high on drugs and it is five months later; and she saw the whole bloody business as beautiful. The lasting impression of this quite subtle study is horror at the girl's sick vision of the injured, moaning driver:

> He was lying there. His skin was translucent.
> There were rubies threaded in his hair, spilling
> from his mouth, and crystals beading his fore-
> head.
>
> I leaned forward and kissed him. Oh God. Then
> I closed the windows round him.

(pp. 173-74)

The sickness of one part of pakeha society, it is implied, is more shocking than the impulsive violence of the two Maoris.

The two stories that repeat the themes of *Pounamu, Poumamu* are less successful. In "The Gathering of the Whakapapa" Nanny Tama manages to keep himself alive till he has pieced together the whakapapa of his whanau, and dies when he has done it. As he closes his eyes the rising sun bursts across the hills, and this probably implies a musical analogue, the equivalent of a Chopin chord, rather than a suggestion of supernatural intervention. But the 'effect' is a distraction, it will take more than the whakapapa to keep the whanau together. "The Greenstone Patu" is also told in the first person by an observer not central to the action. A lost patu, important to the whanau, is found to be in the possession of unrelated Maoris at Porirua who will not part with it. But, as the determined spokeswoman for the rightful owners insists on her claim, the sun glows on the patu in the glass cabinet and the patu is seen to swim, twisting and gliding, towards the claimants, calling its name. The glass cracks and Auntie Hiraina seizes the patu. It is not clear whether we are meant to infer a miraculous intervention on behalf of one family against another—perhaps Mr. Ihimaera had in mind a literary effect like the anonymous Old English poet's vision in *The Dream of the Rood* of the Cross sailing through the air and telling the story of the crucifixion. Perhaps there is a realistic explanation: a combination of optical illusion and Auntie Hiraina's trickery. Either way the outcome is perplexing, and seems to be a tacit admission of the inadequacy of the human fortitude the greenstone has symbolised, the persistence of the old rural virtues.

The last seven stories of this collection end in perplexity, poignant regret, anger, or disappointment. There is hope in the rainbow that Grandfather sees after his twenty years in the emerald city. The other hope is in the optimism of Ihimaera and the initiative of Maoris themselves, who have had great experience in adaptation. The flexibility which has enabled Witi Ihimaera to handle urban and rural themes with comedy, pathos and seriousness, he has related to the meeting house at Rongopai marae, near Waituhi (now being restored), built by the followers of Te Kooti. Ihimaera has explained: 'It is one of the few painted meeting houses in the country which combine both traditional Maori motifs and contemporary scenes (for 1888), like a boxing match, and racehorses galloping neck and neck! The important thing is that this dual spirit—of tradition and modernity, of seriousness and "irreverent wit"— has been carried over into my writing. I try to capture the spirit and beauty of Maori life, but also feel bound to criticism of it where necessary.'

In a careful and sympathetic essay Norman Simms [see excerpt above] evaluates Ihimaera as spokesman of a Maori heritage quite distinct from the European heritage in New Zealand. It is notable that both he and R. S. Oppenheim, from quite opposed points of view, find Ihimaera disappointing. Using such recent analogies as black American jazz, Yiddish theatre, or the Irish folk tradition, Oppenheim thinks the current Maori arts movement is not supported by any substantial folk tradition and that Ihimaera's *Pounamu* stories lack 'the energy which is the essential feature of ethnic literature'.

Dr. Simms, on the other hand, uses the analogies of several historical examples of vernacular language on folk tradition elevated into great literature such as (more recently) Gorky's autobiographical works or the novels of Faulkner and Hardy. He assumes, of course, that the current Maori tradition is a strong one. He finds that in the end Ihimaera does not achieve the necessary grasp of 'the archetypal rhythms of Maori myth and ritual' to enable him to create 'sharp and moving images of . . . the truth of Maori experience in the modern world'. I think both these critics are judging Ihimaera in terms of intentions he does not profess. He has stated his position several times. He said in 1971: 'I eventually want to be known as a writer—not just as a Maori writer', in 1973 he regretted that such was the emotional separation between Maori and pakeha he would never be able to call himself a New Zealand writer; 'I will simply remain a writer, Maori, who just happens to live in New Zealand.' In 1975 he said, 'being Maori is of more importance to me than being a writer', and earlier in the same year, 'I'd like to think I could go back (to Waituhi) to live; it's my dream. But I know I can't go back because that would negate everything my parents have hoped and worked for.' These statements do contain contradictions and uncertainties, but they are consistent in reflecting both the amphibious state of many modern Maoris, and the desire to be free of the uneasy tension between the two cultures. There is an urge, not towards separatism or nationalism, but towards an integration, in which the Maori component has its due satisfaction: 'I don't believe in Maori apartheid; I would rather foster *te manaaki*, mutual respect among Maori and pakeha for each other's values and attitudes. Witi Ihimaera's aim has been to alert Maoris to what they are in danger of losing, to educate pakehas in the meaning of Maori tradition in the hope that they might rediscover its human sources in themselves, and to express some of the pain and the joy of being Maori in an alien world. He has seen his work as a contribution to a wider recognition of the Maori element of New Zealand culture, and if he finds some other occupation that better satisfies that aim he may yet, like his predecessors in *Te Ao Hou*, give up writing in favour of that. (pp. 174-76)

Bill Pearson, "Witi Ihimaera and Patricia Grace," in Critical Essays on the New Zealand Short Story, *edited by Cherry Hankin, Heinemann, 1982, pp. 166-84.*

TIM ARMSTRONG

Last year's Booker Prize winner, Keri Hulme's *The Bone People,* was widely acclaimed as a Maori novel. Witi Ihimaera's massive work [*The Matriarch*] is more genuinely that: instead of the romantic and essentially individualistic version that Hulme provided, this is a novel rooted in a still-living tribal tradition, dealing both with one individual's place within his tribe, and with the overall struggle of the Maori people to achieve a measure of justice from the 'pakeha' (white-faced) race. The novel's action consists of the attempts of the central character, Tama Mahana, to understand the destiny mapped out for him by his grandmother Artemis, the Matriarch who had raised him out as a child. . . . Gradually the novel unfolds the labyrinthine power-struggles within his family and the tribe, as well as the character of Artemis herself: brilliant, ruthless, dominating, relentless in her determination to preserve the future of her people.

The story is skilfully presented through a series of layered narratives, reconstructed events, memories and documents, circling around a climactic encounter on a Marae (tribal meeting place) in Wellington, reminiscent in its virtuosity of Salman Rushdie's work. There is a good deal of ground to be covered for the English reader: Maori cosmology, Pacific migration, the importance of imbedded cultural values like 'mana' (inherited and personal power) and the spiritual relationship of the Maori with the land; but this is passionately presented, and Ihimaera makes use of an obscure episode in Artemis's past to construct a running comparison of Maori struggles with those of the Risorgimento (perhaps a little strained). The book ends rather inconclusively—there is obviously a volume to follow. But overall, this is a brilliant performance: a milestone in New Zealand literature and a novel to be recommended to anyone.

> Tim Armstrong, in a review of "The Matriarch," in British Book News, *September, 1986, p. 545.*

C. K. STEAD

I remember Witi Ihimaera as a shy, charming and handsome student at Auckland University when I was a young lecturer in the early Sixties. He was one of a generation of Auckland students which included David Lange and a number of his present Cabinet. A few years later Ihimaera's fiction began to appear. He was the first Maori writer to give an account from the inside of tribal life and rituals. His novel *Tangi* was widely read and admired, and it was followed by another, *Whanau,* and by two collections of stories. At least one of his stories revealed that he was under pressure to become 'political', to lend his skill and his *mana* to radical Maori protest—a pressure which at that time he resisted. Then he announced that he was not going to write anything more for some time—and he stuck to that. Now, after nearly a decade, he has produced *The Matriarch,* a 200,000-word blockbuster edited down by his publishers, I'm told, from a considerably larger typescript. The Ihimaera of sensitive, lyrical, rather plangent evocations is gone. In his place we have the novelist as warrior, the novel as *taiaha* or *mere,* the reader as ally or enemy.

The matriarch of the title is Artemis Riripeta Mahana, grandmother of the narrator, Tamatea Mahana, who closely resembles the author and clearly draws upon some of his family history. The matriarch sees herself as heir to two Maori power-figures: Te Kooti, the rebel and religious prophet who fought a guerrilla war against the Pakeha for a number of years and survived to be pardoned, and Wi Pere Halbert, a 19th-century Maori politician who conducted from the floor of Parliament his campaign to preserve Maori land under Maori control. The novel moves back and forth across a great sweep of time. As the matriarch instructs her favoured grandson, Tamatea, to whom her power will pass, we are instructed with him in everything from the Maori creation story, through the myth (presented as history) of the arrival of the Great Fleet from Hawaiki bringing the Maori to New Zealand, and in particular of the canoe Takitimu bringing both the Maori gods and the forefathers of Tamatea's tribe. We are also given an account of Te Kooti's (probably wrongful) detention on the Chatham Islands, his escape, and his guerrilla war against the settlers and the Maoris who supported them; and of the rise and fall of Wi Pere Halbert as Maori politician.

As he tells us all this, Tamatea is already an adult, married, as Ihimaera is, to a Pakeha, and with two daughters: so as well as taking us back in time to history and prehistory, the narrative is going back and forth from the present to the narrator's childhood, and to the doings of the matriarch with whom he lived for some of his early years. Family and tribal rivalries are revealed. Artemis is opposed by tribes within the larger federation to which her own belongs. Her power is resented in the family. Her own husband schemes against her. Tamatea is envied, and his *mana* challenged. But through all vicissitudes the matriarch triumphs. She is presented as a figure of power, light, mystery, fortitude, cunning and beauty—Tamatea's protector, instructor and friend, the source of his own skill and power.

The mixture of elements, all the way from the domestic to the divine, is as extreme as is the chronological sweep. In style, the novel moves from conventional fiction, to expository prose, to rhetorical argument, to historical record (including many pages of Hansard). The tone swings back and forth between the grandiose and the banal. All this puts a great strain on any sense of artistic unity. But if it fails (and for me it certainly does fail), that is not only because of its formal inadequacies.

My quarrel with the book's 'content' can be dealt with first, and most simply, by asking what exactly it is that the matriarch achieves. She is represented as triumphant against all odds, having to call up magical forces as well as her powers as orator and as tribal and family politician to defeat her and Tamatea's enemies. What the outcome of all this effort appears to be is the protection of the *mana* of Tamatea. But Tamatea has little identity in the story except as its narrator, and recipient of these benefits. For that reason it is almost impossible to see him as separate from the novelist, which in turn makes the whole work appear to be a gross piece of personal mythologising. The matriarch is great because the novelist tells us it is so; and Tamatea/Ihimaera is great because the novelist inherits her powers.

Beyond the family and tribal rivalries we are told that 'like Te Kooti' the matriarch 'decreed war on the Pakeha'—but where in the novel does this occur? There is a protracted scene, returned to at intervals, in which she is shown claiming against opposition the right to speak on a *marae,* and giving some sort of public embarrassment to a prime minister. If anything followed from that meagre triumph, the novel doesn't tell us. . . .

The novel repeatedly, and in the end tiresomely, asserts the stature of the matriarch. The language ('amazing', 'breathtakingly stunning', 'an incredible beauty', 'a blinding presence', 'charismatic', 'extraordinary', 'astonishing') becomes florid as if with the effort to conjure into being a greatness that has no foundation in fact, nor even, perhaps, in the imagination of the novelist. At no time did I really believe in the greatness of Artemis. Worse, I was never entirely persuaded that the novelist believed in it either. (p. 20)

[Several] overwritten passages (and they occur at intervals throughout) diminished my sense of the reality of the figure whose stature they were meant to enhance.

The Matriarch also sets out to rewrite episodes of New Zealand history from what I suppose Ihimaera would claim was a Maori point of view. So Te Kooti becomes a hero, and what has been known hitherto as the Matawhero Massacre is renamed the Matawhero Retaliation—it being Te Kooti's retaliation for his wrongful (if it was wrongful) detention on the Chatham Islands, and for the fact that he was hounded by the law after his escape.

I don't think with hindsight anyone disputes that it would have been better if the authorities had left Te Kooti alone—though he might in any case have decided to launch an attack on the settlers. But to recount in a gloating, triumphant tone the details of the killings—skulls crushed, babies beheaded in their cradles, parents bayoneted or shot in front of children, children in front of parents—and then to make a hero out of the Christianity-crazed Maori who ordained, because he believed he was the Prophet come to lead his people out of Egypt, that it should happen: this seems to me intellectually puerile and imaginatively destitute. Further, the justification offered for Te Kooti's killings is followed by a tone of moral indignation . . . at the revenge taken at Ngatapu, where a number of Te Kooti's followers were shot at the top of a cliff. But the account conceals—surely deliberately—that these murders were also the work of a Maori, Te Kooti's enemy Major Ropati, whose name I think occurs nowhere in Witi Ihimaera's novel.

There are some rare but important moments in *The Matriarch* when the political posturing stops and the true work of fiction—to make us see—is done. (p. 21)

There momentarily is real life—and you might say that there also is the motive and the justification for indignation, rhetoric, myth-making. But it happens almost inadvertently. The curtain closes, and we are not shown anything like it again. It simply remains in the mind as a measure for all the rest—so much more direct and true and powerful than all that windy stuff about the matriarch with her spiders and her recitative.

On page 370 Ihimaera repeats Te Kooti's cry: 'We are still slaves in the land of Pharoah.' It is a strange cry to come from a man much honoured in his own country and now serving as New Zealand Consul in New York: but whatever the facts, in the mind it may be so. And if that is the case, freedom can only be achieved in the mind. No external power can confer it. My own view is that the kind of picking over old wounds and ancient evils that this novel represents is not the way to go about freeing the mind. The past doesn't have to be forgotten: but its rights and wrongs belong to those who lived them, not to us. There is an egotism of defeat, just as there is of victory. The sense of having been wronged can become, like alcohol, a way of life. The Irish seem to have lived for centuries off moral indignation—is that what Ihimaera wants for his people? His proper task was the craft of fiction. He owed it to himself to write a more considered novel—one which used the language more scrupulously. Everyone would be better served by a more truthful image. (pp. 21-2)

C. K. Stead, "War Book," in London Review of Books, *December 18, 1986, pp. 20-2.*

P(hyllis) D(orothy) James

1920-

English novelist, short story writer, nonfiction writer, essayist, and critic.

James is a respected crime and mystery writer who is credited with expanding the scope of the genre: Although she makes use of elements of traditional detective fiction, James is particularly concerned with establishing realistic situations and exploring the psychological motivations of her characters. According to Norma Siebenheller, James possesses the "ability to put herself in the other person's mind, to feel his emotions and predict his actions. Such is her power of description that the reader will often sympathize with a 'bad' character because he has been made aware of the complex motivations that lie behind every action." James is also noted for her sophisticated prose style, highlighted by literary allusions and quotations, and her vivid, realistic characters and settings.

James's early novels, *Cover Her Face* (1962), *A Mind to Murder* (1963), *Unnatural Causes* (1967), and *Shroud for a Nightingale* (1971), evidence her interest in realism. Although structured in conventional "whodunit" fashion, these works rely on rounded, credible characterizations that "move James's novels away from the highly artificial form of their predecessors and toward a realistic fiction," according to Erlene Hubly. Scotland Yard detective Adam Dalgliesh is the protagonist in each of these books. A published poet as well as a police inspector, Dalgliesh is portrayed as a detached and devoted professional who is acutely sensitive to the emotions and motivations of the individuals he encounters in his work. The developments in Dalgliesh's private and professional life are regarded as engrossing subplots to the novels in which he is featured. *The Black Tower* (1975), set in an institution where Dalgliesh is recovering from mononucleosis, recounts his attempts to prove that a series of seemingly natural deaths at the hospital were actually murders. *Death of an Expert Witness* (1977) takes place in a forensic science laboratory where Dalgliesh studies the death of an antipathetic doctor. Critics attributed James's convincing settings and her close attention to detail in *The Black Tower* and *Death of an Expert Witness* to her experience as a hospital administrator. In *A Taste for Death* (1986), Dalgliesh investigates the murder of two men in the vestry of a church. Anita Brookner remarked that with this book, "P. D. James takes her place in the long line of those moralists who tell a story as satisfying as it is complete."

In *An Unsuitable Job for a Woman* (1972), James introduced Cordelia Gray, a female protagonist who is considerably different from Adam Dalgliesh. While Dalgliesh is an older, experienced Scotland Yard detective, Cordelia is a young, inexperienced private investigator who cannot rely on the resources of a police department. *An Unsuitable Job for a Woman* chronicles Cordelia's first investigation, in which she uncovers a murder originally believed to be suicide. Cordelia Gray reappears in *The Skull Beneath the Skin* (1982). Set on a remote British island, this novel focuses on the mysterious murder of an actress Cordelia is hired to protect.

With *Innocent Blood* (1980), James departed from the traditional detective story. In this novel, a woman who was adopted

as a child locates her real parents and discovers that her father was a rapist and her mother was a murderer. In addition to her novels, James has published several short stories in various mystery and detective publications and, with Thomas A. Critchley, coauthored *The Maul and the Pear Tree: The Ratcliffe Highway Murders, 1811* (1971), a nonfiction volume analyzing a series of notorious nineteenth-century murders.

(See also *CLC*, Vol. 18; *Contemporary Authors*, Vols. 21-24, rev. ed.; and *Contemporary Authors New Revision Series*, Vol. 17.)

NORMA SIEBENHELLER

"Civilized," "literate," and "complex" are just a few of the adjectives that are frequently used to describe P. D. James's writing. Her style is all of that; it is very English, very intelligent, and above all very readable.

Central to the whole concept of the mystery is, of course, plot. Is it logical? Believable? Clear, or muddled? The success of the story depends to a great degree on the answers to these questions. Agatha Christie became the most popular mystery writer in history on the basis of her convoluted plots and surprise endings, although she was not a great writer in the usually accepted sense. That didn't matter. She excelled in the one area where excellence is demanded.

While P. D. James does not create the same kind of plots as Christie did, James too excels in this all-important category. All the other writing skills she possesses—and they are many—would not have saved her as a mystery writer if she didn't build tight plots.

The mystery format demands that there be a crime, several suspects, numerous clues scattered here and there, and a detective capable of finding, analyzing, and interpreting them. If, along the way, the reader finds himself following some false trails, so much the better.

From her very first novel, James has succeeded in this difficult task. *Cover Her Face* is a typical mystery, its murder taking place early and the solving of it proceeding step by tiny step. The reader attempting to follow Dalgleish's thinking may find himself distracted by the third-person narrative style, for James is as often describing the thoughts of the suspects as she is her detective's. Carefully worded thought sequences can (and do) divert attention from the real culprit.

A Mind to Murder is even better done, as two separate crimes are made to seem related and thereby throw suspicion entirely upon the blackmailer—Nagle—and away from Marion Bolam, the murderer.

Shroud for a Nightingale, An Unsuitable Job for a Woman, and *Death of an Expert Witness* are equally well plotted, with clues abounding, but false leads constantly tempting the reader away from the main path. When the solutions are presented, they seem to be the logical results of the various characters' personalities; they are, therefore, essentially believable as opposed to just possible.

Unnatural Causes and *The Black Tower* are not so well constructed, and both suffer from melodramatic excess. Oddly enough, however, it is these two books that contain some of James's very best characterizations, especially those of ill or handicapped people, and the slightly imperfect plots are carried along on the strength of these character studies. (pp. 129-30)

For nearly everyone,. . . James's writing is a pleasure to read: colorful, clear, precise, ample without being padded, often dryly humorous, insightful, compassionate, kind. That she understands her characters, there is never any doubt. It is obvious, too, that she has a psychologist's comprehension of human nature, with an ability to put herself in the other person's mind, to feel his emotions and predict his actions. Such is her power of description that the reader will often sympathize with a "bad" character because he has been made aware of the complex motivations that lie behind every action. She does not sketch in black and white; indeed, her character studies might be titled, "Variations on a Shade of Gray." There's good—and bad—in everyone. (p. 139)

Perhaps most indicative of James's own mood is the generally upbeat way in which she ends her stories. Hers are not the kind of mysteries that build up to an O. Henry twist on the final page and leave the reader breathless. On the contrary, the action moves to a climax, the mystery is solved, and then the story winds down gently, with all loose ends tied. There is an almost nineteenth-century nicety about the way she puts everything in place at the end. And in almost all cases the bad

are punished, and the good, if not rewarded, at least left to continue their lives in peace. (pp. 139-40)

As recently as *The Black Tower,* her sixth book, there is a very positive ending, with a strong hint of a future relationship between Dalgleish and Cordelia. Only *Death of an Expert Witness* fails to reflect James's generally optimistic outlook on life. Since the publication of that book James has stepped beyond the narrow confines of the mystery form to write *Innocent Blood,* a novel that deals with crime but is not in itself a mystery. She is now squarely in the mainstream of popular fiction. Her great commercial success in that area, however, will not put an end to her mystery career. (p. 140)

> *Norma Siebenheller, in her* P. D. James, *Frederick Ungar Publishing Co., 1981, 154 p.*

JULIAN SYMONS

[P. D. James's *The Skull Beneath the Skin*] finds an actress, Clarissa Lisle, her husband, her ex-lovers and her stepson gathering at a castle on an island off the Dorset coast, where Clarissa is to star in a one-night amateur performance of *The Duchess of Malfi.* Off the Dorset coast? It cannot be many miles from that other island off the Devon coast where the cast of suspects and victims assembled in Agatha Christie's *Ten Little Indians.* There is no question of one writer's using another; it is simply that an island offers a convenient setting for the classic closed-circle detective story. A closed-circle tale, however, is not perfectly suited to Miss James's talents. Christie characters can and do tumble like ninepins, leaving us emotionally unruffled, but Miss James creates people who live and suffer, and when her private-detective heroine, Cordelia Gray, thinks, "We are here together, ten of us on this small and lonely island. And one of us is a murderer," we feel uneasily that this is artificial. (pp. 9, 32)

[Cordelia's] job at Courcy Castle is to look after Clarissa, who has been upset to the point of drying up on stage by some typewritten notes, all in the form of quotations stressing the inevitability of death. Cordelia is hired by Clarissa's husband, Sir George Ralston, to intercept any further notes, take telephone calls, check the stage set and generally protect the actress from emotional disturbance. Clarissa proves to be even more unpleasant than is traditional for actresses in fiction, and several of the party have reason to detest her.

The tale's progress is at first leisurely. . . . In fact the pacing is admirable. After the murder, which comes almost halfway through the book, the story speeds up through a series of dramatic revelations and confrontations to a climax that gains in effectiveness from the uneasy calm of the opening chapters.

It is the interplay of character that most concerns P. D. James, the lasting effect of a casual piece of cruelty, the deliberate rasping quality of a police interrogation, the moments of cowardice and betrayal that may mark an otherwise blameless life. All of these enter the story, and the treatment of the people involved is impeccable in everything that does not directly affect the crime. But simply because she has created such convincing characters, one has to complain at the end that the cat's cradle of guilts she offers us (it is not possible to be more specific) is not plausible. One doesn't believe that some of these people would have done what they are made to do.

This is judging P. D. James by the highest standards, those her best books have set. Beginning with the fine story that introduced Cordelia Gray [*An Unsuitable Job for a Woman*], her work went from strength to strength, up to the masterly *The Black Tower* and *Death of an Expert Witness*. These two books are surely among the finest crime novels of the past decade. Like other modern crime writers, Ruth Rendell included, Miss James is intent on extending the boundaries of the crime story, and her most recent book, *Innocent Blood*, was a serious but at times overstrained and overambitious crime melodrama that offered no mystery.

The Skull Beneath the Skin is perhaps an acknowledgment that she had reached too far, a deliberate step back in the direction of orthodoxy. It is a disappointment to the extent that the criminal results don't flow as they should from the stated motives, but this is still an absorbing story, paced and written with fine calculation, a work quite beyond the scope of more than a very few of her contemporaries. (p. 32)

> Julian Symons, in a review of "The Skull Beneath the Skin," in The New York Times Book Review, September 12, 1982, pp. 9, 32.

ANNE COLLINS

The second Cordelia Gray novel has at last made its appearance. But in *The Skull Beneath the Skin* James's own interest has been caught in working out an extremely ordinary formula—house party, remote island, loathed guest meeting appropriate fate, whodunit?—and not in further explorations of the fascinating Cordelia. This time the heroine marches off as bodyguard and companion to the middle-aged and venal actress Clarissa Lisle in a "fawn pleated skirt in fine wool" and matching "cashmere two-piece." Cordelia may now live in a 1980s loft on the top floor of an old factory building in central London, but in this book she seems as resolutely 1930s as the formula itself.

James has always been a solid plotter whose murders took place in confined and carefully controlled situations. Character has always been what set her apart from the run-of-the-mill mystery writer, and in this book, too, her people take definite and intricate shape. . . .

The Skull Beneath the Skin is full of . . . beautiful bits and pieces, which do not come together in the tight warp and woof of character and crime that make a classic of detective fiction. James's careful plotting, despite the macabre elements, comes close to plodding. The worst letdown, though, is Cordelia herself, who solves the murder with all the panache of a good and clever girl scout—the kind who would not even wear perfume, let alone be aware of the impact of her own interesting scent. (p. 55)

> Anne Collins, "When Plotting Becomes Plodding," in Maclean's Magazine, Vol. 95, No. 39, September 27, 1982, pp. 54-5.

ERIKA MUNK

[*The Skull Beneath the Skin*] fails through lack of blatancy. The book's at cross purposes; replete with conventions, it doesn't cherish them, or play with them, or do battle with them, but instead treats them with a kind of flat contempt. The ingredients are almost comically familiar: that sturdy private detective Cordelia Gray (from the grand *An Unsuitable Job for a Woman* . . .) is hired to keep an eye on an actress who has been receiving anonymous threats in the form of quotations from Shakespeare and the Jacobeans. . . .

But James's heart isn't in it. Over and over, she deserts the genre for Real Novel Writing—but a setup like this is meant to be unreal. All she can squeeze out is lyric description (very impatient making) and the sense of confrontation in Cordelia, who represents a humane, stringent, daily morality which sets itself against histrionics of all kinds like garlic against vampires.

The book doesn't, however, set itself against the great themes it pretends to address. [*The Duchess of Malfi*] has only the dimmest existence as a mechanism far in the background. Quite likely James finds it repulsive, even trashy; but she flees its horrifying sensibility without entering it first. The evil in her story takes easier, more melodramatic forms; the villains are mere quotidian liars and psychopaths, not actors acting. A book like Michael Innes's *Hamlet, Revenge!* which is as old as I am and even more self-indulgent, found ways to integrate a similar ploy—quotations used as threatening letters—with the mechanics of Elizabethan staging, the history of acting, the idea of the play, and the very idea of criminal illusion—all in an ironically conventional form. Here all this is missing. It's missing because James doesn't like or trust the genre she's employing, so she misguidedly tries to use it as a vehicle for Higher Things. But the whole point is that this kind of writing should be intelligent, witty, scary, perceptive, you name it, but it's not truth, and it's not art. It is satisfaction. There are a lot of lively mysteries around—maybe it's theater that's dead?

> Erika Munk, "Last Exits," in VLS, No. 11, October, 1982, p. 17.

THOMAS SUTCLIFFE

In her last novel, *Innocent Blood*, P. D. James made some rather serious errors for an established writer of murder mysteries. To start with, her characters were psychologically credible; they had motives for what they did and said rather than just for murder, and their mental life was both complicated and unresolved. The setting for the novel too was a recognizable location, in which the extraordinary had to be conveyed against the pressure of the ordinary and familiar. Strictly speaking there was no murder and the central theme of inherited guilt and revenge was properly regarded as having no ready solution. Most serious of all, perhaps, the novel was clearly sceptical about the idea of conclusive blame. This was not the sort of thing for which P. D. James had been appointed Queen of Crime.

Some, but not all, of these problems have been overcome in *The Skull Beneath the Skin*. As though to reassure readers unnerved by that last dereliction, James has produced a lavish version of a classic country-house murder mystery, crowded with well-researched props and creaking but much-loved stage machinery. Those dismayed by *Innocent Blood* should not be worried by the epigraph from Eliot's "Whispers of Immortality". This is a literary thriller, so all the characters have a talent for vulgar quotation. . . . [Though] all the details are rendered with affection and accuracy and no ingredient is missing there is a feeling that James has become a little uncertain about the form. The trick still works triumphantly, but the patter is uneasy and even, perhaps, a bit doubtful that the routine is worth pursuing.

"This is a story-book killing", says one of the characters halfway through the book, "A close circle of suspects, isolated scene-of-crime conveniently cut off from the mainland, known *terminus a quo* and *terminus ad quem*. It should be perfectly possible to tie it up—that's the jargon isn't it—within a week." In other words we shouldn't imagine that James is taking herself too seriously. . . .

The style too shifts uneasily between knowledgeable parody and sincerity of description which undermine each other. Much of the action is narrated in a Lustgarten prose, full of ominous terminations and dark collusive hints to the reader. It is as much a collector's item as the Gothic Victoriana which fills [Courey Castle], but it is combined here with a different voice, James's own, a simple clarity used to describe Cordelia's emotions and doubts. The combination gives rise to a degree of uncertainty about whether the novel is meant to be a bit of fun, risibly slavish in its adherence to the forms, or whether it is expected to carry some substantial reflection on morality and retribution.

James places her clues scrupulously, and the solution is satisfyingly surprising without being outrageous, but there are too many moments when the novel goes beyond the limits of country house crime, including lines which aren't decorous enough to take part in the playful narrative of an action without feeling. Good writing and genre literature don't mix particularly well, perhaps because one of the qualities of good writing, an honesty about the complexity of events and people, is just an irritating delay to the satisfactions of crime fiction. *The Skull Beneath the Skin* contains the resolution required by the genre and the irresolution of a better book, but it proves, I think, that the ambition to write well and the ambition to write a conventional thriller can't both be fulfilled at once.

> Thomas Sutcliffe, "Stage-Managing Murder," in The Times Literary Supplement, *No. 4152, October 29, 1982, p. 1197.*

HARRIET WAUGH

A new P. D. James novel is an event that aficionados of straight detection look forward to with uncontained glee. Not only does she set puzzles where readers are forced continually to change their opinion as to the culprit, but she usually provides at least one extra corpse along the way. Mounting death is as necessary to the detective novel as a heart massage to a man with a cardiac arrest. In her new, excellent novel *The Skull Beneath the Skin* she adds another method to keep the reader's adrenalin high. She allows you to know who is the intended victim, but the victim does not cop it for some time. It is the possible fashion of the death that engages the interest of the reader as much as the identity of the murderer. P. D. James is not, however, the reigning queen of the genre merely because she tells a good knotty murder story, for others do that just as well, but because her writing and the independence of her characters are in themselves such a pleasure. It is also particularly pleasing to welcome *The Skull Beneath the Skin* as it heralds the return of Cordelia Gray, who is the most attractive and sympathetic detective in modern fiction.

> Harriet Waugh, "Thrillers," *in* The Spectator, *Vol. 249, Nos. 8058-59, December 18, 1982, p. 43.*

ERLENE HUBLY

Readers of P. D. James's novels have consistently placed them in the classical detective tradition, comparing them to the novels of such writers as Dorothy Sayers, Ngaio Marsh, and Margery Allingham. (p. 511)

Only recently have critics begun to question this classification of James as a mystery writer in the classical tradition. Norma Siebenheller, for example . . . , argues that James departs from this tradition in significant ways [see excerpt above]. Stressing neither plot nor detective, James's novels are concerned not just with a puzzle—murder—but with the "corrosive, destructive aspect of crime," the way it shatters the lives of all it touches, a theme that finally "sets James apart, not only from those women writers with whom she is most often compared, but from other mystery writers as well," taking her finally "beyond the mystery novel into the realm of general popular fiction." And Bill Ott . . . contends that James's world, realistic and untidy, is the antithesis of that presented by such writers as Agatha Christie. . . . It is with these last critics that I would like to side, arguing that although James's novels may appear, on the surface at least, to be cast in the mold of the classical detective story, on a deeper level they contain elements which challenge that form. (pp. 511-12)

A dialectic between innocence and guilt, good and evil, the classical detective story is . . . a moral fable that proposes the reassuring idea that the world is basically a good and orderly place, that evil, when it does occur, is only a temporary aberration. In P. D. James's novels, however, the reverse is true. In James's novels the world is basically a disorderly and evil place, in which good, when it does occur, is the temporary aberration. And as this idea is so fundamental to the novels of P. D. James, I would like to explore it, examining one of her novels, *The Black Tower,* in some detail, making references to others, in order to see how she modifies the classical form. (p. 513)

[*The Black Tower*], with its setting, cast of characters, puzzle to be solved, and murderer to be exposed, would seem to be a novel written in the classical mode. And yet, I would argue, its surface features are deceptive, for underneath its basic structure lies a view of reality at odds with the very form that contains it.

The classical detective story, as I noted earlier, is a very rigid form whose purpose is, on one level, to present a puzzle to be solved and, on another level, to propose a certain moral view: that the world is basically a good and orderly place. In order for these two things to be accomplished, certain conventions must be observed. The form's three basic elements—setting, character, and plot—must be of a certain kind and must be held in a precise relationship. The characters, for example, must be stereotypical, two-dimensional, undeveloped, mere vehicles for advancing the plot, which is the dominant element of these tales. Similarly, the setting cannot be developed but must function merely as a backdrop for the more important plot. Characters and setting thus tightly controlled and limited so as to emphasize plot, these novels are finally highly artificial constructions from which the complexity and confusion of the larger social world have been deliberately removed. (pp. 513-14)

This, of course, does not describe what James does with the form. Instead of using it as a means for abstracting her novels from reality, James uses it as a means of examining reality. It is a decision, to acknowledge the realities of life, that James makes as early as her first novel, *Cover Her Face,* when she locates the real mystery of the story in the personality of its victim, Sally Jupp: "At the heart of the mystery, the clue which could make it all plain," Adam Dalgliesh observes, "lay the complex personality of Sally Jupp." By focusing on Sally's character, as much of the novel does, James breaks down the characteristic relationship between character, setting, and plot and makes character as important as plot; indeed, character here *becomes* plot. It is a practice that will move James's novels away from the highly artificial form of their predecessors and toward realistic fiction. . . . (p. 514)

If, then, as early as her first novel James introduces elements of realism into the classical form, with her second novel, *A Mind to Murder,* she continues this movement toward realism, extending it to cover not only character but setting as well. Placing the novel in a psychiatric clinic, she peoples it with patients whose mental disorders range all the way from mild neuroses to chronic schizophrenia, and with psychiatrists who oppose one another over the issue of which kind of therapy to use, some favoring conventional Freudian, others committed to electro-convulsive. Setting her novel, then, in a realistic milieu, peopling it with complex characters who are involved in complicated personal relationships, James opens it up to all the complexities of the social scene, a move that has certain consequences for the novels to follow. For it makes it increasingly difficult for her to sustain the two assumptions upon which the classical detective novel is based: (1) that the world is a limited place in which all things can be known and explained; and (2) that the world is a good and orderly place.

If we return to *The Black Tower,* we can observe James's characteristic milieu at its best. Set in a home for the chronically ill and disabled, peopled with characters whose lives reflect all the confusion and disorder of life as we know it, James gives us a world that is very different from that of the classical detective story. Unlike that world, James's world here is one in which all things do not tend toward order, is one in which all things cannot be known or proved. Indeed, this last idea, that the world is a place whose reality cannot be easily penetrated, is so prevalent in the book as to become one of its major themes. For at every turn James seems to be saying that man, with his limited and erring intelligence, cannot fully understand the reality around him.

The novel begins with this very fact. Physicians, confronted with an ailing Adam Dalgliesh, have misdiagnosed his illness, have told him that he has acute leukemia, and have thus prepared him for death when, in fact, he has nothing more serious than mononucleosis. Another failure to read reality correctly lies at the heart of the book, behind the very origins of Toynton Grange where the story takes place. Told by his physicians that he has multiple sclerosis, Wilfred Anstey makes a promise to God: if He will enable Anstey to regain his health while on a pilgrimage to Lourdes, Anstey will endow and maintain a home for the chronically ill and disabled. Anstey, while at Lourdes, is, indeed, cured, and upon returning to England establishes Toynton Grange as a memorial to the power of God. Whereas the Grange, then, would seem to owe its existence to a miracle of God, the truth is somewhat darker. For unknown to Anstey, his doctors had misdiagnosed his illness, had told him he had multiple sclerosis when, in fact, he had nothing more serious than "hysterical paralysis." What would seem to be a miracle of God is nothing more than an error of man.

If reality confounds the physicians in the novel, it also confuses others who try to penetrate its secrets. The forensic pathologists, for example, supposedly experts in their field, do not correctly determine the causes behind any of the four suspicious deaths in the novel. (pp. 515-16)

The detectives in the novel are equally inept at reading reality. Sergeant Varney, the local policeman at work on one of the cases at Toynton Grange, the death of Victor Holroyd, feels that Holroyd's death "was a clear case of suicide." . . . The sergeant is, of course, wrong. For Victor did not kill himself but was pushed off a cliff by Dennis Lerner. Inspector Daniel, Varney's superior, is also wrong about the case he is investigating. Discussing Maggie Hewson's death, Daniel sees it as "straightforward enough," a clear case of suicide. She has, of course, been murdered by Julius Court.

If the two local policemen are incorrect in their analyses of events at Toynton Grange, Adam Dalgliesh, the expert from Scotland Yard, does not fare much better. Visiting the Grange at the invitation of one of its inhabitants, Father Baddeley, and involved in events only accidentally while trying to recover from mononucleosis, Adam must still try to make sense out of a number of deaths that occur while he is there. Continually confronted with deaths, all of which appear to be the result either of natural causes or of suicide, Adam, suspecting foul play, must try to prove that these deaths are, in fact, the result of murder. And continually Adam fails at his task. Adam, the supreme rationalist, a man trained to reduce all mysteries to observable facts, becomes increasingly frustrated by a reality that will yield no evidence. (p. 516)

Adam, of course, throughout the novel, is in a weakened state, recovering from an illness, and things that normally would be easy for him to do are here difficult. And yet the difficulty of finding evidence, the impossibility of establishing the truth, is so great as to go beyond Adam's illness, to remain unexplained by his weakened condition, to become almost a philosophical statement. For in this novel James seems to be examining the very nature of reality, to be saying that there are some things that exist but that cannot be proved. (p. 517)

If James in *The Black Tower* challenges one of the basic assumptions behind the classical detective story—that the world is a place where all things can be known—she also challenges its second assumption. For by portraying it as a place characterized by complexity and disorder, she is also saying that it cannot be reduced to "the Great Good Place" of the classical form. . . . [James's places] do not provide a contrast to the evil that occurs in them, but rather seem embodiments of that evil. James's places often seem good, but it is a goodness James undercuts with terrible, and sometimes humorous, ironies.

The place where *The Black Tower* is set, Toynton Grange, for example, seems to be a place literally founded on God's love. In its very origins, it would seem to reflect a special connection between God and man. And yet as we have already noted, Wilfred Anstey's miraculous cure was nothing more than a doctor's error, his crippling disease nothing more than temporary paralysis. Life at the Grange, deliberately patterned after that in a monastery, would seem to be a reflection of its spiritual model. Anstey and his staff, for example, while performing their duties around the Grange wear brown monks' robes in celebration of the spiritual life. . . . And one of the residents of the Grange takes special care to mock Anstey's practice of wearing a monk's robe, wearing one of them himself when he, a murderer, kills his various victims. Twice a year Anstey and his crippled charges make a pilgrimage to Lourdes. Enthusiastically supported by the inhabitants of the Grange, in particular by Julius Court, whose efforts in large part make them possible, these pilgrimages turn out, however, to be nothing more than a cover for a drug ring, a means whereby Court can bring back into England, undetected, drugs from France, hidden in the handgrips of the patients' wheelchairs.

And then there is the black tower itself, standing on the edge of a cliff high above the sea, built by Wilfred Anstey's great grandfather in the mid-nineteenth century as a testament to his religious faith. . . . Anstey retreats to the tower not, as he would have others think, in order to meditate upon the wonders of God but in order to contemplate the perversions of man, for he goes to the tower in order to read the pornographic magazines and books he keeps hidden there. (pp. 517-18)

James presents a fallen world, a world in which man is cut off from his true source of power and knowledge. James is, I would argue, a religious writer, "religious" in the sense that she believes there is an order behind the universe, but that it is an order of which modern man has lost sight. In *The Black Tower* there is an image that is central to her work: a Pre-Raphaelite stained glass window portraying the expulsion of Adam and Eve from the Garden of Eden decorates the entrance hall at Toynton Grange. It is an image that hovers over all of James's novels—man expelled from Paradise. Hers is a world peopled with invalids and cripples, the diseased and dying, where life itself, as one of her characters says, is "a progressive incurable disease." (p. 519)

Characterized by disorder and chaos, by unnatural passions and immoral acts, James's world, unlike that of the classical detective novel, is finally one in which order cannot be restored, it having never existed in the first place. (pp. 519-20)

In their endings James's novels seem more like the hard-boiled novels of Raymond Chandler and Ross Macdonald than those of the classical form, with James's detective Adam Dalgliesh often left at the end of a case, as are Philip Marlowe and Lew Archer, with a profound sense of disillusionment and failure. Although Adam does not share the hard-boiled detective's toughness or his cynicism, he does share certain of his other attitudes: his passionate devotion to justice and to truth; his adherence to a strict moral code; his fierce desire to protect a society that is in need of protection; his ultimate realization that the world is chaotic, imperfect, maybe even doomed; and the sense of disillusionment that accompanies this realization.

Belonging to the Romantic tradition, Adam, like the hard-boiled detective, is a knight who must do battle against evil as well as find truth. And yet like the hard-boiled detective, Adam, at the end of his quest, must accept only partial victory. Because guilt and crime are general and diffuse and have no single source, because the dragon seems to encompass all, there can be no redemption. Seeing evil everywhere, Adam, like the hard-boiled detective, can deal only with a small part of it. Succeeding in his quest to find the murderer but failing to achieve the Holy Grail, Adam, like the detectives of the hard-boiled school, experiences none of the admiration or satisfaction that accompanies the classical detective's success. For he has solved little, cured nothing. (pp. 520-21)

James has spoken, in an interview, of being in London during the Second World War when the Germans were bombing that city. . . . James's world is the world that has known that war, a world that has lost its innocence, that finally cannot be compared to the quieter and more stable ones presented by Agatha Christie and Dorothy Sayers. Although James draws upon these earlier writers, using their basic pattern—the presentation of a murder that has to be solved—in order to structure her novels, she rejects the basic assumptions and attitudes that underlie this pattern. Filled with the stuff of reality, with its chaos, confusion, and ambiguity, portraying a world that does not move inexorably toward resolution and order, ending as they

often do in the spirit of the hard-boiled school, with disillusionment and a sense of failure on the detective's part, James's novels are finally something other than the classical detective novel, are finally a curious blend of several forms—the romantic and the realistic, the classical and the hard-boiled. That she makes such a hybrid form work—indeed, has produced several masterpieces in the process—is finally a tribute to her skills as a writer, to her considerable gifts of persuasion. (p. 521)

Erlene Hubly, "The Formula Challenged: The Novels of P. D. James," in Modern Fiction Studies, *Vol. 29, No. 3, Autumn, 1983, pp. 511-21.*

ANITA BROOKNER

P. D. James's excellent novel [*A Taste for Death*] begins with the discovery of the mutilated bodies of two men in the vestry of a Romanesque basilica in Paddington. It ends with a siege in a flat in Notting Hill Gate. These specific locations give a voluptuous amplitude to an already loaded story, proving yet again that the conscientious novelist is not someone who merely sits at a typewriter but who paces out the territory, gets the timing right, is observant of weather, is an inventor of architecture, a creator of interior appointments, a provider of life histories, of families, of chance or habitual encounters. Above all, the superior novelist—and P. D. James is just such a novelist—is a withholder of information, urging the reader along, although that reader, half willing, half baffled, might like to stop and consider matters, until such time as the author thinks it wise to release a few more facts, a partial explanation, a clue picked up from a couple of hundred pages back, or revives a suspicion which has lain dormant for an even longer period of time. The tight control that this implies is not inherent in the idea when it first comes to mind. In the present instance the idea itself is of such complexity that one marvels at the urbanity needed to unravel it, and, more important, to keep the reader waiting until the time has arrived for a final accounting. . . .

It seems unfair, ungrateful even, to urge P. D. James to hurry on with her text, but as soon as one has reached page 454 of *A Taste for Death* one yearns for the security of another volume. She is an addictive writer, whose own acquisitive attitudes are passed on to the reader. It seems to me that she has gained authority with this novel. The quality of intelligence was always there, but now in addition we have a genuine curiosity about character, and an ability to describe the density of little known lives. Above all, there is that sense of place. It is to the greater and lesser Victorians that one is referred throughout this long narrative. And if the Gothic horrors are present together with the sense of justice, one is only confirmed in one's view that P. D. James takes her place in the long line of those moralists who tell a story as satisfying as it is complete.

Anita Brookner, "The Loss of Sir Paul," in The Spectator, *Vol. 256, No. 8240, June 14, 1986, p. 28.*

JAMES CAMPBELL

A Taste for Death resembles *Moby Dick* in that if your only interest is in the story you may as well flick from the first chapter to the last and find out who killed whom. The author's main concern is with what happens in between, where the society of the novel's inhabitants is dissected. Indeed, if there is a faint dissatisfaction at the close, it is only because the one thing which does not fit squarely into this comedy of manners is the deed that is the excuse for the making of it.

Admirers of Dalgliesh will be pleased to learn that he is in stronger form than ever. He has not written a poem for four years, but he can still quote Crabbe over a corpse, pick up references to Plato in a dead man's letters, distinguish the good and bad in Lawrence and mutter a remark from Sartre. Cold fish though he is, he understands the irony of Berowne's death side by side with a tramp, which the family are incapable of doing. He has an insight into the dead man's spiritual crisis which Lady Berowne lacks. . . .

Is Dalgliesh a man, or merely a representative of Justice in its ideal form? James avoids making him infallible by presenting him as an inadequate person, but his instincts as a detective are almost perfect. Although he experiences pity and fear, these emotions are subsumed by his desire for the good. His sympathy might be aroused by the plight of the defeated or the desperate, but it is his job to lock them up if they've done wrong.

The antics of Dalgliesh apart, the best thing in *A Taste For Death* is the partnership with which the book opens, between dear, shy, old Miss Wharton, a church helper, and the mischievous, and in many ways unchildlike, ten-year-old Darren: "After the third visit he had, without an invitation, walked home with her and shared her tin of tomato soup and her fish fingers . . . he had become necessary to her." Other writers might have been tempted to build an entire novel around this recognizable pair; P. D. James can afford to spend them on a sub-plot.

She takes less trouble with those she dislikes. Sir Paul's mother, the dragonish Lady Ursula Berowne, is less a character than a mouthpiece for a set of unlikeable attributes of her class. This, like the upstairs-downstairs atmosphere, is a fault of the genre, whose conventions James seems happy to obey, and of which she is one of the best living exponents. In earlier novels, such as *Cover Her Face* (1962), these conventions threatened to squeeze out her other talents, but here she has made room for them all while still writing what is basically a detective story. James often seems less interested in putting forward a convincing explanation of why one person should plot and carry out the killing of another than in dramatizing all the fuss surrounding it. Sometimes she is too fussy: in her long descriptions of interiors, the studied backgrounds to minor characters' lives, where the background is adequately suggested by the character alone. The alternative view is that the seemingly endless flow of minor characters and sub-plots . . . makes *A Taste For Death* an even more lavish entertainment than usual, and a more serious entertainment than most.

James Campbell, "Looking into the Murky and Murderous," in The Times Literary Supplement, *No. 4343, June 27, 1986, p. 711.*

NICK KIMBERLEY

P. D. James's novels are entirely earthbound: a crime is committed, the suspects' alibis must be broken, the investigator (usually Commander Adam Dalgliesh) gets to the bottom of it—not without a certain ambivalence. None of us is innocent, after all. Dalgliesh makes an unlikely policeman, with a connoisseur's taste in art and several published collections of poetry. Even more unlikely than his writing poetry is the fact that people actually read it and, in *A Taste for Death,* bemoan his current writer's block. Dalgliesh's life is fleshed out in the interstices of a convoluted plot; a brief glimpse of him, aged 15 at his mother's deathbed but unable to mourn, opens up possibilities for easy psychologising which James doesn't always ignore.

James tracks Dalgliesh's investigations in detail, displaying an intimacy not only with routine procedures (autopsies, the dreaded forensics) but also with the vast literature built up around criminal investigation. Her love of human frailty saves her from any complete commitment to the rule of Law—it is the police, not the criminals, who have a taste for death. That same commitment leads her to prolix elaborations: *A Taste for Death* runs to 450 pages, twice the length that McBain and Raymond find appropriate. The most interesting encounter here is between Dalgliesh and his new subordinate, Kate Miskin. Miskin, we are told, was an illegitimate child: is James saying something about the place of women in police work, in fiction, in life? No doubt; and no doubt Miskin will reappear, replacing, I hope, at least temporarily, the by now rather tiresome Dalgliesh.

Nick Kimberley, "Open Verdicts," in New Statesman, *Vol. 112, No. 2884, July 4, 1986, p. 28.*

PATRICIA CRAIG

[Although] *A Taste for Death* is in many ways a classic detective novel, it doesn't include the dumbfounding of the reader as a crucial part of its plan. The identity of the killer, once it's disclosed, probably won't come as much of a surprise to anyone.

The book conforms to the classic pattern by containing a victim who numbers a cutthroat among his closer acquaintances, and by allowing the enquiry to focus on each of these acquaintances in turn. . . . The ambience of nearly every person in the book, whether suspect, police-worker or onlooker, is very carefully established, so that we have a good deal about the tastes in interior decoration displayed by each: 'Above the sofa was a line of watercolours; gentle English landscapes, their quality unmistakable . . .' Every character, too, comes complete with his or her *curriculum vitae,* and the resulting stories form an accompaniment to the main story, that of the murder, without necessarily being interconnected with it, or with each other. This arrangement wouldn't have suited the age of jigsaw detection, when the puzzle was paramount: but it is perfectly in keeping with the freer modes of the present, and besides, P. D. James understands the part played by digressions, and even loose ends, in conveying the sense of anxiety and disruption which co-exists in her books with the exhilarating tackling of a problem.

We find such items, in *A Taste for Death,* as an enlightening smudge of blood and the clue of a half-burned match (about which the author doesn't take a humorous tone); these hark back to an earlier variety of detective fiction, but they are only trifling decorations, inserted, perhaps, to remind us of the conventions, even while these are being more or less eschewed. Dalgliesh, whose character has been built up throughout the series, is notable for the bleakness, detachment and purposefulness of the way he goes about things: but he isn't incapable of unbending. He unbends, for example, on page 203, when he brings as a gift for a book-collecting woman friend a treasure entitled (as he has it) *Dulcy on the Game.* 'Don't be naughty, Adam,' comes the reply. '*Dulcy plays the game.* How lovely! . . . This completes my pre-1930 Brazils.' Unfortunately there is *no* pre- (or post-, for that matter) 1930 Angela Brazil story called *Dulcy plays the game*. *Margaret plays the game,* yes: but that's by a different author, Winifred Darch. Is this a slip, or is P. D. James playing games, testing the alertness of her readers? It's a moment of levity, in any case, and welcome in a book—albeit a continuously entertaining one—full of blood, malice and other disquieting particulars. (p. 23)

Patricia Craig, "Open That Window, Miss Menzies," in London Review of Books, *August 7, 1986, pp. 23-4.*

ROBERT B. PARKER

[*A Taste for Death*] is about murder and the way murder changes everything. It is about the deaths of a senior Goverment minister, Paul Berowne, and a stumblebum, Harry Mack; it is about the investigators, the perpetrator, the bystanders and witnesses. It is also about the human condition in London today, enlarged by a sense of the British past that stretches back like a rich and barely dwindling perspective. And it is graced by one of the most felicitous prose styles I know. Ms. James is simply a wonderful writer.

She is working on a broad canvas in *A Taste for Death,* but the figure that gives her work its focus is that of the detective, Adam Dalgliesh. . . . While Ms. James's narrative is quite sophisticated, the point of view shifting from Dalgliesh to his colleagues Kate Miskin and John Massingham, it is Dalgliesh to whom we return, who makes our compass just.

The victims are found, their throats cut, in a London church. Dalgliesh and his detectives must try to find a connection between the two disparate men—to explain why they died. But no good book is simply about the plot, and *A Taste for Death* is about several things. It is about the relentless repercussions murder generates, washing over people and changing their lives. When it bobs to the surface, it drags with it the paraphernalia of pretense by which people have managed a life that is too much for them. Privacy died with the victim, and the conceits of civilized life shrivel in the hard light of an investigation. The crime is a kind of contaminant, and it poisons everyone who touches it. . . .

Ms. James, who now serves in London as a magistrate, spent 30 years in the British Civil Service, including the police and criminal law departments of the Home Office. She brings that expertise to bear in this as in her other books, and so we come into possession of a slowly accumulating collection of data, simultaneously internal and external. The technical matters of blood tests and autopsy procedures are entirely convincing. The clues that surface are unstartling and credible. The behavior of the suspects is appropriately motivated and the motivation is psychologically acute. The progress toward resolution grows out of the technical matters and the clues and the behavior of the suspects, noticed and understood by determined, intelligent detectives.

A Taste for Death is very shapely, very seemly—at the end everything seems back in place. . . . The order restored is real, but it is an order in which failure and guilt are as natural and permanent as triumph and contentment. Ms. James knows this. Perhaps most of us do. But reading her novel, we know it better.

Robert B. Parker, "Adam Dalgliesh Sees Everything," in The New York Times Book Review, *November 2, 1986, p. 9.*

Elizabeth Jolley

1923-

English-born Australian novelist, short story writer, dramatist, critic, and scriptwriter.

Jolley writes darkly humorous experimental fiction in which she explores such themes as loneliness, aging, homosexual love, and the relationship between imagination and reality. Through disjointed, self-reflexive narratives, Jolley often depicts lonely or alienated individuals who have been uprooted from their accustomed environment. Many of her protagonists use their imagination as a means for pursuing freedom and happiness. In examining this recurring character type in Jolley's work, A. P. Riemer observed: "[The] protagonist in a number of the stories is a writer or at least a person professionally concerned with writing. Through this we may approach . . . the central emphasis of her work—an examination of the viability, the nature, the implications of culture, of writing, of a concern with literature in a world where the connotations of such pursuits are alien." After establishing herself as an important figure in contemporary Australian literature, Jolley gained recognition outside her country in the mid-1980s. Critics praise her witty and disciplined prose, her inventive techniques, and her precise, colorful characterizations.

Jolley first received critical attention in Europe and North America with the publication of *Mr. Scobie's Riddle* (1982). A blackly humorous work set in St. Christopher and St. Jude's Hospital for the Aged, this novel focuses on Mr. Scobie's longing for the life he enjoyed before being admitted to the nursing home. After two unsuccessful escape attempts, Mr. Scobie realizes that his only means of leaving the hospital is death. Reviewers lauded *Mr. Scobie's Riddle* for its subtle and sensitive mixture of humor and pathos. Jolley's next two novels, *Miss Peabody's Inheritance* (1983) and *Foxybaby* (1985), utilize the story-within-a-story framework to explore the relationship between fiction and reality. In *Miss Peabody's Inheritance,* a friendless spinster, Dotty Peabody, writes a fan letter to novelist Diana Hopewell and receives in return the author's novel-in-progress about a strong-willed heroine and her lesbian lovers. Through Hopewell's romantic tale, Miss Peabody escapes her cheerless life and, in the words of Joan Kirkby, "takes up the mantle that Diana has offered her, the mantle of imagination, of creator." *Foxybaby* chronicles the experiences of women attending the "Better Body through the Arts" course at a weight-loss clinic. When the women act out scenes from the instructor's novel, they begin relating to the characters and subsequently reconsider their own lifestyles.

In her next novel, *Milk and Honey* (1986), Jolley incorporates Gothic elements to create a somber examination of cultural discord. In this work, Jacob, a first-generation Australian, recalls his years as a boarder with the Heimbachs, a family of Central European immigrants. Refusing to adjust to Australian culture, the Heimbachs rigidly maintain their traditional customs and values. Jacob eventually marries their daughter and gradually becomes mired in the family's isolated world. *The Well* (1986) details the deterioration of a relationship between two women of disparate age. Driving home from a party, the women hit a man walking in the road. They dispose of the body in a well next to their house and are soon driven apart

Simon Cowling/Rapport

when the younger woman insists that the man is still alive. Bob Halliday observed: "*The Well* combines the sleekness of a parable with the dynamic of a finely crafted horror story to explore a theme that is at the center of much of Jolley's most interesting writing: the disastrous effects of failed or mutated love."

In addition to her novels, Jolley has written three collections of short stories: *Five Acre Virgin and Other Stories* (1976), *The Travelling Entertainer* (1979), and *Woman in a Lampshade* (1983). In her short stories, which are praised for similar qualities as her longer works, Jolley further examines the lives of lonely and displaced characters.

A. P. RIEMER

Reading one's way through Elizabeth Jolley's books is a pleasantly disconcerting experience. Characters, situations, phrases, images recur throughout the novels and stories until they come to seem like old friends—we observe their transformations, how they are expanded or contracted, the manner in which they are presented from various perspectives. The germ of some larger work is discovered in a story a few pages long; an independent tale is absorbed into a quite different story; one work "explains" puzzling ellipses, odd references in another. Some of the stories coalesce into long structures which, though lacking the consistency of a continuous narrative, form a unity not unlike the sonnet-cycles of an earlier age.... In all this Mrs Jolley displays the mark of an admirable literary talent, a range of interests and sympathies both complex and consistent, personal yet abstract, and a command of narrative techniques which identifies her as a writer of considerable standing.

Her readers will, no doubt, discover different appeals (and perhaps different causes of irritation) among her writings. Some will be drawn to what appears to be a concern with, perhaps a celebration of, "alternative lifestyles". She is obviously interested in—though I am not certain that she advocates—various fashionable preoccupations of the last two decades. She seems to subscribe to the current assumption that women's sensibility is intrinsically different from that of men; she explores the possibilities of love between women—rather gushingly in the novel *Palomino,* with fine poise in **"Grasshoppers"** (*The Travelling Entertainer*). The mandatory sympathy for the scorned and the rejected is displayed, as is the predictable condemnation of suburban propriety. But even where her writing engages with the clichés of modern society it seldom descends into cliché or bombast; rarely, if ever, is it entirely polemical or obsessive. The few instances of pretentiousness (as in **"Adam's Bride"**, *Woman in a Lampshade*) are outweighed by the wit, wry humour and surprising twists of the imagination we encounter in most places.

This essay examines what is for me the most interesting aspect or facet of her writing, a concern which transcends social, sexual and psychological issues, though these preoccupations are important to the articulation of this concern. I refer to the sense encountered in much of Elizabeth Jolley's work of the individual adrift between two worlds, between opposed possibilities of being or of becoming. I suggest that in this respect she has made an individual, significant, and in my opinion, lasting contribution to "Australian Literature", especially in her most recently published novel, *Mr Scobie's Riddle*.... (pp. 239-40)

[The] experiences which her fiction records are presented in terms of an awareness of rival claims, rival possibilities. Many of her characters have "come" from somewhere else.... They live, mostly, on the outskirts of a city or in the hinterland, a world of dry grass and cruel heat which they observe, at times, through the distorting lenses of eyes used to Alpine meadows and soft light. Their responses to this environment are ambivalent and perplexed—at times contemptuous like the Torbens in *The Newspaper of Claremont Street,* whose name is "too hard for you stupid people to say, so we change to easy TORBEN", at times resigned or accepting.... A sense of displacement, or of half-belonging, informs most of Mrs. Jolley's work; in *Mr Scobie's Riddle* it reaches complex, metaphoric embodiment.

In some of the stories this concern is explicitly present.... Elsewhere it is distorted in order to highlight the perplexity of these displaced and puzzled sensibilities. Notable in this regard is **"Paper Children"** (*Woman in a Lampshade*), a story which repeats its major conceit once too often, perhaps, yet serves well as an illustration of this important aspect of Mrs Jolley's art. Clara Schultz, retired Director of a women's clinic, travels from the Lehar Strasse in Vienna to visit her daughter Lisa, who had been smuggled out of wartime Vienna as a small child, and is now living with her farmer husband in Australia. At the end of the story we learn that Clara's voyage was never accomplished, that the several confusing and contradictory "reunions" are flashes of fantasy or hallucination experienced by the dying Clara during the last moments of her life in her Viennese flat. These fantasies survey various possibilities of disappointment: Lisa is, by turns, victim and predator, her husband brutal and cowed. Their farm is impoverished or merely prosaic, the house decayed or commonplace.... The reader, like Clara, is perplexed, without direction, lacking the key to unlock the nature of this world; the clash of rival possibilities, the confusions of perspective rise ... [to the] surface of the fiction. (pp. 241-42)

[*Palomino*] seems to me the least successful of Mrs Jolley's works; I find its purposes curious and puzzling. I do not object to the concern with idyll between an older and a younger woman, but I find the mixture of "elevated" prose and melodramatic material unfortunate, given that Laura, the older woman, is a deregistered doctor who had been imprisoned for murder, and Andrea, the younger, is bearing her brother's child. Perhaps, as the novel consists entirely of first-person narratives, letters and extracts from diaries, the intention is ironic—though if that is so, *Palomino* is merely another instance of the operation of the imitative fallacy. Yet the novel has some interest because it sharpens, and in a sense translates into metaphor, that clash of cultures which informs much of the other work. (p. 242)

Such material may also be encountered in **"Winter Nelis"** (*The Travelling Entertainer*). Once again, the main interest of the story seems to be the lack of understanding and compassion between the sexes. Leonora Brown and her husband Desmond have sunk into the tolerant indifference of married life, but the newly married couple next door, the Banks, appear to be on the verge of disaster when Leonora overhears the younger woman's uncontrolled sobbing. She persuades herself that the Banks need the Browns' help, though when the two couples meet she realizes that the Banks have already succumbed to suburban lethargy. Another strand runs through this story, puzzlingly so unless one picks up the "key" or reference contained in Leonora's repeated incantation "I had not known Ludwig many months before he decided to make me the heroine of his opera...." Leonora's fantasies about her namesake, the heroine of *Fidelio,* establish a contrast between Australian dullness and European romanticism, between the void of suburban marriage and the heroic dedication of a Leonore and a Florestan recalling, perhaps, the "nameless joy" of the great duet in Act II, and contrasting it with Mrs Banks who, for all her sobbing, is yet able to offer her neighbours the conventional hospitality of suburbia. The ironies of this story are quite extensive: Mrs Jolley establishes contrasts which are meaningful, suggestive, but not at all prescriptive or illustrative. We may not be sure whether Leonora's memory of *Fidelio* extends to the recognition that, within the conventions of *Singspiel, Fidelio* deals, in a way, with sexual ambivalence.

In this manner, social, psychological and cultural concerns are transformed into images, metaphors. Mrs Jolley's interests extend beyond recalling and recording the clash of cultures, the perplexity of the displaced individual caught between two worlds. Significantly, the protagonist in a number of the stories is a writer or at least a person professionally concerned with writing. Through this we may approach what is for me the central emphasis in her work—an examination of the viability, the nature, the implications of culture, of writing, of a concern with literature in a world where the connotations of such pursuits are alien. This concern receives magnificently wry expression in *Mr Scobie's Riddle*. . . . (pp. 243-44)

[*Mr Scobie's Riddle* is] a novel of surprising complexity, written with a lightness of touch and an admirable restraint. The inception of the novel was, in all probability, "'**Surprise, Surprise!' from Matron**" (*Five Acre Virgin*), where we encounter the setting, a "home" for the elderly, and in embryo, some of the characters. In this wry but often disturbing (and at times, strangely poignant) novel the nursing home becomes a powerful emblem of some of the preoccupations examined in the first part of this essay. Here a collection of senile, in some cases demented, "patients" endure the last days of their lives under the watchful and at times brusque supervision of the "staff", while (in the background, or the underworld) a sinister nocturnal game of poker rolls on, involving some members of the shadowy Morgan family; the fortunes of the establishment are at stake (we eventually learn) each night in the dinette. In this bizarre setting, the novelist establishes and expands an icon of those concerns with alienation, lack of direction, with the conflict of opposed worlds which are familiar from many of the shorter works. (p. 245)

[The] material of the novel is so arranged that the reader is reminded, subtly but firmly, that this world is but a symbol within an abstract, perhaps allegorical framework. The shape of the work—the "fact" of the book in which the "novel" is printed—reveals the degree of abstraction to be encountered here. *Mr Scobie's Riddle* begins not with a conventional epigraph, but with something that is revealed later to be a "facsimile" of one of the character's *pensées*. . . . (p. 246)

This is followed by a section entitled "A Guide to the Perplexed", a series of snippets, either quoting or describing highlights of the narrative that follows. . . . Thus far *Mr Scobie's Riddle* has been notably lacking in the distinguishing marks of a conventional novel: facsimile and "A Guide to the Perplexed" replace epigraph and table of contents. Turning the leaf, and coming on a significantly numbered first page, we find further evasions of "realistic" procedures. There follows a collage of notices concerning the administration of the hospital and a spectral conversation conducted between Matron Price and the Night Sister, M. Shady, in the pages of the hospital's report-book. It is here that we first learn of the gambling in the dinette, involving some "pats." unknown to the Matron (but recognizable from the earlier story), which is finally to settle the fortunes of St Christopher and St Jude. (pp. 246-47)

These unusual procedures alert the reader to Mrs Jolley's displacement of conventional narrative modes; they pave the way for the novel's entering into a symbolic, near allegorical world. In this manner St Christopher and St Jude is capable of being perceived as a microcosm of a particular view of the world, a "little room" into which the examination of a complex society is concentrated. This is a convent, a closure from which the only escape is the answer to Mr Scobie's Riddle—death. It is not the real world of activity and at least illusory freedom, but a place for wayfarers and for hopeless cases, a retreat in which the rules of "normal" life do not apply, whose inhabitants long for a remembered or perhaps imagined world. So Mr Scobie dreams of his house and of the mysteries of the hill, familiar yet inviolate, on the other side of the road, and more prosaically, Mr Privett longs for his house (now victim to developers) and for the fowls and ducks which inhabit the demented doggerel of his songs. In other words, these old

people long for a former, known life which fast assumes for them the status of ideal and myth. . . . The inmates of St Christopher and St Jude are wayfarers without hope, marooned on their island at the intersection of three roads where accidents occur, and therefore needing the special services of one of the hospital's presiding saints—while both may be required in the case of that wayfarer who is brought to mind by the crossing of three roads. The routine established by Matron Price and the housekeeper Mrs Rawlings (who is in reality the consort of the Matron's estranged husband) seems to these yearning "pats." illogical and incoherent, yet they themselves are incapable of conforming with the demands of society, the differently ordered world outside.

The nursing home is, therefore, a place of dislocation. The inmates are perplexed, confused, trapped between two worlds; they long for their habitual way of life, yet they are incapable of pursuing it either "outside" or in this world where they are given lunch at 11 a.m. and are made to bathe at all manner of inconvenient times, where they are "voided" in the small hours of the morning. The novel is very precise in its use of the conceit of the nursing home: as in reality, such practices are prudent and sensible; the inhabitants of St Christopher and St Jude are incontinent and incompetent. Matron Price's régime, for all its apparent inhumanity, is a necessary condition of such a world. Yet the sense of outrage is firmly held; we are made to feel, without mawkishness, that these people are denied necessary courtesies.

Two of the patients—in many way the most complex characters in the novel—introduce memories or fantasies of a cultured life which is basically European in origin and therefore quite alien to the world of St Christopher and St Jude. They are Mr Scobie, a retired music-teacher, and Miss Hailey, disgraced school-mistress. . . . The case of Mr Scobie is the simpler. He keeps in his room a cassette-player and a few tapes of what Miss Hailey contemptuously regards as middle-brow music. . . . In this way Mr Scobie remembers a time which has no truck with the time present. . . . (pp. 247-49)

The lightly sketched-in history of Mr Scobie is paralleled by the much more complex account of the fortunes of Miss Hailey, the source of the novel's "epigraph" from Horace's sixth ode. In the course of the novel her alarming personal history is pieced together. . . . We learn that she is a novelist (though her work remains unpublished), and she demonstrates the extent of her cultivation when she refers to *la petite phrase* and to *A l'ombre des jeunes filles en fleurs*. Elsewhere she displays a familiarity with German literature and music: at one point she spends several hours outside a public lavatory (waiting for the already absconded Mr Scobie to emerge) "performing" the *Eroica* symphony; later she attempts to adumbrate the characters in *Götterdämmerung* (while worrying about the number and position of the umlauts). Wagner seems, at least indirectly, responsible for her fall. We learn that Miss Hailey had conducted a fashionable and lucrative girls' school until an indiscretion with a pupil whom she had taken to Bayreuth ruined her, thus causing her person and her financial affairs to be placed in the custody of Hyacinth Price, Matron of St Christopher and St Jude. As with Mr Scobie's fall from grace, we are led to wonder where, if at all, this refined academy flourished—are Australian headmistresses able to take favourite pupils to Bayreuth?

Miss Hailey, then, is an artist *manqué*. The other inmates and the staff do not know what to make of her litanies of European culture, just as they are singularly unimpressed by Mr Scobie's familarity with Holy Writ. Their horizons are bounded by the trivia of life in the hospital where three roads meet: the routine of meals and showers, the memories of fowl-yards, the strange goings-on in the dinette and the mysterious allure of the caravan down the back. Whimsically but surely, Mrs Jolley makes the resident madwoman into the custodian of a heritage entirely alien to the denizens of St Christopher and St Jude. I would suggest that it is through Miss Hailey and the playful serious-ness with which she is depicted that this novel makes some not at all unimportant statements about the predicament of the artist, the condition of the hopeless wayfarer in a world seem-ingly dedicated to the materialistic "order" for which the hos-pital is a vital image, notwithstanding the sinister underside revealed by the night-world of the dinette. In this manner we may recognize in *Mr Scobie's Riddle* not merely some of the preoccupations of recent Australian fiction, but also an allusive, parodistic image of the novelist who, through the very pursuit of an "art" which finds its inception, and perhaps, proper milieu in another world, is as "crazy" as Miss Hailey herself. (pp. 249-50)

Mr Scobie's Riddle brings together many preoccupations of recent Australian fiction. Patrick White, too, is concerned with the perplexed individual caught between the demands of con-tradictory worlds—personal, sexual, and cultural. Like Miss Hailey's incantations of little phrases and memories of girls in a budding grove, the opening section of *The Twyborn Affair* has elements of a fantasia of Proustian themes and modes. In a different (and for my tastes rather slick) manner, Murray Bail's *Homesickness* explores Australia in search of a cultural heritage. Mrs Jolley's novel is an important landmark in what, I believe, will come to be seen as a vital tradition of Australian writing. That is why her emblems of the nursing home and its resident sibyl are capable of assuming quite abstract implica-tions.

I have merely touched on some elements in what is a most complex and enigmatic novel. *Mr Scobie's Riddle* is simulta-neously suggestive of larger contexts and precise in its concern with a local habitation and a name. More than Mrs Jolley's other writings, it subsumes its "themes" within the particu-larities of a sharply imagined world. (pp. 251-52)

A. P. Riemer, "Between Two Worlds—An Approach to Elizabeth Jolley's Fiction," in Southerly, *Vol. 43, No. 3, September, 1983, pp. 239-52.*

THOMAS M. DISCH

There are few readers who don't suppose that with time, a typewriter and a bit of practice, they, too, could be novelists—and there are *no* novelists who were not once just such readers. In this respect the existence of any novel is in itself a message of hope, a letter from the royal Cinderella. . . .

[In *Miss Peabody's Inheritance*] the Cinderella/novelist pre-sumed to be responsible for half the book's text is called (or chooses to call herself) Diana Hopewell. She is the author of a lesbian romance, *Angels on Horseback,* set in an Australian girls' school. Continents away in London, Diana's novel has found its ideal reader in Miss Dorothy Peabody, a Cinderella "on the wrong side of fifty" to whom no prince has ever come. When she is not at work as a typist in a London office, she must care for her tyrannical, bedridden mother, a comic mon-ster of Dickensian proportions. But one night, when this gro-tesque hand puppet of a mother is asleep, Miss Peabody writes to her idol. . . .

The idol replies at wonderfully immoderate length, favoring her guileless reader with the first draft and working notes of a new novel. . . .

Mrs. Jolley has written a wonderful duet of stories, so carefully balanced and alternated that she maintains our equal interest in both. Indeed, the novel is at its best at the moments it seesaws between novelist and reader, Hopewell and Peabody. . . .

The consequence, in *Miss Peabody's Inheritance,* of so much self-reference is not, as one might fear, that of attending a seminar on postmodern fiction. Mrs. Jolley has a cheery disdain for literary theory; her motive for exploring the complex, three-way bond between novelists and readers and the "characters" of fiction would appear to spring from an old-fashioned concern for morality, in this case the morality of imaginative experi-ence. At a time when some feminists are urging that pornog-raphy be banned as a violation of their civil rights, Mrs. Jolley's concern is timely—a canny reminder that fantasy may be the last redoubt of freedom and, as such, should not be meddled with. The double narrative ends with a flourish (indeed, with a Miss Flourish) of perfect closure that further develops and rounds out the book's themes, but to say how would spoil Mrs. Jolley's best surprise. . . .

[*Mr. Scobie's Riddle*] is a satire of great verve and acerbity, set amid the horrors of the grotesquely squalid and oppressive nursing home of St. Christopher and St. Jude, a kind of geriatric Dotheboys Hall. As in *Miss Peabody's Inheritance,* the focus of our sympathy is someone at the very bottom of all pecking orders, an endlessly abused sufferer. Mr. Scobie is dying the death we all fear may await us if we outlive friends and family. To the predatory determination of Matron Hyacinth Price, bent on having him sign over pension and property to her nursing home, Mr. Scobie can oppose only his feeble and unheeded demur. It is a conflict as stark in its contrast between a farcical evil and a lyric, helpless good as the persecution of Little Nell by the dwarf Quilp in *The Old Curiosity Shop*. . . .

Scobie is not so artfully self-reflecting a tale as *Peabody,* its most innovative distancing device being a prefatory "Guide to the Perplexed," wherein the author provides explanatory notes on certain passages of the text to come. Yet the two books read in tandem do have a palimpsestuous fascination over and above the stories they have to tell, good as those stories are—not because of the literary legerdemain in itself, but because of Mrs. Jolley's insistence that we should understand what she has to say. That is the reason for so much textual self-reference; that is why "the novelist" is always on hand as commentator.

Perhaps a better way to put this is that Elizabeth Jolley is one of those novelists, like Diana Hopewell, whose books come like letters from a faraway friend, a friend who can tell a good joke or convey a home truth without effort or condescension. A friend to whom one can only reply, in Miss Peabody's words, that her story has given great pleasure and a wish for more of her wit.

Thomas M. Disch, "'Bound, Gagged and Left in the Pantry'," in The New York Times Book Review, *November 18, 1984, p. 14.*

JOAN KIRKBY

Elizabeth Jolley's novel *Miss Peabody's Inheritance* is, to bor-row words once applied to Virginia Woolf's *Orlando,* 'doused in wit, a rollicking consideration of profound questions about gender and love'. It is a tale of release and regeneration, both erotic and imaginative, through art. Miss Peabody's inheritance is vision, energy, and a rite of passage from England to Australia; Elizabeth Jolley's legacy is a comic erotic novel of the first order.

The link with *Orlando* is not surprising; like the work of other female modernists, *Miss Peabody's Inheritance* sets out to upend preconceived notions about gender and sexual attraction. Far too often the social and political implications of modernism are forgotten or ignored; dominant critical practice has encouraged us to look at the high art rather than the radical social critique of modernist works. However modernism was not just a reaction against the tyranny of language and literary convention; it was also a reaction against the tyranny of social codes and conventions, not the least of which was sex role stereotyping and the artificial construction of gender. . . . Love outside the gender system, love between women, the radical questioning of gender, sexual exuberance, freedom, laughter, imaginative release and the possibility of radical social transformation were among the ingredients, cultural styles and possibilities of modernism.

Miss Peabody's Inheritance both taps and extends this energy, but with poignant immediacy, for Miss Peabody's erotic, imaginative awakening is also a rite of passage to Australia. The novel highlights the modernist strand of Jolley's writing, the formally complex, anti-linear, self-conscious experimentation with point of view, and the representation of inward states of consciousness. This is not to deny the powerful realist impulse of Jolley's fiction; as one of her characters says 'a poet is one to whom the visible world is real', and some of her stories in this mould have a genuine sense of the tragic. However, *Miss Peabody's* mode is celebratory, exuberant and unmistakably modernist.

The novel's structure is a disconcerting delight with rapidly alternating frames which sometimes leave the reader floating out of frame. The reader just begins to settle into the mock realist frame of Diana Hopewell's omniscient novel within the novel, about the erotically entangled lives of Arabella Thorne, Gwenda Manners and Edgely, only to be catapulted into the rival mock realism of the Peabody household. . . . (pp. 484-85)

Diana Hopewell writes her novel before our eyes, with characters and incidents colour coded, clichés underlined and notes to the uninitiated on the finer points. . . . The mode of the novel, both the novel within the novel and the frame novel, is a stylised realism in which stylised figures commit unstereotypical acts in deft, precise and minimal but telling detail.

The reader, like Miss Peabody, is drawn compulsively on, not the least because of the novel's exuberant eroticism. This is the novel's great surprise—from the first motel water fight ('You exquisite naughty. Oh indecently exquisite.') to the orgasmic night in Vienna when Miss Thorne finally beds Fräulein Valkyrie for a night of passion that is 'idyllic, tender, hilarious, and ludicrous. There was laughing and the trying not to laugh.' This combination of laughter and love should not be as unexpected as it is; again there is the echo of *Orlando*—'She loved her and they laughed.' (pp. 485-86)

The spirited correspondence between novelist and fan is also part of the narration. At first disconcerted, Miss Peabody is soon excited by the novelist's attention and unexpected questions, 'Have you a small straight brave back? And are you in love?' In response to the novelist's descriptions of Australia (the novelist is an invalid confined to a nursing home), Miss Peabody sees her 'dismounting from her horse at sunset to open the gates leading to her property,' or 'charmingly dressed, mounted on her horse and galloping, with passion and grace, alongside a fence made with round poles, like the one written about in the novel.' (p. 486)

It is very much a story of the new world exciting the old. Diana's writing gives Miss Peabody a concept of other possibilities, alternative modes of being, new ways of living, not the least of which is a concept of love outside the forms and norms she has hitherto experienced—love outside the gender system, outside the mould of the office romance. . . . Diana's gift of three coloured sheepskins for Miss Peabody's hard to please recipients is the first nurturing act of kindness she has known and she glows with the warmth of it. That this warmth might have something to do with sexuality is a revelation (reinforced by Diana's novel), so narrow, so heterosexually and genitally prescribed, have the clichés and platitudes of her life been. The riotous coloured sheepskins become an emblem of the vibrant land where many expectations might be overturned. Australia, for Miss Peabody, is a land of enchantment.

Miss Peabody, fired by Diana's writings, is awakened to the visible world around her and she relishes it, addressing cryptic questions to her fellow workers such as 'Has anyone heard a curlew lately?', which set her apart as mystic and inspired. Jolley's skill also allows the reader to perceive the disconcerting burden Miss Peabody's awakening is to her fellow workers who see her as 'tight' or 'mad'. She becomes aware of herself and her body. Inspired by Thorne and Snow she takes long baths and admires Miss Truscott's gunmetal grey stockinged legs. She longs for Diana. (p. 487)

Through Diana, Miss Peabody herself is transfigured. The English spinster doffs the costume of dutiful daughter and takes up the mantle that Diana has offered her, the mantle of imagination, of creator. . . . Diana has been mother and muse to Miss Peabody, as her creation Miss Thorne was for Gwenda, taking her on a 'pilgrimage to bring out in the gel a true appreciation of beauty in all its forms'. There are similarities here with the role of Mrs Ramsay for Lily Briscoe in Woolf's *To the Lighthouse*, Stella for Edith in Hanrahan's *The Albatross Muff*, or Emily for the narrator of Lessing's *Memoirs of a Survivor*. All are concerned with the power of female bonding and visionary, imaginative release.

In *Miss Peabody's Inheritance,* with its intermingling of imagination and eroticism, all sorts of stereotypes are exploded, including those associated with the words 'spinster', 'invalid', 'headmistress'. Instead we have images of woman as indomitable, voyaging, powerful. By the end of the novel, the figures of Hopewell, Thorne and Peabody conjure up Mary Daly's glorious hags, crones and spinsters weaving their cosmic tapestries, or the images of the spinster that Nina Auerbach unmasks in *Woman and the Demon*. Auerbach reveals that a prominent nineteenth century image of the spinster was of a free, untrammelled, buoyant, voyaging consciousness associated with immigration to the new world and prophetic of new social orders. She was 'a specially endowed being for whom the large and changing world is home'. She was threatening to the family and the patriarchal social order because, like the fallen woman of Victorian mythology she exists amorphously beyond women's traditional identities as daughter, wife and mother, and like her is associated with the promise and terror of the new world; she is 'a preternaturally endowed creature who taunts conventional morality and seeks the glory of her own apotheosis'.

Just such a woman is Elizabeth Jolley's larger than life Dr Arabella Thorne, the travelling Headmistress whose entourage leaves behind it 'a trail of broken beds'. Armed with a favourite quote from Johnson, or was it Boswell. . . . Miss Thorne sets out to initiate herself and her gels into all that may be experienced of this manifold earth, age, sex and physical comeliness notwithstanding. (pp. 487-88)

Of course, Arabella Thorne exists only in Diana Hopewell's novel of female eroticism and laughter, the space that the novelist creates outside the gender system. And if in one sense she is but the fantasy projection of a crippled woman in a nursing home (and if in another Miss Peabody only exchanges an English typing pool for an Australian nursing home), this does not detract from the creation. In her novel, Diana speaks the unspeakable and makes visible the invisible, that which is silenced, covered over and made absent in society. Hopewell's fantastic narrative explodes and subverts the tyranny of discourse and gender, all that would prescribe who should be attracted to whom and when and where and at what age.

Love between women, the interplay between memory and imagination, and a compelling response to the Australian continent are motifs of several of Jolley's works. In *Miss Peabody's Inheritance* these are the source of joyous release, but in other works they have led to tragedy. Some of her women must kill for their visions. Laura of *Palomino* is for years in love with a woman with whom she has corresponded (foreshadowing the correspondence of Hopewell and Peabody); she looks forward to their meeting, dreaming of the sweet cool fragrance of Esme's back and breasts and thighs. When they meet Laura is repelled by the short, stout, shrill ageing Esme. . . . Though Laura is aware 'I should have loved you for the pleasure you had in living', she kills her. (p. 489)

Miss Hailey of *Mr Scobie's Riddle* is a darker version of Diana Hopewell and her creation Miss Thorne. Like Diana Hopewell she is a novelist in a nursing home; she weeps over her characters and recites poetry in parks. However, ultimately Miss Hailey is a much sadder figure, an ex-headmistress left with memories of her school and her too fond attachment to a pupil which ultimately left her bereft of everything and incarcerated in the nursing home. She is also beset by sad memories of her 'impassioned mouse' of a secretary (shades of Edgely) and an earlier relationship with Matron Price. Desperately afraid of being revolting when old ('We'll both be revolting . . . We have no choice.'), she weeps for the lack of any real tenderness. Nevertheless Miss Hailey's vision, energy and receptivity to the life around her are potentially redemptive. She is alive, like other of Jolley's artists, to the immense possibilities of transfiguration and new ways of living. (p. 490)

The Newspaper of Claremont Street and the just published *Milk and Honey* (actually written much earlier) are also, like *Miss Peabody's Inheritance,* concerned with rites of passage to Australia and the impact of imaginative surrender to a new land. Like Miss Peabody, Weekly [in *The Newspaper of Claremont Street*] comes from the Old World, the Black Country, and a life of suppression. . . . However, after a lifetime of service, she finally buys land in Australia and the black cockatoos come, bringing to the place 'a quality of strangeness, of something unknown, as if they had some other knowledge, something to do with another kind of life.' Transfigured, Weekly dances in celebration of her new land, like the dancers in Hawthorne's tale 'The Maypole of Merrymount'. Both are dances of assimilation, of drawing oneself into relation with the earth. However, even as Hawthorne's dancers are interrupted by emis-

saries of the Old World, the grim bearded Puritans, so Weekly is encumbered by an emissary from the Old World in the form of the parasitic Nastasya Torben. . . .Nastasya Torben must die before the rite of passage to Australia can be achieved. The old world must be shed before assimilation to the new world is possible.

Milk and Honey recounts a less successful tale of assimilation. Jacob, a first generation Australian . . . , is sent to learn music and board with an old European family. Gradually he, like them, becomes incarcerated in the modes, lifestyles and values of the old world. He has a sense of 'the invisible, inescapable power drawing me into the household'. His will is suppressed, paralysed by ceremony. Almost involuntarily he is betrothed to the daughter, wearing rings of her hair on his fingers, and then he is married to her. 'I was a bird in a snake's eye.'

Jacob's immature affair with Madge, an older woman, short and plump and puffy eyed, is his bid for autonomy and escape from the stifling devotion of the European household. In a sense Madge is, at least in the eyes of the European family, the new world, brash, common, shallow, a gold digger who plays the violin for money rather than art. However, Jacob's uncontrollable obsession with Madge is no match for the family's determination to protect and preserve all that belongs to them.

It is a powerful Gothic tale of incarceration, incest, insanity, murder and mutilation—all in large measure provoked by the difficulties of assimilating to a new land. . . . The land of *Milk and Honey* drives the refugees to madness and murder, and at the end of the novel the family's only survivors are all inmates of an asylum in the new world. Jacob, however, does come to an understanding of the fear that isolated, distorted and eventually destroyed the family and has a sense that something radiant and glowing might grow from the waste and desolation. Even as the wasteland on the way to the mental hospital has been transformed into an ornamental park, 'Perhaps the terror and failure of my life could, in some way, be smoothed over like the swamp had been levelled and rained and combed and planted.'

Miss Peabody's liberating rite of passage to Australia and the exuberant comic achievement of *Miss Peabody's Inheritance* are all the more remarkable when seen in the full awareness of the dark possibilities of Jolley's themes. (pp. 490-91)

Joan Kirkby, "The Nights Belong to Elizabeth Jolley: Modernism and the Sappho-Erotic Imagination of 'Miss Peabody's Inheritance'," in Meanjin, *Vol. 43, No. 4, December, 1984, pp. 484-92.*

JOANNA MOTION

In the increasingly impressive work of . . . Elizabeth Jolley, the patterns have an old-fashioned stamp of Central Europe, struggling to adjust to the relative undress of Australia. With five novels behind her, it is clear that hers is a remarkable talent: bleakly comic, awkward to categorize, original and rewarding. Her preoccupations recur; a passion for music and the natural world are constant elements. A related series of disappointed, more or less lesbian, professional women stalk her pages. The dense skirts of a Viennese inheritance swing through her rooms. But she reappraises these constituents from different and enlivening angles.

The passionate horsewoman whose love and anguish are tackled head-on in the obsessional first-person narration of *Palomino* is slyly sent up in the wonderfully named Diana Hopewell (author of *Angels on Horseback*), the novelist-within-the-novel of *Miss Peabody's Inheritance*. The powerful headmistress who is an entertaining central feature of the same novel, lending her magnificent dressing-gown cord for the costuming of the school *Othello*, makes a pathetic appearance in the gallery of ageing characters who enact the grimmish comedy of *Mr Scobie's Riddle*. But the richest, the darkest and the most unexpected of Jolley's novels to date is *Milk and Honey*, in which she provokes the most daring collision between the old world and the new, exploring to see where a synthesis becomes possible.

The first-generation immigrant Jacob, speaking with "the exaggerated Australian accent of the central European who is trying to fit in", is drawn into a cloying refugee household where he is to foster his talent as a cellist. Outside, the Australian sun is beating down, but he is trapped in a house of aunts and rituals and hand embroidery, silting over on a diet of sweet wine, Polish cucumbers and sugar biscuits. Within the house he is, with dignity, Jacob. At the orchestra he meets crude, natural, Australian Maggie (who plays for money, not for art) and to her he is Jackyboy. Jacob's attempt to combine the conflicting elements of his life within a single dream house turns out to be a fairytale, built on magic money. His ambitions collapse into disaster, but out of the desolate aftermath a sort of resolution and reconciliation grow. *Milk and Honey* is a self-conscious and present novel, mysterious, disturbing and genuinely risk-taking. There is no knowing where Elizabeth Jolley will go next, but the journey is one to follow.

Joanna Motion, "Patterning the Stuff of Life," in The Times Literary Supplement, No. 4255, October 18, 1985, p. 1173.

ANGELA CARTER

In Elizabeth Jolley's delicious and sustaining new novel, *Foxybaby*, as in *As You Like It* and *The Tempest*, a random collection of human beings find themselves in a remote place and there discover unfamiliar and surprising things, to return to the world changed in some way. A group of blue-rinsed matrons gathers under the tutelage of a middle-age spinster, Miss Alma Porch, to improve their minds and diminish their flesh, attending a "Better Body Through the Arts" weight loss course on a rundown campus. They are lonely, loony, unhappy, existentially deranged. Some, eventually, are consoled.

And—two for the price of one—the mode of pastoral comedy in which *Foxybaby* is conceived, accommodating as a magic handbag, finds ample room inside itself for another narrative of an altogether more somber kind, even if capering bucolics are apt to interrupt the proceedings with raucous song and laughter.

The campus is a Trinity College, which is neither in Cambridge, England, nor Dublin, nor Connecticut, but in a place called Cheatham East. (Say it: Cheat 'em, and relish the mild, Dickensian pun.) (p. 1)

Not so much dwarfed by as subtly at odds with their exotic surroundings, the seekers after art and weight loss—and pastime, and company and even love—grapple with the dramatic interpretation of a work-in-progress, an unfinished novel, the eponymous *Foxybaby*, under the tutorship of its author, Alma Porch. Miss Porch has made a film treatment of her novel,

which her students act out. It turns out to be a bizarre form of psychodrama.

It is Miss Porch who articulates the rigorous moral vision that gives all Elizabeth Jolley's work the cutting edge beneath the seductive surface. Miss Porch meditates, "It is right to feel pain." This piercing categorical imperative sticks uncomfortably in the mind like a splinter but, in common with Grace Paley, a writer she somewhat resembles, Mrs. Jolley takes occasional recourse in a distracted winsomeness that camouflages an acute emotional insight that might otherwise seem too cruel. Miss Porch "knew too that this profound despair was a part of the loneliness which accompanied writing. Added to this was the emotional stress of offering a partly-written work to a group of people who were concerned chiefly with losing weight."

Part of Mrs. Jolley's comic method is to juxtapose profound feeling with low farce, high camp with agonized lyricism. *Foxybaby* is a deeply and, I suspect, intentionally disorienting read.

As solitary and as mysteriously self-contained a spinster as those in Patrick White's fiction—perhaps it is an Australian type—Miss Porch at first finds Trinity College, with its regime of lettuce leaves and herb tea, scarcely supportable. She gains comfort from the heartening presence of Meridian Viggars, whose very name is synonymous with vigorous middle age.

Mrs. Viggars it is whose enthusiasm gives life to the class. With her portable wine cellar, she presides over sumptuous and illicit midnight feasts, bulky in her tweeds and trouser suits or else "resplendent in manure-coloured brocade." Mrs. Jolley's language often hits this high pitch of the fastidiously bizarre, as when Mrs. Viggars offers "an excellent Spätlese, quite a lively little wine with naughty thighs and a cheeky nose." It is Mrs. Viggars, with her capacity for selfless love, who conjured up at last, upon a stormy shore, the physical reality of the desolate characters from Miss Porch's novel, and bids Miss Porch walk bravely out to meet them.

The Trinity College part of the novel is an anarchically ramshackle comedy of manners, a ragged daisy chain of disconnected people and events, often deliriously funny, veering giddily between slapstick and gallows humor. The course, as such courses are, is attended mostly by the lonely, the loony and the unhappy. Miss Porch's nights are disturbed by an unwelcome roommate, Mrs. Castle, she of the crushed-strawberry bikini bought for the keep-fit classes, and the Midnight Beetroot lipstick. "Miss Porch began to hate Mrs. Castle and to feel deeply sorry for her at the same time."

Mrs. Castle's family have sent her off to Trinity, all expenses paid, so they can take a holiday from her habitual gentility; Miss Porch imagines the son-in-law celebrating granny's absence by "spending whole days in the bath drinking brandy and walking about the house without any clothes on." Of course! you think; that's just what he *would* do. Then you remember you've never met this person, that he doesn't exist, that he doesn't exist as a character in the novel; he only exists in the imagination of one of the imaginary characters in the novel. (p. 36)

If genteel lewdness is rife among the middle classes, riotous impropriety is the order of the day among the staff. Miles, the factotum, conducts endless, noisy amours, chasing wife and mistress in and out of the orchard, crying: "Get your knickers off sweetheart!'' He discombobulates the cut-glass-and-crochet Mrs. Castle with his lewd refrains.

But more than simply being there in all his reassuring earthiness, Miles seems to function in the plot in something of the same way that Papageno does in *The Magic Flute*. Papageno fails all the tests of virtue and courage but he gets his happy ending all the same because for him happiness is the same thing as simple, immediate, sensual gratification. He is appetite, not ethics, like a child. So is Miles. And it would *not* be right for Miles to feel pain. It would be as senselessly dreadful as the suffering of a child.

The suffering of children is the theme of the novel-in-progress inside *Foxybaby*. We find out about this novel in a stylized, indeed positively Brechtian way. Miss Porch's students mime episodes of the film treatment while she reads the appropriate sections aloud to an accompaniment of cello and tapping-sticks provided by Miss Peycroft and her stupid sidekick, Miss Paisley. This accompaniment, in its incompetence and pretension, says all that need be said about Miss Peycroft's commitment to the arts. Miles is supposed to film all this but soon sells the video camera. It is as though Mrs. Jolley is making it as difficult as possible for us to become emotionally involved with the red-haired runaway whom her father calls Foxybaby. (pp. 36-7)

[The] girl whom Miss Porch has picked out to impersonate her heroine unexpectedly gives birth to a daughter. The students prepare bootees and small garments. Now it is time for an outing to the sea on a day of storm. . . . Beside the sea, Miss Porch goes out to meet the red-haired girl and the man with the baby in his arms. The atmosphere darkens, as though childish things have been put away, as the fictions fuse.

Or do they? There is a teasingly enigmatic coda suggesting that Mrs. Jolley has not really brought us to a conclusion. There are no conclusions in life, after all, so why should we fake them up for the sake of art? Instead, she has taken us to the point where the novel we have just read is about to have been written.

Or perhaps Miss Porch was dreaming all the time. There is a suggestion she might have dreamed the main body of the novel, including, presumably, her own work-in-progress, while dozing on her journey to Cheatham East and, indeed, the novel is structured with all the numinous inconsequence of the dream. It is hard to know what to make of it. My response was to turn to the beginning and start reading all over again. (p. 37)

Angela Carter, ''Dreams of Reason . . . and of Foxes,'' in The New York Times Book Review, *November 24, 1985, pp. 1, 36-7.*

LESLEY CHAMBERLAIN

Anyone straying into Trinity College, somewhere remote in Australia, could be forgiven for judging culture a perversion. Alma Porch, unmarried, unsure, ugly and indeterminately middle-aged, agrees to tutor a creative drama course for obese and aspiring women, and opens a Pandora's box of unsuppressed, ill-chosen passions, midnight feasts and loneliness. . . . [*Foxybaby*] is something beyond the mixture of Barbara Pym gentility and sexual farce it might first appear to be; it becomes an exploration of the intricacies of the imagination. Miss Porch stops being the Writer as Unconvincing Person and begins to read aloud from her drama-in-progress. She chooses Anna from among her pupils to act the part of her female protagonist, but at heart the choice is fascination, and was made not that day

in class but some time before, on first sight. The pale, half-ugly pregnant woman unconsciously gives birth to the character she plays, with Miss Porch as confidante-midwife. The real Anna never speaks.

In the fictionalizing mind of an otherwise diffident and hardly imaginative spinster, art and life enter into a sustained, confused, uncontrollable erotic embrace. . . .

The technique of framing a work-in-progress with a story about its writer and another about its audience tended to drag in *Miss Peabody*, where the inner tale was mildly pornographic and thin, but it excels in *Foxybaby*, because Miss Porch's tale is gripping. A lonely man in love with his drug-addict daughter tries, on a desperately brief motel holiday, to help her and her baby. Jolley's change of tone in the telling at first seems bathetic. But the drama exerts on the pupils a Socratic magic, drawing out their prejudices and drawing in their emotions. The drama course, so fake in the commercial world, becomes real in the inner life of the pupils because of the quality of the script. Particularly spellbound is the powerful, likable, rich Mrs Viggars, who is moved to offer a home to the forlorn ''real'' Anna. Her dependence on the drama presses a sometimes despairing Miss Porch to keep writing, and therewith comes one of the many passing erotic messages of *Foxybaby*: the fascinated reader, through her interest, engages the author in a slavish bond of admiration and dependence.

Yet the epigraphs, and a car accident early in the novel, point to a dream, in which the writer is trying to sort her relations with the world, and to distinguish art from culture. What takes place then is essentially a traumatic vision, illuminated and relieved by expressionist flashes of antipodean landscape. Thus it is when Miss Porch has first immersed herself in her work, after the first ''reading'', that she looks into the pinkish-mauve Australian twilight and sees at once the necessity of her solitude and her writing and has a private vision of Gethsemane. The comic streak, the light touch and the homely blurb of this book all belie the fact that it is an unusual novel about the genderless erotic adventure of writing.

Lesley Chamberlain, ''The Embrace of Art,'' in The Times Literary Supplement, *No. 4341, June 13, 1986, p. 645.*

PETER ACKROYD

[*Milk and Honey*] is written in the form of a monologue—the voice that of Jacob, a quondam cellist whose hand has been so badly charred in an accident that he is now forced to earn a precarious living as a door-to-door salesman. The mood of the book, therefore, is one of bleakness and frustration, and almost at once Jacob's unhappy narrative reverts to ''the shuddering, muttering, mocking nightmare which belongs with childhood.'' This is a nightmare from which he has never been able fully to awake, however, and the opening sequences cast their shadows across the entire novel.

George Orwell once said of *David Copperfield* that its vision of childhood was so accomplished that, as a boy, he vaguely believed it ''had been written *by a child*''; the childhood sections of *Milk and Honey* have the same simple, mysterious assurance. Jacob is taken from the vineyards of his Australian farm to be educated by a family of displaced Central Europeans, the Heimbachs. . . .

All this is depicted so naturally that only in retrospect do the macabre aspects of the story acquire their full significance:

Jacob believes himself to have killed the young idiot son of the family and, partly in recompense, he is inveigled into marrying the young Louise Heimbach. At this point, the beginning of his adult existence, his life divides; he becomes obsessed with Madge, an Australian, but once he moves outside the household he comes close to being destroyed. Eventually, his double involvement provokes an inexplicable tragedy.

This is the outline of the story, and no doubt it will come as a surprise to Elizabeth Jolley's admirers. She has in previous novels chronicled the lives of the isolated and unhappy, but she has done so with spry, sometimes even insouciant, social comedy.... [In] *Milk and Honey* her tone is darker, richer and more complicated. This is the first time that she has abandoned the omniscient third-person narrative, so valuable as a protective lace curtain, and has chosen instead to employ the resources of monologue; and it is as if the fall into the consciousness of another person has broken open her style, rendering it more haunting and ultimately more profound....

We are accustomed to Australian writers making their way to England, where their style often seems exuberant and grandiloquent, somehow managing to undermine the usual restrictions of conventional English by which they feel themselves to be imprisoned. But Elizabeth Jolley has traveled in the other direction. She has made her own journey *to* Australia and, as a result, her prose has become tighter and sharper—it is almost as if all its energy were being compressed by the sheer size and weight of her adopted country. In a brief prologue to *Milk and Honey* she writes of certain debris that is swept up by the high winds of Europe and deposited in "another hemisphere"—and how it does not rest on this alien soil but settles with other European fragments in order to preserve itself and to "remain unchanged for as long as possible." This is an approximate version of her own situation as a novelist.

But it is also the condition of the characters in *Milk and Honey*. The household of the Heimbachs is insulated from the rest of Australia, and as long as Jacob remains within it, playing his cello, he also remains untouched. So the book is concerned with two cultures—or, rather, it depicts the intensity that one culture can acquire when it is torn up and planted elsewhere....

Nevertheless, the abiding images of this novel are those of mortality or decay; its narrative is striated with emblems of burning, of sickness and death. If Elizabeth Jolley was once close to Barbara Pym, on this occasion she is even closer to Edgar Allan Poe, and the prose of the book is slow, mournful, incantatory. Hers is the poetry of the grotesque—and she has a poet's ear, also, in her ability so to control the cadences of her writing that their movement becomes a necessary part of the story. There is something perhaps too stark about it, as if she had for too long been separated from the community of meanings that makes up the European inheritance, but the starkness lends the book a hallucinatory quality that lingers in the memory. In that sense *Milk and Honey* seems closer to fable or folk tale than to the conventional novel—its European images have been placed in an Australian setting where their shadows become darker and longer, more difficult to understand but also more difficult to resist.

Peter Ackroyd, "Two Cultures, One Transplanted,"
in The New York Times Book Review, June 15,
1986, p. 12.

BOB HALLIDAY

Like many of her fellow Australian novelists, Elizabeth Jolley is fascinated by loners and outsiders.... Jolley's characters are generally stunted, truncated types whose deviations are impressed on them by various forms of confinement. Her work is rarely depressing, however, because Jolley mines the sometimes monstrous situations she describes for humor, and even her darkest passages will suddenly flash with a hint of macabre craziness going on behind the scenes.

A strong element of autobiography can also be sniffed out in her fiction. Displaced Europeans like her own family inhabit many of Jolley's books. Certain incidents, specific landscapes and family situations are repeated verbatim in novels and stories written over the years, and Jolley brings them across to the reader with the force of direct memory....

[*The Well*] combines the sleekness of a parable with the dynamic of a finely crafted horror story to explore a theme that is at the center of much of Jolley's most interesting writing: the disastrous effects of failed or mutated love.

The book's central character, Miss Hester, is a spinster who lives with her father on a large piece of land in rural Western Australia. One day, while visiting the general store for provisions, Hester spots a young orphan girl.... Hester is drawn to the girl and acquires her, bringing her home together with the groceries. (p. 10)

The two lead a reasonably happy existence together, but things change when Hester decides to sell her land, and the purchasers throw a party to which they invite the two women.

Katherine is excited by the dancing, and when Hester permits her to practice her driving on the way home she is reckless. She hits a man walking in the road.... Once home, the two women dispose of the body down a deep, disused well next to the house. Soon afterward they find that all of Hester's cash, which she keeps in the house, has been stolen, and it becomes evident that the dead man was the thief.... Hester tries to force Katherine to climb down into the well and retrieve the money from the corpse, threatening her with jail if she refuses. The girl, on the other hand, claims that the man in the well isn't dead, and sits for hours at the edge of the pit, conversing with him. He has proposed marriage to her, Katherine claims, and is begging piteously to be rescued.

The horrific conclusion Jolley contrives for the tale is arrived at as neatly as the recapitulation at the end of a Haydn sonata movement, and even while shuddering at the cruelty of it, readers will admire the deftness with which it weaves together the strands of symbolism which thread their way through the story.

The same virtuosity of form that gives *The Well* such a bite sometimes sabotages the stories collected in *Woman in a Lampshade*. Jolley uses her stories as laboratories in which she tests out experimental techniques and tinkers around with certain symbols, mostly drawn from nature, which intrigue her. Often the same symbol will appear in identical form in several stories.... When everything works out, the stories that result are both innovative and memorable. **"One Christmas Knitting"** uses a gentle, wistful surrealism to put a dreamlike aura around childhood memories of events in a transplanted Austrian household, and the mood possesses the reader entirely. In **"Pear Tree Dance,"** one of the very best pieces, an eccentric woman transcends her narrow and absurd life by purchasing a piece of land, and in nine pages Jolley somehow manages to communicate the woman's complex character and the significance of her transformation.

But other stories have the feel of trial runs where dramatic life is drained away by too much attention to technique. ["**Woman in a Lampshade**"], in which a woman writer is so preoccupied with killing off a young man in a story she is writing that she fails to respond to the real despair of a youth she spends the night with, is so deliberate an exercise in irony that the characters stay dead on the page. One would gladly sacrifice cleverness of design for more of the naturalness the premise of these stories requires.

A similar problem infects . . . *Milk and Honey,* a bizarre novel tale which rivets without really satisfying the reader. (pp. 10-11)

Jolley is so caught up in writing a Gothic novel that credibility is sacrificed. All of the trappings of Gothic horror are there in extreme form: incest, hints of insanity, a family idiot hidden away in a secret room, unexplained disappearances, but the psychological support for such a structure is never adequately filled in. Jolley relies too much on nudges and dark hints to the reader. . . . The perverse, highly wrought atmosphere evaporates and it becomes evident that the characters act the way they do because they inhabit a Gothic novel. . . .

Anyone who picks up *Milk and Honey* looking for a good read will not be disappointed. It has a creepy fascination that succeeds in holding the reader fast even as it fails in its larger ambitions. But the way to experience Jolley's powers at full throttle is to start off with *The Well* and then try out several of the stories in the *Woman in a Lampshade* volume or the earlier novel, *Mr. Scobie's Riddle.* For all the comparisons that have been made of her work with that of Muriel Spark and Flannery O'Connor, Jolley really resembles neither. She is an Australian original who deserves a wide American audience. (p. 11)

Bob Halliday, "Elizabeth Jolley's Well of Loneliness," in Book World—The Washington Post, November 2, 1986, pp. 10-11.

ROBERT COOVER

Elizabeth Jolley seems to have a lot of fun when she writes. She lets herself go, laughs a lot, cries a lot, dances every chance she gets (women—women of all ages—dancing, dancing properly or crazily, most often crazily, or at least in delicious uninhibited celebration, is a profoundly Jolleyan motif), gets playfully inventive, then spooks herself with the uncanny, celebrates outrageous behavior and eccentric voices, mocks Paradise, eats an apricot, throws a goofy wedding party, commits a murder or two, hovers about hospitals and old folks' homes because she loves the people there, loves people everywhere, to tell the truth, though there's no hope for them, sadly enough, crippled as they are with guilt and poverty and stupidity and mortality, no hope and not all that much dignity either, but they *are* a treat to listen to. And what an ear she has for them! (p. 1)

"Yo' should 'ave seen the mess after the Venns' Party," the cleaning lady known whimsically as "The Newspaper of Claremont Street" (Ms. Jolley has published a novel by this name—[in *Woman in a Lampshade*] she appears in the story "**Pear Tree Dance**") shouts out to her employer. "Broken glass everywhere, blood on the stairs and a whole pile of half-eaten pizzas in the laundry. Some people think they're having a good time! And you'll never believe this, I picked up a bed jacket, ever so pretty it was, to wash it and, would you believe, there was a yuman arm in it . . ." (pp. 1, 44)

[There are scores] of inimitable voices in *Woman in a Lampshade,* many of them drawn, it would seem, from close personal experience. When Ms. Jolley first moved to Western Australia from the English Midlands nearly 30 years ago, the publisher's note tells us, as though to make of the author one of her own inventions, "she worked as a nurse, a door-to-door salesperson and as a flying domestic amongst other things, and now cultivates a small orchard and goose farm."

There's also here, for example, philosophical Uncle Bernard who "travels in macaroni," plants potatoes destined to die of the frost in the hard clay. . . . There are murderers and idiots and dear Anti Mote the kleptomaniacal nudist and the marvelous Mrs. Morgan, heroine of several of these stories, also a cleaning lady and the mother of two dropouts, who dreams in "**The Last Crop**" of writing a book. . . .

[In *Woman in a Lampshade,* the] charmingly dotty lady writers, no doubt often meant as ironic self-portraits, are as central to Ms. Jolley's fictions as clowns and ringmasters are to circuses. The most notable one here is the lampshade-wearing Jasmine Tredwell of ["**Woman in a Lampshade**"] who takes her typewriter and dance music to bed with her, along with her newest Muse in the form of a hiccupping young hitchhiker, in the hopes of resolving her current plot problem. . . .

Eccentric lady writers with disorderly plots and original voices dominate three previous Jolley novels as well, novels that are all memorable for their innovative narrative devices, their elaborated fictions-within-fictions, their rousing sense of humor, and their themes of love between women and the fearful but grimly comic processes of aging.

Miss Peabody of *Miss Peabody's Inheritance* is a lonely English spinster, well past her prime, who sends a timid fan letter to the exotic Australian romancer Diana Hopewell, thereby initiating an elaborate correspondence between the two women in which the novelist in effect seduces the spinster with details of her work-in-progress about three elderly lesbians traveling through Europe with a young schoolgirl. When Miss Peabody starts confusing fiction and reality, she is asked to take a leave of absence from her secretarial job, whereupon she flies off to Australia to meet her idol. But too late. She has died ignominiously, a sick old woman, in a nursing home. Miss Peabody is left with the projected novel, her "inheritance.". . . .

Foxybaby is in reality the title of a work-in-progress by the novel's central character, Alma Porch. (p. 44)

Miss Porch's painful if somewhat parodic tale of a father's desperate and sensual love for a hysterical daughter embroiled in drug addiction and other cruel attachments is set within the hilarious and bawdy frame story of the crazy summer camp, which in turn seems to be Miss Porch's anxiety-driven dream *about* the camp on the bus ride going there. Central to the camp story is Miss Porch's initiatrix (rather like an experienced upper-former at a girls' boarding school), Miss Mabel Harrow, yet another goofy lady novelist given to grand gestures and astonishing flights of breathless rhetoric.

This Jolleyan archetype, though still present like a kind of tucked-in signature, fades into the background in her newest and most spellbinding work to date, *The Well,* only to assume her familiar ringmaster's role at the last moment. Near the end of the book, the main character, Miss Hester Harper, runs into an unnamed lady writer in the general store, where she has earlier seen her shopping for a square plastic bowl to soak her feet in, and we are led to suppose that their encounter may well have inspired the book . . . that we have just been reading.

The Well is an exquisite story, a parable of sorts, as stories of wells are apt to be, especially bottomless wells with dead—or mostly dead—men dropped down them. The style reflects this fairy-tale quality. . . . (pp. 44-5)

Once again, the forging and severing of bonds between women are at the heart of the plot: crippled Miss Harper's childhood adoration of her governess, Fräulein Hilde Herzfeld, the only real love of her life until now; her servant Katherine's adolescent friendship with Joanna, her mate from the orphanage (always about to arrive, never quite getting there); and, above all, the passionate mistress-servant relationship that develops between crotchety old Miss Harper and the excitable orphan girl who so generously and tenderly serves her.

This affair with young Kathy is itself, at least from Miss Harper's perspective, a kind of impossible fairy tale, as if the world, which grants no wishes, had momentarily forgot its true nature. Fearful of losing Kathy to this world, once it gets its senses back, she withdraws from it, taking Kathy with her as though to sequester a secret treasure. Rapidly declining fortunes

ensue, but this is a small price to pay for the momentary recovery of that magical garden thought lost in childhood. She is somehow suddenly, old age, lame leg and all, beautiful again. Lovable. Desirable. Even though, as she knows when the migraines overtake her, it can't last. . . .

Elizabeth Jolley's writing, even at its best, it should be said, seems ultimately somewhat slight, her great gifts devoted on the whole to entertainments more witty than profound. There is a recurring familiarity about her characters and themes, and she has an appetite for plots that tend to erase themselves, in the way that punch lines erase their jokes, thereby weakening our emotional attachment to them. There is even on occasion a writer's-workshop feel about her stories, a touch of the O. Henrys.

But she is a relaxed and appealing storyteller with a great sense of humor and a wonderful ear, an elegant and compassionate voice. Her lines literally radiate with the pleasure she's had in writing them. She's having all this fun so, since she's sharing it, why shouldn't we? (p. 45)

Robert Coover, "Dotty and Disorderly Conduct," in The New York Times Book Review, *November 16, 1986, pp. 1, 44-5.*

Ken (Elton) Kesey

1935-

American novelist and short story writer.

A transitional figure linking the Beat generation of the 1950s with the counterculture movement of the 1960s, Kesey is best known for his first novel, *One Flew over the Cuckoo's Nest* (1962). This book is considered a masterpiece of contemporary American literature for its disjointed, colloquial prose style, its tightly constructed plot, and its exposition of modern social ills. Although many critics faulted Kesey's portrayals of blacks as sadistic agents of institutionalized cruelty and women as either emasculating shrews or good-hearted prostitutes, the novel has elicited diverse critical interpretations and has achieved overwhelming popularity among young adults. Like most of Kesey's fiction, *One Flew over the Cuckoo's Nest* focuses on alienated or nonconformist individuals who attempt through love, hope, and humor to retain their sanity and self-respect while rebelling against repressive authority figures.

Kesey received his bachelor's degree from the University of Oregon and later attended creative writing classes at Stanford University during the late 1950s. Shortly after accepting a job as a night attendant at the Veterans Administration Hospital in Menlo Park, California, Kesey volunteered for a series of government-sponsored experiments involving such psychoactive drugs as LSD, psilocybin, and mescaline. Kesey's hospital and drug experiences inform *One Flew over the Cuckoo's Nest,* portions of which he wrote under the influence of peyote. Set in a mental facility in the northwestern United States, the novel utilizes the viewpoint of Chief Bromden, a schizophrenic half-breed Indian from the Columbia River region. Chief Bromden feigns being deaf and dumb to avoid being "worked on" by the hospital staff and other enforcers of what he calls the "combine," a word which suggests, among other meanings, a brutal agency of normative control designed to alter or "correct" deviant or undesirable behavior. Chief Bromden views existence as a humorless cartoon filled with pain until the arrival of McMurphy, a swaggering ex-marine who submits to psychotherapy to avoid a sentence of hard labor at a state work farm. By demonstrating to the disturbed patients of the ward the value of laughter as a source of sanity and as a weapon of derision, McMurphy becomes engaged in a power struggle with Nurse Ratched, an efficient administrator of sterile, institutionalized conformity who manipulates patients into attacking one another to maintain her control. McMurphy is later angered to learn that his term, unlike those of other patients who volunteered for therapy, is of an unspecified duration, and his release is dependent upon Nurse Ratched's approval. Unable to live by the rules of the ward, McMurphy makes an unsuccessful attempt to escape and finally assaults Nurse Ratched for her role in an adolescent patient's suicide. McMurphy is subsequently lobotomized to demonstrate to the ward the power of Nurse Ratched's authority. Chief Bromden, irrevocably changed by the incident, smothers McMurphy in order to deny Nurse Ratched her victory and to accept responsibility for the role he and the other patients played in contributing to McMurphy's downfall. Chief Bromden then escapes to Canada as a sane individual.

Photograph by Brian Lanker

Kesey returned to Oregon to prepare his next book, for which he interviewed loggers during their trips to and from work and at night in local bars. *Sometimes a Great Notion* (1964) is set in the logging town of Wakonda, a region on the Oregon coast with an extremely high suicide rate. More complex and ambitious in scope than *One Flew over the Cuckoo's Nest,* this book alternates between first- and third-person narrative and contains such devices as italics, parentheses, and capital letters to reflect the confusion of contemporary life and the absurdity of the notion of absolute truth. Ostensibly the story of Hank Stamper, an individualistic logger who defies neighbors and union organizers by continuing to work during a strike, the novel also concerns Hank's half-brother, Lee. As a boy, Lee witnessed Hank in a sexual encounter with his biological mother; as an adult, he determines to seek vengeance upon Hank by seducing his wife. The brothers, despite their capacities for reckless self-indulgence, come to realize their helplessness and interdependence, as Hank's logging operations fail and Lee's revenge proves unfulfilling and guilt-provoking. Although *Sometimes a Great Notion* received praise for its regional accuracy and stylistic complexity, the book attained neither the popularity nor the acclaim of Kesey's first novel. Both *One Flew over the Cuckoo's Nest* and *Sometimes a Great Notion* have been adapted for film.

Kesey's literary output diminished after 1964. Stating "I'd rather be a lightning rod than a seismograph," Kesey announced in 1966 that he was giving up writing to live his life as though it were a work of literature. With hipster philosopher Neal Cassady and many others, Kesey initiated an antic comic-book existence and promoted drug use and social revolt. Calling themselves the "Merry Pranksters," Kesey's group introduced to California the LSD "acid tests" described by Tom Wolfe in his book *The Electric Kool-Aid Acid Test*. The experiences of the Merry Pranksters are also chronicled by Kesey and his friends Ken Babbs, Kenneth Barnes, and Keith Foster in *Kesey's Garage Sale* (1973), a collection of magazine articles, interviews, and satiric essays presented in the grandiose, mock-epic style of Marvel comic books. Replete with illustrations, photo collages, and unusual typography similar to those of early Beat magazines, the collection also includes Kesey's unproduced screenplay *Over the Border*, in which he describes his experiences in Mexico after leaving the United States to avoid prosecution for possession of marijuana in 1967. In this work, the near-death of his son due to inattention forces Kesey to temper his belief in spiritual transcendence through drugs with a realization of their destructive potential.

Demon Box (1986) is a collection of short stories, articles, essays, and interviews which have appeared in various periodicals since the late 1960s. Most of the stories, featuring as their narrator Kesey's alter ego, Devlin Deboree, and written in a style of free association which reminded several critics of New Journalism, balance Kesey's nostalgia for the mirth of the 1960s with his growing awareness of the negative aspects of counterculture lifestyle. In the essay "Demon Box," Kesey applies the concepts of physicist Sir James Clerk Maxwell to psychology, suggesting that the superego allows pleasant ideas to enter the mind while shutting out unpleasant thoughts. Modern consciousness, according to Kesey, is the result of entropic decline, a mixture of good and bad ideas which ironically presents to us a more inclusive picture of reality than that associated with "sanity." Although *Demon Box* received largely mixed reviews, critics particularly praised Kesey's mastery of style and language.

(See also *CLC*, Vols. 1, 3, 6, 11; *Contemporary Authors*, Vols. 1-4, rev. ed.; *Contemporary Authors New Revision Series*, Vol. 22; and *Dictionary of Literary Biography*, Vols. 2, 16.)

M. GILBERT PORTER

[*In the essay excerpted below, Porter analyzes stories and articles written by Kesey for various magazines prior to their republication in book form as* Demon Box.]

Kesey's two novels [*One Flew Over the Cuckoo's Nest* and *Sometimes a Great Notion*] are finished works of art, products of a skilled craftsman carefully realizing his vision in appropriate forms. What Kesey has titled *Demon Box* and described as "form in transit" appears to be a very personal assessment of selected steps and missteps that have led him to midlife and to uncertainty about his art. Like Dante, Kesey seems to have found himself meandering in a murky wood away from the straight path, and, like Hemingway, he apparently feels he can liberate himself from his personal demons by writing them away, most recently through a kind of new-journalistic auto-biography. There is a free-style unburdening of self in many of these pieces that is more reportage than fiction, and the up-beat, media-keyed forms run together in a frothy mixture em-

ployed, it seems, as much to scour the artist as to polish his art. The problem years seem mainly to be those between the publication of *Sometimes a Great Notion* in 1964 and Kesey's move to the farm in Pleasant Hill in 1968. Troubled areas from those years come up repeatedly in the new work: the experiments with drugs and group living that sometimes exploited family and friends, the vision of altering consciousness and establishing revolution, the lure of power, the scrapes with the law, the rasping polarities of freedom and responsibility, the frustrating attempts to establish universal connections. The tone in these pieces shifts from self-indulgence to self-criticism to self-congratulation, but underlying every movement is an intense quest for understanding, for direction, for form.

The optimism that enabled Kesey to resolve positively the tensions between the strong and the weak in the McMurphy/Bromden, Hank/Lee pairings appears much more tenuous in the later work. In "Abdul and Ebenezer," for example, there is a sinister, brooding tone of death. The setting is pastoral, Kesey as central figure is folksy and rural, but nature is more Tennysonian—"red in tooth and claw"—than Wordsworthian—"apparelled in celestial light"—and the American Adam on the frontier watches his cows "begin to despair" and "stand ass to the wind and stare bleakly into a worsening future." The creative gusto of a series of bulls leads only to their destruction. The conception of the cows leads as often to pain and death as to the creation of new life. Floozie's calf lives, but Floozie dies from the infection of her own partially passed afterbirth. The cow named Ebenezer survives a difficult birth, but, frightened by crazy people, she tramples her calf to death. The dominant image at dawn on the farm is the shiny truck from Sam's Slaughtering.

The prevalence of death and the dark side of nature have always been important themes in Kesey's fiction, evidence of his realistic and comprehensive vision and a measure of his heroes' romantic transcendence, but in the later work these negative elements are more pronounced, more insistent. The dark forces do not necessarily prevail, but they prevent—or at least vitiate—Kesey's characteristic celebration. They tend toward disintegration, blocking the formal wholeness otherwise permitted by the vision of a world in which destructive forces are matched by creative ones. (pp. 79-81)

Kesey's personal tribute to Neal Cassady ["The Day After Superman Died"] comes from Devlin Deboree, Kesey's fictive alter ego. He offers a semi-fictional account of his activities and feelings on the day he learns of Cassady's death. Cassady died in 1968 from exposure, pneumonia, and an overdose of drugs, but Kesey sets the "story" in 1969 in order, apparently, to treat the death of Cassady and the end of the decade as symbolizing the death of an era: perhaps the demise of idealism, of revolutionary zeal, of creative social experimentation, maybe even of innocence and optimism. In a quirky way, this memoir tries to be an apologia for Cassady's life. In a quirky way, it succeeds, but the justification of the charismatic Cassady, whom Kerouac called "the Holy Goof," is strained by the death and degradation that surround his life in the story and in the decade. The elegiac salute is sincere, but the fear and trembling accompanying it dominate the piece. (pp. 81-2)

While looking in his barn-loft study for his rose-tinted sunglasses in order to answer Larry McMurtry's question "What has the Good Old Revolution been doing lately?" Deboree recalls his morning confrontation with two Woodstock returnees, Blondboy and Blackbeard, both spaced-out bums from California parading themselves as "beautiful people." Bad breath, bad vibes, bad company—they are abusive to Deboree and his dog. Deboree sends them slinking away, snarling. Sandy Pawku, once one of the Merry Pranksters, immediately arrives with the news that Houlihan (Cassady) died yesterday. Formerly skinny and frantic, this dog-killer and bearer of bad tidings is now fat and frantic, as well as self-indulgent, cruel, crude, and pushy. With mindless hilarity she tells the stunned Deboree that Houlihan's last words in the Puerto Sancto clinic were "Sixty-four thousand nine hundred and twenty-eight," the number of railroad ties he had counted when he passed out. As Sandy roars off to town for supplies and "connections," Deboree goes dutifully to the pasture to bury a newborn lamb mysteriously killed in the night. Trembling with mourning and fear, he buries the lamb near the swamp, as ravens watch. (p. 82)

[Deboree is later] awakened by the return of the bums with the drunken Sandy, who, as she passes out, abandons herself to group sex with the scrofulous pair of fellow Californians. As Deboree watches the grubby scene before him, he tries to transform his memories of Houlihan's triumphs and defeats into something significant, something that "counts." In some desperation, Deboree decides at last that Houlihan's final words were not mechanical numbering, but "counting," a psychological gathering of forces in preparation for renewed advances upon the vicissitudes of the contemporary world. Deboree ends the tale with a similar exercise of his own, ticking off the "names" of the decade and invoking the spirit of some kind of renaissance. The spirit he invokes, though, is more fearful than inspiring, and thus his invocation—"come back, go away"—is as timid as the decade was tense.

Deboree does not find the rose-colored glasses he sought at the beginning. Therefore, he has nothing to mitigate the events of the day or the decade. In the "year of the downer," he can only respond to McMurtry's question about what the Revolution is doing with the mental answer "losing." The most painful loss for Deboree was Houlihan, who was a superman mainly through his extraordinary physical and verbal energy, and who was a symbol of the Revolution largely through his substitution, in his life and at his death, of movement for direction. Circularity, not a new order, was the only revolution ultimately connected with Houlihan, despite Deboree's anguished attempts to make it appear otherwise. Beginning and end in a circle are common, said Heraclitus, and no matter how many one counts, railroad ties are never anything more than railroad ties, and the tracks eventually turn back on themselves. The mysteriously slain lamb surrounded by ravens is clearly intended, then, to stand as a symbol for Houlihan, the burned-out boy-man prematurely destroyed by dark forces he could neither understand nor control. Deboree's lament for his friend evolves into a chronicle of fear over these dark forces, embodied in the story in the images of the slaughtered lamb, the ravens, the swamp, the crushed and twice-shot bitch whose pieces are nibbled by her pups, and the bestial coupling of Blackbeard and Blondboy with the swinish Sandy.

Kesey's memorial to Cassady becomes at last a cry for the "beautiful people" gone astray, a jeremiad for the aborted Revolution. Among the names listed in Deboree's concluding litany is Charles Manson, a symbol of the Revolution run amuck and a man whose crime in August of 1969 provided a terrifying end to the sixties. The crime also revealed a sobering vision of the destructive potential of the drug-induced attempts to alter consciousness that characterized the decade. (pp. 83-4)

["The Thrice-Thrown Tranny-Man, or Orgy at Palo Alto High School"] is a series of twelve verbal snapshots in a memory album bringing together two trips Kesey took to Puerto Vallarta in the years after the events in *Over the Border*. In the first trip Kesey (Deboree), with his wife and children, encounters a fifty-year-old tourist from Portland, Oregon, who is stranded in the Mexican town with his wife and dog while he awaits the arrival of a new transmission—his third replacement in a new car—from Tucson, Arizona. In the second trip, Kesey and his brother take their dying father to Puerto Vallarta for a last vacation. Because Kesey reminds the tourist of his son—and because he is a fellow American—the Tranny-man confides in him and solicits his assistance. Because the Tranny-man is a frightened and displaced figure hidden under stereotypical behavior, Kesey observes him closely and reflects on his condition and the qualities that he shares with his own father. The juxtaposition of images and reflections provides a meditation on rites of passage: a wife's coming to awareness, the end of the Tranny-man's marriage, the dying of a father, and the passing of full responsibility from one generation to another.

The Tranny-man is a Babbitt/Archie Bunker figure, jingoistic, sexist, racist, materialistic, often irrational, not always tactful, and frequently irascible. When his rented Toyota has a blow-out in the left rear tire, he drives the car back to town on the flat, telling his calmly quizzical wife, "I'm going to *drive* the sonofabitch *back* to the sonofabitch that rented me the sonofabitch and tell him to shove this jap junk up his greaser ass!" This from the man whose Dodge Polara has dropped two transmissions in five thousand miles. Tired of being snapped at and treated like a thing, his wife leaves him. But Kesey perceives beneath the Tranny-man's bluster all-too-human fears—of change, of aging, of death. . . . [The Tranny-man and Kesey's father] merge in the narrative memory as older Americans on their way out. Deboree can help the Tranny-man get back in motion, but he cannot still his fears. Kesey can get closer to his father through love, attentiveness, and a brief "flash" with dope, but he can neither save his life nor evade responsibility for the life his father relinquishes to him:

> "You guys better know what gear you're jam-
> ming into, though," he said in a voice unlike
> any he'd ever used when speaking to Buddy or
> me . . . "because if you don't it could be the
> End of the Universe as we know it."

Soberly, Kesey acknowledges under the benediction of his father that experimentation must not lead to madness or "universal anarchy will reign." . . .

'["The Thrice-Thrown Tranny Man, or Orgy at Palo Alto High School"] is a five-finger exercise, lightly comic, shading off into the elegiac. The subtitle is a throwaway reference to a film of a nude party shown without censorship to the faculty and students of a Palo Alto high school, a sign, apparently, of rapidly changing times. One section of the story recounts some personal money problems Kesey once had, but mainly the focus is on Americans coping imperfectly with ineluctable change. (pp. 89-91)

If one lingers overly long on the eccentricities of Kesey's recent work, it is possible to feel some dismay over what appears to be an artistic decline. . . . [A cavalier] mood accounts for the strained affirmation of "The Day after Superman Died" . . . [and] the casual pencil sketches in "The Thrice-Thrown Tranny-Man" . . .—accounts, that is, for the present shape of *Demon Box*. Except for the presence of some of the same characters and the common theme of a widespread moral disintegration in human affairs, there is no clearly discernible principle of order linking the parts of *Demon Box,* and Kesey insists upon deferring closure of the work indefinitely.

It is easy to make too much of these vagaries. What they probably amount to, finally, is nervous skylarking before the big game, or intellectual calisthenics to keep muscle tone ready for the next major challenge. It is more important to remember what Kesey told John Pratt explicitly and what he has demonstrated resoundingly in two fine novels—that he is "a serious artist." That he is also a serious moralist is equally clear from his best writing. . . . A fellow writer who found Kesey in "articulate and vital spirits" reported Kesey's conviction from the talk that "the writer has an ethical purpose. He must 'stand between the public and evil. A good story needs a good villain—one that is evil, not just bad'—and the writer must find a way to 'draw a bead' on that character or quality. The good writer, in [Kesey's] opinion is a person of 'power' and character who guards faithfully that axis of human choice." In *Demon Box,* . . . Kesey is striving—however uneven the results—to remain faithful to his vision of the good writer's purpose.

Kesey is a skilled writer of character and power with a chest full of purposeful tools. We can believe with confidence, I think, that the serious artist he is will enable him to overcome the various imps of the perverse, within and without, distracting him from significant forms and will compel him again to the performance of what he does best: the imaginative creation of lively and well-formed stories about who we are and who, with grit, we might become. (pp. 100-02)

M. Gilbert Porter, in his The Art of Grit: Ken Kesey's Fiction, *University of Missouri Press, 1982, 102 p.*

CHRISTOPHER LEHMANN-HAUPT

So many signals of health and power come with *Demon Box* that for a while you think that Ken Kesey . . . has found his voice again. He's survived the 1960's, the flower children gone to seed, and the hallucinogenic bus trip described in Tom Wolfe's book *The Electric Kool-Aid Acid Test.* He's served his "dope sentence" and is "back in Oregon on the old Nebo farm with my family—the one that shared my last name, not my bus family." While so many of his followers have crashed, he seems to have bounced. . . .

It *looks* like a new Ken Kesey, but we can't be absolutely certain. There are also times when he gets nostalgic for the 1960's. There are places where he takes cheap shots at straight America. There are still a lot of drugs and alcohol going down. And then there's the problem of whether the book is fiction or nonfiction. The copyright page informs us that "some of the essays in this collection were previously published, in slightly different form," in [various magazines]. . . . But everywhere in *Demon Box* people are given fictional names, even when the author is clearly on assignment. Is Mr. Kesey sending us the old counterculture message that nothing is real, life is a trip, "Strawberry Fields Forever"?

All the underlying issues raised here remain in doubt until the penultimate essay, **"Demon Box,"** a piece somewhat in the spirit of Hunter Thompson's "gonzo journalism," about Mr. Kesey's relations with mad people, their keepers and a counterculture guru named Dr. Klaus Woofner, who runs the Big Sur Institute of Higher Light. Here the matter of the book's form becomes a major source of irritation, because the author invokes the spirit and authority of a major counterculture figure of the 1960's and 1970's—Fritz Perls of the Esalen Institute—without allowing us to exercise our own views of Dr. Perls and the school of gestalt therapy he founded.

Very well, then; so we have to deal instead with Dr. Woofner's ideas, yet another view of psychic life that invokes Newton's second law of thermodynamics. The human mind is Sir James Clerk Maxwell's demon box, in which the superego plays the demon, letting the good thoughts in and shutting the bad thoughts out. The problem, according to Dr. Woofner, is that, like all other systems, this one, too, is subject to entropy: the superego demon is losing energy; the randomness of the mind's organization is increasing; the bad thoughts are getting mixed up with the good ones; the world is growing increasingly crazy.

What is Mr. Kesey's attitude to this? At his Promethean moment of guilt, a crazy comes to save him. In a scene too charming to be believed, an inmate where the movie version of *One Flew Over the Cuckoo's Nest* is to be filmed recognizes the author and his problem, and snaps him out of his despair. So once again the inmates appear to be saner than the outmates; we are back where Mr. Kesey began in his first novel.

But what is really his point? That people judged to be crazy by our society are in fact more in touch with reality than the sane? That may be the meaning he intends, but his entropic metaphor backfires. His book is the box; he himself is Maxwell's demon. He is what is losing energy—it is he who is having trouble separating the crazies from the sane. As for his readers: we are on our own. Energy need not necessarily flow into a given system. Let mine be the force that directs yours elsewhere.

Christopher Lehmann-Haupt, in a review of "Demon Box," in The New York Times, *August 4, 1986, p. C18.*

HENRY ALLEN

[Kesey's *Demon Box* is like] that feeling when you're a kid on a carnival ride and they cut the power. You think to yourself: "We're still going as fast as ever." But you're slowing down, horrible gravity luring you to a halt. . . .

[Kesey is] still going strong," you think. And, sure enough, there are moments that carry you along, rushes of the energy that teased with despair in *One Flew Over the Cuckoo's Nest* and *Sometimes a Great Notion;* and the descriptions:

In a piece about a marathon in Peking, he describes a room where a Chinese family watches television: "The only light there would be the flutter of the tiny screen beating at the dark like the wings of a black and white moth."

Or: "The wash hung tense in the smoky air, like strips of jerky," he writes of a bad day at his farm outside Eugene, Oregon. . . .

There's plenty of cause for optimism, especially at the beginning of the book, with a lean, clear piece about Kesey leaving jail after his six-month sentence following a marijuana bust. Then there's a series of discomfiting vignettes about the Tranny Man, a disappointed American tourist with transmission problems in Mexico. Then a piece about a bull named Abdul, followed by **"The Day After Superman Died,"** about Kesey's grief when he learned that hip avatar Neal Cassady had been found dead, and full of barbiturates, by a railroad track in Mexico.

It's a terrific piece, a smog of despair, a diary of a day during which Kesey gets stoned, gets drunk, throws a couple of evil hitchhikers out of his yard, looks for his rose-colored sunglasses (literally!) and remembers the promise of his youth. He comes to fear that he was wrong about Cassady, the non-stop-talking, ex-con amphetamine addict who had enchanted Jack Kerouac and Allen Ginsberg back in the '40s. He worries that Cassady's madness was not some higher American wisdom vindicating every romantic excess, but had "all been a trick. . ., only the rattle of insects in the dry places of Eliot, signifying nothing." Kesey ducks answering his own question by hinting at significances too huge or obvious to explain, and leaving it at that.

As in most of the pieces, real people are given fictional names. Cassady is "Houlihan," Kesey is "Devlin Deboree," and so on. Would we want to read about them all if we didn't know who they were? In any case, this is a book that's mostly about Kesey and his friends. The problem is that Kesey doesn't have a whole lot to write about except what it's like to get stoned, travel a little and be Kesey. . . .

Nowadays, the new consciousness is a souvenir, a dead flower that's less interesting than the old Kesey novels that we're apt to press it in. But Kesey can't let it go. The action in this collection keeps revolving around "Devlin Deboree" and his friends getting stoned, and however brilliant the writing, there's something missing. In **"Killer,"** for instance, he describes getting stoned on a drug called STP and diving into a pond to pull out a barrel. It's the best description anyone will ever write of pulling a barrel out of a pond, but all Deboree has done is get stoned and pull a barrel out of a pond. Kesey keeps failing to turn these events into microcosms or epitomes, maybe because significance always seems self-evident when you're stoned.

This is a book that you enjoy as long as you're enjoying it, if you know what I mean. But as Kesey says, "When you got nothin' to say, my Great-Uncle Dicker advised me once in a kind of Arkie ode to optimism, go ahead and say it."

Sometimes he does. He comes off the way he always has, as a big, strong, charming, failed, talented, childish, self-indulgent and now middle-aged man trying to fight back despair with main force. He doesn't seem to want to change—maybe that's why he's taken so many drugs. But maybe the power will switch back on and he'll finally give us the legendary novel he's supposed to be writing about Alaska.

Henry Allen, "Ken Kesey On the Road Again," in Book World—The Washington Post, *Vol. XVI, No. 32, August 10, 1986, p. 9.*

DANIEL PYNE

In his strong, lucid new collection of stories and essays, *Demon Box,* Ken Kesey wrestles with those 20 years—with the contradictions that the last two decades have engendered—and with the terrifying possibility that he came away from his Great Quest empty-handed. Empty-handed! Or, at least, not with the kind of universal truths and solutions that Kesey seemed to be seeking:

"I know now that it isn't my fear that chains me back," Kesey writes in [**"Demon Box"**].

It's the bleak and bottomless rock of failure. . . . The air is thick with broken promises coming home to roost, flapping and clacking their beaks and circling down to give me the same as Prometheus got . . . *worse!* Because I sailed up to those forbidden heights more times than he had. . ., but instead of a flagon of fire, the only thing I brought back was an empty cocktail glass . . . and I broke that.

Everything in *Demon Box* revolves around this theme—around the Promethean struggle of modern man to simply sort out and try to *understand.* No longer is Kesey the mad genius of the magic bus, with a potion for every pain; in the stories of *Demon Box,* his thinly disguised alter-ego is Devlin Deboree, a middle-aged writer with a wife and kids and a farm with cows and ducks and a psychotic goat; a man with a celebrated past that is rapidly losing its context, and an uncertain future in what he has come to understand as the context of contradiction.

Deboree, like Kesey, is "afraid of running empty."

For Kesey, at least, this book is proof that he hasn't.

From the subtle, understated first-person narrative of the opening, in which Deboree is released from county jail and reflects on the many faces of Time, Kesey seems to be as much rediscovering his own creative powers as he is uncovering the simple, personal truths and realities that are the soul of this material.

Kesey is a fine writer, neither superficially trendy nor smugly stylish—one may tend to forget that Kesey of [*The Electric Kool-Aid Acid Test*] is colored by Wolfe's amphetamine prose; Kesey's own writing is spare and exacting, with a keen sense of the rhythms of both narrative and dialogue, and a perverse precision of character. . . . (pp. 1, 6)

Through Deboree's eyes, we see a world that embraces its contradictions, from the Great Pyramid in Egypt, and the Great Wall of China, to the back pasture of his Oregon farm, and the lascivious trespasses of a promiscuous Angus bull. That these stories have autobiographical roots becomes unimportant; ultimately this isn't a book about Ken Kesey at all.

Perhaps *Demon Box* isn't the book that all the neo-pranksters and Kesey groupies and folks who care about that kind of thing have been keening for like some kind of literary Holy Grail. There are missteps, sputters and lapses; a section of goofy songs/verse (appropriately entitled **"Demon Briefs & Dopey Ditties"**) smacks of self-indulgence, however harmless. But here is, it would seem from this collection of work, the profit of a gifted writer striving to regain his vision; to uncloud it, to refocus it.

"I do not have a cure for your problems . . ." says the mystical crippled shrink who tells the theory of the Demon Box—a divided mind made weary by the constant contradictions it must hold in balance. "I refuse to offer temporary solutions. . . . All I can do is bring you to your senses here, in the present."

It might as well be Kesey's line, because that's what the *Demon Box* offers: illumination.

Of course, this is an old role for the Merry Prankster. His original role. It's where he started, as a young Stanford creative writing fellow, banging out this timeless tale of mental hospital heroics. Illuminating. (p. 6)

Daniel Pyne, in a review of "Demon Box," in Los Angeles Times Book Review, *August 31, 1986, pp. 1, 6.*

Oliver Harris, "Away a Long Time," in New Statesman, *Vol. 112, No. 2898, October 10, 1986, pp. 30-1.*

OLIVER HARRIS

While the Kesey legend has been maintained by his fans, it is only in the last few years that he has emerged from the sidelines and backwaters, his soft Oregon drawl now to be heard on the reading and lecturing circuit. Perhaps the last dust of Sixties fallout had to settle before *Demon Box* could appear. But Kesey has always been a cryptic guru and the new work, returning to the past as much as catching up with the present, raises more questions than it answers. The Prankster project had been 'transcending the bullshit', so it is with a provocative irony that *Demon Box* finds Kesey mainly down on his Oregon farm, knee-deep in bulls and shit. (pp. 30-1)

His tales from animal farm revel in a cute anthropomorphism. Foxes emit 'yips of ornery delight', his cattle don't moo, they talk back. Cows struggle in labour and bulls rampage on heat. *Nostalgie de la boue?* It is all uncomfortably folksy, as are the homespun parables attributed to 'Grandma Whittier'. This is particularly tiresome since *Demon Box* does contain some very fine writing indeed. Kesey is at his best when out of Oregon on magazine assignments abroad, producing comic masterpieces of New Journalism on location in Egypt and China, or when returning to mourn the fallen idols of the Sixties.

Conscious of the inherent dangers in any memorial to John Lennon, Kesey insists that **"Now We Know How Many Holes It Takes To Fill The Albert Hall"** is not a 'nickel valentine to a dead superstar'. The piece concludes by tying together the tensions addressed in the book as a whole, between Sixties idealism and Eighties cynicism. Kesey admits to having heard no 'Pollyanna pie-in-the-sky promises' lately, while Hunter Thompson confirms the spirit of the times: 'Today's wiseman has too much brains to talk himself out on that kind of dead-end limb.'. . .

In **"The Day After Superman Died"** Kesey reports the death of Cassady, who enters the pantheon of comic-strip heroes that makes up Kesey's mythological America. It is an exemplary story of great emotional intensity based on Cassady's enigmatic last words: 'Sixty-four thousand nine hundred and twenty eight.' Kesey deciphers the numbers as the heroic counting of railroad sleepers between two Mexican towns, so satsifying his need for some 'comforter of last-minute truth' from his old partner in pranksterism.

In China Kesey deprecates the image of the 'Bigtime Writer' abroad, signalling his resistance to a return to the glitter of the literary game. So, in *Demon Box,* Kesey revisits the Sixties and Literature in order to come to terms with them. Fittingly the collection concludes with his last encounter with the barbarians on bikes in **"Last Time the Angels Came Up."** The Magical Mystery Tour peters out in brute pointlessness, echoing the down-beat ending to Wolfe's documentary: 'WE BLEW IT!'

Demon Box seems to be a reprise and a prelude, a promotional recollection announcing Kesey's return to centre stage. 'I been away a long time,' were the last words of *Cuckoo's Nest.* Kesey is back and *Demon Box,* with its faults and its hard-won triumphs, its unexpected novelties and puzzling mix of genres, is another, cooler, prank. (p. 31)

STEPHEN SCHWARTZ

[The stories and articles in *Demon Box* may explain] the fading of Kesey's star. Their intention is unvarying—they present a series of nostalgic homages to the spirit of the 1960s, the decade in which Kesey rose to prominence as an author and as an aspirant to the title of hippie messiah, a notable rival of Timothy Leary, Allen Ginsberg, and John Lennon. But unlike Ginsberg, the bad poet, and Lennon, the popular songwriter, Kesey, as a novelist originally of some seriousness, could not easily convey his message of revelation through his creative work. *Cuckoo's Nest,* although having as its subject such quintessential sixties themes as madness, the romanticized underclass, and Western regional sentiment, didn't blow any minds, to use the quaint locution. (p. 48)

Nobody can deny that Kesey was a talented writer. I would even say that in the beginning he was a fine writer. But today, at least, he is a talented writer only, and no more; a capable worker, no better or worse than he who writes press releases for Drano or Pampers. His particular sell involves himself, his dreams about the sixties, and flashes of sophomoric philosophizing about prisons, or hitchhiking, or mental hospitals. In the end, he is a salesman of myths. But as this latest collection shows, the myths have become shopworn.

The main effect of these dozen meandering pieces is to prove once and for all that excessive drug consumption leads the writer not to greater imagination or insight but to a wallowing in the inconsequential. In most cases, any conclusion is lost in the void; if it is rescued, it proves to be trivial. One of the essays, **"Oleo: Demon Briefs and Dopey Ditties,"** consists of some musings on his child's failures in school followed by some stoned and predictably idiotic song lyrics. . . . The connection between the lyrics and the problems of his child is not made but perhaps is obvious, embarrassingly obvious.

Another piece, on the death of the erstwhile driver of his drug-bus, Neal Cassady, is incomprehensible for one who does not know the history of Kesey and Cassady. Even those sketches that might have turned into short stories, rather than bursts of literary swamp gas, find the author mired in the banal once it is informed with chemical meaning. . . .

Cuckoo's Nest remains interesting because its characters are brilliantly derived from the real-life subculture of the Pacific Northwest. Every character, with the possible exceptions of Big Nurse and McMurphy, is a recognizable human type, of interest because truthfully drawn. But the Kesey of *Cuckoo's Nest* is absent from *Demon Box.* There are no human types here. His portrait of the fictional Chief, a mentally disturbed American Indian, in *Cuckoo's Nest* had more life than his eulogistic sketch of his close friend Cassady. Have intimacy and grief dulled his pen? I think not; rather it is that once upon a time Kesey ceased being a writer and became, instead, an ideologue of the anti-America subculture, celebrating a drugged oblivion; a peculiar transmutation of the Buddhist priest role so many of the literary rebels of the 1950s coveted. (p. 48)

There has always been a heartlessness to Kesey, but Kesey the comic writer—as opposed to Kesey the silly writer, his most recent incarnation—could make his attitude work as literature. Today all that is left is the heartlessness. Everybody along

Kesey's path is described with a certain tone of contempt. ["**Demon Box**"] describes his fear of having people need anything from him, particularly the patients in the mental hospital where the film of *Cuckoo's Nest* is to be made. Kesey—the outcast and the friend of the prisoner, the advocate of reform in the mental health industry—finds the modest inquisitiveness of real patients unnerving and distasteful. The real Kesey doesn't cotton to mental patients—they have what he calls here "the loser's profile."

At any cost, Kesey wants to avoid being seen as a loser; indeed, a number of the essays in this book center on his difficult attempts to divest himself of psychotic hippie burnouts who have gathered unto him in the wake of his sixties exploits. But that Kesey himself is a loser is proved by this terrible book; *Demon Box* is important only as testimony to the enormous capacity for self-waste to which so many gifted Americans succumbed in the 1960s. To those who did not themselves go through the sixties it will be, without doubt, obscure and baffling. To those who did, the book is a cause for discomfort if not a certain shame. (pp. 48-9)

Stephen Schwartz, in a review of "Demon Box," in The American Spectator, *Vol. 19, No. 11, November, 1986, pp. 48-9.*

Tanith Lee

1947-

English novelist, short story writer, author of children's books, and scriptwriter.

A prolific author of fantasy and science fiction who originally wrote for a young adult audience, Lee is praised for her imaginative characterizations, her vivid portraits of fantastic worlds, and, most notably, her expressive yet disciplined prose. Michael Swanwick commented that the strength of Lee's narrative style "lies in the marvelous joinery of her sentences. Her prose practically shimmers on the page." A frequent concern in Lee's work is the search for identity, a theme addressed in her first adult novel, *The Birthgrave* (1975). In this book, a goddess who is unable to recall her past must come to terms with her lack of identity. Lee chronicles the adventures of characters introduced in *The Birthgrave* in the sequels *Vazkor, Son of Vazkor* (1978; published in Great Britain as *Shadowfire*) and *Quest for the White Witch* (1978).

Two of Lee's other adult novels, *Don't Bite the Sun* (1976) and *Drinking Sapphire Wine* (1977), chronicle a young woman's search for love and meaning in a hedonistic and technologically advanced society. Following a duel in which she kills a man, the woman is exiled and subsequently establishes a new society. In both books, Lee provides a glossary to assist the reader in understanding the vernacular used by her characters. Reviewers compared Lee's *Tales from the Flat Earth* series— *Night's Master* (1978), *Death's Master* (1979), *Delusion's Master* (1981), and *Delirium's Mistress* (1986)—to the stories of *The Thousand and One Nights* because of its rendition of myths and legends and its moral content. Set in an imaginary period when the earth is thought to be flat, these books incorporate many elements of sword and sorcery fiction and relate the interaction of demons and human beings.

Lee has published several popular science fiction and fantasy novels during the 1980s. In *Day by Night* (1980), which involves the framing of a story within a story, the entertaining tales of a fabulist writer become reality on the other side of her planet. *Sabella: or, The Blood Stone* (1980) is a sensuous tale of vampirism, and *The Silver Metal Lover* (1982) concerns the love affair between a woman and a robot. In *Days of Grass* (1985), the appearance of alien creatures forces the human race into underground cities. This novel focuses on Esther, a girl on the verge of womanhood who leaves the safety of the cities to confront the aliens. Lee has also contributed numerous short stories to science fiction and fantasy magazines. Many of these pieces are collected in *Dreams of Dark and Light: The Great Short Fiction of Tanith Lee* (1986).

(See also *Contemporary Authors*, Vols. 37-40, rev. ed. and *Something about the Author*, Vol. 8.)

Don't Bite the Sun is written in the first person. The author displays a sparkling style as we follow the adventures of a dissatisfied, strange and darkly beautiful woman through her world. Although the age class lives (and *must* live) for pure pleasure, the heroine searches for some vague thing . . . or meaning . . .

The heroine is a product of her world, it reflects her, and we see it through her perceptions, with special impact. The desert blossoming scene and its aftermath culminating in a tender and bittersweet, although pathetic, attempt at affection; and her failure to grasp real love, are truly moving. The novel has deep insights. A pleasure to find a real science fiction novel which succeeds in making its ideas seem fresh.

Unquestionably one of the most fascinating books I have read in years. (p. 35)

> Paul G. McGuire, "Angel, Don't Bite the Electric Imperial," *in* Science Fiction Review, Vol. 5, No. 3, August, 1976, pp. 34-5.

PAUL G. McGUIRE

Originality in treatment and style is the something extra that gives Tanith Lee's *Don't Bite the Sun* a special dazzle. . . .

RICHARD E. GEIS

Lee's previous novel, *Don't Bite the Sun* set the scene for [*Drinking Sapphire Wine*]. So the back cover says. I've tried sampling these novels, but can't get hooked.

You want a reaction to Tanith Lee's prose? Shallow, fast-paced dialog (of which there is a lot of) and self-consciously adult, which makes it smart-aleck juvenile. But she has her admirers, so. . . .

She has invented a whole slang language which has to be defined in a glossary.

This one is about a he/she human thrown out of a future heaven-like city, who fights back and triumphs over the robots.

> *Richard E. Geis, in a review of "Drinking Sapphire Wine," in* Science Fiction Review, *Vol. 6, No. 2, May, 1977, p. 16.*

DAVID A. TRUESDALE

Even given Tanith Lee's talent in giving us a truly fantastical dreamworld filled with dastardly demons, gibbering Drin, imaginative sorceries and evil curses, there is something wrong with [*Night's Master,* an] interwoven series of short stories. The problem appears to be in the first draft quality—off and on—throughout the entire book, offset with the oh so obviously beautifully written remainder. This unevenness lends the at-mosphere of quickly written sketches to what would otherwise be well detailed and rounded stories, and a hastily compiled series of combined "morality" tales and weird magics is not what we have come to expect from the author. . . . (p. 49)

[Despite] the sketchiness of some of the prose, if you like curling up by the fire on a cold night to read about a maiden's tears turned into a dazzling necklace sought by the Prince of Demons, or how because this same Prince of Darkness cannot have the beauty of a mortal he changes her lover into a hideous monster, or how Azhrarn seduces and makes love to a beautiful male child he has taken from its dying mother—then buy this book. (p. 50)

> *David A. Truesdale, in a review of "Night's Master," in* Science Fiction Review, *Vol. 8, No. 3, May, 1979, pp. 49-50.*

ROLAND GREEN

Tanith Lee continues her output of unconventional fantasy and sf with [*Sabella: or, The Blood Stone,* a] short novel of a young female vampire's search for a way to live in a human world. The author's gifts for characterization and realistic detail are particularly noteworthy. While the tone of the book is per-sistently grim and there are some fairly explicit scenes of sex and vampirism, it remains a compellingly powerful work. . . . [The] book should appeal to many readers of straight horror fiction who do not normally read much sf.

> *Roland Green, in a review of "Sabella; or, The Blood Stone," in* Booklist, *Vol. 76, No. 21, July 1, 1980, p. 1596.*

PUBLISHERS WEEKLY

Tanith Lee is a prolific writer who still manages to turn out work of high quality. [*Day by Night*] is one of her longest and most ambitious, with a complicated plot involving mirror ex-istences on the bright side and dark side of a planet that does not rotate. Vitra Klovez of the night side is a Fabulast, a creator of stories (recorded directly from her mental images) for the pleasure of the miserable, poverty-stricken masses. Her latest story is of a woman on the other side of the planet, much like

herself, who is framed by a rejected suitor—a vicious, char-ismatic man—for his attempted murder.

> *A review of "Day by Night," in* Publishers Weekly, *Vol. 218, No. 13, September 26, 1980, p. 119.*

RICHARD E. GEIS

I hope it's a compliment to say that when she writes of magic and evil sorcerers, of invincible heroes and flawed courtesans, Tanith Lee is better than Robert E. Howard. Her fiction is so sensuous, muscular, disciplined and taut that it is a pleasure to read her. . . .

[*Unsilent Night*] contains two stories and ten poems.

The stories, "Sirriamnis," and "Cyrion in Wax" are familiar: the strange slave girl who worships a distant, evil goddess and who practices shape-changing and who makes a noble youth her victim. Her death is ironic. The story of Sirriamnis is told by an old slave in ancient Greek times.

"Cyrion in Wax" tells how a superior, highly intelligent young man outwits and kills a seemingly all-powerful, evil sor-cerer. . . .

I have a feeling *Unsilent Night* would be a good acquisition: I think Tanith Lee will endure as a writer far beyond her time.

> *Richard E. Geis, in a review of "Unsilent Night," in* Science Fiction Review, *Vol. 10, No. 3, August, 1981, p. 11.*

PETER STAMPFEL

Nowadays the fantasy field is a light industry for which I have little use. However, yet and still.

Is there ever an exception, and her name is Tanith Lee, Princess Royal of Heroic Fantasy and Goddess-Empress of the Hot Read. The third and latest volume in what she calls her Flat Earth series, *Delusion's Master,* just came out, along with a reprint of the first volume, *Night's Master.* The series will probably be six books long, and I can't wait. The last series I read that gave me comparable thrills was Roger Zelazny's five-volume Amber saga.

Lee's series is inspired by *The Arabian Nights* and the fairy tales of Oscar Wilde, as well as all the myths that have ever strode and stormed through the mind and soul of mankind. The earth is flat here, the gods are aloof, and Demon Princes take great delight in tormenting mankind with epic wickedness. There is also sex of every description, and sensuality unsur-passed in the fantasy field. And mythic-level rage, lust, and revenge. And jewel-like writing that dazzles and intoxicates.

This is not the mindless babbling of first love. I have read 17 of Lee's novels. They run the spectrum from science fiction to horror to children's books. I've read *Night's Master* three times and will go back for a fourth, at least. *Death's Master,* the second volume, I have read twice. The new volume can be read on its own, but I recommend picking up *Night's* and *Death's* and starting with them.

The series is episodic, and although that's usually a criticism, in this case the approach is perfect. . . . The jeweled labyrinth of a plot is best discovered by the reader; *Delusion's Master*— and the whole series—reveals a brilliant writer at the top of her form.

Peter Stampfel, in a review of "Delusion's Master," in VLS, No. 1, October, 1981, p. 6.

ROGER C. SCHLOBIN

[*The Silver Metal Lover* is one of Tanith Lee's] excursions into the world of the future, and while Lee is usually more effective as a fantasy writer, this effort is worthy of attention. It is marked by her always striking prose and her ability to endow her characters with persuasive humanity. Readers should not be fooled by the early chapters, which introduce the initially vapid and superficial protagonist, Jane. Ruled by an authoritarian and wealthy mother, Jane is the perfect consumer of the future, her very physical structure and appearance scientifically determined. She is preoccupied with the usual sophmoric concerns that make the young so egocentric and boring, so much so that there's a strong temptation not to continue reading. The turning point for Jane and the reader is when she falls in love with a robot, a Silver Ionized Locomotive Verisimulated Electronic Robot, "S.I.L.V.E.R." (pp. 17-18)

Both Jane and Silver change, and in their doomed relationship there is joy and growth. From the white cat who curls up on the brass bed to their street singing for the sometimes too-human audiences, Lee successfully creates a real relationship for the reader. While many may find the ending too supernatural, the novel is nonetheless a chronicle of a poignant love that is highly engaging and powerful.

Lee continues to distinguish herself with her ability to bring flesh and blood to the worlds of the future. (p. 18)

Roger C. Schlobin, in a review of "The Silver Metal Lover," in Science Fiction & Fantasy Book Review, April, 1982, pp. 17-18.

DAVID A. TRUESDALE

From Tanith Lee we have come to expect the unexpected as well as the beautiful, and none of either is in much evidence [in *Cyrion*]. The prose is choppy, off-rhythm, hurriedly penned as if it were a first draft and, in some cases, hard to follow without a quick re-reading, which destroys reader flow and which, in turn, crumbles the concentration and ultimate absorption into the various fantasy(s).

And what about the fantasies? Are there intriguing moral dilemmas predicated by the situations, magics or evil machinations against which Cyrion must wrestle, or resolve in order to extricate himself? No. Time after time we see Cyrion thrust into an improbable situation and after ho-hummedly rolling his tongue around cliché dialogue—be it with monster or human beguiler, an obligatory scene or two of alternate glitter and gore—emerge the victor. After the first three stories I was tired, following the next four I was irritated and bored, and it took herculean effort to force myself through the final third of the book, a novella titled *Cyrion in Stone*.

David A. Truesdale, in a review of "Cyrion," in Science Fiction Review, Vol. 12, No. 2, May, 1983, p. 19.

MICHAEL E. STAMM

[*Death's Master*, a] complex tale of Uhlume, Lord Death, and Zhirem and Simmu, magical children of different mothers, is full of strangeness and dark sensuality. The prose is very rich, reminiscent of Clark Ashton Smith's, and at novel length must be read slowly lest the reader find it indigestible; it will not appeal to every taste. The story is good, the product of an amazing imagination, though it is not one of Lee's very best; this edition will necessarily appeal most to bibliophiles and Lee collectors, who will miss something very fine if they overlook it.

Michael E. Stamm, "Strangeness and Dark Sensuality in Beautiful Lee Reprint," in Fantasy Review, Vol. 8, No. 4, April, 1985, p. 25.

ROLAND GREEN

This superb anthology of short pieces by the ubiquitous Tanith Lee [*The Gorgon and Other Beastly Tales*] features a collection of marvelous and mostly legendary beasts. Of the 11 stories, particularly noteworthy are "**Draco, Draco,**" a sensible tale about dragon slaying; "**The Hunting of Death: The Unicorn,**" a beautiful novella that can also be interpreted as a religious allegory; and "**Sirriamnis,**" a historical tale of love, slavery, and death. Lee's imagination and her command of the English language are as brilliant as ever.

Roland Green, in a review of "The Gorgon and Other Beastly Tales," in Booklist, Vol. 81, No. 16, April 15, 1985, p. 1162.

GREGORY FROST

[In *Days of Grass*, Tanith Lee] gives us a post-holocaust world; . . . the catastrophe has been brought on by the arrival of an alien race who have driven the last vestiges of mankind to burrow into makeshift underground worlds.

Early descriptions of the aliens, called "Spiders," remind one immediately of the martian tripods from Wells' *The War of the Worlds*. They even scream upon attack, an inhuman shriek that again echoes Wells. The main character in Lee's book is Esther, a young woman who has broken a taboo of her underground domain and ventured up to the surface. Esther is a woman in turmoil, maturing from girl to woman both physically and in spirit, eventually becoming leader of a people for whom she feels nothing, as if they and not the unseen beings who have taken over her world were the real aliens. The flaw here is that the subterranean background is barely imagined, so that the reader comes away with a sense that, as in a stage play, the sets have all ceased to exist the moment the spotlight leaves them. This vagueness hurts the book, which begs for a hard-edged reality in the first half to offset the phantasmagoric second part, where Esther is taken into the alien city to meet the master of the "Spiders." *Days of Grass* is a flawed book, and a despairing novel, but at the same time one that sinks deeply into the substance of myth.

Gregory Frost, "Spider Woman," in Book World—The Washington Post, December 22, 1985, p. 8.

MICHAEL R. COLLINGS

Fantasy writers manipulate language to create a universe in which the laws of our objective universe are suspended. Writers may achieve this effect by assertion; they may merely incorporate into the fantasy world references to beings and situations alien to our experience. In the *Deryni Chronicles*, for example, Katherine Kurtz defined an alternate universe peopled with both humans and Deryni, human-appearing beings who wield particular powers that we as readers must define as magical. Magic occurs in the *Chronicles* largely because Kurtz defined Gwynnedd as a place in which magic is viable.

Yet language is forceful and capable of multiform effects. In fantasies the style of the prose itself may lend credence to the fantasy universe. Or alternatively, the writer may use a style consonant with the reader's expectations but, by giving common words new meanings, create a fantasy universe. In either case if the wording, the sentence structures, or the denotations and connotations of key words were altered, the fantasy universe would collapse into the mundane. . . .

In Tanith Lee's *Death's Master* language is, from the opening paragraph, consciously elevated and antiquated, creating the emotional effect in the reader of suddenly being immersed in an unfamiliar world. (p. 173)

[In *Death's Master,* language functions] in transporting us from conventionality to the fantastic. The stylistic differences between the language of *Death's Master* and our everyday patterns of speech and thought are apparent in the opening lines of the book:

> Lady Plague wore her yellow robe, for the sickness was a yellowish fever, yellow as the dust that swirled up from the plains and cloaked the city of Merh and choked it, yellow as the sinking mud to which the wide river of Merh had turned. . . . The bedchamber of the queen of Merh was this way: Burnished weapons of hunting and war hung upon the walls which were painted with scenes of hunting and war.

The sentences are elevated in style and structure, with a formulaic repetition of words and phrases (particularly the conjunctive *for*) and a strong sense of the archaic and the exotic, as, for example, in the highly evocative word *Burnished.*

In addition, the language of *Death's Master* distances us from the conventional by aligning itself with traditional epic devices. *Death's Master* uses figurative language and epithets and similes that reflect the epic impulse; phrasing is woven largely from familiar words but is nonetheless compatible with a world inhabited by demons, demiurges, and heroes. Throughout the novel, for example, Lee employed the Homeric device of allowing the coming of dusk or dawn to signal transitions between scenes, and she was rarely content merely to say that the sun came up or went down. Instead, she formalized her descriptions, creating formulaic communications within the image and establishing implicitly the relationship between the passage and the context. Chapter 5 of part 1 begins: "The sun had risen above the forest of petrified cedars. Its arrows had not pierced the black spreading canopy; the sun had gone away, and the blue dusk had followed. And the dusk permeated the forest as the sun had not been able to." This passage provides an ideal fulcrum between Narasen's conjuring of the witch of the House of the Blue Dog and the queen's subsequent sexual coupling with a magically animated corpse. The birth of her child is described, and her own death adumbrated, in the next description of time: "The third day came. It rushed on slippers of silk, this gentle day, in at the palace gates. And just behind the day rushed another, less gentle, and through another door." In subsequent passages Lee continued to blend image and plot through a subtle evocation of the epic sense, for example: "It was the moment of the sun's death, and the whole camp bloody with it. In the red glow, the three brothers hastened to find

their father the king, and they threw the child smelling of lions before him."

Even more overtly, Lee built her novel on episodes that, through their evocation of the mythological universe of classical epic, succeed in pulling us farther from our world and into one in which Death, Night, and multiple divisions and subdivisions of subservient demons interact with the realms of humans (who are themselves both terrestrial and submarine). Achilles's invulnerability provides an analog to Zhirem's through the agonies of the well of fire; Simmu's quest for the Garden of the Golden Daughters closely parallels Gilgamesh's quest for immortality; and the wanderings of Simmu and Kassefeh, culminating with their arrival at the immortal city of Simmurad, suggest the wanderings of Odysseus.

To emphasize the other-worldliness of the epic impulse (and thereby to distance us as readers from the fantasy universe in which *Death's Master* takes place), Lee employed linguistic patterns to capitalize on the epic characteristics of the plot; the vocabulary and sentence structure parallel plot development. For example, Simmu is described in a passage that suggests strongly the epic simile, both in being an explicit comparison and in being complex, formed of several levels of comparison: "For Simmu there began then a time of near humanness, a time of near forgetting. As the tree was dormant in the winter, empty of fruit and leaves, so was Simmu. Spring woke the tree; a spring would come also to wake Simmu, but Simmu's spring was yet far off."

The language of the novel is archaic, exotic, and elevated; words such as *burnished* (in the opening paragraphs) further emphasize the sense of antiquity Lee was weaving while suggesting the formulaic language of traditional military epics and sagas. Words interweave to create scenes evocative of the landscapes of epics: "Here grew exotic malformed trees with fruits that shone like brass, and here, on the wide, melanotic shores of the lake, unicorns had been known to dance, to fight, and to couple. And this night the unicorns came, as if they were the sigils of a man's terror and craving." Lee defined a landscape in which the sudden intrusion of the unicorns is not only possible but eminently fitting, while limning a counter-Eden, a garden of darkness and fear particularly appropriate to the plot at this point. Perhaps not coincidentally, Lee's garden strongly suggests John Milton's Paradise, including a meandering fog and fruits that "shone like brass." (pp. 176-77)

[For] Lee language is external, imposed upon plot and character, and consciously elevates the world of the novel beyond our own, while still retaining its essential credibility. We accept the fantasy universe precisely because it is *not* defined in familiar terms, because the words do *not* fit together as we might expect. The language functions in ways foreign to our expectations; we are thus more amenable to the vision of a universe that similarly functions in ways foreign to our expectations. (p. 181)

Michael R. Collings, "Words and Worlds: The Creation of a Fantasy Universe in Zelazny, Lee, and Anthony," in The Scope of the Fantastic—Theory, Technique, Major Authors: Selected Essays from the First International Conference on the Fantastic in Literature and Film, *edited by Robert A. Collins and Howard D. Pearce, Greenwood Press, 1985, pp. 173-82.*

JOAN GORDON

The Birthgrave shows Lee's interest in myth and exemplifies her characteristic reshaping of mythic elements. A goddess awakens, without memory, in a volcano. She seeks identity and memory, experiences power in healing and death, becomes a warrior and a victim. This woman, with her struggles, her power, and her adventures, seems to partake of archetypes of death and nurturing, as if she were both Pluto and Demeter in the old stories. Herein lies one of the novel's great strengths.

Its other strength is its full realization of the world through which the goddess travels. It is, as we expect of heroic fantasy, a primitive world, but one imagined with a variety of cultures and customs. The characters are vivid mixtures of good and evil, convincing both as people and as types. This is a powerful book.

It is not a flawless one. Some of its massive detail, such as specifics of fashion and decor, and some of its motifs, such as character doubles and color coding of cultures, confuse more than they clarify. Later novels are clearer because more spare.

Still, Lee is always worth reading and this, with its companion volumes, belongs in most collections.

Joan Gordon, "Out from Under the Volcano," in Fantasy Review, *Vol. 9, No. 4, April, 1986, p. 25.*

MICHAEL E. STAMM

Delirium's Mistress is the long-awaited fourth novel in Tanith Lee's Flat Earth series, which began with *Night's Master* (1978) and continued with *Death's Master* (1979) and *Delusion's Master* (1981). The title character is the daughter of Azhrarn, demon lord of Night. . . . Azhrarn's daughter—with the help of a mortal—escapes her island exile in the underworld, and renounces her father—and the name which marked her as his—in favor of the name Sovaz, the witch: Delirium's mistress.

The novel is full of memorable characters—Oloru, favorite of the priest-magician Lak Hezoor, whom he betrays to the Hounds of Night who harry the souls of dreamers; the shadowy Eshva, whose expressions and gestures are so eloquent they seem to speak aloud; and many more. The Flat Earth novels are reminiscent of the *Thousand and One Nights* in their beauty, strangeness, eroticism, and cruelty.

Tanith Lee has published at least two dozen books in her career, 11 since *Delusion's Master* appeared. But the quality of her work is not lessened by its quantity. The prose in *Delirium's Mistress* is as luxuriant as ever, imparting some of the qualities of a fever dream; it is not read easily (though her style in other books can be very different). These books should be read gradually, but they should be read, and they will be enjoyed.

Michael E. Stamm, "Hothouse Fantasy," in Fantasy Review, *Vol. 9, No. 7, July-August, 1986, p. 30.*

MICHAEL SWANWICK

Dreams of Dark and Light is subtitled *The Great Short Fiction of Tanith Lee*. This is serious bragging, and it's a pleasure to report that the contents of the book back it up.

Tanith Lee writes fantasy for adults. It is darkly, lushly romantic stuff, with silvery veins of eroticism and sinister beauty. In **"Nunc Dimittis,"** for example, the aged and dying servant of a vampire princess recruits his replacement from the criminal underworld. The story is shot through with sexual tension, even perversity, and a fey sympathy for the wild creatures that exist beyond the bounds of human law. Yet, at the same time, it is a simple and touching tale of love and loyalty.

Strange sexual undercurrents run through all of Lee's work, often coupled with dark yearnings toward death. Her favored characters alternate between the poles of obsession and seduction, and the sole true sin (as in **"Black as Ink,"** her elegant modernization of the swan maiden fairy tale) is not to give in to the romantic impulse. The heroine of **"Bite-Me-Not or, Fleur de Fur,"** chooses her demon lover over comfort, luxury and fulfillment of her childhood dreams, and, despite the heavy price she pays, is right to do so. Her tragedy ends in a moody and evocative tangle of sex, salvation, death and love. The shopgirl's obsession with a beautiful paralytic in **"Margritte's Secret Agent"** is not at all healthy, nor is it meant to be. Other stories flirt with bestiality, patricide, and even necrophilia, though always in disguised, submerged form.

But the strength of Tanith Lee's work lies in the marvelous joinery of her sentences. Her prose practically shimmers on the page. What would in the hands of a lesser writer—a merely *good* writer—collapse into purple fustian, Lee makes work. **"Elle est Trois, (La Mort)"** is a tour de force of writerly skill. The only fantastic element is death itself, represented by three avatars that could justly be taken as simple metaphors. Yet she handles them like a dark conjurer, trading off voices and personas with the skill and sophistication of Lady Death herself toying with carnival masks.

These are stories best read in the evening, amid expensive surroundings, a snifter of fine brandy by the elbow. I read several in the bathtub, a bottle of beer in my hand, with undiminished pleasure, but I felt guilty about it afterward.

Michael Swanwick, "Tanith Lee: The Allure of the Sensual and Decadent," in Book World—The Washington Post, *July 27, 1986, p. 4.*

José López Portillo (y Pacheco)

1920-

Mexican novelist and nonfiction writer.

The President of Mexico from 1976 to 1982, López Portillo is also the author of two novels, *Quetzalcoatl* (1965) and *Don Q* (1969). In *Quetzalcoatl,* a provocative allegory, López Portillo modifies Mexico's national myth surrounding Quetzalcoatl, the white-feathered serpent god of civilization who established peace and then left Mexico, vowing to return on a specific date to supplant his rival, Tezcatlipoca, the god of human sacrifice. Edmund Fuller described *Quetzalcoatl* as "close to poetry in richness of imagery and force of emotion." López Portillo's second work, *Don Q,* is a witty, philosophical novel of ideas in which an impatient and imperceptive young lawyer engages in obfuscated discourse with Don Q, an eccentric intellectual tutor reminiscent of the title character in Miguel de Cervantes's *Don Quixote.* López Portillo has also written several nonfiction works on political topics, including *Génesis y teoría general del estado moderno* (1958).

UPI/Bettmann Newsphotos

PUBLISHERS WEEKLY

[In ***Don Q***], Pepe Seco, a young lawyer, recounts his circular adventures with Don Q, a philosopher who deals with eternities and finds it difficult to get to the point. There is no action in this fiction; forward movement comes from the motion and development of ideas: talk is everything. But what entertaining, maddening and provocative talk it is, as the dialogue progresses from ideas about self, memory, words and music to considerations of heaven and hell, pride, will, sin, guilt and time. Sly allusions to Goya, Cervantes, de Saint-Exupéry, Beethoven and Wagner enrich Lopez-Portillo's narrative and the argument, often carried on parenthetically by Pepe in his academic way and Don Q in his mystical fashion, provides contrast and food for thought.

A review of "Don Q," in Publishers Weekly, *Vol. 210, No. 14, October 4, 1976, p. 63.*

PUBLISHERS WEEKLY

[*Quetzalcoatl*] is a retelling and reweaving of the legend of Quetzalcoatl, the ancient god and ruler of the Toltec in Mexico, a figure represented by the plumed serpent. Quetzalcoatl (a name rich in meanings), the god of civilization, has a body of legend associated with him. The author takes these tales, interweaves them, and incorporates, too, the stories and teachings of other great religious leaders throughout history. Good and evil, the struggle between them, have much to do with this updating of ancient stories, and of course Quetzalcoatl—"the plumed serpent"—is to be taken as a symbol of Mexico itself.

A review of "Quetzalcoatl," in Publishers Weekly, *Vol. 210, No. 14, October 14, 1976, p. 63.*

EDMUND FULLER

[Lopez Portillo's two books] are probably best called novels, though each is of an uncommon sort. *Quetzalcoatl* . . . is close to poetry in richness of imagery and force of emotion. Its narrative style is swift and spare but at appropriate moments has a high incantatory tone.

It is a variation on the national myth of the Feathered Serpent, the white god from the East who drove out the dark god of human sacrifice, bloody Tezcatlipoca. Quetzalcoatl fostered civilizing arts, initiating an era of humane worship with flower offerings in place of torn-out hearts. After the 52-year cycle into which ancient meso-Americans believed time to be divided, he was expelled by Tezcatlipoca and sailed eastward, promising to return at a precisely designated time. In one of history's most incredible circumstances, Hernan Cortes landed on the Mexican coast on the exact day on which the worried Emperor Moctezuma (often spelled Montezuma) and his seers expected the return of Quetzalcoatl, a coincidence which gave a psychological advantage to the Conquistadores though the Aztecs quickly discovered that the Spanish were not divine.

This Quetzalcoatl, big, white, with golden hair and beard, is washed up on the coast, bound to a cross, amnesiac. The people call him a plumed serpent from his mane of hair and declare him a god. He says, "I cannot be a god. I am barely a man and I have already sinned. I do not want blood. I have come to give my own.'' Yet he promises, ''I will give your souls the science of sin and of redemption, and I will teach you the science of the earth to improve your lives.''

He establishes Tula, seat of the Toltecs. These builders are ambivalent; they wish to worship him, but to control and limit him. Under his teaching they flourish, but tragedy and mystery lurk always. He goes on a mission to the primitive Chichimeca, who wound and seize him. Rescued, he explains his benevolent purpose to some captive Chichimecs: ''I will give you security, well-being, rest. . . .'' The Chichimecs reject him: ''Give us freedom, not abundance! . . . We do not want the servitude in which the Toltecs live in order to provide themselves with what you call a good life.'' . . .

This cryptic, poetic book will appeal to all who are interested in pre-Columbian Mexico. In an author's note, Sr. Lopez Portillo discusses the traditions from which he has wrought his vision, laden with enigmas of life and history.

Utterly unlike [*Quetzalcoatl*] in tone and content is *Don Q* . . . , a comic philosophical novel, wholly cerebral. It is a monologue by a young attorney, Jose Guillermo, about his baffling dialogues with the elderly Don Q, who variously addresses the narrator as Pepe Seco, Pepe, Josefo and other names. Don Q at different times claims to be a nephew of Miguel de Unamuno, Spanish philosopher, a cousin of Antoine de Saint-Exupery, and also the nephew of Antonio Machado, Spanish poet. He himself may be Don Quixote redivivus, with a touch of Quetzalcoatl.

A wry, antic wit suffuses the book. It abounds in Parkinsonian phrases such as ''absolute squander,'' or, ''The Law of the Universal Disproportion of Efficiency.'' Don Q is ''continually and personally battling the infinite.'' He talks much of ''Ieity'' (rhyme with ''deity''), the self as God, originating with Lucifer. ''The human genre was created after that experience, full of large and small I's, all potential rebels, seed of great protests. . . .'' At times, listening to Don Q's discourse, ''I clearly heard his brains squeak.''

One wishes good fortune to this subtle, witty, cultivated, feeling man, and his nation, as he takes up the burdens of head of state.

> Edmund Fuller, ''Uncommon Novels by Mexico's New President,'' in The Wall Street Journal, December 1, 1976, p. 20.

JOHN MELLORS

[*Quetzalcoatl* concerns] a bearded white man, found washed up on a cross on Mexico's eastern shore. He preaches a new religion containing elements of Christianity and communism. The native Indians are persuaded to give up the old gods, who demand blood, and Quetzalcoatl teaches them sin and redemption and 'the science of the earth to improve your lives.' Merit, not murder, is what the new god wants.

At first, the people prosper, but the desire to improve others' lives, by force if necessary, leads to imperialism and a revival of the old, more spectacularly satisfying rituals. Quetzalcoatl leaves, as he arrived, naked, in the sea: 'the serpent is biting its tail.' It is an undeniably powerful and exotic story, but I found *Quetzalcoatl* an indigestible mixture of myth, allegory and sermon.

> John Mellors, ''Scent and Smell,'' in The Listener, Vol. 97, No. 2466, February 17, 1977, p. 221.

FRANCIS KING

Many years ago, the *Spectator* (or it may have been its rival) set for its weekly competition 'The least enticing invitation'. . . . If a similar competition were to be held for the least enticing blurb—a blurb is, after all, a form of invitation—that for José Lopez Portillo's *Don Q* would win hands down. 'A mordant exercise in rhetorical obfuscation . . . A novel wholly without action . . . *Don Q* finds it difficult not so much to keep to the point as to reach it in the first place . . . The result is a dialectic loaded with diversions and pauses. . .'

Unfortunately, I find it impossible to improve on this description. The book abounds in exceptionally tedious passages, with Don Q going on and on about what he calls his 'Ieity'; but there are also, it must be admitted, occasional shafts of sunlight through the gaseous clouds, when some sharp aphorism or some amusing paradox irradiates a page. It is greatly to the credit of the Mexican electorate that the author should be President of that country. The British would never forgive a politician a work so uncompromisingly 'intellectual' in intention.

> Francis King, ''Unholy Grail,'' in The Spectator, Vol. 240, No. 7818, May 6, 1978, p. 28.

DEREK STANFORD

I would call José Lopez Portillo, President of Mexico and author of the strange novel *Don Q,* a rococo philosopher were it not that this suggests conceptual superficies and the prettification of Reason adapted to the ears of a *dix-huitième saloniste*. Instead, we have in Don Q—the monologist who holds captive the young literal-minded lawyer recording his conversation—an exuberantly singular Knight of Ideas, a somewhat Hegelian Quixote. Like the hero in Wyndham Lewis's *Tarr*, he is drunk on 'the laughing gas of the Infinite'. As Don Q tells his legal Boswell, 'wherever I turn my head, I find an enigma and many answers . . . It's in me to look for answers to my inexhaustible eagerness to pose questions'. This is a novel of talk, of table talk—of an endless sending up of ideational balloons, few of which are retrieved. Other characters feature very little, though I was taken with Don Lu who refused Communion on the ground that it was too egalitarian for him. A novel for a minority—for those choice spirits who find in ideas not a faith, a fortress or a strait-jacket, but an everrenewable legerdemain—*Don Q* will surprise and delight the right reader. (p. 44)

> Derek Stanford, ''Time Games,'' in Books and Bookmen, Vol. 23, No. 11, August, 1978, pp. 44-5.

STEPHEN RENO

[In *Don Q,* Lopez Portillo] pits a word-bound young lawyer from the Universidad Nacional Autonóma de México, Pepe Seco, against a Rabelaisian, Indian philosopher from whom the book takes its title. In a series of Socratic exchanges, the venerable Don Q leads his 'Ieity' (a combination of the words 'I' and 'deity') or what is known as the 'dynamic ability to propose oneself as a motive of meditation'. . . Don Q sums up Pepe Seco's problem as one of suffering from a 'quasi-solemn scholasticism' in which an 'ill-fated and aggressive tendency towards distinctions and subdistinctions' has led to his being a 'mediocre glosser'. Throughout, Pepe Seco's impatience, condescension and lack of perception prevent his following Don Q's rapturous flights of imaginative inquiry into the problems of free will and human definition.

With aggression and lack of compromise, Don Q portrays what happened when Aztec religion, with its sense of responsibility for the maintenance of cosmic order through discipline and sacrifice, was replaced by Christianity.

> I want you to understand well what happens to a people when you suddenly take away the highest responsibility that any human race could ever have imposed on itself. Imagine the deafening silence in the Indian world when it turned out that not only did they not have the responsibility, they had not the right to personal salvation, because their sins had already been redeemed by the blood of a son who had an amorous, sweet, tender mother.

In part, what accounts for the attractiveness of [*Don Q* is Lopez Portillo's] portrayal of the synapse between modernity and antiquity, between rigid intellectualism and aboriginal wisdom. (p. 590)

Stephen Reno, ''Don Juan and Don Q,'' in The Listener, *Vol. 100, No. 2584, November 2, 1978, pp. 589-90.*

THE NEW YORK TIMES BOOK REVIEW

Quetzalcoatl: In Myth, Archeology and Art [by José López Portillo, Demetrio Sodi, and Fernando Diaz Infante] offers a historical, psychological and literary survey of the cults of Quetzalcoatl and the civilizations those cults took root in. . . .

Perhaps the most arresting section of the book is an imaginative re-creation of the Quetzalcoatl story [*Quetzalcoatl*] in a text by Mr. López Portillo, the former President of Mexico. . . . In bringing together certain fragments of the myth, Mr. López Portillo has created a story of real dramatic power. His version is idiosyncratic, to be sure, and it has some obvious and current political purposes; but it is characteristic of myths of the Toltecs, Mayans and Mixtecs that they require a personal interpretation. The former president is doing what many another poet and scholar has done with these stories and he does it in an interesting way. (p. 25)

A review of ''Quetzalcoatl,'' in The New York Times Book Review, *December 12, 1982, pp. 24-5.*

Charles Ludlam

1943-1987

American dramatist, actor, and director.

A prolific comic dramatist who also directed and performed in his off-off-Broadway productions, Ludlam was one of the founders of the "Theater of the Ridiculous." According to Ludlam, this theatrical style "synthesizes wit, parody, vaudeville farce, melodrama, and satire, giving reckless immediacy to classical stagecraft." The typical Ludlam play is fast-paced and usually contains elements of camp and burlesque. In writing his plays, Ludlam extracted dialogue, characterizations, and scenes from such diverse media and literary sources as popular songs, vintage films, radio and television programs, and classical drama. In the manner of the medieval Italian commedia dell'arte, with which his productions have been compared, Ludlam's scripts allow the players freedom to improvise and to speak directly to the audience. While some critics view Ludlam's comedies primarily as entertainments, Joel G. Fink maintained that Ludlam "perceptively underlies the surface of slapstick and farce with real and complex . . . issues and questions."

Ludlam graduated from Hofstra University with a degree in dramatic literature in 1965. He became disillusioned with the established theatrical community in New York City and joined the Playhouse of the Ridiculous, an experimental acting company based in Greenwich Village. Following a number of acting roles, including the first of many female impersonations, Ludlam wrote his first play, *Big Hotel* (1967). Loosely based on such films as *International Hotel* and *The Grand Hotel,* this play is nearly devoid of plot and allows for much improvisation. The performances, which were marked by their chaotic disorder and anarchic humor, differed considerably each night. During rehearsals for his next play, *Conquest of the Universe* (1967; revised as *When Queens Collide*), disagreements surfaced within the troupe, and Ludlam left to form the Ridiculous Theatrical Company. This group's early productions, which incorporated as well as lampooned outmoded theatrical traditions, were performed in a movie theater and attracted a devoted, primarily homosexual following. *Bluebeard* (1970) was the first of the company's plays to be widely reviewed and is considered one of Ludlam's finest achievements. More conventionally structured than his earlier works, *Bluebeard* centers on a scientist's attempts to create a third genital. Mel Gussow observed: "Charles Ludlam has apparently seen, adored, laughed at, been scared to death by and memorized every mad-doctor movie ever made. *Bluebeard* . . . is a distillation of that ghoulish genre, and serves as both a loving paean and a lunatic parody."

Critics have noted that several of Ludlam's works produced during the 1970s are more disciplined and less chaotic than his early plays. *The Grand Tarot* (1969; revised, 1972) involves a magician's encounter with real-life tarot symbols, and *Corn* (1972) chronicles the legendary feud between the Hatfields and the McCoys. *Camille: A Tear-Jerker* (1973), which Ludlam regarded as the play that brought him a larger and more mainstream audience, combines elements of the classic Alexandre Dumas novel, the Giuseppe Verdi opera *La traviata,* and the George Cukor film. In this play, Ludlam cast himself as the tragic heroine, Marguerite Gautier. Reviewers lauded both Ludlam's performance and the play's mixture of camp and

Photograph by Fred W. McDarrah

pathos. *Hot Ice* (1974), a satire of Hollywood gangster films, examines the controversy surrounding cryonics. The play revolves around a group of cryobiologists who begin freezing deceased human beings in an attempt to "stamp out America's number one killer—death." Ludlam adapted *The Ventriloquist's Wife* (1977) from the film *Dead of Night,* in which a ventriloquist's life is increasingly controlled by his demonic wooden puppet. In Ludlam's version, the puppet covets the ventriloquist's wife.

Ludlam wrote several noteworthy plays during the 1980s. In *Reverse Psychology* (1980), humorous complications occur when husband-and-wife psychiatrists Leonard Silver and Karen Gold begin having affairs with their spouse's patients. *Galas: A Modern Tragedy* (1983), in which Ludlam again assumed the female lead, recounts the life of opera diva Maria Callas. *Le bourgeois avant-garde* (1983) is based on the Molière play *The Bourgeois Gentleman* and lampoons Manhattan's art community. In *The Mystery of Irma Vep: A Penny Dreadful* (1984), which parodies both Victorian novels and gothic horror films, Ludlam and another member of the Ridiculous Theatrical Company performed all seven roles. *The Artificial Jungle* (1986) is a spoof of the film version of the James M. Cain novel *Double Indemnity.* In this play, a pet shop owner's unfaithful wife recruits a piranha to help her and her lover murder her husband so that she can collect on his insurance policy.

Ludlam was also well regarded for his work in children's the-ater, having adapted such classics as *Jack and the Beanstalk* and *Punch and Judy*. In *The Enchanted Pig* (1979), Ludlam borrowed from *Cinderella, The Frog Prince,* and *King Lear* to relate the tale of a princess and her marriage to a pig.

(See also *Contemporary Authors,* Vols. 85-88, Vol. 122 [obit-uary].)

DAN SULLIVAN

[*Conquest of the Universe* is described by the Playhouse of the Ridiculous Repertory Club, Inc.] as "a para-moral study of these space-intoxicated times" and "a supreme comedy of The End."

All right, if you say so, boys and girls. But the first thing an outsider notices about this avant-camp spectacular is that it's even bawdier than the group's last one, *Gorilla Queen*. Persons who found that particular music-drama a bit much even for the modern liberated sensibility should be warned that *Conquest* is even more so. You don't have to be a prude not to like it.

On the other hand (take this as testimony of one prude who did like it) the play contains nothing that can't be found on some of the racier Greek vases or in the darker verse of Jonathan Swift.

At any rate, conventional and unconventional sex is not the only theme of *Conquest*. Digestion also gets some graphic attention as does infanticide. There is even a parody of Mary Martin in *Peter Pan*. Can irreverence go further? . . .

If Charles Ludlam's script for *Conquest of the Universe* some-times seems merely mindless, the director, John Vaccaro, and his actors generally make it seem really outré, which is some trick in the unshockable 1960's. And Mr. Ludlam's script is not without virtues of its own, making excellent sport of pulpy science fiction flicks, bloody Elizabethan melodramas and bad rock 'n' roll as well as Miss Martin. . . .

As barbarous and nihilistic as *Conquest of the Universe* looks on stage, there is clearly discipline behind the scenes. Are they secret traditionalists after all?

> *Dan Sullivan, " 'Supreme Comedy' of the End Opens,"*
> *in* The New York Times, *November 27, 1967, p. 60.*

MEL GUSSOW

Charles Ludlam has apparently seen, adored, laughed at, been scared to death by and memorized every mad-doctor movie ever made. *Bluebeard* . . . is a distillation of that ghoulish genre, and serves successfully as both a loving paean and a lunatic parody.

The root of this *Bluebeard* is that old 1935 Charles Laughton movie, *Island of Lost Souls*—with infinite revisions and elab-orations by the devious Ludlam. There are intimations, for example, of *Faust,* and Bartok's *Bluebeard's Castle* is playing as the entertainment begins.

Ludlam's hero-villain is the Baron Khanazar von Bluebeard, and that K in Khanazar is as hard as a pile-driver. In one of Ludlam's consistently amusing linguistic conceits, characters occasionally rasp K's where there are no K's, just as, occa-sionally, they intentionally drop their Transylvanian accents for New Yorkese. Ludlam khids himself as well as Khana-zar. . . .

Any innocent female, such as the mad doctor's nubile niece Sybil, who visits Bluebeard's island, is almost immediately wooed, then wedded to a laboratory table for experimentation.

The plot is complicated and digressionary, and great fun to follow—from boudoir (a blatantly lewd, hilarious seduction of Sybil's billowy guardian by the irrepressibly lascivious Blue-beard) to laboratory. No corny burbling decanters there, just a tinny chair that looks like an exploded box spring—placed on stage simply so that Ludlam can maniacally heave it off stage.

> *Mel Gussow, in a review of "Bluebeard," in* The
> New York Times, *May 5, 1970, p. 58.*

MEL GUSSOW

That mad comic genius, Charles Ludlam, plays a mad comic fool in *The Grand Tarot,* the Ridiculous Theatrical Company's latest voyage into hypno-mystical-magical theater. . . . [Al-though] the play is not as precise or as funny as Mr. Ludlam's *Bluebeard* . . . it too is charged with cosmic comedy and the-atrical energy.

At the end of *The Grand Tarot,* director-author Ludlam has one of his . . . [characters] announce that this is "a work in progress—the plot is still trying to emerge from the mire of the playwright's mind." I admire the mire.

There is an emergent plot of sorts, about The Magician . . . seeking truth, meaning, and his sister, The High Priestess . . . , and encountering a stageful of tarot symbols, including The Hermit, Death, The Moon, The Star—and The Fool who finds his role as the prat-falling butt of all boots.

At times the show seems as much about old movies or the Ridiculous Theatrical Company itself as it does about tarot. The actors step out of character to relate personal experience as it relates to the entertainment. This is one area of the show that needs further definition. . . .

As conjuror-creator, Mr. Ludlam riffles the deck—absurd rid-dles, terrible jokes, movie taglines, old pop tunes (Bing sings), mind-reading in the audience. Not everything works, but with an epic sweep he soon moves to new Tarot-tory.

> *Mel Gussow, in a review of "The Grand Tarot," in*
> The New York Times, *March 4, 1971, p. 28.*

MEL GUSSOW

[*Eunuchs of the Forbidden City*] is a comic epic about Tsu Hsi (1834-1908), dowager Empress of China. . . .

In *Eunuchs* we follow her from her start as a humble concubine through her victory in competition for the hand of The Son of Heaven, a simple-minded monarch. . . . In her fiendish climb to supremacy, which includes killing her son and fomenting the Boxer Rebellion, Tsu Hsi ("Toots" for short) is surrounded largely by devious eunuchs. "We have no power to love," reasons one eunuch. "We must love power." . . .

The words are a heady blend of movie taglines, puns, cartoon balloons, pop-tune lyrics, perverse anachronisms, fabricated Confucianisms ("The upkeep of woman is the downfall of man") and pure Ludlamisms ("Boredom is the absence of yum-yum''). No excerpt can convey the giddiness of the dialogue, and I'm not sure that a reading of the script could convey it either.

Eunuchs indisputably belongs to the Ridiculous Theatrical Company, which has refined itself and its style over the years. Even the most grotesque events are underplayed, which in the case of *Eunuchs*, allows the troupe to mock debauchery as well as chinoiserie.

The indirect approach leaves room for humorous digression. There are sardonic discourses on jade, revolution and the uniqueness of eunuchry, as well as interpolations of dance and song including one disarming moment when two empresses . . . cuddle a newborn prince and croon in unison, ''Chingalingalee. Chingalingaloo. You're my Chinese baby.''

The play is long . . . and the author does not quite know how to end it. After . . . [Ante Hai's] hilarious execution, *Eunuchs* subsides. But this is an exuberant and robust work, one of Ludlam's most polished and comic inventions.

> *Mel Gussow, in a review of "Eunuchs of the Forbidden City," in* The New York Times, *April 7, 1972, p. 27.*

MEL GUSSOW

Corn is a change of pace and of face for Charles Ludlam's Ridiculous Theatrical Company. Instead of the baroque grotesqueries of *Bluebeard* and *Eunuchs of the Forbidden City*, Ludlam now transports us to country-western territory for ''a finger lickin' good'' musical hoedown. The self-spoofing, admittedly cornpone, material does not liberate Ludlam's feverish playwright's imagination—he is more at home in Transylvania than on the farm—but it still provides a thoroughly enjoyable entertainment.

Ludlam has chosen the prototypal hillbilly yarn—the Hatfields and the McCoys—and seasoned it with a dash of Woodstock and a dose of faith-healing. A world-famous singer, Lola Lola, needs a wide open space for a free concert and for the sake of adjoining farms she wants to bring the feuding families together. . . .

The backdrop is a quilt; Ridiculous has gone homespun. The fun is not primarily in the script, but in the performance.

> *Mel Gussow, in a review of "Corn," in* The New York Times, *November 24, 1972, p. 43.*

MEL GUSSOW

Charles Ludlam has brazenly cast himself on Garboed waters, playing Marguerite Gautier, La Dame aux Camelias, herself, in his own free adaptation of [Alexander Dumas's *Camille*]. . . .

The limitations of the Dumas play form the limitations of Ludlam's rerun. As a playwright and director he is inspired by the grotesque. The monsters, demons and fools who usually populate his fantastical works (such as *Bluebeard*) expand his comic imagination. In contrast, *Camille* serves largely as an excuse for a lighthearted spoof of a sentimental classic. . . .

As with all *Camilles* this one builds toward the death scene. . . . Once again, poor Camille dies, but this time we laugh.

> *Mel Gussow, in a review of "Camille," in* The New York Times, *May 4, 1973, p. 24.*

WALTER KERR

When, in the Ridiculous Theatrical Company's production of Charles Ludlam's *Hot Ice*, a policeman rises from his card game to urinate, *he* urinates: unzips, delivers, rezips all by himself. . . .

To tell you the truth, I was a bit surprised upon visiting the Ridiculous Company after an abstinence of several years to find Mr. Ludlam's group still so much concerned with this sort of candor. When does daring begin to realize that it has been duplicated too often, and are we really to take fresh delight in the spectacle of bald, full-breasted hermaphrodites camping as before? The fact that *Hot Ice* has to do with cryo-surgery may suggest that it is as up to the next moment as, say Woody Allen's *Sleeper*. Lamely and lamentably, it is no such thing. Though the evening boasts a certain number of cryo-type jokes (''Where is the cryo-bus?'' ''Just around the coroner''), it contains just about as many direct quotes from an old James Cagney film, *White Heat*.

Now this is puzzling on several counts. What are all these references to a film made in 1949 (I've just checked the date) doing in what is presumably the farthest-out of fresh forms? Nobody laughed at any of them, possibly because they are merely quotes, not twists. Just as possibly, the audience . . . may not have been looking at late television recently and, as a result, mayn't have the faintest notion of what that mother-gangster relationship is all about. In any event, I had the rather uncomfortable feeling that I was the only auditor present whose memory went far enough back to keep up with Mr. Ludlam. . . .

[There] are hints, here and there, that a bit is *going* to be funny. I found myself interested in a narrator's disquisition on an earlier text, the ''Ur-Hot Ice,'' which had proved so successful that audiences were not only riveted to their seats, they were unwilling to leave them after a performance—which meant that each subsequent performance had to be given in some other theater. But before the whimsy could be developed beyond the first upturn of a smile, the narrator was back in his corner, playing with his Yo-Yo, and policemen in red crash helmets were charting the course of an auto through Times Square, Herald Square, and enough other Squares to provoke an onstage wag to wink at us and remark, ''They must be taking the square route.'' I've warned you.

> *Walter Kerr, "Kerr on 'Hot Ice'," in* The New York Times, *Section II, March 10, 1974, p. 3.*

CLIVE BARNES

That fine hairline between comedy and tragedy is lovingly and most skillfully etched in Charles Ludlam's *Camille*. . . . Mr. Ludlam describes his work, with more pride than modesty I suspect, as ''a tear-jerker,'' and in a strange way it is oddly touching. It is also one of the most hilarious and unbuttoned camp evenings in New York.

You can, and possibly will, laugh until the tears run down your cheeks—but remember to question yourself whether all the tears are those of laughter. Mr. Ludlam says his play is ''freely adapted from *La Dame aux Camelias*, but it has also had a certain help from Verdi's opera and Garbo's movie.

The key to the production is the performance of Mr. Ludlam himself as Camille. Now this is no ordinary drag act played for laughs. . . . He is a completely convincing Camille. . . .

Of course, the sentiments of the Dumas are comic today—a comedy driven away in modern terms by such various devices as Verdi's music, Ashton's choreography or Garbo's magic. Here they are not driven away, but are left like a raised eyebrow glancing at affectation. It is very funny to have the poetic flights of the piece dashed to earth by an intonation, or, at times, a wild, naughty but always apt anachronism.

> *Clive Barnes, "Touching 'Camille'," in* The New York Times, *May 14, 1974, p. 31.*

MEL GUSSOW

Charles Ludlam's *Stage Blood* is *Hamlet* with a happy ending, which is of course, ridiculous—as in Ridiculous Theatrical Company. In Mr. Ludlam's latest comic invention . . . , a seedy troupe of actors is in Mudville, U.S.A., preparing to open *Hamlet* without an Ophelia. . . .

[A local girl] wins the role and the show goes on. As Mr. Ludlam's lovely new toy-top of a revolving stage merrily spins, we see *Hamlet* between the scenes, which includes hanky-panky in the dressing room, a death by hatchet-in-the-neck (could it possibly be a suicide?) and two ghosts of Hamlet's father vying for the spotlight.

Laughs are freefalling, but the play is less wild and untidy than usual Ludlam. There is a slight loss in madness and nonsense but a gain in structure and discipline. This is a crisply wrapped comic package, with a clear plot and smart staging.

The pun in the title is apt. *Stage Blood* is The Theater that gets into an actor's veins and also bottled paint slapped on fake wounds. . . . It is seasoned with Mr. Ludlam's comments on the art of artifice (for him, acting is "seeming not being") and valuable theatrical information. Did you know that the plays of Shakespeare were not written by Shakespeare but by another playwright of the same name?

> *Mel Gussow, in a review of "Stage Blood," in* The New York Times, *December 9, 1974, p. 54.*

MEL GUSSOW

If Charles Ludlam had lived 50 years ago, he might have been a vaudeville headliner, but he would have never lost his sense of the Ridiculous. Fascinated by ventriloquism, he has created a diabolically comic coup de théâtre entitled *The Ventriloquist's Wife*. . . .

Mr. Ludlam recycles the detritus of our culture. Just as his *Bluebeard* was influenced by the movie *The Island of Lost Souls* and his *Camille* by Garbo, *The Ventriloquist's Wife* draws wattage from that 1945 Michael Redgrave horror movie, *Dead of Night*. As you may remember, that was the movie in which a ventriloquist's life was taken over by a wooden dummy. . . .

[The plot revolves around] an actor down on his luck who buys a wooden dummy in a pawn shop, names him Walter Ego, and becomes his straight man. Walter—cute, cuddlesome, and as nasty as W. C. Fields was to Charlie McCarthy—artfully upstages his master and covets his wife. Walter is both the child in the house and the fiendish rival for the lady. . . .

Because the show has evolved in rehearsal and in performance, it still needs some polishing, particularly toward the trick Pirandello ending. But the script is one of Mr. Ludlam's most inspired creations. . . . *The Ventriloquist's Wife* raises ventriloquism to a high comic art.

> *Mel Gussow, " 'Ventriloquist's Wife' Is Presented," in* The New York Times, *December 28, 1977, p. C13.*

MEL GUSSOW

[*Utopia, Inc.*] transports us through the pseudoscientific Bermuda Triangle into a curious subterranean kingdom that seems to be a comic combination of Shangri-La, *The Tempest* and that Bing Crosby-Bob Hope movie *The Road to Utopia*.

The hero of the play . . . is a smuggler who traffics in "ha-ha weed." He and his mate . . . are "shipwrecked on an uninhibited island," thickly populated by other members of Mr. Ludlam's Ridiculous troupe. . . .

The story is one of passion, intrigue, plunder and vengeance; in other words this is a Ridiculous comedy. As usual, Mr. Ludlam borrows freely—from himself and from others. *Utopia, Inc.* is a thesaurus of movie taglines, vaudeville jokes and outrageous plays on words, enough, as the author observes, to send us to the "punny farm." The sources are as various as Mike Nichols, Elaine May, Herman Melville and Claudette Colbert—or was it Albert Schweitzer who first said that the secret of a long life was good health and a short memory? Some of the lines are clever and perhaps even original. Other lines are awful—and hoary with age.

To underscore his lack of seriousness. Mr. Ludlam offers the audience the following advice: "Don't look for deeper meaning. Just take it at farce value." But Mr. Ludlam must be measured against himself, and by Ridiculous standards, *Utopia* is a Grade-B effort—an evening of lackadaisical Ludlam.

It lacks the monstrous lunacy of Mr. Ludlam's lascivious *Bluebeard*, the rabid romanticism of his hairy-chested *Camille*, the hayseed ebullience of the country-western *Corn*, the blissful virtuosity of *The Ventriloquist's Wife*. Each of these was a travesty of a specific genre. *Utopia* is more general—and also indiscriminate. . . .

This time, the evening's pleasures are more visual than verbal. . . . Egg cartons, teabags, aspirin bottles and pie plates are recycled into an imaginative ensemble of the familiar and the grotesque. . . . [We] laugh more at the show's millinery than we do at its dialogue.

> *Mel Gussow, " 'Utopia, Inc.' from Charles Ludlam," in* The New York Times, *December 5, 1978, p. C7.*

MEL GUSSOW

Imagine if you can a cross between *King Lear* and *The Frog Prince*, with a slipper from *Cinderella* and a twist of *The Three Sisters*, and you have an approximation of *The Enchanted Pig*, Charles Ludlam's delirious new merriment. This comedy . . . is clean and camp-free. It should appeal both to wide-eyed adults and sophisticated children.

King Gorgeous III is Mr. Ludlam's version of Lear. . . . Marching off to still another battle, handsome Gorgeous tells his three nubile daughters that in his absence they can have the run of the castle, except that they are not to venture into one particular room, referred to with dungeon intonations as "that room!"

Of course, this is the first place they go. In "The Room!" they discover a book of prophecies. The eldest daughter will marry a prince from the East; she glows with pleasure. The middle daughter will marry a prince from the West; she glows in anticipation. The youngest and prettiest daughter . . . awaits her fate with trepidation. Then comes the prophecy: She will marry . . . a pig from the North.

Shortly after, the suitors arrive, and the marriages take place. . . . From here on, it is a Ridiculous free-for-all, a giddy sendup of fairy tales and picaresque odes. . . .

This time, Mr. Ludlam limits himself to writing and directing. . . . His play is a pun-filled romantic adventure that cribs from a diversity of sources, spoofing but not debasing material. *The Enchanted Pig* has that spontaneity that we associate with Mr. Ludlam at his most effervescent. In his long Ridiculous career, he has had his ups and downs. *The Enchanted Pig* is definitely an up, easily in a class with such vintage Ludlam extravaganzas as *Bluebeard* and *Camille*.

> Mel Gussow, "Black-Eyed Susan Wed to 'Enchanted Pig': Ludlam's Cure for Snout," in The New York Times, April 24, 1979, p. C10.

JULIUS NOVICK

[Charles Ludlam's] new piece, *Reverse Psychology*, amounts to very little. The doughty author-director who has parodied Marlowe, Shakespeare and Wagner here subdues himself to the limits of twentieth-century sex farce. Dr. Leonard Silver . . . is married to Dr. Karen Gold; both are psychiatrists. Leonard is carrying on with Eleanor, who turns out to be Karen's patient; Karen is carrying on with Freddie, who is Leonard's patient and Eleanor's husband. The complications are endlessly tedious, the satire on psychiatry is rudimentary and hackneyed. . . . Though the self-conscious writing and acting put everything in quotation marks, *Reverse Psychology* is not really a parody; it comes nearer to being a crude imitation of a bad old-fashioned Broadway flop. Only for a few minutes in the second act, when the other three members of the cast—two women and a man in drag—hurl themselves lustfully at Ludlam, is there a hint of the old Ridiculous extravagance.

But even the old Ridiculous extravagance has not, in my experience, been free of this company's characteristic failings. Ridiculous writing and Ridiculous acting are typically noisy, strained, clumsy, often desperately lacking in wit. (pp. 355-56)

Clurman says of the true "theater" that "Its very idea of craft, its methods and its manner of organization are calculated to voice its human aim." This is true of Ludlam's theater. The noisy crudeness of its work is not inadvertent; it is part of the giddy anarchy that is the company's "human aim." But badness on purpose is not, in effect, much better than badness of any other kind. It dulls and diffuses the company's impact. Where would the Ridiculous Theatrical Company be if Ludlam's critics and audiences demanded more from him—higher standards, less self-indulgence, more discipline in his anarchy—and he in turn demanded more from himself and his colleagues? We will presumably never know. (p. 356)

> Julius Novick, "Reverse Psychology," in The Nation, New York, Vol. 231, No. 11, October 11, 1980, pp. 354-56.

FRANK RICH

Having spent the past few seasons impersonating neurotic middle-aged men, Charles Ludlam has decided to jump into wom-en's clothes again. But not just any woman's clothes. . . . [In *Galas*] Mr. Ludlam has wrapped himself in the extravagant gowns and furs of Maria Magdalena Galas—a larger-than-life opera diva whose dramatic singing career is matched only by her tumultuous offstage adventures with the rich and mighty Greek shipping tycoon Aristotle Plato Socrates Odysseus (known to his friends as "Soc").

"I *am* music!," proclaims Galas shortly after we meet her. . . . [Galas] may not be music and she may not always quite be womanly, but she surely is a comic creation of a high order. . . . Mr. Ludlam gives us the regal Maria Callas of legend and gossip: a narcissistic superstar who orders her maid to adopt "a manner of excessive politeness," who brings the impresarios of La Scala to their knees, who dismisses Pope Pius XII (here called Pope Sixtus the Seventh) as "just another bishop."

He even gives us the Callas of those final, bitter years—a sobbing, lonely lady of leisure who rattles around in her Paris apartment bemoaning the fact that all her friends are "either dead or in Monte Carlo" and that there is "nothing particularly good on television" to distract her from the demise of her career and love life. *Galas* is subtitled *A Modern Tragedy,* and while that's an overstatement, the evening does end with a played-for-keeps whiff of *Madame Butterfly.* . . .

The text itself has its limitations. "The characters in the play are real," writes Mr. Ludlam in a program note. "Only their names have been changed to protect the playwright." He speaks the truth. *Galas* actually is a fairly factual, if broad, account of some high points in Callas's life, starting with her first marriage to a brick tycoon. And Mr. Ludlam is not unsympathetic to his subject. "To have everything and lose it—now, that isn't funny," says Galas at the end. Ludlam the actor gets a laugh on the line, but Ludlam the playwright isn't entirely kidding.

To the extent that *Galas* tries to speak seriously about its heroine's suffering (especially in Act II), the writing suffers, too. But if Mr. Ludlam's biting style and unsparing social observations are sometimes cramped by his biographical comprehensiveness, he just as often gives in to the urge to be rude. There are some very funny, not to mention tasteless, jokes scattered throughout, involving topics as varied as Galas's contempt for the public, Eva Perón's philosophy of government, the merits of Wagner and the dietetic uses of tapeworms.

> Frank Rich, "'Galas,' New Play by Ridiculous Company," in The New York Times, September 16, 1983, p. C3.

CLIVE BARNES

[*Galas*] is based, quite avowedly, on the glorious and unhappy career of the Greek-American *diva,* Maria Callas, one of the few indisputably great singers of our century. (pp. 86-7)

Ludlam calls his piece "a modern tragedy," but in fact it is a camp comedy—but a comedy about Callas? The idea itself is enough to make a brick walla wary. Yet what emerges is not a comedy and not a tragedy—it is a pure slice of Ludlam at his exquisitely poised finest. . . .

Galas is—as a play—badly constructed and not especially well-written—it is a vehicle and would, as would be simply proved, be impossible to envisage even without Ludlam and his cohorts. But with them it has a sad, funny and touching way of its own. Ludlam is a caricaturist who exaggerates to tell the truth, but the underlying line is bold and clear, and the final effect unforgettable.

More than most of Ludlam's shows this is absolute and solid Ludlam—it is the nature of the piece. It has been built like a *bel canto* opera, with just about as much dramatic persuasiveness. At one point Ludlam's Galas says: "I must be first woman—that is what *prima donna* means.". . .

Yet it is the over-bearing, over-weening, over-reaching Ludlam who raises feelings of pity and compassion that seem to go beyond the play's scope, but are, in fact, obviously its ultimate purpose. (p. 87)

> Clive Barnes, "'Galas': Tragedy Turned Comedy," in New York Post, September 26, 1983. Reprinted in New York Theatre Critics' Reviews, Vol. XXXXIV, No. 18, Week of December 12, 1983, pp. 86-7.

JOHN HOWELL

Charles Ludlam's Ridiculous Theatrical Company has sent up every imaginable target. . . . The most recent object of Ridiculous wit is the "avant-garde," shrewdly chosen at a time when a '60s-based performing-arts avant-garde has achieved unprecedented and widespread public notice. Of course, artistic director Ludlam is experimental and "avant" too; his rewrite of Molière's *Le Bourgeois Gentilhomme*, in a script of stinging wit, bad jokes, topical references, and deliberate banalities, is itself a traditional avant-garde maneuver, a reworking of a classic in contemporary terms.

[*Le Bourgeois Avant-Garde*'s] opening is a mock theatrical quote and an all-around metaphor for what follows: after three knocks of a staff on the stage floor, cheap and tacky chandeliers are jerkily pulled to the ceiling of the equally cheap and tacky drawing room-ranch house set. The particular avant-garde which is this production's main target is the '60s-rooted, serious, brainy performing art that not incidentally defined the milieu in which the Ridiculous Theatrical Company was originally formed. So when Mr. Rufus Foufas . . . , millionaire businessman, hires a composer, a choreographer, and a poet for the production of a truly avant-garde event to aid him in seducing a beautiful avant-garde actress, there's lots of banter about creating "pieces, not plays," "movement, not dance," and "sound, not music"; about "saying something without meaning anything"; and about abstraction, minimalism, and ontology in theater. . . . (p. 73)

As the latest installment in Ludlam's repertory, *Le Bourgeois Avant-Garde* is good, not great, Ridiculous. But this kind of play acting, at once buffoonish and sophisticated, presents its own pleasures even when the action falters, shticks go on too long, or when wit simply flags. A whirligig of theatrical references and styles, Ludlam and Company finally create their own original synthesis of subversive comedy out of an ideological performing stance willing to take on any subject at hand (like the card-carrying avant-garde theater they both satirize and belong to); ultimately the virtues and flaws of a given production seem less important than the constant process of performance as an exploration. The Irish like to say that the most serious people are those who laugh the most; on this scale the Ridiculous enterprise is in the category of the sublime. (p. 74)

> John Howell, "'Le Bourgeois Avant-Garde,' The Ridiculous Theatrical Company," in Artforum, Vol. XXII, No. 2, October, 1983, pp. 73-4.

JOEL G. FINK

[Plot] is not the essence of *Le Bourgeois Avant-Garde*. Over the years, The Ridiculous Theatrical Company has nurtured a presentational style of popular theatre often resembling a Punch and Judy Show come-to-life. . . . Synthesizing many styles of comedy, Ludlam's work is more akin to the rough hewn spirit of Commedia Dell'Arte than to the precise clock work of French Farce. Whether using direct asides or indirect "in" jokes, the company's immediacy and intimacy with its audience is equally as important as any on-stage dramatic relationship. Though very different in theme and content, Ludlam's plays have a generally similar construction and style. Although always working for a laugh, Mr. Ludlam, as both author and director, perceptively underlies the surface of slapstick and farce with real and complex (in this case "artistic") issues and questions. When "avant-garde" is defined as "French, for bull-shit," and artists describe themselves as "post-talent," the *serious* and the *ridiculous* meet to create satire. (p. 104)

[There is] a structural problem in *Le Bourgeois Avant-Garde* that has also been apparent in several of Ludlam's previous works. Although the first act establishes *situation* and *character*, the second act stumbles at efforts toward thematic development. Comic bits . . . tend to be prolonged and labored, and the production's second half is only rarely as entertaining as the first. . . . Ludlam's many production roles undoubtedly make a clear cut directorial perspective difficult, and the lack of consistent dramatic structure and rhythm finally works against much of the production's rich comic potential.

It should be noted, however, that it is possible, and even likely, that the company's continued success is founded on exactly this lack of "careful" and polished production values. Even the occasional lapses into truly bad taste must be taken into account as integral for the "ridiculous" overall effect intended. (pp. 104-05)

The Ridiculous Theatrical Company has had both a steady and an impressive output of productions. It is a mark of Charles Ludlam's unique talents that the company has grown and evolved, while still keeping strong roots in the theatrical sensibilities that originally informed it in 1967. Although in the last several productions the company has shown its comic energies in need of a target worth hitting, they seem to have fixed on a mark, in *Le Bourgeois Avant-Garde,* which both focuses and inspires their ridiculous theatrical talents. (p. 105)

> Joel G. Fink, in a review of "Le Bourgeois Avant-Garde," in Theatre Journal, Vol. 36, No. 1, March, 1984, pp. 103-05.

DON NELSEN

As is often the case with the Ridics, [*The Mystery of Irma Vep*] is a parody of an established genre. This time: Gothic horror. Imagine elements of *The Wolf Man, Dracula, The Mummy* and *Jane Eyre* held together in the overall story of *Rebecca*. . . .

My favorite creature in *Vep* is Nicodemus Underwood, the one-legged, buck-toothed caretaker of Mandercrest on the moors who doubles at night as a werewolf. At one point, he encounters Jane Twisden, Mandercrest's maid.

"How come," asks . . . Twisden, "you're not still a werewolf when the moon is still full?"

"I am in remission since a cloud passed over the moon," he replies.

Ludlam is brilliant at burlesquing a character enough to make it funny but not enough to render the character unbelievable. In fact, it's commonplace for the Ridiculous Theatrical Company to make you believe anything because, at bottom, there is a great deal of truth in what they are playing.

This does not prevent their plays from occasionally lapsing into boredom. There were stretches in *Vep* when yawns rather than laughs were the proper reaction because Ludlam tends to over-write.

But *Vep,* which leads us on an eerie odyssey from an English manor house with a dark secret to the tombs of the pharaohs in Egypt, is certainly one of the best performances the Ridiculous has mounted in some time. For inspired parody, there is no theater I know of that can match the RTC.

> *Don Nelsen, " 'The Mystery of Irma Vep', but That's Really Ridiculous," in* Daily News, *New York, October 8, 1984. Reprinted in* New York Theatre Critics' Reviews, *Vol. XXXXV, No. 15, Week of November 19, 1984, p. 164.*

DAVID STERRITT

The Mystery of Irma Vep isn't hard to solve. Just rearrange the letters of the last two words and you have a certain supernatural creature that's known to lurk in gothic novels and old horror flicks, among other habitats.

And don't be angry that I've given away the ending, because I won't give away what really counts—the dozens and dozens of laughs that tumble through the Ridiculous Theatrical Company's latest offering, proudly subtitled *A Penny Dreadful.*

Though its name invites laughter even before the curtain rises, the Ridiculous troupe is a solid and experienced company that has been refining its comic vision for almost 20 years. Its backbone is the versatile. . . . Charles Ludlam.

The story begins and ends in a mansion on the moors, and hops to Egypt for the second act. The characters include rich Lady Enid Hillcrest and a servant named Nicodemus Underwood, as well as the mysterious title character and an oversize vampire right out of the *Nosferatu* movies.

These figures are parodies, of course, not people. And that goes double for the women, played with flouncing hilarity by the all-male cast. . . . The play is ridiculous, to be sure, but it's sly as well as silly. . . .

Irma Vep doesn't have the insane inspiration of a first-rate Ludlam classic like *Bluebeard,* but it's the next best thing.

> *David Sterritt, "As 'The Mystery of Irma Vep' Unravels, Laughs Come Tumbling Out," in* The Christian Science Monitor, *November 13, 1984, p. 50.*

FRANK RICH

The Artificial Jungle is Mr. Ludlam's omnibus reply to *Double Indemnity, The Postman Always Rings Twice* and *Little Shop of Horrors*—with a little of Zola's *Thérèse Raquin* tossed in for added kicks in Act II. . . . Both as writer and director, Mr. Ludlam remains our master of the ridiculous, if not yet of

suspense. . . . [The] pastiche, hard-boiled dialogue crackles with an authenticity as tightly monitored as the Gothic Victorian diction of *Irma Vep.* . . .

The Artificial Jungle isn't always top-rung Ridiculous, but, with this troupe, second-rung is more than funny enough. . . .

The Artificial Jungle means to be more than merely a Mel Brooks-style spoof of a genre that has already been parodied too much. What the author is after instead is a deconstruction of the form that mocks its underlying pretensions even more than its hoary pulp-fiction clichés.

Unlike David Mamet, who missed the joke by highlighting ponderous psychosexual implications in his screenplay for the remake of *The Postman Always Rings Twice,* Mr. Ludlam seeks to remind us that a good chiller may be simply that and no more. The most biting passages in *The Artificial Jungle* include those in which the characters explain the titular metaphor ("Everything preys on some other living thing, it's the law of the jungle") or wax philosophical ("We killed him to escape the tackiness of existence") or practice sex as an athletic existential sport. Much as Mr. Ludlam kids Cain and Raymond Chandler, he's even tougher on anyone who confuses toney melodrama with life or high art.

Not for the first time, Mr. Ludlam's scrupulous faithfulness to his sources leads to overlength. *The Artificial Jungle* might be riper at 70 minutes without an intermission than at 100 minutes with one. But the lulls (generally of plot exposition) are balanced by some genuine, at times shriek-inducing surprises.

> *Frank Rich, "Ludlam's 'Artificial Jungle'," in* The New York Times, *September 23, 1986, p. 13.*

MOIRA HODGSON

[Charles Ludlam's] latest fable, *The Artificial Jungle,* is a hilarious play inspired in large part by James M. Cain's *The Postman Always Rings Twice.* It takes place in a pet shop (all done up in Day-Glo), owned by Chester Nurdiger . . . , whose wife Roxanne . . . is just as bored and restless as she can be, suffocated by the daily routine of feeding piranhas and cleaning out rat cages. As Mrs. Nurdiger . . . , her mother-in-law, says, "Pet people have to handle things in a day that would put most people in a dead faint." Thursday nights it's dominoes and cold cuts with Frankie Spinelli . . . , a policeman who is their regular visitor.

Enter Zachary Slade . . . , a balding drifter clad in Brando T-shirt and fake snakeskin jacket. . . . Roxanne, who didn't get her gorgeous lips "from sucking doorknobs," immediately falls for him. "Love is a disease," she says, "and you gave it to me."

There is murder, suspense—and an amazing acrobatic tour de force by Chester's mother-in-law. . . . [The] set, complete with snapping piranhas and Last Supper kitchen clock, is delightful. But no one is more delightful than Ludlam himself, [in the role of Chester], sitting up in bed, his rubbery face under an ice bag, reading 3-D comics. (pp. 618-19)

> *Moira Hodgson, in a review of "The Artificial Jungle," in* The Nation, *New York, Vol. 243, No. 18, November 29, 1986, pp. 618-19.*

David (Alan) Mamet

1947-

American dramatist, scriptwriter, and essayist.

Mamet is highly praised for his accurate rendering of American vernacular, through which he explores the relationship between language and behavior. According to Mamet, "the language we use, its rhythm, actually determines the way we behave, more than the other way around." Terse and pointed, his dialogues are often compared to those of Harold Pinter, whom Mamet has cited as an early influence. Thematically, Mamet examines such topics as loneliness, responsibility, communication, and the dichotomy between reality and social myth. Although critics have faulted Mamet for failing at times to create dramatic conflict and for excessive use of profanity, they generally agree that he is one of the foremost contemporary American dramatists.

Mamet's first play to receive attention, *The Duck Variations* (1972), displays features common to much of his work: a fixed setting, few characters, a sparse plot, and dialogue that captures the rhythms and syntax of everyday speech. In this play, two elderly Jewish men sit on a park bench discussing a plethora of unrelated subjects. Mamet's next play, *Sexual Perversity in Chicago* (1974), examines confusion and misconceptions surrounding relationships between men and women. While some reviewers found this work offensive and misogynistic, Julius Novick contended that the play "is a compassionate, rueful comedy about how difficult it is . . . for men to give themselves to women, and for women to give themselves to men. It suggests that the only thing to fear, sexually, is fear itself." This play was adapted for film as *About Last Night . . .* In *American Buffalo* (1975) and *The Water Engine: An American Fable* (1977), Mamet explores contradictions and myths prevalent in the business world. *American Buffalo,* for which Mamet received the New York Drama Critics Circle Award, is set in a junk shop where three men plot to steal a valuable coin. A lack of communication and understanding causes the men to abandon their efforts. The protagonist of *The Water Engine* creates an innovative engine but is murdered when he refuses to sell his invention to corporate lawyers.

A Life in the Theatre (1977) offers a stark and wryly humorous view of the theatrical world through the performances and backstage conversations between a veteran actor and a novice. Edith Oliver remarked: "Mamet has written—in gentle ridicule; in jokes, broad and tiny; and in comedy, high and low— a love letter to the theater." *The Woods* (1977) involves a young couple who discover the darker realities of their relationship while vacationing in an isolated woodland cabin. Mamet followed *The Woods* with three short domestic dramas in which he places considerable emphasis on dialogue. In *Reunion* (1977), a woman and her alcoholic father come to terms with their twenty-year separation; in *Dark Pony* (1977), a father relates a story to his young daughter as they drive home late at night; and *The Sanctity of Marriage* (1979) concerns the separation of a married couple.

Glengarry Glen Ross (1982), Mamet's most acclaimed work, is an exposé of American business. In this play, four Florida real estate agents in competition to become their company's

© Thomas Victor 1987

top salesperson victimize unsuspecting customers. Although Mamet portrays the agents as unethical and amoral, he shows respect for their finesse and sympathizes with their overly competitive way of life. *Glengarry Glen Ross* was awarded both the Pulitzer Prize in drama and the New York Drama Critics Circle Award. Mamet's next play, *Edmond* (1982), involves an unhappy businessman who leaves his wife and ventures into the seamier districts of New York City. After being beaten and robbed, the man turns to violence and is imprisoned for murdering a waitress. Gerald Weales viewed this play as a chilling example of how "we become part of our destructive surroundings." *Prairie du chien* (1985) and *The Shawl* (1985) are companion pieces in which Mamet employs supernatural elements. The first play centers on a bizarre, unsolvable murder, while the second concerns a psychic's fraudulent efforts to obtain a client's inheritance.

In addition to his work for the theater, Mamet has written several screenplays. The first, an adaptation of James M. Cain's novel *The Postman Always Rings Twice*, is generally considered Mamet's least successful effort. In *The Verdict*, based on Barry Reed's novel *Verdict,* a downtrodden, alcoholic lawyer battles injustice within the judicial system to win a malpractice suit for a woman who suffered brain damage during childbirth. Reviewers extolled Mamet's terse dialogue, citing the lawyer's jury summation as a particularly powerful sequence of the film. In his recent screenplay, *The Untouchables,* Mamet incorporates elements from federal agent Eliot Ness's memoirs and from the popular radio and television series. Set in Chicago, the film focuses on Ness's struggle to uphold the Prohibition law and bring mobster Al Capone to justice. Although David Denby found the script substandard for a writer of Mamet's talent, he called *The Untouchables* "a celebration of law enforcement as American spectacle—a straightforward, broadly entertaining movie."

(See also *CLC,* Vols. 9, 15, 34; *Contemporary Authors,* Vols. 81-84; *Contemporary Authors New Revision Series,* Vol. 15; and *Dictionary of Literary Biography,* Vol. 7.)

DAVID DENBY

Frank Chambers, the narrator-hero of James M. Cain's much adapted 1934 novel, *The Postman Always Rings Twice,* is an amoral young drifter, easily tempted and easily mastered, a realist who becomes a sap. Soon after starting work at a hamburger joint near Los Angeles, Frank climbs into bed with Cora, who is trapped in an unhappy marriage to the owner, Nick Papadakis, a drunken, boorish immigrant. Cora is ravenous—in Cain's terms, a caged animal. She provokes Frank into becoming brutal enough to dominate *her* ("Bite me! Bite me!" she cries on page 9) and then to kill Nick. Ungovernable female sexuality working on men's violent impulses—this was the juicy paranoid premise of so many novels written by the men of the "hard-boiled" school of the thirties and forties (Hammett, Chandler, Cain, etc.), and it was carried over into the dozens of movies made from their books or influenced by their books.

Cain's work has a glib, trashy energy that makes it fun. But that's not the way playwright David Mamet and director Bob Rafelson (*Five Easy Pieces*) see it. . . . [Their version] is a very solemn piece of work. Mamet and Rafelson have turned Cain's entertainingly steamy pulp classic into a grim, primal fable—Greek tragedy in the American Depression. Funereally paced, humorless, grindingly naturalistic, this *Postman* has been made in defiance of what people have always enjoyed about the material. I think the movie is a disaster—almost unbearable—yet the moroseness, the claustrophobia, the messy, "dirty" sex will probably earn it some rave reviews. God knows it doesn't look like ordinary commercial entertainment. . . .

Mamet and Rafelson betray Cain in another way, making him heavy and slow. They deal with the story as if it were written by Sophocles or O'Neill yet add nothing that deepens the material. The result is baffling—a call girl bizarrely dressed in sackcloth. (p. 39)

Mamet has dropped the vulgarities and the pulpy animal-woman talk that Cain wrote for Cora, but he hasn't put anything in their place. She's hungry, and that's about all she is; one gets a little tired of that mouth hanging open. When this Cora is matched with . . . Frank there's no wild romantic tension: He's a squalid, aging failure, and when he dominates her, Cain's meaning gets reversed; she can't "destroy" a man who is already finished. (pp. 39-40)

The fifteen-rounds-to-a-knockout sex scenes feel ludicrously forced, almost as if the lovers were punching and kicking because they couldn't really make it together. This *Postman* isn't deliriously dangerous, it's just messy and sordid—a movie about depressing losers. (p. 40)

> David Denby, "*Return to Sender,*" in New York Magazine, Vol. 14, No. 13, March 30, 1981, pp. 39-41.

STANLEY KAUFFMANN

David Mamet, who wrote the adaptation [of *The Postman Always Rings Twice*], has poured out theater plays in the last five or six years, two of which—*The Water Engine* and *American Buffalo*—were good enough to raise expectations here. Dashed. Admittedly, Cain's novel is not so good as one remembers: some of the writing lapses out of tension into slush. ("I kissed her. Her eyes were shining up at me like two blue stars. It was like being in church.") But it has two qualities that still hold. The structure is like an arrow flight, except for the episode with the puma-hunting girl (which is worsened in the film). And Cain is careful to make his lovers pathetic—not sympathetic, which would kill it—but pathetic victims of moral weakness. Mamet's screenplay hashes up both these qualities. The structure is tugged out of shape (an episode in a bus station, for instance); the line of the lovers' involvement is zigged and zagged; and nothing of the woman's past is clarified. Puppets are what they start as and remain. And some of the dialogue is quaint. "You scum," [Cora] says to [Frank], the man with whom she has planned and committed her husband's murder.

And the "twice" of the title is left out. The quintessential irony of the story is that a man who commits murder and gets away with it is later found guilty of a killing he did not commit. (It's the same twist as in C. S. Forester's *Payment Deferred,* which was written earlier.) But this film ends with [Cora's] accidental death in a car smash, with nothing of what follows. The implication is less than faint that [Frank] will be arrested for murdering her, will be tried and executed.

But maybe that castrated ending was the director's idea, not Mamet's. (p. 26)

Cain's story, if you've forgotten, is about a Depression drifter who is hired as a mechanic by the Greek owner of a garage-cum-diner in California. The Greek has a wife younger than himself and not Greek. (In the novel she has a lot of ethnic loathing for her husband which at least helps to characterize and motivate her.) Cain wasn't concerned to show the hell into which two lovers plunge themselves by murdering the woman's husband, which was what Zola had done in *Thérèse Raquin,* he wanted to dramatize the immorality of egotism, the fact that there is no reliable bar between gratification-as-ethics and murder. Rafelson and Mamet reduce the lovers to objects of our smirking recognition ("Oho, so that's the setup!") . . . All the people involved here, laboring diligently together, have turned out an empty and odious film. (p. 27)

> Stanley Kauffmann, "*Still Ringing,*" in The New Republic, Vol. 184, No. 3457, April 11, 1981, pp. 26-7.

JOHN SIMON

A Sermon, written and staged by David Mamet, is a spoof of an Episcopalian sermon, delivered by a swinging young priest . . .

to an affluent congregation uneager to hear hard-nosed theology or fire-and-brimstone fulminations. So our homilist provides resolutely lay moralizing, scarcely more than chatty *non sequiturs* with the following schema: major premise, irrelevant minor premise, rhetorical pause posing as a conclusion. At first, this is mildly diverting, but we soon master the formula and want more than mealymouthed moral attitudinizing. If this unnamed priest were a character in a play—e.g., in *Mass Appeal;* or if the satire had more bite to it—e.g., as in *Sister Mary Ignatius Explains It All for You,* very well. But this unmuscular Christianity without a plot and characters is not enough: The sermon-playlet ends, the priest departs, and we forget everything we heard. (p. 71)

> John Simon, *"Einstein in the Woods," in* New York Magazine, *Vol. 14, No. 44, November 9, 1981, pp. 70-2.*

STEVEN H. GALE

David Mamet's plays are about relationships. Throughout dramatic history, of course, the theme of interpersonal relationships has been a primary concern, yet Mamet's examination of the intercourse between individuals is more intimate and more human than that of most of his forerunners or his American or British contemporaries. In part this is because he is extremely perceptive and in part it is because he is an accomplished craftsman.

Well grounded in theatre history and theory, Mamet is also gifted in bringing common experiences alive for his audience. His situations are sometimes realistic and sometimes symbolic, but they all contain a universal kernel around which the action is built and with which the audience identifies. In addition, he creates characters who are both believable and human; and the phrasing, clichés, and cadences of his dialogue are so accurate that when his plays first opened in New York, many reviewers compared his work to that of Harold Pinter. He is not just an American Pinter, though. While there are similarities in content and technique, essentially Mamet's approach is less intellectual, philosophical, or theoretical than Pinter's as his narrower focus generally deals with the superficial aspect of his subject. By this I do not mean to denigrate his work, for he is extremely successful at what he does, and his writing is far more easily accessible than is much of Pinter's—and he is still a young dramatist developing his skills. Where Pinter deals with the deepest levels of the psyches of characters who have desperate needs in order to expose those needs and the strategies employed to fulfill them, Mamet shows ordinary human beings caught in the immediacy of stipulated needs for various kinds of social interaction. As a result, Mamet's plays are not as deep and dark as Pinter's; at the same time they ring truer for a less sophisticated audience.

The Duck Variations was first staged [in 1972]. (p. 207)

The play deals with two men in their sixties. They often come together during lunch to talk—about life and death, the perils of leadership, fate, sex, the environment and pollution, or whatever else comes to mind. Because of their age they have the wisdom and perspective on their subjects that comes with experience, but sometimes they are the butt of their own societal satire, too, and exhibit the foolishness of those whom they both envy and find ridiculous.

Each of the fourteen variations is about a different topic, though they are all connected by the common denominator of the ducks and each is somehow related to the preceding variation and prepares for the variation that follows.... The opening line or two establish the topic for each variation, as the men link a series of clichéd stories and commentaries about ducks that become allegories for serious protests about life, nature, mankind, and society. As Emil and George alternate in setting the topic, they try to top one another and their personalities emerge; ultimately, the seemingly slower-witted George is seen as the more perceptive. The characters become believable, recognizable; they remind us of our favorite grandfathers. In spite of the fast delivery of short one-line dialogue, the characters know each other well enough to communicate, sometimes responding to unfinished thoughts, though ironically, too, sometimes not being able to pick up the most obvious clues.

While the philosophical stances assumed by George and Emil regarding their numerous, shifting subjects carry revelations about the nature of the universe and man's place in it, ultimately the importance of their conversation lies not in occasional insights but in the fact that they are conversing. When they come together it is clear that they know each other and that they have met here previously, perhaps for years. They are familiar and they use their familiarity as a basis for much of the mental gymnastics that they engage in. They have achieved a stable relationship, one that is vital to their mental well-being. Every day at lunch time they meet to talk, to share the time together, to create an imaginative break in their mundane day. Indeed, this may be the high point of their day—the companionship that both need and relish. As Emil says in the "Seventh Variation," "A man needs a friend in this life." (p. 208)

At first glance [*Sexual Perversity in Chicago*] seems less mature than *Variations*. The language is certainly coarser, being filled with four-letter words, and the sexual imagery that abounds is sophomoric in tone. The subject, too, seems to be more college blackout material than the earlier drama: two young men talk about their sexual exploits and describe the women they see as sexual objects in very graphic, though limited, terms. Actually, however, the play is more subtle than a simple plot summary suggests, for the sex is not important *per se* as it really functions metaphorically to carry the author's meaning. The physical act supplies Mamet's terms for discussing his underlying theme. While he comments on the relationships between one man and another and between one woman and another, this is incidental and only a by-product of his main concern. His focus is on the relationship between men and women.

There are two couples involved, though the members of each recombine with a member of the other to form two additional pairings. Dan and Bernie are filing clerks; Dan is twenty-eight and Bernie somewhat older. They are paralleled by Deborah, a twenty-three-year-old illustrator, and her older roommate, kindergarten teacher Joan. As the play progresses, Dan and Deborah pair off, as do Bernie and Joan. From the composite conversations between the members of the various groupings, together with occasional monologues, the individual nature of each character emerges.

Although there are few direct statements of theme, a Gestalt forms from Dan and Bernie's constant comments and observations about women in general and their sexual relationships with women. It is important to note that the drama opens with just such an exchange:

DANNY: So how'd you do last night?
. . .
BERNIE: Are you fucking kidding me?
. . .

BERNIE: So tits out to here.

There follows an improbable Pinteresque story of Bernie's exploits that winds up with the suggestion that the girl involved can be sexually stimulated only if a friend she telephones makes noises like an anti-aircraft battery while she and Bernie have sex—and the climax comes when she sets the room on fire and sings "Off we go into the Wild Blue Yonder." This scene is countered by one in which Deborah and Joan conclude that men are "all after only one thing." But amusingly, "it's never the *same* thing."

The two commentaries come together in the next scene when Joan and Bernie meet at a singles bar. He tries a line on her, claiming to be a meteorologist for TWA, but she rejects him— "I do not find you sexually attractive." Bernie fights back, calling her names and forcing her to realize that just as he treated her as a sex object, she has treated him the same; and, now that she can see an individual behind her easy categorizing, she realizes that he is as much a person as she is, and that she has hurt him.

This recognition may be the high point in the relationship between the sexes in the play, for thereafter everything is largely downhill. In the next scene, for instance, Bernie details one of his fundamental principles of life: "The Way to Get Laid is to Treat 'Em Like Shit." As Danny observed earlier, "Nobody does it normally anymore." Herein lies the key to the play. The relationship between the sexes, Mamet says, is not natural. It may be that this stems from the very setting of modern urban society, something implied in the drama's title. It may be that life in a big city causes people to become perverted as a consequence of sharing lodgings with members of the same sex, artificially separating the sexes and reenforcing their biases and prejudices about one another through the kinds of bull sessions that fill the play. Whatever the reason, male bonding and female bonding have replaced heterosexual relationships and understandings.

The thematic content is most clearly expressed through the characters of Dan and Bernie. The themes are reflected through Deborah and Joan, too, though Mamet either does not understand women's fears of men as well as he understands men's fears of women, or he feels that he is making his point through male characters and that since the females' fears are the same, they can be seen mirroring those fears without much development. Thus, the theme of the play is simply fear of trusting the opposite sex. This fear leads to feelings of bitterness, pain, resentment, and, finally, to despair and desperation. Bernie, the older male, talks around the subject of women and meaningful (i.e., more than purely sexual) relationships with them and he tells stories about women degraded by men (as in his tale about King Farouk's habits), yet the way he talks about the things that he talks about indicates the importance of what he cannot talk about. He resorts to clichés, the idiom of the barroom, the barracks, and pornographic movie houses to avoid straightforward communication. He cannot express his needs and fears. We hear him talk about how he treats women (the radio-throwing episode, for instance), but when we see him with Joan his actions do not match his words.

What we have, then, is a picture of a man who wants and needs a relationship with a woman, but whose experience has shown him that he cannot trust them. Unfortunately, his need makes him vulnerable to rejection, and it appears that there have been frequent rejections. So he cuts himself off from others in an effort to avoid a repetition of previous pain, thereby isolating himself further as the vicious circle progresses He lies to others because he has been lied to. He sets up self-protective walls, defense mechanisms, in the form of rituals and clichés. He plays roles in attempting to conquer women, who are worthy of nothing more, but they do not respond correctly, so he gets madder. Sex becomes an instrument of revenge. . . . Bernie's thoughts, couched in the terms of the *Playboy* mentality, seem immature. Seen as a reaction to the source of his vulnerability and humiliation and to his powerful fear of rejection, however, these actions are understandable.

Joan, as Bernie's counterpart, fears being "used" sexually. This is a different fear from Bernie's, but essentially it is the same; she fears rejection as a person. Dan and Deborah are younger, so they have not met as much rejection, but it exists, as is apparent in Dan's patterns of noncommitment or exposure in his relationship with her: "So, look, so tell me. How would you like to eat dinner with me tomorrow. If you're not doing anything. If you're not too busy. If you're busy it's not important."

Bernie and Joan are harder, more fearsome, than Dan and Deborah. They serve as mentors to the younger pair—who are too shallow to perceive the mistakes of their instructors, who will follow the older pair's lead, and who will probably end with similar attitudes and approaches in their relations with the other sex. (pp. 209-11)

[*American Buffalo*] became Mamet's first play to appear on Broadway. . . . It won the New York Drama Critics Circle award for best play of 1977 and Mamet received an Obie as best playwright.

The plot is simple. In Act I, Don, owner of the shop where the action takes place, and his gofer Bob discuss a burglary that Bob plans to commit. The intended victim had visited the shop earlier and bought a buffalo-head nickel for ninety dollars, and Don thinks that the customer's apartment may be filled with valuable coins. A friend of Don's called Teach becomes involved in the planning session and tries to persuade Don to use him for the job. There is little action and the play's interest derives from psychological tensions and the constant flow of slang and the strong language used (certainly a natural idiom for these circumstances and characters).

Act II might be subtitled "Waiting for Fletcher," since most of the tension until the end of the drama revolves around whether the mysterious Fletcher will appear and the burglary be committed. Ultimately, the three men turn on each other; Teach strikes Bob in the head with a piece of junk and the play ends with the two older men about to drive Bob to the hospital.

In an interview, the dramatist claims that he meant for the play to be an indictment of the American business ethic and that his hoodlum characters are lower-class representatives of the levels of corporate employees. "We excuse all sorts of great and small betrayals and ethical compromises called business," he says. The basis for this drama, then, is that "There's really no difference between the *Lumpenproletariat* and stockbrokers or corporate lawyers who are the lackeys of business. Part of the American myth is that a difference exists, that at a certain point vicious behavior becomes laudable."

The play definitely can be read in this light, and it makes sense, though it is not sufficiently developed or epic enough to be as convincing as it might be. However, the concept of relationships is again crucial. Where *Sexual Perversity* was about the fear of establishing relationships, *American Buffalo* is about the fear of losing a relationship.

Essentially, Don is concerned with the business venture at hand. His relationship with Bob is business oriented, though there is affection displayed—he treats Bob kindly, offers Polonius-style advice, and trusts him to perform his function adequately; he lends Bob money, shows some concern over the young man's drug habits (getting upset when Teach refers to "the kid's . . . skin-pop"), and worries about the blood coming out of Bob's ear. Don makes distinctions, however, as he points out to Bob early in the play, "there's business and there's friendship." This distinction allows Don to deal with Bob in a way that does not involve a change in his relationship with Teach. Furthermore, Don's emotional range is limited to pride that his shop is a focal point for activity in the neighborhood. Otherwise he is passive. Apparently his relationship with Teach has never been verbalized and he is too contented and unconcerned to worry about it now. That he is not overly involved emotionally with Bob is demonstrated by his lack of a vehement reaction to Teach's attack.

When Teach enters, there is a change in tone. Teach perceives his relationship with Don as threatened by Bob, if Bob and Don have gone so far as to form an alliance for the burglary, and Teach's seeming anger at the way Grace and Ruth treat him really masks his feelings about Bob. His immediate reaction when he enters the shop is to begin a tirade deriding the two women, but when his explosion comes, near the end of Act II, it is directed against Bob—because of the implications of the newly emerging relationship between Bob and Don.

Teach has his definition of friendship: "I pop for coffee . . . cigarettes . . . a *sweet roll*, never say word . . . and [I] don't forget who's who when someone gets *behind* a half a yard or needs some help . . . or someone's sick." And he insists on certain distinctions: "We're talking about money. . . . We're talking about cards. Friendship is friendship, and a wonderful thing. . . . But let's just keep it *separate*." In the final analysis, Teach wants to maintain the *status quo*. Whether his relationship with Don is based on business or friendship, it demands the exclusion of Bob.

Bob is caught in the middle. He both works for and likes Don, as evidenced by his distress at having bungled the job and his buying another coin to please his boss. He is not perceptive enough, however, to realize his position vis-à-vis either Don or Teach, whatever the basis of the competition that he is unwittingly engaged in with Teach. Ironically, he is a threat to Teach only in Teach's mind.

That none of those relationships is as fully developed as that of George and Emil in *Duck Variations* is evident from the characters' dialogue, which is incomplete. These characters are more futile than those drawn by Mamet previously, and their fragmented dialogue reflects their lives. It also indicates that their thoughts and words are relatively insubstantial or unimportant, so they do not bother to finish them.

The title of the play is interesting. Obviously it may refer to the coin, which serves as a plot device and has little intrinsic value, regardless of the consequences of its existence. It might also refer to American business, which because of its excesses may be on the verge of extinction, as the buffalo has been. Or it may have significance in reference to the characters, for buffalo are large, bumbling, fairly unattractive animals and normally we do not attribute to them the same emotions and sensitivity that we might project onto other creatures. Don,

Bob, and Teach end up as innocents in regard to their planned crime. But the crime is incidental anyway. More important is their innocence in terms of being able to recognize relationships, emotions, or the connection between relationships and emotions.

The Water Engine was written in 1976 as a radio drama for National Public Radio's *Earplay*. (pp. 211-13)

The Water Engine is probably Mamet's weakest full-length published work, amounting to little more than a 1930s radio melodrama. Subtitled *An American Fable*, *The Water Engine* is epitomized by the quotation that preceeds the published text: *"The mind of man is less perturbed by a mystery he cannot explain than by an explanation he cannot understand."* Mamet's basic premise is that business is willing, even desperate, to suppress inventions that otherwise are beneficial to mankind if they endanger profits. There is a whole subgenre of popular literature that supports this theory, of course, and the dramatist has drawn on all of its clichés. Essentially he is dealing with public distrust of business and the business ethic.

In Act One it is disclosed that a young inventor, Lang, has "built an engine which used distilled water as its only fuel." After some pseudoscientific gobbledygook that is supposed to support this possibility, there are two sources of tension in the play. Briefly there is concern over whether Lang will be able to make his marvellous machine available to the public. At the end of Act One and throughout the second act the tension gains momentum as the concern becomes whether Lang and his sister Rita will be murdered by business interests in order to silence them. By the end of the play Lang's laboratory has been wrecked, he has been lied to and cheated, and he and Rita are kidnapped and murdered.

Throughout the play there are three thematic threads. First is the pervasive undercurrent of rumor ("Lindbergh came in with this *Doctor's* bag") that reflects the intermixings of society and suggests that public speculation is wildly imaginative and completely inaccurate—but is contrasted with events in the play. Many of these expressions are Whitmanesque or Sandburgian in tone. Second is the linking of trust and money in American business, as evidenced by Lang's need to pay his patent attorney, thereby insuring the lawyer's honesty—but naturally he is sold out to a higher bidder. This theme is carried by the voice over Chainletter . . . and the Soapbox Speaker, who points out that business gets its authority from its victims: "The power of the torturers comes from the love of Patriotic Songs . . . where is the *wealth?* . . . The ownership of the land. / These things do not change. / They don't change with give aways and murals." The corruption and malevolence of business is ironically apparent in the contrast between Murray's expounding on "the great essential strength of the Free Market" and the Speaker's rhetorical "What happened to this nation? Or did it exist? . . . It was all but a myth. A great dream of avarice." The third thematic thread is the connection between trust and the survival of civilization. As stated in the chainletter, "All civilization stands on trust. / All people are connected. . . . Technological and Ethical masterpieces decay into folktales."

Water Engine is Mamet's most ambitious work in terms of the large number of characters (there are eight main roles and thirty-two supporting parts) and the interweaving of subplots and themes. It is almost epic or heroic in its treatment of society and in the actions of Lang. It is also more accessible and more acceptable to a general audience than most of the playwright's pieces since *Duck Variations*. The theme is traditional, shallow, and melodramatic (with a thirties' tone; B-grade Odets), and relatively straightforward. It is cinematic in nature, possibly because of its radio origins; there is more action, a different kind of suspense and general tone, almost like a Charlie Chan movie. And the language is not flavored with Mamet's typical spice of four-letter words.

Where in all of this are the interpersonal relationships? Nowhere. Not every play has to be a serious endeavor and for Mamet this drama was an exercise rather than a statement. It lacks the emotional intensity and involvement of his other works. The style is diffuse and there is little significance in the play, but the author probably enjoyed writing it, just as he enjoys working on children's dramas. (pp. 214-15)

[*Reunion*] is the playwright's most affecting and human work since *Duck Variations*. The situation is simple. After a separation of twenty years, fifty-three-year-old Bernie is reunited with his twenty-four-year-old daughter, Carol. As they talk about their lives and bring each other up to date, it is evident that the father needs and wants to reestablish a relationship with his daughter and the daughter needs and wants to reestablish a relationship with her father. Mamet's drama beautifully depicts the touching way in which they communicate, hesitatingly, as a renewed bond is formed.

The conversation realistically bounces from thought to thought about the past and the present. The two are not sure what they have in common or whether the other will reciprocate emotionally. We learn a lot through the play's fourteen scenes: Bernie was a machine gunner in World War II, he was hospitalized for back trouble, worked for a van line and the phone company, he had a second wife and a son, is a Democrat, has friends, works in a restaurant, was an alcoholic, and is thinking about remarrying; Carol has been married for two years to a man who already had two sons, but she is unhappy in the marriage because her husband is "a lousy fuck." More vital, though, is their need for each other. Naturally they display curiosity about what the other is like and has been doing, but the crux of the play is that they need to overcome their separation. (pp. 215-16)

The final scene is appropriate. Out of his love for his daughter Bernie has gotten her a gold bracelet. Human fallibility intrudes, for the present is marred—there is an error in the inscription. Yet despite the flaw, the message is clear; the gift is intrinsically too valuable to be damaged by superficialities. . . . It is fitting that the time of the play is early March, the beginning of the season of renewal, for the relationship between father and daughter has been reestablished. (p. 216)

[*Dark Pony* is very] short, it is a sketch consisting of a father telling his four-year-old daughter a story about an Indian and his friend Dark Pony as they drive home at night.

As in *Reunion,* the two characters are very human and the play is a powerful theatrical moment. The father and daughter have shared the ritual of this story in the past—they announce the brave's name simultaneously when it is time to do so in the story. The daughter is a typical four-year-old—literal minded; when Rain Boy is described as running "like a deer," she wants to know if he hopped. The father becomes engrossed in his mythmaking and is moved by the plight of an Indian who thinks that he has been deserted by a magical horse, a feeling with which the father identifies.

On the one hand, the play shows the closeness of the father and daughter. On the other, the generation gap is apparent, for the daughter's involvement in the story ceases when she recognizes that they are almost home, but she does not realize her father's emotional reaction. He is concerned with the need for a father-like companion who helps when needed, she with the security of home. The father's final words, "Dark Pony, Rain Boy calls to you," may be a call for help in the dark—and his daughter's final words may be the answer: "We are almost home."

A Life in the Theatre premiered . . .on October 20, 1977. Its critical reception was more enthusiastic than for any of Mamet's other plays—perhaps due to its subject matter, the theatre. Because of this favorable reaction, the drama became the first of the playwright's plays to be filmed. . . .

In twenty-six scenes the dramatist displays veteran actor Robert and relative newcomer John solo and interacting, on stage during performances and off-stage between scenes, performances, or productions. Ostensibly about the theatre, the day to day life of two characters, the play obviously uses its subject to discourse dramatically on life in general, the role of art in society, the relationships between teacher and pupil, the generations, and man and man. Throughout the play a number of statements clearly draw superficial parallels between the theatre and life. (p. 217)

Related to the theatre as life theme is the teacher/student subtheme. Besides the phenomena control idea, Robert tries to impart wisdom on a wide variety of subjects. He speaks about self-control, initiates John into the theatre's superstitions (knocking on wood), holds forth on the importance of developing voice control and keeping a straight back, reflects middle-class values in his comment about his younger colleague's admirable care of his tools, and offers advice about whose advice should be heeded. Robert is basically a contemporary Polonius. Conservative, a traditionalist who opts for law and reason in the theatre and in life, his lessons are essentially inconsequential. He affects a liberal artistic stance, yet he decries artistic experimentation. As a result, his role as teacher is a hollow one.

As was the case with *American Buffalo,* though, there is both less and more to this play than might be assumed from the foregoing. It is too episodic and sketchy to develop the theatre/life metaphor fully. Some critics have complained about the stereotypes, clichés, and superficialities, and there is an incompleteness about the characters because they are always playing roles, on stage and off. At the same time, while there is no specific indication of the passage of time, taken together the scenes create a time-lapse montage that is sufficient to trace the stages of development in the relationship between the two men. When the play opens John is in awe of Robert. He does not know the other actor well enough to predict his reactions, but he wants to please the older man. The conversation regarding the doctor scene in that evening's performance exposes John's uncertainty and his shifting evaluation of an actress's looks betrays his toadying attitude. Caught off guard by Robert's responses, John makes a comment about the table scene that is much less expansive, for he is apprehensive and wants to know which way to jump before he commits himself to either praise or criticism. Robert postures through this and many of the following scenes, alternately playing with and patronizing John, though it is not until scene seven that he is willing to antagonize his younger companion when he reacts defensively to the other's actions on stage, and even then this is done under the guise of offering a neophyte advice based on the wisdom of experience. In scene nine, however, Robert's grand posture is weakened when he confuses a line on stage and John saves him. By scene thirteen John is beginning to find Robert's pose tiresome and is unimpressed by the insights that the older man gleans from the lifeboat script; the opening scene's atmosphere of ingratiation is gone by scene seventeen when John can yell at Robert to stop his inane babbling. At this point the relationship begins to shift again. Robert has taught John about snobbery and decorum by example and by declamation; now he relates John's ''breach of etiquette'' not just with society and by extension with the theatre but also with ''our personal relationship with each other.'' In scene twenty-two that relationship appears to be becoming an unhappy one when Robert reacts jealously to some of John's reviews and John responds in a pique, and scene twenty-three reenforces this assessment as John is put out by Robert's watching him rehearse from the wings. Robert's attitude is different from what it has been, though. In this scene his concern with the ongoing traditions of the theatre becomes personalized and he watches with the fondness of a proud father as John performs. Scene twenty-five reveals that John likewise is genuinely concerned with Robert when the older man cuts himself. In the final scene even petty jealousies over each other's lives outside the theatre have been put aside as the relationship has matured and the men can part for the evening with shared respect and affection.

In part *A Life in the Theatre* delineates the decline of one actor and the concurrent rise of another, but more importantly through a variety of circumstances and over a long period of time it shows how two men overcome obstacles to form a solid relationship. Scene twenty-four serves as a miniature of the play and of the relationships: there are muffed lines, attempts to help each other, displays of misplaced self-confidence, and anger: As in life, in the theatre parts run over into other plays and into life itself. But through it all there is an underlying sense of good humor and, ultimately, proportion that binds the men together.

The Woods was first produced . . . on November 11, 1977. In it Mamet returns to the theme of relations between the sexes that operated in *Sexual Perversity,* but this play has been tempered by the theme of love that moves through *Reunion* and *Dark Pony,* producing a more intimate, personal, and closer view than that of *Sexual Perversity*. As a result, the characters and situation are more fully drawn and the rendering is more accurate—and maybe more typical.

The three scenes follow the logical construct of thesis, antithesis, and synthesis. In scene one, we learn what the characters want and need from a relationship and that their desires are similar. Nick has brought Ruth to his family's cabin in the woods. She is in love with him and enthusiastic about life. We find out in scene two that Ruth believes that his having brought her means that he is committed to their relationship and she is expansive and philosophical: ''So little counts. . . . Just the things we do. . . . To each other. The right things.'' The cabin is a pleasant sanctuary where she finds security and happiness in her lover's companionship. (pp. 218-20)

Scene two takes place at night. Now the needs of the two are patently at odds. Ruth is still verbalizing her dream. . . . Nick's dream, ''we would meet and we would just be happy'' is more barren in detail and he has begun to tire of her constant talk, so he tries to take what he wants—and she has given freely previously. He tries to force her sexually. When she rejects

his physical attack, Nick complains that there is nothing to do in the woods, even though Ruth has been cataloguing activities throughout the play. She has become a sexual objective for him and he cares about little else, thus becoming frustrated, bored, and uninterested in her. Ruth responds that he cannot force something merely because he wants it and that he does not treat her with respect; Nick tells her that she talks too much. Ruth tries to reverse the mood, presenting Nick with a gold bracelet as a symbol of her eternal love, but he rejects her. When he refuses her offer of sex as proof of her love, she feels that she must leave.

Reconciliation is at the heart of scene three. Nick does not want to break off the relationship completely, but Ruth does. Having wanted to know all about him, she now knows too much: ''The worst part, maybe, is just learning little *things*. . . . about each other.'' One thing that she learns is that the basis of his relationship with her is limited: ''I want to fuck you.'' This statement brings a tirade from her in which she accuses him of not being a man, of having ''bizarre'' fantasies, and of being afraid; and in anger she tries to strike him with an oar. Instead, he strikes her, knocking her off the porch. This is the turning point in the play. The recognition of his physical violence causes Nick to regard Ruth as human again and for the first time he can expose his own vulnerability. His shock at having hit her brings a revelation of his dream which parallels the one that she articulated in the first scene. . . . [Nick] claims that he needs time to separate himself from the influence of the city, that he needs her and he equates being alone with death. Having expressed this understanding of himself, Nick admits that he brought Ruth to the cabin because he loves her and he can finally say ''I love you.'' Ruth can now accept him and the relationship and the play ends with them hanging on, partly in love and partly in a desperate need to be together. The title of the play is taken from its setting, of course, but it also has reverberations with the Grimm fairytale of the two children who become lost in the woods and huddle together in each others arms in a vain attempt to comfort and support one another as they die. (pp. 220-21)

Mamet is still young . . . , yet his work is consistently more imaginative, sensitive, and technically superior to the dramatists of his own generation and it surpasses in promise that of the previous generation. In the eight years that he has been writing he has produced several minor gems as well as a body of solid work. Clearly his style improves as he becomes more certain of his major themes. As he progresses, his plays reflect a more and more accurate and personal rendering of interpersonal relationships. As he becomes more concerned with his characters as people and less concerned with them as symbolic representations, his dramas become less abstract and more moving. His characters become less desperate and as a result more normal and real. And it is here that Mamet's greatest promise lies, for he has had an ability to write effective theatre from the beginning. His future looks bright; he is likely to become a standard against which his contemporaries will be measured. (pp. 221-22)

Steven H. Gale, ''David Mamet: The Plays, 1972-1980,'' in Essays on Contemporary American Drama, *edited by Hedwig Bock and Albert Wertheim, Max Hueber, 1981, pp. 207-23.*

FRANK P. CALTABIANO

One of the unfortunate consequences of exhuming, or discovering, and publishing later early works of art practitioners who have achieved some status or notoriety is that a lot of unworthy material gets exhibited which otherwise would not have been given a second viewing. . . . *Lakeboat,* by popular American playwright David Mamet, first staged in 1970, is the present case in point. . . .

Lakeboat contains some early indications of this talent but is nonetheless an uninteresting play which should have been either rewritten or forgotten.

The setting and the situations in the play promise more than is delivered. Several hands on a commercial vessel which ferries cargo across Lake Michigan are seen in twenty-seven blackout scenes and sketches which are supposed to reveal the hearts, minds, aspirations and frustrations of these socially and psychologically locked-in shipmates. Instead of doing so, they lapse into predictable exchanges sustained only by the foul language so common to Mamet characters. Such language is here conveniently appropriate, of course, because these are rough men engaged in very rough work. The verbal color, however, does not thicken the play's substance. It is a work which at best could be made into a mildly entertaining evening by a group of interesting actors.

Part of what limits Mamet, in my view, and what separates his from the more substantial works of Sam Shepard and Ronald Ribman is that Mamet has no real vision for raising the sights or bettering the plight of the ordinary guy caught in the wake of the dissolving American dream. Where Shepard, Ribman and, to a degree, Lanford Wilson have worked toward the evolution of some kind of survival action for their major characters, Mamet chooses merely to record their present state in much the same way that television sitcoms do.

> *Frank P. Caltabiano, in a review of "Lakeboat," in* World Literature Today, *Vol. 56, No. 3, Summer, 1982, p. 518.*

ROBERT BRUSTEIN

Edmond is a remarkably cruel play—ruthless, remorseless, unremittingly ugly. Written in that terse banal naturalism that has become Mamet's staccato trademark, it follows the spiritual journey of a stocky middle-class young man who wakes up one morning to tell his wife that he is deserting her. Leaving the safety of his home, he embarks on a terrifying odyssey through the urban landscape, looking for sexual and other satisfactions but instead finding violence and fraud. Beaten up and robbed, he buys a knife for protection; mugged by a pimp, he turns on his attacker and kills him.

In his developing madness, Edmond becomes one with the hostile world he has invaded until in a particularly brutal scene he stabs to death a waitress who has taken him home. His whole being is now riddled with hatred—of blacks, of women, of humankind itself: "This world is a piece of shit. There is no law. There is no history."

Eventually, Edmond is apprehended and imprisoned. His cellmate, a gigantic sleepy-eyed black man, listens stoically to Edmond's philosophizing before unzipping himself and forcing Edmond to commit an act of fellatio. . . . In the final scene, Edmond is on the lower bunk talking to his cellmate above about the nature of God and the universe ("Maybe we're here to be punished. . . . Do you think we go somewhere when we die?"). When he is finished with this primitive, oddly affecting metaphysics, he reaches up, in the last gesture of the play, to kiss goodnight the man who sodomized him and hold his hand.

What Mamet has written is a version of *Woyzeck* in the modern city, displaying not only Buechner's hallucinatory power but also the same capacity to show compassion for lowly, inarticulate wretches without mitigating their awful fates. He has pushed our faces into a world which most of us spend our waking hours trying to avoid, finding a kind of redemption in the bleakest, most severe alternatives. I don't think he will be thanked much for this, but I for one want to express gratitude. . . . (p. 24)

> *Robert Brustein, "The Shape of the New," in* The New Republic, *Vol. 187, No. 2, July 12, 1982, pp. 23-4.*

FRANK RICH

According to a fortuneteller who appears in the first scene of David Mamet's *Edmond,* everything in life is "predetermined." If you can buy that, you just may believe Mr. Mamet's play, which tells of a respectable New York businessman who walks out on his wife to explore Manhattan's sleaziest wild side, and, ipso facto, plunges into degradation, madness and murder.

But theatergoers who take a more skeptical view of the powers of fate, especially as employed by playwrights, may have a different reaction to *Edmond.* They may conclude, as I did, that on this occasion Mr. Mamet is spinning hooey and neglecting his valuable gifts. In plays like *American Buffalo, Sexual Perversity in Chicago* and *The Water Engine,* Mr. Mamet has demonstrated an uncommon ability to hear the voices of inarticulate Americans and to limn the society that oppresses them. Though the thematic concerns are similar in *Edmond,* the author's ear has gone tone-deaf, and his social observations have devolved into clichés. . . .

[The language] sounds just like that in another ill-fated Mamet effort, *The Woods.* All the characters in *Edmond* have the same diction—even down to their choice of obscenities. It's a clipped, vague form of speech that approximates the manner of Beckett (and, at times, Büchner), but leaves out the substance and spice. Simple declarative sentences are repeated needlessly; questions are answered with evasions or other questions. Yet whenever Mr. Mamet wants to come to a point, he just announces it—in authorial lines like, "The world seems to be crumbling around us," or "You can't control what you make of your life," or "There is no law, there is no history—there is just now."

Mr. Mamet dishes out his stylization as if he, too, were a three-card monte dealer: it's a shell game designed to distract us from the fact that he's not playing with a full deck. Look closely, and even the play's premise doesn't add up. Why is Edmond, a New York resident, such a naïve rube that he's shocked or bilked by nearly every stereotypical street hustler he encounters as soon as he leaves his home? Why does he then, without any visible transition, turn from a milquetoast into an avenger as fearless as Charles Bronson in *Death Wish*? "Predetermination" isn't a satisfactory answer. Neither is the play's underlying, knee-jerk sociological bromide that the dehumanized urban jungle reduces all who enter it into beasts.

Eventually, God also gets some blame—He must create a new world "where people are kind to each other"—but not before Mr. Mamet plays God himself by finding the redemptive side to his protagonist's behavior. As the author has it, Edmond's acting out of his darkest impulses allows him to achieve a liberating spiritual breakthrough; he discovers who he really is, which makes him finally understand that everyone he hates (women, blacks, homosexuals) are "people, too." This allows the evening to end with an unearned sentimental tableau in which the hero holds hands with the cellmate who had earlier raped him.

Because Edmond is a device, not a character, and because Mr. Mamet will toss off any fortune-cookie message to paper over the play's various narrative, philosophical and psychological shortcircuits, *Edmond* can, by the end, mean almost anything you wish.

> *Frank Rich, "Mamet's 'Edmond' at the Province-town," in* The New York Times, *October 28, 1982, p. C20.*

STANLEY KAUFFMANN

David Mamet, an occasionally interesting playwright, adapted the screenplay [of *The Verdict*] from a novel by Barry Reed, which I haven't read. The script has a nice pop-cynical tone, and it comes through when it absolutely must deliver: [Galvin's] summation to the jury. This speech is terse and pungent: the powerful have the power to convert all the rest of us into victims and that condition probably cannot be changed, but must it *always* prevail?

The script has its bumps, though. Would [Galvin] have turned down a hefty settlement offer without consulting his clients, the woman's sister and brother-in-law? Would he have opted for trial without a deposition in hand from his key witness? Would his new lady-friend have carried telltale evidence in her pocketbook? And would the bishop be willing to blink, as he does, at the fact that a surprise witness has shown the hospital to be truly criminal? Would he have been willing to shield the guilty behind the legal technicality invoked?

The film's firm qualities themselves make these flaws stand out. The visual texture and the acting are so thorough that the plot mechanics obtrude especially, as if we could spot cracks in the scenery of a gripping theater melodrama. (p. 24)

> *Stanley Kauffmann, "Trial and Tribulation," in* The New Republic, *Vol. 187, No. 3544, December 20, 1982, pp. 24-5.*

DAVID DENBY

Like all courtroom dramas, *The Verdict* is at times hokey and manipulative and implausible. No matter how many twists and surprises are thrown in, the trial format always feels rigged and a little constricted—perhaps because it requires more clearly defined answers than other kinds of art and also a certain overdramatization of themes. Yet this is certainly one of the finest courtroom movies ever made. Working from a novel by Barry Reed, David Mamet has constructed a terse, elliptical screenplay with some of the best dialogue heard on the screen this year. Mamet brings a satisfyingly rough edge to the sardonic lawyers' chat, to the rancid jokes and malice of a corrupt judge showing off in his chambers. The sharp, nasty talk becomes even more tonic and necessary when we realize that Mamet has involved us in an essentially religious conception of the law. For Galvin is like nothing so much as a parish priest who has lost his faith. He's gone past cynicism, and yet he's not quite dead. The spirit of the law has died in him, but he knows that it's still alive in other people. As he explains

to Laura . . . , the shady lady with the hurt mouth who becomes his lover, the system may favor the powerful and the rich, but as long as judgment is left to a jury—twelve ordinary men and women—it can never be completely corrupt. Galvin believes in what Marcel Ophuls, in his documentary on the Nuremberg trials, called "the memory of justice"—the notion that everyone carries an ideal of true justice around in him, an ideal that occasionally becomes law. The movie shows how he redeems himself by reaching for that ideal. . . .

Part of the reason we're caught is that the filmmakers are smart enough not to treat us like slobs. This isn't the kind of upbeat movie in which the hero sweeps the empty bottles into the garbage one morning, squares his shoulders, and staggers out to face the rising sun. Galvin undergoes many moments of panic, doubt, weakness. (p. 62)

Corruption has indeed become [Mamet's and] Lumet's great subject. In a modern corporate state, good and evil may not be clear, and many people wander around in a fog of compromise, torn between ambition and guilt. . . . But Galvin's soul isn't nearly so tormented. . . . He saves himself by making a leap of faith. . . . Galvin's making himself clean is a genuine moral triumph. (p. 64)

> *David Denby, "Rough Justice," in* New York Magazine, *Vol. 15, No. 50, December 20, 1982, pp. 62, 64.*

GERALD WEALES

[*Edmond*] is uncharacteristic in a couple of ways. For one thing, its view of contemporary society is darker, more savage than anything else Mamet has written, although the implications of *The Water Engine* as *An American Fable* (its subtitle) or even the screenplay for *The Verdict* before the happy ending sets in indicate Mamet's grave distrust of economic and institutional power. In *Edmond*, the corruption is universal, a societal malaise—sleaze, more accurately—that infects everyone. To depict that condition, Mamet abandons his customary use of completely conceived characters and writes a skeletal descent-into-hell drama that suggests nothing so much as a play like Georg Kaiser's *From Morn to Midnight*. Although Mamet's hero has a name, he is a representative figure like Kaiser's Cashier, and the rest of the characters, as in Kaiser, are identified by relationship (wife) or function (hotel clerk) or place of encounter (man in a bar). Edmond walks out on his loveless marriage and, in a series of short scenes, loses his middle-class identity, becoming first a victim, then a victimizer. Mamet's choices are almost all from the ugliest side of urban life (pimps, con men, whores), and one of the limitations of the play is that this milieu has to stand for other layers of society which *Edmond* seldom deals with directly.

Mamet's indictment is more complex than that of Kaiser, for the American playwright's concern is with the ways in which we become part of our destructive surroundings. "And every fear hides a wish—a wish that the worst would happen, putting a stop to our anxiety and our responsibility," Mamet told the *Christian Science Monitor*. "That's the basic point of *Edmond*." The remark is a paraphrase of one of Edmond's lines, spoken after he has been imprisoned for murder and before he is forced to go down on another prisoner. The amorphousness of Edmond's remarks and his almost headlong plunge into the abyss that has brought him here seem to confirm the connection between fear and wish, but the "basic point" seems to me obliquely related to that. One of the most effective scenes in the play is the one in which Edmond, bleeding from a brutal beating, stumbles into a hotel in search of a phone and the clerk cannot bring himself to answer a simple plea, not for help but for information. "Do you want to live in this kind of world?" Edmond asks, and the play seems to answer *yes,* for Edmond too. (pp. 604-05)

The *Monitor,* in an indirect quotation from Mamet, reports "an upbeat twist at the end" of *Edmond,* although I find it hard to see. It is true that Edmond seems to have found shelter, a home of sorts, in his prison cell and that his relationship with his fellow prisoner is apparently closer than that with his wife. This is not the crucifixion with which *From Morn to Midnight* ends, but I can find nothing but irony in the final scene, both in its coziness and its anchorless philosophical discussion of Hell and Heaven. Besides, the final image . . . is one of isolation. Edmond steps up on his bunk and kisses his cellmate in the bed above; he then gets down and, as he settles in his own bed, their hands, which have been touching, slowly separate. Only disconnect. (p. 605)

> Gerald Weales, "American Theater Watch, 1982-1983," in The Georgia Review, *Vol. XXXVII, No. 3, Fall, 1983, pp. 601-11.*

CLIVE BARNES

Mr. Mamet is at his best in miniatures—plays poised like operas on a sea of musical words, and containing the kernel of an idea—poetic fortune cookies floating with drama.

Even the biggest of them are small-scaled. But in [*Prairie du Chien* and *The Shawl*] . . . miniaturization has been taken beyond any natural limit.

Prairie du Chien is nothing but an incomprehensible tall story told by a traveler on a train, while two other men play an antiphonal game of poker which erupts into unexpected violence. Why?

The more substantial, or at least longer, *The Shawl,* concerns a medium who insists to himself and his mysterious assistant that his psychic powers are fake, but is quite conceivably the real thing. Why?

The plays, slices of atmosphere rather than life, have much the same purposeless attitudinizing that afflicted Mamet's earlier dialogue for sad lovers, *The Woods.*

When Mr. Mamet is pretentious he can become exceedingly tedious, and as a playwright he seems to lack self-criticism more than self-discipline, for even his apparently empty plays have their vacuums well-crafted, with their vacuity actually given a certain verbal style.

And his plays must be fun for actors and directors alike, because the most elusive and wispy of them, like these two, breathe theatricality like oxygen. (p. 96)

> Clive Barnes, "Lincoln Center Reopens: 2 by Mamet," in New York Post, *December 24, 1985. Reprinted in* New York Theatre Critics' Reviews, *Vol. XXXXVI, No. 18, Week of December 23, 1985, pp. 95-6.*

FRANK RICH

Mr. Mamet can be one of the best writers we have, but [*The Shawl* and *Prairie du Chien*] are trivial, largely humorless ef-

forts—the Mamet of *Mr. Happiness* and *The Woods,* not *American Buffalo* and *Glengarry Glen Ross.* . . .

[*The Shawl*] is the more substantial of the pair, but it never gathers any of the metaphorical force of Mr. Mamet's best spooky play, *The Water Engine.* It tells of a flimflam artist, a middle-aged psychic named John . . . who might be a cousin to the salesmen of *Glengarry.* In a few brief scenes set in his threadbare parlor, we watch John attempt to cheat a grieving woman . . . out of her inheritance even as he tries to retain the affection of his restless young male lover, Charles. . . .

John wants to teach Charles the tricks of his phony trade: Explaining that "divination" is only "common sense," the fortuneteller demonstrates how anyone can guess a gullible customer's secrets with the aid of deduction, psychotherapeutic questioning and library research. But Mr. Mamet seems to be saying, rather sentimentally, that "a world without mystery" is a world without romance. The play's narrative twists, more contrived than surprising, leave us with the observation that, in telepathy and love alike, trust and a heap of faith can make one's wishes come magically true. . . .

Set in an old-time night train running from Chicago to Duluth, [*Prairie du Chien*] unfolds two violent tales simultaneously: One is a lengthy anecdote of jealousy and murder recited by a mysterious stranger . . . ; the other is a contentious onstage gin game conducted by two of the car's occupants. . . . The links between the two tales are schematic, as is the contrast set up between the cynical, insomniac storyteller and an innocent little boy . . . who sleeps through the adult nefariousness around him.

There is little sense of menace or tension, as there must be, to the mostly static action of a play in which we're told that "murder is in the air."

> Frank Rich, "Lincoln Center Presents 2 One-Acts," in The New York Times, *December 24, 1985, p. C11.*

ROBERT BRUSTEIN

[David Mamet's] two short plays, *Prairie du Chien* and *The Shawl,* which while miniature, provide a bigger lift than most things I've seen lately. (p. 26)

Prairie du Chien began as a radio play, and it unravels on the stage like a Faulkner short story. . . . But this gothic vignette has intriguing supernatural overtones. When men come to investigate the murder of the hired hand, they find no one in the house except a glowing fawn and a pretty red dress, burning in the closet. Three years later the sheriff himself is discovered in a rocking chair, wearing a red gingham dress and saying, "Please help him . . . there in the barn . . . please help him." The play ends with an outburst of violence on the part of one of the card players, who pulls a gun on the partner he believes to be cheating him.

This atmosphere of unearthliness in a naturalistic setting is even more intense in the companion play, *The Shawl.* This concerns a middle-aged medium named John preparing, with the aid of his black male lover, Charles, to swindle a young woman who has come to him for counsel. (pp. 26, 28)

All . . . is spoken in that terse, elliptical style—replete with interrupted sentences—that is the hallmark of Mamet's writing, but the new element is the suggestion of the supernatural and the mystical, all the more haunting for its quotidian context. . . .

The Shawl reminds me of one of Yeats's few contemporary prose plays, *Word Upon the Windowpane,* another story of a fake psychic unexpectedly possessed by a spirit (in her case, that of Jonathan Swift). Mamet is on a fascinating new trip that promises to open up whole new countries; it is characteristic, but no less cause for celebration, that his first tickets to mystery should be such a modest pair of ghost stories. (p. 28)

Robert Brustein, "The Infidelity Play," in The New Republic, Vol. 194, No. 6, February 10, 1986, pp. 25-6, 28.

RICHARD CHRISTIANSEN

The 30 pieces collected in David Mamet's [*Writing in Restaurants*] contain everything from random thoughts to firmly held convictions, but they all exhibit the author's singular insights and moral bearing. . . .

Even the most amusing of these short observations—and **"True Stories of Bitches"** is quite funny—are infused with Mamet's desire to build strong, intelligent relationships with his fellow man.

Many of the essays have to do with drama, naturally, but whether he is talking to a group of critics or to fellow workers in the theater, Mamet is always urging his audience to go beyond craft and into a proud, dignified, loving commitment to their art and to the people with whom they work. . . .

His sense of humor saves Mamet from being a ponderous preacher, but unquestionably he *is* a preacher, damning the corrupters of the marketplace and exalting the pure in heart who would join with him in creating a theater of committed artists.

The passionate bonding of souls is what attracts Mamet to the scenes of pool halls and poker games, where he can absorb and celebrate the style and intensity of the participants. He deplores the loss of faith in religion; he despises meaningless, amalgamation holidays, and he exults in the rituals of the Super Bowl and Academy Awards, both occasions that truly unite the people who are watching them. . . .

The rootlessness of modern man, the break-up of loving relationships, the tragic human waste caused by greed, the pride in professionalism, the love of theater, and the desire for a world of serenity and confidence—all these themes have been vividly, specifically dramatized in Mamet's *American Buffalo, Glengarry Glen Ross, Edmond* and *Sexual Perversity in Chicago.*

They are all here, too, in these graceful, fanciful, hortatory essays of a profoundly moral writer of our time.

Richard Christiansen, "'Writing in Restaurants': David Mamet's Passionately Moral Notes on Our Time," in Chicago Tribune, January 18, 1987, p. 7.

DAVID DENBY

[*The Untouchables,* a] staunchly heroic chronicle of gangbusting in the early thirties is filled with shiny, flat-topped cars and blazing tommy guns. It's a celebration of law enforcement as American spectacle—a straightforward, broadly entertaining movie, though not nearly as interesting as you would expect from David Mamet (screenwriter) and Brian De Palma (director). Their smartest move was to make the murdering Capone an essentially public man—a sententious thug, vain of his prowess as an after-dinner speaker. In public, Capone is merry: He knows that he titillates the journalists, pols, and society types who gather to pay him tribute, so he ravishes his audience with veiled threats against enemies. And when he talks to gangsters, he's a tease, expounding his theories of crime with sweet reasonableness—and then committing acts of violence so outrageously lurid that even the pomaded hoods are shocked into silence. . . .

In the arts, evil is irresistible, virtue often dull. Mamet and De Palma, telling the story from the good guys' point of view, have succumbed to this syndrome. Ness the family man, holding hands with his wife; Ness the man who won't take a drink because it's against the law. . . . We look for a touch of irony, a subversive intent. But there isn't any. . . .

In his plays and movie scripts, David Mamet has created classic portraits of American thieves, hucksters, and weaklings. But Mamet may lack the imagination of goodness. When we first see Ness, he's a proper young Treasury officer who speaks in wooden sentences, a brave, incorruptible man who knows nothing of violent Chicago methods. How can you lick Al Capone if you're the kind of G-man who worries about a rolling baby carriage in the middle of a shoot-out? (p. 68)

David Denby, "Big Caesar," in New York Magazine, Vol. 20, No. 23, June 8, 1987, pp. 68-9.

TERRENCE RAFFERTY

In *The Untouchables,* De Palma unleashes his strangely moving sense of perceptual dread in the big violent scenes, and he gets the effects he wants. Actually, the picture comes closest to achieving some kind of emotional depth in its showiest and most overdetermined moments. . . . But the emotions are transient, because Mamet's script doesn't give them a coherent context. Although formally *The Untouchables* is an exceptionally straightforward old-Hollywood narrative, Mamet's just a bit too hip, too ironic to pin himself down to a classic gangster-movie tone. The movie isn't sentimental and street-tragic the way the Warner Brothers pictures of the 1930s were . . . (Capone, though funny and charismatic, is clearly a monster, and his henchmen are grotesque). It comes nearer to the other available convention—the righteous, heroic, government-authorized mode of F.B.I. movies—but Mamet clearly isn't comfortable with that, either. He keeps us aware throughout that the law Ness and his men are enforcing, Prohibition, is a stupid one, and, at various points, suggests that the battle against Capone is a game, a play, a ritual. It's scrupulous of him to acknowledge this, and also too easy: it separates the audience's (contemporary) consciousness from the characters'. Whatever suspicions the Untouchables may have about the value of their mission, the moral ambiguity never seems to affect their behavior as characters, to have any dramatic consequences. Mamet tries, halfheartedly, to re-establish the mythic verities of good versus evil by portraying Ness as a family man bent on protecting the innocent, decent middle-class home from the indiscriminate fury of the gangs. But he can't quite put over that old-movie corn, either—he keeps snickering about what a boy scout Ness is, and obviously relishes stripping him of his scruples in the course of the picture. (p. 901)

Mamet's script provides a solid movie-action framework for the material without supplying a fully satisfying attitude toward it. His treatment is neither simple enough to be purely rousing nor complex enough to be disturbing: this evasiveness keeps *The Untouchables* from being a classic. (pp. 901-02)

Terrence Rafferty, in a review of "The Untouchables," in The Nation, *New York, Vol. 244, No. 25, June 27, 1987, pp. 900-02.*

PAULINE KAEL

[With *The Untouchables* Brian De Palma is] making a self-consciously square movie. He works within the structure of Mamet's moral fable, and Mamet is a master of obviousness. This writer is all deliberation—his points are unavoidable. Yet his characters have a fullness: you get what you need to know about each one. His dialogue is pointed; it has tension. And the scenes have a satisfying economy. He's a good engineer, and his construction provides De Palma with the basis for reaching a broad audience. (p. 71)

There's no getting around it: though *The Untouchables* is De Palma's only measured film, it's a blood thriller. It works for an audience because of the excitement you feel when the four heroes overcome their misgivings and their tremors, and go in for the kill. The Old Testament language is, finally, preparation and justification for attacking the mobsters with the only means at hand. And when, near the end, Ness arrests the mob's white-suited enforcer, Frank Nitti, and Nitti taunts him, saying that he'll be let out by the courts, and then tells a spiteful lie about Malone, we can see Ness's need to release his anger. . . . [The] audience wants it to happen, *needs* it to happen. Ness says at the beginning that he will do anything "within the law" to destroy Capone's grip on the city; the point of his character is that as he gets to know himself better he learns he'll do more.

This is too programmatic. The way Mamet designs his celebration of law enforcement, Ness's giving in to his vengeful impulse completes the plan. It's what is supposed to show that he's human—that he's grown. For some of us, this takes the air right out of his actions, and he's left a little wooden. Mamet doesn't allow the characters enough free will. But, in an impressive, four-square way, he fills out the audience's expectations. He gives you revenge—an eye for an eye—and makes it seem just and righteous. It's a relief when the film doesn't take itself so seriously—when it tosses in such burlesque stunts as a judge's ordering a jury that Capone has suborned to switch places with the jury in the courtroom next door, and then has Capone's counsel changing his client's plea from not guilty to guilty without consulting him. It's as if the stern Mamet had left the room and the kids were playing.

The Untouchables is not a great movie; it's too banal, too morally comfortable. The great gangster pictures don't make good and evil mutually exclusive, the way they are here. (Even Ness's deliberate violence, when he turns judge and executioner, is meant to be good: he's carrying out Biblical law.) But it's a great audience movie—a wonderful potboiler, like *I Pagliacci.* It's a rouser. And if people laugh and cheer when the gangsters get their heads blown off they're probably not cheering real death. These gangsters aren't the lawless aspect of ourselves—the sly, manipulative part, the killer part. They're just sleazeball monsters. (p. 72)

Pauline Kael, "Broad Strokes," in The New Yorker, *Vol. LXIII, No. 19, June 29, 1987, pp. 70-2.*

Timothy Mo

1950-

Hong Kong-born English novelist, journalist, and critic.

Mo is best known for his seriocomic novels revolving around the lives of expatriates. Drawing much of his material from his own English and Chinese heritage, Mo examines the problems immigrants encounter while adapting to foreign cultures. He is praised by many critics for his authentic dialogue and his descriptive talent, and his insider's perspective on the cultural clash between Eastern and Western society has prompted several critics to label his novels as original and insightful. Mary Hope commented: "With a foot in both camps, Mo keeps his Chinese tongue firmly in his British cheek with devastating effect."

The Monkey King (1978), Mo's first novel, is set in Hong Kong and centers on the life of Wallace Nolasco, a young man from the Portuguese colony of Macao who marries into a large, traditional Chinese family headed by the domineering Mr. Poon. Shunned by his in-laws, Wallace struggles to maintain his cultural identity. He secures a position in his father-in-law's business and is assigned to manage one of Mr. Poon's mainland properties, where he begins to accept the traditional ways of the Chinese and earns the respect of Mr. Poon, who eventually names him heir to his business empire. Mo's second novel, *Sour Sweet* (1982), chronicles the lives of the Chens, a working-class Chinese immigrant family living in London, and their attempts to retain their cultural values. The Chens gradually learn to embrace the social customs of their new country when they open a restaurant and begin to interact with their English patrons. Interwoven with the Chens's story is that of the Hungs, another immigrant family involved in such criminal activities as drug trafficking and racketeering. Most critics lauded Mo for his vivid depiction of London's Chinatown district and for his deft handling of several family crises. Jonathan Yardley remarked that "nothing about the novel is so clear as that Timothy Mo deeply loves these eccentric and spunky people he has created. He has given them qualities that are distinctly Chinese, and qualities that are distinctly human, and what he has to tell us is that the two are exuberantly the same."

An Insular Possession (1986) marks a change of direction in Mo's fiction. A historical novel that took him five years to complete, *An Insular Possession* is set during the First Opium War between China and England and concerns two young American journalists who campaign to halt the British-backed importation of opium into China. Mo includes excerpts of letters, diaries, and newspaper clippings to add to the authenticity of his story. Most critics found the novel very demanding in scope and difficult to read in various sections, yet Gillian Wilce contended that "once you slow to its pace, surrender to the leisured orotundity of its language, relish rather than skip the apparent digressions, then you may well find yourself closing it with regret."

(See also *Contemporary Authors*, Vol. 117.)

© Jerry Bauer

MICHAEL NEVE

Hongkong appears in one of two ways in contemporary novels. There is the Hongkong of the *tai pan*, the heroic Western figure striding against an exotic background, achieving great feats of capitalist accumulation against overwhelming odds. . . . The other, more recent Hongkong owes its existence to the Vietnam War, which brought American soldiers enjoying "rest and recreation" and a new place for Hongkong in fiction: an international espionage centre, complete with lingering colonialism and a vast drug trade. . . .

Timothy Mo breaks new ground with *The Monkey King*. He writes from within, from real acquaintance with the feeling that sweeps the local population as a typhoon draws across the South China Sea; he has swum at Repulse Bay in the early morning; he has tasted the unique half-orange flavour of Green Spot. His central character, Wallace Nolasco, begins the story at odds with himself and Hongkong. He is from Macau, part-Portuguese, and about to make a business marriage into the family of Mr Poon. It is the family that Wallace must deal with, all of them strange to him, not least his "wife", May Ling. . . .

Gradually Wallace begins to fit. His half-marriage and his ethnic outsiderness become resolved in the middle section of the book, when he and May Ling spend time on the Chinese border. Here, Poon's dissenting urban family is exchanged for a vision of the old China, with its village headman, struggles against natural disaster, and various priests. Wallace becomes involved in a feud over the siting of shrines and the draining of paddy fields: all taking place within the subtle Chinese idea of *fung shui,* or appropriate siting of the works of men within nature. He intervenes effectively, and returns to the Poon family and the city to take up his proper place. But the trap has been laid, and the family claim him. The funeral of Mr Poon is also Wallace's funeral, as well as his assumption of responsibility. The monkey has survived but also been caught.

The book captures the sense of familial claustrophobia well, and has a flat prose that seems appropriate. There is also, however, a bizarre kind of overwriting at work, which is hard to read. At the same time as he seals the fate of his central character, Mr Mo leaves himself in a linguistic confusion. Is it ironical, or just a version of the Chinese baroque, to say "The crowd hissed corroboration"? Smart sentences such as this one lie heavily on the plot, interfering with our view of Wallace as he disappears into a tight, morally empty, noncommunist Hongkong. The bits of overwriting do not harmonize with the best, because sparest, insights. Not least of these, in the proper Chinese fashion, is the absence of sex.

> *Michael Neve, "The Hongkong Beat," in* The Times Literary Supplement, *No. 3979, July 7, 1978, p. 757.*

MARY HOPE

Comparisons are, I see, already being made between Timothy Mo and V. S. Naipaul. These do justice to neither writer. Mo's talent and concerns are quite different. *The Monkey King* his first novel, is the story of Wallace, a 'Portugese' from Macau, who marries into the Hong Kong household of the despotic Mr Poon. Submitting at first to the poor food, the hierarchical tortures, the taunts of unmarried sisters-in-law, he finally out-Chineses the Chinese, turns exile in one of the New Territories villages to dazzling entrepreneurial advantage and returns to take over the extended family.

With a foot in both camps, Mo keeps his Chinese tongue firmly in his English cheek with devastating effect. From the first, when you read that Mr Poon's house 'was furnished in two basic styles, classical Chinese and government surplus', you can guess at the ironies you are to encounter.

None of the events is funny: all of them are hilarious. The laconic refusal to treat tragedy as sad treads a fine line between cynicism and endurance; the daughter-in-law Fong, attempts the traditional escape route from family oppression; a suicide attempt lands her in hospital: 'The lacerations on her neck and wrists had been quick to heal, but the fractured ribs and concussion she sustained when the ambulancemen dropped her on the staircase were more serious . . .' Like those ambulancemen, Mo has a fine way of picking you up and dropping you when you least suspect it.

> *Mary Hope, in a review of "The Monkey King," in* The Spectator, *Vol. 241, No. 7827, July 8, 1978, p. 26.*

JAMES BROCKWAY

When I picked up [Mr Mo's] book I didn't really feel much urge to read it. . . . *The Monkey King* was about a poor, partly Portuguese youth, Wallace Nolasco, from Macau, who marries

into the family of a Cantonese businessman, Mr Poon, and thereafter has to live with that family and his unattractive, almost imbecile girl wife, May Ling, in Hong Kong. And what's Hong Kong to me or I to Hong Kong?

How mistaken I was. Timothy Mo has written about this large Chinese family and the multinational, but largely Chinese community in which it contrives to exist in so vivid and engaging a manner that I now feel I've been to Mr Poon's house at Robinson Path in the bustling Western District of Hong Kong and still have the smell of the place in my nostrils. (p. 50)

There's little 'plot'. Nothing really dramatic or awful happens in all 269 pages. . . . Instead we follow Wallace's career, which, after Mr Poon's death, leads to his unexpected accession to wealth, authority and—most unexpected of all—fatherhood.

Yet two things of the greatest importance do, indeed, happen between these covers. Life happens, real, fantastic yet credible life. *And* Mr Mo proves himself to be a true novelist. Here I cannot go into much detail, though I would wish to, but must be content to point to, first, the splendid and highly entertaining character-drawing of almost everyone in the novel, but particularly of Mr Poon and a rich woman friend, Mabel Yip, a wonderfully absurd and amusing creation; and second, to the very funny English these people use—a main source of Mr Mo's humour. . . .

The novel is so good that Mr Mo's own occasionally peculiar or mistaken English ('unillusioned', 'innured', 'malintention') is regrettable. Also his adoption of some of the ugly and pretentious clichés beloved of British politicians and the press. . . . He also overloads his descriptive passages with polysyllabic words such as 'placatorily', 'formulaic' and 'exsanguination' and even writes of 'factionalism' and '*ad hoc* conventions' among footballers and of 'symbiotically indistinguishable' paint. This can be funny—until it is overdone.

Whether the source of these blemishes was the University of Oxford, *The New Statesman, Boxing News* or *The Times Educational Supplement,* all places where Mr Mo has studied or worked in England, is hard to say, but I have the feeling we, and not he, are to blame for them. Anyway, a genuine writer, which with this book he has proved himself to be, has no need of verbal cosmetics. His book is worth every penny. . . . (pp. 50-1)

> *James Brockway, "Timothy Mo: A True Novelist," in* Books and Bookmen, *Vol. 24, No. 2, November, 1978, pp. 50-1.*

CHARLES R. LARSON

[*The Monkey King* is] a true example of the imaginative art. Though . . . the story is rather plotless, Mo's main characters have a vibrancy and a convincing quality. . . .

Timothy Mo explores the colorful nature of the Poon tribe with all the skills of a comic storyteller. As his publisher asserts, Mo is the first novelist (in English) to look at Hong Kong with an adroitness similar to V. S. Naipaul's treatment of Trinidad. There are, in fact, a number of similarities between *The Monkey King* and Naipaul's masterpiece, *A House for Mr. Biswas,* notably the darker overtones of the story. Mostly, *The Monkey King* is a novel to be read and enjoyed, and, I suspect, Timothy Mo is a writer to watch in the future.

Charles R. Larson, in a review of "The Monkey King," in World Literature Today, Vol. 53, No. 4, Autumn, 1979, p. 626.

PETER LEWIS

Part of the considerable appeal of Timothy Mo's first novel, *The Monkey King* (1978), lay in the novelty of its subject. . . . *The Monkey King* was frequently comic without being a comic novel, and claims that Mo was doing for Hong Kong what V. S. Naipaul had done for Trinidad in his early novels were almost inevitable.

In his second novel, with the punning title of *Sour Sweet,* Mo again concentrates on Chinese society, though on this occasion the setting is not the Far East but England in the 1960s, when peculiarly oriental forms of gang warfare rooted in the notorious Triad Societies were still occurring among the Chinese community. Mo writes about a world within a world, that of Chinese immigrants from Hong Kong who are intent on retaining their national and cultural identity while being economically dependent on their host country in various ways, both legal and illegal. As in *The Monkey King,* Mo provides us with an inside view of an unfamiliar social milieu, but by placing the narrative firmly in London he achieves a new *frisson.* What is startling is the apparent discrepancy between location and action, between modern England and a largely self-contained and alien society functioning within it.

The main plot of *Sour Sweet* concerns the small family unit of Chen, his wife Lily, their young son Man Kee, Lily's sister Mui, and (in the later stages) Mui's illegitimate daughter and Chen's father. Mo traces the fortunes of this family over several years, during which Chen gives up his job as a waiter in a Soho restaurant to set up his own "take away" business in suburbia. Mo depicts the family relationships and tensions with a delicate balance between comic distance and emotional involvement. While being far too sympathetic for satire, Mo's treatment of the Chen household, as he charts their attempts to establish a modus vivendi with what they regard as an inferior and relatively uncivilized people, is often humorous; misunderstandings and cultural collisions abound.

Yet for all the comedy, the final effect is far from comic. Interwoven with the narrative concerning the Chens is another about the operations of one of the Triad Societies in London, the Hung Family, which bears a strong resemblance to the Mafia. In addition to its protection rackets and drug trafficking, the Family is engaged in a power struggle with a similar organization, and this sometimes erupts into incidents of murderous brutality. . . . [It] is Chen's misfortune to come into direct contact with it briefly when he urgently needs money. Subsequently Chen goes to great lengths to keep as much distance between himself and the Family as possible. There is therefore a grim irony in the unexpected and arbitrary way the Family finally eliminates him, not because he has committed a punishable offence but because he is a suitably innocent scapegoat needed by one faction in an internecine power struggle.

Mo excels in handling domestic situations, relationships between men and women in families, and the subtle manoeuvrings by which women control their men while maintaining the appearance of subservience; he has a very sharp eye indeed for the nuances of behaviour in close-knit social units. By comparison, his treatment of the Hung Family is more superficial; the main participants in the Family are stereotypes. . . . Yet

even the Chen narrative would have benefited from some tightening up: Mo needs to beware of too leisurely a mode of narration.

Peter Lewis, "Hong Kong London," in The Times Literary Supplement, No. 4127, May 7, 1982, p. 502.

PHILIP CONSTANTINIDI

The prevailing theme of [*Sour Sweet*] is the unwillingness of Chinese society to adapt to English ways; the Hung family looks to Hong Kong for authority, and feuds only with other Chinese; Lily Chen organizes her life on precepts learned as a child in China and does not wish to change. To emphasize this alienation, Chinese characters are prone to speak in a kind of pidgin English, but inconsistently, so exposing the artificiality of the convention. It would require extraordinary finesse to establish comprehensible speech-patterns for non-English-speaking characters, when writing in English, without intending to be funny. But an incident where humour is intended, involving a Chinese grandfather, a group of English old age pensioners, and a coffin, fails to cause even the faintest smile. There is something very unfunny in the way Mr. Mo describes people falling into the culture gap, where he most often chooses to be light-hearted; the clinical tone becomes a little supercilious. (p. 19)

Philip Constantinidi, "Monosodium Glutamate," in Books and Bookmen, No. 322, July, 1982, pp. 18-19.

JONATHAN YARDLEY

Sour Sweet is, on every level that really matters, a work filled with wonders, surprises and rewards—a novel that, at the risk of using a word cheapened by familiarity and abuse, can only be described as enchanting.

Timothy Mo is the son of an English woman and a Cantonese man, and in this novel he has chosen to write about the clash of those cultures from which he himself has been formed. He has settled a little Chinese family in London in the early 1960s, found a house for them in a most unprepossessing neighborhood, set them up in a carryout-Chinese-food business, and let their lives unfold in ways that are often unpredictable but always illuminating. In certain respects *Sour Sweet* is, as its title suggests, a sad book, for life is not always easy for the Chens and in the end something terrible, though not insuperable, happens to them; but far more than that it is a wry and joyful book, packed with life and loaded with uproariously funny scenes.

At first there are three of them: Chen, the husband, a stolid and rather taciturn man who works as a waiter in a restaurant in London's Chinese quarter; Lily, his wife, a woman of demure demeanor but great willpower and inner strength; Man Kee, their infant son. . . . Soon they are joined by Mui, Lily's spinster older sister, who at first refuses to leave their flat and forms, from incessant watching of television, dire impressions of the country in which she now lives. . . .

What happens to the family, in brief, is that troubles back in China force Chen to take a substantial loan so he can send money to his relatives there. This loan he acquires through an unscrupulous representative of a Triad, a "family" based in Hong Kong that is part Mafia and part benevolent ward boss. Chen fears the Triad, and decides to leave the Chinese quarter in the somewhat unrealistic hope that it will forget about him.

He and Lily—who is ambitious and has long wanted him to go out on his own—find a house in an industrial area, hard against a car-repair shop, and open business there. (p. 3)

Observing her customers Lily remarks to herself that "there was no question how superior Chinese people were to the foreign devils," and furthermore: "They all looked the same to her. And how quickly their pink skins aged. How few types of face there were compared to the almost infinite variety of interesting Cantonese physiognomies: rascally, venerable, pretty, raffish, bumpkin, scholarly." While the English wallow in "lurid orange sweet and sour pork with pineapple chunks," the Chinese in their greater wisdom taste the delights of "white, bloody chicken and yellow duck's feet." These lapses in British taste are all about them, but Lily and Chen can only sigh, comment upon the great mystery of them, and go about the business of their lives.

When it comes to the education of Man Kee, though, England presents grave difficulties. At the age of 5½ he goes off to a British school, but to Lily it is entirely unsatisfactory; he seems to do nothing all day except play, and for lunch is served "mince, jam tart and custard," which into the bargain he has the effrontery to like. This is all wrong. . . .

So once a week Lily packs Man Kee off to a Chinese school for immersion in the eternal verities, but she can't escape the inevitable: England is having its way with Man Kee, just as it is with all of them. And the way it is having is not, Lily must reluctantly acknowledge (if to no one save herself), entirely bad. . . . Mui, in particular, bursts forth from her cocoon and becomes positively cross-cultural, with results that often shock the ardently traditionalist Lily.

While all of this goes on, there is yet another story, that of the gradual evolution of the marriage of Lily and Chen. It begins, as so many marriages do, in mutual ignorance of each other's essential nature, but over the years it slowly ripens, often in ways that surprise the parties to the marriage as much as they do the reader. . . .

If anything, indeed, *Sour Sweet* is a book about love. Its humor comes from the confrontation of alien cultures, but it's great tenderness comes from the depiction of a family that is in this thing together. . . . Nothing about the novel is so clear as that Timothy Mo deeply loves these eccentric and spunky people he has created. He has given them qualities that are distinctly Chinese, and qualities that are distinctly human, and what he has to tell us is that the two are exuberantly the same. His book—a work of absolute originality, written with beauty and quiet energy—is a wonder. It is also entirely irresistible. (p. 8)

Jonathan Yardley, "Dinner at the Chinese Restaurant," in Book World—The Washington Post, *March 31, 1985, pp. 3, 8.*

MICHAEL GORRA

The young Anglo-Chinese novelist Timothy Mo's second book has some of the same objectivity as Narayan's [*Under the Banyan Tree*], and I think for the same reason. But the real comparison is with V.S. Naipaul—not the jaundiced traveller, but the novelist who has lamented that "experimentation, not aimed at the real difficulties" has robbed the novel of conviction, so that "the world we inhabit, which is always new, goes by unexamined, made ordinary by the camera, unmeditated on"; the Naipaul who in the great comic realism of his early novels of Trinidadian life revealed a piece of that world we

had not seen before. Mo's achievement in the Hawthornden-prizewinning *Sour Sweet* is of a similar order: not the creation, like Gaddis, of his own world, but of a world that he makes a part of everyone's. In its chronicle of the lives of Chinese immigrants in London in the early 1960s, *Sour Sweet* extends the range of material with which the novel as a genre can deal. Mo has, of course, been helped in having by birth access to a realm of experience with which the English novel has not before dealt. And yet to make accessible to others the world one knows, to do it so completely that the reader accepts the characters' point of view and begins to see London as an alien place—that is a great achievement.

Yet *Sour Sweet* makes no attempt to compete with Maxine Hong Kingston's accounts of the Chinese interior landscape, concentrating instead on its characters' lives in the world, and above all on their work. The novel tells two stories in alternating chapters. The first is that of the Chen family, who run a take-out counter selling food that "bore no resemblance at all to Chinese cuisine." . . . The second story describes the operations of the London branch of Family Hung, a Chinese secret society that, from its start centuries ago as a religious fraternity built around the martial arts, has grown into a criminal confederation, linking Hong Kong to Chinatowns around the world. The two narratives touch only twice: once when Chen goes to the Hung for money to pay his sick father's hospital bills in Hong Kong; once again at the end of the novel when the time comes, as one knows it must, for him to discharge that debt. Yet if Chen's final meeting with the Hung does have a certain inevitability about it, it seems the inevitability of life itself, and not that of a thriller; hedged by accidents and contingencies, seemingly determined not by the requirements of literary form, not even by those of the turn-of-the-century naturalism that *Sour Sweet* resembles, but simply by the fact of being Chinese in a particular place at a particular time. I suppose an American analogy would be a novel about an Italian family trying to avoid the Mafia, but we don't have that novel, have only shelves of formula fiction and an unironic *Godfather*. Perhaps the American novel, with its emphasis on self-creation, is essentially unsuited for dealing with immigrants, with what ought to be the great American story. For immigration, as Mo suggests, reminds one not so much of the person one might become, as of the person one already inescapably is. *Sour Sweet* shows, at any rate, that those least able to adapt to English life are those infected by the spirit of what, along with chopsticks, most represents China to the West—the martial arts. Lily Chen's father, disappointed that he had no son, taught her Chinese boxing when she was a girl. And Ma Lurk Hing is the secret society's enforcer and leader, a fighter who believes guns beneath a serious warrior's dignity. Both remain intransigent before English life, and both suffer because of it. Lily's insistence that Chen continue to send his parents money makes the Hung able to find him in an age when they can trace every letter that passes between Hong Kong and London; and Mo suggests she'll lose her son Man Kee as well, not to the Hung, but to English life itself. Ma doesn't recognize that street-fighting must be a last resort in the West, that one should do business with rivals rather than kill them. And his inflexibility leads to his betrayal, and his crippling by a shot-gun blast. (pp. 671-72)

[The] novel is filled with moments of odd incidental beauty as well, with the pains and above all the comedy of ordinary life in an alien land: Chen trying to learn to drive, and failing; Lily, who does learn, realizing that you can bribe your way out of a traffic ticket in London, as you could out of almost anything in Hong Kong; Man Kee puzzled and upset when his teacher at school accuses him of fighting "dirty," when all he has done is use some of the kicks his mother has taught him. Naipaul says the camera has made the world ordinary. And yet the film critic Siegfried Kracauer speaks of film's achievement as the revelation—the redemption—of the reality that passes unnoticed before our eyes. The realistic novel at its best has always offered that redemption as well. With *Sour Sweet,* Timothy Mo joins the company of those who have enabled it to do so. (p. 672)

Michael Gorra, in a review of "Sour Sweet," in The Hudson Review, *Vol. XXXVIII, No. 4, Winter, 1986, pp. 670-72.*

RIVERS SCOTT

[Many] readers will open Timothy Mo's *An Insular Possession* in hopes of . . . [an] injection of familiar nostalgia. It is certainly a blockbuster of thoroughly commercial proportions—593 pages, many of them in very small print. It has its share of bloodletting, scandal and mild romance, clashes of conscience about the infamous opium trade, and the gory battles of the First Opium War itself. But—warning—it is not what it seems.

In the first place, it disdains old-fashioned narrative. Nothing could be further, in treatment or technique, from the conventional saga-novel than this choppy affair, in which hardly has the third-person chronicler started to get up steam than his story is interrupted by a letter from one of the participants (or two, or three, of them) or an extract from the fictitious *Lin Tin Bulletin and River Bee* or its philistine rival the *Canton Monitor* (this is where the small print comes in). Alienation effect? It will drive many people potty.

Mr Mo would argue, I believe, that this is just what he intends. Hong Kong born, he is trying to teach us benighted Westerners, used to linear narrative which goes from point A to point B and a time scale to match, to stretch our sensibilities and sample an Eastern mode. . . .

I am not saying that *An Insular Possession* goes the whole way with this theory. But it does go part of the way. And in doing so, in my view, it falls between two stools. The characters are not developed, and the events which go on around them are not strong enough to make up for this. Too many of them are uninteresting and the dialogue is often forced. The newspaper parodies become obvious and overlong. . . .

Yet certain passages in this book are remarkable: a scene in which a coolie is fatally bitten by a king cobra and one of the characters provokes a riot by sketching the corpse; a Portuguese Jesuit praising the Chinese for their gift of faith; and a very funny episode in which the American traders in Canton, having abused the British for engaging in the opium trade, decide to do a U-turn and join in the game themselves. . . .

Most of all, perhaps, Mr Mo shows his mettle in a wonderful description of the first Jardine steamer—in fact, the first steam-powered paddle boat of any sort—[to appear] at the mouth of the Canton River, to the utter consternation and panic of the Chinese. 'Gongs are beaten, flags are brandished, tiger-masks flaunted.' In vain. The devil-ship coughs, sneezes and clanks, wheels flashing, flames and smoke belching, as it makes its way slowly upstream in defiance of tide and wind.

This novel moves slowly, and sometimes to good effect. But I hope it is not just insensitive Western barbarism to say that in the end one is left feeling becalmed.

Rivers Scott, "Eastern Eye," in The Listener, *Vol. 115, No. 2959, May.8, 1986, p. 25.*

GILLIAN WILCE

[*An Insular Possession* is] a Western novel in that it flows through time, from 1833 to 1841, from the squabbles of the Western trading companies battening on to the south coast of China with the Chinese authorities into the first Opium War and on to the lease and settlement of Hong Kong. . . . [The] text is almost evenly divided between narrative and extracts from diaries and letters, from the conservative, pro-British *Canton Monitor* and its rival *Lin Tin Bulletin* founded by young Americans Eastman and Chase, who deplore the British trade in 'drug'.

Eastman and Chase—with Irish painter Harry O'Rourke, Jesuit Father Ribeiro and other tangential figures—are as much the eyes and ears of the novel as its protagonists. It is as if the convention whereby 'our Western novel . . . addresses itself rather to the individual as hero or heroine, from the delineation and resolution of whose dilemmas, material and moral, most of its energy and interest springs' had been turned inside out. The focus is our group of friends, but the energy comes largely from the wider events influenced by public figures, Company bosses, naval commanders, Chinese Governors, whom we watch through their eyes. . . .

A deceptively gentle book, it is nevertheless very demanding of its reader: it asks time, patience, carefulness. It may appear at first overly educational with its long passages on the coming of steam, essays on painting, recipes for the practice of heliogravure, fables told to personages and rumours of events in the UK and US. But once you slow to its pace, surrender to the leisured orotundity of its language, relish rather than skip the apparent digressions, then you may well find yourself closing it with regret, not only better informed, but sorry that your imaginative participation in another time, another place has come to an end with the parting of friends.

Gillian Wilce, "Slow Boat," in New Statesman, *Vol. 111, No. 2876, May 9, 1986, p. 27.*

BRIAN MARTIN

[*An Insular Possession*] is a first-class historical novel of tremendous sweep, mainly embracing life in Canton and Macao just before and during the first Opium War, 1839-42. The background is provided by the Chinese Empire of the Manchu dynasty in its declining years, and by the awful new power of the British Empire under Victoria, whose advance was made inexorable by the inventions of the Industrial Revolution, the steamship, and, in military terms, weaponry such as Sir William Congreve's rocket.

The success of an historical novel depends on how well the author convinces us of 'the concrete reality' of the past, as Eliot put it. Timothy Mo penetrates in detail the world of south China in the 1830s and 40s. He writes in the present tense which involves the reader immediately in what is happening and lends urgency to his action. (p. 36)

Embroiled in the bitter squabble between the Chinese and the intruding Western barbarians, the Portuguese, the Dutch, the

Americans, but mainly the British, are the two heroes, Eastman and Chase. The novel follows their fortunes as employees of the American commercial house of Meridian and Co. When the company announces its intention to take part in, and its share of, the opium trade, in which opium from India was bartered with Chinese merchants mostly in exchange for tea, they resign and establish a newspaper, *The Lin Tin Bulletin and River Bee*. . . . The suitability of the title is fixed upon after some debate: Lin Tin Island was where the opium-hulks anchored, and, as Eastman explains, the river bee 'collects clover and can sting'. At odds with the western merchants making fortunes out of the drug trade and with some sympathy for the imperial Chinese administration on this point, the two Americans become, with their critical publication, the William Cobbetts of the Macao Roads.

Their attack on the opium trade is without quarter. They object to the enrichment of the few and the degradation of the huge majority: they castigate the missionary clergy who 'go up the coast in opium-clippers and distribute Bibles with the drug! What a cruise of humbug is this! The wares of death dealt impartially with the word of life'; and they clarify the equivocating position of the British government, somewhat similar perhaps to that of today's government adopted towards the tobacco industry. . . . At every turn, Eastman's Macao-based *Bee* opposes the views of the British-established *Canton Monitor*: 'We deplore the truck in poison on which your masters' fortunes and your own journal are established exclusively'. Such forthrightness leads eventually to a pistol duel in which the *Monitor's* editor has his teeth knocked out by Eastman's bullet. (pp. 36-7)

No attempt in a review can do justice to the scope and range of this novel. It is rich in observations, whether Timothy Mo is describing the billiard-room of Meridian and Co's factory in Canton, or the godowns (warehouses) of Macao, whether he is in the battle-trenches of the Manchu warriors, or on board a British warship. There is a wealth of colorful detail: the Canton River at its mouth 'stains the clear blue sea yellow-brown, the colour of tea as drunk in London'; camped in the grounds of a temple the sepoys of the Madras Native Infantry prepare their breakfast and defecate (let this come as no surprise to health-food fanatics), 'bright yellow ropes of excrement . . . the product of their diet of pulses'. On a broader plane we see the profound effects of new technology, not only the harnessing of steam power, but of daguerreotype: 'both photography and journalism, offspring on the sinister branch of art and literature, were the most powerful agents in this novel passion for the actual and the real, alliance made yet more potent where the photograph might be reproduced as an article of news itself.'

Timothy Mo tells his story by many devices: he uses straightforward narration, directly recorded dialogue, extracts from letters and journals, and newspaper reports. They help the book gain its enormous range. . . . *An Insular Possession* is a marvellous, monumental achievement, highly intelligent, witty, and having the gravitas of true historical insight. (p. 37)

Brian Martin, "The Clash of Empires," in The Spectator, *Vol. 256, No. 8235, May 10, 1986, pp. 36-7.*

HERMIONE LEE

[*An Insular Possession*] ought to be a magnificent novel. Its subject, the nineteenth-century opium wars between Britain and China, is sensational, and like the materials of J. G. Ballard's *Empire of the Sun* or Salman Rushdie's *Midnight's Children* or Peter Carey's *Illywhacker*—comparably large-scale amalgams of fact and fiction, also treating the legacy of imperialisms—it has the advantage of not being a fictional commonplace. Timothy Mo has written two very good earlier novels; and this massive historical recreation has taken him five years.

In its way, the detail of the reconstruction is dauntingly impressive. . . . He takes us through the few years of rapidly growing hostilities to 1841, with the British attack on the Bogue forts and China's ceding of Hong Kong as an 'insular possession' for secure British trade. The novel ends just before the 1842 Treaty of Nanking. . . .

The narrative boggles the mind with facts, figures, details, scenes, incidents, and the weight of words. It is in love, like a Kipling story, with how things work: printing presses, guns, warships, cameras. It is addicted to specificity (200 chests of opium imported in 1700; 40,000 in 1838) and to grotesque minutiae, like Chinese barbers scraping the inner eyelids of their customers. It has a passion for set pieces: a duck shoot, a coolie stung dead by a snake, a visit to a waterborne brothel, a wrestling match between newspaper editors, and, for climax, two phenomenally detailed battle scenes. It is lavish with its geography, from the ambiguous waterways of the South China coast to the sight of Hong Kong in its first squalid splendour.

Characters are not the main point. The emphasis is on . . . bitter historical irony. . . .

It is also a highly self-conscious and inordinately slow-moving narrative, and this is where doubts set in. Journalism, painting, photography and drama are all incorporated . . . and the relative merits of literal reproduction and artistic invention are discussed. Fictions masquerading as fact, like Poe's *Arthur Gordon Pym*, are cited. Linear Western art is compared to the Chinese prose romance, which is circular and full of redundancies, a lake as opposed to a river, an organic growth and not a ticking clock. By the end we have collected a compendium of alternative ways of representing history, and a conclusion which underlines the self-conscious methodology of the whole. . . .

Mo's decision to couch the whole novel in an alienating, mock-heroic manner compounds the insistence on artificiality. Everyone, including the narrator, talks like a funny, pompous early-Victorian. . . . There are yards and yards of this flat talk, of portentous newspaper leaders and stiff correspondence. Slowly, slowly, the prolix, leisurely, redundant freight moves on, deeply engrossed in a particular history and in how to tell it. It makes a daring and confident journey, but not all its readers are going to get to the finish.

Hermione Lee, "Saga of the Opium Wars," in The Observer, *May 11, 1986, p. 24.*

John (Patrick) Montague

1929-

American-born Irish poet, editor, short story writer, translator, and critic.

A prominent figure in contemporary Irish poetry, Montague focuses upon personal as well as social concerns and explores such diverse subjects as alienation, love, death, family life, and the disintegration of traditional Western culture. The history and mythic qualities of Ireland are also dominant features in many of his poems and are developed in part through Montague's blend of Irish colloquialisms and the forms and patterns of Gaelic poetry. Critics note that Montague often investigates and recounts Ireland's history to comment upon the contemporary "troubles" in his country. Although sometimes faulted for using historical examinations to voice his own political beliefs, Montague is praised for his careful craftsmanship and vivid imagery.

Montague was born in Brooklyn, New York, to Irish-Catholic immigrants who had been forced to leave Northern Ireland in 1925 due to the political activities of Montague's father. Montague and his siblings moved to the Republic of Ireland in 1933 to live with relatives. *Poisoned Lands and Other Poems* (1961), Montague's first major volume of poetry, details his youth in Ulster and his later experiences in the cities of Dublin and Paris. Evident in this collection is Montague's love-hate relationship with Ireland, a theme which recurs in much of his work. Montague contrasts the natural and historical beauty of his country with its current violence and social unrest. Reviewers especially lauded "Like Dolmens round My Childhood, the Old People," a poem depicting Irish cultural decline. In the collections *A Chosen Light* (1967) and *Tides* (1970), Montague further examines the relationship between Ireland's past and present. He also offers in both volumes several personal poems, some of which center on marital and familial crises. For example, in "The Road's End," Montague mourns the passing of his youth, and in "Last Journey," he addresses the death of his father.

The Rough Field (1972), an eighty-page poem that incorporates pieces from his earlier collections, is Montague's most widely discussed work and his most profound analysis of Ireland's social and political condition. Beginning with the seventeenth century, when the English invaded Northern Ireland and forced Irish Catholics from their land, Montague details the oppression and exploitation that has occurred throughout Ireland's history. He employs a variety of traditional and experimental poetic structures and integrates fragments of historical documents, newspaper accounts, local dialect, and even graffiti into his verse. Benedict Kiely described *The Rough Field* as Montague's "most remarkable book and one of the most interesting statements made in this century about Ireland past and present." In *A Slow Dance* (1975), Montague continues to examine Ireland and his life in relation to his country, focusing upon subjects of loneliness and death. Some of the poems in this collection were compared to the verse of William Butler Yeats.

Photograph by Fergus Bourke; reproduced by permission of John Montague

Montague's poems in *The Great Cloak* (1978) reveal a shift from political topics to more personal concerns. Divided into three sections to create an episodic structure, this collection examines the failure of Montague's first marriage, the beginnings of a new relationship, remarriage, and the birth of his first child. In his next volume, *The Dead Kingdom* (1983), Montague recounts his travels from the Irish Republic to Northern Ireland for his mother's funeral. During this journey, Montague reflects upon his life and family and mourns the secular and religious division of Ireland. Bernard O'Donoghue commented: "*The Dead Kingdom* reminds us of Montague's eminence, reclaiming for him his place among the leading modern poets." Montague has also published *Selected Poems* (1982) and *Death of a Chieftain and Other Stories* (1964), a collection of short fiction that chronicles the lives of Irish farmers and townspeople. In addition, he edited *The Faber Book of Irish Verse* (1974; republished as *The Book of Irish Verse: An Anthology of Irish Poetry from the Sixth Century to the Present*).

(See also *CLC*, Vol. 13; *Contemporary Authors*, Vols. 9-12, rev. ed.; *Contemporary Authors New Revision Series*, Vol. 9; and *Dictionary of Literary Biography*, Vol. 40.)

DOUGLAS SEALY

A reference to Lenin on the jacket of Montague's [*Patriotic Suite*] might lead the unwary to expect an incisive analysis of Ireland's ills; instead the author comments with urbane irony on what has caught his poet's eye: council houses below a railway viaduct, patriotic relics in a museum, a self-drive car on the Atlantic coast, the ruins of Coole Park, and other graceless by-products of our time. Our attitudes towards revolution, towards our native language, towards our presence in the Congo and towards folk-music receive a sardonic glance. Mr. Montague does not too obviously take sides which takes the sting out of his bite or the bite out of his sting; he is on the whole content to present us with the *corpus delicti* and to leave us to notice the smell if our nostrils are as sensitive as his. For himself he is chiefly concerned with imponderables. . . . Every revolution is taken over by the bourgeois, pace Lenin. Mr. Montague regrets the inevitable in readable verse but offers no new synthesis. The poet's job is not to answer questions, but ask them, someone said once. Mr. Montague has it in him to ask more startling questions than those he has lightly touched on in *Patriotic Suite*. (pp. 99-100)

> *Douglas Sealy, in a review of "Patriotic Suite," in*
> The Dublin Magazine, *Vol. 6, No. 2, Summer, 1967, pp. 99-100.*

THOMAS LASK

In *Death of a Chieftain,* John Montague . . . has laid bare the lives, the hopes, the folkways of North Irish farmers and small townsmen. His book is a series of vignettes, and though the characters in each are individually drawn, we are more likely to remember them as part of the dour and restricted landscape of the world they live in.

Mr. Montague may not have intended it, but his picture is one of small communities, suspicious, intolerant, savage, narrow, slaves to the soil, full of periodic violence and prejudice. The interiors are dark, smoky and too often foul; the outside foggy, murky and damp. The spirit of the people mirror all these qualities. It is interesting to see how his tales fall into the old formula for Irish stories: "Rum, Romanism and Rebellion." . . .

Mr. Montague's tone is deliberately flat; he builds his stories by slow accumulation of detail. There are no climaxes, as if the absence of high points is due to the lack of color in the lives of his characters. Only in ["**Death of a Chieftain**"] does he show a different side. It is set in Central America and has to do with an Irishman's search for the missing link between the shadowy Celtic civilization and the hidden civilizations of the Indian. In a strange twist he finds it—in himself. It is a story we might call a romance and it shows what the author can do when he gets away to more exotic and warmer climates.

> *Thomas Lask, "Three But Not of a Kind," in* The
> New York Times Book Review, *March 23, 1968, p. 29.*

MICHAEL LONGLEY

[*A Chosen Light*] is an impressive book and with it John Montague steps quietly into the front ranks of contemporary poets. His clear purpose is to create poems whose statement and movement are uncluttered, poems which combine a discreet suggestiveness with maximum verbal efficiency: as a result his poems often exhibit that finality of form, that feeling of inevitability which marks a first-rate talent; and sometimes as in his poems about love and friendship his work is, quite simply, very beautiful.

Indeed, the love poems of the first section please me the most. Here—and this is not always the case later in the book—the reticence of Montague's poetic personality has something to shape and make recognisable, to be truly tactful about. The aesthetic control and the quietness of the tone of the voice are the symptoms and the fruits of real tensions whereas elsewhere they occasionally seem little more than the products of accomplishment and a fine professionalism. Perhaps even in **"All Legendary Obstacles"**, one of the loveliest pieces in the whole collection and a poem which in itself may suggest possible new directions for Irish poetry, the enjambment ("All legendary obstacles lay between / Us . . .") and the untypical heavy stresses of "great flanged wheels" betray an obtrusive knowingness. These minor flaws, which seem to me the products of a rhythmical literal-mindedness, might well have been carried by the iambic measure and the English language's rhetorical tendencies which Montague has chosen to jettison: but these same flaws might then have blossomed into damaging dishonesties at deeper imaginative levels.

This is why we should salute the new rhythms and the experiments of this book. In the best poems they are brave and honest. Montague has learned from and developed the short line and the cadenced near-prose of the Black Mountain poets. Their methods are ideal for mapping a tone of voice; but very little can be encompassed by tone of voice alone, and Black Mountain poetry lacks stamina, staying power. (pp. 93-4)

[Montague's] new methods work perfectly in the more occasional poems, but in the set pieces they inhibit resolution, deny climax. To transcend and to affirm one must raise one's voice, and this is what Montague at the moment cannot do. Impressive as this book often is, I can't help feeling that except for the finest pieces it marks an interim stage, the main failings of which are an aesthetic rootlessness and a lack of affirmation, real pressure, that *joy* Yeats said was essential. (p. 94)

> *Michael Longley, in a review of "A Chosen Light,"*
> *in* The Dublin Magazine, *Vol. 7, No. 1, Spring, 1968, pp. 93-4.*

M. L. ROSENTHAL

The Irish poet John Montague is one of the most interesting now writing in English. He tells a story, paints a picture, evokes an atmosphere, suggests the complexities and torments of adult love and marriage—all in the most direct, concrete, involving way. The poems come out of a deeply human speaking personality for whom language and reality are more than just a source of a plastic design of nuances. Montague does have a highly developed sense of the craft; he is a real poet, who works at his desk and drinks of the tradition. But he brings all his engagement with his art directly to bear on the world of our common life, as Frost and Williams so often did, and thus makes immediate contact with his readers. He thinks and talks like a grownup man, and that fact alone makes him better literary company than most of his poetic contemporaries.

The poems of *A Chosen Light* fall naturally into four large groups. The first ones we encounter, and with some exceptions the most striking, have to do with love. More particularly, they deal with love in a marriage that, it is suggested, has suffered a grievous, unnamed wound and yet survives with a unique meaning and purity. The group includes at least five truly memorable pieces, chief among them **"All Legendary Obstacles,"** a poem about the troubled reunion of lovers after long separation. (p. 632)

A second grouping has to do with rural Ulster. . . . Local realities of landscape, personality and indigenous experience are sharply sketched in with a bitter yet tender truthfulness reminiscent of the older Irish master poet Austin Clarke. Unlike Clarke, though, Montague has lived much of his adult life away from Ireland, mostly in Paris. His poems have a distancing and a nostalgia peculiar to this situation and not uncharacteristic of much modern Irish writing that grows out of the self-exiling of many Irish writers. (pp. 632-33)

Montague's Parisian experience constitutes the center of the book's third section. Although this section brings his political awareness, Irish interests and marital situation into play again, its true concern lies in his situation as an artist of this moment. The brief title sequence [**"A Chosen Light"**] moves into this focus of sensibility with a special accuracy and beauty. . . . The final group of poems ranges among primal and broadly symbolic motifs that place this guiding sensibility in the widest possible context. With this book John Montague reinforces his position among the humanly genuine poets now writing. (p. 633)

> *M. L. Rosenthal, "Poet of Brooklyn, Ulster & Paris,"*
> *in* The Nation, *New York, Vol. 212, No. 20, May*
> *17, 1971, pp. 632-33.*

FRANK KERSNOWSKI

Forms of Exile, though published in 1958, shows the temper of the early 50s, as well as the early development of John Montague's poetry. The first, and larger, part of this first volume consists of almost unqualified rejection of Ireland. The subjects, though, are not those of Yeats; for the young man who wrote these poems had, at that time, only a bookish familiarity with the Anglo-Irish. To a quite unsurprising extent, the book is priest-ridden. Some of the best, and most controversial, of the poems concern the debilitating effect of the Church on life in Ireland. **"A Footnote on Monasticism: Dingle Peninsula,"** written by 1953, presents an old ruined monastery and then musingly recreates the past as the poet imagines himself one of these silent, worshipful men. . . . (p. 15)

Like many other young Irishmen of his time, John Montague, though never coerced by his family, was encouraged to consider a vocation. Perhaps for that reason, these early poems so often speak from the persona of the priest.

"Soliloquy on a Southern Strand," completed after Montague's return to Ireland in 1956, examines another part of a priest's life: the end when he must sum up his achievement. The poem is spoken by an old priest as he sits on a beach in Australia and thinks back to his youth in Ireland. A country boy, he had been shy, somewhat inept. So in school with the more sophisticated, he willingly accepted the security offered by the cloth. After years of continence, he has come to a slow and gentle life surrounded by young sun-worshipers who must consider him alien and irrelevant. He himself finds scant more significance in his life. . . . The contrast in this poem is between vital life in a young, active culture and one that meditates on a dying past. (pp. 15-16)

[Several poems] contrast Irish life with that of another country. In **"Rome, Anno Santo"** the bleakness of Ireland forms a small

dark cloud in the splendor of Rome, the harshness of Irish pilgrims contrasted with the humanism of Rome. Still the Church is not condemned, only Irish Catholicism. In **"Song of the Lonely Bachelor"** and even in a poem called **"Prodigal Son"** Montague condemns the Jansenist-charged Catholicism of Ireland for allowing the people no more than a slow telling out of beads.

Though distinctly Roman Catholic in many of the poems, Montague does not deny the importance of the Anglo-Irish past to him. In a series of poems written before [his] trip to the United States, he alludes to a series by Yeats with his title: **"Rhetorical Meditations in Time of Peace."** Rhetorical diction, rather than Montague's later conversational one, indicates his following Yeats, the Anglo-Irish and English tradition. The progress of diction in this tradition may well be toward the language that men speak, but the men who speak usually have a most uncolloquial choice of words. Even in the final ominously despairing section of his poem, Montague's words soothe the reader rather than involve him in the grit of the experience. . . . (pp. 16-17)

Whether or not Montague matured into his own style during the three years he was in the United States or whether he expanded his understanding of poetry by meeting poets from another tradition seems inconsequential. . . . Though few, the poems he wrote about this period indicate a new understanding of poetry. Even **"Soliloquy on a Southern Strand"** has a glitter to it not found in the earlier poems. The glitter in the poems specifically about the United States, however, is that of a sloganed world, as in **"Downtown, America"**:

> NEWS OF THE LATEST TRIAL—THE
> WINNING HORSE—TROOPS HAVE LANDED—
>   COMMISSION'S
> REPORT IS THROUGH
> These are normal things and set the heart at rest.

Intending to condemn the brashness of the culture, Montague in his quotations has considerably expanded the technique of his poetry by including the brash, colloquial writing of the journalist. In later poems, such as *The Bread God,* the technique will return to add complexity to more mature poems.

In a three-poem sequence called **"American Landscapes,"** he again used a quotation: "A loud-speaker car drones through the streets, / Calling JOIN THE U.S. MARINES." but the poem itself becomes part of the gentle rhetoric he used so well. In the last two poems here he evokes the particular in all its brash and futile urgency. **"Bus Stop in Nevada"** gives our mobile culture to us with smell and sound. . . . In the last poem, **"Hollywood and Vine,"** a nearly brutal life tears through the fabric of Montague's trained poetic with force comparable to **"Downtown, America."** Young men solicit on the street. . . . Though slanted, these poems do not tell the reader how to react; and the young poet himself seems a bit unsure of how he should react. (pp. 18-19)

[Montague] has yet to decide whether to let the colloquial increase its importance in his poetry or to pursue the more rhetorical mode of the past. No poem in *Forms of Exile* attempts to solve all these problems. After the brash newness of the United States, Montague returned to Ireland, consciously looking for the past. Six months after returning, he wrote **"The Sean Bhean Vocht,"** which shows he is aware answers exist to his problems. (p. 20)

When he wrote this poem in 1956, Montague could not without qualification accept the past which he had only been able to piece together from pieces of flotsam. . . . Yet he was drawn to see what part of himself answered when the past called. . . . Though knowing little at this time of either Jung or the history of ancient Ireland, Montague readily acknowledged that past as alive in him and communicatable to others in the present through a persona. The immediate effect on his verse is to increase attention to specific details and to increase the colloquial even to the extent of quoting Irish, something rarely done by the strongly internationalist poets in the mid-50s. These techniques had been apparent even in the quite traditional poems written before the trip to the United States and were dominant in the poems written about that trip. But in **"The Sean Bhean Vocht,"** the two approaches find their best amalgamation. Over one-third of the poem is dialogue, and the rest is tightly structured colloquial speech. (pp. 20-1)

Poisoned Lands, Montague's second volume, shows a further investigation into poetic forms. Dominant, however, is the sound and attitude of poetry from the fifties: elegance, irony, compression, and formal eloquence. More often than in *Forms of Exile,* the sound of local idiom appears, shattering the carefully wrought forms. Or a savagely ironic ending will make paradoxical what had been a cleanly rhetorical poem. . . .

The necessities of publishing partially mutilated the structure of the book as Montague had planned it, but the three parts are still evident: country, sickness, healing. Although most of them are new, several of the very good poems earlier appeared in *Forms of Exile.* (p. 22)

Since the country section of the book follows some people away from Ireland, such good poems as **"Rome, Anno Santo"** and **"Soliloquy on a Southern Strand"** fit well. The sense of loss of all the people when separated indicates the poet's view of the time: live in Ireland or live in meaningless exile. . . . But this theme, carried over from *Forms of Exile,* is only part of *Poisoned Lands.* The important new poems in this section present the country and its people with great attractiveness and, often concurrently, distrust. **"Like Dolmens Round My Childhood, The Old People"** gives five examples of Irish country life, one, "Wild Billy Harbison who married a Catholic servant girl," unmistakably Ulster. Like all in this poem, Wild Billy is the victim of creeds and old hatreds which destroy life and joy. (p. 23)

Many of these early poems show Montague's desire to comprehend the origins of his culture, but his instinctual awareness of the importance of the past far outdistances his information. **"Wild Sports of the West,"** for instance, investigates the class structure in nineteenth-century terms with the characters of landowner, bailiff, and peasant-poacher. Their roles are fixed for all time, but Montague does not here go into their ancient prototypes. When confronted with monuments of the far past, though, he wrote poems lean and rich with a blend of the colloquial and rhetorical. **"A Royal Visit"** is about Tara, and the pun of the title places English rule of Ireland into the forepart of time, where it belongs. (pp. 24-5)

Ireland has not been found appealing in the first part of *Poisoned Lands:* ruined lands inhabited by ruined people, the flotsam of a wrecked culture. Yet, as true in *Forms of Exile,* no other place offers artistic refuge. In **"Stills"** he sets an emblem of modern corruption, showing with photographic exactness "Four suave and public men, in braided uniforms." Men of this kind have set administrative patterns into action which make even

the warrior obsolete: "Softly swords rust in warriors' hands. . . ." From them exudes nothing natural. Death and birth become the same. . . . In the poem **"Poisoned Lands"** country people censure a land owner for his practice of putting out poison meat to kill predatory animals. . . . So evil and unnatural does he seem, the country believe him to be the devil incarnate. . . . No utilitarian purpose motivates this modern extermination, but instead a malignancy. The poems of illness show a corrupted modern world, and even Ireland stuck on the backshelf of Europe has been touched.

The book in its original structure would have conformed to the mythic pattern of sickness and rebirth. Even in Montague's printed version, though, the fertility rite appears. In the last section, the country mummer-poet finds more complex and sophisticated forms; for art itself becomes the king who can destroy the blight. **"Cultural Center"** from *Forms of Exile,* now entitled **"Musée Imaginaire,"** becomes with its new setting and title a compendium of art past and present. The description of "Room III," beginning with the Catalan crucifix no longer censures America's jumbled taste, but asserts art's healing grace: "A complete abstraction judges us, / From its clean white wall." (pp. 26-7)

Though Ireland is often the scene, . . . Montague has no intention of becoming a local bard. He will be neither plowboy gadfly nor self-determined remnant of the Literary Renaissance. In **"Regionalism, Or Portrait Of The Artist As A Model Farmer,"** Montague announces his preference for "fierce anonymity" rather than the more clearly defined character of some: "Wild provincials / Muttering into microphones / Declare that art / Springs only from the native part." Montague neither then nor now, however, rejected Ireland as a subject. In **"The First Invasion Of Ireland"** he makes a tentative inquiry into ancient Irish history. Developing a scene from *Leabhar Gabhála, The Book of Conquests,* he tells of three men and fifty-one women, refused admittance to Noah's ark, who land in Ireland. Here Montague ironically contrasts that occasion with the present condition of Ireland:

> Division of damsels they did there,
> The slender, the tender, the dimpled, the round,
> It was the first just bargain in Ireland,
> There was enough to go round.

Concerned with accuracy, Montague now considers changing the word *first* to *last.* Though clever in conception and nimble in diction, this poem is stilted, much more so than will be Montague's later revivifications of Ireland's ancient past. (pp. 27-8)

Well settled in Paris when writing *A Chosen Light,* he looked at Ireland from the distance of the Irish writer in exile, with memory sharpened by frequent visits. Both the organization of the volume and the manner of its publication reflect Montague's multicultural concerns. The first section was published separately at the Dolmen Press in Dublin under the title *All Legendary Obstacles.* **"The Country Fiddler,"** the second section, was published with poems from **"The Cage"** and two unpublished poems as *Home Again* by Queen's University of Belfast.

A Chosen Light, structured as it is, leads the reader to understand the magic of art and life in the final section, **"Beyond the Liss,"** by making him, in the first section, **"All Legendary Obstacles,"** aware of dangers that can inhibit life. The passing answer of simple people is given in **"The Country Fiddler,"** the second section; while **"The Cage,"** the third, tells of the traps in our modern world. However, this sectional division seems intended to help the reader enter the distinctive world of an Irish poet become European. The same theme runs through all: the struggle of an Ulster Catholic to find cultural referents for his own affirmation of gentleness, love, and compassion. (pp. 37-8)

A Chosen Light does not deal directly with political problems, but the poet as persona of the country reveals its problems. Montague explores the harsh meanness and violence that can be readily associated with any part of the world that has lost or not achieved an ordered structure. **"Country Matters"** tells of a pretty young girl pursued by men until "no one 'decent' / Or 'self-respecting' would touch her." She probably is found everywhere; but in rural areas she is seen so often as to be a type: brief careless joy leading to a dull, sad life. Though life is often loose in the country, morality is strict, love a luxury. . . . (p. 38)

Montague makes the destruction of a trivial person emblematic of a general state of pain and loss. He knows the lack of language, the loss of speech that creates the easy world of clichés in which none needs think or struggle. In **"Obsession"** he tells of a recurring memory that stuns him and strikes him inarticulate; and ordeal and trauma are often subjects in this volume, especially in the first section. **"That Room"** exemplifies a frequent technique. The poet tells that within a room two people found an understanding which changed their lives. Specific causes are omitted, for Montague here charts a pattern and does not describe an event. (p. 39)

The poems describe the difficulties of a person growing from a childishly simple society into an adult one. **"Return,"** the title being a frequent subject for Montague, summarizes the duality:

> Seeing your former
> self saunter up the garden path
> afterwards, would you flinch,
> acknowledging
>   that sensuality,
> that innocence?

Quite likely, one can see the problems and peculiarities of another culture better than those of his own. However, outside Ireland flesh and joy do not seem to cause such intense or long-lasting torment.

That Montague treats his and others' fleshly difficulties without comedy differentiates him from most of his predecessors and many of his contemporaries. As Vivian Mercier has shown in *The Irish Comic Tradition*, sex and death both arouse such fear and awe in the Irish that they have traditionally been the subjects of comedy. Even though Montague's treatment of sex avoids the usual humor, the fear is frequently there. **"The Trout,"** for instance, is a thinly described description of masturbation and was called "a love poem" by Montague on the cover of a record album, *The Northern Muse*. . . . (p. 40)

Another reason for the Irishman's typical reaction to the sexual may well be his view of women. Robert Graves in *The White Goddess* has, with the agreement of many, established matriarchy as the structure of ancient Celtic society. Believing in racial memory, as he does, Montague's presentation of the woman as muse and goddess may well be a conscious recreation of ancient mythic patterns. In **"The Gruagach"** Montague tells of the way a mountain recalls to the minds of locals the ancient Scottish Gaelic goddess, "the brute-thighed giantess. . . ." Even

more commonplace events elicit a similar response from Montague, as, for instance, in **"Virgo Hibernica"** in which trudging "docile" by a woman's flank he feels "the gravitational pull / of love." Increasingly, Montague's lyrics attempt to express the ritual giving significance and form to the details of experience. To enter into that ritual is often to accept a nonrational (perhaps mystical) union of self and mythic order and identity.

The terror-evoking power of even young women in Montague's poems becomes the essential identity of old women. They often appear as hags used by the neighborhood to frighten children into behaving. Actually, though, they only frighten because their extreme old age separates them from the present. They touch the past in their remembered experiences. Because they provide an entry to a more stable time for Montague, they often resemble the Sybil. (pp. 40-1)

These old women removed from easy identification with the present seem to lead Montague to find a correspondence between himself and them. By his vocation and by his ready sympathy for the misplaced, the outsiders, he appears ill at ease in the order of the modern European world. He does, however, understand it and reflect in his poems some of its natural beauty as well as its mechanical regularity.

A considerable part of Montague's concern in this volume is with his adjusting to living in Paris. (p. 42)

Though Montague finds that his life and his beliefs allow him to share the experience of a wide variety of people, there continues to be a kernel of identity in him that is forever Ulster. In **"Waiting,"** life in Paris takes him back to wartime Ulster with its German prisoners, its air-raid alerts, and the bombing of Belfast, "the grit / Of different experience, of shared terror / No swift neutral sympathy can allay," when the fire engines came from the South to help put out fires in bombed Belfast. Hopefully accepting any sign of a united Ireland, Montague celebrates an act of human kindness.

Montague's accustomed way of presenting Ireland is through the experience of his acquaintances or family. In **"The Road's End,"** another poem about returning to his childhood home, he describes the decline in population: "Like Shards / Of a lost culture, the slopes / Are strewn with cabins, emptied." Especially in writing about country people, Montague makes heavy use of place names and family names: the Blind Nialls, Big Ellen, Jamie MacCrystal. The simple, leisurely people of the country become expendable in the efficiency of the modern world, as Montague suggests in **"The Hen House"** and in **"Hill Field."**

Perhaps because he writes mostly about country people, Montague generally writes of the Irish as bitter, flawed, or failing. Two family poems illustrate the theme. In **"The Cage,"** he describes his father, an Irish exile in New York, as "the least happy / man I have known." In part, exile itself cost him happiness; but the poem also stresses that Irish narrowness encloses minds as tightly in exile as at home. The Ulster tendency to hold its own tightly, even unto death, is the theme of **"Family Conference."** (pp. 42-3)

Often in Montague's poetry the present has been rejected, but not simply because it is different. He has opposed what limits the human being to dullness, what denies joy. . . . Repeatedly in this volume, Montague designates art as capable of bringing life. Implicit always is a social order which grants to the artist a persona he must struggle to fit. Art and order exist together and ideally strive to create personal happiness and social stability. *Ideally* must be stressed. For the individual's struggle with a persona never ends, and dissonance is eternal.

In **"Beyond the Liss"** Montague presents an analogy of the poet through "Sean the hunchback," who steps into the world of faery. Believing that all poets have quirks, deformities, which separate them from the rest of the population, Montague shows the difficulty of such a person. Though capable of transporting himself beyond commonness, beyond deformity, into the magic world of beauty, he cannot continue in such happiness. Montague's similarity to the confessional poets of contemporary America is evident here. But unlike them, he chooses to employ a persona rather than his own bare psyche.

The poems in *A Chosen Light* vacillate between inquiries into personal and social difficulties and unpleasantnesses and celebrations of joy when the poet has found a pleasing persona. The last poem, **"The True Song,"** sums up Montague's attempt to assume the persona. For emblems of beauty, death, and victimage, he has a swan, a lady, and "a stricken one":

> For somewhere in all this
> Stands the true self, seeking
> To speak, who is at once
> Swan
>   lady
>   stricken one.

Here all is myth and metaphor. And undoubtedly, Montague intends many of his specifically Irish poems, such as **"The Siege of Mullingar,"** to exist in the same metaphoric state. However, that achievement must ultimately be judged by history.

Yeats was able to use place names, particular events, and specific individuals mythically for at least two reasons: he was a conscientious systematizer, and he drew his attitudes and personae from an established literary tradition. But for the contemporary poet, such as Montague, the personal, even the individual trauma, is frequently the subject. The thing is important in itself, not because of metaphoric association. The personal involvement of the poet in the poem, without benefit of persona, and his desire to achieve a persona demand that the critic distinguish between the two and understand the reason for both.

Essentially, today's poet cannot step comfortably into the world of legend as he would like it to be. Modern scholarship has made the past all too immediate for him. And those ancient times seem more like the flawed present than the ideal lands poets have always wanted them to be. Kinsella's translation of the *Tain,* for instance, shows heroic Ulster to have much in common with strife-ridden Londonderry. Montague in his attention to detail in describing scenes and people attempts to present the ritual underlying them. At times, the details are so specific that one can simply say, that is the thing itself. Usually, this occurs when he writes about Ireland rather than about France. Whether because the subject is limiting in itself or readers are often limited, one often steps into specifically Irish poems with difficulty. However, an internationalist poet such as Montague must consider the culture of present-day Ireland as valid a subject as that of any other country. (pp. 44-6)

Tides, like Montague's earlier verse, is essentially concerned with describing the rituals giving form to the details of life. However, the individual poems within the structure of the whole volume have a greater psychic fury than the earlier. This is not to say that they are all among the best poems Montague has written. Many are, but the volume itself gives added strength to individual poems because it is so tightly unified by concern with death and destruction. . . . The poetry is not morbid, for all its dwelling on the subject, because Montague tries to give "an answer to death." Curiously, the structure of the volume resembles that of the traditional elegy.

"Premonition," which opens the volume, presents a by-now-obsessive image in Montague's poetry: the nightmarish carving up of a woman's body. As in **"Obsession,"** which began *A Chosen Light,* one infers that dreamer and tormentor are the same. But here the ending gives added concern:

> On the butcher's block
> Of the operating theatre
> You open your eyes.
> Far away, I fall back
> Towards sleep, the Liffey
> Begins to rise, and knock
> Against the quay walls.

The image of pain is part of a pattern in which death and life, pain and joy, rise and fall as necessarily as the tides. The pattern continues in all of life and may be traced in the details even of lovers' quarrels. **"Summer Storm"** tells of such anger and its exorcism in a garish scene as two people squash mosquitoes on each other. Both become dominated by the rising and falling pattern manifest in the woman's body. Identification of sea and woman's body occurs frequently in mythic literature and here prepares for the last section of the book, **"Sea Changes,"** in which Montague presents the patterns without obvious recourse to the human. . . . Like **"The Gruagach"** in *A Chosen Light* these poems present monolithic earth forms which evoke awe because they have the fixity of fundamental forms of creation.

"The Wild Dog Rose" and **"The Hag of Beare"** are the two most likely in the whole book to be complete in themselves. . . . Taken as companion poems, they show how the sexual experiences of two totally different women transform Christian figures into beauty and love, in contrast with the frequent austerity and antagonism of Christianity in Northern Ireland. Again, Montague's concern is with transformations in people who are touched or controlled by patterns which give shape to all creation.

"The Wild Dog Rose" begins with a description now familiar in Montague's writing: "that terrible figure who haunted my childhood. . . ." The old women of **"The Answer"** and of **"Waiting"** occur again here. And like them she is a crone, so old she belongs to another time, existing now as a reminder of the past. For many, she seems a wicked creature, a hag akin to Kali the goddess of death. Her age and ugliness remove her from general experience, but these it seems most draw Montague to her. He writes, "Memories have wrought reconciliation / between us. . . ." Her deformity brings them closer, "lovers almost," suggesting Montague's obsessive concern with the artist's own deformity. This separates him from active people, those at ease in the company of strangers. But in the company of people he does not feel the need to deceive, Montague is a different creature. Then the deformity becomes his entry into another's pain.

The old woman's loneliness, terrifying in itself, becomes accentuated after a drunk attempts to rape her. Through his friendship with her, however, Montague understands that her loneliness and later her abuse have led her to create beauty. During the attack she prayed to the Virgin Mary, whom she credits with saving her. Living alone in the country, the old woman creates her own objects of worship from her surroundings. "Each bruised and heart-shaped petal" of the wild dog rose reminds her of the Virgin Mary and "all she suffered." The virgin becomes in this creation beautiful, human, and understanding. And the old woman's ugliness is only the sign of her separation from the people around her, ones quite likely to regard her as evil and the Virgin as a battlecry. Both are the rose whose beauty comes from suffering in life and from a love that becomes faith.

"**The Hag of Beare,**" a version rather than a translation, has a quite different woman as narrator. But like the one in "**The Wild Dog Rose,**" her life shows the large pattern of joy, loss, and beauty. She too creates from love that has become belief. But this old woman knew and loved the world. She, an aging courtesan, mottled in skin, one eye gone, and infirm in all ways, remembers the homage she was once paid, when she lived by her skills, developed into arts. Now she finds neither the way nor the will to practice them; mean and petty days have come, and she has no hope either of their return or the return of her youth.

The hag, at whatever time in her life, made a transformation as important as aging when she came to Christ. But even in this quite schematized ritual, she both viewed and accepted him in her own terms. . . . However, in presenting Christ as a desirable man, she has created a companion religious figure to the human Mary in the preceeding poem. The pairing of these two in an other than mother-son relationship would not be out of the ordinary in many religions based on the fertility cycle. (pp. 47-51)

Clearly, Montague presents Christianity within the framework of Celtic belief. . . . Though Montague is concerned to show "the struggle between paganism and Christianity, between worldly pleasure and the doctrine of salvation through repentance," as important to him is the contemporary significance of the poem. In part of *The Rough Field*, Montague will return to the theme of the psychological struggle between Christian and pagan identity in a woman to arrive at the same conclusion as in these two poems. His poetry is centered on celebration of the muse, the ancient goddess who occurs in three phases: mother, lover, destroyer. Though he does not deny the importance of Christianity, he stresses the physical love and the celebration of the ritual of the year which it should share with those religions it most resembles.

After having expressed the appeal and continued force of mythic identity and patterns in the first section ["**The Wild Dog Rose**"], Montague then explains the dangers. The tides before were at the ebb, bringing memories of past days; they are now the tides that wreck, that bring terror and destruction. (p. 51)

Emphasis in this section continues to be on pain, the exonerating quality of it generally more obliquely stated than in "**Pale Light.**" Two prose passages are especially difficult, being as they are unexplained images of suffering. "**Coming Events**" describes a man being flayed alive. . . . In "**The Huntsman's Apology,**" another prose piece, a killer justifies his acts by contrasting them with those of the scavenger, who preys on weak and wounded animals. Though the kill gives him belief in his power, the scavenger is actually like one who woos the muse with his own unhappiness rather than the joy of life, death and birth. The power of the cycle is so great and dominating that one must either celebrate it or maliciously resist the flow by structuring the natural into unnatural forms. Montague writes of both possibilities. (pp. 52-3)

Before opening the pattern of the tides to its widest, Montague narrows to reveal a personal and immediate obstacle (though he might prefer the vaguer term of condition): the past and present of Northern Ireland as they affect his life. Here the first poem ["**The Northern Gate**"] gives title to the section and . . . sets the tone as Montague recalls the hoot of an owl, "clearing his throat / somewhere behind me," only to be drowned out by "a sigh of airbrakes / from a morning lorry." In the conversational tone of the internationalists, Montague uses a traditional death bird, the owl, to announce the death of wilderness and nature as the mechanical world expands control. Though the tone of this section is consistently deathly, there is complexity in the variety of transformations possible. In "**To Cease**" Montague considers erratic humanity becoming a natural monolithic monument. Though he may envision such a state, Montague himself is not close to entering it. He has not moved completely into a new order, in part because the world around him has not and in part because he has not completely freed himself from old limitations.

In two elegiac poems, he writes of that past. "**Last Journey**" considers the death of his father. . . . The death of the father does not completely sever Montague from the past. As much as humanly possible, the death of his grandmother, who raised him, and is described in "**Omagh Hospital,**" does. The old woman, delirious and dying, asks her grandson to take her home. He remembers her house, "shaken by traffic / until a fault runs / from roof to base." The "fault," if one remembers Montague's poem with the same words for title, achieves metaphoric value for him. Like the land, he too is flawed, broken by weakness and strength as well. He can bury emblems of the past, but must force his mind away from contemporary entanglements to break the domination of that past. However, he does not seem willing to abandon his country and his time during the great turmoil of Ulster. (pp.55-6)

[In the last section of the volume, "**Sea Changes,**"] the ocean and its inhabitants, including man, find themselves controlled by a complex, unifying pattern.

The subtitle to this section, "A Sequence of Poems for Engravings by William Hayter," stresses Montague's concern with a general, even abstract pattern, as William Hayter's etching on the front of *Tides* shows. Though more objectively realistic than some of Hayter's, the etching represents his concern with rhythmic, wavelike forms.

The merging of female form into waves, though, does not dominate "**Sea Changes.**" In fact, after the initial poem, only one specifically sexual distinction is drawn. In "**Boats,**" Montague continues his search for unions between Christian and pagan belief. "**Remous**" stresses another of Montague's themes in this volume: the ecstatic and cataclysmic possibilities of sexual love. (p. 57)

Somewhat distracting, because of frequent occurrence, is Montague's stressing of the cataclysmic. In "**Lame de Fond,**" perhaps the strongest poem in this last section, he reiterates a foreboding theme: relentless, inevitable power. Earlier in the poem was a seemingly more hopeful view: "Die or devour! But / Everything dies into birth." Describing the life of sea creatures, Montague presents again the cyclic order in which death but prepares for life, in which the past lies inert, though nutritive, under the present. However, one wonders if the most powerful wave of all moving silently across the bottom of the ocean can not throw all before it into havoc. Would it follow ancient patterns and obliterate a life not in accord with it? destroy all? The same problem comes to mind when I read Montague's poem **"A New Siege"** in *The Rough Field*. Is Ulster, and Ireland in general, captured in an ancient destructiveness? Will there be enough to build on? An optimist, like Toynbee, would say, "World War III will not destroy all life." Perhaps only the old, the hags for instance, can face mindless destruction so calmly.

Montague makes clear in this book, as he has before, that his concern is with historical as well as psychological and physical patterns.... Even [in **"Wine Dark Sea"**], a poem that seems so studiedly calm, anxiety enters minds entangled with history in a prediction of nothingness. Yeats, for instance, regarded man's release from the cycle of death and rebirth as the ultimate good. Perhaps in his seventies Montague will too, but now such release only seems an end to entanglements that may lead to knowledge but not to single happiness. Ambivalence is stressed repeatedly. In **"Filet"** the nets dropped over boats become symbolic of purpose which makes life possible and also that which ensnares instincts in "a tourniquet of death." (pp. 57-8)

Though Montague's concern with politics has been constant throughout his writing, his contemporaries generally regard him as a writer of love lyrics, probably because Montague's political concern has been oblique, an implicit examination of political and cultural conditions as they shape friends and family. Understandably, then, many people reacted with surprise and irritation as *The Rough Field* began to appear in pointedly political parts. The general approach in this long poem is one anticipated by Montague's other poetry.... [The] poems in *The Rough Field* examine the particular disintegration of Ulster's culture through the example of people close to the poet.

By the time *The Rough Field* is into print as a complete volume, all sections of it will have appeared in some form before except for two. This examination of Ulster by a poet after many years of exile reasonably begins with a version of **"Home Again,"** after which **"The Leaping Fire"** concentrates specifically on his family.... In **"The Bread God,"** which must be considered one of the strongest sections of the whole long poem, family and the culture of the North are openly related to one another. Also in this section, Montague develops a form of sufficient complexity to present the multilevels of reality which constitute the religious and political history of the North. The poem is presented as a "lecture with illustrations in verse" which is transmitted by radio and frequently interrupted by "pirate stations." These surreptitious stations attempt to drown out Montague's portrayal of Catholic life in the North with Protestant war cries, such as *"'Cromwell went to Ireland / TO STOP / The Catholics murdering Protestants!'"* Here history is reversed. (pp. 59-60)

The violence of Penal Times is only suggested in **"Penal Rock/ Altamuskin,"** as Montague recalls a country grotto that served as a place of worship for Catholics denied their churches. He visits this place that once was a shelter for his family, now all dispersed, and imagines them at services.... Omitted is any direct reference to militancy among Catholics today; but this poem was published in 1968, before the violence in the North had become a way of life. (p. 61)

In the next three sections of *The Rough Field*, Montague will add two that have not yet been published: **"The Severed Head,"** which concerns the change from Irish to English as the language of Ireland, and **"A Good Night,"** which presents a boisterous

night in a pub that turns harsh as the men get drunk. Between these is **"The Fault,"** which expands and elaborates the poem by the same title. In all three, Montague investigates a culture cut off from its source: the ancient Celtic language and culture. And each presents a people grown brutal and purposeless after the linguicide.

But the condition of Northern Ireland today cannot be simply described as the result of centuries of conflict with England. In **"Hymn to the New Omagh Road,"** Montague shows the destruction of the land with its attendant cultural associations, as modern industrial progress justifies its power by exercising it. Montague develops a form to present contemporary practices and aberrations and at the same time to recall a simpler and less-troubled past.... Since progress and profit today remove all blame for any action, Montague gave his poem appropriate form when he made the first long section a balance sheet. Under **"Loss"** occur items—"primrose and dogrose"—one would hope, but not expect, a builder to value. The ironic "unlawful / assembly of thistles" indicates the tone of the whole section, and is carried over as well into **"Gain."** Here Montague itemizes the small economic advance, an increase of ten miles per hour of average speed, which sometimes sends the driver straight into Garvaghey Graveyard. (pp. 62-3)

Two sections appear before the final one, **"The Wild Dog Rose: "Patriotic Suite"** and **"A New Siege."** Both of these depict the effects of the 1916 Uprising in contemporary Ireland, the first in the South and the second in the North. Montague describes the theme of **"Patriotic Suite"** as "Decay in the South"; but the poem itself presents a somewhat more hopeful view of life in the Republic. The poem begins by merging the ancient battle music of the Celts with a sound from nature, "the wail of tin / whistle" and the "lost cry / of the yellow bittern." So begun, the poem establishes an innate, racial quality of resistance in the Irish.

Poems II and III describe the absence of spirit in art following the Revolution: "The mythic lyre shrunk to country size." Though this poem is entitled **"Traits and Stories,"** alluding to Carleton's stories about the North, the difficulty of post-Yeatsian Irish poets is accurately described. After the fervor and grandiose action of the Irish Literary Renaissance, poetry and life in the South often seemed trivial.

Obviously, much of **"Patriotic Suite"** must deal with the leaders and events of the 1916 Uprising. In **"Revolution"** Montague makes clear where his own sympathies lie:

> The bread queue, the messianic
> Agitator of legend
> Arriving on the train—
> Christ and socialism—
> Wheatfield and factory
> Vivid in the sun:
> Connolly's dream, if any one.

Connolly's socialist ideal appeals to Montague because, if put into practice, it might have kept the state from the boring sameness and bureaucratic structures of middle-class life— "the antlike activity of cars"—that Montague shows in **"Enterprise."** In the case of the hill tribes described in **"Tribal Dance,"** the warriors are discarded by the population after the battles are over. The impersonal description of death and disaster of those who have become useless, even detrimental to the quiet business of peace, marks the failure of the revolutionary spirit to continue after the revolution. (pp. 64-6)

"**Annus Mirabilis, 1961**" is generally colloquial in diction, though contemporary may be the more exact term, for reserve and control necessitate a traditional structure. The poem is a gentle ironic castigation of Ireland for belittling its revolutionary fathers. Spirit and freedom become unimportant in a state that measures its value in terms of "trade expansion" and neglects an intrinsic idea of self, one that has inspired revolutionary movements for hundreds of years.

"**1966 and All That**" stresses again the new complacence of Ireland in the midst of a much more energetic modern world. The poem ends by recalling the opening of "**Patriotic Suite**" from the point of view of someone who has spent some time, and some poems, examining modern Ireland: "the herring gull claims the air / again, that note! / above a self-drive car." Though he seems to lack optimism, Montague actually intends to make Ireland aware of its course, not to condemn it. . . . [We] are to believe that the spirit which took Ireland from under the wing of Mother England can take her to dignity and strength, but only if the people do not allow themselves to be lulled into passivity by the new and minimal prosperity.

The insubstantiality of Ireland's new image becomes evident in "**A New Siege.**" (pp. 66-7)

The contention that the violence in Ulster is part of a wider process of change is repeated by Montague throughout the poem. In one stanza he cites the uprising on college campuses which occurred so often in America during the late 50s and through the 60s. But this poem remains tied closely to the North and closer still to Londonderry, as seems stressed in Montague's dedication of the poem to Bernadette Devlin with the hopeful inscription: "Old moulds are broken in the North."

The sound of the breaking mould has been heard in rifle, grenade, and bomb. I await the sound of the new and must pessimistically wonder if Ireland in general, the North in particular, can escape the political lethargy that followed partition. Only a solution to Irish violence on categorically different grounds can, it seems to me, assure a country that will have a cultural existence which belongs to the present. The poets, especially, have brought to Ireland news of change, of new joy and pain; but the plain people of Ireland remain in the world of the 1950 American swing and have not heeded often enough their artists, the signalers of the process of man. Violence sweeps over, as poets write in avant-garde terms of radical solutions.

In particular, I must wonder if John Montague has tied his talent to a culture that cannot respect it; to wonder if his poetry would not be furthered by his total rejection of Ireland, which he did not even do in the 50s. At least it is possible to observe that Montague's poetry grows in technique as he increases in vulnerability. In *The Rough Field*, especially "**A New Siege**," he risks much by believing contemporary Ireland is worth writing about. Only the sound of a new, peaceful order will prove him right. (pp. 68-9)

> *Frank Kersnowski, in his* John Montague, *Bucknell University Press, 1975, 72 p.*

NICOLAS JACOBS

After such a statement as *The Rough Field* anything else on the subject will seem like an afterthought, and that is the first impression the reader has of *A Slow Dance*. But the richness of John Montague's basic themes leaves plenty of material to be worked on, and it would perhaps be more illuminating to

see the latest collection as a sorting-out of themes arising from *The Rough Field*, and a preliminary survey, of the kind represented by *A Chosen Light* and *Tides*, towards a further sustained statement. Certainly there are close connexions with the earlier work. ["**A Slow Dance**"] takes up (one is tempted to think) the implication of the need for ritual which emerges from the epilogue to *The Rough Field;* it can be read as enacting the relationship between man and the soil to which he belongs, in a sacred dance in which the numinous and the sexual enmesh. . . . (pp. 31-2)

It is as though the myth given a decent burial at the end of *The Rough Field* is being resurrected in a form more universal because associated with the fact of man's physical existence rather than a particular cultural context:

> A circle of stones
> surviving behind a
> guttery farmhouse,
>
> the capstone phallic
> in a thistly meadow;
> Seskilgreen Passage Grave.
>
> Cup, circle,
> triangle beating
> their secret dance
>
> (eyes, breasts,
> thighs of a still
> fragrant goddess).
>
> ("**Seskilgreen**")

What is expressed here can be seen, according to one's point of view, as a statement of the power of God as it informs the whole world, or of the necessity of paganism. We find something similar given expression by David Jones in "The Tutelar of the Place" and by George Mackay Brown in many of his Orcadian poems; the point is emphasized in the litaneutical form of "For the Hillmother". It may be fanciful to see here a formal echo of the hymn *Anima Christi*, yet such a syncretism, if remarkable in 'puritan Ireland', would seem so neither in its mediaeval predecessor nor in Mackay Brown's mythicized Orkney. Where myth and religion meet, there may be a way beyond the problems stated in *The Rough Field*.

The second section of the book appears to return to the old themes. . . . [The] exact significance of Montague's poetry often takes time and the developing patterns of context to become fully clear. At the moment, it is not plain that the poems are, or are meant to be, an advance on *The Rough Field*. (pp. 32-3)

The third section, beginning with the sequence "**The Cave of Night**," appears as a further examination of myths in their destructive aspect. It is hard to determine whether the section represents a simple revulsion from the nightmare world (extending from the human sacrifices of pagan Ireland to those of Christian Belfast) it pictures or a pessimistic acceptance that the destructive side of myth might be the necessary price for its life-giving aspects. "**Killing the Pig**" is the crucial poem here, and its significance is ambiguous:

> A child is given
> the bladder to play with.
> But the walls of the farmyard
> still hold that scream,
> are built around it.

After so much celebration of rural Ireland it is a little difficult to read into this poem the condemnatory tone which its symbolism might seem to require; is there here an acceptance of some kind of violence, and, if so, where would that leave the serene mythopoeia embodied in the slow dance? Again we may have to wait and see; but in the closing sequence, **"Coldness,"** the heritage of violence is merely noted, certainly not accepted.

If there is the germ of an argument in the third section, the fourth returns to the documentary mode: the descriptions and images of family recall *A Chosen Light* and *The Rough Field.* As in any good set of variations, the poet cannot be said in any derogatory sense to repeat himself; as an example of a powerful detail giving point to a recurring theme one might take the end of **"At Last,"** where the poet's father, coming home from America, finds communication possible with his son at last when they listen together to a recorded broadcast by the son himself. It remains to be seen where these poems lead. Nor is it obvious that the last sequence, **"O'Riada's Farewell,"** is meant to have a thematic connexion with the rest. On the face of it an elegy for a dead friend and a meditation on an artist who destroyed himself, it might be made to correspond in some way to the state of Ireland; but again it is far too easy for a commentator at this stage to see 'meanings' that are no part of the poet's intention. To grope for that intention is all the honest critic can do. I should prefer in any case to wait for a further instalment of John Montague's work in the hope that, as with *The Rough Field,* the development of the ideas into new patterns will give substance to the emerging questions and suspended judgements of *A Slow Dance,* and provide rather more evidence of what the poet is about in these impressive, but evidently provisional sequences. (pp. 33-4)

> *Nicolas Jacobs, "John Montague," in* Delta, *England, No. 55, 1976, pp. 22-34.*

PAUL MARIANI

[*The essay from which this excerpt is taken was originally published as "Fretwork in Stone Tracery (John Montague)," in* Parnassus, *No. 1, 1979.*]

John Montague published *A Slow Dance* and *The Great Cloak* three years apart, though their subjects—old laments and modern loves and their different musics—cover the same five-year period in his life. . . . *A Slow Dance* is by far the stronger of the two books and I cannot read it without thinking of the old, pre-nineteenth-century Irish tunes that belong to a primitive world with its convoluted melodic line, dirgelike and unearthly. Only Seamus Heaney among Irish writers today can compare with Montague when it comes to evoking this old Irish music with its vigor, its subtle webbing, its rainsoaked landscape of gray rock and burren, hedgerow and hawthorn and bog. And if *A Slow Dance* is not Montague's most ambitious book—that honor belongs to his earlier sequence on the Irish troubles, *The Rough Field* (1971)—then it is still his strongest and most satisfying to date, touching a world aligned to Ireland's distant past: somber, unrelenting, pagan, aristocratic, like fine fretwork in stone tracery.

It is Yeats who stands behind this music, though Montague has managed to come close to the unadorned, stubborn ground of Ireland's being without Yeats's Romantic overlay and without recourse to his vatic posturing and Romantic rhetoric. At its best, Montague's language is more attuned than Yeats's to the rare phosphorescence of Ireland's ancient past. There is in Montague a clearing of the field, a greater knowledge of the past understood in its own uncompromising terms, with less guesswork, less anxiety over generating all-encompassing Irish

myths. What we hear are the old instruments resurrected: the shrill and beat of tin whistle, fiddle, harp, *bodhrán* and bones. . . . (pp. 203-04)

Yeats claimed to be among the last Romantics, yet forty years later we have still not escaped his valedictory note. Nor is this any less true for Montague. The difference, however, between his Romanticism and Yeats's is that he has cut his Romantic stance closer to the bone, making it more of a tribal affair, grafting his own line onto Yeats's late wintry branch: that stark, disconsolate, percussive line we find in the last plays and poems.

Besides the melodic line there is in Montague the realist's lens, images heightened and isolated by the jagged contours of the lines themselves. . . .

A Slow Dance reveals a great deal about how Montague takes hold of a subject and finds a style to work it with. He claims a field and marks it with his own scratches the way animals stake out territorial prerogatives. He wrestles forms—a wide variety of them, both closed and open—and makes them his own, even if it means twisting their necks into submission. He has used the sequence to ride over a sixty-four-page format. . . . (p. 205)

And these *are* true sequences. *A Slow Dance,* for example, begins with a seven-poem section celebrating the old blood-hungry gods of Ireland. The section salutes the old dolmens and stone circles that dot the Irish and English countryside, dating back to a time before Ireland's memories of England turned so violently bitter. . . .

The poem's last section closes like a diptych. Lining up with the opening sequence, this powerful, elemental lament is for Ó Riada, the Irish composer who worked so successfully in the old Irish musical tradition and who died in 1971. It is an antiphon calling across to the slow dance at the beginning of the volume, Ó Riada's impersonal, tormented music merging with Montague's sad lines. . . . (p. 206)

For the most part, Montague maintains an icy control over his subjects; syntax chafes against line break and the chiseled images pluck pizzicato against eye and ear. But sometimes, ever the Irish republican, he slips over into sentimentality, especially when he tries to deal with human love. For if Ireland has its proud, aloof blind bards strumming the golden hairs of ancient harps, their visions blazing into the dark skull as words begin to tumble into the thin air, she also has her tradition of beerhall and pub, where patriotic ballads recall the old tragedies and stir us in spite of ourselves. No less a figure than James Joyce was wary of this all-devouring, sentimental popular music, with its come-hithers and "Wild Colonial Boys." Only by turning the tradition on its head and keeping a safe distance from those sirens was he able to escape that sentimentality which sometimes catches up Montague. (p. 207)

In Montague's world the passage of time is an allusion, for the old terrors still dominate his landscapes. So in one poem he recalls a night spent in a Belfast high-rise hotel, where "jungleclad troops" ransacked the Falls area, running down the "huddled streets" in search of terrorists, until the "cave of night" bloomed "with fresh explosions." Ireland's landscape of nightmares is like Bosch's fevered vision, where a "woman breasted butterfly / copulates with a dying bat" and a "pomegranate bursts slowly / between her ladyship's legs," her eggs "fertilizing the abyss."

A man racked with nameless guilt and a stiff pride, so his poems tell us, Montague is at home, finally, with bog and farmyard, tides and rivers, seagull and wren and curlew, with phallic tumuli and stone outcroppings, death and the scent of death, the release afforded by strong whiskey and copulation . . . all bought at the cost of the knowledge of his own mortality. He has not escaped his Jansenist background, though we know from these poems he has tried. Out of his struggle for some sort of order and his willingness to surrender himself to some kind of primordial fate, he has created a slow dance, a somber music, set to a few dark chords to which he clings as to a birthright. (p. 208)

Paul Mariani, "John Montague," in his A Usable Past: Essays on Modern & Contemporary Poetry, *University of Massachusetts Press, 1984, pp. 202-13.*

A. K. WEATHERHEAD

John Montague is agnostic about the validity of conventional poetic form: he questions it, but he needs it there to be questioned, rather as Thomas Hardy needed the idea of God. He is divided in loyalty between formal patterns which are associated with the past and the values of an organic living present with its strong claims against conserved convention. He is the poet of exile, literal and metaphorical, recognizing the conflicting claims of the old country and the new—claims, that is, of Ireland and New York and of old and new Irelands. He responds to the losses and gains incurred in the renunciation of a tradition or, in [*The Great Cloak*], in the alienation of one love and the adoption of another. (p. 97)

His verse reflects his ambivalence not only in its substance but in its manner. . . . The prodigal son in a poem so titled in *Poisoned Lands* returns once a year to a landscape and a village that is "Unchanged in age or shape since childhood. . . ." The figure in **"Murphy in Manchester,"** on the other hand, lives with "Half-stirred memories and regrets. . . ." The poet himself knows the condition of exile: born in Brooklyn whither his father had emigrated from Ireland, he subsequently returned to the ancient turf.

The conflict of this exile, in the poetry and no doubt in life, is that between the conditions that made it "right" for the poet's father

> to choose a Brooklyn slum
> rather than a half-life in this
> by-passed and dying place

and, on the other hand, the appeal of home *because* it is home and ancient Ireland is the poisoned land which indirectly gives title to the early volume. (pp. 97-8)

[In] *Contemporary Poets of the English Language* the poet says:

> . . . my effort to understand as much of the modern world as possible serves only to illuminate the destruction of that small area from which I initially came, and that theme in turn is only part of the larger one of continually threatened love.

And throughout all the poetry love is associated with an enclosed place, though it is insecure there. . . . (p. 99)

The need for an enclosed place intensifies through the volumes of this poet as the threats of violence from outside become more dangerous. The latest volume, *The Great Cloak,* is itself

such a sanctuary: the epigraph begins, "As my Province burns / I sing of love . . ." . . . . (p. 101)

The complex of ambivalent attitudes toward Ireland and the enclosed scene of love—the desire for home, the recognition of the father's need to emigrate, and the sense of vulnerability—these may be taken as an index of the poet's complex attitude toward traditional order and, in turn, toward the order of formal verse structure. The early poems are mostly in regular metrical form, tightened on occasion by rhyme. But the form is flexible: metre can give way to free verse; if there are rhymes, they are rarely in a single pattern. Later the form becomes even more flexible: the poet-exile leaves the ordered poem as he left the ordered and archaic world. By 1972 Montague expresses an attitude to form which is not consonant with his own earlier practices and for which there is a parallel, partly no doubt a cause, and certainly an apt metaphor in his sojourn in America where apparently along with the husks of the Prodigal he was fed some of the new poetic principles. (p. 102)

For the most part, Montague had not up to . . . [this time] made functional use of his margins. In *Tides,* however, in the poem **"Life Class,"** he shows some good husbandry in deriving effects from the space at the edges of the page as he moves the short-line text across and back into three different positions in order to indicate different attitudes to the subject, the nude woman posing for the class. In the first eight stanzas, which adhere to the left margin, the body of the model is considered structurally—the hinge of the ankle bone, the calf's heavy curve, and so on. The second part, of about the same length but centered on the page, surveys the subject lustfully; the third, eight stanzas, again, set against the right margin, considers her humanly, as "a mild housewife / earning pocket money. . . ." Then in two more shorter sections the poem moves back to the left margin, combining the attitudes that have been individually declared. **"The Cave of Night"** in *A Slow Dance* similarly shifts the margin as the topic or perspective shifts. (p. 103)

[In *The Rough Field*] the poet has occasional recourse to the collage as a substitute for the logical ordering of a poem. In Part I the description of the poet's homecoming to Garvaghey is counterpointed by excerpts from the *Ulster Herald,* set in the margin, recalling the arrival of Lord Mountjoy at Omagh. Then opposite a description of the poet's grandfather, a marginal note quotes the announcement of the appointment by the Lord Chancellor of John Montague, among others, to the Commission of the peace for Tyrone County.

Some of the other parts of the poem have similar notes commenting directly or obliquely on the main stream of the verse. But it is noticeable that the collage technique is used most extensively in those parts which deal with formal disruption of one kind or another, whether the despoliation of nature for the making of a highway or the civil turbulence that attends denominational differences. Part III, **"The Bread God,"** subtitled "A Collage of Religious Misunderstandings," is concerned with such disorder. Here is a miscellany of passages of prose and verse: a letter to the prime minister deploring the entry of the United Kingdom into the Common Market, Carleton's description of Christmas in Tyrone, a letter from the poet's uncle a Jesuit priest, and . . . a communication the poet had received after being put on the mailing list of an extreme Protestant organization. . . . (pp. 103-04)

Part VII, **"Hymn to the New Omagh Road,"** also makes use of the collage technique. It opens with two lists, in prose, one titled, "**Loss,**" the other "**Gain,**" the titles being in Gothic type. They itemize the disadvantages and the advantages of the new road. Then there follows a passage called "**Glencull Waterside,**" in which verse describing the construction of the road alternates with lines of a pretty poem of an earlier date, reprinted in reduced type. . . . This part of *The Rough Field* closes with "**Envoi: the Search for Beauty,**" a little poem in a William Carlos Williams vein which mentions a farmer who, being drunk, bought "a concrete swan / for thirty bob," to deposit "on his tiny landscaped lawn," an anecdote which contributes ironically to the complex theme of beauty in the collage.

As D.E.S. Maxwell has noticed, the unity of *The Rough Field* is not imposed from an exterior scheme but grows with its composition, organically. . . . And this suggests that unity, the pattern, has been discarded, in part at least, so that the poem may accommodate protest, as if the artificiality of poetic order must give way before real grief. . . . We may note the parallelism here between Montague's strategy and the whole ambivalence of his attitude to Ireland: as by constraint he is exiled from the country and from the enclosed place of love and order, so he leaves the patterned poem for the collage, relinquishing an order to which, all the same, he repeatedly shows commitment.

In its substance, *The Rough Field* reflects the quandary of the returned exile, who wants the past for its orderliness—the world, as he puts it, "where action had been wrung / through painstaking years to ritual"—but who recognizes also that such a world, on account of its harshness, "only a sentimentalist would wish to see . . . again."

The exile has returned in this poem, however, in order to fulfill the need of self-determination. In its various parts, Montague encounters his grandfather, uncle, father, mother, and other figures out of his past who together constituted his ordered childhood. In other parts of the poem, particularly Part III, the "**Collage of Religious Misunderstandings,**" he presents parts of the feuding, past and present, that caused exile.

The loss, though, is not just Ireland, but by extension the loss of childhood innocence. In Part VI, "**A Good Night,**" the poet remembers how once he climbed to the source of a mountain stream until he came upon "a pool of ebony water / Fenced by rocks. . . ." Here, at the source of the stream and the source of his own being, he tried and failed to catch the "Ancient trout of wisdom" that legend declared inhabited the pool. But now memory itself irradiates the present; and, so it seems, "the burden of the mystery" is lightened. . . . (pp. 104-06)

[In *A Slow Dance*] his commitment to the homeland has become stronger. In the opening and title poem, ["**A Slow Dance**"], he moves back to his origins and in a slow cleansing and healing dance he is reborn from the Irish earth. In this volume he repeatedly returns to Ireland's mythic past. And the historic Ireland, also, still has its romantic appeal and the present it claims. "**The Errigal Road**" parades local memories, irradiated by the imagination but due to be effaced by the Troubles, which have perhaps sharpened them in the first place. They are shared now with an "old Protestant neighbour"—"old neighbours / can still speak to each other around here." But love is threatened and so is the enclosed place of order: "Soon all our shared landscape will be effaced." In "**Dowager,**" another thoroughly Irish anecdote, an old woman relates memories and reports the satisfactions of age. If she is not a symbol for Ireland as the Cailleach was in *Tides* she surely embodies

it; she and her situation as described (notwithstanding reminiscences of William Carlos Williams) could exist nowhere else. Most of the lines are end-stopped and suggest the limitations of age; but the enjambment between the last two stanzas and the emblem on her Rolls Royce suggest the constantly springing life of the spirit in the old satisfied body. . . . (p. 108)

After the earliest volumes Montague's poems are less lyrical. In *A Slow Dance*, they are more formal than some in *The Rough Field;* there are no unstructured items of protest that have resisted form. Often the poet is talking in verse which, though not by any means flat, does lack the intensity of the earlier lyrics. Sometimes the talk comes in the voice of Yeats, an element of the past of Ireland that Montague is not about to relinquish, which we hear with every use of the word pride. . . . Sometimes the verse reminds us of the conflict expressed earlier between "emerging order" and protest: the talking becomes uncertain as if the poet had failed to settle whether to present facts in their own bleak facticity or, with a little "leisure for fiction," to hold them to a more intense poetic pitch with figurative expression. . . . The poems in this volume depend often on the juxtaposition of clear-cut images presented without intensity and deriving from each other no more than the slightest incremental meaning that this technique frequently offers. There are some short simple poems using this technique, such as "**Sawmill, Limekiln**" and "**Homes.**" In other poems juxtaposition is more complex and used with more advantage. "**The Cave of Night**" in six separate sections combines Irish myth—the horrors of human sacrifice in the enclosure of a dolmen circle—with contemporary Irish history—lovers frightened in the night by bombs and nightmares. Proceeding on the similar principle of the juxtaposition of parts without editorial comment is "**Wheels Slowly Turning,**" a poem indebted to the memories of a medical orderly friend of the poet's, "who helped to clear many battlefields." The poem has five six-line sections distinctly separated by asterisks, and then an *envoi.* The first of the five parts presents the image of an overturned army lorry with "Wheels slowly turning." In the following are images of corpses; these become "bridegrooms of death . . . 'knee-deep in knight's blood, / hip-deep in the blood of heroes'." Then death appears as a woman, love making is war, and then as a Black Widow goddess. The lightly pitched *envoi* describes how the orderly lost a leg in a battle but lived to tell how its wooden replacement attracted women. . . . There are many mutually enriching relationships between the parts of the poem: the overturned lorry is like a beetle; death is a black widow; a destroyed battalion is a "crushed centipede." The knight's blood and the blood of heroes relate across the gap to the orderly's hunter's weapon; and death's love-making, of course, to that of the "toothsome ladies" in the *envoi.* . . . It is not in itself sinister that death, the sinister mistress, is so lightly traded off in this poem for an aphrodisiacal wooden leg, when the wheels have turned. But the transaction contributes to a sense that horrors have become such unsensational daily events as to be accommodated into our lives with no more than the insouciant raised eyebrow. (pp. 108-11)

But death, a regular preoccupation, is not always treated easily. The contemporary Ireland as pictured in a number of the poems, "**The Cave of Night,**" for one example, (and, of course, as pictured in the newspapers) is no longer an enclosure of love and order; and some kind of mental accommodation of death is no doubt an aching need. (p. 111)

With this volume the face of Montague's verse has become lined. It is concerned with death and, even more perhaps, with loneliness. The poet anticipates loneliness in **"The Errigal Road"** as the shared landscape is diminished; he feels the pathos of a friend dying alone and of a "heart locked in"; he knows the "secret shell / of loneliness" and the sense of loneliness when cars pass each other at night on the long country roads. . . . In these recent poems the place of order has become constricted and fearful. Meanwhile outside, everything, the great globe itself, swims in solitary vacancy.

The latest volume, *The Great Cloak,* confirms the ambivalence of this poet who is unwilling to relinquish what he has repudiated. It is, in itself, as suggested above, a deliberate withdrawal from the war-torn Province, where ignorant armies clash. The poet of "Dover Beach" called for human love as a haven in a torn world; Montague's haven, on the other hand, is apparently the poetry itself. The poems, which are to be read as a unified sequence, come in three parts, the first covering "libertinism"; the second, the disintegration of a marriage; the third, the growth of a new relationship. But in this last part, in **"The Point,"** the poet still turns back to his former wife as in earlier poems he turned back to the "bypassed" Ireland. . . . In the last poem of the volume, **"Edge,"** the poet has found a "sheltering home," an Edenic place with the uninsistent symbols of garden, lighthouse, vast lifting Atlantic tides, and harbour arms, where he and his new wife may rest. They are blessed. And yet the poem offers no sense of permanent security: the two people are there out of good luck, and fate relenting, and at last only on the edge. . . . (pp. 112-13)

A. K. Weatherhead, "John Montague: Exiled from Order," in Concerning Poetry, *Vol. 14, No. 2, Fall, 1981, pp. 97-113.*

EDNA LONGLEY

John Montague's imaginative persona combines the love poet, the evoker of "memoried life", and the cultural anatomist. This last role, culminating in the grand if imperfect design of *The Rough Field* (1972), has received most attention. Yet the force of that sequence as an exploration of Northern Irish "tribal pain", of "the pattern history weaves / From one small backward place", lurked in the precisely captured Tyrone scenes and portraits of *Poisoned Lands* (1961). There the sensuous self-immersions of Seamus Heaney are anticipated in poems such as **"The Trout"** ("To this day I can / Taste his terror on my hands") and **"The Water Carrier"** . . . . But Montague's "original townland" is more inhabited than Heaney's, and its violence and mystery more directly express "Ancient Ireland". . . . [**"Like Dolmens round My Childhood, the Old People"**], together with other figures from *A Chosen Light* (1967), were later to give *The Rough Field* its communal backbone; while the darker side of Montague's early imagery—petrification, putrefaction, superstition—perhaps unconsciously tapped the Ulster unconscious.

More conscious and programmatic, *The Rough Field* sometimes trades immediacy for formulaic *leitmotifs*. . . . Nevertheless Montague on the whole discovers in his home ground ("Garvaghey" means "the rough field") a plausible microcosm for Ulster's complications of race, place and language. . . . Douglas Dunn has criticized his historical determinism, the acceptance that "Once again, it happens". But, besides the inevitable fatalism in most contemplations of the Irish question, Montague's natural inclination runs to dignified elegy rather than political argument or the "positive art" recommended by Louis MacNeice in the face of fragmentation.

The Rough Field mourns not only **"A New Siege"** in Derry, but also the way in which "the New Omagh Road", on top of the Plantation, has bulldozed the past. . . . The layout of *The Rough Field,* as published by the Dolmen Press, once superbly supported this "bardic" formality. Now, unfortunately, many of Montague's longer poems suffer strange blanks due to excessive space left at the bottom of their first pages. And *The Rough Field,* already weakened by the restoration of certain poems to their former contexts, loses its sections and its separate identity in Part II of the *Selected Poems.*

Even before *The Rough Field* "pattern" and "ritual" were becoming favourite words of Montague's. . . . Stylization advances in *A Chosen Light,* where **"A Bright Day"** celebrates "a slow exactness / which recreates experience / By ritualizing its details". Always a poet of statement as well as imitation—the root of his dilemma—Montague stylizes and ritualizes more effectively through rhetoric than through imagery. In recent collections his verse often renounces momentum in favour of stilted, statically posed images: "Beneath, white / rush of current, / stone chattering / between high banks." Although some of these images are beautiful—cattle "lashing the ropes / of their tails / across the centuries"—this seems a wilful attenuation, reflecting the French and American influences (and influences from the visual arts) which succeeded Montague's initial Audenesque exuberance. The short line, that potential enemy of the dynamic, denies his later love poetry the rhythmic and verbal dash of the celebrated **"All Legendary Obstacles"**. . . . The retrospects on divorce and remarriage in *The Great Cloak* (1978) lack this tension and intensity; just as Montague's "Irish" poems after *The Rough Field* tend to collapse into a kind of celtic *chic*. . . .

But if the poet, or his intention, sometimes overlies individual poems, John Montague's *Selected Poems* are none the less indispensable. He began to write in the early 1950s when not only Irish politics but Irish poetry could be regarded as a "struggle with casual / Graceless unheroic things, / The greater task of swimming / Against a slackening tide". More than any poet of his generation he opened up channels between the Irish and English literary traditions, between regional and cosmopolitan allegiances, between Ulster and Irish perspectives. The fact that tides have turned, bringing in an unexpected shoal of younger Northern poets, must not obscure his achievement.

Edna Longley, "The Pattern History Weaves," in The Times Literary Supplement, *No. 4137, July 16, 1982, p. 770.*

JOHN LUCAS

[John Montague] makes clear that his concern with place customarily yields a poetry that's the opposite of escapist.

Montague is very much an historian, even an archaeologist, of Ireland. . . . This sense of stumbling across an Irish past is vital to much of his best work, but it also creates a problem. For everyone and everything is likely to turn into a cultural artefact ('Another emblem there!'); and in such poems as **"The Sean Bhean Bocht"**, **"Country Matters"**, **"Lament for the O'Neills"**, there's a sense of individuals being put on parade in order to demonstrate their Significance. Being human isn't enough. Of course, so intelligent a poet is aware of this danger and can turn it to advantage, as he does in a fine early poem, **"Like Dolmens Round My Childhood, the Old People"** . . . .

Yet even this presumed laying of ghosts allows for their continued presence. And indeed in a way they are, to use the Yeatsian term, presences. Moreover, the very fact that they *are* presences means that they testify to that deeply-troubling tension between continuity and discontinuity which repeatedly surfaces in Montague's work, as it perhaps must. For the past out of which the presences emerge is infected by the particular history of Ireland, which can't be off-loaded. This is partly a matter of language. In several poems Montague introduces Gaelic words, but they thrust up self-consciously, shards of a lost culture. . . .

Everywhere the past breaks in, but never as simple consolation. There is, for example, the bitterly cunning **"Poisoned Lands"** with its wicked last line, in which the poet imagines the landowner saying 'If you too licked grass, you'd be dead today'. The colonised must toady to their masters, but having to lick what rhymes with grass is to come near to destroying yourself. (And somewhere behind the line, no doubt, is Spenser's wonderment at those Irish people he saw reduced to eating grass.) Montague evokes the brutal implications of such life in several good, mordant poems, and one is rather more than that. **"The Wild Dog Rose"** is a rich, powerful poem about an old crone whom the poet has known since childhood, whose place and appearance he keenly evokes, and who tells him a terrible tale of how she was nearly raped by a drunk who broke into her cottage. . . . [The] subtly-cadenced lines voice a sense of generous vulnerability, even of love, and it is surely all-important that Montague here uses unmetred verse, for its unemphatic, hesitant rhythms mean that he doesn't run the risk of improper shaping or emphasis. I imagine that he's learned a good deal from 20th-century American poets, in particular William Carlos Williams and (less valuably) Robert Creeley, and the consequence is that in manner his best poems usually enact discoveries; they do not feel as though an issue is being forced. It is a virtue of such a manner that it requires Montague to forgo the grand, heroic gesture or pose. What we have instead is the kind of balanced, impartial-it-may-seem voice that he imagines for the seagull:

> What a view he has
> of our town, riding
> inland, the seagull!

And although Montague's balance is hard-won, because he is committed to an Ireland from which the seagull can flap away, the poem's lean humour typifies his sceptical but not ungenerous temperament, and embodies the exactness of vision which he speaks of in **"A Bright Day"**, . . . and which is present in the best of his love poems (especially **"All Legendary Obstacles"**). To have sustained this vision so successfully makes the publication of this *Selected Poems* an important occasion. (pp. 20-1)

John Lucas, "Pleading for the Authenticity of the Spirit," in New Statesman, *Vol. 104, No. 2682, August 13, 1982, pp. 20-1.*

EDWARD LARRISSY

John Montague's *Selected Poems* makes one wonder why more of the Irish had not made it into [*The Faber Book of Modern Verse*]. Nothing between Yeats and Heaney, unless you count a few Anglos. Montague is a fine poet, and could certainly pass muster. He has the usual post-Yeatsian fear of rhetoric: 'Enlarged profile, gun and phrase,' as he nicely puts his association of posturing politics and language. He praises Tim,

'the first horse I rode', for 'denying / rhetoric with your patience, / forcing me to drink / from the trough of reality.' And again in **"A Bright Day"** we are told of what seems to Montague 'The only way of saying something / Luminously as possible.' . . . This is something Montague can achieve, often finely. In this respect he is often reminiscent of the later Heaney (or is it the other way round?) Not of early Heaney: Montague lacks that earthy sensuousness of perception and language. His is rather a tough urbanity of stance and diction which seems somehow characteristically Irish and, rhetoric or not, invites a comparison with Yeats, albeit a limited one.

There is something to be said for a good ear and for fine phrasing. Sometimes the rhythm of a Montague poem is impossible to decide on: the effect is awkward and unprepossessing, lame rather than deliberately rugged. . . .

These *Selected Poems* are divided into two parts. The second begins with *The Rough Field* (1972) and with that renewed political awareness which everywhere accompanied the resurgence of nationalism in the Six Counties. Before this, Montague had looked with a kind of passionate detachment at intense moments of his own experience of living in Ireland. With *The Rough Field* there is a renewed interest in the tragedy of Irish history. . . . **"Lament for the O'Neills"**, **"A Lost Tradition"**, **"Sound of a Wound"**, all deal with the embittered Irish knowledge of having been disinherited from the great and extraordinary Gaelic culture. **"A New Seige"**, which looks at Derry past and present, is conscientious stuff, but little more. **"The Cave of Night"** gives a dark view of the violence on both sides of the present Troubles, switching between legendary pre-Christian Irish child-sacrifice and the bombing of children in a community centre. This poem achieves a fine nightmare intensity.

Formally Montague has moved towards a greater use of fluent, run-on short lines. This seems to help him to discipline his rhythm, though his voice hasn't changed much. One must beware of the tendency to think that poems which look sparse on the page really are terribly precise and imagist. Montague could hardly be described as an imagist—and no harm done. Nevertheless he has always been able to startle with a precise impression. (pp. 62-3)

Edward Larrissy, "Judging, Knowing and Making," in Poetry Review, *Vol. 72, No. 3, September, 1982, pp. 61-3.*

THOMAS PARKINSON

Montague is more immediately attractive than Kinsella, and he often writes poems that would excite the envy and admiration of any poet, from **"All Legendary Obstacles"** through **"Edge."** His poetry works with most charm when affection moves toward passion. As a love poet he is comparable to Lawrence and Graves, with Graves serving as his master. Graves functions well for him, especially since his immersion in French and American poetry leads him to modulate the standard forms that Graves mastered. Montague's ear is not entirely reliable, but he does not fall into the conventional line that sometimes plagues Kinsella. When he moves beyond the personal and erotic poem, Montague shows an extremely varied control of prosodic vocabulary. The section chosen from *The Rough Field* (1972) indicates his power of bringing together deeply personal family love with his indignation at oppression, uniting all under the common wild dog rose. These poems [found in *Selected Poems*] form a good entry into his work.

Scholars will have as merry a time with Montague's texts as they do with those of Graves. But the poems just cited are far less than half of those originally printed in *The Rough Field*. The book under review is highly selective, and I regret that a poet who so carefully composed his books is not presented more fully. Perhaps, like Wallace Stevens, Montague thought a more inclusive Collected Poems to be a preamble to death.

[*Selected Poems*], then, should be read as an introduction to an extremely fine poet, and a sensible reader will seek out the individual volumes from which it is selected, especially *The Rough Field* and *The Cloak*. . . . Although the *Selected Poems*, including some hundred and twenty-five poems, is not just the tip of the iceberg, it omits a great deal of splendid work. The problem it confronts—the wide range of Montague's work—is even greater for a reviewer with limited space: How to suggest the qualities of a poet who writes savage political poems, poems of familial affection and loss, poems with a lustful passion as attractive as it is startling, poems evoking natural landscapes with rich overtones of charged emotion, tender eloquent elegies for the gifted who die too young, and all these with an increasing command of the traditions and innovations of centuries of human experience? It cannot be done. . . . (pp. 665-66)

> *Thomas Parkinson, "Poetry Is Alive and Well in Ireland," in* The Georgia Review, *Vol. XXXVI, No. 3, Fall, 1982, pp. 662-68.*

BERNARD O'DONOGHUE

[John Montague's *Selected Poems*] anticipated five of the poems in this new volume, *The Dead Kingdom*. Already some interesting changes have been made in these five (which are among the most memorable poems in the book). Some of these changes are just slight, felicitous verbal adjustments: for instance, **"At Last"** describes the poet's father's return to Ireland from America (we remember him from the earlier poem **"The Cage"** as 'the least happy / man I have known'). While the son is driving him home, they stop at a pub and listen to a radio broadcast by the poet which revives their closeness. 'Well done', the father said in the version in the *Selected;* 'Not bad', he says now, more expressively. There are more substantial changes which answer to the different setting of poems in the two volumes, as in the case of the verbally precise **"The Well Dreams"**; some changes in diction there tighten up the poem's delicate music, but it has an altogether different resonance in *The Dead Kingdom* where its ageless stillness is the culmination (italicised throughout) of the second volume's five sections, **"This Neutral Realm"**. . . .

The theme of [*The Dead Kingdom*] is the tension in, and between, the two parts of Ireland as the poet has experienced them. . . . The book is the most compelling treatment yet of Montague's subject, famously well summarised in *Irish Poets in English* by Maurice Harmon: 'reaching inward and homeward, to family life, to history, to the lost and vanishing culture, to whatever details may be detected in the personal, familial and national past to account for actual experience and for the individual artistic vision'. But [it] is all expressed with Montague's incomparable wit and lightness; his poetry is fastidious, exact, lucid without ever calling attention to itself, and it covers subjects of great diversity: the horror of the bus-burning in **"Northern Express"** (reminding us that we are reading one of Muldoon's inspirers); the pastoral clarity of **"The Well Dreams"**; above all the spare, painful emotion of his family poems. . . .

The appearance of this book reminds us of two things: first, discussion of politics (even Irish politics in English poetry) can be direct and still unhectoring, as in **"The Black Pig"** section. . . . Secondly, and more obviously, *The Dead Kingdom* reminds us of Montague's eminence, reclaiming for him his place among the leading modern poets. (pp. 70-1)

> *Bernard O'Donoghue, "Picking and Choosing," in* Poetry Review, *Vol. 74, No. 3, September, 1984, pp. 70-2.*

DOUGLAS DUNN

That talent for organization and the placing of parts which distinguished *The Rough Field* again underlies the success and interest of Montague's *The Dead Kingdom*. . . . Considered free of their sophisticated setting, many of Montague's poems are simple and moving. Poems on his mother and her death, his father, relatives, childhood, the Troubles, places, mythology and ancient history are juxtaposed within five titled sequences and played off one against the other.

At times, the book seems intended to contrast an affectionate elegy for his parents with a bitter and reluctant mourning of the matter of Ireland. Intimate and public sorrows, private grief and public calamity, encourage an uncomfortable medley of feelings in a reading of *The Dead Kingdom*. The death of the mother seems a larger than personal loss, while the proximity of **"Northern Express"** (a description of an incident from Ireland's contemporary violence) to **"Gravity"**, **"Intimacy"**, **"A Muddy Cup"** and other personal poems is surely a deliberate ploy.

Where Montague's design fails is in those poems that inflate the feeling of the book as a whole rather than serve it. **"Invocation to the Guardian"** and **"Deities"** introduce an overblown faith in mystique and antiquity. It is almost as if they represent an effort to graft on the loftiness that the plainer idiom of the rest of the book resists. Not so, perhaps, the two other poems related to them, the panoptic **"What a View"**, a more realistic soaring of imagination, and **"The Well Dreams"**, which sets off "the hidden laughter of earth" and the nature of Ireland free of history and inhabitants. . . .

Without the contemporary hyperbole of **"Deities"**, *The Dead Kingdom* would be wonderfully unified, its narrative movement, its marriage of public and private realms, of curse and blessing, little short of tremendous. I doubt if Montague has ever been so controlled and touching as he is here in such poems as **"The Music Box"**, **"Family Conference"** and **"The Locket"**. Melody and imagery may have been sacrificed to narrative and feeling, but Montague's art in *The Dead Kingdom* is to make us not miss them.

> *Douglas Dunn, "The Dance of Discontent," in* The Times Literary Supplement, *No. 4253, October 5, 1984, p. 1124.*

SEAMUS DEANE

Writing in Sean O'Faolain's *The Bell* in 1951, John Montague called for a caustic, Swiftian voice 'to clear this apathy from the air'. He also demanded of his generation that it reflect Catholicism as a living force in Irish life. For a long time it has been customary to associate the Catholicism of the new state and the apathy of the thirties and forties as natural allies and there is no denying a certain coincidence between them.

But the 'other' Irish Revival, which included Austin Clarke, Denis Devlin, Patrick Kavanagh, Frank O'Connor and Sean O'Faolain among its best-known figures, was a movement which confronted and absorbed the political and cultural force of Irish Catholicism, sometimes with hostility and sometimes with sympathy, and always with a consciousness of its difference from the preceding generation of Yeats, Synge and Joyce.

This movement, or series of interlinked movements, made a virtue of its localism, of its deep insider's knowledge of the life of the mass of the Irish people, contrasting this with the shallower if more cosmopolitan attitudes of the Revival.... John Montague began his career at a moment when the dispute between the attractions of a bogus cosmopolitanism and a native loyalism had reached a point of exhaustion. The marks of that struggle have remained in his poetry ever since.

Born in New York, brought up in the family home in Tyrone in Northern Ireland, educated in Dublin, he spent long periods in the United States and in France before returning to Ireland. Montague's experience seems designed to enforce and reconfirm the legitimacy of that dispute. In one respect he is decisive in resolving it. Return to Ireland is a return to closure, oppression; exile from it is an escape to openness, energy, freedom. While this is by no means the whole story, it remains an important feature of it. Ireland, in one of its guises, is a maimed and maiming place. It makes exile inescapable, return, in the full sense, impossible. Montague remembers Patrick Kavanagh's 'baffled fury' as that 'of a man flailing between two faded worlds, the country he had left, and the literary Dublin he never found'. He fears this fate of being caught in the interval between two worlds but he also seeks it and feels sought by it. Home is lost, exile is temporary and no solution, only writing, founded on the experience of being neither wholly national nor wholly international, remains. Dislocation, in its etymological sense, is his obsession. Whatever he returns to—Tyrone, Dublin, Paris, the sites of childhood or of love, he finds them broken and out of their brokenness tries to recompose the wholeness of feeling which they once represented. Specific places matter a great deal in his poems and he concentrates on their detail with a miniaturist's care, seeing in every part the presence of the whole. His melancholy thus refines itself into a connoisseur's art. The history of feeling is captured in the exquisite detail. From *Forms of Exile* (1958) to *Tides* (1970) Montague reads his own plight as an encounter between an aesthetic sensibility and an unforgiving history, the position of the exile who returns to find his home incomprehensibly the same and yet, because of that, suddenly anachronistic, fossilized.

Yet the stress of the relationship between his country and his art is not to be understood as an enervating struggle between natural opposites. The fragile, almost anorexic, form of his poems is founded on something other than a wish to distinguish his art from its contrastingly farouche origins. It arises also from the wish to incorporate this uncivil element, to achieve some kind of truce with it without ever going so far as to compromise or to be compromised by it. **"Like Dolmens Round My Childhood, The Old People", "The Sean Bhean Bhoct", "Speech for an Ideal Irish Election", "Old Mythologies"** and **"Virgo Hibernica"** are poems in which, in a variety of different ways, Montague attempts to come to terms with the local and the legendary elements of his past, trying to take the weight of it in his verse without being brought low by it. History is important but, to be manageable, it has to be shaped and stylized into images. The image thus becomes more than a representation of the past; it is also a mark of the poet's triumph over it. It is familiarized into his own idiom. (pp. 146-48)

The image, in its finality, conquers narrative so completely that there are times when the narrative appears to be little more than the excuse for the production of the image. The capacity to master the Irish past is so pronounced that the reader may not feel the strength and risk of the dark forces that have been so expertly contained. The stylishness therefore courts the danger of reducing the feeling. The poise, we may feel, would be more impressive if we had a stronger sense of the imbalances which it has so narrowly escaped. In relation to history, Montague keeps a certain distance. Yet this impression is countered by what may be called the explanation for this distance which is, at one level, the fear of being infected by an easily available rhetoric. (pp. 148-49)

There is a temptation to speak of Montague's poetry as petering out into silence but this would be inexact. Instead, what he does is to exploit all the possibilities of muteness in which, in the absence of speech, there is gesture—of the body, of landscape, or objects in a room. This is most clearly seen in his love poetry in which, time and again, the feeling rises towards muteness and is then transferred from speech to the pathos of gesture. So, in this respect, the elegance and the refinement of the poetry is not an evasion of feeling but a means of handling its power to strike the writer dumb. He defers to gesture in order to achieve the distance he needs.

Between 1958 and 1970, from *Forms of Exile* through *A Chosen Light, Poisoned Lands* (1961) to *Tides,* Montague maintained this distance in the two kinds of poem which dominated his work—poems about Irish and poems about private experience. Almost all the latter were love poems; almost all the former were strategic containments of his culture and of its past. The love poems are sensual and candid enough about the physical aspects of love. But they are not erotic. The love relationship is bathed in the light of appreciation and of memory and the heat of desire is thus subdued. The observation is not voyeuristic, dwelling on detail, but rather regretful, dwelling on the passing moment.... [In **"The Same Gesture"**], the final lines ... have that intonation of a courteous farewell which lends pathos to all the love poems while, at the same time, preserving their tender (and stylish) distance. The first personal pronoun is usually 'we', not 'I'. The experience is not only shared, but has been shared in a mute past to which the witnesses are objects, actions. The community of the two lovers leaves no more than a faint impress on the surrounding world. The watermarks of privacy haunt those reimagined bedrooms and gardens where the lovers had once been, but there is a decisive sense of removal, of a life lived intensely in exile. So the relationship of the love poems to those directly concerned with the common and shared past of Ireland is a mute one too. The two kinds of poem have a stylistic harmony, but Montague appears at this stage to be seeking a thematic unison between them. He is still marked by the old dispute between Ireland and his art, between being a poet and an Irish poet.

The dispute returned with renewed force after the outbreak of the Northern troubles in 1968. Old moulds were broken, indeed, as far as the political situation was concerned but, in poetry, new opportunities offered themselves very quickly. Montague's response to these events was to reassert his position as an inheritor of the Northern crisis. His poetry, and his volume of short stories, *Death of a Chieftain* (1964), had registered the early symptoms of the collapse. The notion of literature as an Early Warning System gained fresh currency for a time. At this point, in the early seventies, Montague revised much of his past work in the light of the new situation and produced two volumes *The Rough Field* (1972) and *Poisoned Lands* (1977) in which he finally confronted the history which he had for so long distanced. . . . The effect was that Montague enforced a new reading of his work, offering his poems now as interlinked moments which had at last discovered their origin and purpose. (pp. 149-51)

In these volumes, then, the exile returns to the home ground only to find it riven ever more deeply by division and dislocation and to discover in himself and in his family the same division and its characteristic consequence—dumbness, muteness, aphasia. But now the poems of exile, of disengagement, of style based on the achievement of distance, all move together in the magnetic field created by the immense political current of the crisis. In addition, the poems now are flanked, in the margins, by the languages of the hustings, of folk-song and folk memory, of government report, of family record. Tyrone now becomes the site of devastation. The English invaders, the Protestant settlers, overlay the former Gaelic culture. The twentieth century violates the densely woven relationships of geography and history in its haste to create an urban wilderness. The Montague family, gaining some small prestige in the nineteenth century, nevertheless loses its inherited gifts—music and language—so that they now remain in the mute form of the decayed fiddle, in the half-mute form of the poet's flawed speech. A whole culture has undergone the experience of aphasia in losing its language, and then has painfully grown another tongue, the English tongue, which nevertheless remains marked by the political and social crises attendant upon its birth in the severed head of Irish Gaeldom. All around are the habits and stories of a degraded people and the desolate landscapes of a vanished civilization. The power of Montague's material, and the effect of his careful arrangement of it, are of themselves sufficient to make it memorable. Along with Denis Devlin's *The Heavenly Foreigner*, Patrick Kavanagh's *The Great Hunger* and Thomas Kinsella's *Nightwalker*, it is one of the most remarkable narratives in modern Irish poetry. (pp. 151-52)

History, although a potent force in Montague's work, is, finally, a maiming influence. It attracts him by the thought of community which it holds within it; it repels him by the spuriousness of the communal sense which it finally offers. *The Rough Field* is, in its way, a magnificent error, for it is founded on the notion that the individual poems of the earlier books will be liberated by the historical continuum in which they are placed. In fact, they are encumbered by it. The problem is intensified by the fact that the North and the South are historical territories which do give release to many of his contemporaries and their presence there seems to shadow his own—Kinsella in the South, Heaney, Mahon and others in the North. A pathfinder who discovers that the territories he broke into have been settled by others, he feels deprived of his imaginative preserve and is left to forage where others feed. This is a problem of psychic space, always a pronounced one in Ireland but knowable anywhere.

In a way, Montague was forced into a confrontation with the North, and with history, not only by the crisis but also by the emergence from it of a group of other writers who laid an unassailable imaginative claim to it. But this may have been his good fortune. The dependence of his poems on a series of syncopated images, on pleated phrasings, one folding over another, their connectives hidden, almost disqualifies them from the confrontation with history with its demands for extended

narrative. Narrative in Montague's poetry provides no more than a stage for the ballet of dainty interchanges. . . . (pp. 152-53)

In *A Slow Dance* (1975) and *The Great Cloak* (1978) Montague restores to his poetry the loneliness which is, paradoxically, its proper home. He can endorse his homelessness by imagining a community in which it would be healed but he does not violate it by laying claim to that community, by attempting to possess it as his own. . . . In *The Great Cloak,* the keenest poems show the pain of a man whose marriage has broken and who discovers 'that libertinism does not relieve his solitude'. Even when a new marriage restores him, the lovers find themselves in the solitude of one another's arms while Belfast falls to pieces around them. This feeling of solitude is the source of the aristocrat in Montague. His connoisseurship, his refinement, the easy elegance of his verse are infinitely preferable to the sentimentality, the plebeian togetherness which mars it when he cancels his solitude and believes he can dissolve it in camaraderie. In the end, nothing can dislodge the spear of isolation. It is the hurt that gives his work its distinctive feeling. (p. 153)

Montague remains a profoundly political poet. . . . But the more enduringly political aspect of his work lies in grieved admission that, although nothing can break in upon his solitude, the longing for relief from this plight is a legitimate and permanent one. It is no accident that he has championed two writers, Kavanagh and Goldsmith, both of them examples of the artist surviving almost impossible conditions. In his introduction to *The Faber Book of Irish Verse* he envisages an international poetry which has national roots, a definition of Irish which arises from a negotiation between the English and the Gaelic traditions. As in the poetry, the search is for a reconciled community, the refusal is to accept as inevitable the burden of solitude. Goldsmith's deserted village, Kavanagh's hungry hills, Montague's ruined Tyrone, are all abandoned places, victimized by history, repossessed as a possibility in poetry. But they are none the less lost, for all that. This Montague would not accept. But, as the later poems in his *Selected Poems* (1982) demonstrate, the acceptance has begun to grow. (p. 154)

Montague has finally come to see the dead kingdom of history and accepts his exile from it. But rather than see this exile as an aristocratic aloofness—which he recognizes to have been his attitude at one time—he now sees it as a strange form of presence, even protection, in the culture from which he has become separated. In the poem "Mount Eagle" (from *The Dead Kingdom*) the aristocratic bird finds that the moment has come to leave off his flight over the world and meet a different destiny in his mountain world. It was 'to be the spirit of the mountain'. This is a figure for Montague's own destiny. He has twice revised his career. Once, between 1968 and 1978, he rewrote his poems against the Northern crisis. Now, since *The Great Cloak,* he has begun to rewrite them again, but on this occasion against the experience of the solitude which the North bore in upon him. This remaking of his own poetry, his refashioning of the once exhausted notions of self and community, of art and country, is a transference to a new plane of one of the unchangeable features of modern Irish experience. It is as close to reconciliation as anyone has come, but the price paid has been high. . . . (p. 155)

Seamus Deane, "John Montague: The Kingdom of the Dead," in his Celtic Revivals: Essays in Modern Irish Literature, 1880-1980, *Faber and Faber, 1985, pp. 146-55.*

Alberto Moravia

1907-

(Born Alberto Pincherle) Italian novelist, short story writer, essayist, critic, dramatist, translator, scriptwriter, travel writer, editor, and journalist.

Moravia is one of the foremost Italian literary figures of the twentieth century. His depiction of existential themes, based upon mass indifference and the selfish concerns of the bourgeois world, predate the writings of Jean-Paul Sartre and Albert Camus. Deeply informed by the theories of Karl Marx and Sigmund Freud, Moravia's work commonly focuses upon such subjects as politics, sexuality, psychology, phenomenological philosophy, and art. In his exploration of humanity's conceptions of reality, Moravia presents a world of decadence and corruption in which individuals are guided primarily by their senses and sex serves as a comfort for spiritual barrenness and the inability to love. Because these themes have been repeatedly explored and reworked in his writings, some critics fault Moravia as a writer of limited range who has done little to advance the techniques of the novel or the short story. Most, however, appraise Moravia as an artist who realizes the full potential of his subjects and uses classic storytelling devices to examine the preoccupations of modern civilization.

Moravia's sensibility was shaped in part by a battle with tuberculosis that left him bedridden and isolated during his adolescent years. He spent much of this time avidly reading and writing and achieved major success with his first novel, *Gli indifferenti* (1929; *The Time of Indifference*). A realistic picture of middle-class corruption that flaunted the ruling fascist government's policy of idealistic formalism in art, the novel depicts sex as a basic psychological need and the most significant human activity. In a world of isolation and apathy, the characters in *The Time of Indifference* use sex, money, and politics as means toward achieving happiness, but their lives are plagued by lovelessness. Moravia drew praise for his psychological insight and his portrayal of a world approaching total disillusionment.

As an antifascist in the 1930s and 1940s during Benito Mussolini's regime, Moravia's actions were subjected to careful scrutiny, and he came precariously close to being labeled an enemy of the state. In the fiction he wrote at this time, including *Le ambizioni sbagliate* (1935; *The Wheel of Fortune*, later republished as *Mistaken Ambitions*), *La mascherata* (1941; *The Fancy Dress Party*), and the short stories collected in *I sogni del pigro* (1940) and *L'epidemia* (1944), Moravia depicted characters who abused others as a means of self-satisfaction, but he cloaked in allegory and satire what could be construed by censors as allusions to fascist politics. Due to the increased government pressures that accompanied the Nazi occupation in 1943, however, he and his wife were forced to flee Rome and live for several months among peasants in rural Italy.

Following these events, Moravia's fiction became more socially conscious, displaying Marxist elements and expressing sympathy for the lives of common people. In *Agostino* (1943)—published together with *La disubbidienza* (1948) in English as *Two Adolescents: The Stories of Agostino and Luca* (1950)—Moravia relates the story of an adolescent who loses his in-

nocence when he becomes increasingly aware of both his sexuality and the plight of the lower classes. *La romana* (1947; *The Woman of Rome*) portrays the experiences of a working-class girl who discovers strength, love, and acceptance through her difficult life as a prostitute. In *La ciociara* (1957; *Two Women*), which is widely regarded as one of Moravia's most poignant statements on the redeeming nature of human suffering, a shopkeeper and her daughter endure the brutal effects of war by overcoming their inability to experience compassion and grief. The short stories Moravia wrote during the postwar decade, like his novels from this period, are influenced by his preoccupation with populist concerns. In the short fiction collections *Racconti romani* (1954; *Roman Tales*) and *Nuovi racconti romani* (1959; *More Roman Tales*), Moravia depicts commonplace occurrences in the lives of working-class characters and uses colloquial language.

By the 1960s, Moravia had strayed from Marxism and had begun advocating intellectual solutions to world problems. In such novels of this period as *La noia* (1960; *The Empty Canvas*) and *L'attenzione* (1965; *The Lie*), ideology takes precedence over the narration of plot. The protagonists of both novels are artists who suffer intellectual, creative, and sexual crises. Moravia resolves his characters' dilemmas through basic Freudian and phenomenological principles. In *Io e lui* (1971; *Two: A Phallic Novel*), the humorous running dialogue between the protagonist and his penis, commonly interpreted as the ego and the id, provides a study of man's self-perceptions. Further collections of Moravia's short stories include *L'automa* (1962; *The Fetish and Other Stories*), *Una cosa e una cosa* (1967; *Command and I Will Obey You*), and *Il paradiso* (1970; *Paradise*).

Many of Moravia's later works center upon the dehumanizing effects of society and technology, the alienation of the human psyche, and the breakdown of personal communication. William Slaymaker observed that several of Moravia's novels published since 1960 feature characters who "learn through suffering to see the nature of their own personal and cultural reality and learn to escape the narrow confines of their own personal desires and modern cultures which exploit them as means to ideological ends." In the novels *La vita interiore* (1980; *Time of Desecration*) and *1934* (1982), Moravia again concentrates on the obsessive qualities of politics, money, and sex. *Time of Desecration* examines modern terrorism, while *1934* contrasts Germany's active acceptance of totalitarianism with Italy's passivity during Adolf Hitler's rise to power in Germany. In *L'uomo che guarda* (1986; *The Voyeur*), a middle-aged university lecturer preoccupied with nuclear war and sex struggles with feelings of ambivalence toward his father while attempting to salvage his marriage. In this novel, Moravia is also concerned with the voyeur/exhibitionist relationship between reader and author and between author and characters. The short story collections *Un'altra vita* (1973; *Lady Godiva and Other Stories*) and *Cosa e altri racconti* (1985; *Erotic Tales*) continue Moravia's examination of alienation and sexuality as well as his exploration of the female psyche begun in *Paradise*.

In addition to his fiction, Moravia has published collections of essays and travel pieces. Among his best-known nonfiction volumes are *L'uomo come fine* (1954; *Man as an End: A Defense of Humanism; Literary, Social, and Political Essays*), *La rivoluzione culturale in Cina ovvero ill convitato di pietra* (1967; *The Red Book and the Great Wall: An Impression of Mao's China*), and *A quale tribu appartieni?* (1972; *Which Tribe Do You Belong To?*). Many of his novels, including *The Woman of Rome*, *The Time of Indifference*, and *Il conformista* (1951; *The Conformist*), have been adapted for film, and he has also written a number of plays, most notably *Beatrice Cenci* (1958).

(See also *CLC*, Vols. 2, 7, 11, 18, 27 and *Contemporary Authors*, Vols. 25-28, rev. ed.)

THOMAS G. BERGIN

[It] would hardly be saying too much to call Moravia Italy's leading novelist. For this alone he would merit our attention; but the popularity of his translations hints at something more—implies, I think, that he has more than regional significance and belongs by right of achievement to that rather select international group of writers who have something to say that other men, regardless of national barriers, want to hear. To understand why he should have such an international appeal, we shall have to glance at the matter and manner of his work.

First of all, his roots are firmly fixed in what we might call traditional realism. Some of the short stories are "surrealistic"

or fantastic and the shortest of his full-length novels has an exotic background, but in the main his world is the middle-class society of Rome; which is to say, of a European metropolis; which again is to say, a class reproduced with only minor variations from Vienna to San Francisco. It is the world with which, in its superficial aspects, we are all familiar, a world made of taxis, cigarettes, suburban villas, and the tensions of civilized urban living. In this Moravia differs from many of his Italian contemporaries who are faithful to the regional tradition, whether of the romantic or naturalistic sort. There is enough detail in his novels to let us know we are in Rome, but only just enough; of local color there is very little and, as a matter of fact, in the early novels, the fondness for rain and cloudy skies could easily lead us to believe that the author's scene is Liverpool or Cleveland rather than Italy's sunny capital. So the reader who is a part of this general Western culture, whether he be from Bologna or Boston, will have no trouble recognizing the world of Moravia. Indeed, to many American readers it may well be more familiar than, let us say, Yoknapatawpha County. The denizens of Moravia's urban habitat are also recognizable, though perhaps at times we could wish they weren't. A typical cast may be found in **Wheel of Fortune**, which contains a middle-aged woman, temporarily estranged from her husband and anxious for reconciliation—not out of love, but out of hurt pride; a husband torn between his sensual desire for a young siren and his uncomfortable awareness that his wife has all the money in the family; a young girl, aggressive and self-confident, who intends to marry a journalist and build up a career for him; the journalist, *ipse*, who is more resigned than enthusiastic about his future and is led to break his engagement because he wants to redeem the aforesaid siren (or is it that he wants to build up the picture of himself as a fine fellow?); a moon-struck youth in the throes of adoration for the middle-aged woman; an older man, father of the boy, full of vanity and anxious to retain his prestige as an intellectual; and the young siren herself, around whom the plot revolves, avid for only one thing: plenty of money. The characters are of our times and of our kind, their motives readily understandable. A great deal of Moravia's appeal lies in the naturalism of his characters to which the complications of his interlocking plots lend, as it were, an extra fillip.

But that is not all. The Moravian character has his own identifying stigmata, and they too, deepening the personality described and hence justifying the interest of the perceptive reader, are at the same time illustrative of the preoccupations of the age we live in. The type that recurs most frequently in his works and which has won him most acclaim is the adolescent. And Moravia's youths are something special, something which only our own times, with the preparation of Freud, Dostoievski, and perhaps Gide, could have produced. The one thing they have in common is insecurity. The Moravian adolescent is a far cry from Stover at Yale or Willie Baxter; his nearest American counterpart is the protagonist of Salinger's *Catcher in the Rye*, but Moravia isolated the specimen nearly twenty years ago and has had all the time in between to define and, shall we say, to mount his catch. His first novel, **The Indifferent Ones**, contains a pair of young people, slightly post-adolescent in years but containing in germ all the elements of the more authentic species to follow. Their insecurity springs from a disgust with their family background, specifically the shoddy behavior of their mother. Their purpose is revolt, but revolt can only take the form of further degeneration or, in the case of these young people, moral indifference. At the same time they long earnestly for respectability and action. And act they can and do, but respectability on examination turns out to be either false or unattainable. (pp. 216-18)

Luca, in the story **"Disobedience,"** is overcome with such a profound world-weariness that he attempts a kind of progressive withdrawal from life which eventually brings on him a serious illness. Luca is saved by initiation into sexual experience, and as he is the only one of the adolescents in Moravia's gallery who really wins to salvation, there is an allegory here that is significant and of which more is to be said. In their solitude, their revolt against circumstances, and their dim suspicion that society is false and evil, all these young characters are at first glance simply romantics. (Moravia has admitted that his first novel at least was born of a "strongly romantic" mood.) But their outlook is anything but romantic; the sources of their distress are emotional as well as psychological, but their calculation and self-awareness are mature beyond anything the romantics ever dreamed of. They are flesh and blood, to be sure, but the color of their crisis is intellectual—coldly intellectual, one might say.

Yet for all that, the underlying romantic attitude is Moravia's true strength, even if it is not immediately apparent. For, taken all together, what do these adolescent crises signify if not a revolt against society and its cheap pretenses? Were it not for this thesis—and such it is, though never overtly expressed—Moravia would not have the appeal for his readers that in fact he does. For he is *in fondo*—very much *in fondo*, if you will—as much of a moralist, as much of a wistful idealist as any nineteenth-century champion of Rousseau or Shelley. Two short stories—as yet untranslated—may buttress the argument here. In one, called **"Metamorphosis,"** a young man goes to a fashionable reception and at a certain moment as he looks at the throng, he remarks that every guest has lost his human face and head and has taken on the features of an animal, reptile, or insect. He observes that there is a preponderance of asses, rabbits, and goats. In another story, and a very good adventure story it is too, a young courier, waylaid and robbed of his jewels, falls in with the girl bandit who, in order to win his sympathy, tells him a long story of her early innocence and betrayal and the like. She also, as a matter of course, seduces him. He is ashamed of "taking advantage of her," but the author (Moravia is never reluctant to interpret his characters) steps from behind the curtain and informs the reader that their only true relationship was in love, and the young man falling back on the conventional pattern of hypocritical bathos was in effect trading honesty for pernicious illusion. Such tales as these, underlined by the allegory of Luca's experience, give us the key to the meaning of the novels, which are on the political side anti-bourgeois, and in the spiritual realm truly desperate assertions of the need for integrity in human relationships, and affirmations of the values of natural instinct as against the frustrations of middle-class society.

In a way it is surprising that the political aspect does not loom larger in Moravia's works, for surely his basic thesis was intensified by the shabby pretenses of Fascism, to say nothing of his own personal suffering under the racial laws. And indeed *The Fancy Dress Party* contains elements of anti-Fascist criticism, while *La Speranza (Hope)*, written in 1944 when every one in Italy was speculating on the shape of things to come, views Communism with a good deal of sympathy, although with the reservations we should expect from an intellectual. And *The Conformist*, which the author thinks—as do others—his best novel, is the strongest indictment we have yet had of the confining and distorting effect of dictatorship on the human

soul. Yet for all that, *The Conformist*, is not merely an anti-Fascist novel, *The Fancy Dress Party* can be read on its own merits without reference to time or place, and *Hope* is unique among his works. For Moravia is too complicated a personality and too pure an artist ever to become a propagandist *tout court*.

In truth, for the most part, whatever element there may be of specific criticism of the political régime under which his characters have their being, it is overshadowed by the deeper significance of the implied melancholy estimate of society in general. For what is at the base of the maladjustments so painfully and clinically examined by the author—and it rings true enough to convince the reader—is a dissatisfaction with the materialism and vanity of middle-class society as he sees it. . . . I believe it is because, taken in the mass, the characters of Moravia echo the uneasiness of many citizens of the Western world in the face of social conventions that seem no longer acceptable and yet cannot easily be replaced, that he has had such general recognition. (pp. 218-21)

As for the manner of the telling, there are certain virtues in Moravia's style which surely have had much to do in getting him a hearing. Basically his style is rather conventional, close to the documentary if not to "journalese." His manner might even be considered old-fashioned in that it consists of alternating passages of conversation and commentary. His characters speak fluently enough and one might say at times too freely, but their speech is always a little literary in flavor; they talk indeed very much like characters in a book—and not a twentieth-century book, either. But the author is not content to leave them alone. His novels abound in descriptions of rainswept streets or drab hotel rooms or suburban villas. Such characteristics, to be sure, are not necessarily virtues, but from the point of view of simple communication Moravia has an advantage over many of his contemporaries in Italy and elsewhere who have gone in for elliptic conversations, impressionistic descriptions, and a very irregular narrative line. With Moravia, however disturbing some of the activities of the characters may be, the reader never has to ask what the author is trying to convey, and the narrative, not always fast moving, none the less does proceed along a trajectory that can be plotted without the aid of critical or philosophical exegesis. In the full-length novels there is very little humor, but there are not infrequent passages admirable either for pictorial beauty of description or for the graceful economy with which a concept or an observation is expressed. It is in effect not a style that pampers the reader, but it does not tease him either. Perhaps it is too simple to say that Moravia is one of the relatively few who still consider what they have to say more important than the striving for an original manner of saying it; yet such is the impact of his prose, an effect which at once helps the reader to understand the content and convinces him of the seriousness of the author's message. (pp. 221-22)

[Moravia] informs us that at the time he began *The Indifferent Ones*—in 1925—he had written a number of short stories and two novels, all of which were derivative and that *The Indifferent Ones* itself reflects the decadent realism "of the preceding quarter century." It is a phrase, of course, that could mean anything to the "influence" hunter, and perhaps like many writers Moravia is unaware of any specific literary inheritance. The character of his prose, hard, documentary, and urgent as it is, is distinctly reminiscent of Stendhal, as is also his combination of cool observation and romantic fancy. The relentless and probing dialogues, along with an almost morbid interest in the origins of motivations, are at once suggestive of Dostoievski. Such influences may well have come to him directly or may equally well have come through his reading of the works of his compatriots of a generation earlier: in all probability G. A. Borgese, whose *Rube* was a curious kind of Italian *Red and Black,* has left his mark on Moravia; and Pirandello and Bontempelli he must have read and can hardly have ignored. These, of course, were masters available to all of his generation, and Moravia is not the only contemporary writer in whom their doctrine is apparent. Yet he is the one disciple who seems to have profited most from that particular tradition, many of his generation having preferred the sentimental tradition of D'Annunzio or the experimental Americans, e.g., Hemingway, Faulkner, or Steinbeck, or the conventional regionalism of the Verga school.

Moravia's place in the history of Italian letters may be, and indeed will be, fixed no doubt with reference to the determinants we have mentioned. His significance both for his country and for the world at large is a different matter and seems already measurable. Defects he has, a kind of aridity in presenting the vicissitudes of his characters, a notable lack of compassion in the early novels, a predilection for the morbid, a lack of humor. I would be inclined to say that if he had remained the kind of precocious prober who wrote *The Indifferent Ones* he would not have had any especial claim on our attention save as an illustration of a state of mind universally prevalent in the early years of our century. But I think that beginning with *The Fancy Dress Party* and to an increasingly marked degree in the successive novels, *The Woman of Rome* and *The Conformist,* we may well find in him not only the accurate observer of the passing scene but an artist who combines rare technical skill with true sympathy for the afflictions of contemporary humanity. Most critics have tended to see in Moravia only one manner; *The Indifferent Ones* was in its way a perfect novel and, according to the common thesis, he has served us nothing new since. One of Italy's leading critics compares his career not to a road leading in any particular direction, but to a roller coaster which after a series of vertiginous swings brings us back always where we started. And, as far as manner and content are concerned, I am inclined to agree. It is the attitude in the later novels that seems to me to give evidence of a growth in compassion and understanding. (pp. 223-24)

I think that if Moravia had written only the early novels he would have to be reckoned with both as an authentic artist and a perceptive critic of our world. Now that he has added as well the extra-dimensional depth of compassion I believe that one can predict true greatness for him. Certainly he has won the right that very few novelists of his generation may claim to speak for all of us in the Western world who were born in the first decade of this introspective century; and there seems no reason to doubt that whatever he may yet have to offer us, enriched by his growing depth of understanding, must command our attention and respect. (p. 225)

> *Thomas G. Bergin, "The Moravian Muse," in* The Virginia Quarterly Review, *Vol. 29, No. 2, Spring, 1953, pp. 215-25.*

WILLIAM SLAYMAKER

While Moravia's fiction is full of dark portraits of human lives which lack guiding ethical ideas and cultural ideals, it is not true that his art is totally negative and pessimistic. His fictional images of humanity are positive in the sense that he believes, as a realist, that he is naming and seeing things as they are.

He summarizes his position in an essay devoted to realistic fiction where he repeatedly emphasizes that realism is the writer's courageous and humanistic act of describing what men are really experiencing and how they are managing to exist. Man's existence in a modern neocapitalist society may be bleak, yet the realistic revelation of it, being true, makes the aesthetic image somewhat positive even if the method of capturing that image is negative. (p. 81)

It is in *Man as an End,* and in particular the main essay which has given the book its title, that we find Moravia's most complete and eloquent statements about the plight of humanity in the modern world. This long essay, completed in 1946, makes it clear that Moravia is concerned about the use of man as a means or tool to accomplish ideological ends. His essential argument is that man is an irreducible irrational being not definable in precise terms. But reason in the modern world has attempted to reduce man to an ideological concept. Moravia believes the modern world cannot tolerate man as an end in himself because reason cannot tolerate human individuality and freedom. However, Moravia's attack on reason in the twentieth century should not be seen as a rejection of humanism. His attack is, rather, a critique of a conception of humanism too narrow to allow man an adequate arena of irrational behavior. (p. 82)

Although Moravia acknowledges . . . that "literature is by its very nature humanist", it is nonetheless difficult to find the positive aspects of his neohumanistic fiction. More frequently one sees the negative qualities of the lives of his characters. His fictional protagonists experience "boredom, disgust, impotence and unreality" in addition to the "nothingness" which Moravia perceives as the hallmark of contemporary Western culture. In spite of this negativism, the major protagonists also experience a kind of conversion at the end of a Moravia novel. The conversion experience turns suffering and frustration into a dim illumination of love, freedom and dignity. A brief look at the novels published since 1960 will show that, though there are no . . . [vigorously positive character] portraits, there are those who learn through suffering to see the nature of their own personal and cultural reality and learn to escape the narrow confines of their own personal desires and modern cultures which exploit them as means to ideological ends.

The novel *The Empty Canvas* (1961; *La noia,* 1960) is concerned with an artist who has reached a crisis. Dino can no longer paint. His creative energies have dried up. He suffers the classic symptoms Moravia outlined in **"Man as an End"**: boredom, impotence, unreality and nothingness. His boredom and disgust with the flatness of life pervade his account of his life. Even sex does not interest him at the beginning of the novel. Life, like his painting, is empty of significance.

This state of boredom changes when Dino meets Cecilia. What attracts him to her is her impenetrability as a human being. She becomes his mistress, but even in this close relationship, he cannot fathom the mysteries of her motivations. Her reasons for existing and acting are opaque to Dino. He discovers she has another lover, but he cannot convince her to give him up. Nor can he discover why she continues to come to him. He cannot buy her love with his wealth. He is unable to convince her to marry him. She cannot be bought; she simply loves him in her unique uncommitted way. . . . The opacity of her personality, the inability to reduce her to a common denominator (wife) or an object (prostitute), drives Dino to extremes. He inflicts cruelties on her to elicit some emotional or passionate response. His inhumanity always brings the same results—

Cecilia's passive and naive behavior. Since he cannot absorb her into his world of boredom, disgust, unreality and nothingness, and since he cannot dehumanize her, Dino attempts suicide.

It is in the epilogue section, just a few pages in length, that Dino emerges as a human being. He has done all in his power to resolve his dilemma by negating himself. Suicide was his last desperate act to remove his humanity. Now he feels that he can live a serenely resigned existence without hope. More positively, he learns, by contemplating a tree outside his hospital window, to accept other objects in a world in which he is but an object. He learns to value the love and happiness of other independent existences. He knows that Cecilia is enjoying herself with her lover while he recuperates from his suicide attempt. In an astonishing revelation, akin to a religious conversion, Dino discovers that by dispossessing Cecilia, she becomes fully existent as a human being. He does not know whether he will reestablish a relationship with her or not, but he knows he loves her in a new way. And he knows he will go back to the studio and start painting again—to fill in the empty canvas. (pp. 82-4)

For Dino, reality has reestablished itself as something to confront and bump into. And with the reestablishment of reality comes the reestablishment of his self as a human object which despairs but is not disgusted; which lives without hope but is not bored; which loves but is not possessed by love. . . .

Moravia's novel *The Lie* (1966; *L'attenzione*, 1965) is a Gidean novel of mirrors. It is a diary about the writing of a novel. Like *The Empty Canvas*, the protagonist, Francesco, is an artist who has reached a crisis in his intellectual and personal life. He feels the need to write a novel about reality, but reality gets in the way. As a result, he separates from his wife, Cora, in order to devote his creative energies to writing. As in the earlier novel, the impotent artist experiences a sudden sexual awakening. In *The Lie*, Francesco discovers an incestuous attraction for his step-daughter, Baba. He believes he loves her because she is an object and a nothingness. He derives a perverse pleasure from the thought of buying Baba from Cora. The objectification of human sexuality and the value it gains as an object is a well-developed theme in this novel, as it is in most of Moravia's fiction. Linked to the concept of sexual objectification is the metaphor of automatism. Sexual attraction, repulsions and other human physiological changes occur in this novel in ways that make human life resemble machines or puppets which have lost willful self-control and moderation.

In *The Lie*, Moravia adopts rudimentary Freudian and phenomenological explanations for these sexual and physiological phenomena. His depictions of automatic human behavior are also analyses of the effects of modern neocapitalist culture on human beings. Given both the repressed sexual instincts and a modern oppressive cultural superstructure, the novel becomes an investigation into the problem of human action and existence. (p. 84)

Moravia's next novel, *Two: A Phallic Novel* (1972; *Io e lui*, 1971), comes forth in comic costume. Moravia himself as well as his critics have compared some of his narratives to the tales of Apuleius, Boccaccio, Rabelais and Goldoni. In *Two* we find the tradition of the ribald tale continued, but more accurately, the comic sensibility of this novel comes closest to that of Erasmus' *In Praise of Folly*. . . .

Two is a postmodern *Satyricon* of sexual misadventures and perversions. The battle of the sexes in *The Empty Canvas* and

The Lie becomes the battle of the sex in *Two*. The protagonists are the artistic intellectual Federico, the narrative "I" ("Io"), and his gargantuan penis, the "he" ("lui"), with whom he carries on a hilarious dialogue about power. Federico, or Rico, wants to sublimate his sexual machinery, elevate his creative genius and deescalate his insistent and potent companion. Rico perceives that all great art and thought are sublimated sex, and he wishes to join the ranks of great artists. Thus he abandons his wife Fausta in order to escape his sexual serfdom. He has sold his sex to Fausta and he wants out of the contract.

Rico wants to devote his energies not only to art and thought, but also to social causes. Social revolution seems another way to raise his personal and social position. He resents the fact that his efforts in the name of revolution have not been taken seriously by his revolutionary acquaintances. By transferring his sexual potency from the bedroom to the political arena, Rico hopes to establish his superiority and get "on top" of those who have dismissed his revolutionary ideas. (p. 86)

By the end of the novel Rico has given up his search for sublimation. In the concluding comic section, Rico returns to his wife primed and ready to do his sexual duty. Fausta leads him off by the penis like Apuleius' ass. . . . While Federico's problems are a grotesque caricature of human sexuality, the thrust of the novel is obvious. The humane ego ("I") wins a battle against the violence and tempests of the sexual self ("he"). The educated, intelligent and reasonable person, Federico, overcomes the mythical, mystical and sexual urges of the irrational self.

While the battle between self and sex obviously points to the follies of human weaknesses, of all of Moravia's novels *Two* contains the most positive portrait of a human being. To some extent, this is made possible by the narrative's grossly exaggerated comic effects which make human reality acceptable. The darkness of human sex drives and other foolish ideas such as sublimation are enlightened by the moderating and balancing effects of humor.

The sense of comic relief evident in *Two* is absent from Moravia's recent novel *The Time of Desecration* (1980; *La vita interiore*, 1978). Like *Two*, the novel is a dialogue between the body and the moral will. Unlike *Two*, the sex drives of the body are perverse and devoid of humor. Moravia's emphasis on sex has been the primary cause of negative critical responses to his narratives. His response is that sex is a means of analyzing the relationships of human beings to their reality. While the confrontation with reality by means of sexual encounters is common in all Moravia's fiction, the detailed descriptions of sodomy, oral sex, and masturbation in *The Time of Desecration* display a gratuitous violence rarely found in his writing.

At the beginning of *The Time of Desecration*, Moravia tells the reader that the novel is an interview given to the narrator who remains an unnamed "I" throughout. The narrator recounts his dialogue with Desideria and reports the inner dialogue between her consciousness and her "Voice." Like Rico, who carries on a comic dialogue with his penis, Desideria attends to an inner Voice which guides and commands her. Moravia's novel is an analysis of a neurotic, schizophrenic adolescent who attempts to find freedom through personal rebellion and social revolution. She engages in both sexual and social actions which assert both her own and the Voice's antiauthoritarian thoughts and feelings. The Voice is a prolongation of masturbation—the self communicating with the self, the consciousness communicating with the body. The Voice is, in part, the feminine foil of Rico's Rex—a part of the body, sexual in nature, which commands. Yet the Voice is also a moral consciousness that asserts its concept of duty by calling for revolution as an actual and symbolic demonstration of a conscious rejection of bourgeois morality. The Voice commands and Desideria obeys for she fears returning to the state of an unconscious inhuman lump of flesh. (pp. 87-8)

In the conclusion to the novel, Desideria abandons not only the narrator but also her Voice. She asserts her self as an end detached from the machinations of the Voice. The Voice is both an inner sexual and a conscious drive to rebel, but it is also brutal, exploitative, and unloving. (p. 90)

Moravia's most recent novel *1934* (1982; *1934*, 1983) rehearses the familiar themes of his previous novels, but it does not continue the narrative experiments begun in *The Lie* and concluded with the publication of his open-ended dialogic narrative *The Time of Desecration*. Like all of Moravia's thesis novels, the protagonist of *1934*, Lucio, pursues one major philosophical or psychological problem. He seeks an answer to the question: how is it possible to live in despair and not wish for death? Desperation and suicide cast their long shadows throughout the novel making it another of Moravia's dark portraits of human existence. However, Lucio's death wish and pessimism are countered by his ardent desire to "stabilize" melancholia by turning it into a Stoic, rational acceptance of life. He attempts to transform his darker side into a genuine love of reality. (pp. 91-2)

1934 is a very perplexing novel to read despite its conventional narrative structure. The novel requires the reader to ascertain the true identities of major and minor characters, and the truth content of their statements. For example, Lucio learns that Beate, the German actress he meets on a boat to Capri, has a twin sister, Trude. Beate is a melancholic spiritual presence who wishes to conclude a death pact with Lucio. Trude is a lively sexual creature who confesses a fascination for Lucio. Paula, Trude's companion and, perhaps, lesbian lover, reveals to Lucio that his love affair with Beate is a joke. Beate and Trude are the same person acting out a dual role in order to trap an unsuspecting Italian Casanova. Lucio has fallen victim to the trap, and now he must discover (as must the reader) who or what it is that he really loves. Is it Beate the German actress, Beate the ideal feminine counterpart, or a Beate-Trude combination of the ideal and the real? The complexity of the situation is increased by the possibility that Paula is lying in order to break off the affair which may ruin her own love relationship with Trude. These Pirandellian puzzles about the nature of reality and truth are mirrored in another important aspect of the novel, the dual relationship of German and Italian politics and culture.

The title of the novel indicates not only the year of this morbid and puzzling love affair, but also points to the political and cultural events which have contributed to Lucio's sense of despair. Lucio, as well as the antifascist Italy he represents, is threatened by the militant shadow of Germany. . . . The relationship of Germany and Italy is the analogical equivalent of his relationship with Beate and Trude. They represent the dissociation of his sensibilities between the decadence of German Romanticism and the balance of the Italian Renaissance.

Lucio intends to stabilize his life by writing a novel about a hero who commits suicide. The novel will aesthetically purge his death wish and allow him to live a moderated life. As his love affair with Beate and Trude develops, he hopes to arrange a similar purgation of his desperation by finding in both sides of one woman the depolarization of despair and desire into one perfect and unified ideal. The final consummation of this perfect love is denied to Lucio by political events. Hitler's Night of the Long Knives destroys Beate's husband. Unwilling to live without him, she commits suicide with Paula who cannot live without her and her other self, Trude. The double suicide and suicide note repeat the famous suicidal deaths of Kleist and his lover Henriette Vogel.

In the concluding chapter of *1934*, there is no revelation of Lucio's intention to lead a different life or return to a former life with a renewed and more positive perspective. In this way, the novel differs significantly from the *Empty Canvas, The Lie,* and *Two*. In the last few pages of the novel, Lucio describes his dream of the consummation of love with Beate which ends in frustration and disappointment as he awakens to reality. Lucio has resigned himself to living for the memory and fantasy of his dream love, knowing that it never existed and never will exist. The fact that he returns to his family's estate rather than commit any desperate act shows his final resignation and acceptance of the ambiguity of life and his love for it. He writes a novel as an aesthetic explanation and purgation of his suicidal tendencies and tragic death of his beloved Beate. The political and cultural decadence and personal despair of the year 1934 are recorded in Lucio's novel. Through the medium of art, the abject pessimism of his desire for death is replaced by a Stoic acceptance of the impossibility of human happiness. (pp. 92-3)

Nonetheless, Moravia's commitment to a revelation of reality, however bleak it may appear on the surface, is an affirmation of his stated belief in the possibility of social, political, and personal change. Love, freedom, dignity, reasonable moderation and tolerance for the follies of human life are concepts that his characters realize imperfectly but strive for. Even *The Time of Desecration*, the most negative of his recent novels, holds out the remote possibility for a realization of these concepts. (p. 94)

> William Slaymaker, "Holograms of Humanity: The Negative Reality of Alberto Moravia's Postwar Novels," in South Atlantic Review, Vol. 49, No. 2, May, 1984, pp. 80-95.

MIRANDA SEYMOUR

Moravia has been identified with sex ever since the runaway success of *Woman of Rome* in 1947 established him as Italy's best-known novelist. The sex-scenes in his last-but-one novel, *Time of Desecration*, were of such a singular nature that the French translators complained, the Italian Mary Whitehouse rose in wrath, and the Germans, not usually known for their puritanism, flatly refused to publish the book.

The title [*Erotic Tales*] is a misnomer. There is plenty of sex in the tales, but nothing erotic. Suggestions that they are obscene or pornographic are equally misleading. The bodies Moravia exhibits in precise and often terrifying detail are presented in a way which is more likely to chill than to titillate. Anatomically, they are grotesque. One aspect, legs, breasts, buttocks, whatever, is singled out for the protagonist's obsession and magnified as if seen through the distorting lens of his vision. Moravia is also an avid film-goer and critic; his written representations are strikingly cinematic. Behind the camera, out of sight, he is the analytic observer, detached, dispassionate. As a script-writer, he takes us into the dream-world of

Freudian obsessions, blurring the line between reality and imagination.

The dreamlike stories are the ones whose images linger to haunt and tease the reader. Sometimes, as in the story of a man's quest among the illusory images of Venice at carnival time, and **"The Hands Around the Neck"** where a man responds to his wife's provocative urges to play at strangling her, it is impossible to tell where reality takes over, and to what extent. Others record the fantasy lives of isolated men, tempted by the devil (synonymous always with sexual urges in this author's work) in the form of a girl-child whose innocent smile contradicts the perverse pleasure she offers. Each tale carries a scorpion-sting of paradox in its tail. 'I was a good, conscientious nurse, with a vice,'' says the virgin whose hands were always sliding under the patients' blankets. 'I became a sane, normal woman, and a murderess.'

'I am an old devil, very old, it's true, but I'm not a good devil and even less a poor devil,' boasts the narrator of the longest and best of the tales. Here, reminding me of Bulgakov at his wittiest and most fantastical, Moravia shows the devil falling hopelessly in love with the scientist he has lured into signing a Faustian pact. But for once the devil has met his match. No matter how alluring a form he assumes, the professor always sees through it. Satan's gain is the devil's loss, on this occasion.

Miranda Seymour, "Neither Obscene nor Pornographic," in The Spectator, Vol. 255, No. 8210, November 16, 1985, p. 37.

LORNA SAGE

The first two stories [in *Erotic Tales*] review fantasies of phallus-worship that belong to the infancy of porn. **"The Thing"** involves two women and a pony (Kurt Vonnegut says somewhere this is the world's oldest dirty postcard), and **"To the Unknown God"** features the clinical caresses of a starched hospital nurse.

How does one extract anything but a comic *frisson* from these banalities? Moravia's answer is to write the pony story from the point of view of a woman (why not of a pony?) and to pose as an eavesdropper on the nurse's own confessions—thus adding an extra dimension of *literary* perversity, the writer as transvestite and so on. But this ploy, while it gives a certain teasing obliquity to the sorry sideshow, also poses another embarrassing question: whose pleasure is it anyway?

The English title **"Erotic Tales"** (in Italian it seems to have been called bluntly after **"The Thing"**) sounds indeed like a boast—or a confession. And this, if you like, is the dilemma of the genre (one man's fetish . . .). Sex may seem the great equaliser and comforter—'while it's impossible to replace a face, the genitals, on the other hand, have certain physical similarities, are interchangeable,' thinks one sad widower missing his wife—but in story after story it's the isolation and loneliness of characters following through their particular obsessions that one's left with. Not to mention the loneliness of the writer, and the reader. . . .

There is, of course, some of the kind of caressing detail you'd expect—'my tongue, like a lovesick snail, left a slow, damp trail'—but not enough to distract you for long from the spectre of emptiness. And many of the stories (**"A Bad Memory Block,"** **"In My Dream I Always Hear a Step on the Stairs"**) deal in greyly Kafkaesque moments when the guilty act itself is lost on the past or the future, and tension and anxiety prevail. One

grimly comic piece, **"The Devil Can't Save the World,"** gives a new twist to the Faustian pact: the demonic sting of desire inspires a scientist to the discovery that will end the world, but when the Devil (who is a woman for this purpose, and in love) tries to undo the damage by offering him real sexual satisfaction, she finds herself dissolving, 'becoming the same impalpable stuff that phantasms and dreams are made of. . . .'

Back to square one, and the book's 'real' theme, the dreadful certainty of returning to oneself. As someone said, Hell is repetition.

Lorna Sage, "Hollow Desire," in The Observer, December 22, 1985, p. 19.

STEPHEN KOCH

[The stories in *Erotic Tales*] are about a number of things, mainly unpleasant, beyond mere desire.

They're a bit like mere desire itself in that respect. The stories are of course about wishing, wanting and (mainly not) having; they are also about guilt, domination, damnation, obsession, power, and self-surrender. They are not, I regret to say, particularly engaged with anything that might be called having fun, or for that matter even having pleasure. But more of that later. Sustained by Moravia's tone of genteel non-judgmental intelligence, they traffic in devils and fetishes and black ecstasies, and unfold in a haunted rhythm that turns them into dream stories.

Now, the successful creation of a dream state on the page, despite a lot of very silly talk on the subject, is very difficult to accomplish and very rarely done. But Moravia is wonderfully skilled. I can't think of any recent prose that so effectively catches dreamstate: the oneiric trance, the uncanny link between strangeness and the familiar, and the true dream rhythm.

This is a world of desire as dream and dream as a code for a nightmarish real life. Here people make love to horses, sell their souls (in two stories at least) to devils, and chase girls dressed as death across the Piazza San Marco. In **"The Thing"** an amiable Lesbian—serenely disdainful of the "normal" world's harsh nasty phallic tyranny (that's "the thing")—visiting a friend in another female couple, finds herself hypnotically drawn, like some Sapphic Alice, into an all-female anti-Wonderland of bestiality, domination, and a paradoxical inverted phallus worship. In **"Even the Devil Can't Save the World,"** a nuclear physicist sells his soul to the devil, who is cleverly disguised as a saucy schoolgirl without underpants. In **"The Woman in Black,"** a man who had been able to find satisfaction only in a quite special routine with his late wife goes looking for a substitute, and when he finds his wish come true, all cloaked in black, perversely fails to keep their rendezvous.

We are also, I am afraid, never far from the darker side of the phallic preoccupation. True, in a gentle tale called **"To The Unknown God,"** the ruling bleakness seems to give way before a decorous account of a shy virginal nurse who consoles herself and her male patients with a mild inoffensive intimacy (just one sweet little squeeze through the sheets as she makes her rounds)—until the story ends with a patient dead in his bed and the nurse in flight and despair. While the point of view is thoroughly cosmopolitan, it is also, not surprisingly, very masculine and Italian. The sense of damnation is quite specifically Catholic; virginity is a major trope and trouble; and even in **"The Thing,"** a story with an all-female cast ("they were more than ever worshipers of the member . . ." though beyond "even the blind, brutal humanity of male aggression'') feels to me as if written from a male point of view. The politics of the stories are much engaged in the question of masculine domination, but the perspective is not in the least feminist, I suppose because Moravia's view is really too dark for feminism's innate progressivism. All is lost, and in advance—as in **"Even the Devil Can't Save the World,"** where even the temptress is really male, the heavy-breathing but disguised Satanic Adversary himself.

Yet for all the sex, the stories are too genteel to be urgent. And as anyone knows who's listened to other people's dreams over breakfast, their very mystery can grow dull. The stories in *Erotic Tales* either work or they don't, and when they don't, they are really quite yawnsome. Despite odd lapses, **"The Thing"** is a minor but haunting erotic tour de force. Meanwhile, some of the best things in the book are the very concentrated (four to five pages), little emblematic tales in the back of the book—something like the very Freudian, impressive **"What Use Have I Got for a Carnival"** (that's the one where the guy chases the girl across the Piazza San Marco). I especially liked a story (really more political than sexual, linked to the days of '70s terror in Italy) called **"In My Dream I Always Hear a Step on the Stairs."**

The general view is fastidious, mildly beguiled, and thoroughly pessimistic. Nobody ever has any fun at all, or even much plain pleasure. One begins to yearn for just a little humor. As in a dream, Moravia's characters are always in the grip of some welling erotic something that fills their supine minds with an obsession beyond their power and certain to spell disaster. At best, like the Sapphic Alice in **"The Thing,"** they escape the lethal fetishistic Red Queen and return to a life of some equilibrium, some decency. Some, not much. In Moravia's world— at least what he shows us here—there is no such thing as sexual liberty, leave aside fulfillment. I wouldn't want to live—God knows—in a world where love, dreamed or undreamed, really was what Moravia says it is. Happily, I don't believe it is. But these stories are dark warnings.

> Stephen Koch, ''Moravia's Satyricon: Tales of Pleasure and Pain,'' in Book World—The Washington Post, *January 26, 1986, p. 8.*

ROBERT WELLS

[*The Voyeur*] reflects an apparent belief that people have no existence apart from the situation they are in, and that the first fact of that situation is the body. Moravia indicates his characters by a twitch of the nostrils, fleshy fingertips, even by the disposition of pubic hair; and shows them drawn together— along with himself and his reader—in the calculating complicity of voyeur and exhibitionist.

Edoardo, the narrator, is a survivor of the generation of 1968. He belonged, as he repeats somewhat rhetorically, to "the protest movement", but is now, peaceably enough, a university lecturer. He describes himself as "an intellectual, an animal that's dying out", and his nickname appropriately is Dodo. Two connected obsessions dominate his life: the exercise of a strong visual sense (events are related almost entirely in the present tense) and compulsive thoughts about nuclear war. The novel's Italian title is *L'uomo che guarda;* the intellectual is revealed as the man who sees and cannot understand. Understanding has been outdated by the Bomb.

Edoardo is baffled too by his domestic life. His refusal to own property means that he and his wife, Silvia, must live in the flat belonging to his father, a famous professor, whom he claims to detest as standing for everything that his own generation rebelled against. Silvia has friendlily, but inexplicably, cleared out, and the action of the novel—such as it is—is mainly concerned with Edoardo's fumbling attempts to find out why and to get her back. This, it turns out, means untangling his feelings about his father and facing the likelihood that the "solemn commitments" by which he flatters himself he has lived are little more than personal resentments in a stalemate of sexual rivalry.

Though Moravia's characters express themselves chiefly through a series of erotic encounters, sex is valued rather as a kind of gluttony, an impersonal expression of vitality which succeeds, where the intellectual's understanding fails, in challenging the crushing anticipation of catastrophe. Edoardo discovers to his cost that his father, fighting old age, has known this all along. But he is also helped by the realization that his wife's betrayal of him makes her "all the more vital and free" in his eyes.

The deadpan directness of Moravia's sexual preoccupation reminds one of Auden's remark that "Italian men have to make sure you know they've got a penis", but *The Voyeur* is saved— disheartening and inconclusive fable though it is—by Moravia's dry, unironic intelligence.

> Robert Wells, ''The Dying Out of Dodo,'' in The Times Literary Supplement, *No. 4363, November 14, 1986, p. 1290.*

LORNA SAGE

The plot-arrangements of [*The Voyeur*] have a joyless (though not unfunny) economy about them. Moravia's narrator Edoardo, a dedicated and devious looker-on and an obscure professor of French literature, lives with his wife Silvia in a flatlet inside the Rome flat belonging to his father, who is a famous professor of physics. . . . Edoardo (who has never recovered from 1968 and all that) thinks about two main things: the nuclear threat, and sexual power-games—fissures and fission, as he says. . . .

[*The Voyeur* is] the sort of novel where you're meant to 'see things coming' quite some way off, and be surprised only by the actual feel and texture and *look* of what happens. As well, of course, as the shamelessness of the author, which with Moravia after all these years is something of a routine surprise. He teases one with occasional Rome exteriors, cityscapes that suggest space, variety, growth. . . . But it's not to be. The fission/fissure obsession—'The idea of a harmless, lovable reality that can transform itself in an instant into an inferno'—undermines the very notion of life going on and branching out. Everything narrows down to the contents of the flat and the inside of our narrator's head.

Sex with Silvia seems to work very nicely ('for every voyeur there's an exhibitionist' thinks Edoardo smugly), so why does she pack her case and leave one morning? And what is it about the 'other man' that reminds him of mental pictures (of his parents' lovemaking) that he'd rather forget? Well, he puts things together at last, helped out by a beautiful black woman who seems to have stepped out of his favourite obscene poem by Mallarmé ('A negress possessed by the devil') expressly for the purpose (it's not the erotic descriptions that are 'shocking' in this book, but the nakedness of the authorial manipulation). The black woman makes love to him in the dark, and tells him things that only Africans and post-Freudian analysts know, such as 'The son doesn't possess the truth, only the father possesses it.'

But does knowing the truth about father make you somehow free? At the very last Moravia seems to be offering himself and his reader a choice, for once. Again, the wise woman from Zaire supplies the imaginative cue, telling him a bush story about a man living in the world of the dead, who 'starts feeling homesick . . . and goes back up to the living'. . . . It ends up an oddly moving book about Moravia's determination (pushing 80) to evade authority and respectability to the last.

Lorna Sage, "Sex in the Head," in The Observer, *November 23, 1986, p. 30.*

LUCIA RE

Nicknamed Dodo like the extinct flightless bird, the protagonist of [*The Voyeur*] feels that he too belongs to a dying breed. At the age of 35, now that his few remaining friends from the 1968 student movement have either gone underground or left Italy altogether, Dodo is resigned to a quiet life as an assistant professor of French literature at the University of Rome. His students are apathetic and his job bores him. His wife, Silvia, is just a pretty woman from the Roman middle class, indifferent to Dodo's increasingly vague left-wing ideals. They have, however, a seemingly idyllic relationship involving a daily routine of afternoon lovemaking, dining out in neighborhood restaurants and pleasant conversation. Theirs is "a discreet, reasonable, domestic intimacy which resembles Silvia herself." But domestic intimacy in Mr. Moravia's novels is never quite what it appears to be.

The housing shortage in Rome and Dodo's low salary are apparently the reasons why the couple have to share quarters with Dodo's father, a well-off and well-known physics professor. He represents everything Dodo despises: the "establishment," bourgeois wealth and reactionary politics. Although they live under the same roof, Dodo treats his father as a complete stranger. This domestic setting is the basis for yet another of Mr. Moravia's ironic tales about the sexual mores of the Italian middle class. For besides being a disenchanted intellectual, Dodo is a voyeur whose life is full of doors left ajar and windows left open. . . .

Since the narration in *The Voyeur* takes the form of Dodo's "intimate journal," the reader is ironically placed in the position of voyeur as well, along with, of course, Mr. Moravia himself. This endless doubling of the voyeuristic perspective is the governing strategy of the novel and its principal theme. . . .

The climax of the skillfully constructed plot hinges (predictably enough) on the recollection of a primal scene, and on a variation of the Oedipal fable that plays with the theme of Oedipus' blindness and insight. While the novel . . . will not disappoint Mr. Moravia's admirers, its graphic descriptions of male sexual fantasies, female anatomy and an encyclopedic variety of erotic positions and dispositions may appear tasteless and even ludicrous to many readers. Mr. Moravia tries to forestall such objections by referring throughout *The Voyeur* to texts by well-established writers—such as Mallarmé and Proust—that belong to "that genre normally referred to as obscene," thus legitimating his own practice of writing. "What matters most in a writer," Dodo says, "is not the things he writes, but how he writes them." Exactly. Mr. Moravia cannot, unfortunately, compare with either Mallarmé or Proust; even at his best, he is more like a second-rate Roman version of Henry Miller.

Lucia Re, "Peeping Dodo," in The New York Times Book Review, *March 29, 1987, p. 15.*

Vladimir (Vladimirovich) Nabokov

1899-1977

(Also wrote under pseudonym of V. Sirin) Russian-born American novelist, poet, essayist, short story writer, dramatist, critic, translator, biographer, autobiographer, and scriptwriter.

Nabokov is recognized as one of the greatest literary stylists of the twentieth century. His intricate, self-conscious fiction investigates the illusory nature of reality and the artist's relationship to his craft. Nabokov maintained that "art at its greatest is fantastically deceitful and complex," and by emphasizing stylistic considerations above notions of moral or social significance, he championed the primacy of the imagination, through which he believed a more meaningful reality might be evoked than that of actual life. Viewing words not just as vehicles for meaning but also as significant objects in themselves, Nabokov made use of intellectual games involving wordplay, acrostics, circular time frames, and multilingual puns to create complex, maze-like narratives. Although some critics fault Nabokov for his refusal to address social and political issues, many maintain that beneath his passion for "composing riddles with elegant solutions," as he himself stated, his fiction conveys a poignant regard for human feelings and morality.

Nabokov was born into an aristocratic family in St. Petersburg, Russia. The Bolshevik Revolution forced the Nabokovs to move to England in 1919, and Vladimir soon began to study Russian and French literature at Cambridge University. The death of Nabokov's father, who was killed by right-wing extremists at a 1922 political rally of Russian exiles in Berlin, Germany, greatly affected Nabokov, and elements of the experience recur throughout his work. He lived for several years in Berlin until the threat of war necessitated his move to Paris in 1937 and to the United States in 1940. Nabokov was a professor of Russian literature at Cornell University from 1948 to 1958. He settled in Switzerland in 1960 after the popular success of his controversial novel *Lolita* (1955) enabled him to become a full-time writer, but he retained his American citizenship. The effects of his abrupt departure from his homeland, as well as his peripatetic life, often emerge in Nabokov's writing in the form of a lament for a lost past and an awareness of the threat chaos poses to order.

Nabokov's novels written in Russian, many of them under the pseudonym V. Sirin, are generally regarded as more autobiographical and less significant than his works in English. In these and later novels, Nabokov focuses on alienated and compulsive protagonists whose complex aesthetic imaginations and quests for self-knowledge render them social misfits. The chessmaster Luzhin in *Zashchita Luzhina* (1930; *The Defense*), for example, strives to discover his identity through chess but loses interest in his wife and family as the game becomes an obsession. After removing himself from society and losing his sanity, Luzhin commits suicide; his last glimpse of the world reveals an enormous chessboard on which he must play an endless game. In *Octchayanie* (1936; *Despair*), a darkly humorous murder story, a schizophrenic chances upon a vagrant who bears a striking resemblance to himself. The man plans with his wife to kill the vagrant in order to collect on his own insurance policy, but the plot proves unsuccessful, and he escapes to France. There he writes a story berating the

world for ignoring his cunning and expertise and gradually becomes insane. Nabokov's final novels written in Russian are looser in plot and display a wider range of invention. *Priglashenie na kazn'* (1938; *Invitation to a Beheading*), a novel which prompted critical comparisons to the stories of Franz Kafka for its dreamlike plot, setting, and characters, relates the final days of a rebellious young man sentenced to death for the capital crime of "gnostical turpitude." Many critics view this work as an allegory describing the artist's determination to remain free from collective social pressures. Nabokov's last novel in Russian, *Dar* (1952; *The Gift*), is usually considered his greatest work in his native language. Through five distinct stories which bear no integral relationship to one another, the novel brings its concerns together in the manner of a mosaic composed of strongly contrasting individual sections. While following the growing moral and artistic awareness of his protagonist, Fyodor Godonuv, Nabokov also addresses such topics as Russian literature, love, and politics. *The Gift,* according to Andrew Field, "is the greatest novel Russian literature has yet produced in this century."

In Nabokov's first novel written in English, *The Real Life of Sebastian Knight* (1941), the narrator writes a biography of his recently deceased brother, novelist Sebastian Knight, in an attempt to reveal his true character. The narrator's efforts crumble, however, amid a confusion of identities, as he mistakenly pursues a man whom he believes to be his brother. *Bend Sinister* (1947), one of Nabokov's few novels to deal overtly with political themes, relates the struggle of a world-renowned philosopher to uphold human values against a tyrannical police state intent on eradicating individuality. Unable to control himself when his son is accidentally killed by the regime during a kidnapping scheme, the philosopher is shot in an attempt to murder the country's dictator.

Nabokov became a literary celebrity with his notorious novel, *Lolita.* Rejected by four American publishers due to its pedophiliac subject matter, the book attracted a wide underground readership upon its publication in France and became a bestseller when published in the United States in 1958. The plot revolves around the disastrous passion of Humbert Humbert, a brilliant, middle-aged European professor and aesthete, for Dolores Haze, a promiscuous twelve-year-old schoolgirl whom he pursues to compensate for the loss of a love during his adolescence. Dolores, whom he idealizes as "Lolita," is representative of the superficial and earthy American culture that Humbert views from a sophisticated European perspective. In addition to its satirical vision of American morals and values, the novel also examines the effects of the artist's asocial impulses. *Pnin* (1957), one of Nabokov's most complex yet accessible works, centers on the bumbling attempts of an exiled Russian scholar to adapt to life at an American university.

Nabokov's next book, *Pale Fire* (1962), was praised by Anthony Burgess as "the first major formal innovation in the novel since *Finnegans Wake.*" This work consists of a playful, parodistic exegesis of a complex 999-line poem about death, immortality, and art written in rhymed couplets and attributed to John Shade, whom Nabokov called "the greatest of *invented* poets." Noted for its rhythmic variations and sympathetic narrator, "Pale Fire" is considered one of the twentieth century's greatest poetic achievements. The novel also includes a critical foreword, commentary, and index attributed to the pseudonymous Charles Kinbote, whom Nabokov identifies as an unbalanced American scholar. The contrasting personalities of Shade and Kinbote serve simultaneously to celebrate authorial judgment and to parody critical explication. Nabokov's later works, *Ada; or, Ardor: A Family Chronicle* (1969), *Transparent Things* (1972), and *Look at the Harlequins!* (1974), parts of which function as allegories of his life as an artist, recapitulate his major themes relating to alienation and mortality.

In addition to his novels, Nabokov was also noted for his critical observations and scholarly pursuits. Of these works, he is probably most highly revered for his translation of Alexander Pushkin's *Eugene Onegin.* Several volumes of memoirs and essays have been published posthumously, including *The Nabokov-Wilson Letters: Correspondence between Vladimir Nabokov and Edmund Wilson, 1940-1971* (1979), which provides insight into Nabokov's theory and method and illuminates his long professional relationship with Wilson. Such volumes as *Lectures on Literature* (1980), *Lectures on Russian Literature* (1981), and *Lectures on Don Quixote* (1983) represent his years in academia. Nabokov's recently translated novel, *Volshebnik* (1939; *The Enchanter*), is considered a preliminary sketch for *Lolita.* Unlike that work, however, *The Enchanter* functions as a cautionary moral tale in which a pedophiliac is destroyed by his desire to consummate his love for an adolescent girl.

(See also *CLC,* Vols. 1, 2, 3, 6, 8, 11, 15, 23, 44; *Contemporary Authors,* Vols. 5-8, rev. ed., Vols. 69-72 [obituary]; *Contemporary Authors New Revision Series,* Vol. 20; *Dictio-* *nary of Literary Biography,* Vol. 2; *Dictionary of Literary Biography Yearbook: 1980;* and *Dictionary of Literary Biography Documentary Series,* Vol. 3.)

EDMUND WHITE

This book is being billed as the European *Lolita,* and indeed *The Enchanter* is a short story on a related theme that Vladimir Nabokov wrote in Russian in 1939 in Paris. He then sailed for the United States, where, 10 years later, the real Lolita, *our* Lolita, first began to make her presence felt to him. . . .

[In *The Enchanter*], a 12-year-old girl, never named, excites a man in his 40's, also never named, one day while she's roller-skating through a park and he's sitting on a bench watching her with scorching desire. To gain access to her he marries her sick, impoverished mother, who dies conveniently soon afterward. The girl and her new stepfather drive (actually, are driven by a chauffeur) to a Riviera hotel, where he molests her while she's asleep. She wakens at the height of his ecstasy and screams; he runs into the traffic and dies.

The story, like *Lolita,* is a heady combination of passion, humor and beauty, but whereas *Lolita* is a descendant of Pushkin's sparkling novel in verse, *Eugene Onegin, The Enchanter* is more akin to Gogol's eerie story "The Overcoat," with its molelike protagonist and surrealist conclusion.

Nevertheless, the story's humor does anticipate the novel's. In *The Enchanter* the pedophile, thrilled to be so near his prey, notices in a blur that a newspaper is "dated the 32nd." Later, he grotesquely considers poisoning his new wife, but he fears an autopsy ("They'll inevitably open her up, out of sheer habit"). Confused by desire, he sees out of the corner of his eye a "black salad devouring a green rabbit." . . .

These are roguish bits of buffoonery reminiscent of Humbert Humbert, if less urbanely ironic. [*The Enchanter*] also anticipates, though seldom equals [*Lolita's*] lyricism, especially in the ecstatic descriptions of the child's nascent beauty. Indeed, every detail in the story is triggered to release its cache of that spooky, ethereal poetry always hiding just below the surface of Nabokov's best prose.

There are more differences than similarities, however, between the two texts. Lolita is a fully realized character, enchantingly vivid with her coarse cries, pink lipstick, crushes on actors, stylish but ineffectual tennis game and soft myopic gaze, whereas the girl in *The Enchanter* is a nerd. She's docile, has flecks of dandruff, black stockings, horrible steel skates and a bad case of *pudeur.* Something about her reminds us of wet wool and heavy braids; her American cousin, by contrast, is brash, adores gooey fudge sundaes, flirts with bellhops and walks with that heartbreaking freedom only American women possess.

Similarly, the protagonist of *The Enchanter* is a balding, thin, dry-lipped jeweler with a hard heart and calculating loins, whereas Humbert is a magus of yearning blessed with a "clean-cut jaw, muscular hand, deep sonorous voice, broad shoulder," not to mention a capacity for tenderness held in check only by his extreme sexual ambitions. The Enchanter is an earthbound erotic empiricist, whereas Humbert is an inspired prophet of nympholepsy.

Technically the biggest difference is that [*The Enchanter*] is narrated in the third person, whereas [*Lolita*] is in the first person. The eloquent or choked voice of Humbert—sometimes lying, alternately lucid and lurid, always intelligent, cultured and funny—is the engine that powers *Lolita*, the 20th century's *Anna Karenina.* Humbert's complexly orchestrated voice, juxtaposed with the jazz of American slangy dialogue, allows Nabokov to play European subtlety against American forthrightness. The tension between French and American culture (Humbert is Swiss-French), dramatized by Humbert and Lolita's painful incompatibility, has no parallel in the story, which robs *The Enchanter* of resonance.

Nabokov always referred to Humbert as a monster, a pervert, while we can think of him only as a sympathetic hero hounded by the Eumenides of lust. Curiously, the Enchanter seems more a textbook sociopath. Perhaps in being developed, the character of the child molester ran away from its creator, eluded his intentions to become an emblem of that blend of imagination and reality that love—and art—always represent in Nabokov's fiction. . . .

If *The Enchanter* is not so fully realized as *Lolita*, it is nonetheless suspenseful, funny and shocking. The concluding seduction scene, if less grave and dreamlike than the corresponding moment in the novel, is even more obsessively erotic. Almost 10 years after his death, Vladimir Nabokov has provided us with the literary event of the season.

Edmund White, "*Imagine Lolita as a Nerd*," in The New York Times Book Review, *October 19, 1986, p. 7.*

LLOYD ROSE

The Enchanter isn't exactly a "lost" Nabokov story. Scholars have been aware of it for years, under the title "**The Magician**"; Andrew Field even translated a couple of passages in *Nabokov: His Life in Art.* It is known as the prototype of *Lolita* which Nabokov discusses in the afterword to that book: a nameless protagonist (Nabokov calls him "Arthur" in the *Lolita* afterword, though he is nowhere named in the story), entranced by a twelve-year-old girl, marries her ill, widowed mother in order to have a chance to seduce the child. The mother conveniently dies and he takes his chance; the result is not at all what he had hoped. (p. 133)

As the germ of *Lolita*, *The Enchanter* offers some of the pleasures of a puzzle—one of which is speculating how this status, unthought of during its composition but inevitably imposed on it by the later book, would have pleased the puzzle-maker of genius who created it. Throughout *The Enchanter*, glints of *Lolita* flash at us like reflections from a fragmented mirror.

Here is the nymphet sitting on a bed clasping her drawn-up knees, but with no pretentious American mother to tell her in execrable French not to expose herself. Here is the potential seducer, moving through the house with a tune on his lips, foreshadowing Humbert the Hummer. Here is the scene in which he sees the girl again after a separation and for a moment feels no sexual desire for her, only compassion. The maid she will never see again waves good-bye; a cornucopia of gifts is promised (though not delivered till *Lolita*); a traffic accident resolves a plot problem. In the most beautiful image, the girl first appears on skates—a harbinger, to roll on into the full-grown book—"Once a perfect little beauty in a tartan frock, with a clatter put her heavily armed foot near me upon the

bench to dip her slim bare arms into me and tighten the strap of her roller skate. . . ." This is all that is left in *Lolita* of the nameless little girl in *The Enchanter*, who is more akin to the gentle Annabel who was Humbert Humbert's childhood love than to the vulgar bobby-soxer Lolita.

In his afterword to *Lolita*, Nabokov explained that "the initial shiver of inspiration" that produced *The Enchanter* "was somehow prompted by a newspaper story about an ape in the Jardin des Plantes who, after months of coaxing by a scientist, produced the first drawing ever charcoaled by an animal: this sketch showed the bars of the poor creature's cage." This is certainly a description of *Lolita*, with its ape-artist hero Humbert delineating in voluptuous, hellish detail the tale of his love and obsession. *The Enchanter* is told in the third person, in the ironic tone that came so easily to Nabokov and that can be one of the less attractive qualities of his writing. *The Enchanter* has some of the nastiness of *Laughter in the Dark*—essentially, it's an ugly joke on its protagonist, who, after going to the trouble of marrying the widow in order to be near to her daughter, not only fails to seduce the child but ends up throwing himself under a truck. Nabokov rather despises the poor sap, while for Humbert he has a certain pity and empathy that cut the sourness of his contempt. In *The Enchanter* the thwarted child-molester muses on lust and love:

> Often I have tried to catch myself in the transition from one kind of tenderness to the other, from the simple to the special, and would very much like to know whether they are mutually exclusive, whether they must, after all, be assigned to different genera, or whether one is a rare flowering of the other on the Walpurgis Night of my murky soul. . . .

He never finds the answer to this question, but years later Humbert does. Standing on a mountain slope listening to the cries of children at play in a mining town below, he realizes that "the hopelessly poignant thing was not Lolita's absence from my side, but the absence of her voice from that concord." At this moment Humbert turns the joke of his relationship to his stepdaughter, and the reader's cynicism, inside out: he becomes Lolita's father. He will go on to kill the man who has stolen her, the libertine playwright Clare Quilty (author of *The Enchanted Hunters*), his monster-self—a liberation denied the suicidal Arthur. *The Enchanter* is exquisitely written. What it lacks is *Lolita*'s moral beauty.

The distancing, superior attitude of the author of *The Enchanter* toward his creation is familiar to anyone who has read Nabokov's interviews, with their mandarin pronouncements on art. He despised Dostoyevskian emotionalism and literature that "means something." No modern author has tried harder to disclaim the sentimental attractions of his work and to celebrate style as substance, and no other modern author has had the dazzling skill almost to bring it off. Even after acknowledging that Nabokov's greatest English-language novels—*Lolita, Pnin, Pale Fire*—are his most heartbreaking (his greatest Russian novel, *The Gift*, is, at least in translation, buoyantly vital, lighthearted, *smart*; a young man's book, though he was thirty-eight when it was published), one is still left with that extraordinary style, jeweled and gleaming. Texture is his text; the brilliant play and reflection of words contain as much "meaning" as the ostensible story. In Nabokov's hands words become not just bearers of meaning but things in themselves, objects. He was, after all, a skilled lepidopterist, and as a writer he is the poet as scientist. He pins the English language to a board, dissects it, studies its structure, and reassembles it in a fabulous way—his sentences are unicorns and griffins in the bestiary of English prose, as muscular and supple as the humbler beasts of burden he parodies in his *Lolita* afterword: "'He acts crazy. We all act crazy, I guess. I guess God acts crazy.'''.

Even now, when he is generally spoken of as one of the greatest English-language writers of this century, there are readers and critics (admirers, presumably, of the spare style mocked above) who are uneasy with him. His prose isn't clean-lined and democratic, his irony is detached rather than "savage," and he doesn't work up a sweat; his verbal acrobatics are as graceful and effortless, and as *dry*, as a Fred Astaire solo. Such a highly self-conscious style is always in danger of falling into artificiality, and it has served Nabokov best when used in the first person, reflecting the rococo imaginations of his various odd protagonists, few of whom are native English speakers.... The word order and phrasing run merrily free of the boundaries of common English rhythm. This is partly why Nabokov can be so *surprising*, and why he has the stamina and control to go on adding phrase after phrase to a sentence without ceasing to astonish and please us.... (pp. 133-34)

The Enchanter is a product of the late thirties, the period during which [Nabokov] wrote his first English novel, *The Real Life of Sebastian Knight* (1941). We cannot have it as he would have presented it to us, alchemically transformed from his first language to his second; what we have is his son's translation, in which, in his own words, "I have tried hard to stick to the Nabokov rules: precision, artistic fidelity, no padding, no ascribing."... The prose of *The Enchanter* is Nabokov's, then, yet still not quite finished. Missing is the gloss he would have given the literal translation, the wit and shimmer of the work that he did in English and in the translations (by Dmitri Nabokov and others) that he oversaw.

But there are many felicities and beauties. For lovers of Nabokov's work, the following passage, written sixteen years before *Lolita* was published and reaching us only now, nine years after Nabokov's death, has an impact and poignance it would not have had—could not have had—in 1939. Watching his child-love skate, the intellectual pederast wonders,

> Was it concupiscence, this torment he experienced as he consumed her with his eyes, marvelling at her flushed face, at the compactness and perfection of her every movement (particularly when, having barely frozen motionless, she dashed off again, pumping swiftly with her prominent knees)? Or else was it the anguish that always accompanied his hopeless yearning to extract something from beauty, to hold it still for an instant, to do something with it— no matter what, provided there were some kind of contact, that somehow, no matter how, could quench that yearning?

This is not merely Nabokov the conjurer transforming the erotic into the abstract, fusing the physical with the metaphysical; it's a description of the longing that impels his art. It is he who has drawn, with all the skills of a great painter, the bars of his own cage, the cage of the world, what he refers to in *Speak, Memory* as "the prison of time." In *Lolita*, Humbert determines "to fix once for all the perilous magic of nymphets." His creator worked all his life to fix the perilous magic of existence, spread its wings, pin it down, preserve it forever

in an image of flight, and free the shadow of art, more real than what cast it, to fly on in a reflected sky. (pp. 134-35)

Lloyd Rose, "From Beyond the Bars of Time," in The Atlantic Monthly, Vol. 258, No. 5, November, 1986, pp. 133-35.

STEVEN G. KELLMAN

It is only by a considerable stretch of the generic imagination that *The Enchanter* could be considered a novel, and by an ingenious allocation of pages that it has become a book. With generous margins and chapter breaks, the tale itself is a mere seventy-four pages in the original typescript. The text is supplemented by: an excerpt from the afterword to *Lolita* that Nabokov first published in French, in 1956; part of a letter we are told he sent to his American publisher in 1959; a translator's note; and a lengthy postcript by the translator, who also happens to be the author's only son. Shades of Charles Kinbote, the psychopathic assembler of scholarly apparatuses in *Pale Fire?*

Portions of the original Russian typescript, along with Vladimir Nabokov's handwritten corrections, are, we are informed, reproduced as the endpapers of this posthumous discovery. I ascribe no sinister significance to the fact that Dmitri Nabokov was born the same year, 1934, that his father published a novel titled *Despair*. And I have no reason to doubt the filial translator's curious insistence that "no literary adventurer would have a leg to stand on if he were to question the authorship of *The Enchanter*."

I do not invite amputation, but I do note that on the back flap of this new book we are instructed [that Dmitri Nabokov] ... "is writing a pseudonymous novel." "Play! Invent the world! Invent reality!" urges the Baroness Bredow in *Look at the Harlequins!* (1974). And its sly author, whose *Invitation to a Beheading* (1938) begins with an invented epigraph by an invented Frenchman, one Pierre Delalande, delighted in pulling the legs of his readers, even out from under them. He might have enjoyed the suspicion that Dmitri, who was a 5-year-old in 1939, when *The Enchanter* is said to have been written, is using Vladimir Nabokov as his pseudonym. The coy master himself appended the name V. Sirin to his earliest fiction, including, according to Dmitri, *The Enchanter*.

It would be delicious to believe that *The Enchanter* is the greatest familial literary hoax since Thomas Hardy wrote his own biography and signed it with the name of Florence Emily Hardy, his second wife. Or else it would be reassuring to be able to believe that *The Enchanter* is not being published merely as the fossilized droppings of a literary lion, that it would be of compelling interest even if written by an unknown.... But *The Enchanter* is a novella whose chief appeal is as a rehearsal for *Lolita*, Nabokov's own favorite.

It is, in brief, the story of a 40-year-old man who asks himself: "What if the way to true bliss is indeed through a still delicate membrane, before it has had time to harden, become overgrown, lose the fragrance and the shimmer through which one penetrates to the throbbing star of that bliss?" He becomes so enamored of a roller-skating 12-year-old nymphet he encounters in a park that he marries her ailing widowed mother in order to gain access to her. When the mother finally dies, he whisks the child off to a rural hotel, where a pathetic attempt to take possession of her ends in disaster.

In the appendix to *Lolita* . . . , Nabokov describes its prototype as a "short story some thirty pages long" in which "the man was a central European, the anonymous nymphet was French, and the loci were Paris and Provence." Not only is *The Enchanter* a few pages longer than remembered, but its local habitations and names are refined into abstraction. The main character could be studying to be Humbert Humbert, but, though Nabokov recalls him as "Arthur" in his 1950s afterword, he remains anonymous, and moves in a vaguely European, but unspecified, setting, throughout *The Enchanter*. . . .

Lolita begins with a celebrated apostrophe to its elusive eponym by playing on her name. . . . However, the *fille fatale* of *Ur-Lolita* is given neither a name nor a nationality. *The Enchanter* is *Lolita* without first-person narration, without the landscape of American popular culture, without Clare Quilty, without the inventive brio and without the exquisite tragicomedy.

What the two works do have in common is the once risqué, now reprobate theme of child molestation. And, though one was written in English and the other, Dmitri asserts, in Russian, they share the language of the baroque. When Vladimir Nabokov advertised the lost Russian novella to Putnam's as "a beautiful piece of Russian prose, precise and lucid," he was being arch in hopes of a contractual triumph. At least in its English version, which offers us "fleeting glimpses of incidental ephemera," *The Enchanter* is too finely nuanced even to be clear. Niceties of style prevent us from ascertaining essential facts of the plot, like what exactly is the dire fate that befalls our girl-crazy protagonist when, surprised in sin, he rushes barefoot out into the street. We do not even know his occupation except that it is "a refined, precise, and rather lucrative profession" and "a limpid, elegant profession." He is given "the keen eye of an appraiser of facets and reflections," but that could as easily make him an author of Nabokovian prose as a jeweler. (pp. 676-78)

I eagerly await Dmitri Nabokov's next book. (p. 679)

> Steven G. Kellman, "Paler Fire," in The Nation, New York, Vol. 243, No. 20, December 13, 1986, pp. 676-79.

JOHN UPDIKE

The Enchanter arrives in the reflected glow of *Lolita,* and does, like it, begin with a middle-aged man's passion for a twelve-year-old girl. Its nameless heroine is first seen in a Paris park, on roller skates. . . . The nameless hero (whom Nabokov remembered as being called Arthur and hailing from central Europe) is a rather pale monster, though at one point, we are told, he "flashed a tusk from beneath a bluish lip" and at another, . . . he notes "the rancid emanations of . . . wilted skin." His profession, several times coyly alluded to, might be that of a diamond-cutter. Unlike Humbert Humbert, in *Lolita,* he is not the narrator of his love story, but we are made intimately privy to his heavy-breathing observations of the nymphet's "large, slightly vacuous eyes, somehow suggesting translucent gooseberries," "the summery tint of her bare arms with the sleek little foxlike hairs running along the forearms.". . . She is never more than the sum of such details, however, since events contrive to keep her elsewhere even when her admirer marries her mother. When the stepfather and the child are at last thrown together (by the mother's death, as in *Lolita*) nothing happens equivalent to the complex and robust mixture of seductiveness, defiance, filial dependence, and comradely cockiness with which Dolores Haze meets Humbert Humbert's

desire. The great superiority of *Lolita* to *The Enchanter* resides, above all, in the rich character of Lolita—her Americanness, her toughness, her resilience, her touching childishness as it shades erratically into treacherous womanhood. The pedophilia of *The Enchanter* seems nastier for having a limp and silent body as its object. The courtship of the mother seems grimmer than the acquiescent conquest of crass Charlotte Haze, and her death sadder. The hero's lust is less ethereal and more genital, and there is not the relieving circumstantiality, in the vague France of *The Enchanter,* of the novel's amazingly and uproariously well-observed Americana. And the redeeming, splendid, headlong, endlessly comic and evocative English of *Lolita*—the apologetic and manic voice of Humbert Humbert—has no equal in this translation, though there are indications that the original Russian was heavily worked, toward a feverish jocosity that might make its central topic palatable. Nabokov may have been knowingly wrapping up, with a terminal flamboyance, his days as a Russian writer. . . . (pp. 125-27)

During the author's lifetime, his son, Dmitri, born in Germany but raised in the United States, was his best translator of the Russian works into English, producing versions that additionally benefitted from the paternal author's extra touches and refinements. Here Dmitri had to work with an abandoned text whose "virtuosity," he says in his afterword (or "postface," as he puts it), "consists in a deliberate vagueness of verbal and visual elements" and wherein "VN, were he alive, might have exercised his authorial license to change certain details." In a few spots (such as the "high-speed imagery of the finale," which comes through smashingly) the translator has dared venture away from "a totally literal rendering" that would have been "meaningless in English." Often enough, the English version feels strained and even unintelligible. . . . One doesn't know how much to blame the translator's very Nabokovian insistence on rigorous fidelity or the author's Nabokovian fondness for "double- and triple-bottomed imagery" that may ripple through the Russian but rather clots the derived English. Dmitri elucidates some "compressed images and locutions" in his afterword, as well as indignantly repelling some recent trespassers upon his father's reputation; but "precise and lucid" seem odd words to describe *The Enchanter*. Not only is there a fog of namelessness and verbal overload but ambiguity enshrouds such turns of plot as whether or not the hero sleeps with his bride on the wedding night and whether or not he goes into a pharmacy to buy poison for her.

The Enchanter, in short, is a squirmy work whose basic idea was tenacious enough to inspire a masterpiece on another continent a decade later. It is remembered, in *Lolita,* by the name of the hotel, The Enchanted Hunters, where Humbert and Lolita first sleep together. Or, rather, she sleeps while he stays awake, in one of the most beautifully described of the many insomnias in Nabokov. . . . In the same bedded situation where these magical sentences evoke the drifting Tristan and his underage Iseult, *The Enchanter* has its cruel, obscene, and cacophonous climax. The transformation is one of the miracles of modern fiction. (pp. 127-28)

> John Updike, "Old World Wickedness," in The New Yorker, Vol. LXII, No. 43, December 15, 1986, pp. 124-28.

MARTIN AMIS

Nabokov variously referred to [*Volshebnik*] (*The Enchanter*) as 'a prototype' of *Lolita,* 'a kind of pre-*Lolita* novella,' 'a dead scrap' and 'a beautiful piece of Russian prose.' The long short story had to wait 20 years before it fulminated into the famous novel, and another 30 before its triumphant resuscitation. *The Enchanter* is quite a discovery. After this, 1987 will be all downhill.

What exactly do the two works share? Elements of the same obsession, one or two crucial joists in the plotting, a verbal surface of the highest tautness and burnish. But as reading experiences they remain sharply distinct. You read *Lolita* sprawling limply in your chair, ravished, overcome, nodding scandalised assent. You read *The Enchanter* on the edge of your seat, squirming with fearful admiration and constant resistance; you are always saying no, no, no. *Lolita* is comedy, subversive yet divine: somehow, it describes an ascent. Whereas *The Enchanter* is a moral horror story, the last twitchings of a dead soul.

Like Lolita, the girl [in *The Enchanter*] is 12. Her effect on [the protagonist] is immediate. . . . But it is not passion that emboldens him, only circumstance, a glimpse of the possible laxity of future events. The world will have to let it happen. He befriends the girl's mother (a widow), who is promisingly sickly and may have only a year to live. He forms a plan, or he lets it form, or it forms itself.

In *Lolita,* however inadvertently, Lolita is the enchantress. Here, the ravisher assumes that role—or he tries. In fact he enchants nobody, except himself. For all its lucidity, the world of *The Enchanter* is affectless, morally dead. The main characters are nameless (though this is done so artfully that you scarcely notice); the settings of time and place (the Thirties, Paris and Provence) are unimportant, indeed drearily incidental. *Lolita* is, among other things, a landscape novel, satirically fixed in its period. The turpitudes of *The Enchanter,* it seems, can happen anywhere, at any time. Unlike Humbert, with his crooner's mug, his 'ad-eyebrows,' his 'striking if somewhat brutal good looks,' the enchanter is quite faceless, except when he leers; he is just subtly sub-human. And the girl has nothing but her ordinary innocence, her freshness, her brand-newness.

Grimly the enchanter courts the girl's ailing mother. He listens 'to the epic of her malady'; he makes 'mooing sounds of consolation' and false tenderness; he 'wordlessly compresses or applies to his tense jowl her ominously obedient hand.' Ironically, in the fairytale scheme of the story, she is the 'monster,' with her hairless wart, her cold brow, her surgeons' scars, seemingly pregnant 'with her own death.'

On their wedding night, the enchanter bluffs and stalls; yet, 'in the middle of his farewell speeches about his migraine' he suddenly finds himself next to 'the corpse of the miraculously vanquished giantess.' The successful copulation, with its dire presentiment, occurs only once. Soon, the wife is dead for real, and the enchanter is heading south for the union with his little princess.

Only at this point does he fully immerse himself in his sexual plans for the girl. 'The lone wolf was getting ready to don Granny's nightcap.' These four pages of drooling reverie—and they have a radiant ghastliness—constitute the enchanter's inexpiable moral trespass: salacious, savage and gruesomely sentimental. And it is for this, rather than for the actual molestation, that the enchanter is so roundly punished. The sexual spasm is still cooling on his mackintosh when he receives his spectacular and sanguinary retribution. Thrice-orphaned, the girl is left behind, as she was always left behind, humanly unregarded.

Some readers may find the moral starkness of *The Enchanter* somewhat Russian Orthodox, when set against the decadent complexity of *Lolita*. Certainly, it belongs to Nabokov's Berlin period, more specifically to the line of antic cruelty which runs from *King, Queen, Knave* to *Despair*. In any event it is a little masterpiece, witheringly precise and genuinely shocking. Special praise must go to the translator. It may be that Nabokov's death has paradoxically liberated his sometime collaborator, for *The Enchanter* is seamlessly Nabokovian.

The evident persistence of the nympholepsy theme is striking, but only because the theme is striking. It is no more persistent than Nabokov's interest in doubles, mirrors, chess, paranoia—and much less persistent than his interest in the *artiste manqué*, with which, however, it is importantly connected.

Martin Amis, "Lolita's Little Sister," *in* The Observer, *January 4, 1987, p. 22.*

ALAN JENKINS

In mood and moral atmosphere *The Enchanter* is closer to *Despair* or *Laughter in the Dark* than *Lolita*. It is narrated in the third person, though from the protagonist's point of view—we see the world heightened or distorted by his delirium, and we have access to his gloomy, joky introspection. He is unnamed. His stratagems are more diabolical than Humbert's, which are always tinged with desperation. He is forty, "thin, dry-lipped" and a jeweller; though the locations—never specified in the story itself—are Paris and Provence, he has none of Humbert's gallicized sophistication, none of the dilettante *littérateur*'s manic allusiveness, and, where Humbert's self-lacerating ironies are playful and complex, the earlier protagonist's merely lacerate. What he and Humbert share, though—as do Albinus and Hermann—are the financial resources and freedom to pursue their obsession, and, an opportunity once presented, the determination, the insane indifference to "normal" constraints which characterize the pursuit.

The enchanter of the title is the pursuer himself, though he mostly sees himself in a less flattering light ("the lone wolf was getting ready to don Granny's nightcap"); the title may recall The Enchanted Hunters motel-lodge in *Lolita,* and the girl whom he attempts to bring under a grotesque kind of spell is also his prey. If the enchanted hunter has here some of the ghastly self-awarenessness of his later, infinitely richer embodiment, the girl herself is an extremely pale shadow of Dolores Haze. She is still very much a child. There is no suggestion that she shares the aura of "innocent" depravity which surrounds Lolita. Her presence is almost purely physical. . . .

There is also something poignant or pathetic about the girl, deriving mainly from her semi-orphaned and farmed-out state (too much of a threat to her mother's health, she lives a loveless existence with family friends in the provinces), but for the most part the book has a sustained undertone of horrific farce, half precipitated by, half the raw material for, the protagonist's cynical manipulations. His seduction of her mother, the mother herself ("tall, pale, broad-hipped", "with a hairless wart near a nostril of her bulbous nose"), the details of consummation (with both mother and daughter), the steady progression towards disaster—also farcical, when it comes—and most of all the mental processes of the enchanter, alternating between semi-appalled analytical detachment and entranced fantasy, have a sombre, cruel hilarity, which was carried over into *Lolita*'s more nightmarish moments. Humbert's account of desire *in extremis* is driven by the need to explain, and, overwhelmingly, to share: his love, his pain. The enchanter shares with us principally a sick joke: reality remade in the image of his madness, sometimes thwarted, sometimes abetted, as Dmitri Nabokov says, by Fate. The sense of doom is heavy, and we are reminded of McFate, abetted by Clare Quilty, in *Lolita.* For the enchanter there is no such accounting; retribution comes in a bravura climax (the climax after the climax).

It is hard to imagine how any other book this year will give such sentence-by-sentence pleasure as this tale of a melancholy monster, who says "I know that I would be a most loving father in the common sense of the word" and act out, to his destruction, the uncommon sense of it, who is briefly cheered by giving, to a "toddler", an absentminded smile, since "only *humans* are capable of absentmindedness", whose shudders and throbs of yearning are unlike those most of us know only in their object, and in whose story (thanks, perhaps, to translator's hindsight—or hind-hearing—and sleight-of-hand) we catch frequent pre-echoes and stirrings of a much more flexible, inventive, alert, caressing and humane voice. . . .

Alan Jenkins, "First Throb of the Enchanted Hunter," in The Times Literary Supplement, No. 4372, January 16, 1987, p. 55.

JOHN BAYLEY

[*The Enchanter*] has been translated—and very brilliantly translated, in the master's own style—by his son Dimitri. The author's original instinct may have been right. Yet it remains a wholly successful short story, because it deals so curtly and so deftly with its theme.

That theme, as the author surmised, needed the relaxed, humorous, untidy treatment possible in a novel. Humorous above all. There is plenty of humour in *The Enchanter,* as in all of Nabokov's stories, but it is a stylised, self-regulating humour. It does not put on carpet slippers and let its hair down, as it does in *Lolita,* where humanity is marvellously and invisibly restored by its presence. True humour is never wholly under the author's direction, or does not seem to be; and the humour of *Lolita* (whose true heroine is 'big Haze') seems to evade the somewhat too pertinacious pursuit of its effects by the narrator and his creator. A good novel is funnier than its author knows. *The Enchanter* should really be called 'The Magician', which is a more accurate rendering of its Russian title *Volshebnik,* but Nabokov himself called it *The Enchanter,* no doubt because enchantment sounds more rapt and poetical than magic, more suited to the nymphet's effect on her would-be owner, and the owner's lyrical description of her.

But there is the irony, for it is he himself who is the enchanter or magician—a failed magician, who 'starting little by little to cast his spell, began passing his magic wand above her body . . . until she made a faint motion, and turned her face away with a barely audible, somnolent smack of her lips.' There, however, the resemblance between *Lolita* and *The Enchanter* ends. Both have these wonderfully hilarious, slow-motion physical pictures: the nymphet comes 'clamping' along on her roller-skates; a quick knitter 'now and then, with a lightning motion, adjusted the trailing tail of her woollen foetus'; and both—like most of Nabokov's stories—have their ritual moment of romantic disillusion: after the fantastic peepshow of love comes the awakening on the cold hill side. But whereas the wretchedly comfortable and comic Humbert, the 'I' of Lolita, finds that his nymphet is already entirely knowing and sardonic about the absurdities of masculine desire, the enchanter's victim man-

ifests the conventional appalled response, and the end of her anonymous would-be rapist (a jeweller by trade incidentally) is an equally conventional nightmare one.

In both cases, of course, the rich texture of the writing serves to point up the deadliness of the fixation. A consummate artist, Nabokov was justified in implying that such art has no need crudely to draw our attention to the pathos and horror of its subject. As empirical technician, moreover, he would be justified in pointing out that the alternative treatment of the subject in *Lolita* and *The Enchanter* faithfully reflects what occurs in real life. Some girls might be devastated, some merely amused. The child abuse, which hovers in the background of Dostoievsky's novels, is given the same slant by him in the nightmare of Svidrigailov in *Crime and Punishment,* who finds his little victim looking up at him with a knowing leer. For all his expressed contempt for Dostoievsky Nabokov certainly got a lot from him.

The sheer play of the artist's intelligence, perhaps a little overblown by the time of *Lolita,* appears here with masterly economy. Nabokov's Russian is probably never self-indulgent, as his English can be. His son, who contributes a most engaging and perceptive afterword, has done a superb job, no doubt with some original help from father. The story should probably be read first very quickly, and then very slowly, when the reticent way in which the creator has got inside his jeweller's mind will be fully clear. . . . The nymphet's mother, whom the jeweller marries for his pathetically fell purposes, is sketched with Shakespearian certainty, and—as of Nabokovian right—the direness of the poor creature's situation is taken for granted. When she dies unexpectedly after an operation the jeweller's first reaction is one of acute disappointment. Though fate has given him exactly what he wanted, her death means that the nymphet will not come home 'that night', as her step-father had carefully planned. Another stroke of psychology worthy of Shakespeare is the jeweller's wholly justified confidence that he has made the last months of the nymphet's mother comparatively happy ones. Things like this put the story in the top class of Nabokov's work: the jeweller is a character comparable to the chess-player Luzhin, of *The Defence,* or to the hero of his very first and one of his best novels, *Mary.* (pp. 28-9)

John Bayley, "A Writer and a Gentleman," in The Spectator, Vol. 258, No. 8273, January 31, 1987, pp. 28-9.

FRANK KERMODE

Since [*The Enchanter*] is about a middle-aged man's lust for a prepubescent girl, or 'proto-nymphet,' as D. Nabokov calls her, and since he marries the girl's mother to get access to his prey, the connection with *Lolita* is plain enough; and since publishers enjoy selling books it will not be underplayed in the publicity. On the other hand, it is also necessary to establish that the tale has virtues of its own and is not a preliminary sketch for the novel: so D. Nabokov insists that although his father said the anonymous girl of *The Enchanter* was 'the same lass' as Lolita, she is so 'only in an inspirational, conceptual sense'. D. Nabokov normally writes a testy, conceited critical prose imitated from his father's, and is very severe on the 'inane hypotheses' of some commentators: so 'only in an inspirational, conceptual sense' is uncharacteristically hazy. Still, the point is made: *The Enchanter* and *Lolita* are both about middle-aged paedophilia, but differ in treatment, much as one would have expected.

D. Nabokov undertakes to explain some of the difficulties facing the reader of this complicated stretch of prose. . . . He is keen to show that Nabokov had no special interest in little girls; he wrote studies 'of madness seen through the madman's mind', and the madman might be a musician, a chess-player or a paedophile. He goes out of his way to deny that there was ever a further story on a similar theme called "The Satyr", as Field claims. In any case, crazy nymphet-lovers didn't in themselves interest Nabokov: what mattered were the 'combinational delights' he could derive from them as from other subjects, the disinterested play of light and shadow over them. Nevertheless it is also claimed that the morality of the tale is perfectly sound. The protagonist is represented as 'cynical, contemptible', and gets his due reward when run over by a truck. He is credited with an occasional 'yearning for decency', and his feeling for the girl is not simply lecherous but partly paternal. These thematic ambiguities are reflected in the prose, and the translator offers explanations of certain passages so knotty that he himself had difficulty in understanding them. I have to admit that in some cases the explanations left me just as baffled as before. . . . So as not to follow too far those 'parallel primrose paths', the resemblances to *Lolita,* we need to remind ourselves that the girl in the story, unlike Lolita, is not already corrupted; it is the violence of her horrified response when she wakes in the hotel bedroom to see him plying his magician's wand that causes him to rush out to his destruction. The unnamed protagonist . . . repudiates any idea of Oriental debauchery: his is a 'unique flame', he is totally obsessed with one little girl, lovingly and intimately described, and totally repelled by female maturity, as represented by her forty-year-old mother. He gets as big a kick out of her rollerskates as Humbert does from Lolita's tennis racket. The thought of the girl is like cocaine melting in the loins. Does he really feel like a father, or is he using his position as stepfather to acquire ready access to bliss? Is what he feels 'healthy shame or sickly cowardice', concupiscence or 'aesthetic anguish'? You can see

that here, as in *Lolita,* there are serious questions about the differentiation of blisses. Anyway Arthur comes to a bad end, like Humbert, which is a way of settling the moral aspect of the problem.

The story is very heavily written, and requires to be read with a certain devotion. The same can be said of *Lolita,* but there the effect is different: the text jokes with us and with itself, the rascal lover is obsessed not only with the girl but with an alien culture and an alien language, and in all sorts of ways he interests us as much as the trickery of the book's design. It seems to me that *The Enchanter* lacks these charms. The complexities of its language (the English certified as very close to the tortuous Russian) are oppressive rather than enlivening. What does seem worthy of Nabokov is the rendering of the detail of the girl's body, and of the man's intense desire. There are other good things—for instance, his devious and sometimes absurd progress towards climax, symbolised by his inability to find his way back to the hotel room where the girl lies asleep and unprotected.

The Enchanter might have looked less disappointing as "The Enchanter", a story in a volume of stories; dressed up as a book and ambiguously hyped as elder sister of *Lolita* it is given a false eminence, and subjected to unavoidable comparisons. It also seems to testify to an obsession with a particular manic obsession, more timidly expressed, less blissful, than in its successor. Lionel Trilling, in a famous review, pointed out that *Lolita* was not pornographic but insisted that it was shocking— a complex act of transgression that only success in shocking could justify. *The Enchanter* is neither pornographic nor shocking in the necessary way: it is, in a curious way, too weighed down by conscience.

Frank Kermode, "Protonymphet," in London Review of Books, *February 5, 1987, p. 13.*

St.-John Perse

1887-1975

(Pseudonym of Marie-René-Auguste Alexis Saint-Léger Léger; also published under pseudonyms of Saintléger Léger and St.-J. Perse) French poet.

Perse is a significant contemporary poet and Nobel laureate whose verse reflects his perception that humanity is universally subject to alienation. Perse's focus on despair is tempered, however, by his acceptance of both the negative and positive facets of existence. This dualistic philosophy is demonstrated in his vivid descriptions of exotic landscapes and kinetic language praising the spiritual and physical aspects of life. Often prosaic in appearance, Perse's poetry is written in the free-verse style of verset which, with its heavily cadenced, incantatory rhythms and reverential content, resembles portions of the Old Testament as well as the poetry of Walt Whitman and Paul Claudel. Although Perse is also linked with the poets of the French Symbolist tradition, his highly imaginative works defy conventional categorization.

Perse was born on St. Leger-les-Feuilles, an island owned by his family in the French West Indies. As a child, Perse was exposed to the lush foliage and natural disasters—hurricanes, tidal waves, and earthquakes—indigenous to the tropics. His childhood nurse, a worshipper of Siva, the god associated with destruction and regeneration in the Hindu triad, introduced Perse to a culture vastly different from his own. These elements provided him with a knowledge of botany, natural history, and diverse religions—especially Roman Catholicism—all of which are amply displayed in his verse. Financial difficulties caused by a massive earthquake eventually forced Perse's family to sell St. Leger-les-Feuilles and relocate to France. After an education encompassing medicine, law, and the arts, Perse, under his real name of Alexis Saint-Léger Léger, embarked upon a career as a diplomat. As secretary of the French Embassy in Peking, China, he befriended Chinese philosophers and became familiar with Asian culture. His esteemed career climaxed when he was appointed Secretary-General of the French Foreign Ministry in 1932. Before this promotion, Perse had already authored *Éloges* (1911) and *Anabase* (1924; *Anabasis*) but had foresworn publishing future poems while in public service. He did continue to write, however, and reputedly amassed several volumes of manuscripts that were confiscated by Nazi soldiers in 1940.

Major segments of *Éloges* were first published in *La nouvelle revue française* under the name Saintléger Léger in 1909 and 1910 and were reprinted in book form in 1911. An expanded second edition of *Éloges* appeared in 1925 under the pseudonym St.-J. Perse. In many of these poems, Perse evokes memories of his childhood and details life in the tropics through the use of sensuous and precise language. The sequence "Images à Crusoe" ("Pictures for Crusoe"), inspired by Daniel Defoe's prose work *Robinson Crusoe*, presents Crusoe as an emblem of solitude and loneliness. Similar themes pervade all of Perse's work.

Anabasis is perhaps Perse's most celebrated composition. According to Octavio Paz, this work "is an account of the peregrinations and movements—in space, in time, and in the secret

enclosures of the dream—of races and civilizations, a celebration of the founding of cities and laws.'' *Anabasis* centers upon a nomadic tribe that explores and civilizes an arid, windy area similar to the Gobi Desert. Once the land is settled, a sense of longing provokes another excursion into the desert to repeat the process. While alluding to the restless nature of humanity, *Anabasis* also serves as a metaphor for the poet's struggles with language.

After *Anabasis*, Perse abandoned publishing to concentrate on his diplomatic responsibilities. His refusal to collaborate with the Vichy government following France's collapse in 1940 led to his removal from office, his emigration to the United States, and revocation of his French citizenship. Perse's poetry from this time documents his world view of the physical and spiritual expatriation of humanity. The pieces in *Exil* (1946; *Exile and Other Poems*) recount the desperation of exile in images that are derived from contemporary and personal situations but are universally applicable. Perse claims that he was redeemed from this bleakness through the inspiration and creation of poetry. *Vents* (1946; *Winds*) traces the destructive results of human knowledge on the development of modern civilization. The winds refer on one level to those created by the atomic explosion at Hiroshima, which to Perse represented the culmination of amoral learning and positioned the present age on a historical cusp that will necessitate the moderation of knowledge with wisdom.

Perse's last major volumes, *Amers* (1957; *Seamarks*) and *Chronique* (1960), focus on the affirmative qualities of life. Of *Amers* Perse wrote: ''I have striven to exalt, in all its ardour and pride, the drama of that human condition . . . that so many persons today take delight in debasing and belittling to the point of depriving it of all meaning, of all supreme connection with the great forces that create us, that use us, and that control us.'' Critics have commented that *Amers* contains some of the most beautiful descriptions of erotic love in contemporary poetry. In *Chronique,* Perse meditates on his life's experiences and freely alludes to his previous works. Other works by Perse include *Oiseaux* (1962; *Birds*), a collaboration with the artist Georges Braque, and *Chant pour un equinox* (1977; *Song for an Equinox*).

Perse was awarded the Nobel Prize in Literature in 1960, confirming his international status as ''one of the greatest pioneers of modern poetry,'' as the Nobel committee stated. His work has been translated into many languages by several honored individuals, including T. S. Eliot and Dag Hammarskjöld. While critics recognize the sometimes difficult nature of his verse, most acknowledge the perceptiveness of Perse's poetry and concur with Wallace Fowlie's assessment: ''[Perse's] work relates the secular and the spiritual efforts of man to see himself as a part of the natural world, to tame the hostile powers of the world, to worship the endlessly renewed beauty of the world, to conjugate his ambitions and dreams with the changes and modifications of time.''

(See also *CLC*, Vols. 4, 11 and *Contemporary Authors,* Vols. 13-16, rev. ed., Vols. 61-64 [obituary].)

VALERY LARBAUD

[*The preface excerpted below was originally written for the 1926 Russian edition of* Anabasis *and was published in* La nouvelle revue française, *January, 1926.*]

How many French poets were read between 1895 and 1925? Possibly a hundred, of whom thirty at least seem worthy of attention and qualified to add something to the ensemble of French poetry.

The period was one of feverish activity. Poets were completing the dislocation of the Alexandrine, freeing this measure from classical tyranny of versification. Free verse was in the process of invention. The laws of the ''*verset*'' were being explored. Experiments were being conducted with a view to combining the rhythms of prose with the rhythms of lyric poetry. A host of craftsmen were copying the monuments of the past, trying to rejuvenate them.

What remains of all this effort? How many lasting monuments did all this labor add to the sum of French poetry? They may be counted on the fingers of one hand.

We have the enormous lyrical and dramatic monument of Paul Claudel which dominates the entire group; that of Paul Valéry; that of Francis Jammes . . . ; that of Léon-Paul Fargue . . . ; and finally, the more recently added, and still unfinished, monument of St.-John Perse: his *Eloges* and his *Anabase*. . . .

In thirty years, then, we have five monuments, as against some fivescore buildings which stand in ruins about them or which have crumbled to dust. What a terrible and silent Judgment!

Yet all these attempts were not in vain. Noble fragments of some of them persist which, in the years to come, will interest such rarely privileged archeologists as can appreciate their beauty, regardless of the historic value of documents. The fact remains, however, that only the works of Claudel, Valéry, Jammes, Fargue and St.-John Perse endure today and will continue to endure.

(When all is said and done, did the age of Henry IV, one of the most productive of literary eras, bequeath us a greater number?)

A personal poetic thought is perforce a novel thought, indeed a foreign thought. Faced with Claudel's earliest works, many belated literati—I mean men not sufficiently well-lettered— felt that they were reading translations and imitations of foreign works. Today it is obvious that nothing could possibly be more French than the matter and form of Claudel's writings. The same will hold true of St.-John Perse's poetic vision and of his prosody, based on the Alexandrine.

Indeed, what he has brought to French lyricism, what he has described and what he has introduced into French poetry is very novel and very personal. He has offered geographic, historic and human visions of the lands in which he has lived (the West Indies, where he spent his childhood, and China, where he resided several years). In *Anabase,* he gives the chronicle of an ascent from the shores of the sea to the deserts of Central Asia. . . . (pp. 101-03)

But what a vast progress, what a renewal, and what a gain in lyric depth since the day of Chateaubriand's descriptions! Those of St.-John Perse are at once more exact and precise, they are more highly charged with sense and meditation. These landscapes of his lie within himself; he beholds them in a mirror which rests in the core of his consciousness; he sees them and is astonished; he takes possession of them yet he feels himself alien; an alien on the human plane, not nationally speaking. He is a man to whom our planet will forever be a thing of wonder. It is as if some part of him could not accept the conditions in which he is forced to live as conditions which are his, and made for him, and the only possible ones. Even that ''colour of man'' which he loves, he perceives and feels as an alien thing.

The language and rhythm, which he compels to express his thought, he treats with the same detachment, a detachment more immaterial and intellectual than haughty. In his hands the language of French poetry is like some splendid thoroughbred he is riding; he uses its qualities but forces it to move at a gait new to it and contrary to its habits.

It is as though he said to the language:

''You shall describe what you never described before I came . . . you shall patiently enumerate objects and actions and men that neither Scève nor Ronsard had observed and that Malherbe and La Fontaine would have considered outside your province . . . you shall set your scale to the scale of this huge Continent, of this far-flung expanse which has nothing to do with the land where you were born and where you grew up. . . .''

Already in *Eloges* St.-John Perse had made this language describe the seas and islands of the tropics. Now, with *Anabase,* he achieves the conquest of Asia, the vast roof of the world.

Yet it is the tongue of Scève and Ronsard and La Fontaine and Racine, and it is the line created by Malherbe, which he employs and marshals for his conquest.

Accordingly, if we pause to survey the various architectural units set up in the other great linguistic fields, where shall we find any to match this planetary monument of poesy? (pp. 103-04)

> *Valery Larbaud, in a preface, translated by Jacques Le Clercq, to* Anabasis: A Poem *by St.-John Perse, translated by T. S. Eliot, revised edition, Harcourt Brace Jovanovich, 1949, pp. 101-04.*

HUGO von HOFMANNSTHAL

[*The essay excerpted below originally appeared in German in the* Neue Schweizer Rundschau, *May, 1929.*]

Anabasis has a heroic background which in its lighter aspects is reminiscent of the severe delicacy of Poussin. The action itself dispenses with historical, ideological or social allusions. The precision that we consider as almost synonymous with the French spirit is eliminated. Less, however, than with Mallarmé do we find the parallel of musical expression: instead of the mirroring-word material so rich in sensual significance, thanks to which the appearance of objects seems to be wrapped in music, we experience great reserve and hardness. Evocative of purity and severity, of domination and self-control, the following words occur again and again: scalebeam; pure salt; the pure idea; the cleansing and sanctifying qualities of salt—*les délices du sel*. The deliberate harshness of transitions, the brusque and repeated disruption of images, the capricious evocation of the Orient—the combination of these qualities constitute a work which alternately offers of itself as much as it withdraws. On closer investigation we find it a poem full of beauty and strength; a work created, moreover—although we cannot say precisely why—in the spirit of our day, that alert and heroic spirit of contemporary France which is giving birth to new saints and founding a new colonial empire before its southern gates. (pp. 106-07)

> *Hugo von Hofmannsthal, in a preface, translated by James Stern, to* Anabasis: A Poem *by St.-John Perse, translated by T. S. Eliot, revised edition, Harcourt Brace Jovanovich, 1949, pp. 105-07.*

T. S. ELIOT

[*The preface excerpted below was originally written for the 1930 British edition of* Anabasis.]

I am by no means convinced that a poem like **Anabase** requires a preface at all. It is better to read such a poem six times, and dispense with a preface. But when a poem is presented in the form of a translation, people who have never heard of it are naturally inclined to demand some testimonial. So I give mine hereunder. (p. 9)

For myself, once having had my attention drawn to the poem by a friend whose taste I trusted, there was no need for a preface. I did not need to be told, after one reading, that the word *anabasis* has no particular reference to Xenophon or the journey of the Ten Thousand, no particular reference to Asia *Minor;* and that no map of its migrations could be drawn up. Mr. Perse is using the word *anabasis* in the same literal sense in which Xenophon himself used it. The poem is a series of images of migration, of conquest of vast spaces in Asiatic

wastes, of destruction and foundation of cities and civilizations of any races or epochs of the ancient East.

I may, I trust, borrow from Mr. [Lucien] Fabre two notions which may be of use to the English reader. The first is that any obscurity of the poem, on first readings, is due to the suppression of "links in the chain," of explanatory and connecting matter, and not to incoherence, or to the love of cryptogram. The justification of such abbreviation of method is that the sequence of images coincides and concentrates into one intense impression of barbaric civilization. The reader has to allow the images to fall into his memory successively without questioning the reasonableness of each at the moment; so that, at the end, a total effect is produced.

Such selection of a sequence of images and ideas has nothing chaotic about it. There is a logic of the imagination as well as a logic of concepts. People who do not appreciate poetry always find it difficult to distinguish between order and chaos in the arrangement of images; and even those who are capable of appreciating poetry cannot depend upon first impressions. I was not convinced of Mr. Perse's imaginative order until I had read the poem five or six times. And if, as I suggest, such an arrangement of imagery requires just as much "fundamental brainwork" as the arrangement of an argument, it is to be expected that the reader of a poem should take at least as much trouble as a barrister reading an important decision on a complicated case.

I refer to this poem as a poem. It would be convenient if poetry were always verse—either accented, alliterative, or quantitative; but that is not true. Poetry may occur, within a definite limit on one side, at any point along a line of which the formal limits are "verse" and "prose." Without offering any generalized theory about "poetry," "verse" and "prose," I may suggest that a writer, by using, as does Mr. Perse, certain exclusively poetic methods, is sometimes able to write poetry in what is called prose. (pp. 9-11)

But *Anabase* is poetry. Its sequences, its logic of imagery, are those of poetry and not of prose; and in consequence—at least the two matters are very closely allied—the *declamation*, the system of stresses and pauses, which is partially exhibited by the punctuation and spacing, is that of poetry and not of prose.

The second indication of Mr. Fabre is one which I may borrow for the English reader: a tentative synopsis of the movement of the poem. It is a scheme which may give the reader a little guidance on his first reading; when he no longer needs it he will forget it. The ten divisions of the poem are headed as follows:

    I. Arrival of the Conqueror at the site of the city which he is about to build.
   II. Tracing the plan of the city.
  III. Consultation of augurs.
  IV. Foundation of the city.
   V. Restlessness towards further explorations and conquests.
  VI. Schemes for foundation and conquest.
 VII. Decision to fare forth.
VIII. March through the desert.
  IX. Arrival at the threshold of a great new country.
   X. Acclamation, festivities, repose. Yet the urge towards another departure, this time with the mariner.

And I believe that this is as much as I need to say about Perse's

Anabasis. I believe that this is a piece of writing of the same importance as the later work of James Joyce, as valuable as *Anna Livia Plurabelle.* And this is a high estimate indeed. (pp. 11-12)

T. S. Eliot, in a preface to Anabasis: A Poem *by St.-John Perse, translated by T. S. Eliot, revised edition, Harcourt Brace Jovanovich, 1949, pp. 9-12.*

S. A. RHODES

The poetry of St.-J. Perse comes from the hazy reality of a mystic past, like a radiant image out of a mirror. The mist vanishes, the glass melts, and from its mysterious waters rises a winged creature. This marvelous being has the fragrance and the colors of flowers; it has the sensitiveness of winged insects. It seems nurtured and suckled with earthly fruits and celestial elixirs. When its heart and mind are intoxicated to the limit of human endurance, it breaks forth into a pure, aërial song of joy and sorrow. It is over soon, and it then relapses into a silence forever. The wings are folded again; the waters are crystallized back into glass. Only the reflection from the mirror— its poetry, pure, diaphanous, infinite—remains to attest the miraculous metamorphosis.

St.-J. Perse is divided in his allegiance to the spirit. Though life plays an irresistible melody upon his heart strings, he bathes the realities of the earth in the beaming enchantment of his poetic eye. He struggles for the voluptuous strength of nature, the secret communion between dumb animal and silent skies. He strives to enter as a partner into their peaceful understanding. He sees with disquieting fortitude the disruptive character of our earthly condition. The unknowing impulse of all life towards light is a measure of a contrary blind urge towards decay. Withal, spirit and matter commune in a reintegration of transcending harmony. The poetry of St.-J. Perse is the embodiment of a moment of such harmony. (pp. 28-9)

A wistful mood pervades many of the early poems in *Éloges.* The book opens with a cantata entitled: **"Pour Fêter une Enfance,"** which sings a dream childhood. Its subtitle could well be: "A la Recherche d'un Paradis Perdu"—The Quest of a Lost Paradise. It evokes the vision of a blessed antiquity, a high condition of purity in human nature and feature. It is difficult to determine whether we are in the presence of a recollection from childhood, or from a lost Paradise—a golden Atlantis sunk beneath the sea of oblivion, "a world swaying between sparkling waters, . . ." It is both, perhaps. The poet himself is uncertain. Do these fabulous impressions pertain to this or to another age? (pp. 29-30)

In *Éloges,* as later in *Anabase,* the poet is in quest of the same lost paradise. If **"Pour Fêter une Enfance"** formulates it, the later poems are its development. The first five cantos of the poem **"Éloges"** speak clearly of a child's wondrous voyage towards legendary islands. (We get a sight of these promised lands in a later poem.) In this one, the atmosphere on board the phantom ship bathes the mystic quest in the glowing colors of reality. The bridge is washed by waters that seem to surge from a dream. The morningtide comes down from the sky to meet the poet's transport of spirit and senses. His song reaches a high degree of unadulterated purity, expressive of the sense of the spiritual journey on which he is bound. (p. 31)

But the tone of the poetry alters swiftly. A desert wind seems to scorch the sea breeze. The soft sail gives way to the hard earth. The poet submits the angularities and malformations of the clay that entombs the soul of man to the erosive wear of his poetic passion. His poetry takes the quality and texture of an emotional convulsion. The reality of a vision is reduced to its ultimate and simplest expression through the simultaneous projection of two divergent streams of consciousness upon it: the intellectual and the intuitive. Reality appears then unearthly, or ideal, and irreality takes on a positive and yet transparent density. We get a dizzy and even dangerous spinning of flesh and spirit about the moving center of the poet's thaumaturgic perceptions. The ground shifts places with the sky under his feet. He ceases to feel terrestrial; he becomes empyreal. . . . He sees man, creature of dust, sunk in the wide morass of loneliness and grief, of chaos and strife. He descends to its bowels to explore its darkness, but it is always with an inner harmony to guide him. By a miraculous catharsis, his poetic desire finally disperses all the buried clouds. The radiance of his quest returns to illumine the universe he explores. Chaos is metamorphosed into order, hell into heaven. "O winds! . . ."; the poet sings. "Truly I inhabit the bosom of a god."

The cause of his sorrow is transmuted in this manner into a source of ecstasy. The most persistent impression one gathers from the swift notation of somber and happy moods in this poetry is one of light. "O joy inexplicable except as light!" he observes. That strikes the keynote to the symphony of **"Éloges."** Involved as he is in every conceivable way within the turmoil of a delirious world, the poet marches steadily and unwearily out of it towards another reign of the spirit. Poetically, he has no other impulse than to go forward towards that light. It is not without reason that the eighteen cantos end upon a note of renunciation. "Now, leave me," he warns. "I set out alone."

"La Gloire des Rois," the poem that follows **"Éloges"** in the book, as it succeeds to it spiritually, though both are dated 1908, is written in the form of a concerto—a symphonic poem in three movements and two themes. (pp. 31-2)

"The Glory of Kings" is a fiction of the soul's journey through the lures of earthly and unearthly ways. It is the recital of a spiritual cruise upon the swelling tides of passionate experiences; the log of an arduous navigation through the crosscurrents of desires, and of the arrival to the envisioned port. It is a legend, a confession and a dream; a symbolic fusion of the Homeric, the Baudelairian and the Rimbaudian themes; the *Odyssey, Le Voyage,* and *Illuminations* converging into a lengthening and perpetuating stream.

All erotic expression in this poetry is characterized by cognition and apprehension. But sentimental and intuitive immediacy does not preclude a distinct and inherent feeling of disillusion and frustration to permeate it. First, however, the poem fairly glows with the emanations of sensuous fervor. Its flame burns with consuming splendor. The recitative in praise of a queen is an invocation to Venus that recalls the glory of Rimbaud's *Soleil et Chair.* It is a song for the garden of Priapus. Seldom has erotic poetry been at the same time so voluptuous and so pure. The taste and fragrance of the flesh permeate the words and give them an inebriating virtue. But the poem is no more lascivious than is the *Song of Songs.* A current of lyric exaltation pervades it, and acts as a purifying catharsis upon subject and diction. It clothes the instincts with the poetic, and hence translucent, cloak of beauty. (pp. 32-3)

Perse transmutes into words the coursing torment of passion laboring the body, the keen pain of unrestrained desire. He casts no moral cloud over the burning sun of love. The magic of his poetry provides the necessary moly against the spell of the flesh. Morally, that is to say, intellectually, spiritually and emotionally, the poetry of Perse is an antidote to all lustful urge, precisely because it recognizes no other guiding code than the poetic. (p. 34)

The second part of "**La Gloire des Rois,**" its second movement—"**Amitié du Prince**"—is a spiritual biography. It divulges the efforts of the soul to divorce itself from its marriage to the flesh, and from subservience to it. From the inn of pleasure, on the highway of desire, where the Poet had stopped first, he passes, satiated but unappeased, to the cell of the anchoret. He deserts the Queen, the "lofty inn of flesh", tentacular and tantalizing, for the "very thin and very subtle" Prince.

We may accept as an effective principle of the poetic nature of Perse that, his docility to the enchantments of the earth notwithstanding, his spirit remains unintoxicated with them. It avows the passionate abandon of the heart which tarries on the way; but its eyes are turned towards the "halls with whitewashed walls", intent upon the "invisible sign of dream". His Prince is nurtured with the fruits of the earth. But his ready detachment from them is incantatory. The sense and rhythm of this incantation penetrate the spirit of the poet and his words. He sees in him the Healer and the Assessor and the Enchanter at the sources of the spirit. His power over the heart of man is a wonderful thing, he believes, and his freedom among them very great.

The extent and the freedom of this power in the poetry of Perse is a revelation. In this one as in no other of his poems, he exhorts his spirit to ever greater disincarnation; here as nowhere else his lyricism rises to a wonderful degree of purity. (p. 35)

The conjuring property of such writing is to be ascribed in part to its strong simplicity. Rhetorical trappings are cast off in favor of poetic confessional. Here is a soul enamoured of the ideal that begs no other grace from it than that it sublime the heart. For Perse, all earthly fulfillments must be conditioned upon their being diaphanous. His poetics contain the proviso that no experience may conceal or congeal the spirit. However tyrannical they may be for a while, in the end they must subordinate their claim to that of the spirit. Their intoxication must yield to its serenity; their eloquence to its silence.

Of such a nature is the apology of the poet and his quest. His Prince is a soul in poignant wrestling with its human incasements, and instigating, as he says, "at the highest point of the soul a great quarrel." So moments of the most sensuous iridescence alternate with others of azure and mystic purity in this poetry. (p. 36)

"**Images à Crusoe**" are the pictured recollections of the poet's lost paradise. They are alluringly unfolded to the exiled vision of Crusoe—alias Perse—when he is deeply engulfed in the spleen of his cultivated prison. They recall—in the realm of poetry, and to those who wander that way—the lamentations of the soul, cast out from its own inner Arcadia into a suffocating, barren Gehenna.... The "**Images**" of Perse present the pictorial concept of an imprisoned flight. They bespeak a soul trapped in the brumal regions of terrestial odysseys, a soul cornered and in plight. The poet's evocation, in summation, loses all earthly quality; it becomes mystic. He seeks to rediscover the ways he knew once in his luminous exile, ways God had once revealed to him, and more distant now, he fears, than the passing storm. Crusoe thus attests to his sense of bewilderment. He is Adam distraught outside his Eden home.

The confusion of his earthly sojourn has not dimmed in him the memory of his sideral peregrinations. He gropes for the path that leads out of the world. He longs to come again upon the revelation vouchsafed by God to him when he was, he says, addressing him, "fed with the salt of your solitude, witness of your silence, of your shadow and of your thundering voice." As with the Prince in "**Amitié du Prince**," Crusoe also turns then to the illuminated words written on the pages of his inner life to re-read their lucid message. He runs the wrinkled finger of his experience over the memories and prophesies recorded there. And thus, in inspired trance, he waits for the rising wind that will set him free, all at once, "like a typhoon," he says, "dividing the clouds before his expectant eyes."

As we pass, then, from one poem of St.-J. Perse to another, we come closer and closer to a perception of the reality his inner gaze has discovered in the absolute heavens—we come closer and closer to the mystery of a poetic transfiguration.

Finally we come to *Anabase,* a poem that exhilarates the senses and the spirit as mountain air does, for here the poet comes upon the object of his quest at last. It is an epic of the highroads and the highseas. Its movement is an ascending one; its tempo mounts from the earthly and temporal to the cosmic and spiritual. (pp. 38-40)

Anabase unfolds fascinating vistas of long wanderings upon boundless steppes.... Its ten chapters develop the thunderous adventures of proud nomads upon high plains, the clashing advance of conquering horsemen through vast deserts, and always their renewed departures for vaster heavens....

Nothing, however, is more gripping in *Anabase* than the poet's at times frantic celebration of the nubile earth—his glorification of the growth, resurgence, and fragrance of the seasons. An ambience exhaled, it seems, by those "scented girls clad in a breath of silk webs", envelops the poem. It penetrates every pore of the sentient organism, physical, moral, and intellectual, until the reader himself is submerged in it, as though he were encamped at the feet of those selfsame hills, and soothed by those same "scented girls". And they do soothe, or the poem does. For Perse does not condescend to win his reader over by sentimental or intellectual suasion or coercion. He hypnotizes him first emotionally and psychologically, and has him then at his mercy spiritually. (p. 40)

This poem of Perse is, as he himself says, " a history for men, a song of strength for men." It is, in places, a triumphal hymn to happiness. And though it evokes Asiatic plains and Eastern caravanseries, it conveys also, and effectively, the sense of a mystic quest. It uncovers the travail of the human entrails that spreads pestilence even into the human heart; withal, that "solemn odour of roses", of which the poet speaks, rises like an incense from it. Through the purity of this quest, this poet is a modern Parsifal to the modern soul, just as by its dramatic and spiritual qualities, his poetry is close to the music-drama of Wagner. A state of thrilling expectation pervades *Anabase*. It voices with intense beauty the agitation and intoxication of action. But as though aware that each and every action is only an earthly illusion, to each and every such momentary illusion corresponds in it a vision of other realities—moods of unrest and yearning of victories more delectable to the spirit. The worldly laurels can wither away then this side of reality. On the other side of the world, the most vast, there is a compensating power. The poet scatters upon the sands and the waters of all the rivers he traverses his passions and his thirsts. He marries his desires to all earthly allurements. The hymen belabors his being, "as a ferment of black grape." It raises his fever to the pitch of the unearthly; he knows no respite with himself. So he envisages the journey beyond his body. One can follow the progress of the spiritual longing upon him with almost mathematical certainty through his journey and his poem. (pp. 41-2)

Anabase, then, is more than the story of "migration, of conquest of vast spaces in Asiatic wastes" [see excerpt by T. S. Eliot above]. It is an expedition of the soul in search of self-knowledge and renunciation. It is, in the end, an ascension to the millenial heights of Oriental revelations. St.-J. Perse begins with the rationalism of the West, and ends—like so many poets before him—with the wisdom of the East. He moves with hungry spirit through the fertile and reasonable Occident as well as through the sterile and mystic Orient, until he strikes what he calls the "lieu dit de l'Arbre Sec." (p. 43)

This is the poetry of St.-J. Perse: the revelation of a soul that thirsts to know itself in the midst of the confusion of life—a thirst quenched, at last, by the light and music of pure knowledge, which is pure beauty. (p. 45)

St.-J. Perse is one of the purest poets of his generation. He has no ethical or political ax to grind with his time. He is a poet, not a prophet. His poetry, unlike that of Baudelaire, is not furrowed with the gnawing pains of good and evil. He is no Lucifer cast to earth. Unlike that of Rimbaud, it is not seared by flames from forbidden heavens. He is not Prometheus bound. And unlike that of Mallarmé, it is not stilled by the awful ring of the absolute Word. He is not Logos. He is a pure poet. And those few souls in the world who still look to poetry for new revelations to beautify their earthly lives, can turn to him with hope. They will not be deceived. (p. 50)

S. A. Rhodes, "The Poetry of St.-J. Perse," in The Sewanee Review, *Vol. XLIV, No. 1, January-March, 1936, pp. 25-50.*

ALAIN BOSQUET

[*The essay excerpted below originally appeared in German in the review* Das Lot *in 1948.*]

St.-John Perse proved himself, in his very first writings, to be the poet of solitude and of a prophetic gift, one of those who tower above the men and things about which they sing but with whom they come into contact only after a slow and strenuous conquest. (p. 154)

[*Éloges*] is a collection of poems that praise the world and life:

I honor the living—

says the poet. It is a book of childlike astonishment, about the discovery of colors and forms. Birds, beasts and plants are there in abundance, and in it one discovers already a nostalgia for distant isles, vanished relatives, legends, monarchs of whom one knows little but whose prowess one sings. The earth is praised there, together with all that it bears. Fleetingly, even mystery and the unknown are greeted:

The world is like a pirogue which, turning and turning, no longer knows whether the wind wanted to laugh or cry.

In such a pantheistic and jubilating atmosphere, the poet too has his place, presumably in the shadow of the things and beings that he glorifies. But the poet is conscious of

the obscure birth of speech

and

of things said in profile . . .

and he can already see his duties take shape, for duties these are indeed, to report on mystery and to be the intermediary between the Prince and Beauty, between the Regent and Language. French literature offers us but few other works where one might discover an affinity with *Éloges.*

When *Anabasis* was published in 1924, this long epic poem inspired, among the few writers who dared comment on it, as much controversy as fearful admiration. One is not accustomed to discovering, in a French poem of such length (*Anabasis* has more than forty pages), only the emergence of mysterious beauties and of purely lyrical notations. Critics sought a key to all this but found only forbidden treasures. They began to suggest that the regions of the poem corresponded to those where the poet, in actual geography, had indeed been; or that Rabindranath Tagore might offer more explanations than any Western man of letters; or that only such other French poets as Paul Claudel or Victor Segalen had experienced mysteries of the same nature. All critics agreed, however, in praising unreservedly the tone of the poem, its amplitude and dignity. (p. 155)

The poem concerns itself, quite rightly, with an expedition, a prince, and with founding; but to want to attribute a definite intention to a poem that names no dynasty, no continent and no date, this would seem to be a vain task indeed. The poem tells of a vision, of a state of mind and a conflict, rather than of a stroy or plot. (p. 156)

This *Anabasis,* far more than any parable or exemplum, is, as it were, the youthful expedition of a conqueror, an adventure where action and thought go hand in hand and the landscape reveals itself as man moves through it. In the purest sense of that word, it is a caravan in which image and proclamation are almost one and the poem arises from a decree published by a prince who is both captain and prophet, merciless as the former and, as the latter, pain-racked. But a song also arises in the margin, so to speak, of the poem:

But tidings there are of my brother the poet: once more he has written well. And some there are who have knowledge thereof . . .

This brother who is barely known and, as it were, neglected or disdained, becomes one with the prince, in *Exile,* though but seventeen years later. Henceforth, prince and poet are identical, and the conquest of the landscape becomes that of language while the labyrinth of the soul is patterned on the meandering courses of the desert streams. (pp. 156-57)

Exile heralds, in the work of St.-John Perse, a series of poems where crystallization is complete, where the fusion of poet and human being, of diction and imagery is fully achieved. Henceforth the man who writes is the one about whom one writes, and what one describes is that whereby one describes. The man in exile is, at one and the same time, both the exiled prince, who has lost his power and his kingdom, and the poet in exile, who is no longer master of his poem. This exile has suspicious shores where birds and syllables are myriad, sands that seem suspect and threatening caesuras. But this exile is also to such an extent necessary, as is any flight or movement, that one can almost say that it is awareness. It makes presence precious, it summons inspiration and is the source of suffering and therefore of the poem too. . . . (p. 157)

Finally, the poet resigns himself to his fate of singing only of exile, just as the prince resigns himself to that of reigning there only, for this is after all a way of mastering that which is changeless and of being great in the storm.

Thus does it become apparent that the elements of nature, when they move, offer the most appropriate subjects for St.-John Perse's inspiration, so that he no longer speaks of water but of rain and snow, no longer of earth but of sands, no longer of air but of wind, no longer of fire but of lightning. For these shifting elements determine the shifts of man and of the poet.

After exile or, so to speak, the tempest, there come **"Rains."** Instead of shattering the poet and driving him forth, they strip his soul to the quick and reveal the friendly or unfriendly details of his life. . . . (pp. 157-58)

Then come the **"Snows,"** white and light, slow but thick. They may lash less painfully than the rains, but they are not as quickly gone and they gain in discretion what they lose of liveliness. They are a sign of sadness and of aging. . . .

Vents (*Winds*), first published in 1946, consists of a single poem of more than a hundred pages and sets us, with over-powering greatness, the problem of man subjected to the most contradictory and violent passions. The rains were incisive and loud, the snows were lovely but cheats. The winds are more dangerous, warm at one time and, at another, cold; they whistle and sing, they stroke and strike. They are capricious and invisible, so that they disarm whoever resists them. They mean strife, war and panic. Mankind's misfortune is their proudest attribute. . . . (p. 158)

Exile had been the poem of solitary man who discovers greatness in renunciation. *Winds* is the poem of man subjected to the whims of war and peace, whether within himself or without, both of which he fears, because he knows not how to prevent war nor how to maintain peace and loves both because he knows that both are born of himself. Few works of recent years are both as beautiful and as tragic, as lofty and as moving. A critic, speaking once of the year 1946, defined it simply as the year in which *Winds* was published. This critic did not yet suspect that the influence of Perse's poem would spread far beyond such limits because his poetry can brook, as its frontiers, only those of language itself, a language which it rejuvenates by forcing it back to its origin.

This conquest in reverse is also costly. One climbs the slope of Perse's works painfully, like those Himalayan slopes that lead to the Tibet of the spirit where this poetry was born. It is a poetry of whose existence one can become aware only in solitude or exile, and in a state of grace which demands the talents of the prince and of the conqueror. One catches a true glimpse of it only after having completed an anabasis that closes itself like a circle and which therefore exists perhaps only at it own purest peak. One finally reaches this poetry after having suffered under many rains more sharp than the spears of battle, many snows more white than blindness, many winds that discourage and counsel hate; and one possesses it at last in a state of plenitude which admits the fragility and supreme serenity of a heroic weakness. (p. 160)

> Alain Bosquet, "The Works of St.-John Perse," translated by Alain Bosquet, in *Exile and Other Poems by St.-John Perse, translated by Denis Devlin, Bollingen Series XV*, 1949, pp. 154-60.

ARCHIBALD MacLEISH

[*The essay excerpted below originally appeared in the* Saturday Review of Literature, *July 16, 1949.*]

Perse's poems are difficult of course. But difficulty is only a fault in an artist when he intends it, or when he is not artist enough to overcome it. Perse's "difficulty," as Roger Caillois points out, is the result neither of ineptitude nor of willfulness but of the opposite of both: an extreme precision and richness of language and a vocabulary capable of extraordinary reverberations of intellectual and emotional meaning. Those who regard words as the mathematical equivalents of dictionary definitions may consider Perse "rhetorical," but his "rhetoric" is as precise as the language of the makers of sails and the navigators of planes, and its sonority is not in the thorax but the mind. . . . (p. 313)

Perse is too much of an artist to accept the promptings of the subconscious as perfected poetry, and too intelligent a man to write private letters to himself for public distribution. His "difficulty," in other words, is not the difficulty usually associated with the word modern. But the fact is that only in the real—not the snobbish—sense of that ambiguous term can Perse be classified as a modern poet. He belongs to no clique and has never been a partisan in the literary wars. ("On the subject of literary doctrine," he once wrote, "I have nothing at all to state. I have never relished scientific cooking.") He affects none of the fashionable literary maladies of the time: not even the chronic malady of the mirror: not even the despair which that malady produces in poets as in foreign secretaries and unoccupied women.

Perse's modernism is a function of time, not of aesthetic theory. If he is one of the first of those who have brought new life to Western poetry—one of the half dozen great innovators and creators who have renewed the phoenix in an altered age—he owes his distinction, not to the acceptance of aesthetic formulas and fashions, but to the writing of poems which have pushed forward the sensibility of his generation as well as the frontiers of his art. Like the best work of Yeats and Rilke and Eliot and Pound, the best work of Perse is a Discovery of This Time. Unlike the others, however, Perse has pushed his discovery outward into the world of earth and men. The time in which he journeys is the time which passes over the generations of mankind, and the hero he seeks is the hero who inhabits, not the shadows of the mirror, but the eternal earth. Of Perse's contemporaries, only Sandburg, whose male and vigorous art has wholly different purposes, faces the same quarter of the sky, and only Pound, in his first few, long-deserted Cantos, has inhabited even briefly the same ground.

It is this difference in the orientation of the compass which underlies the peculiar quality of Perse's work. Perse almost alone among the major poets of this generation is capable of the act of praise—the ceremony of the love of earth and men—the celebration of the sea and of the herb and of the dry bone and the living bone. From the beginning of his work, through the years of his greatest personal happiness, and through the years of an unhappiness such as few contemporary writers have been obliged to endure, the love and praise of the beauty of the world have commanded his mind. *Éloges* was the title of his first book, and the refrain which ran through the poems of that collection was the phrase *"Oh, j'ai lieu de louer."* But praise and the occasion of praise were not merely the passion of his youth. They are still, to this day, the law of his art and the charter of his life. Even now, his public career destroyed by the Nazis, his closest human relationships broken off by a long and painful exile, his property confiscated, his books and manuscripts lost or burned, Perse can say that he is "sworn, in defiance of our time, to take nothing from it but joy, free and freely given."

From another man, from a closeted intelligence ignorant of the true nature of this time, from a literary poet occupied with the imitation of academic models rather than the discovery of a great and tragic age, such words might well be suspect. From Perse they have an indelible accent of candor: an unbearable simplicity. For Perse knows this time of ours. . . . And what he finds in it to praise, he finds not by sentiment or delusion but with a seeing eye, a poet's eye, an eye that dares to see and to believe. . . . [Though] Perse's world now is the world of exile his new poems are not—"Exil" itself included—poems of estrangement from life. The exile of which Perse writes is, in poignant part, his own physical exile from the France he loves, and in part the spiritual exile from certain aspects of his time ("the threshold of Lloyd's where your word has no currency"), of the poet ("precarious guest"), and of all those others on all the shores of the world who must *"porte à l'oreille du Ponant une conque sans mémoire."*

But the poem **"Exil"**—and this I think is its supreme achievement—is something more and different. It is a poem *about* the poet and about his relation to that companion of his exile, his art, which goes closer to the nerve of truth than any but the very greatest poetry can go. Perse was not only exiled from political France: he was also confronted in his exile, after many years of silence, with the demands of the art he had put aside. (pp. 314-16)

Read in **Exil** the catalogue of the Princes of Exile—of the most intense moments of man's experience as man—of those occupations and actions of man which are most himself show him most himself—and you will find three things. You will find the portrait of a poet. You will find the portrait of *the* poet. And you will find poetry itself.

No one more than Perse detests the literary ritual. No one more than he despises the comparison of incomparable beings. Nevertheless it is impossible to put down this book without asking oneself where among living men—in what nation or what tongue—a poet equal to this poet may be found. (p. 317)

Archibald MacLeish, "St. John Perse," in his A Continuing Journey, *Houghton Mifflin Company, 1968, pp. 313-17.*

ALLEN TATE

[*The essay excerpted below originally appeared in* Poetry, *January, 1950.*]

In spite of the synesthetic imagery of much of Perse's poetry, and the superficial likeness not only to Whitman but to Rimbaud, we have [in **Vents**] . . . a series of powerful poems the units of which resemble, in structure, the historic verse-paragraph which was the most original rhetorical invention of John Milton.

These parallels in English, even if they be just, will possibly bore the French reader; but it would be a mistake for a critic in English (or, at any rate, for the present writer) to try to look at Perse from inside his own traditions. We must use both French and Anglo-American poetry, and allow for mistakes of reference. . . . It is beyond my capacity, as it would be an impertinence on this occasion, to discuss Perse's relation to Valéry and Claudel, the only French poets of his time who to the eye of an American reader seem to be his peers. Perse once made a remark to me about Valéry in connection with a long formalistic poem of my own. It was to the effect that the greater concreteness and intractability of English imposed certain formal necessities upon our poetry. The less physical French language tended too easily to attract formal effects, and that possibly Valéry had exhausted, for our age, the French formal limits. A return of the French language to the sensibility, and of poetic rhythms to inchoate verse, had become a necessity.

How far any poet may be trusted to deliver objective judgments on the verse of other poets (I suspect my own) will remain an unsettled problem. I have mentioned Perse's comment on Valéry only to observe that his sensitivity to language, both French and English, is wonderfully acute, and that his knowledge of English poetry is so broad and exact that quite possibly a large general English influence must be acknowledged in a poet completely French. Is it not thoroughly French to assimilate a wide range of cultures, ground them in the French sensibility, and forget that they ever came from over the frontier? There are, for example, two Poes: one is named Poe and the other Poë. The Frenchman Poë would not recognize his American counterpart should they pass each other in the street.

It seems to me inevitable that **Vents** will take its place with "Le Cimitière Marin" as a landmark in modern poetry in any language. How long a poem will "last" nobody had better try to decide. Yet **Vents,** with the two other poems, **"Pluies"** and **"Neiges,"** which likewise develop with great power meteorological imagery, establishes for our generation a location of the spirit that once known must be returned to again. Here we have man under the elements, and the elements in man, who yields to them. But the broadest of these powerful symbols which reach us through the sensibility rather than the intellect, is the wind: at one level it is the Dantesque wind of the Second Circle; it expands into the driven spirit of man in his present distress. It would be a mistake if we stopped, at that point, our exploration of the symbol: we should be stopping at its romantic implications. The beautiful symmetry of the form, the precision of image, and the presence of a cold and passionate intelligence combine in a quality of insight which is not of the provincial rationalism of our time. It reaffirms the greater tradition of the tragic consciousness. (pp. 79-81)

Allen Tate, "Homage to St.-John Perse," in his Memoirs and Opinions: 1926-1974, *The Swallow Press, Inc., 1975, pp. 76-81.*

THE TIMES LITERARY SUPPLEMENT

St.-John Perse had called his first book **Éloges,** and he told Gide that no other title could be better suited for what he had in him to write. He is a poet moved to his depths by the perfections of creation . . . , and he numerates created things with the gravity and magnificence of liturgical chant. . . . He is dazed and enraptured by this prodigal beauty. He takes us with him into a universe of splendour and violence; we explore islands thronged with dazzling birds and gigantic flowers, washed by milky seas, scorched by the burning sun and freshened by cool airs at nightfall. Yet he never disputes the presence of a mean and horrifying degradation in things—he accepts this *laideur* and transforms it. . . . He perceives the smallest details, the inscape of a horse or sails in the wind. His voice extends without effort into the dimensions of space at noon or when,

at nightfall "le silence [multiplie] l'exclamation des astres so-
litaires." If his syntax strikes and pierces and clangs like a
gong ("That dolphin-torn, that gong-tormented sea") he can
also intercept the murmur "douce comme la honte qui tremble
sur les lèvres, des choses dites de profil." Such is the paradise
which Perse never ceases to celebrate wherever his journeys
take him in time or space, but we must be careful not to see
it in terms of conventional exoticism, a sort of family album
decorated by Gauguin. It is always a re-creation of that childhood paradise which all men secretly cherish. *Éloges* extols
the time of the child—"l'enfance irréfutable"—in order that
its reflection may illuminate the richness of the phenomenal
world: these poems are archives of immemorial childhood.

St.-John Perse looks at the world with a synoptic vision which,
as Roger Caillois noticed, is closer to Dr. Toynbee than to
Hegel. All civilizations appear simultaneously imprinted on
the mind's retina. The figures on the Acropolis mingle with
those of the Bayon d'Angkor, the skyscrapers of New York
under snow take on the monstrous outlines of Tyre, Thanksgiving Day is another Panathenaea. . . . The imagery takes us
from the solitudes of Central Asia to slagheaps and smoking
iron foundries; across "vastes plaines sans histoires enjambées
de pylones." The poet also seeks to save the most perishable
things from the shipwreck of civilizations—things so denuded
of meaning that they are little more than signs of human in-
digence in the world's profusion. (p. 233)

The whole *oeuvre* of Perse, as we come to know it, is an
attempt to find the way back to a beginning and to communicate
with the sources of life. His first poems discover the unappeased longing for a lost paradise, and this desire grows in
scope and depth in all he has subsequently written. . . .

[*Anabase*], Perse's second book, is a poem of successive migrations. Many commentators, haunted by memories not only
of Xenophon but of Alexander the Great and Genghis Khan,
have described it as primarily a celebration of conquests and
triumphs, and indeed the poem has moments of pride and
violence which appear to confirm this interpretation. The abrupt
vigour of the first strophes promise that a city will be established. . . . But if we listen attentively we begin to be aware
of a peculiar vibration in the writing, like minute particles of
sand brushed against the silence of abandoned cities. Time
traces its enigmas on the *tabula rasa* of the desert, and the
Prince sets out once more to discover the meaning of these
runes.

Anabase is sustained by the double movement of arrival and
departure. The city is established and abandoned, the walls are
built and they fall in ruin; there is joy and bitterness, abundance
and famine, vigour and accidie, pride and humility—and always the insatiable thirst for uncontaminated space. The direction of the poem would not be so poignant if it did not spring
from Perse's uninhibited delight in the evidence of beauty.
Even in the bleakest of continents he finds the traces of his
paradise. . . . The overture to the poem is like the notes of a
flute insinuating themselves into the monotonous cadences of
daily living. . . .

The will to conquest is perhaps nothing more than an excuse
for going elsewhere; to reach a destination has ceased to have
any importance, and it is enough to depart with the taste of
dawn in the mouth. "Je m'en irai avec les oies sauvages dans
l'odeur fade du matin." These soldiers are not campaigning
for booty, they are seeking to discover the sources of existence.
They can scarcely be thought of as an army of warriors. . . .

They pause to build cities in the desert but this cannot divert
them for long from their purpose. How can those who are
compelled to lay bare the mystery of the origin bind themselves
to the exigencies of earth—as if life received its only sanctions
from clay on the potter's wheel, the harvesting of fields or the
treasury of precious stones? How can they stay for long in the
pleasures of abundance when the sudden scent of a flower can
subvert an empire by reminding them of the perpetual exile in
which they live? Only the desert is empty enough for them.
The nomad departs, and ahead of him stretch the "pays d'her-
bages sans mémoire, l'année sans liens et sans anniversaires,
assaisonnée d'aurores et de feux."

Exil, the third sequence of poems, plunges even farther into
this obsessive search for that which lies behind history; yet
these poems, written after twenty years of silence, are themselves the product of a particular moment in history. Perse,
who experienced this moment with great anguish, refused to
be dominated by it and transformed it into a symbol of universal
exile. Words and images become transparent, to suggest the
fragility of a world doomed to destruction. Frequent alliteration
suggests the slipping and sliding of everything into nothing.
Such phrases as "à l'orient du monde," "avant l'aube," "avant
le jour" recur, as if the poet is trying to discern points of
stability in the common disruption. In the end nothing remains,
the possibility of significance ebbs away and the Exile is left
murmuring: "Qui sait encore le lieu de sa naissance?" . . .

"Pluies" calls on the rain to inundate the world, to wash away
all its garnered possessions: the great libraries, the works of
art, laws, chronicles, monuments, inscriptions. . . . The poet
seeks the uncontaminated face of the earth under the débris of
history in order that he may give it a new orientation.

The same theme is taken up in "Poème à l'Étrangère", written
in 1942. It is an invocation of France, engulfed in the miseries
of the Occupation. . . . But behind the haunting refrain of "Rue-
Gît-le-Coeur" which restores the vision of a lost Paris the
invocation is, in fact, to another country, always unknown, of
which France is but a shadow. The daily and intimate grief of
this loss is not permitted to distract the poet from his quest.
Once more he departs, "chantant l'hier, chantant l'ailleurs,
chantant le mal à sa naissance."

Only the falling snow, purer and softer than rain, can mitigate
this endless torment. Perse watches the first flurries of it from
a high window in New York—the snow which effortlessly and
inexorably effaces that *laideur* which is man's legacy to the
world. He had called on the rain to scour all the illusions of
knowledge and wisdom from stone and marble and parchment.
Now, in *Neiges,* he asks that the human countenance imposed
on the world should be blotted out; he wants the snow to
smother tools, workshops, factories, and to purify every place
touched by man. The world, it seems to him, must turn to a
new, blank page. He would like to discover the sources of
language where all words, purged of accretion, might communicate primeval wonder. . . . The search is profitless because
it is contrary to the *meaning* of language. But the poet will not
relinquish the impossible hope of perceiving "au matin, sous
le plus pur vocable, un beau pays sans haine, ni lésine, un lieu
de grâce et de merci pour licencier l'essaim des grandes odes
du silence."

The long poem *Vents*—vast in its scope—carries the quest still
farther. It is too complex for short analysis; all that can be
done here is to suggest a few points of reference. *Vents* is the
epic of a new Columbus, a journey towards the sun which sets.

It is not any the less a search for origins. For Perse, born in the Antilles, the west was his first home, and now, retracing his steps, he recovers the place of his childhood on the threshold of the future. . . .

His latest poem, *Amers,* has only recently been published in its definitive form. It is a conclusion—if there can be any conclusion—to Perse's long search for the beginning, the sources of life. . . . *Amers* is a poem in praise of the Sea. . . . How is it possible to recover the childhood whose presence in us is so strong that even the dawning consciousness of infancy seems already to hold the memory of it? The Sea, matrix of life, is "antérieure à notre chant," it is voiceless. The child of the islands, the young Crusoe, the conqueror of *Anabase,* the new Columbus interrogate the Sea for the last time: "la mer immense et verte comme une aube à l'Orient des hommes," to show the way to the Eternal Source.

Whatever the end of this quest, its course has been extraordinarily consistent. Perse is haunted by entropy, by a universal decline and exhaustion; he hastens, therefore, to gather up what remains that nothing be lost. He seeks to transfigure the fragile anonymities of the world before they are engulfed in night, to endow the indigent with magnificence. The young poet's response to the world was that of wonder; then, as he came to perceive everything under the doom of age and death he grew more imperious and his incantations took on the urgency of anguish. His poems are the meeting of opposites—the tension between the richness of the world and its poverty, between the celebration of splendour and the necessity of detachment, between the pride of life and grief at its dissolution. The poetry receives its astonishing resonance from these tensions; because of them it is learned and subtle, but not obscure and impenetrable. Its themes are simple and their repetition would be monotonous if Perse had not used all the resources of language with such mastery. It is an elemental poetry, not merely because it invokes the forces of nature but because it is faithful—in spite of its complex refinement—to universal emotions.

Crushed beneath the strata of millennial cultures man, in the poems of St.-John Perse, finds himself as naked as in the first ages of the world. He has been enslaved to an abundance without significance and, prince-beggar, he turns with anarchic violence to the primeval Origin. But however far it is possible to journey upstream the Source is never discovered; there is always a final barrier, like a sword which turns every way. This brilliant and bitter poetry, transfused with a religious fervour from which God is absent, carries the undertone of *Ecclésiastes.* Like that great biblical poem it belongs to a moment of transition and judgment for the world. (p. 234)

"St.-John Perse: Poet of the Far Shore," in The Times Literary Supplement, *No. 2931, May 2, 1958, pp. 233-34.*

W. H. AUDEN

The first test of any poet is his ability to create a world which is unique but credible to a reader because he finds he can inhabit it. It may be a very small world, like A. E. Housman's, or a very peculiar one, like Constantine Cavafy's; its laws may be quite different from the laws—natural, social or grammatical—of the public world so long as the beings which compose it and the events that occur in it are consistent with each other. The distinction between the minor and the major poet is largely a matter of size; the greater the poet, the bigger his world, the greater the number and variety of its inhabitants, the wider the range of possible events.

If one reads through all of the poems of St.-John Perse, one is immediately aware that each is, as it were, an installment of one great oeuvre. He is one of those fortunate poets who discovered both his vision and the proper linguistic means to express it quite early. Both in its properties and in its style, *Éloges,* published in 1910 (in America in 1956), already contains in germ everything that was to flower so magnificently in its grander successors. . . .

Only the poet himself has the authority to say what his literary influences have been, but a reader may legitimately say, "To me the poems of A seem to have a certain kinship with the poems of B but are totally alien to the poems of C." Thus, St.-John Perse's imagery seems to me to have an affinity with the imagery of Arthur Rimbaud's *Les Illuminations.* Then, not only his fondness for catalogues but also the way in which he organizes his longer poems recall Whitman, particularly a poem like "Passage to India." But in spirit his work makes me think first and foremost of Pindar. His psalms of praise share with Pindar's odes an aristocratic poise and a personal anonymity which is foreign to Whitman, and his metaphors are generally more elaborately developed than Rimbaud's.

The world in which Pindar lived and which he celebrated was a small locality in which the significant individuals, their family histories and their deeds were known to all his audience. The only modern poet who grew up in anything like the same sort of world was W. B. Yeats, but in our time Ireland is, or was, the exception while in Pindar's time history on the parochial scale was the norm. But St.-John Perse has quite deliberately set out to sing of the whole globe and of Man the Maker of World History. For this formidable task his own history has made him unusually well qualified. . . .

[One] of the first characteristics of his world is the complete absence of proper names. Landscapes are vividly described but no indication is given of where they are situated. As befits a modern world in which historical knowledge has made all the past present, the events which occur in St.-John Perse's poem could be taking place in any historical epoch. Its inhabitants have neither names nor genealogies; they have functions.

There is suffering and death in this world, but not tragedy. What the poet celebrates, that is to say, is not the refusal of the noble individual to live at any price, but the inexhaustible power of life to renew itself and triumph over every disaster, natural or human. What he looks for and tries to express in every one of his poems is the sacredness of being. (p. 1)

W. H. Auden, *"A Song of Life's Power to Renew,"* in The New York Times, *July 27, 1958, pp. 1, 12.*

JOSEPH H. McMAHON

The award of the Nobel Prize in Literature to Alexis Léger, the poet-diplomat who writes under the evocative pseudonym of Saint-John Perse, is an honor of more than passing interest and concern to this country, for it is a reminder of some of those basic American values we tend to forget in the tangle of discussions on organization men, lonely crowds and ascending or declining prestige. (p. 407)

[The poems Léger] had published prior to his decision in 1924 to give no further public dimension to his work so long as he was actively and importantly involved in the French Foreign

Office, had frequently alluded to a kind of geographic cultural dynamism, a shifting of cultural centers from one place to another, both because the spread of civilization was seen as a responsibility and because, under the pressures of outside threats, civilizations could be destroyed. In the poems [*Eloges, Anabase,* and **"Amitié du Prince"**] this movement was personified in the Prince, a kind of generalized protagonist in whom the various threats and promises found expression. Underlying the Prince's activities was a pervasive belief in the value of his mission, an optimism that faith in man would be productive, and a deposit of patience and endurance sufficiently strong to allow him to carry on until the day when the faith and the belief would join as the basis of the flourishing human enterprise civilization should be.

Washington in 1940 must have struck the exiled poet curiously. There he found the personal solitude he had so often used to characterize his protagonist, and there he found, too, a kind of scandalous haven momentarily spared the destruction visible elsewhere.

That place, Washington, and those years, 1940 and after, were clearly a refuge for the fertilizing forces of civilization; if deductive analysis could not, under the pressure of events, point to this truth, activity could. In the sudden spurt of foreign language publications, as in the sometimes exaggerated appeals of MacLeish himself, could be found the evident marks of a perhaps limited but nonetheless determined effort to remember and continue the complex values of Western civilization. But at the same time Washington was also the center in which was being daily planned the most destructive war ever fought and, because of this, it represented a frightening paradox.

It was, quite simply and yet quite terribly, a question of man and his works, and of man and his works Alexis Léger had had some fine things to say, inspired from the very beginning of his career with a profound distrust of power philosophies and a deep commitment to the kind of ideal that had been wrought into literary splendor by the seventeenth century classicists. The war clearly imperilled these closely held beliefs, just as his own dismissal from the Foreign Service and his ensuing disgrace by the Vichy government which stripped him of his French citizenship seemed to make a mockery of the idea of human excellence his poetry had limned.

His poetic vision had sought to pay homage and honor to the human experience and, in so doing, both to continue the valuable development of that experience and to rescue French poetry from the fascination with sterility it had fallen victim to at the end of the nineteenth century. In the months after his arrival in [the United States], all this must have seemed sham and folly; civilization, whatever might be the eventual outcome of the war, must have seemed clearly doomed to the dictatorship of destructive technocracy; the humanist gesture must have seemed a futile, fluttering pose, a weak protesting hand raised against the unstoppable on-rush of immensely powerful forces.

The irony . . . was a noble one. It was also a multi-faceted one, for if the poet found himself in a situation hauntingly similar to that he had sometimes evoked in his poetry, he found himself also in a place very much like some of those he had alluded to in his poems: a new land, being visited ever more frequently with reminders of its place in a larger, more diversified world, and yet strangely a land which could easily and perhaps too facilely be identified with the dangers of technocracy to its own detriment and the detriment of that larger world to which it so clearly belonged. (pp. 407-08)

His first "American" poems—stimulated, he tells us, by an unwanted voice come back to stir him out of firm resolutions—are personal debates, tortured inner dialogues designed to measure at once the extent to which values proclaimed in earlier poems have any merit and the possibility of any continued worth for poetic statement itself.

The drama in a poem like *Exile* is quite simply the tension between despair and hope, with the scales tilting uncertainly in search of some measure which will justify the poet's exile. No conclusion is drawn, except perhaps the decision to continue the investigation into the function of the poet and the sense of possibly pervasive values in the tradition of poetry.

This investigation continues in the ensuing poems—**"Rains," "Snows"** and **"Poem to a Foreign Lady"**—and from it emerges not so much an optimism as a responsibility. The poet, we learn, sees things differently, not only because of the peculiar perspective located by his insights, but equally because, through his statements, he confers a valuable kind of organization on what otherwise might be a chaotic world; he gives it, in a limited but important sense, a symbolic power because he sees and understands the extent to which its qualities can become hopelessly enmeshed and so confused with its defects.

The poetic act—he is reminded of this by the Foreign Lady's plea—is not simply a means of forging personal and impenetrable armor against the assaults of the world; it also is a public responsibility to give that world a sense unseen by the technicians, not easily expressed by purely discursive minds and their methods. (p. 408)

The noble irony, once the continued power of poems to make uniquely valuable statements had been accepted, could then allow a return to the preoccupations expressed in the poems of the 1920's. But the return would necessarily involve change both in expression and in emphasis.

The threats and menaces which had served mainly as principles of tension in those earlier poems assume, with **"Winds,"** a disturbing reality the poet must deal with on terms not necessarily of his own creation. It is almost as though the slowly and deliberately articulated expression of faith in the poet's ability to impose sense on the world was being undermined by the realization that other forces are empowered with a similar capacity. There is no single way to organize human experience, but several, and because of this the task of poetry is subtly altered from that of imposing order to that of imposing values.

This fact, I suspect, rather than sheer infatuation with rhetoric, is what explains the amplitude of the poem; quite simply, the old declarative register no longer has power. Stating that things *are* such a way does not make them *be* that way; the poem can no longer be bare statement but must be transformed into argument; it must seek in its complex, dense and sometimes obscure structure to become a symbol of the dense, complex and obscure situation it describes. (pp. 408-09)

[The United States] serves as the backdrop to *Winds*. In its physical vastness, in the variety of its habits, people and occupations, as well as in the many values which struggle against each other in its almost boundless confines, the poet seems to have found the appropriate locale for the problem he is situating—appropriate both because it does genuinely represent many contradictory and conflicting things and because in a curious way it is at once a sampling of and a promise of continuity to European civilization.

The poem operates simultaneously on several levels, evoking both the current destructive forces sweeping through the world and the old destructive forces which, in the past, have been responsible for the discovery and exploration of the United States. It is the poem which confers unity on these different moments, not by seeking a solution to the insoluble problem of chronology but by seeking to find the imprint of man in the uncommitted forces of the winds. The winds symbolize power; but in themselves they have no value. It is to man that this task falls, and he can accept it either worthily or viciously; he can use power either to advance or to destroy himself.

The poem's search for this excellence—and it must be remembered that it is a vast poem—encounters a unique kind of crisis in the problem of the atomic bomb. Here the excellence of the human imagination and the ingenuity of human intelligence seem to have combined in an act of thorough nihilism, using important values to create a most serious threat and impediment to the continued expression of those same values. Under the force of the vast light and powerful wind created by the bomb, human experience is thrown into an almost irremediable darkness, an obscene irony—the cold which Edith Sitwell called the highest human idea, but the cold which, she hastened to add, is nothing.

Faced with this predicament, the poet is again on the testy fringe of despair, as he had been in *Exile*. But, as was true in that poem, so here the very polarity of the situation indicates the way to some kind of solution.

What is involved in the bomb, like what was involved in his own exile and the inexplicable tyranny it seemed to confer on the absurd, is the kind of awful situation which has allowed man, throughout the history of the West, to see the threads of his dignity in a sometimes terribly shabby fabric. The force of the poem must become the complement to this other force, the thread of light in the cloth of darkness.

The poet's voice must serve to remind men of their dignity and potentialities even as it presents them with a clear picture of the perils. The poem itself must serve to create the second half of a dualism found in man by attracting him to the merit which the other half of the dualism persistently threatens. The poet becomes the witness for man, the poem his testimony in behalf of human excellence.

What is this excellence? It is, Léger seems to say, the movement through which man defines himself by giving values to his civilization. But the definition is not easily made, because it depends on the willingness to accept pain, to elect the unpleasant but productive choice rather than the pleasant and destructive one.

Despair—the sort of succumbing to fate that might have been so easily possible and so very attractive in wartime Washington—is really the choice of an easier way. The hell of life is in carrying on despite the forces that would engulf us at every moment; but the anguish and the pain are not without their compensations. Men do win victories; they do attain to excellence; they do bring continuity to their civilization; they do articulate ideals.

Men are, in short, free to elect the path they wish to follow, and they are urged along that path by the various impressive ceremonies human endeavor has learned to celebrate in its effort to arrive at understanding: the act of love, the desire for achievement, and—certainly not the least important—the sort of reflective statement and accomplishment brought about by

a continually vigorous poetic presence. In poetry—this is seen clearly in Léger's two most recent poems, where the ground charted in **"Winds"** is developed and man's accomplishments celebrated—there is a paradigm of the human condition, for out of the imprecise tangle of obscure insights and fleeting impressions the poet, aware of how much pain and effort are the conditions of his own work, creates a humane object of enduring beauty which, in its loveliness, offers a challenge and a counter-balance to the forces of destruction and inhumanity.

So I, at least, read Alexis Léger. It is undoubtedly an honor to this country that he has chosen to live and write here, and that he has found in this nation sources for his poetic statements. But it is an honor which contains its own sobering suggestion. The way to human excellence, Alexis Léger reminds us, is a painful way; by avoiding the pain and the uncomfortable responsibilities it represents, we may be avoiding the achievements it leads to. (p. 409)

> *Joseph H. McMahon, "Saint-John Perse: A Question of Man," in* Commonweal, *Vol. LXXIII, No. 16, January 13, 1961, pp. 407-09.*

OCTAVIO PAZ

Rereading Perse's books, one notices that a single verbal stream flows uninterruptedly from *Eloges* to *Chronique*. Perse's language swallows up events, transmutes them and then, so to speak, redeems them. Everything that has taken place over the last fifty years—including the poet's personal life—is fitted into the work. Discords, schisms, exiles, love and love affairs, atrocities, the annihilation and birth of cities, the emasculation of language, unbearable fevers in the western sky—all these are the images and rhymes of an enormous poem. The dispersions of our world finally reveal its living unity. Not the unity of some system that wipes out contradictions and is never more than a partial vision, but that of the poetic image. . . . Anyone interested in what took place in the first half of this century had better avoid the dubious accounts of it in our newspapers. Let him get hold instead of a key group of poetical works. One of them would be that of St.-John Perse. (p. 522)

Each of Perse's books is a stanza in a single poem; and each of these long stanzas is itself an isolated poem. Unity and multiplicity.

What is the theme of Perse's poem? What story is recounted in the stanzas called *Eloges, Anabase, Exil, Vents, Amers, Chronique*? The work opens as a kind of chant, a eulogy of the natural world and the first age of man. Sea, sky and land seen through the troubled eyes of a young boy. Praise and farewell to childhood, to its "magnanimous myth" and the rich fare at its table. The first book, the first stanza, is an announcement of the voyage to come: "All the roads in the world feed from the hand" of the young poet. It was a short step from *Eloges* to *Anabase*. Perse took it without nostalgia, determined from then on to live as the Stranger. There is no road that leads back to the country of his birth. *Anabase* is an account of the peregrinations and movements—in space, in time, and in the secret enclosures of the dream—of races and civilizations, a celebration of the founding of cities and laws, the evocation of great birds of passage: "Fertile land of the dream! Who speaks of building?" From *Anabase* on, the Stranger's lot is made one with the rain, the snow and the wind, images of change and migration, powerful concretions of the word *Exile*. Histories of our age, they are at the same time the account of an exile that has no end, because all of human history is a history of exile. The planet itself is a migrant body.

Perse's adventure is anything but a circumnavigation; each stop becomes a new point of departure, a moment's respite before continuing the journey. The geometrical figure that describes this universe is not a circle but a spiral. Perse's poetry should be read as an exercise in spiritual intrepidity. His poems offer a man no shelter from the night and bad weather; they are themselves an encampment under the open sky. No roots here: wings. His theme is singular and plural: time, the times. History minus any characters, because the only real character in history is a nameless and faceless being, half flesh and half dream: the man all we other men are and aren't. Voyage without map or compass or the names of countries, because cities, ports, islands, all that marvelous geography, dissolve the moment that we touch them. Chronicle of storms and balmy days, annals of the wind, book of seas and rivers, stone tablet of the sky inscribed with good and bad years, like the symbols in a *stela*. Perse's poetry penetrates beyond optimism and pessimism, indifferent to quarrels over names or grubby controversies about morality and meaning. His morality is something other, like his enthusiasm and terrible energy. Perse's theme is time, our very substance. The poetry of time, which buries and banishes us. Insofar as we are men, we are a metaphor for time. A migrant image. (pp. 522-23)

Although Perse's poetry abandons the horizontal method of narration, his material remains epic. Using an abundance of examples, which in itself indicates the richness of his historical experience, he dazzles our eyes with a display of the wonderful and laughable diversity of man's works, occupations and activities. Rejecting the intercession of philosophy, he brings us face to face with the direct meaning of history: we must create or perish. The poet presents, he doesn't prove. . . .

The poet is the chronicler of rainstorms, the historian of blizzards. The pomps of history encompass physical phenomena. Thunder, lightning, the wild heat of summer are all part of his Romance. Or is it just the opposite: that Perse thinks of history as an event in nature? Most likely neither. The vision here is total: history and nature are both dimensions of the human, extremes of the same contingency. And man? Contingent also: a wager that life has made with itself (p. 523)

Perse's poetry culminates in a song that celebrates the very act of singing: not an exaltation of this or that particular action but of the essential act itself, in all its purity, using words that tremble with creative energy. Is it any wonder that he would make a final song in praise of the highest activity known to man: the poem? As a celebration of language, Perse's poetry is a return to the origin of the poem: the hymn. An exclamation in the face of life, an affirmation of existence, a eulogy. Poetry which ignores the gods but bathes itself in the fountain of the sacred: "Surely I live in the throat of some god." This terrible age of ours produces more than doubt and negation. A poet may still accept it in its totality: "Great age, you form this praise." No real poet was ever a Manichean. Good and evil, darkness and light are not separate entities but the two sides of Being—that eternal Sameness which is never the same. The poet "turns from contention." His song is praise. (p. 524)

> Octavio Paz, "St.-John Perse: Poet as Historian," in The Nation, New York, Vol. 192, No. 24, June 17, 1961, pp. 522-24.

KATHLEEN RAINE

[*The essay excerpted below originally appeared in* Encounter, *October, 1967.*]

Like most of my generation I read *Anabase* because it was translated by T. S. Eliot, in 1930. Even in this early poem (first published in 1924) and indeed in the earlier *Eloges*, [Perse's] inimitable style ('Innumerable the image, and the metre prodigal') was already formed. But I remember being puzzled where to fit this poet into the picture my generation was at that time building up of what modern poetry was and should be. Surrealism was easy to understand, being little more than *avant-gardism* as such; Joyce and Proust had obvious contemporary points of reference, but its very originality made the *Anabase* seem the more strange. Its theme—the setting-out of a nomadic prince on an expedition of conquest—was in no obvious way related to contemporary experience, even though the images (exotic in the style of Gauguin) were, as such, pleasurable. The great sweep of the rhythm had no obvious similarity (other than not being confined within any traditional metrical form) with the free verse of Pound or Eliot; it is in fact nearer to Claudel. It was not clear what affinity such poetry had with Eliot's own theory and practice as a poet; nor do I even now know the answer to that question.

Twenty years were to pass between the first publication of *Anabase* and the appearance of *Exil*, "Poème à l'Etrangère," "Pluies" and "Neiges" in 1942. These poems were written in the United States, and first published in Buenos Aires, and in France on the presses of the Resistance, without the name of the author. During the intervening years the diplomat had kept 'his brother the poet' in abeyance. We shall never know (unless those lost manuscripts should be recovered) how St.-John Perse developed from the author of the romantic epic *Anabase* into the poet of *Exil* and that greater poem of exile, *Vents*, written in the United States and published in 1946. With these poems, the poet and the times moved into conjunction; what had formerly been a personal voice became a voice of the age. If *Vents* is his greatest poem this is surely so in part because the vision of these 'very great winds over all the faces of this world', whose storm tore down the edifice of European civilization and carried the poet into the New World was experienced so immediately by 'his brother the prince', Alexis Léger; as Dante, Milton, Byron and Yeats, whether as rulers or as exiles, played their part in and shared the suffering of their cities. No more than these is he a political poet; but like them political concern and knowledge is part of the structure of his thought, giving authority to his prophetic speech. There is no longer, in 1945, any question of how St.-John Perse's poetry relates to the contemporary experience. The migrant tribe is ourselves, the country we must leave, our own past, and Western civilization; whether as conquerors or exiles—and there is little difference—we must set forth again into that future open alike to all. 'All to be done again. All to be told again. And the scything glance to be swept across all man's heritage.' The state of exile, in many cases physical, but above all spiritual exile, is the typical condition of poet and prince alike in the new dark age of barbarism and the reversal of the natural hierarchies with all their values; the state to be explored.

Claudel, writing of *Vents*, pointed out that whereas the *Odyssey* is an epic of home-coming, *Vents*, an epic description of the fall of the civilization whose beginnings Homer scarcely saw, is a poem of setting-out; as that other epic, *Finnegans Wake*, ends, like the *Götterdämmerung*, with a purification by re-immersion in the source. But for St.-John Perse, this purification, re-immersion and setting-out is not cyclic, but at every moment to be enacted as life moves always into its future.

He chooses for his symbols those freely-moving elements which traverse and unite all times and spaces—seas, winds, birds, the perpetual setting-out of migrant swarms, flocks, human tribes; an 'open' poetry in which all spaces and times co-exist in a single present. No theme could be more true to one of the as yet unformulated experiences of this time. The scope of his poetry is coterminous with the earth in its single indivisible space-time. (pp. 176-78)

Our generation has become intellectually, but not imaginatively, habituated to the retrospect of natural evolution, to the new spacious simultaneity of the relativity of time and place. In reading the poetry of St.-John Perse we experience this new freedom, familiar to the scientist, which poetry has been slow to enter. Plato called the world a happy and immortal animal, one immortal joy sweeping through its myriads of component lives; and all Perse's poems are (as one is entitled) praises, *éloges*, of this 'moving image of eternity'. His prodigality of image both illustrates and suggests the infinitely various and inexhaustible fecundity of one life in all. (p. 179)

For St.-John Perse it is true, as Blake claimed for himself, that 'I see everything I paint In This World'. Blake also said that 'to the Eyes of the Man of Imagination, Nature is Imagination itself'; and that the world perceived by the senses is the fourth region of consciousness, externalized by the illusory philosophy of materialism, 'although it appears without, it is within, in your imagination'. In the poetry of Perse, the sensible world is restored as a region of the imagination; for the content of his imagination is 'nature' itself.

The unbounded nature of the poet's theme, free in time as it is uncircumscribed by space, determines the prodigality of his metre. Accustomed as we are to minimal vision, our attention solicited by, and for, the pathological, the criminal, the immature, the uneducated, the ignorant, and the unskilled of all sorts presenting the articulations of ignorance as communications of knowledge and achievements of art, we have all but lost the capacity for the total response his poetry demands. The 'self-expression' of the individual (always more or less handicapped in one or more of the above ways) has no place in his art. Claudel called him 'a Mont St. Michel immensely accentuated in an ebbing tide'; and if this mountain is generally unnoticed in postwar England this may well be because, by standards designed for measuring mole-hills, mountains are unperceived. Yet his unbounded vision of 'the visible and tangible world of which we are a self-conscious part' is a liberation offered to whoever is willing to entrust himself to the great open sea ('*le mouvement même de l'Etre*') of St.-John Perse's poetry.

As against the continuous and relentless attrition, the dwindling of knowledge, the coarsening of sensibility, the abdication in thought, feeling and conduct of even the conception of the best, tacitly demanded and too often accorded in deference to the all-too-common common man, he summons to an expansion of consciousness, to a total realization of being. He speaks as the 'free man of high caste', reminding those who prefer to forget how great are the demands made by the aristocratic view of man, which alone protects and fosters the highest human potentialities: knowledge, and the freedom to translate knowledge and imagination into action (the prince) and into art (the poet, who is 'brother' to the prince). For Perse, as for Plato, and Manu, the superiority of the 'man of high caste' lies not in his status but in his quality of being; his superior knowledge and freedom of action whether as acknowledged leader, or as exile from a fallen civilization, 'the superior man' remains such by virtue of what he is. The prince-poet has given himself

totally to the fullest attainable human experience by accepting those hard terms upon which alone freedom of act and thought are given. We are again reminded of Conrad, whose heroes also were free men of high caste, and of his phrase about 'the unknown disciplines of the self-imposed task'. Sex and the dead, Yeats somewhere said, are the only matters serious enough to engage the thoughts of an ageing poet; and erotic love and death are the frontiers which alone bound the world of St.-John Perse's prince-poet. Mortal, we are possessed by, but cannot possess, the immortal life which the sexual mystery confers, and death takes away; no other limitations can take away the freedom of act and thought of whoever fears neither the loss of life nor of possessions. Courage, magnanimity, and knowledge—the aristocratic virtues—are the fruits of this proud detachment. The plebeian whine comes from those (of whatever social class, since caste and class are not coterminous) who have not looked at life and death. The experience of immortality is lost precisely when we seek to bind it to our transient selves. '*Il faut que vous mettez la tête dans la gueule du lion*' was the memorable advice the poet once gave me; for such is the condition accorded by reality itself, that lion's-mouth ever open before us.

> One same wave throughout the world, one same wave since Troy
> Rolls its haunch towards us. On a far-off open sea this gust was long ago impressed.

The sea, ancient and universal symbol of material flux, impressed by the 'breath of life' in the beginning is an image from *Genesis* acceptable alike to Platonist and evolutionist. (pp. 182-84)

'One law of harmony governs the whole world of things.' The amplitude of that harmony, of the free-flowing 'wave throughout the world' characterizes the cadences of the verse of St.-John Perse; for verse it is (so he insists) though of very long lines, and in no way to be confused with prose-poetry; or, in England, with the cadenced poetic prose of David Jones. (Readers of Proust will remember that the two maids at Balbec were incredulous when Marcel, reading *Éloges*, told them that this was 'poetry'.) It is difficult to attune a foreign ear, not to the sweep of the larger pattern, but to the very subtle internal cross-patterns, again like waves, whose regularity of rhythm breaks down into such variety of rhythm, assonance, even internal rhyme. The ruling pattern is liturgical, with returning phrases which, as in an Introit psalm, define and continually re-affirm the theme. (p. 184)

No two poems are alike, nor their imagery interchangeable. A superficial reader of Perse will be impressed by the consistency of his inimitable style, his 'breath', but a closer reading reveals the architectural unity of theme, imagery and even metre within each. (p. 185)

St.-John Perse's existentialism (if such it is) might seem opposed to the symbolist tradition which (under whatever name) stems from some form of Platonism. Neither poetic practice can be detached from that view of the nature of things in which it is grounded. The symbol presumes multiple planes of being linked both by cause and by analogy; without understanding of this metaphysical ground, symbolist poetry becomes meaningless. In Perse's existentialist use of the image a metaphysical ground is no less implicit, by his own confession. No less than the poetry of Yeats his work must remain opaque to vulgar positivism, for he too uses the term 'divine', though for him divinity is existentially implicit. Perhaps the two apparently opposite modes may be compared to different phases of waves; at their point of intersection we have the existential image; at the limit of their amplitude, the analogies and resonances of the symbol. And like the symbolists, St.-John Perse not only assumes but affirms and uses as the instrument of his art the law of harmony which subsists in and unifies the cosmos; his universe is neither arbitrary nor indeterminate, and governed by that symmetry, unity, and accord in which Plotinus discovers the essence of 'the beautiful'.

The symbol is, besides, itself rooted in nature, and in that reading of the great Bible of the world which precedes all written books, those remote copies of the intrinsic meanings of things. I was myself dramatically reminded of this when in the summer of 1966 I saw flying over the Temple of Aesculapius at Epidaurus (of all places) an eagle with a writhing serpent in its beak. This symbol, first used as a metaphor by Homer, has accompanied European poetry and symbolic thought throughout its history, gathering on its way the symbolic associations profound and various. The alchemists made of eagle and serpent figures of their mythology; Ovid, Spenser, Blake and Shelley have in turn clothed the image in literary form and symbolic connotations. But seeing the thing itself (as if a piece of writing in the sky torn loose from all these books) I thought of St.-John Perse; whose poetry re-immerses all our used images in 'that original night' of Orpheus, contemporaneous with every period of history and every moment of life, and gives back to us a world at every moment newly created. (pp. 191-92)

Kathleen Raine, "St.-John Perse, Poet of the Marvellous," in her Defending Ancient Springs, *Oxford University Press, London, 1967, pp. 176-92.*

John Cowper Powys

1872-1963

English novelist, poet, critic, autobiographer, philosopher, essayist, nonfiction writer, and author of children's books.

Powys is perhaps best remembered for his series of novels set in Wessex county, the region intricately developed and expanded upon in the fiction of Thomas Hardy. Like Powys's other fiction, these novels—*Wolf Solent* (1929), *A Glastonbury Romance* (1932), *Weymouth Sands* (1934), and *Maiden Castle* (1936)—employ mythical and supernatural elements to explore various aspects of human consciousness, morality, and sexuality. His protagonists often embody introspective and romantic qualities and possess a deep affinity for the natural elements that surround them, enabling Powys to convey his dualistic philosophy of the universe. Powys's writing is usually divided into three periods: his early novels of contemporary life; his historical novels; and the futuristic, allegorical fantasies of his later years. Thematically linking the stories of these three eras is Powys's belief that modern civilization deters the individual from examining thoroughly the complexities of life. While Powys is often faulted for the prolixity of his prose, he is praised for his evocative rendering of rural scenes and human emotions.

Powys was raised in Dorset and Somerset, areas prominently featured in his novels. His father was an Anglican minister, and his mother was a descendant of poets John Donne and William Cowper. The eldest child of the family, Powys was the first to distinguish himself in letters. His brothers Theodore and Llewelyn also wrote several noted works of fiction, and four other siblings published books of their own. After graduating from Corpus Christi College, Powys gained recognition as a lecturer at British universities and on the American Chautauqua circuit, where he displayed his extensive knowledge of literature and philosophy.

Powys was more than forty years old and still lecturing extensively when he published his first fiction. Reflected in the dedications of his first two novels—*Wood and Stone* (1915) to Thomas Hardy and *Rodmoor* (1916) to "the spirit of Emily Brontë"—are two dominant influences on Powys's early style. These books, as well as the posthumously published *After My Fashion* (1980), written in 1919, and *Ducdame* (1925), are often described as romantic tragedies. Each work centers on a male protagonist who broods upon the nature of his existence and dies after being manipulated by natural and human forces. While these novels were generally well received when published, most contemporary critics regard them primarily as apprentice works for his Wessex novels.

The Wessex novels are characterized by their immense length, their philosophical protagonists, and Powys's often mystical descriptions of the English countryside. In contrast to the heroes of his previous works, the characters in Powys's Wessex novels are ennobled and enriched by life. *Wolf Solent* details the experiences of the title character after he withdraws from teaching in London to his family's native village. Given to bouts of intense contemplation, Wolf examines his purpose in a universe that is often detailed in explicit, anthropomorphic terms. Powys explained: "The inmost being of the book is the

necessity of opposites. Life and Death, Good and Evil, Matter and Spirit, Body and Soul, Reality and Appearance have to be joined together, have to be forced into one another." *A Glastonbury Romance,* considered by many critics Powys's masterpiece, encompasses such elements as the Holy Grail legend, the Crucifixion, and Communism to express the multifarious properties of the world. Both *Weymouth Sands* and *Maiden Castle* exhibit Powys's knowledge of the occult. In the former novel, the supposedly insane Sylvanus Cobbold voices many concepts from alchemy and other ancient supernatural beliefs, while in *Maiden Castle,* the magician Uryen Quirm searches for relics from an antiquarian religion.

The Wessex novels evidence Powys's growing interest in and knowledge of Wales. While writing *Maiden Castle,* he set up permanent residence there, and his subsequent novels are imbued with Welsh history and legend. *Morwyn; or, The Vengeance of God* (1937) depicts a journey through hell by a group of Welsh people who encounter the legendary bard Taliessen and the magician Merlin. *Owen Glendower* (1940) reenacts the Welsh uprising against Henry IV and focuses on Glendower's visionary qualities. Of this novel Louis B. Salomon commented: "Mr. Powys has woven the myriad and many-colored threads of history into a shimmering tapestry which, for all its faults, has a tragic beauty and grandeur that few historical novels of today can match." *Porius* (1951), set in Arthurian

Wales, revolves around conflicts and battles between various cults and nationalities during the Dark Ages. This novel features many characters from the *Mabinogion,* Welsh history, and Arthurian legends.

In his later years, Powys turned to writing fantasies. In the short novels *The Inmates* (1952), *Atlantis* (1954), *The Brazen Head* (1956), and *All or Nothing* (1960), as well as such collections of shorter fiction as *Up and Out* (1957), *Real Wraiths* (1974), *Two and Two* (1974), *You and Me* (1975), and *Three Fantasies* (1985), Powys continued to explore the contrariness of the world and vituperatively condemned scientific experimentation on animals, an issue first introduced in *Morwyn.*

In addition to his fiction, Powys wrote several volumes of poetry, excerpts from which are represented in *John Cowper Powys: A Selection from his Poems* (1964). Several nonfiction works, including *The Complex Vision* (1920), *The Meaning of Culture* (1929), and *The Enjoyment of Literature* (1938), established Powys as an insightful philosopher and literary critic. Powys's *Autobiography* (1934) is noted for its candid treatment of such topics as sex and sadism.

(See also *CLC,* Vols. 7, 9, 15; *Contemporary Authors,* Vols. 85-88; and *Dictionary of Literary Biography,* Vol. 15.)

THE NEW YORK TIMES BOOK REVIEW

Mr. Powys is what might rather vaguely be described as a philosophical novelist. He draws the pattern of [*Wood and Stone*] upon certain basic convictions, or assumptions, as to the fundamental forces in human life and lets the evolution of his story show those forces at work, inexorable and dominating, even if they are, to all seeming, simple and weak. These basic assumptions in his philosophy of life, as he sets them forth in his preface, where indeed, he seems a bit hesitant concerning them as compared with the surety with which he makes them manifest in the progress of his drama—these basic assumptions are that sacrifice rather than power and love rather than pride are the forces that exert the dominant influence upon human life, that are, in the last analysis, the secret of the universe.

The man who has the courage to set up this contention in a world given over, in both life and fiction, to the adoration of power and the cult of the superman deserves attention for that fact alone; and when to this is added the quite to be unexpected fact that, having both an unconventional idea and a philosophic turn of mind, he yet can write a story possessing the feel of life, dramatic interest and subtlety and nimbleness in the portrayal of character and you have a book worth reading—if you are not too particular as to certain of its phases. . . .

The centre of interest in the tale is a great hill of tawny sandstone, its quarries owned by a man of immense wealth and a Machiavellian dexterity in the exercise of his love of power. His beautiful daughter has inherited his lust for dominance, but while he depends upon his wealth for its instrument she finds hers in the lure of her sex and beauty. Across their path falls the shadow of a shy, pale, fluttering little woman, and then the opposing forces of sacrifice and love and power and pride are pitted against each other. The list of actors in the drama is very long, comprising most of the people of the countryside and the village, and they reveal the greatest variety of conception and true and graphic colors in their portraiture.

Mr. Powys is evidently a keen observer of life and responsive to all its phases. His story shows a rich background, not only of observation, but also of philosophy and of imagination. (p. 527)

> *"Dream and Reality in Recent Stories," in* The New York Times Book Review, *December 26, 1915, pp. 527, 530.*

THE NATION, NEW YORK

On his title-page Mr. Powys calls [*Wood and Stone*] a romance, and in his preface an eccentric story. He further explains it as an attempt to controvert the Nietzschean theory of the ill-constituted and the well-constituted; to trace "the curious labyrinthine subtleties which mark the difference—a difference to be observed in actual life, quite apart from moral values—between the type of person who might be regarded as born to rule, and the type of person who might be regarded as born to be ruled over."

After that, the reader might expect to find himself in for almost anything in the way of philosophy veneered with dialogue. But a criticism obligingly composed by the publisher has already caught his eye, before he has so much as opened the volume. "Following the lead of the great Russian Dostoevsky, he proceeds boldly to lay bare the secret passions, the unacknowledged motives and impulses which lurk below the placid-seeming surface of ordinary human nature." To be a Dostoievsky in art while routing Nietzsche in philosophy would seem a rather large order. Luckily, when one really gets into the book itself, all this thundering in the index is readily enough forgotten. The scene is laid in Thomas Hardy's country, the book is inscribed to him. For a time it threatens to be nothing more than a fresh ruling of that strange law which ordains that people who turn the novel into a vehicle for realism or philosophy, or any other abstraction, commonly end by celebrating Priapus. . . . On the whole, the book brings to mind not Dostoievsky, or Hardy, or any modern, but Landor, or, perhaps more truly, Peacock. Mr. Powys's heroine, if he may be said to have one, is the slender pathos and passion and charm of feminine youth. Over this embodiment of the Will to Love he broods, as Peacock did, with gentle irony. One thinks of Peacock also as these characters meet to talk, and talk so comfortably in character. Quincunx the recluse, Taxater the theologian and lover of good wine, are of Peacock's quizzical brood; and something like his is the atmosphere of humane speculation which marks the book as a whole. Whether or not this is strictly a story, even an eccentric story, it is that rarer thing, a book of distinctive flavor. (pp. 46-7)

> *A review of "Wood and Stone," in* The Nation, New York, *Vol. CII, No. 2637, January 13, 1916, pp. 46-7.*

THE NORTH AMERICAN REVIEW

Rodmoor is a story of fatal, too human, passions, of blind soul struggles, set in a little village on the East Anglican Coast. For unity's sake the scene is carefully harmonized with the inner motive of the story. It is worth remarking that the kind of unity that is most highly prized by a certain type of writer is the unity of effect conferred by landscape and environment; and this leads sometimes to a kind of childishness, a kind of old-womanish superstitiousness, a Castle-of-Otranto-like romanticism. Mr. Powys does not altogether escape this tendency. In his story Nature sometimes ceases to be an Arctic void and is suspected, like any old witch, of "exercising a malign influence"; the sea (which is really the chorus in the drama) is accused of hypnotizing otherwise sane persons, with its ceaseless, terrifying voice; at critical junctures fiery clouds point threatening fingers at poor bedeviled mortals. An owl pecks at a dead woman's eyes, merely to remind us that Nature may be as gruesome as a folk story.

But it would be a mistake to suppose that *Rodmoor* is merely a study in the effect of environment upon sensitive spirits. The meaning of the tale goes deeper than any "call of the wild" or than any of those psychological hypotheses that in the hands of certain writers lend themselves so agreeably to dramatic development. It delves down into the irrational, into the sub-human, and it finds awful realities just under the skin of consciousness.

It is perhaps not worth while to summarize the story; for in summary it could appear hardly otherwise than as a rather violently romantic drama of passion, played by oddly chosen characters, and ending rather confusedly in death and in unexplained gloom. The qualities to note are the extraordinary and disturbing reality of the thing; its awful plausibility; its terrible success in rousing sympathy and in quelling it; its insane humor and its humorous insanity. What could be more amusing than Dr. Fingal Raughty's Micawber-like whimsies? What sweeter or more assuring than Mr. Traherne's glorious Platonism? And yet these people make us afraid. (p. 945)

Perhaps this story of Mr. Powys' is just a pathological study; but perhaps it is something more: it possesses at least that thrill of the unknown which is also the thrill of beauty, and this gives it a claim. Pragmatically the world must decide whether negations can have a "human" meaning, whether the irrational can be domesticated in popular literature. Imaginably, we may become positivists, in fiction at least, and shut out the unknown. But probably not. Probably a story that takes us so thrillingly and dizzily over the verge of what we call sanity as does this of Mr. Powys' will always be welcomed. (p. 946)

A review of "Rodmoor," in The North American Review, *Vol. CCIV, No. 733, December, 1916, pp. 944-46.*

THE TIMES LITERARY SUPPLEMENT

The immediate effect of [*Ducdame*] by Mr. John Cowper Powys though powerful, is as confusing as that of the supposed Greek, or Celtic, invocation from which he has taken his title. The forcible union of idea and situation is disturbing. The author has not disengaged himself sufficiently from the bewilderment of his hero, Rook. The new Squire of Ashover, Rook, to whom we are first introduced, meets his brother, Lexie, a man doomed by disease and his own thoughts to an early death, at midnight and by weird moonlight, in the ancestral graveyard, where, in an environment that seems the more unnatural as it is appropriate, they discuss problems of morbid love, the succession of the family, and the black craft of the vicar. Rook, for no very apparent reason beyond that of obstinacy and fictional needs, has brought his mistress, the pathetic Netta Page, to live in the hereditary home, despite the very reasonable objections of his mother. Rook, "a megalomaniacal subjectivist," and his enfeebled brother are the last of the Ashovers, unless, by bend sinister, we count a deformed and horrible progeny hidden among gypsies and peasants. Against Netta, who is sterile, the mother of Rook and his cousin Lady Ann,

driven by an instinctive idea that the line must not perish, conspire. The much hinted insistence of the dead themselves is brought into uncomfortable reality by the obsession of the vicar, William Hastings, who, believing in total extinction of mankind, directs, as an experiment, his thought and black practice against the Ashovers. This remarkable situation is rendered more difficult by the emotional dissatisfaction of Rook, introspective to a degree hardly sane, and troubled by the various influences of Netta, his cousin, and the little wife of Hastings. . . .

The scene is laid in Dorset; but it is a country of the mind, and by a compelling pathetic fallacy nature echoes and completes the narrow ring of moods. . . . There is sound workmanship and constructive power in the book, but the dual mode is uncertain. We are left with the impression of a harsh plot forced into a narrow mould of ideas.

A review of "Ducdame," in The Times Literary Supplement, *No. 1230, August 13, 1925, p. 532.*

THE SPECTATOR

Everyone realizes how important it is that novels should begin well. The reader knows that it is the novelist's duty to rouse his interest with his first sentence; and the novelist himself seems nowadays to feel his responsibility so deeply that he moves heaven and earth to find a brilliant opening. Mr. Powys succeeds admirably. The sentence and the situation with which he begins [*Ducdame*] would catch and hold the most wandering attention:—

> Some of the most significant encounters in the
> world occur between two persons one of whom
> is asleep or dead.

And he does not keep us waiting long to learn what it is all about. Rook Ashover, the twenty-first possessor of an English country house, and the only heir of the family except for an invalid brother, is endangering the continuance of his line. His mother is trying to force him to marry a cousin; but all the interplay of human relationships which centre in his childlessness affects him disagreeably. He continues to live with a more or less unmarriageable woman, always trying to find out, in some rather baffled, pessimistic way, a reason or justification for the universe as he conceives it to be.

In some sense, of course, the problems Rook Ashover sets himself are also Mr. Powys's own. There are two opposed schools of countryside novelists. One of them, like the fine ladies and gentlemen of eighteenth century France, sees a Boucher or a Watteau in every rural prospect, swards smoother than plush, dotted with carefully laundered lambs; on the grass human beings of a more than mortal sweetness disport themselves with idyllic grace. The other school, more serious and respectable but equally prejudiced, sees, when it looks over the landscape, a menace in every cloud, a snake in every orchard, and Nature hovering with bloody and malicious claws over all animal, vegetable, and human life. Mr. Powys belongs most definitely to the second class. He writes:

> The gamekeeper and his wife were engaged in
> feeding the fowls, assisted by their idiot son.
> This child, whose half-articulate utterances and
> facial distortions would have been horrible in
> a city, fell naturally into his place among wilt-
> ing hemlocks and lightning-struck trees and birds
> eaten by hawks and rabbits eaten by weasels.

The falseness of this pessimistic attitude is plain, since all hemlocks are not wilted nor all trees blasted by lightning: nor is an idiot child any less saddening in a village than in a town. It really is a falseness, a patent desire to be romantic and gruesome at any cost, since in his best passages Mr. Powys shows himself peculiarly sensitive to

the scent of young leaves and the new-grown grass. . . .

There has been a surfeit lately of gloomy and distorted books about villages, and a fashion for cheap and shabby-black magic in all of which the desire to startle is obvious. One tires very quickly of bogies, born of a muddled and lazy philosophy; and Mr. Powys must forgive his readers if they grow impatient with his idiot-boy and "the oozy stalks of half-dead bluebells," and refuse to be really impressed. There are many ugly things in life, under the hedgerows or elsewhere, but so gifted and sensitive a person as this author need not go out of his way to dilate on them when he can equally well exalt us instead with a vision of that beauty and rightness in life in which he himself believes so strongly. He never convinces us that he believes in the existence of a malignant blight on the world's face. And when he follows his intuition and relies on his sensitive perceptions without being sidetracked into gloom, he can suggest the subtle degrees and half-tones of many diverse and enthralling kinds of human emotions amazingly well, and write vividly and with power. He is, in fact, so able and in many ways so likeable a writer that one is impelled to quarrel violently with him for his quite unnecessary errors of judgment, since **Ducdame** is, in spite of everything, a good and intelligent novel, and the story of Rook Ashover's final surrender to family claims is, some crudities excepted, well imagined and ingeniously told.

"Gloom in the Hedgerows," in The Spectator, *Vol. 135, No. 5064, August 22, 1925, p. 313.*

V. S. PRITCHETT

The pleasure of the reader of modern studies in the fantasia of consciousness is the pleasure of the diver. But it has the diver's limitations; the time spent below the surface must be relatively short. The fresh, reviving air is, by an annoying irony, on the surface of life! The moral is, that while the universe itself may not be large enough to hold the tortured and exultant sensibility of a **Wolf Solent,** and while the conflict between his body and soul can be dramatized in a seemingly infinite number of sensations, six hundred pages is far too much to give him. The submersion is too long. It is a sad fact that Wolf Solent, child of "this segment of astronomical clay, stretching from Glastonbury to Melbury Bub," a god, a poet, is also a school teacher and a bore. His sensibility gets in the way of everything. "In the violence of this action an earthenware jug of water— and Wolf had time to notice the mellow varnish of its surface— fell with a crash upon the floor." That parenthesis betrays him. He is cursed with the sensibility of our generation and its insidious self-love. When we were advised to love our neighbours as ourselves it could hardly have been anticipated that we should love ourselves so well! Yet **Wolf Solent** is a stupendous and rather glorious book. Wolf is a clumsy mystic who, returning to his native Dorset as the secretary to a satanic old squire, falls in love with the almost incredible bodily beauty of Gerda, and with the pallid, more spiritual Christie, almost simultaneously. He marries the former and craves for the latter. His body or heart is satisfied; his soul is hungry. This conflict is fought against the beautiful and *macabre* background of the

rainy Dorset country and, in such descriptions as the wooing of Gerda, in Wolf's tragic disillusion when Gerda is unfaithful to him and his sense of magnetic oneness with the earth is lost in the death of Christie's incestuous father, Mr. Powys rises to passages of amazing beauty. The world we see through Wolf's too piercing eyes contains a most startling collection of lecherous men who though pitiably twisted by evil are yet vouchsafed the sight of the stars. Mr. Powys in his passionate reverence for all natural things finds that nothing *is* evil. He propounds and accepts the paradox of man with his feet in the pigsty experiencing the sacrament of love before the altar of majestic death.

If this sounds high-flown—and Heaven knows the book is at times an orgy of self-consciousness—there are some sardonically drawn characters to show what Mr. Powys can do when he comes to the surface. Gerda's father, the stone-mason, is hot, red and alive; Lob, her young brother is cut richly out of Dorset soil; and other "lewd forefathers of the hamlet," such as Bob Weevil, the butcher, are excellently drawn. Each consciousness has its own symbols; and it is not without effort and struggle that one fights a way into this prolix book and grasps the symbols of Mr. Powys. "Poison and sting . . . the furtive coil and the sex-clutch; yes a spasmodically jerking, 'quivering ego-nerve, pursuing its own end—that was what was behind everyone." This is Wolf Solent's world and there is no character to whom one can fly for relief from him. The book is as beautiful and strange as an electric storm, and, like the thunder on Sinai, it is somewhat of a sermon. (pp. 197-98)

V. S. Pritchett, "Below the Surface," in The Spectator, *Vol. 143, No. 5276, August 10, 1929, pp. 197-98.*

NEW STATESMAN

As one plunges deeper in the wilderness of [**Wolf Solent**], it becomes increasingly difficult to keep in mind that it is not the first novel of a very young man indeed. All the usual signs are there: the complete absence of objective grasp; the interminable soul-searchings of the hero; the megalomaniac inconsequence of the plot; the feverish effort to get everything in. To these generic defects Mr. Powys adds a conscience condemned, by the lack of fixed principles, to constant overwork, and a style of such unsophisticated badness as becomes, in the long run, almost endearing.

Wolf Solent is a man of thirty-five, whose inner life, through a prolonged or rather petrified adolescence, has been entirely in day-dreams, to which he attaches a mystical significance and which, his adult acquaintance having presumably outgrown them, he believes peculiar to himself. This belief the author seems, unfortunately, to share. Wolf's return to his native Dorset, and his experiences there, drive him out into reality a little, but how far the reader may be left to decide; for none of Wolf's irrelevant and repetitive musings are ever spared him, and they resemble each other very closely from first to last. The book is full of the grandiose beginnings, loose ends and meaningless gestures of the amateur. It is, on the whole, heavy reading, for Mr. Powys does not attempt to select—his aim is to transcribe. This is no doubt a form of sincerity; but still, sincerity is only a means; and an accumulation of detail merely puzzles the mind, as the ear is puzzled by a succession of unrelated sounds. A novelist, besides, must leave out something. Mr. Powys's method is to leave out the difficult things. Important transitions, the growth of relationships, he passes over in silence, assuming in the next chapter that they have taken place, and leaving the how and why for ever a mystery to the astonished reader.

To say that a book is without selection, proportion, or logical development, is to condemn it at once as lacking the qualities of mind. Now there may be art-forms in which the will and the intellect have a subordinate place, but the novel is not one of them. The novelist must know his own mind before he can advance a step; otherwise, concerned as he is with life directly and as a whole, he is obliged to put everything in. Anything that presents itself may, for all he knows, be the essential thing, and besides, if he leaves it out he feels it will be lost for ever. Great novels are based on principles; and Mr. Powys, for lack of them, is a prey to all the bugbears of the imagination.

Wolf Solent has two bugbears—will and energy. They take in his mind the forms of modern civilisation and sex. The first he escapes, though it continues to haunt him at intervals, by returning to Dorset and living in a small workman's villa: beautiful houses are apparently too voluntary and coherent for him. Sex he cannot escape, being as much attracted as repelled by it. Sex, therefore, is what the book is about. It is treated with a mixture of pedantry and superstition hard to describe; indeed, Mr. Powys quite loses his head over it. (p. 606)

[Wolf] is in a continual state of shock; shocked at his friends, shocked at himself, shocked still more when he is not shocked; shocked by sex particularly, but not exclusively. . . . He torments himself unflaggingly over his ideals without having any clear notion what they are, or any impulse to sit down and think them out. In fact, Mr. Powys has rediscovered the hundred per cent romanticism of *Sturm und Drang*—and he does not appear to entertain the least suspicion that it has been discovered before.

His moral sensitiveness, indeed, and patience in recording impressions might give his book some value if he had command of English enough to do them justice. Unfortunately, he has not. At the end of a long, serious, introspective sentence, suddenly you come upon an exclamation mark: it strikes on the ear like the blunder of a too-genial guest at a genteel and rather strained tea-party. This hearty symbol, however, recurs so often that one comes to take it in the right spirit, as a mere confession of inadequacy. Mr. Powys's literariness is a more consistent shock. "Miss Gault's face," he says, "was like an ancient amphitheatre full of dusky gladiators." Faces, interpreted by Mr. Powys, are seldom without some monstrous oddity. Smiles are reflected in them like bunches of honeysuckle. In fact, the book is so strenuously over-written that it was hardly possible it should be expressive. It has been grossly over-praised. (pp. 606, 608)

"*A Question of Selection*," in New Statesman, *Vol. XXXIII, No. 852, August 24, 1929, pp. 606, 608.*

PERCY HUTCHISON

Although *A Glastonbury Romance*, by the author of *Wolf Solent*, is printed as a single volume, it is in reality a two-volume novel bound as one. In the first part Mr. Powys is engaged in assembling his cast of some forty men, women and children, in setting his stage, in invoking to his aid the subtle psychological forces and the exterior compulsions that are to operate in the playing-out of the piece, and, most of all, in acquainting his reader with his own personal philosophic point of view that is to govern the entire story. In the second part these disparate ingredients are kneaded together into a more homogeneous whole, with a dénouement of no little power. The writing of *A Glastonbury Romance* must have been a herculean task. In his assembling of selected individuals Mr. Powys has given representation to the multiple factors in community life; not only do his characters act and react on one another, they also are to be seen in all their reciprocal relations with a locale and an environment.

There is one preliminary matter on which Mr. Powys lays stress—he would have it understood that his town of Glastonbury is purely fictitious. It is not the Glastonbury of Arthurian romance, although Arthurian legend is to play an important part in his story. But it is as legend in general—as a dead hand out of the past—rather than as particularized legend, that the ancient story is to operate. Arthur, Merlin, the Grail—these are for Powys symbols for whatever may belong to the past, but which has influence (or might have influence) over a later generation. Thus, in setting a revival of Grail worship against communism imported from Russia, as Mr. Powys does in this narrative, he is staging a satire of proportion. . . .

A Glastonbury Romance is to some extent a study in good and evil; with its clever contrasting of ancient and modern, it becomes a social study; and, finally, it is an investigation into the physical and the spiritual where these two so merge into each other that the result is what is generally known as mysticism. Clearly Powys would have us regard him as a modern mystic.

The story takes its start in the reading of the will of the late Canon John Crow, who has ignored both his issue and his collateral heirs to bestow his wealth on his former secretary-valet, John Geard. The money eventually comes to its more rightful inheritors—that is, such of it as is left after Geard's protracted experiment in reviving a cult of the Grail. But as a matter of fact the money is of less importance in Powys's scheme of the novel than is Geard's Grail excursion, which, with its mystic implications, is one of the two preoccupations of the book. The other is the communism already referred to. . . .

The publishers are at pains to advise the curious that there is abundance of melodrama in the book; indeed, they inform us—somewhat blatantly—that there are "six major love-affairs, one murder, three births and two deaths," one of which is by suicide. . . .

[There] is a certain carelessness of relationship among Powys's Glastonbury people (both before and after marriage) that endows the book with bucolic piquancy; the murder, however, is so long prepared for, there are so many cries of "wolf," that the effect, when reached, is considerably weakened. But Powys, as one eventually perceives, is in actuality far less interested in the murder as committed by old Codfin than he is in the vicarious enjoyment of the act of killing on the part of his Welsh character, Owen Evans. A bit noisome, on the whole, this sadism of Owen Evans, an excursion into the erotic which will in no wise enhance the attraction of the book for many readers. Previous to this final experience—this experience de luxe—in cruelty, Evans had enjoyed himself by representing the crucified Christ in a Glastonbury passion play. The reader will answer the question as to the Welshman's probable madness as he sees fit. If we understand Mr. Powys, in his opinion Owen is not mad. (p. 7)

On the other hand, it must be recognized by those who might criticize Mr. Powys on his adventure into abnormal psychology, that he has the right of all dramatists not to be called to account for any of his characters. It must also be remembered that mysticism, in which the physical and the spiritual blend indistinguishably, has by most students of the subject usually been held to contain a large element of sex. Owen Evans, then, is to be taken in the same detached way that one takes the jealous Othello or the incestuous Oedipus, namely, as an objective fictional creation invoking a plenitude of horror together with something of pity. On the whole, however, Powys (and this applies to his entire work) is nearer to Poe than he is to Shakespeare or the Greek dramatists, in that the amount of pity he is able to arouse is not commensurate with the horror he has invoked. That this is a confession of at least partial failure in those portions of the story in which the author follows a tragic vein is obvious.

On the whole, however, it is evident that *A Glastonbury Romance* is to be regarded as comedy rather than tragedy; that when we have had set before us Evans's religious mania, and the many other manias of the book, we are really bidden to witness a gigantic Walpurgis Night orgy.

It is a pity that Mr. Powys's grandiose satire should, however, have its sharpness blunted by the excess of philosophy and psychological analysis which clutters his pages. The mysticism on which the author spends so much time and labor is overworked. Mr. Powys might credit his readers with more acumen than he appears to grant and not lecture them so much. His mysticism is easily understood without the repetitions in which he indulges, and when it is not understood (as is frequently the case) his repetition makes it none the clearer.

On the vastness of his canvas, on the complications of his pattern, on that pattern as picturing a Somersetshire pastoral scene, rich in its flavoring, Mr. Powys can receive only commendation. The flood which at the end sweeps in from the sea to engulf the Glastonbury of his imagination is as full and stirring a flood as fiction has yet produced. The book also is to be commended for its humor—scattered here and there is much humor. The march of the characters through the pages—this also is no mean feat on the part of the author. Why, therefore, when John Cowper Powys, can, when he wishes, show such prowess solely as a teller of tales, does he feel himself under compulsion to exhibit himself so persistently as psychologist and philosopher? His admixture of vibrations, nerves, ultra-refinements in impulses, and so on, detracts from rather than augments the real achievement of this book. And so insistent is the sex-motif that one feels that while Powys started as a Dostoievsky he ended merely as a D. H. Lawrence. (pp. 7, 24)

> Percy Hutchison, "John Cowper Powys's Fictional Carry-All," in The New York Times Book Review, March 27, 1932, pp. 7, 24.

FERNER NUHN

Less intimate than *Wolf Solent,* with its characters more impersonal and more subdued to action and setting, a formidable romance [*A Glastonbury Romance*] still is: mustering through 1,174 tall pages a whole village-full of people in a cycle of modern loves and quests. Backstairs and drawing-room are equally represented—loafers, capitalists, Communists, laborers, children, and petite bourgeoisie; miserables, saints, and sinners. For metaphysical accompaniment to this interplay Mr. Powys calls upon almost every known form of belief, from the most primitive animism to communistic impersonalism—in-

cluding ancestor-worship, idolatry, Christianity, worship of sun and moon, exorcism, self-immolation. It is one of Mr. Powys's most flavorous qualities, this seemingly innocent hospitality toward any sort of channel of the human spirit. Just as it is his engaging practice to enter into as with joy every kind of vagrant human impulse—of dalliance, lust, love, passion, obsession, mania.

In all this matching of an unseen platonic form with every physical event, it cannot be said, however, that Mr. Powys is uniformly persuasive. There are times when the confluence of seen and unseen strike one as somewhat routine, out of the author's standard position rather than from a newly felt intuition. But in a work of such length pages of duller sensibility are to be expected. And there are many scenes when the landscape, the weather, the spiritual background, and the passions of people do merge with powerful effect. Hardly another writer today has so intense a feeling for English earth, a feeling which again and again gives to particular places—river thickets, hillsides, fields, and even particular trees and stones—a loving evocation such as children wrap about the familiar features of their dooryards. No reader will forget the tremendous picture of Stonehenge which appears in the early pages of this book.

And what redeems Mr. Powys's insistent platonism—disarming, I should think, even to a behaviorist—is a certain puckish humor, a gleeful aberration, which allows to intrude upon the most exalted moments some earth-returning detail. . . .

Naturally the reappearance of various Arthurian features in a modern story sets the author very difficult projects, not the least of which is the portrait of a Merlinish sort of prophet. With this "Bloody Johnny" Geard, an extraordinary phlegmatic, hydrocephalic individual who usually manages to be absent, or absent-minded, during the most crucial occasions of the story, I think he has been extremely successful. It is Geard who gives a hint of the meaning of the Grail in this modern narrative, and it is one which should be something of a shock to Lord Tennyson in his grave. For it has to do a good deal more with human love than with divine aspirations.

But I believe I am right in seeing that this meaning has already been exemplified in the various love affairs which thread the story, and which, in spite of the heavy fanfare of super-naturalism, are the real heart of the book. What it takes "Holy Sam," the Galahadish youth, a vision of the Grail to make clear to him, John Crow and Tom Barter and Lady Rachel and Owen Evans have already proved to themselves in successful mating. It is a modern sort of ideal of mutual joy and respect in sexual union, relieving women as much from the ethereal emptiness of idolization in a tower casement as from the debased couch of merely momentary satisfaction. This, I think, is Mr. Powys's modern version of chivalry, objectified in *A Glastonbury Romance,* as it was more personally recorded in *Wolf Solent.* And it is a conception which I suspect has had more than a little to do with the reconciliation of this occult Piltdown Man to the modern world. Certainly it has given weight to these last two books.

> Ferner Nuhn, "A Modern Cycle of Chivalry," in The Nation, New York, Vol. CXXXIV, No. 3485, April 20, 1932, p. 474.

ARCHER WINSTEN

For those to whom John Cowper Powys is already guide and philosopher extraordinary, *A Glastonbury Romance* adds 1174 pages drawn from those "primordial wells of deep delights" which have yielded so heavy a flow in his previous work. . . . If not the longest novel ever written, at least it is the longest-winded. (p. 201)

One can say that Mr. Powys has an excellent and catholic taste in literature, that his mind is powerful and retentive, and that he is not squeamish about taking what he can make his own. What cannot be said is that he shares the excellences of his models. Everything he touches is stamped with the unique impress of his vision.

He has fashioned a complicated plot, turning upon social, sexual, mythological, historical, religious, and mystical conflicts, which cannot be squeezed into the ordinary limits of a synopsis. It includes one murder, two deaths, three illegitimate children, and seven love affairs. There are also a flood, two miracles . . . , a Passion Play, and a communistic experiment. Mr. Powys has created a host of characters, each one placed in his niche in this cross-section of English society. He ranges down to the bald-headed madwoman, Bet Chinnock; he rises to the Marquis of P.; in between there are the servants, a communist, an industrialist, an anarchist from the Scilly Isles, a Welsh antiquary, doctor, priests, cuckolds, lechers, a thief. Not content with only plot and character, Mr. Powys deals intermittently but at length with the Cymric, Druidic, Arthurian, Saxon, Norman, Christian and Modern influences resident in Glastonbury. Arthur's sword, resembling what John Crow had heard of the "so-called Cosmic Rays" fell into the river while he was looking at a drowned cat from the Pomparlès bridge; Sam Dekker saw the Holy Grail with a fish in it, possibly a tench; and Philip Crow's airplane drones a modern note in the air over Glastonbury. It finally becomes a performance of amazing virtuosity in which Mr. Powys never falters.

The purpose of all this has been well stated both by the author and his publishers. He wishes to gather his characters into a "straining knot of psychic relations"; the book offers a series of "mystical intimations". He has succeeded perhaps too well. For the value of *A Glastonbury Romance* rests entirely upon its psychic and mystical revelations. If Mr. Powys is not a major prophet, his characters become meaningless, their actions insignificant, and the whole book an over-inflated bladder of nonsense.

Let us consider Mr. Powys's ever-present First Cause. Now the First Cause is double-natured, has a personality, resides beyond the darkness which is beyond the astronomical world, sends forth black and white vibrations to act on mortals, has two eyes, one pouring forth good, the other evil, and receives prayers from earth. "A certain delicious shudder" in the First Cause is what mortals recognize as Sex in animal, vegetable, and human life. If one prays at noon-day, it should be to the sun; if at midnight, to the moon. The best time to appeal to the First Cause is at either the morning or evening twilight. There is less chance of psychic interference then and the results are better.

In humbler vein, there are other jewels of mystic revelation which are much funnier. (pp. 202-03)

When downright silliness shows as the heart and core of a book of such monumental proportions and imaginative vigour, it is no matter for laughter. Mr. Powys writes with a creative prodigality which is admirable. His insight into the human emotions is often most convincing. His descriptions and setting leave little to be desired. What a pity, therefore, that he must be essentially a self-hypnotized Houdini of psychic literature, al-

ways the destroyer of his undoubted gift. He is befouled in the immense dragnet of his psychic imagination. Small wood-louse and universe, tree and religious prophet, are all lost in equal nebulosity. And to make matters even worse, this is the identical mysticism the author has promoted since the First Cause only knows how long. (p. 203)

Archer Winsten, in a review of "A Glastonbury Romance," in The Bookman, *New York, Vol. LXXV, No. 2, May, 1932, pp. 201-03.*

PERCY HUTCHISON

In *Weymouth Sands* John Cowper Powys has again proved his ability, so markedly shown in *Wolf Solent* and *A Glastonbury Romance,* to place before the reader a diversified human story, albeit the attention is focused within a fairly circumscribed locale, and the span of time held to a minimum. In other words, Mr. Powys's interest and method are precisely the opposite of the method and interest of the "saga" writers; and particularly is this so in *Weymouth Sands.* One is not to look here for broad and sweeping narrative. The novel is, instead, a keen study and a richly variegated portrayal of many lives which either are closely commingled or in momentary contact. It is a novel of loves, and near-loves; a novel in which there is at least one deeply rooted hate. Moreover, it is a novel which only a Powys could write, and this not merely because it is of the Powys country, Dorsetshire scene and Dorsetshire people, but because, for all the keenness of analysis, there is throughout that brooding pity, that gentle humaneness and that whimsical tolerance which are characteristic of the writings of these three literary brothers, Llewelyn, "T. F." and John Cowper. Let others argue about right and wrong, they seem to say. People are; they act thus and so. They feel, they love, they aspire; or they do not aspire, but work like moles in the ground. Human behavior is what a Powys sees when he looks about him, and *Weymouth Sands* is an intricate, provocative and living example of the novel which takes people as it finds them.

If any characters assume in *Weymouth Sands* greater prominence than others those characters would be Adam Skald, generally called "The Jobber"; Cattistock, wealthy and miserly, and a girl from Guernsey, Perdita Wane; for it is over the lives of these three that love and the premeditation of murder exercise sinister control. Yet to those who know the several writings of John Cowper Powys and the general tenor of his philosophy it is apparent that the character of Sylvanus Cobbold, a mystic thinker, probably held the greatest interest for the author. Indeed, Mr. Powys's publishers state that he "'confesses that into the mystical personality of Sylvanus Cobbold he has flung many of the most secret manias and superstitions of his own nature." But let us stop here, for in this passage there is a valuable key. There is no other living author who winnows his words more assiduously than does the novelist of *Weymouth Sands* or who refines them to such ultimate meanings. Hence when Mr. Powys talks of his "secret manias" and his "superstitions" one must not see in the first word the crude insanities of the mentally deranged, or in the second anything like rude tradition. From the point of view of the townsfolk, the police especially, Sylvanus, going up and down the sands spouting his philosophic niceties, is indeed sadly cracked. But for Powys, we venture to say, he is the sanest of them all.

And if we follow a bit further we see just how valuable as a key is this "confession." Ultimately Sylvanus is arrested and committed to the insane asylum for alleged immoral relations with young girls. That these alleged relations were of the mind and not of the body is, of course, wholly beyond the comprehension of traditionally rooted court authorities, and we see the sardonic grin on Powys's face as he hands his modern Socrates a modernist's substitute for the cup of hemlock. Secret manias and superstitions—we see what Mr. Powys means here, what he means throughout the book; the world is the same today as in the time of Socrates and of Christ; the idealist is the one who is pilloried.

John Cowper Powys is often likened to Thomas Hardy, and in certain respects there is resemblance, even after we have discounted the fact that both write about the same section of England and the same segment of the English population. Especially is it true in the degree to which both novelists integrate their people and their story with the natural scene. (p. 8)

Fundamentally, however, and this is of deep importance, Powys bears no resemblance to his great Wessex predecessor; the sweep of narrative, above all, the immense clarity which so distinguishes *Return of the Native, Tess* and *Jude* have no counterpart in *Weymouth Sands*. Clearly, Powys, had he been so minded, could easily have whipped his book into a concentrated drama of "The Jobber," Cattistock and Perdita. But he did not wish so to do. . . . Powys is like an artist who is equally proficient in dry-point and in impressionistic coloring, and he mingles the two arts most subtly; *Weymouth Sands* is both disconcertingly sharp and mercifully blurred; Powys is more merciful both to his characters and to his readers than is Thomas Hardy. Is he, possibly, more true to life? Not necessarily, for what may seem to readers of this generation to have been cold-blooded literary "plotting" on the part of Victorian novelists was, with such writers as Hardy, Thackeray, George Eliot, at least, the clearing away of what seemed to them non-essentials rather than a heartless compulsion of marionette characters.

And it is what seemed to the Victorian novelists as being nonessential that a writer like Powys is likely chiefly to stress. In *Weymouth Sands* the reader is never quite clear as to why it is that Skald fails in the end to carry out his murderous intent on Cattistock. True, he is passionately in love with Perdita, and she has left him because he has made his intent known to her. But she takes no steps to keep him from committing the murder, and it is a general weakening of his will after her desertion which prevents the deed, not any definite change in him, either mentally or morally.

And this is the Powys purpose, the Powys interest, throughout—not to place before the reader a grandly progressing narrative, a trampling tale. Instead, in exquisitely refined prose, fortified by an imagination which can penetrate the most baffling recesses of the human personality, John Cowper Powys says in effect; "Here is the human pattern as I see it, darkness and light swiftly interchanging, trifling emotions occupying the entire life of some, the entire life of others devoid of a single emotion. Is my pattern bizarre? Then it is because life itself is bizarre. And it is yours to take or leave, as you choose."

No, life is not all the time a Walpurgis Night; but much of the time it is. For the rest, it is a pure marriage, a decent burial, lazy indolence, well-directed or futile struggle. And Mr. Powys, impersonally surveying the personal scene, smiling sardonically the while, attaches no moral to his tale, reads us no lessons. The cool, calm impersonality of *Weymouth Sands,* and the author's all but diabolical power to peer beneath the surface, combine to make it a book of moment. (pp. 8, 21)

Percy Hutchison, "A Tolerant View of Humankind," in The New York Times Book Review, *February 25, 1934, pp. 8, 21.*

MARK VAN DOREN

[*Weymouth Sands*] is the third large novel which Mr. Powys has written about the doings of two little gods. He does not invoke their names, but he so frequently employs their epithets—erotic and neurotic—that we know who they are all right, even though the better-known of them has been disguised. The cheeks of Eros are neither round nor red, he carries no quiver, and he does not move by wings. He is as pale-faced as his brother, as loathsomely deformed, and as much under the necessity, when he wants to proceed from one place to another in that portion of southern England which Mr. Powys has chosen for the scene, of slithering on his belly. The two of them together have Mr. Powys's human world completely under their power. Not a man or a woman in Weymouth, not a boy or a girl, not even a ghost but writhes in the grip of some irregular and distorted passion, or grows steadily more grotesque under the influence of an insane illusion.

The author of *A Philosophy of Solitude* and *In Defense of Sensuality* is at some pains to make it clear that the whole world either is or ought to be this way, and to suggest that he is so creating it here in protest against a scheme of things whereby science will soon have "killed God, tortured the last animal to death, suckled all babies with machines, eavesdropped on the privacy of all souls, and made life to its last drop an itch of the blood and a weariness of the will." Or it may be that he has set out to create a special world which will be a horrible example of what science, etc., can do to us. I doubt it, though. I think he has proposed to show us, in the face of the various belittling analyses we have made of human nature, how grand and terrible it is after all, and how it is possible that powerful personalities shall continue to exist. If his personalities are not actually powerful, and I find this to be the case, then the explanation may be that science already has triumphed, leaving only such gaunt simulacrums of greatness as Sylvanus Cobbold and Dogberry Cattistock, to take only two of Mr. Powys's people who have failed, I take it, to be what he wanted them to be.

But of course another explanation would be that Mr. Powys is not a first-rate novelist. In spite of the fact that he writes with a richness which I like and is nowhere really uninteresting, I am afraid that this second explanation is the more plausible one. It seems to be the simplest way of accounting for the further fact that the several stories he has interwoven in Weymouth do not come off. They ought to come off, it would seem. The setting is always gorgeous, the people have vast potentialities, and Mr. Powys is continually promising us crises and disclosures of gigantic moment. But when the crises arrive we somehow miss in them the one telling stroke we had expected, and the disclosures have a strange way of limiting the world of Weymouth instead of enlarging it, so that we suddenly perceive it to be more like the little life we live than we had been led to suppose it was. We discover merely that Mr. Powys has been trying to read into life something which is not there. We might wish it were there, but we know that Mr. Powys is not the man to convince us that it is. . . .

[The characters], in spite of Mr. Powys's very ably phrased vaunts as to their immenseness, are never anything but husks with artificial hair whose complicated stories move us neither to pity nor to terror. I heartily wish it were otherwise. Surely there was never a man who desired more deeply that Mr. Powys does to write a great novel, or who made more elaborate and admirable preparations. Few novelists have possessed so many of the required qualities without possessing the one quality— I cannot name it—which is essential. Mr. Powys is not without his fascinations, and he can be read with an absorption which one by no means experiences every day. But so far he does not seem to be a great novelist.

> Mark Van Doren, "Eros and Neuros," in The Nation, *New York, Vol. CXXXVIII, No. 3583, March 7, 1934, p. 280.*

PERCY HUTCHISON

[*Maiden Castle*] is another story the scene of which is laid in "Wessex," the Dorsetshire first made familiar by Thomas Hardy and since exploited by John Cowper Powys through a series of novels of which this is the latest. *Wolf Solent, A Glastonbury Romance* and *Maiden Castle* do not, however, form a sequence. In fact, they have little in common except their general background and the author's unflagging interest in the psychology of men and women, individually, or in contact or attrition with one another. Forty years ago Hardy would have been classed as a psychological novelist. We fancy that Mr. Powys feels that he has carried on the Hardy tradition. And that in compensation for a decrease in objective drama he has deepened psychological effectiveness, largely through his knowledge of Freud.

None of this will be news to Mr. Powys's already large reading public. But it may help those now coming upon him for the first time to orient themselves in a novel certain at the outset to be bewildering because of its apparently complete lack of movement. If they read far enough they will discover that there is movement; forces subterranean, slow, sinister, driving Dud Noman on, and Wizzie Ravelston and Enoch Quirm, quite as inexorably as Hardy's "President of the Immortals" drove Tess on. Whether or not the reader will like *Maiden Castle* will depend largely on whether he cares to see himself turned inside out through the turning inside out of fictional characters, or whether he prefers to live independent of disturbing exhibitions. Is the psychologist indisputably right? he will ask.

John Cowper Powys has long been devoted to the results of antiquarian research, taking an especial interest in the pagan antiquity of his native Dorset country, with its Druidic remains, and in the traditions of Wales, whence his family originally came. It is Mr. Powys's conviction that people are deeply under the influence of the past. This may be true in lands in which there is a lineal past. But it is less true in America, or only sporadically true. We have no Maiden Castle—Celtic, Mai-Dun Castel—so that it becomes a trifle difficult for the American reader to assent to Enoch Quirm's great absorption in the tradition of Maiden Castle, an absorption so deep that under its overwhelming influence his mind becomes unhinged. If Mr. Powys had taken a leaf out of *Wuthering Heights* he would not have labored his point to the degree he does. Not that Mr. Powys fails entirely to produce his eerie effect. But if he could master the short, stabbing art of Emily Brontë he could make a reader's flesh creep and his hair to rise as now he does not do. His Enoch Quirm is more a case from a psychiatrist's files than he is the disembodied, sinister, not to say supernatural, force Mr. Powys sought to create. . . .

Mr. Powys so densely crowds each of his canvases as to become the despair of any reviewer. But it is never the story, main plot and sub-plots, which is of importance in considering this gifted, but frequently exasperating, author. John Cowper Powys is to be read primarily, not as a novelist, but as a psychologist who uses the medium of the novel rather than the medium of straight-out exposition, to set forth his creeds and to enlarge upon them. One reads him for his nuances of meaning. With him a feather turns a character's psychological balance one way or the other. One reads him for his revelations of the hidden springs of intellectual motivation or emotional florescence. John Cowper Powys, one might venture to say, arouses more diversified reaction among readers than almost any other novelist. Perhaps that is why he is widely read. Mr. Powys stimulates, either to aversion or antipathy. And *Maiden Castle* sustains this conclusion.

> Percy Hutchison, in a review of "Maiden Castle," *in* The New York Times Book Review, *November 29, 1936, p. 7.*

LOUIS B. SALOMON

If the neatly boxed two volumes of *Owen Glendower* do not quite live up to their promise, it is certainly not because of any lack of romantic glamour in the subject: that fifteenth-century rebel-hero who hoisted the banner of the red dragon for Welsh independence and, allying himself with the mighty Percys of Northumberland, shook the English throne under its usurping occupant, Henry Bolingbroke. . . .

Instead of the pompous old charlatan who in Shakespeare's *King Henry IV* boasts that he can "call spirits from the vasty deep" and that at his birth "the frame and huge foundation of the earth shaked like a coward," [Owen Glendower] is here presented as a magnetic personality with a fatal strain of mysticism in his make-up, a dabbler in magic arts, to be sure, but one whose real sorcery consists not so much in necromancy as in his ability to "exteriorize" his soul while his body remains in a state of cataleptic trance (readers of Mr. Powys's *Wolf Solent* will recall that young man's "mythology"). One feels from the very first that Glendower is a man fated to perform mighty deeds with a tragic end, like the ancient Celts of whom it was said, "They went forth to battle, and they always fell."

Considering, however, that I had anticipated a genuine literary thrill in the treatment of this dazzling figure by so distinguished a stylist, psychologist, and antiquary as Mr. Powys, the book disappointed me. Despite a plethora of murders, feuds, burning loves, alarms and excursions, it seemed to me unconscionably long-winded; and on top of a style which is unaccountably labored, especially in the first volume (where the central romantic figure is constantly referred to as "our hero" or "our young friend"!), it is overlaid with a dank miasma of Celtic mysticism which seems to emanate more from the mind of the author than from the circumstances of the story, even though the drama is played out by Welshmen against a backdrop of the very hills and forests of Arthurian legend, of Bran and Myfanwy and the chimerical heroes and heroines of the *Mabinogion*. Part of this crepuscular haze arises from the fact that Mr. Powys, himself steeped in Welsh history and folklore, strews his narrative prodigally with dark allusions to bygone Cambrian celebrities without a vowel to their names, the symbolical significance of which cannot but mystify the overwhelming majority of modern readers.

On the credit side, he has effected an astounding reconstruction of the spirit and trappings of a turbulent epoch.... Where Shakespeare, in his two *Henry IV* plays, merely stages a spectacle of martial pageantry as a background for the clowning of Jack Falstaff (who appears in *Owen Glendower* under his true name of Sir John Oldcastle), Mr. Powys has woven the myriad and many-colored threads of history into a shimmering tapestry which, for all its faults, has a tragic beauty and grandeur that few historical novels of today can match.

> Louis B. Salomon, "Red Dragon of Wales," in The Nation, *New York, Vol. 152, No. 4, January 25, 1941, p. 103.*

R. ELLIS ROBERTS

In Mr. Powys's [*Owen Glendower*], interminably verbose, over-accentuated, pompously and vaguely mystagogic, and with its adolescent emphasis on sexual cruelty, the historical figures are stirred to life only occasionally. Owen Glendower, a warrior, a scholar, and a patriot is drawn now more than life-size, now removed from humanity, and now reduced to a crazy pattern of uncontrolled impulses.

In this last he resembles nearly all Mr. Powys's major characters—a little crazy, vastly unpleasant in their off moments, and with a most unanimous interest in the infliction or endurance of pain. Now pain, and even sexual cruelty, can be subjects in imaginative literature—from Aeschylus to William Faulkner imaginative artists have used them: but it is fatal, if the romancer wishes to avoid the repulsion of the normal reader, to present them not as things done or suffered, but as spectacles watched. There is a delectation in prying and whispering and analyzing in this novel which for me makes much of the book frankly disgusting.

Apart from Owen the book's hero is Rhisiart, half-Welsh, half-Norman, a young man just down from Oxford in 1400, a grave and grey-headed judge at its end in 1416: certainly, as he had to go through Mr. Powys's novel, this premature senility is not unnatural. Throughout his life in the book Rhisiart is unable to distinguish between love and cruelty; when he watches a vile lady, with opulent curves, scold obscenely at her helpless and rejected lover, Rhisiart hates her and yet something about her "made that hatred quiver and vibrate with a craving to hug her till she cried out under his grip."

This Alice is a lady whom Rhisiart really detests: what he feels toward those he likes I must leave the reader of the book to discover. Mr. Powys spares neither fancy nor paper in conveying the information....

In the many scenes of fighting, public or personal, Mr. Powys's gusto is a little less morbid: Mars is certainly less repulsive than Venus.

Mr. Powys derives—this book makes it quite clear—from the old school of horror story. Today if we are to have horror, it must be imaginative and spiritual as in Julian Green's work, or some books of Kafka's. Mr. Powys's bullies and bogies, brutes and maniacs, mouthy seers and boastful bards are but painted cardboard; and they move in a fifteenth century of the novelist's own invention. Mr. Powys takes no pains to make his period references accurate; I admit his right to use modern language—though one jibs a little when Rhisiart uses such expressions as "dangerously hypnotic" and "mass-obsession"—but his ignorance of the period, especially in matters of religion, is so great that the book loses all pretensions to

being an historical novel, except in certain details of decoration.

> R. Ellis Roberts, "Warrior, Scholar, Patriot," in The Saturday Review of Literature, *Vol. XXIII, No. 15, February 1, 1941, p. 10.*

JOE LEE DAVIS

The best of John Cowper Powys' romances—*Wolf Solent, A Glastonbury Romance,* and *Owen Glendower*—have been massive feats of a weird, sombre, elemental imagination. So is [*Porius*] in its attempt to tell all that took place in the Valley of Edeyrnion in North Wales from October 18 to 25 in 499 A.D.

These seven days were crucial ones in Arthur's reign and in the personal history of the hero, Porius. The intrigues of Arthur's life-hating, war-mongering, sex-fiendish nephew, Medrawd or Modred, and the resentment of tribal dignitaries against Brython-Roman domination led to a conspiracy to yield the Valley to the invading Saxons of Colgrim. Porius, the heir of the local ruling family, married his bethrothed, Morfydd, possessed and lost during frenzied hours of fertility ritual and massacre the daughter of a giant, and came into his princehood with the passing of his father.

Despite the emergence of these two lines of action and the limitation of time and setting, the effect of diffuseness is well-nigh overwhelming. Porius is the centre of narrative reference for only some of the chapters. Other characters bewilderingly usurp his place. The cast the reader has to keep straight numbers over fifty. The range is truly that of the saga, of myth on the grand scale, including everybody from Arthur himself and Nineue and Myrddin Wyllt or Merlin to Gog and Magag, with the poet Taliessin as part of the elaborate portentous machinery and with the Mithraic Bull and the Pelagian Heresy hovering in the remote theological background....

Mr. Powys' at once dinosaurian and dionysiac prose is appropriate to such a vision.

> Joe Lee Davis, "A Grand Scale Myth," in The New Republic, *Vol. 126, No. 17, April 28, 1952, p. 22.*

GEORGE D. PAINTER

There are few experiences available to the contemporary reader so strange and rewarding as the descent into the Platonic cavern of a Powys novel. The cave is the material world; the enormous and terrible characters who inhabit it seem shadows cast by good and evil and the Comic Spirit from a real world outside. Mr. Powys is our only twentieth-century descendant of the great nineteenth-century romantics, of the line of Dostoevsky, the later Dickens and the later Hardy. He is, I believe, and confess that so far this is a minority view, one of the two living English novelists of genius (the other being Mr. Henry Williamson), in the old, dying and real sense of the word. If he is scandalously neglected, it is because in the marching column of present-day writers he is almost the only one in step. "Monsieur Poop thinks him a fool," as Stevie Smith has said, "but this old man is wise and sly, he knows the truth, he tells no lie." There is, to my mind, no living sage better qualified to teach his grandchildren to suck the egg of the universe.

The Inmates is Mr. Powys's first novel since *Maiden Castle* (1937) to be set outside Wales and in the modern world. "What I've tried to do in this tale," he says in his preface, "is to invent a group of really mad people who have the fantastic and grotesquely humorous extravagance that, after all, is an element in life,'' and ''to defend the crazy ideas of mad people as against the conventional ideas of sane people.'' It is an old man's novel, but that is one of its special pleasures and powers; he walks with a stick, which he also uses to lay about him; he is now more interested in ideas than in persons. His characters are embodiments of the unaccepted but disquietingly true-seeming beliefs that have put them behind walls; yet they have an overpowering physical presence.

One may succeed in forgetting the philosophies of Mr. Lordy, Mr. Pantamount and the rest, but one is unlikely ever to forget what it was to sit with them, among the warders, at asylum-tea. The inmates compulsorily inhabit a looney-bin called Glint (''this cosmic hall''), which is surrounded, like Tartarus, by a wall and a river. They are prodigiously comic and alarming characters, as touching as they are touched. There is a strange and beautiful love-story between a typical Powys hero and heroine: a hero, that is, who is bony-faced and cunning, like his author, and sees everywhere in the phenomenal world intimations of spiritual power, enjoyment and danger; and a heroine who is at once a projection of the hero's desires, and an emanation of the powers he cultivates. There is a series of appalling encounters (though these, too, like the characters, tend to be comic) with derangement and evil; and depths of the soul to which only Mr. Powys knows the entrance are plumbed, possessed and colonised. But the main purpose of the work is the chain of dialogues with the mad. To the lunatic alone does the world of matter become, by privilege, non-existent or symbolic; everlasting truths begin where everyday sanity ends; the inmates are sound philosophers, and it is the vivisecting Doctor and the sadic warder who are stark, raving mad, unfit to be let out. Only after this symposium, when each patient has had his full say, and a kind of anthological metaphysics of the insane has thus been constructed and roofed in, tile by loose tile, do they all escape to America in a largish helicopter before which Freud would have blanched and blushed. Monsieur Poop would not think *The Inmates* a good book; it breaks all the rules and reaches all the sources. I have relished no novel so intensely since the same writer's *Porius*.

> *George D. Painter, in a review of ''The Inmates,'' in* The New Statesman & Nation, *Vol. XLIV, No. 1113, July 5, 1952, p. 21.*

THE TIMES LITERARY SUPPLEMENT

[Of his two new stories in *Up and Out*] Mr. John Cowper Powys himself writes:

> The feeling, for it is more than a doctrine or an idea, underlying both these stories, is that there is nothing in the universe devoid of some mysterious element of consciousness, however small, queer, ridiculous, or whether animal, vegetable or mineral, such a thing may be.

This feeling pervades all Mr. Powys's writings; and it is perhaps this that has held up the understanding of them. He has been writing now for more than forty years and during the past twenty-five his output has been prodigious; and yet, though authentic voices have never been wanting to assert his genius, the prevailing critical mood of the past two generations has been strangely lethargic in response. . . .

Mr. Powys is never obscure; and his large works, with their long and classically modulated periods, their wealth of vocabulary and allusion, their strange assurance and utter independence of what most of us would say that he ought to be writing, pursue us with the unhurrying and unperturbed pace of Francis Thompson's God in ''The Hound of Heaven.'' Escape has proved impossible, and we are today watching the steady rise to full recognition of one of the outstanding writers of our century. (p. 601)

A Glastonbury Romance was a great act of courage; and Mr. Powys's *Autobiography,* in which he claims to recognize the presence of the sadistic instinct within himself, was an even greater. The power of *A Glastonbury Romance* matures from its controlled survey of good and evil as balanced and artistically accepted principles within the universe and within man. But, this acknowledged, we may next suggest that Mr. Powys's genius, his extraordinarily wide and deep comprehension of human instincts and potentialities, derives from his own intimate experience of a terrible evil; through accepting without surrendering to it he has gained an inclusiveness known to few in immediate contact with the origins, beyond good and evil, of creation. And surely, it is this very acceptance, as an intimate and personal experience, of the deepest and most fearful cleavage and antagonism of opposing principles within and yet intrinsic to the cosmic scheme, which enables him so uncannily to focus the secret life of sticks and stones, recognizing in them what theologians would call the immanence of the Deity.

This dispassionate balancing of good and evil, and in particular the evils of cruelty, could scarcely be, on all occasions, maintained. When an evil is too pressingly known, there is also the compulsion on the artist to descend into the arena, to fight; and for many years Mr. Powys has engaged himself strenuously against his main horror, vivisection. This campaign found its most satisfying projection in *Morwyn,* a richly compacted ''Inferno'' where, among others, the majestic figures of Taliessin and Merlin appear as powers of good.

The novels of Welsh history, *Owen Glendower* and *Porius,* completed Mr. Powys's weightier works. Since those appeared, we have been aware of an easier, more buoyant manner in the Homeric *Atlantis* and medieval *The Brazen Head.* These later books take us directly to a world of myth and enchantment which allows a new freedom in the handling of the animistic properties of nature, as in the delightfully argumentative Fly and Moth of *Atlantis* and the parts played, in both narratives, by certain peculiarly wise trees. . . . And here we are brought to the threshold of the two new stories published together under the title *Up and Out.*

We have Mr. Powys's own authority for regarding the animistic insight as their key; but this is not necessarily a happy insight. Indeed, it is just because he makes no distinction between the sensitivities of animals and men that his horror of vivisection is so great. The first story opens with an attack on this recurring horror, in comparison with which the subsequent brief and unsensational announcement that the world has just been destroyed by atomic warfare comes, with a typical stroke of Powysian individualism, as an anti-climax. Four survivors voyage on a fragment of Earth into space. The fantastic adventure shows us the slaying of Time, conceived as an amorphous slug, and its swallowing by Eternity; an even more repellent creature which next swallows itself. The stars, through Aldebaran as representative, elect to commit general suicide. Representatives of Oriental, Greek, and Welsh mythology and religion accompany these remarkable events by argument and comment. Finally the four survivors meet God and Satan in friendly colloquy, after the manner of Goethe's *Faust,* and hear God's personal account of the creation which has proved so disastrous and his plan for a new attempt without either animal slaughter or free-will. The book's hero suggests instead that they all—God, Satan and the four survivors from Earth—attempt a plunge "up and out" into the new "dimension" sometimes discussed by philosophers. The attempt is made, but it leads only to extinction for all concerned.

The story constitutes an attack not only on vivisection and the lust for scientific knowledge, but also on all avenues of escape offered by such abstract concepts as "eternity," "dimension" and "the Absolute," or any fixed theology. And yet the apparent pessimism is countered by so irrepressibly buoyant a style and so lively a play of humour that it can scarcely be regarded as final. The characterization of God is particularly attractive and entertaining. Never was there a more well-intentioned deity: simple-minded, unpretentious, courteous, kindly, indeed wholly lovable, and, in effect, rather like the God of *Green Pastures,* surprisingly convincing. It almost seems as though Mr. Powys is nowadays at his happiest when speaking through the voice either of God himself or of some insect or inanimate object.

The two narratives are published, and may have been conceived, as complementary; certainly they should be read together, like the "Everlasting No" and "Everlasting Yea" of *Sartor Resartus.* The second is by far the happier. This fantasy takes us to the Moon, and is filled by heterogeneous persons and events, moving with a dreamlike inconsequence which yet holds together as a pleasing unit. Among its constituent elements are some exciting meditations on the mystery of life, a stick in telepathic communication with a club, and a Moon-giant who possesses a collection of "Milestones of Terrestrial History" (e.g. a fragment of the Ten Commandments, Achilles's heel, Nero's fiddlestring, a white feather from the Dove of the Ark, a piece of one of King Alfred's burnt cakes, the half-bitten apple-core from Eden, &c.). Among the Moon-dwellers we find an academically minded and clairvoyant spinster and her friend, a professional, but baffled, philosopher; and from Earth we have a Welsh lady whose soul visits the Moon's soul in sleep. A romantic conclusion shows us the young hero, successor to the young heroes of *Atlantis* and *The Brazen Head,* climbing "up and up and up" to find union with the daughter of the Moon and Sun on the ridge of the Moon's mountains which divides its known from its unknown face.

The fantasy, carried in a style of purity and charm, is wholly pleasing. The mysteries of "space" and "infinity" are metaphysical positives coming under no such condemnation as did "time," "eternity," and "the Absolute" in the previous tale: indeed, the contrast is stated. Most vivid of all is the dance of the Terrestrial Milestones and the characterization of the Dove's White Feather as she finds union with her long-lost love, a Raven's Black Feather from the Raven which did not, according to the account in *Genesis,* return to the Ark. No person of fiction was ever created with more masterly a touch, nor more warmly convincing in life and speech, than this fascinating White Feather. A few pages only, but the miracle is performed. Again, a line or two and a few scattered phrases endue a piece of quartz dancing "ecstatically" down a slope with a lovable, semi-human vivacity surely new to our literature.

Here rather than in Mr. Powys's denials lies his true genius, and its meaning for us to-day. Rationally, he has always maintained a certain agnosticism, even scepticism; and yet each book in turn is saturated in a sense of the occult, of magic, of some hinterland to the phenomenal world of prodigious strangeness and importance. In his latest work this divergence appears to be widening. . . . [Powys urges us] to transfer finally our more numinous speculations from the altar to the earth, to the observable universe and all its children. And yet the more uncompromising his religious scepticism becomes, the more his narratives are charged with a sense of the miraculous. Perhaps he would say that when once we have touched the living magic of creation, then all the rest, our immortalities and eternities and dimensions and theologies, will be handed back to us, if we still want them; but not till then. . . . [Perhaps] it is not fantastic to see in the poignant love-intercourse of our White and Black Feathers some delicate intimation, some feather-light whisper, hinting an answer. If so, it is an answer which Mr. Powys has not as yet explicitly formulated. His latest fantasy moves in advance of the main body of his teaching. (p. 602)

"Cosmic Correspondences," in The Times Literary Supplement, *No. 2902, October 11, 1957, pp. 601-02.*

THE TIMES LITERARY SUPPLEMENT

With scarcely a single earthly acknowledgment, *All or Nothing* transcends the world of appearances and offers a key to other space-time continuums with their different qualities and experiences. It can be regarded as a metaphysical discourse, a mockery of rationalism, meta-fiction or space poetry.

It is set out in the form of an imaginative saga, recording the adventures in body and spirit of two children, John o' Dreams Nu and Jilly Tewky Nu, who live nominally in an English village. Governing their actions is the perpetual struggle between a fossilized skull and "what looked like a petrified flower-bowl", known as Bubble and Squeak, and standing respectively for All or Nothing, that is to say the desire to fill the universe to its furthest extent, or to destroy everything. Among the heroic adventures are space visits to the Milky Way and the centre of the sun, clashes with giants, slugs and worms, all animistic and often anthropomorphic, and meetings with an Arch-Druid and Boadicea.

Abandoning any connecting thread, Mr. Powys relies on boisterous imagination to carry along the jumble of erratic incidents, symbolism and blind-alleys. The diffusion detracts from the book's obvious merit as a great energetic outburst, for there is much that seems to belong to the worst sort of fairy story, wilful and childish. At moments when the imagery becomes poetic deliberate silliness is liable to intrude, and the use of cerebral whimsy as a means of exposing the dullness of the human race occasionally degenerates into petulance. It is too often as if Beowulf was overlaid by Peter Pan.

But Mr. Powys is pointing out the dullness that comes from a trammelling of the human spirit by some of the bug-bears accompanying life: inertia and triviality and routine. *All or Nothing* sweeps them away into outer space, flourishing as an essay in imagination which is its own, and Mr. Powys's, justification.

"Outside Appearances," in The Times Literary Supplement, *No. 3042, June 16, 1960, p. 381.*

VALENTINE CUNNINGHAM

The importance for modern English literature of the publication of this "lost" novel [*After My Fashion*] that John Cowper

Powys wrote in the immediate aftermath of the First World War can hardly be exaggerated. We had all wondered over "John the Talker", the revivalistically inspired ranter, next in force only to D. H. Lawrence, falling so fictionally silent after his *Rodmoor* (1916). How odd a nine-year gap before *Ducdame* (1925). Perhaps it really had taken him that long to warm himself up for the hugely unstoppable outpouring of the later 1920s and 1930s that gave us in rapid-fire succession *Wolf Solent, A Glastonbury Romance, Weymouth Sands* and *Maiden Castle*. . . .

Well, at last we know: he wasn't stumped Coleridgeanly for words, he hadn't gagged on the richly forced Pantagruelian gruel of New York. *After My Fashion* isn't precisely the huge panorama of America or New York that some readers of Powys have desired. But its generous biting off of the bitter matter of New York not only affords it a front rank in the process of English authors "imagining America", it also places it foremost among world literature's modern efforts to cope—one thinks particularly of Kafka's *Amerika*—with American impressions.

After My Fashion is by no means as long as *A Glastonbury Romance*—perhaps no novel, not even *Glastonbury,* should be. But the signs of that awesome "Druidic hypnotism of speech" which Powys attributed to John Geard in that novel, of the endlessnesses, the "gibberish", the sheer ranting abundance to come (Powys got "extraordinary pleasure from reading aloud" *Finnegans Wake*), are very clear. Adjectives roll off the page in the excessive clusters that stuffed the lecturer's hours. . . . Like D. H. Lawrence, he repeats himself gladly. Metaphors, tags, phrases, adjectives, situations that take his fancy (like the central male character Richard Storm's continually going down on his knees before the laps of women), are sure to come back again and again. Words mesmerise more than they inform.

One much repeated word is "queer". Powys seeks to entice and shock the reader into a view of the world as skewed, queered. A major queerer has been the First World War—and *After My Fashion* must surely be placed alongside our great post-Great War fiction, like *Jacob's Room* and *Mrs Dalloway*. From rural Sussex to raw New York the War's horrific pressure is felt. . . . Post-War sexual relations are freer. "The youth of these after-war days" are ready to be excited by the "great new art" of Elise Angel (she's based on Powys's friend Isadora Duncan), an art, it's suggested by the Communist Karmakoff, that will go down even better in revolutionary Russia. Clearly, too, Powys's sense of "the calamity" of the modern—modernism rings like a litany through the book: "You modern writers", "these modern authors", "modern city", "modern way"—"the calamity of being alive at all on this harassed earth", is connected with Storm's assertion that "The war can never really end". The war chimes in with—it doubtless helped to mature—Powys's feeling for the universe as a masocho-sadistic place, a veritable destructive element. . . .

This strangely violent world is queer, too, because its author peoples it deliberately with odd types. He liked to claim affinities with the weird among writers, with Dostoevsky, Nietzsche, Blake. He called himself a "Welsh Rasputin". . . .

The "evocation of a strange marginal purlieu": it is on the edge where the borders of opposed worlds edgily smash and collide, that Powys believes "glimpses" into "the very secrets" of things are permitted. And *After My Fashion* shows that his mastery of frontier insights was early on superbly achieved. To be sure, one of his most reiterated dualistic sets now seems rather heavy-handedly done: this novel's people are altogether too fond of generalizations about the dichotomous ways of men and women ("'Men and women want different things of each other', he muttered, 'and always will'"). But the border-clashes between good and evil selves ("luckless humanity, torn and divided between the two natures"), between good and diabolic forces (Storm's inner critical demons, the Revd Moreton's yen for black masses), between God and Christ (that is between Lucifer "the Infernal Power of malice" and Lucifer the Light-Bearer), as well as the hints of mysterious meanings bursting sacramentally through the physical, material world ("life extending a little further than the five senses"), are all rendered as skilfully as anywhere else in his work. What's more, it is of special interest in this early novel, by an established critic who was turning himself into a fictionalizing visionary, that Storm, the renowned litterateur and critic, should be shown straining to channel his energies into a visionary poetry. . . .

Just so, he's torn (and he's a greater tearer-up, especially of letters) between France and England, and England and America. England's untheorizing instinctiveness, its innocence and rurality, its sturdily commonsense hostility to new poetry and new politics, its drawing-room stuffinesses, are all put down in comparison with France. . . . But once he is in New York, with its overpowering buildings ("huge erections", "iron and marble monsters"), its painted women and swamping crowds, its nightmarish subways, its soft drinks and Ebstein's laundry, Storm endorses Nelly's English longings for Hardy landscapes, Sussex Downs and rainy fields. . . .

As Powys himself eventually did, the novel settles finally amid English landscapes, English weather, pragmatism and softness. But much of its power undoubtedly consists in its persisting scepticisms about England, and the irresolute, liminal attractions that it keeps animating for the new arts of Europe, the new politics of Russia, and the new grandeurs of New York that somehow sum up all those new worlds: the Woolworth Tower, the Stuyvesant Theatre, the Pennsylvania Station. "Here at any rate was a beauty and nobility that had something in common with [the] Sussex Downs."

Valentine Cunningham, "A Bite Out of the Big Apple," in The Times Literary Supplement, No. 4031, June 27, 1980, p. 726.

JOHN MELMOTH

In extreme old age (he died in 1963, aged ninety) Powys amused himself with a string of romances sufficiently rule-less and self-regarding to be in little need of readers. That Glen Cavaliero, who wrote the afterword to [*Three Fantasies*], categorizes them as "the juvenilia of old age" indicates not only their resistance to classification but his own unease at their so abruptly being made public. His assurances that they should not be mistaken for "the playthings of a literary senescence" do nothing to enhance the reputation of a writer whom he obviously admires.

Performing the kiss of life on stone-dead ephemera is by no means a self-evidently charitable action. Powys's "heroic and elemental" conception of literature, his "instinct" for those things which are "distinguished, heroic and rare" may be little more than windy rhetoric, but he was right to insist that his gifts needed the space and scope of large novels. The reservations which he expressed about "the abominable art of the short story" put *Three Fantasies* in a worrying perspective.

"**Topsy Turvy**" (1959), indulging a Powys fascination with the inanimate, stages an *affaire du coeur* between a door handle and a child's painting. Aside from expressions of mutual respect and affection, the sweethearts spend much of their time in "the Dimension of Truth" above "a rock-a-bye ocean of drifting clouds", discussing problems of philosophy, in a state of undress, with famous pairs of lovers: Dido and Aeneas, Robin Hood and Maid Marion, Sir Henry Irving and Ellen Terry, Dick Turpin and Black Bess. So far, so straightforward. The only problem is how seriously to take these wranglings with the niceties of sense data, the problem of other minds and the relationship between soul and body. On the one hand, the dialogues are sufficiently convoluted to pass as philosophy proper—it is as though Powys were putting an insipid neo-Platonism in the mouth of the most repressed logical positivist; on the other, the disputants' glib pantheism is amateurish and without rigour.

"**Abertackle**" (1960), very much in the manner of *All or Nothing* which Powys published in the same year, is both bleaker and more bizarre. At first sight, its "philosophy of escape" is more reasonable than the tawdry maunderings of its predecessor: "Life is a frantic struggle to escape from the old traditional legacies and myths and customs and convictions and symbols and ideas and moralities and ethics and religions and idolatories and beliefs." The villagers of Abertackle are seasoned if rather high-toned gossips, ever ready to mull over the worship of the machine, sexuality, the theatre and speculative physics. However, any suspicion that Powys has ceased from wackiness is swiftly dispelled by the introduction of Gonflab, a dwarf with no body, whose arms and legs grow out of his head and who subsists on a diet of bats plucked from the air.

The first sentence of "**Cataclysm**" (1960) unerringly sets the tone: "In the little town of Riddle in the county of Squat in the west of Bumbledon there was a young man called Yok." Young Yok, his Auntie Zoo-Zoo (a gigantic reincarnation of the earth goddess Gaia) and a number of other assorted oddities wage war from an aeroplane on the crew of an expedition bound for Venus to capture animals (principally badgers) for purposes of vivisection. Not entirely without sense—"I would sooner be shot dead by a murderous burglar than have scientific treatment from a scientific doctor"—it betrays a profound confusion of values in the way it cheerily blows its enemies to bits, reducing the would-be vivisectors to a dust cloud of whirling fragments.

Cavaliero is on record as discerning evidence of "genius at play" in all three pieces. Powys may have been closer to the truth in dismissing them as "suckfist gibberish", "manic", the product of an "obsession". Indeed, it is their obsessiveness that gives them such momentum as they have. Powys's problems with sexuality and violence present the psychoanalytical critic with an embarrassment of symptoms. Two of the stories terminate in cannibalism; the author disposes of his characters with a hit-man's insouciance. Although "**Cataclysm**" is relaxed and informative on the joys of masturbation, Powys's feelings about the "secretive violence" of copulation are more problematic: it is identified at best with rending and bloody defloration and at worst with straightforward rape.

John Melmoth, "Suckfist Obsessions," in The Times Literary Supplement, *No. 4289, June 14, 1985, p. 677.*

Katharine Susannah Prichard

1883-1969

Fijian-born Australian novelist, short story writer, poet, dramatist, editor, journalist, nonfiction writer, and autobiographer.

A prominent and influential figure in Australian literary history, Prichard was one of the foremost writers to insist on the use of Australian subject matter as the foundation for a national literature. Prichard traversed much of Australia to authenticate the various settings of her novels, which include the bush country of Victoria, the opal fields of northern New South Wales, the karri forests of the southwest, and the cattle stations of the west. Combining romantic, realistic, and idealistic sentiments, Prichard is noted for her lyrical narratives, her courageous, steadfast protagonists, and her predilection for social commentary. Recurring motifs in her fiction include nature, work, and mateship. Above all, Prichard extols the virtues of the Australian people who live off the land and whose simple values she admires.

Prichard's first novel, *The Pioneers* (1915), won a prize offered by her publisher for the best novel of Australian life. Set in the bush country during the early nineteenth century, this book traces the paths of immigrants and ex-convicts who settled the region. Prichard's next novel, *Windlestraws* (1916), is a *Robin Hood*-type story involving a romance which takes place in London. This book is one of only two of her works that is set outside of Australia.

Prichard's abhorrence of the social injustices she witnessed as a journalist in England and in her homeland led her to study the doctrines of Friedrich Engels and Karl Marx. In 1918 she began attending political discussion meetings, and in 1920 she joined the Australian Communist Party, for which she spoke and wrote pamphlets. *Black Opal* (1921) is Prichard's first novel to display her socialist ideology. This work depicts the struggle between opal miners and Armitage, an American opal buyer, for control of the field. Armitage is depicted as a capitalist villain who would stifle the miners' freedom. A subplot of this novel concerns Sophie Rouminof, a miner's daughter with a beautiful singing voice who accompanies Armitage to the United States to perform. She becomes successful and rich but hates the fast-paced American lifestyle and eventually returns to her simple life in Australia, which Prichard portrays as the superior existence. *Working Bullocks* (1926) also contains socialist elements but concentrates on the conflict between nature and humanity. Against the background of the karri forest of southwestern Australia, Prichard relates the love story of Red Burke, a bullock driver, and Deb Colburn, a boarding-house worker. Nature and animal imagery are abundant in this work, as humans and animals together work the colossal forests, and environment and humanity become fully integrated. Prichard's social and political beliefs are conveyed through Mark Smith, who leads the lumber mill workers to strike when an accident takes the life of one of their group.

Coonardoo: The Well in the Shadow (1929) was the first sympathetic study of an aborigine woman in Australian literature and is regarded by some critics as Prichard's finest work. The novel revolves around the concealed love between the aborigine

Coonardoo and Hugh, the son of the cattle station owner for whom Coonardoo works. Feeling guilty for loving what white tradition tells him is a subhuman creature, Hugh rejects Coonardoo and marries a city woman who eventually leaves him. The lives of the protagonists begin to deteriorate when Hugh assaults and then banishes Coonardoo from the station because she has been seduced by his neighbor. At the book's end, both die tragically. Critics praised Prichard for the deep understanding and sympathy with which she depicted aboriginal customs and feelings, and John Carter asserted that *Coonardoo* "stands as a forceful piece of social documentation and bids fair to do for Australia what *Uncle Tom's Cabin* did for America." Prichard traveled across Australia with Wirth's Circus to gather material for *Haxby's Circus: The Lightest, Brightest Little Show on Earth* (1930). This novel portrays a family circus owned by Dan Fay, who forces his children to perform dangerous stunts in order to ensure the success of his show. The plot centers on Fay's daughter Gina, who is a talented bareback rider until she breaks her back during a performance. Gina displays determination and courage by protecting her mother and younger siblngs from her father's obsession and by eventually taking over management of the circus. In *Intimate Strangers* (1937), Prichard explores new middle-class moral attitudes and awakening social consciousness through a study of the deteriorating marriage of Greg and Elodie Blackwood.

Prichard regarded the Goldfields trilogy as her most significant literary achievement. Comprising *The Roaring Nineties: A Story of the Goldfields of Western Australia* (1946), *Golden Miles* (1948), and *Winged Seeds* (1950), this social history presents the evolution of the goldmining industry. *The Roaring Nineties* depicts the pioneer days of the mines as well as the incipient hostility between companies and individual prospectors. *Golden Miles* portrays the domination of the industry by corporations and the subordination of individual miners. Prichard also traces the growth of mining unions in this novel. *Winged Seeds* carries the history through the Depression to the end of World War II. While some critics contended that the trilogy is overly didactic, with characterization subordinated to social criticism, others found Prichard's account to be well-drawn and accurate, blending realism and lyricism. Prichard's last novel, *Subtle Flame* (1967), is generally regarded as one of her weakest works. In this book, a Melbourne newspaper editor quits his job to work for world peace after his son is killed in Korea. Critics complained that the narrative consists mainly of dogmatic proselytizing and that its characters serve as symbols rather than fully realized individuals.

In addition to her novels, Prichard was prolific and well regarded in other genres. *Clovelly Verses* (1913) and *The Earth Lover and Other Verses* (1932) collect her poetry. *Brumby Innes* (1927) is a play in which she depicts the callous treatment and sexual exploitation of Australian aborigines. Prichard's short story collections include *Kiss on the Lips and Other Stories* (1932), *Potch and Colour* (1944), *N'Goola and Other Stories* (1959), and *Happiness: Selected Short Stories* (1967). Set chiefly in the outback, the pieces in *Kiss on the Lips* range from experimental fiction to conventional short stories. The works in *Potch and Colour* are based on tales that had been told to Prichard by gold prospectors, while *N'Goola* is an eclectic collection of amusing character studies and stories in which Prichard presents her socialist beliefs. *The Wild Oats of Han* (1928) is a novel for young adults about Prichard's childhood in Tasmania, and *Child of the Hurricane* (1963) is her autobiography. Prichard also wrote nonfiction, including *The Real Russia* (1935), in which she relates her impressions of her visits to the Soviet Union, *Marx: The Man and His Work* (1922), and *Why I Am a Communist* (1950).

(See also *Contemporary Authors*, Vols. 11-12 and *Contemporary Authors Permanent Series*, Vol. 1.)

THE ATHENAEUM

Declaring itself on its title-page to be an Australasian prize novel which gained for its author 1,000*l*., Miss Prichard's work [*The Pioneers*] excites some curiosity about the failures in the competition out of which it has emerged triumphantly. For, though *The Pioneers* is a stirring example of sensational fiction, it is not a first-rate work of art. The scene is laid in Australia in the days when convicts were transported to Van Diemen's Land, and the author in an arbitrary but effective fashion shows the heroic nature of the gratitude awakened in an escaped convict by a young married woman who aided him and his wounded companion. At a later stage we are presented with two young lovers in the son of this good Samaritan and the daughter of the grateful convict, and for a villain we have a sort of colonial Jonathan Wild. . . . The story, with its details of scrub fire,

"cattle-faking," and convict life, may at least pass as a representative colonial work; the author's character-drawing shows talent, and we fancy that, with greater attention to veracity of general effect, she may produce a thoroughly satisfactory novel.

A review of "The Pioneers," in The Athenaeum, *No. 4585, September 11, 1915, p. 174.*

THE NEW YORK TIMES BOOK REVIEW

The prize novel, like the prize play, is often a very saddening affair. Not infrequently it leaves the reader filled with dismay at thought of what the other manuscripts submitted must have been like, if this was the best the judges could find, or else wondering whether those judges were recruited exclusively from a home for the feeble-minded. And so . . . [*The Pioneers*] is at once a pleasure and a restorer of confidence, for, although by no means without faults, it is unquestionably a worth-while book, interesting, with plenty of spirit and a good deal of significance.

As its name implies, it is a story of pioneers, of men and women—and especially of a man and a woman—who went to Australia as emigrants, hoping to find in this new country the peace and home and fortune they had been denied in the old. Donald Cameron, a Scotchman, of course, and his wife, Mary, herself a native of that other land of mists and moors, mountains and heather—Wales—appear in the first chapter, making their toilsome way through the foothills to a spot the man has already chosen, with all their household goods and other belongings piled on a wagon, and a cow and her calf as the nucleus of the splendid herds of which the man is already dreaming.

But they are workers as well as dreamers, this sturdy, shrewd, silent Donald and his brave wife, and before long the first rude hut has been built, a paddock made, land cleared and plowed. Then one day Donald is obliged to go for supplies to the distant Township of Port Southern, leaving his wife and baby alone there in the wilderness, with no friend near save the dog. But before he goes he gives his wife a shotgun and teaches her how to use it, warning her that blacks may come, or escaped convicts from "the Island," desperate men, ready to commit any crime rather than return to the hell on earth from which they have fled. . . . For a day or two she goes in fear; and yet when the thing she has so dreaded actually happens, when two gaunt and ragged men really stand there in the doorway, she meets the situation with fine courage. It is from this event, from the meeting between Mary Cameron and "the taller and shaggier" of the two men, that much of the subsequent history develops.

But Mary Cameron is not the only nor even the foremost heroine of the book. That place belongs to Deirdre Farrel, loving, loyal Deirdre, who was willing to pay the highest possible price in order to shelter the blind "Schoolmaster" she loved so passionately, but when she found she had been cheated, refused payment in a way which, though justified not only in the eyes of all men but by her own conscience, left a cloud of pain and horror over all her life. For Miss—or is it Mrs.?— Prichard is no sentimentalist, and her book is very far indeed removed from the rose-colored, spun-sugar fiction with which we are all so wearisomely familiar. The fate of the "Schoolmaster," a man worth all the other men in the book put together, the pitiful collapse of poor broken Steve, the death of Conal, the Fighter—there is tragedy and grim truth in each of these. Not that *The Pioneers* is in any way a sorrowful or a joyless novel; there is happiness in it and successful love, courage, both moral and physical, hope and promise for the future of those destined by inheritance to be pioneers. . . .

There are parts of the book in which the author's control of her tools leaves something to be desired, and we feel that so shrewd and so successful a man as Donald Cameron would scarcely have allowed McNab to entangle him in his web, especially as he knew what sort of creature that cunning, spider-like person was. But on the whole the book is well written, it has plenty of drama and exciting moments, and a good story told with spirit. Davey is a sufficiently likable jeune premier, and the two women, Deirdre and Mary Cameron, are portrayed with tenderness and insight. Moreover, it gives a graphic picture of a life very strange and far away to most of us, yet one closely akin to the existence led by those of our forefathers who came to this country in the early days, or later drove their prairie schooners out into the wilderness. This prize novel, in short, presents an author whose future career should be an interesting one.

> "A Prize Novel," in The New York Times Book Review, *January 23, 1916, p. 26.*

THE NEW YORK TIMES BOOK REVIEW

"Red" Burke is a primitive creature with bulging muscles and ready fists, who drives men and oxen with equal mercilessness and effectiveness. His temper is sullen, his "love" (this is insisted upon again and again) is sheer animal appetite. Only one disinterested or kindly act, if we except a race that he allowed to be "pulled" through fear of blackmail, is recorded of him, and it is rather significant of the obsessions that have overtaken current fiction that he should be propounded by Miss Katharine Susannah Prichard for our admiration and esteem in *Working Bullocks,* an impressive, realistic novel from Australia.

Literature does not reach us in any appreciable bulk from the Antipodes. But those who open this latest offering with the hope of finding it suffused with the charm of an unfamiliar country are likely to be only partly repaid. Barring a few terminologies—"brumbies" and "brush," "township" and "timber"—the action of the story might very well pass in any of our Western States. As one reads on the conviction grows that the pioneering of the Anglo-Saxon race, in extending its activities over the greater part of the unclaimed and temperate zones of the earth, has evolved and standardized a society that is only remotely affected by its political loyalties. Even when all credit has been assigned it for its effectiveness, this society remains a bleak and arid affair, more crudely material in its perspective and less colored by idealism than any community since paganism. (p. 8)

No detail of life in an Australian mill town is spared by Katharine Prichard to build up a picture of squalid, unrelieved dawn-to-dark toil which we can only hope is not typical of the youngest of the Commonwealths. The ramshackle huts in which women and children die of pneumonia; the roaring mill, where defective machinery takes its toll of the men's lives and limbs; the boarding houses into which the unmarried mill men shamble to eat, ravenously and silently; the sprees and sports meetings and abortive strikes which are the only alleviation to this drab existence, are drawn with a power that one feels must come from some deep dissatisfaction with the things that make national trade balances and the deprivation that is the price of material prosperity. Evangelical Christianity, it may be noted, makes but one momentary incursion into Karri Creek, and that

as grotesque and futile as even the editorial board of the Mercury could desire.

In spite of a sort of fog of animalism that covers its psychology and which may itself be in the nature of a protest. *Working Bullocks* is a startling and unusual novel. . . . (pp. 8, 14)

> "Australian Realism," in The New York Times Book Review, *April 24, 1927, pp. 8, 14.*

CAROLINE B. SHERMAN

From the moment he crashes through the forest on to the front page [of *Working Bullocks*], driving with crack of whiplash and buoyant shouts of encouragement his teams of struggling, straining bullocks with their load of giant timber, to the moment he drives his bullocks slowly off the last page into the forest again, the stalwart figure and shouldering personality of Red Burke dominate this stirring tale of the Australian bush. Whether asserting his lordship over the kings of the Karri forest or reduced to sudden ignominy by unseen forces too subtle for his battle, Red Burke's is the figure that, above all the many types pictured by his creator with bold, telling strokes, typifies the rude, pulsing life of the Australian Southwest.

We may not know the country or the people, or the life there, but no one can read this story of the working bullocks, whether beasts or men, without feeling with clear certainty that our author knows her bush country and her forests to the furthest reaches, knows the kind of men and women that they breed—men and women fitted to compete with the bush and the forests—as well as the kind of human scum they inevitably attract, as is the way with all new and developing countries.

With sure and unsparing hand Miss Prichard writes of powerful and elemental things, of rude conditions and brute forces. Yet over it all she pours the golden sunshine of Australian skies; the peace of starlight and the calls and songs of birds; the calm of cool, green forests and the cleansing storms of blinding rains and witching mists. We find ourselves, from the first, in a country where every wild flower, every tree and almost every bird has a name new to us, where spring comes with November, and sports and festivities are strange but indigenous. The bullock, the whim, the axeman's heart, fit themselves into our mental vocabularies before many pages are turned, and before we have been swept half through the book we have definitely added this corner of Southwest Australia to the known quantities of our universe. Not only is the whole story set close in the very sinews of the country, but occasional short paragraphs of pure description relieve the tenseness of the human tale like lyrics in a dark tragedy, and telling, local similes link the two elements throughout the pages.

> Caroline B. Sherman, "Australian Forest," in New York Herald Tribune Books, *May 29, 1927, p. 2.*

THE TIMES LITERARY SUPPLEMENT

In spite of the preliminary help of a glossary, there are perhaps too many native words in *Coonardoo*, by Katharine Susannah Prichard, for the ordinary reader's comfort. This novel . . . is a record of the speech and peculiarities of a vanishing people, the Australian aborigines; and the student of folk-lore will delight in the songs which Mrs. Prichard has collected and her first-hand description of the native ceremonies. The story is a vivid and moving study of the blacks in relation to the whites, and in particular of the lovely and faithful Coonardoo—whose name means "the well in the shadow"—playmate, lover, and devoted servant of Hugh Watt, and the mother of his only son. Mrs. Prichard has the trick of making her characters come alive; and the heroic, battling figure of Hugh's mother . . . is impressive in its strength. Hugh, too, is a human and lovable person, less fortunate in his wife, Molly, than in his mother. Molly, indeed, deserts him, with her five small daughters, after the hardships of the pioneer life have worn down her weak character, and he is left with Coonardoo to look after him, and Winni his half-breed son to delight his heart and his pride. But he never again takes the native woman whom he deeply loves, as his wife, and from this springs her tragedy and eventual ruin.

The story covers a long period of years; Phyllis, Hugh's eldest girl, grows up with her grandmother's spirit and love for the land, and comes back to Wytaliba to become almost a son to her father until the inevitable conquering young man appears, and she unwillingly recognizes her mate, and goes off with him to make her own life. Hugh's second loneliness is worse than the first, and he is half unconscious how much the mere presence of Coonardoo about the place makes up for everything else. The north-western life is pictured vividly in all its aspects and seasons with what seems to be an unexaggerated emphasis.

A review of "Coonardoo," in The Times Literary Supplement, *No. 1433, July 18, 1929, p. 574.*

JOHN CARTER

The name of Katharine Susannah Prichard must be added to the list of distinguished women who are writing of the inarticulate dark-skinned races of the world in their tragic contacts with the whites. Much as Julia Peterkin has revealed the "bluegum" negroes of the Carolinas in her *Green Thursday* and *Scarlet Sister Mary*, and as Sarah Gertrude Millin has studied the blacks of South Africa, so has Miss Prichard, in [*Coonardoo*], a moving story of Northwest Australia, added to the richness of English literature and to our sympathetic appreciation of those tragedies of the colored peoples of the earth which we conveniently term and forget as "problems."

Coonardoo was a native woman of the Gnarler tribe, settled at the Wytaliba cattle station in the arid ranching country of West Australia. She was, in the vernacular, an "abo," a "gin" and as such was fair prey for any white man who desired her. However, Mrs. Bessie Todd, owner of Wytaliba, had other plans for Coonardoo. She desired to train her to look after her son Hugh, heir to the great ranch. The poor little native girl is trapped between two loyalties: between her tribe—"she was theirs by blood and bone, and they were weaving her to the earth and themselves, through all her senses, appetites and instincts"—and her devotion to her white masters. . . .

So simple a story of docile beastlike devotion is of universal interest but is lacking in dramatic interest. The merit of [*Coonardoo*] lies less in the story or even in the characterization, which is regrettably uneven, than in the picture [Prichard] gives of the sun-parched desolate plains of Australia's wild west, with the camels, horses and cattle, the rare rains and the terrible droughts, the cockatoos and crested pigeons, and the strange aboriginal tribes dying of civilization as though it were a deadly disease, as perhaps it is.

The native customs, the corroborees and pink-eyes, the moppingarras or medicine-men, the cooboos lying in their scanty ginaginas, crowded in the uloos or dancing on the mulga,

singing bucklegarro songs to the chorus of "Poodinyooba mulbeena," here is an entirely new patois and another idiom, as distinctive and compelling as the wigwams, moccasins and papooses of North America or the Afro-American locutions of Uncle Remus. If one may make a criticism, it is that this new dialect is administered to the reader in strong doses, without a context which would make its meaning sufficiently clear and that hence it necessitates a glossary. The aboriginal lingo, moreover, suffers, as Dr. Traprock observed of the Polynesian, from vowel-complaint and is apt to strike the American ear as absurd.

In structure, the story of *Coonardoo* is a little incoherent. Time, in particular, flows at an uneven rate through its pages, and there is no especial point of reference which ties the tale to any era. The style, though congested with local idioms and unfamiliar locutions, is vigorous and straightforward.

The foreword assures us that things have changed for the better, that natives are often paid for the work they perform for their white masters and that "there has recently been a regulation to prevent white men taking rooms for a gin, or half-caste, in a hotel." Nevertheless, *Coonardoo* stands as a forceful piece of social documentation and bids fair to do for Australia what *Uncle Tom's Cabin* did for America and Mrs. Millin is doing for South Africa—to make the white race face the facts of its treatment and study of the black descendants of the aborigines, through an authentic piece of national literature which raises a parochial problem to the level of the universal.

John Carter, "In the Back Country of Australia," in The New York Times Book Review, *March 16, 1930, p. 7.*

HARRIET SAMPSON

There is an amazing honesty in [*Fay's Circus* (published in Great Britain as *Haxby's Circus: The Lightest, Brightest Little Show on Earth*)]. . . . The theatricality, the vagabondage, the hovering danger are there, but they are all in the day's work to Daniel Fay and his family. And [Prichard] respects these honest folk sufficiently to show them as they are—"tough and straight—and game as you make 'em."

This is really the story of Gina, the second daughter, a brilliant bareback rider, whose good nature and pluck led her to take upon herself too much of the drudgery of camp life. One hot evening her foot slipped and she fell to the sawdust, her back broken. Three months in a plaster cast at the hospital improved her native astuteness and taught her the fundamentals of hygiene. She emerged with the use of her legs (small consolation to one no longer a stunt rider) and with a slight deformity, sure to increase with hard work. Hard work was the only thing hereafter of which the Fay family thought her capable. There was a new baby, Lin, and Gina cared for and protected him as her own. When five years later she learned that there was to be another she earned enough money telling fortunes to take her mother to a hospital. On her return when she found that Lin, whom her father had insisted upon "working," although he was afraid of the trapeze, had been killed, she left the circus and supported herself by washing in a mining town. Here she kept her mother and baby sister for six years in comfort and tranquillity with the prospect of romance in the offing. But Lotty Fay missed the familiar life and when her husband discovered her, was ready to believe she ought to ask for forgiveness and help build up the disbanded circus. Gina again submerged herself in the show. There she stayed until by an unexpected legacy she made herself master and succeeded her father in authority. . . .

The story is Gina's, but the tradition and power that make Gina are her father's. Dan was a born showman, careless of everything but the success of the show, devoted to his children, but willing to risk their lives for a better spectacle, faithful to his wife, but incapable of imagining her needs. He permitted no cruelty to animals, no drinking or swearing on the lot. He kept his daughters secluded after public appearances. He could talk the crowd into amiability, even play the clown if advisable. He was unsparing of himself and his courage was magnificent. As an old man he entered the cage after a lion had mauled his keeper and commanded the beasts into submission, although his only experience had been a brief period years before with a toothless old Nero, too decrepit to snap at a rabbit.

Katharine Susannah Prichard has herself traveled with Wirth's, the famous circus of Australia. She knows intimately of what she writes, and it is easy to believe that she shares the gallantry of her characters.

> Harriet Sampson, "*Among the Circus Folk,*" *in* New York Herald Tribune Books, *April 12, 1931, p. 24.*

THE NEW YORK TIMES BOOK REVIEW

Novelists have found it fatally easy to surround the circus with an aura of false glamour. We have all heard a great deal—too much, in fact—about the lure of the big top and the nostalgic smell of sawdust. As for that long procession of broken-hearted clowns, it would be kinder not to mention them. Consequently, when *Red Wagon* appeared last season, Lady Eleanor Smith was rightly praised for achieving an authentic, unsentimentalized picture of circus life.

Much the same claim can be made for this book by Katharine Susannah Prichard [*Fay's Circus*]. . . . Even if one had not been told by an obliging publisher that Miss Prichard, bent on exactitude, travelled across Australia with Wirth's Circus, it would be obvious that she knows her material. She seems to be less saturated with the atmosphere of the ring than Lady Eleanor Smith, but she is no less conscientious in her details. Unfortunately, despite this praiseworthy realism, she has written a rather dull book. Reprehensible as the admission may be, it does not make nearly as good reading as the unabashedly romantic yarns of such a writer as William J. Locke.

Fay's was a small family circus which rattled across the Australian back country in shabby wagons. Dan Fay, to whom his show meant everything, raised his numerous children, from babyhood, to be performers. He drove them hard—so hard that he was partially responsible for the tragic accident which changed young Gina from a beautiful, gypsyish bareback rider into a drab cripple. After that accident she became a reproach to him, and a reminder to the other artists of the dangers they faced daily. Only Rocca, the sensitive dwarf, had any sympathy for her sufferings, and so great was his resentment on her behalf that he was obliged to leave the circus lest he actually murder Dan Fay.

The rest of the book follows the development of Gina. The death of a cherished little brother—this time undeniably caused by the willfulness of Dan—hardens her and wakens her from her hopeless lethargy. She practically kidnaps her own mother so that she may bear the newest baby in a hospital rather than in a jolting wagon. At Gina's insistence, they leave the circus and stay away for six years so that the child, Maxine, may grow up safe and strong. On their return, Gina helps to reorganize Fay's and battles resolutely with her father when he attempts to sacrifice his family to the god of his devotion, the show. . . .

There is, undoubtedly, good stuff in this long-winded story—good descriptions of circus routine, accurate accounts of the curious psychology of circus people. Why, then, is the effect so tedious? Partly because Gina is not really a very convincing or full-blooded character; partly because much of the novel reads like straight exposition; chiefly, perhaps, because Miss Prichard lacks some vital quality of imaginative lift. Her prose is adequate but not in any way distinguished. There is no magic in her writing, no exuberance. One feels that she is temperamentally not particularly suited to the kind of theme she has chosen.

> "*Circus Life,*" *in* The New York Times Book Review, *April 12, 1931, p. 7.*

M. BARNARD ELDERSHAW

In my critical analysis of Prichard's work I propose to discuss first its premises and second its style and matter. These premises I take to be in the order of my antithesis, individuality, idealism, socialism. (p.24)

[Prichard's] novels are definitely Australian. The great continent is a sort of presiding genius. The author strives to isolate its essence. In each novel she takes a phase of Australian life—the opal fields, the timber getters' camp, or station life in the far north-west. She is a specialist in background. Her local colour is no cosmetic. She has lived in the north-west, stayed in the opal fields and in the timber getters' camp, has even, I have been told, travelled with Wirth's Circus to get the right atmosphere for *Haxby's Circus*. She believes, as individualists must, that environment makes the man. So she builds her characters up from their environment. Her narratives and her characters are founded on their background and grow out of it as trees from the soil. . . . [Prichard's books draw their light] from the environment and circumstances in which her group finds itself. (p. 25)

Prichard, who is individualist, draws with a bold, often stark outline. She compresses and curtails. She is not portraying life or any universal conflict. She is telling a story that is localized and definite.

Since the Americans got at it one feels that it is necessary to strip the word 'idealism' of some of its associations before one uses it. To say that Katherine Susannah Prichard is essentially an idealist is not to accuse her of sentimentality or of the least trace of didacticism. No one is less of a sentimentalist. The world of her books is harsh and hard, but it is not hopeless. Underneath lies faith in the courage and steadfastness of man. Even in the most sombre of her books Coonardoo triumphs over the fate that overtakes her because, despite everything, she has kept the fidelity of her loving heart. Prichard's men and women . . . have qualities indestructible by anything that life can do to them. The brave are never wholly conquered; they still have their valour. Potch, Michael, Sophie, Deb, Coonardoo and Gina are each in their own way victorious, they transcend circumstance.

Each novel has its central idea, its core of idealism which shines through it and gives it poetry and unity. In *Black Opal* it is comradeship, in *Working Bullocks* it is fertility and staunch every-day courage. In *Coonardoo* it is fidelity and in *Haxby's Circus* courage again.

Comradeship is loyalty to the ideal of the brotherhood of man; fertility is loyalty to life and its purposes; fidelity is loyalty to an individuality, so that all Prichard's books are animated by the great individual virtue of courage and the great social virtue of loyalty. And both are the children of steadfastness, the strength and the will to set at least one thing above life and never, come what may, to let it go.

In calling socialism one of the premises of Prichard's work, I do not refer to her politics but to the social feeling that informs her books. Her men and women are gregarious, the stories are of their group rather than of their individual life. Each novel tells the story of people bound together by common work and common interests, the opal mines, timber getting, the circus. In no instance are her characters drawn at hazard from the professions and trades and bound together only in their emotional life. Her groups have the solidarity of occupation. They are grouped as in Soviet Russia according to trade. Work always has its place in her novels as it has in life. Her people are not allowed to escape the commonplace. Emotion is everywhere balanced by necessity. Her books display a sort of artistic preference to unionists.

The democratic tradition is strong in Australian letters. Prichard is carrying it on, but she is too great an artist to grind axes in the sight of her readers. Only in *Black Opal* does she enunciate a social theory. This book is the work of an avowed idealist and democrat and breathes a passionate insistence on individual rights. It paints a Utopia of common men in Fallen Star Ridge opal fields. The miners are poor, their life is hard, but they eat the bread of freedom. Armytage, who wishes to syndicate the mines and put the miners on a secure wage basis, is the villain. He symbolizes the capitalist world that would stifle freedom with plumbing fixtures and motor transport. Sophie's mother, dying, begs Michael to keep Sophie safe at the Ridge, and Sophie leaving it, though Michael has sacrificed his honour to prevent this great harm befalling her, finds success and heartsickness. The life of the miners at Fallen Star Ridge is painted as the good life. The rich Americans who take Sophie up for the sake of her beautiful voice are depraved tyrants of the poor. This is an idealism that ennobles the commonplace and extols the homely virtues of simple people. It is a little naïve and as an artist Prichard has travelled a long way since, but the same ideas, modified and matured, underlie all her books.

Having discussed the premises, I find I have but little to say about the style, so closely are the two woven together. (pp. 25-8)

[Prichard's novels] fall into a circle, *Haxby's Circus* marking a return to the kindliness of *Black Opal* after the harshness of *Working Bullocks* and the stark tragedy of *Coonardoo*.

Black Opal is a remarkable early novel. It has most of the characteristics of the later books but is much more transparent in its technique. It is all the more interesting for that, as it gives us the opportunity to observe the working of the author's gift before she achieved the artistry to hide it.

Sophie, the motherless daughter of a worthless father, has a beautiful singing voice. Armitage, an opal buyer, tempts her to leave the Ridge and become a singer. Michael Brady, who looks on Sophie as a sacred trust from her dead mother, steals and holds her father's opals so that she will not have the money to go away. Arthur Henty, a squatter's son whom Sophie loves,

has not the courage of his love, and Sophie, sick with disappointment, runs away with Armitage. She finds success but not happiness. She frets until she loses her voice and comes back, tired and broken, to the Ridge. She is received as a beloved prodigal and in the fidelity of Potch and the companionship of her own people finds happiness and her voice again.

Of the book's social idealism I have already spoken. It has a further ideal background in its symbolism. The opal symbolizes love, a force dark and bright, irrational and yet natural, that draws man from his orbit into follies not his own. Even the noble and selfless Michael feels the opal fever and stoops to an action that is not in his character. Sophie is like an opal. The comparison is insisted on. She has the power to draw men out of their orbits. She and the opals between them make something very like a thief out of Michael. Arthur is brought to his death.

Sophie is a troubler. (pp. 28-9)

[Sophie] is displayed to us with much care, taken slowly as it were like one of the opals from its wrappings and displayed in candlelight. We catch a glimpse of her first at her mother's funeral and then hear nothing more of her until the whole scene is laid. Then we are given the picture of Sophie, 'the girl in the black dress on the fine chestnut horse, the children with the flowers and the young man standing beside them.' I do not know of any other character in Prichard's books who is treated as tenderly and produced as carefully as Sophie. For Katharine Susannah Prichard scorns glamour and other adventitious aids. One feels that it is the love and beauty of which she is the symbol, not the fallible Sophie, on whom this care and tenderness, as of something precious, are lavished.

The characters in *Black Opal* are kindly drawn with a gentleness that we do not see again until *Haxby's Circus*. Even Armitage is more wrong-headed than bad, and Jun Johnson, the 'bad man,' is brought to naught.

Working Bullocks is a much more ruthless and less obviously poetic book. The poetry and the idealism are still there, but they are, as it were, driven into solution. The timber getters' life is hard and dangerous. Deb sees her two brothers killed by their work, Chris crushed by a heavy log as they haul the trees from the forest, Billy even more cruelly sacrificed, the machinery of the sawmills catching him and leaving him nothing but 'bloody pulp.'

The book is deeply embedded in life and in work. There are magnificent descriptions, close, circumstantial and living, of the felling and hauling of trees, of catching and branding the wild brumbies, and of breaking them to the saddle, Red working with 'loverly patience' to gentle them, of the sawing of timber at the mills, of milking cows and bottling jam. Everything is exact, concrete, circumstantial, even technical. That concreteness gives a solid basis of reality to the overshadowing sense of the unity of life which permeates the book. Through his work man is linked to life. He is part of a universal creation—the same life force works in him as in all other created things. (pp. 29-31)

In such a life love, too, is a primitive force. There is no place for pretty flirtations. Tessa's girlish wiles fall very flat. 'What was to be expected of a girl who made a bird's nest of her hair and powdered her face to look like the face of a corpse?' Red returned to his half-hearted wooing of her only because 'I got to let that cow Gaze know he can't go 'round clapping his brand over mine,' but he is disgusted by her flirtatiousness. (p. 31)

It is Deb who is his true physical mate and they come to their mating in the end as simply as the animals. Red had hoped to own his own bullocks again, but after all their striving Deb and her young husband can only begin where their parents began before them. There is no compensation for losses in that life. Life has not beaten them and it is only the outer shell of their happiness that has gone. There is no nicely finished end, no happy solution as in *Black Opal*.

In *Coonardoo* the background dwarfs the characters. In *Working Bullocks* Nature was an enemy to man but casual and unconscious. In *Coonardoo* there seems to be more than a trace of positive malevolence in the immensity and loneliness of the background. At the end of the book only the spark of Coonardoo's fidelity is left; all else is utterly stamped out. Man's cruelty is added to Nature's cruelty. The story is bare and simple, the prose bleak. It is significant that in this, the most tragic of her books, the story is more individual and less social than in any other. Hugh lacked courage and so he was ruined, and with him Coonardoo and the station and all. It is a negative epic of courage and a positive epic of fidelity. It represents in the cycle of Prichard's novels a sort of black winter of sorrow.

In *Haxby's Circus* the winter is over and we are back again among kindly people and kindly scenes. Tragedy is not lacking. Gina is crippled and receives all the burdens and little of the happiness of life. But she has the courage to conquer her circumstances and herself and at last, as Rocca did before her, to make of her deformity itself a means of self-expression. Although in no sense a sequence, the qualities of the earlier novels knit together in *Haxby's Circus*. The comradeship of *Black Opal* unites the circus folk; the vitality of *Working Bullocks,* the will to go on and to live without repining, is their backbone, too; the fidelity of Coonardoo, of Potch and of Michael, is in Gina.

Prichard has written three other books which stand a little outside this orbit. One is her first novel, *The Pioneers,* written in 1915, an obvious first book, and bearing little mark of the genius that was to flower later. It is a melodramatic story of a marriage bargain to save a father's life, of betrayal and death. It is interesting to us now, in the light of Katharine Susannah Prichard's later work, to find in it the first obscure traces of a feeling for the authentic flavour of the Australian bush, its challenge to the hardihood of man, and the symbolic quality she was to find in it. (pp. 32-3)

Another of these minor books is *Windlestraws,* written and set in London, which is not generally considered by critics to be in her best vein. The third is a book for, or at least about, children, *The Wild Oats of Han.*

More important than these is the volume of short stories published in 1932 under the title of one of the stories, *Kiss On The Lips.* The thirteen stories that make up the volume are both uneven and varied. . . . There is much that is fine and memorable in the collection. It would seem to be the slow distillation of years and to recognize fully the difficult and intricate art of the short story. There is nothing casual or haphazard about the stories. Each one is finely bred, made and shaped, sometimes to the point of artificiality, but always by the hand of an artist. They are etched, bitten into copper with acid, finished and permanent, hard, clear, distinct. There is understanding but no softness in them. Their subject-matter is what is, not what might be.

Each story is separate and stands on its own merits and yet there are strong links of unity making the book a whole. There is the author's style, which is so mature and so strongly individual as to give to each story a colour in common that outweighs differences of subject-matter, like a family likeness binding together individuals however divergent they may be on the surface. Behind this is the preoccupation with one theme which holds good for the majority of the stories. Lastly, they are all cut out of the same attitude of mind—poetic realism.

The style is terse and brilliant. The expression sometimes has a dramatic roughness and verisimilitude which is not naturalism but an aesthetic adaptation of natural rhythms. "The Curse," the most experimental in form of the stories, shows this quality most strikingly. The story of a man who, ruined by the noxious weed, Patterson's Curse, degenerated, took to petty thieving, and was sent to jail, is indicated rather than told in alternate passages of anonymous dialogue and of descriptions that read like *vers libre.* The whole is like a pattern on beaten metal. The descriptions have a sculptured lushness, as a fluency portrayed in stone; the dialogue is like a row of nails. (pp. 34-5)

There is a thrusting, economical truthfulness about all the descriptions in this book, but they have as well a brittle and artificial quality. They are always art as well as Nature. They compose, they are heightened, they have firmer edges than fluent Nature ever had. Here is a descriptive passage from the middle register.

> The tree grew, tall and spindling, in front of a house which shrank a little from the street, its windows dim in the shadow of those dark, oval leaves. The house held itself together, taking advantage of the tree, white moons of its bloom level with the balconies, but brackish soon, their fragrance of lemon blossom and musk failing, turning sour in the hot stale air, breath of a sick and filthy animal which came from the house: all the houses in Magnolia Street.
>
> ("Kiss On The Lips")

These descriptive passages are scattered through the narrative and the dialogue, always short and pointed, striking the note to which both narrative and dialogue conform. It is in the descriptive passages that the individuality of each tale is rooted. They give, with a strong sharp reality of their own, the tone to the work. No story is without a snatch at least of this quality. In one only, and that probably the weakest, "The Cow," there is a feeling of vagueness, relaxation, even flabbiness.

The theme with which so many of the stories are preoccupied, the book's second source of unity, is happiness. This on the surface may seem paradoxical, but it is true. Perhaps happiness is too paltry a word, but I can find no other to fit it better. The author conceives happiness as a mystery, the flowering of the spirit, the search for a spiritual well-being that has little to do with outward circumstance. Here the pursuit of happiness is shown in its negative as well as its positive phase, but it is there at the core of almost every story. In "The Grey Horse" it is glimpsed and lost, the achievement of the horse in his sphere is measured against the achievement of the man in his; the horse is fulfilled according to his nature, the man is unfulfilled. It is there that happiness is lost. This is repeated under another guise in the story "Happiness." Nardadu, the gin, plucking over the offal of a dead bullock, is happy. Her life has achieved its simple ends, content flowers in her and is beautiful. The long, complicated and exasperated quarrel between the sister and the wife at the station, life jangling from discontent to disaster, is a story which she apprehends but which passes over her head. She has found a comfortable place in life, they have not. **"Kiss On The Lips"** is a story of happiness—the good life—in an unlikely place. In the squalor of a slum Charley Nielsen achieved the impossible. 'There wasn't nobody ever like him, Charley. Tender and true . . . too good . . . he was, that's all . . . a kiss on the lips. . . .' His death could not destroy that, though life went on and in its routine and mediocrity half obliterated it. In **"White Kid Gloves"** there is a mystical flowering of happiness at the end. In **"The Cooboo'** a gin, with the realism of her simplicity, chooses the kind of happiness and fulfilment she wants, though it means the killing of her baby—a brief, telling, convincing story this. In **"The Cow"** a woman adjusts herself, finds a northwest passage between the needs of her nature and of her spirit. In **"Two Men,"** perhaps the subtlest of the stories, happiness is needlessly lost because two people are inarticulate, because both want to give and cannot understand the other's manner of giving. In **"An Encounter"** there is a delicately drawn picture of an old man who is happy, whose life has reached a balance. (pp. 36-8)

In **"Mrs. Jinny's Shroud"** there is, as in **"The Cooboo,"** the choice, the sifting out of happiness from everything else. Mrs. Jinny keeps it and throws away the rest. And so it goes on.

Of Katharine Prichard's poetic realism I have already said something in the discussion of her prose style and of the stilled and fashioned world she creates as background. It is there not only as a picture but as a symbol. She lends to what she describes a spiritual as well as a physical significance. She is too good an artist to use her symbols very obviously. Half the time the reader gathers no more than a fleeting sense of a deeper meaning. The desired impression is made on his mind without his knowing whence it comes. For instance, the magnolia tree in **"Kiss On The Lips"** is the symbol of Charley's life flowering in evil surroundings, its sweetness soon quenched. Whether this is explicitly realized or not makes little difference, it is part of the quality of the story, its bouquet. There is another tree in **"Dark Horse of Darran."**

> 'You never see anything like that tree outside Todd's store them dry years!' Steeped in his reminiscing, Jo was caught again by the vision of that blossoming tree in the dingy, sun-blasted little town. 'Covered all over with flowers . . . sort of weeping willow . . . white flowers tumblin' down into the street. And smellin' so as you'd look around to see if a flash Jane from the city was about.'

The acacia is not only a tree, it is the persistence of life even in the face of drought, it is a promise like the rainbow. **"The Grey Horse," "Mrs. Jinny's Shroud," "White Kid Gloves," "The Cow"** are each saturated in this kind of symbolism. They have a foot in each world. Poetry grows in realism as mysteriously as happiness in life. (pp. 39-40)

> *M. Barnard Eldershaw, "Two Women Novelists,"*
> *in his* Essays in Australian Fiction, *1938. Reprint by*
> *Books for Libraries Press, 1970, distributed by Arno*
> *Press, Inc., pp. 1-40.*

MUIR HOLBORN

It is our creative artists who are the true discoverers, who convert life from a mere grubbing for physical necessities into rich and meaningful experience. It is they who explore and re-explore our landscape and our people, show us what is to be cherished in our common life and make us credible to other nations. What would we be, for all our vaunted wool-cheques, our expanding secondary industries and our novel system of multi-gauge railways, had we no Lawson, Furphy, Paterson, Bernard O'Dowd or Katharine Prichard? These are the people, not the pastoralists nor even the Chambers of Commerce and Manufactures, who convince us that Australia and the Australians, despite all the contrary evidence that might be adduced from the seeming chaos of contemporary life, are more than worthy of our passionate love and fidelity.

And the influence of our writers, our true discoverers, is not limited to the pathetically small number who actually read their works. Their ideas, moods and images, bearing the impress of powerfully creative minds, and released from their imprisonment between the covers of books by all but the most solitary readers, permeate much more widely throughout the populace than is usually imagined.

Of all our contemporary discoverers, Katharine Susannah Prichard is probably the most widely travelled, geographically and intellectually. In a rhapsodical prose poem published in 1934 in the Magazine *Home* and beginning with the words 'It is true that I love every inch of Australia . . .' she describes in glowing prose the beauties which she has found in this country, from Cape Howe to Broome and from Cape York to the Leeuwin. Her affectionate pride in Australia and in all things Australian, whether they be commonplaces or unique and exotic, cannot fail to give direction, definition and significance to the reader's usually vague though genuine feelings of attachment to the land of his birth. (pp. 233-34)

In a long literary life extending over roughly thirty-five intensely active years, and encompassing the production of twelve novels, two volumes of short-stories, two of verse and a book of essays on life in the Soviet Union, Katharine Prichard has opened up vast tracts of Australia for literary visitation. Lawson and Furphy had dug deeply on small selections, Sydney, the Turon-Cudgegong goldfields, the Western plains, the Riverina. Katharine Prichard has moved from the coastal cities to the opal fields of Lightning Ridge, to the far North-West of Western Australia, to the karri forests of the South-West and the goldfields of Kalgoorlie and Boulder.

All these wanderings from place to place would be, of course, devoid of interest if they produced nothing more than travel jottings or semi-literary Baedekers, or if they had been adventitiously embarked upon in the search for marketable local colour. Despite a relative prolificacy, Katharine Prichard takes a serious view of the functions of the creative artist. She wrote years ago, in an article intended for the guidance of youthful authors: 'People should write only when they can't help writing; have something definite to say, some rage or vision of beauty they are bursting with, some knowledge or passion or a good joke to share with others and laugh over.' It is a dictum which reminds us of Auden's assertion that a good joke can be poetry. Even the powerful impulse is not enough; love and care must be present in the act of composition. Nettie Palmer wrote in the *Woman's Mirror* in 1927 that each of Katharine Prichard's books 'represented as much devotion as many writers would give to ten.'

The key to the variety of locale in her work may be found a little later in the article already quoted: 'I dream of a literature to grow up in this country which will have all the reactions to truth of a many-faceted mirror.' We cannot understand Australia if our knowledge of it is limited to a few streets in Sydney or Melbourne plus a vague, general concept to cover all the rest. We must have an appreciation of the intimate details which comprise the lives of all its peoples and localities; from these we can work towards a more valid idea of the whole. Katharine Prichard's works are a particularly notable and generous contribution towards this broader vision. H. M. Green has written that 'no novels or set of novels by any one author give a better idea of this country than those of Katharine Susannah Prichard'.

Her approach in all her major books, when beginning to write about a 'new' area (unlike that of some regional novelists who simply give an unusual, local setting to a story that might as well have happened in half a dozen places) is rather to reveal the threefold aspects of life—people and environment, with work as the nexus; for she is concerned to show how human character and behaviour are moulded by day to day surroundings and occupations. English novels so specialise in leisured characters or in exhibiting people during their moments of leisure, that practical-minded persons may be forgiven for wondering how anything serious ever manages to get done at all in the world of *fainéants* which they encompass. Those with a background of English fiction are, consequently, often struck by Katharine Prichard's detailed and brilliant presentations of human labour. 'Her interest in other people's jobs is only equalled by her devotion to her own,' Nettie Palmer writes, and it is well known that each of her novels dealing with a fresh terraine has been preceded by a long period of residence in the selected area and of participation in its daily life and effort.

The evidence of vivid, first-hand experience is manifest in all her major books. In *Coonardoo* all that goes to comprise the fabric of daily experience, the mustering, the branding, the rites and the song-making of the aborigines, is handled with a wealth of understanding. Nor, I would venture to suggest, have the details as well as the drama of life in the mines been anywhere presented with greater power and authenticity than in the early chapters of *Golden Miles,* the second volume in the goldfields trilogy.

Yet what is important is not the work as work, but its relationship to the rest of life. Background is quite as significant and the human response paramount over all. In *Working Bullocks* we feel the constant impersonal presence of the forest, neither sinister nor benign, cutting short the span of man's life and being in turn mastered by humanity, the mastery being achieved through the workers' devotion to the art and science of forestry, felling and hauling. It is hard to think of any English-speaking novelist in whose work is felt so constantly the struggle, the tension, the active relationship between man and nature, with man's arts, his physical and intellectual powers being developed and strengthened in the combat. . . . Katharine Prichard's chief characters will not acknowledge defeat even in the midst of desolation. They remain resolute in their faith and integrity. Coonardoo, shorn of all hope or consolation, is broken; she is one of the few genuinely tragic figures in our literature who reminds us no little of Hardy's Tess on the way to execution. 'Missus Sally,' the magnificent central figure of the goldfields trilogy, is likewise undefeated. War, struggle and the passing of the years have swept away her husband, her children, her friends; but, retaining her memories and her confidence in the Australian future, she has riches still.

Katharine Prichard is a realist within the main stream of Australian letters, a peculiarly dynamic realist. We are deceived if we imagine that her novels are solely concerned with giving

photographic accounts of the selected landscapes and their communities. (pp. 234-36)

[Prichard's trilogy of the Western Australian goldfields, comprising *The Roaring Nineties, Golden Miles,* and *Winged Seeds*], contains an enormous amount of information which the author has gained from years of conscientious and skilled research. . . . Katharine Prichard's purpose is (as novelist) to describe and (as poet) to draw us imaginatively into the teeming, complex life of the goldfields. She aims to cover a period of more than fifty years, and her method of revealing the relationship of people, work and environment is basically the same as that of all her major novels. Whereas many authors would focus attention upon the long and interesting development of the principal characters, merely sketching in a shadowy background, that is not Katharine Prichard's way. Characters, she feels, cannot be separated from their history and background, and these must be accurately revealed or not at all. What actually happens, when the trilogy is read in full, is that we find her people and her world so alive and so compelling that we are eager for all the information that we can get. Some of what is given has to be re-read and thought over. This slows up the action, undoubtedly, but it stimulates mental activity in a way thwarting to readers who have not mastered a somewhat primitive craving to discover 'what'll happen next'.

Too much of the data is perhaps conveyed through the conversation of old hands reminiscing, or ruminating aloud over the contents of newspapers and official reports. We would prefer, particularly in reading the final volume, to be at the centre of things, rather than among the spectators or those summing up after the event. Yet the Western Australian story has been so eventful that it is difficult to see how the field could have been otherwise covered in a work of reasonable proportions. And to those who would ask, 'Why cover it anyway?' we can only answer, 'Because the resulting work of literature heightens our understanding and appreciation of Australia and the Australian character.' It is hardly true however that the author intrudes unduly with personal comment, a device momentarily out of vogue but once favoured by more notable authors than one has here space to mention.

For those acquainted at first hand with the Western Australian goldfields, or through the work of writers from 'Dryblower' Murphy and 'Prospect lood' Ophel to Jules Raeside and Gavin Casey, there can be no doubting the veracity and strength of Katharine Prichard's account. The intense privations of desert-pioneering, the growth of Kalgoorlie and Boulder from typhus- and dysentery-ridden shanty towns to modern cities, the predatory attacks of the large mining companies upon the privileges of the alluvial prospectors—all are drawn with remarkable power; while into this rich fabric are woven the lives of characters such as Sally Gough and Dinny Quinn, whose endurance, sanity and good humour are remarkable in an era of fiction in which the positive characters are usually so upstaged by neurotics, rapists, sadistic spivs and tortured professors, that we feel embarrassment in the presence of a novel in which useful, kindly and intelligent people are predominant.

Yet perhaps the most signal achievement of *The Roaring Nineties* and its successors lies in their revelation of poetry in a terraine which the most unenterprising prospector might be forgiven for dismissing as unpromising.

Throughout all the author's principal works we find persisting in manifold forms a governing belief that is here elaborated into a poetic truth from which the whole work springs and draws its strength. This belief is, in essence, that beauty is not an exotic luxury to be sought in remote places and cultivated under hot-house conditions; and that poetry, which involves the perception and communication of beauty, is not an activity which can only proceed satisfactorily in studies or boudoirs or upon romantic crags. Beauty and poetry are present throughout the natural and human worlds—they are immanent in deserts and withering climates and among poor and humdrum people. They thrive wherever there is mateship, love, pity, struggle in the cause of human ideals.

This theory, which has affinities with one of the less studied branches of Wordsworth's philosophy of life and letters, has become so important to Katharine Prichard's outlook that the whole trilogy is a symbolic expression of it. As beneath the remorseless sun and 'sterile sierras' of Kalgoorlie we can win, if we have the will and understanding, riches of gold; so in the everyday lives of her mining community, we can hit upon beauty, provided that our love of humanity is such that we are not initially repelled by indifferent exteriors or by attitudes and beliefs in conflict with our own.

The trilogy is full of symbolism of this kind, quietly and subtly employed, such as the winged seeds of the Kalgoorluh nut breaking over the grave of the aboriginal woman, the last of the goldfields tribe: a message of youth and strength, of life eternally renewing itself in spite of all frustration and suffering.

The poetry is not found in this use of symbolism only, nor in isolated felicities of style; it is apparent in the form, the carefully wrought history, the skilful repetition of particular themes which add a further dimension to the main events. The reappearances of the aborigines, once numerous, virile and robust, who dwindle away as Kalgoorlie swells to a city of trams and municipal gardens, provide not only an intense poignancy, but a silent and powerfully ironic commentary upon the smash-and-grab methods and mentality of the invaders.

The trilogy may be regarded as the culmination of Katharine Prichard's work to date. It lacks the literary compactness and the tragic intensity which set *Coonardoo* high in the ranks of world fiction. Yet it is perhaps her most representative work, vast in compass, rich in incident and character, a criticism of all that is ruthless, corrupt and degrading in contemporary life, but radiant with a passionate love and hope for working humanity: the courageous answer of an intrepid and highly creative mind to the challenge of material, brutally intractable.

The three goldfields books are particularly valuable today, not only for their discovery of new territory, but as a fresh affirmative of our basic tradition which, as has often been stated in recent years, is realistic in method, democratic in temper, and spiritually buoyant. There is room for books of other kinds, experimental, introspective or veering to fantasy; but our indigenous tradition, while wholesome and vital, is also unique to this country, is *us*, and deserves study and preservation. (pp. 238-40)

> *Muir Holborn, "Katharine Susannah Prichard," in*
> Meanjin, Vol. X, No. 3, September, 1951, pp. 233-40.

G. A. WILKES

"I dream of a literature to grow up in this country which will have all the reactions to truth of a many-faceted mirror. People should only write when they can't help writing; have something definite to say, some rage, or vision of beauty they are bursting with . . . Strindberg says: 'Put the truth on paper, and you have

Art'." This declaration, made in the year of publication of *Coonardoo,* almost defines the singularity of Katharine Susannah Prichard among Australian novelists. If not the first to insist on the use of Australian material as the only foundation for a national literature, she has now become the foremost of that school, the novelist who has striven most consistently to make the continent articulate through her writing. The claim would be justified not only by the "coverage" of Katharine Prichard's novels, but also by the power and the starkness that her representation has achieved—by no one else has this theory of a national literature been so ruthlessly applied.

Yet to look back now on her earliest work is to realise how slowly Miss Prichard formed her purposes and awakened to her individuality. [Written in 1908 but not published until 1928, her] first book, *The Wild Oats of Han,* was a sympathetic story of her Tasmanian childhood: though it retains a certain appeal for its delicacy and tenderness—qualities too rarely encountered in her writing afterwards—no one could have predicted from it what the author's later development would be. *Windlestraws*, a romance with a Russian prince for its hero and the convention of imposture as the mainstay of its plot, was such a novel as any other freelance journalist might have written in London before the first war, under the necessity of supporting life by his pen. The adroitness of the plotting shows that Katharine Prichard at this time could do well enough, if she chose, what was not worth doing. [Written after *Windlestraws* but published before it, her] third novel, *The Pioneers,* winning the Australian section of the Hodder and Stoughton Dominions Competition in 1915, is a sad commentary on the standard of the other entries. Although in a sense *The Pioneers* discloses the general theme of all the books that follow it, the novel itself rather belies its title, for the pioneering phase of the story soon passes into a treatment of settled community life in Gippsland—Han now reappearing as Deirdre. The use of intrigue to sustain the structure—Mary Cameron's secret, the plots of McNab to ensnare Davey and Conal, the convict past of the Schoolmaster and Steve—is also foreign to the later work.

The first novel in which Miss Prichard seems to find her feet is *Black Opal* (1921). This initiates the series of books that draw their strength from the environment against which the story is projected—in this instance the opal-mining community of Fallen Star Ridge. And the history of Michael Brady, Sophie Rouminof, Arthur Henty and Potch is now used by Miss Prichard as the vehicle of a further theme: the conflict of the system of individual ownership of mines on the Ridge with the system of company exploitation Armitage wishes to introduce, putting the independent miners on a wage and increasing the output of the field. The exoneration of Michael from Heathfield's charges is presented both as a personal triumph for him and as a vindication of "the law and ideals of the Ridge" against Armitage's capitalist project.

The author of *Black Opal* clearly possesses social sympathies which had not been entertained by the author of *The Pioneers.* Her attitude to the industrial question hints at one article of the later creed, while her attitude to life as it is lived on the Ridge suggests another. The value set on the life of the Ridge is emphasized when Sophie returns to Fallen Star in a revulsion from the emptiness of high society in the United States, to which her operatic success has won her admission. Towards the end of the book Sophie confides to Potch some advice given her by an American negro:

> "One thing he said has always stayed in my
> mind: 'Keep close to the earth!' It was not

good, he said, to walk on asphalted paths too long . . .''

"Keep close to the earth?" Potch mused.

"In tune with the fundamentals, all the great things of loving and working—our eyes on the stars."

In the novels that follow *Black Opal*, Katharine Prichard tries to work out this principle in fiction.

While, in characterization and psychological range, *Black Opal* makes little advance on *The Pioneers*, it does present one relationship of some interest. This is the attraction of Sophie to Arthur Henty, the subtle chemistry that seems to draw her helplessly to him, in spite of her decision to marry Potch. The crisis comes when, at the ball at Warria, the two go outside into the darkness. "There was no hesitancy, no moment of consideration. As two waves meeting in mid-ocean fall to each other, they met, and were lost in the oblivion of a close embrace . . . He murmured into her hair, and then from her lips again took a full draught of her being, lingeringly, as though he would drain its last essence." Though Miss Prichard is here still using the conventions (and the language) of the romantic novel, there is a sense of a more elemental feeling breaking through that framework. It is most nearly defined when, after Henty's suicide, the Ridge folk ponder on "how different both their lives would have been if Sophie and Arthur had been true to the natural impulse of their lives, that instinct of the mate for the mate."

Black Opal is developmentally significant, yet as Katharine Prichard's third novel it could have done little more at the time than confirm the mediocrity of her talent. The sudden achievement of mature power and assurance is reserved to *Working Bullocks* (1926) and its successor *Coonardoo* (1929)—with these two books Miss Prichard reaches her full stature. Discarding involution of plot, she now leaves the novel to be sustained by the native force of its theme. *Working Bullocks*, set in the giant karri forests of Western Australia, is informed by the most sensitive apprehension of environment in all Katharine Prichard's work. It is not the gauntness of Australian scenery that is reflected here, but its primitive beauty and colour. (pp. 220-22)

A critic who applied to *Working Bullocks* the new American technique of analysing the imagery of novels as well as of poetry would find that in the early chapters the images are all of fecundity, vigour, and burgeoning growth. The leaves of the saplings have "ruddy and amber sap in their budding tips", the tree Deb admires at Lalganup siding is "robust and growing to its prime", and the arm with which Red grips his whip, "sleeve torn from it, bare to the arm-pits, red and brown with sunburn, glint of fire in the hair on it, muscles and sinews strung out, flung its challenge." This quality in the imagery (an index to the temper of the whole book) intimates that Katharine Prichard has now discovered her special terrain as a writer—the cult of the primitive.

Indeed, *Working Bullocks* could be summed up as a study of those who "keep close to the earth . . . in tune with the fundamentals, all the great things of loving and working." The philosophy is reflected in the exact description of activities like the yarding and breaking of brumbies or the hauling of logs by the bullock team, as also in the splendid physical exertion of Neil Hansen at the wood-chop or of Red Burke exultantly pitting his strength against the Marri in flood. Sometimes the

emphasis is less on the activity itself than on the deep satisfaction the character draws from it. . . . (pp. 222-23)

This "cult of the primitive" has more important consequences, perhaps, in the psychology of *Working Bullocks*. Entering into a fuller possession of her powers, Katharine Prichard develops a new awareness of the submerged workings of impulse and instinct—of the undercurrents that move blindly below the surface of ordinary consciousness. The "instinct of the mate for the mate" that had irresistibly drawn together Sophie and Arthur in *Black Opal* is now developed in the relationship of Red Burke and Deb Colburn, in the elemental sympathy that flows between them. The new primitivism may be felt—to name only one episode—on the occasion when Red, drowsing in the forest at noon, with Deb asleep at an arm's-length from him, first awakes to his feeling for her: in the breathlessness of the forest, the sun drenching both their bodies, his senses draw him into the rhythm of nature itself, until he seems to hear the sap flowing in the trees.

To seek to communicate experiences of this order is to run the hazard of artistic insecurity. Miss Prichard does not always seem alert to the risks. The parallel maintained in *Working Bullocks* between the relationship of Red Burke and Deb and the mating of the chestnut stallion can lead to such writing as this:

> He was a brumby, Red told himself . . . He remembered the Boss and the way he had gone to his mate, and she had stood to him, tremulous, eyes dilated, squealing with delight as he bit her flanks.
>
> He would take his mate like that when he wanted her, Red told himself . . . he would bite her flanks and she would spring to his passion, cry with delight as he held her. And she would be a woman like this girl, strong, with animal instincts, undaunted.

Although Katharine Prichard is writing quite earnestly, it is hard to suppress the smile as one reads.

If *Coonardoo: The Well in the Shadow* (1929) attains a higher level than *Working Bullocks*, it may be because here the effort to "keep close to the earth" is absorbed into the novel in a more artistic way. The description of the arid climate of the north-west, the drought-stricken plains and withered trees, and of the strenuous work of mustering and branding on a cattle-station, is necessary for showing the conditions by which the psychological development is partly determined, while the account of aboriginal ceremonies that weave Coonardoo to her race by her senses, appetites and instincts is basic to an understanding of her behavior in the later stages of the story. The more likely reason for the superiority of the second book to the first, however, is that the tragedy of Coonardoo is a finer vehicle for a novel than the history of Red, Deb Colburn and Tessa Connolly could ever have provided.

As *Coonardoo* has never lacked for praise, one may perhaps turn from "adjectival commendation" to one or two problems arising from it. This novel certainly shows that, as Katharine Prichard has become more conscious of her individuality as a writer, so has her code of values become more decided. It was plain in *Working Bullocks* that a woman like Deb Colburn, in tune with the fundamentals of working and loving, is more admirable to Miss Prichard than a woman like Tessa Connolly, with her fluffy hair, her cosmetics, and her appealing ways;

just as the virile Red Burke is more worthy of regard than Leslie de Gaze, the remittance man of aristocratic pretentions, with a penchant for gentleman-farming. This discrimination persists into *Coonardoo*, until we become aware of an unconscious standard by which Miss Prichard is measuring her characters—especially her women characters. Mrs Bessie, who accepts the hardships of Wytaliba and works the station on her own, bears the stamp of the author's regard; on the other hand Jessica Haywood, whom Hugh brings from the city to visit Wytaliba as his future wife, is viewed with some animus. Constantly described as "a slight pretty creature", "very delicate and blossomy", she is made to dress in "a white frock sprigged with little flowers" and sit at the piano singing sentimental songs, and when Hugh escorts her about the stockyards, she "stepped daintily beside him in a white muslin frock and white shoes, holding a pink silk sunshade over her head"—the persecution is never relaxed. Miss Prichard's code of values is beginning to produce bias—possibly unconscioius bias—in her portraiture.

Again, the presentation of elemental behavior in *Coonardoo*, despite the raw power it lends to the novel, occasionally seems to oversimplify the motivation. The relationship of Billy Gale to Phyllis is unsatisfactory in this way: her marriage to him from primitive compulsion ("I've got to. Out here, you can't live alone. You can't live on yourself") leaves one with the misgiving that the problem is really more complex than Miss Prichard's solution of it suggests. To be a little more querulous, the episode when Hugh "takes" Coonardoo is not entirely convincing: as he watches her from the other side of the campfire, "deep inexplicable currents of his being flowed towards her . . . Awakened, she came to kneel beside him, her eyes the fathomless shining of a well in the shadows. Hugh took her in his arms, and gave himself to the spirit which drew him, from a great distance it seemed, to the common source which was his life and Coonardoo's." But what of the "boy with a swag of ideals", as Mrs Bessie has recently described him; what of Hugh's own determination to disprove Geary's taunt? Miss Prichard is oversimplifying the issues. When we come to Coonardoo's surrender to Geary ("male to her female, she could not resist him. Her need of him was as great as the dry earth's for rain") it is hard to resist the feeling that the novelist now has a formula that can dispose of awkward problems in motivation. The feeling is strengthened by the manner of May Hallinan's capitulation in *Brumby Innes*, the play written in 1927.

But *Working Bullocks* and *Coonardoo* together mark the first peak in Katharine Prichard's development, a peak given greater salience by the declivity of *Haxby's Circus* (1930), which followed. The coda to this achievement is the volume *The Earth Lover and other Verses* (1932), where in such poems as "Lips of my Love" and "Love Philtre" the erotic strain of *Working Bullocks* and *Coonardoo* finds a clearer and more sensitive expression, and in ["The Earth Lover"] the personal creed by which the two novels are sustained is explicitly stated:

Let me lie close to the earth,
Battened against the broad breast
Which brings all things to being. . .
For I am an earth child,
An earth lover,
And I ask no more than to be,
Of the earth, earthy,
And to mingle again with the divine dust.

The decade following the appearance of *Haxby's Circus* is a period of transition in Katharine Prichard's career. *Kiss on the Lips*, the volume of short stories, appeared in 1932, and then came the trip to Soviet Russia which led to a renewed output of the social pamphlets begun with *The New Order* in 1919: *The Real Russia, Who Wants War?*, *Marx, the Man and his Work*. From this transitional period emerged two novels, *Intimate Strangers* (1937) and *Moon of Desire* (1941). The second, dealing with pearling at Broome, leaves a fainter impression than the first, which does add materially to the work of the previous phase.

With *Intimate Strangers*, something of the delicacy of Katharine Prichard's verse filters through her prose. This novel, in the setting of a summer holiday by Calatta beach, is a study in disenchantment. Greg and Elodie Blackwood, after some years of marriage, have reached the point of wondering whether there is now anything steadfast and inviolable in their relationship, or whether it has become no more than a domestic arrangement: to each other, they have become intimate strangers. Elodie's subconscious regret is that marriage has meant the sacrifice of her music, while Greg is exasperated by his wife's ability to withdraw her mind from him so that her thinking becomes an enigma—a withdrawal he tries angrily to conquer by physical possession. (pp. 223-26)

Intimate Strangers is unlike anything else Katharine Prichard has written. Much more of the action is passed through the minds of the characters than elsewhere, and in exploring the relationship of husband and wife, she seems to have come to value events (to adopt Conrad's formula) not for themselves, but for "their effect on the persons in the tale." The situation is held still while Miss Prichard contrives occasions for analysing it: Greg's infatuation for the beauty of Dirk Hartog, which represents "every man's grasping after an idealisic illusion"; the tolerance of this feeling by Elodie, which annoys him more; and especially Elodie's attraction to Jerome Hartog, the uncanny affinity between them offering her "an invitation to rebirth." As she traces the ebb and flow of their relationship, Katharine Prichard exhibits a control of indirection and nuance unparalleled elsewhere in her writing—she is working now in the "finer vibrations" of experience. (p. 227)

The years between *Haxby's Circus* (1930) and *Moon of Desire* (1941) are an interval of diffusion and uncertainty in Katharine Prichard's development. The return to sustained endeavour comes with *The Roaring Nineties* (1946). The genesis of the goldfields trilogy is to be sought first in the social pamphlets of the thirties, which supply the determining philosophy, and second in the collection *Potch and Colour* (1944). The short stories assembled here deal chiefly with the goldfields of Coolgardie and its environs, and are based on the reminiscences of the old prospectors: "authentic fragments of the life of our people— yarns that have been told to me, for the most part in the mining districts and wheat-growing areas of Western Australia." The trilogy itself comes from a more thorough working of the same lode, combined with strenuous research. . . . (pp. 227-28)

Miss Prichard has herself acknowledged the dual purpose of the series by confessing that "in this story of the goldfields of Western Australia, I have tried to tell, not only something of the lives of several people, but to give also the story of an industry." It may be said at once that the second objective is more successfully achieved than the first. Katharine Prichard has always needed some framework in her novels against which the human story may be developed, and *The Roaring Nineties* manifests again her ability to give the very feel and texture of living in conditions removed from city life, and her flair (in dealing with such institutions as "the roll-up", for instance) for bringing out the underlying principles on which such a mode of living is based. The picture of the prospecting days in *The Roaring Nineties* passes into the era of company management in *Golden Miles* (1948), and the third volume, *Winged Seeds* (1950) carries the narrative from the Depression to the end of the second World War. The whole history of the fields is given, from the early struggle for alluvial rights and the "wild-cat" schemes of the first speculators to the mechanization of the mines, the fight for collective bargaining, the traffic in stolen gold—the epigraph to the last volume is eloquent with hope for the future.

The aim of giving "the story of an industry" may have been realized, then, but what of the aim to tell "something of the lives of several people"? From this standpoint, the trilogy is a monument of lost opportunities. The portraiture is all done by *assumption*. Miss Prichard assumes that the characters are as well known to the reader as they are to herself from the outset, and that he also shares her attitude to them. Dinny Quin and Sally Gough are fully-developed characters from the moment they enter the story: after that, we simply observe their repeated appearances. In observing, we are of course meant to admire—in the author's estimation, these two are the really sterling figures in the book. Looking for the attributes which her approval has led us to expect, we find she has not displayed them—she has displayed her admiration instead. Unless a special value is to be set on the feminine capacity for cooking, dishwashing, scrubbing and carrying water, Sally must be pronounced an unremarkable person, while Dinny Quin emerges as a much less emphatic personality than Frisco Joe Murphy. The minor figures fare even worse than the principals. There are a score of people whose names are repeated from page to page, while they themselves do not develop, or even live—rarely have a novelist's obligations to her characters been so signally neglected.

Perhaps the worst form of this neglect is Miss Prichard's peremptory treatment of the mental and emotional life of her people. Whenever a problem of motivation demands analysis (as when Morris foresakes Sally on the Lake Darlot rush) it is brushed aside; whenever a relationship requires probing further (like the affinity of Sally and Frisco) the exploration is declined. The characters are simply passed from one situation to another, any treatment of emotion that is required being left to the method of *assertion*. Morris pauses to kiss Sally as they trek to a new field, and we are told "It was a delirious moment." When no delirium is communicated, the bare statement is useless. Yet this now becomes Katharine Prichard's constant resort. Later Sally is "swept by a desire to throw everything to the winds and go away with Frisco"; she suffers "anguish" at the outbreak of war; on receiving news of Lal's death "her mind whirled crazily in her rage and grief"—the author is content to *tell* what happened, instead of showing it actually happening. She is not above notifying developments that have not occurred, as when after Lal's death it is suddenly reported that he was always Morris's favourite son, or when after the death of Marie Robillard we learn that "Marie had understood her best of all." It is by these methods that such psychological force as the trilogy possesses is steadily drained away.

As the narrative wears on, it also becomes manifest that, beyond the two purposes Miss Prichard has professed in the chronicle, lies a third that eclipses them both. From her treatment of the issue of alluvial rights, the struggle for trade union

principles, and the war against "fascism" it is clear that she is writing not merely the story of an industry, but a chapter in the history of the Australian democratic crusade. The goldfields saga is a novel *à thèse*.

Of itself this need cause no alarm, as the thesis novel—witness Irwin Shaw's *The Troubled Air*—is not by definition a failure. But Katharine Prichard's earlier attempts in this line do not inspire confidence. In *Black Opal* she had romanticized Michael Brady as "the little father, the knight without fear and without stain, of the Ridge"; in *Working Bullocks* she had fallen into the same error with Mark Smith, and had contrived a spurious mill strike so that he might air his socialist doctrines; and in *Intimate Strangers* the entry of Greg and Elodie into the working-class cause all but made nonsense of the book. The interesting thing is that in none of these experiments had Miss Prichard shown any awareness that the thesis novel is one of the most delicate and exacting of art-forms. When she comes to write a trilogy on the principle, she is like an infant playing with blocks.

It is bewildering that so experienced a novelist should prose so intolerably about conscription, profiteering, and trade unionism without taking care to embody the issues in the psychological processes of the action, making them the conditions under which these processes are worked out. In *Golden Miles* and *Winged Seeds*, Miss Prichard treats all the technical hazards of the novel *à thèse* as though they did not exist, and repeatedly the thesis breaks loose from the novel and acquires a life of its own. The cudgel that the author wields in the second volume becomes a sledgehammer in the third, as for page upon page she explains the issues at stake in the Spanish Civil War, the true nature of the Russo-German Pact, and the vital importance of the battle of Stalingrad. As these issues are forced into the dialogue, it turns into a kind of basketball, and Dinny Quin comes to unite the worst features of the armchair strategist and the club bore. It must surely be an axiom of the thesis novel that the reader cannot be interested in the "further implications" of the action unless the action itself is satisfactory to him: it is only by fulfilling this first condition of his art that the novelist may fulfil any others. *Golden Miles* and *Winged Seeds*, failing of their purpose at this primary level, fail inevitably at the secondary levels also.

The goldfields trilogy is indeed an embarrassment to the admirer of Katharine Prichard. It is possible to commend the chronicle for its huge dimensions, or for the labour that has gone to its making—but these are non-literary judgments. To commend it as reportage is a possible solution: to the objection that this is to damn with faint praise, the reply must be that if the trilogy were to be judged by purely literary standards, it would have to be damned irretrievably. It seems preferable to base Miss Prichard's reputation on those portions of her work that are best qualified to sustain it—*Working Bullocks, Coonardoo,* and *Intimate Strangers*. (pp. 228-31)

> G. A. Wilkes, "The Novels of Katharine Susannah Prichard," in Southerly, Vol. 14, No. 4, 1953, pp. 220-31.

JACK LINDSAY

[In Katharine Susannah Prichard's first published novel], *The Pioneers,* we meet her bias to a broad canvas and a realistic representation of the world of work; but it is with *Black Opal* that she grows more assured in method and reveals her originality, the lines in which her definition of the Australian scene is to develop. From the outset she is deeply interested in the problems of the commonfolk, in their struggles to make themselves at home in the Australian earth. But that interest alone would not have necessarily turned her into a great writer. Her specific contribution appears in the scope of her vision, her way of thinking and feeling always in terms of the group. And for her the group is always the productive group: men and women united concretely in labour-process. It is the concreteness of the situation that absorbs and kindles her. And this means that, with all her group-focus, she does not belittle or underestimate individuality. For, in the naked and simple relations of the concrete labour-process, a man is shown for what he is, for what he is truly worth, without any chance of appealing to adventitious aids or disguises.

But the values of the concrete labour-process can plainly and powerfully pervade a group or a community only in its pioneering stages, before the forces of the cash-nexus have effectively invaded the scene. Once that invasion occurs, the situation becomes highly complex; labour-power itself becomes a thing bought and sold, and the clear relationships of men working together in definite ways for definite goals are obscured. K.S.P. in her work has set herself the problem of defining the pioneering group in its early phases when the man-to-man relationships still substantially rule, and life, however crude and difficult, is operated on generally understood bases. She has then to go on and depict the pangs of change as the rule of money comes in, gradually and violently upsetting and perverting the original systems. In doing so, she has to show further how the element of comradeship, obvious and dominant in the early phases, is not destroyed despite the distortions, but reasserts itself in new forms, which slowly become adequate to the changed situation and finally threaten the values of the cash-nexus.

I do not mean that she started off fully-equipped with this purpose in mind. What she aimed at was a representation of the pioneering community which she loved and respected. But, step by step, she has been forced into the struggle to understand the nature and significance of the forces perverting the community of brotherly work, and to find out where the conflict between the comradeship and the cash-nexus is leading. Thus, her political conclusions have not been imposed upon her material, but have organically grown through the depth and force of her penetration into the human situation.

In *Black Opal,* which tells the story of a community of opal-miners in New South Wales, we see how she derives from the work of Lawson and the others who directly expressed the mateship of pioneering days and who had also reacted against the money-rule that was breaking down the man-to-man values. What is new in her work is the way in which she brings to bear on the situation a steady and comprehensive view of conflict and development. She shows in detail how the simple systems of goodfellowship, coöperation, and trust, which sufficed an industry in its first stages, cannot stand up against the impact of big business and the world-market. There is no hope for the old pattern of individual initiative expressed in partnerships of two or three men and involving the coexistence of an indefinite number of small units of production. K.S.P. then has to show the break-up of the pioneering spirit of damn-all independence and the painful emergence of new forms of collective resistance to the State and to Monopoly. At the same time she is aware that the creation of the new forms is no easy matter and that the old modes of thought can inhibit as well as help the new forms forward. The stubborn individualism of the pioneer, which works harmoniously with the concept of mateship, can find wily ways of accommodating itself to the world of the cash-nexus as well as opposing that world with its need to level the mass of workers inside the wage-system.

That is how K.S.P. comes to see the situation and its problems as she goes on grappling with it. But in *Black Opal* she is as yet only dimly aware of the complexity and confusion that evolve with the active intrusion of large scale capital. In a note, written in 1946, she remarks:

> The miners' struggle to maintain control of their industry indicated a trend of thought which has broadened and developed. Primitive methods sufficient for mining opal cannot be applied effectively to coal and gold mines, requiring mass production and mechanisation, and therefore control in the interests of the nation. Michael Brady [the novel's hero] would be the first to say that men of the Ridge are behind scientific progress in industrial organisation which has that objective.

This is a rather heavy way of putting the fact that the opal-miners think they can maintain the values and methods of small-production despite the manifest demonstration of the impossibility of so doing—and that the author at this time shares their illusions. But it is precisely because she has so thoroughly entered into their world and taken into herself the pioneering values that she develops in her creative method and outlook the great dynamic force which is to carry her on. Her mood here is indeed rather on the anarchist level, profoundly suspicious of everything whatever connected with the State and with Law, and finding its solutions in the direct democracy of the small group who can hold mass-meetings to make their own decisions and declare their own law. Again, this is no weakness. It is because K.S.P. feels with every fibre of her being the values and virtues of this direct democracy that she has an unfailing touchstone as she adventures into the more veiled and entangled world of capitalised industry.

She has a total sympathy with the rough tough workers and is able to define them in all the vivid variety of their strong and often gnarled characters. She enters into their world with a loving acceptance, which does not need to call on the least idealisation or falsification. The goodness of a community nakedly based on concrete labour-process is such, she knows, that that goodness will come through all the limitations and crudities of circumstance. The bad characters stand inevitably out as the exceptions, the flouters of the common bond. At the same time two negative aspects are important. The cultural level of the community is sure to be low, since the struggle to keep alive and carry on is overwhelming; outside the world of work the interests are narrow and there is a down-dragging circuit of confined activities. And inside many members there are present the unpleasant qualities, temporarily held down or limited by the common bond, which will emerge more actively with the inroads of the cash-nexus. . . . The problem of developing such a community beyond its pioneering levels without loss of its finest elements is acute; and this difficulty is expressed in the way the author presents the character of Michael, a studious withdrawn person, a great reader, the only miner with knowledge and ability to give leadership in large issues. The gap between Michael and his mates is a genuine reflection of the weakness in the situation, but it also brings out certain weaknesses in the author herself. The ordeal that Michael undergoes through suspicion of theft from a mate symbolises the ordeal of the community under the attack of the cash-nexus—an attack carried out by American big-business, the form of economic organisation about as far removed from that of the Ridge as could be. His triumphant clearing links with the new unity of the group under the stress of the attack. But the symbolism is not effectively related. Michael's victory reaffirms the old mateship, but does not carry it onto a higher level.

A similar confusion or weakness appears in the story of Sophie whom Michael has brought up and who goes off with the son of the main American buyer. She has ambitions to become a great singer, but in the end is disillusioned by the American social scene and returns to marry the humble miner Potch. Here the novel wavers on sentimentality. We see that it is no longer sufficient to oppose the values of the uncorrupted work-community to those of the sophisticated money-world. To persist in such a position leads to a sentimental Rousseauism. The elements of such a position in *Black Opal* run counter to the realistic depiction of the mining community both in its general bearings and in its individual members.

Michael is shown as a man marked and apart; and this tendency to oppose politics and life as irreconcilables—at least at any level beyond that of the simple direct democracy of the pioneering community—carries on to a certain extent through K.S.P.'s work. There is no such cleavage at the pioneering level; the immediate reactions to injustice and crime, expressed by the mass-meeting, are not felt as something separate from the ordinary run of life, as political protests or activities. They are the spontaneous forms by which the work-community protects itself from alien intrusions and irritations. But once the forms of direct democracy are rendered impossible by the intrusion of the State as guardian of the cash-nexus, politics and life lose their unconscious unity. If there is to be an effective resistance to the disruptive forces, a thought-out strategy and a knowledge of history, of the economic set-up and the socialist goal, is required. Only a few persons are ready to make the effort to acquire the new knowledge and to devote themselves to the difficult and often crushing struggle. Hence the gap between the Michaels and the mass of workers. But it is a gap that must be steadily broken down if progress is to be achieved. In *Black Opal* it is presented as a fact, but without any attempt to bring out the problems it raises.

Here however K.S.P. has started off on the trail that leads to the trilogy. Indeed many other problems and relationships, which keep reappearing in her work, are already present. Sophie with her ambitions as a singer anticipates Elodie of *Intimate Strangers* and Violet of *The Roaring Nineties*. Further, the questions she raises have their links with the characterisation of Sally and Laura, women who, used to much more civilised conditions, settle down in different ways to the crude pioneering world. Michael in his relations with Mrs. Ruminoff is a sketch of Tom in his relations with Nadya Owen. K.S.P.'s way of returning to certain images and relationships throughout her work is not, however, a sign of poverty of imagination and craftsmanship. On the contrary, it derives from her dogged resolve to get ever more inside those images and relationships which from the outset have struck her as profoundly typical and significant of the scene she is seeking to understand.

In *Black Opal* we may then say that a new stage of the Australian novel has been reached. K.S.P. builds on the levels already consolidated, carrying on both their main strengths and some of their weaknesses. At the heart of the whole picture is the deep binding sense of mateship born out of community of work under pioneering conditions. The weaknesses appear as a strain of sentimentality, a belief that the old forms of mateship can be sustained in a nostalgic way without an all-out effort to realise what they are up against and how they are being sapped in a situation of strong capitalist penetration. The strengths include the warm and intimate portraits of the miners in all the oddities and humours born from their hard way of life. But what gives artistic unity and force is the insight whereby the various characters and episodes are brought together in a comprehensive concept of the community of work. The loose and yet powerful link between individual oddity and communal spirit is richly realised; and we see the author already grasping the way in which concrete labour-process involves a vital relationship to nature. Nature is both landscape and inscape, a friend and a foe, pervading all human experience and at the same time pervaded by human hopes and fear; it never is a mere background, something vaguely added-in now and then. In *Black Opal* many of these positive qualities are still slight in comparison with the developments to be made in later novels, but they are sufficiently present for us to claim that the work raises the Australian novel to a new level and clears the ground for a fuller expansion of its themes.

In her next two books K.S.P. triumphantly carries on the promise of *Black Opal*. *Working Bullocks* deals with the timber-getters of the West. Here the novel does not base its tale on a compact group such as the opal-miners of the Ridge; but the theme of the community of work is still central. An effect of massive simplicity is gained, which depends on the simple and yet profound conception of the book, and on the direct and yet subtly heightened style. There is the unity of a lyrical poem, a love-poem; and at the same time this lyrical outburst is controlled and given weight by the merging in a single focus of sexual emotion, the energies of work, and the omnipresent sense of union with nature. The story is straightforward, simple. Red Burke falls in love with Deb Colburn, and in the end she comes to him despite her mother's opposition. Obstacles have to be surmounted. Chris, Deb's brother, has been killed while working with Red, and Red has been entangled with another girl, Tessa; but from the start we know that nothing can hold the pair apart. The extraordinary compact weight of the book comes on the one hand from the very ordinariness of the material and on the other hand from the new depth given to that material, the richness of perspective developed out of the dynamic unity of the fundamental elements I have indicated. Hence the classical quality that the book possesses. All is inevitable; we feel that we are touching the pure essences; all is deeply moving and fresh. New dimensions open on the common scene.

It has often been remarked that K.S.P. is both a realistic and a poetic writer; but how this fusion of opposed qualities has been brought about has not been analysed. The key, it cannot be overstressed, lies in her understanding of labour-process. Her realism does not halt at a down-to-earth clarity and an often merciless precision. . . . K.S.P. shows her commonfolk in all the grime and the constricting pressures of their environment; she endows them with no virtues that do not spring from their hardy, adventurous, yet extremely limited way of life. If there were no other factors in her representations, the result would be a pedestrian and documentary record. But other factors are strongly present as a leaven; and these, which saturate her realistic account with poetic values, derive from her grasp of the social essence of work. In the pioneering conditions both the individual contribution and the social essence are plain, understood intuitively by the workers themselves and gathered without contradiction in the philosophy of mateship. But the social essence includes more than the cooperative and communal elements in thought and feeling which go to make up that philosophy. It involves also the living relationship to nature, the ultimate unity of labour-process and natural process. And it is by her deep comprehension of all this that K.S.P. achieves her full artistic force, her human richness, her transformation of realism into poetry. She is enabled to make working companions of a sober matter-of-fact statement and a lyrical impetus. For a further point emerging from her dialectical triad of people-work-nature is that she sees sex also in its social essence: the most intense flowering of the individual body, but a flowering which in the last resort gains its mysterious richness from the labour-process that unites men dynamically with nature.

In *Working Bullocks* she steps at a stride into her full kingdom. The various elements of her new synthesis are present in *Black Opal*, but often in tentative and uncertain forms, and still in some degree tied down to more conventional systems of thought and feeling. Now all her hesitations go and every trace of sentimentality is burned out. The result is the classical solidity, the fine relation of parts to whole, the simplicity born of a deep and sure realisation of her theme at all its levels.

Early in the book, before the explicit comparison is drawn, we are made to feel that the timber-men are also 'working bullocks', and that, as such, they are both vitally merged with the world of work and nature, and yet submerged by exploitation so that they must struggle to regain their humanity. In their bullock-status they still hold the potentiality of enhanced human values, so that the conflict is between their bullock-selves and the humanity struggling to be born out of them and looking beyond the world of alienating exploitations. This inner struggle of theirs is one with their struggle against the economic and political factors that stupefy and hold them down. At the same time men must fight to hold their own in the dangerous world of nature as well as to keep alive in the crushing world of the cash-nexus, and so a duality enters into their relationship to nature. On the one hand is their aggressive impulse to master and conquer it; on the other hand is an impulse of love and fellowship. The image of the first impulse is one of violence and war; that of the second is one of wooing and mating. This dual aspect of the relation to nature is subtly brought out by K.S.P.'s treatment of the love-affair. Deb herself is imaged as a young tree.... The whole of this chapter is of the first importance for the understanding of K.S.P.'s method. The inner conflict of men poised between impulses of aggression and needs of harmony is expressed by the mixture of tenderness and violence in Red's reverie over the young tree which is Deb. (pp. 367-75)

With *Coonardoo* (1929), K.S.P. expands her method and brings in the aborigines. The story, set in the deserts and cattle-country of the northwest, is more extended than that of *Working Bullocks* and cannot be expected to maintain the latter work's strong simple proportions; but in dealing with a long period of time and with changing relationships among its characters, it preserves the same foursquare solidity and certainty of aim. Here the unit is the station where Hugh and the aboriginal girl Coonardoo grow up together; and it is the aborigines in general who bear the brunt of exploitation. It is on them that the dehumanised and dehumanising forces of the world press most fully and cruelly; but in the process the dominant whites are themselves distorted and dragged down by the powers they wield. The relationship of the two groups is expressed by the relationship between Hugh and Coonardoo. What could have been a union of inspiring love becomes a frustrated and tragic connection, which brings both of them down. Even that which is good in Hugh is poisoned and turned into a destructive thing, as his daughter Phyllis realises. 'Just a good ordinary little man who's tried to make a Galahad of himself. And his repressions have rotted in him.' The aborigines retain an element of true humanity, despite all the corruptive pressures, for they still retain much of their old tribal attitudes and relationships; but the whites are distorted deep within by their position of power. (pp. 376-77)

The aborigines have been in part demoralised by the effects of the whites upon them: as is expressed here by Coonardoo's helpless surrender to the vicious Geary, which brings Hugh's wrath upon her. But there survives in them the human solidarity which the whites have lost. They cling to their tribal unity, despite the way in which the whites have broken it without putting anything adequate in its place, and they preserve largely intact their sense of a harmonious union with nature. Their culture is thus essentially richer than that of the whites. The rejection and final demoralisation of Coonardoo through Hugh's false 'pride', his whole complex of false ideas about the necessary relations of white and aboriginal, is in effect the expression of the loss of all natural harmony by the whites: their loss of the brotherly communion of work and its unity with natural process. (p. 377)

As in dealing with the workers, K.S.P. depicts the aborigines with complete realism; and for the same reasons as with the workers, she irradiates them with her poetry, using the threefold focus of personal character, work, and relation to nature.

Now come two works which have many virtues, but lack the sustained penetrating power of *Working Bullocks* and *Coonardoo*. No doubt K.S.P. was to some extent marking time and extending her techniques, in preparation for another large adventure. *Haxby's Circus* (1930) deals with a show wandering over much of eastern Australia. K.S.P. has mastered the details of the circus and brings out the charm and squalor of the feckless nomadic life. Haxby, a generous hearty hard-living man, who can be callously mean and cruel to his family in his devotion to the show, is well drawn. Gina, his daughter, has been crippled in the ring, and fights him in the name of her mother and her brothers and sisters. But she cannot escape the spell and ends by using her crippled form in order to give the show the clown that it needs. The symbolism does not quite come off.... She has saved her personal hurt; she accepts the cruel and uncomprehending laughter of the spectators; she has overcome tragedy by seeing and feeling in her own fate the grotesquerie and absurdity of human life. This may be an existential solution for herself; but in the sense that *Working Bullocks* and *Coonardoo* would give to the term 'the order and harmony of the world', the circus holds up a mirror only to some aspects of reality, not to the whole. Still, as a parable of the artist's acceptance of tragedy and absurdity, there is force in *Haxby's Circus,* even if not the unity of multiple levels that gives such depth to the preceding two novels.

Intimate Strangers appeared ten years later. Between had come the depression of the 'thirties, the rise of fascism, the returning threat of war; and K.S.P. had visited the Soviet Union. She wants to bring home the ominous condition of the world and turns from the pioneering wilds to the tamer world of the contemporary urban middle-class. As in *Haxby's Circus*, there are many virtues, and, for different reasons, a certain incompleteness. For once K.S.P. fails to achieve a structure capable of expressing her ideas. The main part of the book deals with the slow breakdown of Elodie's marriage and her falling in love with the adventurer Jerome. But underlying this is the theme of middle-class frustration and the discovery of what is wrong with the world; which implies the discovery also of the working-class as the sole force able to break through the impasse. Elodie gives Jerome up and finds a new basis for living with Greg through their shared discoveries. . . . But Elodie has been shown arriving at this idea through the experiences of Greg and the girl Dirk rather than through her own; and the developments of Greg and Dirk are not treated at length as her love-emotions are. They come into the story episodically and tangentially. There is thus a failure to bring about a full fusion of the theme of a breaking-up middle-age marriage and that of deep social pressures making for frustration and dead-end, of which Elodie and Greg are almost wholly unconscious at the outset. The struggle for socialism is represented by the fisherman Maretti, for whom the upper-class girl Dirk, long unawakened, at last discovers her love. And here again we feel the socialist viewpoint as something strange, almost foreign and exotic, set over against normal Australian life. Elodie, like Sophie, is a musician who gives up her career for domestic reasons. Greg too is an artist who has failed to find himself, forcing himself into an uneasy niche in the money-earning world. Whereas Sophie's return to the Ridge expressed, however sentimentally, a rejection of the corrupted culture of the cash-nexus, here in *Intimate Strangers* the failure of the art-impulse in Elodie and Greg is not clearly correlated to the wider issues. In a general way one feels that their middle-class system of living has broken their dreams of finding their individual outlets of self-expression; but whereas Greg's breakdown is linked with his loss of a job and the economic depression, Elodie's romantic dreams of escape are treated rather in their own terms, simply as a matter of englamoured emotion, and she stays on with Greg out of compassion, not out of a shared awakening to the return of their world. Still, there is a brilliant evocation of the seaside scene; and all the elements of a powerful work are present, even if some are implied rather than developed out.

But whatever cavillings there may be about these last two works, no one can deny that K.S.P. gets into her full creative stride with the trilogy. The mass of material which she has here sifted and controlled must have taken long to gather, partly drawn from documentary sources, partly from the tales and traditions of the miners themselves. The three books—*The Roaring Nineties* (1946), *Golden Miles* (1948), *Winged Seeds* (1950)—constitute a single narrative, centred on Sally Gough, and must be considered as such, though each work has a difference in form and method, which links with the difference in material, in the stage reached by the mining industry. In the first novel we have the prospecting and pioneering stage; in the second, the stage where large scale capital has taken over and the miner sinks from free prospector and alluvial-worker to wage-slave; in the third, the stage where capital has definitely triumphed and the miners are proletarians—though the old dreams of independence can still be stimulated by memories like that of the Larkinville rush. The second stage is broken by the first World War; the third by the second World War. Each war is shown as the culmination of factors which the working-class, if sufficiently militant, could have controlled and defeated. The War-breaks are thus no extraneous irruptions; they are bound up with the economic and political problems directly hitting the miners—especially as gold plays so important a rôle in international capitalism. As a result, in the second and third books of the trilogy the international relations of the Australian

gold-mines play an increasing part. While local events and problems keep the main limelight of the story, they are more and more linked with world-issues; and this fact determines much of the changing methods and perspectives brought into play.

There is a vast gallery of convincing and warmly-realised miners; but continuity and clarity are assured through the key rôle played by Sally and the persons most closely connected with her—her luckless aristocratic husband, her children and grandchildren, the stalwart Dinny, the swashbuckling unscrupulous Frisco, the wholly-corrupted Paddy Cavan. The deploying of the enormous mass of material so that a clear pattern is kept, is itself a literary feat of a high order. The work is a social history, a record of the mines, and an epical novel. Inevitably there are points where the first two aspects threaten to swamp the third; but, taken as a whole, the plan comes off. The story of the mines is told in human terms. The endlessly crisscrossing lines of narrative fall into an easily recognisable pattern, so that a clear significance and an impression of swarming complexity are simultaneously conveyed.

The Roaring Nineties is the most artistically satisfying section. For here K.S.P. deals with the pioneering world she knows and loves so well: the phase when concrete labour-process dominates the scene and the cash-nexus plays a minimal part. Her triadic movement of people-work-nature is able to express itself with a magnificent fullness; and because she feels so entirely at home, she controls the intricate design of comings and goings, prospecting and rushes, failures and successes, without the least fall into confusion. Sally stands at the centre, growing in stature, and yet presented without any undue attention to her problems which would distract the reader from the bustling changing scene. We are given the story of Sally, but at the same time, because of K.S.P.'s unifying focus, we are given the story of the gold-mines. The gold-mining is not the background to Sally's life; the dialectical triad of people-work-nature ensure that the old manipulations of 'private life' against a back-canvas, a social setting or landscape, simply have no relevance to the creative method.

With *Golden Miles* a new problem comes to the forefront: that which has been showing up in embryonic forms in Matthew, Mark, and Tony Maretti of previous novels. How is one to bridge the development from independent pioneer to proletarian, from intuitive revolt based on mateship to organized resistance based on trade-union brotherhood? The novelist needs to show the transition from one way of life to another which is in many ways its opposite; to show the difficult pangs of consciousness involved by the change, the new forms of organisation required, the new kind of leadership. National and international elements which the pioneer could safely ignore must now be taken into consideration; the complex of relationships in which everyone is entangled grows infinitely larger; the play of external forces on each individual grows vaguer, yet more hard to defy and resist.

K.S.P. shows the new strains and stresses mainly through the development of Sally's children and grandchildren. Dinny is one of the old miners who develop a fighting proletarian outlook; but it is in Sally's son Tom that we are made to see the slow and often painful growth of a revolutionary consciousness. Strongly affected by the inspiriting example of Nadya, he becomes a sturdy fighter for socialism. Sally's divided state, between Tom's uncompromising views and the more conservative position of her husband, helps to keep the struggle of ideas tethered to common life and to bring out the confusions and resistances which are generated.

There are still many hangovers from the past among the miners. The passion of the fight for alluvial rights in the latter part of *The Roaring Nineties* has shown how the men still see themselves as pioneers able to stand outside the capitalist net which in fact has long snared them. And now the widespread practice of gold-stealing from the mines persists as a form of protest against the net. Here the individual lawless protest plays into the hands of the most corrupt side of capitalist enterprise; and in her handling of this aspect of the situation K.S.P. goes to the heart of the complicated process whereby the rebellious miner, chasing a mirage of independence, is forced into the pattern of the cash-nexus. (In the pioneering days the mad dream of wealth is purged by the actual hardships and endurances, the bitter manual work; but in itself it nourishes all that is most anti-social at the heart of the work-community with its mateship. What K.S.P. depicts is the working-out of this extreme contradiction and its resolution in the fight for socialism.) The problem for Tom and his fellows is to transform the aimless resentment expressed in the thefts into a conscious effort to regain spiritual independence, self-initiative, and fraternity on a new level, without the inner contradiction that betrays and rends.

K.S.P. integrates the general aspects with the tale of the Gough family through Paddy Cavan's scheme to get his own back on Sally's son Dick, of whom he is jealous, by planting gold in the house. But the more purely political side of things, especially that connected with international affairs, is often dealt with through discussion; and though the arguments are always in character, they are a poor substitute for the full working-out of a theme in action. In part the use of discussion stems from the need to introduce a number of aspects of gold, international connections, which would take an inordinate amount of space if dramatised out. But we feel also that the author is not as easily at home in the trade-union sphere, in the world of the proletariat, as she is in the world of pioneers. The social relationships have in many respects become stretched thin; abstract labour (in Marx's sense) has clamped down over concrete labour; the alienating process has considerably advanced. It is no longer possible to show the triadic movement of people-work-nature in the dynamic and poetic method that organises *Working Bullocks, Coonardoo,* and *The Roaring Nineties.*

The thinning-down of the close texture and of the countless converging factors of action is in part inevitable. But it does mean that the family-chronicle and the march-of-history begin to some extent to be opposed, rather to be seen as different facets of the same process. The crowding-in of political issues which do not arise immediately from the milieu of the Goughs and their friends means that many matters are not fully digested, dramatised out, presented with the full impact of inner and outer tensions. To take one example: the gold-planting in *Golden Miles* is developed as an exciting and significant episode, seen throughout in terms of character-conflict and yet symbolising the historical situation; in *Winged Seeds* a few lines only are given to the period of communist illegality early in the second World War, when Sally again has to hide things and is almost involved in much trouble through a comrade in panic dumping a printing-machine in her grounds.

All events indeed in such a long and complicated story cannot be told at length, with a full working-out of tensions and effects; but the above comparison does point to a certain fullness and solidity in the earlier part of the trilogy, which is lacking in the later part. And yet such a comment is not altogether valid; for it fails to take into consideration the changing method of the narrative as time goes on. The sort of event that is extremely important at one phase is something taken without much fuss and bother at another. In *Winged Seeds* K.S.P. is dealing with the least resilient and active period of her miners. She is concerned largely with the growth of Bill, Sally's grandson, as a political fighter, and with the break-up of Cavan, now Sir Paddy. The two aspects are brought together by the love of Bill and Pat, Cavan's stepdaughter; and Pat and her sister Pam are used to bring in a direct impact of world events, such as the Spanish Civil War. Despite Cavan, the girls have come through their intellectual interests to share in the anti-fascist enthusiasms of the 'thirties. As Cavan represents the most corrupted aspect of pioneering days which has now merged with the finance-connections of gold in the international sphere, the girls represent the anti-fascist movement stirring the generous youth of the world. The three of them thus provide the links that educe the wider meaning of Bill's struggle and the way in which Australian gold-production plays an important part in the capitalist world-economy. Without displacing the Goughs from the centre of the picture, the girls and Cavan determine the general perspective of *Winged Seeds* and the angle from which many of the problems are approached. Thus, the more that one considers the structure of each book of the trilogy, the more one finds that the artistic method and the psychological focus are closely related to the social stage which is being defined. Each book has its own character, determined by the inner structure of the gold-mining industry and its world-connections; and apart from minor criticisms one must admit that the tone, perspective, and structure of each book alter effectively in accordance with the general plan. The deeper changes in people are conveyed by the changes in artistic method and focus. Thus K.S.P. is able to express both the gradual changes and the sudden expansions into new levels, to seize the subtle variations of tone, the new unity of outlooks, which come about at moments of decisive change in the experiences, the ways of life of individuals and groups. (pp. 378-84)

I have not dealt with the short stories, which have been gathered into three collections: *Kiss on the Lips* (1932), *Potch and Colour* (1944), *N'Goola* (1959). Though some are merely slight sketches or anecdotal jottings, a large number show the author's finest qualities, her mingled feeling for people, work and nature. At their best they have the same classical quality, the lyrical force and weight, of *Working Bullocks*. In one sense they show the rough material that has gone to the making of her novels, but in another they are satisfying art-works in themselves, compressed as a folktale that generations of tale-tellers have worn down to its essentials, casual as an anecdote told in a pub or round the campfire. At times we get in pure form the poetic quality I have attempted to analyse, as in **"The Cow"** or **"The Curse"**. But K.S.P. is essentially a worker in big patterns. She needs space in order to obtain her fullest and most characteristic effects. (p. 385)

[Prichard] builds on the Australian tradition, on the best elements that have come out of the expressions of the pioneering days; but she adds a massiveness, a consciousness of interrelations, a breadth of conception, which are all her own and which have lifted the Australian Novel to a new level. . . . Because of her clear and solidly-based grasp of the part played by the labour-process in human life, she achieved an essentially Marxist approach long before she could have heard the name of Marx or known anything of his work; and indeed I have the feeling that she has fought her way through to an understanding of all that Marx meant by alienation and the struggle against it, without any theoretical aids from outside. From the outset her creative intuition grasped the unity of the life-process, the function of concrete labour, the living relationship with nature which is of the essence of human freedom. It seems to me that she learned her direct political comprehensions from Marxism, especially as to the forms of economic and political struggle necessary for the overcoming of the contradictions and distortions of class-society; but her creative grasp of all that is humanly implied by the struggle for freedom and brotherhood is entirely her own. Her work can in no sense be described as an intelligent application of Marxism; only in its lesser aspects could that description be used. Rather it is a creative development of the Marxist concepts of what humanises and what alienates, born out of an artist's deep sympathy for, and understanding of, her fellow men. Such a development could only occur in a country like Australia, at the time of K.S.P.'s early years of growth and maturing, for only in such a country would it be possible to observe and live through the rapid change from a pioneering man-to-man world into a world of capitalist monopoly. And thus it is that her work becomes an important contribution to world-literature as well as to the literature of her homeland.

There are obvious affinities with the best of Soviet work; but as I have said, K.S.P.'s development is independent and has virtues all its own. I am most reminded in some ways of Sholokhov, who has epical breadth and the same sort of feeling for the unity of human and natural process. But his work, dealing with the Russian Civil War or its aftermaths, has a dramatic quality which we cannot expect in the slow unrolling of an industry's history over more than half a century. K.S.P. is capable of dramatic writing with tragic tensions, as above all the latter part of *Coonardoo* shows, but in many ways the lyrical compactness of *Working Bullocks* is more characteristic of her bent. Where necessary she can bring considerable analytic powers to bear on her theme, but she is above all an integrative writer, with her main strength deriving from her deep feeling for natural harmonies. Because of that deep feeling of hers, she had been able to tackle the task of exploring all that breaks the harmonies, and thus to build her largescale pictures of extended struggle, ordeal, and endurance. Her fusion of realism and lyricism works out as enabling her to sustain a lyrically integrative vision over long spans of individual and social experience. Her realism ensures that she will keep closely in touch with the actual contours of life, the actual levels of development among the commonfolk; her lyricism ensures that she will accept for her criterion no compromises, no half-measures—nothing but the truly good life where men are fulfilled in love and work, and are in harmony with the earth from which they have sprung. (pp. 385-87)

> *Jack Lindsay, "The Novels of Katharine Susannah Prichard," in* Meanjin, *Vol. XX, No. 4, 1961, pp. 366-87.*

CHERRY WILDER GRIMM

If we judge by the career of Katharine Susannah Prichard, the novelist committed to communism or its ideals in Australia must wage an extraordinary fight between the demands of art and those of propaganda. Her true, native yet specialised talent has been poured out for more than half a century in the service of her ideals, her country and the cause of world peace. The themes and qualities which remain most constant in her work have been subject to the greatest changes in critical esteem.

Her simple gravity is as unfashionable as her nationalism, her politics or her romantic interpretation of sex and nature.

Many critics, hypnotised perhaps by those literary prizes, insist that her work is overpraised. It is left to Marxist writers such as Jack Lindsay to give a coherent, percipient, tightly-knit appreciation of her work [see excerpt above]. That this account is as specious as any other piece of special pleading is beside the point: Katharine Susannah Prichard, by temperament, by the political and intellectual climate of Australia, by the nature of her adherents, has been urged further and further left. Her creative imagination and technical ability have been unable to keep pace with the rising tide of her convictions. Her work has culminated in *Subtle Flame,* a long novel, which has been several years in preparation.

The story concerns David Evans, editor of a Melbourne newspaper. After the death of his son in Korea he is impelled to throw up his job and work for world peace. He goes among the people, questioning, exhorting and learning a simpler way of life. He is sustained by friendship with other peace workers, helped by a tough girl journalist, despised—and rejected—by other editors, beaten up by policemen and half-killed by a mob of hecklers. He regains his health with the aid of the young communist girl he has grown to love, and the novel ends on a note of hope and tranquillity.

Embedded in the narrative, sometimes as dialogues or meditation, there are many passages of pure dogma. The reader comes up against revelations concerning the Korean War, the description of printing processes, considerations of the essential goodness of humanity, homilies on atomic warfare and the joyful description of a peace conference. These passages are not well integrated. They have the air of set pieces, often tendentious and over-bearing in tone or full of that proletarian delight in approved activities which inspired Russian novels on such themes as "How We Built the Pipeline through the Urals". In the context of the present novel even the most timeless reminders—on the futility of war, for instance—have lost all power to persuade.

Balanced against this mass of material the actual narrative might still have compelled attention, but it does not. The flimsy characterisation, the loose, scanning time-schedule, the superficial emotionalism, above all the continual infelicities of style: the vintage clichés and vintage slang, mark out *Subtle Flame* not as an unsuccessful novel or a minor work, but as a book quite monstrously bad; the final debacle in a notable career.

The author's greatest affinity is with the far reaches of Australia: landscapes and ways of life distant now in time as well as in space. The present urban setting has proved a defeat. We can only look back to those distant landscapes, the solid and sometimes beautiful achievements of her past, bearing in mind that as Australians we create, and destroy, our own novelists.

> *Cherry Wilder Grimm, "Partial Eclipses?" in* Australian Book Review, *Vol. 6, No. 11, September, 1967, p. 175.*

DEREK WHITELOCK

[In *Subtle Flame,* few of Prichard's] characters are credible, least of all Evans, her dreary Quixote. His change of heart overnight from peppy editor of a popular newspaper to down-and-out for peace is hurriedly described and inadequately explained. He is no more than a creaking transmitter of Miss

Prichard's opinions. [The young communist girl] Sharn, emoting over violets when she is not incompetently rehashing Bertrand Russell, is but dogma on two legs. As for Miss Prichard's villains, men like Bagshaw, "professional soldier, British trained, Indian Army, north west frontier and all that", are ludicrous caricatures. Occasional flights of vintage Prichard prose, one or two moving or exciting passages, struggle for life like wild flowers in a rubble heap of propaganda.

This is not to say that Miss Prichard's message is unimportant, or to deny the courageous originality she has shown, at her age, in writing a long novel to protest about the madness of the arms race. An Orwellian satirical bite, some Dickensian humour, might have made all the difference, might have allowed Miss Prichard to proselytize with effect among the multitudes she is so desperately trying to reach: but she is numbingly earnest throughout. Again, a personal statement from a writer of her stature might have had a considerable impact. As it is, the unappealing character drawing, love interest and dialogue seem intrusive, like clowns performing at a sermon.

If *Subtle Flame* concentrates, to an embarrassing degree, Miss Prichard's faults as a writer, the anthology of her short stories, chosen by herself under the title of *Happiness*, show her at her exultant best. Selected from her three previously published volumes of short stories, *Kiss on the Lips* (1932), *Potch and Colour* (1944), and *N'Goola* (1959), they reveal Miss Prichard at the height of her powers, through the literary medium perhaps most stimulating to her wry, eccentric, potent talent. (pp. 297-98)

Here is the taut, tragic perfection of "The Cooboo", probably the finest Australian short story. "His Dog", which shows Lawson, at his drollest, a clean pair of literary heels, "The Cow", "The Curse", "Painted Finches", "The Siren of Sandy Gap", goldfield stories like "Luck" and "Jimble", "The Grey Horse", "Happiness" itself, a minor *Coonardoo*, eighteen all told, and every one of these brilliant sprints is worth a dozen toiling marathons like *Subtle Flame*. . . .

These beautifully-controlled stories are quick with the power, the lyricism, the deep compassion and the sense of place which distinguish Katharine Susannah Prichard's finest work. (p. 298)

> *Derek Whitelock, "Happy and Unhappy," in South-
> erly, Vol. 27, No. 4, 1967, pp. 296-98.*

Mordecai Richler

1931-

Canadian novelist, essayist, scriptwriter, journalist, critic, short story writer, editor, and author of children's books.

Among the most prominent figures in contemporary Canadian literature, Richler is best known for his darkly humorous novels in which he examines such topics as Canadian society, Jewish culture, the adverse effects of materialism, and relationships between individuals of different backgrounds. Richler left Canada at the age of twenty and lived in Europe for more than twenty years; he usually sets his fiction in the Jewish section of Montreal, where he was raised, or in European locales. The typical Richler protagonist is an alienated, morally disillusioned individual who finds inner stability and self-knowledge difficult to attain. As G. David Sheps observed, Richler's heroes "insist that salvation lies only in the adoption of personal values, but they are not sure which personal values to hold." Although Richler is sometimes faulted for excessive vulgarity and for being overly judgmental of both Canadian nationalism and Jewish culture, he is widely praised for his outrageous sense of humor and his skill at blending realism and satire.

Richler's first novel, *The Acrobats* (1954), is devoid of the humor of his later works. Set in post-World War II Spain, this book recounts the experiences of a young Canadian expatriate. Naim Kattan commented: "*The Acrobats* is in itself a mediocre novel, but, though it has all the pretentiousness and all the imperfections of a beginner's work, it reveals qualities which could equally well be those of a clever craftsman or those of a true writer." Richler's next two novels, *Son of a Smaller Hero* (1955) and *A Choice of Enemies* (1957), evidence a progression toward a more satirically humorous tone. In *Son of a Smaller Hero*, Richler recreates the Jewish community of his childhood and chronicles Noah Adler's attempts to liberate himself from the religious, economic, and familial pressures of his past. As the novel ends, Noah departs for Europe, still searching for his identity. Richler's stark, unsympathetic depiction of Jewish culture in this novel drew charges of anti-Semitism, a reaction also provoked by much of his subsequent work. *A Choice of Enemies* focuses on Norman Price, who, like many of Richler's protagonists, is faced with a moral dilemma. Living in London with a group of American and Canadian expatriate artists, Norman must ally himself either with his bohemian friends or with a young communist whom the expatriates reject. Norman eventually realizes that both options are undesirable.

The Apprenticeship of Duddy Kravitz (1959) established Richler as a major literary figure and humorist. Frequently compared in theme and plot to Budd Schulberg's *What Makes Sammy Run?*, this novel chronicles Duddy Kravitz's rise from Montreal ghetto-dweller to prominent landowner. Although Duddy is driven by greed and his means of acquiring land are ruthless and exploitative, Richler depicts the surrounding society as equally immoral. John Ower asserted: "[To] some extent, Duddy represents (and also becomes increasingly aware of) the incurable evil and sickness of man and society, a nastiness which must be faced, if we are to be at all realistic and honest, and coped with if we are to survive." Richler followed *The Apprenticeship of Duddy Kravitz* with two caustic satires.

© Jerry Bauer

The Incomparable Atuk (1963) derides the materialistic values of contemporary society through the experiences of an Eskimo poet who achieves wealth and popularity when his work appears in a series of Canadian advertisements. *Cocksure* (1968), a black comedy that ridicules popular culture and the entertainment industry, details an unscrupulous movie mogul's takeover of a British publishing company. Although several Canadian and British booksellers refused to carry the book because they found some passages offensive, *Cocksure* received a Canadian Governor General's Literary Award.

In *St. Urbain's Horseman* (1971), Richler returned to the less trenchant humor of *The Apprenticeship of Duddy Kravitz*. This work centers on Jake Hersh, an affluent man who believes that his success is largely unmerited. To relieve his sense of disillusionment and remorse, Jake fantasizes that his cousin Joey is the Horseman, a heroic figure who fights against Jewish oppression. *St. Urbain's Horseman* also won a Governor General's Literary Award, and many critics consider it Richler's most successful book. His next novel, *Joshua Then and Now* (1980), is composed of extensive flashbacks detailing the prominent events and personal crises in the life of Joshua Shapiro, a prominent Jewish-Canadian author. By depicting Joshua's marriage to an upper-class gentile, Richler explores problems inherent in relationships between individuals of different upbringings and social positions. Reuben Shapiro, Joshua's smooth-talking father, is regarded as Richler's finest comic creation.

Richler is also a respected essayist and scriptwriter. In his essays, which are collected in *Hunting Tigers under Glass: Essays and Reports* (1969), *Shovelling Trouble* (1973), *Notes on Endangered Species and Others* (1974), *The Great Comic Book Heroes and Other Essays* (1978), and *Home Sweet Home* (1984), Richler employs an acerbic, humorous style and focuses on Canadian topics. Norman Snider remarked of *Home Sweet Home:* "In his familiar, sturdy, sober prose, piquantly spiced with colloquialisms, Richler has rendered a definitive version of Canada's recent history." *Hunting Tigers under Glass* was Richler's third book to receive a Governor General's Literary Award. Richler's screenplays include an adaptation of John Braine's novel *Life at the Top* as well as *The Apprenticeship of Duddy Kravitz* and *Joshua Then and Now.*

(See also *CLC*, Vols. 3, 5, 9, 13, 18; *Contemporary Authors,* Vols. 65-68; *Something about the Author,* Vols. 27, 44; and *Dictionary of Literary Biography,* Vol. 53.)

DAVID MYERS

Richler is a first-rate satirist and humorist, blessed with a highly articulate sense of what is ridiculous in human behaviour and the imagination to invent fast-moving plots inspired by a zany fantasy. As for characterisation, Richler has created anti-heroes who are both pathetic and hilarious, villains who are thoroughly scurrilous, an authentic panorama of Jewish types, and galleries of incidental caricatures and miniature parodies. Finally, Richler's satiric themes are contemporary, relevant, and probing, and in his latest novel, *St. Urbain's Horseman,* he has succeeded in combining satire, fantasy and farce with moments of near-tragic intensity.

[*Son of a Smaller Hero*] is not primarily a satire; it is more a moral drama of Noah Adler's quest for truth and the maturity to temper this truth with compassion. There are, however, some very successful comic and satiric scenes in the novel. They are found predominantly outside the central relationships between Noah and Miriam. . . . One thinks of the ghoulish crowd glugging coke while they goggle at the excavation for Wolf Adler's body. The varying tone and pace in the scene is masterly. . . . Richler presents the scene tautly and with a minimum of intrusive comment. Some moments are frankly funny, as in the shop-sign "Mexican money is accepted in Mexico. Here, cash will do fine." Other moments feature a wit that is harsh and abrasive; for example, the hypocritical rent-collector from Outremont is described as a "man who did not take his employer's name in vain and who had honoured his father and mother ever since they had died." The whole scene culminates with a delicious irony of fate that mistakenly makes Wolf a folk hero and earns an opportunistic poet considerably more money for his ode to Adler than he had reaped for his ode to Sacco and Vanzetti years before. . . . Richler reveals the two prime preoccupations of his wit in *Smaller Hero:* jewishness and sex. It is hilarious farce when Noah steals the sign reading "This beach is restricted to Gentiles," but for condensed satire this episode must yield to Theo Hall's academic party where the glib witticisms and sexual flirtations barely gloss over the hollowness of the merry-makers and in a fittingly grotesque climax to the

occasion Mrs. Hall puts the stop-watch on her daughter-in-law's latest adultery.

In *Smaller Hero* it is evident that Richler feels much sympathy for the noble aspirations of his protagonist-hero, Noah, and this is why the satiric mood is reserved primarily for the background. In [*The Apprenticeship of Duddy Kravitz*], however, the ambitions of Duddy are materialistic and his methods more than dubious. But Richler chooses not to mock Duddy; in fact he elicits a great deal of sympathy from the reader for the fierce, unapologetic hustling of his anti-hero, and turns his derision instead on the mediocrities and oddities whom Duddy leaves churning in his wake. . . . In his apologia for Duddy, Richler appeals to the pathos of poverty and family ties and contrasts Duddy favourably with condescending, moralizing intellectuals, North American businessmen like Cohen and the hideous Boy Wonder in particular. Not that Richler lets Duddy off scot-free. Uncle Benjy's moving letter to Duddy, begging him to be a *mensh* not a *behemoth*, states the novel's ethical theme; it is this theme that raises the novel above the level of clever farce and gives the concluding lines their full ironic impact. Duddy marvels at his new economic and social status and forgets, at least temporarily, that this success has cost him Virgil's friendship, Yvette's love, and his grandfather's moral approval. Duddy's ethical foils are Mr. MacPherson whose liberal idealism is derided by society at large and Yvette, whose touching need to give love is so horribly misunderstood by Duddy that he offers her money as a bribe to keep quiet about the land around the lake. Mr. MacPherson tried to be a *mensh* and so did Yvette, and that Richler chose to write tragically of their different failures lends poignancy and an ethical counterpoint to the social satire. (pp. 48-50)

The great variety of moods in this novel suggests that Richler's *forte* as a writer is satiric farce with a tragic undertone. The satiric point of view prevents him from lapsing into bathos, and a potentially tragic perspective obviates the emergence of merely trivial farce. In this respect, *Duddy Kravitz* clearly anticipates *St. Urbain's Horseman.*

Richler's later works feature many techniques that are typical of the satirical genre. As John Carroll points out about *The Incomparable Atuk,* the first of Richler's unabashed satires: "Richler sets up his game with a classic manoeuvre of the satirist: put a savage in civilization, and then let the audience decide who is savage, who is civilized." This is the same technique as Huxley used in *Brave New World.* Richler varies it in *Cocksure* with humour of inversion. The civilized hero, whose only sin is to be old-fashioned, and therefore civilized, is isolated in a mod world of swinging savages. But this world of savages is painfully recognizable as our contemporary society. In order to identify with the decent underdog we are obliged to admit the insanity of the society we live in. (p. 51)

As a satirist and black humorist, Richler, like his contemporaries Joseph Heller, John Barth, and Kurt Vonnegut Jr., owes a great deal to Nathanael West. Richler and West both depict the world as a madhouse and the people in it as sick, perhaps irredeemably so. Protagonists like Mortimer Griffin and Jake Hersh, and Miss Lonelyhearts and Tod Hunter before them, are partially victims of the sickness around them, but mainly passive agents of their authors' satiric hostility to the sordid, futile world they live in. West is more bitter and pessimistic than Richler. Mortimer and Jake Hersh try to withdraw and seek refuge in family stability and passive liberal concern. But West had already rejected this kind of solution when he had

Miss Lonelyhearts scorn a normal, suburban marriage with Betty as an ignoble escapism.

In his representation of an insane world, West is more economical, more sardonic, and more grotesque than Richler. Many of his characters are repulsive and vicious. . . . Richler's characters are on the whole more frivolous. Dingleman and the Starmaker are repulsive enough, it is true, but mainly in the sense of comic-book caricatures. Characters like Polly and Shalinsky in *Cocksure,* and Mr. Friar and Max Kravitz in *Duddy Kravitz* have more to do with humorous fantasy and farce than they do with the grotesque.

Most of Richler's satire is light-hearted and farcical in tone, is outrageously explicit on race, religion, and sex, and draws on an apparently inexhaustible supply of contemporary and topical bêtises. Richler's techniques range from soft-core pornography and sick humour to Freudian farce, a zany comic fantasy that is most successful in his imaginary film scripts, an impish pleasure in turning established conventions upside down to reveal the absurdity of our prejudices, and the gift of a mimic in parodying the most varied cliches and jargons. . . . When Richler satirizes Hollywood in *Cocksure* he is unable to resist the temptation to wander off into a spoof on Jewish-Negro-Wasp relationships in swinging London. What he does have to say about Hollywood, however, is more than worthy of comparison with West's picture of Hollywood in *Day of the Locust. Cocksure* is a vitriolic fantasy in which the great American dream of effortless beauty, luxury, and instant satisfaction is transformed through Polly into a surrealist farce of frustration and through the Starmaker into a nightmare of obscene artificiality. Of course, *Cocksure* is not intended to create the mood of bitterness and brooding that overwhelms the reader in *Day of the Locust.* It is more a zany burlesque. (pp. 52-3)

As a black humorist Richler has considerably enriched the satiric tradition of Ambrose Bierce and Nathanael West. Take the story of Mrs. Fishman in *Cocksure.* Mrs. Fishman was the one-millionth Jew to be burnt in the furnace-chambers of Treblinka, Richler tells us, and the halls were festooned with "gaily coloured Chinese lanterns" for the occasion. The survivors of this "sentimental barbecue" commemorate it as one of "the most ring-a-ding nights in the history of the Third Reich." Any laughter that one feels here at the witty incongruity of the word-choice is stifled by the blackness of the humour. . . . Such sick jokes remain funny only because they are set in the world of nonsense fantasy where Richler is so very much at home.

Richler's imaginative world might be fairly described as one where twisted Gothic gargoyles copulate obscenely with fiendishly grinning amoretti, where the horrifying is promiscuously linked with the sexually trivial. This creates a scrappy bits and pieces impression but in those anecdotes in which Richler does succeed in combining sex with wit, the result is inspired nonsense. Ziggy says of his girlfriend, "She's thoroughly middle-class, actually. What I mean is she goes with dogs, but stops at great danes." Woodcock calls these "bawdy jokes" "adolescent" and suggests that "part of the humour they evoke is based on the incongruity of such primitive jests appearing in a novel that in other respects is very sophisticated." What sophisticated satire there is in *Cocksure* is directed largely against trendiness; the most mockery is aimed at the people who are with it in the latest fashion in the sexual revolution, progressive education, racial and ethnic exploitation of the guilty white liberal conscience, and American big business methods in the film and publishing world. (pp. 54-5)

Richler prefaces *St. Urbain's Horseman* with a quotation from Auden which suggests that he does not wish to be read as a mere entertainer, a fanciful farceur. Auden's lines evoke a mood of cosmic despair illumined only by a rare "affirming flame." What is there in the *Horseman* that would justify us regarding it as such a flame? Certainly the despair that we find there is serious enough; the world around Jake Hersh is sordid and vile. Jake himself despairs and lapses into neuroticism and paranoia as he struggles to defend the few liberal ideals he has salvaged from his war with an insane world. Confusedly he holds to his notions of artistic integrity and family loyalty, and worries ineffectually about social injustice and the starving millions. His is hardly a great flame, for he is not meant as a hero, but rather as someone who is representative of the helplessness of so many of his readers, who long for a saner world but don't see how to go about attaining it. And so Jake clings to his comic-book fantasy of the horseman as righter of all wrongs and at the very end of a novel, which had begun farcically, we understand his need for this romantic escapism and dismayed by the injustice that has been done him, we are overwhelmed by tragic pity. (p. 56)

[Richler] accords sympathetic treatment to only two characters in his novel, Jake and his wife Nancy. They are shown to feel a very deep love for one another and the loyalty of this love under duress provides the ethical counterbalance to the sordidness, instability, lack of integrity, injustice, and grasping materialism that Richler is satirizing in this book. The central satirical targets are rich middle-aged Jews who have sullied their youthful idealism and their vows to remember the Spanish civil war and Auschwitz, and who are now guiltily intent on guarding the ignoble privileges of their affluence by making hypocritical claims to be liberal. . . . Jake has too much intellectual integrity to forget or to be hypocritical. But this means that his conscience troubles him all the more because he is only too aware of the inhuman gap between his own affluence and the poverty of millions. . . . Indeed it is almost as though he is unconsciously punishing himself for being happy and well-off and that is why he passively allows Harry to get him into the whole mess. But Jake is not satirized. It is true that he speaks of himself with ironic deprecation, but this inferiority complex combined with his love for his wife and the touching, humorous scenes he has with his children only increases our sympathy with him. (pp. 57-8)

As for Harry, he is an altogether revolting character and was presumably not meant to win our "respect and concern," but rather our fascination and ultimately our loathing. It is more than enough for Harry to be what he is, a voyeuristic, paranoid, sordid, super-intelligent, self-deluded socialist who really suffers from nothing more than galloping envy, sexually and financially. Harry has a curiously contradictory role in the novel. He is presented as a nasty blackmailer and pervert, but on the other hand one feels that his attacks on the capitalist social order have a lot of truth to them. . . . This truth is undoubtedly good for us, the readers, but for Harry himself it is not good; he is consumed by rancour and resentment at what he has discovered. His intelligence has ruined him for the enjoyment of life.

It is pointless to ask whether Joey is an "achieved character," for he is not meant to be realistically convincing. He is shrouded in mystery and rumour because his function is almost a supernatural one, namely to express the absolute dividing line between corruption and purity, cowardice and courage. That is to say that cousin Joey is to a large extent what you are yourself.

People who are themselves corrupt are satisfied that Joey is nothing but a liar, a blackmailer, a cruel terrorist, smuggler, shit-disturber, card-sharp, and maybe even murderer. But to Jake, who stands for "decency, tolerance, honor," cousin Joey is the horseman, "his moral editor," a projection of the exacting standards of his own conscience, a vision of a fighter for justice who answers Jake's cry for a "revelation."

Romantic visions of Joey form only one part of Jake's interior monologue, which is also given over to travestied anxiety about his family's security and health, and an obsessive preoccupation with ribald sexual fantasies and reminiscences. The question is are these sexual fantasies anything more than entertainment for an avidly voyeuristic public? The answer is a decisive yes. Richler is very much the leader in the comic division of today's revolutionary army for free sexual expression and wide tolerance, and is astonishingly inventive in his parodies of pornography. His skits are marked by a brilliant staccato pace, a Rabelaisian explicitness of language, and an unfailing sense of what is both titillating and ridiculous. These sexual skits are only one part of the *Horseman's* extraordinary concoction of anecdotes, tall stories, montages, and fantasies. Such a potpourri cheerfully flouts the conventional novel's laws of form and leaves an impression of exuberant and chaotic fullness.... In range of topic, technique and mood, *St. Urbain's Horseman* presents a bewilderingly rich picture of contemporary Western society.... With this novel Richler has established his satiric stature as comparable to that of both Nathanael West and Evelyn Waugh. (pp. 58-60)

> David Myers, "Mordecai Richler as Satirist," in
> Ariel, (*The University of Calgary*), Vol. 4, No. 1,
> January, 1973, pp. 47-61.

KERRY McSWEENEY

Richler once explained that his novels "break down into two categories readily. There are the naturalistic novels and the straight satires.... I guess my ultimate interest is in the novel of character really." This terminology is unfortunate: 'the novel of character'' is useful enough, but the other two designations are misleading. Properly speaking, none of Richler's novels is either naturalistic or a straight satire. The former is presumably meant to cover books like *A Choice of Enemies* and *St. Urbain's Horseman,* which are realistic in setting and technique, moral in theme, and in which a central figure comes into conflict with himself and with aspects of his society in ways whereby character and values are explored. By the latter term Richler doubtless meant to designate *The Incomparable Atuk* and *Cocksure.* The first of these is a satirical entertainment which collapses into farce; much of the content of the second is satiric: but neither is formally speaking a satire.

In any event, recognition of generic differences among Richler's novels is not more critically important than recognition of their thematic and presentational similarities. Take, for example, the "naturalistic" *A Choice of Enemies* (1957), and *Cocksure* (1968), a "straight satire." Norman Price and Mortimer Griffin, the central characters of each novel, both live in London and are professionally connected with the city's artistic and creative worlds. Both are Canadian WASPS of good family; both have in the past acquitted themselves with distinction on the battlefield, a heroism associated with the traditional conservative values of their upbringing. In the present, however, such values have come to seem vestigial, what the earlier novels calls "the fossil[s] of a sillier age, like the

player-piano." Both Norman and Mortimer have come to espouse enlightened liberal values and to move in like-minded left-wing circles. (p. 122)

In each novel, events come to undermine the foundations of each character's enlightened values, a destabilization influenced in each case by Jewish shadow figures, Karp in *A Choice of Enemies,* Shalinsky in *Cocksure.* As the sands shift under them, Norman and Mortimer both become at odds with their liberal friends, whose communal beliefs are shown to have become solidified into a new orthodoxy, conformist rather than openminded, intolerant rather than humane. As a result of the clash between individual and group, both become increasingly isolated, ineffectual and value-less; and both finally come to a bad end.

A Choice of Enemies is an intelligent, inventive and rather undervalued novel, on the whole a stronger and more engaging, though a much less professionally polished performance than *Cocksure.* (p. 123)

[What] remains most vividly in the memory concerning *A Choice of Enemies* is its dark negating vision, which ultimately leaves shattered the novel's humane and moral concerns. It is of course possible to read *A Choice of Enemies* in such a way as to discern the constructive moral seriousness and the positive conclusion which are for some critics the hallmarks of an artistically successful fiction and the substance of their critical discourse. Take, for example, Bruce Stovel's introduction to the New Canadian Library edition of the novel. Stovel finds at the end of *A Choice of Enemies* a positive conclusion to Norman Price's "apprenticeship": he "fights his way back to an honest self-scrutiny, to a separate peace, to a determination to struggle for success in his marriage and his work." But what I find is a worn out, morally numbed man passively sinking into a marital limbo with a shallow, opportunistic and ugly wife; in the novel's final sentences, Norman's mind plays host to an utterly banal thought while he pours himself a stiffer drink. (pp. 123-24)

This deconstructive power is also present in *Cocksure,* and it has not gone unremarked by Leslie Fiedler, who describes the novel as "a book which seems always on the verge of becoming truly obscene, but stops short, alas, at the merely funny" [see *CLC,* Vol. 5]. The black humour strain in *Cocksure* is principally found in one of the novel's two narrative lines: that involving Richler's most fantastic invention, the Star Maker, the malign demiurge of the film industry who aspires to divine status through self-reproduction, who is destroying humane literary values, and who—in the high point of the novel's dark exuberance—recalls how Jewish Hollywood entrepreneurs of the 1930s came to perfect the manufacture of handsome WASP robots for the screen, mechanical images of desire for the masses.

But as Fiedler intimates, this strain does not infect all of *Cocksure,* which in its other narrative line is in the main content to be not blackly comic or absurdist but wickedly funny about a number of the excesses of contemporary programmatic liberalism. But while *Cocksure* is not on the one hand a black farce (though with elements of such which at times approach the obscene), it is not on the other hand a satire because it does not imply a standard of values against which deviations and perversions can be measured. Indeed, one of the few ways in which the Canadianness of *Cocksure* might be pointed up is to note that while the American Leslie Fiedler was complaining that its obscenity was intermittent, the English critics Philip

Toynbee and John Wain were complaining about the work's unsatisfactoriness as satire. . . . (pp. 124-25)

In its failure to be neither fish nor fowl *Cocksure* ultimately disappoints as a serious work of fiction. One reason why the castigation of contemporary mores part of the novel does not solidify into a satire is clear: the inconsistent treatment of Mortimer Griffin, the central character. Mortimer is alternately a target of the satire and, as both naif and reliquary of traditional values, the lens by which the objects of satire are focused. The gap between Mortimer's penile chart on the one hand and his Victoria Cross on the other is enormous and no attempt is made to bridge it.

The reasons why the "obscene" tendencies of *Cocksure* keep collapsing back into the "merely funny" are less apparent, but I can offer one hypothesis. It has to do with Richler's growing fixation with gamy sexuality (it is even more pronounced in *St. Urbain's Horseman*). This fixation is insufficiently assimilated into the texture and themes of *Cocksure,* and its instances remain rather gross adhesions to the text. George Woodcock relates these features "to the world of sexual fantasy and bawdy jokes that beguiles adolescent boys" and lets the matter go at that. But the fact that part of Richler's imagination seems arrested at the level of the highschool lavatory wall is an important matter. One is not arguing that his imagination is tainted by preoccupations he should have outgrown and that he should clean up his act. One's complaint is exactly the opposite: that Richler has been too genteel to allow the lewd and the gross fully to possess his imaginative processes, come what may. To do so might lead to a discomforting shifting of the sands for a writer habituated to satirical and moral themes; but it might also be salutary. On the one hand it might lead to their transformation into the truly obscene; on the other it might be liberating and allow Richler finally to overcome one of his most serious weaknesses as a writer of realistic fiction: his self-confessed inability (as pronounced as Hemingway's) to create convincing female characters. In any event unless some imaginative transformation of these fixations occurs, one will continue to be tempted to apply to Richler Irving Howe's comment on Philip Roth: that his is "a creative vision deeply marred by vulgarity."

All of *Cocksure* was written in one of the interstices in the composition of *St. Urbain's Horseman* (1971), the long-gestating novel that should have been Richler's major achievement to date. The novel gives evidence everywhere of technical maturity and full stylistic control, and combines the subjects, themes and modes of Richler's earlier novels in ways that suggest—as does the high seriousness of its epigraph—that Richler was attempting a cumulative fictional statement of his views on the mores and values of contemporary man. But while *St. Urbain's Horseman* is a solid success on the level of superior fictional entertainment, on the level of serious fiction it must be reckoned a considerable disappointment. It doesn't deliver the goods and simply does not merit the kind of detailed exegesis it has been given by some Canadian critics.

The center of the novel is a crisis point in the life of Jake Hersh, a successful thirty-seven year old "alienated Jew. Modishly ugly" with a "gorgeous wife" and three children. A Canadian living in London and connected with the city's artistic worlds, of liberal convictions and sensitive conscience, Jake is clearly meant to be the definitive portrait, this time Jewish, of the Norman Price / Mortimer Griffin figure. There are two generic components of Jake's crisis: (a) the advent of the mid-life crunch (Samuel Johnson is cited in this regard), which is

triggered by a sense of professional unfillment and intimations of mortality; (b) the cumulative malaise of Jake's "American generation"—"Always the wrong age. Ever observers, never participants. The whirlwind elsewhere"—with its attendant feelings of guilt (Jake even feels a "burden of responsibility" over enjoying a "singularly happy marriage"). Both of these components are called attention to throughout the novel and are rather too neatly summarized in the long last chapter of its third part. (pp. 125-27)

The thematic skeleton of *St. Urbain's Horseman* is, then, solid and substantial; it is in its incarnation that the weakness of the novel lies. Everything depends on the presentation of Jake, especially of his mental life and the deeper reaches of his character, and on the intensity of the reader's sympathetic involvement with him. Unfortunately Jake is characterized rather too superficially. One is told, for example, but never shown, that he is charged with contradictions concerning his professional life; and for all the time devoted to what is going on in his head he doesn't really seem to have much of a mental life. Despite the big issues he is said to be struggling with, *St. Urbain's Horseman* can hardly claim serious attention as a novel of ideas. (pp. 127-28)

Another serious shortcoming is that Jake is treated with too much indulgence. I do not mean to say that he is idealized. It is of course true that he is shown to be drolly neurotic, irrationally insecure, resentful, and ignoble; and he is not spared the demeaning affliction of "a cherry-sized hemorrhoid." But on the whole Richler seems to have assumed that Jake's sensitivities, difficulties, needs, and muddled liberal values are so inherently appealing and widely shared that only a few broad strokes . . . will suffice to secure the reader's sympathetic involvement.

Richler does indirectly try to supply Jake with a dark underside, but he is unsuccessful in giving the reader a convincing sense of the twisted self within. (p. 128)

Another important point is that while Jake's story is the single narrative line in *St. Urbain's Horseman,* it in fact takes up only about half the novel's pages. The rest of the material, related only tangentially to his *crise,* is crisply deployed and excellent as entertainment, but its very abundance tends ultimately to work against the novel's serious aspirations and keep it at the level of what Roger Sale calls "a raconteur's story, shaggy and timed, incapable of testing anything." (pp. 128-29)

The Jewish Montreal world is . . . an integral part of Richler's best novel, *The Apprenticeship of Duddy Kravitz* (1959), which is the story of a Jewish boy's making it. But however memorable, *Duddy Kravitz* is hardly a masterpiece. Published when Richler was only twenty-eight, the novel is rough-hewn in style, technique and characterization. The chapter in *St. Urbain's Horseman* describing the mourning for Issy Hersh, for example, is a much more effective realization of Richler's time and place than anything in the earlier work. Indeed, it is hard not to think it unfortunate that the novel did not come to Richler at a later stage of his career, when his talents had matured and he was fully in control of them. Had this been the case the story of Duddy Kravitz might have been able to withstand comparison with, say, V. S. Naipaul's *A House for Mr. Biswas;* as it stands, however, it is different neither in kind nor degree from novels like Schulberg's *What Makes Sammy Run?* (p. 129)

Much of the critical comment on *Duddy Kravitz* praises the novel for its mixture of slice-of-life realism (an authentically observed time and place) and serious moral concern. But I would myself argue that the world of the novel is marred by presentational crudities (including reliance on stereotype and caricature) which are not wholly made up for by the powerful characterization of Max, Duddy's father, and by the fresh invention of the Marxist Bar-Mitzvah film. I would further suggest that the moral pattern is rather too schematic and clear cut, is hardly a challenging fictional subject—it is that of hundreds of North American novels and films—and is in fact one of the weaker features of a novel that might well have been a stronger performance had it been more thoroughly naturalistic in technique and eschewed the moral overlay.

Had it been so, the major source of the strength of *Duddy Kravitz* would have been more readily identifiable: the raw drive of the title character, who is Richler's most forceful and memorable creation at least partially because he is an incarnation of the deconstructive, negating energy of Richler's imagination. Duddy may be placed in a moral context but the frame is ill-adapted to the picture. Duddy is a grating amoral force who is all undirected drive and aggression. His needs are deep and compulsive but because he does not know what they are he does not know how to satisfy them. For most of the novel the object of his desire is possession of the secret lake and its environs—in one scene his gaze remains fixed on them even while he is making love with Yvette. At moments, however, Duddy seems obscurely to sense that the source of his deepest needs lies elsewhere and is connected with his father and mother. But his father is emotionally empty, a defensive failure, a pimp and a dope, with nothing to give; and his mother is long dead. Duddy's deepest needs will never be satisfied no matter how hard he runs (though they do become more and more covered by the garish scab of material success). It is this demoralizing psychological datum, much more than his imputed moral failure, that stunts and ultimately withers Duddy's humanity even as it fuels his aggressive, destructive personality, and which makes him (when he reappears in *St. Urbain's Horseman*) speak deeper than he knows when he exclaims "How in the hell could anyone love Duddy Kravitz?"

One may close with a prediction. In the years before him Mordecai Richler the novelist will continue to offer superior fictional entertainments informed by moral concern and leavened with satiric bite, but unless his gamy fixations are transformed and the rough beast at the nadir of his vision can only again shoulder its way into the pages of his fiction, he will not be able to offer more. (pp. 130-31)

> *Kerry McSweeney, "Revaluing Mordecai Richler,"* in *Studies in Canadian Literature, Vol. 4, No. 2, Summer, 1979, pp. 120-31.*

NORMAN SNIDER

The best of [*Home Sweet Home*'s] pieces are the most personal. **"My Father's Life,"** written on the occasion of the death of Moses Richler, is deeply felt but unsentimental, and **"St. Urbain Street Then and Now"** is in the writer's best nostalgic vein. **"Making a Movie"** is a sardonic account of the arduous journey of his well-known novel, *The Apprenticeship of Duddy Kravitz,* to the screen. Richler, a connoisseur of slights given and received, recalls a Hollywood reception at which his *Duddy* screenplay won an award for "Best American [sic] Comedy Adapted From Another Medium." He was piqued not for reasons of nationalism but because no one associated with the picture offered to buy him even a celebratory soda water. (p. 64)

But when Richler has no personal stake in the material, the results are more pedestrian. He is deeply interested in federal politics, the Montreal Canadiens and the politics of Quebec, but ballet, the Canadian Football League and the city of Toronto fail to arouse his best efforts. Confronted with such topics, he sleepwalks through the writing like a film star waltzing through a cameo turn in a bad movie.

Still, while Richler seems remarkably passive as a reporter and almost never uncovers material unknown to other journalists, his gimlet-eyed judgments are invaluable. More than most writers, he possesses a shrewd knowledge of what is truly good about Canada—fresh Winnipeg goldeye, the writings of Morley Callaghan—and what is really awful, former PC leader Joe Clark. At his most scathing he can make a Canadian want to pack his bags instantly and flee in shame to New York, London or Upper Volta. Skeptical of both Canadian nationalism and Quebec separatism, he finds much to admire and criticize in both Prime Minister Pierre Trudeau and Quebec Premier René Lévesque. (pp. 64, 66)

In his familiar, sturdy, sober prose, piquantly spiced with colloquialisms, Richler has rendered a definitive version of Canada's recent history. . . . [In] *Home Sweet Home* Richler proves himself an incomparable critic of his home and native land. (p. 66)

> *Norman Snider, "True Patriot Ambivalence," in* Maclean's Magazine, *Vol. 97, No. 19, May 7, 1984, pp. 64, 66.*

RONALD BRYDEN

Home Sweet Home offers several lamentably funny studies of Canadian desperation. . . . Mr. Richler visits the home of Karsh of Ottawa—the only home outside the United States, he's informed, ever visited by Edward R. Murrow on "Person to Person"—and watches an acolyte tape-record the *pensées* of the photographer who built a career making executives look like Churchill and Schweitzer. He attends a Mr. Universe contest in Montreal whose short, bulging contestants all receive medals as consolation for watching the title go to Mr. America. He even turns his satire on himself. Lured to the Academy Awards ceremony by an Oscar nomination for *The Apprenticeship of Duddy Kravitz,* he's ignored by its distributors, loses to Mario Puzo and brings away only a Writer's Guild award for "the best American comedy adapted from another medium.". . .

In some ways, he's Canada's Sinclair Lewis, guffawing with despairing scorn at the Babbittry and boosterism of a new, uncertain society. That may be part of his secret; though Canada admits to no Middle West, the nerve he touches runs all the way down Middle North America. But he's a truer writer than Lewis; he manages to produce caricature that is truthful. Lewis achieved laughter by exaggeration. Mr. Richler's specialty is the exaggerations people have perpetrated on themselves, whose absurdity betrays the truth they wished to hide. His two best pieces are almost pure pathos. One is a memoir of his father, a lifelong loser whose one tragicomic gesture against anonymity was spotting errors in the movies he drowned his Sundays watching. . . . The other is a requiem for the greatness of the Montreal Canadiens, lost in the rush to sell one of Canada's rare glories, ice hockey, as a commerical sport to the Sunbelt.

He has a Canadian love of the underdog who seizes his day—small boys who cheerfully disrupt parades, jokers who put out tongues at the camera, the man in Arctic Yellowknife who, asked what social institution would most improve the town's quality of life, replied "A whorehouse." Ultimately, his humor is absurd with a capital, philosophic A—cartoons of small figures asserting themselves ludicrously in a huge, cold space too vast for names or postures to carry across it. Perhaps that's his real secret. His Canada looks not unlike the universe.

Ronald Bryden, "Northern Light," in The New York Times Book Review, *June 3, 1984, pp. 32-3.*

GEORGE GALT

[*Home Sweet Home*] exhibits the intelligence, wit, and polish [Richler's] followers admire, also the bitterness and breeziness sneered at by his critics. Richler's scathing impatience with fools and deadly skewering of hypocrisy are delivered with such fluency, such a delicious mix of barroom banter and elegant high prose that anyone who enjoys language must in some way warm to these essays. (p. 13)

Richler writes at his best when he can personally inject himself into his story, at his worst when he feels called upon to make pronouncements on the state of the nation. **"My Father's Life,"** the most impressive essay in this collection, may surprise readers who expect a running patter of sly one-liners. Despite its unusual earnestness, his biographical sketch of Moses Richler draws on the author's long-cultivated strengths: the keen and particular memory, attention to significant detail, an exceptional talent for the rendering of dramatic cameos, and an unbending sense of who he is and where he comes from. The comic public commentator unmasks himself, revealing a painful and embittered childhood; the angry love a tough Jewish kid felt for his gentle, inept father; and the beginnings of this author's iconoclasm—first on St. Urbain Street and then in the world beyond. It's a confessional piece of the best kind, escaping the sentimentality and self-aggrandizement that can easily sink such a memoir. What he has written is a miniature map of his own psychology, and a street-wise eulogy to the father who helped shape it.

"My Father's Life" . . . leads a group of seven essays linked by their autobiographical form. **"Pages from a Western Journal"** . . . is the slightest, offering no more than the title advertises, disjointed impressions from a 10-day flying visit to Brandon, Winnipeg, and Edmonton. **"St. Urbain Street Then and Now"** . . . has the grit and tension of rich childhood memories juxtaposed against the middle-aged nostalgia of eyes wandering their old neighbourhood. **"Making a Movie"** . . . gives us the jaundiced and jaded cosmopolitan screenwriter up against Hollywood hubris—and winning. . . . **"On the Road"** . . . is the standard essay on the perils of an author's promotional tour, though Richler writes it better than most. **'North of Sixty,"** . . . an essay on Yellowknife, reaches the excellence of the St. Urbain Street memoir. Sourness and vitriol, ladled out so generously in the pieces on southern Canada, are foregone here. Instead a sense of wonderment and celebration propel the writing. (pp. 13-4)

"Home is Where You Hang Yourself," . . . which opens the book, announces its tone and substance. . . . [He] has always felt deeply ambivalent about his homeland, one part of him loving it and relying on it for source material, another despising its middlebrow mediocrity. The ambivalence is, or has been, essential to the success of his work, as this essay demonstrates. He rarely misses the chance to take a shot at the parochial, as if the bright, ambitious Jewish kid inside him still suffered a

claustrophobic need to escape the cultural narrowness of Montreal's ghetto and middle-Canada's small-mindedness. On the other hand Montreal, with all its faults, is the place he knows most intimately and loves best. . . . His displeasure with anglophone Canadians, whether Jew or gentile, implicitly characterizing them as crude, uncultivated, and unimaginative, allows him the critical detachment he needs and in turn supplies this book with many of its strengths. . . .

Apart from the pieces with a personal touch, there are three sports essays that shine, and a comic ditty expertly puncturing puffed-up Yousuf Karsh. Then there are the political pieces.

In his article on the October Crisis the author concludes: "But at the day's end, at the risk of appearing callous, I must say damn little actually did happen in 1970. In an American year in which there were 13,649 homicides, eighty cops were killed, and Weathermen blew up banks and university buildings, in Canada a politician was murdered and a diplomat kidnapped, later to be freed. Everybody in the house, not only Trudeau, overreacted. To some extent, I think, out of issue-envy.". . . Richler's essay is a cute interpretation of our major political shitstorm since the war, but in more ways than one it just doesn't wash. . . .

"'Pourquoi Pas?'—a Letter from Ottawa" . . . quickly takes our political pulse, and examines at some length the cultural currents of the day. Always wary of nationalist sentiments, scornful of the protective and affirmative action such sentiments often inspire, Richler here points to the Independent Publishers' Association's 1973 suggestion for Canadian content quotas in book stores to support his distaste for the whole movement. He ridicules this idiotic proposal deservedly and well. . . .

But it's an example of a position either ill-considered or sloppily researched. . . . One of Richler's peculiar habits as an essayist is to focus on a single foolish act—proposed content quotas in book stores, for example—and use it as the clincher in an argument. The truth that was sacrificed for wit is that the IPA proposal was an aberration in a persistent and mostly enlightened lobbying by the IPA and others. This led to a publications program administered by the federal department of communications, providing funds that many publishers of Canadian books would be hard put to forgo. (p. 14)

"Language (and Other) Problems" . . . discusses the origins of French Canada's malaise and the foibles of the PQ administration since 1976. Mostly it's solid reportage but says nothing new to anyone who has followed public affairs over the past decade through major Canadian newspapers. Some of Richler's interpretations are unfortunate. He compares Quebec's public and para-public payroll of 342,000, for example, to California's 320,000, about as facile a conservative putdown of the PQ's social-democratic tendencies as can be imagined. In the next breath "an all-but-comprehensive health plan here" is acknowledged, but exactly how many thousands of doctors, hospital workers, and administrative employees this would subtract from the total is not offered. (pp. 14-5)

There are careless slips in the final political piece as well. **"O Canada"** . . . tells us twice that the Foreign Investment Review Agency was put in place at the same time as the National Energy Program in 1980, which must have surprised any of Richler's American readers whose applications FIRA rejected in the previous six years. The Tories' Ottawa leadership convention was held in 1982 according to this essay, making the one held last year a charity benefit. Minor points, of course,

but curiously slapdash for an author of Richler's high reputation. Half a dozen of our best political journalists could have
written these political pieces more convincingly, not to say
more accurately.

To be fair, every essay here offers entertaining reading. As he
has grown older, Richler has turned the volume down on his
Canada-bashing rhetoric, though the caustic bitterness is by no
means entirely muffled. I find a monotony and predictability
to his treatment of Canada as a country of hopeless yokels,
but even in his political journalism there remain many moments
of intelligent laughter. We will never have enough of that.
(p. 15)

George Galt, "Having It Both Ways," in Books in
Canada, *Vol. 13, No. 7, August-September, 1984,
pp. 13-14, 16.*

MARK ABLEY

The publication of *Home Sweet Home* affords sour proof of
Richler's sheer inadequateness as an interpreter of Canada to
the English-speaking world. A collection of nineteen articles
written over the past quarter-century, the book includes essays
on such disparate topics as broadcasting and body-building,
the trials of life as a script-writer and the tribulations of Montreal's professional baseball team. The only unity comes from
Richler's awkward, acerbic style and from his passionate de-
nunciations of Quebec nationalism.

Born and brought up in a Jewish, working-class district of
central Montreal, he spares little love for the Anglophile captains of industry and culture who flourished in the city he knew
as a child forty years ago. But he reserves his scorn for the
new masters of Quebec, the *indépendantistes* of the Parti Qué-
becois who seek political sovereignty for the province, along
with some form of economic association with English-speaking
Canada. Richler describes the PQ as "an abomination" and
compares one of its ex-ministers to Torquemada. . . .

His zeal to discredit the PQ leads him to play fast and loose
with the facts. Discussing the government's language legis-
lation, for example, he states "Bill 101 ruled that wherever a
child came from—abroad, or even from another Canadian province—it had to be educated in French, unless one of its parents
had been to an English school in Quebec." In fact, the law
allows a child who was receiving English-language education

in the province in 1977 to finish his schooling in English, and
it grants the same right to any younger brother or sisters. . . .

Richler knows next to nothing about western Canada or the
Maritime provinces, and his travel articles in *Home Sweet Home*
can be disconcertingly inept. . . . But more important than mere
clumsiness is his recurrent inability to carry on an argument
for more than two paragraphs without resorting to snide digressions or witty irrelevance. "Canada is enduring bad times",
he announces portentously; but the evidence moves swiftly
from unemployment statistics to a discontented American who
pitches baseballs in Toronto, and to the failure of Canada's
best ice-hockey players to defeat the national team of the
USSR. . . .

The subject of Canadian nationalism provokes in Richler a
telling unease. He dedicates *Home Sweet Home* to his publisher
Jack McClelland, who served as co-chairman of the Committee
for an Independent Canada—which Richler prefers to dismiss
as "a hard-line nationalist faction". ("Hard-line" and "faction" are both, of course, terms that convey an unearned derision.) Rather than facing up to the issues which the CIC
addressed, especially the economic domination of Canada by
American business, Richler tries to blacken the nationalist
movement by focussing on a few of its wilder and sillier off-
shoots. His rhetorical position resembles that of worried North
American men who still seek to disparage feminism by mocking the women who once burned bras. For all its jauntiness
and buoyancy, his own prose sometimes betrays the insecurity
of the colonized. In an essay on the National Ballet of Canada,
he can find no better way to describe its quality than by quoting
the critics of the *New Statesman*, the *Guardian*, the *Observer*
and the *New York Times*, as if the only proof of artistic excellence were international esteem.

Like Canada's National Ballet, *Home Sweet Home* has met
with approval in the USA and Britain. But it is still an annoying
and unreliable book, every page of which needs to be approached with a sceptical, alert intelligence. Its most rewarding
essays are two personal memoirs, **"My Father's Life"** and
"St. Urbain Street Then and Now", which have a warmth, a
freshness, and a depth of understanding absent from Richler's
political and social commentary. If he would stick to what he
comprehends, his name would appear in print less often. But
the rest of the world might have a clearer vision of Canada.

Mark Abley, "Oh God, Oh Montreal," in The Times
Literary Supplement, *No. 4264, December 21, 1984,
p. 1470.*

Theodore (Huebner) Roethke

1908-1963

American poet, critic, essayist, and author of children's books.

Roethke is among the most celebrated American poets of the twentieth century. His work conveys through dynamic, descriptive imagery the physical essence of nature and the human body. The concrete language of Roethke's poetry serves to present his personal themes as archetypal experiences, resulting in a highly original, symbolic body of work charged with semantic associations that must be intuitively comprehended by the reader. The implicit content of his poems prompted Richard Allen Blessing to note: "When Roethke is at his best, 'meaning' is a complex of forces, a musical expression growing out of the pre-conscious resonances of the language, out of the play of sound against sound, out of the energy of primitive rhythms, out of the extension of sense through ambiguity, out of the explosion of sense through paradox, out of the telescoping and juxtapositioning of images."

Roethke was raised in Saginaw, Michigan, where his parents operated a large floral greenhouse and produce business. His ambivalent relationship with his father, as well as the greenhouse and the Michigan environment, figure prominently in much of Roethke's most critically appreciated work. The recurring spells of mental illness from which Roethke began to suffer during the 1930s and the landscape of Seattle, Washington, where he later resided, are also crucial elements of his verse. Roethke's first volume, *Open House* (1941), was enthusiastically received by W. H. Auden, Louise Bogan, and Yvor Winters, among others. Containing poems mainly written in traditional forms and meters, *Open House* has since been faulted for its frequently imitative and derivative qualities. While Roethke continued to evidence such influences as Wallace Stevens, William Blake, and Dylan Thomas, he developed a style in his later verse that more subtly integrated his own abilities and concerns.

Roethke's second collection, *The Lost Son and Other Poems* (1948), represents a strengthening of his poetic expertise and is generally considered a significant contribution to contemporary American literature. In explaining the stylistic changes in *The Lost Son,* Roethke wrote, "I am trying to loosen up, to write poems of greater intensity and symbolic depth." By relaxing his dependence upon conventional structures and experimenting with free verse, Roethke evolved a form capable of examining his own psychic and sexual growth, as evidenced in two of his most memorable sequences, "The Greenhouse Poems" and "The Lost Son." In *Praise to the End!* (1951), Roethke depicts nature as an extended metaphor for his subconscious.

Roethke published several retrospective collections late in his career. Both *The Waking: Poems, 1933-1953* (1953), which was awarded the Pulitzer Prize in poetry, and *Words for the Wind: The Collected Verse of Theodore Roethke* (1958), which won the Bollingen Prize and the National Book Award, combine new poems with a selection of older material. The posthumously published *The Far Field* (1964), winner of the National Book Award, contains "North American Sequence," one of Roethke's most praised pieces. *The Collected Poems of Theodore Roethke* (1966) provides an overview of his distin-

guished career. These books evidence Roethke's craftsmanship in complex verse forms and his skill in creating love poetry and expressing philosophical concerns.

Although his output is relatively small in comparison to other major poets of the twentieth century, Roethke is appreciated for creating such painstakingly detailed popular poems as "My Papa's Waltz," "The Waking," "Four for Sir John Davies," "Elegy for Jane," and other frequently anthologized works. Critics have often disagreed, however, in their attempts to classify Roethke's poetic style. His deeply personal images and the manner in which he utilizes nature to explore psychological territories have prompted scholars to associate Roethke's verse with either the Confessional or the Romantic school of poetry. Nevertheless, many would agree with Stanley Kunitz's assessment: "Roethke belongs to that superior order of poets who will not let us rest in any of their poems, who keep driving us back through the whole body of their work to that live cluster of images, ideas, memories, and obsessions that constitutes the individuating source of the creative personality."

(See also *CLC,* Vols. 1, 3, 8, 11, 19; *Contemporary Authors,* Vols. 81-84; *Contemporary Authors Bibliographical Series,* Vol. 2; and *Dictionary of Literary Biography,* Vol. 5.)

ROSEMARY SULLIVAN

If one were to search for the persistent pattern which unifies Roethke's work, making it such a coherent body of work, one would have to settle on the pattern of rebirth. "All my poems seem to be about dying and being reborn again and again," Roethke said. The poems record a perpetual "journey to the interior," most often a regression to the foundations of the psyche and a subsequent re-emergence of the self reconstituted and participant in new forms of unity. A poet's identity is to be found in the habits of feeling and insight which are particularly, almost obsessively, his own and which distinguish his work from all others. The starting point of Roethke's work is this passion for rebirth, to strip away encumbrances in order to get back to first things. This impulse might possibly be connected with the manic-depressive pattern of his own personal experience, with its violent oscillations between extreme states of joy when the sense of being gained greatest access, and unendurable anxiety which threatened the very stability of the self. These oscillations clearly undermined any sense of continuity of self which Roethke might have been able to secure. The self was for him something that had to be perpetually recreated. It was an extremely tenuous concept since it had to be based on assurances of spiritual identity, and confidence continually wavered. Roethke called himself a perpetual beginner. Each time in each new poem, it was as if he had to begin over again, no previous gain being sufficient in the arduous process of self-definition. His work is therefore completely autobiographical in the broadest sense—a compulsive and continual reassessment of the nature of identity. "The human problem," Roethke wrote, "is to find out what one really is; whether one exists, whether existence is possible." For many this self-consciousness is the source of the intensity and depth of his poetry, since it is seen as central and radial to contemporary sensibility. For others, it provokes only charges of narrowness and egocentricity.

Judging from the multiple articles and reviews of Roethke's poetry, the heresy of the egotistical sublime presents a formidable hurdle to appreciation. M. L. Rosenthal writes: "For the most part Roethke had no subject apart from the excitements, illnesses, intensities of sensuous response, and inexplicable shiftings of his own sensibility" [see *CLC*, Vol. 3]. . . . The consensus is that Roethke is not one of the poets in whose work we encounter the whole range of life, primarily because we do not encounter there the whole range of the living.

There are two arguments involved here: first that Roethke is an egocentric poet, his theme remaining entirely and only himself; and second, that his poetry is unable to enter into the world of public relationships, that he has little or no feeling for life as a "dynamic engagement in time, in place, in history." The criticisms are clearly separate if related problems, and it is often due to a failure to distinguish between them that Roethke's poetry suffers. The first and most important complaint is that he is an egocentric poet. It is felt that he chose to record the agonies and frustrations of his personal experience, particularly as derived from mental illness, and yet failed to give them an imaginative, poetic order. His musings remain simply private problems, and as such relatively uninteresting.

M. L. Rosenthal is Roethke's most astute critic. In a review of *The Far Field* called "The Couch and Poetic Insight," he insists that Roethke's poetry has always been the expression of an unresolved hysteria in the face of the demands of actual life. His only source of energy is his uncontrolled riotous psyche—the heights of pure manic recklessness, and the depths of painful and disturbing dejection. Moreover he used himself up after the first wild orgies of feeling in his early poems. Such criticisms seem to depend on the idea that Roethke's poems are simply the expression or regurgitation of unconscious drives. Roethke, as it were, found his vein in *The Lost Son* and the *Praise to the End!* sequences in his uncanny sensitivity to the fluctuations of his own psyche. He proceeded to make of poetry a couch for the rehearsal of his psychological problems which remain largely opaque and impenetrable to the outsider. This confessional mode, reduced to a kind of psychic recharging, became redundant and self-repetitious in his poetry. This is to assume that Roethke's is a poetry of therapy, of raw ego: "little more than a rehearsal of common paranoia."

The feeling, it would seem, is that he made no attempt to ensure that his intensely personal investigations into the unconscious self would be expressed in terms of universal predicaments. This is to underestimate his deep sense of poetic tradition and the fund of conventional imagery from which he drew in the creation of his poems. From a close reading of the poems, particularly of the *Praise to the End!* sequence, it becomes apparent how continuously he refers the reader to a heritage of poetry—to Blake, to Wordsworth, to Sir John Davies, to Eliot—which at once defines the cultural or emotional ambience in which the work must be understood and moves the poem beyond the opaque and gratuitous to the realm of general concern. The poetic ancestors seemed to have been an immediate aspect of his experience. In fact, it is remarkable how little sense of pastness is involved in his idea of literary tradition. The ancestors were part of a living present tradition which could be called upon for assistance in his attempts to clarify private themes.

Moreover Roethke was deeply sensitive to problems of opacity and suspicious of the personal poem which might depend upon too private, too febrile emotions. But he also knew that the very process of interior probing could constitute an exploration of general experience if the poet remained faithful to what was most universal in himself. He had read Rimbaud, Maud Bodkin's *Archetypal Patterns in Poetry,* and Jung, each of whom confirmed the possibility of a personal poetry concerned with archetypal experience. Rimbaud was particularly important to Roethke with his theory of objective poetry, postulating as it does an unconscious level of experience which the poet might exploit for its archetypal patterns. . . . In his early sequences Roethke was able to turn his themes, particularly his relationship to his father and the impact this had on his attempts to evolve an independent identity, into fundamental human concerns by confronting them at the archetypal level of meaning where the magical notions of father and authority accrue. His poems were not structured after a specific myth but created their own myth of the "Lost Son," recording a *Prelude* or spiritual autobiography of the quest for identity. His search for the father thus came to involve metaphysical questions such as the search for essential order and authority. In his last years, Roethke turned to a study of mysticism to extend his quest for identity. . . . The suspicion of Roethke's interest in mysticism has been increased by the attempts of some of his sympathetic critics to tie his poetry rigorously to orthodox mystical processes. Roethke never claimed that he had reached the final stages of mystical illumination. He was interested in mysticism as a psychological process that terminates in an undefinable but somehow potent sense of illumination. Such an analysis offered him a means to objectify his search for spiritual identity within a structure that is universally recognizable, but this structure always had to be justified in personal terms. His mystical poems actually record the desperate struggle for belief, rather than a formularized ritual.

In both his early and late poetry, if Roethke took the problems of the self as his theme, he was neither egocentric nor narcissistic. The self in his poetry becomes a symbol, interesting to him only when it impinges on representative concerns and not otherwise. In fact he is the least confessional of modern poets. His poems are never private complaints, the record of domestic misfortunes which move for their human content but seem never to exceed themselves. Yet he never evaded the personal either. His poems show how the violence of the self—the problems of alienation, discontinuity, and homelessness—can be written about with subtlety and passion.

Roy Harvey Pearce put the matter most eloquently when he said that he took Roethke's life work to have been directed toward "enlarging and deepening the sense of the authentically personal." He added that Roethke's poetry "controlled the wide and deep areas of the personal, the widest and deepest, I am persuaded, in the work of any contemporary American poet."

This does not, however, answer the complaint of the lack of breadth and inclusiveness in Roethke's poetry. If he is not egocentric in the pejorative sense, his obsessive preoccupation with the generic self is remarkable. (pp. 190-95)

Pearce writes that Roethke had achieved a marvelous command of the personal. "For him the world was first I, then (from the minimal to God) thou—but not yet, as with Blake, he, she, or they." Rather, "to have revealed the sacredness of the second person, of all persons (and places and things) as they in truth are second—this is Roethke's achievement." Had Roethke had time, Pearce feels he would have moved into a more objective world into which he might have been able to introduce an awareness of the concrete and particular conditions of modern life.

John Wain reluctantly asserts that of the various kinds of illumination a human life needs, Roethke's poetry pursues only one kind. It does not enter the ordinary world where social concerns have their effect. The human world, however palpably present in Roethke, is limited to

> an old woman with her life running down, a
> child being weaned, a man making love to a
> woman or listening to the wind in the trees—
> these things are memorably and truthfully cap-
> tured: and, beneath them, the basic subject of
> the human being as a creature. But there are
> other areas—of memory, of history, of personal
> relationships, of opinion, of custom—which we
> ordinarily inhabit and which Roethke's poetry
> does not allow us . . . to revisit.

The balance of opinion in these and other essays is that Roethke's commitment is to the intensely private and personal, leaving untouched the intermediate range of sentiments of ordinary life—the social and historical. Roethke was acutely aware of this. Throughout his notebooks one can see him trying to write poems of a more general or public human concern. A few of these appeared in **Open House** and **The Lost Son**: poems like **"Dolor," "Last Words," "Highway: Michigan,"** and **"Judge Not."** Ralph J. Mills prints some of them in the **Selected Letters.** Others never emerged from the notebooks: poems which try to reproduce a circle of friends, or a social milieu, even political pastiche.

For the most part, such poems are failures. As Denis Donoghue put it, Roethke had no sense of life as a "dynamic engagement in time, in place, in history." For him all problems centered in the self. He was not interested in the possibility of social forces assisting or thwarting individual identity; in his poems, ambush is always interior—self-aggression or despair. The major premise of his work is the conviction that only when the self is fully in control of its inner world can it turn outward. In this the pattern of his **"North American Sequence"** is epitomal—the wounded self withdrawing from human society in search of renewal.

The whole question of Roethke's instinctive ability to admit the value of social criteria with reference to the self might be seen against the larger perspective of American poetry. Many critics—one thinks in particular of Richard Poirier in *A World Elsewhere* and Tony Tanner in *The Reign of Wonder*—have remarked the extraordinary visionary tendency in American literature. So often American poets choose to concentrate on the realities of consciousness and the struggle of the self for a congenial environment of the imagination, while rejecting any social definition of the self. There is a persistent conviction that the idealized self can never function in a world of social and economic systems, so that the retreat from any historically formed environment to a primitive timeless world where there is no encumbrance to the expression of the true inner self—denudation as a prelude to discovery—has become one of its most formidable archetypal patterns. Such terms as "the eye," "nakedness," "childhood," for example, carry highest value in American poetry because its goals have almost always been visionary—the omnivorous eye of the poet discovering relationships, integrating the parts of his vision. Society, even the society of others, is an interference, a distraction, in the compulsive drive to discover an original relation to the universe.

Roethke quite clearly accepted this attitude as part of his literary heritage. What we do not find in his work is double consciousness, a commitment to a visionary dream of the self that can simultaneously accommodate the buzz and din of ordinary life. Instead his poetry is a healing process taking place in isolation, apart from society; the self retreating into itself before returning newly constituted and ready to participate in new relationships. Roethke described the archetypal pattern of his poetry when he wrote of his last poems: "They begin at the abyss, at the edge of being, and descend finally into a more human, more realizable condition. They turn away from loneliness to shared love." His sensibility quickens at opposite extremes of the spectrum, either in spontaneous, inchoate, germinal experience—the unconscious world of the fish, the slug, the frog—or in the intuitive intensity of mystical experience, the soul moving beyond itself.

Roethke also knew that a concerted effort to develop a social or public sense might have violated his gift. As Wallace Stevens remarks in *The Necessary Angel:*

> What is the poet's subject? It is his sense of
> the world. For him, it is inevitable and inex-
> haustible. If he departs from it he becomes ar-
> tificial and laborious and while his artifice may
> be skillful and his labor perceptive no one knows
> better than he that what he is doing, under such
> circumstances, is not essential to him.

The fundamental point is whether a poet has a sense of identity at all. With Theodore Roethke, the pressure of his own imagination, the inescapable presence of his own individuality, is always recognizable in the depth of his penetration into the interior processes of personality, and in his acute sensitivity to the subliminal, irrational forces of life. (pp. 195-98)

> *Rosemary Sullivan, in her* Theodore Roethke: The Garden Master, *University of Washington Press, 1975, 220 p.*

JAY PARINI

Roethke was a great poet, the successor to Frost and Stevens in modern American poetry, and it is the measure of his greatness that his work repays detailed examination. Roethke saw himself as working within a great tradition, modifying and extending it after his own fashion. Specifically, Roethke was a Romantic. His work abounds in references to Blake, Wordsworth, and Yeats, especially, but my stress is upon the American quality of his Romanticism with Emerson and Whitman as primary ancestors, with Stevens as a strong contemporary influence. Without impugning his originality, one can read all Roethke's work as a continuing conversation with his precursors; he was a poetic ventriloquist of sorts, able to speak through masks of those whom he called "the great dead." Still, there is a voice at his core which is unmistakably his own. He has his special province, a landscape so personal and distinct that no amount of imitation or writing-like-somebody-else, as he called it, disturbs the integrity of his voice. (pp. 3-4)

[The] genius behind any imaginative work has something to do with imagery. Roethke's verse from *Open House* to the posthumous *The Far Field* displays a consistent and vivid imagery found only in the greatest writing. His images derive from the dream world of his Michigan childhood, and one soon finds that a few key symbols operate throughout his work, most important the Father (who is alternately the poet's biological father, Otto Roethke, or God), the greenhouse, and the open field (where illuminations generally occur). There are minor symbols in this cluster, too—the wind (spirit), the stone (associated with transcendental experiences) and the tree (selfhood). The image of Woman as mother, lover, or sister is present from the beginning, taking on greater significance in the middle and later periods. The central figure in all the poems is Roethke in his mythic projection as the "lost son." Indeed, the **"Lost Son"** sequence . . . represents this poet's most permanent contribution to modern poetry. . . . Roethke is a poet of the egotistical sublime (to use Keats's description of Wordsworth). He appropriates for himself those parts of the world that make up the imagery or world picture at the back of his mind. These images became the signposts of his secret planet, and we can know Roethke best by knowing his entire work, by following his personal development from unrealized potential to self-discovery and, ultimately, self-transcendence.

Roethke's poetry will never be properly understood unless read within the context of Romanticism in its American manifestation. The work of recent critics has been invaluable in showing the breadth and continuity of the Romantic movement from its origins in eighteenth-century Germany to the present. What seems constant in this nearly intractable movement is the recognition that every man is cut off from nature; given this state of affairs, art becomes indispensable in the process of reconciliation between self and nature (subject and object). Every man has either to make his peace with nature or wage his own "war between the mind and sky" (as Stevens called it). (p. 4)

Emerson's far-reaching influence on some later American poets has been demonstrated, but not for Roethke, although his ten-

dency toward idealism in the later poetry can be traced directly back to Emerson's essays. Nevertheless, Roethke's attraction to the world of objects was undiminished by his belief, which he took from Emerson, that nature was the symbol of the spirit. Indeed, few poets have evoked the physical world in such concrete terms. In this, Roethke seems closer to Thoreau than Emerson, for Thoreau's nature was at once sensuously concrete *and* spiritual. (p. 5)

Roethke was devoted to both Yeats and Stevens, acknowledging his debt to them many times. His quest for the greenhouse Eden, as Louis L. Martz called Roethke's childhood dream world, imitates the quest patterns of the other great Romantics, although the greenhouse has more in common historically with Blake's Beulah (where nature is threatened by chaos and darkness) than Yeats's Byzantium or Stevens's wholly fictive realm, where nature is left behind.

To long for a purity not available *within* nature or the natural processes is a common Romantic urge, and Roethke does not escape its pull. . . . Like Stevens, [Roethke] believes that "the greatest poverty is not to live / In a physical world. . . ." He seeks out "that anguish of concreteness"—a total immersion *within* nature. In the early poem **"Epidermal Macabre,"** Roethke . . . wishes the body away, but the spirit he longs for remains carnal:

> And willingly would I dispense
> With false accouterments of sense,
> To sleep immodestly, a most
> Incarnadine and carnal ghost.

Yeats makes a similar wish in *The Tower,* and Roethke is as much a Platonist as his Irish master. His one pure expression of the body-spirit dichotomy occurs in the late poem **"Infirmity"** where the gradual separation of these previously integrated elements is acknowledged: "How body from spirit slowly does unwind / Until we are pure spirit in the end." But this unwinding comes only after the body ceases to provide joy, in either old age or sickness. For the most part, Roethke accepts his physical state as something worthy of celebration. The body is the source of all energy. It is part of the natural world and, in the highest state of consciousness, self and other intermingle. (pp. 5-6)

Like Wordsworth, Whitman, and Yeats, Roethke was writing the poetry of autobiography, working with the materials of his own life and shaping them into a personal myth or mythos in Northrop Frye's sense of the term as a general organizing principle of literary form. Coming well *after* the discovery of psychoanalysis, Roethke had available a vocabulary and technique for invading the unconscious dimension. When he became interested in psychoanalysis through Kenneth Burke, his colleague at Bennington in 1942, his poetry moved into the arena of greatness. But *Open House* did not suggest the beginning of a major career. With the advantage of hindsight, one can go back and find in it themes that flow into Roethke's later vein, but at the time no one knew what was coming. (pp. 6-7)

One cannot understand the original method of Roethke's poems after 1948 without seeing how he adapted the techniques of analysis in a special way, relating them to Romantic poetics, to extend if not complete . . . the historical movement called Romanticism.

One central source of conflict for Roethke was his father's death when he was fifteen. He returns to this painful experience of loss throughout his career, always seeking that final atonement where conflicts are abolished and harmony is restored. I doubt whether he attained this goal, but perhaps he didn't really want to; this conflict proved a wealthy source of poetry. From this single life-crisis, Roethke generated his mythos, a world of luminous personal symbols. Otto, the father, lords over this dream world; he is the ''garden master'' (as Rosemary Sullivan has called Roethke himself in an excellent book) [see excerpt above]. Otto metamorphoses into God in the later poems, but this God is curiously like Otto: loving and terrible at once, a symbol of immense power and wrath, more like the Jehovah who punished Job than the gentler Elohim who visited Adam and Eve in the garden. Otto Roethke's father had come from Prussia in 1870 to Saginaw, Michigan, and started the greenhouses which caught the poet's imagination. (p. 8)

The greenhouse as a symbol was obviously rich in possibilities. In the journals, Roethke explores its full meaning: ''What was this greenhouse? It was a jungle, and it was paradise; it was order and disorder. Was it an escape? No, for it was a reality harder than the various suspensions of terror.'' There is an ambivalence here; this ''greenhouse Eden'' is not William Blake's Eden, wherein all the natural processes are completed, the contraries resolved. Again, it seems closer to Blake's lower paradise, Beulah, that ''married land'' sung of by the prophet Isaiah. Far from the transcendental state of resolution, the greenhouse stands for process, for generation. It is paradisaical in its lushness, its proliferation of beautiful sights and smells, and its perfectly controlled atmosphere, protected from the wilderness outside its walls. But this paradise remains unnatural, artificial. Only the massive effort of the florist-father keeps it going through winter. It is analogous with the family itself, that hothouse where a child matures in the constant temperature of parental protection. . . . The jungle aspect of Roethke's paradise cannot be avoided; the rubbery shoots that dangle and droop, the vines that reach out for something to wind around: these terrify the child. To press the analogy one step further, family affection threatens the child's tender ego with extinction; the father-son struggle witnessed in Roethke becomes part of the son's efforts to establish identity. Because Otto died at a crucial stage in young Theodore's development, the son never had the chance to complete this primal warfare.

What fascinates me is Roethke's willful plunge into the unconscious to find the symbols that would ground his poetry in a reality that is at the same time particular and mythic, autobiographically true and metaphorically resonant. We may gain insight into how Roethke achieved this balance by looking into Emerson's important essay, ''The Poet.'' He writes:

> The poet . . . puts eyes and a tongue into every dumb and inanimate object. He perceives the independence of the thought on the symbol, the stability of the thought, the accidency and fugacity of the symbol. As the eyes of Lyncaeus were said to see through the earth, so the poet turns the world to glass, and shows us all things in their right series and procession.

If Roethke's greenhouse was nothing more than a personal detail of one man's life, it would cease to interest us; instead, he has turned the greenhouse world into a symbol for all that is miraculous, lovely, and threatening about the life cycle. . . . Roethke has allowed each symbol to stand naked in all its ''anguish of concreteness,'' and this allows the reader a special burden of interpretation. It was Ezra Pound who warned the apprentice poet never to say ''dim lands of peace''; ''dim

lands'' must suffice, if the poet knows how to write. Roethke did know how, of course; his greenhouse poems, especially, are among the most concrete (and symbolically charged) that have been written in this century. (pp. 8-10)

• • • • •

Certainly the desire to explore consciousness in its entirety is fundamentally a Romantic impulse. It would be foolish to say that Roethke achieved as much as this; yet he did search dim regions of the subjective mind with uncommon persistence. He found in the recesses of memory those images which perhaps could liberate him from the ruin of his own past. His world view was deeply Romantic, following from Blake and Wordsworth on one side, from Emerson and Whitman on the other. Like his great contemporary, Wallace Stevens, he was writing ''the poem of the mind in the act of finding / What will suffice.'' But unlike Stevens, he was willing to settle for nothing less than mystical union with the Divine Presence. In this ambition, he seems closer to Emerson, who wanted his ideal poet to claim *everything*. . . . (p. 187)

Roethke's specific connections were Romantic, especially with the American visionary side. More so than any other contemporary poet, he carried on an exhaustive dialogue with his precursors. . . . There will always be critics ready to dismiss Roethke with a backhanded swipe: ''He's an imitator.'' The response to this is, simply, that he *is;* but he uses imitation as a technique for liberating his own strongly original voice. ''In a time when the romantic notion of the inspired poet still has considerable credence,'' he wrote, ''true 'imitation' takes a certain courage. One dares to stand up to a great style, to compete with papa.'' Roethke has this courage, competes, and—sometimes—wins.

In all, *The Lost Son* remains the central volume, this poet's most durable achievement, and the key to his work. This is not to dismiss the love lyrics of his middle period or the best of his later meditative sequences, which deepen and extend the autobiographical mythos at the core of all his best writing, the quest for the greenhouse Eden. The cycles of death and rebirth are crucial here, providing the contrarieties that generate creative energy. The long poem sequences, Roethke's favorite medium, make constant use of this pattern; the poet's most basic movement is from desolation and fear to consolation and joy. In this, Roethke becomes a meditative poet par excellence.

It looks clear now that Roethke has earned a permanent place in the literature of American Romanticism. Finally, it is Roethke's fierce honesty with himself that illumines his best work; when he succeeds, it is because he has managed to speak directly about his most personal and, often, disturbing experiences. When he fails, it is because of self-deception or affectation. (p. 188)

Jay Parini, in his Theodore Roethke: An American Romantic, *University of Massachusetts Press, 1979, 203 p.*

GEORGE WOLFF

The question concerning Roethke's contribution to American poetry is even harder to answer than the question of why his stature has not yet been accurately assessed. There is one important way in which Roethke failed to contribute what might have been expected of him. He did not join in the immense dialogue that the best of his peers, such as Eliot, Auden, and Lowell, carried on with the past. These poets openly addressed many of their poems to writers of earlier centuries, while Roethke rarely did so. A glance through the titles of Auden's and Lowell's poems turns up many names of writers that they are speaking to or for. The only poet actually named in a Roethke title is Sir John Davies. Although Roethke studied and formed deep attachments to earlier poets, he did not seem to make his soul out of them or to bring them as openly into the thoughts in his poems as did the others. This lack of a full and explicit communication with the traditions of American, English, and European poetry is the most serious limitation in Roethke's work. (p. 132)

But what did he contribute? What are the essential qualities of Roethke's best poems? What is it that makes them specially his? He described in the most loving yet honest detail the beauty and ugliness of the world he knew best—his father's greenhouse and portions of the northern United States landscape. In his role as lonely, meditative observer, he found other cares than those pressed on him by society and history. The passing of World War II does not make a ripple in his poetry. More importantly, his taste in poetry was the widest possible: he learned from everybody. And in doing so, he demonstrated that a poet does not have to commit himself to one kind of poetry. He can pass freely across the defense perimeters of the warring camps, whether the traditionalists or experimentalists of Roethke's early career or the "university poets," the writers of "open poetry," or the poets of "the deep image" of a later day. Associated with this nondogmatic receptiveness of Roethke's was his lack of pretension. In most of his poetry and in all of his prose, be it notebooks, letters, reviews, or essays, he expresses himself with exuberant frankness. Finally, and most importantly, he never ceased living out the search for his father. As Auden pointed out at the beginning of Roethke's career, he transformed his personal pain, his loneliness, his grief over the loss of his father, into an emotional and spiritual journey with which others could identify. (pp. 132-33)

Roethke liked the "raw" poet William Carlos Williams more than he did the "cooked" T. S. Eliot, but as a poet Roethke resembles Eliot much more than he does Williams. And the special point of the resemblance lies in their sense of tradition, their caring about the past. Eliot and Roethke cared more than did Williams for their American, English, and European poetic ancestors. It is not so important whether Eliot or Roethke was, at a given point in his career, attacking or praising a seventeenth-century poet as that he cared about that poet. Eliot's and Roethke's caring was often an inseparable mixture of liking and disliking, as in Roethke's ambivalent feelings about Eliot himself and in Eliot's even more complicated feelings about a poet with whom he shared so much, John Milton. Eliot almost turned a generation of readers against Milton, despite the fact that Eliot resembled the earlier poet in many ways. Only a "classroom" poet, like Roethke, would care to ponder such a sentence as this one of Eliot's:

> There is more of Milton's influence in the badness of the bad verse of the eighteenth century than of anybody's else: he certainly did more harm than Dryden and Pope, and perhaps a good deal of the obloquy which has fallen on these two poets, especially the latter, because of their influence, ought to be transferred to Milton.

Who cares? Williams did not care, and neither do his poetic descendants, like Allen Ginsberg. But Roethke did care, and the kind of poetry he wrote reflects that caring. (pp. 133-34)

George Wolff, in his Theodore Roethke, *Twayne Publishers, 1981, 152 p.*

LYNN ROSS-BRYANT

Theodore Roethke's poetry comes out of the slime, out of the primordial unity that human beings leave—with anticipation and regret—when they begin the struggle to become persons in the world. From these small beginnings Roethke develops a poetry that explores the furthest reaches of the spiritual dimension of human life. From first to last the poetry achieves moments of affirmation of shared life that are grounded in the given, immanent world. The intention of this study is to enter fully into this "poetry of the earth" in order to explore Roethke's vision of the rootedness of human beings in the natural world and the necessity of relationship for the life of the spirit.

The importance of rootedness in the earth and shared life are revealed in several ways. First and always, there is the present actuality of the things of the earth with which he acknowledges his kinship by paying loving attention to their particular manifestations, whether as person or plant or animal. In this sharing of life one both experiences and learns about the dimension of spirit because of the correspondence that exists between all living things. This respect and care for the earth are obviously important in a time when we are reexamining our relationship to and use of our threatened natural world.

The rootedness also involves a psychological dimension as it reveals the archetypal connectedness of human beings with primordial reality. Archetypal roots involve both the mutuality of human experience and the evolutionary continuity and recapitulation of all life. Thus, ancestors are important in Roethke's poetry: whether they be those from the mire or from the cultural tradition or from the personal family, they are part of who we are.

The affirmation one comes to in Roethke's poetic world through acknowledging and experiencing the shared life of the things of the earth is not without its times of darkness. In this respect his vision is once again of special relevance to the contemporary world. He neither denies nor attempts to escape from the darkness that is part of human experience and humans themselves. With insights we can trust both psychologically and theologically, Roethke reveals that from the darkness of the depths of experience we can learn to see. This is not a seeing that abolishes the depths; rather, it comes to know them as necessary to wholeness of life.

Roethke's poetry, then, offers us a vision of spirit that is firmly rooted in the earth and in the relatedness of life. I wish to explore this dimension of the poetry and the religious implications it has for our world as it offers a grounding for meaning and action based on the connectedness that is given in the nature of things. Wholeness of human life and meaningful action, then, depend on life lived in relation.

This affirmation of the earth is made in a poetry that moves through a number of different forms, beginning with the most basic and minute perceptions and from these moving outward, never forgetting its origins, to encompass increasingly greater ranges of human perception. What can be seen as a spiritual journey begins in the greenhouse with the search for the self; moves out to others; and, finally, explores the ultimate dimensions of human experience and fullness of the life of the spirit.

The poetry generally follows a chronological development both in terms of the order in which the poems were written and presented and in terms of the life of a person: the early poems are those of the child who must find his place in the world; the final poems are those of the old man who must face the inevitability of leaving this world. There is, however, an additional dimension to the poetry that is in opposition to the linearity of this chronological movement. There is a *circularity* in the life of the natural world with its cycles of decay and renewal and a *spiraling* in its recapitulating evolutionary movement. This pattern is reflected in the continuing movement from darkness to light and again to darkness and to light that is the controlling organization in many poems. Roethke describes the early poetry (in terms of both form and theme) as having a cyclical movement: "There is a perpetual slipping back, then a going-forward; but there is some 'progress.'" The poetry as a whole seems to follow this spiraling development. It is also evident in the repetition of certain images that accumulate new dimensions of meaning each time they appear so they both are and are not the same images throughout the poems. This thematic and formal repetition and progress provide links that connect the stages of development as well as individual poems. Thus a whole world of meaning is gradually created. In this coherent world the early poems take on new meaning in light of the further stages of the journey. And the final poems are their richest when they are experienced as the final stage of the journey that began in the greenhouse. (pp. 3-5)

[With] the poems of *The Lost Son* Roethke discovered the form and approach through which he would write his best poetry. *Open House* seems an experiment, a tentative expression. Although the concerns of this poetry—most basically the identity and assertion of the self—are important throughout Roethke's work, his means of expression in the early poems are traditional lyrical forms and his tendency is to explain, to tell, to convince. He seems at this point too unsure of himself as a poet and of his world as a viable subject to let the poetry reveal the world as it does in later poems. The sense of mystery and concreteness that emerge together when he is successful in creating an image that reveals the human and the natural worlds at once simply cannot be contained by this form. W. H. Auden, a friend and counselor to Roethke throughout his career, wrote in a review of *Open House*: "Both in life and art the human task is to create a necessary order out of an arbitrary chaos. . . . The order realized must . . . have been already latent in the chaos, so that successful creation is a process of discovery." He goes on to say that perhaps Roethke was "trusting too much to diction, to the poetic instrument itself, to create order out of chaos." Poetry is only an instrument; it cannot widen the area of experience with which it deals. It may be that this is the lesson Roethke learned following these first poems. Although he also seems to be trusting himself and his poetic instrument more in moving into new, yet unexplored areas, perhaps the crucial difference is trusting the world itself, trusting the chaos not to destroy. By accepting its existence and giving it its due, he discovers in it an order that is beyond his willing or understanding but which he can accept and affirm.

The real starting point and continuing renewal point for the poetry is the greenhouse world of the poet's childhood. The minute particulars of nature, observed with the wondering, open eyes of the child, form the beginnings and the foundation for the possibility of an affirmation of all life. It is through an acceptance of the natural world in all its mystery and fecundity that the poet is able to affirm himself in this world and to move to an affirmation of other individuals and, finally, of the sacred.

With the greenhouse poems the formal rhyme scheme and the more intellectual attitude that accompanied it are gone. Roethke seems to have opened himself to that given, concrete world and apprehended directly its powerful life. The world has been considerably enlarged not only because of the freedom of form but also through a much richer, livelier vocabulary and a greater use of alliteration. He creates a world of which we are an integral part not only because there is a similarity between the growth of a plant and the growth of the spirit, although this is extremely important, but also because we are made to feel our kinship with Roethke's root cellar and his flower dump—that darker side of life. He is beginning here to call on the basic unity of all things on which the poems depend for their power and coherence. He trusts that this will work not only because of his poetic skills but also because this connectedness actually exists. William Meredith says of the *Lost Son* poems, "Instead of ordering experience, these poems attend on experience with the conviction that there is order in it. . . . This *revealed* order was the only one Roethke served from this time on."

The longer poems of *The Lost Son* and *Praise to the End!* in which Roethke attempts to create the return to the world of the child, also depend heavily on the assumptions of the fundamental connection between the things of the earth. The poems of this period require a form that is extremely open and variable and a language that defies our normal patterns of speech in order to reflect both the chaotic world of the child and the mysterious logic that governs our first perceptions of the world. It is through the openness of the child—and of the poems—that this world becomes something to be affirmed.

The primary organizing device for these poems is the circular pattern that is repeated, with some movement forward in each poem and in the sequence as a whole. This pattern is based on Roethke's notion that "to go forward as a spiritual man it is necessary first to go back." The form, then, and the content are the same. There is an attempt to return to one's origins, to the time of childhood or before. Roethke tries to re-create this experience of the primordial for us so that we too will be able to experience the movement to light, the new creation of the self in the world. But in Roethke's world this light comes only after the very real experience of darkness. Roethke's fidelity to his vision and his technique are revealed here as he places himself before a great darkness in the *faith* that order will emerge. The light comes, if it does, through the objects of the natural world. Through "long looking" and acceptance of what is, he experiences the world in such a way that affirmation is the natural response—an affirmation both of the world with all its terrors and all its delights and of the self with its capacity for joy and despair, love and anger, life and death.

In the poems following *Praise to the End!* the apparently irrational and formless structures disappear. They were necessary to recapture the moment of chaos and the childhood conflicts, but through them a self was established that was able to face and come to terms with its past. In the poems that follow, then, there is generally a return to a more traditional form and language, though remnants from this past life recur throughout the poetry. They serve, as do many of the repeated images, to create a sense of an entire world in which the past is not forgotten but is a constant, creative force in the continually new present.

With their more traditional forms and Roethke's increased sense of personal and universal order, the poems of *The Waking* and *Words for the Wind* add to this growing poetic world Roethke's version of the social—his love poems. These two volumes contain the poetry of the mature adult who, having come to an affirmation of himself and his world, is able to reach out to another person and share the joys and sorrows of existence. But with the other also come the double dangers of the desire for total unification and the fear of loss of self to the other, both of which must be avoided if real relation is to occur. This adult consciousness also brings with it an awareness of death. The joys of the body, the natural world, and love are in the process of passing even as they are most fully experienced. Once again, it is only through an acceptance of the totality of life, which includes separation and death, that finite existence can be affirmed.

In the final volume of poetry, *The Far Field,* the poet builds on his concrete experiences of nature and other people to make explicit what has been present from the beginning—the dimension of spirit. Two quite different approaches are used. **"North American Sequence"** is in many ways similar in technique to the poems of the earlier volume, *Praise to the End!* Memories from childhood appear, the things of the natural world dominate, and each poem and the sequence as a whole develop from a time of darkness to a new sense of meaning and a rejoicing in the light. However, significant differences separate the earlier and later poems. The memories that are recaptured are no longer those from the primordial past. The self has been gained; the question is now one of spirit. There are also differences in technique. Although the poet still uses the device of creating a series of images that then settle into a unified vision, this has been significantly modified to suit the new dimension of human experience. Roethke has extended his idea of correspondences so that a whole catalogue of things or events from the natural world or the world of childhood experience is explored to reveal, through its likeness, the human spirit. In addition, both the natural and the human are brought to a fullness as together they compose a new spiritual center. He immerses himself in the sights and sounds and silences of America, and through the experience of their endless variety he comes to the vision of the unity of the "rose in the sea-wind" at the end.

In **"Sequence Sometimes Metaphysical"** he still attempts to preserve the tension, the variety, and yet to discover the unity. However, instead of the expansive, flowing verse of **"North American Sequence,"** we find the tightly compacted lines of **"In a Dark Time."** It is contraction that dominates here. Within a strict form and with end-stopped lines and bare, often monosyllabic language, Roethke tries to create, almost as a single image, a direct, intense experience. Despite the tremendous difference in form, however, the poems seek the same reality of the self in its fullest spiritual dimension within and through the natural world.

This is the goal of the striving, the exploring, begun in the greenhouse, which, while reaching far beyond the greenhouse, never leaves behind the close attention and openness to the mystery of the natural world in which all Roethke's poetry is firmly grounded. Through the experiences of the life that is presented in the poetry—from the seeking of the self, to the other, and, finally, to a more inclusive "Other"—the fullness of the life first found in the flowers and dirt of the greenhouse is realized and made a part of the man. (pp. 5-8)

> *Lynn Ross-Bryant, in her* Theodore Roethke: Poetry of the Earth . . . Poet of the Spirit . . . , *Kennikat Press, 1981, 211 p.*

JOHN LUCAS

However sympathetically we study Roethke's writing, it is impossible to avoid the feeling that some of it springs from an effort of will. Certainly his determination to be a 'philosophical' poet often rings false. Besides that, there is his insistence that a poet is to be identified by his separateness. In his own case, as is well known, this was the recurrent and humiliating mental illnesses that he never managed to shake off. He came to see these as intimately connected with his gifts. . . . Reading, say, **"A Tirade Turning"**, one is inevitably reminded of the atmosphere that surrounded the poetry and career of Dylan Thomas, a poet for whom Roethke felt much sympathy. There is the same mixture of the genuine and fake, the same hysterical shouting, the same blurring of lines between being a poet and acting the part. (pp. 48-9)

The pity is that Roethke became so bound up in his role-playing that it extended beyond the bounds of his public image to his actual writing. Time and again he writes prose that makes you wince for its overblown insistence on his powers. Nor does the poetry escape. For example, the notorious Yeatsian stance of the later poems remains a problem in spite of all the defences that have been made of it. I do not think that Roethke steals more than he borrows, and I cannot see in the work a monarchical invasion of Yeats' rights—let alone those of Stevens' or Eliot's. This is not to deny that Roethke has his successes; but we can hardly avoid recognising that he frequently puts on the Yeatsian singing-robes in order to insist on his own stature. Nor do I think we have accounted for his borrowings when we have called them 'deliberate', as some of his more abject admirers do. Indeed, my guess is that this mistaken defence has been in large part responsible for the dismissal of Roethke in some quarters. The plain fact is that however deliberate the borrowings were, the question of their propriety has still to be settled.

Roethke knew this himself. In **"How to Write like Someone Else"** he defended his policy of imitation and borrowing on the grounds that it could help him to discover his own identity. Equally important, though he doesn't say so, it helped him discover who he wasn't. As his first volume, *Open House* reveals, that included Allen Tate, Stanley Kunitz, Emily Dickinson, Elinor Wylie, Leonie Adams and Auden. (pp. 49-51)

["**The Premonition**", from *Open House*], is a poem about death. . . . More particularly, it is about the fear of dissolution, which the poet connects with his father and which exists for him as a present threat. Without doubt, this fear haunted Roethke all his life. It recurs again and again in his work and is responsible for much of his finest poetry. One way of trying to cope with it was by burrowing back into those days of another summer, to see if he could drag out into the open the roots of the dark terror that fastened onto his mind. Hence, his next volume, *The Lost Son.*

There are those for whom the poems of *The Lost Son* represent Roethke's finest work. I am not entirely happy with this judgement, but I have no wish to underestimate the enormous power and originality of the volume; and any attempt to write about recent American poetry without taking it into account is an act of lunacy. *The Lost Son* is divided into four sections, and Roethke's genius emerges only in the first and last. But all four have their parts to play in building up an image of the lost son. The first is about the stages of life up to adolescence, which becomes the subject of the second section. The third section tries to build on the insights and discoveries of the first in recognising the cyclic course of life—water to water; and the fourth, armed with this recognition, explores the ways in which the poet is linked to the past and may through knowledge escape its tyranny. (The volume's title suggests not only that the past is unrepeatable but that it is gladly abandoned.)

It is in the first section that we meet the new Roethke. In only one poem, "**Moss-Gathering**", is there an undue dependence on another voice, and Roethke's poem is uneasy in its debt to Lawrence's "Snake". But the rest is triumph. (pp. 52-3)

As we all know, Roethke grew up surrounded by greenhouses, and the poems of the first section of *The Lost Son* concern the poet's identification with the processes of nature as a way of delving into his own growth. The identification goes beyond the level of literary metaphor; it is sustained by a deep and valid awareness of growth, of becoming, in which all living things participate. (Which is why his use of the present tense in these poems is so vital to his effort to discover and render the process of growth.) (p. 54)

[It] is worth emphasising that the poems of the first section of *The Lost Son* resist any abstraction of "theme"; they are neither fables, allegories, nor metaphors, and only in and through their texture is their meaning discoverable. For the poems are not so much about growth as involvements in it. The same can hardly be said of the poems in the second section. They are very obviously 'about' something; the ennui and melancholia of adolescence, the pretentious sadness of youth and the 'pricklings of sixteen-year-old lust'. The poems are also, in a very limited and limiting sense, aware of the social-political world; and in this they correspond to the Audenesque poems of *Open House*. More than one critic has noted Roethke's lack of interest in anything beyond himself, and it is true that the world of men engages him very little. But it needs to be said that he made a wise decision in deciding to abandon the effort to look outward, even if that produces an inevitable monotony in his work. For his efforts to engage with the social world are at best pallid and derivative, at worst disastrous. The second section of *The Lost Son* shows that all too clearly.

The third section is even less rewarding than the second. The poems here are simply declarative or explanatory goings-over of what had been so finely rendered in the first section. . . . "**The Cycle**" is a flat retelling of the processes of life, and the poems of this section have a hand-me-down diction, especially in the use they make of Freudian and Jungian symbolism (as though Roethke feared that the poems of the first section would prove too opaque). . . . I want to suggest that Roethke is never at his happiest when his reading shows through. At different points in his career he owes far too much to Jung and Tillich. But this is something to pick up later. First, I have to speak of a masterpiece.

The fourth section opens with the long title-poem, which is quite unlike anything that has gone before. It is a poem built of extremely disturbing material—presumably a severe mental crisis and the need to trace this to its root. It is worth examining this poem in some detail, because its difficulties repay close attention, and also because it holds the clue to what I regard as a real weakness in Roethke's poetry as a whole. "**The Lost Son**" uses very varied means—fragmented memories, nursery-rhymes, scraps of nonsense verse—as ways of tunnelling back into the cause of the illness, so that there can be a rebuilding towards health. For the need to move forward is a constant theme with Roethke, from first to last: 'many arrivals make us live', he says in a late poem, and that includes self-arrivals. But the first section of "**The Lost Son**" is all regression. (pp. 55-6)

[Up to section three, "**The Gibber**"], "**The Lost Son**" is magnificent. It is difficult, certainly, but not unjustifiably so, and Roethke has a sure control over his material. At great pain, I would think, he has managed to create a meaningful poem of terrific honesty and intelligent self-exploration. But the section ends with the weakest lines in the poem. Roethke himself spoke of these lines as '"rant" almost in the manner of the Elizabethans'. If this is so, he must have had very minor Elizabethans in mind, for the lines are not only literary, they are extremely inept:

> These sweeps of light undo me.
> Look, look, the ditch is running white!
> I've more veins than a tree.
> Kiss me, ashes, I'm falling through a dark swirl.

The interesting question is, why should these lines be so bad? In terms of the movement of the section, disgust at sex has here reached a point where the poet breaks down completely. He does not manage to cope with his sense of guilt at discovered sexuality, instead it overwhelms him. But this is not dwelt on: the 'rant' is so perfunctory and weakly written that it suggests Roethke couldn't bear to acknowledge the reason for the breakdown, or even that it had occurred. We have, then, to look to the fourth section to see what develops from this breakdown. For up to this point the poet has been trying to break through to the acceptance of his sexuality which will allow him to shake off the dread of his father's ghost. But when we turn to the fourth section, "**The Return**", we find that the problem of acceptance has been shelved. True, the section is about the attainment of a new calm and sanity, but this comes about not because of a breakthrough but from a turning away. In fact, at this point the poem ceases to move forward and turns back on itself, no matter how the structure and general intention suggest the opposite. . . . The title of this section is unintendedly suggestive, I think. Roethke clearly means "**The Return**" to suggest a return to sanity, to identity; but it *feels* as though what has happened is a return to that womb from which he had insisted on the need to escape.

I am certain that Roethke knew, no matter how obscurely, what was happening to this poem. In the fifth and final section, "**It Was Beginning Winter**", he tries to disguise its reversal of direction by offering new—and unjustified—grounds for the breakthrough he has claimed in the fourth section. . . . In this section Roethke tacitly suggests that the youth's new mental health is due to an accession of spiritual grace. But if this is so, the first three sections become pointless, since they have been concerned with a psychological process. For the poet to make his earthly father suddenly melt into a heavenly one is plainly cheating. Roethke destroys the integrity of his own poem, I think, because in spite of recognising the need to move forward, he cannot finally come to terms with his own sexuality. It is impossible to know why this should be, but I suggest that it is closely connected with that terror of dissolution that came regularly to him, as so many of his poems reveal. The fear of breaking away from his parents into adult freedom—which would include the freedom to give himself to another person—involved too great a threat to selfhood. (pp. 59-61)

In the poems that make up the remainder of the volume there is a fundamental evasiveness. "**The Long Alley**" and "**A Field of Light**" have fine moments, but they lack a genuine coherence, and in reading them you have a persistent feeling that they come to something without knowing why—the something being, of course, a new calmness of spirit. I also think that Roethke begins to use the technical innovations of "**The Lost**

Son" as a way of blinding himself, and perhaps the reader, to his own evasions. There is a sense that vast battles are being fought and won; but in the end little seems actually to have taken place.

This charge must extend to his next volume. The poems of *Praise to the End!* at first sight seem disturbingly honest in their apparent willingness to pursue the truth. Indeed they do pursue it up to a point—which is always the same one, of onanistic guilt, connected with father fear. Then come the familiar hiatus and the assertion of new maturity. For this reason, I find the quasi-therapeutic nature of these confessional poems pretentious in a quite literal sense. They offer much more than they achieve. They are also extremely repetitive in structure and linguistic means, both of themselves and of the poems of the final section of *The Lost Son,* and although they customarily receive high praise, they seem to me near failures as works of art. For one thing, they rely far too heavily on Jung and Freud. (Carolyn Kizer's statement that when Roethke wrote these poems he had read neither strikes me as incredible.) For another, they are a bit like cyphers. Once you have puzzled out their meanings there seems little else to do with them. I am not much tempted to re-read the volume.

Most of the language of *Praise to the End!* is impenetrably private. A former pupil of Roethke's has said that the line 'a black scow bumping over rocks' represents the unborn child's impression of its mother's heartbeats. I do not see how we can be expected to guess this. In addition, there are many reminiscences of Dylan Thomas; a typical instance is:

Later I did and danced in the simple wood

Nor is this just a matter of diction. Dylan Thomas is very important to Roethke's volume, in terms of subject—the opening section of **"The Shape of the Fire"** presumably owes something to "If My Head Hurt a Hair's Foot"—and as a more general influence. Much of Thomas's work struggles with the pain of adult sexuality and the irrecoverable joys of childhood, and this is precisely the territory of *Praise to the End!* But as in **"The Lost Son"**, Roethke never manages to break through, and although he does intermittently understand this, I think—particularly in the title-poem—it is hardly satisfactory, because it undermines his intention. For the poems of *Praise to the End!* form a sequence, much in the manner of the previous volume. Nearly all of them drive back to the earliest memories and sensations, but they move progressively nearer to maturity, or towards that moment which forms for Roethke the barrier to maturity. (pp. 61-2)

The Waking is aptly titled. It contains, moreover, two of his most beautiful poems, **"Elegy for Jane"** and **"An Old Lady's Winter Words"**. Both of these poems face up to the anguish of life, and yet both are celebrations beyond anything he had managed in *Praise to the End!* (p. 66)

["**Four for Sir John Davies**"] focuses on sexual love, and it enquires into the possible consequences of involvement with another person. In **"Elegy for Jane"** the poet can keep a certain distance from his subject because the girl is dead, and because, as he himself says, he is 'Neither father nor lover'. But **"Four for Sir John Davies"** is about himself, and for this reason is less unquestioning in its celebration of the way love wakes the individual to full life and creates harmony between the microcosm and macrocosm. I say this, recognising that the poem is customarily seen as one of unhesitating celebration. I do not believe it is, because reading his work I cannot think that Roethke ever managed to stamp out the fear of involvement

which he saw that love demanded. Temporarily, yes, and he has his poems of praise; but they do not define his position any more surely than poems of disgust. **"Four for Sir John Davies"** is a better poem if we admit its hesitancies and doubts; significantly, its worst section is one of insistent celebration. Also significantly, the poem is full of questioning. In his admirable essay on Roethke, John Wain has said that these questions all expect the answer Yes. I am not so sure. (pp. 66-7)

In 1953 the poet married Beatrice O'Connell, and as Carolyn Kizer has said, there followed a five-year honeymoon, resulting in the wonderful love poems of *Words for the Wind*. In these poems of praise, the cadence 'taken from a man named Yeats' shows itself most unmistakably and, I would say, justifiably. Because although the debt can become burdensome, as Roethke's borrowings so often do, I don't find his own voice inhibited; at least, not often, though there are occasions when the cadence is too derivative, as in **"The Pure Fury"**:

Dream of a woman and a dream of death.

This is pointless, a mere habit of mind that also shows itself in the semi-quotation from Webster in **"I Knew a Woman"**. But we can admit the occasional failure and still accept the fact that Yeats allows Roethke to find his own voice. It may be against all the rules, but it works, finely in **"The Dream"**, but most in **"Words for the Wind"**. It would be quite wrong to think of this poem as merely a lyric celebration of love. It is that, but it is much more besides. As with **"Elegy for Jane"** it declares belief through the amazing resourcefulness of technique and vision that give authority to its assertion that all who embrace, believe. It establishes the harmony of correspondences that **"Four for Sir John Davies"** had queried:

The sun declares the earth;
The stones leap in the stream

It is so astonishingly alive in its responsiveness that you readily forgive the few moments of strain (they are mostly lapses of language). Certainly, if you have read steadily forward through Roethke's work it is extremely moving to come on the measured gratitude of the final lines:

[I] see and suffer myself
In another being, at last.

Yet, it did not last. As **"Four for Sir John Davies"** suggests, Roethke could not always avoid the possibility that love involved self-destruction, that the lover was merely the ladle rattling in an empty dish. In a poem called **"The Beast"** the poet refuses the chance to see and suffer himself in another being.... Why? The answer, I think, is to be found in a powerful poem, **"The Sensualists"**. This is about disgust at sexual involvement and the fearful recognition that a living woman cannot be Dante's Beatrice, that a dream of woman is better than the real thing. (pp. 69-70)

["**The Sensualists**" reveals] that a psychological problem is at the root of his difficulties in accepting involvement with another person (though at the beginning of the last stanza he does admit that dream of a woman is a dream of death).

It is important we grasp this because I think that much of Roethke's failure as a poet lies in his misunderstanding or misinterpretation of his difficulties. He is neither a metaphysical nor a philosophical poet, although these roles have been claimed for him by Peter Levi and others. When he tries to construct a metaphysical argument from his psychological problems he becomes not only bad, but repetitive—many of his poems are an attempt to systematise or 'fix' mood. This point bears particularly on his posthumous volume, *The Far Field*. Here, moods are captured and held fast in a way that makes for a great deal of bad verse. Only two sections need concern us, the first and last. With the exception of two touching and graceful poems, **"Wish for a Young Wife"** and **"The Happy Three"**, the love poems of the second section are dull, and although the third section, **"Mixed Sequence"**, has its successes, they do not seem to me many or considerable.

The opening section, **"North American Sequence"** is about death. The poems try to find a mode of accepting the dissolution of identity, the inevitable future extinction of self. There is one fine poem, **"Meditation at Oyster River"**, and the other poems in the sequence try to recapture its success by repeating its mood of calm resignation. The result is that they seem to be written to formula. As usual where Roethke is trying to convince himself, these poems are dressed in borrowed robes. . . . I confess to finding [**"The Far Field"**] almost totally fake. Partly it is because of the blatant echoes of Stevens and Eliot, the sense I have that other poets are providing Roethke's insights and protecting him from his own. But there is also a real incongruity in combining Eliot and Stevens as Roethke does. (pp. 72-4)

What is noticeable about this and other poems of **"North American Sequence"** is that they do not rage against old age. Apparently, Roethke told Ralph Mills that he expected *The Far Field* would be his last book and unmistakably he is concerned to make a good end. That may sound disrespectful, but **"The Far Field"**, **"The Rose"** and most of the other poems of the opening section seem very much projections of an "image". This is not true of **"Meditation at Oyster River"**, which with nearly total success authenticates a mood of reverie, of some longing for renewal and finally of acceptance of imminent death. . . . Yet though **"Meditation at Oyster River"** is a fine poem, there is no doubt that it is a minor one. The feeling is clear and thin; it is a poem from which the mire and blood have been drained away; and without being impertinent, it does seem to me that Roethke here is not only settling for death but settling into it. (p. 74)

The poems of **"North American Sequence"** open the volume, but I am reasonably certain that they must have been written after the **"Sequence, Sometimes Metaphysical"**. For in the fourth section of *The Far Field* there is still an effort to cope with human involvement. But the poems are muddled; they are looking for a way out of the involvement, even if they don't recognise this. To put it brutally, the agony of suffering himself in another being has simply become too much for

Roethke to bear. The two key poems of the section are **"In a Dark Time"**, probably the most widely praised poem he ever wrote, and **"The Marrow"**, also much admired.

"In a Dark Time" presents perhaps the easier problem. As I see it, either you believe what Roethke says or you don't, and I don't. It seems to me that so much in this poem has to be taken on trust that we need to have absolute faith in Roethke's honesty, and I am not sure he warrants it. He says:

> I know the purity of pure despair

and for all Stanley Kunitz's defence of the 'oracular abstraction' of the style I am not persuaded that anyone who felt such despair would put it quite that way. Nor would he be likely to go on to ask rhetorically:

> What's madness but nobility of soul
> At odds with circumstance?

Madness can, after all, be a good many other things. This is not to deny that the poem has impressive lines, nor is it to underrate the intensity of Roethke's personal anguish. It is, however, to argue that he has too readily converted his psychological difficulties into a rather book-worn language of mystic intuition. The language of Dante and St. John of the Cross feels too easily adopted. . . .

> The mind enters itself and God the mind
> And one is One, free in the tearing wind.

These and other lines read to me as the language of a poet who is determined to convince himself that he has shared an experience for which he produces little actual evidence. . . . It would be crude to say that **"In a Dark Time"** repeats the confusion of **"The Lost Son"**, in substituting reconciliation with a heavenly father for an earthly one, but I do think that essentially the same problem and confusion undermine both poems. (pp. 75-6)

Only very rarely did [Roethke] break through to the severest self-knowledge. But this is not to belittle his accomplishment. It does no good to overpraise Roethke if only because that leads to an unfair reaction against his work. But whatever we can say against him, the fact is that at his best he is a wonderful and original poet, who has produced some of the most distinguished work to have come out of America since the second world war. (p. 79)

John Lucas, "The Poetry of Theodore Roethke," in his Moderns & Contemporaries: Novelists, Poets, Critics, *The Harvester Press and Barnes & Noble Books, 1985, pp. 46-79.*

John (W.) Saul (III)

1942-

American novelist.

A prolific and popular author of horror fiction, Saul blends elements of the traditional gothic tale with those of the psychological thriller. Children often assume the roles of both victims and victimizers in Saul's novels, which are typically set in close-knit, often isolated small towns. The impetus behind Saul's plots is ostensibly that of revenge for acts of injustice; yet, according to Saul, "in my books, the psychological makeup of the characters is at the root of what's taken place. . . . When they're read very carefully, the occult is seen to exist more in the mind of the villain, and that may be as supernatural as they get." Although his novels have been faulted for weak characterizations, repetitious plots, and graphic descriptions of violent acts, Saul is generally praised for his ability to create eerie moods and to maintain suspense.

In his first novel, *Suffer the Children* (1977), Saul depicts the emotional traumas of a girl whose seemingly caring father attempts to rape her and whose sensitive sister undergoes a sinister change in personality. Whether demonic possession or the psychological history of the characters has caused the transformations is uncertain at the novel's end. *Punish the Sinners* (1978) concerns the attempts of Dominican priests to lure a young male high school teacher into their sybaritic sect. This group engages in perverse homosexual activities and may be responsible for the suicides of girls at the parochial school where the protagonist teaches. In *Cry for the Strangers* (1979), two married couples move to a seemingly pleasant fishing village. However, visitors to the town begin to die in mysterious and violent ways during fierce storms, their fates linked to ancient events. In *Comes the Blind Fury* (1980), a blind girl who was accidentally killed by jeering children returns as a ghost to take revenge on their descendants. *When the Wind Blows* (1981) is a psychological thriller depicting the brutal emotional relationship between a tyrannical mother and her daughter. This novel is set in a mining town where an Indian burial site is linked to a supernatural legend and numerous deaths.

In his later novels, Saul often makes use of science fiction elements. *The God Project* (1982) focuses on the controversial topic of genetic engineering. In this novel, a mother rejects the medical pronouncement that her child died from Sudden Infant Death Syndrome and uncovers a conspiracy in which doctors and scientists are performing secret experiments on children in an effort to improve the human race. In *Nathaniel* (1984), Saul concentrates on the psychological effects of a disturbed family on a young boy who may be driven to murder by another boy's spirit. *Brainchild* (1985) details how a Mexican-American surgeon takes revenge for the murder of his ancestors by rebuilding a young accident victim's brain and "programming" him to kill. Saul's recent novel, *Hellfire* (1986), revolves around an autocratic New England family whose wealth was acquired by unscrupulous means and who are haunted by a vengeful ghost.

(See also *Contemporary Authors*, Vols. 81-84 and *Contemporary Authors New Revision Series*, Vol. 16.)

© Milkie Studio. Courtesy of Jane Rotrosen Agency.

HENRY ZORICH

This spooky melodrama [*Suffer the Children*] has plenty going for it thanks to the solid storytelling ability of [Saul], who keeps us on the edge of suspense from the first page to last. We go along on the story picking up pieces here and there, wondering about certain things which happen to the principals. Then Saul nicely delivers a windup which ties all the loose pieces together. We get to know and understand the relationship of Jack and Rose, his obvious indifference to his wife's sexual needs, his own impotence, although he and Rose have sired Sarah and Elizabeth, two very strange children. Sarah is different from most children, quiet, *weird* and eventually she is shaken into a psychotic state of shock by the attempted rape and beating of her own father. What came over Jack? Even *he* doesn't really know, but something strange did happen. . . . And Elizabeth is beginning to change from a sweet little girl into a domineering, frightening monster! Sarah comes home one day totally shocked to the very realities and is confined to a mental home. The years pass and Jack and Rose are dead now, having drowned aboard their boat, an apparent suicide yet no one really knows. Elizabeth is now the mistress of the home and Sarah is to be released from the institution. Although Sarah is now in good spirits and in apparent perfect mental health, something happens which puts her back into her mental state. Saul never wavers in his story, always adding a little color and dimension as he moves along.

*Henry Zorich, in a review of "Suffer the Children,"
in* West Coast Review of Books, *Vol. 3, No. 5,
September, 1977, p. 65.*

CAROL K. CAREY

[*Punish the Sinners* is a] fair-to-middling shocker that centers
on young Peter Balsam, who faces the challenge of teaching
psychology in a parochial school. As if that weren't horrible
enough, an outbreak of mass hysteria strikes his adolescent
pupils. One slashes her wrists in the tub; another attempts
suicide in the locker room. Balsam, a former student priest,
is also drawn into the Society of St. Peter Martyr, a group of
sybaritic priests who favor drug-induced orgies. Barely up to
either assignment, Balsam fails miserably as both teacher and
defender of the Faith. Saul's concept of small-town malevolence is a fascinating one, but it fails to realize its potential—
the plot lags and his characters behave with uniform predictability.

*Carol K. Carey, in a review of "Punish the Sinners,"
in* Library Journal, *Vol. 103, No. 11, June 1, 1978,
p. 1200.*

NEWGATE CALLENDAR

Most writers dealing with the subject of the clergy and the
church take a—shall one say—deadly serious point of view,
and so it is with John Saul in his *Punish the Sinners*. . . .

Mr. Saul, a skillful writer, turns to an isolated small town in
the eastern Washington desert for his locale. He gives us a
priest who would have loved it had he been in charge of the
Spanish Inquisition, and contrasts him with a new teacher (Latin
and psychology) in the parochial school. Psychology is a daring
subject to introduce in the curriculum, and while the kids love
it, many parents object. Soon there is a rash of suicides among
girl students. Naturally, the psychology teacher is blamed.

There is a touch of the occult in *Punish the Sinners*. The fanatic
priest has some strange powers. At the end there is a chilling
resolution and a surprise or two. This is a grim book and, in
the narrow circle of crime and occult fiction, it could be a
controversial one. Even in the church, justice does not always
triumph.

*Newgate Callendar, in a review of "Punish the Sin-
ners," in* The New York Times Book Review, *June
11, 1978, p. 34.*

PUBLISHERS WEEKLY

[In *Cry for the Strangers*], residents of Clark's Harbor, a small
town in the Pacific Northwest, have no use for outsiders. No
one manifests this sentiment more obviously than Harney
Whalen, the surly police chief, who advises all strangers to
leave town. Artist Glen Palmer and his wife, who move to
Clark's Harbor when they discover that the sea miraculously
cures their son's extreme hyperactivity, decide to stay despite
the natives' antagonism. They are befriended by Brad and
Elaine Randall, who have ignored warning signals and moved
to the town, where Brad, a psychiatrist, hopes to write a book.
Frequent violent storms coincide with bizarre occurrences: a
fisherman's wife apparently hangs herself after her husband
drowns; a young man (whose brother loses his life when their
boat is mysteriously set adrift) is strangled to death on the
beach; and Palmer's wife is found dead of a broken neck. All

of the victims are outsiders whose fates are linked to events
that occurred long ago. Terror and suspense are trademarks of
Saul . . . and there is plenty of both in his latest chilling tale.

A review of "Cry for the Strangers," in Publishers
Weekly, *Vol. 215, No. 17, April 23, 1979, p. 79.*

RICK ERICKSON

In a fishing village [the setting of *Cry for the Strangers*], non-
natives begin dying, apparently accidentally—a lone fisherman
drowns and his wife hangs herself, after warning others. Natives ignore it all, but a transplanted artist and a would-be
writer escaping the city are disturbed and threatened. Through
the artist's children we begin to suspect a natural source of the
deaths; but a grim, ominous twist follows the apparent end of
the killer, for a first-rate conclusion. The plot does require us
to witness a storm per night, and a biorhythm theme is patched
on at the end, but overall the book is skillfully done.

*Rick Erickson, in a review of "Cry for the Strangers,"
in* Library Journal, *Vol. 104, No. 12, June 15, 1979,
p. 1359.*

PUBLISHERS WEEKLY

[In *Comes the Blind Fury*, Saul] has forged a story more eerie
in concept than in execution. The setting is the small seaside
town of Paradise Point, a suburb of Boston. The ghost of a
12-year-old blind girl (who, 100 years before, had been brought
to her death by taunting schoolchildren) returns to wreak havoc
on the community's 12-year-olds. Five children meet horrific
deaths: two tumble off the bluffs to the sea, one is crushed by
a boulder, and the remaining two die at school. Unfortunately,
similar events precede each fatal accident, dispelling most of
the suspense. It is only at the end, when the complete legend
of the ghost's vengeance comes to light, that the tale takes a
chill turn. For this readers will have to wade through much
mumbo jumbo, including overly simplistic scenes devoted to
the marital problems of the novel's key couple, and to the
emotional paralysis of the town doctor.

A review of "Comes the Blind Fury," in Publishers
Weekly, *Vol. 217, No. 4, April 11, 1980, p. 75.*

JACKIE CASSADA

[In *Comes the Blind Fury*, a] little girl's ghost, an old man's
revenge, and a doll from the past converge in a horrifying tale
set in Paradise Point, a New England coastal town. June and
Cal Pendleton's dreams of starting a new life are shattered
when the ghost of a long-dead child transforms their 12-year-
old daughter Michelle into an avenging angel. An accomplished
fashioner of the simple horror story, Saul combines sympathetic
and skillful characterization with evocative use of atmosphere
to create a well-crafted, although predictable, chiller.

*Jackie Cassada, in a review of "Comes the Blind
Fury," in* Library Journal, *Vol. 105, No. 10, May
15, 1980, p. 1190.*

PUBLISHERS WEEKLY

[*When the Wind Blows*] is most assuredly not for the weak-
hearted. Diana Amber, a childlike 50-year-old who suffers
from spells of amnesia, is brutalized by her despotic mother

Edna, an expert in emotional terrorism. The Ambers own a mine in which the Indians bury their stillborn children. When the engineer of the mine dies, his lamblike, nine-year-old daughter Christie is bequeathed to the Ambers. As Saul gruesomely dramatizes, Diana is compelled to repeat the mistakes of Edna, and in the chilling epilogue one wonders if Christie will be her foster mother's echo. The author does a fine job of maintaining suspense, and although readers may try to preserve a protective skepticism, they will find that the events of the story haunt them even during the waking hours.

A review of "When the Wind Blows," in Publishers Weekly, *Vol. 219, No. 24, June 12, 1981, p. 52.*

NEIL K. CITRIN

Using an Indian legend to suggest supernatural overtones to a mining accident, [Saul] gets his novel [**When the Wind Blows**] off to a promising start. As the story drags on, however, the promise withers.

In the opening scenes, Amos Amber dies in his mine with many other citizens of Amberton. His wife, Edna, is giving birth to an unwanted child as an eerie wind sweeps down off the Rocky Mountains. Fifty years later, another accident claims the life of a man trying to reopen the mine. His daughter goes to live with Edna Amber and her daughter Diana. Edna objects, knowing how the wind affects her daughter. Diana adopts Christie Lyons anyway, beginning a break from her mother that brings her under the wind's influence.

Despite the focus on Diana, Edna Amber dominates this book. Her possessiveness of Diana and her treatment of the helpless Christie is somewhat tempered by the knowledge that her fears have some basis in reality. Despite this, and [Saul's] effective handling of Diana's progression from relative sanity to insanity, the novel fails. It drags on, pulling the reader through a series of mundane miniclimaxes to a routine climax.

Neil K. Citrin, in a review of "When the Wind Blows," in West Coast Review of Books, *Vol. 8, No. 1, February, 1982, p. 50.*

JOSEPH D. CHIBIRKA

[**The God Project**] is the sixth novel written by John Saul and looks like another bestseller. He again has children as primary characters, involved in frightening circumstances, eliciting very real and sometimes unique responses and reactions.

In an idyllic small town in rural New England, the Montgomery family lead a happy, prosperous, perfectly normal life. One night their healthy six month old daughter dies, apparently of Sudden Infant Death Syndrome, (SIDS), but Sally Montgomery refuses to believe any of the doctor's explanations. She combines her talent as a computer analyst and the maternal intuitions of a neighbor whose son is mysteriously missing, and produces a strange set of facts involving missing children, a high degree of SIDS, and facts about the observation of their children by a research institute in Boston.

The novel deals with a conspiracy of scientists, doctors and an obscure institution performing experiments upon unsuspecting children.

Sally Montgomery and Lucy Corliss, whose son is abducted, suffer deep maternal grievings over the loss of their children. . . . They discover that Lucy and Sally's older sons both

have incredible health, never a cold or sickness between them; with the help of one town policeman and a young doctor, they compile facts involving selected "perfect" children. . . . This conspiracy has been hidden through the bureaucracy and computerization of medical and school records, and the women are frightened there is no way to uncover or to stop the outrage.

There is little development of the character of Steve Montgomery, Sally's husband, who is easily convinced by the doctors that Sally is having neurotic problems getting over the death of their daughter, but Saul does give us some unexpected twists in the plot, creating an interesting and exciting psychological thriller.

Joseph D. Chibirka, in a review of "The God Project," in Best Sellers, *Vol. 42, No. 7, October, 1982, p. 262.*

NEIL K. CITRIN

Saul's weakness as an author, displayed to me in [**When the Wind Blows**], discouraged me from wanting to tackle [**The God Project**]. Yet, as I began reading it, I realized that Saul had improved in his development of characters and structuring of plot. Sadly, however, his handling of the main theme of the book made it less than satisfying.

The novel begins with the loss of Steven and Sally Montgomery's infant daughter to sudden infant death syndrome (SIDS). Unwilling to accept her doctor's statement that no one understands the disease, Sally sets out to find the real cause of the death. At the same time, however, another child, a playmate of Sally's son, mysteriously disappears. The mother cannot accept the official verdict of her son as a runaway and begins her own investigation. The two women become united in an effort to uncover a conspiracy of sorts that reaches all the way to the top levels of the U.S. government.

Saul's craftsmanship cannot be questioned here. Though his characters remain sketchy, they do react convincingly to the problems facing them. The big problem is the underlying moral. No one knows the cause of SIDS, the author tells us with a conspiratorial wink. It must be a government conspiracy that involved genetic experimentation, computers and the invasion of individual privacy. The results of this experimentation, he adds, will be the creation of mutants. Saul's playing to the audience's fears without offering a realistic answer disappoints.

Neil K. Citrin, in a review of "The God Project," in West Coast Review of Books, *Vol. 8, No. 6, November-December, 1982, p. 43.*

BILL COLLINS

[Saul's first five novels] have so far escaped my notice. After reading [**The God Project**], his latest, I'm not sure that I will take a lot of time to search them out. But, confronted with a cross-country plane ride, I would certainly trust picking one of them up to read on the trip. Saul is an obvious master of the craft of telling a gripping story—gripping while it's being read, amorphous a day later. . . . He knows what buttons to push, how to involve the reader quickly and thoroughly, and permits most of his characters to exhibit more than a usual amount of intelligence and courage as they face the almost inexplicable ramifications of the novel's unfolding plot.

The first grabber occurs almost immediately, with the understandable emotional reaction of suburban housewife Sally

Montgomery to her infant daughter's death from Sudden Infant Death Syndrome (SIDS). Many of us have experienced this tragedy, either directly or through the grief of a friend, so Saul's choice of it bespeaks a clear eye for instant reader identification with the protagonist. When Lucy Corliss's subteen boy Randy is kidnapped by a mysterious woman, and in rapid succession it appears that Randy's best friend, Jason Montgomery, may have been responsible for his infant sister's death, it's too late; the reader is hooked for the duration.

Perhaps the best thing about Saul's writing is his knowledge of when to double-cross the reader who has begun to settle into the novel's cinematic formula. Sally's husband, Steve, remains through most of the book the equivalent of the sheriff in low-budget SF films who says "Shoot them!" when confronted with giant cockroaches eating Tucson. But the small-town lawman of the novel (with a Polish surname, perhaps to further confound lovers of stereotypes) exhibits uncommon insight in realizing that paranoia and conspiracy theory are indeed the only logical approaches to the seemingly unrelated events that gradually begin to weave together in ever more threatening ways.

Without giving away too much to prospective buyers, I must observe that Saul has also shown a keen eye to the box office in his choice of the potentially most popular villains of the '80s, genetic engineers. In fact, his only real miscalculation lies in making them so soulless that compared to them Joseph Mengele would be a candidate for humanitarian of the year. But, at the last, Saul doesn't pander to formula taste by tying things up in a comfortable package. His conclusion is as chilling as it is, in retrospect, inevitable, further attesting to his mastery of the craft.

I have used "craft" twice now, and "art" not at all. This omission is deliberate, but not a denigration. Saul has written an entertaining thriller with an SF basis, which should provide almost any reader with an enjoyable evening or two wallowing in escapism. (pp. 45-6)

Bill Collins, in a review of "The God Project," in
Science Fiction & Fantasy Book Review, *No. 16,*
July-August, 1983, pp. 45-6.

NEIL K. CITRIN

With the still rich resources of American folklore at his fingertips, [Saul] had the opportunity to create a gothic horror masterpiece; however, [*Nathaniel*] fell short of this critic's expectations.

Mark Hall's mysterious death, following an unexpected visit to the home of his parents, brings his wife and son to Prairie Bend. The community works to welcome them as they make the transition from city to country, but two elements upset this cozy situation: a sister and a farm that Mark had never mentioned. Trying to work out the solution to this problem, Janet uncovers a few family secrets. She also discovers, unwillingly, that her son plays a key role in an ongoing drama that revolves around an old folk tale.

Saul clearly knows how to tell a good story, and in the eerie tale of Abby and Nathaniel he had an excellent foundation for a real corker. Instead of developing it properly, however, he uses it as a smokescreen for a naturalistic explanation with a touch of the supernatural. Weak characterization, a major flaw with this writer, makes the subtle plot points difficult to follow.

Neil K. Citrin, in a review of "Nathaniel," in West
Coast Review of Books, *Vol. 10, No. 5, September-*
October, 1984, p. 55.

WALTER ALBERT

[*Nathaniel*] is declared on the front cover to be [Saul's] "new bestseller." . . . A nondescript style and the ability to turn out fat novels that are far too long for their meager content seems no obstacle to popular success, and Saul will no doubt continue to please the audience that finds him readable.

After Mark Hall is killed in an accident during an unannounced visit to his parents' farm, Janet Hall and her son Michael come to the isolated community where the funeral is to be held and meet, for the first time, Mark's parents, Amos and Anna Hall. Janet finds their apparent concern for her comforting and, to Michael's dismay, decides not to return to Manhattan to their apartment. Mark has never told Janet why he suddenly left his parents' home, but it is not long before Janet becomes aware of dark undercurrents that lie beneath the surface of the peaceful setting. Michael is beset with visions of strange and disturbing events that he cannot understand and hears the voice of a long-dead child, Nathaniel, who seems to be reaching him from beyond the grave and urging him to acts that he finds increasingly difficult to resist.

None of the adults is drawn convincingly, but Saul has a modest ability to capture some of the instability and fears of children. Michael is the center of the action of the novel and is gifted, or cursed, with second sight and a psychic strength that he uses at first reluctantly and then with real malevolence. *Nathaniel* is more the study of a disturbed family and its effects on a child than a novel of supernatural terror. The psychic horrors are less real and less disturbing than the violations of Michael's sense of security and psychological stability. There is little of the imagination that characterizes the work of some of Saul's contemporaries, like Stephen King and Peter Straub, but the claustrophobic isolation and psychological dependency of characters unable to break out of destructive family patterns occasionally give the novel some interest. This interest, however, is only intermittently aroused and Saul's flat, cliche-ridden language is, finally, incapable of sustaining this slender thread.

Walter Albert, "Fat Novel, Thin Tale," in Fantasy
Review, *Vol. 7, No. 9, October, 1984, p. 34.*

PUBLISHERS WEEKLY

Saul has added a touch of science fiction to the now familiar elements (multiple murders involving teenagers and children in small-town settings) that have made his novels [bestsellers]. . . . When 16-year-old Alex Lonsdale has a near-fatal car accident [in *Brainchild*] in La Paloma, Calif., he is saved by the computer-assisted brain surgery of Raymond Torres at Palo Alto's Institute for the Human Brain. Torres despised the *gringos* of La Paloma during his childhood, and rebuilding Alex's mind "in the demonstration of his own genius, he would have his own revenge." The *idiot savant* contradictions of the "new" Alex, super-intelligent yet minus memories and emotions, confuse and disturb the youth's parents and friends. Then the murders begin. Reminiscent of Ken Grimwood's thriller *Breakthrough* and Robert Silverberg's *The Second Trip*, *Brainchild* falls short of Grimwood's taut suspense and detailed brain-surgery research, and it lags far behind Silverberg's mastery of psychological science fiction. The quirks and oddities of

Alex, however, maintain interest, despite the predictable plot turns of this overlong tale.

A review of "Brainchild," in Publishers Weekly, *Vol. 227, No. 26, June 28, 1985, p. 71.*

MICHAEL STAMM

Brainchild is the story of teenager Alex Lonsdale.... Alex suffers brain damage in an accident and is put back together again by surgeon Raymond Torres, 4th-generation Mexican-American, most of whose aristocratic ancestors were murdered when America acquired California in 1850. The story's implication—at best misleading and at worst dishonest—is that a boy who survived that massacre has somehow 'returned,' via the convalescent Alex, and is out for revenge.

When I finally began to learn what was *really* going on—and how little sense it made—I realized that *Brainchild* is as ephemeral as I had anticipated a John Saul novel to be (though it is somewhat better written than his others).

When the gimmick of the novel was revealed, I laughed aloud. Full of two-dimensional characters who evoke no belief or sympathy in the reader, and marred finally by a *Friday the 13th*-style non-ending indicating that what the reader thought was happening all along will *really* happen—now that the book has ended—*Brainchild* has nothing to say and is not enjoyable even in its failure.

Michael Stamm, "This Child Is No Good," in Fantasy Review, *Vol. 8, No. 10, October, 1985, p. 20.*

PUBLISHERS WEEKLY

A small New England town with a dark secret and a guilty memory is the setting of [*Hellfire*].... The autocratic Sturgess family's dark 19th century mill stands as silent testimony to the wealth it built on child labor. While the restless, vengeful spirit of young fire victim Amy waits in the mill, the present-day Sturgesses are, under their good manners and impeccable breeding, every bit as monstrous as their ancestors. Matriarch Abigail and her bad seed granddaughter Tracy make life hell for Philip Sturgess's new wife and her daughter by a previous marriage. If there is an inevitability about much of the novel, the bloody, tantalizing plot rushes forward, the setting and historical background are well drawn and Tracy is memorably, startlingly nasty.

A review of "Hellfire," in Publishers Weekly, *Vol. 229, No. 26, June 27, 1986, p. 82.*

FLEMING MEEKS

[*Hellfire*] is set in a sleepy Massachusetts town, long dominated by the wealthy Sturgess family. Stereotypical New England WASPS, grandmother Abigail Sturgess, son Phillip and granddaughter Tracy live in an imposing mansion, overlooking the village and the long-abandoned shoe factory—the factory from which their fortune was derived.

But all is not well in the Sturgess home. The widowed Phillip has remarried, bringing his wife Carolyn and her amiable 11-year-old daughter, Beth, to live at Hilltop. Tracy, who has been spoiled into a state of near pathological snobbery, resents their intrusion and conspires with her grandmother to drive them out.

Enter Amy, the ghost of an 11-year-old killed with seven other children in a fire in the mill 100 years ago. Amy, whose entrances are accompanied by the smell of smoke, befriends Beth, and the nasty secret of the Sturgess family is revealed: The children all could have been saved, but Samuel Pruett Sturgess sealed them behind a fire door, saving the mill instead.

And Amy wants revenge.

Beth, in the meantime, has come to be regarded as something of a nut case. When one of Tracy's friends takes a fatal fall down a set of stairs at the mill and lands on a pickax, Beth claims that Amy did it, because he'd been nasty to her. But the accident closely resembles the one that killed Abigail's first son, 40-odd years ago, and prompts her to reconsider her husband's repeated warnings about the mill: "It's an evil place," and his last words: "She's there ... She's still there and she hates us all." ...

If this plot sounds a bit overwrought, consider the following: *Suffer the Children*—an evil deed of 100 years ago is being punished, children are disappearing; *Brain Child*—after an accident, a child is brought back from death and is revenging a terrible deed from 100 years ago; *Nathaniel*—a new kid in town takes over the spirit of a 100-year-old legend that haunts the town; *Comes a Blind Fury*—a new girl in town seeks revenge for the torments a blind girl suffered before her death 100 years ago. ...

[Saul] seems to have wrung all of the terror out of his plot long ago, the result being that the most frightening element of *Hellfire* is not the supernatural nor the ample number of "accidental" deaths, but rather it's the unrelenting adolescent nastiness of the jealous step-sister.

Fleming Meeks, in a review of "Hellfire," in Los Angeles Times Book Review, *August 10, 1986, p. 6.*

Bernard Slade

1930-

(Born Bernard Slade Newbound) Canadian-born dramatist and scriptwriter.

In his plays, Slade presents humorous examinations of different types of romantic love and familial commitment. His protagonists are usually involved in unlikely situations which Slade renders believable through his engaging characterizations and language. Slade is often praised for his pointed jokes and puns, which hint at deeper truths about the human condition. His works have been compared to the romantic comedies of Noël Coward and Neil Simon for their witty depictions of the perils of love.

Slade's first Broadway production, *Same Time, Next Year* (1975), is considered his most accomplished work. Doris and George, the only characters in the play, meet accidentally at a California motel and begin an affair. Although both are happily married, they continue to meet one another each year at the same location. As the play progresses, Doris and George develop as individuals and as a couple during the next twenty-five years. Slade also offers a social chronicle of the United States from the early 1950s to the mid-1970s by providing for a montage of popular songs and newscasts between acts. At every rendezvous, the changes in Doris's and George's political beliefs, language, and physical appearance reflect America's shifting social climate.

Slade's next play, *Tribute* (1978), is more serious in content, addressing the subject of death and the importance of familial relationships. The play revolves around Scottie Templeton, an unsuccessful scriptwriter and Hollywood public relations man who charms everyone except his own son. When it is revealed that Scottie is dying of leukemia, his friends rent a theater and pay homage to him, while Scottie tries to win back his son's love. John Simon noted that Slade "mixes laughter and tears with almost supernatural skill, always sidestepping ultimate frivolity, always teetering back from the abyss of mawkishness into the happy pratfall of farce."

Slade's subsequent works have met with less enthusiasm. *Romantic Comedy* (1979) follows several years in the stormy relationship between two collaborating dramatists. *Special Occasions* (1982) returns to the two-character format of *Same Time, Next Year,* exploring a couple's increasing understanding of each other after their divorce. Slade also wrote the screenplays for film adaptations of *Same Time, Next Year, Tribute,* and *Romantic Comedy* and has written extensively for Canadian and American television.

(See also *CLC,* Vol. 11; *Contemporary Authors,* Vols. 81-84; and *Dictionary of Literary Biography,* Vol. 53.)

RONALD BRYDEN

On the surface, *Tribute* may seem as all-American as [*Same Time, Next Year*], but inside is a very Canadian play indeed.

In New York, *Tribute* will seem no more than a sentimental hymn to star-spangled showbiz. In a format blending elements of Hollywood roast, the Academy Awards dinner and Armistice Day, it pays homage to all the unknown soldiers of *Variety*'s obituary pages, summed up here by Scottie Templeton. Scottie is a failed screenwriter, sitcom producer and flack, but to his peers he's a prince, a hero of Algonquin Hotel legend: the man who sends friends strippers on birthdays, plays hoaxes by phone and mistakes Zanuck's wife for a party girl. And for tonight, he's a star. . . .

In case that's not enough, he's also dying of cancer. So one by one old drinking partners, discarded wives and nostalgic call girls step up to tell of his famous pranks and the heart that lurked beneath the shallow stream of old Hollywood jokes. Only one person holds out, the one Scottie cares for most. No analyst of his sexual history will be surprised to learn that it is another male: his son Jud . . . , still bitter about his parents' divorce and something nasty he saw in a Beverly Hills cabana 15 years ago.

Here's where the Canadian play surfaces. Jud's mother has remarried and moved to Canada, where Jud has been reared. As a result, he is a stiff, puritanical youth, given to wearing white shirts, ties and a spinach-green prep-school pullover, who prefers the Museum of Modern Art to wrestling nude 42nd Street ladies with Dad. "Before I die, I want to try and teach him how to have fun," says Scottie. He does more than that. By the end of the evening, the boy confesses his hang-up has always been envy of Dad's glittering life. He doesn't want to be Canadian. His spiritual home is Beverly Hills too.

It's an honest statement of how a good many Canadian artists and writers feel deep down. The play's less honest in concealing its debt to a finer comedy than itself, Noel Coward's *Present Laughter*. Scottie is a bagels-and-lox version of Coward's Gary Essendine, beating debutantes from the hem of his dressing gown with his cigarette holder. But where Coward justified Gary's life solely and arrogantly by his talent, Slade needs leukemia to justify Scottie's want of it. Coward's apology for his life is a proud non-apology. Slade's is Canadian. It reeks of guilt.

Ronald Bryden, "Bernie Slade Knows Us Better than We Think," in Maclean's Magazine, *Vol. 91, No. 10, May 15, 1978, p. 80.*

JOHN SIMON

I am not sure about how good a play *Tribute* is; what I know is that it is extremely clever and likable, which is as unusual a combination in plays as it is in people. But that combination is what we got from Bernard Slade before, in *Same Time, Next Year,* and that is what we get from him this year. . . .

Do you realize what a *coup de théâtre* this is? First of all, Scottie . . . actually addresses us with "You are my friends and you are the greatest audience a man ever had." We have been flattered from the stage before, but not without the star's having to step out of character and start throwing prefabricated kisses at us. Here it is all part of the play: *We* are this man's friends, *we* are giving him this farewell tribute, *we* have somehow become his therapists and earned his moist-eyed gratitude. And here he is, much cleverer and wittier than the rest of us, but it is *our* love that has made him tongue-tied—as inept as we are. O ineffable joy! And then the touching way in which words are restored to him: but I can't give that away.

There is more. *Tribute* is a play about reconciliation between parent and child; who in this Gilead of ours, with more physicians and less balm than ever, does not find uplift in that? A play, moreover, that mixes laughter and tears with almost supernatural skill, always sidestepping ultimate frivolity, always teetering back from the abyss of mawkishness into the happy pratfall of farce. A play that takes the sting out of adultery, divorce, prostitution, failure in business, nonachievement of artistic aspirations, family in-fighting, and, best of all, death itself! *Tribute* is the most comforting news this side of a cure for cancer.

So whatever a captious critic might say, this *comédie larmoyante* is destined to become a crowd pleaser, and who could begrudge it? For, along with the cleverness, there is something very nice about *Tribute:* You have the happy feeling that the many very genuine witticisms in it are not, as usual, made at the expense of other people. Nobody is made a fool of; nothing is attacked in a scalding, humiliating, irrevocably damaging way. Only a nice man could have written *Tribute,* and to spend a couple of hours in his company is a privilege and a pleasure. What, for me, sets Bernard Slade above a Neil Simon (even if Simon's jokes come a bit faster, and certainly thicker) is that Slade's characters are not interchangeable: They speak, think, jest as themselves, and not as so many indistinguishable mouthpieces of their author. And that is both clever and nice, both imaginative and self-effacing. (p. 74)

If there is a serious omission in *Tribute,* it is that it never quite shows us the nature of the anxiety Scottie is trying to hide. Oh, we all know it well enough from our own experiences; still, we want the playwright to illuminate it for us. A gnawing hunger persists at the core of the play, but you may easily overlook it amid the plenty. (p. 77)

John Simon, "Assent for 'Tribute'," in New York Magazine, *Vol. 11, No. 25, June 19, 1978, pp. 74, 77.*

BRENDAN GILL

Tribute bases its plot on a gimmick: Friends of Scottie Templeton, the hero of the play, have rented a theatre in which to pay tribute to him; we in the audience . . . are in that very theatre and are, in effect, among his dear friends. Toward the end of the play, after Scottie, his ex-wife, his son, a couple of girlfriends, and a close business associate have acted out what amounts to a version of the old TV show "This Is Your Life," Scottie is discovered seated in a box at the [theatre]; he comes down to the footlights and thanks us, his old companions, for . . . well, for what? Certainly not for the tribute that we are supposed to have been paying him, because, having been told again and again by his admirers onstage that he is among the wittiest and most charming of men, we have had demonstrated to us only that [Jack Lemmon] is among the most resourceful of actors; it is *his* charm [in portraying Scottie] that we find ourselves applauding. For Scottie Templeton is a dying man, understandably at the end of his emotional tether; he is making a frantic attempt to establish a relationship with his priggish son, who, on the evidence of his lines, is wholly unworthy of his mischievous scamp of a father. The playwright wishes us to see that Scottie's attempt is proof of an authentically unselfish and loving parental impulse, but as the role is written we are apt to conclude that the attempt springs from the fact that the son is the only person alive upon whom Scottie's implacable winsomeness has failed to have an effect. It is not love unrequited but narcissism outwitted that has brought Scottie to the brink of breakdown.

Brendan Gill, "In Praise of Lemmon," in The New Yorker, *Vol. LIV, No. 19, June 26, 1978, p. 51.*

JOHN SIMON

Romantic Comedy is Bernard Slade's hardheaded attempt to write a romantic comedy in the manner of post-Hays Office Hollywood, with a sprinkling of Shaw and a dash of Coward. It is his bow to nostalgia, which, as we have all noticed, is sweeping the country. Still, I regret that the wry author of *Same Time, Next Year* and the still controlled sentimental maker of *Tribute* should have leaped on that backward-hurtling bandwagon where the cart is always set before the horse.

Worse yet, he has opted for that hoariest of cliff-hangers, the three-act coitus interruptus. Jason Carmichael is a brilliant playwright in collaboration, but has lost his partner to the movies. Phoebe Craddock, a shy young New England schoolteacher who has sent him a dramatic manuscript, walks in by accident on Jason's wedding day; our stranded George S. Kaufman type looks at the MS and promptly, besides taking a wife, takes Hart. Jason and Phoebe proceed to collaborate on numerous hits and some flops. Phoebe loves Jason unavowedly but obviously; he loves her even less avowedly, indeed unconsciously. Whenever they might come together, something prevents it. . . . But fourteen years later, by Act III, Scene 3, Jason and Phoebe end—well, not quite engorged with bliss like your Cary Grants and Irene Dunnes (a few concessions to our hardened hearts must be made), but almost.

Who steals Iago's purse steals trash; who gives away this plot gives away nothing essential. Mr. Slade, however, is a fellow of, perhaps not infinite but, surely, definite jest: *Romantic Comedy* almost makes up in comedy what it lacks in romance. . . .

Well, isn't the comedy enough? Not quite, when there are no convincing characters, merely manipulable counters. Certainly Jason is a consistently sophisticated, witty curmudgeon and Phoebe a basically passionate but repressed clever woman. Yet their behavior belies their intelligence in the interest of keeping the slender plot unwinding a little longer. And, in a sense, these two are too consistent: Even their quirks are the appropriate ones for the cunning automata that sport them; Phoebe and Jason never become independent of their creator, never sprout idiosyncratic lives of their own. And the supporting characters are even more schematic: the wisecracking Follies girl turned agent with a heart of gold (the whore's legacy to the huckster); the understanding but ambitious wife who chooses a solid career over a shaky marriage; the nice Other Guy who always does the decent thing, even unto his undoing; the Hollywood star who doesn't know which end is up—or which side of her dress is out. . . .

[Somewhere] en route to *Pygmalion* and *Private Lives* via Old Hollywood, Slade bogs down rather badly—all the more so since he cannot convince us that the trip was necessary.

> John Simon, "Slow Burn," in New York *Magazine,*
> *Vol. 12, No. 46, November 26, 1979, p. 90.*

JACK KROLL

Bernard Slade's *Romantic Comedy* isn't very romantic, and it's funny only in a forced, clenched way that greatly lacks charm. Slade has tried to do a "take" on the old genre of romantic comedy—he's tried to write a romantic comedy for a time that's not very romantic. The many references to Noel Coward, to Philip Barry, to Kaufman and Hart, are Slade's way of smuggling his play into that company while at the same time telling us he's so sophisticated that he knows you can't write that kind of play anymore. The result is that Slade outsmarts himself but isn't smart or daring enough to go all the way and write an antiromantic *Romantic Comedy* that would really make us laugh at these unromantic times.

Slade's hero, Jason Carmichael . . . , the successful Broadway playwright, is not a likable guy, but he's unlikable not in an interesting contemporary way—he just seems like a minor-league version of those self-absorbed, abrasive curmudgeons that used to be played by George Sanders, Monty Woolley and Clifton Webb. His collaborator, Phoebe Craddock . . . , is like those small-town girls who make it as writers in the big city, who used to be played by Jean Arthur, Claudette Colbert and Irene Dunne. Slade makes all sorts of switcheroos on the genre—there's a nude scene, for example, that's played not by [Phoebe] but by [Jason]. The result is a play that seems half anachronism, half just plain not good enough, hardly measuring up to Slade's *Same Time, Next Year.* . . .

[Several of the minor characters are] given little buffing-up touches by Slade, but they remain tired clichés in a quasi-updated old format. In the end, you just don't care about these two eccentric blooms, Jason and Phoebe, grinding out plays in their hothouse in Jason's ritzy New York City digs.

> *Jack Kroll, "Once More, with No Feeling," in*
> Newsweek, *Vol. XCIV, No. 22, November 26, 1979,*
> *p. 75.*

CLIVE BARNES

Bernard Slade writes plays about love. Or perhaps he doesn't write them. Perhaps they write themselves, and Slade merely provides the theme, punctuates it with jokes and lets his typewriter do the talking. They are . . . seemingly so painless, painlessly so seamless. . . .

The first, *Same Time, Next Year,* was about tactfully adulterous love, the second, *Tribute* concerned filial love, while the third *Romantic Comedy* suggested mistimed love. Now with *Special Occasions* Slade has given us a play about divorced love.

He has returned to the formula—two characters and a time span—that worked for him so well in *Same Time, Next Year.* At the beginning of the play Amy and Michael are celebrating their 15th wedding anniversary and planning their divorce. It is what experienced playgoers will recognize as a piquant yet totally unlikely situation. Such situations are Slade's forte, and he never plays them pianissimo.

Because they both write successful Broadway comedies Bernard Slade is frequently compared with Neil Simon. There is a big difference. Simon writes about life as it is, whereas Slade is far more concerned with life as it should be. His plays are frequently funny—and like Simon his jokes are not all merely wisecracking one-liners—yet Slade tends to trivialize serious situations—although this was not true of his most seriously felt play, *Tribute*—and to sugarcoat realities.

The present play celebrates Amy and Michael's 10-year divorce following their 15-year marriage, and the special occasions of the title are those family gatherings, a burial here, a baptism there, that continue to bring them together. Also, over the decade, we can see their development as people (although they are as tediously superficial at the end as they are at the beginning, even if both the tediousness and the superficiality are different) and their establishment of a loving friendship.

Superficial Amy and Michael might be, but they are not un-amusing, and Slade milks their situation with the same kind of hearty, yet effortless gusto that has characterized his other plays. Here he gives us an evening that works on its level of slick quaintness—for example, joke surprises come regularly like the chirping of a cuckoo clock. But for anyone wanting more weight with their wit and more depth to their comedy, *Special Occasions* will probably seem a case of too much fluff surrounding too little stuff. . . .

[The glossily gift-packaged characterizations of Michael and Amy] underline the basic weaknesses of the play. Why should we be interested in these people in the first place? And, even given interest, why did they ever marry in the second. They are a couple monstrously unsuited for anything other than divorce.

Slade's typewriter still keeps clacking out its jokes and occasional felicities. But the clacking sounds more insistent and less spontaneous than hitherto. Perhaps it is simply better at adultery than divorce, or perhaps it just needs a vacation, or at least a new ribbon.

Don't get me wrong—*Special Occasions* is not a bad evening in the boulevard theater, undemanding and provocative only to the point of the hidden cliche. But it is not, by any stretch, a special occasion.

> *Clive Barnes, "Nothing Special Funny about 'Occasions'," in* New York Post, *February 8, 1982. Reprinted in* New York Theatre Critics' Reviews, *Vol. XXXXIII, No. 2, Week of January 11, 1982, p. 378.*

FRANK RICH

Special Occasions is an attenuated television play that uneasily mixes the conventions of the situation comedy and soap opera. . . .

A two-character work, *Special Occasions* revamps the premise, but not the structural gimmick, of Mr. Slade's *Same Time, Next Year.* In that earlier comedy, a pair of illicit lovers carried out a series of yearly assignations designed to prove that a married man's best friend is his mistress. In the new play, a just-divorced couple keep meeting in a series of similar, calendar-leaping scenes so that we might learn that an ex-married man's best friend is his ex-wife. There's one other change as well: Unlike the one-set *Same Time,* this play requires two turntables of scenery to show us the weddings, funerals and high school graduations that bring the couple together. . . .

The heroine and hero announce their personality traits early on and rarely develop more depth than posterboards. Amy Ruskin is an aggressive go-getter who is defined by her tendency to smoke, drink and use "curse" words to excess. . . .

Her former husband of 15 years, Michael, is a television-writer-turned-playwright who has trouble expressing emotions and instead houses his "deep-seated rage" in migraine headaches and lower back pains. . . .

[Many of the dozen-odd scenes] contain roughly the same elements. First, we are told what special occasion has brought Amy and Michael together. Then we are told of some putatively shocking bombshell that has occurred in their lives since the last scene—a death in the family, a new marriage or dissolution of same, a major medical or psychological crisis. Finally we are brought up-to-date on the goings-on of an increasingly large and indistinguishable group of never-to-be-seen supporting players. . . .

Though it often seems that much of *Special Occasions* is taking place offstage, Mr. Slade does have one variation up his sleeve: In no fewer than four scenes, the action is quite literally phoned in. We also get a scene in which the climax is played over a tape, cassette, as well as one which consists of watching Michael listen to his telephone-answering machine. At such times, *Special Occasions* might as well be recited by a pair of Western Union messenger boys.

> *Frank Rich, "Slade's 'Special Occasions'," in* The New York Times, *February 8, 1982, p. C13.*

JOHN SIMON

I liked Bernard Slade's first Broadway play, *Same Time, Next Year,* but my approbation has been diminishing with every subsequent Slade offering. The latest, *Special Occasions,* which closed after one performance, was a sort of recycling of *Same Time, Next Year,* or, more precisely, that play turned inside out. I could clarify this aperçu, and would have done so had the play lasted, but, as things are, let's just leave it at that. *Special Occasions* was really designed-for-television comedy coming from what may become known as the American branch of the Slade School of Design: here and there a genuine wisecrack, surrounded by others that are less wise than cracked. And there were considerable stretches during which the play deluded itself into trying to get along on no gags at all. . . .

Still, it was bracing to hear the vaguely autobiographical hero, a TV writer turned playwright, confess: "I had a minimal talent. I stretched it as far as it can go." I just hope Mr. Slade did not expect us to contradict him. At the same time, I wonder just how our producers select a play. Do they look for merit? Not likely. Or do they ask: "How many sets? How many actors? What stars are currently available?" There is nothing wrong with boulevard comedy (though there is nothing great about it either), provided it too is chosen for its quality, not merely for its economics. (p. 54)

> *John Simon, "Making the Lowly Lowlier," in* New York *Magazine, Vol. 15, No. 8, February 22, 1982, pp. 52-4.*

ROSALIND CARNE

Take one intelligent, assertive, but deeply insecure woman. Give her an emotional plank of wood for a husband. Turn him into a mildly successful playwright, and the inevitable result is alcoholism and divorce. Author Bernard Slade wisely skips this dismal preamble and opens his unusual and, in many ways, endearing comedy [*Special Occasions*], on the night of their fifteenth wedding anniversary.

Recuperating after the party, steeling themselves for separation, they survey the piles of gifts that surround them. How will they announce the divorce, wonders Michael? "Thought I'd mention it in the thank you notes," replies the resourceful Amy. With dialogue like this, the couple stand a good chance of sustaining our interest as they take us through the next seven years of not-quite severance, emerging from their respective homes to meet on those special occasions, weddings, funerals, accidents and so forth, that punctuate all our lives.

Amy gives up the booze and remarries, much to Michael's faintly disguised jealousy and disgust. But she soon tires of her devoted, pear-shaped solicitor, just as Michael tires of Julia, Marion, Olivia and all the others he hopes will fill the gap of loneliness. Deep down they still want each other. . . .

What appears to hold them together, apart from their offspring, is their shared history, and on this point the play rings true. Free of the trammels of marriage, they are able to look at each other more clearly and to reach beyond antagonism to friendship.

As this is a two-hander, we never meet the children, friends and in-laws who occupy so much of their attention, but the writer covers the ground exhaustively and we come to know them all well. A little too well, for the play's worst fault is its excessive attention to detail, its inability to let matters rest and the fact that it simply goes on too long. With no particular sense of danger, no climax or catharsis, it palls after the first half. The original concept might have been better realised as a series of half hour slots on TV or, considering the lack of visual excitement, radio.

Rosalind Carne, "'Special Occasions': Ambassa-dors," in Plays & Players, *No. 365, February, 1984, p. 32.*

W(illiam) M(ode) Spackman

1905-

American novelist, essayist, and critic.

Spackman writes ornate novels about the romantic affairs of upper-class men and women. These works typically involve adulterous relationships between a middle-aged man and two women, one younger and one nearer to himself in age. Spackman asserted: "My only real literary interest is the high-style novel," and his work revels in the sensuousness of language and its ability to evoke the beauty of women, classical values, cities, and food and wine. His writing contains dialogue featuring idiosyncratic rhythms, indirect discourse, and frequent exclamations, through which he reflects the syntax of upper-class colloquial speech. Although some critics fault Spackman for simplistic characterizations, others regard him as an impressive novelist of manners.

Prior to his writing career, Spackman was a Rhodes scholar at Balliol College, Oxford, and a professor of classics at New York University and the University of Colorado. His first novel, *Heyday* (1953), elicited comparisons to F. Scott Fitzgerald's "Babylon Revisited" for capturing the social and spiritual climate of the generation of affluent young Americans during the Depression of the 1930s. Following a twenty-five-year hiatus, Spackman published *An Armful of Warm Girl* (1978). In this novel, an aristocrat who has been abandoned by his wife travels to New York to reestablish an old love affair and in turn is pursued by a young actress. John Leonard noted: "[Except] for one seduction and one surprise, not much happens . . . and yet everything happens: romance, wit, intelligence, geniality, culture without the politics that spoiled it after 1959, sex without tears, a genuinely lovable character."

Spackman's novels following *An Armful of Warm Girl* explore conflicts inherent in adulterous love. *A Presence with Secrets* (1981) examines the dalliances of a womanizing artist from the perspectives of the protagonist, his libertine female cousin, and his closest male friend. Edmund White observed that "Spackman's characters reveal what people feel when love is free, uncoded. These feelings turn out to be sweetness, sensuality, loneliness, and an amazement at the appalling otherness of others." Henry James's *The Ambassadors* served as a model for *A Difference of Design* (1983), in which a wealthy American mother dispatches a diplomat to France to liberate her son from a seductress. The diplomat, however, becomes entangled with his Parisian cultural guide and the seductress he had intended to confront. In *A Little Decorum, for Once* (1985), Spackman explores through long, witty conversations the generational differences in extramarital behavior. Christopher Schemering called the book "a whirly, madcap battle of the sexes, updating those light, frothy turn-of-the-century operettas in which merry makers chase themselves into a lather of irony and infidelity." Spackman has also written a collection of critical essays, *On the Decay of Humanism* (1967), and has contributed articles to such magazines as *Parnassus, Canto,* and *Esquire.*

(See also *Contemporary Authors,* Vols. 81-84.)

JAMES KELLY

Mr. Spackman aims his first novel [*Heyday*] at the lonely generation of the vulnerable Thirties. A member of the Princeton class of 1927, he freely admits, in a publisher's quote, that there is quite a parallel between the intent of *Heyday* and Fitzgerald's "Babylon Revisited," which had a vintage ten years earlier. It is, he says, "the spiritual biography of a generation, a statement about American values, an elegy upon the immemorial loneliness of man, a statement about the young American upper class in that era of its disaster, the 1930's." Pretty large claims for this nostalgic and singleminded chronicle of Greenwich Village sex-capades, featuring nubile ivy-leaguers whose hearts belonged to Eighth Street even during sidetrips to Paris, France, and Coatesville, Pa. Regrettably, therefore, one must judge *Heyday* by how close it comes to the author's elaborate intentions, which is not very.

Webb Fletcher, the narrator and omnipresent total-recaller of *Heyday,* begins to think about the past when news reaches him at his wartime ONI desk that Mike Fletcher, cousin and Princeton '27 classmate, has been killed in the Coral Sea action. He had not known Mike very well, even though they had resembled each other in looks, behavior, and taste for the same women during terrible, desperate Depression years. . . . Using Mike as the touchstone, [Webb] returns in his mind to entwined campus memories, to misty, drunken adventures, and (inevitably) to the libidinous solace of Kitty, Stephanie, Jill, Barbara. How do you compose a suitable obituary for somebody like Mike, a shadowy hero who always rejected more than he accepted and never knew for sure what was offered? Webb has a try at it, anyhow, giving himself nearly equal billing.

By 1931, Webb is in New York after a hitch on the Paris *Herald* and idyllic *Tender is the Night* adventures with Barbara, afterward his wife. Mike, now an unemployed advertising man, and Webb, now transferred to *The Sun,* move in the same restless, partying group. When Barbara is sentenced to prison for seven years following an accident with her car, the two voluptuaries settle down to a geometric, sensuous pattern [of love relationships]. . . . Webb finally resolves his pattern in genuinely poignant scenes with Barbara, returned from prison and ready to begin again. For Mike, no answer until the Coral Sea. And Mike's obituary becomes at last an obituary of the shattered generation to which he belonged—a sobering reminder for the man who puts it together.

If Max Bodenheim, Scott Fitzgerald, and Ezra Pound had at one time pooled their forces (shocking thought) to write a definitive Depression Novel, the chances are it would have turned out something like this parodiable amalgam of classical allusions, large social observations, and explicit sexual vignettes. As a one-man tour de force, *Heyday* is remarkable. Mr. Spackman faithfully reports the bedroom habits of his characters, much as if he were an anthropologist invited to attend a Melanesian ceremonial. He expertly records colloquial talk and city sights. Lovingly, and with great attention to literary style, he weaves his material into dirge-like passages which are as full of dramatic posturings as a Greek chorus. It is not enough, though. His people have small significance beyond their assigned roles as erotic symbols. And the convoluted, thesaurus-haunted connective tissue of the story seldom advances beyond the beguiling designs of word embroidery.

James Kelly, "'Tween-Lost Folk," in The Saturday Review, New York, Vol. XXXVI, No. 8, February 21, 1953, p. 19.

WILLIAM PFAFF

[*Heyday*] is the story of two men from the class of Princeton, 1927. . . . The narrator looks into the past twenty years to tell his own story and that of a classmate and friend who died in the war.

Their time gave them only two years of the iridescent kick of the twenties, and then there followed the windy decade of depression. That is where most of the story takes place. New York City during the depression. The gay and rich were broke and on the lip of hysteria. So Mr. Spackman's book is a lush and emotional story of how people lived on salaries which gave them sandwiches and neuroses.

A tragedy forms the single hard line in this soft web—the narrator's wife spends the decade in prison on a manslaughter charge, having killed some children in an automobile accident. Otherwise the story is an impassioned involvement in the past, sometimes quite moving, sometimes just a bit silly. It is quite erotic, again occasionally to a faintly absurd degree. And it is always very readable. Mr. Spackman quotes the lines "with a casual smile / saunter round corners to their doom," and he has tried, I think, to write such an account of his period, but

he has not the Eliotic quality of distillation, of muscle, which makes the distinction between interesting and fine. (pp. 631-32)

William Pfaff, "Young Men and Expensive Company," in Commonweal, Vol. LVII, No. 25, March 27, 1953, pp. 631-32.

FRANCES TALIAFERRO

At last, after all the novels of fornication, a novel of seduction. The title [*An Armful of Warm Girl*] is far too cute for the contents: Spackman is a very Fabergé among novelists, and this novel is not fluffy but mannered, elegant, enameled. New York and the more feudal provinces of the East are the setting; the time is the late 1950s, epoch of a glamour hitherto unnoticed but here perfectly credible. The hero is Nicholas Romney, fifty, recently severed from his Main Line Philadelphia milieu and wife (in that order). Imagine Ovid an alumnus of Princeton ('31), with a fondness for his own epigrams, Bach, and crème aux marrons, baching it in his dear little townhouse hung with Copley portraits. Such is Nicholas Romney.

His vocabulary is seignorial; his cadences, when they don't sound like La Rochefoucauld, are echoes of G. M. Hopkins. He is the most original literary creation of the decade. . . . Only a barbarous Boeotian could fail to be tickled by the amorous intricacies of this delightful book. It is Watteau's *Embarcation for Cythera* rendered as a fugue by Cole Porter: an incomparably civilized trip.

Frances Taliaferro, in a review of "An Armful of Warm Girl," in Harper's, Vol. 256, No. 1535, April, 1978, p. 83.

JOHN LEONARD

The time in W. M. Spackman's delightful novel [*An Armful of Warm Girl*] is 1959. The place is New York, to which our unlikely hero has come in a rage. Our unlikely hero is Nicholas Romney, Princeton '31, Philadelphia banker and libertine, 50 years old and in a rage because his wife wants a divorce. In New York he will pursue a married woman, Victoria, with whom he had an affair 17 years ago, and he will in his turn be pursued by a 20-year-old actress, Morgan, who may or may not be his daughter. (We never find out.). . .

Nicholas, you see, is well-educated, and *An Armful of Warm Girl,* you see, is a very literary comedy of seduction, full of references to Dante, Shakespeare, Racine, Henry James, T. S. Eliot and Immanuel Kant, although the two most important writers in the book, besides, of course, Mr. Spackman, are Homer and Ovid. Nicholas identifies temperamentally with Ovid, another "man of sensibility" whose Latin couplets he renders into colloquial English when it suits him, and Mr. Spackman seems to have written a French boudoir farce, set in New York in 1959, according to Homer's literary technique in the *Iliad.* I think so; I'm not really sure. But Nicholas does explain to the stricken Morgan:

> . . . take the Iliad: the Iliad it often appeared was like a ballet, matched heroes dancing forward at each other in opposing pairs to fling their antiphonal taunts and spears, then dancing back, and then after a choral movement of the ordinary infantry another pair coming on, another pas de deux; and this he said was how it often seemed to be with love, the shafts of

women's transfixing beauty ran him through,
their sighs answering his antiphonally in turn,
and if it was ever-changing and new still was
it each time any the less utterly a death?

That describes *An Armful of Warm Girl,* all right: opposing
pairs and pas de deux, all antiphonies and antistrophes....
With the exception of two big parties, almost every scene in
the novel involves an irreducible pair.

This does not, alas, explain why almost all the men in the
novel are bankers who go to Geneva in August in order that
their wives may conduct affairs in Paris and Rome. Nor does
it justify the incessant gormandizing: "Mrs. Barclay wished
he had somehow learned to distinguish between a woman and
an entree." Nor does it excuse the promiscuous literary criticism: "Eliot, that Pindar of the prie-dieu, *wonderfully* lyric
and readable on there's-nothing-to-be-done-about-any-
thing."...

But I could be wrong. One thinks also of Shakespeare's comedies, Georges Feydeau, the roundelay, *Smiles of a Summer
Night,* psychoanalysis, *Lolita,* "bavarois with kirsch-soaked
strawberries piled round in crimson dunes" and other "fragments of sob-mangled rodomontade." The point is that, except
for one seduction and one surprise, not much happens in *An
Armful of Warm Girl,* and yet everything happens: romance,
wit, intelligence, geniality, culture without the politics that
spoiled it after 1959, sex without tears, a genuinely lovable
character....

It is as if Randall Jarrell had written *The Merry Widow.* I think
W. M. Spackman is probably a classicist and antiquarian who
must be around 70 years old by now, and I hope he has retired
to Crete to eat olives and goat cheese because he reminds me
that once upon a time there was a civilization.

> John Leonard, in a review of "An Armful of Warm
> Girl," in The New York Times, *April 10, 1978, p.
> C21.*

JEAN STROUSE

Imagine a modern Don Juan playing the lead in *Women in
Love,* directed by Nabokov with lyrics by Cole Porter, and
you'll have a rough—if somewhat overblown—estimate of *A
Presence With Secrets.*... [In this book, Spackman has] constructed an elegant, erudite, witty play on the verb "to know"
in all its sexual and secular conjugations.

Lest that sound too abstract, listen to this account of an incipient
affair: "They blandly lingered . . . over the splendors of his
salmon, the cool cheeses, the crimson dunes of wild strawberries on their palliasses of bright leaves...." (p. 78)

The "he" whose salmon they linger over is Hugh Tatnall, a
famous American painter living in Florence, "impeccably upper-class Philadelphia," artist-in-residence at Smith and virtuoso at the craft of seduction. Spackman presents him in three
takes. In the first, seen through Hugh's own eyes, he has taken
refuge from a rioting mob in a luxurious Florentine *pensione*
with a delectable, terrified, just deflowered young woman named
Rosemary, who wants him to explain her to herself and says
things like, "she'd never imagined one would feel sort of 'well,
Italian-second-person-singular about you'." (pp. 78-9)

In the second, narrated by Hugh's female equivalent, a libertine
cousin with whom he encounters Breton separatists and murder
on a weekend fling, he asks, "Why did you come with me?"

and she thinks, "Oh heaven as if I *knew,* and I said, 'But
Hugh darling I love you, even after all this time I love you, I
never stopped,' with my soft look at him under my eyelids to
make sure he believed me."

And in the third, at Hugh's funeral, his closest friend Simon
Shipley ponders, "as one marauding male about another,"
Hugh's life, his art, his girls....

A sense of humor about sex is a rare thing in contemporary
writing, and Spackman drenches these dalliances in laughter
and light. He also shows, without moralizing, the masculine
romanticism that cloaks women in draperies of enchantment.
Some will find this too ornate.... That, of course, is a question
of taste: on finishing *A Presence With Secrets,* I turned right
back to page one to read it again. (p. 79)

> Jean Strouse, "Rake's Progress," *in* Newsweek,
> *Vol. XCVII, No. 2, January 12, 1981, pp. 78-9.*

EDMUND WHITE

For anyone who aspires to a style that can wheel dramatically
close to its subject for a pore-by-pore inspection, then track
inexorably through the parting dancers or place an unsmudged
glass before a window silver with sunstruck rain; for anyone
eager to write a single sentence that holds in suspension particles of wisdom and nonsense, action and observation, lust
and loveliness; for anyone who is curious about the verbal art
of picturing things and maneuvering a reader, as distinct from
such less elusive aspects of fiction as plot, suspense, symbolism, and "message"; for this dwindling but avid crew of devotees, Spackman's new novel *A Presence with Secrets* will
come as a great clarification. It is the most stylish, vital, and
worldly book to emerge—well, since his last book, *An Armful
of Warm Girl.*

The style owes a debt to both Henry Green and Ivy Compton-
Burnett. It was Green (inspired in turn by Charles M. Doughty's *Travels in Arabia Deserta*) who devised a written language
that strikes us as "artificial" only because it approximates the
flexibility, the concreteness, and surprising syntax of spoken
English. We like to assure ourselves that no distinction exists
in English between spoken demotic and written hieratic....
But in fact there *is* a gap in English (and American) so great
that we can't hear the quaint music, the oddly placed stress in
many sentences in Green or Spackman unless we say them out
loud.

I'm not suggesting that Green or Spackman chart the trackless
wastes of ordinary chatter or render its mindlessness and feeble
energy. Quite the contrary. These writers have contrived a
literary manner that is hard, condensed, often epigrammatic,
but that does draw for its effects on the repetitions of speech,
the gliding elisions, its illogical leaps, inversions—the stut-
tering of thought and feeling....

From Compton-Burnett, Spackman has learned how to pay
unblinking attention to the balletic intricacies of refined small
talk, conversation that epitomizes her novels and his with its
emphasis on originality of presentation and perfect conventionality of subject....

The temptation to fill up my pages with quotations from Spackman attests to his accomplishment. He has done away with
tiresome exposition at the outset and philosophical musing for
the wrap-up. There is no merely mechanical filling in of obligatory scenes, no unsavory ponderings of the meaning of events,

no throat-clearings, no characters nor situations foreign to his understanding or ungrateful to his talent. Like the first painter who realized he could do away with the holy family and concentrate on the landscape or eliminate the diners and render the peaches and napery, Spackman has stripped away everything irrelevant to his genius. He seems the sort of artist who makes his decisions by depending on goose-bumps. . . .

If judged by his own standards, Spackman receives high marks; he's certainly not guilty of "the arrogance of a settled way." His first novel, *Heyday,* is packed with incidents and characters and covers many years, a capaciousness he will reject in the later two novels. The tone of *Heyday* is an unsettling mixture of the factual and the fabulous. We must work our way through circumstantial accounts of court trials, job prospects, money troubles, and infidelities-in-the-interest-of-career, in order to arrive at those magical passages that seem the pale sapphires in overly busy mounts—the nostalgic visit to Wilmington, for instance, or a tete-a-tete luncheon of martinis for him, whisky sours for her, pure pleasure for us. And the voices of the young women—they have the authentic Spackman ring of well-bred strategic vagueness. These are voices we'll be hearing again. (p. 37)

In *A Presence with Secrets,* Spackman has reduced the anecdote to its simplest elements in order to give himself room for the delights of rendering; just as Morandi chose to paint nothing but bottles, Spackman has restricted himself to romance. But the love he portrays is not the sort we're used to reading about. In most bourgeois novels (most novels, that is), the love is hopeless, one-sided, doomed from the start; if the love is to flower at all, it must do so by virtue of a miracle, since the lovers come from different classes, races, from warring families or warring nations, and so on. (pp. 37, 39)

In Spackman's novels the lovers do not reach for each other across a social chasm. The romances do not dramatize large social conflicts nor produce an illusory solution to real tensions. Instead, the lovers are all privileged and physically beautiful. Moreover, they all subscribe to the same code: that the institution of marriage is unlikely to house for long such a bird of passage as passion; that passion itself is not brutal or even primarily biological but rather tender and civil; that the only way to survive the sadness of living and loving is with a reckless gaiety of spirit. Spackman's men and women are all co-conspirators, libertines willing to propitiate the deities of convention in order to secure the joys of dalliance. Spackman's lovers do not suffer. Whereas most fictional lovers suffer, I'd say, in an *exemplary* way (their torments are emblems or scaled-down versions of society's inequities), Spackman's characters reveal what people feel when love is free, uncoded. These feelings turn out to be sweetness, sensuality, loneliness, and an amazement at the appalling otherness of others. Which is what the title means; another person, one's lover, is a presence with secrets. . . .

Like many writers (Shakespeare, for instance), Spackman makes birth a condition for civility, but any time at all spent with the actual rich or well-bred convinces the reader that Spackman's vision is utopian, a glimpse of what people, freed from poverty and ignorance, might become. Yet even in such an Edenic state, people will remain pregnant with secrets. As the narrator tells us, "even a lover is an ally against loneliness who still hasn't claim enough to encroach upon my solitude for me to 'know.'" . . .

Of course, if solitude is accepted, measured, cherished, and if the inevitable distance between two people is turned from des-

olation into coquetry, then life regains its enchantment and becomes once again practicable—or at least endurable. . . .

But of course that is what art—or at least Spackman's art—surely must be, the very distillation of enchantment, the consolation for life. (p. 39)

Edmund White, "A Goose-Bump Genius," in The Village Voice, *Vol. XXVI, No. 3, January 14-20, 1981, pp. 37, 39.*

J. D. O'HARA

[There] truly *is* a way in which men can exploit women, and women men, and the other combinations, and it's *all right.* Let me get hastily to a for instance. It's by W. M. Spackman, whose *An Armful of Warm Girl* I must've praised before. This novel . . . is *A Presence with Secrets.* It tells about Hugh Tatnall, a skilled and wealthy American painter resident in Europe and the U.S., and begins with a scene in which a very recently seduced young woman laments to him what she has done with him. Hasty passages:

> "And when don't you see I'd never so much as called you by your first *name* even, before I simply—Oh *how could I!*" she mourned. "And it wasn't even partly your fault!" she accused him, choking.
>
> (pp. 459-60)

There, polished to an even brighter shine, is the style of *An Armful of Warm Girl,* the intricate, knowing, precious style that Henry James might have risen to if he possessed sexuality and a sense of humor. It is the artificial and unreal style for which Restoration comedy had such a desire, the style in which words might express the human longing for sensuality fulfilled and accompanied by its verbal equivalent. (Most readers have never felt such a longing, of course, and after a page of Spackman they stumble thick-tongued back to their Dreiser or D. H. Lawrence or even Mailer.) It is a style of wish-fulfillment, evoking a society in which both men and women are in control of themselves and yet passionate too, emotional and yet intellectual too, full of animal desires and yet cultured too. And Spackman composes marvelous music in this style. Yet in this novel he has gone further and has done what seems impossible. The young lady's sexual encounter was improvisto because it was caused by an Italian political riot; a bloody political killing occurs later; the hero himself is killed; the self-centeredness of self-satisfaction is made clear . . . and yet the style lives on, the dream remains dreamable. (p. 460)

J. D. O'Hara, in a review of "A Presence with Secrets," in New England Review, *Vol. 3, No. 3, Spring, 1981, pp. 459-60.*

ANATOLE BROYARD

Everybody seems to admire W. M. Spackman's novels. . . .

As much as I'd like to, I can't be quite so unqualified about *A Difference of Design.* . . . While I'm grateful, almost uncritically so, for characters who believe in love, romance, gallantry, manners, elegance and all the other refinements that men and women used to bring out in each other, it seems to me that Mr. Spackman gives us too much of those good things. To use the current idiom, his love lacks the sadness and pain that makes us believe in it.

Sather, the protagonist of the book, is a cultivated, handsome 50-year-old businessman who is sent to Paris by the mother of a young man who seems to be dangerously embroiled with a French woman. The theme is from Henry James, but Mr. Spackman copies James by chewing, as Edith Wharton put it, more than he bites off.

Two women in their 20's fall in love with Sather, practically at first sight. One is Maria, the beautiful and clever founder of an expensive escort service. She is a bilingual American who will shepherd Sather, who doesn't speak French or know France, through the intricacies of the culture and the cuisine. . . .

No sooner does Maria fall for Sather than she begins analyzing her reactions to him and his to her. Her conversation is reminiscent of what used to be called the New Criticism, in which every aspect of a novel or poem was scrutinized ad nauseam. Poor Sather, who seems to be a lusty, easy-going fellow, shows a remarkable patience with Maria's didactic passion, which to any less forgiving man would surely have had a dampening effect.

Perhaps it does, for he soon finds himself trying to steal the Countess Fabrienne, also a young beauty, who is already tired of the American lad Sather has come to rescue. Fabrienne exhibits all the virtues and vices of upper-class French culture. She thinks in categories and the subtlest of vernacular French phrases, so that Sather rarely knows what she's talking about.

Most of her talking she does to herself, like a woman thinking about a party she is planning for 20 people. What will she wear, how will she dissemble her feelings, how can she seize the advantage over Sather? Unlike Maria, who lets it all hang out in American style in spite of her Francophilia, Fabrienne is like a queen in a Court of Love, worrying like an erotic casuist every least nuance of love. It often seems that she enjoys her language—a veritable dictionary of the untranslatable idioms that educated French women use to deal with amorous males—more than anything those males might do if they were encouraged. Fabrienne's love is a structure by Levi-Strauss, a strategy, a conundrum in human relations.

I don't see how Sather can bear either one of them. If I were in his place, I'd catch the next plane back to New York City and find a woman who has what is vulgarly known as spontaneity and who also speaks a common language.

Anatole Broyard, in a review of "A Difference of Design," in The New York Times, *June 16, 1983, p. C19.*

STEPHEN KOCH

A Difference of Design is an exceedingly elegant and exceedingly short . . . novel by a writer whose reputation lately has been burgeoning in certain sectors of the literary intelligentsia. Quite deservedly so. Mr. W. M. Spackman is a phenomenon, all right. His art will prosper. For one thing, his delicious short sketches of the loves of the sublimely rich really are amusing. For another, Spackman is irresistible—catnip, as he might say— to critics, who are drawn to his prose very much as Spackman's Fascinating Women are drawn to the Marvelous Men who stroll so confidently into the three-star restaurants of his world. In truth, every Spackman page is an ideal example of some much-argued critical point about The Novel, and for all their elaborate languor, these novels occupy a self-conscious position on the critical chessboard. In *A Difference of Design* Spackman has

made that position explicit by proclaiming his book a forthright steal from his literary ancestor, Henry James. *The Ambassadors,* to be precise. With a difference of design.

Not that this novel is in any way theory-laden or academic. On the contrary, *A Difference of Design* is a fluffy and extremely easy read. Henry James, T. S. Eliot remarked, "had a mind so fine that no idea could violate it." That is exactly the spirit of Spackman's prose. What this means in practice is that from first to last a Spackman novel is dominated not by ideas or observation or conflict or even passion, but by an elaborately relaxed, elaborately lightweight *style.*

Unlike Henry James, however, Spackman is a romantic. That is, he is absorbed in the power of language and the romantic reverie to conjure another realm. A somewhere else ruled by beauty, with roughly the same relation to your and my world as a high-fashion photograph has to your and my clothes: i.e., Zip. To be sure, Spackman is no fantasist: no Borges, or Calvino, or Burroughs. His cities are not invisible, but dreamy variants on the real New York and Paris and their very richest suburbs. In truth, his romantic somewhere else is *wealth,* which he doubtless sees as one of his links to James. This is a realm of the rich: rich men, rich women, rich love, where people forever are having a perfectly *lovely* luncheon on the terrace, and citing Ovid and musing on Madame Récamier and adoring each other.

Because Spackman's romantic feet just barely graze the ground of the actual as he wafts through his prose, what we are left to notice first, last, and always is, precisely, the prose. It is often beautiful, and I predict it will one day be parodied and imitated and become a touchstone: People will hold their breath on a golden terrace and think of a Spackman moment. (p. 3)

Actually, the Style is a sophisticated confection of the table talk and bedroom sights and, to be blunt, more affected pretensions of the American upper classes, a mélange of fractured French and lots, just heaps and heaps, of darlings and sweets and perfectly awful moments, simply heavenly people, and damned annoyances.

Now, I have no objection to Mr. Spackman finding his poetry in the lightweight language of the upper crust, but as his reputation grows, I think the shallowness of his sources is worth noting. Spackman may indeed be an heir to James (though not in his romanticism); he may indeed use the much-abused high modern method of the stream-of-consciousness with great skill. But finally this gossamer has been spun from little more than the asinine lockjaw drawls of Muffy and Wingate III. If it is high style, it is also High Prep. Very high. (pp. 3, 5)

Spackman's subject is always the same: Love. Triangular love, to be precise, which in Spackman always has much the same design. A man, usually of a certain age, is simply irresistible to (at least) two women. He thus is obliged to, sort of, choose. . . .

In *A Difference of Design,* The Man is named Sather (based, most improbably, on James' Lambert Strether). The Woman is the beautiful countess who, until Sather's arrival, has been playing with the playboy Sather has been dispatched to bring home. The Girl (well, not quite a girl) is the young woman who has been hired as Sather's guide. (Oh, come on, now. Guide?). Both of these women, I need not add, adore, but hopelessly adore, The Man.

More than a little garden-variety masculine wish-fulfillment runs through these pages. Well, why not? In Spackman's world it is wishing and love, sweet love, that rule. Life is a dream, and money has made it come true. It is not reality, and it is not, contrary to claims, Nabokovian artifice either. It is not ironic enough, not sufficiently attuned to disaster, for that. In Nabokov, the power of artifice kills. People die in Nabokov. In Spackman, all adored, they drift. We drift with them, and as the pillow talk of the love and sex murmur on, it seems not to matter whether we believe. It is all so . . . harmless. Yet to my mind it lacks passion, and lacking passion, truth. Even the sex, so lovely and discreetly handled, strikes me, frankly, as sexless sex. In a review of *An Armful of Warm Girl* John Leonard called it "sex without tears" [see excerpt above].

Well, fair enough. (p. 5)

Stephen Koch, "Love among the Rich," in Book World—The Washington Post, *August 14, 1983, pp. 3, 5.*

GARY DAVENPORT

One of the classic American treatments of the public-private dichotomy—particularly as it assumes the form of the seduction of an individual away from a mundane role created for him by his society—is *The Ambassadors,* and a contemporary re-working of that James novel is of interest here. W. M. Spackman's *A Difference of Design,* with characters named Chad Newman, Lewis Lambert Sather, and Maria Godfrey, is manifestly such a retelling of James's story, set implausibly in the 1980s. Readers of Spackman's curious collection of essays, *On the Decay of Humanism* (1967), may wonder at this apparent interest in James—to whom he condescends in a long essay in that volume—and especially at his use of *The Ambassadors,* a novel in which he "cannot find anything to admire." (Readers of James who join me in finding a very great deal to admire in *The Ambassadors* may be mildly surprised by the hubris, or the quixotism, of this attempt to set the record straight.)

Spackman has said that his only literary interest is the "high-style novel," and that is what he has written—or rather what he is at pains to write, for I would describe the style as affected rather than high. . . . He seems especially concerned to eschew ideas or "meaning," and he is usually successful—although undigested prejudices appear with great frequency. There is for example no effort to conceal a contempt for the Great Unwashed . . . , for "liberated" women (or rather *girls, love-lies, angels, things,* and *creatures,* as the adult females of the novel are likely to be called), or for the vulgar present (one sympathetically portrayed character muses about "how straightforward being alive must once have been, au grand siècle," when "the scenario was dans les règles and fore-seen"). Whatever one thinks of such sentiments, they are, as the novel presents them, too thinly literal, too stereotypical to be the fabric of interesting fiction. A reader may also suspect that the author is using his novel as a medium for the public unpacking of a well-stocked mind: at one point quotations from Rostand, Musset, Fontenelle, and Constant occur within the space of some twenty lines of text.

But the real shortcoming of *A Difference of Design* is that it dispenses with (or throws into nearly total eclipse) the very quality that makes James's version of the story so powerful: a sense of the conflict between the potential individual destinies of the Americans in Europe and the mundane social destinies designed for them by the Americans back home. There simply are no individual personalities in the book capable of engaging the interest of a mature reader. Their motives are transparent: the women gush and tease, and the men charitably allow them-

selves to be seduced. If one wished to argue that there is no American cultural soil in which the traditional novel of manners can flourish, he could do worse than choose *A Difference of Design* for text: it is a truer exemplar of the tradition than any other American novel I can call to mind, but it is instantly recognizable as a product of the hothouse. (pp. 134-35)

Gary Davenport, "The Two Worlds of Contemporary American Fiction," in The Sewanee Review, *Vol. XCII, No. 1, Winter, 1984, pp. 128-36.*

WENDY LESSER

Reading *A Little Decorum, for Once* is a bit like sitting in a cafe and overhearing a rather pretentious but nonetheless riveting conversation at the next table. On the one hand, you can't believe that people really talk like that. On the other, you're thrilled at having acquired this stolen bit of "real life."

W. M. Spackman's brief novel contains exactly those contradictions. His style is at once strikingly artificial and persuasively realistic, consisting almost entirely of broken bits of dialogue that flow into their narrative surroundings. The tone is light but intelligent, careful but colloquial, and the overall effect is one of witty disregard, making *A Little Decorum* the type of work one can easily imagine people describing as a *jeu d'esprit.*

Mr. Spackman's characters speak breathily and effusively, in fits and starts, with interjections inserted at odd points in their sentences. These sentences, in turn, are often expressed as indirect quotation, further eliding the distance between author and character. "Yes, well, he said mildly, after a moment, yes the heart unit had, he'd of course concede, been something of a memento mori, how did those splendid duty nurses stand it, hour after hour?" This is the musing of the novel's central character, a novelist named Scrope Townshend, as he converses with his former and soon-to-be-reclaimed mistress, Laura Tench-Fenton, about his recent heart attack. Nor is Scrope the only one with such eccentric speech patterns; the novel itself speaks in this fashion, with author barely separable from character, dialogue from description. Even the quoted bits from Scrope's fiction sound exactly like Mr. Spackman's own Scrope-encompassing novel.

As a character, Scrope Townshend earns his central position by virtue of his age as well as his wit. A sixtyish grandfather, he is viewed by the novel's other characters as both the voice of experience and something of an innocent. His and Laura's affair, which has intermittently engulfed them over the course of many years, lends *A Little Decorum* its deepest emotional elements and provides the frame for all the other relationships. . . .

Mr. Spackman's novel gives far greater weight to perceptions than it does to plot. A slight story line holds the work together: Sibylla (Scrope's daughter) and Charles (the live-in lover of Sibylla's best friend, Amy) fall in love and into an affair. This affair of theirs, in its actual and suspected manifestations, provides the major conversational material not only for the older generation (Scrope and Laura), but also for the younger. . . . To complicate matters further, Sibylla is married to Laura's stepson, Alec. The Sibylla / Charles affair, in its consummated form, takes up remarkably few pages in the novel. Most of the book is instead devoted to discussions of its ramifications by the two participants and their Greek chorus of onlookers.

If this begins to sound a lot like *The Golden Bowl* or another of Henry James's *jeux d'esprit*, that is not a fact that has escaped the author. At one point Mr. Spackman has Sibylla say, "But oh Charles you *know* this, you're not like those fumbling Howells-ish characters in Henry James who have to have minor characters explain things to them all the time." But while the felt intensity of withheld material and the tightness of the author's social universe may recall *The Awkward Age* or *The Wings of the Dove*, the degree of character development does not. Mr. Spackman's creations can be annoyingly flighty.... And even at their best, as in Scrope and Laura, the people in *A Little Decorum* just don't spend sufficient time on stage to touch one with any depth. Perhaps because of the work's brevity, there isn't room enough here for the creation of intense feeling—which is why Mr. Spackman's latest work of fiction seems more like delicious coffeehouse gossip than a substantial novel.

> Wendy Lesser, "Adultery with Discussions," in The New York Times Book Review, *October 20, 1985, p. 14.*

CHRISTOPHER SCHEMERING

The naughty world of W. M. Spackman is located somewhere between a scoop of Evelyn Waugh and a very un-McCarthy-like Gropes of Academe. In *A Little Decorum, For Once* the witty exchanges between lovers are caresses, avenues of sensuality, while the sexual skirmishes are farcical, irrelevant. Set on and off the Princeton campus, *A Little Decorum, For Once* is a whirly, madcap battle of the sexes, updating those light, frothy turn-of-the-century operettas in which merry makers chase themselves into a lather of irony and infidelity.

Virtually plotless and filled with loose ends, the comedy employs a three-tiered structure to give its readers their bearings. At a "still marauding sixty plus," novelist Scrope Townshend and his ex-paramour, high-fashion editor Laura Tench-Fenton, are suddenly tossed in a tempest: his married daughter Sibylla and her "huge" stepson Alec are courting marital disaster. Sibylla is enchanted by Alec's best friend Charles, and Alec finds himself in another quandary: Charles' girlfriend Amy has the hots for Alec! Serving less as a Greek chorus than a daffy

peanut gallery is Scrope's grandson Richard and his freshman bed mate, Mimi, who gets around, to put it mildly. (p. 3)

Spackman, the author of *An Armful of Warm Girl,* is such an eccentric stylist that he may be considered an acquired taste. (The continuous exclamations, odd rhythms, and run-on nature of the sentences take some getting used to.) But he's never so off the beat that one loses the beat. ("Black chiffon isn't to sleep in, it's to sleep with in.") The characters' exchanges are so long and dense and intricate that it's easy to get lost in all the verbal haranguing. From pillow talk to luncheon gab, the "delicious" girl-women take center stage and hold court to lounging hunks who come up with an occasional grunt or even a less occasional rejoinder like "which side of this dizzy debate with yourself are you planning to end up losing!"

The lack of narrative push also contributes to the lack of focus, but surely this is Spackman's point and forte: everything and everyone is slightly off, daft. But the marvelous Spackman dialogue, with its ironic asides, stream of consciousness nonsense, and brackets of affection should be patented. It begins with a sneeze of a conceit, then erupts into a full rip-snorter, taking surprising turns and unexpected dives until it disappears down a madhatter's chute:

> "My blessed woman," (Scrope) besought (Laura) "hasn't it even occurred to you that one of *the* bonds of long and happy understanding between us mayn't be that simply we find it natural to be in love with two people at once, provided one of them is the other of *us*? It's what we did!—what's more, if everybody else did too, don't we privately think la condition humaine would be as happy a state as ours has been? Dammit, if I ever decided to rearrange the past with an autobiography, I'll say so! (By the way, I've a splendid title, *Bygones, Begone!*)."

This is the crucial passage in Spackman's roundelay. Nothing is resolved in his celebration of the roving eye; only the chaser, the chased, and, happily, the chase remain. (p. 10)

> Christopher Schemering, "W. M. Spackman: Games of Love and Language," in Book World—The Washington Post, *November 10, 1985, pp. 3, 10.*

Norman (Richard) Spinrad

1940-

American novelist, short story writer, editor, essayist, critic, and scriptwriter.

Spinrad gained recognition during the late 1960s as a contributor to the "New Wave" movement in science fiction. Like J. G. Ballard, Michael Moorcock, and Harlan Ellison, who are categorized as New Wave writers, Spinrad utilizes tenets from psychology, sociology, and linguistics and employs such devices as interior monologue, satire, and black humor. Spinrad categorizes his work as speculative fiction, which, he asserts, is "the only fiction that deals with modern reality in the only way that it can be comprehended—as the interface between a rapidly evolving and fissioning environment and the resultant continuously mutating human consciousness." Spinrad's plots are usually set in the near future and are often based on extreme examples of present-day conditions. Social and political turmoil, media manipulation, legalization and mass use of drugs, violence, and sex are recurring elements of his fiction.

Spinrad's first novel to gain critical attention was *The Men in the Jungle* (1967). Amid explicit scenes of sex and violence, this novel details the exploits of an opportunistic mercenary who travels from planet to planet to incite revolutions in order to head a new regime. In *Bug Jack Barron* (1969), Spinrad tests the limits of traditional science fiction by including stream-of-consciousness narrative, obscenities, and detailed sexual encounters. Set in a near-future United States, the novel centers on Jack Barron, a popular television personality who investigates an accusation about the Foundation for Human Immortality, a privately-owned operation that sells immortality treatments to its clients. He exposes a scandal, becomes a hero, and runs for President. Some critics disapproved of *Bug Jack Barron* because of its scatological language and nihilistic tone, while others praised its effective portrayal of the power of television to shape human thought. Spinrad's next novel, *The Iron Dream* (1972), is based on the premise that Adolf Hitler emigrated to the United States in 1919 and became an author. Hitler's pulp science fiction novel, *The Lord of the Swastika*, is related in the course of Spinrad's book. The strength of *The Iron Dream*, according to Ursula K. Le Guin, lies in its irony and its penetrating examination of fascism. *A World Between* (1979) is about an idyllic society whose standards of individualism, pluralism, democracy, and sexual equality are threatened by two alien factions trying to take over the planet. A bitter propaganda war ensues, through which Spinrad satirizes extreme political views and defines an ideal male-female coexistence. The novel's theme is underscored in a subplot detailing the conflict that arises between lovers who are swept into the ideological battle.

Spinrad's next novel, *Songs from the Stars* (1980), depicts a postnuclear holocaust tribal civilization that has rejected technology and other "black sciences" and lives by the hedonistic law of "muscle, sun, wind, and water." The novel centers on a technocratic villain who threatens the serene existence of the idealistic inhabitants. *The Mind Game* (1983), a mainstream novel, revolves around the underhanded dealings of a pseudoscientific cult. *The Void Captain's Tale* (1983) is a futuristic

story about the relationship between a male starship captain and a female pilot whose sensual impressions are integrated with the ship's circuitry. In this work, Spinrad employs extensive symbolism and a futuristic language containing words from various twentieth-century cultures. *Child of Fortune* (1985), which takes place in the same universe as *The Void Captain's Tale,* is a retrospective coming-of-age tale narrated by fictional novelist Wendi Shasta Leonardo. The book details Wendi's *wanderjahr*, a rite of passage during which adolescents travel from planet to planet as "children of fortune" attempting to discover and establish their identity. A noted feature of this novel is Spinrad's depiction of lushly detailed, diverse settings.

Spinrad has also written several volumes of short stories. The first of these collections, *The Last of the Golden Horde* (1970), includes pieces written between 1963 and 1969, several of which first appeared in science fiction magazines. The stories in *No Direction Home* (1975) present bleak and sometimes horrifying views of the future. These works center on such topics as drugs, rock and roll, scavengers in the ruins of the United States, combat football, and motorcycle gangs. *The Star-Spangled Future* (1979) gathers previously published and new stories as well as a series of annotations and essays in which Spinrad discusses upon the significance of speculative fiction and science fiction in contemporary American literature. Spinrad has also written scripts for the television series "Star

Trek'' and has edited two science fiction anthologies, *The New Tomorrows* (1971) and *Modern Science Fiction* (1974).

(See also *Contemporary Authors,* Vols. 37-40, rev. ed.; *Contemporary Authors New Revision Series,* Vol. 20; and *Dictionary of Literary Biography,* Vol. 8.)

ROBERT W. HASELTINE

[*The Men in the Jungle*] is a difficult novel to assess, for it is written on two quite different levels. The first lends itself to a science-fiction setting, recounting the adventures and problems of an amoral character who foments a revolution to gain power. The characters of this story are finely drawn; the three main characters, Bart Fraden, his mistress, and his chief of staff, are well defined, and their actions stem from their personalities. They are, therefore, quite believable. At this level the jungle of the title is on the planet Sangre, and is the base of operations for the overthrow of the sadistic rule of the Brothers of Pain. Their power structure admits only men to power, all others are animals—and animals are eaten by men. The action is fast, bloody, sexy, and compelling. The second level is the psychological, and the jungle is man's mind. The theme seems to be that, given an environmental setting where the finer parts of man's character cannot develop, the sado-masochist will be in the fore.... The end of Sangre is one of rioting, sex, and cannibalism, as Fraden, making his getaway with only his mistress—his chief of staff has become like one of the natives and has been killed by them—leaves Sangre in far worse shape than he found it.... It is very well-done, and should be made available to readers.

> *Robert W. Haseltine, in a review of ''The Men in the Jungle,'' in* Library Journal, *Vol. 92, No. 5, March 1, 1967, p. 1033.*

THE TIMES LITERARY SUPPLEMENT

In this intelligent novel [*Bug Jack Barron*] set in America a decade or so from now Mr. Spinrad writes about two of the most potentially dangerous elites: the super-television inquisitors and the men with the scientific power to control and extend human life for ever.

Jack Barron, a fast-talking, highly-sexed television tycoon has a weekly show—Bug Jack Barron. People get on their videophones (''everybody has one'') to him in the studio to tell him about a problem that's bugging them. Barron then links up his videophone with the ''bugger'', in a manner of speaking, and a triangular discussion takes place with Barron in the chair and an audience of over a hundred million people. One night a Negro calls in to say that the Foundation for Human Immortality is anti-black. Now the Foundation for Human Immortality is a nice little privately-owned operation—no sign of Medicare yet—where you pay your $50,000 for a freezer contract and get frozen until the big defrost day, by which time scientists at the Foundation will have discovered how to keep their clients alive for ever.

Jack Barron starts an investigation of Mr. Deep Freeze himself, the owner of the Foundation, one Benedict Howards.... There is a mammoth, no-holds-barred struggle between the two men on all levels—personal, professional and political—which reaches a climax when Barron discovers what the Foundation is *really* up to. And what it is really up to is not very nice.

Mr. Spinrad writes with verve and has a lively ear for current idiom. His ''political science fiction'' has a deadly plausibility.

> *''White Frost,'' in* The Times Literary Supplement, *No. 3552, March 26, 1970, p. 328.*

JAN SLAVIN

Spinrad has potential as a writer, but he lacks the control, judgment, and sensitivity of a well-developed author. [In *The Men in the Jungle*, he] started with a good idea, and sufficient ability, but has failed to combine them properly, and the result is about as appetizing as a ruined souffle....

This book is a paradox. The description is vivid, but disgusting. The pace is reasonably fast. The plot is basically an adventure-type but it develops twistedly, so horribly. The characters are real, but they are loathsome, sick, and sub-human. If there is any point or reason in this tale, it is lost amid sado-pornographic scenes.

Perhaps Spinrad was trying to satirize the sex-sadism books that are growing ever-popular. Perhaps he is trying to hold up a mirror to the great amount of violence, perversion and even blood-lust that is present in the world today. But that mirror seems warped, and rather than reflecting or shocking into action, it appears to me that it only disgusts, or titillates, depending on your sensibilities. Instead of a valid protest against ruthless violence, it is merely a collection of obscene descriptions.

> *Jan Slavin, in a review of ''The Men in the Jungle,'' in* Luna Monthly, *No. 14, July, 1970, p. 27.*

LEONARD ISAACS

The themes of nuclear apocalypse and of precognition are separately treated in Spinrad's ''**The Big Flash**'' and ''**The Weed of Time**'' [collected in *No Direction Home*]. ''**Flash**'' is an ongoing countdown from T minus 200 days to ... well ... the big flash, and is handled through an accelerating series of first-person vignettes. The story plays upon the paranoia and trauma of late-sixties America as a freak-rock group called ''The Four Horsemen'' changes in the reader's eyes from an amusing put-on to a pawn of the contingency planners to the actual catalyst for Armageddon. The reader quickly senses what the outcome will be, but sees it so inextricably tied up with the fabric of modern-day America that he himself is implicated. (p. 57)

''**The Weed of Time**'' is an exploration of a consciousness that is 110 years in length and limitless in duration. A single act at age 20 has given the narrator precognition of his entire life, so that at every instant—including the period from birth to age 20—all moments of his existence are equally and eternally present for him. There is a long sf tradition of dealing with the paradoxes of travel or perception in time, and Spinrad has contributed an imaginative and compelling addition to that company. The narrator explains and repeats the nature of his dilemma, begging the reader to understand. Here is an endlessly tortured soul, grabbing at the reader's lapels. He doesn't wait to be properly introduced, but he makes his reality damnably difficult for the reader to dismiss. (pp. 57-8)

The most memorable entry in the Spinrad collection is **"The Lost Continent"**; here Spinrad . . . offers up a vision of what follows environmental cataclysm. On the most immediate level, Spinrad depicts a ravaged future America, a society living— just barely—amid the ruins of the Space Age. This, in itself, is very convincingly done; the society is not barbarian or feudal, it is merely second rate. Spinrad succeeds in evoking for the reader the full paradox of twentieth century America. It is accomplished by indirection, by probing the effects of the American legacy upon 22nd century descendants (white) and successors (black). Racial tension threads the story like an electric cable, and the small details add on increments of charge. There is no sense of authorial intrusion as a visiting African academic contributes a bit of description of desolated Manhattan under its Fuller Dome ". . . composed of relative darknesses of blue, much as the world under the canopy of a heavy rain forest is a world of varying greens." (p. 58)

[*No Direction Home* is a] mixed bag: of the remaining entries, three are simply ballast, two more are impossibly sentimental, and two are excellent. **"The Conspiracy"** is an avant-garde filler of the *New Worlds* sort, while **"The National Pastime"** and **"In the Eye of the Storm"** are traditional fillers of the American-pulp variety. **"Heirloom"** unintentionally trivializes the agony of Vietnam by implying that a Terran expeditionary force sent to preserve the planet Bornok for democracy can be made to withdraw within two weeks by the simple expedient of the natives' ignoring the existence of their protectors, even at the cost of a few individual executions. **"Heroes Die But Once"** sets up an incredibly naive image of what an ideal marital relationship is like and then strives for tragic effect by having it destroyed when the couple realize that each member was willing to sacrifice the other to save the self. Perhaps there is at work in the sf universe a Law of Conservation of Cliché, so that all the ones that never appeared in the collection's best pieces had to surface here. The action in **"Heroes Die But Once"** centres around a cold, inhuman intelligence carrying out your usual unspeakable tortures upon an idyllic young couple in the name of experimentation. This one made for truly embarrassing reading. (p. 59)

"No Direction Home" (the title story) and **"All the Sounds of the Rainbow"** are just slightly dated now in that both focus on psychedelic trips, but in each piece the theme is treated so imaginatively and persuasively that the story's erstwhile topicality is the briefest of distractions. Here, Spinrad is in full control of acid-head clichés; he doesn't so much avoid them as alter their chemistry for unexpected effects. In **"Rainbow"** the character with the power of synesthesic projection is an aging, opportunistic ex-beach bum who wishes he hadn't fallen off his surfboard. And in **"No Direction Home"** Spinrad effortlessly accomplishes what I regard as the essential task of science fiction—to give the reader a glimpse of a previously unseen facet of reality by illuminating it from a novel perspective. (pp. 59-60)

> *Leonard Isaacs, "Ivied Walls and American Graffiti," in* Foundation, *Nos. 11 & 12, March, 1977, pp. 55-60.*

ALGIS BUDRYS

[In *A World Between,* the] free world of Pacifica finds itself contended for by Earth's Femocracy on the one hand and the interstellar technocracy of the Transcendental Science movement on the other. Spinrad makes a serious attempt to represent real present-day ideologies and find a middle ground. Since both philosophies also have had or are having their day as fashions in sf, Spinrad's construct has that additional level of relevance. Couched in a narrative that does not quite founder in its own details of plot-twist, this book is serious and significant reading for old hand or novice.

> *Algis Budrys, in a review of "A World Between," in* Booklist, *Vol. 75, No. 13, March 1, 1979, p. 1043.*

PAMELA SARGENT

Norman Spinrad has written some short story gems, as a look through his recent collection, *The Star-Spangled Future* . . . , will demonstrate. If Spinrad has a distinctive theme, it is power; his characters struggle for it or try to figure out how to use it. His latest novel, *Songs From the Stars* . . . takes place a few centuries after an atomic war; the two main characters, Clear Blue Lou and Sunshine Sue, are on the verge of a discovery which could radically change their society. Spinrad takes these familiar science-fictional elements and creates an original and entertaining story, his best novel so far.

Lou and Sue live in Aquaria, a land on the west coast of the former United States. Aquaria has rejected the "black sciences" of advanced technology, living by the law of "muscle, sun, wind and water," but radioactive power cores have been found in several radios used by the Sunshine Tribe's Word of Mouth network. Lou, a Perfect Master of the Clear Blue Way (who functions much like a circuit-riding judge), must travel to the town of La Mirage to confront Sue, head of the Sunshine Tribe. Sue, however, has a secret ambition. Having learned of the ancient art of "media" from old writings, she dreams of a worldwide communications network. The two do not realize that they are pawns in the plan of a "sorcerer," Arnold Harker, who wants to send a spacecraft to an abandoned space station.

To tell any more would spoil the story. The book is written in a trendy patois which could have been annoying except that it is so perfect for depicting these characters. There is a message in the novel, but it never gets in the way of the story. Spinrad is best at detailing the society of Aquaria and its customs, less convincing when he adopts a second-person, present-tense style to convey an alien and transcendent vision, and his descriptive passages can veer toward the purple. But *Songs From the Stars* is, as a whole, a lively, humorous, lusty, well-plotted, and often poetic book.

> *Pamela Sargent, "Imagination in Orbit," in* Book World—The Washington Post, *Vol. X, No. 30, July 27, 1980, p. 9.*

DENNIS LIVINGSTON

Norman Spinrad is one of the more provocative science-fiction authors. He lives up to his reputation in this complex novel of strange doings on the planet Pacifica [*A World Between*]. In an entertaining and witty context, Spinrad brings together several of the most important topics that have preoccupied his colleagues in recent years.

Most obvious is the issue of sex roles. As its name implies, Pacifica is blessed with a benign environment and a relatively small population of 30 million, descended from human colonists. The Pacificans have developed their own unique culture in which men and women are formally equal in all spheres of life, although women tend to predominate in political and economic affairs, while men often take the lead in family and sexual matters. This is not simply a reversal of the present on Earth, since the individualistic Pacificans (whichever path they choose) treat each other with respect and tolerance.

Also unique to these people is their mastery of the media of the future—the combination of cable television, computer conferencing, and interactive data banks that seems to be just around the corner here and now on Earth.

Again, the media do not fit into a hierarchical political system. On Pacifica they are used as the foundation for an electronic democracy, in which media access is guaranteed to all and citizens may take part in votes of confidence in their leaders.

To this decentralist utopia come two opposing groups engaged in an ideological battle to gain cultural predominance over the human worlds. The Transcendental Scientists are pushing for a male-dominated elite that will guide humanity, through the use of high technology, to mastery of the universe. The Femocrats control a war-weary Earth and seek to reduce men to the status of breeders in the name of an all-embracing Sisterhood.

Each group aims to polarise the sexes on Pacifica and thereby gain control of the planet. To achieve this, they will spread their propaganda by making full use of the media-access rights granted them.

Spinrad brings in aspects of various present Earthly debates in what may seem a satirical manner, but shows his skill by not scoring easy points. All three opposing forces are represented by a couple. Each of these six people, in their different ways, feels the pull or repulsion of the competing ideologies. It is clear that Pacifica poses a challenge for both Scientists and Femocrats, yet even the Pacificans learn some uncomfortable truths about themselves in the process.

Spinrad deals with questions about the social control of technology, the rights of any culture to interfere with another in the name of its own 'higher good', and the interplay of gender with sociopolitical environment. (p. 426)

> *Dennis Livingston, "Culture Clashes," in* Futures, *Vol. 12, No. 5, October, 1980, pp. 426-27.*

ALLEN VARNEY

Spinrad's new (and little publicized) mainstream novel [*The Mind Game*] is of marginal SF interest, since it deals with a pseudo-scientific pop cult based on Scientology, which has been called a "science fiction religion". Spinrad's creativity would be more impressive were his book's "Transformationalism" not so obviously a stand-in for Scientology and its founder not a duplicate of L. Ron Hubbard; but clearly this novel gains much of its power from its horrible resemblance to reality.

Jack and Anne Weller are a loving Hollywood couple who are abruptly separated when she is drawn into the clutches of Transformationalism. With his wife spirited away by the church to parts unknown, Jack pursues every course of action imaginable to regain her, but finally he has to play along and undergo Transformational "processing" himself. He plays a "mind game" with the Transformationalist movement to convince them his conversion is sincere while avoiding being "programmed"....

As always with Spinrad's novels, it's easier for me to find reasons why I shouldn't have liked the book than reasons why I did. In *The Mind Game* the characters are two-dimensional—though the Hubbard figure is imbued with a certain charisma despite his boozy, con-man approach—and the prose includes occasional boners like "he had been too inside his own head to notice" . . . and "bubbling alchemist laboratories". . . . A major secondary character suddenly disappears without explanation 160 pages into the novel and the plot's single unbelievable coincidence is a dilly, as Jack stumbles upon a Transformationalist "Master Contact Sheet", potentially damaging to the movement, simply lying around on a desktop.

Yet these flaws, however serious, do not diminish the absorbing development of the novel. Weller is not strongly characterized, but he becomes an Everyman we sympathize with as he fights to retain his own thought processes while relentlessly bluffing his way up through the cult hierarchy. "Processing" is the key. . . . Spinrad's books are entirely concerned with *process*. He chronicles, with absolute integrity and an unequalled sense of pace, the slow transformation that comes with (to borrow the title of his earlier mainstream novel) "passing through the flame".

> *Allen Varney, in a review of "The Mind Game," in* Science Fiction Review, *Vol. 10, No. 1, February, 1981, p. 56.*

DARRELL SCHWEITZER

Songs from the Stars reads like it was written in 1968. Had it actually been published then, I imagine most critics would have pronounced it datedly trendy. Perhaps by 1981 it would have become a period piece antique, like *The Butterfly Kid*. Right now it might best be called a historical reconstruction. (It is also simply a rather good novel, but more on that later.) One of its premises is that, after an atomic holocaust, there flourishes in what was once California a society based on 1960s back-to-nature utopianism. The place is called Aquaria. The main characters are named Sunshine Sue and Clear Blue Lou. The people are divided up into tribes and live in communes. They follow "The Way" and are all very Zen. They talk in language that would have been very hip ten or so years ago. Worse yet, the early sections of the narrative itself are written in such language, which means the author's voice is constantly intruding, reminding the reader that he is reading a story. . . .

There are so many shrieking implausibilities in the first few chapters that I nearly gave up then and there. Fortunately, I persisted. Once the action leaves Aquaria, the novel gets a lot better. (p. 28)

In some ways, *Songs from the Stars* provides the clearest example of how *not* to handle social extrapolation that I have ever seen. The society of the novel is a descendant of our own, yet Spinrad would have us believe that after the destruction of nearly everything, a minor social trend, which has *already* peaked and reversed, will shape society, while much older and more massively entrenched elements will have no effect whatever. Actually, most of Spinrad's major assumptions are sensible enough. I can well believe that a low-technology, post-atomic society would try desperately to keep the environment clean, and that atomic energy would be feared as sorcery of the worst sort. I can even believe the tribal setup, the communes and the presence of guru-like figures who pass judgment by inspiration. But I cannot believe that the people are going to be 1960s style hippies. I suspect they would be something entirely different, their beliefs shaped by the traumatic experiences of their ancestors. If they remember anything of the old society, it would surely be some remnant of its most important aspects, probably very distorted. Spinrad's overall plan is okay, but he has all the details wrong.

Be that as it may, once past the opening chapters, the novel keeps you reading. It has the raw power characteristic of Spinrad novels and a certain amount of grace. There are even moments of considerable beauty. The hero and heroine are led, by convoluted means, to collaborate with "black scientists" on an attempt to launch a space shuttle. It seems that just before the cataclysm, a space station had picked up an extra-terrestrial signal. Obviously this is the key to mankind's future. There is one more descent into cliche as the characters fake an alien landing to make the Aquarians unite out of fear . . . , but in the interplay between the hero and heroine and their scientist guide and the sequences on the space station itself, we get quite an intelligent tale of the effects of power (particularly media power, a long-running Spinradian concern) on individuals, the balance between science and mysticism and finally, a vast cosmic vision worthy of anything in Stapledon. That the "black scientist" should be cold, soul-less and ultimately unable to cope with this vision is hardly a surprise, but somehow Spinrad manages to transcend the stereotype and make him humanly convincing.

Clear Blue Lou is less successful a character, too much a wish-fulfillment. The writing itself is more versatile than you might expect from the first few chapters, moving from slangy trendiness to lucid descriptions to cadenced, near poetry toward the end. The author is clearly in control. The failures must be attributed to deliberate, wrong decisions. The successes are considerable. [*Songs from the Stars*] is, ultimately, at war with itself, and I think the right side won. (pp. 28-9)

> *Darrell Schweitzer, in a review of "Songs from the Stars," in* Science Fiction Review, *Vol. 10, No. 3, August, 1981, pp. 28-9.*

H. BRUCE FRANKLIN

Adolf Hitler's best-known science-fiction novel is, of course, *Lord of the Swastika,* which won the coveted Hugo award at the 1955 World Science Fiction Convention. Hitler, who had dabbled in German politics before emigrating in 1919 to New York, where he became one of science fiction's most respected figures, here reveals the wild audacity of his imagination and the full sweep of his political vision. This is the exotic premise of Norman Spinrad's *The Iron Dream,* first published as a highwater mark of New Wave science fiction in 1972 and now reissued in paperback. . . .

The Iron Dream consists mainly of *Lord of the Swastika,* Hitler's sword-and-sorcery extravaganza in which a thousand years after a thermonuclear holocaust, a gigantic blond superhero restores the Manifest Destiny of his homeland Heldon by forging a fanatical party and an invincible army, sterilizing or exterminating all genetic inferiors, wiping out the subversive Dominators, conquering the vast sinister power east of Heldon that had coordinated the worldwide Dominator conspiracy, and eventually cloning a race of genetically pure blond male giant supermen to take over the universe. Spinrad's alternative history, a fantasy in which Hitler is merely a novelist, also includes notes about the colorful author's importance to science fiction and its fans, as well as a crucial document in the form of an "afterword" by "Professor Homer Whipple."

At the very least, *The Iron Dream* must be admired as a remarkable tour de force, a dazzling display of ingenuity and originality. But it is much more than that, for it forces us to confront elements of fascism within our own culture, low and high.

The Iron Dream denies us the sweeter pleasures of most fiction. We are not allowed to identify with the characters, who are all disgusting, especially the brutish supermale superhero; we are not permitted to lose ourselves in the action and adventures, for they grotesquely parody the sadistic megalomania of sword-and-sorcery science fiction; we can hardly enjoy the plot, which is a replay and extrapolation of the history of Nazism. No, our pleasure is mostly cerebral: we identify all the parallels between the events imagined by Hitler the novelist and those produced by Hitler the Fuehrer; we note that the hero's invincible weapon resembles a gigantic phallus; we recognize the similarities between his brutal omnipotent maleness and the diseased fantasies of both fascism and the latest sword-and-sorcery epics. Then, when we get to Homer Whipple's afterword, we find that the very process of intellection we had to use to comprehend the novel is now replicated and parodied.

But of course Whipple missed the main thrust of the book, for to him Hitler's bizarre fantasies merely prove that the author is demented. . . . Professor Whipple, however, as much as he loathes this sickening picture, is just as passionate as Hitler in his own "feelings of fear and hate toward the world communist menace," which in his world of 1959 is resisted only by a despairing America and its staunch ally Japan, gloriously strengthened in its defense of "freedom" by its "time-hallowed traditions of Bushido." Thus Whipple admits that the unscrupulous ferocity of Hitler's all-conquering hero "seems somehow perversely refreshing," for "In these dark times, who in his heart of hearts does not secretly pray for the emergence of such a leader?" The astute reader is left wondering about the responses of the urbane, liberal American intellectual to actual fascism, militarism, and genocide. Unhappily, *The Iron Dream* seems at least as timely today as it did a decade ago.

> *H. Bruce Franklin, in a review of "The Iron Dream," in* Book World—The Washington Post, *July 25, 1982, p. 11.*

ALBERT I. BERGER

[Spinrad's] early novels, particularly *Bug Jack Barron,* are nothing if not touchstone artifacts of the sixties and the hot-house creativity which so marked so much writing in that wondrous decade. Yet they still strike home. When struck, humans howl in pain and rage, and the howl of the State is suppression. Spinrad's work has twice been the target of suppression in allegedly democratic states: a British parliamentary attack and major distributor's ban against Michael Moorcock's *New Worlds* in 1968 for publishing excerpts from *Bug Jack Barron* and a 1982 ban on the sale of the first German-language edition of the devastating 1972 examination of fascism, *The Iron Dream.* (p. 31)

These are good times for [*The Iron Dream*]. Spinrad's craft is sure and imaginative. He makes astonishingly good and thoroughly logical and consistent use of an old science fiction device, the parallel time-track, to examine the individual and mass psychology of fascism. On this alternative track Adolf Hitler gave up on right-wing German politics early and migrated to the United States to become a science fiction illustrator, and then a Hugo award-winning hack writer of such classics as *Emperor of the Asteroids, Savior From Space, The Triumph of the Will,* and so forth. His most popular book, for which he wins the Hugo posthumously, is *Lord of the Swastika,* which *The Iron Dream* republishes, ostensibly in tribute, along with the obligatory, adulatory introduction and mandatory academic afterword.

"Hitler" writes his fantasy version of the rise and fall of the Third Reich without the intervention of the western democracies and the inconveniences of the Russian winter. (pp. 31-2)

"Hitler" is no artist; the book is repetitive and the gory, fantastic, oversimplistic rendering of World War II as sword-and-sorcery too thin to be interesting once the basic situation has been set up. It eventually is nothing more than a pornography of violence in which the titillating episodes follow each other in escalating intensity, with only the thinnest (and shortest) intervals for separation and plot. But, of course, that is exactly the point. "Hitler"'s fantasy and fascism are shown as the sublimation of sexuality into violence as well as the infantilization of all human relations through the categorization of all human relations through the categorization of people into monolithic masses shaped as the reflection of a charismatic individual. There is only one woman, in a reference so fleeting as to *seem* accidental. While sexuality is absent, imagery of dominance and homosexual fetish abound. (p. 32)

The foreword, reporting the unrecognized hack's posthumous following, largely for a book ground out on a six week contract, and the impact of his fans and their Nazi convention costumes, nicely ties Spinrad's examination of Nazism to contemporary popular culture; while the afterword similarly skewers the easy academic acceptance of fundamentally barbaric principles if they can be made to fit preconceived notions or anti-communist cant. The critic, "Homer Whipple," pre-empts nearly everything that can be said about *Lord of the Swastika,* including the judgment that the author's personality is, by the evidence of the novel, seriously deranged. He attributes the novel's appeal to people's desire for a strong leader in parlous times. . . . Although Whipple sees the derangement of "Hitler"'s vision, and recognizes it for the brutal power fantasy it is, he also celebrates its freedom from doubt and its ability to mobilize the masses. He believes Jaggar's popularity to be a yearning on the part of Americans for [a blond "superman"] leader and is glad that the Aryan giant is only the fantasy creation of a warped science fiction writer whose influence on the world at large was so small.

And there, the circle is complete; for it was, in reality, no fantasy at all. Nor is it now. It is perhaps enough simply to note the deluge of sword-and-sorcery novels and films inundating American popular culture lately. . . . And the West German government which bans *The Iron Dream* (on the grounds that the impressionable would miss the satire and see it as pro-Nazi) has no problem with their home-grown "Peacelord of the Universe," Perry Rhodan.

As uncritical, entertainment fiction, *The Iron Dream* probably runs as thin as "Hitler"'s artistry. On the other hand, as a thoughtful, incisive satire on the roots of fascism and an example of the thoroughgoing fashion in which Spinrad maintains the internal logic of his parallel time-track to serve his ends, *The Iron Dream* belongs in any serious science fiction collection. (pp. 32-3)

Albert I. Berger, in a review of "The Iron Dream," in Science Fiction & Fantasy Book Review, *No. 8, October, 1982, pp. 31-3.*

HOWARD WALDROP

Norman Spinrad has written some good books, some great idea/too-bad books, and a couple of unreadable novels. Now, with *The Void Captain's Tale* . . . he has come up with an idea, a style and a narrative that perfectly fits his talent.

There is the Southern California/starship syndrome: lots of hedonists and gourmands on interstellar flights, drugs, decor and our old science fiction friend, the Jump, whereby a ship in one place jumps to another, through some hyperspace or other dimension, circumventing all the relativistic effects of trying to go faster than light.

There have been jumps in science fiction before, most notably Cordwainer Smith's "Game of Rat and Dragon" (1955). Spinrad explores new ground in the mechanism for the Jump; in this case, the Jumps are triggered by the orgasms experienced by the Void Pilots, specially-trained women whose enhanced sensory experiences take the ships across three-light-year leaps.

In other hands, or even from an earlier Spinrad, all this would be just too much. But the sex, though ever-present among the crew and Honored Passengers, is understated. The tale, narrated by the Void Captain, becomes one with ever-deepening levels of meaning and symbolism.

Spinrad has the complications start when the Void Captain meets and talks with the Void Pilot, a rare event in the society he posits. (All the other Void Pilots seem to be, from hints dropped about them, the futurological equivalent of shopping-bag ladies.) From this point we enter the closed world of the starship *Dragon Zephyr* and its worlds-hopping passengers, some of whom have never made a planetfall in their lifetime, but got from ship to ship between ports. We also start the slow and inevitable realization by the Void Captain of what is going to happen, what he's going to do.

For this jumbled future, Spinrad has created one of those synthetic languages (a sort of pig-Earth, a use of polyglot phrases from dozens of locales around the world) which causes a little reader discomfort for the first few pages, but slowly and gradually comes to seem almost right.

I don't like to use an adjective to describe one writer's work that contains the name of another, but Spinrad has written a very (Barry) Malzbergian book, dark and somber in tone, subject matter and method. That his other long works have been poles away from this is a sign that he is growing, and in interesting ways. All the blurbs I've seen are right: this is Spinrad's best book.

Howard Waldrop, "Lem, Le Guin and Spinrad: Other Worlds, Other Times," in Book World—The Washington Post, *February 27, 1983, p. 10.*

TOM EASTON

Norman Spinrad has done some remarkable work by any standard. Much of it has been risky experimentation of one form or another, and some of it, such as *The Iron Dream,* has succeeded admirably, at least in its own terms. Sometimes he fails, though not for lack of ambition.

I have one of those failures here. It's *The Void Captain's Tale,* and it is by no means all bad. (p. 101)

The flaw is in the style. Spinrad has given his characters a roundness of phrasing, a fulsomeness, that makes them all sound as if they are on the verge of throwing up. Actually this tone suits his story's world, one of decadent self indulgence. More serious is his attempt to portray a future evolution of language by absorption into English of words and phrases from many tongues (largely the familiar ones of German, French, Spanish, and Latin). The trouble is that foreign words often— if not usually—creep into a language to express the inexpressible. Spinrad violates his own intent by using the foreignisms largely as asides, as nonessentials, as in "und so weiter," and so on. For example, see the hero's confession of "a certain secret pride in having chosen the vision absolute over the quotidian vie humaine." On the few occasions when an alien word is not likely to be known to a modern, it is usually clear in context. Unfortunately, the effect is fulsome; it reminds of antique bad writing, sprinkled with pretentious displays of false erudition. It fails to feel futuristic, and it does a lot to spoil the tale for me.

Will it do the same for you? Maybe. Maybe not. The answer depends on how much you dislike the antique style Spinrad reminds me of and on how much you focus on plot instead of style. You may be more willing to forgive the style, for Spinrad presumably limited his linguistic invention in the name of making his prose accessible to modern readers. You may love [*The Void Captain's Tale*] for there is much in it to love. (pp. 101-02)

> Tom Easton, in a review of "The Void Captain's Tale," in Analog Science Fiction/Science Fact, Vol. CIII, No. 4, April, 1983, pp. 101-02.

GERALD JONAS

The title of Norman Spinrad's latest novel [*The Void Captain's Tale*] is a tip-off. This is science fiction as self-conscious art— perhaps "artifice" would be a better word. On Mr. Spinrad's Void Ships, interstellar travelers are kept alive by artifice— not just physically by life-support systems but also psychologically. A never-ending round of esthetic, intellectual and sexual *divertissements* guards both passengers and crew from a mind-shattering encounter with the reality of the Void through which they are passing. Only one person on board actually confronts the Void: the Void Pilot, a woman whose nervous system is plugged directly into the ship's circuits. Each time the ship jumps instantaneously through light-years of space, the Void Pilot experiences an orgasm beside which normal fleshly delights pale. Like all such such pleasures, it ends too soon— but under certain circumstances, so the rumor goes, the Pilot's orgasm can become literally endless.

The Pilot in *The Void Captain's Tale* seduces the Captain into betraying his trust with what might be described as the ultimate indecent proposal: pleasure everlasting. Mr. Spinrad does not shrink from the passages of sexual evocation his plot demands. Yet he never descends to the merely pornographic. Having established that his characters speak a futuristic language in which words and concepts from many 20th-century cultures are blended—they say things like "Vraiment, meine kleine" and "Racial seppuku may be an aesthetically pleasing fini"— he has available an erotic vocabulary that is neither too explicit nor too private.

As with all artifice, *The Void Captain's Tale* depends on the cooperation of the audience for its effects. Norman Spinrad, like his characters, takes great risks; the rewards for readers willing to meet him halfway are commensurate. (pp. 37-8)

> Gerald Jonas, "Inside Elsewhere," in The New York Times Book Review, May 22, 1983, pp. 15, 37-8.

GARY K. WOLFE

Norman Spinrad's major novel so far [*Child of Fortune*] returns us to the universe of his 1983 *The Void Captain's Tale*. . . . This universe bears notable resemblances to that of Cordwainer Smith and, like Smith, Spinrad is able to invest even the most bizarre imagery with enough metaphorical weight to appeal to readers way beyond the usual science fiction audience. . . . I think there is little doubt that *Child of Fortune* will be received as one of the major SF novels of the year. . . .

[The second title page of *Child of Fortune*] tells us it is "A Histoire of the Second Starfiring Age," by Wendi Shasta Leonardo. "Histoire" is important; Spinrad's polyglot style combines familiar phrases of various Indo-European languages, Homeric epithets ("the far-flung worlds of men"), and a vaguely archaic diction to create an effect which, at best, contributes strongly to the texture of Spinrad's imagined world. At worst it sounds like Miss Piggy.

The narrative is the coming-of-age tale of Wendi Shasta Leonardo, the daughter of an inventor and a "tantric adept" (sex is viewed as both an art and a science in this society, but Spinrad does not quite succeed in overcoming a traditional male-oriented, heterosexual model of it), who with the aid of sexual techniques learned from her mother and a ring invented by her father to electronically magnify this sexual prowess, sets out on her "wanderjahr" to find herself. She first visits Edoku, a planet entirely remade for recreational purposes, where she joins a group of neo-hippies led by the near-mythical figure of Pater Pan (Wendi? Pater Pan? Get it?) Under his tutelage, she begins to learn the art of tale-telling, and when he departs, she accompanies another lover to the planet Belshazzar, famed for its psychotropic drugs. On Belshazzar is the most truly impressive image of the novel—a continent dominated by gigantic trees and flowers exuding such powerful psychotropics that few can enter the "Bloomenveldt" and return. Wendi's successful return gives her the epic material for her own story, and the novel finally focuses on the narrator learning her art. A last encounter with Pater Pan underlines this in a surprising and satisfying way.

Despite echoes of Cordwainer Smith—as well as Henry Miller, Baudelaire, and perhaps even Octave Mirbeau—*Child of Fortune* is a highly original work and one of considerable merit. . . . I hope the book achieves the audience it deserves.

> Gary K. Wolfe, "Spinrad's Magnum Histoire," in Fantasy Review, Vol. 8, No. 7, July, 1985, p. 24.

GERALD JONAS

Norman Spinrad's ambitious *Child of Fortune* . . . is set in the same universe as his brilliant novel, *The Void Captain's Tale*. . . . It is a far-future, far-flung universe of dazzling scientific and artistic achievements, held together by faster-than-light "Jump ships." . . . In his new book, Mr. Spinrad follows the adventures of a young girl of good family who, like most of her contemporaries, journeys from planet to planet in search of her true calling. Imagine a civilization wealthy and wise enough to encourage its youth to sample *all* of life's possibilities— sexual, esthetic, occupational—before making choices. Mr. Spinrad's heroine has just the right combination of spunk, self-awareness and naïveté to benefit from this experience. The book is big . . . and it needs to be; to place the heroine's final choice in proper context, we have to know what she rejected.

Unfortunately, the opening chapters are the least interesting. Instead of enthralling us with a universe of marvels seen from the heroine's perspective, Mr. Spinrad offers list after list of guidebook wonders that fail to stir the imagination. Perhaps readers unfamiliar with the earlier novel will feel differently, but I had the impression that the author was dutifully laying the foundation for what was to follow, and I became impatient. Then, with no warning, the *real* story begins—and it is marvelous. The heroine and her lover of the moment come to a planet where a vast forest has evolved with giant blooms and fruits that rely on mammal-like creatures for pollination. Through an array of individually tailored psychotropic perfumes, the alien flowers offer a lifetime of mindless pleasure in exchange for services performed on Earth by bees and birds. As experienced by the human lovers, this is by no means an unattractive choice. How the heroine regains her freedom—and discovers her true calling—by wielding the peculiarly human weapon of speech—is the core of the story.

To convey his vision, Mr. Spinrad has concocted a patchwork language studded with phrases from many different Earth tongues and neologisms like "ruespieler" and "ruegelt." This potpourri takes some getting used to, but the effect is worth the effort, if only so the reader can appreciate the ease with which the author brings together in one sentence, in the book's last chapter, the locutions "tantric expertise" and "chutzpah."

Gerald Jonas, in a review of "Child of Fortune," in The New York Times Book Review, *September 8, 1985, p. 28.*

TOM EASTON

In *Child of Fortune,* Norman Spinrad returns to the cosmos of *The Void Captain's Tale.* On his last visit, I criticized his heavy use of foreign words and phrases, sprinkled throughout his prose in a way that reminded me of the false erudition of decades ago. After my review [see excerpt above], he wrote me a lengthy letter objecting to my blindness—he had been striving to invent or simulate an evolved version of English, with generations more of borrowings from other tongues. That much was clear, but I did feel that his simulation was too heavy-handed to be successful. Now I wonder if he had second thoughts, for though he does the same thing again, he does it with a lighter hand, and the effect is far more friendly to the modern reader. He gives the flavor of a much-evolved language without burdening our eye. At the same time, he has not totally given up; he speaks of the language of his tale's time as if everyone has his or her own personal dialect or "sprach of Lingo," and occasionally he tosses in a character whose sprach is as impenetrable as ever.

So much for surface. What is the story? Spinrad gives us a picaresque novel that may well be SF's equivalent of Fielding's *Tom Jones,* a long, witty, wonderful tale of maturation told by his protagonist as she looks back from her position as a successful novelist (or the future equivalent). (pp. 177-78)

Moussa's wanderjahr takes her, without excess parental support, to a world of inbred confusion, a carnival, and a psychotropic jungle. She learns to manipulate people with a new-found gift of gab and begins to learn the trade of ruespieler (storyteller) for ruegelt (pay). She loves and loses, goes hungry, taps a wealthy meal-ticket, blows her mind, and regains it thanks to an awesome determination. As we see her, she is a charming waif who emerges to adulthood by pursuing the vision of the Yellow Brick Road (of wandering, of striving).

It is tempting to read into *Child of Fortune* something of autobiography. Spinrad *is* a child of the sixties, and it is easy to speculate that, like Moussa and her friends, he was once concerned with no more than getting high and laid, with perhaps half an eye, half the time, on finding himself. Surely, he too felt the drive to become a ruespieler, and as he pursued that particular Yellow Brick Road, he in time came to his present estate, honored elder of the ruespielers' tribe. I do not hesitate to recognize his status, and then to say that I enjoyed *Child of Fortune* immensely. I recommend it to you. (p. 178)

Tom Easton, in a review of "Child of Fortune," in Analog Science Fiction/Science Fact, *Vol. CV, No. 13, December, 1985, pp. 177-78.*

George Szirtes

1948-

Hungarian-born English poet and critic.

Szirtes is frequently described as a "painterly poet," reflecting his complementary interests in painting and poetry and his ability to capture subtle meaning in imaginative and original descriptions. In his poetry, Szirtes renders his personal responses to the everyday world in an often quirky, surreal style. Blending intense imagery and witty observations, Szirtes approaches the ordinary with delight and wonder while examining themes related to love, art, and politics. When Szirtes was eight years old, his family emigrated from Hungary to England, and critics have suggested that his verse expresses an Eastern European sensibility within the order and clarity of English poetic forms.

After having concentrated on painting during his youth, Szirtes began publishing poetry in magazines and pamphlets during the early 1970s. His poems and etchings were exhibited at the Victoria and Albert Museum in 1978. Critics noted the painterly qualities of the pieces in his first collection, *The Slant Door* (1979). Alan Brownjohn commented: "Several of the early poems are about moments of time in the lives of people, caught as a painter or a photographer would catch them, with some philosophical reflection worked in." Szirtes's second volume, *November and May* (1981), also reflects his fascination with visual detail and his ability to evoke surreal elements in descriptions of the commonplace. Szirtes stated that *November and May* is "dominated by two conflicting themes: an interior world animated by horrors and hauntings, and an external one full of beauty." Reviewers noted a sense of menace in this work, particularly in the poem "The Birdnesters," which tells of an atrocity committed by three shepherds through their innocent desire to please a newborn god.

Many of Szirtes's poems collected in *Short Wave* (1984) are concerned with the contrast between reality and imagination and the difficulty of using language to adequately express emotion and recreate experience. More technically formal than his earlier verse, these pieces place less emphasis on surreal imagery. Critics detected a greater complexity of meaning achieved through Szirtes's command of meter, stanzaic form, and rhyme. Like much of Szirtes's work, *Short Wave* was praised for displaying clarity, wit, and originality. Szirtes's visit to Hungary in the early 1980s provided a unifying theme for *The Photographer in Winter* (1986). In this collection, Szirtes makes allusions to George Orwell's novel *1984* while exploring such topics as tyranny and exile. The title poem, based on his parents' life in Budapest, evokes an atmosphere of terror and totalitarian surveillance, creating an allegorical fantasy in which Szirtes examines what he terms the "illusion of reality." In "The Courtyards," Szirtes recreates the eerie and mysterious feelings and the horrors associated with several famous European courtyards. In his review of *The Photographer in Winter*, Peter Porter echoed the opinions of several critics: "In the end, [Szirtes's] triumph is his ability to wring lyrical language from grim subjects without averting his eyes."

(See also *Contemporary Authors*, Vol. 109.)

Photograph by Say-Woon Low. Courtesy of George Szirtes.

PETER PORTER

[George Szirtes is] interested in lighting up the homely and quotidian. . . . His poems domesticate the presence of the gods, in their local Palmer-like incandescence. His early works were full of surrealistic incoherence, but *The Slant Door* manages to reveal the excitement of strange juxtapositions while ordering language with great efficiency.

Szirtes chooses words like pigments, as though they could be modified in their mixing, but he keeps closer to Chardin than to Chagall. There is plenty of sober truth in his writing. . . . The poet's knowingness is gentle and ritualistic: it is a way of bestowing a blessing. . . .

His wit is quiet and chromatic, and he has a striking benevolence of imagination. He is one of the poets writing today of whose future I have great confidence.

Peter Porter, "Transformations," in The Observer, August 19, 1979, p. 37.

ALAN BROWNJOHN

George Szirtes is a painter as well as a poet, but *The Slant Door,* a substantial first volume, impresses the more it moves away from some habits of using the painter's eye for intriguing detail to get poems off the ground and employing a rather garish surrealist fantasy. Several of the early poems are about moments of time in the lives of people, caught as a painter or a photographer would catch them, with some philosophical reflections worked in. . . . Where he doesn't get bogged down in a muffled sort of allegory they are at least attractive, and one of them is moving: **"At the Dressing Table"**, where he shakes off his tendency to allegorise and brings off a poignant juxtaposition of past and present. Szirtes goes in for fairly rich and elaborate developments of his themes, and sometimes the form or in some way the ''mould'' he has chosen for the ideas draw a poem out into inflation or vagueness. . . . (p. 75)

Nevertheless, *The Slant Door* moves very steadily towards a greater confidence, clarity, and originality of outlook. The sense of the indefinable mystery in certain small moments of time is finely conveyed in **"At The Sink"**, where he feels himself almost called to construct a religion from the act of pouring milk into a jug. . . . And better still, **"Anthropomorphosis"** finds exactly the right kind of metaphor for his obscure sense of expatriation (he was born in Hungary and came to England when he was eight) in, of all unlikely ideas, the ''gob of spit'' launched by a ''foreigner'' seen from a bus:

> It was as if I'd seen it all before—
>   . . . the afternoon
> Rearranged itself around his act. . . .

By the end, *The Slant Door* is beginning to show signs of a considerable and enterprising new talent. (pp. 75-6)

Alan Brownjohn, ''Cosmic, Comic, Casual, Careful,'' in Encounter, Vol. LIII, No. 5, November, 1979, pp. 70-7.

WILLIAM PALMER

George Szirtes has achieved in *The Slant Door* that rare thing— a book that cannot be wrapped in a five hundred word review and dropped to oblivion. It is one of the best first books of poetry to be published in the past few years, that is, if we judge by successful poems and not by promise or critically adduced intentions.

This, of course, is to take the book as a whole, and in an unusually meaty book, with poems crowded together on the page, there is a fair amount of XXth century poetic stock:

> Sunlight laces the book
> The dying light shudders
> The trees fling their doily patterns high

The last line is from one of those poems about the pathos of old age that now seem obligatory in any young poet's book. But there is also this:

> Look, it has snowed in the night
> And the roads are bright as skin
> Lit by the moon: the snow *is* moonlight
> And there will be no morning ever again,
> We shall live in white like brides
> Never stirring, nor shall light be over
> To discover the bed unmade or the windows thrown wide
> Or the street stopped in its course like a river.

This may appear slight at first, and this is the whole poem, but it is a whole poem and shows a quite unforced balance and subtlety of thought and rhythm as the language is moved through modulation and oppositions, moved to that last line and held there. It has mastery and fitness; the scene is general, we can supply the detail; what is left out is the presence of the poet; for its duration we exist in the poem. . . . George Szirtes knows poems are made of words, that words make ideas and not the other way around, and it is not only from the jacket's information that he was born in Budapest that I think one could infer the wide intellectual concern and peculiarly East European tenderness without sentimentality in the face of horrors that most young Englishmen have not come even geographically close to. . . . (pp. 68-9)

William Palmer, ''A New Slant,'' in Poetry Review, Vol. 70, No. 3, December, 1980, pp. 68-70.

JOHN LUCAS

November and May is full of vital perceptions. George Szirtes has an unfakeable sense of the epiphanic; and reading through his new collection one repeatedly comes across poems which register an almost numinous sense of the variousness of things. . . . Yet I think he doesn't work hard enough at his poems. If you're as gifted as Szirtes you shouldn't need to lapse into such clichés as 'the summer heat is stifling'; nor should you be so wordy as to say that 'the room is heating / to a mid-morning equilibrium, a bright / clarity of statement, positively forthright . . .' And he can be unaccountably prosaic, as in **"The Phylactery"**, where at least two stanzas don't earn their keep. But when you have said all that you have to add that his best poems make delightful and rewarding discoveries. (p. 19)

John Lucas, ''Opening Prisons,'' in New Statesman, Vol. 103, No. 2650, January 1, 1982, pp. 18-19.

SHIRLEY TOULSON

[The] most approachable poems in [Szirtes's *November and May*] are those in which he exercises his talent in order to evoke a peopled landscape. So I would advise anyone coming new to his work to look first at **"Sheep Shearing at Ayot St Lawrence"**, a poem that presents a detailed picture of men and beasts, while subtly implying a criticism of those who turn to the fallacy of the picturesque. The other poems in this collection, especially those that take up the theme of the title and explore the patterns woven by light and shade, youth and age, are much more difficult. Like the ghostly figure in **"Half Light"**, they make 'darkness luminous' by emerging out of the most elusive attributes of time, space and perception itself, as the poet draws his readers into an exploration of the territory that lies beneath conventional outlines. For, despite their strong visual quality, these are subjective poems, which are primarily interested in the way human reactions are affected by the physical setting in which they occur. . . . They reach their finest achievement in the three poems of **"The Weather Gifts"** sequence which give precision and meaning in human terms to the vaporous movements of the clouds. This is George Szirtes's second collection, and it well confirms the acclaim which greeted his first. (pp. 253-54)

Shirley Toulson, in a review of ''November and May,'' in British Book News, April, 1982, pp. 253-54.

TIM DOOLEY

George Szirtes's first collection, *The Slant Door,* opened with a poem about the naive Yugoslav painter Generalic and contained another called **"Salon Des Indépendants"**; such pieces not only signal what marks off Szirtes from his British contemporaries—his natural recourse to analogies from painting rather than from literature—but also offer clues to his particular qualities as a writer. The effect Generalic produces by his representation of the human figure does not differ significantly from that of a painter like Léger. The difference between the two is the difference between an artist who breaks the conventions of realist representation in a knowing way and one who does it innocently.

It is tempting to see a parallel here with Szirtes's own position. The disruptions of expectation and the unusual visual intensity in his poems might suggest a common strategy with the poets of the Martian school, but he is unlike them in that it is difficult to detect in his work a systematic interest in pursuing a particular aesthetic method. The quirks and surprises in Szirtes's poems are not the result of originality of manner, but of originality of vision, something which qualifies him to exhibit his work among the true "indépendants" and which makes his new book *November and May* unusually arresting.

The power of the imagination to create alternative versions of reality is referred to directly in several of these poems. . . .

Two major sequences of poems in this collection—**"Misericords"** and **"The Dissecting Table"**—are grouped under titles which suggest artistic exercises or indulgences. While these poems allow Szirtes to exercise his taste and talent for verbal and visual puns . . . this is not done at the expense of the poems' subjects, for which Szirtes communicates a mixture of affection and awe. He retains a painter's sense of the importance of attending to externals, so as to represent the world honestly, but also so as to understand it, and himself, more thoroughly. . . . Thus Szirtes leads the reader from the mysteries of art back to the problem of life, a puzzle that the foreign language of poetry repeatedly fails to explain.

Typically, Szirtes is more interested in evoking the sadness involved in attempting to explain than in offering explanations. This is demonstrated in the strangest and most menacing of the poems in *November and May,* the semi-narrative **"The Birdnesters"**. The opening stanza's precise use of dates, names and geographical detail gives to the poem a documentary tone oddly out of key with the fiction that follows. Three nineteenth-century French shepherds believe they have witnessed a new Incarnation, in a stable, "Exactly as in the Bible story". They decide to return the next night to check whether what they think they have seen can in fact be true. On the way, one of the shepherds hears what he takes to be roosting wood-pigeons and suggests that if they could capture enough to make a pigeon-pie:

> It would be a suitable present for
> The new-born God, supposing he exists
> And we are not all touched with August madness.

The remaining two-thirds of the poem is dominated by a painful and detailed description of the clubbing to death of the birds, which turn out to be doves, and the reactions of the shepherds who, seeing the carnage for which they are responsible, return home with no further reference to their original quest, "in a mood of deep tranquillity". The moral dimension of the tale is left to the reader to state for himself. The result is an extraordinarily haunting piece of writing which stands out, even

in as finely written a book as this, as a work of unusual integrity and authority.

Tim Dooley, "The Death of Doves," in The Times Literary Supplement, No. 4135, July 2, 1982, p. 720.

ALAN JENKINS

The poems contained in George Szirtes's *November and May* are largely concerned with propitiating the grimmer or less manageable gods and with trying to wrest a quirky, by no means comforting morality—in both senses—from the already quirky occurrences of the everyday and the domestic. The epigraph from MacNeice's "Snow" ("There is more than glass between the snow and the huge roses") suggests that Szirtes has sensed the limitations of meticulousness, starkness, cleanliness, a strong visual quality, unblurred impressions, confidence and clarity—the terms in which his previous volume was praised—and begun instead to look out for the "mundane apparition", the unattended moment of mystery or menace; to look out, too, for the words and rhythms that will evoke this malady of the quotidian with oblique forcefulness, deadened, remote decorum of manner. . . . (p. 58)

The rhythms in some poems here may owe something to MacNeice; this numbed serenity of tone while giving utterance to a disturbing and discomfiting vision, and the tendency to turn the arresting perception into a pretext for speculation, are vaguely reminiscent of the Fullers, *père et fils*. But Szirtes's language is neither as fluent nor as subtly resonant as theirs. It is, though, sometimes agreeably odd. . . . Perhaps the strangeness has something to do with the fact that to Szirtes English was, and perhaps in some residual way remains, a foreign language. It is crucial, anyway, to what his poems convey: bits of a world seen up close, with time infinitely slowed—as in the ambitious sequences **"Misericords"** and **"The Dissecting Table"**—shot through with flashes of a cryptic, distinctly foreign wisdom.

For the most part, "The hybrid language serves and makes the point", as in the poem **"A Reunion"**; occasionally Szirtes's ear fails him, and the cadences refuse to be other than stiffly inert. This surely excessive flatness and clumsiness mars what is otherwise the most memorable piece in the book, **"The Birdnesters"**: "It was a miracle they had not clubbed / Each other into insensibility." Elsewhere in the same poem we have an exceptional delicacy and power, corresponding to a very different order of seeing:

> Except one bird that seemed perfectly still,
> Hovering, glacial, directly above
> The blurring figures of Jean and Henri
> Like some strange and dangerous benediction.

It is for these strange and dangerous benedictions, and for its subtle paradoxes and contradictions, that Szirtes's poetry should be read. (pp. 58-9)

Alan Jenkins, "A Barbarous Eloquence," in Encounter, Vol. LIX, No. 2, August, 1982, pp. 55-61.

RODNEY PYBUS

George Szirtes' second collection [*November and May*] is curious, in both senses of the word: puzzling, in that he often effects almost surreal transfigurations of 'ordinary' observable reality, not so much making connections as showing us that we can't explain the inexplicable, that things are nearly always other than their appearances, and that our sixth sense is the imagination; but his language and rhythms seem shy of appearing to exert influence on the reader by conveying a feeling of pressure in his own acts of exploration, sometimes as if the conjunction of the matter-of-fact and the mysterious were enough. Nevertheless, his vision is certainly curious in a positive way, inquisitive of and probing that area he refers to in an epigraph from Louis MacNeice's 'Snow': 'There is more than glass between the snow and the roses.' The world is 'incorrigibly plural' and 'various', as MacNeice said, and this is Szirtes' central theme. . . . I can see that the would-be thrust of much of *November and May* is towards discovering hidden forms in the everyday, but the actual poetic processes seem at variance with this.

'The imagination feeds on what it gets', he says in **"Homage to Postman Cheval"**, but it's what happens after the imagination has been fed that's important, and I'm not entirely convinced that Szirtes has found quite the right forms for his imagination to work in at full stretch. He has a tendency to let his iambics develop a rather pedestrian beat (more than half the poems here use the metre in some form), and to become too wordy, so that the overall effect of a poem becomes, to use one of his artist's terms that appears once or twice here, 'scumbled'. But at his best his strong visual sense combines in a most attractive and intelligent manner with his talent for creating and suggesting the mysterious in the everyday. When that mysteriousness comes 'naturally' it stays, aching somewhere out of reach of bare semantics. And poems like **"Brimstone Yellow"**, **"Kin"**, **"Low Tide"** and **"May Wind"** are admirably various, but have in common a leanness of syntax and a compression which make them, in the best sense, exciting. (pp. 75-6)

*Rodney Pybus, in a review of "November and May,"
in* Stand Magazine, *Vol. 24, No. 2, 1983, pp. 75-6.*

JOHN LUCAS

There is more than a trace of Geoffrey Grigson in the manner of George Szirtes' relish for the observable world. Describing a bullfinch perched on a lilac flower, he says that the bird's weight 'bothered the lilac, she bent / a little, her small tent / of pleasure collapsing / inward with the swaying'. Although those lines could never be mistaken for Grigson, the weighting and positioning of rhyme and phrase owe something to his example. In *Short Wave*, notation becomes poetry: 'Tired, you slumped into the chair / and shade and water burned a stain / across the colour of your coat.' That comes from a poem called **"Against Dullness"**, whose sentiment Grigson would certainly echo. But the lines also make plain Szirtes' very individual gifts. Yes, he takes a painter's delight in registering surfaces, but even when he is at his most 'visual' there is about his work a sense of imagined, guessed-at worlds, which is radically different from Grigson's delimited precisions. . . .

Many of his poems start from, and are about, lives which cross his sight path and which, as they do, seem to flicker with meaning that hints at withheld significance. Such lives, such meanings, cannot be reduced to order, to a fixed design. Szirtes is hostile to the chill perfection of still life. In a lovely little poem, **"A Girl Sewing"**, which might almost serve as his credo, he lets go of his right to those aesthetic discriminations that hold the transitory in a kind of verbal amber: 'Whole days like this can eat away a life, / leave tiny bones, half powder

and half shadow, / freeze the creases of a finished garment / or find perfection in imagined girls.'

The neatly judged cadences of those lines show that Szirtes' imagination is not of the aggressive kind which insists on finding a poem in everything. He is altogether more diffident, and thus receptive. Accordingly, his best poems are a tactful negotiation between experience and words. He uses a variety of stanza forms and rhyme patterns but not, I think, out of wilful experimentation. It is more that he wants to honour the particularity of what the eye and the mind register, and the result is that *Short Wave* is a truly original volume of poems. It is witty but in no superficial sense; for the wit is directed by, indeed *is*, an angled vision that is at once strange and compelling, so that once we have read a Szirtes poem we are likely to say, 'Oh yes, I *see*.'

That is true of **"Captain Haddock"**, of **"Sea Horse"**, **"Skeleton Crow"**, **"The Claude Glass"** and, above all, [**"Short Wave"**]. And although Szirtes' ear sometimes lets him down— there is never a chance that the ten syllables of 'And we are shaken by the light in the street' will become the five-stress line he requires, and he should not have let through so clumsy a line as 'The bird cannot exactly be said to be dead'—it would be wrong to make much of these lapses. *Short Wave* is easily the most enjoyable new volume of poems I have read this year. (p. 24)

John Lucas, "Sight Lines," in New Statesman, *Vol. 107, No. 2756, January 13, 1984, pp. 24-5.*

PETER PORTER

Eliot's suggestion that a poem may communicate before it is understood has been used to dignify some pretentious works, but he must have meant that there is something immediately attractive over and above meaning in poetry. It is hard to imagine any successful verse totally devoid of sense or wholly hermetic, but a good poem may still circle meaning rather than present it directly. Such happens from time to time in *Short Wave,* though George Szirtes is so committed to reality that when he is mysterious you feel that he has earned the right to be so.

People find Szirtes's poetry attractive because they recognise in it a basic understanding of human feeling and a proverbial sense of language. Now he has added a patina of strangeness which excites the reader's attention and draws him into the depths of a poem. In some ways the new complexity of mood is a surprise, since this new book is technically more traditional than Szirtes's earlier work: regular metrical lines, rhymes and stanza-forms dominate. His subject matter is very much his own—he moves without strain through domestic scenes and canons of great art. Home thoughts from Hertfordshire and Goya's Chamber of Horrors ask for understanding of the same intelligence—and invariably get it. Some of these poems have a splendid solemn music about them. It is a music of ideas— traditional, but offered up at a slight kilter. . . . Though he avoids archaisms, Szirtes has a Jacobean imagination. For him, words are either very sharp or wonderfully upholstered—he is a Tourneur or Webster put down on the M1. The difficult poems—**"The Parrotfish,"** **"Assassins,"** **"The Dog Carla"**— yield to poems of great luminosity, such as **"Flemish Rain"** and **"Porch."** . . . *Short Wave* is a book of considerable accomplishment. Szirtes's voice is now completely his own.

Peter Porter, "The Music of Ideas," in The Observer, January 22, 1984, p. 53.

ANDREW MOTION

Once in a while, or maybe only once in a lifetime, most of us want to write love poems. And most of us, especially if the love we want to write about is happy, find it dismayingly difficult. Why? The most obvious reason—or at least the most commonly given, and the one made famous by Larkin—is that 'happiness writes white'. . . .

Short Wave, George Szirtes's third collection, contains a large number of love poems which clearly centre on a happiness so relaxed and trusting that it's likely to write very white indeed. . . . The intimacy here is both advertised and guarded, and anyone complaining that it involves a lack of focus on particular objects and events would be failing to appreciate that discretion is an important part of the emotion's strength. Poem by poem, this justification works for a good deal of the book (in which the palpable world is regularly relayed merely as shadows, light, reflections, windows, and so on), and it ensures that we hear a tone which is never less than intelligent and humane. But while these qualities are not to be gainsaid, and are admirable in themselves, they can hardly help creating a sense of blandness when the collection is considered as a whole. Nor can they help compromising the commitment that he so obviously and excellently feels.

The problem is not so much one of monotony (Szirtes is too vigilant a craftsman for that) but of too easily rationalised restraint. Around the book's central core of contentment stand a cluster of dilemmas that are treated with the same sort of control he uses to govern the difficult question of intimacy in love. Szirtes's most characteristic position is to be caught between two possible versions of an event, dreaming of both—so that the event itself remains out of reach. . . . [In] many of the love poems his attention is split between the significance of the visible world, and the sense that 'It's what we feel that's mortal, tender, and paradoxical'; and in the long poem **"The Kissing Place"** he actually admits that his subject is immanence rather than tangled poetic involvement: the kissing place is an 'interregnum'—a place 'the god / prepares for us before his passion'.

In Szirtes's first two books, his imagination was quickened by a tendency to view the world in complicatingly surrealist terms. The surrealist element survives in *Short Wave*—most successfully in **"The Moving Floor"**—but is deployed less concentratedly, and only rarely deepens into mystery. That's to say, his poems register the mystery, but too invariably choose to 'leave that dark and keep our noses clean'. The purpose is a sympathetic one—as he says of Art in his poem to Peter Porter, 'She'll hear the scream but make it learn / A civilised and formal turn / Of speech, so that the scream may earn / A living coinage'—but it confines him to a poetry which for all its obvious virtues is too strictly legal, decent, honest and truthful.

Andrew Motion, "Too True," in Poetry Review, Vol. 74, No. 1, April, 1984, p. 64.

SIMON RAE

George Szirtes [the author of *Short Wave*] is probably tired of reading reviews of his work which start by reminding him he is a painter by training, but, whether he is framing his family in **"The Claude Glass"**, exploring the ironies of still life in

"A Pheasant" or contemplating **"A Girl Sewing"**, his poems do tend to assemble like pictures. Or perhaps a truer analogue, given the narrative element in many of his poems, would be the photographic collages [of] David Hockney . . . , with their brilliant incorporation of activity and the passage of time in a static image. As with Hockney's "joiners", Szirtes's poems are only too happy to fragment and distort, disrupting preconceived ideas of what a representation of reality should be. But, unlike Hockney, whose photographic experiments are designed to show the world more "like it is" than orthodox representations could, Szirtes upsets the conventions of the realist mode in pursuit of an alternative version of reality. As the title of his first book, *The Slant Door,* suggested, his imagination meets the world at an angle, and his poetry is open to the hallucinatory and the completely bizarre (**"Slow Tango for Six Horses"**). Twists of fantasy, convoluted shards of narrative and snippets of historical detail are shaken together and served with surrealist relish. . . .

However, to adopt the controlling image of the title poem [**"Short Wave"**], it is not always easy to know whether one is on the right wavelength ("You tune in but the voice is out of reach / and seems merely to flirt with meaning"). Of course the reader realizes he is being teased with his own stolid hungerings after paraphrasable meaning and quantifiable significance ("Preferring always what's predictable"). And should he raise the question of "seriousness", he can be referred to **"John Aubrey's Antique Shop"**, where the presiding antiquary muses: "As I've forgotten who once said of Andrewes, / his sermons were too playful. I believe it. / 'Here's a pretty thing, and there's a pretty thing' / argues a serious lack of seriousness." The question recurs in **"Postscript: A Reply to the Angel at Blythburgh"**, in which Szirtes engages Peter Porter in debate. This is not an altogether successful poem, and Szirtes's wilful skittishness ("Christ sways on his slender Cross, / St Sebastian, scandalous / In loincloth, sways like Diana Ross, / Supreme, appalled") offers no real challenge to Porter's more weighty approach.

The problem of tone arises with regard to another poem, **"Long Nose Tragedy, Short Nose Comedy"**, written to show that "It is quite possible to preach a sermon / on the limitations of a nose". But the "playfulness" Szirtes brings to the pulpit seems to have no self-regulatory mechanism to screen out a stanza like this:

> Was it a nose that led Jews to their death?
> They couldn't cut it off to spite their face
> but others are always willing to do it for you.
> If it offend thee pluck it out. But what of the space
> remaining? It can take away your breath.
> You'll never stick it back with Super Glue.

Lapses of taste like that certainly can take away your breath.

Simon Rae, "Less than Serious," in The Times Literary Supplement, No. 4235, June 1, 1984, p. 610.

RODNEY PYBUS

Domestic interiors, often peopled by his family or other less recognisable figures, occur frequently in [*Short Wave*] and earlier books by George Szirtes. Such scenes are rarely straightforward, however grounded in the actual: scarcely ever Vermeer, more likely to be closer to the macabre side of Goya or the troubling paradoxes of Ernst. However, Szirtes' own brand of surrealism seems to be changing. Where earlier it appeared to spring from pain and anxiety, it now seems generally more willed, with the kind of jokiness that can compare St Sebastian, 'scandalous in loincloth', to Diana Ross.

Among the most satisfying and accomplished poems, in which his elliptical vision leads to writing of real achievement and the familiar is intriguingly and disconcertingly defamiliarised, are **"Flemish Rain"**, a number of the **"Kissing Place"** group . . . , and the four poems in the excellent title group which cleverly evoke Szirtes' concerns: that 'frequency that's unfrequented' where 'You tune in but the voice is out of reach / and seems merely to flirt with meaning. . .'. This is perhaps only to confess to a preference for those poems with some clear connection with the observable world, as opposed to the bizarre fantasy of **"Slow Tango for Six Horses"**.

What disturbs me more about *Short Wave* than Szirtes' proper refusal to let his imagination be wholly constricted by the 'real' is a tone, sustained in part by the prevalent iambic rhythms, which suggests that his earlier disquiet (as in **"The Birdnesters"** in *November and May*) might be settling into something rather more mannered, that his 'slant door' view of the world has become more habit than a genuinely-felt exploration of his own responses to the strangeness of the "given". . . .

Rodney Pybus, in a review of "Short Wave," in Stand Magazine, *Vol. 26, No. 3, 1985, pp. 64-5.*

BARBARA HARDY

The entire volume, *The Photographer in Winter,* reads like a sequence, since the poems mostly deal with a recent return journey to Hungary. Its subjects blend a personal sense of exile, nostalgia, and guilt, with sharp and tough political narrative and imagery. . . . [**"The Photographer in Winter"**] offers a powerful epigraph and model of ancestral allusion. It is a quotation from *1984,* attributed to author but not text, laconically insisting on Orwell's novel as a key text for the time which we must all know. The poem itself—like others—deals with terror, courage and tyranny, passionately uses allegory and fantasy in Kafka-like images. The poems are sometimes reflexive, never narrowly literary. Art emerges as a life-and-death theme. The art of colouring photographs, for example, images the difficulty of turning nature into art, producing vivacity, 'glowing / pink and white', and inertness, 'showing / No signs of having lived'. It also looks into the attempt to reach, leave and place the dead and the past. . . .

[Szirtes's] witty and austere iambics sometimes recall Auden's sestinas, and like Auden he has a capacity to write long poems whose inventiveness is fertile and flexible. These are poems which are always turning corners to enlarge or shift story and feeling. **"The Swimmers"** has this gift of resilience, used shockingly. The poem begins with the crowds of dead in an English parish church, startlingly imaged as swimmers, fluid, dissolving, packing history, 'dear small girls, their sisters, mothers, / Husbands, families, their towns, whole countries'. After coming to an illusory elegiac close, 'Tread lightly here, respect the concentration / Of these verbose and delicate people', the poem swerves powerfully into a foreign history, to conclude with the narrative of a drowned girl shot and thrown into the Danube, in 'the last week of the Terror'. The body seems, grotesquely, to swim, and is finally seen, truly, to swim in stubborn survival and continuity, 'The ripples spreading grey and red and white / From the small body, echoing in the stone.' The politics of anger and compassion makes one feel superficial

in wanting to admire such structural skills, but the form is a form of feeling, neither imposed, showy, nor clever.

Szirtes has spent his adult life in [England], but the experience, and the gallows-humour and fantasy of his poems, are European. He is entertaining as well as shocking and polemic. . . . Throughout the volume you get a solid, often terrifying, sense of the substantial environment in which the tyrannies and violences occur. This is poetry of the urban world, where to describe tenements, streets, stairs, apartments, lifts, and trains is to sound surreal. There is a love poem, **"Meeting, 1944"** where the inextricability of the personal and public life is the subject. There is a simple poem—a classic—about innocence and experience, **"A Small Girl Swinging"**. There are poems like **"The Birds Complain"** which use natural images for political argument, with ease and agility. There are grimly comic and strongly rhythmical verses which are like Brecht but wholly individual, especially **"The Button Maker"** and **"Changing Names"**. The volume ends with three translations by Szirtes from the Hungarian. They give a special sense of complicity and closure, balancing the Orwell quotation, but placing the poet with his compatriots. He belongs with them, but he lends a strong voice to English poetry. (p. 22)

Barbara Hardy, "Twisting Myths," in Books and Bookmen, *No. 366, April, 1986, pp. 21-2.*

PETER PORTER

George Szirtes has made a unique contribution to the debate about the insularity of contemporary English poetry. He has taken England into Europe. *The Photographer in Winter* is recognisably English, but it concerns itself with a wider European experience. . . .

Unlike Joseph Conrad, whose writing always has a foreign accent to my ear, Szirtes remains in full command of modern English: it is his sensibility which has reverted to Europe.

The central poem of his new book is **"The Courtyards,"** where he compresses into a hundred lines the history of those implacable buildings out of which despair, neurosis, revolution and terror have come in a dozen European capitals. Mozart, Kafka, Imre Nagy and the postwar film lie behind his sharply incised vignettes. . . . Several poems, including [**"The Photographer in Winter"**], are based on events in the lives of his parents in Budapest. Here the photographer stands for the illusion of reality and the evasiveness of truth. What seemed settled on film changes at a stroke to fortune or disaster—the click of the shutter gives a lying permanence to the circumstances it records. Congruent with such poems are ones about changing names and considering the child the poet never was.

These cross-currents are sometimes presented comically, as in **"Cultural Directives"** in which propaganda muddles its examples and speaks of 'Michelangelo, the great Italian composer,' 'the English artist Shakespeare' and 'Mozart, the Swiss poet.' Humour, in Szirtes, is too humane to be called black (though that is what his name means in Hungarian)—rather, it is emollient of the harshness of life under constant surveillance.

He is also a dab hand at the folksy fable, sending up its Brechtian sententiousness, as in **"The Button Maker's Tale."** In the end, his triumph is his ability to wring lyrical language from grim subjects without averting his eyes.

Peter Porter, *"Shadows of Budapest," in* The Observer, *June 1, 1986, p. 22.*

SIMON RAE

A church interior is George Szirtes's starting point in **"The Swimmers"**, one of the most successful poems in [*The Photographer in Winter*]. The polished church floor reminds him of 'black ice', and sets off a train of thought about the past generations, trapped like 'dead swimmers' beneath that impenetrable surface. . . . History's 'prodigality with numbers' is a theme that transcends the confines of a parish church in England, and Szirtes is taken back to his native Hungary: 'Some forty years ago a girl was drowning / In the icy Danube, one of a great number / Shot that day in the last week of the Terror.' The girl dies hard, like a cat, while 'Those who remained below grew slippery / And featureless'. . . . **"The Swimmers"** is a fine poem, and neatly illustrates Szirtes's dual allegiance, to his English experience and his Hungarian heredity. (p. 133)

With its epigraph from Orwell, and its impersonal tone of implicity threatening intimacy, the title poem, **"The Photographer in Winter"** (dedicated to 'M.S. 1924-1975'—presumably the poet's mother, who was herself a photographer before the family fled the Russian tanks), creates a brooding atmosphere of totalitarian surveillance. Poet as secret policeman—'I'm watching you. / You cannot get away. I have been trained / To notice things': the paradoxes of the photographic process—to preserve the living moment, you have to 'freeze' it into stasis; and a dulling emphasis on a cold so deep it seems to inhibit life at its very core—'The whole era has been sealed in ice'—are some of the thematic threads combining to make this a rich but disturbing poem. With **"The Courtyards"**, another eerily atmospheric poem imbued with a sense of history without any precise references (and in ways reminiscent of James Fenton's "A German Requiem"), **"The Photographer in Winter"** sets the tone for the whole book—sombre, enigmatic, bleak, with the predominant imagery drawn from the extremes of cold. (pp. 133-34)

Szirtes tends to see the past frozen into stone, petrified into a photographic image that cannot develop or be changed, but only assimilated—by art—into some sort of pattern. . . . (p. 134)

Simon Rae, *"Prayer and Privacy," in* London Magazine, *n.s. Vol. 26, Nos. 5-6, August-September, 1986, pp. 132-35.*

LACHLAN MACKINNON

What most of the poems [in *The Photographer in Winter*] share is a subject: dislocation. . . . Szirtes's alien perspective shows the glamour of insularity, but it also contains an implicit criticism of much recent English poetry for its inwardness, its political isolation. The problem is that Szirtes's own poems are markedly English themselves, sometimes disablingly so.

Two long poems, **"The Photographer in Winter"** and **"The Courtyards"**, both contain striking lines set in mysterious circumstances. . . . **"The Photographer in Winter"** is reminiscent of Andrew Motion's *Secret Narratives* in its refusal to disclose its occasion fully while telling a tantalizingly oblique story. Lines like *"The whole era has been sealed in ice"*, "The elderly keep slipping into graves", "The gods of gracious living pass us by"—the last in "their motorcade"—tie together, in the second instance wittily, the political and the climatic. The atmosphere of terror and ignorance may suit the evocation of a totalitarian society, but it can also indicate poetic self-regard.

Both poems use the same six-line stanza, two couplets enclosed by a third. This symmetry resists the drive of narration and invites us to contemplate, just as the forward tramp of the internal couplets is cradled and stilled by the outer one's embrace. What could advance inexorably leaves us unsettlingly poised between commitment and detachment. The stanzas are often moving, but the poems too static.

The same cannot be said of the other pieces in the book, except for the rather tired dream-analogy **"Notes of a Submariner"**.

Lachlan Mackinnon, *"A Dislocated View," in* The Times Literary Supplement, *No. 4365, November 28, 1986, p. 1355.*

Paul Theroux

1941-

American novelist, travel writer, short story writer, critic, and poet.

An American expatriate living in England, Theroux vividly captures in his fiction and travel books the experiences of displaced individuals and the cultures of exotic lands. Like Joseph Conrad, Graham Greene, and V. S. Naipaul, with whom he is often compared, Theroux frequently explores conflicts between Westerners and third-world inhabitants. An important motif in Theroux's work concerns the outsider who can discover his identity only in a foreign land. Other recurring concerns include economic and social dissolution in England and the aberrations of postcolonial life in such places as Malawi, Singapore, and Honduras. Reviewers praise Theroux's works for his meticulous attention to detail and his polished, realistic style.

After graduating from the University of Massachusetts, Theroux joined the Peace Corps and was sent to Malawi, in southeastern Africa, to teach English. However, his involvement with a group of political leaders who were disenchanted with the prevailing regime, coupled with allegations of spying, led to his deportation in 1965. Theroux subsequently lived and taught in Uganda and Singapore before settling in England. His first travel book, *The Great Railway Bazaar: By Train through Asia* (1975), garnered enthusiastic critical attention and became a best-seller, a rare accomplishment for this literary genre. In this work, Theroux presents caustic and dispassionate observations of the land and people of Asia. David Roberts remarked that Theroux's account "represents travel writing at its very best—almost the best, one is tempted to say, that it can attain." In *The Old Patagonian Express: By Train through the Americas* (1979), Theroux chronicles a trip from Massachusetts through the southernmost regions of South America. Among Theroux's other well-regarded travel volumes are *The Kingdom by the Sea: A Journey around Great Britain* (1983), *Sailing through China* (1984), and *The Imperial Way: By Rail from Peshawar to Chittagong* (1985).

In such early novels as *Fong and the Indians* (1968), *Girls at Play* (1969), and *Jungle Lovers* (1971), Theroux focuses on the troubles that arise from the differing temperaments of Westerners and Africans in post-imperial times. The characters in these works experience disillusionment in foreign countries and, in turn, develop an unfavorable opinion of the values of their own society. The Peace Corps volunteer in *Girls at Play* and the insurance salesperson in *Jungle Lovers* are shaken by the discovery that the standards of conduct they intend to dispense are morally inadequate and potentially destructive. Many of the short stories in *The Consul's File* (1977) and *World's End* (1980) feature protagonists who gain insight into their homeland as well as the countries they visit. Another of Theroux's prominent interests involves the artist who tries to comprehend situations beyond his control and who often turns to violence to impose his own order. This theme is demonstrated in such novels as *Waldo* (1967), *Saint Jack* (1973), *The Black House* (1974), and *Picture Palace* (1978).

According to most critics, Theroux's most fully-developed character is Allie Fox, the hero of *The Mosquito Coast* (1981).

A mentally unstable inventor disgusted with America's decadence and materialism, Allie moves his family to Honduras to begin life anew. There he constructs a huge machine that makes ice, but it self-destructs and emits toxic chemicals into the atmosphere. Allie's ambitions exceed his capabilities and result in personal and environmental destruction. William J. Schafer saw Allie's death as "a metaphor for the slow death of technology." *The Mosquito Coast* was later adapted for film.

Half Moon Street (1984) consists of two novellas, *Doctor Slaughter* and *Doctor DeMarr*, which emphasize the dangers of leading dual lives. In *Doctor Slaughter*, which was adapted for film as *Half Moon Street*, a graduate student joins a call-girl organization to earn money for her education and unwittingly becomes entangled in an assassination plot. In *Doctor DeMarr*, a man assumes his twin brother's identity after finding him dead of a drug overdose. This piece highlights the paradoxes as well as the comic aspects of duality. With *O-Zone* (1986), Theroux uses the conventions of science fiction to portray a near-future America decimated by technology and seized by fundamentalism and xenophobia. Led by a fifteen-year-old computer expert, a group of wealthy New Yorkers travel to what is known as the O-Zone, a quarantined nuclear wasteland in the Midwest which has ironically evolved into a paradise. The New Yorkers learn from the citizens of O-Zone that such traditional values as love and courage lead to happiness. Most critics contended that Theroux was unsuccessful in adopting the mechanics of science fiction to his own style and faulted him for repetition, predictability, and bathos. Theroux is also the author of *Sunrise with Seamonsters: Travels and Discoveries, 1964-1984* (1985), an acclaimed collection of essays on travel, family, literature, celebrities, and railways.

(See also *CLC*, Vols. 5, 8, 11, 15, 28; *Contemporary Authors*, Vols. 33-36, rev. ed.; *Contemporary Authors New Revision Series*, Vol. 20; *Something about the Author*, Vol. 44; and *Dictionary of Literary Biography*, Vol. 2.)

W. SCOTT MORTON

Paul Theroux sailed 1,500 miles down the Yangtze River, and he brings the experience to life in this short and highly anecdotal account [*Sailing Through China*]. He has done his homework well, and his observations gain much from the accounts he has included by two former river captains. . . . His descriptions of his traveling companions—most of them American millionaires—are devastating. Watching the Chinese pulling junks upstream, one comments, "They don't care about television—couldn't care less if the Rams are playing tomorrow." Another, looking across the river at the sunlight on the steep cliffs, exclaims, "What a place for a condominium!" The Chinese are depicted as drab, tired, practical, materialistic, baffled and hungry, and Mr. Theroux sees little hope for their future. He cheers up slightly when he can talk to a few in English. But he presents both the Chinese and the rich Americans as without imagination. *Sailing Through China* is both informative and amusing. . . .

> W. Scott Morton, in a review of "Sailing through China," in The New York Times Book Review, *April 22, 1984, p. 15.*

KATE CRUISE O'BRIEN

Laurel, the egocentric, clever and completely unreflective heroine of Paul Theroux's *Doctor Slaughter,* is doing her best [to become like the men she deprecates]. Laurel is an American Fellow at the Hemisphere Institute of International Studies in London, studying the Persian Gulf. She is overworked and underpaid and she doesn't want to live in a small flat in Brixton with a frozen toilet. When Laurel receives a videotape—anonymously—in the post, about a high-class whore service posing as an 'escort agency', she is delighted to discover that plainer women than she can earn up to £500 a night with the Jasmine Agency. The traditional wisdom that teaches that whores are exploited by men is not part of Laurel's creed. She is the one who will do the exploiting, 'sex often made her feel like a ravishing witch, for after they had come they were small and weak, and they would need her again to make them strong: the crude magic worked'. But Laurel's 'crude magic' is less potent than she imagines. The powerful effects of cynicism have gone to her head. This sexual snob is merely the tool in A Plot—of vague, amorphous, and Middle Eastern dimensions involving the murder of a peace-making peer, Lord Bulbeck, one of Laurel's kindlier clients. *Doctor Slaughter* is an oddly leaden attempt at black humour. Paul Theroux is at his best when he is making fun of things that don't matter very much: British snobbery, embassy dinner parties and political gossip inspire his light, spiky wit. But some things—assassination, prostitution and the Middle East, for instance—simply aren't funny at all and no invocation of irony on the part of the usually light-hearted Mr Theroux will make them so. (pp. 25-6)

> Kate Cruise O'Brien, "Sexual Rejects," in The Listener, *Vol. 111, No. 2861, June 7, 1984, pp. 25-6.*

PETER KEMP

The heroine of Paul Theroux's *The Picture Palace* was elderly and ailing, indifferent to her world-wide reputation as a photographer, happily addicted to junk foods, a plain near-virgin whose personal handicaps spurred her into creative achievement. Moving as far to the opposite extreme as possible, Theroux places at the centre of his new novel, *Doctor Slaughter,* a character who is the antithesis of all this. Young and pulsing with animal energy, obsessed by wealth and success, fanatically finnicky about her food, Lauren Slaughter is attractive and promiscuous, trading on her physique in a way that relentlessly cheapens her.

Mordantly portraying different kinds of exploitation, *Doctor Slaughter* is markedly similar in tone and tenor to the stories in Theroux's *The London Embassy*. In fact, it seems to owe its genesis to one of them, **"Fury"**: a piece about a couple of girls—one an American graduate in economics who turns to high-price prostitution, the other a vegetarian physical fitness fanatic—who have been merged to produce Lauren. *Doctor Slaughter*'s background resembles that of *The London Embassy,* too: London, murky in more ways than one, a dank, dirty labyrinth of snobbery, rapaciousness and monied savagery. And there's the same concern with documenting flaccidity and corruption in terse prose kept healthily crisp with ironic metaphor.

Finally, the narrative—full of unsuspected traps—swivels round to deliver a come-uppance to Lauren. She finds she's been bought and used for ends she never dreamed of, and is involved in a scenario more perverse than any of those she knowingly acted out. To emphasize the point that the independence, power and sophistication she prided herself on were pathetically illusory, Theroux cranks his plot in a rather mechanical and melodramatic way into a story of political assassination. The book's heated, *grand guignol* closing scenes, however, carry less real force than the earlier episodes, with their glacially funny vignettes of contemporary London life and icy, exhilarating probings into greed and impoverishment.

> Peter Kemp, "Meat for Money in the Murky Market," in The Times Literary Supplement, *June 8, 1984, p. 632.*

LEWIS JONES

There is as much in the way of tourism in Paul Theroux's fiction as in his books about long railway journeys. Along the iron rails of that reliable and agreeable legacy of the 19th century, the conventional narrative, he has steamed around the world, to the Far East, Africa, South America and Europe. His heroes are American expatriates—research students, teachers and diplomats, pimps—drawn by romance and distracted by the sordid. Theroux's theme is the relationship of the two, and his master is Graham Greene.

This discipleship is most evident in *Picture Palace* (1978), in which Greene makes an appearance. The novel is about Maude

Coffin Pratt, an elderly American photographer, who intends Greene to be her final subject. He takes her out to dinner, reminisces about travel and tarts and persuades her to abandon photography for autobiography. He inspires the novel, then, and doing so says something that stands as Theroux's artistic credo: 'Greene said, "Only the outsider sees. You have to be a stranger to write about any situation."'

Doctor Slaughter, Theroux's latest novel, is an examination of this credo. It is about Lauren Slaughter (*née* Mopsy Fairlight), who has come to London to do research on the Arabs at the 'Hemisphere Institute of International Studies'.... (p. 24)

Lauren is beautiful and healthy (she is a jogger and food faddist) but she is poor. She has to live in a bedsit in Coldharbour Lane, Brixton—in hateful contrast to Mayfair, where she studies....

Her circumstances and attitude make her unusually receptive to a videotape, sent to her anonymously, of a documentary about the Jasmine Escort Agency, Shepherd's Market, which is a front for prostitution....

Confident of her superiority, Lauren visits the Jasmine Escort Agency and, with the help of Madame Cybele, Captain Twilley and an Arab called Karim, she is soon a successful tart, with a flat in Half Moon Street. She specialises in Arabs, with whom she can converse easily on economic matters and from whom she learns much of value to her academic work. She is also a favourite of Sam Bulbeck, a Labour life peer who is involved in Middle East peace talks.

Lauren enjoys her double life as student and tart: 'She was two people'. But after a time she ceases to be a stranger and learns that she is not a free agent, harmlessly exploiting the exploiters, but the bait in a complicated political trap. The novel ends with her removal to France, where she discovers the true nature of her private life on the front pages of the newspapers.

Like Theroux's earlier London fiction—*The Family Arsenal* (1976) and the short story collections, *World's End* (1980) and *The London Embassy* (1982)—*Doctor Slaughter* is full of the peevish observations of the tourist, about smelly phone boxes and so on.... It is interesting to see one's country through a tourist's eyes and delightful to pounce on inaccuracies...; but Mr Theroux has lived here for some time now, and his observations are not as fresh as they were. More interesting, perhaps, is his treatment of prostitution and its 'small hot secrets'—the sexual equivalent of tourism.

But *Doctor Slaughter* is clearly intended as something more than a fictional Baedeker. Though there are other discernible influences on the novel ('Why did the French seem to take such pleasure in giving a person bad news?' seems straight out of *Gentlemen Prefer Blondes*), the strongest, one is tempted to call it the overpowering influence is again that of Greene. The title, the brevity (137 pages) and even the book's jacket (with its absence of biographical detail and its talk of 'an entertainment of a very high calibre') invite comparison with *Doctor Fischer of Geneva*, that perverse allegory of greed. So, to an extent, does the plot....

Like *Doctor Fischer*, *Doctor Slaughter* is a realistic fairy tale about pleasure and power, the personal and the public. As might be expected, Theroux is not flattered by the comparison: the detail of his novel is not so telling; the spareness of the narrative, lacking the resonance of Greene's, begins to look like thinness. Leaving the invited comparison aside, *Doctor Slaughter* is a highly accomplished and sometimes amusing exercise; taking it into account, it is best seen as a tribute to a great master. (p. 25)

Lewis Jones, "Pale Greene," in The Spectator, *Vol. 252, No. 8138, June 30, 1984, pp. 24-5.*

CHRISTOPHER LEHMANN-HAUPT

[The two novellas in *Half Moon Street*] are tricky, dazzling performances....

Though *Doctor Slaughter* has amusing things to say about sex and *Doctor DeMarr* is penetrating on the subject of twinship, the stories are not as ambitious as his last novel, *The Mosquito Coast* (1982), which in its scope and depth represented a climax in Mr. Theroux's multiform development. One might call them entertainments, part thriller and part social commentary, and as such they are more than satisfying, although if I had to carp I would fault *Doctor Slaughter* on the one hand for the vagueness of its conclusion, and *Doctor DeMarr* by contrast for its overtricky resolution.

Still, as amusing as they may be, it's interesting to consider how the two fictions reflect Mr. Theroux's career as a writer and his preoccupation with identity and alienation. If we reverse the order of the pieces, they can be seen as telling a version of their creator's own story. In *Doctor DeMarr*, a New Englander suffers from his own redundancy. Being a twin, he lacks distinction. He tries to exile himself from his brother's life, but he's tricked by his death and drawn fatally back to the ambiguity of being a twin. What Gerald should have done is gone abroad, though of course then Mr. Theroux would not have had his particular story to tell.

Lauren Slaughter has taken that step, changed her name (from Mopsy Fairlight) and assumed the role of an artist-impostor whose survival depends on tricking men into realizing their fantasies. But it doesn't work. Where she thinks she's in control she's really being controlled, and at the end of *Doctor Slaughter* she is forced to return to America.

Does *Half Moon Street* then reflect despair at the impossibility of finding one's identity even in exile? No, because Gerald DeMarr and Lauren Slaughter can't do one special thing that would have rescued them from their respective dilemmas. Neither of them can *write*. Gerald can't write drug prescriptions, so it's impossible for him to play his dead brother's role once he discovers that George was a doctor.

Lauren's career at the Institute is limited by her inability to produce a paper....

Sometimes when Lauren "was trying to write it was as if she were trying to invent the written word—like originating language itself. Impossible. And what about spending every night with those men? She was strong but she did not have time enough to write and also live her other life."

Paul Theroux, by contrast, can write. He can soar and he can dig. He can go anywhere he wants in the world and take his talent with him. For him there is no exile or loss of identity. In *Half Moon Street* he observes what happens to those who lack his ability. But he's also celebrating his gift.

Christopher Lehmann-Haupt, in a review of "Half Moon Street," in The New York Times, *October 1, 1984, p. C16.*

ALICE McDERMOTT

In fiction, a female character who is ambitious and amoral, confident, intelligent and given to considering the wealthy men she uses "bewildered boys" is somewhat akin to the young soldier in a war movie who passes around a sweet photo of his pregnant wife: one senses immediately that sooner or later they're both going to get it. . . .

It would seem that a novelist as talented as Paul Theroux could make the story of Lauren's double life yield better irony than: smart girls can be wild in bed, or smart girls aren't as smart as they think. *Doctor Slaughter* [one of two novellas in *Half Moon Street*] lacks much of what Mr. Theroux does best (London, for instance, is surprisingly under-described) and the characters here—the kinky Arabs, the sweet Lord Bulbeck, the mysterious Van Arkady who masterminds Lauren's career, and certainly sexy (and unbelievably energetic) Lauren herself—never become more than figures in an adult cartoon. It's too bad—Mr. Theroux can do so much better.

He does do better, in fact, in *Doctor DeMarr,* in which character is so skillfully defined that even the broadest strokes of the plot (and it does run rather thin and broad toward its conclusion) seem believable, even inevitable.

George and Gerald DeMarr are American twin brothers who have not seen one another for nearly half a lifetime until "Out of nowhere and after years of silence, George showed up one July day and put his face against the screen door and said, 'Remember me?' He was clowning in that way that desperate people sometimes do."

George *is* desperate, and sick, and he asks Gerald only for a place to stay. Gerald had believed, hoped, his brother was dead, but still he gives him his house near Boston and then leaves for a vacation on Cape Cod. When he returns a week early, he finds George dead of a drug overdose. His reaction is peculiar: "For Gerald, George's death was more like an amputation—one that had been successfully carried out on his own body. It was as if a diseased and disfiguring part of himself had been cut away. It was a horror, and yet he could not think about it without feeling a little sentimental." Gerald disposes of his brother's body but then begins a casual investigation that leads him, almost inadvertently, to an impersonation of his twin and an attempt to both take on and amend his brother's life.

All this might seem a bit far-fetched, a bit too obviously Jekyll and Hyde, were it not for the way Mr. Theroux manages to make the animosity Gerald feels for his brother seem a natural consequence of having a twin, "a reflection, or an instance of human repetition, or a small bodily stutter." The identical clothes and haircuts and faces, the interchangeable names, the single gifts marked, "To Gerald and George," "the hackneyed upbringing of being twins—the freakishness of it, the puppet show," are all furiously described. "They knew that most people lived with the satisfaction that they were single and unique; but it was the fate of twins to be always weighed and compared. For the whole of their early life they were unhappily chained together, and it was torture to them, for the few likenesses they saw seemed like nothing more than ugly parody."

Given this premise, so wonderfully defined, Gerald's desire to see his brother dead, his feeling of living his own life as a shadow, someone buried alive, is completely convincing, as is his subsequent sidestepping into George's life and the identical fate he finds within it.

Neither of these short novels is as good as Mr. Theroux's best fiction, but, in true Jekyll and Hyde tradition, what is good in *Dr. DeMarr* can serve as antidote for what is bad in *Doctor Slaughter.* Return to *The Mosquito Coast* or *Picture Palace* to discover what is better still.

Alice McDermott, "Ravishing Witch, Ph.D.," in The New York Times Book Review, October 28, 1984, p. 35.

WEBSTER SCHOTT

The British tend to know a good thing in literature when they see it. They got *Half Moon Street* first [published in England as *Doctor Slaughter*] and made it a best seller. They also discovered Paul Theroux first.

We Americans may be realizing at last that Theroux . . . is among the best American writers. *Half Moon Street* is his 22nd book and it shows some of the reasons why. It's nearly everything fiction should be—diversion, psychological revelation, and social news. Furthermore, it is written in radiant language.

Half Moon Street consists of two short novels—*Doctor Slaughter* and *Doctor DeMarr*—about identity, power, and the fatal dangers of the world we live in.

Stories about lonely people who want more and find trouble, they see strangeness and evil drifting through English-speaking society like a change of weather. Sinister processes are at work in the service of personal separation and cultural discord. Decay lies beneath the surfaces of social ritual and institutional facade. Humane qualities like compassion and affection are smothered by urgent drives for control and sensation. Not everything in Paul Theroux's tales is black. But nearly everything is seen as if at 2 in the morning.

The first novel deals with a young American scholar [Lauren Slaughter] in England who falls into a ring of international blackmailers and assassins while believing she is merely doing for money what comes naturally. . . .

Theroux's vision in these two novels is of conspiracies in which the ultimate victims are those who while manipulating others are manipulated themselves and drawn into violence. . . .

The assumptions and conceits of *Doctor DeMarr*—double identity, criminal intelligence, social decay, the guilty as victim—are almost exactly those of *Doctor Slaughter.*

Gerald DeMarr, a middle-aged failed economist in a Boston suburb, hasn't seen his twin brother George in decades. Suddenly George turns up one day, sick and desperate, pressing his face against the screen door and asks Gerald for a place to stay.

Reluctantly, Gerald agrees and leaves for a vacation at Cape Cod. He was once inseparable from George. Too many personal failures, too much festering envy, too many years of separation between young manhood and middle age have turned his feelings into indifference or hostility toward his lost brother. Gerald tells George to be gone from the house when he returns.

Instead, George is dead. Gerald finds him sitting upstairs in a chair, his arm full of punctures, drug paraphernalia nearby. Gerald buries the body in a landfill to avoid trouble and decides to trace his brother's recent past by means of a laundry ticket. He discovers that his twin was a successful impostor of a medical doctor who sold prescriptions to addicts and was on the verge of detection.

Gerald assumes George's identity. Despite its problems it's a better life than his own. He enjoys the dignity of being a "physician." The patients respond. He may even be better at it than George was. And he makes gestures toward correcting his brother's failures. But he slips.

Doctor Slaughter seems by far the better of the two novels. Gerald Demarr's motivation is almost mythic. Lauren's is concrete. *Doctor DeMarr* is just barely credible. *Doctor Slaughter* is as real as an escort service classified advertisement in the *International Herald Tribune*.

But each is successful. In *Half Moon Street* Paul Theroux combines unlikely elements—mystery, character study, the Gothic nightmares of industrialized society—in fiction that shimmers with implications, possibilites, and warnings.

> Webster Schott, "Beyond the Pleasure Principle,"
> in Book World—The Washington Post, December
> 9, 1984, p. 5.

MICHIKO KAKUTANI

Whether he is writing fiction or nonfiction, whether he is writing about Africa, the Far East, England or the United States, Mr. Theroux always has a distinct point of view. He is detached and observant—by turns amused, appalled and fascinated by the oddities and incongruities of the country—or city—he happens to be visiting. Like an anthropologist, he notices the ironic, the incongruous and the obvious that most people overlook. He notices the huge number of law students studying on the subway—"all these lawbooks in this lawless atmosphere." He notices the militaristic organization of so many antiwar groups—"the people who object to ROTC end up marching many more miles than the sophomores on the parade ground." And he notices that patronage works best when both patron and recipient have what the other lacks. . . .

Although most of the pieces in [*Sunrise with Seamonsters*] could be categorized as literary essay (Hemingway, V. S. Pritchett, Graham Greene), travel article (on Afghanistan, Nyasaland, Burma, Cape Cod and India, among other places), or profile (John McEnroe Jr., V. S. Naipaul, S. J. Perelman), they are not arranged by subject, but by date. And the chronological order, oddly enough, ends up making perfect sense, for taken together, the pieces form a sort of ongoing portrait of Mr. Theroux himself—his coming of age as a writer and a man. The earliest sketches, written when he was a Peace Corps volunteer in Africa, show a gifted but callow writer—a young fellow fond of cosmic speculation. . . .

Later, he says he learns the art of skepticism from V. S. Naipaul; and, in fact, the more mature pieces contain echoes of that writer's iconoclasm and impatience: Mr. Theroux dismisses "the average tennis champion" as "a pathetic oaf"; the "whole idea of manhood in America" as "pitiful"; most pacifists as "cowards" who are frightened of dying. Recalling an outrageous example of racism in Mozambique, he writes, "It was grotesque, it was outrageous, it was the shabbiest, darkest kind of imperialism. I could not believe my good luck."

If he is adept at making acerbic witticisms, however, Mr. Theroux also possesses a certain generosity of spirit: he is skilled at celebrating such disparate writers as Kipling, Perelman and Henry Miller; he can locate satisfactions in even

the most arduous of tasks—riding the subways of New York for a week, say, or sailing around Cape Cod in a tiny rowboat.

Perhaps, in the end, what makes Mr. Theroux most persuasive as a writer is simply his willingness to put himself on the line, to monitor his own emotions and give us a report. He tells us what it feels like to go back, 20 years later, for a high school reunion. . . . He tells us what it feels like to be an anxious reporter, waiting to interview John McEnroe Jr. . . . And he tells us what it feels like to be a recent college grad, trying to figure out what to do with his life:

> I had joined the Peace Corps for what I now
> see were selfish reasons: I had thought of responsibilities I did not want—marriage seemed
> too permanent, graduate school too hard, and
> the army too brutal. The Peace Corps is a sort
> of Howard Johnson's on the main drag into
> maturity.

"All anyone can do," Mr. Theroux writes, is to "try to be honest about what he feels, what he's seen or thinks he's seen," and in these essays, he does just that. While he does not make the noisy gestures of a Mailer, does not offer the agonized introspection of a Didion, he is—in his own, low-key way—just as gusty, personal and astonishing a writer.

> Michiko Kakutani, in a review of "Sunrise with Sea-
> monsters," in The New York Times, June 5, 1985,
> p. C24.

COLIN THUBRON

Monsters are never far from Paul Theroux. They loiter opposite him on railway carriages and buttonhole him in down-at-heel provincial towns—outlandish gargoyles of tourists or just repulsively ordinary folk. He greets them with glee, of course. Eccentrics parade through his novels; and readers of his travel-books—regaled by yet another succession of mendicant grotesques—may momentarily wonder if he ever encounters anything admirable on his journeys at all.

But his *Sunrise with Seamonsters* gives us a rather different Theroux. These 50 short essays and articles, written between 1964 and 1984, include travel pieces, interviews, autobiographical sketches and literary appreciation, often fused together. The monsters are still here, of course, but kept decently in place. What emerges is a kindlier, more celebratory writer—his delight in photographs, in boating, in maps; his love of family and literature. The needle eye and mind are still alert, but his (often scathing) book reviews are omitted in favour of studies of favorite authors, and several of his autobiographical pieces are revealing. (p. 3)

His earliest essays—descriptions of Africa which he now finds "a little forced and clumsy"—are tinged with a romanticism, a striving for poetic effect, which he later eliminates. His autobiographical **"The Killing of Hastings Banda"** already shows him in command of a black-humored scenario which sees him thrown out of his Peace Corps teaching job in Malawi for unwitting involvement in a blunderous coup.

After his time in Africa, his articles mingle a deepening taste in literature with reflections on travel and with a few telling personal memoirs. The illuminations of his childhood (essays on **"Being a Man"** and **"Traveling Home: High School Reunion"**) were not written in the frailty of adolescence or young manhood, but in his successful maturity. From this bastion he attacks *machismo* with the virulence of somebody hurt, during more vulnerable years, by the sheer crassness of the high school masculine ethic. . . . The same anger lingers behind his essays on Hemingway and on the failed sensibilities of whites in Africa, in **"Tarzan Is an Expatriate."**

Most of the writers he loves are conversely humane, skeptical, intelligent. His tributes to V. S. Pritchett, Henry James and V. S. Naipaul contain generous critical praise: precise and imaginative. There is an affectionate memoir of S. J. Perelman, an appreciation of Joyce Cary, and a lovely essay on Graham Greene's shadowy (to Greene) female traveling companion during his African *Journey Without Maps*.

Sunrise with Seamonsters is uneven—but what such anthology isn't?—partly because these pieces were responses to editorial commissions. But even when an article does little more than assemble some loosely related ideas, Theroux papers over the cracks so beguilingly, and the ideas are so pungent, that it scarcely seems to matter. Incidental felicities include a swinging attack on patronage ("When patronage is extensive, who indeed needs readers?"), an arresting study of the Exotic, and a discourse on the trials of writing, which is bitterly familiar.

Curiously, the weakest pieces of this mosaic are those about travel, especially train journeys. His accounts of train-hopping to Chittagong, or wanderings in Corsica or Burma, are fragmented and slight, better suited to absorption into the picaresque expansiveness of a travel book. His account of the London-Paris train-ferry is the soggiest patch in the book, and his overview **"Stranger on a Train"** takes too long to say rather little. In his chapter on Afghanistan (dropped from *The Great Railway Bazaar*), he dismisses "the Afghans" (a meaningless ethnic label, anyway) as "lazy, idle and violent," after spending only a few days in their country, mostly with hippies. This is precisely the kind of Tarzan expatriate attitude which he condemned as a younger man in Africa.

On the whole it is Paul Theroux's rootedness, not his vagrancy, which he celebrates most strikingly in this rich and various collection. (pp. 3, 10)

> Colin Thubron, "On the Road with Paul Theroux,"
> in Book World—The Washington Post, *July 7, 1985*,
> pp. 3, 10.

MARK ABLEY

Halfway through *The Old Patagonian Express*, Paul Theroux stopped to analyse his reasons for travelling. Other writers might seek fresh perceptions of a foreign culture; the strange delights of a new landscape or language; the comfort of strangers. Theroux's motives are unashamedly selfish: "I craved a little risk, some danger, an untoward event, a vivid discomfort, an experience of my own company, and in a modest way the romance of solitude." He travels not to learn, to comprehend, or to report the truth about foreign parts; he travels to dispel boredom.

There is, of course, a handsome literary tradition of solipsistic treks. The travel writer, A. W. Kinglake observed in the preface to *Eothen*, "must, and he will, sing a sadly long strain about Self; he will talk for whole pages together about his bivouac fire, and ruin the Ruins of Baalbec with eight or ten cold lines". Likewise Theroux. In **"Making Tracks to Chittagong"**, an essay [included in *Sunrise with Seamonsters*] about travelling on the Indian sub-continent, he devotes a total of eight reluctant lines to the city of Agra ("The town is nothing")

and four of its buildings ("The Agra Fort is substantial . . . the Taj Mahal is something else"); yet the railway stations of Barog, Dhumdanj and Solan Brewery spur him to eloquence.

Although Kinglake conceded that a traveller's egotism can become shameless and obtrusive, he insisted that it "must still convey some true ideas of the country through which he has passed . . . if you bear with him long enough, you may find yourself slowly and faintly impressed with the realities of Eastern Travel". Like so many travel writers before him, Theroux takes a sour joy in those sooty realities. "There is", he admits, "something in feeling abject that quickens my mind and makes it intensely receptive to fugitive impressions." The justification for the abjectness is the quality of sight, or insight, to which it can lead.

Travel, in Theroux's eyes, becomes a synonym for imaginative exploration. It is, he writes, "never easy: you get very tired, you get lost, you get your feet wet, you get little cooperation, and—if it is to have any value at all—you go alone". A foreign culture merely provides the fuel on which his solitary imagination blazes. He explains our renewed passion for reading books of travel in terms of a need to find an antidote for the bland poison of mass tourism. . . . Theroux refrains from exploring the implicit conflict between such a traveller and a travel writer; for by exposing to the world's hungry eyes the wonders he has found on his journeys, a writer risks destroying what has most inspired him. If each man kills the thing he loves, a travel writer's words can be particularly lethal. . . .

As Theroux knows, some areas of the world have seen their culture all but interred by tourism. Overseas travel is never neutral; as surely as they bring sun-tan lotion and foreign currency, tourists also bring changes. In the context of any Third World country—and in many parts of the first and second world too—travel means power. It implies an extraordinary wealth, and an even more extraordinary leisure. Theroux castigates the hippie travellers of a generation ago, but without allowing for the motive that lay behind some of their follies: a desire to experience an exotic culture in a direct, immediate way, free of the artificial glamour of tourism and its transparent power. He likes to have it both ways, attacking sanitized and unsanitized travelling alike.

Theroux's well-known scorn seems to me, after a few hundred pages, little more than an annoying tic. He has the dangerous habit of expressing gloomy opinions in the guise of self-evident truths: "Afghanistan is expensive and barbarous", he proclaimed in an essay for *Harper's* in 1974. "The Afghans are lazy, idle and violent." He wrote the piece to appear in *The Great Railway Bazaar*, was persuaded to omit it, and deleted from that book almost everything about Afghanistan except fierce generalizations. Unlike his friend—and, in a sense, his master—V. S. Naipaul, Theroux rarely grounds his scorn in political understanding. While he has a gift for finding charged, complex images of a country or city, the implications of these images sometimes appear to elude him. . . .

It comes as something of a relief to turn from the travel-pieces in *Sunrise with Seamonsters* to his literary essays, where his sense of appreciation and delight far outweighs his spleen. Oddly, though, he inserts a few paragraphs from two venomous, ephemeral book-reviews into his introduction, perhaps in case anybody should suspect him of going soft-hearted in middle age. (Novelists who don't happen to review books, by the way, "I find lazy and contemptible".) He has a fine understanding of the architecture of fiction; his tributes to Naipaul and Joyce Cary are both generous and astute. An essay on *What Maisie Knew* has a particular interest, for it shows Theroux struggling to define the pleasure and value of a novel with which he is clearly not in full sympathy.

Sunrise with Seamonsters is packed with small revelations about its author; by alluding to his own beliefs and practices even in essays concerning other writers, he makes his literary "discoveries" as autobiographical as his travel writings.

> Mark Abley, "Sneers on the Way," in The Times Literary Supplement, No. 4296, August 2, 1985, p. 863.

SUSAN FROMBERG SCHAEFFER

At the beginning of *The Mosquito Coast,* before the soon-to-be-psychotic Allie flees what he believes is an imminently doomed America, Paul Theroux describes his protagonist's philosophy: "It's the empty spaces that will save us. No funny bunnies, no cops, no crooks, no muggers, no glue sniffers, no aerosol bombs." Mr. Theroux, it seems, has an equally intense faith in the redemption of empty spaces, and O-Zone, "the large sealed-off territory in the midwest," a supposedly uninhabitable zone created after a disastrous leakage of nuclear wastes, is one of those empty spaces and gives its name to his new novel.

O-Zone is set approximately 50 years in the future. It begins when seven wealthy men and women and one teen-age boy, Fizzy, a computer genius and what we would call a nerd, fly to O-Zone for a New Year's Eve party. They come from New York City, "a terrible place" filled with aliens—Skells, Starkies, Trolls, Diggers, Roaches (not the exotic beings their names imply, but illegal residents of the city). All seven adults live in fortresslike towers and are so fearful of the city they rarely go outside. Fizzy, the boy, whose life becomes the battleground on which the struggle for change and happiness will be fought, lives in a room without windows and, until he is 15, does not venture onto the streets. When he does, he finds them heavily patrolled and is incessantly stopped at checkpoints. New York protects its citizens by destroying anyone who appears to be dangerous; the price of safety is a kind of anxious imprisonment, the city itself a luxurious jail.

Although Mr. Theroux does not explicitly say so, alienation from nature is responsible for the immense decadence and decay of the city's unhappy citizens. . . .

In this world, O-Zone (the outer zone) is, as Mr. Theroux himself says, a complex image or symbol. . . . (p. 12)

As the first people allowed in in 15 years, the eight travelers look forward to an exotic experience. The surprise is that O-Zone turns out to be neither unpopulated nor uninhabitable. Godseye, a murderous, governmentally sanctioned group reminiscent of the Ku Klux Klan, has, without telling anyone, dumped undesirable characters, or "aliens," into the zone, wishing upon them slow death from cancer and radiation. But the area itself has mutated into a peculiar version of paradise—a cross between the Garden of Eden and Love Canal. It not only supports life, it nourishes it, and restores the humanity of its inhabitants. Fizzy discovers the existence of the survivors, and on an investigatory expedition one of the partygoers shoots and kills two of them. On New Year's Day, the party returns to Manhattan, subdued, chastened and changed, and the remainder of the novel . . . charts and explains the nature of these changes. *O-Zone* explores the way we live now to diagnose the ills of our times, and to suggest ways we might find our way back to the "paradise" that the zone represents. It is, at heart, a profoundly didactic book.

O-Zone belongs to that category of novel we once called science fiction but now call "futuristic." A futuristic or apocalyptic novel carries a special burden: it must not only—like any other novel—create its own world, it must also be as accurate in its assessment of present troubles as it is convincing in its portrayal of the future. *O-Zone,* however, does not create a coherent vision of the present or the future. The New York of the novel exaggerates to absurdity what already exists: the slums are worse, the gulf between the rich and poor is wider. The future may, of course, turn out to be a terrible caricature of the present. But nothing in *O-Zone* explains why the lunatic or horror fringe of our society becomes the norm. Why does Mr. Theroux seem to assume that in the future all "fortyish" men will be impotent and therefore murderous? Why assume everyone will be as emotionally empty as a gourd?

Mr. Theroux demonstrates a touching faith that men in a state of nature will become, if not noble savages, at least admirable human beings, fully biological creatures who can do what all living things are meant to do—grow. Fizzy, who rejects the city in favor of the zone, becomes the prototype of the "new man" who must eventually solve the problem of how to combine a truly human life with the inhuman technology men have created. As he matures, he becomes the good savage equipped with technology—the kind of man who can lead humanity out of the double wilderness of emotional alienation and dehumanizing science to achieve, in himself, a desperately needed symbiosis between the two. This is why it becomes so important for all the major characters to come to love the initially despised Fizzy, no matter how unlikely that transformation may be.

More serious than the naïveté of Mr. Theroux's philosophy is his seeming inability to create characters in whom we can take an interest. They are one-dimensional, each embodied with one, sometimes two distinguishing traits. Moura, for example, is rich and bored. Holly is sex-starved and then, when sated, has a "roasted" look. Rinka, a friend of Holly's and Moura's, has no distinguishing traits. Hooper and Hardy, two central characters, are, for hundreds of pages, defined only by their professions. Fizzy himself is an O-Zone in human form. . . . But crucial as he is to the scheme of the novel, he is sloppily drawn: he is forever "squawking" and "honking" and boring everyone (including the reader) with his endless explanations of natural and technical phenomena. When he is "snatched" by the aliens, the other characters feel little regret; neither does the reader.

The plot—a kidnapping, a rescue attempt and a "surprising" resolution—deadens because it is so entirely predictable and repetitive.

In the end, *O-Zone* is a kind of neo-Thoreauvian, Rousseauean work, a *Lord of the Flies* in reverse. It is as if Mr. Theroux were asking us to contemplate the bright side of nuclear pollution. After all, without the spill of radioactive waste, we would not have the redemptive space of O-Zone. When one of the characters stumbles upon a little town, he finds what he has searched for all his life. People "still cut the grass, and weeded the flowers, and put up the flag." The truth then strikes him: *"This is the past."* And so we and the characters learn that the past could become our future. In other words, the past *is* the bluebird of happiness, to be found in our own backyard.

This is a popcorn apocalypse, easy to swallow in large amounts, providing little nourishment, animated by sentimentality rather than sentiment. *O-Zone* finally espouses all the virtues of Norman Rockwell: we learn that we ought to love better, that courage can save us, that imaginary fears are worse than real ones, that we all need to be needed, need people to love. Apoplectic rather than apocalyptic, *O-Zone* tells us what we already know. But it does not tell us this well, or interestingly, or vividly. Mr. Theroux makes none of this new—and his menacing future rattles at us like a badly made plastic skull. (pp. 12-13)

> Susan Fromberg Schaeffer, "Nerd of Paradise," in *The New York Times Book Review, September 14, 1986, pp. 12-13.*

JOHN CLUTE

O-Zone may be a novel about a near-future corporate-state America, gripped by xenophobia and fundamentalism, where Owners zap 'aliens' with ray-guns for the fun of it, but no one on reading the book could mistake Paul Theroux for a writer of science fiction. This is perhaps deliberate; it surely seems almost inevitable. When mainstream writers decide to try their hand at science fiction, the likes of *O-Zone* are all too often what they end up producing.

This is not to say that the second half of this enormous novel is particularly bad, and there are indeed long sequences, set in boondock America, where Paul Theroux, once he gets his dander up, comes very close to delivering the goods. It is the disdainful amateurishness of the first half that marks the author as being ill at ease with the sleek, efficient, pulpy conventions of the genre, so that in establishing the terms of his future America he seems at times unbearably coquettish, fatally condescending. (p. 29)

All of this takes 200 too many pages to tell. Like a slightly prurient virgin, Theroux will time and again touch on an sf convention—hi-tech weaponry; ubiquitous computer interfaces with the world; fundamentalist vigilantes terrorising 'aliens' from gunships; rococo fashions and decadent sexual practice among the rich Owners of a moribund, balkanised America—only to shy away from actually allowing it to inform his ample creative imagination. By failing to use these conventions competently, however arbitrary they may seem to a 'literary' mind, he creates a world of numbing exiguity. Only in O-Zone itself does he come to life.

Fisher is an inspired creation, a gawky, savage, creepy mathematical genius, not too dissimilar (one might hazard) to a certain American chess wizard. His gradual coming to manhood in the real world may be an old theme, one at the heart of a thousand sf juveniles, but in Theroux's hands it is given a darkly comic complexity that almost redeems the novel. Here, with wit, panache and considerable satiric punch, Theroux finally makes one able to believe in the seamy, fractured nightmare of his fascist America; he grasps the nettle of his vision. Those who put up with the earlier ramblings will feel rewarded for their persistence. (p. 30)

> John Clute, "Off Limits," in *New Statesman, Vol. 112, No. 2899, October 17, 1986, pp. 29-30.*

STEFAN R. DZIEMIANOWICZ

[The] true antecedent for [*O-Zone*] is not novels like *A Canticle for Leibowitz* or *Alas, Babylon,* but *The Kingdom by the Sea,*

Theroux's own depressing travelogue on the crumbling remnants of empire in rural Great Britain. This time, though, it's America and its dream that are scrutinized.

Theroux's apocalypse doesn't begin with a bang but with the whimper of an ailing world that can't tell where it hurts. Under the government-fostered impression that a leak of radioactive waste has contaminated the heartland, American society has concentrated in New York, where it is being slowly strangled by misguided priorities and mindless distractions. Its minorities and homeless, dubbed "aliens," have become subhuman scapegoats for everything wrong with the country. Its economy has divided the lucky into an elite trapped in their hermetically sealed environment and a bureaucratic service sector that's second cousin to Big Brother.

O-Zone, which turns out to be surprisingly lush and viable, is the last best hope for saving the country from its own inertia. A new frontier capable of generating its own mythology, it serves as land of potential opportunity for the story's three main characters: for environmental architect Hardy Allbright it offers a chance to restore the country to geographic wholeness; for his businessman brother Hooper it holds out the possibility of a new sense of values gained through his love for an O-Zone alien; for Fizzy, the computer genius and emotional cripple, it means a shot at being shaped into a complete and capable human being. When Fizzy's kidnapping by O-Zoners makes convergence of the two worlds inevitable, we wait to see if both will benefit or one will destroy the other.

The outcome would have been more satisfying had Theroux not made his characters such obvious products of their environment. As he labors to show that O-Zone is really a consequence of narrow opinions and conditioned responses, the reader is very aware of being set up for Great Changes In Individual Thinking that portend Monumental Changes for Society In General. If anything, though, characters become so monolithic and the threat of O-Zone so overwhelming that victories seem too personal, almost self-indulgent. As nothing in this cautionary tale indicates that Theroux feels the situation is so hopeless, one can only surmise that a surer grasp of the milieu, or perhaps avoiding it altogether, would have allowed the author to better express his intentions.

> Stefan R. Dziemianowicz, "Waste-Watchers," in *Fantasy Review, Vol. 9, No. 10, November, 1986, p. 34.*

JOHN SUTHERLAND

It is odd to find Paul Theroux writing an imaginary voyage. One's first thought is that the author has run out of exotic countries to visit. Perhaps the Theroux passport has expired. Or perhaps he is simply tired of the road and has decided to make up his faraway places. For whatever reason, *O-Zone* is, as its publisher warns, 'unlike anything Paul Theroux has ever written'....

[*O-Zone*] may be a new world for Theroux, but it's been mapped out by any number of SF writers. Among many other stories, Tom Disch's *334* and J. G. Ballard's *Highrise* are echoed in *O-Zone.* And in the later sections there's more than a suggestion of William Nolan's *Logan's Run.*

Given the vast length of *O-Zone* (compared to the wafer-slim novella *Doctor Slaughter*), one has to assume that Theroux means it seriously: 469 nine on ten-point pages can't exactly have been thrown off. But it's hard to believe that Theroux wants permanent membership of the Science Fiction writers' club. One assumes the work belongs with the sizeable library of one-off SF works by non-SF writers: *The Old Men at the Zoo, Lord of the Flies, 1984, Clockwork Orange, Ape and Essence*. *O-Zone* is not as good as any of these (nor as good as Theroux's previous best). But it's good enough. The conventions of dystopia give some fresh scope to the author's fixed ideas about civilisation and barbarism. And the plot element dealing with the evolution of the odious Fizzy from nerd to manhood is gripping. The main fault is that the idiom of the work too often strikes the ear as unconvincing. This is particularly so with the future slang Theroux coins. (p. 14)

John Sutherland, *"Fiction and the Poverty of Theory," in* London Review of Books, *November 20, 1986, pp. 14-15.*

SUSAN LARDNER

A new novel takes getting used to, even when the reader and the writer have met before. With a novelist like Paul Theroux, whose subject is being a stranger, each new venture involves a change of scene and point of view, and the reader needs time to adjust to the new guise of a familiar psyche. The opening line of Theroux's latest novel, *O-Zone*, sums up the difficulty: "The first thing these people always asked, whenever they went out was where were 'they'?" Where is Theroux, this time out? (p. 108)

Theroux has specialized in travel facts and dreams for twenty years, and the props, the costumes, and the rhetoric of science fiction are just devices for reworking ideas about safety and risk which he has dealt with in straight accounts of his own journeys. . . . In *O-Zone*, genetic engineering makes fatherhood passé, and the principal explorer is a bumptious fifteen-year-old named Fisher, or Fizzy, who rediscovers America without having to love it or leave it. Adjacent story lines center on sex and family life, aspects of the unknown covered in the novels *Picture Palace*, *The Black House*, and *The Family Arsenal*, among others.

Five hundred and twenty-seven pages is a lot of paper, however, and, despite the apparent abundance of plot and the flexible metaphors, *O-Zone* bulges with paraphrase and repetition. Familiar Therouxvian syntax ("Murdick's gabbling fear made

him giddy," "Their isolation . . . had given her a glimpse of the past and made her truthful") too often encountered ("Desire made him solitary," "Inexperience made him dumb," "Fear made him quarrelsome") loses its charm. The word "strange" is put in play more frequently than it should be, and the same goes for "wild," "dangerous," "secret," and "dark." Chapter 1, Part I, contains such a solid account of the literal and figurative features of the setting that the recurrence of words and phrases in subsequent chapters and Parts leaves a reader ill-disposed to confront, on page 378, the proposition that O-Zone is "a byword for everything unknown and unfathomable and empty and strange." Like a man under a strange and unfathomable spell, Theroux elaborates, further asserting that O-Zone "was associated in the American mind with such strange imagery," and making it perfectly clear that "saying the word was less like mentioning a part of the United States than a distant island or another planet." How do I gloss thee, O-Zone? Let me count the ways. Whether he is writing a detached third-person narration, as in *O-Zone*, or a close first, as in *Saint Jack*, Theroux is inclined to pontificate. He likes to nail his points down with pithy observations and asides rather than let meanings dangle. In *O-Zone*, as if doubtful of the force of his invention or of the reader's ability to decipher it, he tackles the story at every turn to comment, until his own adventure in exegesis becomes the main event.

The tendentious manner and a feeling for the drama in life make Theroux a throwback to the nineteenth century. Closer temperamentally to Poe than to Thackeray, he is not a social critic, except in passing. The redundancy of *O-Zone* is laced with striking passages of ominous description ("The heavy black sky had slipped down against the orange bar of sunset and narrowed it to a red line and squeezed it into the far-off hills") and bursts of perverse wit ("I lack inexperience"). The irony of familiar future/mysterious past leads nicely through the concept of this world as a richer version of outer space into the notion of space travel as a vulgar fad: "What a bore he was, waiting his turn for the rocket." Romantic and cynical impulses combine to produce Theroux's distinctive thorny style, and even this overwrought novel is worth exploring for its surprises. (pp. 108-09)

Susan Lardner, *"Familiar Future," in* The New Yorker, *Vol. LXII, No. 52, February 16, 1987, pp. 108-09.*

John (Barrington) Wain

1925-

English novelist, poet, short story writer, critic, editor, biographer, autobiographer, and translator.

With the publication of his first novel, *Hurry On Down* (1953), Wain was linked with the "Angry Young Men," a group of post-World War II British writers whose work expressed disenchantment with the constraints of England's class structure and disdain for cultural pretentiousness. Although his early fiction and poetry is similar in content to works by other authors categorized as Angry Young Men, including Kingsley Amis, John Braine, and John Osborne, Wain discounts critical attempts to interpret his work as part of any literary movement. In his fiction, Wain clearly delineates the moral values of his characters and employs straightforward narration. His early poetry is conventionally structured and, like his fiction, is praised for displaying wit, clarity, and poignant satire. In his later verse, Wain incorporates various experimental techniques and reveals his growing interest in topical political and social issues.

In his early novels, Wain explores through satire the traits necessary for survival in a difficult and frightening world. The protagonists of these books are directionless young men striving to retain their individuality amid what they perceive to be the excessive class consciousness and phoniness of contemporary English society. *Hurry On Down* is a picaresque novel in which Charles Lumley moves from one unsatisfying job to another. Wain satirizes social presumptions through exaggerated depictions of the class associations Lumley encounters in each of his positions. Dan Wickenden noted that "[Wain's] satire, though devastating, is not so much savage as exuberant." Wain also utilizes the picaresque mode in *Living in the Present* (1955), which centers upon a despairing teacher who decides to kill the most hateful man he knows and then commit suicide. Wain portrays a farcical chase through Europe in which humorous circumstances foil each attempt to perpetrate the murder. The teacher eventually falls in love, marries, and then wonders why he ever contemplated suicide. In *The Contenders* (1958), Wain exposes the absurdity of obsessive male rivalry and the relationship between business and art by depicting the overzealous competition between two friends—a businessman and an artist—from the viewpoint of a narrator who serves as the voice of moderation. In *A Travelling Woman* (1959), Wain appropriates elements of Restoration comedy to portray shortcomings of modern marriage.

With *Strike the Father Dead* (1962), Wain's novels began to display a more serious tone. This book centers on the conflicting values which strain the relationship between a classics professor and his son, a jazz musician. Wain's pessimism, always a factor in his novels, is strongly evident in *The Young Visitors* (1965) and *The Smaller Sky* (1967). The former shows how ideological conflicts between East and West affect the love relationship between an Englishman and a Russian woman, while the latter examines society's harsh attitude towards nonconformity by depicting an unhappy scientist who leaves his wife and family for an isolated existence. *A Winter in the Hills* (1970) focuses upon an English philologist who becomes embroiled in a dispute between a Welsh bus company and a pro-

© *Jerry Bauer*

spective buyer who plans to sell the company to a large English corporation. The philologist learns the value of social commitment by helping the Welsh workers retain local ownership of the business.

Many critics regard *The Pardoner's Tale* (1978) as Wain's finest novel. In this work, he develops a complex novel-within-a-novel structure revolving around Giles Hermitage, a deserted husband who is writing a book about a man contemplating divorce. As the two stories intertwine, the reader observes how the circumstances of Hermitage's life are reworked into fiction and how the novelist's imagination influences his view of reality. D. A. N. Jones observed: "The two stories are ingeniously linked. . . . [The] linking method has been deliberately designed to make it difficult for Wain's narrative to carry conviction, to suspend the reader's disbelief: he has met this self-imposed challenge and succeeded triumphantly."

In his short stories, Wain further expounds upon themes developed in his novels, including the ethical value and implications of individualism. His short fiction has been collected in four volumes: *Nuncle and Other Stories* (1960), *Death of the Hind Legs and Other Stories* (1966), *The Life Guard* (1972), and *King Caliban and Other Stories* (1978).

Wain began publishing poetry while attending Oxford University during World War II. There he met Kingsley Amis and

Philip Larkin, with whom he shared similar poetic values. In 1953, Wain was named editor of ''First Reading,'' a British Broadcasting Corporation radio program that featured promising young writers. Such poets as Wain, Larkin, and Amis, as well as D. J. Enright and Donald Davie, all of whom read from their work on ''First Reading,'' are collectively categorized as belonging to ''the Movement.'' This group of poets repudiated what they perceived to be the obscurity and pomposity of the modernist verse of Ezra Pound and T. S. Eliot in favor of clarity, precision, and plain language. The poems in Wain's first two volumes, *Mixed Feelings* (1951) and *A Word Carved on a Sill* (1956), focus on such personal themes as love and isolation. Beginning with *Weep before God* (1961), Wain's poetry becomes more loosely structured and addresses social and political topics. *Wildtrack* (1965) marked a radical change in Wain's technique, as he experiments with verse form to create a lengthy, kaleidoscopic poem that investigates human interdependence. In *Letters to Five Artists* (1969), Wain pays tribute to artists who have influenced him. *Feng* (1975), a long retelling of Shakespeare's *Hamlet* from the perspective of Claudius, Hamlet's stepfather, compares the corrupting forces of power in medieval times with contemporary abuses. *Poems, 1949-1979* (1982) contains Wain's best early verse as well as new poems.

Wain's numerous nonfiction works reflect his versatility and prolificacy. His literary criticism is praised as cogent and accessible, and he has edited a number of respected poetry anthologies. In *Sprightly Running: Part of an Autobiography* (1962), Wain recalls how his traumatic childhood experiences helped form beliefs which surface in his writings; he also discusses literature, criticism, and academia. His second autobiographical volume, *Dear Shadows* (1986), consists of profiles of nine influential figures, including Marshall McLuhan and E. H. W. Meyerstein. Wain has also authored three biographies, most notably *Samuel Johnson* (1974), for which he was awarded the James Tait Black Memorial Prize. Critics generally regard this work as one of Wain's greatest achievements. While depicting his life, Wain explicates Johnson's views and compares them with modern literary and intellectual precepts. Wain also offers his own opinions on these subjects and laments the passing of such values as faith in reason and respect for tradition.

(See also *CLC*, Vols. 2, 11, 15; *Contemporary Authors*, Vols. 5-8, rev. ed.; *Contemporary Authors Autobiography Series*, Vol. 4; and *Dictionary of Literary Biography*, Vols. 15, 27.)

R. D. CHARQUES

Mr. Wain's first novel [*Hurry On Down*], an up-to-date essay in the comic picaresque, is inventive, impulsive, cogitative and often very funny. His hero, Charles Lumley, the product of an exemplary upbringing and the foot-loose possessor of a university degree, suffers a brain-storm of alcoholic decision and sets out on the quest for a living wage determined to shed ''his class, his *milieu*, his insufferable load of presuppositions and reflexes.'' He becomes, by turns, window-cleaner, export delivery car driver and dope runner, hospital orderly, chauffeur, bouncer at a night club and radio gag-writer. His misadventures in each of these several capacities hover with breathless calm on the lunatic fringe of the strictest provincial realism.

Terse and uncomplicated in his vein of absurdity, loose-muscled and witty in style, Mr. Wain scores most freely at his most anarchic moments of dissent from current social moralities. The fooling is sometimes a little weak, the wit of the dialogue is not always in character, and here and there, rotating on the axis of school and university, Mr. Wain stretches the long arm of coincidence. But he has made a very good comic start.

> *R. D. Charques, in a review of ''Hurry On Down,'' in* The Spectator, *Vol. 191, No. 6536, October 2, 1953, p. 380.*

THE TIMES LITERARY SUPPLEMENT

Mr. John Wain has written a fresh and amusing novel [*Hurry on Down*] about the adventures of a young *petit bourgeois* hero attempting to escape from the restrictions of class and cash. The manner Mr. Wain adopts in describing his hero's adventures as window cleaner, lorry driver, drug runner, hospital orderly, chauffeur and member of a radio script-writing team is somewhere between that of early Waugh and early Linklater: but this is a Linklater with a purpose and a Waugh with a difference. Charles Lumley is in flight from his parents (with whom his relationship remains undefined throughout the book), from academic culture and gentility, from a manner of speech and a way of living. . . . During his career as window cleaner Lumley makes certain resolutions. ''He must form no roots in his new stratum of society, but remain independent of class, forming roots only with impersonal things such as places and seasons.'' The demands of such ''realism'' force him to acquiesce in the murder of an acquaintance who is about to expose his part in a drug-running organization, and later to behave with brusque inhumanity towards a working-class girl who has fallen in love with him. Yet Lumley is unable to compete on equal terms with those who are ''really at home in the parish of grimacing and licking'': when at the end of the book he is about to succumb to the lure of the highly polished fancy woman for whom he feels an urgent longing, it is with the awareness that she is calling him out into the human jungle, and that in the jungle he will die.

All this is perhaps too solemn: or at least it ignores Mr. Wain's grasp of comic effects, which range from some fine inconsequential farce, through skilfully treated social irony to an uncomfortable facetiousness. The best farcical scenes are those in which the twitching provincial highbrow, Froulish, outlines the plot of his ''Work in Progress'' to a literary society, and in which a young mechanical maniac tests out his home-made racing car; but the lightly borne social irony runs through the whole book, helping to touch off excellent impressionistic views of a dance hall, a variety of public houses, a working-class domestic interior with figures. *Hurry on Down* shows at times a clumsiness of hand and of conception natural in a first novel; but it reveals also considerable powers of observation and a great fund of comic invention.

> *''Matters of Conscience,'' in* The Times Literary Supplement, *No. 2697, October 9, 1953, p. 640.*

DAN WICKENDEN

A wind blowing out of the eighteenth century, when English fiction was young and boisterous, invigorates *Born in Captivity* [published in England as *Hurry On Down*], a picaresque comedy set in England today. But the hero of this richly entertaining first novel might puzzle such illustrious forebears of his as Tom Jones and Roderick Random.

Charles Lumley, fresh from a provincial university, embarks on his career as a latter-day picaroon in rebellion against the prison house of middle-class respectability—not quite intact after two world wars but still unbearably stuffy—into which he has been born. His desire to wear no label, remain unattached, to be wholly his own man, is contemporary in its acute self-consciousness. And there is "the mushroom-shaped cloud that lived perpetually in a cave at the back of his mind."...

Basically serious, bearing (I think) the unmistakable hallmark of literature, *Born in Captivity* is besides, satirical, exciting and often wildly funny. Along the way it conjures up the poetry, the anguish, the incidental absurdities of a man's first passionate love. And it is thronged with sharply drawn characters, most of them disreputable, few of them pleasant, but all of them wonderfully alive.... This is realism made fantastic, heightened by spirited caricature.

Although the author may owe a little to Anthony Powell, and certainly owes something to his coarser, more extrovert eighteenth-century models, he has written a highly original novel. His sinewy prose, full of strong verbs and fresh, witty images, is a joy to read. And his satire, though devastating, is not so much savage as exuberant: what fun that there are so many balloons to pop!

John Wain . . . is as hard-headed, as devoid of romantic and sentimental illusions, as any of his contemporaries: but he most refreshingly writes like a young man glad to be alive and rejoicing in his youth.

> Dan Wickenden, "Here, in a Manner of Speaking, Comes Tom Jones Again," in New York Herald Tribune Book Review, *March 21, 1954, p. 3.*

EDMUND FULLER

[In *Born in Captivity*] we run into the problem of what happens when a notable comic talent addresses itself to a subject that isn't funny. The result is a book occasionally hilarious, always interesting, but essentially unsatisfactory. Into the fairly formal convention of the lightly satirical novel it injects jarring elements irreconcilable with its general tone.

Born in Captivity expresses Charles Lumley's feelings toward the middle class in which he has been nurtured. Just out of college, he is aimless. To discard all the stigmata and obligations of class is his chief wish. (p. 5)

The flaw in the pattern is found early in Charles' attitude. Instead of being lightly feckless, amiably inept or unconcerned about conformity, he sees himself as having "been equipped with an upbringing devised to meet the needs of a more fortunate age, and then thrust into the jungle of the Nineteen Fifties." At the deep level, he is sorry for himself, which is not good for comedy.

Only at the end is his real wish laid bare to him—neutrality, the wish not "to take sides in all the silly pettiness that goes on." Inevitably this neutrality extends into the moral field. Early in the story Charles finds himself involved in a dope ring and is ashamed, but does nothing. Chance got him into it and chance gets him out. The comic integrity of the book is destroyed from there on.

We laugh at foibles, blunders, peccadillos—but Mr. Wain lets Charles become contemptible, and at that we do not laugh. It requires the huge derision of a Rabelais to achieve this—the target must be defined at once as contemptible and then laughed to scorn. Charles is intended to be sympathetic, we are to identify ourselves with him. He is not seeking something, he isn't even doing a competent job of escaping. Charles is drifting, and that, too, is not funny. (pp. 5, 20)

Mr. Wain writes well, but failed to decide clearly what *kind* of book he was writing. (p. 20)

> Edmund Fuller, "The Unhappy Drifter," in The New York Times Book Review, *March 21, 1954, pp. 5, 20.*

THE TIMES LITERARY SUPPLEMENT

Mr. Wain's first novel, *Hurry on Down*, was picaresque in the sense that its form was purely serial: the hero stumbled from one situation into another. Its great novelty, as Mr. Angus Wilson perceptively said at the time, was that a novelist had at last admitted to his pages the expense-account world which had grown up since the war. Mr. Wain's second novel, *Living in the Present*, widened the hero's wanderings and introduced an artificial quest theme: bent on suicide, the hero was first to kill the most hateful man he knew. Mr. Wain's third [*The Contenders*] is a "straight" or "serious" novel in the sense of being concerned primarily with a character-situation. It is also serious in the sense of not making us laugh. At the same time, the old *picaro* is not quite banished, either from the narrator's temperament or from the style of writing which Mr. Wain has lent him.

The narrator is a fat, easy-going young man called "Joe" Shaw. He presents himself as at school, in a North Staffordshire pottery town, with two friend-enemies, Ned Roper and Robert Lamb. Mr. Wain himself was brought up in Stoke-on-Trent; but Shaw, Roper and Lamb belong to a generation almost ten years older than his own. At an unrepresentative if not impossible age Roper becomes an industrial tycoon. Lamb goes to London and, with a no less unrepresentative suddenness, though not at so youthful an age, is acclaimed as an artist. The rivalry between the two eventually centres upon a top fashion model, the emblem of what not only all men but all women may be supposed to want. She marries Lamb, but then leaves him for Roper. Lamb acquires and then leaves a marvellous Italian girl, with whom, in the end, Shaw (the narrator) falls in love and whom he rescues, tiring of his role as a mere spectator.

For the most part, Mr. Wain manages his plot with a springing vitality, though his earlier chapters could be thought either not substantial enough or not really necessary: the book (which is quite long) could in fact, with advantage, have been either longer or shorter. The characters lack certain kinds of distinctness. We are told that Lamb is dark, stocky and explosive; and that Roper is tall, fair and suave. Their physical presence nevertheless so little appears in the writing that one is forced to visualize both as portrayed on the hideous jacket. They exhibit behaviour which is not out of character, but which is never quite beautifully and is sometimes crudely rendered: one dreads Lamb's next fit of tantrums because of the routine way in which he will scowl, bang and shout.

The narrator rarely seems just what he is supposed to be. A provincial journalist, he yet knows the metropolitan-literary smart talk, while his slang idiom belongs rather to Mr. Wain's generation than to his own.

"Fairly Serious," in The Times Literary Supplement, *No. 2924, March 14, 1958, p. 137.*

MAX COSMAN

Somewhat autobiographic, it would seem, **The Contenders** is another attack on our social set-up. More specifically, it is a sour look at England's competitiveness and, by implication, at competitiveness anywhere else. Training for careerism in his country, as Wain reports it, begins early. Pitted against each other throughout school days, English males never get over their indoctrination. The contest's the thing. As a result, Robert and Ned, the main antagonists of the book, continue to square up to each other even when they are adults.

Myra, a model of beauty but no model otherwise, is the symbolic as well as synthetic prize in their final contest. So pervasive, Wain continues, is the spirit of competition that Joe too, eternal uncle that he is and a most reluctant antagonist, in a sense has to stand up eventually—against his admired Robert. His award, incidentally, is the equally symbolic though more desirable creature, Pepina. . . .

For all its exploration of personality, **The Contenders** is notable not for the characters in it but for its own character. Like its predecessors [**Hurry On Down** and **Living in the Present**] it is a cross between burlesque and melodrama. But its significant core is really the author's contempt for what is about him. His satiric animus misses nothing, whether it be national mores or crockery designs, Bohemian life or Philistinism, guests of a celebrity or a Chelsea love-nest, an art patron or a dining-car steward. All get their denigratory quietus.

Whether such disapproval of the human scene owes much or little to Sartre-Camus, it is none the less native in Wain. Basically he is an inquisitor of belief and an irrepressible censor of behavior. But at the same time he is a writer fallible in his craft, still apt to contrive when he should perceive, and to verbalize when he should be subtle.

Max Cosman, "John Wain Attacks Competitiveness in Our Society," in New York Herald Tribune Book Review, *April 27, 1958, p. 7.*

WHITNEY BALLIETT

Mr. Wain, who is an unbridled and highly skilled clown, has patched together [in **The Contenders**] a genuine comedy about three men, born and raised in the English Midlands, out of old vaudeville routines—slapstick; the woman talking interminably in the phone booth; funny dialects; the fat man—and a pure, unabashed sense of the ridiculous. But he does it with the freshness of the inventor, and not as a borrower: "Myra held out her hand to me with one of the gestures they taught her in ballet classes when she was sixteen. I didn't know whether I was meant to shake it, kiss it, or get out a box of matches and light it for her." He is also a fearless writer who, unlike many of his English contemporaries, doesn't consider style an aberration; his prose is awash with inspired metaphors and similes, and, in the manner of Rebecca West, he occasionally allows them to grow into small fantasies that both illuminate and decorate. . . .

Mr. Wain is secretly busy with an extremely difficult feat—a convincing portrait of a wholly good man, an extended joke

that is not revealed until the end of the book. It starts on the first page, where Mr. Wain sidelines his real hero, Joe Shaw, by making him a raconteur about to tell the story of a complex, twenty-year relationship between his two oldest friends. Mr. Wain further dismisses him as a fat, genial, inconspicuous man who grows up full of self-pity and without an inch of ambition. The two friends are Ned Roper, a tall, cool extrovert who views life as a series of easy problems in logic, and Robert Lamb, a short, dark, self-centered rebel who never has anything under control except his talents as a painter. Both become celebrated and wealthy—Lamb as a painter and Roper as a pottery manufacturer. But they are driven by an uncontrollable need for oneupmanship that eventually becomes the mutual magnetism of hatred. They use Shaw as an unwieldy but essential mirror for their egos, as well as for a combination referee, Dorothy Dix, and Boswell, summoning him to London at all hours from their home town, where he has become a newspaper reporter. (p. 94)

But Shaw's patience runs out. His side of his relationship with Roper and Lamb—as a blue-ribbon jury that examines, judges, and rules on all the greed, meanness, and phonyness they gradually reveal to him—puts an unbearable strain on his stoicism. It is at this point that one realizes that just as Mr. Wain has intended, Roper and Lamb are only symbols—nicely fitted out with a wide assortment of standard human characteristics—of the war between Business and Art. It is Shaw who, like an enormous balloon in descent, has been slowly filling the sky. In what appears to be a final act of self-effacement, he dashes off to London once more to rescue a beautiful Italian servant girl Lamb has deserted (a replacement for his wife, whom Roper has stolen), and finds her after a nightmarish search. . . . (pp. 94, 96)

Shaw tells the girl *he* is taking her home with him, she agrees, and in a fit of grateful self-revelation he tells her his true first name ("My Christian name isn't really Joe [he has said at the start of the book]; it's an absurd name that I always detested and wouldn't let anybody use"). It is Clarence, a stolid synonym for the venerable strengths of provincial England, which, like China, eventually absorbs all evil without a ripple. (p. 96)

Whitney Balliett, "The Emergence of Clarence," in The New Yorker, *Vol. XXXIV, No. 15, May 31, 1958, pp. 94, 96-7.*

ROBERT GUTWILLIG

John Wain's new novel, **A Traveling Woman,** is, to put it bluntly and mildly, familiarly disappointing and disappointingly familiar. . . .

A Traveling Woman is the story of common, everyday adultery, about which the author takes a very dim view. It all happens this way. There are these three couples and one bachelor. The first couple is George and Janet Links. He's a solicitor. At least it says he is, but he might just as well be a milkman or a third baseman. She wears peculiar spectacles, but her heart's in the right place. Then there's Barbara and Evan Bone. She's a pretty nitwit and he's a jealous lout. Bone's problem is that he "married a too pretty wife, married for her prettiness, and was unsure of his power to hold her."

And if it's depth the reader wants, there are the Cowleys, Edward and Ruth. Edward has written *The Discovery of Faith,* which he promptly loses. He is a large, voluble man, bulging with free advice and chock full of creamy goodness. (p. 309)

And then there is, of course, the bachelor, Frederic Captax. Freddie's a flabby pathologist who starts the whole messy business by persuading George to come up to London to see a psychiatrist. Not that George wants to see Mr. Volumnis, not that Captax cares either, but they both figure that George will have to stay in town nights and have an opportunity for his nasty philandering. . . . In the end, they all live unhappily ever after, except the Cowleys. They're just numb.

It's not just that *A Traveling Woman* is a bad novel, clumsily plotted, carelessly written and peopled with ciphers. Anyone can write a bad novel; it's not a felony. But the point is that John Wain, one of the really good English novelists, poets, and critics, has dropped a dreadful clinker. For some reason, Mr. Wain has not been able to apply his usually formidable and uproarious imaginative pressure to his characters and situations. Symptomatic of this failure is a potentially marvelous scene in which Captax impersonates Volumnis before Janet. But somehow the scene just isn't funny, and soon Janet reveals she wasn't convinced for a moment. Nor was the author apparently. (pp. 309-10)

Robert Gutwillig, "An Off-Told Tale," in Commonweal, Vol. LXX, No. 12, June 19, 1959, pp. 309-10.

ROBERT O. BOWEN

[*Living in the Present*] is fast-moving, funny and even somewhat pertinent as social comment on a rather dreary English world.

The tale is a simple one: Edgar Banks decides to flee his schoolmaster's life via suicide. As a grand gesture, he intends taking along the most worthless oaf available. Naturally all of this fails through Edgar's whimsical sallies, as the action moves on with all the swoop and clatter of a night train through the Alps, where the story carries us.

Edgar's victim-to-be is an ideally repulsive and bungling neo-Nazi named Rollo Philipson-Smith. The novel is a comedy of manners, concocted of current snobberies, ideas and personality types. . . .

The plot is a pseudo-picaresque chase in which the hero dashes about the Continent trying to stage his murder-suicide. Each attempt is thwarted by some comic situation, and most often the situation involves social satire of a lively if unoriginal sort. If Mr. Wain had pretended to seriousness, the stock quality of his characters and their situations would constitute a true failure. In a farce that pretends to nothing else, a reader is no more offended at these than he would be to find in a run-of-the-mill Western the good cowboy on the side of right against a corrupt range boss.

Robert O. Bowen, "Suicide with Motive," in The New York Times Book Review, March 6, 1960, p. 38.

MAX COSMAN

[Though Wain, in his preface to the American edition of *Living in the Present*, is] a perceptive self-critic—he recognizes that the weakness of his book lies in its undue adherence to plot—he does not put his finger on what is fundamental: his lack of empathy. Like many a critic-turned-novelist (recently he has himself written this of Edmund Wilson) his vision of personalities, particularly those different from his own, is critical or expository rather than imaginative; to use Colin Wilson's term,

Wain is very much an outsider. He sees his people only in their peripheral aspects; that is, in their oddities or reprehensibilities, which means that he must treat them, willy-nilly, as humors, as characters in a 17th-century sense, rather than as whole human beings.

Thus Rollo Philipson-Smith is no more to Wain than a stumpy neo-fascist, McWhirtner a lustful poet-*manqué* constantly ready to soak up liquor, and the Crabshaw family an assortment of pestiferous creatures right down the line from hen-pecked husband to *enfant terrible*. Even those Wain approves of, Marabelle, the free-living soul, and Catherine, the loving one, are beyond him as flesh-and-blood creatures.

Nevertheless, *Living in the Present* has much to offer. It is fast-moving, a noticeable part of it done in what Wain has himself accurately called "a tearaway picaresque manner." It is also unafraid to name abuses and, in a period like ours, when anarchy is apt to be considered normal, makes the rather important effort to order life.

Since the medium is melodramatic farce, the execution is necessarily light, but the intent is serious enough as two key statements indicate. The first, at the beginning of the book, says: "Death destroys a man, but the idea of death saves him." The second, virtually at the end, reads: "Death destroys a man, but the idea of life saves him." The change in phrasing is slight, but tremendous in implication.

Living in the Present is the story of Edgar Banks, who despairs of life and wants to make his suicide worthwhile by ridding the world of Rollo Philipson-Smith at the same time. Poisoned whiskey fails because of an unexpected circumstance; other opportunities are nullified by Banks' personal weaknesses. The best chance of all is lost when he chooses instead to save the life of an obstreperous child. In this emphasis on an immediate, homely good in preference to a distant and grandiloquent one, Wain obviously is on the side not of ideologists but of humanists. In so doing he justifies a somewhat guarded comment in his preface that more is intended in his novel than meets the eye. (p. 24)

Max Cosman, "Three British Novels," in The New Leader, Vol. XLIII, No. 16, April 18, 1960, pp. 24-5.

FREDERICK T. WOOD

John Wain's fourth novel, *A Travelling Woman*, proves disappointing. The 'travelling woman' of the title is presumably Janet Links, the wife of a partner in an old-established firm of solicitors, whose husband, after four years of marriage, begins to wonder what he saw in her in the first place, and embarks upon an illicit love-affair with the wife of one of his partners. Indeed, the story, which is rather diffuse, is made up of several matrimonial or extra-matrimonial complications that criss-cross each other, but the point of it all is not very clear. A study of human nature of a certain type in very ordinary people? Possibly, but one cannot be sure. The publishers' blurb calls it 'a novel which points no moral, but from which readers may draw one if they wish'; but with all the wishing in the world the difficulty is finding one to draw. It is amusing, gay, light-hearted and serious by turns, and it has the saving grace of not being too long, but the characters, all of whom are rather pathetic creatures, seem lacking in depth. The most moving part of the book comes at the end. We cannot feel that it adds very much to John Wain's reputation as one of the foremost novelists of the present generation. (p. 341)

Frederick T. Wood, "Current Literature, 1959: Prose, Poetry and Drama," in English Studies, Netherlands, Vol. XLI, No. 5, October, 1960, pp. 340-46.

GENE BARO

[John Wain's *Nuncle and Other Stories*] is a somewhat disappointing performance. True, this book bears the stamp of intellectual clarity that one has come to associate with Mr. Wain's work; but this short fiction, for the most part, lacks the insight of the poetry, the down-to-earth vigor of the essays, or the satirical point of the novels.

To be sure, the best stories in this collection are grounded in the precise observation of lower middle-class British life that has been one of the factors in Mr. Wain's reputation. In such stories as "**Christmas at Rillingham's**," "**Rafferty**," and "**The Quickest Way Out of Manchester**," the author engages real people in a believable context. . . . In these stories, there is more than meets the eye. There is the suggestion of a life that lies beyond the immediate situation pictured, a life and a system of values that exert pressures and produce tensions all too germane to the behavior of the characters.

A number of the other stories, however, do not have the effect of involving particular situations and characters in a shaping context. They tend rather to be abstract ideas, literary notions, worked out in fictional terms. Too often, the effect is merely of an exercise intelligently done.

Gene Baro, "Mr. Wain in New Form," in Books, September 10, 1961, p. 10.

HALLIE BURNETT

The short stories [in *Nuncle and Other Stories*] vary from simple character study, as in "**The Two Worlds of Ernst**," to fantasy, as in "**Master Richard**" and "**An Address to the Literary Philosophical Society**," but all have one element in common: each rushes pell-mell to whatever destruction, or state of grace, or planned fulfillment seems inevitable for the character pinpointed by the angry pen of the author. Each is driven by an anachronism inherent either in the individual or in the situation to some perfectly logical jumping-off place in life, and whether he or his world is any better off for it is unimportant. The quality of Mr. Wain's writing is of an order to convince one of his logic, and although, with one exception, there is plot in each of the stories, it is character with its inconsistencies—even its hallucinations—which hold the reader's attention. . . .

In "**A Few Drinks with Alcock and Brown**" a young man, "who ought to have learnt how to rule his life," tries to ignore a letter in his pocket from an ex-fiancée. Masterfully understated, the tension grows through the young man's drinking at a bar, the senseless threat of a fight with a stranger, and ends with his obeying a "public duty" to inform the police. Thus the letter is ignored for awhile longer. Yet "as he stood, glass in hand, he thought of the first time he had kissed Ellen . . . the only real thing in his life," and the portrait of a young man is complete. In "**Rafferty**," also, the nuances of sentiment and speech are subtly and accurately described; the story ends with "life's so full of unexpected things, it pays to cultivate a taste for them"—as the young man goes on his way, leaving a girl who took too long to make up her mind.

In the stories of fantasy there is conflict between the real world and the deeper need of the individual for escape to another altogether. . . .

There are lesser stories and also better stories in the book. "**Nuncle**," in which a once-famous novelist who has become a drunken has-been tells of his rejuvenation by marriage to a pretty girl and then of losing her to her own father, develops unexpectedly, with sinister undertones and Freudian implications, to an inevitable but surely happy ending. This is perhaps the finest story in the book. John Wain is at his best in slower, more controlled pieces in which subtle irony and the hidden, destructive urges of his characters are savored by both author and reader, but there are vigor and imagination in all of the stories, and a point of view that is consistent and thoroughly contemporary.

Hallie Burnett, "It Takes All Kinds to Make a Tale," in Saturday Review, Vol. XLIV, No. 37, September 16, 1961, p. 31.

D. J. ENRIGHT

There is a remarkable consistency about John Wain's writing. It is always very personal, it never leaves you in doubt as to what you are meant to feel. There is no nonsense about the writer standing back from the subject. Indeed this writer tends to trample his subject. Mr. Wain is a romantic, he is always *feeling*: he is always, in an unusual degree, writing autobiography.

This 'part of an autobiography' [*Sprightly Running*] is something of a poser. The reviewer can hardly complain that the author's personality looms too large. There are no dealings in statecraft or public life to be scrutinized and questioned. There cannot be much doubt as to the author's sincerity. And there would seem little to be gained from quarreling with his responses to external reality: they are as they are, and that's that. But even a reviewer has a right to responses. I found myself sometimes bored by this book, often irritated, less frequently charmed, and occasionally cheered.

It is generally recognized that those horrors from which the Channel might seem to have saved the Englishman have already been visited upon him in his schooldays. Mr Wain portrays the bullies who afflicted his schooldays in terms of the Nazi leaders and the playground ethos in terms of the Moscow Trials. 'The parallel,' as he says, 'is not mere fancy.' But all the same there is a lot of rather agreeable distance in between those parallel phenomena. Mr Wain writes as if no one had ever been bullied before; and as if no one else had suffered the agonies of calf love: 'I rotted in that emotional dungeon until the door rusted off its hinges.'

This attitude lends freshness and force to his narrative: everything is at first hand: feelings and situations, it is all pioneer experience. But the inability to relax, to smile at himself, seems to me to produce a very unhappy effect. . . . That effect shows itself in the heavy gibes at the teaching profession—it failed to understand the young Wain—and in his 'Open Letter' to the Soviet Union. I can believe every single word he utters in his 'Letter', but his tone is such as to suggest that communism was invented solely to annoy John Wain. Is it a feeling that the reader will anyway discount much of its weight which leads Mr Wain to wield such heavy language? Words do sometimes need to be weighed. . . .

We also note that Mr Wain displays a self-awareness which hitherto his readers may not have credited him with. His vision of life he terms 'apocalyptic'. He admits to a degree of paranoia. In recounting his wholesale adopting of Johnson's stoical pessimism, he points out rather endearingly that Johnson spoke as an old and sick and battered warrior, whereas John Wain was 20 years of age and suffering only from an eye complaint which at least enabled him to stay at Oxford. . . .

Mr Wain is an inveterate teacher: he must instruct, rectify, warn or denounce. He doesn't have much faith in his pupils: he starts from scratch: he doesn't take much for granted. 'I do not believe in a Destiny that shapes human life, but now and then one feels the presence of something that is hard to explain in other terms.' This quotation demonstrates, as does every page of the book, how dissimilar and increasingly dissimilar its author is from his supposed stablemate, Kingsley Amis, who has always taken a good deal for granted. Mr Wain was probably right in deciding to be a full-time writer. There is a lot of truth to be told. The danger is, the best of truths can be discredited in the telling.

D. J. Enright, "Strong Feelings," in New Statesman, *Vol. LXIV, No. 1644, September 14, 1962, p. 323.*

SAMUEL HYNES

Strike the Father Dead, Wain's newest novel, is not his best, but it is typical of what he does well, and of what he does badly. The time of the novel is the years during and just after [World War II]; the scene moves between a provincial university town and the darker, black-market-and-jazz side of London (with a side trip to Paris). The principal character, Jeremy Coleman, is a jazz pianist, an adolescent when we first see him, in revolt against his father, a Professor of Classics, and the values which his father represents. We follow Jeremy as he leaves his father, enters London's Bohemia, and finally finds a substitute father in an American Negro jazz musician.

This sketch of the action of the novel should be enough to show how paradigmatic the whole thing is. Jeremy rejects a complex including the provinces, a maiden aunt, a tradition-minded father, the classics, and English patriotism, and chooses instead jazz, draft evasion, Bohemianism, and a Negro. Clearly the past he is denying is a version of the traditional English past, and the world which he elects to enter is a version of the English present.

The past is rigid, repressive, and obsolete; the present is creative, international and free. Since we are all, presumably, in favor of creativity and freedom, and opposed to repression, we must take Jeremy's career to be a progress, and the ending of the novel to be a happy one. And if we have any doubts as to what it's all about, Jeremy tells us: "All I could do was to get away from the things that had influenced me, as I had already got away from my father. It was all part of the search for an identity and a way of life."

Anyone familiar with the jargon of modern criticism will recognize some old friends in that question: the Flight from the Past, the Search for Identity, the Quest for a Father—these are commonplace phrases for commonplace modern themes. Now obviously there is nothing wrong in writing a novel with familiar themes, but there is a danger, when you deal in commonplaces, of slipping out of reality into convention, and this Wain has unfortunately done. Jeremy's father, for example, has literary, not human ancestors, and is as conventional as

the Cruel Stepmother. So is Percy, the simple-warm-hearted Negro—he's not Uncle Tom, but he's just as unconvincing. Wain's concern to demonstrate the Search for Identity has led him to write a book with real names and unreal characters.

This is not to say that there are not many excellent things in the novel. The places are good—the Soho clubs, the rock-and-roll dance halls, the pubs; and the atmosphere is wonderfully realized—that odd impermanent dreariness that was London after the war is as real as soot and bomb sites. And the ideas with which Wain is dealing are serious, important ideas. But still the words that one must use to describe his achievement are not words that a novelist will be pleased with. His book is a serious, intelligent, conscientious piece of work, but that is not quite enough to make it a good novel. (pp. 48-9)

Samuel Hynes, "Pitfalls in the Search for Identity," in Commonweal, *Vol. LXXVII, No. 2, October 5, 1962, pp. 47-9.*

HONOR TRACY

In [*Strike the Father Dead*], Mr. Wain covers ground which has been covered before, "not once now and then, but again and again": he tells us a number of things we knew already and a number of others we may not by any means accept; but he does it with such zest and humor and simple starry-eyed pleasure that we shall have to forgive him. Indeed, he writes so well that the end of the book may be reached before these drawbacks are perceived.

His theme is the revolt of the child against parent and its gradual melting into compassion and understanding as youth goes by and a new generation appears, to begin a rebellion of its own. Professor Coleman has the Chair of Classics in a minor university. . . . His wife is dead. His son, Jeremy, is the tedious little egocentric all too familiar to readers of the present-day English novel: his only interest outside himself is jazz, on which he discourses at length and with a mirth-provoking solemnity. (p. 45)

Mr. Wain's method is to allow the members of the family in turn to tell the story each from his or her point of view. It might have been effective if he had really explored the minds of all three and held a fair balance between them; but in spite of humane endeavors to do so, he identifies himself with the son so plainly that the other figures remain shadowy and unconvincing. Such as he is, Jeremy appears in the round, while the Professor and Aunt Eleanor reveal themselves only in their relationship to him or by their attitude to what he has done.

Mr. Wain's own attitude to the Professor is arbitrary and arrogant, as is shown by his choice of a title from the lines in *Troilus and Cressida:*

> Strength shall be lord of imbecility,
> And the rude son shall strike the father dead.

The "imbecility" of the father here consists of being true to his ideal of duty and service and to the classical tradition of civilized Europe, that Europe which Paul Valéry defined as "*la partie précieuse du monde*"; and, of course, failing to "understand" his detrimental child. The "strength" of the rude son consists in living entirely for and to himself and feeling essentially a man of his time. He suffers from a common delusion of to-day, the off-shoot perhaps of political democracy, that all activities are of equal value if only we choose to say so. He despises the Professor's niggling over details of syntax or palaeography because he is unable to see that scholarship is built on such niggling, or to understand scholarship's place in civilized life. Jazz, on the other hand, strikes him not as an atavism, an echo from the mindless chaotic jungle, but as a virile 20th Century mode of expression, an art with the charm, denied to other arts, of not requiring a great deal of grind.

Nevertheless, when we have done shaking our heads at the author's addle-pated perversity, when we have tut-tutted over his facile Freudian approaches and his contemporary clichés, have requested him kindly to spare us the Sunday-newspaper moralizing and wondered why the dickens he has to use that bastard American idiom, we still have a lively, fresh and impressive book, and one that is often extremely funny. The highest tribute that I could pay was to read it straight through without any sense of grievance. . . . (pp. 45-6)

> *Honor Tracy, "Lord of Imbecility," in* The New Republic, *Vol. 147, No. 16, October 20, 1962, pp. 45-6.*

JAMES GRAY

The "Angry Young Men" of contemporary English letters held the attention of susceptible readers for a tense moment a few years ago when they seemed about to make literary history. They attracted this interest more because they were puzzling than because they were impressively challenging figures. It was difficult, in fact, to make out what they were angry about.

The fragment of autobiography offered by John Wain under the title *Sprightly Running* may, therefore, have seemed important to its publishers as an elucidation of what made the young men angry. However, although the author has been considered to be of that company from the beginning of his career as critic, teacher, poet, and novelist, he has never, in his own mind, been one of them. Years ago he publicly disavowed association with the cult, and here he is able to explain with great precision why he rejects that, or any other, literary trade-mark.

What he has always wanted to be is a creative artist. As such he knows what Sigrid Undset pointed out long ago, that literature is "concerned with that timeless thing, human nature." It is the task of the writer to evoke a way of life and to call into reality certain individuals as they try to cope with the complexities of a microscopically examined fragment of existence.

No better proof of John Wain's right to his ambition could have been brought forward than the success he has had in this evocation of himself. Every word has the crystal ring of authenticity, so unlike the clatter of vehement self-deception to be found in the exhibitionistic performances of the great confessors like Rousseau. Within the limits of reticence, properly set by sensibility, John Wain is utterly candid, quite without pretense, earnestly yet always humorously persuasive. . . .

The character that emerges from this study is neither wholly admirable nor wholly attractive. But what matters is that the reader feels the presence of a man whose spirit has been refined by suffering, by insight, by the determination to be honest and, finally, by the benign influence of a mature, ironic outlook. Wain has gained in stature by this modest examination of his far from angry purposes.

> *James Gray, "Never in Anger," in* Saturday Review, *Vol. XLVI, No. 20, May 18, 1963, p. 29.*

DAVID LITTLEJOHN

[Wain's autobiography, *Sprightly Running,* surveys] the first thirty-five years of his three score and ten. He obviously, and intelligently, felt the need for a personal taking stock in mid-journey: but whether it was necessary or useful for him to share it all with us remains to be asked. Autobiography-as-personal-therapy, especially for a professional writer, may be a fine and healthful thing; but a book must be justified on quite other grounds for the general reading public.

"I have often thought," wrote Wain's (and my) favorite author, Samuel Johnson, "that there has rarely passed a life of whch a judicious and faithful narrative would not be useful." Still, laboring through the first hundred pages of *Sprightly Running,* one wonders just how "useful" can be the hundredth retelling of the cradle-to-college torments of an English boyhood. . . . [It] is all so embarrassingly uninteresting. . . .

Wain is too anxious to find *meanings* in it all, to make every street fight prefigure the war, every bully a portent of Hitler, to find the springs of his present (and genuine) tragic vision in the loneliness of a misfit adolescent. . . .

Fortunately (for us), John Wain survived all this, and went up to Oxford in 1944, rejected by the Army (he is careful to explain) for poor eyesight; and his loving reflections of those four years make up the book's most admirable chapter. . . .

Here he found Charles Williams, Nevill Coghill, his tutor C. S. Lewis; most outrageously, E. H. W. Meyerstein, Wain's minor contribution to the list of eccentric and unhappy English immortals. His thirty-five-page portrait of this mad and magnificent failure is the finest thing in the book. . . . Not only does he bring this paranoic mountain of a man triumphantly to life; he is also able to analyze both Meyerstein and his relationship to him with an artistry that is at once sympathetic, honest and keen.

The fifth chapter—"A Literary Chapter"—is almost as good, as readable (and as long) as the chapter on Oxford. There is here—and this is not its best feature—a good deal of angry editorializing, which was perhaps to be expected from a man who frankly makes his living by literary journalism. (p. 75)

In this chapter too comes our glimpses of Wain's milieu, of the English literary world, half-academic, half-journalistic (since he has been both), of Leavis and the Leavisites, C. S. Lewis' postwar coterie, the *genuine* Angry Young Men, "The Movement," the *New Statesman,* the B.B.C. It bears the passing and small fascination such pictures afford. More important, more serious, is his defense of leaving teaching for writing, coupled with uniquely perceptive commentaries on both professions . . . ; his discussions of the university's role, of academic psychology, and of critical versus creative writing, the latter of which strikes me as almost a Last Word on the subject.

The book declines from here on into more rambling journalese, largely his "Impressions" of America and Russia. He surveys the whole of American social history in an extraordinary single paragraph . . . , and goes on to lament our want of a settled tradition, our "reliance on material profusion" and our frightful neighborliness. (pp. 75-6)

[The] Oxford and Literary chapters make up almost half the book, and they are fine: for what the evidence is worth, I am eager to read them again. Here is the man that matters: the writer, the lover of men and life and letters who has never let his premature, self-indulged "tragic vision" get in the way of his zest for living, his commitment to writing, his delight in the eccentric and wonderful in man. (p. 76)

David Littlejohn, ''The Misfit at Home,'' *in* The Nation, *New York, Vol. 197, No. 4, August 10, 1963, pp. 75-6.*

RICHARD MAYNE

The Young Visitors is an attempt to make something of [the Cold War]; and because Wain's by intent a serious writer, not prone to pin a social comedy on a 'topical' issue, I think it's worth attending to, even if—as I believe—it fails. The opening is full of promise. A group of Komsomol members, students at the university, arrives at London Airport; and through the words of one of them, Elena, we gain their first impressions. The soil of The West, home of imperialism, is solid beneath their feet at last. Students from France neck shamefully on the airport bus. Along the route are 'double houses'—semi-detached—split down the middle with a blank wall and no connecting doors. There's an immense amount of traffic—what a contrast with the unfilled streets of Moscow. Huge advertisements parade cigaretts and drinks. All this, on a journalistic level, is well-observed. It's when the 'plot,' the intrigue, begins that things go wrong.

Wain's plan was evidently to confront as forcefully as possible the quality of two ways of life. His Komsomol student is a sympathetic enough character, imbued with Party slogans, but impulsive and likeable within the limits of the possibility of 'getting to know' her. To meet her, he produces an English communist, freer than she is—and that, of course, means also freer to be corrupt. Wain had in mind, I imagine, some such paradox as he found in India—that if you want a free society you must put up with inefficiency and dishonesty. So the English communist, 'Jack Spade', is more of a wide boy than an idealist; he's merely learned up the Party slogans and the pat responses, and his real name isn't even 'Jack Spade'. With him, I think, the book takes a wrong turning. In order to make his political point, Wain has avoided what would otherwise have been the normal confrontation, between Elena and a genuine English communist. That might have produced some interesting discords—although it might also have made for a gawky, dialectic-ridden book. As it is, the wide boy (who takes over the narration from Elena in alternate chapters) more and more dominates the idiom and feeling of the tale; and from an imaginative essay on East and West, *The Young Visitors* swerves back to one of the main themes of John Wain's fiction—a 'picaresque' character who comes to grief because real human beings can't sustain indefinitely the carefree picaresque role.

Spade the seducer falls in love with Elena once they've slept together: she, tipped off about his real character by the local Party secretary, decides to have her revenge by pretending that she's going to defect to the West. But before this plot has a chance to work itself out, another member of the visiting party eludes the escort, and Elena and her friends find themselves *incommunicado* in the Soviet Embassy, awaiting the plane for Moscow and whatever retribution they deserve. The closing scenes, revealing the dark side of Elena's world and the tensions between hers and an older generation, recapture the focus of interest from Spade's racy fluency; but they leave the larger artistic problem unresolved. So do some of the picturesque extras—including an old-style communist agitator, comico-pathetic, who's clearly intended to carry more significance than his minor role here allows. Finally, too, I couldn't help won-

dering how it was that the visitors were left so free so long from Embassy 'guidance'—a minor point of plotting that highlighted the book's artificiality. (p. 528)

Richard Mayne, "Travelling Man," *in* New Statesman, *Vol. LXX, No. 1804, October 8, 1965, pp. 528-29.*

WALTER ALLEN

John Wain has written a consistently entertaining novel [*The Young Visitors*], he has written it in a style that is intelligent, inventive, and never dull. Yet it is unlikely to compel the reader's complete belief.

A party of young Russians arrive in England to study local government. Their initial assumptions and misinterpretations as they encounter London are amusingly rendered—and one accepts, for the sake of the fun, the notion that their image of English life is derived entirely from a literal acceptance of Dickens.

They end their first day watching a television interview with Jack Spade, a Communist who runs the Rebellion Theater Group, and are so impressed by his defiance of capitalist values (in ''the very center of the government propaganda organization,'' the B.B.C.) that they pour into a taxi and pay their homage to him at his headquarters, the Rebellion Cafe in Soho. One of them, Elena, is indeed so inspired that she pays him a second, secret visit. . . .

Basically, this story of a confrontation between East and West seems to me of great interest. But it is less than satisfying because of a curious bias that creeps in (I am sure against Mr. Wain's intentions). It is the consequence of his narrative method. He tells his story in chapters that alternate between Elena's voice and point of view and Spade's.

Elena is an ordinary, conventional young woman, accepting the assumptions of her society without question and coming to England in the wake of an unhappy love affair. Out of simple-minded zeal for Communism she becomes the victim of a plausible, nasty young man. Of course she captures our sympathy.

Spade, however, is just a crook. Communism is his racket. He lives on the royalties of a novel (*Leprosy*) he has published in Moscow that purports to be a dissection of English life. Mr. Wain quotes from it. It is very funny, but so grotesque as to make it impossible to believe it could be issued from Moscow, even for the crudest propaganda purposes. The wholly conscious hyprocrite—a character it is never easy to accept—Spade exposes himself with every word he utters. Given the conscious hypocrisy, the self-exposure, it is impossible to believe in his sudden conversion, or to accept the radical change roused by his love for Elena.

The overt moral of *The Young Visitors* seems to be that nice young Russians shouldn't go to Britain because if they do, they will be conned by crooks posing as Commies. Mr. Wain cannot really have meant this. I think his novel is the product of conflicting impulses. On the one hand, it satirizes professional literary Communists in the West. On the other, it tries to get inside the skin of contemporary Soviet youth. This latter he does brilliantly. But, in terms of fiction, the two impulses cancel each other out.

Walter Allen, "London Had Changed since Dickens," in The New York Times Book Review, October 24, 1965, p. 52.

JOSEPH EPSTEIN

[The subject matter of the pieces collected in **Death of the Hind Legs and Other Stories**] cuts across class, age, and sex lines, dealing as it does with hustlers, housewives, and scholars, with the feeble-minded and the highly cerebral, the young and the very old, the unfaithful and injured. The same amplitude characterizes their construction. Wain easily switches from a first- to a third-person technique, from a male to a female point of view. His range is such as almost to bring the reader up short as he ends a story told in the openly sentimental voice of an aging postman only to begin another told by a confidently cynical businessman; leaves off another about a young intellectual and his girl sharing digs in London to take up still another told by a veteran dresser in an old burlesque house. There is a craftsman at work here, and a virtuoso. (p. 4)

Wain's stories are about cruelty: the cruelty of men to each other and to their women and children; the cruelty—one might say the almost inevitable cruelty—of time and aging on people.

In writing about cruelty, it should be made clear, Wain is not dealing with anything so stark and simple as evil. For the most part, the cruelty at the center of his stories is not directly perpetrated by or on anyone; rather it is often unconscious, almost always inadvertent, and sometimes even random. A number of Wain's stories are narrated by the very agents of the resulting cruelty; with the exception of the title story, in fact, it is good to be able to report that there isn't a sensitive narrator or anti-hero in the house. It is out on the blurry borders of the indirect and the unintended where the sad acts of these stories take place. Callousness, not malice, is generally the villain. Interestingly enough, **"Down Our Way,"** a story about a lower-middle-class London family that doesn't want to rent their extra room to a Negro, is the only one whose characters' intentions are directly malicious, and also the only really inferior one in the collection.

In **"Manhood,"** a father insists his son become an athlete in disregard of the boy's nature and, although the boy goes along with it, the relationship between father and son is wrecked. A nervous young man in **"A Visit at Tea-time"** returns to the house in which he was born in order to look at a tree planted by his now-dead father to celebrate his birth. Not only has the tree been cut down—it gave no shelter and cut off the sunlight—but the young man is treated to a stilted Freudian interpretation of his motives by the wife of the current owner. In Wain's stories people are always foisting their ideas and interpretations off on others, usually intending to be helpful though almost invariably with damaging consequences. (pp. 4, 19)

The most brilliant story in **Death of the Hind Legs,** however, is the one entitled **"Steam."** It's about that most subtle and vicious kind of cruelty—the cruelty of indifference. The story centers around one Mr. Greeley, a retired steam-locomotive engineer in an age of Diesels. Mr. Greeley, who lives with his daughter and son-in-law, is what the English, with chilling exactitude, call a superfluous man. He lives in and for the past; each day he visits an obscure museum in London, where the relics of the steam locomotive age are stored, among them the elegant old engine that he drove in his last active years. Where he is not completely overlooked, he is taken as an eccentric, a nut, a troublesome old kook. When, at the story's end, his

heart fails, his son-in-law, not really a bad sort, expriences a feeling of relief. Mr. Greeley's bedroom can now be made over into a rumpus room for the kids. Otherwise, the old man's death, as Wain describes it, is a matter of monumental indifference to everyone. . . .

Taken together, the stories in **Death of the Hind Legs** constitute a delicate and remarkable probe of the modern heart of darkness. Their author is a writer of considerable subtlety and no little importance. (p. 19)

Joseph Epstein, "Sins of Omission," in Book Week—The Washington Post, Vol. 4, No. 12, November 27, 1966, pp. 4, 19.

T. O'HARA

How seriously can we take John Wain? Since his early, forced inclusion in the Angry gaggle to his present virtuosity evidenced by Shakespeare criticism, autobiography, novels both petulant and mature, essays on America, poetry: lyrical and ersatz epic, reviews that show a factual backlog usually the product of older minds, and his sporadic short stories, his stance has reflected the tonal ambivalence of a confirmed literary prankster.

In this collection of eleven stories [**Death of the Hind Legs and Other Stories**] once in a while an emotion is exposed legitimately and with an intensity and precision that cuts, but too often a flatulence and gross sentimentality perdures, reminiscent of the Monday through Friday scenarios that keep housewives from getting familiar with reality. What, then, is he trying to pull? A writer's awareness of his varied poses of condescension can normally be detected. Think of *Dubliners* whose readers know that Joyce is thoroughly in control of the superior laughter directed at the gyrations of his bumptious Irishmen. But Wain isn't writing irony and he's not a parodist. There are too many embarrassments to allow the happy conclusion that the fictional affairs are under the command of a gifted and sly general.

In **"A Visit at Tea-time,"** for instance, we expect from the regressive yearnings of a man confronting his boyhood house and garden something more than the old replay about you can't go home again threaded with a few castrative and narcissistic strands. And isn't it painfully clear that a story hinging on such a tenuous plot as girl-stands-before-mailbox-to-retrieve-vile-letter-to-lover needs a treatment far removed from a *Redbook* discussion by the mailman and the girl on the machinations of love?

"Goodnight, Old Daisy" follows an old man in his Lear period to a museum where the train he once operated is stored. His thoughts tell us of the symbolic identification so essential to his soul and the good, distant days when he and Daisy ripped through the world. His death at the end offers no relevant comment on the nature and meaning of his existence. The tragic fatuity of his mechanical obsession is hinted at but loses its imaginative strength under the ordinary prose. (p. 538)

There are exceptions. **"Darkness"** tells of a frightened man's archetypal journey through the blackness of a Spanish village and blends comedy and fear in a way that is above Wain's other maneuvering of technique, and **"King Caliban,"** the opening story, details the destruction of a simple and loving wrestler whose muscular innocence is manipulated by his venal wife and brother. These don't compensate, however, for the rest. The recurrence of defeated men and women, the desolution motifs, the dislocated relationships and the cultural and institutional collapses point out Wain's ambition. It is to explore that force that through the green fuse drives. Regrettably he failed to achieve it. (p. 539)

T. O'Hara, in a review of "Death of the Hind Legs," in Commonweal, *Vol. LXXXV, No. 18, February 10, 1967, pp. 538-39.*

THE TIMES LITERARY SUPPLEMENT

John Wain has developed an ingenious idea into a shapely novel, slim to the point of thinness. He seems to know and understand the environment he is discussing (a fact which gives *The Smaller Sky* an advantage over his last novel, *The Young Visitors*) and he may stimulate further thought on a question of current concern—the way in which people are labelled "mad," and the result of that labelling. The labelled person here is a dull and prudent man, successful in his scientific career, who finds that certain inner tensions are more than he can bear. Leaving his job and family, he becomes a "dropout", in the dullest and most prudent way he can conceive. He lives in the railway hotel at Paddington Station and spends his daylight hours on the platform, hoping that he will be mistaken for the steady commuter he used to be.

He is assaulted by the late-night layabouts. . . . [The] worst menace comes from the world of mass communications. He is hunted down . . . through the agency of a scoop-hungry television journalist, attempting a kind of *Man Alive* programme. The deep hostility which the author expresses for this villain, the detestable motivation which he ascribes to him, suggests that the novel is intended as a moral fable—seeking a single element in society as blameworthy for the general discontent. . . . The author's treatment of the television man unbalances his story, suggesting that an attempt to narrow down that vague conflict between "the individual and society" has been vitiated by unfairness.

The narrative is swift and readable, the dialogue sound and well-selected; but there seems to be a serious lack of point. John Wain appears to be claiming that this novel is a commentary on "the modern world": if so, readers may find it somewhat shallow and pretentious.

"Dropping Out," in The Times Literary Supplement, *No. 3423, October 5, 1967, p. 933.*

JOHN HEMMINGS

One of the ways of measuring how civilised a society is would be to estimate the extent to which it tolerates the solitary eccentric. Other eras outclass ours; the heyday was perhaps the late 18th century. Nowadays we can stand deviation from the norm only if the deviants go around in droves: a single flower person would be certified. When Geary, the anti-hero of *The Smaller Sky,* is accused by a friend of being 'incapable of behaving in a rational manner', his retort is no less pertinent for being obvious: behaving in a rational manner means, in common parlance, behaving like everybody else.

Mr Wain's fable is—or could have been—just as pertinent, if only he could have brought himself to believe in his own argument. Geary has decided that his marriage is a failure and that his work no longer interests him; so he quits his wife and chucks his job. What could be more rational? He takes a room in a station hotel and spends his days entirely on the station.

Again, what better place than a terminal for a man who has come to the end of his personal road? Here he can sit still or stroll about unnoticed, like Baudelaire's *promeneur solitaire et pensif* who is in the crowd and yet not of it. And what more appropriate terminal than Paddington, so eccentrically designed 'as if Brunel liked trains better than human beings'? Geary is calm, contented, capable, affable to the acquaintances he runs across on the station, affectionate towards his ten-year-old son who pays him a worried visit, diplomatic even with the psychiatrist who is sent to sniff at him. But he can't convince Mr Wain of his sanity. We are told about some drums that beat in the poor chap's head whenever he leaves the station; so he really is off his chump, and *The Smaller Sky* loses its point. When Geary, escaping from the television cameras, falls from the roof and breaks his neck, he is neither victim nor martyr, but a sick man the doctors didn't get to in time; and the novel, if not an outright failure, is a downright disappointment.

John Hemmings, "Certified," in The Listener, *Vol. LXXVIII, No. 2011, October 12, 1967, pp. 476-77.*

MALCOLM BRADBURY

A Winter in the Hills is Wain's eighth novel, and obviously (it's 384 pages long) an ambitious one. It's a 'new life' story about a 40-year-old philologist, Roger Furnivall, who has just lost an injured brother whom he has tended since the war. Roger now decides to widen both his philological and sexual scope, setting his sights on a job at Uppsala ('His motive for going there was that he liked tall, blonde girls with perfect teeth and knew that in Uppsala there were a lot of them about'). Less a professional sexual athlete than a hard-working amateur, his way to his business is to learn Welsh. He takes off for North Wales, where the book is set, and gets involved in the struggling life of the area. An economic battle is going on; a local operator is trying to buy up the one-man bus-services and sell them to a big English corporation; Roger identifies with the small independent man and ends up collecting fares and fighting off the strong-arm methods of the opposition. He also falls in love with, and takes over, the wife of an economist at the local university, who shares the opposition philosophy. The book ends as he wins out: the buses sold back to the small men, the sense of locality and sexual satisfaction neatly interfused, the new life gained. Admittedly on ambiguous terms, since the forces of economic centralisation are still massing; nonetheless, a comic festival of Celtic-fringe poetry stirs up the thought of a new cultural thrust against the counting house on top of the cinder-heap.

In some ways it is the old axis of the Fifties novel (which always had a fondness for Wales). But the terms have changed and grown bigger. Now those characters with 'English of that fluting, narrow vowelled kind that suggested the Home Counties', detested by Fifties heroes as a matter of natural right . . . have large associations with economic, even linguistic, and cultural, exploitation. Compensatorily, the yeomen virtues have to feel their roots right back to tough, hard-gained, Welsh speakers subsisting in the hills. The story pulls out Wain's liberal integrities, turning the pieties, towards a kind of local nationalism. But though the theme is capable of this symbolism, Wain plays it in the end as a plotty narrative of action. The cost here is loss of symbolic density; the gain a social and emotional density, a lived-out sense of the Snowdonian community where he sets his action. He ends up with a celebration of the small victories of self, which are worth having even if the larger drift of history goes against you. What is salvaged is the emotional life, and the sense of actuality in the book is enough to give that meaning—even if, one feels, some corners are cut on the way. And the result is a modest victory for Wain's own kind of novel over the adjustments it has had to make.

Malcolm Bradbury, "Welsh Wain," *in* New States-man, *Vol. 79, No. 2042, May 1, 1970, p. 632.*

PAUL WEST

In his previous novel, **The Smaller Sky,** John Wain used as his central structural image London's Paddington railroad terminal, and the result was an engrossing fusion of documentary and allegory. It seemed that what happened in Paddington stood for almost anything under the sun—at least, it could if you wanted it to. In **A Winter in the Hills,** an altogether more pastoral novel, something of the same takes place (or, since Wain's insinuations are diffident even at their strongest, can be made to). The setting is Caerfenai, a university town in North Wales, but the book's true context is the Welsh hills and the geological strata underlying them—so much so that Roger Furnivall, the naïve philologist who is its quasi-hero, can lie on a couch and intuit himself into terra firma....

How refreshing and heartening it is to find an English novelist for once going out of his way to reveal Britain as a chunk of the planet, Englishmen as members of the species, and the mind itself as something other than a gadget for identifying mores. John Wain, in fact, has challenged himself to press social and comic minutiae into the texture of a comprehensive, quietly registering vision, which means that he must demand much of himself stylistically speaking. Not that he forces apocalypses out of provincial Welsh fatuities or plumps for a geological-ecological-cosmic prose poem; instead, he patiently and meticulously adds detail to detail, divining things through Roger's pedantic but increasingly elastic mind until the book develops a ripple, then a ground swell, which the reader can sense for himself after about fifty pages. In other words, every word is a world with a special, ascertainable history (as Roger the philologist knows only too well). So it would be inaccurate to say that there are many passages in the novel in which layers of being—modes of humanity, phases of *Homo sapiens*—overlap and interact; what really happens is that Wain sets up an evocative continuum to which the reader can relate quite casually, never having to brace himself for a page of heavy meditation or the anticlimax of the parochial coming hard after the prodigious. **A Winter in the Hills** does almost insidiously what T. S. Eliot summed up as dreams crossing and moments in and out of time: Roger Furnivall discovers the race he belongs to, as well as its breadth, its beginnings, its variety, and its frightful, arbitrary power for good and evil alike.

The novel's pretext, however, is some rather trivial knockabout in which Roger helps himself to a local bus and then becomes involved in its owner's feud with what looks like the omnibus division of the North Wales Mafia....

An ironic point emerges: Roger, who came to Caerfenai to study Welsh in order to prepare himself for a job at the University of Uppsala where blondes offer to divulge their Swedish tanning-secrets, enlarges himself by becoming involved with a small community. Petty and shallow to begin with (as well as being forty, about which the book strikes a recurrent elegiac note), he opens up, becomes a part of the main. It's a familiar enough rite of passage, but John Wain, although at rather wearisome length, makes it new by stressing its anthropological aspect. English reviewers praised the book's portrait of a little market town, which is like praising *Candide* as a travel book. What they seem to have missed is Wain's first venture onto the Golding standard, according to which Men evoke Man rather than quaint, esoteric codes by means of which the gentlemanly ones can be distinguished from the boors.

Paul West, "Eisteddfodder," *in* Book World—Chicago Tribune, *September 13, 1970, p. 15.*

MARTIN LEVIN

At the end of the closing short story in this collection of John Wain [**The Life Guard**], the narrator asks: "Does anything ever, really change?" The answer abstracted from Mr. Wain's stories might be: yes and no. The roles change. But the human frailty remains constant.

Wain began writing angry young postwar fiction when "Establishment" was still a synonym for upper-class hegemony. But now, through a spokesman, the author finds himself cluck-clucking and tut-tutting, like any élitist, at the new existential establishment of proles and young folks.... In other stories, Wain observes the meanness and bad character of some lower middle-class siblings, and the sinister vibrations emitted by everyday life. The old Wain comes through in one admirably lean short story: **"Wait Till the Sun Shines,"** in which an agricultural worker attains enough upward mobility to reach the farmer's wife. Some things change less than others.

Martin Levin, *in a review of "The Life Guard," in* The New York Times Book Review, *March 19, 1972, p. 41.*

RICHARD P. BRICKNER

The wonderful title story of Wain's collection [**The Life Guard**] gives us a lifeguard at a down-and-going British resort, eager to show how safe for swimming the ocean is under his eye. But a demonstration-emergency he sets up soon gets out of hand and turns into a real one. Wain is very good at rendering panic. By the time the story is over, its title has undergone a convulsion, a complicated battle, physical and psychological, fought between its very words: "life" loses because "guard" wins. It is a complete story, exciting, subtle, and resolved—resolved in resounding dilemma. We've gotten used to this sort of resolution. Dilemmas are often answers; often there is nothing beyond but them....

In Wain's **"Wait Till the Sun Shines,"** shallower than **"The Life Guard"** but a pleasure for the immediacy of its tension, a tractor driver hays a treacherous hill where a predecessor has been maimed. I'm not giving everything away by telling that the driver passes the physical test: The physical climax is not the ending, which involves a tainted moral victory with repercussions that extend the story outside itself in time.

Wain has the knack of keeping the reader reading. When he disappoints, we are likely to be more disappointed than we would be if his motive were not quite so much to keep us reading. Some of the stories in this new collection are slickly slighter than they need be. Wain will settle for casual glances where scrutiny is called for. In his last novel, **A Winter in the Hills,** the same difficulty emerged—a tendency to lift the pressure. In these stories, lifting the pressure takes the form of choosing easy satirical marks or in other ways sticking to the surface of a matter.

At his best, though, as in the two stories mentioned and in one about a musical comedy star gone over the hill before he knows it, Wain is casual in the finest sense: His natural narrative voice has tricks down its throat that are as surprising as men and women are. He also satisfies our urge for tension, our urge for unforeseen predictability, and our urge for reverberant resolution. (p. 23)

Richard P. Brickner, "Two in the Modern Tradition," in The New Leader, *Vol. LV, No. 10, May 15, 1972, pp. 23-4.*

DALE SALWAK

Wain is clearly an accomplished novelist. In the tradition of the eighteenth-century novel, he fulfills most effectively the novelist's basic task of telling a good story. The techniques of modern novelists—placing biased and implicated characters close to the center of action in order to make for complexity of perspective, foreshortening of plot to allow for dramatic concentration, and jumbling narrative sequences to involve the reader in a struggle for the meaning of events—do not figure in Wain's books. They move along at an even pace; he avoids stylistic experimentation and relies upon a simple, tightly constructed, and straightforward plot; clarity; good and bad characters; and a controlled point of view. We need only think of Joyce, Kafka, and Eliot, and the contrast is clear. What many of his novels ask from us is not some feat of analysis, but a considered fullness of response, a readiness to assert to, even if not to agree with, his vision of defeat.

Wain also has the seriocomic touch. With varying success, Charles Lumley, Edgar Banks, Joe Shaw, and George Links are all creations of the comic spirit, characters who are cherished as samples of the immense variety of human behavior. But here as elsewhere Wain tries to be a balanced writer. There is a serious, almost tragic dimension even to these more lightly presented characters. And there are, of course, other characters in whom the tragic element dominates: Arthur Geary, for example, in *The Smaller Sky,* or the unhappy Giles Hermitage in *The Pardoner's Tale.*

If his methods of characterization are consistent, his success with his creations is not. In the early novels, for instance, the subject matter seems trivial at times, and only with difficulty do we summon that kind of involvement with character and situation which presses upon us in the best of Wain's work. In these early novels everything is controlled by Wain's personal vision of life; we feel the characters and events are allowed to stiffen into mere illustrations of ideas. In the later novels, by comparison, we find most remarkable the psychological verisimilitude: the majority of characters in *The Young Visitors, The Smaller Sky, A Winter in the Hills,* and *The Pardoner's Tale* are credible. Although we are still aware of the presence of a mind shaping the contours of the plot, we also sense that the author is allowing the characters a measure of autonomy and idiosyncratic existence.

Wain is also accomplished in his creation of place and atmosphere. In *Strike the Father Dead* he fully captures the grayness of a London day, the grayness of lives spent under its pall, the grayness of the people who wander its streets. When Wain describes an afternoon in which Giles Hermitage forces himself to work in the subdued light at home; when Arthur Geary walks the platforms at Paddington Station; when Charles Lumley walks in on a literary gathering; when Roger Furnivall makes his way home through the Welsh countryside—at such mo-

ments we encounter Wain's ability to develop and control the setting and atmosphere. Encompassing this ability is the memorable way in which the novels celebrate a central conviction of Wain. They affirm the significance of the seemingly commonplace life and of the seemingly commonplace man.

The themes communicated through Wain's criticism and novels are, like his method, consistent. It is clear that he sees the eighteenth century as a time of dignity, pride, and self-sufficiency—qualities lacking in the twentieth century. Like Samuel Johnson, Wain defends the value of reason, moderation, common sense, moral courage, and intellectual self-respect. Moreover, his fictional themes of the dignity of the human being, the difficulty of survival in the modern world, and the perils of success have established him principally as a moralist concerned with ethical issues. In later works, the value of tradition, the notion of human understanding, and the ability to love and suffer become the chief moral values. In all his novels, his own feelings are primarily concerned with the problem of defining the moral worth of the individual. For these reasons, Wain is recognized as a scholarly and poignant observer of the human scene.

One last word about Wain's capacities as a novelist. Clearly, the spiritual dimension is missing in the world he describes: God is, if not dead, absent. And yet there is frequently the hint or at least the possibility of renewal, which is the closest Wain comes to any sort of recognized affirmation. Charles Lumley, Joe Shaw, Jeremy Coleman, and Roger Furnivall are all characters who seem to be, by the end of their respective novels, on the verge of rebirth of a sort, on the threshold of reintegration and consequent regeneration. In each case, this renewal depends on the ability of the individual to come to terms with himself and his situation, to confront and accept at a stroke past, present, and future, and to accept and tolerate the contradictions inherent in all three. (pp. 131-33)

Above all, what he shows us in his fiction is the imponderable variegation of human experience, in an ultimately unjust world. Joy and sorrow intermingle, as do the lovely and the grotesque, sanity and dementia, love and lovelessness. Wain's vision is one of disenchantment with the values of modern life, and more deeply, it asserts the power of that "injustice which triumphs so flagrantly in the destinies of men." In allowing himself to respond so sensitively to the tragic aspects of the life which he sees around him, Wain is of course doing nothing new. To Shakespeare, to Sophocles of old, and to the writer of the Book of Job, human misery was an old story. But his deep compassion for human suffering and tenderness for the unfortunate denote a sensibility more needed than ever in an age when violence, brutality, and cynicism are all too prevalent. (pp. 133-34)

Dale Salwak, in his John Wain, *Twayne, Publishers, 1981, 155 p.*

PETER LEWIS

The narrator of John Wain's [*Young Shoulders*] is a seventeen-year-old schoolboy, Paul Waterford, who is suddenly precipitated from the condition of privileged teenagerdom into responsible adulthood when a disaster befalls his family. His younger sister Clare is killed in an aeroplane crash in Portugal while on a school holiday, and Paul's young shoulders are called upon to carry a weight of grief and misgiving, partly on behalf of his estranged (though not separated) parents. Atlas-like, he responds, and is himself transformed by the experience.

The events of the novel take place within little more than twenty-four hours, during which time Paul accompanies his parents to Portugal to participate in a communal form of mourning in the English Church at Lisbon. Paul confronts death and loss for the first time, although his sense of loss is not total; he feels the presence of his dead sister, and seven "reports to Clare" alternate with the eight main sections of the narrative.

Paul finds relief in his fantasy of a utopian never-never land, the World Free Zone, but this idealistic mental construct cannot withstand the impact of reality once the process of initiation is fully under way. *Eros*, not *thanatos*, presides over Paul's short stay in Lisbon, and in the company of Gerald Worplesdon, the father of one of the dead boys, he descends into the underworld of nightclubs and brothels where he discovers the transfiguring power of his own sexuality—without losing his virginity. He also learns much about the varieties of human love, and is able to return to his parents, especially his mother, with new insight into their vulnerability and needs.

Young Shoulders is full of mythic and archetypal resonances, yet John Wain has not exploited these in the manner of, say, Iris Murdoch; he may even have introduced them unconsciously. . . .

Young Shoulders works quite well as a realistic treatment of an adolescent suddenly growing up at a moment of crisis (although the time-scale makes the action in some ways more "dramatic" than "novelistic"). Yet is also seems to aspire to an artistic condition that it does not attain.

> *Peter Lewis, "Rites of Passage," in* The Times Literary Supplement, *No. 4150, October 15, 1982, p. 1141.*

SHIRLEY TOULSON

Paul Waterford, a 17-year-old sixth former from a Berkshire comprehensive, accompanies his alcoholic mother and depressed, ineffectual father on a 24-hour visit to Lisbon in order to attend the memorial service of his 12-year-old sister Clare and the other children from her boarding school, who were killed in an air crash. Within its strictly classical framework of limited time and place, *Young Shoulders* . . . tells how Paul shakes off the idealistic but arrogant dreams of adolescence, and grows through the tragedy of his immediate circumstances into the responsibilities of adult life.

The transition is a positive one, conclusively belying the reputation for anarchic iconoclasm with which John Wain has too often been hag ridden. . . .

Unlike the somewhat older Charles Lumley of [*Hurry On Down*], whose long struggle towards authenticity led him to drift away from any honourable commitment that smells of respectability; Paul Waterford is a boy with a well worked out life plan. . . .

The novel is interspersed with Paul's reports to Clare, as he expounds on his original plans for a World Free Zone, in which people can develop as full, compassionate human beings, unrestricted by the tensions of competition and convention. This Utopia is largely an escape from his mediocre, middle-class background, and the dissatisfaction he feels with his parents and the wreck of their marriage.

Before he can grow up, this dream must be abandoned. The loss is not caused by the tragedy of Clare's death, but by the over-powering realization, in an up-market Lisbon night club, that the compulsions of sex can dwarf any other consideration.

Given the straight choice between establishing the World Free Zone and having the girl he lusts for, he knows "I wouldn't hesitate, I'd have the girl".

There is no choice, the one alternative is as impossible as the other, but, shocked by this knowledge of himself, he walks out into the night, penniless and with no notion as to the whereabouts of his hotel; leaving behind him the seedy little journalist who had decided to show the boy the town, pathetically using Paul as a substitute for his dead son.

A loner among the bereaved parents, the wretched Gerald is cloaked in the same thick-skinned, egocentric superficiality as Adrian Swarthmore, the television journalist of *The Smaller Sky*, a novel which also has to do in part with the relationship between father and son. Yet even he is an object for compassion, and as Paul comes to realize a new love for his own parents, and to understand the frequently bizarre expressions of grief around him, he perceives that "everybody in the world is wounded", and so enters into the experience of human responsibility.

John Wain is a novelist who can get inside people's heads, where the real feeling is, and show how it can be expressed in behaviour that is often both terrible and comic. In *Young Shoulders,* this balance between the internal and the external world is beautifully maintained. It gives Paul Waterford an assured place among the few memorable adolescents of our literature.

> *Shirley Toulson, "Watching Wounded," in* The Times Educational Supplement, *No. 3463, November 12, 1982, p. 23.*

BRYN CALESS

Few writers who have advanced beyond middle age are able successfully to capture the mental images and slang idiom of the teenager, but Wain does it brilliantly [in *Young Shoulders*]. The long sustained passages where Paul communes with himself, and with the spirit of Clare whom he feels to be close to him, are consummately done. . . .

This is not merely about the trauma of grief: it is a tightly organized story that follows Paul's growth to self-knowledge, his abandonment of childish fantasies (his 'World Free Zone' utopia), his cruelly honest observation of his parents' estrangement and sadness, his own attempt to understand death and loss, his growing compassion and sympathy for women, this last symbolized in his meeting with a young prostitute while walking home.

Rarely, too, it is a novel about reconciliation, of coming together to solve problems, of co-operation rather than antagonism. It is a *hopeful* book, not of the Patience Strong variety, but about rugged, hard-earned experience which tells you that life is worth living and going on with. This is an important, compassionate, gentle and humorous novel.

> *Bryn Caless, in a review of "Young Shoulders," in* British Book News, *May, 1983, p. 328.*

NEIL BERRY

Didacticism, together with an unfashionable strain of stoic moralizing, has remained a feature of Wain's fiction and criticism. But though he never wastes a chance to denounce cars and juke-boxes, he has become less strident and touchy over the years. *Dear Shadows,* his latest book, a slim volume of reminiscences, is mostly free from the breast-beating of *Sprightly Running.* . . . In the present volume, the title of which he takes from Yeats's elegy ''In Memory of Eva Gore-Booth and Con Markiewicz'', Wain writes about himself incidentally. Comprising nine pen-portraits of people, famous or otherwise, who have been important to him but who are now dead, this is a comparatively modest and restrained piece of writing.

The chapters vary in size and quality. Some suffer from an excess of piety. Those on Nevill Coghill and on Wain's father, for example, belong to a style of moral portraiture—the exemplary character sketch or panegyric—which reads awkwardly in the late twentieth century. Others seem—to this reviewer at least—to be of limited public interest. At the centre of *Dear Shadows,* however, is a lengthy reminiscence of Marshall McLuhan which alone is almost good enough to justify the book. Wain writes memorably about this eccentric Canadian Catholic whom he knew as a literary academic some years before McLuhan's books on media turned him into one of the 1960s' most talked-about gurus. The author of the *Gutenberg Galaxy* is glimpsed in a series of vivid snapshots: sitting on a bar-stool stifling his dyspepsia while in full verbal flow; beating the back of his neck with a strange implement to stimulate his cerebral cortex; briefly diverting his manic mental energy into playing with his children; overwhelming his audience with oracular pronouncements (''Incidentally, John, it's no accident that after 1850 English prose becomes a p.a. system'').

The book's other big section might have benefited from some of the humorous touches which enliven the McLuhan portrait. In it Wain recalls the American journalist Harvey Breit, the jazz musician Bill Coleman, and Robert Lowell and Elizabeth Hardwick who once, after a convivial evening, invited Wain to join them in bed. The piece conveys, if nothing else, the intoxicating effect that American abundance and vitality could have on an Englishman with the memory of austerity fresh in his mind. But its digressiveness strains the reader's patience. . . . Careful construction is not among the virtues of *Dear Shadows.* The final chapter, ostensibly concerned with Richard Burton, says as much about Nevill Coghill and his embattled position as a champion of student drama in wartime Oxford—ground already covered at the beginning of the book.

Self-indulgence has been a weakness of this sincere and, at best, stimulating writer. So, too, has emotional hyperbole. Though *Dear Shadows* contains nothing so extravagant as the claim in *Sprightly Running* that his childhood taught him the nature of modern totalitarianism, Wain can still resort to the wild and gratuitous comparison—as when he likens the distress caused him by the breakdown of his first marriage to the madness of John Clare. This is a book which looks back to a time when leisurely anecdotal writing, punctuated by moralizing and displays of authorial sensibility, still enjoyed a captive readership. But John Wain is not alone among his angry contemporaries in having proved rather more of a traditionalist than he first appeared.

Neil Berry, ''Leisurely Older Man,'' in The Times Literary Supplement, *No. 4334, April 25, 1986, p. 445.*

FRANK KERMODE

In the poem which provides John Wain with the title of [*Dear Shadows: Portraits from Memory*] Yeats is addressing the dead Gore-Booth sisters and telling them, quite tenderly at first, that now they're dead they know it all—

> all the folly of a fight
> For a common wrong or right

—so that it seems dying has enabled them to catch up with him, for he knew it and stayed alive. The strength of feeling is unmistakable—

> the innocent and the beautiful
> Have no enemy but time

—and at the end of the poem fuels an incendiary fantasy: all their efforts to achieve a common right amounted to no more than the construction of an aristocratic folly, fragile and, in the long run, a waste of life and beauty. I doubt if Wain wanted the whole context to be considered, and none of his dear shadows dirtied upper-class hands in popular causes: but the living, contemplating the completed lives of dead friends, will often feel sadness at what seems evidence of waste of effort, frustrated intentions, avoidable unhappiness in a world now past, a world in which happiness seemed more possible than it does at present. There is something of this sadness in Wain's account of the men and women he summons—or rather is visited by, since he lacks that peremptory Yeatsian touch, calling this person, summoning that one, and putting them to work in poems.

When Yeats surrounds himself with ghosts he is always the boss, but Wain here is always the observer, meeting and listening to interesting people, representing himself as 'a willing pair of ears'. He tells us that this volume may be taken to be the sequel to his autobiographical *Sprightly Running,* published in 1962, but he does himself an injustice, presenting himself merely as a compliant fellow who had the luck to run into various peculiar, talented and amiable people to whom he had very little to give. His book may therefore be taken to confirm the view that he and others who started out in the Fifties were grey-faced youths who hated Mozart, abroad, metropolitan high jinks and Modernism. It is a view no more accurate than Isherwood's pretence that he was an impassive observer of all the goings-on he reported from Berlin. In fact, the wild, funny and curious young Wain was the magnet, and the distinguished as well as the commonplace filings fell irresistibly into line. However, he could hardly say this; and in any case to have given himself a vivid part in the séance wouldn't have suited the gently nostalgic tone of the older Wain's remembrance.

He is a survivor; he chose quite deliberately to be a man of letters, one to whom no genre of writing was alien, knowing that he did so at a time when the profession was dying. His model was Arnold Bennett. . . . Wain had an easier start than Bennett, his fellow townsman, but the second stage was harder. No serious young writer in the Fifties could possibly be as rich and free to move around as Bennett had been. In 1950 you couldn't take more than £25 out of the country, and there were no credit cards. So Bennett's Parisian life was not available to Wain: but eventually he did work in Paris and in New York (always on the understanding that Stoke and Oxford were his true homes) and he did write novels, plays, memoirs and reviews without giving up verse. In fact, he has been very prolific, though no more a recluse than his model, and with a gift for friendship Bennett would have admired. *Sprightly Running* will be remembered, if for nothing else, for the superb chapter on a wholly improbable friend, E.H.W. Meyerstein.

The comparable chapter in this book is on Marshall McLuhan. Wain knew him long before he was famous, even before the publication of *The Mechanical Bride,* which brought on the first stirrings of the cult. He took an interest in McLuhan's ideas, but it was the man, with his completely individual profile, that enchanted him: large and gauche, usually towing a priest along, constantly saying astonishing or absurd things (his 'probes', as he called them), an authoritarian father whose strictures were ignored by his children, he was exactly the mixture of enthusiastic amateur and professional pedagogue Wain has always admired. . . .

There is some mention here of a television interview I did with the sage in January 1967. It was produced (for *Monitor*) by Jonathan Miller, and Wain was present. He says he understood nothing of the conversation, and the BBC presumably agreed that it was unintelligible, for it was never transmitted. . . . Miller later wrote a book about McLuhan for a series I edit, and the book may have helped to reduce the subject's reputation. Wain reviewed it favourably, so all three of us were involved in a performance he regarded as at least mildly treacherous. . . . [It] is somehow pleasing that Wain should make amends for us all by addressing McLuhan's shade with such evident affection and understanding of his true qualities.

Wain could have been a don and a very good one; the point of his piece about Nevill Coghill is that it tells us what sort of don he would have been. Dons aren't always very lovable and colleagues were nasty to Coghill, a very agreeable man whom I remember best from a photo showing him perched on his chaise-longue like a huge faun. He believed in teaching students about Shakespeare by producing the plays, which seemed wicked to the other teachers; and 'the hard-nosed professionals', as Wain calls them, sneered at his scholarship, which was much more ingenious and original than they allowed. In the matter of scholarship, what Wain requires is a subtle combination of gentleman and player, a Coghill who inhabits an academy innocent of competition, self-serving and self-display. It may seem a utopian fancy, but I think Wain locates it in a magical, rather Arnoldian Oxford that somehow existed alongside the real one, in the good old days.

The old days, indeed, preoccupy him more and more. In Shottery, not yet swamped by tourists, he lived in theatrical lodgings run by a wise raffish landlady, and now meditates the advantages to art of small towns like Weimar or Salzburg or even Shakespeare's London. The Potteries of his father's youth are also the object of his piety: but so are the jazz clubs of Paris, London and New York and the trumpet of Billy Coleman which, I am prepared to believe, had a sort of primitive purity. Famous names—Pound and Lowell, for instance—flit through these pages, but nobody is there because he or she is famous, only because Wain in his wanderings bumped into them and found them worth his time or his affection.

This seems a very relaxed book, but just when you think you can predict the next bit because you've formed a notion of the author as a testy past-praiser living on old fruit preserved as bland sweet jam, just then he may confound you with an unexpected view of someone, or with the hidden side of some idea. The range of intellegence is great; not deep the poet sees but wide.

Frank Kermode, "Past-Praiser," in London Review of Books, *June 5, 1986, p. 10.*

Alice Walker

1944-

American novelist, short story writer, essayist, poet, critic, and editor.

Best known as the author of the Pulitzer Prize-winning novel *The Color Purple* (1982), Walker writes powerful, expressive fiction depicting the black woman's struggle for spiritual wholeness and sexual, political, and racial equality. For Walker, the black American woman is a universal symbol representing hope and resurrection; through her female characters, she advocates the importance of bonds between women who contend with negative social mechanisms. Although most critics categorize her writings as feminist, Walker rebuffs the label, describing her works and herself as "womanist." She defines this term as "a woman who loves other women. . . . Appreciates and prefers woman's culture, woman's emotional flexibility . . . and woman's strength. . . . *Loves* the spirit. . . . Loves herself. *Regardless*." Some critics have faulted Walker's fiction for its unflattering portraits of black men. However, most applaud her lyrical prose, her sensitive characterizations, and her gift for rendering beauty, grace, and dignity in ordinary people and places.

Born into a large family of tenant farmers in rural Georgia, Walker usually sets her fiction in the deep South. Her first novel, *The Third Life of Grange Copeland* (1970), introduces many of Walker's prevalent themes, particularly the domination of black women by black men. In this book, which spans the years between the Depression and the beginnings of the civil rights movement, Walker chronicles three generations of a black sharecropping family and examines the effects of poverty and racism on their lives. Because of his sense of powerlessness, Grange Copeland, the family patriarch, drives his wife to suicide and neglects his children. When Grange deserts his family to seek a better life in the North, his legacy of hate and violence is passed on to his son, Brownfield, who eventually murders his wife. At the conclusion, Grange returns to his family a broken man and attempts to reconcile his past transgressions with the help of his granddaughter, Ruth. For Grange, Ruth symbolizes hope because she has survived her family's history of brutality and despair. Some critics accused Walker of reviving stereotypes about the black family, while others praised the book for its intense, descriptive language.

Walker's next work of fiction, *Meridian* (1976), is a study of personal development and sacrifice set during the civil rights movement that is regarded by many critics as one of the best novels depicting that era. In this book, Walker explores conflicts between traditional black values handed down through slavery and the revolutionary polemic advocated by the black-power movement. Meridian Hill is a college-educated woman who commits her life to aiding southern blacks in their struggle for political and social equality. She joins an organization of black revolutionaries but is forced to leave the group when she refuses to condone its violent actions. However, Meridian continues her activist work and later becomes a legendary heroine resembling such historical figures as Harriet Tubman and Sojourner Truth. Walker also addresses sexual politics within the movement in a subplot involving Meridian, her lover and compatriot Truman, and Lynne, a Jewish activist whom Truman

eventually marries. While several critics admonished Walker for depicting Meridian as a mythic figure, Marge Piercy responded: "Is it possible to write a novel about the progress of a saint? Apparently, yes. With great skill and care to make Meridian believable at every stage of her development, Walker also shows us the cost."

The Color Purple placed Walker among the most influential contemporary American writers and made her a literary celebrity. Presented in an epistolary style, this novel chronicles thirty years in the life of Celie, a poor southern black woman who is victimized physically and psychologically by both her stepfather and her husband but manages to survive her ordeal and emerges as a stronger person. While in her teens, Celie was repeatedly raped by her stepfather, who sold the two children she bore him. Celie is later married to a widower named Albert, whom she addresses as "Mister," and who for the next three decades subjects her to domestic slavery and periodic beatings. Celie writes letters describing her ordeal to God and to her sister Nettie, who escapes a similar fate by working as a missionary in Africa. Celie eventually finds solace through her friendship and love for Albert's occasional mistress, Shug Avery, a charismatic blues singer who helps her gain self-esteem and independence. At the novel's end, Celie is reunited with her children and with Nettie. Although Walker received unanimous praise for *The Color Purple,* especially for her accurate rendering of southern black vernacular and her vivid characterization of Celie, the book generated much controversy, particularly for its negative portrayal of black males. Trudier Harris charged that the book "gives validity to all the white racist's notions of pathology in black communities," and Darryl Pinckney unflatteringly equated Walker's novel with Harriet Beecher Stowe's classic, *Uncle Tom's Cabin.* Pinckney stated: "Like Stowe's, Walker's work shows a world divided between the chosen (black women) and the unsaved, the 'poor miserable critter' (black men), between the 'furnace of affliction' and a 'far-off, mystic land of . . . miraculous fertility.'" Nevertheless, Peter S. Prescott echoed the opinion of most critics when he called *The Color Purple* "an American novel of permanent importance, that rare sort of book which (in Norman Mailer's felicitous phrase) amounts to a diversion in the fields of dread." *The Color Purple* was adapted for film in 1984 by Steven Spielberg, and many critics regard this popular motion picture as the catalyst for Walker's subsequent rise to literary and national prominence.

In addition to the reputation she has garnered for her novels, Walker is also considered an accomplished poet. Darwin Turner described Walker's verse as "moderately open forms which permit her to reveal homespun truths of human behavior and emotion." Walker's first collection, *Once* (1968), includes poems she wrote during the early 1960s while attending Sarah Lawrence College in New York City. Some of these poems reveal the confusion, isolation, and suicidal thoughts Walker experienced when she learned in her senior year that she was pregnant. In her second volume, *Revolutionary Petunias* (1973), Walker addresses such topics as love, individualism, and revolution while recounting her years in Mississippi as a civil rights activist and teacher. *Goodnight Willie Lee, I'll See You in the Morning* (1979) contains verse that celebrates familial bonds and friendships. Michael Dirda commented that Walker's poems "sometimes . . . address the reader directly; often they carry morals and are written as allegories, somewhat reminiscent of Stephen Crane's little symbolic story poems." Walker's recent collection, *Horses Make a Landscape Look More Beautiful* (1985), focuses upon contemporary social issues.

Walker has also published two volumes of short stories, *In Love and Trouble: Stories of Black Women* (1973) and *You Can't Keep a Good Woman Down* (1981), both of which share the thematic concerns of her novels. *In Search of Our Mothers' Gardens: Womanist Prose* (1984) collects Walker's essays from the past twenty years and features several autobiographical pieces. In her review of *You Can't Keep a Good Woman Down,* Carol Rumens summarized Walker's achievements: "Walker's work should be admired . . . not because it represents a flowering of black or female consciousness, but because at best it brings to life the varied scents and colours of human experience."

(See also *CLC,* Vols. 5, 6, 9, 19, 27; *Contemporary Authors,* Vols. 37-40, rev. ed.; *Contemporary Authors New Revision Series,* Vol. 9; *Something about the Author,* Vol. 31; and *Dictionary of Literary Biography,* Vols. 6, 33.)

In this volume commentary on Alice Walker is focused on her novel *The Color Purple.*

GLORIA STEINEM

There must be thousands of people scattered around this country, each one of whom thinks only she or he knows how necessary and major a writer Alice Walker is.

Even "writer" may be too distant a word. Traveling and listening over the years, I've noticed that the readers of Alice Walker's work tend to speak about her as a friend: someone who has rescued them from passivity or anger; someone who has taught them sensuality or self-respect, humor or redemption.

"I've been a much better person," said an angry young novelist to a roomful of his peers, "since I've been under the care and feeding of Alice Walker's writing." (p. 35)

"While I'm reading her novels, I'm completely unaware of her style," said a literary critic who is a writer herself. "It's unpretentious and natural, like a glass that contains whatever she wants you to see. Yet I can read a few paragraphs of hers and know immediately: That's Alice." (pp. 35, 37)

I've heard many such comments over the past decade or so. . . . I don't hear the usual celebrity question: what is Alice really like? Readers feel they know her personally from her writing. But lives touched by her work form a small secret network on almost every campus and in many cities and towns.

Of course, the existence of such readers, even unknown to each other, means that Alice Walker is not a secret writer. Her two novels, three books of poetry, and two short story collections have sold and been reviewed respectably. . . .

But her visibility as a major American talent has been obscured by a familiar bias that assumes white male writers, and the literature they create, to be the norm. That puts black women (and all women of color) at a double remove. Only lately have writers like Toni Morrison or Maya Angelou begun to escape those adjectives that are meant to restrict, not just describe. Toni Cade Bambara, June Jordan, Paule Marshall, Ntozake Shange, and other valuable current writers are still missing from the mainstream (and the mainstream is missing them) because of this bias against the universality of what they have to say. So are all the Zora Neale Hurstons and Nella Larsens of the past whose works have been allowed to pass out of print and out of mind.

Even with Black Studies, Women's Studies, and other new courses now trying hard, it's going to take many years to change academic habits that still expect American readers to cross boundaries of country, time, and language to identify with Dostoevsky or Tolstoy, but not to walk next door and meet Baldwin or Ellison; that still assume women can identify with male protagonists, but that there's something perverse about the other way around.

As usual, however, the people are way ahead of their leaders— and readers are ahead of their book reviewers. It's true and important that a disproportionate number of people who seek out Alice Walker's sparsely distributed books are black women. . . . But white women, and women of diverse ethnic backgrounds, also feel tied to Alice Walker. The struggle to have work and minds of our own, vulnerability, our debt to our mothers, the price of childbirth, friendships among women, the problem of loving men who regard us as less than themselves, sensuality, violence: all these are major themes of her fiction and poetry. (In *The Third Life of Grange Copeland,* her first novel, she exposed violence against women by their husbands and lovers. It was 1970, years before most women had begun to tell the truth in public about such violence, and her novel paid a critical price for being ahead of its time.) In fact, she speaks the female experience more powerfully for being able to pursue it across boundaries of race and class.

And she never gives in. No female character is ever allowed to disappear behind a sex role, any more than she would allow a black character to sink into a stereotype of race.

As the young novelist said, "I've become a much better person . . ." and that seems to be a frequent reaction of her readers who are black men. They comment on her clear-eyed rendering of the rural black South in which many of them grew up, her loving use of black folk English, and her understanding of what goes right and wrong between men and women.

It's true that a disproportionate number of her hurtful, negative reviews have been by black men. But those few seem to be reviewing their own conviction that black men should have everything white men have had, including dominance over women; or their fear that black women's truth-telling will be misused in a racist society; or their alarm at her "lifestyle," a euphemism for the fact that Alice was married for 10 years to a white civil rights worker. (p. 37)

As for white male readers, the main problem seems to be a conviction that her books "aren't written for us." Given the fears expressed by those black male critics, it's ironic that white men's reactions often center on the increased understanding of black rage, and a new conviction that they themselves have been deprived of seeing the world whole. In fact, Susan Kirschner, an English professor who made a study of all the reviews of *Meridian,* concluded that the only critic to examine seriously the moral themes of the novel, not just respectfully describe its plot, was Greil Marcus, a white reviewer writing in *The New Yorker.* (pp. 37, 89)

I've suspected for a long time that a convention of all the atomized Alice Walker readers in the country might look surprisingly big and diverse. It might look something like the world.

In fact, her readers may be about to find each other, and discover their numbers greatly increased, in the light of new public attention. *The Color Purple,* Alice Walker's third and latest novel, could be the kind of popular and literary event that transforms an intense reputation into a national one.

For one thing, the storytelling style of *The Color Purple* makes it irresistible to read. The words belong to Celie, the downest and outest of women. Because she must survive against impossible odds, because she has no one to talk to, she writes about her life in the guise of letters to God. When she discovers her much-loved lost sister is not dead after all but is living in Africa, she writes letters to Nettie instead. The point is, she must tell someone the truth and confirm her existence. . . .

The result is an inviting, dead-honest, surprising novel that is the successful culmination of Alice Walker's longer and longer trips outside the safety of Standard English narration, and into the words of her characters. Here, she takes the leap completely. There is no third person to distance the reader from events. We are inside Celie's head.

And Celie turns out to be a no-nonsense, heartrending storyteller wih a gift for cramming complicated turns of events and whole life histories into very few words. Like E. L. Doctorow in *Ragtime,* the rhythm of the telling adds to the momentum of suspense—but what he did with an episodic style and pace of chapters, Celie can do with the placement of a line, a phrase, a verb. . . .

Reviewers should also understand why Alice Walker has always preferred to describe her characters' speech as "black folk English," not "dialect"; a word she feels has been used in a condescending, racist way. When these people talk, there are no self-conscious apostrophes and contractions to assure us that the writer, of course, really knows what the proper spelling and grammar should be. There are no quotation marks to keep us at our distance. Celie just writes her heart out, putting words down the way they feel and sound. Pretty soon you can't imagine why anyone would bother to write any other way.

The second pleasure of *The Color Purple* is watching people redeem themselves and grow, or wither and turn inward, according to the ways they do or don't work out the moral themes in their lives. In the hands of this author, morality is not an external dictate. It doesn't matter if you love the wrong people, or have children with more than one of them, or whether you have money, go to church, or obey the laws. What matters is cruelty, violence, keeping the truth from others who need it, suppressing someone's will or talent, taking more than you need from people or nature, and failing to choose for yourself. It's the internal morality of dignity, autonomy, and balance.

What also matters is the knowledge that everybody, no matter how poor or passive on the outside, has these possibilities inside. (p. 89)

By the end of the novel, we believe that this poor, nameless patch of land in the American South is really the world—and vice versa. Conversations between Celie and Shug have brought us theories of philosophy, ethics, and metaphysics; all with a world vision that seems more complete for proceeding from the bottom up. The color purple, an odd miracle of nature, symbolizes the miracle of human possibilities.

In the tradition of Gorky, Steinbeck, Dickens, Ernest Gaines, Hurston, Baldwin, Ousmane Sembene, Bessie Head, and many others, Alice Walker has written an empathetic novel about the poorest of the poor. . . . But, unlike most novels that expose race or class, it doesn't treat male/female injustice as natural or secondary. (And unlike some supposedly feminist novels, it doesn't ignore any women because of race or class.) Just as unusual among books about the poor and powerless, it is not written *about* one group, *for* another. The people in this book could and would enjoy it, too.

It's hard to imagine anyone in the country this novel couldn't reach.

But will it? (p. 90)

Gloria Steinem, "Do You Know This Woman? She Knows You: A Profile of Alice Walker," in Ms., Vol. X, No. 12, June, 1982, pp. 35-37, 89-94.

TRUDIER HARRIS

The Color Purple has been canonized. I don't think it should have been. The tale of the novel's popularity is the tale of the media's ability, once again, to dictate the tastes of the reading public, and to attempt to shape what is acceptable creation by black American writers. Sadly, a book that might have been ignored if it had been published ten years earlier or later has now become *the* classic novel by a black woman. That happened in great part because the pendulum determining focus on black writers had swung in their favor again, and Alice Walker had been waiting in the wings of the feminist movement and the power it had generated long enough for her curtain call to come.... While it is not certain how long Alice Walker will be in the limelight for *The Color Purple,* it is certain that the damaging effects reaped by the excessive media attention given to the novel will plague us as scholars and teachers for many years to come.

The novel has become so popular that Alice Walker is almost universally recognized as a spokeswoman for black people, especially for black women, and the novel is more and more touted as a work representative of black communities in this country. The effect of the novel's popularity has been detrimental in two significant and related ways. Response to its unequaled popularity, first of all, has created a cadre of spectator readers. These readers, who do not identify with the characters and who do not feel the intensity of their pain, stand back and view the events of the novel as a circus of black human interactions that rivals anything Daniel Patrick Moynihan concocted. The spectator readers show what damage the novel can have; for them, the book reinforces racist stereotypes they may have been heir to and others of which they may have only dreamed.

The other, equally significant, detrimental effect is that the novel has been so much praised that critics, especially black women critics, have seemingly been reluctant to offer detailed, carefully considered criticisms of it. While that may be explained in part by the recent publication of the novel and by the limited access black women critics traditionally have had to publishing outlets, these possible explanations are partly outweighed by the fact that the novel has been so consistently in the public eye that it takes great effort not to write about it. *The Color Purple* silences by its dominance, a dominance perpetuated by the popular media. Those who initially found or still find themselves unable to speak out perhaps reflect in some way my own path to writing about the novel. From the time the novel appeared in 1982, I have been waging a battle with myself to record my reaction to it. For me, the process of reading, re-reading, and re-reading the novel, discussing it, then writing about it has reflected some of the major dilemmas of the black woman critic. To complain about the novel is to commit treason against black women writers, yet there is much in it that deserves complaint.... After all, a large number of readers, usually vocal and white, have decided that *The Color Purple* is the quintessential statement on Afro-American women and a certain kind of black lifestyle in these United States. (p. 155)

When I started asking black women how they felt about the book, there was a quiet strain of discomfort with it, a quiet tendency to criticize, but none of them would do so very aggressively. We were all faced with the idea that to criticize a novel that had been so universally complimented was somehow a desertion of the race and the black woman writer. Yet, there was a feeling of uneasiness with the novel. Instead of focusing upon the specifics of that uneasiness, however, most of the black women with whom I talked preferred instead to praise that which they thought was safe: the beautiful voice in the book and Walker's ability to capture an authentic black folk speech without all the caricature that usually typifies such efforts. They could be lukewarm toward the relationship between Celie and Shug and generally criticize Albert. However, they almost never said anything about the book's African sections until I brought them up. Do they work for you? Do you see how they're integrated into the rest of the novel? Does the voice of Nettie ring authentic and true to you? Only when assured that their ideas would not be looked upon as a desertion of black femininity would the women then proceed to offer valuable insights.

For others, though, silence about the novel was something not to be broken. One Afro-American woman critic who has written on contemporary black women writers told me that she would never write anything on the novel or make a public statement about it. Quite clearly, that was a statement in itself. Her avowed silence became a political confirmation of everything that I found problematic about the novel.

But shouldn't black women allow for diversity of interpretation of our experiences, you may ask? And shouldn't we be reluctant to prescribe a direction for our black women writers? Of course, but what we have with this novel is a situation in which many black women object to the portrayals of the characters, yet we may never hear the reasons for their objections precisely *because they are black women.* (pp. 155-56)

In Gloria Steinem's article on Alice Walker and her works, especially *The Color Purple,* which appeared in *Ms. Magazine* in June of 1982 [see excerpt above], Steinem reflects her own surprise at Walker's achievement; her response is condescending at times to a degree even beyond that latitude that might be expected in such works. She praises Walker for generally being alive, black, and able to write well. (p. 156)

Steinem focuses on the language and the morality in Walker's novel. The language I have no problem with, but then I am not one of the individuals who assumes that black women have difficulty with folk idiom. Celie's voice in the novel is powerful, engaging, subtly humorous, and incisively analytic at the basic level of human interactions. The voice is perfectly suited to the character, and Walker has breathed into it a vitality that frequently overshadows the problematic areas of concern in the novel.... The form of the book, as it relates to the folk speech, the pattern and nuances of Celie's voice, is absolutely wonderful. The clash between Celie's conception and her writing ability, however, is another issue. I can imagine a black woman of Celie's background and education talking with God, as Mariah Uphur does in Sarah E. Wright's *This Child's Gonna Live,* but writing letters to God is altogether another matter. Even if we can suspend our disbelief long enough to get beyond that hurdle, we are still confronted with the substance of the book. *What* Celie records—the degradation, abuse, dehumanization—is not only morally repulsive, but it invites spectator readers to generalize about black people in the same negative ways that have gone on for centuries. Further, how Celie grows and how she presents other characters as growing is frequently incredible and inconsistent to anyone accustomed to novels at least adhering to the worlds, logical or otherwise, that they have created.

When I read lines such as "... I'm so beside myself," "She look like she ain't long for this world but dressed well for the next," "Look like a little mouse been nibbling the biscuit, a rat run off with the ham," and "Scare me so bad I near bout drop my grip," I felt a sense of déjà vu for all the black women who made art out of conversation in the part of Alabama where I grew up.... That part of Celie I could imagine. And one might even understand, at least initially, her fear of her stepfather and the underdeveloped moral sense that leads to inactivity in response to abuse. Her lack of understanding about her pregnancy is also probable within the environment in which she grew up; as many black girls/women during those years were taught that babies were found in cabbage heads or in hollow logs. But those years and years and years of Celie's acquiescence, extreme in their individuality, have been used too readily to affirm what the uninformed or the ill-informed believe is a general pattern of violence and abuse for black women. That is one of the dangerous consequences of the conceptualization of that powerful voice Celie has.

One of the saddest effects and the greatest irony of that voice is that, while it makes Celie articulate, it has simultaneously encouraged silence from black women, who need to be vocal in voicing their objections to, as well as their praises for, the novel. As Celie's voice has resounded publicly, it has, through its very forcefulness, cowed the voices of black women into private commentary or into silence about issues raised in the novel.

The voice led to Steinem's celebration of the wonderful morality in the novel, yet what she finds so attractive provides another source of my contention with the book. Steinem asserts that morality for Walker "is not an external dictate. It doesn't matter if you love the wrong people, or have children with more than one of them, or whether you have money, go to church, or obey the laws. What matters is cruelty, violence, keeping the truth from others who need it, suppressing someone's will or talent, taking more than you need from people or nature, and failing to choose for yourself. It's the internal morality of dignity, autonomy, and balance." What kind of morality is it that espouses that all human degradation is justified if the individual somehow survives all the tortures and uglinesses heaped upon her? Where is the dignity, autonomy, or balance in that? I am not opposed to triumph, but I do have objections to the unrealistic presentation of the path, the *process* that leads to such a triumph, especially when it is used to create a new archetype or to resurrect old myths about black women.

By no means am I suggesting that Celie should be blamed for what happens to her. My problem is with her reaction to the situation. Even slave women who found themselves abused frequently found ways of responding to that—by running away, fighting back, poisoning their masters, or through more subtly defiant acts such as spitting into the food they cooked for their masters. They did something, and Celie shares a kinship in conception if not in chronology with them. (pp. 156-57)

I found so many white women who joined Steinem in praising the novel that I read it again just to recheck my own evaluations. Then, since I was on leave at The Bunting Institute at Radcliffe and had access to a community of women, the majority of whom were white, I thought it would be fitting to test some of my ideas on them. Accordingly, I wrote a thirty-three-page article on the novel and invited women in residence at the Institute to come to a working paper session and respond to what I had written. My basic contentions were that the portrayal of Celie was unrealistic for the time in which the novel was set, that Nettie and the letters from Africa were really extraneous to the central concerns of the novel, that the lesbian relationship in the book represents the height of silly romanticism, and that the epistolary form of the novel ultimately makes Celie a much more sophisticated character than we are initially led to believe. . . .

During that session, I discovered that some white women did not like the novel, but they were not the ones controlling publications like *Ms.*. One white woman commented that, if she

had not been told the novel had been written by a black woman, she would have thought it had been written by a Southern white male who wanted to reinforce the traditional sexual and violent stereotypes about black people. That comment affirmed one of my major objections to the thematic development of the novel: The book simply added a freshness to many of the ideas circulating in the popular culture and captured in racist literature that suggested that black people have no morality when it comes to sexuality, that black family structure is weak if existent at all, that black men abuse black women, and that black women who may appear to be churchgoers are really lewd and lascivious.

The novel gives validity to all the white racist's notions of pathology in black communities. For these spectator readers, black fathers and father-figures are viewed as being immoral, sexually unrestrained. Black males and females form units without the benefit of marriage, or they easily dissolve marriages in order to form less structured, more promiscuous relationships. Black men beat their wives—or attempt to—and neglect, ignore, or abuse their children. When they cannot control their wives through beatings, they violently dispatch them. The only stereotype that is undercut in the book is that of the matriarch. Sofia, who comes closest in size and personality to the likes of Lorraine Hansberry's Mama Lena Younger and comparable characters, is beaten, imprisoned, and nearly driven insane precisely because of her strength.

The women had fewer comments on the section on Africa, but generally agreed that it was less engaging than other parts of the novel. I maintained that the letters from Africa were like the whaling chapters in *Moby Dick*—there more for the exhibition of a certain kind of knowledge than for the good of the work. (p. 157)

Other women from that session also commented on Walker's excessively negative portrayal of black men—not a new criticism leveled against her—and some thought the lesbian relationship was problematic. There were others, though, who couldn't see what all the fuss was about, who said that they had simply enjoyed reading the novel. I had no trouble with their enjoyment of the novel as a response to reading it; my problems centered on the reasons for their finding it so enjoyable. Those who did generally mentioned the book's affirmation: that Celie is able to find happiness after so many horrible things have happened to her. That is a response that would probably please Walker, who has indicated that the character Celie is based on her great-grandmother, who was raped at twelve by her slaveholding master. In reparation to a woman who had suffered such pain, Walker has explained: "I liberated her from her own history. . . . I wanted her to be happy." It is this clash between history and fiction, in part, that causes the problems with the novel.

On the way to making Celie happy, Walker portrays her as a victim of many imaginable abuses and a few unimaginable ones. Celie is a woman who *believes* she is ugly, and she centers that belief on her blackness. While this is not a new problem with some black women, a black woman character conceived in 1982 who is still heir to the same kinds of problems that characters had who were conceived decades earlier is problematic for me—especially since Celie makes a big deal of how ugly she believes she is. But, you may say, how can a woman affirm any standard of beauty in an environment in which men are so abusive? Allowance for the fact that Celie is "living" in the 1940s really does not gainsay the criticism about this aspect of her conception. I would say in response that Nettie was there during Celie's early years, and Nettie apparently has a rather positive conception of herself. If Celie believes her about some things, why not about others? Instead, Celie gives in to her environment with a kind of passivity that comes near to provoking screams in readers not of the spectator variety who may be guilty of caring too much about the characters. Before she can be made to be happy, Celie is forced to relive the history of many Afro-American women who found themselves in unpleasant circumstances, but few of them seem to have undergone such an intuitive devaluation of themselves. . . . I can imagine Celie existing forever in her situation if someone else did not come along to "stir her root life," as Jean Toomer would say, "and teach her to dream." It is that burying away of the instinctive desire to save one's self that makes me in part so angry about Celie—in addition to all those ugly things that happen to her. Plowing a man's fields for twenty years and letting him use her body as a sperm depository leaves Celie so buried away from herself that it is hard to imagine anything stirring her to life—just as it is equally hard to imagine her being so deadened. Ah—the dilemma.

Celie does have an awareness of right and wrong that comes from outside herself—as well as the one she will develop from her own experiences. She knows that Albert's abuse of her is wrong just as she knew her stepfather's sexual exploitation of her was wrong. And she does go to church; whether or not she believes what she hears, certainly something of the Christian philosophy seeps into her consciousness over the years. There are guidelines for action, therefore, to which she can compare her own situation and respond. Also, considering the fact that she cannot have children with Albert, the traditional reason for enduring abuse—one's children—is absent in her case. So why does she stay? (pp. 157-58)

From the beginning of the novel, even as Walker presents Celie's sexual abuse by her stepfather, there is an element of fantasy in the book. Celie becomes the ugly duckling who will eventually be redeemed through suffering. This trait links her to all the heroines of fairy tales from Cinderella to Snow White. Instead of the abusive stepmother as the villain, the stepfather plays that role. He devalues Celie in direct proportion to Nettie's valuing of her; unfortunately, as an inexperienced rather than an adult godmother, Nettie lacks the ability to protect Celie. The clash between youth and age, between power and powerlessness begins the mixed-media approach of the novel. Celie's predicament may be real, but she is forced to deal with it in terms that are antithetical to the reality of her condition. (p. 159)

The fabulist/fairy-tale mold of the novel is ultimately incongruous with and does not serve well to frame its message. When things turn out happily in those traditional tales, we are asked to affirm the basic pattern and message: Good triumphs over evil. But what does *The Color Purple* affirm? What were all those women who applauded approving of? It affirms, first of all, patience and long-suffering—perhaps to a greater degree than that exhibited by Cinderella or by the likes of Elizabeth Grimes in James Baldwin's *Go Tell It on the Mountain*. In true fairy-tale fashion, it affirms passivity; heroines in those tales do little to help themselves. It affirms silence in the face of, if not actual allegiance to, cruelty. It affirms secrecy concerning violence and violation. It affirms, saddest of all, the myth of the American Dream becoming a reality for black Americans, even those who are "dirt poor," as one of my colleagues phrased it, and those who are the "downest" and "outest." The fable structure thereby perpetuates a lie in holding out to blacks a non-existent or minimally existent hope for a piece of that great American pie. The clash of characters who presumably contend with and in the real world with the idealistic, suprarealistic quality and expectations of fairy-tale worlds places a burden on the novel that diffuses its message and guarantees possibilities for unintended interpretations.

With its mixture of message, form, and character, *The Color Purple* reads like a political shopping list of all the IOUs Walker felt that it was time to repay. She pays homage to the feminists by portraying a woman who struggles through adversity to assert herself against almost impossible odds. She pays homage to the lesbians by portraying a relationship between two women that reads like a schoolgirl fairy tale in its ultimate adherence to the convention of the happy resolution. She pays homage to black nationalists by opposing colonialism, and to Pan Africanism by suggesting that yes, indeed, a black American does understand and sympathize with the plight of her black brothers and sisters thousands of miles across the ocean. And she adds in a few other obeisances—to career-minded women in the characters of Mary Agnes and Shug, to born-again male feminists in the character of Albert, and to black culture generally in the use of the blues and the folk idiom. (p. 160)

I *will* teach *The Color Purple* again—precisely because of the teachability engendered by its controversiality. I will be angry again because I am not a spectator to what happens to Celie; for me, the novel *demands* participation. I will continue to react to all praise of the novel by asserting that mere praise ignores the responsibility that goes along with it—we must clarify as much as we can the reasons that things are being praised and enumerate as best we can the consequences of that praise. I will continue to read and re-read the novel, almost in self-defense against the continuing demands for discussions and oral evaluations of it. Perhaps—and other black women may share this response—I am caught in a love/hate relationship with *The Color Purple*; though my crying out against it might be comparable to spitting into a whirlwind in an effort to change its course, I shall nevertheless purse my lips. (pp. 160-61)

Trudier Harris, "On 'The Color Purple,' Stereotypes, and Silence," in Black American Literature Forum, *Vol. 18, No. 4, Winter, 1984, pp. 155-61.*

BETTYE J. PARKER-SMITH

In her fiction, Alice Walker has called together a meeting of Black women. The place is the South. They are plain women. They grow petunias. They struggle endlessly and are harmless because they know no wrong; mostly just ordinary churchgoing or church-been women who sometimes, in their confused state, amalgamate Voodoo and Christianity. Their tragedies are very personal, very real, and extraordinarily bleak and Black. They keep repaying their dues in their small isolated world fashioned by time and condition. Eventually they all shape into hardened clay. Different though they may sometimes seem, they all push against the same barbed-wired wall of racism, sexism, age, ignorance, and despair. Often they are reduced to a level lower than themselves (frequently analogous to animals and insects), become frustrated, and operate on the level consistent with their reduced state. They are trapped by circumstance and this entrapment is the result of their sense of powerlessness against the structure of the dominant society as well as the fact that they have little understanding of that structure. Therefore, in a day-to-day existence, they carry out a plot constructed by white society (male and female) and choreographed by Black men. Walker's characters mirror allegations about Black women in relationship to their pain and suffering. The claim that Black women's conditions result from an intrinsic weakness is angled more graphically and more consistently in Walker's fiction than in her poetry. It is on this theme within her fiction (*The Third Life of Grange Copeland, In Love and Trouble, Meridian, You Can't Keep a Good Woman Down,* and *The Color Purple*) that this effort is engaged. (p. 479)

Mary Helen Washington, an Alice Walker critic, states that the author is an apologist for Black women. And she uses "apologist" in the sense that Walker "speaks or writes in defense of a cause or a position" [see *CLC,* Vol. 19]. The cause is the liberation of Black womanhood, but, as an apologist, she demonstrates this position basically in the sense of acknowledging. To be sure, she acknowledges the condition, but prior to her most recent novel [*The Color Purple*], she was either not yet ready or willing to go to the level of defense. In *Purple,* on the other hand, she lifts Black women off their knees, uses love as a defense mechanism, and raises Black women to a level of royalty. *Meridian,* her long-standing civil rights novel, does not reach this height. She only acknowledges Meridian's plight. What is clear, nonetheless, is her articulation of the complete Black male-female dialogue in all of her fiction. She captures the exactness of their experiences by using the South as a backdrop. She draws upon the language: a quick, choppy, picturesque recipe of words and phrases. She plays upon the land: open, swallowing, birthrighted, but for the most part unattainable. She builds on the feelings of ambiguity, the love/hate relationships that Black women have for their men; the "no-good son-of-a-bitches," who despite their "triflin'" ways and cruelties, receive their meals and loving on a silver platter. Without a doubt, she transposes her "self" into her writing. In fact, she confessed to Mary Helen that she knew the women she writes about, and while growing up in Georgia, she smelled the burnt of their pain. (p. 480)

[*The Color Purple*] shows Alice Walker's growth as a writer. And, in this masterpiece that exceeds its limits as a work of fiction, she elevates Black women to the height of sovereignty. They wear the royal robe of purple. In her early works, women used their fragile strength to love everybody and anybody except themselves. Now, robed in purple, they receive and accept the *right* to love themselves and each other. Love of self energizes them to the point that they break their chains of enslavement, change their own worlds, time and Black men. They are prepared to fight—eye for an eye, tooth for a tooth. And they remain women—cry when they need to, laugh when they want to, straighten their hair if they take a notion. They change their economic, political, and moral status, with love. (p. 483)

[The] women in *Purple* build a wall of camaraderie around themselves. They share in each other's pain, sorrow, laughter, and dreams. They applaud each other's achievements. And they come to each other's rescue. They are sisters in body as well as in spirit and the spirit *cannot* be broken. They found God in themselves and "they loved *her* fiercely." (p. 485)

[To] transmute any part of the Holy Trinity to female would suggest to these women a lesbian notion, which is not only immoral and unnatural but sacrilegious as well. Walker's women, traditional then, who found solace in the church, accepted the church in the ways that they could best relate to it, time and circumstance playing important roles. Her modern women find that God is within. (p. 490)

Purple opens with a warning: "You better not never tell nobody but God. It'd kill your mammy." This statement introduces a long list of pain-stricken letters to God. Bosom buddy though God may be, she must use her all-knowing power to recognize the writers of these letters because they bear no signatures. For the character-writer, Celie, being omnipotent is quite enough. What she needs is to share her burdens, be taken off the cross, and find a way to save herself. She does find a way and it works because, as she discovers, God *is* herself.

The women in Alice Walker's fiction . . . are a disturbing bunch indeed. For the most part, they do not understand the complexity of their problem, and because their limited worlds cannot assist them they are destined to operate haphazardly. They vacillate between the bottle and the Bible and spend a lot of time on their knees. The distinctive feature of these women is the tremendous quality with which they carry their suffering. Some are generous and proud. Some are forgiving even to the men who mistreat them. Some are trusting and patient. The new women overcome insurmountable odds to change their condition. They are all resilient to a point. All of these qualities contribute to the success of Walker's literary style and effect.

In forcing her readers to face the truth, she carries them beyond the normality or abnormality of an experience. In blowing the breath of life into her characters, she carries the reader to the edge of the cliff—to the point where the balloon is ready to burst. She operates the way of a good gumbo maker; the roux must remain on the fire until the point of burning. It takes skill and know-how to be able to recognize that point. She uses imagery, often intangible, grass-roots form, to connect her characters to the South: flowers, quilts, cotton stalks, wasps' nests. Plant life (often in the form of petunias) is a consistent image in her fiction as well as her poetry. Her sense of humor allows the reader to move through her fiction without becoming overburdened by its pain. Plants, often present in her death scenes or at the end of some tragic moment, have a germinating quality. They symbolize hope. As a major modern writer, Alice Walker continues to water her purple petunias. The height that she can climb as an American literary contributor cannot even be suggested. What is evident, however, is that her women are now finding some peace of mind. (pp. 490-91)

Bettye J. Parker-Smith, "Alice Walker's Women: In Search of Some Peace of Mind," in Black Women Writers (1950-1980): A Critical Evaluation, *edited by Mari Evans, Anchor Press/Doubleday, 1984, pp. 478-93.*

GEORGE STADE

Twice I have heard Alice Walker's novel *The Color Purple* described as "a sacred text," once by a true believer, once by a village aetheist. Certainly the extra-textual evidence is with the true believer: the novel has been a bestseller, first in hardcover and now in paperback; it won the Pulitzer Prize and the National Book Award; many of the reviews were written with a hushed and unctuous reverence. . . . In a collection of essays, *In Search of Our Mothers' Gardens* (1983), Miss Walker explicitly announces the attractive dogma that informs her novel. The subtitle of this collection is *Womanist Prose.*

"Womanist," as Miss Walker defines it, describes (among other things) "a woman who loves other women, sexually and/or nonsexually. Appreciates and prefers woman's culture, woman's emotional flexibility (and values tears as natural counterbalance of laughter), and woman's strength. . . . *Loves* the spirit. . . . Loves herself. *Regardless.*'' Although Miss Walker, in her words, is .''a rather ardent feminist,'' her feminism can be distinguished from her womanism, in theory if not in her practice. Both can be distinguished from women's liberationism.

Feminism, let us say, is a political program based on the reasonable premise that since women are as good as men in fact, they should be equal to them under the law. But womanism is based on invidious comparisons between the sexes; another name for it might be ''female chauvinism.'' Women's liberation, on the other hand, was a crisis cult produced (through antithesis) by what we might as well call the manist sexual ambience of the sixties, which led men to believe they had a right to sex on demand and which undermined the woman's traditional right to say no. In America the red stockings are always blue, or at least purple.

The Color Purple has its deepest tinges of women's liberation at its conclusion, with the establishment of a utopian commune presided over by the heroine and her female lover, although a couple of womanish men are allowed to hang around, so long as they behave themselves. But the novel is not feminist—it does not argue the equality of the sexes; it dramatizes, rather, the virtues of women and the vices of men. (pp. 264-65)

[With] a few telling exceptions [the men] are brutal in the flesh because they are impoverished of spirit. They are pitiless when they are not self-pitying. They are misogynist and they are pedophobic (''he hate children and he hate where they come from''). They are petty, spiteful, ''hurtful,'' and treacherous. They are also arrogant, complacent, lazy, insensitive, incompetent, vain, inartistic, contemptuous of women, but quick to take credit for their work. Above all, they are lechers, mechanical monsters of sexual appetite.

What makes men so awful we never learn. The male characters in this novel, all black, are not, as we might think, made awful by their mistreatment at the hands of whites. Nettie's letters from Africa, where the men are just as awful, make precisely that point. (''Wherever there's a man, there's trouble.'') We do learn that Harpo, against the grain, is awful to women because that is what his father, Mr._____, taught him to be. And then we learn that Mr._____ is awful to women because that is what *his* father forced him to be. Harpo, left to himself, would have been happy cooking, watching the kids, doing the housework for his amazon wife. . . . Celie, in short, redeems these men by giving them the courage to be women, by releasing the woman already in them. But masculinity is unredeemable; masculinity is radical evil, irreducible, the causeless cause of all that's wrong in the world.

Such a view of men informs many recent novels and short stories, tales of a woman who leaves an impossible husband or lover or father, only to suffer further indignities at the hands of other lustful men, finally to find happiness or at least health in the embrace of a career (usually artistic), or another woman, or, in a few cases, in cohabitation with a homosexual male, a man happy to grant the heroine a room of her own, ''preferably one with a key and a *lock*,'' as Alice Walker puts it.

These fictions, written over the last twenty years, since about the time Sylvia Plath's *The Bell Jar* was published, are an advance over their womanist predecessors in at least one way: no glamorous male is awarded to the heroine as a prize for her virtue; the rejection of men and all their ways is at last explicit—is, in fact, the conclusion and climax toward which everything else in these works tends. But these works also, in a number of ways, revert to their predecessors, to their narcissism, their sentimentality, their melodrama, their champi-

oning of domesticity over the public world of masculine power plays, and their nondenominational religiosity (*The Color Purple* is dedicated, ''To the Spirit: without whose assistance neither this book nor I would have been written.'' Celie, Nettie, and Shug all pay their tribute to the Spirit. ''God is everything, say Shug.'')

Frankenstein, or The Modern Prometheus is womanist in this sense. So is *Jane Eyre*. . . . But the long high noon of womanist fiction extended over the two middle quarters of nineteenth-century America. During that period, liberal ministers and Northeastern middle class women joined forces to beget the sentimental firstborn of American mass culture. Such is the argument of Ann Douglas's *The Feminization of American Culture*. . . . As Miss Douglas shows, middlebrow ladies' magazines such as *Godey's, Graham's,* and *Peterson's,* far outsold those for high-brows or men. During the 1850s, any one of the more popular womanist novels outsold all of the works of Hawthorne, Melville, Thoreau, and Whitman published during the whole decade. As one male competitor, his mouth pursed with sour grapes, complained, ''It is the women who read. It is the women who are the tribunal of any question aside from politics or business. It is the women who give or withhold a literary reputation. It is the women who regulate the style of living. . . . It is the women who exercise the ultimate control over the press.''

The kind of writing that brought on this diatribe, in Miss Douglas' words, was frequently informed by ''a massive hatred of the male world,'' by ''narcissistic rage,'' by a need to demonstrate that ''*any* woman is better than *any* man.'' The nonclerical male characters, by and large, are ''either awkward brutes, stumbling amid female subtleties, or wistful would-be transvestites''—which is what Alice Walker's Harpo and Mr._____ turn out to be. Popular as they were, the domestic-sentimental novels of the mid-century are no longer read outside of the classroom with one exception. That exception is *Uncle Tom's Cabin* which according to Harriet Beecher Stowe, ''God wrote,'' and which is the spiritual progenitor of *The Color Purple,* not because of the race issue, the emotional hot spot of neither novel, but because of their shared womanism. (pp. 265-67)

Margaret Mitchell, in *Gone with the Wind,* puts an ice pack on Mrs. Stowe's prurient fever. She describes Yankee women, who ''accepting *Uncle Tom's Cabin* as revelation . . . evidenced what Scarlett felt was a very nasty and ill-bred interest in slave concubinage.''

By then the first great wave of American womanist writing had receded, pushed back by the winds of social change, by literary realism, naturalism, and modernism. Certainly, there were wavelets during the twenties, when the Woman's Christian Temperance Union spearheaded the drive for Prohibition. . . . And now that womanist writing is once again in full flood, Carrie Nation's descendants are spear-heading a drive against pornography—and for the same reasons.

For all that, it would be unseemly for men to grouse about womanist fiction. Whatever else it is, literature, says Kenneth Burke, is equipment for living, although some equipment is better than other kinds. And if womanist fiction helps equip anybody to live, it more than justifies its existence. If men need to equip themselves, there is already more male chauvinist fiction around than anyone could read in a lifetime. Just the same, every contribution so far by American fiction writers to world literature has been an assault on the womanist complex of values. The fiction of Cooper, Poe, Melville, Twain, London, Crane, Dreiser, Stein, Hemingway, Faulkner, and Fitzgerald is all antiwomanist. (The exceptions are Hawthorne,

Edith Wharton, and Henry James, who appropriated womanist sentiments and situations for ulterior purposes.)

So, until recently, was the fiction of Roth, Bellow, and Heller, for example. But Roth's last three novels constitute an extended apology for the treatment of women in his best two novels, *When She Was Good* and *Portnoy's Complaint*. Saul Bellow's last novel has no hero; but its flighty male protagonist . . . is chastened and domesticated by the courage and dignity of his wife and mother-in-law—as the flighty and philandering hero of Joseph Heller's next to last novel is chastened and domesticated by his virtuous wife Belle. There's a failure of nerve there, perhaps even a craven impulse to curry favor, certainly a reknotting of the apron strings these writers had once gleefully cut in the characteristic American male writer's gesture of self-definition. It's too bad, because craven fiction never equipped anybody for anything.

No one can accuse Alice Walker of a failure of nerve—which may be why *The Color Purple* has meant so much more to American readers of fiction, the majority of whom are still women, than have the recent novels of Roth, Bellow, and Heller. For the sake of those contraries without which there is no progression, I would rather have manist writers bare their fangs than hide behind a sheepish grin. They can be sure that womanist writers will no longer pucker up, whatever the manists do. (pp. 268-70)

> George Stade, "Womanist Fiction and Male Characters," *in* Partisan Review, *Vol. LII, No. 3, 1985, pp. 264-70.*

RICHARD WESLEY

Although shut out as a winner at the 1986 Academy Awards, [*The Color Purple*] is easily the best-known and most controversial film of the 1985-86 movie season. Alice Walker, creator of the story, has been praised on one side as a major heroine and giant in American literature, and vilified on the other as a traitor to her race, a marginal talent upon whom praise is heaped because she is a woman, and as a pawn/weapon employed by white men to subjugate black men, whom they view as their natural enemy in the continuing struggle over male power.

In a strange and wonderful way, these wildly divergent reactions are a testament to the power and talent of Alice Walker. Like the best writers of any era, she has probed deeply into the soul of the nation in which she was bred and, in doing so, has brought to light our country's dark secrets.

As an African-American male, I found little that was offensive as far as the images of black men portrayed in either the novel or in the movie goes, though there were times I did think, "Alice Walker doth protest too much."

What angers black men as they read [*The Color Purple*], or watch the film version, is that *all* the black men are portrayed as fools; the women are portrayed as noble and long-suffering. If they have any weaknesses, they are weaknesses seemingly brought about by their long association with these foolish men. Walker had a point to make, and she had no need to include those black men who, with the help of the women in their lives, raised large families, sent their children off to school and into productive lives.

Black people from poor, impoverished southern rural backgrounds can tell endless stories about such men. They were not from middle-class backgrounds, nor did they have much in the way of education. They lived just down the road from where Celie and Mister lived. Many black men were upset that Alice Walker chose to paint a picture in which these men did not exist. I was not "upset," but I was disappointed. (p. 62)

We may understand the sociological conditions that might explain Mister, but there are some black men who are going to be brutes no matter what the circumstances of their lives. Mister behaves the way he does because he can get away with it. He has the power. He reflects the prevailing attitudes of male privilege. As long as black men seek to imitate the power structure that crushes them, as long as black women support this sad act of imitation and intimidation, and as long as black women submit to the idea that they have done something to deserve a lowly status in life and in the eyes of their husbands, then the morbid relationship of Celie, the oppressed, and Mister, the oppressed oppressor, will continue to be played out in homes all across America.

My feelings about *The Color Purple* put me directly at odds with many black artists, social leaders, civic leaders, and ordinary citizens all over the United States who *do* have enormous problems with the novel and with the film. That is their prerogative and I respect it.

What I do not respect, however, is the behavior of others in my community who have taken it upon themselves to be guardians of the black image. (pp. 62, 90)

These image tribunes are most often black males, usually in their thirties and older. They almost always seem to base their attacks on political concepts developed in the community during the turbulent days of the 1960s. For these men, the Black Power ideology of that time has remained sacrosanct and is in no need of revision. Part of that ideology requires black men and women to pull together. However, the unity of black men and women can only exist if the man *leads*. Therefore the woman must "submit": remain silent on sensitive issues. You do not "disrespect" your man in public, that is, criticize him in public, or speak too loudly about things that matter to you, or interrupt him when he is conversing with friends or colleagues on "serious" issues. A woman must always defer to her man and subjugate her will to his.

Few black men in their right minds will come out and couch their objections to Walker's novel in those terms, but you can hear echoes of those sentiments in much of their criticism of her: Walker is airing dirty linen in public. She is reminding many of us men of our own failures. She is reminding women of *their* failures as well. She is saying that Black is Beautiful, but not necessarily always *right*. A lot of people do not want to hear that.

I find all this especially surprising given that in past years when black male authors such as Chester Himes in *The Primitive* or John A. Williams in *The Man Who Cried I Am* decried both directly and indirectly the black woman's lack of faith and support of them, no one said a word. We should never forget that the 1950s and 1960s were a time when many black male authors rose to prominence by writing plays and novels in which black women were portrayed as castrating shrews who stunted their sons' growth by criticizing and denigrating them at every opportunity. The silence at the time was deafening.

If black women writers such as Gayl Jones, Audre Lorde, Ntozake Shange, or Alice Walker are to be hounded from one end of the country to the other for decrying the insensitivity of black men to black women, then should not those black male writers such as Ishmael Reed be brought before some of these "image tribunals" to account for *their* literary transgressions? But more important, there should be *no* "tribunals" at *all*. No one in America—and black America, especially—should be telling writers what they may or may not say. Writers are the antennae of any society. They have to speak when others dare not. The years-long stagnation of the once-vital Black Arts Movement of the 1960s and 1970s is only the latest example of what can happen when ideology is allowed to dominate thought. (pp. 90-1)

Richard Wesley, "'The Color Purple' Debate: Reading between the Lines," in Ms., Vol. XV, No. 3, September, 1986, pp. 62, 90-2.

DARRYL PINCKNEY

The novel and the film of *The Color Purple* are both works of the imagination that make claim to historical truth. The novel is set between the wars, while the film opens with the date 1909, as if someone had decided that the story of a black woman's hard life in the backwater was more plausible in a less immediate social past. . . . In any event, 1909 leaps out from the screen like a correction to the novel, which, with its flat characters, sudden revelations, and moral tags, has a doggedly nineteenth-century quality. . . .

The Color Purple is an epistolary novel. Celie, age fourteen, writes letters to "God." She has no one else to talk to about her troubles, of which she has plenty. . . . Celie is condemned to a life of drudgery because she is ugly, poor, black, and a woman. She is married off to a "Mr._____" . . . who has more brats than he let on. . . . Most of the novel concerns the downs of Celie's life with her new family and her long campaign to free herself.

The agent of Celie's salvation is a "high-natured" blues singer, a woman called Shug, who is Mister's lifelong obsession and who becomes Celie's great love as well. . . .

Celie isn't shy before the Lord. The letters are rendered in a folk idiom, not as someone like Celie would probably compose them, and one wonders why Walker did not let Celie tell her story directly as an innocent narrator.

In addition to Celie's racy missives, the novel consists of letters from Nettie, Celie's beloved little sister who runs away from their pa only to be turned out by Celie's husband after fighting him off. The earnest Nettie writes to Celie from Africa where she has gone to be a missionary with a couple who just so happen also to be the adoptive parents of Celie's two children. However, Mister intercepts Nettie's letters. Celie, with Shug's help, finds Nettie's letters in a trunk and the realization that Mister has kept them from her for some *twenty years* leads her to vote with her feet for freedom.

The use of Africa in the novel points to the programmatic intention behind Walker's design. The motherland is celebrated: "Did you know there were great cities in Africa, greater than Milledgeville or even Atlanta, thousands of years ago?" Blackness per se is also honored. . . . In between descriptions of plantings and other rituals, Nettie is critical of patriarchy, of the limited choices for women in her village, and of the practice of clitorectomy. Walker manages not to miss any bases in the correct-line department, and perhaps that is why Nettie's letters seem stiff when compared to Celie's back-fence gossip with the Lord.

Nettie is also something of a historical anachronism. The American Missionary Association trained most of its black evangelicals in the late nineteenth century. The example of Nora A. Gordon of Spelman College, who was compelled by "Christ's preciousness" to "take the Bread of Life to the poor heathen,"

inspired black women students in the last century not only because being a missionary was a dramatic gesture of racial uplift but also because it was an acceptable expression of ambition, a way out. But funds for and belief in the missionary vocation declined sharply after the turn of the century, and women like Mary McLeod Bethune and Alice Dunbar-Nelson became educators or worked in the black woman's club movement instead. Nettie, not a Garveyite, would have been historically more convincing had she merely gone north.

Mainly, through the lives of Nettie and Celie, Walker means to say a great deal about the liberating possibilities of the bonds between black women. But she also means to say a lot about black men, those boulders obstructing the path to glory. . . .

The black men are seen at a distance—that is, entirely from the point of view of the women—as naifs incapable of reflection, tyrants filled with impotent rage, or as totemic do-gooders. Walker's cards are always stacked against them—"Well, you know wherever there's a man, there's trouble"—even when her polemical intention is confused by her folksy tone. "A girl child ain't safe in a family of men." Contemporary black women's fiction has always contained scenes of domestic tension and even offhand domestic violence. But in *The Color Purple* this violence is on virtually every page. And throughout the novel, the color of the villains has changed, from white society to black men.

The outcome for Celie, equipped with the moral superiority of the victim, is never in doubt. . . . [She] emerges victorious. "You a lowdown dog is what's wrong, I say. It's time to leave you and enter into the Creation. And your dead body is just the welcome mat I need." The woman who has paid more than her share of dues is entitled to considerable bonuses. (p. 17)

Zora Neale Hurston's novel *Their Eyes Were Watching God* (1937), a brilliant evocation of the mores and folkways of the deep South, is clearly one of Walker's models. Hurston's heroine, Janie Crawford, is a subversive in a way that was new in black writing back when other black women novelists, Jessie Faucet and Nella Larsen, for example, were depicting black women who were refined, urban, and eager to hold to convention. . . . But [Walker] has turned Hurston's folk wisdom, with its wry humor and painful good sense, into feminist clichés. Whereas Hurston places her characters firmly within their moment and language, Walker whips around hers a vague tidewater transcendentalism. "But I don't know how to fight. All I know how to do is stay alive." Celie, like Janie, manages to escape from a grinding marriage, but whereas Janie follows her own principles, Celie ends up in a feminist paradise—drinking herb tea, making trousers at home for a living, waiting for Shug, and smoking a little "reefer" when she wants to feel the spirit.

The Color Purple is a didactic narrative, and as such it puts Walker closer to Harriet Beecher Stowe than to Hurston. Like Stowe's, Walker's work shows a world divided between the chosen (black women) and the unsaved, the "poor miserable critter" (black men), between the "furnace of affliction" and a "far-off, mystic land of . . . miraculous fertility." (pp. 17-18)

Many of *The Color Purple*'s themes are examined in her previous novels—the deep South, the black family, social change, the violence of black men toward black women. In *The Third Life of Grange Copeland,* in which the suffering of some of the wives is extreme, the violence is partly understood as frustration with the sharecropping system. In *Meridian,* which is set in the South during the civil rights movement, the martyrdom is more psychological. Physical and psychological suffering merge in *The Color Purple,* and the righteous—black women—are called upon to heal themselves and, by their example, their people. Celie does not turn to the church but to the temple of herself for salvation.

The sense of mission pervading *The Color Purple* comes from Walker's view of the black woman's history as a legacy of "creativity" that found expression only in such chores as gardening, cooking, quilt making. . . . It is debatable whether black women in history were wholly inarticulate or whether their condition was an utter mystery to them. Curiously enough, Walker's role as champion of the victims of the past places her in a position of cultural arrogance not unlike that of white missionaries to black Africa.

Walker has been hailed as a developer of the "womanist process," as an "apologist for black women," as a writer whose fiction "has called together a meeting of Black women" [see excerpt above by Bettye J. Parker-Smith].

Yet much of the appeal of *The Color Purple* does not lie in its text, but, through representing the black woman's experience in the popular feminist vocabulary, in its power as a symbol of the reconciliation between black women and white women in the feminist movement. . . . Alice Walker herself came of age during the debate in the Sixties over whether black women were the punching bags of black men. But Walker is so intent on investing drudgery with romantic properties that she loses sight of the fact that black women simply had to work. The black woman entered the lower professions faster than her white counterpart and this was crucial in a society that kept black men out of the labor force. Indeed the valor of the black woman lay in her history as a wage earner, in what Angela Davis once called "the deformed equality of equal oppression." . . .

That the civil rights movement was deteriorating while American feminism was rising had a strong effect on Afro-American literature. Black women writers seemed to find their voices and audiences, and black men seemed to lose theirs. Black women's concerns had earlier belonged to what was considered the private, rather than the public, as if the kitchen range could not adequately represent the struggle. But it turned out that the concerns of the kitchen were big enough to encompass the lore of struggle and survival. The black woman's story of family, community, so rich in gossip, language, and alive with the romance of discovery, was a welcomed departure from highly publicized apocalyptic writings, such as Cleaver's *Soul on Ice* (1967). Audiences were getting tired of black writers telling off whites. . . .

Ishmael Reed's most recent novel, *Reckless Eyeballing,* is in part a comic rebuttal to this work by black women since the Seventies, like Ntozake Shange's *For Colored Girls Who Considered Suicide When the Rainbow is Enuf* (1977), as well as Alice Walker's novels. These feminist works shared a mood in which black women began to question "myths," like whether freedom was to come first for the black man, or whether black women felt guilty because of the "emasculation" of the black male. (p. 18)

[Reed's novel is] very different from other fictions that approach the subject of sexuality and black life, works in the naturalistic tradition like Richard Wright's *Uncle Tom's Children* (1938), Chester Himes's *If He Hollers Let Him Go* (1945), or James Baldwin's *Another Country* (1962). In these books every psychological brutality could be described so long as it conformed to the sense that even as a fiction, it was part of a documentary truth that reached back to the slave narratives. It is this high ground that Alice Walker herself attempts to claim. But it must be said that she is playing a safe hand, given the acceptability of feminism and the historical conditioning that has the country afraid of black men. (p. 20)

Darryl Pinckney, "Black Victims, Black Villains," in The New York Review of Books, *Vol. XXXIV, No. 1, January 29, 1987, pp. 17-20.*

Dieter Wellershoff

1925-

German novelist, critic, dramatist, essayist, editor, and scriptwriter.

Wellershoff is credited with helping form the *Kölner Schule,* a group of influential West German writers who employ the methods of new realism to create works in the style of the *nouveau roman,* or antinovel. In his own fiction, Wellershoff abandons conventional forms of logic and order to better reflect reality, which he views as a continual series of risks. Wellershoff's novels typically deal with the alienation and aimlessness of humanity, and he often depicts characters whose lives are beginning to deteriorate. Although some critics fault him for confusing narratives, others praise Wellershoff for originality and insight.

Wellershoff's first novel, *Ein schöner Tag* (1969; *A Beautiful Day*), portrays a frustrated and emotionally exhausted family who halfheartedly attempt to change their lives. This work centers on the pervading sense of purposelessness and apathy of an aged father, his resentful spinster daughter, and his irresponsible son. *Die Schattengrenze* (1969) is an unorthodox crime thriller related from the subconscious of a pursued embezzler. The reader is swept into the criminal's paranoia and hallucinations, causing normal perceptions of time and space to become distorted. *Einladung an alle* (1972) recreates an actual manhunt for a notorious criminal who hid and lived in the woods of Germany. The novel, which according to one critic "occupies a territory somewhere between *In Cold Blood* and *Figures in a Landscape,*" is related from various perspectives, including those of the policeman in charge of the search and the hunted man himself. *Die Schönheit des Schimpansen* (1977) traces the life of protagonist Klaus Jung from the time he is expelled from college until he commits murder and suicide. Through extensive symbolism, Wellershoff explores the phases of progressive psychological disintegration caused by the stress of alienation. *Die Sirene* (1980) details a university professor's obsession with a female stranger from whom he receives mysterious telephone calls. *Der Sieger nimmt alles* (1983; *Winner Takes All*) relates how a man's passion for money and power leads to his demise. In this novel, Wellershoff focuses on the psyche of his protagonist while also providing commentary on present-day West Germany and the means and motivation behind the country's economic recovery following World War II.

In addition to his fiction, Wellershoff has won renown in Germany as a radio playwright. *Das Schreien der Katze im Sack* (1970) collects radio scripts written by Wellershoff over a ten-year period and displays his shift in approach from realism to the avant-garde, which is most apparent in his use of interior monologue and his experiments with sound. Wellershoff is also highly regarded for his works of literary criticism. In the essay collections *Literatur und Veränderung: Versuche zu einer Metakritik der Literatur* (1969) and *Literatur und Lustprinzip* (1973), he argues that literature provides an arena for repressed desires, maintaining that "true literature attacks and transforms habitual patterns of perception" and can thus be an instrument of change. He contends that literature must adopt the tactic of "irritation," disturbing a reader's expectations and being transformative rather

than normative. *Das Verschwinden im Bild: Essays* (1981) continues his discourse on literature, offering insight into creativity and the imagination. In *Die Arbeit des Lebens: Autobiographische Texte* (1985), Wellershoff relates portions of his life and conveys the spirit and essence of the post-World War II era in Germany through vignettes, tales, and essays.

(See also *Contemporary Authors,* Vols. 89-92 and *Contemporary Authors New Revision Series,* Vol 16.)

THE TIMES LITERARY SUPPLEMENT

Of late the pouring of ultra-new wine into old bottles labelled *Kriminalroman* has become a literary growth industry in Germany. This newly prestigious minor art form has now attracted Dieter Wellershoff's not inconsiderable talents, and the result is [*Die Schattengrenze*], an intriguing, though only intermittently satisfactory, essay in offbeat writing.

The shadowy frontier of the title denotes both the Federal border the novel's embezzler hero desperately hopes to cross, and the fracture-line of his mind from the dark side of which all events are viewed. The latter device, though effective, is full of pitfalls: on the analogy of playwrights whose characters' sense of ennui only produces boredom beyond the footlights. Herr Wellershoff's attempts at communicating vertigo often come perilously close to giving the reader migraine.

This is not simply a matter of unrelieved recourse to a swaying and downward spiralling "camera eye"; having devised the novel as a superior jigsaw puzzle—or, to quote the blurb, "having simultaneously adopted and burst through the pattern of the crime story seen from the perspective of the hunted man"—the author makes us work gratuitously hard at attaching sequential meaning to haphazardly arranged fragments of narrative.

Those who stay the course, however . . . , will be rewarded by intermittent felicities which compensate for the effort involved: a mordant deadpan reportage on *Wirtschaftswunder* promotion; descriptions of coitus as a drowning individual's clutching at society; motorway landscapes glimpsed from within a car in circuitous, aimless flight, and quite a few more. And yet, at the end of this infold-method whodunit, one cannot help asking why he did it.

> *"Whydunit," in* The Times Literary Supplement, *No. 3511, June 12, 1969, p. 643.*

ROBERT J. CLEMENTS

[*Die Schattengrenze*] is a crime thriller related directly from the subconscious of the pursued criminal, who committed his deed under the pressures of his environment. From the first pages, where he lies about his whereabouts, he confuses hallucination with reality. Throughout the novel he moves in the shadowy, diffuse border between the everyday world and nightmare. The reader is absorbed into the consciousness of the protagonist and swept into the latter's paranoia; normal time and space disappear, transitions take place imperceptibly. As with his earlier *Ein schöner Tag,* Wellershoff is winning praise for the originality and consistency of his narrative.

> *Robert J. Clements, in a review of "Die Schattengrenze," in* Saturday Review, *Vol. LII, No. 7, July 5, 1969, p. 29.*

HANS-BERNHARD MOELLER

Not content with the role of godfather to the "Kölner Schule" group, Wellershoff fathers his own "new novels." *Die Shattengrenze* constitutes his *Dans le labyrinthe* (Robbe-Grillet). The maze through which Wellershoff's protagonist passes is patterned by paranoia. He feels persecuted by an interested barkeeper, guests at a party, his female companion, and his partners in car theft. Presented in the descriptive and flat or surface-directed, nonchronological and repetitive composition of the "new novel," *Die Schattengrenze* ignores its potential to offer insight into the heart and soul of an obsessed person. Even sympathizers of the nouveau roman who are accustomed to absence of characterization, of symbols, and of edification, would find this outside view of a private pathology episodic and monotonous. Wellershoff fails to achieve the skill and the milieu of *Ein schöner Tag,* his previous new-novel view of a neurotic family which, at times, approached the power of Sartre's *No Exit.*

> *Hans-Bernhard Moeller, in a review of "Die Schattengrenze," in* Books Abroad, *Vol. 44, No. 2, Spring, 1970, p. 306.*

THE TIMES LITERARY SUPPLEMENT

[Insight] into the Federal Republic's literary scene is afforded by *Literatur und Veränderung,* a wide-ranging selection of occasional essays and review-articles by the novelist and dramatist, Dieter Wellershoff. . . . Explicitly declining to regard literature purely as sociological material or, on the other hand, as an autonomous "Sache für sich", he sees it rather as a necessary source of vicarious experience and imaginative stimulation. Both writer and reader are compared to an astronaut undergoing simulation exercises, extending awareness without risk. The "transformation" envisaged by Herr Wellershoff encompasses the ways in which the act of reading encourages us to re-inspect habitual responses and attitudes, increases the scope of the imagination, and opens up new avenues of human communication. These sentiments have often been expressed, of course, but . . . there is every need for Herr Wellershoff's declaration of faith.

Literatur und Veränderung does not ignore the commerical aspects of the cultural scene. . . . We are even initiated into the realm of the ubiquitous *Hefte,* available at every German newspaper kiosk, by an instructive and amusing analysis of a "Kelter Arzt-Roman". Here, as elsewhere in the selection, the author shows an awareness of the interplay of literary and social factors, and a humane concern with the world in which readers live. The intellectual vitality of his essays may result, not least, from a knowledge that he is arguing from strength: the "culture industry" of the Federal Republic, with its omnivorous demand for printed and broadcast "material", may need watching . . . ; but it is, at its best, an impressive phenomenon, and Dieter Wellershoff's stimulating book is, indeed, its progeny.

> *"Towards a Wordless Inwardness," in* The Times Literary Supplement, *No. 3577, September 18, 1970, p. 1044.*

MARILYN GELL

It is fashionable these days for German writers to produce works dealing with the alienation and aimlessness of man. Some do this quite well. Heinrich Böll, for instance, is a master of the genre. Wellershoff is not. The three main characters of [*A Beautiful Day*], Carla, Gunther, and their father, are in fact indistinguishable. And "aimlessness" here applies not only to the characters but to the novel itself. There is no real action, no real progress. While this is undoubtedly the point, it leaves the reader with a distinct feeling of frustration, as if he had been trying to construct a puzzle with only half the pieces.

> *Marilyn Gell, in a review of "A Beautiful Day," in* Library Journal, *Vol. 96, No. 18, October 15, 1971, p. 3347.*

PUBLISHERS WEEKLY

[In *A Beautiful Day*] Lorenz, retired naval officer, lives with his spinster schoolteacher daughter, Carla, in Cologne. His life is purposeless, given to drifting in and out of the aimless dreams of the old to the simplest tasks of everyday living. But now there are two out-of-the-ordinary topics to occupy his thoughts, the "Beautiful Day," his own 71st birthday, and his son Gunther's mission to try to recover some of his pre-war money. His son and daughter as well are engaged in the usual apathy of hopeless dreams, and preoccupations with the symbols and mechanics of living. Alienated not so much from others as from life itself, they are sapped of vitality, intellect, emotion. The portrait of two spent generations is moving in its very hopelessness, an ironic and gently haunting novel that probes at the desensitizing qualities of human experience.

A review of "A Beautiful Day," in Publishers Weekly, *Vol. 200, No. 17, October 25, 1971, p. 48.*

THE TIMES LITERARY SUPPLEMENT

The ten years spanned by Dieter Wellershoff's *Das Schreien der Katze im Sack* mark the period which saw major changes in the techniques of *Hörspiel* writing. And although even in his more recent work Wellershoff could scarcely be judged a leading member of the radio's avant-garde, the six plays published in this collection do reveal certain typical shifts in approach. The early pieces have a largely realistic quality. Voices form either interior monologues or constitute the utterances of real characters in a plausible setting. For example, *Der Minotaurus* (1960) neatly contrasts the reflections of a young man and his mistress on the abortion he is forcing her to undergo on the day in question. In his version of things, the doctor is a kind of Minotaur; in her view, the man is.

In Dieter Wellershoff's other radio plays, interior monologues invariably become more confused, giving way to a collection of blurred flashbacks and partially remembered phrases. The past may be a string of leitmotivs and haunting judgments, as it is for the senescent university professor in *Die Schatten*. To the teacher in *Bau einer Laube* it can become a series of verbal indictments, prodding him with memories of an unsuccessful marriage and a mediocre career in a texture of near-paranoia, for which he tries to compensate by labouring away at the intricacies of his fretwork. In the nightclub setting of *Am ungenauen Ort,* sound forms a generally impressionistic medium, as we spend an evening on the town with Viktor and Balduin and experience, through the hostesses' perspective, the interchangeability of all pleasure-seeking visitors to this tinsel nighttown. . . .

The two more recent plays in Wellershoff's collection—*Wünsche* (1969) and *Das Schreien der Katze im Sack* (1970)—depart noticeably from these familiar paths. First of all, they are stereophonic. However, they do not employ this more differentiated sound-system merely to generate a greater sense of aural three-dimensionality. On the contrary, stereophonic permutations are allowed to increase the plasticity of the works' verbal collages and make them, as a result, even more non-referential. In *Wünsche,* a disturbed sexual murderer is haunted by his past. Schizophrenia has a stereometric quality, which can be well portrayed by the use of two independent loudspeakers, splitting the main figure into an active and an analytic self. Hence space can become a symbolic dimension. (p. 1485)

"The New Radio Play," in The Times Literary Supplement, *No. 3639, November 26, 1971, pp. 1485-86.*

JOSEPHINE HENDIN

In Dieter Wellershoff's *A Beautiful Day* a family is glued together in need and irritability, stuck on the fact that no day can be beautiful and forced to see how frustration turns everything into slush. . . . [At] its best Wellershoff's novel is the prose song of a father and daughter who miserably endure.

Old man Lorenz, who spent his prime supported by his energetic wife, now spends his old age cared for by his young but spinsterish daughter Carla, who cannot bring herself to get rid of him. . . .

[Lorenz] is one of those wretches for whom nothing is ever enough. Nothing could be except the realization of this fantasy: he and Carla "would get stuck to each other," and would somehow have their ribs meshed so that "only by coughing would be he able to dislodge them."

Wellershoff's sense of the phlegminess of family bonds, of the nauseating stickiness of human needs runs through the novel. Even when Carla rebels, running away for a vacation alone, she cannot escape it. For life away and outside is only a more forlorn despair than the one at home, where her dusted tables and thickly buttered breakfast bread are at least the marks of satisfaction.

Passivity lies over everyone like a pall; emptiness stretches everywhere. Wellershoff's novel has the heavy beauty of that mindless dreariness where there is no sun, no energy and no hope, but where everyone blindly jogs on.

Josephine Hendin, in a review of "A Beautiful Day," in The New York Times Book Review, *April 2, 1972, p. 6.*

THE TIMES LITERARY SUPPLEMENT

The basis for Dieter Wellershoff's latest novel [*Einladung an alle*] is a manhunt which took place in the Osnabrück region of Germany some years ago. The "man from the woods", as he was called, managed to create mass hysteria in a large section of the public, and we witness some of the mechanics of this process here. The "invitation to everyone" of the title might be thought of as an invitation to join in the hunt: both physically and in spirit. Wellershoff brings out the discrepancy between the popular press's image of this near-ubiquitous bogeyman and the actual hounded human being, largely indulging in little more than breaking-and-entry in order to keep alive. Within ten chapters we enter the minds of a number of people involved in the gigantic, extended search operation, including the prey himself, the detective in charge of the whole exercise and a zealous policeman shot in the performance of his duties. Almost everyone in the novel is depicted understandingly, with a humanity which stands in direct contrast to the mass media's savagery and the frenzy of the hunt.

Einladung an alle occupies a territory somewhere between *In Cold Blood* and *Figures in a Landscape.* On the other hand, it documents its story convincingly. However, the factual material is by no means paraded self-consciously; it is in fact the sensitivity with which Wellershoff describes the region that really gives the novel its sense of realism. On the other hand, the paraphernalia of a documentary (specific dates and locations, quotations and behind-the-scenes perspectives), the detailed character portrayal and even the vividness of the setting are subordinated to a more general concern with society. Both hunter and hunted are depicted as victims. For some the manhunt is society's quest for a scapegoat, an old battle distorted afresh by the tabloids; for others it becomes part of a professional rat-race. There are even Rousseauistic overtones to the "man from the woods", for all the blackness with which the popular imagination is encouraged to picture him.

If all this makes *Einladung an alle* sound like the kind of amalgam of *Kriminalroman* and existential novel which Peter Handke achieves in *Die Angst des Tormanns beim Elfmeter* and which Wellershoff himself gestured towards in his earlier novel, *Die Schattengrenze,* it should be noted that this new work is more a novel of kaleidoscopic effects, of sudden and even deliberately crude contrasts. Genres are mixed but not merged. . . .

Within this spectrum of varieties of realism, contrasting various attitudes and perspectives, Wellershoff can even be found indulging in a rather experimental permutational technique at some points to capture the rambling quality of the hunted figure's thought processes. Yet *Einladung an alle* avoids the stereotypes and commonplaces of both the documentary and the mentally unbalanced "outsider" novel, although it gathers much of its momentum from both of these modes. In essence, it is a work written with great sympathy both for the landscape and the sad figures who move across it.

> *"Whom the Papers Slay," in* The Times Literary Supplement, *No. 3690, November 24, 1972, p. 1415.*

THE TIMES LITERARY SUPPLEMENT

A baby cries: the origin of language. It sucks its thumb: the origin of socialization, conditioning, and culture. The reality principle increasingly gains control, while the pleasure principle is driven back into phantasy and sublimated through culture. Wellershoff sees literature as the realm of the pleasure principle, affording us an arena for our repressed desires; moreover, he maintains [in *Literatur und Lustprinzip*] "true literature attacks and transforms habitual patterns of perception". It can thus be subversive; an instrument of change: like a daydream, it tests out alternatives.

Wellershoff now enlarges on this thesis in his latest collection of essays, *Literatur und Lustprinzip.* As the title suggests, he has called up the heavy artillery of Marcuse's critique of Freud in *Eros and Civilization* to support his argument that the task of literature is to emancipate consciousness:

> We are constantly confined by the pressures of conformity and the routines of social behaviour which canalize our instincts; thus there is embedded in every manifestation of human life a residue of unrealized possibilities, which strive towards an alternative means of realization through phantasy.

As Marcuse has shown, our society has developed the capacity to assimilate and emasculate criticism. But he has also denied Freud's assertion that the imagination, the "constitutive mental faculty" of art, has retained its freedom from the reality principle at the cost of being ineffective in reality.

For Wellershoff, then, the role of literature is vital: to act as "a proving-ground for the intellectual and social flexibility essential to a modern society". To do this, it must adopt the tactic of "irritation": by disturbing our expectations, by being transformative rather than normative. Perhaps unexpectedly, Russian Formalism—with its concept of *ostraneniye,* making the familiar strange—is here enlisted to uphold the social validity of literature, together with a dose of information theory and anti-authoritarian sociology. Parallels, are also drawn with schizophrenia and drug-experiences as extensions of consciousness: literature reverses the process by which our perceptions become atrophied and we lose "information".

To activate our slumbering phantasy and intensify our awareness, literature must be spiced with uncertainty and formal complexity; and it must be in a state of perpetual self-renewal

to continue to excite our jaded sensibilities. Wellershoff shows this in its crudest form where he contrasts romantic and pornographic fiction: the former asserts the reality principle (happy ending, marriage and conformity), the latter claims to assert the pleasure principle (the Reichian Arcadia). But he dismisses pornography as a mere "illusion of liberation", and detects the spectre of sublimation in its patterns of manic repetition and multiple orgasm: instinct is sacrificed to "geometry". More valid is Surrealist automatic writing, an attempt at plugging straight into the unconscious, which Wellershoff sees as the forerunner of other techniques of subverting norms, such as montage and computer poetry—which, he maintains, shows a striking similarity to the writings of the mentally disturbed.

Consistent with current interest in "trivial literature", the central piece in *Literatur und Lustprinzip* is a long essay on the detective novel. Wellershoff analyses the development of the genre from Poe to Patricia Highsmith and traces a gradual shift of emphasis away from the detective and the rational reconstruction of the crime towards a study of criminal motivation. But the traditional—as opposed to the psychological—thriller here merely serves as a foil to what is presented as the model for progressive literature: the *nouveau roman.* While the former is, in the end, merely a normative jigsaw-puzzle, with all the pieces provided, the latter is a hypothetical *recherche,* forcing us to rethink all our certainties, without the guarantee that any clear picture will emerge.

It is striking that Wellershoff generally goes abroad to find examples of the kind of writing he favours. One would expect him to be sympathetic towards Thomas Bernhard, for instance. But on the whole he finds little comfort in the contemporary German scene, which he sees as polarized between political/documentary writing and the white-coated linguistic technicians, whose verbal experiments, he feels, have already become institutionalized. . . .

What standpoint should the writer adopt? After calling a wide range of modish witnesses (from Shklovsky to R. D. Laing) in his case for avant-garde writing, Wellershoff eventually reverses into a decidedly old-fashioned position: subjectivity. . . . [For] Wellershoff—presumably because he is himself a novelist—[subjectivity] is an article of faith. He sees subjectivity not as restriction but as resistance: a schematized picture of reality is corrected and concretized through the writer's individual perception. Hidden impulses, the creative tension between reality and possibility, underlie the act of writing.

Literatur und Lustprinzip is a vigorous defence of the "erotic, utopian elan" of literature against those whose "social guilt", in Wellershoff's view, forces them to proclaim it dead, thereby merely reaffirming that the reality principle is still the dominant ideology. It also contains much stimulating discussion of individual texts. But, ironically, the practice of concocting a "book" out of occasional pieces mirrors the literary techniques that Wellershoff champions: the reader is expected to reconstruct—in this case an argument—out of a pile of disparate material, with overlaps and omissions. Perhaps here too "irritation" is the intention?

> *"The Ideology of Irritation," in* The Times Literary Supplement, *No. 3769, May 31, 1974, p. 582.*

ERNESTINE SCHLANT

The title of Dieter Wellershoff's latest novel [*Die Schönheit des Schimpansen*] refers to the statue of a black chimpanzee.

The chimpanzee is carved in a crouching position staring with fascination but without comprehension at a skull he holds in his hands. Klaus Jung, the protagonist of the novel, acquires the statue at a tourist resort. The event is narrated at the very center of the novel. It radiates its significance retrospectively into the first two parts of the novel and dominates the remaining two parts. The statue is also connected with carefully placed references throughout the novel to the *Tibetan Book of the Dead* and its message that even death is fraught with terror and only nothingness offers true release from suffering.

The novel traces Jung's psycho-history from the time he is dismissed from the university for cheating on an exam paper . . . until he commits suicide in his car by inhaling carbon monoxide. This history concentrates on two phases: in the first phase, following his debacle at the university, he joins a group of peddlers, selling newspaper subscriptions in the satellite cities of industrial areas. Ellen, the boss's girl friend, arranges for their flight. She takes Jung on an extended vacation to the Canary Islands, yet they cannot find a workable relationship. Jung is lost in the absentmindedness typical of psychological repression; Ellen is demanding and disappointed and, from Jung's tense perspective, probably unfaithful. In the second phase, many years later, Jung again travels, this time for a company leasing automats, collecting their revenues. He lives with Ellen in an unhappy, pointless marriage. He decides on a weekend rendezvous with a woman he met by chance and kills her in a most brutal manner. After he has erased all traces of his presence and has left town, Jung commits suicide.

As in his earlier novels, Wellershoff explores stress situations of alienation and phases of progressive disintegration. Yet it is hard to believe that he suggests, seriously, murder as the individual's release from unbearable pressure and suicide as the road to nothingness.

The novel is carefully structured, the symbolic levels are well in evidence, the craftsmanship is immaculate. In perspective as well as subject matter, the novel covers territory that has long been explored by French existentialism and its aftermath, the *nouveau roman* (notably as practiced by Alain Robbe-Grillet and his early adept Peter Handke of *Die Hornissen, Die Hausierer* and *Die Angst des Tormanns beim Elfmeter*). *Die Schönheit des Schimpansen* is, in every sense of the word, a perfect example of epigonic literature.

> *Ernestine Schlant, in a review of "Die Schönheit des Schimpansen," in* World Literature Today, *Vol. 53, No. 1, Winter, 1979, p. 107.*

REINHOLD GRIMM

[It seems to me that Dieter Wellershoff . . . ought to receive more attention in this country. I firmly believe his ideas would appeal to an American public. Wellershoff is unique—and perhaps not only among his compatriots—in that he has produced at least as many works of criticism as of fiction; and though he may not be the greatest of contemporary German novelists, he must surely be hailed as one of the finest and most consistent as well as most stimulating essayists now writing in that language. His restless search encompasses the whole gamut from *Literatur und Veränderung* (*Literature and Change;* 1969) to *Literatur und Lustprinzip* (*Literature and the Pleasure Principle;* 1973); but however far his critical pointer tends to move on the sliding scale of life, he remains safely grounded in his literary experience, both active and passive.

With undiminished acumen and steadfastness, and yet not without grace and serenity, Wellershoff once again offers testimony, in these two new collections [*Das Verschwinden im Bild: Essays* and *Die Wahrheit der Literatur: Sieben Gespräche*], of his range as well as depth as a critic. The seven interviews contained in the . . . [latter] volume are somewhat less weighty, it is true; but this is almost inevitably the case with such "conversations." All the more important, however, are the ten sizable essays assembled under the heading *Das Verschwinden im Bild,* in itself an enigmatic and ambiguous image. The wealth of Wellershoff's insights and suggestions, even in some of those casual talks, can hardly be hinted at in a couple of paragraphs; suffice it to say that his basic concern is always how to intensify and expand—through irritation and, if need be, downright transgression—both his and our subjective sensibilities. Exploring, on the one hand, the creative (and crazy) adventures of the mind and, on the other, wisely exploiting not just traditional genres but the mass media as well, Wellershoff constantly seeks to revive and refine our imagination, to strengthen and broaden the psychic and sensitive realm of what he claims are the boundless possibilities of modern man which are but oppressed and suppressed yet can and must be restored.

Each and every one of his pieces is, in varying manner and degree, centered upon this fundamental problem. Thus one might well call him, drawing on a recent verdict pronounced by Walter Hinderer, an untiring knight-errant, though not so much of "the psyche" alone, but rather of human (and humane) life as such—life, that is, as revealed by, and enjoyed through, the catalyst and simulator of literature.

> *Reinhold Grimm, in a review of "Das Verschwinden im Bild: Essays" and "Die Wahrheit der Literatur: Sieben Gespräche," in* World Literature Today, *Vol. 55, No. 3, Summer, 1981, p. 467.*

S. BAUSCHINGER

Although *Die Sirene,* characterized by its publisher as "the story of an unusual seduction," has indeed an interesting plot and is written in concise language following the classic structure of the *Novelle*, it leaves the reader with a certain feeling of dissatisfaction. Elsheimer, professor of pedagogy, director of an institute, member of important scholarly associations and well-known participant in many TV panels, receives a telephone call from a woman, a total stranger in some sort of personal distress. She immediately begins to occupy his mind more and more. She lives in another city and he tries to see her, but she eludes him, nevertheless continuing her calls. After a last attempt to see the woman, Elsheimer, who has become addicted to her seducing calls and phones her back constantly, does exactly what she tells him to do in her final rejection, which leads to his final humiliation: he goes to a brothel, and the reader might assume that this action at last frees him from the alluring calls of his siren.

Although the woman at least pretends to be in need of psychiatric help, Elsheimer offers remarkably little in the way of analysis. To the contrary, we read about his dreams, and in the course of the narrative the roles of would-be analyst and analyzed are reversed. The caller becomes more and more a therapist questioning the patient relentlessly. Elsheimer, whose deterioration is convincingly described—his relationship to his wife changes, he cannot concentrate any longer on his work, even his appearance changes—is the patient, the victim. The reader, however, never understands why the professor, who is so magically attracted to the mysterious caller, never makes an attempt really to go and see her when he is in Hamburg, which occurs twice. He does have her address. Could it be that, in the end, he is as afraid of her as he is attracted by her? That would be an explanation, but the text does not give enough evidence for such an assumption.

S. Bauschinger, in a review of "Die Sirene," in World Literature Today, *Vol. 55, No. 3, Summer, 1981, p. 471.*

W. V. BLOMSTER

The family whose decline is told in this verbose novel [*Der Sieger nimmt alles*] began as modest producers of condensed milk. One wishes that Wellershoff had condensed his account of their woe as well. The publisher pretentiously suggests that the book introduces a theme hardly considered in German literature: the interweaving of economics and individual existence. Yet the novel often seems a recycled *Buddenbrooks,* complete with a Hanno-gone-delinquent and a still more drunken Christian; at some moments it harks back to the autumnal bleakness of Keyserling's *Abendliche Häuser.* Only decadent detours through today's "dolce vita" document modernity.

The book opens with the despondent death of its nonheroic central figure and then traces his course of self-destruction through the two decades which precede it. The events of this detailed dance around Germany's golden calf are painfully predictable. The integrity of the work lies in this panorama of a family and its enterprise. Indeed, their misery is without the dignity of conscious suffering; they are without pathos and unworthy of discussion from the standpoint of tragedy.

The account of their existence is delivered with the same numbness which disfigures the lives of those who participate in it. The weakness of the book is the absence of an analytic narrator, without whom the critical condemnation of a senseless world ricochets through its many pages without firm impact upon a target. Only in the epilogue is a voice in the first person heard. "I consider the future black," it says. This, at the end of a work of such interminable gloom, is easily the literary understatement of the decade.

W. V. Blomster, in a review of "Der Sieger nimmt alles," in World Literature Today, *Vol. 58, No. 1, Winter, 1984, p. 102.*

REINHOLD GRIMM

An author about to turn sixty may be said to have reached the proper age for autobiographies; yet that which Wellershoff has produced [*Die Arbeit des Lebens: Autobiographische Texte*] is doubtless not an autobiography proper. Its subtitle indicates at the outset that what we are faced with are merely "autobiographical texts." Unlike the classical autobiographer, Wellershoff does not tell the whole story of his life as it gradually unfolds, but instead relates a selection of isolated, though surely not disconnected, portions from it; quite like the former, however, he tries to capture the entire span and spirit of his era as reflected in his own personal growth and development. Furthermore, we learn almost as much about the lives of his parents and family as we learn about him. All of which is to say that [this volume] constitutes a mixture of autobiography, history, and biography, and thus yet another specimen of that hybrid genre which has flourished in German letters over the past

decade and a half and which can be defined as a complex *Lebensdarstellung* in the broadest—and loosest—sense imaginable. . . .

Wellershoff did not aim at creating any narrative unity; rather, he has combined and even blended descriptive and discursive pieces ranging from anecdotal vignettes to full-fledged tales or essays. Nevertheless, there does obtain in his fragmentary work an overall unity. It manifests itself of two thematic levels. The first concerns the ambiguity of meaningfulness in human existence—i.e., the tensions between the superfetation of meaning (*Sinn* as "das stärkste Rauschmittel") and the total lack or loss thereof (*Sinnverlust*). The second refers to the task of the writer and, specifically, autobiographer—i.e., the revolving, indeed revolutionizing, labor of the human mind ("innere Umwälzungsarbeit") necessary to transmute experiences into recollections and recollections into new concepts and ideas. Together, they form the core of Wellershoff's *Arbeit des Lebens,* on the pages of his book as in his real life.

Apart from such generic and general characteristics, mention should be made of the wealth of factual information offered in this multifaceted volume. Not only does it contain a fascinating report on the chaotic last days of World War II, but it also includes a relentless account of the fate of Germany and of Europe at large. Once again Wellershoff has demonstrated his keen awareness of the problems of our modern world, as well as the remarkable degree to which he masters modern German prose.

Reinhold Grimm, in a review of "Die Arbeit des Lebens: Autobiographische Texte," in World Literature Today, *Vol. 59, No. 4, Autumn, 1985, p. 591.*

KIRKUS REVIEWS

[In *Winner Takes All,* a] leading exponent of the German "new realism" school relates in microscopic detail the rise and fall of a cad. . . . This unrelentingly grim novel was a giant bestseller in Germany three years ago.

At age 27, failed medical student Ulrich Vogtmann attends a lecture on finance that turns him inside-out; he leaves believing that money is "the most brilliant creation of the human mind." Determined to amass as much of the magical stuff as possible, he hires on at a canned-goods factory, where he is quickly noticed by the owner, Hermann Pattberg, and promoted to chauffeur and confidant. Vogtmann also catches the eye of Pattberg's bookish daughter, Elisabeth, whom he pledges to wed the very night his old girlfriend, Jovanka, undergoes an abortion. This callous treatment of Jovanka seals his fate; henceforth he is trapped in an upwardly-mobile spiral of cunning deals and broken relations. In his race to the top, Vogtmann runs rampant over his wife, his mistress, his brother-in-law (who kills himself with a shotgun), and his son, Christophe (who turns to kleptomania to blot out his father's obsession with money). Finally, though, Vogtmann's unprincipled ways catch up with him. Called on loans he can't cover, he is fired and deserted by an enraged Elisabeth. Without income or home, he can no longer hold on to mistress or friends. A heart attack ends his sour, sorry life.

Wellershoff writes like a scientist studying alien phenomena, objectively but without compassion. As an exercise in physical and psychological observation, this novel excels; but it neglects to engage the heart, and so, for most readers, will fail both as story and as art.

A review of "Winner Takes All," in Kirkus Reviews, Vol. LIV, No. 16, August 15, 1986, p. 1248.

BOYD TONKIN

A few years back, when streetwise critics picked up a taste for high theory and low cunning, the worst insult you could throw at some plausible piece of fiction was to call it a '19th-century novel'. Dieter Wellershoff's *Winner Takes All* would no doubt fall under this dread rubric. If so, come back Victorian values: all (well, quite a bit) is forgiven.

Despite the bright light of detail it casts over West German society, from the Economic Miracle to the Red Army Fraction, the scope and structure of *Winner Takes All* bring to mind the tragic realism of an earlier age. For Wellershoff takes as his subject the crossroads where capitalism and private life meet. This unholy junction turns out to be a place of sharpened stakes, shallow graves and howling spirits.

During the first rumbles of Germany's post-war boom, a drifting student, Ulrich Vogtmann, catches the boss's eye in the course of his menial job in a condensed milk factory. Quickly he discovers the poetry of money and the art of acquisition: 'Money dissolved everything that appeared solid into movement . . . It was the universal machine that set all other machines in motion.' Like any rising young man from a high bourgeois epic, Ulrich marries his employer's daughter. The patriarch Pattberg remains at root a rich peasant, while Ulrich pushes his food business into the era of posh delis and sprawling hypermarkets. As ambition, love and politics entwine he fights the *angst* that afflicts new capital indebted to old land: 'He was still the man without property, the man who had married into wealth, who had brought in nothing but himself.'

Sliding between wife and mistress down the endless pine-fringed *autobahnen*, Ulrich watches Germany change and its youth— including his shoplifting son—turn against their parents' hollowness. Clutching at everything, he can hold on to nothing.

Nemesis, when it arrives, is fast and squalid. Ulrich overreaches himself in a crooked scam, trying to sell insecticidal capsules to war-torn Zaire. For the second time in modern fiction, European traders project into that region the heart of darkness that lies within themselves. *Winner Takes All* starts and finishes in a scene of fluorescent horror worthy of Fassbinder. Now a bankrupt cadger, Ulrich dies in anguish at a hotel that comes to represent the gleaming new Germany in all its shiftiness and ostentation. Like his country's repressed memories, the corpse is hustled out of sight down the emergency stairs.

Any callow radical can launch a critique of possessive individualism from a safe moral distance; too many still do. But Wellershoff's writing never delivers a judgment where it can dramatise a contradiction. He explores the self-estrangement at the core of the entrepreneurial ethic. Ever eager to fix the future and cancel the past, Ulrich fails to build a home in the present. Few recent novels have grasped as well as *Winner Takes All* the ambiguous pleasure of accumulation: the half-erotic, half-aesthetic thrill that drives Ulrich to clinch his deals.

We need fiction of this quality to unravel the ties that bind passion to profit. . . . (pp. 34-5)

Boyd Tonkin, "Ghost Writers," in New Statesman, Vol. 112, No. 2896, September 26, 1986, pp. 34-5.

MAUREEN FREELY

Dieter Wellershoff's *Winner Takes All* (described as a modern classic that 'took Europe by storm') is about a grim, alienated, empty-hearted and venal young man who marries into a prosperous provincial family. The story is exceedingly dull until the arrival of the devil, about a third of the way into the book, in the form of an international financier.

With Ulrich Vogtmann's descent from the purgatory of middle-aged prosperity into the hell of venture capitalism, the book becomes a masterpiece of *Schadenfreude*. Rarely have the illusory promises of wealth appeared more tantalising. It is not so much an exposé of the capitalist machine as a celebration of its seductive attractions, its power and its contradictions, and as such could be described as the thinking man's 'Red Wedge.'

Maureen Freely, "New Worlds for Old," in The Observer, October 12, 1986, p. 29.

JOHN BROOKS

[In *Winner Takes All*], we spend a lot of time with Vogtmann in hotel rooms, on superhighways in his silver-gray Mercedes and at business and business-social meetings. Many weather fronts pass over West Germany, and the storms they bring are duly recorded. Where American novels of business are apt to glitter with ingenious technical detail but are weak on character and description, this one focuses on the true material of fiction, and properly keeps information on commercial method in the background.

The reader ends with the feeling of having been with Vogtmann, perhaps even of having been Vogtmann, for a time. But the feeling is depressing. One is reminded not, as the publisher hopes, of Thomas Mann's *Buddenbrooks,* but rather of Zola. Mr. Wellershoff . . . offers effective descriptions of furniture and mood and squalor (in this case the squalor not of poverty but of affluence), as well as rather heavy-handed symbolism: Vogtmann, who literally deformed his feet by wearing too-tight shoes in his youth, has deformed his adult soul by making a god of money. But, in literary art if not in life, Zola's time has gone, and the poetry even Zola managed is missing here.

Sociologically, this is surely the dark side of Germany's economic miracle: while West Germany rose with Western aid from the ashes of war to world leadership, greedy, empty men were destroying themselves and all they touched, there as elsewhere. The fact that *Winner Takes All* was a best seller in West Germany suggests that Vogtmann's story has a contemporary resonance in that country.

John Brooks, "The Silver-Gray Soul of Ulrich Vogtmann," in The New York Times Book Review, January 4, 1987, p. 20.

Anzia Yezierska

1885?-1970

Russian-born novelist, short story writer, essayist, and critic.

Yezierska's novels and short stories, published mostly during the 1920s and 1930s, chronicle the early twentieth-century Jewish immigrant experience in the United States. Her protagonists search for the "American Dream" while contending with a new and sometimes hostile environment. The struggle of Jewish women to liberate themselves from the restrictions of their orthodox religion and old-world traditions is an important element in much of Yezierska's work. Although her characters are often disillusioned in their quest for material success and cultural assimilation, they usually find contentment by combining values from both worlds. Critics generally praised Yezierska's unpolished, effusive prose style and her use of colloquialisms to capture the essence of life in the tenements of New York City's Lower East Side at the turn of the century.

Most of Yezierska's fiction is extracted from episodes in her own life. She was born in Plinsk, near the Russia-Poland border, and immigrated to the United States with her family in the 1890s. In America, she performed menial labor during the day and attended night school to learn English; she eventually earned a degree in domestic science from Columbia Teachers College. The young women in Yezierska's works share many of her experiences, while the male characters are usually modeled after two men who played important roles in her life: her father, a respected Talmudic scholar who expected his wife and daughters to support him financially, and the American educator and philosopher, John Dewey, who encouraged her literary pursuits. Yezierska and Dewey became romantically involved when she audited his class in social and political thought at Columbia University. Their relationship, treated fictionally in several of her works, is most fully documented in the novel *All I Could Never Be* (1932).

Yezierska's first published story, "Free Vacation House," appeared in *Forum* magazine in December 1915. This work portrays an immigrant family's pride in their impoverished but honest lifestyle and the insensitivity and condescending attitudes of social workers who offer them assistance. Another early story, "The Fat of the Land," was included in Edward J. O'Brien's anthology *Best Short Stories of 1919*. In this piece, the lonely, affluent elderly protagonist longs for the vitality of her earlier life in the East Side ghetto. The paradox of attaining a better lifestyle but feeling separated from one's heritage recurs throughout Yezierska's fiction. In her autobiographical novel *Red Ribbon on a White Horse* (1950), Yezierska acknowledges having similiar emotions after the publication of her first book, the short story collection *Hungry Hearts* (1920). Film producer Samuel Goldwyn purchased the movie rights to *Hungry Hearts* and offered Yezierska a position as a scriptwriter in Hollywood. Although she became a celebrity, Yezierska realized that she could not write so far removed from the Lower East Side environment, and she returned to New York City in 1921.

Yezierska's first novel, *Salome of the Tenements* (1923), introduces her recurring motif of ill-fated relationships between poor, passionate young immigrant women and wealthy, emo-

tionally reserved American males. In this work, Sonya Vrunsky manipulates others in her determination to marry philanthropist John Manning. She remains unsatisfied after experiencing his lifestyle, however, and eventually finds fulfillment in fashion design and in marriage to an immigrant. Many of the pieces in Yezierska's second short story collection, *Children of Loneliness* (1923), again focus upon insensitive, inept charity workers who attempt to aid impoverished ghetto families. Her next book, *Bread Givers* (1925), is considered Yezierska's most accomplished work and most closely parallels her own struggle for independence. This novel follows Sara Smolinsky's efforts to free herself from her father's restrictive religious dictums and make a place for herself in America. Sara eventually learns to accept and incorporate old-world values into her life as an American. One reviewer lauded *Bread Givers* for its "raw, uncontrollable poetry and . . . powerful, sweeping design."

Yezierska's subsequent novels, *Arrogant Beggar* (1926) and *All I Could Never Be*, were not as well-received as her previous works. Critics noted her lack of stylistic experimentation and the similarities of plot and characterization between these books and her earlier fiction. Following the Depression, Yezierska was unable to find a publisher, and she joined the Federal Arts Project, a branch of the Work Projects Administration, to earn a living. She alters details of these and earlier years in her last work, *Red Ribbon on a White Horse*, to satisfy her literary objective of presenting in microcosm the experiences of the Jewish immigrants she had known.

In the late 1950s and 1960s, Yezierska served as an occasional book reviewer for the *New York Times*. She also published several stories concerning the problems of America's senior citizens and the new immigrants from Puerto Rico. Several of these and earlier pieces appear in *The Open Cage: An Anzia Yezierska Collection* (1979). Although Yezierska lived in obscurity for the last twenty years of her life, contemporary literary scholars have acknowledged her importance as one of the first writers to present the Jewish immigrant experience from a female perspective.

(See also *Contemporary Authors,* Vols. 89-92 [obituary] and *Dictionary of Literary Biography,* Vol. 28.)

THE NEW YORK TIMES BOOK REVIEW

It would be difficult to point to a group of short stories within the covers of a book that makes a stronger appeal to all that is best in the human heart than the ten stories which form this collection [*Hungry Hearts*]. Many realistic tales of New York's Ghetto have been written; but in point of literary workmanship and in laying bare the very souls of her characters, the superior of Miss Yezierska has not yet appeared.

The hunger so vividly and impressively portrayed in this book is not physical hunger, but the hunger of the spirit for better things.

One of the stories, **"The Fat of the Land,"** was selected by Mr. O'Brien as the best piece of imaginative fiction of the year. **"The Lost 'Beautifulness'"** is pathetic in the extreme, and in these days significant also. Hanneh Hayyen's boy was fighting for America in the great war in France; the mother decided to have the kitchen painted as a welcome to him when he came back. . . .

Upon the completion of the work the landlord promptly raised the rent, and a little later raised it again. The boy returned with his honor stripes and a medal for distinguished service.

> All at once he stopped; on the sidewalk before their house was a heap of household things that seemed familiar, and there on the curbstone a woman huddled, cowering, broken.
>
> Good God his mother! His own mother—and all their worldly belongings dumped there in the rain.

"How I Found America" depicts the dark background of the land from which these Russians have fled and their unfaltering determination to become Americans.

> *A review of "Hungry Hearts," in* The New York Times Book Review, *December 5, 1920, p. 18.*

CARL VAN DOREN

Miss Yezierska, most newly arrived of our literary immigrants, does not escape touches of sentimentalism [in *Hungry Hearts*]. Her little book is full of tears that sometimes come too quickly, as if she had not learned that the quickest tears dry soonest. She repeats her formula—an immigrant girl longing for escape

from bitter conditions—too frequently. When she leaves the East Side neighborhood to which her art is native she never quite has the look of reality. And yet she has struck one or two notes that our literature can never again be without, and she deserves the high credit of being one of the earliest to put those notes into engaging fiction. As a nation we have taken, she cries out, the bodies of our immigrants and used them to make the nation. But what of their souls? What of that radiant aspiration—alas, too often disappointed—which has drawn our immigrants hither from the most cramped and wretched corners of the earth? What of the uprush of affection which many of them, yes, most of them, still experience long after they may be thought to have won the right to disillusionment? These are elements in the national wealth which simply must not be wasted. *Hungry Hearts* is a genuine little horde of that wealth, an evidence of the tongue of flame which flickers beautifully above the slums in which we negligently leave some of our truest lovers. (p. 122)

> *Carl Van Doren, "Hungry," in* The Nation, *New York, Vol. CXII, No. 2899, January 26, 1921, pp. 121-22.*

LOUISE MAUNSELL FIELD

The principal interest in this new novel, *Salome of the Tenements,* consists not in what the author has tried to do and apparently believes that she has accomplished, but in what she has done, almost—perhaps altogether—unconsciously. What she has tried and intended to do, she herself states clearly enough:

> Sonya and Manning, tricked into matrimony, were the Oriental and the Anglo-Saxon trying to find a common language. The over-emotional Ghetto struggling for its breath in the thin air of Puritan restraint. An East Side savage forced suddenly into the strait-jacket of American civilization. Sonya was like the dynamite bomb and Manning the walls of tradition constantly menaced by threatening explosions.

This, the intention. But what has actually been done is to show the point of view of the Russian Jewess from New York's lower east side; for it is from this point of view, and this only, that the book is written. . . .

[Sonya] is an illiterate, hot-blooded little savage, tossed here and there by the tempest of her own whims and passions, utterly unscrupulous, yet with a longing which is often pathetic for the restraint and cultivation she so entirely lacks, and tries to convince herself that she despises. The author seems to admire her immensely.

Anzia Yezierska has made of her Sonya Vrunsky a living human being; she is real to us, even when the incidents of her story are far from convincing; real in her ignorances and her crudities, her idealization of Manning and her ardent amorousness, her flaming desires and her complete egotism, her craving for luxuries and beautiful clothes. Sonya is drawn with strong, sure, vivid strokes. But when the author turns from her heroine to Manning her hand falters—the lines are fumbling. She seems to have taken her ideas of the type and its surroundings from the cheaper "movies." There are times when the descriptions more than border upon the ludicrous. . . . In short, much of the book reads like a burlesque. Manning's dislike to having his wife make love to him in public is his nearest approach to the type he is supposed to represent.

But if the novel fails to set forth the contrast its author has intended to present, it is not without value. It has clever moments and some amusing ones; Mrs. Peltz's frank statement of facts at that truly extraordinary reception Manning gave after his marriage provides a refreshing moment and Sonya's feelings are often well described, while she herself is vividly presented. But it is in the point of view of this Russian Jewess that the book's significance consists, a point of view which is evidently the author's own. Manning had poured out his money and lavished his time on the social settlement by means of which he hoped to help the poor he idealized; but Sonya tore the last veil of deception from his eyes: "Why, there would be no fake settlements if they were only openly what they should be; marriage centres—clearing houses for ambitious youth, where live east side girls like me can catch on to men higher up." . . . And indeed, . . . the settlements and charitable institutions are worse than useless. It is interesting to see the point of view taken by Sonya Vrunsky, the east side Jewess, of such work as this. The social workers look "so hard, so ugly," with the "school teacher tightness about their lips, the self-conscious look of virtue in their eyes." The work in the free ward of a hospital is thus described:

> The operation was performed—by inexperienced students, who cut up the poor for nothing to learn how to operate on the rich. They removed his tonsils—and also his voice.

Resentment—resentment of an inferiority which cannot be glossed over or denied away; envy of the education and good breeding ascribed to the "American-born," the "higher-ups," and with it an attempt to belittle all that is so envied, breathes through almost every page of the book. . . .

Manning is "the arrogant Anglo-Saxon"; Sonya's final realization of his "fineness" is a grudged concession. Whether the point of view shown here is one common to many of the east side it is not for the present reviewer to say. But it is certainly an interesting one, and it would perhaps be well for the "American-born" of the educated class to consider the way in which they and their charitable enterprises are regarded by this *Salome of the Tenements.*

> *Louise Maunsell Field, in a review of "Salome of the Tenements," in* The New York Times Book Review, *December 24, 1922, p. 22.*

SCOTT NEARING

A flame—a leaping, scorching, searing flame—that is the impression scarred into the mind by *Salome of the Tenements.* Sonya is young. She loves life. She yearns for the unattainable. One day she starts out in pursuit of it, and the story of that pursuit is the thread of the tale. Really, "Salome" is a misnomer. Sonya Vrunsky might be likened to many classic figures, but never to Salome.

She might, for example, be called the Père Grandet of the tenements as she presses her experience to her bosom, crying: "Mine, mine, mine only and forever!" Or she might be likened to Mr. Bounderby, exploiter and enslaver of men and women. Sonya is the miser and the monopolist—at heart a business-woman, not a vamp. Besides, the traditional Salome was a cat's-paw in the hands of Herodias, while Sonya is a devouring monster. She describes herself as "a soul consumed with hun-

ger for heights beyond reach," but in seeking to scale those heights she does not hesitate to set her feet on the necks of her fellows, as when she destroys Lipkin's happiness, or begs her costume from Hollins, or lays the trap for Manning, her millionaire future husband, or buys her landlord without paying the agreed price. Here she is not a soul but a combination promoter and confidence woman.

Salome is an unwholesome book. With the possible exception of Hollins it contains but one character that stands out clearly against the heaving background, and that character, Sonya, exhibits a depravity of spirit and an incapacity to live and let live that rivals the degradation of Balzac's most admirable villains. The book is vivid. In places, it is well done. The life of Manning wins no understanding from the novelist, but the pictures of the Ghetto are admirable and the suppressed aspirations of the Russian Jewess burst into flame in the form of Sonya Vrunsky. This time Miss Yezierska has created, not a hungry heart, but a yawning abyss, an ego that does not project a single ray of social understanding. (pp. 674, 676)

> *Scott Nearing, "A Depraved Spirit," in* The Nation, *New York, Vol. CXVI, No. 3022, June 6, 1923, pp. 674, 676.*

THE NEW YORK TIMES BOOK REVIEW

The title of the first article in [*Children of Loneliness,* a] collection of articles and short stories, **"Mostly About Myself,"** would have been far more appropriate for the volume than the one chosen. For it is almost always about herself that Anzia Yezierska writes, though in this book she has at least avoided some of the more obvious absurdities of her earlier novel, *Salome of the Tenements,* by keeping, for the most part, strictly to the kind of people and the kind of life she really knows and understands. Her gift is not creative; she is a reporter and an autobiographist rather than a fiction writer. What she has herself seen, felt and suffered—especially suffered—she can set before the reader vividly and with no small degree of force. Her heroes and heroines are all very much alike—passionate, emotional, unrestrained, intensely egotistical, living, it would seem, always on the verge of hysteria, possessed of a really extraordinary belief in their own abilities, and with that "artistic temperament" which Gilbert Chesterton so admirably diagnosed as a disease which afflicts amateurs.

The book contains an interview with the author, seven short stories and three avowedly autobiographical articles, these last being the most interesting portion of the volume. The tale which gives the book its title, **"Children of Loneliness"** pictures vividly that tragedy which is the gulf between the immigrant parents, still clinging to the old ways, and their "Americanized" children. Yankev Ravinsky and his hardworking wife had staked all their hopes on their daughter Rachel. But after four years at college Rachel found her parents' table manners unendurable. "To think that I was born of these creatures! It's an insult to my soul. . . . They're ugly and gross and stupid. I'm all sensitive nerves." . . . Rachel's old parents and their squalid surroundings are clearly seen and reproduced; their pain is beyond all doubt the anguish which has come to many who have found themselves despised by their children. . . .

The book has a value because of the vivid picture it gives of life on the east side, among the immigrants, their hopes and fears and way of looking at things—especially at the hated "charities." It has color and a dramatic quality which, if it frequently slips into melodrama, nevertheless gives effectiveness to many of its scenes.

A *review of "Children of Loneliness," in* The New York Times Book Review, *October 28, 1923, p. 9.*

THE TIMES LITERARY SUPPLEMENT

The impact of race on race must always imply some kind of spiritual drama—perhaps a spiritual tragedy. The immigrant may be absorbed—the Americanization of the immigrant is deliberate and rapid; if he is not absorbed, he will lose everything—except his soul. There is another alternative: he may be absorbed and yet in rare cases save his soul actively alive and devote it to realizing his dream in the service of America.

That is what has happened to Anzia Yezierska, the author of **Children of Loneliness**, a Polish immigrant who has come to see America as "a big idea—a deathless hope—a world still in the making." . . . [In] the ten stories she now gives us she tells once more what her critics have called "her one story"—the story of hunger and loneliness. But she has learnt since she began to write that there is a thing more terrible than the hunger for bread—the hunger for people; and she finds its satisfaction in watching and recording the struggle of the immigrant Russian in America. That is the one theme which fills these vivid narratives of grinding poverty—the bitterness of defeated endeavour, and despairing toil, passionate yearning for a fuller life, but above all of a burning desire for self-expression in art or literature. . . . And in many of these tales Anzia Yezierska shows how these aspiring dreams won success in their very failure. In the moving episode called **"A Bed for the Night"** the outcast of the lodging house did not find the home she sought, but her experience of one night gave her a new life and a new love; and something of the same lesson comes with greater depth of insight from **"Dreams and Dollars."**

A *review of "Children of Loneliness," in* The Times Literary Supplement, *No. 1138, November 8, 1923, p. 748.*

THE NEW YORK TIMES BOOK REVIEW

Bread Givers defines the emotional tone of an immigrant family in the dismal tenement of an overcrowded block of the east side of New York. It is a complex mood of grave joy and bottomless anguish, of Old World standards and New World values, of hope and struggle and defeat and achievement. The very title is significant of the inclusive simplicity, the intensity, the tangibility and the emotional directness of Anzia Yezierska. **Bread Givers** imposes its own vision from the very first paragraph and does not let go of the reader's spellbound attention until long after the last page. It provides a picture of a not unfamiliar family of immigrants, yet it is a particular and a highly individualized family of Polish Jews who exist larger than life in the timeless innocence of Anzia Yezierska's turbulent and colloquial prose. . . .

The Smolinsky family and the flat in which they live is almost painfully actual. The reader is sensible of their physical presences and of all that surrounds them. The Reb Smolinsky, wise in the lore of the Torah, comfortably immured in the seclusion of his learning, calmly collects the earnings of his four daughters and chants of the terrors and the hatreds and the punishments from the Old Testament and the Hebrew writers. His wife worries and scolds and heatedly bargains, alternately glows with the submissive pride of the wife of a wise man and rails

at him for not providing for the family, and relaxes voluptuously in memories of the luxurious and wealthy home of her father. Bessie, the "burden-bearer," grows old before her time with carrying the entire household on her shoulders. Fania's secret is a romantic attachment for a poet, with whom she corresponds in ethereally impassioned letters and for whose sake she studies and reads incessantly. Mashah, "empty-head," loves her own pretty face and spends out of her earnings for clothes and drugstore accessories, to the scandal of her sisters, the disgust of her mother and the outspoken rage of her father. Sara, "blood-and-iron," is possessed of a fierce hunger to lift herself out of her environment, to become a teacher. . . .

One by one the Reb drives away the suitors of his daughters. They are left disconsolate, and his good wife must now apply the goad again. This time the Reb descends definitely and finally from his solitary and immeasurable grandeur. He goes to the marriage broker and brings back husbands—such husbands—for his daughters. . . .

Sara runs away to earn her living and put herself through school. She works by day in a laundry and by night, in a dark, dingy hall bedroom, pores over her books. On a bitterly cold night her mother comes lugging a feather mattress for her warmth and a package of herrings for her food, and inexhaustible wisdom and love for her comfort. It is an appeal to her weakness that Sara resists. She must shut out everything, just as the old Reb has done, but that which means everything to her. She is the Reb translated into the American idiom. She is the beautifully superfluous learning of the Reb chained to use and producing importance. She is his ideal harnessed to a practical purpose.

Sara's chance encounter with her father in his old age, when she stops to pick up the chewing gum she knocked from the tray of a strange peddler and becomes aware of a too-familiar back, a well-known straggling beard, and knows it for the sadly shrunken form of her own father, is one of the poignant moments of the novel. Sara is at the high point of her success, a competent and well-paid teacher and the fiancée of a brilliant colleague in the school. The Reb is at his lowest point. From that instant of the meeting in the street Sara submits herself and subjects her sisters to the old father and their stepmother. They are contributing to that alien household, giving their father money as they used to do. This time it is Sara, who always before had resisted him, who molds herself to his will and brings her young man to learn Hebrew from him and opens her hard-won home to his oblivious and child-like tyranny.

This colorful, almost barbaric tapestry of the east side, this **Bread Givers,** makes us all debtors to Anzia Yezierska, who came here herself an immigrant and made her way much as her Sara did. **Bread Givers** enables us to see our life more clearly, to test its values, to reckon up what it is that our aims and achievements may mean. It has a raw, uncontrollable poetry and a powerful, sweeping design that is comparable only to [a] poem on a similar subject, Lola Ridge's *The Ghetto*. Lola Ridge sees Hester Street as a pageant of the "strong flux of life, like a bitter wine." Anzia Yezierska gives that life an inflection of her own and reveals the inner workings of that passion to be and to assert one's self which has erected skyscrapers upon the frail basis of an armload of garments, a scanty store of this strange English and a voice "like a fire-engine," and an unresting idealism.

"Turbulent Folkways of the Ghetto in a New Novel," in The New York Times Book Review, *September 13, 1925, p. 8.*

JOHAN J. SMERTENKO

A certain measure of achievement there is in [*Bread Givers,* the] new novel of Mrs. Yezierska's: complete and colorful personalities live in it; strange, sordid scenes from the Ghetto depths are vividly depicted here; and the fierce vitality of the author seethes through its pages. But this unharnessed and little directed vitality is the author's undoing.

Like a canoe in the rapids, the frail bark, creative genius, is dented again and again by rocks that may easily be avoided in a quieter current. And Mrs. Yezierska has heedlessly ignored her light craft and her inadequate equipment and trusted herself to the mercy of the foamiest torrent. For she is unmistakably a writer for whom the much abused phrase, *furor scribendi,* seems to have been coined expressly. In fact, I imagine that a certain fury characterizes all her actions and that writing is but one of the manifestations of her superabundant and sweeping virility.

It is obvious that she shares the passionately egocentric attitude evinced by her heroine, Sara, who considers physical training courses at the University an injustice because she earns her way through college by working in a laundry, who startles the bursar out of his wits by asking for a refund of tuition fees on the grounds that she had "paid to learn, not to fail", and who is always amazed and angered when her sudden, unsolicited overtures of love are rather impatiently rejected by the objects of her fugitive affection. Equally evident is the fact that, like Sara, our author is the victim of a purely personal morality which is governed neither by code nor by logic but by the particular circumstance. Hence, while the actual incidents portrayed are in every sense kaleidoscopic, the spiritual pattern is a labyrinth; and while the individual parts of the story are probably honest transcriptions of experiences, the entire work is not a true representation of Ghetto life. . . .

There is other evidence that Mrs. Yezierska was moved to write this novel before she had thoroughly apprehended its problems. She is concerned with "the slice of life" not with life in the round; she plays all her notes *fortissimo* and in a frantic tempo with the inevitable loss of emphasis and shading. In closing my review of *Salome of the Tenements* I quoted some French philosopher to the effect that *la vérité est dans une nuance.* It is as appropriate to sum up the criticism of *Bread Givers* in the phrase, *il y a des nuances dans la vérité.*

Johan J. Smertenko, "From the Ghetto Depths," in The Saturday Review of Literature, *Vol. II, No. 11, October 10, 1925, p. 192.*

THE NEW YORK TIMES BOOK REVIEW

Arrogant Beggar is the story of an imaginative and rebellious girl from the tenements who approaches the larger life promised by organized charity with high hopes of illusion, and turns from it at last, scarred by the experience and richer in wisdom, to find her own place in the scheme of life. It is a vividly told story, rushing pell mell from one episode to the next, seldom pausing for background, characterization, or detail of any sort beyond scattered essentials. One sees that Miss Yezierska knows her theme so well that she feels no need of taking pains with her material—which those who have read her previous books . . . will recall. She seems to have set down this story of Adele Lindner as fast as she could write, until she came to the ending, perhaps, when she felt constrained to arrange an innocuous,

quaint and chintzy happy-ending to what, for the most part, is as much a social survey document as a novel. (p. 18)

"A Social Survey," in The New York Times Book Review, *November 6, 1927, pp. 18, 20.*

THE SATURDAY REVIEW OF LITERATURE

The plot [of *Arrogant Beggar*] is trite, the characterization is thin, and the thought is an elaboration of the obvious. The plot: poor working-girl received into charitable institution nobly spurns its charity and makes her own living, thereby being enabled to marry a genius and establish a happy home. The characterization: one vivid Russian Jewish working-girl (evidently Miss Yezierska herself momentarily disguised), one poor old woman oozing kindness, one diaphanous genius, and several suits of clothes passing as donors of charity. The thought: there is a gulf between the rich and the poor which is difficult to bridge, but members of each class—especially the poor—may be happy if they will only be brave and kind.

Miss Yezierska's hostility to organized charity is as deep as was that of Dickens but it is less courageously presented. Where Dickens, trusting to his hatred, made no attempt to be fair but painted his full-blooded monstrosities with reckless gusto, Miss Yezierska for once tries to hold her emotions in check and to write with even-handed justice: but the result is still satire, however much it masquerades as realism. Before the end a perverse sympathy seizes the reader for the waxen Lady Bountiful and Prince Charming who strive so hard and so fatuously to do right—and who strive still harder and more fatuously to come to life as characters. The faint pathos of a marionette show hovers about the volume.

But surely never was a poor story better told. Miss Yezierska's style goes at lightning speed; the reader is whirled onward from sentence to sentence at a rate that for sheer thrill of movement hardly has its equal. The experience is more exhilarating than the best automobile race or football game. In the fewest of words Miss Yezierska can conjure up the scene or situation that she desires. Both scene and situation are usually of the most familiar, but like an old room newly decorated they gleam beneath their author's furnishings. What could be more trite, for example, than the substance of this description of a moist hand,—but what more deadly than the assonances with which Miss Yezierska drives home her physical disgust? "The damp skin clinging to my fingers felt like a limp fish wriggling against my palm." Old wine in new bottles; old thoughts in a new style; triteness made palatable; plus a Russian warmth and gush of emotion new in American literature;—what is Anzia Yezierska? She is not Shakespeare nor yet Cervantes, but she is pleasant to listen to, even when, as in the present volume, she has nothing particular to say.

A review of "Arrogant Beggar," in The Saturday Review of Literature, *Vol. IV, No. 19, December 3, 1927, p. 405.*

THE NEW YORK TIMES BOOK REVIEW

[Apart] from the original story she had to tell, her own, [Anzia Yezierska's] work as a creative artist has so far been negligible. This last book of hers, *All I Could Never Be,* is no more a new book than a new edition of a previous publication can be called that. Again it is the story she has told before, to no small degree her own story, the tale of the inarticulate but passionate Jewish, immigrant young woman who seeks sympathy and understanding among those who, because of a more austere background, cannot or do not know how to give them. This has been her thesis and theme over and over again; this has also been her plot.

Salome of the Tenements, if the memory of this reviewer be correct, married into the family of a cold-blooded American; Fanya, the new Salome, is thwarted in the fulfillment of her love, but, nevertheless, goes through the same suffering for want of responsive warmth from Henry Scott, the sociologist. Fanya eventually reaches fame and economic independence through virtue of her pen; she is a novelist when the book closes, but her emotionalism and rebellion have not been curbed. She understands Americans a little better, but still she feels that theirs is a sorry kind of humanity.

Apparently from the content of the book and from her own personal history, Miss Yezierska "has a great respect for those who can call themselves writers. It seems a pity, therefore, that she does not respect the art with more devotion. Not only does she fail to create characters or plot—for outside of the heroine no other creature comes to life and the story as such might be a case history—but she is extremely careless in tying up her material.

> "Thwarted Love," *in* The New York Times Book Review, *August 21, 1932, p. 11.*

THE CHRISTIAN SCIENCE MONITOR

Anzia Yezierska has, in large degree, lived the material out of which her novels are constructed. She came to America penniless and unschooled, she worked by day and studied by night. She learned to put into unpolished but vehement words the aspirations, the rebuffs, the disappointments and misunderstandings, the squalor and the glorious dreams of her people. . . .

As a story, **All I Could Never Be** stands up well almost to the end. The writing is more even and disciplined than in Miss Yezierska's earlier work, without any appreciable loss of intensity. She has become less naïve, more self-conscious, and more lenient in her judgment of those who fail to understand her people. A dozen years ago the reader would have been summoned peremptorily to sympathize entirely with the impulsive Fanya and share her violent reactions against those who withdrew from her too extravagant devotion. Now the reader is reminded that Americans of the old stocks have also their valuable heritage—a heritage of steady, well-ordered accomplishment. The novel is a plea for understanding, primarily for an understanding of people like Fanya who wear their hearts on their sleeves and pour themselves out in lavish affection, but secondarily, and perhaps a little grudgingly, it is a plea for understanding on the other side. She wants to say that it is not entirely the fault of those who have been in America longer that newcomers are made to feel that they are on the other side of a social ditch. She concedes that New Englanders, too, have their virtues. When every race knows its own quality and clings to what is real and abiding in its own background, it then rests on a sure foundation.

> "Child of Loneliness," *in* The Christian Science Monitor, *October 8, 1932, p. 5.*

LYMAN BRYSON

It is poverty, according to the ghetto proverb, that becomes the wise man like a red ribbon on a white horse and poverty has never frightened Anzia Yezierska. What she has fought against all her life is doubt of herself and, in this singularly moving autobiography [**Red Ribbon on a White Horse**], she tells how neither poverty nor wealth nor another person's wisdom could help her.

She went out of Hester Street to Hollywood years ago and then rejected being "an author who grows rich writing of the poor." She had other successes, suffered personal rejections, wondering always if she might be too demanding, and she came down at last to the Writer's Project of the W.P.A. Of this she gives a picture that for irony and tears is not likely to be surpassed. . . .

Haunting this journey after money that was not worth having, and fame that was useless, and mere existence in a time of trouble, and the serenity of renunciation which she could not achieve, was the presence of her father. He had no doubts of himself and no faith in her. It was his duty to read the sacred books and hers to bear children and to help a man. She rebelled against his remote, fiercely devoted single-mindedness but she has come at last to see that the "fierce obsession of my will to lift my head up out of the squalor and anonymity of the poor" was really a "poverty of spirit." She has come back to herself and needs nothing else.

The fierceness of temperament that has made life so hard for her shows in her writing, which is nervous, direct, and passionate. Of her writing career, she tells very little because it did not satisfy her, even when it was successful. She often chooses not to be explicit about the details of her story although she has included a number of portraits, brief but telling, of the real persons in Hollywood, in the W.P.A., in the worlds she passed through. She gives a deep pathos to the repeated experiences of being told that she had come at last to live with herself which she knew was truth but could not bring herself to live by. We are loaded down these days with books that tell us how to be happy and rich enough and quiet. Anzia Yezierska found no such escape and offers none; she tells the disturbing truth about her own soul.

> Lyman Bryson, "Haunted Journey," *in* The New York Times Book Review, *September 24, 1950, p. 22.*

W. H. AUDEN

[The essay excerpted below was originally published as an introduction to Anzia Yezierska's book Red Ribbon on a White Horse, *Charles Scribner's Sons, 1950.]*

Reading Miss Yezierska's book [**Red Ribbon on a White Horse**] sets me thinking again about that famous and curious statement in the Preamble to the Constitution about the self-evident right of all men to "the pursuit of happiness," for I have read few accounts of such a pursuit so truthful and moving as hers.

To be happy means to be free, not from pain or fear, but from care or anxiety. A man is so free when 1) he knows what he desires and 2) what he desires is real and not fantastic. A desire is real when the possibility of satisfaction exists for the individual who entertains it and the existence of such a possibility depends, first, on his present historical and social situation—a desire for a Cadillac which may be real for a prosperous American businessman would be fantastic for a Chinese peasant—and, secondly, on his natural endowment as an individual—for a girl with one eye to desire to be kept by a millionaire would be fantastic, for a girl with two beautiful ones it may not. To say that the satisfaction of a desire is possible does not mean that it is certain but that, if the desire is not satisfied, a definite and meaningful reason can be given. (pp. 327-28)

So long as it is a matter of immediate material goods, few sane individuals cherish fantastic desires after the age of puberty, but there are desires for spiritual goods which are much more treacherous, e.g., the desire to find a vocation in life, to have a dedicated history. "What do I want to be? A writer? A chemist? A priest?" Since I am concerned not with any immediate objective good but with pledging the whole of my unknown future in advance, the chances of self-deception are much greater because it will be years before I can be certain whether my choice is real or fantastic. Nor can any outsider make the decision for me; he can only put questions to me which make me more aware of what my decision involves.

Miss Yezierska's book is an account of her efforts to discard fantastic desires and find real ones, both material and spiritual. (p. 328)

[Miss Yezierska's father] had a vocation, the study of the Torah, which involved his being supported by his wife and children. He had expected them to do so in Plinsk, he expected them to continue doing so in New York. But what they had accepted in Poland as an extra burden, worth bearing for the honor in which a learned and holy man was held by the community, was bound to seem intolerable in America, where not only was a nonearner regarded as an idler but also the possibility for the family of acquiring status existed in proportion to their earning capacity.

His daughter, however, as she later realized, was more like him than either of them at the time could perceive. Had she been less like him, had she simply desired money and a good marriage, there would have been less friction between them but she, too, was seeking for a dedicated life of her own, which in his eyes was impious, for all vocations but one were for men only.

"A woman alone, not a wife and not a mother, has no existence." She, however, wanted a vocation all to herself and thought she had found it in writing. She began, as she tells us, with the hope that "by writing out what I don't know and can't understand, it would stop hurting me." At the same time, of course, she wanted money to satisfy her needs. This is any artist's eternal problem, that he needs money as a man but works for love. Even in the case of the most popular writer, money is not the purpose for which he writes, though popularity may be.

So she begins; she writes a book, *Hungry Hearts,* about the life of a poor immigrant, which is well reviewed but does not sell; then, suddenly, the American Fairy—whether she is a good or wicked fairy, who knows?—waves her hand and she is transported in an instant from Hester Street to Hollywood; from one day to the next, that is, suffering is abolished for her. How does she feel? More unhappy than she has ever been in her life. To have the desires of the poor and be transferred in a twinkling of an eye to a world which can only be real for those who have the desires of the rich is to be plunged into the severest anxiety. The foreshortening of time which is proper to a dream or a fairy story is a nightmare in actual life. (pp. 330-31)

With the coming of the depression Miss Yezierska ceased to be a solitary failure and became one of millions who could not be called failures, because the positions in which they could succeed or fail no longer existed. It was surely the height of irony that, in a country where the proof of one's importance had been that one was rich and popular, people should suddenly, in order to prove that they were important enough to eat, have to go to elaborate lengths to establish that they were penniless and friendless. (pp. 332-33)

Among her companions in poverty and comedy [in the Arts Project of the W.P.A.], Miss Yezierska felt once more to some degree that happiness of "belonging" which years before she had felt in Hester Street, though only she realized this after it was over. But belonging to some degree is not enough; one must belong completely or the feeling soon withers. Once again the lack of a common memory of the past and a common anticipation of the future was a fatal barrier, not only for her but for most of her fellows. . . .

Miss Yezierska's autobiography is, literally, the story of an early twentieth-century immigrant, but it has a deeper and more general significance today when, figuratively, the immigrant is coming more and more to stand as the symbol for Everyman, as the natural and unconscious community of tradition rapidly disappears from the earth. (p. 334)

> *W. H. Auden, "Red Ribbon on a White Horse," in his* The Dyer's Hand and Other Essays, *Random House, 1962, pp. 327-34.*

ALICE KESSLER HARRIS

An immigrant, desperately poor and often hungry, Yezierska wrote realistic stories of Jewish immigrant life on New York's Lower East Side. Her tales paved the way to success and adulation: she became the American dream come true. And her fiction illuminates the meaning of the dream.

All of the six books Anzia Yezierska published between 1920 and 1932 are in some sense autobiographical, but none more so than *Bread Givers.* Her constant themes are the dirt and congestion of the tenement, the struggle against poverty, family, and tradition to break out of the ghetto, and then the searing recognition that her roots would always lie in the old world. If in her other work Yezierska offers glimpses of the language and culture of immigrant Jews at the turn of the century, in *Bread Givers* she opens the door wide and leads us through the days of her childhood to the impetuous decision to reject her parents' home. Along the way, she lays open the woman's experience of immigration, revealing the ways in which Jewish women encountered the new world and tried to reconcile it with the old.

Yezierska's old world was like that of many turn-of-the-century immigrants. She was born in a small town—probably a *shtetl* called Plinsk—in Russian Poland about 1885. (p. v)

For the shtetl wife, poverty meant constant work and continuous sacrifice for husband and children. Although women complained often and bitterly, Jewish faith provided both solace and rationalization for their hard life. Only men could study the Torah. Their wives and daughters were destined to smooth the path. A woman's virtue was measured by how well she helped her husband to live a pious existence, free from daily worry and encouraged by her orthodox observance of ritual in the home. To serve her husband and father should be a woman's highest wish, and it was, in any event, her only hope of heaven. (p. vi)

In contrast with the restricted options of the shtetl, America seemed to offer boundless opportunities even for girls. Some of Yezierska's best-known stories are about young girls who dream of America as a place where they can freely meet the ideal lovers who surely await them. (p. vii)

For many women, the transition to America aggravated the tension between their religiously enjoined subservience and their actual economic importance. In the old country strong community sanctions and religious edict kept women in their place despite their economic activity. But now, without the protective cloak of persistent religious observance, women's secondary position in the new world seemed anachronistic: a matter of outmoded custom and tradition. A new world demanded a new rationale for keeping women down. It found it in the strong family structure sustained by women's developing economic dependence. (pp. vii-viii)

Woman who wanted to break out of these old patterns violated not only the expectations of their own immigrant community, but also American social prescription that confirmed dependent roles for women at the turn of the century. Some women, nevertheless, found new outlets for their aggressive energies. Most continued to live their lives through husbands and to sacrifice for children. In the absence of a vital economic need, this became a narrowing pursuit whose results can sometimes be seen in the overly-concerned and child-centered woman we have come to know as the American version of the Jewish mother. (p. viii)

Yezierska's great gift was her ability to capture the ambiguity created by America's consistent temptations. She could write about the warmth and closeness of the immigrant community as she rejected the dirt and poverty that accompanied them. She could describe the pull of prosperity and the urge for adequate food as she warily watched for the trap that the marketplace surely laid. She condemned the endless toil and incessant anxiety that bound America's workers, but she remained eternally optimistic that its promise would be redeemed. She offered no answers, but she was sure that America somehow had them. Her reviewers used to say that she wrote about "life." And she did. Deceptively simple in plot and structure, her work is suffused with the unending trauma of adjustment, with the psychic stress of adaptation, with alternating currents of exhilaration, weariness, fear, self-doubt, self-loathing, and quiet acceptance that were all part of every individual's entry into America.

In his introduction to Yezierska's autobiography [*Red Ribbon on a White Horse*, see excerpt above], W. H. Auden wrote that the book was "an account of her efforts to discard fantastic desires and find real ones." I prefer to see her work as an attempt to reconcile American ideals with Jewish culture. For what seemed to Auden fantastic desires were for Yezierska only the wish to take the promise of America literally. America offered two things, both equally unattainable for the shtetl woman and, Yezierska was convinced, simultaneously available in America. America held out the possibility of love and of satisfying work. Yezierska's task was to find out if they could be achieved without giving up the best of the old culture and without the dreadful pangs of rootlessness that would follow.

Life in America did not begin and end with marriage. It offered the opportunity to reject old roles—to be unlike the women she knew. (pp. xii-xiii)

The road to becoming a person lay through the dangerous territory of Americanization. Yezierska is at her best when she describes the anguished journey. Americans were clean, so immigrants had to get out from under the dirt. But tenement apartments were crowded and dark. Few had running water. Soap cost money and washing took precious time away from sleep or studies. Americans were neat and stylish. But what immigrant girl had the money for clothes? Or the time to remake hats and learn new manners? Americans were soft spoken and educated so the struggle to learn English, to finish high school, even to attend college, became a single-minded obsession for those who wanted to shed the greenhorn image. A jumble of emotions assaulted the poor immigrant who tried to absorb these rules all at once. (p. xiii)

Americanization brought self-assurance and a change in personality that would transform the crude immigrant into a suave native. The tall Anglo-Saxon male appears repeatedly in Yezierska's work. To the immigrant girl he is an inspiring figure. Older and infinitely more sophisticated than she, he appears as the measured and calm epitome of her aspirations. To her, he represents reason and civilization. To become like him, she strives to get away from the Yiddish language and to suppress her displays of feeling. Yet it is precisely these qualities that he admires. To his Anglo-Saxon imagination, she seems, in her roughness, the essence of life. Her emotional energy and excitement draw him. He is captivated by the color and vitality of the immigrant community. His romantic vision of the ghetto leads her to see beyond its poverty and to recognize that her roots lie in the community she is trying to escape. In *All I Could Never Be*, Yezierska explores the conflict between reason and emotion in a love affair modeled after a sad experience of her own. For a while the lovers complement each other. In the end, however, they seem irreconcilable and immigrant and WASP part.

On the way to successful Americanization lay another kind of anguish. Becoming an American cut women off from their culture and their past. It brought the fearful recognition that they were adrift in the world. "I had gone too far away from life and I did not know how to get back," lamented Yezierska. One of her characters, an immigrant's college-educated daughter, echoed the cry: "I can't live in the old world and I'm yet too green for the new. I don't belong to those who gave me birth or to those with whom I was educated." Yezierska offers some possibilities of solace. The educated daughter of immigrants could return to the ghetto in a spirit of love for her people. Together they might forge a new world out of her book knowledge and their knowledge of life.

The best part of America was freedom. As she was obsessed with her own need to be free, she gloried in the country that made it possible. This was a place in which all could aspire to the "democracy of beauty," she wrote in 1922. Yet she saw clearly America's failure to live up to its potential. In the midst of the depression she wrote sadly of her fellow immigrants, "We foreigners are the orphans, the step-children of America. The old world is dead behind us, and the new world— about which we dreamed . . .—is not yet born." And again, "How many get the chance to give to America the hope in their hearts, the dreams of their minds?" Greedy landlords and bosses shared the blame for poverty's distortion of the dream. Still her faith remained intact. Friends described her late in her long life as a woman instinctively opposed to "oppression of the spirit."

Many of these themes, of course, are present in the work of other first generation Jewish immigrants and their children. Poverty, Americanization, family tensions, the ambiguity of success are the painful realities of which immigrant drama was made. The pain surfaces in great novels like Henry Roth's *Call it Sleep*, in forgotten entertainments like Samuel Ornitz's *Haunch, Paunch and Jowl* and in rediscovered sagas like Abraham Cahan's *The Rise of David Levinsky* and Michael Gold's *Jews Without Money*. (pp. xiv-xv)

Yezierska shares with her fellow immigrants the ability to evoke vividly the religion and tradition of the shtetl which she rejects. The intensity of her rejection contributes to the liveliness of her memories. Her heroes and heroines are in constant motion. They do not meander through the streets of the Lower East Side like Ornitz's street gangs. They rush headlong, hunting for a way out and pausing, like Michael Gold, to dwell on the distortions that poverty creates in the personalities of the people they pass along the way. Gold, like Cahan in *Yekl*, comments on the disjuncture between husbands who have found the way to the new world and wives who hang back, comfortable in their old patterns. Yezierska offers another and no less real syndrome: the wife who pleads, threatens, and nags her husband into American ways. Samuel Ornitz's Meyer Hirsch, who became a corrupt lawyer, and Abraham Cahan's David Levinsky, a wealthy cloak manufacturer, take their place alongside Yezierska's Sara Smolinsky as vivid warnings of the abject emptiness of lives lived to someone else's tune. David and Meyer, rich and dissatisfied, fall into the yawning chasm between two worlds. Sara, for whom success was not measured by money alone, is saved by making her peace with her immigrant childhood and her father.

If Yezierska has none of Ornitz's sense of humor or Gold's sense of the absurd, she may more accurately represent the way Jewish immigrants managed to struggle out of the Lower East Side. Relatively few became socialists, like Gold, or petty gangsters. Many nourished themselves on hope while they slaved to educate themselves and their children. And if Yezierska has neither the symbolic depth of Henry Roth nor the epochal power of Abraham Cahan, she offers unparalleled ability to bring life to a neglected aspect of Yiddish culture, plunging us directly into the woman's experience of immigration.

When women appeared at all in the novels of her fellow-writers, they were likely to be creatures of male sexual imagination, manipulative and overly protective mothers, or dependent wives made fearful by their helplessness. Mary Antin's romanticized and sentimental *The Promised Land* provides no antidote to this view. Fannie Hurst occasionally offers glimpses of autonomous women but their freedom is bounded by severe moral constraints. Yezierska, in contrast, offers independent and self-willed women, and she does not hide the psychic pain of their sacrifice. The struggle out of poverty, never easy, posed for women a unique problem. Those who shared the mobility aspirations of a larger society had to violate family and community tradition in order to achieve them. Most women brave enough to risk transgressing drifted towards radical activity where they could more readily find support. Even so, their lives were filled with conflict.

We find bits and snatches of rebellious womanhood scattered in the literature of Jewish labor and socialist leaders. . . . Autobiographies like Rose Cohen's *Out of the Shadow*, Lucy Robins Lang's *Tomorrow is Beautiful*, Emma Goldman's *Living My Life*, Rose Pesotta's *Bread Upon the Waters*, Rose Schneiderman's *All for One* offer poignant testimony to the pain of women who rejected the injunction to marry and rear families as their major responsibility. They indicate that the current of discontent ran deep. Yezierska speaks for all of them and nowhere more fully than in *Bread Givers*.

She later commented of this novel, "I felt I had justified myself in the book for having hardened my heart to go through life alone." Perhaps, in the end, it is the need for self-justification that invests *Bread Givers* with its powerful emotional force. Anzia Yezierska and Sara Smolinsky, the novel's narrator, are emotionally interchangeable. Sara, as a small child, watches her self-righteous father successively drive off the suitors of each of her three sisters, and marry off his daughters to men of his own choosing. The horror and injustice of her sisters' broken lives leads her to vow that she will not become a fourth sacrifice to his rigid conception of Jewish womanhood. So she escapes. But her father's curses ring in her ears and memories of her mother's boundless and forgiving love mock her own self-centered life. Sara, repeating Yezierska's own experience, struggles upward. She drives herself through night school and college, thrusting out of her mind questions about what she was doing and why. Successful at last, she visits her parents, teacher's diploma in hand, to hear her unrelenting father proclaim: "She's only good to the world, not to her father. Will she hand me her wages from school as a dutiful daughter should?" Is there then any reconciliation between the legitimate search for self-fulfillment and duty to family? Yezierska, like Sara, opted for self and built her life around her own authentic needs. She freed herself from a tradition few of her countrywomen could ignore in that first generation, and she did it against the heaviest odds. But she paid an enormous price. This book was part of her attempt to seek absolution.

In the light of the emerging women's movement, *Bread Givers* has become more meaningful than ever. When it was first published in 1925, reviewers praised its blistering intensity, and translucent prose. They talked about its "crisp" quality, its vitality. "One does not seem to read," commented critic William Lyons Phelps. "One is too completely inside." Today these qualities are enhanced by Yezierska's scrutiny of issues that are the subject of wide concern. In her life and in this book Yezierska questioned the limited roles offered to women by traditional families. She rejected the constraints that community pressure imposed on her freedom. She presented the possibility of men and women who could acknowledge each other's legitimate needs. *Bread Givers* makes no judgments of people who choose other paths. For freedom is at the pivot of this book as it was the driving force of Yezierska's life. Half a century after she wrote, the power and intensity of her message remain intact. (pp. xv-xviii)

> *Alice Kessler Harris, in an introduction to* Bread Givers: A Novel *by Anzia Yezierska, Persea Books, 1975, pp. v-xviii.*

JOHANNA KAPLAN

It was Yezierska's ambition to "open up my life and the lives of my people" to American-born readers, "since their life was shut out from such as me." In this, she was practically a pioneer, having been notably preceded only by Abraham Cahan. But he had had the unusual advantage of both a traditional Jewish and a secular Russian education, so that even in his early days as a Yiddish journalist and editor he could proceed from a platform of intellectual sophistication. Yezierska, on the other hand, was apparently just another uneducated immigrant girl, marked out by an intense inner conviction of a special destiny, who was carried forward by her impassioned determination to "make herself for a person." She regarded this as the promise of America. But what she had in mind was not merely to become a very different person from the one she could have been had her family remained in Europe—this was after all, commonplace. More provokingly, Anzia Yezierska wished to achieve distinction, "to rise over the world." Ironically, this entailed separating herself from her family and setting herself apart from the more conventional longings and ordinary satisfactions of her first-generation contemporaries—the same people whose lives she wanted to write about.

Her guilty, embattled, ambivalent ties—to her past, to her family, to her people—remained at the heart of her psychic self-definition all her life and was the theme of her work throughout. At first, in anger, the conflict fueled her. It enabled her to people her stories with characters whose inflamed hopes and hungers might be frustrated and injured, but as long as there were obstacles for them to struggle against, they were not vanquished. Her avid young women protagonists contend with extraordinary energy against poverty, meanness of spirit, and the insult of externally imposed limitations. They wish to be "understood" by Americans, to become visible in dignity. Yet their feelings of aggrievement are not embittering; instead, each setback propels them forward in Yezierska's excited vocabulary of hope: they go on yearning, burning, aching, blazing and soaring. Only success stops them, and with it, even in early stories, comes a vocabulary of retributive chill: choking, stifling, stinging, suffocating, "cut off from air, from life, from everything warm and human." In her stories, these things happen to the "rewarded" parents of successful sons and daughters; in her lifetime, Yezierska appears to have done it to herself. (p. 14)

On the evidence of the work collected in *The Open Cage,* Miss Yezierska's real contribution, and one that should endure, are those very powerful early stories, notably **"The Fat of the Land," "The Lord Giveth,"** and **"Children of Loneliness."** These complex, highly-pitched stories about the rending battles within families betray a very dark vision. The conflicts here are not, at bottom, between tradition and modernity, or between old world and new. In Reb Ravinsky, the angry, unyielding "God-kindled" father who begs forgiveness "for the sin of having placed his hope on his daughter instead of on God," or Hanneh Breineh, the forceful, tempestuous, agitated mother who cries out against her children, "'If I would have had a chance . . . what couldn't I have been?'"—in such characters, Yezierska depicted with eerie, empathic power the pitiless, anguished confusion that mired two generations. In mothers like Hanneh Breineh and fathers like Reb Ravinsky, each so bitterly enlivened by loss and disappointment, Anzia Yezierska saw that there could be in parental love a terrible, haunting descent from envy to malediction. She saw this, but in her life as in her work, could find no way to "rise over" its dooming, predictive reach. (pp. 14, 38)

Johanna Kaplan, "Immigrant into Person," in The New York Times Book Review, *February 24, 1980, pp. 14, 38.*

Appendix

The following is a listing of all sources used in Volume 46 of *Contemporary Literary Criticism*. Included in this list are all copyright and reprint rights and acknowledgments for those essays for which permission was obtained. Every effort has been made to trace copyright, but if omissions have been made, please let us know.

THE EXCERPTS IN CLC, VOLUME 46, WERE REPRINTED FROM THE FOLLOWING PERIODICALS:

The American Spectator, v. 19, November, 1986. Copyright © *The American Spectator* 1986. Reprinted by permission of the publisher.

Analog Science Fiction/Science Fact, v. CIII, April, 1983 for a review of "The Void Captain's Tale" by Tom Easton; v. CV, December, 1985 for a review of "Child of Fortune" by Tom Easton. © 1983, 1985 by Davis Publications, Inc. Both reprinted by permission of the author.

The Antioch Review, v. 35, Winter, 1977. Copyright © by the Antioch Review Inc. Reprinted by permission of the Editors.

Ariel (The University of Calgary), v. 4, January, 1973. Copyright © 1973 The Board of Governors, The University of Calgary. Reprinted by permission of the publisher.

Artforum, v. XXII, October, 1983. Copyright 1983 Artforum International Magazine, Inc. Reprinted by permission of the publisher.

The Athenaeum, n. 4585, September 11, 1915.

The Atlantic Monthly, v. 258, November, 1986 for "From Beyond the Bars of Time" by Lloyd Rose. Copyright 1986 by The Atlantic Monthly Company, Boston, MA. Reprinted by permission of the author.

Australian Book Review, v. 6, September, 1967 for "Partial Eclipses?" by Cherry Wilder Grimm. Reprinted by permission of the author.

Best Sellers, v. 35, June, 1975; v. 42, October, 1982. Copyright © 1975, 1982 Helen Dwight Reid Educational Foundation. Both reprinted by permission of the publisher.

Black American Literature Forum, v. 18, Winter, 1984 for "On 'The Color Purple,' Stereotypes, and Silence" by Trudier Harris. © Indiana State University 1984. Reprinted with the permission of Indiana State University and the author.

Book Week—The Washington Post, v. 4, November 27, 1966. © 1966, *The Washington Post*. Reprinted by permission of the publisher.

Book World—Chicago Tribune, September 13, 1970 for "Eisteddfodder" by Paul West. © 1970 Postrib Corp. Reprinted by permission of *The Washington Post* and the author.

Book World—The Washington Post, June 25, 1972; September 12, 1976; February 20, 1977; July 27, 1980; October 12, 1980; January 18, 1981; May 9, 1982; July 25, 1982; October 10, 1982; February 27, 1983; June 26, 1983; August 14, 1983; November 27, 1983;

Allen, Walter. From *The Short Story in English*. Clarendon Press, Oxford, 1981. © Walter Allen 1981. Reprinted by permission of Oxford University Press.

Auden, W. H. From *The Dyer's Hand and Other Essays*. Random House, 1962. Copyright © 1962 by W. H. Auden. Reprinted by permission of Random House Inc.

Bosquet, Alain. From ''The Works of St.-John Perse,'' translated by Alain Bosquet, in *Exile and Other Poems*. By St.-John Perse, translated by Denis Devlin. Bollingen Series XV. Pantheon Books, 1949. Copyright 1949 by Bollingen Foundation Inc. Renewed 1976 by Princeton University Press. Reprinted with permission of Princeton University Press.

Brophy, Brigid. From *Don't Never Forget: Collected Views and Reviews*. Cape, 1966. Copyright © 1966 by Brigid Brophy. All rights reserved. Reprinted by permission of the author.

Collings, Michael R. From ''Words and Worlds: The Creation of a Fantasy Universe in Zelazny, Lee, and Anthony,'' in *The Scope of the Fantastic—Theory, Technique, Major Authors: Selected Essays from the First International Conference on the Fantastic in Literature and Film*. Edited by Robert A. Collins and Howard D. Pearce. Contributions to the Study of Science Fiction and Fantasy, No. 10. Greenwood Press, 1985. Copyright © 1985 by The Thomas Burnett Swann Fund. All rights reserved. Reprinted by permission of Greenwood Press, Inc., Westport, CT.

Deane, Seamus. From *Celtic Revivals: Essays in Modern Irish Literature, 1880-1980*. Faber and Faber, 1985. © 1985 by Seamus Deane. Reprinted by permission of Faber & Faber Ltd.

Eldershaw, M. Barnard. From *Essays in Australian Fiction*. Melbourne University Press, 1938.

Eliot, T. S. From a preface to *Anabasis: A Poem*. By St.-John Perse, translated by T. S. Eliot. Revised edition. Harcourt Brace Jovanovich, 1949. Copyright, 1938, 1949 by Harcourt Brace Jovanovich, Inc. Renewed 1966, 1977 by Esme Valerie Eliot. Reprinted by permission of Harcourt Brace Jovanovich, Inc. In Canada by Faber & Faber, Ltd.

Gale, Steven H. From ''David Mamet: The Plays, 1972-1980,'' in *Essays on Contemporary American Drama*. Edited by Hedwig Bock and Albert Wertheim. Max Hueber, 1981. © 1981 Max Hueber Verlag. Reprinted by permission of the author.

Garnett, Edward. From a foreword to *The Two Sisters*. By H. E. Bates. Cape, 1926. Copyright 1926, renewed 1953 by H. E. Bates. Reprinted by permission of Jonathan Cape Ltd.

Harris, Alice Kessler. From an introduction to *Bread Givers: A Novel*. By Anzia Yezierska. Persea Books, 1975. New introduction copyright © 1975 by Alice Kessler Harris. All rights reserved. Reprinted by permission of the publisher.

Hofmannsthal, Hugo Von. From a preface, translated by James Stern, to *Anabasis: A Poem*. By St.-John Perse, translated by T. S. Eliot. Revised edition. Harcourt Brace Jovanovich, 1949. Copyright, 1938, 1949, by Harcourt Brace Jovanovich, Inc. Renewed 1966, 1977 by Esme Valerie Eliot. Reprinted by permission of Harcourt Brace Jovanovich, Inc.

Kersnowski, Frank. From *John Montague*. Bucknell University Press, 1975. © 1975 by Associated University Presses, Inc. Reprinted by permission of the publisher.

Larbaud, Valery. From a preface, translated by Jacques Le Clercq, to *Anabasis: A Poem*. By St.-John Perse, translated by T. S. Eliot. Revised edition. Harcourt Brace Jovanovich, 1949. Copyright, 1938, 1949, by Harcourt Brace Jovanovich, Inc. Renewed 1966, 1977 by Esme Valerie Eliot. Reprinted by permission of Harcourt Brace Jovanovich, Inc.

Lucas, John. From *Moderns & Contemporaries: Novelists, Poets, Critics*. Barnes & Noble Books, 1985. © John Lucas, 1985. All rights reserved. Reprinted by permission of the publisher.

Moore, Marianne. From *A Marianne Moore Reader*. The Viking Press, 1961. Copyright © 1961 by Marianne Moore.

Parini, Jay. From *Theodore Roethke: An American Romantic*. Amherst: University of Massachusetts Press, 1979. Copyright © 1979 by The University of Massachusetts Press. All rights reserved. Reprinted by permission of the publisher.

Parker-Smith, Bettye J. From ''Alice Walker's Women: In Search of Some Peace of Mind,'' in *Black Women Writers (1950-1980): A Critical Evaluation*. Edited by Mari Evans. Anchor Press/Doubleday, 1984. Copyright © 1984 by Mari Evans. All rights reserved. Reprinted by permission of Doubleday, a division of Bantam, Doubleday, Dell Publishing Group, Inc.

Pearson, Bill. From ''Witi Ihimaera and Patricia Grace,'' in *Critical Essays on the New Zealand Short Story*. Edited by Cherry Hankin. Heinemann, 1982. © 1982 Cherry Hankin. Reprinted by permission of Heinemann Publishers (New Zealand) Ltd.

□ Contemporary Literary Criticism

Cumulative Index
Volumes 1-46

This Index Includes References to Entries in These Gale Series

Contemporary Literary Criticism

Presents excerpts of criticism on the works of novelists, poets, dramatists, short story writers, scriptwriters, and other creative writers who are now living or who have died since 1960. Cumulative indexes to authors, nationalities, and titles discussed are included in odd-numbered volumes. Volumes 1-46 are in print.

Twentieth-Century Literary Criticism

Contains critical excerpts by the most significant commentators on poets, novelists, short story writers, dramatists, and philosophers who died between 1900 and 1960. Cumulative indexes to authors, nationalities, and titles discussed are included in each new volume. Volumes 1-27 are in print.

Nineteenth-Century Literature Criticism

Offers significant passages from criticism on authors who died between 1800 and 1899. Cumulative indexes to authors, nationalities, and titles discussed are included in each new volume. Volumes 1-17 are in print.

Literature Criticism from 1400 to 1800

Compiles significant passages from the most noteworthy criticism on authors of the fifteenth through eighteenth centuries. Cumulative indexes to authors, nationalities, and titles discussed are included in each new volume. Volumes 1-7 are in print.

Children's Literature Review

Includes excerpts from reviews, criticism, and commentary on works of authors and author/illustrators who create books for children. Cumulative indexes to authors, nationalities, and titles discussed are included in each new volume. Volumes 1-14 are in print.

Contemporary Authors Series

Encompasses five related series. *Contemporary Authors* provides biographical and bibliographical information on more than 89,000 writers of fiction, nonfiction, poetry, journalism, drama, motion pictures, and other fields. Each new volume contains sketches on authors not previously covered in the series. Volumes 1-121 are in print. *Contemporary Authors New Revision Series* provides completely updated information on active authors covered in previously published volumes of *CA*. Only entries requiring significant change are revised for *CA New Revision Series*. Volumes 1-21 are in print. *Contemporary Authors Permanent Series* consists of updated listings for deceased and inactive authors removed from original volumes 9-36 when these volumes were revised. Volumes 1-2 are in print. *Contemporary*

Authors Autobiography Series presents specially commissioned autobiographies by leading contemporary writers. Volumes 1-5 are in print. *Contemporary Authors Bibliographical Series* contains primary and secondary bibliographies as well as analytical bibliographical essays by authorities on major modern authors. Volumes 1-2 are in print.

Dictionary of Literary Biography

Encompasses three related series. *Dictionary of Literary Biography* furnishes illustrated overviews of authors' lives and works and places them in the larger perspective of literary history. Volumes 1-62 are in print. *Dictionary of Literary Biography Documentary Series* illuminates the careers of major figures through a selection of literary documents, including letters, notebook and diary entries, interviews, book reviews, and photographs. Volumes 1-4 are in print. *Dictionary of Literary Biography Yearbook* summarizes the past year's literary activity with articles on genres, major prizes, conferences, and other timely subjects and includes updated and new entries on individual authors. Yearbooks for 1980-1986 are in print. A cumulative index to authors and articles is included in each new volume.

Concise Dictionary of American Literary Biography

A six-volume series that collects revised and updated sketches on major American authors that were originally presented in *Dictionary of Literary Biography*. Volume 1 is in print.

Something about the Author Series

Encompasses two related series. *Something about the Author* contains heavily illustrated biographical sketches on juvenile and young adult authors and illustrators from all eras. Volumes 1-49 are in print. *Something about the Author Autobiography Series* presents specially commissioned autobiographies by prominent authors and illustrators of books for children and young adults. Volumes 1-4 are in print.

Authors in the News

Reprints news stories and feature articles from American newspapers and magazines covering writers and other members of the communications media. A cumulative index to authors and a list of surveyed periodicals are included in each volume. Volumes 1-2, both published in 1976, are in print.

Yesterday's Authors of Books for Children

Contains heavily illustrated entries on children's writers who died before 1961. Two volumes only. Volumes 1-2 are in print.

Literary Criticism Series
Cumulative Author Index

This index lists all author entries in the Gale Literary Criticism Series and includes cross-references to other Gale sources. For the convenience of the reader, references to the *Yearbook* in the *Contemporary Literary Criticism* series include the page number (in parentheses) after the volume number. References in the index are identified as follows:

AITN: *Authors in the News,* Volumes 1-2
CAAS: *Contemporary Authors Autobiography Series,* Volumes 1-5
CA: *Contemporary Authors* (original series), Volumes 1-121
CABS: *Contemporary Authors Bibliographical Series,* Volumes 1-2
CANR: *Contemporary Authors New Revision Series,* Volumes 1-21
CAP: *Contemporary Authors Permanent Series,* Volumes 1-2
CA-R: *Contemporary Authors* (revised editions), Volumes 1-44
CDALB: *Concise Dictionary of American Literary Biography*
CLC: *Contemporary Literary Criticism,* Volumes 1-46
CLR: *Children's Literature Review,* Volumes 1-14
CMLC: *Classical and Medieval Literature Criticism,* Volume 1
DLB: *Dictionary of Literary Biography,* Volumes 1-59
DLB-DS: *Dictionary of Literary Biography Documentary Series,* Volumes 1-4
DLB-Y: *Dictionary of Literary Biography Yearbook,* Volumes 1980-1986
LC: *Literature Criticism from 1400 to 1800,* Volumes 1-7
NCLC: *Nineteenth-Century Literature Criticism,* Volumes 1-17
SAAS: *Something about the Author Autobiography Series,* Volumes 1-4
SATA: *Something about the Author,* Volumes 1-48
SSC: *Short Story Criticism,* Volume 1
TCLC: *Twentieth-Century Literary Criticism,* Volumes 1-27
YABC: *Yesterday's Authors of Books for Children,* Volumes 1-2

Author Index

Author Index

Author Index

Author Index

Author Index

Author Index

Author Index

Author Index

Author Index